# The XML Schema Complete Reference

# The XML Schema Complete Reference

**Cliff Binstock**

**Dave Peterson**

**Mitchell Smith**

**Mike Wooding**

**Chris Dix**

**Chris Galtenberg**

▼▲ Addison-Wesley

Boston • San Francisco • New York • Toronto • Montreal
London • Munich • Paris • Madrid
Capetown • Sydney • Tokyo • Singapore • Mexico City

Many of the designations used by manufacturers and sellers to distinguish their products are claimed as trademarks. Where those designations appear in this book, and Addison-Wesley was aware of a trademark claim, the designations have been printed with initial capital letters or in all capitals.

The authors and publisher have taken care in the preparation of this book, but make no expressed or implied warranty of any kind and assume no responsibility for errors or omissions. No liability is assumed for incidental or consequential damages in connection with or arising out of the use of the information or programs contained herein.

The publisher offers discounts on this book when ordered in quantity for bulk purchases and special sales. For more information, please contact:

U.S. Corporate and Government Sales
(800) 382-3419
corpsales@pearsontechgroup.com

For sales outside of the U.S., please contact:

International Sales
(317) 581-3793
international@pearsontechgroup.com

Visit Addison-Wesley on the Web: www.awprofessional.com

*Library of Congress Cataloging-in-Publication Data*
The XML schema complete reference / Cliff Binstock ... [et al.]
    p. cm
  Includes index
  ISBN 0-672-32374-5
  1. XML (Document markup language) 2. Database management.
  I. Binstock, Cliff.

QA76.76.H94 X4549 2003
005.7'2—dc21                                  2002074383

Copyright © 2003 by Pearson Education, Inc.

All rights reserved. No part of this publication may be reproduced, stored in a retrieval system, or transmitted, in any form, or by any means, electronic, mechanical, photocopying, recording, or otherwise, without the prior consent of the publisher. Printed in the United States of America. Published simultaneously in Canada.

For information on obtaining permission for use of material from this work, please submit a written request to:

Pearson Education, Inc.
Rights and Contracts Department
75 Arlington Street, Suite 300
Boston, MA 02116
Fax: (617) 848-7047

ISBN 0-672-32374-5
Text printed on recycled paper
1 2 3 4 5 6 7 8 9 10—CRS—0605040302
First printing, September 2002

***Cliff Binstock***
*To Amy Lynn, my true love,*
*my best friend,*
*my life partner,*
*my wife*


***Dave Peterson***
*To "Helga"*


***Mitchell Smith***
*To Rick for inspiring me in so many ways,*
*Dan for bringing me to Array and your heartfulness,*
*Jonathan for finally hiring me (and so much more),*
*Shanti, Eliyahu, and Amy for being who you are,*
*and to Yehudis for teaching me so well.*
*Finally, to my wife Barbara who never ceases to amaze me.*
*Thanks for your patience, the time to write this book,*
*and your understanding.*


***Mike Wooding***
*I would like to thank my beautiful wife Linda for all*
*of her support on this and every project.*
*Without her support, I could not disappear*
*for the many long hours that are required to write.*


***Chris Dix***
*To Micah*


***Christopher Galtenberg***
*To Lavinia, my lifeblood*

# Contents

Preface  xxxiii

Acknowledgments  xxxvii

**PART I  XML Schema Overview  1**

**1  Introduction  3**
    1.1  Why XML? .................................................................................. 4
    1.2  Why XML Schemas? ................................................................... 5
        1.2.1  What Is an XML Schema Document? ............................ 5
        1.2.2  Benefits of an XML Schema ........................................... 6
        1.2.3  Drawbacks of an XML Schema ...................................... 6
    1.3  The World Wide Web Consortium (W3C) Recommendations ..... 7
        1.3.1  The XML Recommendation ........................................... 7
        1.3.2  The Namespace Recommendation ................................. 8
        1.3.3  The Infoset Recommendation ........................................ 8
        1.3.4  The XPath Recommendation ......................................... 9
        1.3.5  The Schema Recommendation ....................................... 9
    1.4  Object-oriented Concepts ......................................................... 10
    1.5  Unifying Terminology .............................................................. 11
        1.5.1  Important Terminology Used in This Book ................. 11
        1.5.2  Schema Values .............................................................. 12
        1.5.3  Parallel Concepts and Ignoring Differences ................. 13
        1.5.4  Element Terminology ................................................... 14
            1.5.4.1  (Concrete) Elements ...................................... 14
            1.5.4.2  Abstract Elements .......................................... 14
            1.5.4.3  Elements ......................................................... 15
            1.5.4.4  Element Terminology Summary .................... 15
        1.5.5  Element Type Terminology .......................................... 15
            1.5.5.1  (Abstract) Element Types .............................. 16
            1.5.5.2  DTD-defined Element Types ......................... 16
            1.5.5.3  Schema-defined (Abstract) Element Types ... 17
            1.5.5.4  Schema-defined Concrete Element Types ..... 18
            1.5.5.5  Element Type Terminology Summary ........... 18
        1.5.6  Other Terminology to Expect in This Book ................. 19
    1.6  Thematic Examples .................................................................. 19
        1.6.1  Thematic Example Quality ........................................... 24

vii

1.7 Creating an XML Schema Document .................................................. 24
    1.7.1 Editing an XML Schema Document .......................................... 24
    1.7.2 Validating an XML Instance ...................................................... 24
1.8 Typesetting Conventions ........................................................................ 25
1.9 Online Resources ...................................................................................... 25

## 2 XML Processing    27

2.1 Basics ........................................................................................................... 28
    2.1.1 Entity Managers ............................................................................ 29
    2.1.2 Parsers and Lexical Analyzers .................................................... 29
    2.1.3 Validators ........................................................................................ 30
    2.1.4 Parsing Events, Information Sets, and Applications .............. 31
2.2 XML Structure Before and After Parsing ............................................ 32
    2.2.1 XML Documents ........................................................................... 32
    2.2.2 The XML Information Set .......................................................... 33
    2.2.3 The DOM ........................................................................................ 33
2.3 Schema Processing .................................................................................... 33
    2.3.1 Processing an XML Schema Document .................................... 34
    2.3.2 What Does a Schema Processor Add? The PSVI .................. 34

## 3 XML Namespaces    35

3.1 Uniform Resource Names and Uniform Resource Locators ........... 36
    3.1.1 Creating URIs ................................................................................. 37
    3.1.2 Using RDDL with Namespace URLs ....................................... 37
3.2 Namespace Components ......................................................................... 38
3.3 Declaring Namespaces ............................................................................. 38
3.4 Qualified Names and QNames .............................................................. 39
    3.4.1 Qualified Names as Values .......................................................... 40
3.5 Namespace Scoping .................................................................................. 42
3.6 XML Schema and Namespaces .............................................................. 42

## 4 XPath and XPointer    45

4.1 XPath ........................................................................................................... 46
    4.1.1 XPath Location Paths ................................................................... 47
    4.1.2 Predicates ........................................................................................ 47
    4.1.3 Node IDs ......................................................................................... 48
    4.1.4 Using XPath with Identity Constraints ..................................... 49
4.2 XPointer ...................................................................................................... 51
    4.2.1 Location Sets .................................................................................. 51
    4.2.2 Namespaces .................................................................................... 51
    4.2.3 Subelement Sequences ................................................................. 52
    4.2.4 XPointer Extensions to XPath .................................................... 53
    4.2.5 Using XPointer and XPath to Locate Schemas ...................... 53

## 5 The Structure of Documents and Schemas 57

5.1 XML Documents ................................................................................... 58
5.2 The XML Information Set ....................................................................... 61
  5.2.1 The *Document Information Item* Class ............................................ 62
  5.2.2 The *Element Information Item* Class ............................................... 63
  5.2.3 The *Attribute Information Item* Class .............................................. 64
  5.2.4 The *Character Information Item* Class ............................................. 66
  5.2.5 XML Information Set Summary ....................................................... 66
5.3 Introduction to the PSVI ........................................................................ 67
5.4 Introduction to Schemas ......................................................................... 69
5.5 Schema Documents ................................................................................ 70

## PART II  Creating XML Schema Documents  73

## 6 Overview of an XML Schema Document 75

6.1 The Enclosing schema Element ................................................................ 78
6.2 Namespaces ........................................................................................... 78
  6.2.1 The Default Namespace ................................................................... 79
  6.2.2 The Target Namespace .................................................................... 80
  6.2.3 Namespaces and the XML Instance ................................................... 80
6.3 Scope ..................................................................................................... 81
  6.3.1 Global Components ......................................................................... 81
    6.3.1.1 Referencing Global Components
              from an XML Schema Document ............................................ 81
    6.3.1.2 Referencing Global Components from an XML Instance ............. 81
  6.3.2 Local and Anonymous Components .................................................. 82
6.4 Annotating Elements .............................................................................. 82
6.5 Constraining Elements ........................................................................... 84
  6.5.1 Simple Content ............................................................................... 84
    6.5.1.1 Lexically Constrained Values .................................................. 84
    6.5.1.2 Simple Content and Attribute Types ........................................ 85
  6.5.2 Complex Content ............................................................................ 85
    6.5.2.1 Nested Elements .................................................................... 85
    6.5.2.2 Empty Content ...................................................................... 85
    6.5.2.3 Mixed Content ...................................................................... 86
    6.5.2.4 Element Wildcards ................................................................ 87
    6.5.2.5 Complex Content and Attribute Types ..................................... 87
6.6 Constraining Attributes .......................................................................... 87
  6.6.1 Simple Attribute Values ................................................................... 87
  6.6.2 Named Attribute-use Groups ............................................................ 88
  6.6.3 Attribute Wildcards ........................................................................ 88
6.7 Simple Types ......................................................................................... 88
  6.7.1 Built-in Datatypes ........................................................................... 89

- 6.7.2 Deriving Simple Types by Restriction .................................................. 89
- 6.7.3 Constraining Facets ........................................................................... 89
- 6.7.4 Lists .................................................................................................. 91
- 6.7.5 Unions ............................................................................................... 91
- 6.8 Complex Types ............................................................................................... 91
  - 6.8.1 Simple Content .................................................................................. 91
  - 6.8.2 Complex Content ............................................................................... 92
  - 6.8.3 Deriving Complex Types by Extension ............................................... 92
  - 6.8.4 Deriving Complex Types by Restriction ............................................. 94
  - 6.8.5 Blocking Complex Types ................................................................... 96
- 6.9 Model Groups ................................................................................................. 96
  - 6.9.1 The All Model Group ......................................................................... 97
  - 6.9.2 The Choice Model Group .................................................................. 97
  - 6.9.3 The Sequence Model Group ............................................................. 98
  - 6.9.4 The Named Model Group ................................................................. 98
- 6.10 Substitution Groups ..................................................................................... 99
- 6.11 Instantiability .............................................................................................. 100
  - 6.11.1 Element Type Instantiability .......................................................... 100
  - 6.11.2 Attribute Type Instantiability ......................................................... 100
  - 6.11.3 Simple Type Instantiability ............................................................ 101
  - 6.11.4 Complex Type Instantiability ........................................................ 101
- 6.12 Identity Constraint Definitions .................................................................... 101
- 6.13 Notations .................................................................................................... 102
- 6.14 Imports and Includes ................................................................................. 102
- 6.15 Locating XML Schemas and XML Schema Components ........................... 103
- 6.16 Schema Element IDs .................................................................................. 103

## 7 Creating an XML Schema Document 105

- 7.1 A Simple XML Schema Document Example ................................................. 106
- 7.2 A schema Element with Every Attribute ........................................................ 106
- 7.3 Concepts and Observations .......................................................................... 107
- 7.4 The schema Element ..................................................................................... 108
  - 7.4.1 Attributes of a schema Element ........................................................ 108
    - 7.4.1.1 The attributeFormDefault Attribute of a schema Element ....... 109
    - 7.4.1.2 The blockDefault Attribute of a schema Element ..................... 109
    - 7.4.1.3 The elementFormDefault Attribute of a schema Element ......... 110
    - 7.4.1.4 The finalDefault Attribute of a schema Element ...................... 111
    - 7.4.1.5 The id Attribute of a schema Element ...................................... 111
    - 7.4.1.6 The targetNamespace Attribute of a schema Element ............. 112
    - 7.4.1.7 The version Attribute of a schema Element ............................. 112
    - 7.4.1.8 The xml:lang Attribute of a schema Element ........................... 113
    - 7.4.1.9 The xmlns "Attributes" of a schema Element ........................... 113
  - 7.4.2 Content Options for a schema Element ............................................ 115

## Contents

- 7.5 The `annotation` Element .................................................................. 116
  - 7.5.1 Attributes of an `annotation` Element .................................................. 118
    - 7.5.1.1 The `id` Attribute of an `annotation` Element ................................. 118
  - 7.5.2 Content Options for an `annotation` Element ........................................ 118
- 7.6 The `appinfo` Element ......................................................................... 119
  - 7.6.1 Attributes of an `appinfo` Element ....................................................... 119
    - 7.6.1.1 The `source` Attribute of an `appinfo` Element ................................ 120
  - 7.6.2 Content Options for an `appinfo` Element ............................................. 120
- 7.7 The `documentation` Element .............................................................. 120
  - 7.7.1 Attributes of a `documentation` Element .............................................. 120
    - 7.7.1.1 The `source` Attribute of a `documentation` Element ..................... 121
    - 7.7.1.2 The `xml:lang` Attribute for a `documentation` Element ............... 122
  - 7.7.2 Content Options for a `documentation` Element ................................... 122
- 7.8 The `include` Element ......................................................................... 122
  - 7.8.1 Attributes of an `include` Element ....................................................... 123
    - 7.8.1.1 The `id` Attribute of an `include` Element ....................................... 123
    - 7.8.1.2 The `schemaLocation` Attribute of an `include` Element ............... 123
  - 7.8.2 Content Options for an `include` Element ............................................ 124
- 7.9 The `import` Element .......................................................................... 124
  - 7.9.1 Attributes of an `import` Element ........................................................ 126
    - 7.9.1.1 The `id` Attribute of an `import` Element ........................................ 126
    - 7.9.1.2 The `namespace` Attribute of an `import` Element ........................ 126
    - 7.9.1.3 The `schemaLocation` Attribute of an `import` Element ............... 127
  - 7.9.2 Content Options for an `import` Element ............................................. 127
- 7.10 The `notation` Element ...................................................................... 128
  - 7.10.1 Attributes of a `notation` Element ..................................................... 129
    - 7.10.1.1 The `id` Attribute of a `notation` Element ..................................... 130
    - 7.10.1.2 The `name` Attribute of a `notation` Element ............................... 130
    - 7.10.1.3 The `public` Attribute of a `notation` Element .............................. 131
    - 7.10.1.4 The `system` Attribute of a `notation` Element ............................ 131
  - 7.10.2 Content Options for a `notation` Element .......................................... 132
- 7.11 The `redefine` Element ...................................................................... 132
  - 7.11.1 Attributes of a `redefine` Element ..................................................... 134
    - 7.11.1.1 The `id` Attribute of a `redefine` Element ..................................... 134
    - 7.11.1.2 The `schemaLocation` Attribute of a `redefine` Element ............. 134
  - 7.11.2 Content Options for a `redefine` Element .......................................... 135

**8  Element Types  137**
- 8.1 An Example of a Trivial Element Type ................................................. 138
- 8.2 Concepts and Observations ................................................................. 138
  - 8.2.1 Global and Local Element Types ........................................................ 138
  - 8.2.2 Substitution Groups ............................................................................ 139
  - 8.2.3 Blocking Substitution ......................................................................... 143

# THE XML SCHEMA COMPLETE REFERENCE

    8.2.4 Element Type Instantiability .................................................. 146
    8.2.5 Nillable Element Types ........................................................... 147
    8.2.6 Element Types and Namespaces ............................................ 147
  8.3 The `element` Element ...................................................................... 148
    8.3.1 Attributes of an `element` Element ........................................ 148
      8.3.1.1 The `abstract` Attribute of an `element` Element ......... 148
      8.3.1.2 The `block` Attribute of an `element` Element ............. 150
      8.3.1.3 The `default` Attribute of an `element` Element .......... 151
      8.3.1.4 The `final` Attribute of an `element` Element .............. 152
      8.3.1.5 The `fixed` Attribute of an `element` Element .............. 157
      8.3.1.6 The `form` Attribute of an `element` Element .............. 158
      8.3.1.7 The `id` Attribute of an `element` Element .................. 159
      8.3.1.8 The `maxOccurs` Attribute of an `element` Element ..... 160
      8.3.1.9 The `minOccurs` Attribute of an `element` Element ..... 162
      8.3.1.10 The `name` Attribute of an `element` Element ........... 163
      8.3.1.11 The `nillable` Attribute of an `element` Element ....... 163
      8.3.1.12 The `ref` Attribute of an `element` Element ............... 164
      8.3.1.13 The `type` Attribute of an `element` Element ............. 165
      8.3.1.14 The `substitutionGroup` Attribute of an `element` Element ...... 166
    8.3.2 Content Options for an `element` Element ............................ 166
  8.4 The `any` Element ............................................................................. 167
    8.4.1 Attributes of an `any` Element ............................................... 168
      8.4.1.1 The `id` Attribute of an `any` Element .......................... 169
      8.4.1.2 The `namespace` Attribute of an `any` Element ............ 169
      8.4.1.3 The `processContents` Attribute of an `any` Element .... 170
    8.4.2 Content Options for an `anyAttribute` Element ................... 170

**9   Attribute Types   173**

  9.1 An Example of an Attribute Type ..................................................... 174
  9.2 An Example of a Named Attribute-use Group ................................. 176
  9.3 An Example of `anyAttribute` ........................................................... 177
  9.4 Concepts and Observations Regarding Attribute Types ................. 180
    9.4.1 When to Use an Attribute Type ............................................. 180
    9.4.2 Global and Local Attribute Types .......................................... 181
    9.4.3 Namespaces and Attribute Types ........................................... 181
  9.5 The `attribute` Element ..................................................................... 182
    9.5.1 Attributes of an `attribute` Element ....................................... 182
      9.5.1.1 The `default` Attribute of an `attribute` Element .......... 183
      9.5.1.2 The `fixed` Attribute of an `attribute` Element ............. 184
      9.5.1.3 The `form` Attribute of an `attribute` Element ............. 185
      9.5.1.4 The `id` Attribute of an `attribute` Element ................. 187
      9.5.1.5 The `name` Attribute of an `attribute` Element ............ 187
      9.5.1.6 The `type` Attribute of an `attribute` Element ............. 188

  9.5.1.7 The `use` Attribute of an `attribute` Element ............................... 189
  9.5.1.8 The `ref` Attribute of an `attribute` Element ............................... 191
 9.5.2 Content Options for an `attribute` Element ......................... 191
9.6 The `attributeGroup` Element ................................................................... 193
 9.6.1 Attributes of an `attributeGroup` Element ............................... 193
  9.6.1.1 The `id` Attribute of an `attributeGroup` Element ...................... 194
  9.6.1.2 The `name` Attribute of an `attributeGroup` Element .................. 194
  9.6.1.3 The `ref` Attribute of an `attributeGroup` Element .................... 195
 9.6.2 Content Options for an `attributeGroup` Element ............................ 195
9.7 The `anyAttribute` Element ..................................................................... 196
 9.7.1 Attributes of an `anyAttribute` Element ............................... 196
  9.7.1.1 The `id` Attribute of an `anyAttribute` Element ...................... 196
  9.7.1.2 The `namespace` Attribute of an `anyAttribute` Element ............ 197
  9.7.1.3 The `processContents` Attribute of an `anyAttribute` Element .. 198
 9.7.2 Content Options for an `anyAttribute` Element ................................. 199

## 10   Simple Types   201

10.1 An Example of a Simple Type Derived
  from the Built-in `token` Datatype ..................................................... 202
10.2 An Example of a Pattern-constrained Simple Type ........................... 203
10.3 An Example of a Simple Type Derived from a User-derived Simple Type   204
10.4 Concepts and Observations ........................................................ 204
 10.4.1 Constraining Facets ...................................................... 205
 10.4.2 The Value Space ......................................................... 205
 10.4.3 The Lexical Space ....................................................... 206
 10.4.4 The Canonical Lexical Representation ......................................... 206
 10.4.5 Non-instantiable Simple Types ............................................ 207
 10.4.6 Global, Local, and Anonymous Simple Types ................................ 208
 10.4.7 Blocking ............................................................... 208
10.5 The `simpleType` Element ..................................................... 208
 10.5.1 Attributes of a `simpleType` Element ..................................... 208
  10.5.1.1 The `final` Attribute of a `simpleType` Element ....................... 209
  10.5.1.2 The `id` Attribute of a `simpleType` Element .......................... 210
  10.5.1.3 The `name` Attribute of a `simpleType` Element ..................... 211
 10.5.2 Constraining Facets of a `simpleType` Element ............................. 212
10.6 The `restriction` Element ..................................................... 212
 10.6.1 Attributes of a `restriction` Element ..................................... 212
  10.6.1.1 The `base` Attribute of a `restriction` Element ......................... 213
  10.6.1.2 The `id` Attribute of a `restriction` Element ............................ 213
 10.6.2 Content Options for a `restriction` Element .............................. 213
 10.6.3 Constraining Facets of a `restriction` Element ............................ 215
10.7 The `list` Element ........................................................ 215
 10.7.1 Attributes of a `list` Element ........................................... 216

10.7.1.1 The `id` Attribute of a `list` Element .................... 217
10.7.1.2 The `itemType` Attribute of a `list` Element ............ 218
10.7.2 Content Options for a `list` Element ................... 218
10.7.3 Constraining Facets of a `list` Element ............... 220
10.8 The `union` Element ................................................ 221
10.8.1 Attributes of a `union` Element ...................... 223
10.8.1.1 The `id` Attribute of a `union` Element ......... 224
10.8.1.2 The `memberTypes` Attribute of a `union` Element ....... 224
10.8.2 Content Options for a `union` Element ............... 226
10.8.3 Constraining Facets of a `union` Element ........... 227

## 11 Complex Types  229

11.1 An Example of a Complex Type Specifying Empty Content ............ 230
11.2 An Example of a Complex Type That Adds Attributes to a Simple Type ............ 231
11.3 An Example of a Complex Type Specifying Nested Element Types .......... 234
11.4 An Example of a Complex Type Specifying Mixed Content ............ 237
11.5 Concepts and Observations ........................................ 238
   11.5.1 Explicitly Non-instantiable Complex Types ............ 238
   11.5.2 Implicitly Non-instantiable Complex Types ........... 240
   11.5.3 Adding Element Types or Attribute Types to a Derived Complex Type .................... 244
   11.5.4 Removing Element Types or Attribute Types from a Derived Complex Type ................. 244
   11.5.5 Prohibiting Extension or Restriction of a Complex Type ........ 245
   11.5.6 Shorthand Notation of a Complex Type ............ 245
11.6 The `complexType` Element ........................................ 246
   11.6.1 Attributes of a `complexType` Element ............ 247
      11.6.1.1 The `abstract` Attribute of a `complexType` Element ......... 247
      11.6.1.2 The `block` Attribute of a `complexType` Element ......... 248
      11.6.1.3 The `final` Attribute of a `complexType` Element ......... 250
      11.6.1.4 The `id` Attribute of a `complexType` Element ......... 252
      11.6.1.5 The `mixed` Attribute of a `complexType` Element ......... 252
      11.6.1.6 The `name` Attribute of a `complexType` Element ......... 253
   11.6.2 Content Options for a `complexType` Element ............ 253
11.7 The `simpleContent` Element ........................................ 255
   11.7.1 Attributes of a `simpleContent` Element ............ 255
      11.7.1.1 The `id` Attribute of a `simpleContent` Element ......... 255
   11.7.2 Content Options for a `simpleContent` Element ............ 256
11.8 The `complexContent` Element ........................................ 257
   11.8.1 Attributes of a `complexContent` Element ............ 257
      11.8.1.1 The `id` Attribute of a `complexContent` Element ......... 258

|  |  |  |
|---|---|---|
| | 11.8.1.2 The `mixed` Attribute of a `complexContent` Element | 258 |
| | 11.8.2 Content Options for a `complexContent` Element | 259 |
| 11.9 | The `extension` Element | 259 |
| | 11.9.1 Attributes of an `extension` Element | 262 |
| | 11.9.1.1 The `base` Attribute of an `extension` Element | 262 |
| | 11.9.1.2 The `id` Attribute of an `extension` Element | 262 |
| | 11.9.2 Content Options for an `extension` Element | 263 |
| 11.10 | The `restriction` Element | 264 |
| | 11.10.1 Attributes of a `restriction` Element | 266 |
| | 11.10.1.1 The `base` Attribute of a `restriction` Element | 266 |
| | 11.10.1.2 The `id` Attribute of a `restriction` Element | 267 |
| | 11.10.2 Content Options for a `restriction` Element | 267 |
| 11.11 | The `all` Element | 270 |
| | 11.11.1 Attributes of an `all` Element | 270 |
| | 11.11.1.1 The `id` Attribute of an `all` Element | 271 |
| | 11.11.1.2 The `maxOccurs` Attribute of an `all` Element | 271 |
| | 11.11.1.3 The `minOccurs` Attribute of an `all` Element | 272 |
| | 11.11.2 Content Options for an `all` Element | 272 |
| 11.12 | The `choice` Element | 273 |
| | 11.12.1 Attributes of a `choice` Element | 274 |
| | 11.12.1.1 The `id` Attribute of a `choice` Element | 275 |
| | 11.12.1.2 The `maxOccurs` Attribute of a `choice` Element | 275 |
| | 11.12.1.3 The `minOccurs` Attribute of a `choice` Element | 276 |
| | 11.12.2 Content Options for a `choice` Element | 276 |
| 11.13 | The `sequence` Element | 277 |
| | 11.13.1 Attributes of a `sequence` Element | 277 |
| | 11.13.1.1 The `id` Attribute of a `sequence` Element | 278 |
| | 11.13.1.2 The `maxOccurs` Attribute of a `sequence` Element | 279 |
| | 11.13.1.3 The `minOccurs` Attribute of a `sequence` Element | 279 |
| | 11.13.2 Content Options for a `sequence` Element | 279 |
| 11.14 | The `group` Element | 280 |
| | 11.14.1 Attributes of a `group` Element | 288 |
| | 11.14.1.1 The `id` Attribute of a `group` Element | 289 |
| | 11.14.1.2 The `maxOccurs` Attribute of a `group` Element | 289 |
| | 11.14.1.3 The `minOccurs` Attribute of a `group` Element | 289 |
| | 11.14.1.4 The `name` Attribute of a `group` Element | 290 |
| | 11.14.1.5 The `ref` Attribute of a `group` Element | 290 |
| | 11.14.2 Content Options for a `group` Element | 291 |

## 12  Built-in Datatypes   293

|  |  |  |
|---|---|---|
| 12.1 | Numeric Datatypes | 295 |
| | 12.1.1 The Built-in `decimal` Datatype | 296 |
| | 12.1.1.1 `decimal` Constraining Facets | 297 |

   12.1.1.2 `decimal` Derivation Relationships .............................................. 297
   12.1.1.3 `decimal` Alternatives ................................................................... 298
  12.1.2 The Built-in Floating-point Datatypes: `float` and `double` ................ 298
   12.1.2.1 Floating-point Constraining Facets ................................................ 300
   12.1.2.2 Floating-point Derivation Relationships ....................................... 300
   12.1.2.3 Floating-point Alternatives ............................................................ 300
  12.1.3 The Built-in Infinite Integer Datatypes: `integer`,
    `positiveInteger`, `negativeInteger`, `nonPositiveInteger`,
    and `nonNegativeInteger` ........................................................................ 300
   12.1.3.1 Infinite Integer Constraining Facets .............................................. 301
   12.1.3.2 Infinite Integer Derivation Relationships ..................................... 302
   12.1.3.3 Infinite Integer Alternatives .......................................................... 302
  12.1.4 The Built-in Finite Integer Datatypes: `long`, `int`, `short`, `byte`,
    `unsignedLong`, `unsignedInt`, `unsignedShort`, and `unsignedByte` 303
   12.1.4.1 Finite Integer Constraining Facets ................................................. 303
   12.1.4.2 Finite Integer Derivation Relationships ........................................ 304
   12.1.4.3 Finite Integer Alternatives .............................................................. 304
 12.2 Date, Time, and Duration Datatypes ............................................................ 304
  12.2.1 The Built-in Time-line-based Datatypes: `dateTime`, `date`,
    `gYearMonth`, and `gYear` ...................................................................... 306
   12.2.1.1 Discrete Times: The "Integers" of the *Time Line* ...................... 307
   12.2.1.2 Time Zones ..................................................................................... 308
   12.2.1.3 *Time-line*-based Constraining Facets ........................................... 310
   12.2.1.4 *Time-line*-based Derivation Relationships .................................. 311
   12.2.1.5 *Time-line*-based Alternatives ...................................................... 311
  12.2.2 The Built-in `duration` Datatype ............................................................. 311
   12.2.2.1 `duration` Constraining Facets ..................................................... 313
   12.2.2.2 `duration` Derivation Relationships ............................................. 314
   12.2.2.3 `duration` Alternatives .................................................................. 314
  12.2.3 The Built-in Repeating Dates and Times Datatypes: `time`,
    `gMonthDay`, `gDay`, and `gMonth` ........................................................ 314
   12.2.3.1 Repeating Dates and Times Constraining Facets ......................... 315
   12.2.3.2 Repeating Dates and Times Derivation Relationships ................ 315
   12.2.3.3 Repeating Dates and Times Alternatives ..................................... 315
 12.3 String Datatypes ............................................................................................. 316
  12.3.1 The Built-in `string` Datatype ................................................................. 316
   12.3.1.1 `string` Constraining Facets .......................................................... 317
   12.3.1.2 `string` Derivation Relationships .................................................. 317
   12.3.1.3 `string` Alternatives ....................................................................... 317
  12.3.2 Ordinary `string`-derived Datatypes: `normalizedString`, `token`,
    `language`, `NMTOKEN`, `NMTOKENS`, `Name`, and `NCName` ................... 318
   12.3.2.1 Ordinary `string`-derived Constraining Facets ........................... 320
   12.3.2.2 Ordinary `string`-derived Derivation Relationships ................... 320

            12.3.2.3 Ordinary string-derived Alternatives .......................... 320
        12.3.3 "Magic" string-derived Datatypes:
            ID, IDREF, IDREFS, ENTITY, and ENTITIES ......................... 321
            12.3.3.1 Magic string-derived Constraining Facets ................ 322
            12.3.3.2 Magic string-derived Derivation Relationships ....... 322
            12.3.3.3 Magic string-derived Alternatives ........................... 322
    12.4 Oddball Datatypes ................................................................................ 322
        12.4.1 The Built-in QName Datatype ................................................. 323
            12.4.1.1 QName Constraining Facets ....................................... 324
            12.4.1.2 QName Derivation Relationships ............................. 324
            12.4.1.3 QName Alternatives ..................................................... 324
        12.4.2 The Built-in boolean Datatype ................................................ 324
            12.4.2.1 boolean Constraining Facets ...................................... 325
            12.4.2.2 boolean Derivation Relationships ........................... 325
            12.4.2.3 boolean Alternatives .................................................... 325
        12.4.3 The Built-in hexBinary and base64Binary Datatypes ...................... 325
            12.4.3.1 hexBinary and base64Binary Constraining Facets .................. 327
            12.4.3.2 hexBinary and base64Binary Derivation Relationships .......... 327
            12.4.3.3 hexBinary and base64Binary Alternatives ............... 327
        12.4.4 The Built-in anyURI Datatype ................................................. 327
            12.4.4.1 anyURI Constraining Facets ....................................... 328
            12.4.4.2 anyURI Derivation Relationships ............................. 329
            12.4.4.3 anyURI Alternatives ..................................................... 329
        12.4.5 The Built-in notation Datatype ............................................... 329
            12.4.5.1 notation Constraining Facets .................................... 330
            12.4.5.2 notation Derivation Relationships ......................... 330
            12.4.5.3 notation Alternatives .................................................. 330

## 13  Identity Constraints    331

    13.1 Identity Constraint Example .............................................................. 332
    13.2 Concepts and Observations ............................................................... 338
        13.2.1 Identity Constraint Terminology ............................................ 338
        13.2.2 Selectors and Fields .................................................................. 339
        13.2.3 Limited XPath Support ............................................................. 340
        13.2.4 Value Equality ............................................................................ 342
        13.2.5 Enforcing Uniqueness ............................................................... 342
        13.2.6 Enforcing Referential Integrity ................................................ 343
    13.3 The unique Element ............................................................................ 343
        13.3.1 The Attributes of a unique Element ....................................... 344
            13.3.1.1 The id Attribute of a unique Element ...................... 345
            13.3.1.2 The name Attribute of a unique Element ................. 345
        13.3.2 Content Options for a unique Element ................................... 345
    13.4 The key Element .................................................................................. 346

|  |  |
|---|---|
| 13.4.1 The Attributes of a key Element | 347 |
| 13.4.1.1 The id Attribute of a key Element | 347 |
| 13.4.1.2 The name Attribute of a key Element | 348 |
| 13.4.2 Content Options for a key Element | 348 |
| 13.5 The keyref Element | 349 |
| 13.5.1 The Attributes of a keyref Element | 350 |
| 13.5.1.1 The id Attribute of a keyref Element | 351 |
| 13.5.1.2 The name Attribute of a keyref Element | 351 |
| 13.5.1.3 The refer Attribute of a keyref Element | 352 |
| 13.5.2 Content Options for a keyref Element | 352 |
| 13.6 The selector Element | 353 |
| 13.6.1 The Attributes of a selector Element | 353 |
| 13.6.1.1 The id Attribute of a selector Element | 353 |
| 13.6.1.2 The xpath Attribute of a selector Element | 353 |
| 13.6.2 Content Options for a selector Element | 354 |
| 13.7 The field Element | 354 |
| 13.7.1 The Attributes of a field Element | 354 |
| 13.7.1.1 The id Attribute of a field Element | 355 |
| 13.7.1.2 The xpath Attribute of a field Element | 355 |
| 13.7.2 Content Options for a field Element | 356 |

## 14  Regular Expressions  357

|  |  |
|---|---|
| 14.1 Concepts and Observations | 359 |
| 14.1.1 Unicode Regular Expression Guidelines | 359 |
| 14.1.2 The Latin Character Set | 359 |
| 14.1.3 Perl Regular Expressions | 360 |
| 14.1.4 XML Schemas | 360 |
| 14.2 Regular Expression Syntax | 361 |
| 14.2.1 Metacharacters | 361 |
| 14.2.2 Concatenation | 362 |
| 14.2.3 Alternatives | 362 |
| 14.2.4 Grouping | 363 |
| 14.2.5 Individual Characters | 363 |
| 14.2.5.1 Normal Character | 363 |
| 14.2.5.2 Character Categories | 364 |
| 14.2.5.3 Single Character Escape | 366 |
| 14.2.5.4 Multiple Character Escape | 367 |
| 14.2.5.5 Wildcard Escape | 369 |
| 14.2.5.6 Character Blocks | 370 |
| 14.2.5.7 XML Character References | 374 |
| 14.2.6 Cardinality Quantifiers | 374 |
| 14.2.6.1 One Occurrence | 374 |
| 14.2.6.2 Zero or One Occurrences | 375 |

14.2.6.3 Zero or More Occurrences ............................................................. 375
14.2.6.4 One or More Occurrences ............................................................. 376
14.2.6.5 Explicit Numeric Range ................................................................ 376
14.2.7 Character Classes Expressions ................................................................... 377
14.2.7.1 Positive Character Groups ............................................................. 377
14.2.7.2 Negative Character Ranges ........................................................... 379
14.2.7.3 Character Class Subtraction ........................................................... 380
14.2.8 Precedence ................................................................................................. 380
14.3 Constraining Simple Content ...................................................................................... 381
14.3.1 The pattern Constraining Facet ................................................................. 382
14.3.2 Multiple pattern Constraining Facets (or) ................................................. 382
14.3.3 Constraining Derived Types (and) ............................................................. 383

## PART III    Validation    385

### 15    XML Schema Component Detail    387

15.1 Schemas: The Basic Idea ............................................................................................. 388
15.1.1 Names ........................................................................................................ 390
15.1.2 Annotations ............................................................................................... 390
15.2 Schema (Schema Schema Component) ..................................................................... 391
15.3 Attribute Types ............................................................................................................ 392
15.3.1 Attribute Type (Attribute Declaration Schema Component) .................... 392
15.3.2 Simple Type (Simple Type Definition Schema Component) .................... 394
15.3.3 Constraining Facets ................................................................................... 396
15.4 Element Types .............................................................................................................. 396
15.4.1 Element Type (Element Declaration Schema Component) ...................... 397
15.4.2 Complex Type (Complex Type Definition Schema Component) .............. 400
15.4.3 Attribute Set Models .................................................................................. 402
15.4.3.1 Attribute Use (Attribute Use Schema Component) ...................... 403
15.4.3.2 Wildcard (Wildcard Schema Component) .................................... 404
15.4.4 Content Models .......................................................................................... 405
15.4.4.1 Particle (Particle Schema Component) .......................................... 406
15.4.4.2 Model Group (Model Group Schema Component) ...................... 407
15.4.4.3 Wildcard (Wildcard Schema Component) *Reprise* ..................... 407
15.4.4.4 Element Type (Element Type Schema Component) *Reprise* ...... 407
15.4.5 Simple Type (Simple Type Definition
         Schema Component) *Reprise* ................................................................ 407
15.4.6 Reusability ................................................................................................. 409
15.4.6.1 Named Attribute-use Group
             (Attribute Group Definition Schema Component) ..................... 409
15.4.6.2 Named Model Group (Model Group
             Definition Schema Component) .................................................. 410
15.5 Annotation (Annotation Schema Component) ......................................................... 411
15.6 Notation (Notation Declaration Schema Component) ............................................. 411

## 16  PSVI Detail  413

- 16.1 Schema Validation and Schema Processing ............................................. 414
  - 16.1.1 Kinds of Validation ............................................................................ 414
  - 16.1.2 The Steps of Schema Processing ..................................................... 415
  - 16.1.3 The Results of Validation .................................................................. 416
- 16.2 The PSVI ................................................................................................... 416
  - 16.2.1 The Basic Infoset ............................................................................... 417
  - 16.2.2 PSVI-added Properties ...................................................................... 418
    - 16.2.2.1 The PSVI Element Information Item ....................................... 418
    - 16.2.2.2 The PSVI Attribute Information Item ...................................... 421
  - 16.2.3 PSVI-added Information Items .......................................................... 423
  - 16.2.4 The New PSVI Information Items ...................................................... 424

## 17  Java and the Apache XML Project  427

- 17.1 Apache Background ................................................................................. 428
- 17.2 Java Xerces on Your Computer ................................................................ 430
  - 17.2.1 Downloading Java Xerces 2 Parser .................................................. 430
  - 17.2.2 Exploring the Xerces Package .......................................................... 431
  - 17.2.3 Running the Samples ........................................................................ 432
- 17.3 "Hello Apache" ......................................................................................... 435
  - 17.3.1 Your First Parser ................................................................................ 435
  - 17.3.2 Parsing "Hello Apache" ..................................................................... 439
- 17.4 Critical Xerces Packages .......................................................................... 442
- 17.5 Xerces Java DOM In-depth ....................................................................... 447
  - 17.5.1 The Document Interface .................................................................... 447
  - 17.5.2 Creating DOM Documents ................................................................ 449
  - 17.5.3 The Element Interface ....................................................................... 452
  - 17.5.4 The Node Interface ............................................................................ 454
  - 17.5.5 An Advanced DOM Example ............................................................. 456
  - 17.5.6 DOM Helpers and DOM Level 3 ........................................................ 458
- 17.6 Java Xerces SAX In-depth ........................................................................ 459
  - 17.6.1 The `ContentHandler` Interface ....................................................... 459

## 18  MSXML and the Schema Object Model (SOM)  471

- 18.1 Introducing MSXML .................................................................................. 472
- 18.2 Concepts and Observations ..................................................................... 473
  - 18.2.1 ...MS Stands for Microsoft ................................................................. 474
  - 18.2.2 Proprietary versus Standard ............................................................. 474
- 18.3 XML Schema Examples ............................................................................ 474
- 18.4 MSXML Fundamentals .............................................................................. 474
  - 18.4.1 Using MSXML from Visual Basic ...................................................... 475
  - 18.4.2 Using the DOM .................................................................................. 476
    - 18.4.2.1 `DOMDocument40` ................................................................... 476

             18.4.2.2  Reading XML with `DOMDocument40` ........................................... 477
             18.4.2.3  DOM Parsing Errors .................................................................. 478
      18.4.3  Using SAX2 ................................................................................................ 478
             18.4.3.1  `SAXXMLReader40` ...................................................................... 479
             18.4.3.2  Reading XML with `SAXXMLReader40` ........................................ 479
             18.4.3.3.  `SAXXMLReader40` Configuration ............................................. 482
             18.4.3.4  SAX2 Parsing Errors ................................................................... 482
 18.5  Schema Object Model (SOM) ............................................................................... 483
      18.5.1  SOM Fundamentals ..................................................................................... 483
      18.5.2  The `ISchemaItem` Interface .................................................................... 484
      18.5.3  The `ISchema` Interface ............................................................................ 486
      18.5.4  DOM versus SOM ....................................................................................... 488
      18.5.5  Creating XML Schemas ............................................................................... 488
 18.6  Validation ................................................................................................................ 488
      18.6.1  XML Document Samples ............................................................................. 489
      18.6.2  Validation by Using the DOM ..................................................................... 492
      18.6.3  Validation by Using SAX2 ........................................................................... 492
 18.7  Example: XML Schema Tree ................................................................................. 493

## PART IV  Result-oriented Schemas  505

### 19  Object-oriented Schemas  507

 19.1  Concepts and Observations ................................................................................. 508
      19.1.1  Fundamentals of Object-oriented Development ..................................... 508
      19.1.2  Use of Languages ........................................................................................ 508
 19.2  Object-oriented Concepts .................................................................................... 509
      19.2.1  Encapsulation .............................................................................................. 509
      19.2.2  Inheritance .................................................................................................. 509
      19.2.3  Polymorphism ............................................................................................. 510
 19.3  XML Schemas and Objects ................................................................................... 510
      19.3.1  The Good ..................................................................................................... 510
      19.3.2  The Bad ........................................................................................................ 510
      19.3.3  The Answer .................................................................................................. 510
 19.4  Mapping XML Schemas to Object-oriented Languages .................................... 511
      19.4.1  Complex Types ............................................................................................ 511
             19.4.1.1  Non-instantiable versus Instantiable ........................................ 512
             19.4.1.2  Inheritance and Polymorphism ................................................. 514
             19.4.1.3  Order ........................................................................................... 517
      19.4.2  Element Types ............................................................................................. 518
      19.4.3  Attributes .................................................................................................... 518
      19.4.4  Schemas ...................................................................................................... 518
      19.4.5  Simple Types ............................................................................................... 520
      19.4.6  Annotation .................................................................................................. 521

## THE XML SCHEMA COMPLETE REFERENCE

| | |
|---|---:|
| 19.4.7 Putting It Together | 521 |
| 19.5 Sample Schema: `party.xsd` | 521 |
| 19.6 Design Patterns | 527 |
|     19.6.1 Builder Pattern and XML Schemas | 528 |
| 19.7 Language Examples | 529 |
|     19.7.1 Visual Basic | 530 |
|     19.7.2 C++ | 533 |
|     19.7.3 C# and the .NET Framework | 535 |
|         19.7.3.1 NET XML Schema Definition Tool | 536 |

### 20 Document-oriented Schemas    541

| | |
|---|---:|
| 20.1 Why Use XML for Documents? | 542 |
| 20.2 Creating a Schema for a Set of Documents: Document Analysis | 544 |
|     20.2.1 Scenario: A Document Analysis | 544 |
|         20.2.1.1 The First Meeting: Roughing Out the Structure | 545 |
|         20.2.1.2 Between Meetings: The Anomaly Search | 545 |
|         20.2.1.3 The Second Meeting: "Sorting Sheep" | 545 |
|         20.2.1.4 Moving Onward | 546 |
|     20.2.2 Structures to Look For | 546 |
|         20.2.2.1 Big Pieces | 547 |
|         20.2.2.2 Specialized Pieces | 547 |
|         20.2.2.3 Paragraphs and Things That Break Them | 547 |
|         20.2.2.4 Specialized and Non-obvious Structures | 548 |
|     20.2.3 More Detail | 548 |
| 20.3 Implementing Document Processing | 548 |
|     20.3.1 Help for the Author | 549 |
|     20.3.2 Help for the Editor | 551 |
|     20.3.3 Automating Production | 551 |
|         20.3.3.1 Stylesheet-based Formatting | 551 |
|         20.3.3.2 Formatting-markup-based Formatting | 552 |

### 21 Application-oriented Schemas    555

| | |
|---|---:|
| 21.1 XML Applications | 556 |
|     21.1.1 Fundamentals of XML Applications | 556 |
|     21.1.2 XML Input and Output | 557 |
|     21.1.3 Transport Protocol | 557 |
|     21.1.4 Business Logic | 557 |
| 21.2 Role of XML Schemas | 558 |
|     21.2.1 Validation of Data | 558 |
|     21.2.2 Describing Arguments | 558 |
| 21.3 Describing Applications | 560 |
| 21.4 Application Structure | 561 |
|     21.4.1 Sovereign | 561 |

      21.4.2 Request-response .................................................................. 561
      21.4.3 Routing ................................................................................ 561
  21.5 Transporting XML ............................................................................. 563
      21.5.1 Transport Protocols ............................................................. 563
      21.5.2 HTTP .................................................................................. 564
      21.5.3 XML and HTTP ................................................................. 566
  21.6 Describing Applications .................................................................... 569
      21.6.1 Using XML Schemas ......................................................... 569
      21.6.2 WSDL and XML Schemas ................................................. 570
  21.7 Example Application ......................................................................... 572
      21.7.1 Client ................................................................................... 575
      21.7.2 Server .................................................................................. 580

## PART V    Data-oriented Schemas   585

### 22    Data-oriented Schemas: Datatypes   587

  22.1 XML Schema Design Considerations ............................................... 588
      22.1.1 Patterns ............................................................................... 588
      22.1.2 Whitespace .......................................................................... 589
      22.1.3 Strings ................................................................................. 589
      22.1.4 Decimals ............................................................................. 589
      22.1.5 Floats and Doubles ............................................................. 589
      22.1.6 Boolean ............................................................................... 589
      22.1.7 Time Zones and Their Interaction with gMonth, gYear, and gDay .... 590
      22.1.8 Time Zones and Their Interaction with Other Date/Time Datatypes .. 590
      22.1.9 IDREFS and NMTOKENS Datatypes ............................................. 590
  22.2 General Discussion of Facet Restrictions .......................................... 590
      22.2.1 pattern Constraining Facet ................................................. 590
      22.2.2 enumeration Constraining Facet ........................................ 592
          22.2.2.1 Hard-coded Values ................................................ 593
          22.2.2.2 Separate Table ....................................................... 593
          22.2.2.3 Picklist Table ......................................................... 594
      22.2.3 whiteSpace Constraining Facet ......................................... 597
  22.3 Check Constraints versus Triggers .................................................... 598
  22.4 Datatypes ........................................................................................... 598
      22.4.1 string Datatype ................................................................... 598
          22.4.1.1 CLOB Support in Oracle ....................................... 599
          22.4.1.2 length Constraining Facet ..................................... 599
          22.4.1.3 minLength Constraining Facet ............................. 599
          22.4.1.4 maxLength Constraining Facet ............................ 601
          22.4.1.5 pattern Constraining Facet ................................... 601
          22.4.1.6 enumeration Constraining Facet .......................... 601
          22.4.1.7 whiteSpace Constraining Facet ............................ 601

22.4.2 `normalizedString` Datatype .................................................................... 601
    22.4.2.1 `pattern` Constraining Facet ......................................................... 602
    22.4.2.2 `enumeration` Constraining Facet ................................................. 602
    22.4.2.3 `whiteSpace` Constraining Facet .................................................. 602
    22.4.2.4 `length` Constraining Facet ........................................................... 602
    22.4.2.5 `minLength` Constraining Facet .................................................... 603
    22.4.2.6 `maxLength` Constraining Facet .................................................... 603
22.4.3 `token` Datatype ................................................................................... 603
    22.4.3.1 `pattern` Constraining Facet ......................................................... 604
    22.4.3.2 `enumeration` Constraining Facet ................................................. 604
    22.4.3.3 `whiteSpace` Constraining Facet .................................................. 604
    22.4.3.4 `length` Constraining Facet ........................................................... 604
    22.4.3.5 `minLength` Constraining Facet .................................................... 604
    22.4.3.6 `maxLength` Constraining Facet .................................................... 604
22.4.4 `language` Datatype .............................................................................. 604
    22.4.4.1 `pattern` Constraining Facet ......................................................... 607
    22.4.4.2 `enumeration` Constraining Facet ................................................. 607
    22.4.4.3 `whiteSpace` Constraining Facet .................................................. 607
    22.4.4.4 `length` Constraining Facet ........................................................... 608
    22.4.4.5 `minLength` Constraining Facet .................................................... 608
    22.4.4.6 `maxLength` Constraining Facet .................................................... 608
22.4.5 `Name` Datatype ..................................................................................... 608
    22.4.5.1 `pattern` Constraining Facet ......................................................... 609
    22.4.5.2 `enumeration` Constraining Facet ................................................. 609
    22.4.5.3 `whiteSpace` Constraining Facet .................................................. 610
    22.4.5.4 `length` Constraining Facet ........................................................... 610
    22.4.5.5 `minLength` Constraining Facet .................................................... 610
    22.4.5.6 `maxLength` Constraining Facet .................................................... 610
22.4.6 `NCName` Datatype .................................................................................. 610
    22.4.6.1 `pattern` Constraining Facet ......................................................... 612
    22.4.6.2 `enumeration` Constraining Facet ................................................. 612
    22.4.6.3 `whiteSpace` Constraining Facet .................................................. 612
    22.4.6.4 `length` Constraining Facet ........................................................... 612
    22.4.6.5 `minLength` Constraining Facet .................................................... 612
    22.4.6.6 `maxLength` Constraining Facet .................................................... 612
22.4.7 `ID` Datatype ........................................................................................... 612
22.4.8 `IDREF` Datatype ..................................................................................... 612
22.4.9 `IDREFS` Datatype .................................................................................... 612
    22.4.9.1 Single Column ............................................................................ 613
    22.4.9.2 Separate Table ........................................................................... 614
    22.4.9.3 `pattern` Constraining Facet ......................................................... 617
    22.4.9.4 `enumeration` Constraining Facet ................................................. 617
    22.4.9.5 `whiteSpace` Constraining Facet .................................................. 617

- 22.4.9.6 `length` Constraining Facet .......... 617
- 22.4.9.7 `minLength` Constraining Facet .......... 617
- 22.4.9.8 `maxLength` Constraining Facet .......... 617
- 22.4.10 `ENTITY` Datatype .......... 617
- 22.4.11 `ENTITIES` Datatype .......... 618
- 22.4.12 `NMTOKEN` Datatype .......... 618
  - 22.4.12.1 `pattern` Constraining Facet .......... 619
  - 22.4.12.2 `enumeration` Constraining Facet .......... 619
  - 22.4.12.3 `whiteSpace` Constraining Facet .......... 619
  - 22.4.12.4 `length` Constraining Facet .......... 619
  - 22.4.12.5 `minLength` Constraining Facet .......... 619
  - 22.4.12.6 `maxLength` Constraining Facet .......... 619
- 22.4.13 `NMTOKENS` Datatype .......... 620
  - 22.4.13.1 Single Column .......... 620
  - 22.4.13.2 Separate Table .......... 622
  - 22.4.13.3 `pattern` Constraining Facet .......... 624
  - 22.4.13.4 `enumeration` Constraining Facet .......... 624
  - 22.4.13.5 `whiteSpace` Constraining Facet .......... 624
  - 22.4.13.6 `length` Constraining Facet .......... 624
  - 22.4.13.7 `minLength` Constraining Facet .......... 624
  - 22.4.13.8 `maxLength` Constraining Facet .......... 624
- 22.4.14 `decimal` Datatype .......... 625
  - 22.4.14.1 `totalDigits` Constraining Facet .......... 625
  - 22.4.14.2 `fractionDigits` Constraining Facet .......... 625
  - 22.4.14.3 `pattern` Constraining Facet .......... 626
  - 22.4.14.4 `whiteSpace` Constraining Facet .......... 626
  - 22.4.14.5 `enumeration` Constraining Facet .......... 626
  - 22.4.14.6 `maxInclusive` Constraining Facet .......... 626
  - 22.4.14.7 `maxExclusive` Constraining Facet .......... 627
  - 22.4.14.8 `minInclusive` Constraining Facet .......... 627
  - 22.4.14.9 `minExclusive` Constraining Facet .......... 628
- 22.4.15 `integer` Datatype .......... 629
- 22.4.16 `nonPositiveInteger` Datatype .......... 629
- 22.4.17 `negativeInteger` Datatype .......... 629
- 22.4.18 `long` Datatype .......... 630
- 22.4.19 `int` Datatype .......... 630
- 22.4.20 `short` Datatype .......... 630
- 22.4.21 `byte` Datatype .......... 630
- 22.4.22 `nonNegativeInteger` Datatype .......... 630
- 22.4.23 `unsignedLong` Datatype .......... 630
- 22.4.24 `unsignedInt` Datatype .......... 630
- 22.4.25 `unsignedShort` Datatype .......... 631
- 22.4.26 `unsignedByte` Datatype .......... 631

- 22.4.27 `positiveInteger` Datatype .......... 631
- 22.4.28 `float` Datatype .......... 631
- 22.4.29 `double` Datatype .......... 632
- 22.4.30 `hexBinary` Datatype .......... 632
  - 22.4.30.1 `length` Constraining Facet .......... 632
  - 22.4.30.2 `minLength` Constraining Facet .......... 632
  - 22.4.30.3 `maxLength` Constraining Facet .......... 632
  - 22.4.30.4 `pattern` Constraining Facet .......... 633
  - 22.4.30.5 `enumeration` Constraining Facet .......... 633
  - 22.4.30.6 `whiteSpace` Constraining Facet .......... 633
- 22.4.31 `base64Binary` Datatype .......... 633
- 22.4.32 `QName` Datatype .......... 633
- 22.4.33 `anyURI` Datatype .......... 633
- 22.4.34 `NOTATION` Datatype .......... 633
- 22.4.35 `boolean` Datatype .......... 634
  - 22.4.35.1 Representation of the `boolean` Datatype as True and False .... 634
  - 22.4.35.2 Representation of the `boolean` Datatype as 1 and 0 .......... 635
  - 22.4.35.3 `pattern` Constraining Facet .......... 635
  - 22.4.35.4 `whiteSpace` Constraining Facet .......... 636
- 22.4.36 `duration` Datatype .......... 636
  - 22.4.36.1 `pattern` Constraining Facet .......... 636
  - 22.4.36.2 `enumeration` Constraining Facet .......... 636
  - 22.4.36.3 `whiteSpace` Constraining Facet .......... 636
  - 22.4.36.4 `maxInclusive` Constraining Facet .......... 636
  - 22.4.36.5 `maxInclusive` Constraining Facet .......... 636
  - 22.4.36.6 `minInclusive` Constraining Facet .......... 636
  - 22.4.36.7 `minExclusive` Constraining Facet .......... 636
- 22.4.37 `dateTime` Datatype .......... 637
  - 22.4.37.1 `pattern` Constraining Facet .......... 638
  - 22.4.37.2 `enumeration` Constraining Facet .......... 638
  - 22.4.37.3 `whiteSpace` Constraining Facet .......... 638
  - 22.4.37.4 `maxInclusive` Constraining Facet .......... 638
  - 22.4.37.5 `maxExclusive` Constraining Facet .......... 639
  - 22.4.37.6 `minInclusive` Constraining Facet .......... 640
  - 22.4.37.7 `minExclusive` Constraining Facet .......... 640
- 22.4.38 `date` Datatype .......... 641
  - 22.4.38.1 `pattern` Constraining Facet .......... 642
  - 22.4.38.2 `enumeration` Constraining Facet .......... 642
  - 22.4.38.3 `whiteSpace` Constraining Facet .......... 642
  - 22.4.38.4 `maxInclusive` Constraining Facet .......... 642
  - 22.4.38.5 `maxExclusive` Constraining Facet .......... 643
  - 22.4.38.6 `minInclusive` Constraining Facet .......... 644
  - 22.4.38.7 `minExclusive` Constraining Facet .......... 645

- 22.4.39 gYear Datatype ...... 645
  - 22.4.39.1 pattern Constraining Facet ...... 647
  - 22.4.39.2 enumeration Constraining Facet ...... 647
  - 22.4.39.3 whiteSpace Constraining Facet ...... 647
  - 22.4.39.4 maxInclusive Constraining Facet ...... 647
  - 22.4.39.5 maxExclusive Constraining Facet ...... 648
  - 22.4.39.6 minInclusive Constraining Facet ...... 648
  - 22.4.39.7 minExclusive Constraining Facet ...... 649
- 22.4.40 gYearMonth Datatype ...... 650
  - 22.4.40.1 pattern Constraining Facet ...... 651
  - 22.4.40.2 enumeration Constraining Facet ...... 651
  - 22.4.40.3 whiteSpace Constraining Facet ...... 651
  - 22.4.40.4 maxInclusive Constraining Facet ...... 651
  - 22.4.40.5 maxExclusive Constraining Facet ...... 652
  - 22.4.40.6 minInclusive Constraining Facet ...... 653
  - 22.4.40.7 minExclusive Constraining Facet ...... 653
- 22.4.41 time Datatype ...... 654
  - 22.4.41.1 pattern Constraining Facet ...... 655
  - 22.4.41.2 enumeration Constraining Facet ...... 655
  - 22.4.41.3 whiteSpace Constraining Facet ...... 655
  - 22.4.41.4 maxInclusive Constraining Facet ...... 655
  - 22.4.41.5 maxExclusive Constraining Facet ...... 656
  - 22.4.41.6 minInclusive Constraining Facet ...... 657
  - 22.4.41.7 minExclusive Constraining Facet ...... 658
- 22.4.42 gMonth Datatype ...... 658
  - 22.4.42.1 pattern Constraining Facet ...... 660
  - 22.4.42.2 enumeration Constraining Facet ...... 660
  - 22.4.42.3 whiteSpace Constraining Facet ...... 660
  - 22.4.42.4 maxInclusive Constraining Facet ...... 660
  - 22.4.42.5 maxExclusive Constraining Facet ...... 661
  - 22.4.42.6 minInclusive Constraining Facet ...... 661
  - 22.4.42.7 minExclusive Constraining Facet ...... 662
- 22.4.43 gDay Datatype ...... 663
  - 22.4.43.1 pattern Constraining Facet ...... 664
  - 22.4.43.2 enumeration Constraining Facet ...... 664
  - 22.4.43.3 whiteSpace Constraining Facet ...... 664
  - 22.4.43.4 maxInclusive Constraining Facet ...... 664
  - 22.4.43.5 maxExclusive Constraining Facet ...... 665
  - 22.4.43.6 minInclusive Constraining Facet ...... 665
  - 22.4.43.7 minExclusive Constraining Facet ...... 666
- 22.4.44 gMonthDay Datatype ...... 667
  - 22.4.44.1 pattern Constraining Facet ...... 668
  - 22.4.44.2 enumeration Constraining Facet ...... 668

		22.4.44.3 `whiteSpace` Constraining Facet .................................................. 668
		22.4.44.4 `maxInclusive` Constraining Facet .............................................. 668
		22.4.44.5 `maxExclusive` Constraining Facet .............................................. 669
		22.4.44.6 `minInclusive` Constraining Facet ............................................... 669
		22.4.44.7 `minExclusive` Constraining Facet .............................................. 670

## 23 Data-oriented Schemas: Simple Types   673

	23.1 XML Schema Design Considerations ............................................... 674
		23.1.1 `list` Element Design Considerations ...................................... 674
		23.1.2 `union` Element Design Considerations .................................. 675
	23.2 An Example of a Simple Type Mapping to a Database Schema ............... 675
	23.3 Concepts and Observations ............................................................ 678
	23.4 The `list` Element ........................................................................ 678
		23.4.1 Single Column ........................................................................ 679
		23.4.2 Separate Table ....................................................................... 680
		23.4.3 `length` Constraining Facet .................................................... 682
			23.4.3.1 Single Column ........................................................... 682
			23.4.3.2 Separate Table .......................................................... 682
		23.4.4 `minLength` Constraining Facet .............................................. 687
		23.4.5 `maxLength` Constraining Facet ............................................. 687
			23.4.5.1 Single Column ........................................................... 687
			23.4.5.2 Separate Table .......................................................... 687
		23.4.6 `pattern` Constraining Facet .................................................. 689
		23.4.7 `enumeration` Constraining Facet .......................................... 689
	23.5 The `union` Element .................................................................... 690
		23.5.1 A Simple Example of a `union` of Enumerations ...................... 690
		23.5.2 A Complex Example of a `union` of Single-Valued Simple Types ...... 694
		23.5.3 Mapping a `union` of Single-Valued
				Simple Types to a Database Representation ......................... 695
			23.5.3.1 Single Column Database Mapping of a `union` ............ 696
			23.5.3.2 Multiple Column Database Mapping of a `union` ....... 697
			23.5.3.3 Oracle `SYS.AnyData` Type Mapping of a `union` ....... 702
		23.5.4 `pattern` Constraining Facet .................................................. 706
		23.5.5 `enumeration` Constraining Facet .......................................... 706

## 24 Data-oriented Schemas: Complex Types   707

	24.1 XML Schema Design Considerations ............................................... 708
		24.1.1 `mixed` Attribute ................................................................... 709
		24.1.2 `any` and `anyAttribute` Elements ......................................... 709
		24.1.3 `attributeGroup` and `group` Elements ................................. 709
		24.1.4 `annotation` Element ............................................................ 709
	24.2 An Example of a Complex Type Mapping to a Database Schema ............ 709

24.3 An Example of a Complex Type Mapping Supporting
     Mixed Content to a Database Schema .......................................................... 713
24.4 Concepts and Observations ............................................................................. 718
24.5 `complexType` Element ................................................................................... 719
   24.5.1 Attributes of a `complexType` Element ............................................. 719
      24.5.1.1 `abstract` Attribute ................................................................ 719
      24.5.1.2 `block` Attribute ...................................................................... 720
      24.5.1.3 `final` Attribute ...................................................................... 720
      24.5.1.4 `id` Attribute ............................................................................ 720
      24.5.1.5 `mixed` Attribute ...................................................................... 720
      24.5.1.6 `name` Attribute ....................................................................... 720
24.6 `all` Element ..................................................................................................... 720
   24.6.1 `id` Attribute ............................................................................................ 722
   24.6.2 `minOccurs` Attribute ........................................................................... 722
   24.6.3 `maxOccurs` Attribute ........................................................................... 722
24.7 `annotation` Element ...................................................................................... 722
24.8 `any` Element .................................................................................................... 722
   24.8.1 `id` Attribute ............................................................................................ 723
   24.8.2 `minOccurs` Attribute ........................................................................... 723
   24.8.3 `maxOccurs` Attribute ........................................................................... 723
   24.8.4 `namespace` Attribute ........................................................................... 723
   24.8.5 `processContents` Attribute .............................................................. 723
24.9 `anyAttribute` Element .................................................................................. 723
   24.9.1 `id` Attribute ............................................................................................ 724
   24.9.2 `namespace` Attribute ........................................................................... 724
   24.9.3 `processContents` Attribute .............................................................. 724
24.10 `attributeGroup` Element ............................................................................. 724
   24.10.1 `id` Attribute .......................................................................................... 724
   24.10.2 `name` Attribute ..................................................................................... 724
   24.10.3 `ref` Attribute ......................................................................................... 724
24.11 `choice` Element ............................................................................................. 724
   24.11.1 `id` Attribute .......................................................................................... 727
   24.11.2 `minOccurs` Attribute ......................................................................... 727
   24.11.3 `maxOccurs` Attribute ......................................................................... 727
24.12 `complexContent` Element ............................................................................ 727
   24.12.1 `id` Attribute .......................................................................................... 727
   24.12.2 `mixed` Attribute ................................................................................... 727
24.13 `group` Element ............................................................................................... 727
   24.13.1 `name` Attribute ..................................................................................... 730
   24.13.2 `ref` Attribute ......................................................................................... 730
24.14 `sequence` Element ........................................................................................ 731
   24.14.1 `id` Attribute .......................................................................................... 737
   24.14.2 `minOccurs` Attribute ......................................................................... 738
   24.14.3 `maxOccurs` Attribute ......................................................................... 738

| | |
|---|---|
| 24.15 `simpleContent` Element | 738 |
| 24.15.1 `id` Attribute | 738 |
| 24.16 `restriction` Element | 738 |
| 24.16.1 `base` Attribute | 745 |
| 24.16.2 `id` Attribute | 745 |
| 24.17 `extension` Element | 745 |
| 24.17.1 `base` Attribute | 754 |
| 24.17.2 `id` Attribute | 754 |

## PART VI  A Case Study: The Campus Resource and Scheduling System (CRSS) 755

### 25  The Business Case  757

| | |
|---|---|
| 25.1 Basic CRSS Flow | 758 |
| 25.2 CRSS Requirements | 759 |
| 25.2.1 Frameworks | 759 |
| 25.3 System Users | 759 |
| 25.3.1 CRSS Scalability | 760 |
| 25.3.2 CRSS Technologies | 760 |
| 25.3.2.1 XML Schemas and Testing | 761 |
| 25.4 Extensible Style Language Transform (XSLT) | 764 |
| 25.4.1 Business Uses for XSLT | 766 |
| 25.5 SQL 2000 XML Capabilities | 767 |
| 25.6 CRSS Technical Architecture | 770 |
| 25.6.1 Visual Studio .NET | 770 |
| 25.6.2 XML Spy | 771 |
| 25.6.3 eXcelon Stylus Studio | 771 |
| 25.6.4 SQL Validation Service | 771 |
| 25.7 Summary | 771 |

### 26  The Architecture  773

| | |
|---|---|
| 26.1 System Architecture | 774 |
| 26.1.1 Client Tier Model Revisited | 782 |
| 26.1.1.1 XML Schema Support for Reusable Datatypes | 782 |
| 26.1.1.2 Identifying Reusable Datatypes | 783 |
| 26.1.1.3 Creating XML Schema Reusable Datatypes | 786 |
| 26.1.1.4 Reusable Datatype Review | 789 |
| 26.2 Creating HTML Pages by Using XSLT | 795 |
| 26.3 Sending Form Data | 800 |
| 26.4 Summary | 807 |

### 27  The Server Tier  809

| | |
|---|---|
| 27.1 Database Design with XML Schemas | 810 |
| 27.1.1 Mapping XML to Relational Databases | 815 |

|  |  |  |
|---|---|---|
|  | 27.1.2 Testing the SQL Mapping | 822 |
|  | 27.1.3 Database Mapping Summary | 823 |
|  | 27.2 SQL IIS Configuration | 823 |
|  | 27.2.1 Testing the SQL IIS Configuration | 829 |
|  | 27.3 CRSS Application Requirements | 831 |
|  | 27.4 Updategrams | 832 |
|  | 27.5 Summary | 833 |
| **28** | **The Integrated Solution 835** |  |
|  | 28.1 CRSS Design Review | 836 |
|  | 28.2 Web Tier Construction | 838 |
|  | 28.3 UI Broker Component Construction | 842 |
|  | 28.4 Security Broker Component Construction | 846 |
|  | 28.5 CRSS Broker Component Construction | 847 |
|  | 28.6 Template Query | 851 |
|  | 28.7 CRSS Review | 853 |

## PART VII  Appendixes  855

### Appendix A: XML Schema Quick Reference  857

### Appendix B: XML Schema Regular Expression Grammar  867

### Appendix C: The Thematic Catalog XML Schema  877

### Appendix D: Data-oriented Schemas: Oracle8*i* Datatypes  901

|  |  |
|---|---|
| D.1 General Overview | 902 |
| D.1.1 UTF-16 Support | 902 |
| D.1.2 TIMESTAMP and Time-zone Support | 902 |
| D.1.3 `CLOB` and `NCLOB` Support | 902 |
| D.1.4 `UTL_ENCODE` PL/SQL Package Not Implemented | 902 |
| D.1.5 `SYS.UriType` Oracle Datatype Not Implemented | 903 |
| D.1.6 `SYS.AnyData` Oracle Datatype Not Implemented | 903 |
| D.2 Discussion of the Consequences | 903 |
| D.2.1 `normalizedString` Datatype and Subtypes Derived by Restriction | 903 |
| D.2.2 `dateTime` Datatype | 904 |
| D.2.2.1 `maxInclusive` Constraining Facet | 905 |
| D.2.2.2 `maxExclusive` Constraining Facet | 905 |
| D.2.2.3 `minInclusive` Constraining Facet | 906 |
| D.2.2.4 `minExclusive` Constraining Facet | 906 |
| D.2.3 `date` Datatype | 906 |
| D.2.3.1 `maxInclusive` Constraining Facet | 907 |
| D.2.3.2 `maxExclusive` Constraining Facet | 908 |

D.2.3.3 `minInclusive` Constraining Facet .......... 908
D.2.3.4 `minExclusive` Constraining Facet .......... 908
D.2.4 `gYear` Datatype .......... 909
D.2.4.1 `maxInclusive` Constraining Facet .......... 910
D.2.4.2 `maxExclusive` Constraining Facet .......... 910
D.2.4.3 `minInclusive` Constraining Facet .......... 910
D.2.4.4 `minExclusive` Constraining Facet .......... 910
D.2.5 `gYearMonth` Datatype .......... 911
D.2.5.1 `maxInclusive` Constraining Facet .......... 912
D.2.5.2 `maxExclusive` Constraining Facet .......... 912
D.2.5.3 `minInclusive` Constraining Facet .......... 913
D.2.5.4 `minExclusive` Constraining Facet .......... 913
D.2.6 `time` Datatype .......... 913
D.2.6.1 `maxInclusive` Constraining Facet .......... 915
D.2.6.2 `maxExclusive` Constraining Facet .......... 915
D.2.6.3 `minInclusive` Constraining Facet .......... 915
D.2.6.4 `minExclusive` Constraining Facet .......... 915
D.2.7 `gMonth` Datatype .......... 916
D.2.7.1 `maxInclusive` Constraining Facet .......... 917
D.2.7.2 `maxExclusive` Constraining Facet .......... 917
D.2.7.3 `minInclusive` Constraining Facet .......... 917
D.2.7.4 `minExclusive` Constraining Facet .......... 917
D.2.8 `gDay` Datatype .......... 918
D.2.8.1 `maxInclusive` Constraining Facet .......... 919
D.2.8.2 `maxExclusive` Constraining Facet .......... 919
D.2.8.3 `minInclusive` Constraining Facet .......... 919
D.2.8.4 `minExclusive` Constraining Facet .......... 920
D.2.9 `gMonthDay` Datatype .......... 920
D.2.9.1 `maxInclusive` Constraining Facet .......... 921
D.2.9.2 `maxExclusive` Constraining Facet .......... 921
D.2.9.3 `minInclusive` Constraining Facet .......... 921
D.2.9.4 `minExclusive` Constraining Facet .......... 922

**Appendix E: Glossary  923**
E.1 Objects, Classes, and Instances .......... 924
E.2 Markup .......... 927
E.3 XML Documents .......... 927
E.3.1 Whole Documents .......... 927
E.3.2 Parts of Documents .......... 929
E.4 XML DTDs and Schemas .......... 932
E.5 Selected Datatypes Used in Schema Documents .......... 936
E.6 Miscellaneous .......... 937

**About the Authors   939**
**Index   941**

# Preface

The authoring and editorial teams for this book have worked hard to bring you the cleanest, clearest, and most complete XML schema reference source on the market. Endless sweat, research hours, code testing, tech and definition reviews and counter explanations, e-mail queries, dialogue, and debates passed before this book came to fruition. Earnest efforts, stress-filled moments, and writing deadlines have finally gotten us to press time. Here is what this book means to us.

## The History

There are always new and hot technologies to write about (C++, Java, SQL, .NET, XML Schema, and much more). There are qualified writers eager to write a clear and concise best-seller for your bookshelf. There are millions of software developers eager to learn. There are more than a few publishers to choose from. Ultimately there are several technical books on the market within months of any new product, platform, service, tool, or language's release that seek to describe, explain, clarify, and elaborate on a given technology's importance, utility, and implementation. However, there are very few really *good* books on the "why and when" that will actually teach developers emerging technologies. In fact, the hardest types of books to write discuss emerging technologies, because there really are not many good examples. Furthermore, even the "experts" frequently disagree on what is "right."

We spent many months—full time—writing this book. We collectively have something like 80 years of experience. Some of us are on the W3C Schema Working Group. We believe that this combined experience, as well as the determination writing this book, results in one of the few "really good books" previously mentioned. It takes the right combination of technology, authors, publishers, and readers to pull off a book.

## The Book

There are several, and probably soon to be lots, of books on the market that pertain to XML Schema. Despite this influx, we strongly believe that this book provides details that few, if any, other books provide. Specifically, the overarching goal driving this book is to provide detailed examples of every XML Schema component. In order to detail each component, this book contains an example of the corresponding Schema document element, and all of the associated attributes. Many of the books on the market today provide surface details about Schema components. However, this book provides detailed scenarios. Not only are there many pages and examples of each Schema element, there is at least one example of *every single attribute of every single XML schema document element*. Having accomplished that colossal task, we added example after example integrating with many languages and technologies on many platforms. After all, what good is an XML schema by itself?

## Audience

The primary goal of this book is to provide detailed information about XML Schema. The book opens with a discussion on the background and supporting Recommendations for XML Schema. The book addresses how to create XML schema documents. Additionally, some of the chapters in this book cover integrating XML schemas into other existing technologies such as Java, Visual Basic, and Oracle. The audience of this book is software developers who need to create an XML schema or perhaps integrate one into an application. This book does *not* sufficiently cover aspects of the Schema Recommendation that pertain to writing an XML schema validator.

## Prerequisites

Most of the text in this book requires familiarity with XML. For discussions that apply to various technologies, such as Oracle, the text requires familiarity with the pertinent technology. On the other hand, the book explains the standards that provide a foundation for XML Schema and even XML, such as the XML Infoset, XML Namespace, and XPath. Object-oriented principles apply to XML Schema; the book requires that you have a general understanding of objects and inheritance.

## Organization of This Book

The purpose of this book is to detail how to create an XML schema. Furthermore, various sections of this book discuss how and why you would use such a schema. This book is divided into seven parts:

- Part I, XML Schema Overview
- Part II, Creating XML Schema Documents
- Part III, Validation
- Part IV, Result-oriented Schemas
- Part V, Data-oriented Schemas
- Part VI, A Case Study: The Campus Resource and Scheduling System (CRSS)
- Part VII, Appendixes

Part I of this book opens with a brief discussion of XML and the basis for needing XML Schema. The overview encompasses reasons to use—or not to use—a schema. Part I also covers some general concepts that provide a foundation for this book. In addition, Part I briefly discusses the practical aspects of creating an XML schema document and validating an XML instance against the schema represented by that schema document. An *XML document* is a character string conforming to the grammar of the XML Recommendation (see Section 1.3);

it might be in the form of an input stream, a buffer, a disk file, or any other form. An *XML instance* is an XML document—or potentially even part of a document—whose validity is being determined. Specifically, the validity of this document depends on examining an XML schema specified by the XML instance, or possibly a different schema selected using information not in the document.

> **NOTE**
>
> The term *XML instance* as used in this book is not generic: XML is not a class of which these character strings are instances. An XML document (or a fragment of one) is called an "XML instance" only when it is intended to carry the connotation of a candidate for validation in the context where the term is used.

Part II covers the W3C XML Schema Recommendation, *XML Schema*, in detail. In particular, Part II details every XML schema element type and all of the corresponding attributes. Examples throughout this part of the book demonstrate nearly every feature of XML Schema. Part II serves as a tutorial or a reference manual.

Part III encompasses validation of XML schemas. Some of the chapters in Part III are background information, such as an in-depth discussion of post schema-validation infoset (PSVI). Other chapters are more concrete, containing code examples that demonstrate how to validate XML against an XML schema.

Part IV covers how to apply an XML schema to achieve a particular business goal. In particular, this part of the book addresses the target of an XML instance, such as a document or an application. In other words, Part IV discusses how to create an XML schema such that the schema and corresponding XML instances are helpful in providing the desired solution.

Part V discusses how to mirror an XML schema with an SQL schema. The chapters in this part of the book use Oracle as the target database. Many of the issues covered are generic to SQL schema generation. Oracle9*i* is the specific target of Part V. Note that Appendix D addresses the differences between Oracle8*i* and Oracle9*i* pertaining to XML schemas.

Part VI is a complete case study. This case study, the Campus Resource and Scheduling System (CRSS), integrates XML schemas with Microsoft technology: SQL2000, the .NET Framework, Visual Basic code, and more.

Part VII provides grammars, code examples, and a glossary for quick reviews.

## The Web Site

The http://www.XMLSchemaReference.com Web site corresponds directly to this book. The sole purpose of this Web site is to provide an online reference for developers writing XML schemas. Nominally, the Web site provides a place to download all of the files created while writing this book. These files include not only the XML schemas and the source code in various languages, but also all of the test cases for even the one-line code snippets: All of the code in this book is tested!

The Web site is much more extensive than just a collection of files, however. In addition to the traditionally available downloads, http://www.XMLSchemaReference.com has lots simple online examples of every schema document element. There are tables for each element that indicate what attributes are possible, as well as a brief description. Although this Web site is not a tutorial, it is a fantastic quick reference for those who already understand XML Schema in general, but might forget the specific syntax. It is our hope that the Web site, like the book, becomes real reference material for lots of developers.

## The Value

Our goal is to make it easy to create an XML schema—whether you need a tutorial to write your first schema document, or you just need a reference book to write your 5,000th. Having created a schema, this book also gives you the same levels of assistance to incorporate an XML schema into your application. This book provides as much support as you need, without ever getting in the way. Have fun working with XML schemas—we do!

We invite you now to take a tour through the world of XML schema components, beginning with the introduction provided for you in Chapter 1. We welcome your stories, additions, code samples, questions, feedback, and insights.

Cliff Binstock
cliff@XMLSchemaReference.com

Dave Peterson
davep@acm.org

Mitchell Smith
mitchsmith50@hotmail.com

Mike Wooding
woodinmi@mindspring.com

Chris Dix
cdix@navtrak.net

Chris Galtenberg
c@galtenberg.net

# Acknowledgments

**Cliff Binstock:** Many thanks to my wife, Amy, for putting up with months of work on this book: days, nights, and weekends. Many thanks to coauthor Dave Peterson. Dave's unflagging e-mails and editing, as well as his participation in the W3C XML Schema Working Group, made this book as accurate as humanly possible. Thanks to Shelley Kronzek, executive editor, for providing the opportunity to share some of my knowledge with you. Thanks to Anne Marie Walker, the development editor, for teaching me how to write a book (which, by the way, is very different from all the technical documents I have written over the years). Mostly, thanks to you, the reader, for making this long journey worthwhile. I really hope that this book makes your current and future projects much easier.

**Dave Peterson:** I want to thank my wife, Greta, for putting up with me living in another world for too many months while this book has been gestating. Cliff, it's been fun. And thanks to Tyrrell Albaugh for repeatedly saving our sanity towards the end.

**Mitchell Smith:** I would like to thank my friend Cliff for getting me involved, Shelley and Anne Marie for all of their work on this book, and Dave Buehmann and David Schrader for teaching me the expressiveness of SQL and the capabilities of Oracle.

**Mike Wooding**: My efforts on this book were possible because I had the fantastic support of my wonderful wife Linda and my two daughters, Andrea and Jessica. Thanks for allowing me to disappear into my "cave" to complete this.

**Chris Dix:** I would like to thank my wife Jennifer and my sons Alexander and Calvin; you are my favorites. Thanks to Cliff, Shelley, and the folks at Addison-Wesley for this opportunity.

**Chris Galtenberg:** All my love to my Lady Lavinia . . . and many thanks to "The Year 2001," the most brutal and evolutionary period of my life.

# XML Schema Overview

# PART

# I

Part I provides detail on the foundation of the W3C XML Schema Recommendation. This foundation includes, among other topics, the W3C recommendations that support the W3C XML Schema Recommendation.

- Chapter 1 provides an overview of the various W3C recommendations that are the foundation for the XML Schema Recommendation. The terminology and concepts from the various recommendations coalesce into a discrete set of terms, which provide a handle with which to read the remainder of this book.
- Chapter 2 provides a high-level overview of how an XML parser validates XML. This overview also covers the parser extensions required to validate XML against an XML schema.
- Chapter 3 is an overview of namespaces. This overview includes a discussion of the W3C XML Namespace Recommendation. Namespaces are one of the first considerations when creating an XML schema document.
- Chapter 4 covers a basic description of the respective grammars. XPath locates elements and attributes for Identity Constraints. XPointer locates elements for inclusion in an XML schema document.
- Chapter 5 covers the abstract representation of both XML documents and XML schemas. This chapter also introduces XML infosets, which are the abstract versions of documents on which an XML schema processor operates.

# Introduction

**CHAPTER 1**

## IN THIS CHAPTER

1.1  Why XML?   4

1.2  Why XML Schemas?   5

1.3  The World Wide Web Consortium (W3C) Recommendations   7

1.4  Object-Oriented Concepts   10

1.5  Unifying Terminology   11

1.6  Thematic Examples   19

1.7  Creating an XML Schema Document   24

1.8  Typesetting Conventions   25

1.9  Online Resources   26

XML schemas provide a consistent way to validate XML. The XML Schema grammar specifies a language that constrains and documents corresponding XML. The greatest strength of an XML schema is that each schema defines a "contract." This contract provides the foundation for an application to accept or reject XML data before attempting to operate on the data. Although—or perhaps because—schemas are powerful, they can be time-consuming to create. Once created, however, a schema simplifies the rest of the software development process.

## 1.1 Why XML?

For as long as there have been programming languages, programmers have been trying to simplify ways to transmit data from one section of code to another. The simplification comes mostly in the form of standards. Standardization has evolved from solely technical specifications to standards accepted by a large community. The latter often involves programmatic enforcement. Communicating between sections of code has evolved over the years. At a macroscopic level, the following progression roughly describes the evolution of software development:

1. Linear source code
2. Functions and subroutines
3. Object-oriented classes
4. Distributed processing

In recent years, software solutions have required distributed computing. From the end of the 1980s to the middle of the 1990s, distributed computing was in the form of client-server and then *n*-tier applications. Toward the end of the 1990s, the industry moved to Web applications. The most recent—and extreme—form of distributed applications involves Web services. A sophisticated software solution may encompass Web services from many vendors.

From a software development perspective, there has always been a challenge to correctly coordinate the distribution of data. From a programming perspective—again at a macroscopic level—the distribution of data has evolved in parallel with the previously itemized evolution of computing:

1. Fixed memory locations
2. Registers or stack entries
3. Global variables
4. Local variables, structures, and pointers
5. Language-based objects
6. XML

XML has become the definitive—and perhaps the *de facto*—standard for transmitting data between distinct pieces of software—and computers. XML provides a simple, consistent format that any program—using any programming language—can accommodate. Because the XML syntax is well defined, parsers have quickly become available that are easy to incorporate into a new or existing program. The availability of these parsers has promoted the use of XML as *the* language of choice for transmitting data.

XML is also typically considered "human-readable." That is, a developer (or frequently even a business analyst) can examine an XML stream and know that the stream is correct or, conversely, identify errors. Like any other conglomeration of bits consumed by a computer, the XML for a given communication still has to conform to some known structure. This is where XML Schema comes into play.

## 1.2 Why XML Schemas?

XML provides a grammar for parsing a particular file or stream format. This XML grammar covers basic syntax, the most interesting being that of element tags and attribute specifications. Most applications need far more structure. XML schemas provide a mechanism for specifying more extensive grammar constraints. The ability to guide the layout of an XML document makes that XML document much more predictable. A programmer can examine an XML schema and know exactly what corresponding XML documents look like. Additionally, a program can reject an XML document out of hand when the XML does not conform to the appropriate XML schema.

An XML schema specifies valid elements and attributes in an XML instance. Furthermore, a schema specifies the exact element hierarchy (for nested elements). A schema specifies options (such as limits on the number of occurrences of a type of element) and various other constraints placed on the XML instance. In addition, a schema specifies a range for the *value* of an element or attribute.

> **NOTE**
>
> The value of an element is the text between the start- and end-tags; the value of an attribute is the text between the quotes.

### 1.2.1 What Is an XML Schema Document?

An *XML schema document* is the XML representation of all or part of an XML schema. Specifically, one or more XML schema documents describe an entire XML schema. Most of the elements in a schema document are XML representations of schema components; the other elements support assembling a schema from a set of schema documents.

## 1.2.2 Benefits of an XML Schema

XML schemas provide innumerable benefits to a development environment. Many of these benefits are intangible or economic in nature, indirectly increasing productivity and decreasing time-to-market.

The most important tangible aspect of an XML schema is that an XML schema specifies a contract between software applications or between parts of a software application. A developer creating software to generate XML, or an unfortunate employee who has to manually create XML, knows the target. A developer writing software that receives the XML not only knows what to expect, but can validate the incoming XML against the schema. As a specification of an interface, an XML schema might not be as easy to read as an English document, but it is incredibly precise. Furthermore, the writer can clarify the intent of a schema with XML comments and XML schema annotations—each with embedded English (or any other language).

For software development shops creating large applications, the notion of a contract simplifies modularization, resource allocation, testing, and deployment. Modularizing the code is easier because the boundaries are readily identifiable (each boundary is an XML document). This in turn makes resource allocation easier: Individual developers receive specific tasks, each of which has well-defined inputs and outputs. Testing is also much easier: The developer generating XML ensures that the generated XML validates against the XML schema, and the developer receiving the XML can easily create test XML documents in a common editor. Subsequently, integration testing is usually far more successful than with traditional data (such as passing objects and structures). Finally, even deployment is simpler: Versions of code that generate the XML can be deployed at different times than code that receives the XML—assuming that the schema is stable.

Modern distributed environments compound the issues just mentioned for a development shop. In particular, the developer writing software to process XML might be writing a Web service; anyone on the Internet could potentially generate XML that is sent to the Web service. In the case of a Web service, the XML schema is the crucial piece of documentation. Likewise, the XML schema is the contract by which everyone abides. For example, the developer can change the underlying Web service as long as the XML schema does not change. Likewise, developers know the exact target required by the XML schema.

## 1.2.3 Drawbacks of an XML Schema

From a practical perspective, one of the biggest hurdles for XML schemas is the learning curve. An XML schema is not easy to write; a *good* XML schema is even less easy. A good schema takes into account all boundary conditions—just like a good program.

XML schemas are incredibly precise; they are also verbose. This should come as no surprise to anyone who interacts frequently with the equally wordy plain XML, the foundation for XML schemas.

There is a noticeable amount of overhead to using XML. The XML verboseness just mentioned translates directly into extra overhead for deciphering XML. Understanding XML requires a full parser. A native programming structure (such as a C `struct` or a Java `class`) is much more efficient. XML validates against an XML schema. This validation is time-consuming. Worse, loading an XML schema document also requires parsing XML. As computers get faster and faster, developers tend to ignore the effort required from a processor. Of course, in some cases, the programmer can cache schema information for speed. Even so, a user might perceive the time delay caused by a single validation. Almost certainly, the amount of time required for multiple validations has the potential to annoy users.

## 1.3 The World Wide Web Consortium (W3C) Recommendations

A number of W3C Recommendations (the W3C chooses to call them "recommendations" rather than "standards") involve XML processing. Different people with different guidelines developed each Recommendation at different times. Five Recommendations (including the Schema Recommendation itself), provide context for this book:

- The XML Recommendation, *Extensible Markup Language (XML) 1.0 (Second Edition)*
- The Namespace Recommendation, *Namespaces in XML*
- The Infoset Recommendation, *XML Information Set*
- The XPath Recommendation, *XML Path Language (XPath)*
- The Schema Recommendation, *XML Schema*

Each of these Recommendations warrants significant discussion in this book. See Table 1.1 for an extensive list of URLs that encompass these Recommendations. This book consistently references the informal name (such as "the Infoset Recommendation") of each Recommendation just introduced.

### 1.3.1 The XML Recommendation

The W3C released the XML Recommendation in February 1998. This Recommendation defines the parts of an XML document (tags, elements, content, attribute specifications, and so on), along with some ancillary processing instructions and declarations.

> **NOTE**
>
> The difference between "real" declarations and XML's standardized use of "processing instruction notation" for some declarations is historical: XML derived from SGML and tried to be compatible with SGML and use compatible terminology and notations. In SGML, *declarations* can only be established by the ISO SGML Standard. The SGML developers were not prepared to add new declarations fast enough for the XML developers, so they used SGML processing instructions instead. (One use of processing instructions in SGML is for user-defined declarations. As far as SGML is concerned, the XML developers are "users.")

The XML Recommendation does not attempt to define the "abstract" document. The XML Recommendation defines the XML and Document Type Definition (DTD) grammars. Furthermore, the Recommendation discusses well-formed XML documents (documents that conform to the XML grammar) and valid XML documents (documents that conform to a DTD).

## 1.3.2 The Namespace Recommendation

The W3C released the Namespace Recommendation in January 1999. Namespaces are important during document validation. Different sources provide parts of a DTD (in the same way that one XML schema references another). Namespaces provide a mechanism for avoiding naming conflicts.

For example, a DTD might define a `list` element type designed for ordinary written documents such as a book or magazine article. At some point, someone might want to add the MathML package for standardized mathematical formula markup. Unfortunately, MathML has a distinct `list` element type, with quite different content. There might well be a large body of existing documents, making a change to the document `list` element type difficult. Similarly, changing the MathML element complicates the use of standardized tools to handle math.

The solution is to have one namespace for the document DTD's element types and another for the MathML element types. A namespace-aware processor reads a revision of the original DTD that implies the first namespace, and the new `MathML` element types imply the MathML namespace. The XML DTD-based validator selects the correct `list` element type to validate against based on context. All XML schema-based processors are namespace-aware, and operate this way.

## 1.3.3 The Infoset Recommendation

The Infoset Recommendation is the most recent of the Recommendations, promulgated in October 2001. *Infoset* is a commonly used abbreviation for *Information Set*. The purpose of the

Infoset Recommendation is to standardize terminology by describing an object-oriented data structure that captures the abstract tree structure of elements in an XML document. In an XML document (a string of characters), the structure is a nested partition delimited by tags. Many of the elements described by these tags contain data between start-tags and end-tags. In an XML infoset, an object-oriented structure mirrors the tags in an XML document, with data characters being the leaves of the abstract tree structure.

## 1.3.4 The XPath Recommendation

The XPath Recommendation is one of the earlier XML-related Recommendations, released in November 1999. An XPath is a mechanism for navigating through an XML document hierarchy. The XPath notation is intentionally similar to widely accepted URI path notation—*XPaths are not XML*. An XPath can provide the location of a schema, sets of schema components, or individual schema components. Additionally, a subset of the XPath notation provides a language for specifying elements for identity constraints.

## 1.3.5 The Schema Recommendation

The W3C released the Schema Recommendation in May 2001—before the Infoset Recommendation. Nonetheless, the Schema Working Group, which developed the Schema Recommendation, designed schemas so that a schema processor would operate strictly on an XML infoset rather than an XML document. (The Schema and Infoset Working Groups had members in common and tracked one another's work reasonably carefully.)

Because of the dependence on an XML infoset, a schema processor cannot handle parseable entities: The XML parser must first identify, read, and parse these entities while creating the infoset. The XML parser expands the entities before schema processing begins. Therefore, a document with a nontrivial entity structure must have a DTD that declares those entities, although there is otherwise no reason to have a DTD. Fortunately, a DTD does not need to define the element types in a document unless there is some reason to validate them against that DTD.

The Schema Recommendation is divided into the following three parts:

- *XML Schema Part 0: Primer*, `http://www.w3.org/TR/xmlschema-0`: A tutorial that describes how to create an XML schema.
- *XML Schema Part 1: Structures*, `http://www.w3.org/TR/xmlschema-1`: A comprehensive reference guide that discusses the elements available for writing an XML schema document. It also covers the constraints required to implement an XML parser for validating XML instances against an XML schema.
- *XML Schema Part 2: Datatypes*, `http://www.w3.org/TR/xmlschema-2`: A complete reference for the numerous built-in datatypes.

At this book's publication time, the date on each of these Recommendations is May 2, 2001. `http://www.w3.org/XML/Schema` references many other related documents that might be of interest.

Working just from the Recommendations, you need to read *all* the Recommendations to be able to create an XML schema. Although Part 0 is a fantastic tutorial, the examples are not comprehensive. Part 1 covers everything you need to implement an XML validator; some of that is overkill if you just want to write a schema. The intent of this book is to provide one document that covers all three parts at an appropriate level of detail. This book is for the schema writer, not for the person implementing an XML validator. Unlike Part 0 of the Schema Recommendation, this book provides examples of every construct.

## 1.4 Object-oriented Concepts

One of the foundations of this book is object-oriented technology. Specifically, the foundation of XML schemas is *extensional* object-oriented technology; the foundation of more "conventional" languages such as C++ or Java is *intensional* object-oriented technology. In fact, software that processes XML documents must often process both intensional and extensional objects.

The poignant distinction between intensional and extensional objects is that in an intensional language, an instance exists because of instantiation. For example, you might use `'instance = new(class)'` or some other similar syntax. Extensionally, however, an object simply is or is not an instance of a particular class according to whether or not it satisfies the class's "restrictors." Consider, for example, the XML element `'<taggy />'`. It *claims* to be an instance of a `taggy` element type. Presumably, *but not necessarily*, the schema contains that element type (described by `'<element name="taggy" .../>'`). Furthermore, the XML element must satisfy the structure and attribute constraints specified by that element type in order to qualify as an instance. See Section 1.5.4 for a discussion of element types.

With extensional programming, validation software accepts or rejects potential instances. With intensional programming, an instance is implicitly valid: The software prohibits creation of an instance that does not satisfy the restrictions of its class.

In an object-oriented language such as C++ or Java, there is one inheritance mechanism. The derived class has full control of the functionality. New functionality comes from creating new methods or overriding existing ones. In an XML schema, an *extension* is analogous to creating a method or adding new properties. A *restriction* compares to overriding an existing method or restricting existing properties. The XML schema language—*not extensional programming in general*—prohibits certain derivations that are common in existing intensional languages. For example, schemas do not permit element types in an extension to override (subclass) the corresponding structure type.

## 1.5 Unifying Terminology

Five Recommendations define concepts and create terminology for XML Schema—seven, when you add the ISO standards defining SGML-related equivalent concepts. Unfortunately, this complexity has created divergent terminology for parallel concepts and overloaded terminology for distinct concepts. This introductory chapter cuts through the melee and establishes consistent terminology. Ultimately, despite the strong desire to reuse common terminology, the book presents some new terms in the following four circumstances:

- When an existing term has multiple connotations. For example, *abstract* might mean an abstract schema as opposed to a *concrete* XML schema document. The term *abstract* might also mean a non-instantiable class (versus a "concrete" instantiable class).
- When many similar words are used, perhaps with slight nuances, in which one word would suffice. For example, this book consistently presents the term *specify* instead of *define* or *declare*.
- When different Recommendations use different words for essentially the same concepts, we will select one term for the concept and use it consistently (except when explaining the alternate terminology you might find in a particular Recommendation).
- When different Recommendations use the same words for different concepts, we will generally use the words only one way and establish alternate terminology for the other concepts.

### 1.5.1 Important Terminology Used in This Book

Because of the confusion caused by the issues just mentioned, the subsequent definitions establish some new terms. Of particular importance, this section establishes the concept of various *types*. In most of the discussion in this book, the form of each type is irrelevant.

*Simple type:* A component of a schema; a class whose instances are elements and attributes; it restricts the value of its instances according to rules set forth in the Schema Recommendation.

*Complex type:* A component of a schema; a class whose instances are elements; it restricts the content and attribute set of its instances according to rules set forth in the Schema Recommendation.

*Structure type* **of an element type or attribute type:** The simple type or complex type which is the value of the *type* property of an element type; the simple type that is the value of the *type* property of an attribute type.

*Element type:* A component of a schema; a class whose instances are elements; it restricts the *type name*, content, and attribute set of its instances. It primarily binds a structure type to a name.

*Attribute type:* A component of a schema; a class whose instances are attributes; it restricts the *type name* and value of its instances. It binds a structure type to a name.

*Instantiable* **class:**
1. (General) A class that can directly have instances.
2. A complex type or element type that does not require a derivation or substitution to instantiate directly in an XML instance. Unfortunately (for terminological consistency within this book, we have a different meaning for 'abstract'), explicitly non-instantiable complex types and element types specify an `abstract` attribute—although this is a common use of the word 'abstract'.

*Non-instantiable* **class:**
1. (General) A class that can only have instances by virtue of them being instances of another class derived from this class.
2. A complex type or element type that requires a derivation or substitution to instantiate directly in an XML instance.

*XML instance:* An XML document—or even part of a document—whose validity is being determined. Specifically, the validity of this document depends on examining an XML schema specified by the XML instance, or possibly a different schema selected using information not in the document. The term 'XML instance' as used in this book is not generic: XML is not a class of which these character strings are instances. An XML document (or a fragment of one) is called an "XML instance" only when it is intended to carry the connotation of a candidate for validation in the context where the term is used.

The terms 'element instance' and 'attribute instance' appear occasionally. These terms mean a specific element or attribute in an XML instance, respectively.

*XML validator:* An XML validator is a program—or a module in a program—that examines XML purporting to be an XML instance and validates that XML against an XML schema.

*Base* **type:** Simple types and complex types benefit from object-oriented class inheritance. A *base type* is the simple type or complex type of which there is a derivation. A base type is analogous to what some might call a *superclass* or *archetype*.

*Derived* **type:** A derived type is a simple type or complex type derived from a base type. In an XML schema, derivation occurs by *extension* or *restriction*. Both Chapter 10 and Chapter 11 discuss extension and restriction in detail. A derived type is analogous to what some might call a *subclass*.

*Content pattern:* A content pattern specifies a set of content options available for a specific element in an XML schema. The content pattern loosely follows a simplistic regular expression. Appendix A includes a brief discussion regarding the grammar, or format, of a content pattern.

## 1.5.2 Schema Values

Many of the chapters in this book discuss how to express the XML representation of a particular schema component. Each of these elements—the XML representation of a component—has multiple, often optional attributes. In many cases, the values of these attributes refer to another schema component, perhaps a built-in datatype. The value of an attribute is always a character string. This string must always conform to a datatype, although the type may provide many—or no—constraints on the value in the string. The following definitions illuminate the subsequent datatypes that appear frequently in the discussion of schema attribute values:

*NCName:* An NCName is a name that does not contain a colon character. (The etymology of 'NCName' is from "no-colon name" or "non-colonized name"; however, neither of these terms is in common use.)

*QName:* A QName is a *qualified name*—the combination of a *prefix* (an NCName that in the scope of an appropriate namespace declaration determines a namespace), a colon character, and a *local name* (another NCName). Note that a default namespace might *imply* a namespace for a QName, in which case the prefix and colon is omitted and the QName *is* an NCName. (The QName datatype is a bit more complicated; see Section 12.4.1.)

For example, a QName might refer to a global element type. Attributes of various schema elements require a value that conforms to a QName. Chapter 3 has more to say about namespaces.

*ID:* An NCName that must be unique amongst all attribute (and element) values asserted to be IDs in an XML document. (ID is a DTD-prescribable attribute structure type, and there is a corresponding ID datatype defined in the Schema Recommendation that can be the structure type of an attribute type or element type.)

Almost all schema elements can have an id attribute. The structure type of the id attribute is ID.

### NOTE

ids often clutter an XML schema document. Furthermore, an id has no effect on the PSVI and is not reflected in the corresponding schema component (both of these are discussed in Chapter 2, and in more detail in Chapters 16 and 15, respectively). Many of the examples in this book incorporate an ID to demonstrate how to use the id attribute. In fact, schema document elements should probably not specify an ID unless that ID has an intended use (such as a reference from an external XPointer).

## 1.5.3 Parallel Concepts and Ignoring Differences

XML documents are flat strings of characters. The markup in these documents connotes structure. The process of *parsing* a document finds elements and attributes and constructs an "abstract" image that corresponds to the XML structure. Of course, not only the document but all of these elements and attributes give rise to corresponding objects in the abstract structure. Thus, a parallel exists between the concrete documents and the elements and attributes in it (which are all character strings), and the corresponding abstract objects (which explicitly embody the structure recognized by the parser).

Similarly, a parallel exists between the concepts of DTDs and those of schemas. Both create classes (which are DTD "element types") whose instances are particular kinds of elements. The same parallels exist for other classes having to do with whole documents and parts of elements. If you are familiar with DTDs, being aware of the parallels will make learning schemas easier.

Often the distinction between the concrete and abstract versions of a concept is irrelevant: specifically, after the parser has created an abstract copy of the concrete document. Similarly, the processes of validation against DTDs and schemas are pretty much equivalent except in the details of which properties of the corresponding abstract structures record the results.

## 1.5.4 Element Terminology

This section covers the difference between concrete and abstract elements. In addition, this section introduces some terms specific to elements.

### 1.5.4.1 (Concrete) Elements

Fortunately, the XML Recommendation and the ISO SGML Standard (ISO 8879:1986) use the word 'element' consistently. An element is a string of characters satisfying certain lexical and grammatical constraints described in the XML Recommendation. An XML parser recognizes certain substrings of the element as markup; the remaining characters are data. The XML parser further distinguishes characters within the markup strings as punctuation or metadata.

Elements normally begin with a start-tag and finish with an end-tag. There is a special case in which the element consists entirely of an "empty-element" tag. For the purpose of this discussion, the part of a tag of interest is the (metadata) name immediately following the opening punctuation. This name has been variously called the element's "generic identifier," "name," "element type-name," or "type name." We will use the last. (The XML Recommendation refers to this name as just "the name in the start-tag.")

Everything in this book is an object: character strings and, in particular, elements are objects. So, *element* is a class; element's instances are *elements*; an instance is *an element*. Element (the class) provides a *type name* method. The *type name* of an element, as defined previously, is the value of that *type name* method (or property, if that's your preferred terminology for functions tied to an object—elsewhere in this book, they are "propertyMethods").

### 1.5.4.2 Abstract Elements

For each element, a parser generates an equivalent abstract data structure. The Infoset Recommendation calls such structures "element information items." That is the terminology generally used in this book.

An *element information item* is an object with specific properties, such as a *children* property (for *content*), a *local name* property (for *type name*, in the absence of *namespace* processing), and various other properties as well.

This book uses the phrase 'abstract element' only when necessary to emphasize the correlation with real "concrete" elements; normally the book refers to *element information items*.

### 1.5.4.3 Elements
After a parser has parsed an element and generated an element information item, the distinction between *(concrete) element* and *abstract element* is often immaterial. For the most part, any information embedded in the element is available as a propertyMethod value; the information is available as an explicit property value in the structure tree headed by the element information item. This book refers to an *element* when the distinction between abstract and concrete elements is irrelevant.

### 1.5.4.4 Element Terminology Summary
This section takes the element concepts introduced throughout Section 1.5.4, and provides terminology used throughout this book. These terms include:

*Element:*
1. A character string that conforms to the requirements of being an element, as found in the XML Recommendation.
2. Either an element (definition 1) or an element information item. Used when the distinction is irrelevant to the discussion in context.

*Element information item:* An object created from a (concrete) element by a parser, which reflects explicitly the structure, data, and metadata recognized by the parser while parsing the element.

This book occasionally contains these variants:

*(Concrete)* **element:** Element (definition 1). Used only when, because of context, "element" might be misunderstood as meaning definition 2, or when necessary to emphasize the contrast with abstract element.

*Abstract* **element:** Element information item. Used only to emphasize the correspondence to, or the distinction against, a (concrete) element.

A related term is:

*Correspond:* During parsing, an element information item *corresponds* to the generating element, and vice versa.

## 1.5.5 Element Type Terminology
Element types are abstract; that is, they are not parts of documents. They arise from concrete elements in schema documents. We are more likely to care about the distinction between

abstract and concrete with respect to element types (and all schema components) than we did between elements in concrete and abstract documents, because the correspondence between abstract components and their concrete representations is not quite as one-to-one as the correspondence between (concrete) elements and (abstract) element information items. On the other hand, when discussing (abstract) schema components and their (concrete) representation in schema documents, we are never concerned with the distinction between the concrete and abstract versions of those schema documents.

While the situation just described pertains to all schema components and their representations, in this chapter we will only describe, as an example, the concepts and terminology relating to element types, one particular class of schema component. See Chapter 15 for descriptions of all the schema component classes.

DTD-defined element types arise from the XML and Infoset Recommendations (and have roots in SGML). Schema-defined element types arise from the Schema Recommendation.

### 1.5.5.1 (Abstract) Element Types

An *element type* is a class derived from element. The instances of an element type are elements. Any individual element type corresponds to the elements in an XML document that satisfy certain requirements. For the most part, an element type places restrictions on the content of elements (such as which types of subelements or data characters can appear where), on attributes of the elements (which attributes, by name, are permitted, required, or prohibited and which kinds of values each attribute may have), and on the *type name* (a given element type requires that all instances have the same *type name*).

This book refers to an *element type* as an object with various properties. All element types, being classes, use the values of these properties as parameters for the same algorithms in their restrictors. Those algorithms embody the validation rules given in the XML Recommendation.

Element types and other type classes, such as attribute types, are instances of "type generators." *Element type* is the type generator whose instances are element types.

### 1.5.5.2 DTD-defined Element Types

The XML Recommendation does not describe element types as objects (much less classes). The XML Recommendation focuses on concrete element types. The Infoset Recommendation does not discuss element types at all.

A validating XML processor must validate an XML document against any corresponding DTD. The parser reads the DTD, including all element type declarations and attribute list declarations. For each element type declaration, the parser builds internal data structures that embody the element type; for each attribute list declaration, the parser adds attribute restriction information to the internal data structures. The data structures are simply a proprietary realization of the object called an "element type."

On the concrete side, putting an element type declaration together with any associated attribute list declarations constitutes a DTD-defined *concrete element type*. This terminology is rarely used.

The XML Recommendation implicitly asserts the existence of the *element type* class generator. That Recommendation also implicitly causes the element type class generator to provide various properties whose values in each element type are determined from strings in the corresponding declarations but which do not have standardized names. Chapter 15 describes a corresponding schema-defined structure; that structure provides an adequate mental model that may be used for the simpler structure of a DTD-defined element type.

### 1.5.5.3 Schema-defined (Abstract) Element Types

The Schema Recommendation defines a specific class of objects that play the role of element types. The Schema Recommendation Working Group wanted to avoid using the phrase 'element type' that the XML Recommendation uses for "(DTD-defined) element type"; for better or for worse, they chose 'element declaration schema component'. The primary problem with this choice is that everyone else associates the word 'declaration' with the concrete side of things; for many years (before XML), the SGML community *called* element type declarations in DTDs "element declarations."

Schema-defined element types (or "element declaration schema components") are, therefore, objects that are themselves classes, with properties whose values control which elements are instances. Each element type has a name. This book refers to specific element types by name. These names appear in a monospace font:

> An `example` is an element whose element type has the name 'example'. `example` is an element type.

Note that these monospace names, unlike ordinary English common nouns, are case-sensitive. Therefore, this book maintains the case assiduously, even when English usage would otherwise cause capitalization (as in the second sentence).

The "name" of each schema-defined element type is embodied in *two* properties, because schema processors are required to be namespace-aware. The first property is *target namespace*: Its value is the "namespace name" (the URI, not the locally associated prefix). The second property is *name*: Its value is the "local" name (the "whole" name stripped of the namespace-identifying prefix). An element type's restrictor algorithms use these two properties to ensure that a potential instance expects, by virtue of its *type name*, to be an instance of this particular element type. Other properties directly or indirectly determine the acceptable content—and the permitted, required, or prohibited attributes (and their acceptable values)—of the element instance.

In this book, a schema-defined element type, like its DTD-defined counterpart, is referred to by a name (namespace prefix, colon, and local name, or just local name if context permits); that name is displayed in a monospace font. The interpretation of the notation with respect to element instances is identical.

### 1.5.5.4 Schema-defined Concrete Element Types

A *schema document* is an XML document that describes an XML schema. Generally, elements in the schema document are representations of components in the schema.

The Schema Recommendation describes validating an XML document. Furthermore, it describes the creation of a schema as follows: First a parser creates an infoset by parsing a schema document. Then the schema processor scans that infoset and produces an (abstract) *schema*, which includes the *element type* objects.

The elements in the schema document that are XML representations of element types are elements of type `element` (this name fortunately corresponds to the 'ELEMENT' keyword for DTDs). The content and attributes of each `element` element determine the properties of the corresponding element type. Thus, an `element` is a "schema-defined *concrete* element type."

### 1.5.5.5 Element Type Terminology Summary

This section takes the element concepts type introduced throughout Section 1.8.5, and provides terminology used throughout this book. These terms are:

***Element type:***

1. A component of a schema; a class whose instances are elements; it restricts the *type name*, content, and attribute set of its instances. It primarily binds a structure type to a name.

   Each element type requires that its instances all have the same type name and all satisfy the same constraints on their content and attributes. An element type may originate from an element type declaration in a DTD or from an `element` element in a schema document.

2. An *element type* specifically defined by an element type declaration in a DTD. (This meaning is common, but this book uses "*DTD-defined* element type".)

3. Either an element type (definition 1) or the corresponding element type declaration or `element`. Used only when the distinction is irrelevant to the discussion in context.

***Element type declaration:*** A declaration in a DTD used to define an element type: the XML representation of a DTD-defined element type.

***Element:*** A type of element in a schema document used to define an element type: the XML representation of a (schema-defined) element type.

Occasionally used variants include:

***DTD-defined* element type:** An element type whose XML representation is an element type declaration in a DTD (element type, definition 2).

***Schema-defined* element type:** An element type whose XML representation is an `element` in a schema document.

***Concrete* element type:** An element type declaration or an `element`: the XML representation of an (abstract) element type. Used only when necessary to emphasize the parallel with (abstract) element types.

***(Abstract)* element type:** Element type (definition 1 or 2). Used only when necessary to emphasize the parallel with concrete element types.

***Element declaration schema component:*** Schema-defined element type. Standard notation for the Schema Recommendation; used in this book only when necessary to correlate with material from that source. However, the Schema Recommendation does not adopt the "classes are special kinds of objects" approach; the *class* is only closely related to the element declaration schema component, which is the *object*.)

Related terms include:

***Correspond:*** During parsing and validating, an element type *corresponds* to an `element` or element type declaration, and *vice versa*.

***Describe:*** An `element` or element type declaration *describes* the corresponding element type.

***XML representation:*** An `element` or element type declaration is an *XML representation* of the corresponding element type.

In addition to these specific terms, there is a special notation for specific element types (which have names given by the `element` or element type declaration that is their XML representation). References to a specific type are by name; that name appears in a monospace font. Examples abound in the immediately preceding sections, albeit mostly involving the `element` element type.

## 1.5.6 Other Terminology to Expect in This Book

Many other concepts parallel *element* and *element type*. They categorize the same way, get the same notations, and are described using similar terms. For instance, there are attribute types (which the Schema Recommendation calls "attribute declaration schema components") represented in DTDs by attribute list declarations and in Schemas by `attribute` elements. The instances of an attribute type are attributes, or their concrete equivalents—substrings of the start-tag or empty-element tag of an element, commonly called "attribute specifications."

## 1.6 Thematic Examples

Many sections of this book reference one or the other of two examples: a company catalog or a customer address list. These thematic examples are conceptually extremely easy to understand. This section includes XML instances of a company catalog and a customer list, presenting these examples so that the target for each schema element is clear. The corresponding XML schemas appear in Appendix C.

> **WARNING**
>
> Not all the schema examples conform to the best programming practices. This is intentional because the schemas are designed to demonstrate every XML schema concept.

The catalog contains parts. Each part specifies a database identifier, a name, a part number, and various other properties. Note that there are different types of parts (unit items, bulk items, and assembled items), each of which has some unique properties. For example, only assemblies specify a part list from which the assembly is constructed. Listing 1.1 portrays an example of this catalog.

**LISTING 1.1**  The Company Catalog

```
<catalog>
    <unitPart>
        <unitID>10327</unitID>
        <partName>Unit 1</partName>
        <partNumber>UX001</partNumber>
        <partOption>
            <color>magenta</color>
        </partOption>
        <description>Unit 1 is the thing to buy</description>
        <fullPrice>28.00</fullPrice>
        <includedQuantity>1</includedQuantity>
    </unitPart>
    <unitPart>
        <unitID>10329</unitID>
        <partName>Unit 2</partName>
        <partNumber>UX002</partNumber>
        <partOption>
            <color>Pink Grapefruit</color>
        </partOption>
        <description>Unit 2 lasts longer than Unit 1</description>
        <fullPrice>28.01</fullPrice>
        <includedQuantity>1</includedQuantity>
    </unitPart>
    <bulkPart>
        <bulkID>40000397</bulkID>
        <partName>Bulk 1</partName>
        <partNumber>BLK2088</partNumber>
        <partOption />
        <description>
```

```xml
        This includes 1,000
        <partList>UX002</partList>
        pieces.
    </description>
    <fullPrice>1700.00</fullPrice>
    <includedQuantity>200</includedQuantity>
</bulkPart>
<unitPart>
    <unitID>40004787</unitID>
    <partName>Unit 3</partName>
    <partNumber>UX003</partNumber>
    <partOption />
    <description>
        This is obsolete.. on sale
    </description>
    <salePrice employeeAuthorization="MWS"
            managerAuthorization="ALB">28.03</salePrice>
    <includedQuantity>1</includedQuantity>
</unitPart>
<unitPart>
    <unitID>40004787</unitID>
    <partName>Unit 4</partName>
    <partNumber>UX004</partNumber>
    <partOption />
    <description>
        This is also obsolete.. on clearance
    </description>
    <clearancePrice employeeAuthorization="MWS"
            managerAuthorization="ALB">8.57</clearancePrice>
    <includedQuantity>1</includedQuantity>
</unitPart>
<assemblyPart>
    <assemblyID>40004788</assemblyID>
    <partName>Assembly 1</partName>
    <partNumber>ASM9001</partNumber>
    <description>
        This is made up of both
        <partList>UX002 UX003</partList>
        pieces which makes this assembly
        better than the competition.
    </description>
    <fullPrice>3200.00</fullPrice>
    <includedQuantity>1</includedQuantity>
    <customerReview>
        <customerName>I. M. Happy</customerName>
        <customerFeedback>This is the most
 awesome phat product in the entire.
```

*continues*

```
    world.</customerFeedback>
        </customerReview>
        <partList>UX002 UX003</partList>
    </assemblyPart>
</catalog>
```

Many sections in this book pertain to an address list of customers. A customer list contains both business customers and private customers. Each XML customer node specifies a name, a telephone number, an address, and other properties. Listing 1.2 is an example of a customer list.

**LISTING 1.2**  The Customer List

```
<customerList source="Oracle">

<businessCustomer customerID="SAM132E57">
    <name>Cliff Binstock</name>
    <phoneNumber>503-555-0000</phoneNumber>
    <address>
        <street>123 Gravel Road</street>
        <city>Nowheresville</city>
        <state>OR</state>
        <country>US</country>
        <zip>97000</zip>
        <effectiveDate></effectiveDate>
    </address>
</businessCustomer>

<businessCustomer customerID="SAM132E58"
                  primaryContact="Joe Sr.">
    <name>Joe Schmendrick</name>
    <phoneNumber>212-555-0000</phoneNumber>
    <phoneNumber>212-555-1111</phoneNumber>
    <URL>http://www.Joe.Schmendrick.name</URL>
    <address>
        <street>88888 Mega Apartment Bldg</street>
        <street>Apt 5315</street>
        <city>New York</city>
        <state>NY</state>
        <country>US</country>
        <zip>10000</zip>
        <effectiveDate>2001-02-14</effectiveDate>
    </address>
</businessCustomer>

<businessCustomer customerID="SAM132E58"
                  primaryContact="Ellie"
```

```xml
                  sequenceID="88742">
   <name>Ellen Boxer</name>
   <phoneNumber xsi:nil="true"/>
   <address zipPlus4="20000-1234">
       <POBox>123</POBox>
       <city>Small Town</city>
       <state>VA</state>
       <country>US</country>
       <zip>20000</zip>
       <effectiveDate>2001-02-14</effectiveDate>
   </address>
</businessCustomer>

<businessCustomer customerID="SAM132E59"
                  primaryContact="Lydia"
                  sequenceID="88743">
   <name>Ralph McKenzie</name>
   <phoneNumber xsi:nil="true"/>
   <address>
       <street>123 Main Street</street>
       <pmb>12345</pmb>
       <city>Metropolis</city>
       <state>CO</state>
       <country>US</country>
       <zip>80000</zip>
       <effectiveDate>2001-02-14</effectiveDate>
   </address>
</businessCustomer>

<privateCustomer customerID="SAM01234P"
                 sequenceID="88743">
   <name>I. M. Happy</name>
   <phoneNumber>303-555-0000</phoneNumber>
   <phoneNumber>303-555-1111</phoneNumber>
   <address>
       <street>123 Main Street</street>
       <pmb>12345</pmb>
       <city>Metropolis</city>
       <state>CO</state>
       <country>US</country>
       <zip>80000</zip>
       <effectiveDate>2001-02-14</effectiveDate>
   </address>
</privateCustomer>

</customerList>
```

The schema documents that correspond to Listings 1.1 and 1.2 are lengthy and are not included in this section, although they appear in Appendix C. The book provides detailed explanations of the schema in Part II.

### 1.6.1 Thematic Example Quality

Most of the examples in this book exhibit good design; however, there are a number of exceptions, especially in `address.xsd`. These exceptions demonstrate specific features available in an XML schema. For example, the use of `addressLine`, a substitution group, is questionable. Similarly, having the element types `phoneNumber` and `effectiveDate` global is poor programming practice, although they demonstrate global element types nicely.

## 1.7 Creating an XML Schema Document

Hopefully, you are "chomping at the bit" to write your first XML schema document. Fortunately, many free tools and some great not-so-free tools are available. This section provides suggestions for software for editing XML and XML schemas and for validating XML against those schemas.

### 1.7.1 Editing an XML Schema Document

The quickest way to get started writing an XML schema document is with your favorite editor. Because an schema document is just XML, you can create an schema document in Notepad, WordPad, vi, Emacs, or any other text editor that tickles your fancy. The advantage of using a text editor is that you have zero learning curve (for the editor), and you can create an XML schema document quickly.

The primary disadvantage of using a text editor is that the text editor does not provide any guidance. An alternative is to use an XML schema editor such as XML Spy from Altova or a UML-style tool such as SoftModeler from Softera. These tools guide you through the process of creating an XML schema, more than compensating for their fairly short learning curve. In addition, a schema editor might hide the XML markup, making it easier to focus on the content, instead of the syntax. You must be aware that very few software tools implement every feature specified in the Schema Recommendation. This deficit will most likely improve over time as XML schemas and the corresponding software get more popular. That said, most of the XML schema software tools in existence today implement most of the schema features; they probably implement the ones you need.

### 1.7.2 Validating an XML Instance

The author of an XML instance—or an XML schema document, for that matter—does not need to be concerned with *how* validation of the XML instance occurs. For example, some browsers can directly validate received XML. Tools such as XML Spy permit validation in a stand-alone environment. Apache, Microsoft, and others provide software development kits for embedding XML validation in custom applications. But *caveat emptor*: Because XML Schema technology is just becoming widely accepted, few tools on the market properly validate everything in an XML document against a corresponding XML schema.

## 1.8 Typesetting Conventions

This book uses a few typesetting conventions that are worth pointing out. For example, a word or phrase in the `monospace` font indicates a code snippet. Frequently this font points out a specific type (such as `simpleType`), a specific instance of a type (such as the specification of the custom simple type `street`), or even a specific element or attribute instance (such as the element `street` in an XML instance). The monospace font also denotes code listings:

```
A code listing looks like this.
```

Occasionally, a code listing indicates a variable that would need something substituted for it before using the code. The variable appears in an *italic monospace* font:

```
xmlns:ns="http://www.example.com"
```

This book presents new terms in *italic*, except where they appear as separately formatted definitions.

This book presents SPECIAL CONSTANTS, such as those used in the Post Schema-validation Infoset (PSVI) in small capital letters.

This book consistently *mentions* character strings (words, code, whatever) by enclosing those strings in *single* quotation marks. In the following sentence, 'attribute' is first *used* (to name a particular element type) and then *mentioned*:

> The name of the `attribute` element type is 'attribute'.

Throughout the book, warnings, cautions, tips, notes, and notation notes appear. A *warning* is information that—if ignored—might lead to unexpected results. A *caution* indicates that you should take extra care to ensure desired results. A *tip* is a suggestion that might make coding—or gathering information from the current chapter—easier. A *note* points you to other related sections of this book, or illuminates technical features that might not be apparent from a casual reading of the current section. A *notation note* is similar to a note, except that the thrust of the note is to highlight the way specific terminology is used. ⎯⎯ in code lists indicates a continued line:

```
part of line 1
⎯⎯ remainder of line 1
```

## 1.9 Online Resources

Table 1.1 contains valuable URIs that pertain to the Schema Recommendation. Table 1.1 also contains URIs for locating the XML schema documents referenced throughout this book.

**TABLE 1.1**  Online Resources

| Description | URL |
| --- | --- |
| World Wide Web Consortium (W3C) | `http://www.w3.org` |
| The W3C XML Schema Main Page | `http://www.w3.org/XML/Schema` |
| XML Schema Part 0: Primer | `http://www.w3.org/TR/xmlschema-0` |
| XML Schema Part 1: Structures | `http://www.w3.org/TR/xmlschema-1` |
| XML Schema Part 2: Datatypes | `http://www.w3.org/TR/xmlschema-2` |
| Extensible Markup Language (XML) 1.0 (Second Edition) | `http://www.w3.org/TR/2000/REC-xml-20001006` |
| Namespaces in XML | `http://www.w3.org/TR/1999/REC-xml-names-19990114/` |
| XML Information Set | `http://www.w3.org/TR/xml-infoset/` |
| XML Path Language (XPath) Version 1.0 | `http://www.w3.org/TR/xpath` |
| The XML Apache Project | `http://xml.apache.org` |
| Online XML Schema Reference | `http://www.XMLSchemaReference.com` |
| The Main Catalog Schema | `http://www.XMLSchemaReference.com/examples/theme/catalog.xsd` |
| The Main Address Schema | `http://www.XMLSchemaReference.com/examples/theme/address.xsd` |

# XML Processing

**CHAPTER 2**

## IN THIS CHAPTER

- 2.1 Basics  28
- 2.2 XML Structure Before and After Parsing  32
- 2.3 Schema Processing  33

The XML Recommendation does not prescribe that all XML processing programs must be structured in a specific way. However, having in mind a particular processing model does help in understanding XML. This chapter describes a common processing model that seems to be in harmony with the various XML-related Recommendations that are promulgated by the W3C.

The model of XML processing that is arising from those XML-related Recommendations is necessarily rather fine-grained, so that the interactions between various aspects of XML can be described. In practice, different XML systems will clump into "black box" processors that do not show the internal seams and might even bypass some of the steps in the process. This is perfectly reasonable as long as the output behavior of the processor is what the Recommendations require.

## 2.1 Basics

Processing in an XML environment often involves a cascade of simpler processors, each one feeding on the output of the previous one. You can imagine this as a series of programs, with output of one piped (in the Unix sense) to the input of the next.

Some kind of overseeing program is needed to accomplish all this by treating the others as subroutines and creating the piping; sometimes the overseeing program might be the final one, possibly having the others as compiled-in subroutines. Other times, one program in the cascade might need to influence the internal state of an earlier (upstream) one. For example, a parser (see Section 2.1.2) might need to influence the state of the lexical analyzer so it produces the right kind of token. An input controller (in XML and SGML usually called an "entity manager") might need to be told by the parser when to change the input source.

The usual sequence is to have an entity manager feed a uniform character stream from one or many sources to a lexical analyzer, which feeds system-dependent *tokens* to a parser, which in turn feeds *events* or a single *information set* to a consumer. If that consumer consumes events, it is probably a final application. An information set can go directly to a final application or can first be modified by a validator. There are, of course, many variations on these themes. Most notably, the lexical analyzer might be subsumed into the parser, or (if only one input stream is used) the entity manager might be skipped. Also, any of the adjacent steps may be combined into a black box that does several jobs—possibly without actually creating the intervening now-internal output-to-input data structures.

For example, all the processors except the final application might be subsumed by a black-box "XML processor" that does everything to create an infoset and then provides access to it for the application via a *Document-Object-Model* (DOM)-based API or emits *Simple-API-for-XML* (SAX)-compliant parse-event tokens to the application. It is also possible for one processor, such as the parser, to be broken up into two separate cascaded processors, each simpler than the original. Indeed, from one point of view, that is how lexical analyzers came about: The parser originally took as its input the incoming character stream, and researchers realized that, in many cases, describing the grammar against which the parser worked was easier if the input was first chunked into tokens.

Processing outside an XML context is likely to go through a similar process, although the traditional names attached along the way may be different. For example, a compiler might have a macro processor and `include` preprocessor as its *entity manager* and might call its validator a *semantic processor* and its application a *code generator*.

### 2.1.1 Entity Managers

*Entity managers* (to use the XML-specific term) are responsible for finding the characters that are to be streamed to the parser. In XML, this requires feedback from the parser and lexical analyzer; control information is sent back to the entity manager through an upstream pipe. As the parser reads an entity *declaration* in the DTD, it informs the entity manager of yet another potential source of input characters. When the lexical analyzer encounters an entity *reference*, the analyzer signals the entity manager to begin reading characters from that source. Entities are always sources of characters for input.

### 2.1.2 Parsers and Lexical Analyzers

A *parser* is a program or subroutine that reads a stream of *input tokens* and emits a stream of *output tokens*, generally based on grammatical rules. Sometimes there is just one output token—a complicated tree-structured object that embodies the entire parsed document. Sometimes one parser emits symbols that are read by another. Cascading parsers sometimes make the parsing process simpler to describe or simpler to implement.

A *lexical analyzer* is a very simple parser—it reads individual character tokens and emits one token per word or "punctuation character group," based on simple lexical rules. It must be cascaded with a "real" parser, which reads the words and punctuation against real grammatical rules, to determine the *grammatical* structure of the input character string and to emit tokens that describe that structure. Sometimes even the grammatical parse is simpler when the process is broken up by the cascading of two (or more) parsers that follow simpler rules.

For example, during part of the process of parsing the string of characters that makes up an XML document, the parser might recognize (1) '<', a name, and '>' as forming a *start-tag* (which starts an element), (2) characters as making up the content (possibly parsed into subelements), and finally (3) '</', the same name, and '>' as forming the matching *end-tag* (which ends an element).

If you are familiar with SGML, you will recognize that an SGML parser has to track a lot more things in order to deal with omitted and "short" tags. Indeed, this is the main reason XML does not allow omitted or short tags: The XML designers wanted to make parsing XML simple.

### 2.1.3 Validators

A parser has to keep track of information about the tokens it has already read so that it can properly apply the grammar rules to determine the structure of the input. In the process, the parser also determines if the input can satisfy the rules: The input might simply be unacceptable because it cannot satisfy the grammar. It is also possible to specify *additional* rules that are not needed when determining the grammatical structure but that an application might insist that the resulting structure satisfies. A *validator* is a program that checks additional rules after parsing. In XML, a parser can determine the structure of the document—whether the tags are properly formed, what the component elements and data strings are, and which of these are in the content of which elements. Then a validator can check to see whether the order of subelements and data strings is acceptable with respect to the DTD (or schema). A DTD, from this point of view, is simply more rules (over and above the XML grammar) to be checked, cast in a particular language designed for describing the rules. Similarly, a schema is also more rules to be checked, cast in the form of an XML document of a particular type (a "schema document").

> **NOTE**
>
> The rules for parsing XML are entirely contained in the grammar prescribed by the XML Recommendation. The rules for validating against a DTD are not complete in the Recommendation; they must be supplemented by information in the DTD, which is part of the document. Thus, an XML validator must in effect reconfigure itself on the fly—that is, during the process of parsing and validating the document (during the reading of the DTD or any time thereafter before starting the validation phase).
>
> In contrast, the rules for parsing SGML (because of such things as omitted tags) must include information from the DTD. SGML cannot first be parsed against rules completely contained in ISO 8879 (the SGML standard); the rules for parsing the document instance must be modified on the fly, during or after the parsing of the DTD but before parsing the document element.

Often the rules for parsing can be written in a particular form called a "formal grammar." This makes possible parsers that read the grammar, build the grammar information into internal tables, and then parse against that grammar: new grammars, new parsers—with no new code to write. A variation on this theme is to write a program that reads in the grammar and writes out source code for a program that compiles into a parser for that grammar—new code, but none written by hand. (The Unix utility *yacc* works in this manner.) For various kinds of formal grammars, programs are available that read the grammar and either become parsers (called "syntax-driven parsers") or emit parsers for that grammar ("parser compilers"). Because of this, it is tempting to design languages that use grammars for which one of these programs exists.

Syntax-driven parsers that can modify their syntax rules while parsing can be written and hence SGML could have a syntax-driven parser, but such parsers are not well known and generally are not efficient when compared to the more common ones. Therefore, a design goal of XML was to be "parseable" by the simpler parsers that cannot modify their rules while parsing. The process of checking the structure was relegated to a separate routine that checks the structured data from the parser against the rules embodied in the DTD.

> **NOTE**
>
> A nonvalidating XML parser (one that does not validate against a DTD) need not read the DTD and hence might not be aware of entity declarations for entities referenced in the document element. This can cause the nonvalidating parser to fail to parse some of what is intended as part of the document. There are nonvalidating parsers that read the entire DTD and act on the entity declarations therein, so that even though they do not validate the element/attribute structure, they build a complete document tree. This is the sort of parser needed when the resulting tree is to be validated against a schema. (Any *validating* parser can be provided with an *entity-declarations-only* DTD that effectively causes no validation of the element structure.)

## 2.1.4 Parsing Events, Information Sets, and Applications

When a parser emits many output tokens, these tokens are generally called "parsing events." When a parser emits the entire tree structure of the document in one token, that token is sometimes called an "information set."

> **NOTE**
>
> XML parsers that conform to the SAX specification (http://www.saxproject.org/) emit parsing-event tokens. Parsers conforming to the DOM (http://www.w3.org/DOM/) build an information set that can be queried by the application via an API. Other parsers may build an "XML document information item" (as defined in the Infoset Recommendation).
>
> These three options do not preclude others from emitting proprietary-form parsing events or a proprietary-form information set.

For the purposes of this book, an *application* is a program that accepts as input the output of a parser (often with some additional intervening processing, such as by a validator). Because an information set is typically a tree structure, the receiving application often (though not always) "walks the tree"; that is, it visits each node and leaf in succession, according to a standard algorithm, in an order that usually is the same order in which the parser created them.

Such an application might well be more efficient with a parser that emits parsing events as it parses, providing the information for each node or leaf as it is encountered during the parse. An application that expects parsing events must build its own tree internally if it needs to remember any of the information from one event to the next—such as the subtree of a particular element that for some reason it cannot finish processing until the element is complete, or cross-reference information that cannot be completed until the referenced material is found.

However, because XML schema processing is described in terms of operations on an information set, this book will use that processing model.

> **NOTE**
>
> Although event token-emitting parsers can be made to cooperate with a validator, doing so does complicate matters. Accordingly, because this book is trying to explain schemas, it will generally avoid bringing up the techniques necessary to effect schema validation in a SAX-based or other event-token environment.

> **NOTE**
>
> An event-emitting parser can validate the document against a DTD even if the parser does not build a complete tree structure of the document. Attribute information can be validated as the tag containing it is recognized; the content of an element can be validated against the content model as each data character or subelement is encountered.

## 2.2 XML Structure Before and After Parsing

The process of parsing takes a flat character stream including markup and creates a structured dataset, whose structure is determined by and reflected in the markup. This section describes more of what goes into and what comes out of a schema processor.

### 2.2.1 XML Documents

XML documents consist of elements. We shall assume that *element* is a class and that all elements are instances of that class. *Element* puts restrictions on its instances:

- Each instance must be a string of characters.
- It must begin with a start-tag and end with an end-tag, or it must be an empty-element tag.
- There are various other restrictions as well.

All XML tags contain a *type name* that is used during DTD-based validation to determine the DTD-defined element type against which the element is validated. A DTD-defined element type is a class derived from *element* (so that each instance of an element type is an element).

## 2.2.2 The XML Information Set

The XML Recommendation does not specify the information set that a parser should deliver. However, the Infoset Recommendation defines an abstract data structure called the "XML information set" or "infoset," which could be used as a single output token.

Conforming XML parsers are not *required* to implement exactly this information set, although fortunately many do so in one way or another. In any case, the XML infoset is the generic abstraction used in most XML documents and by many processors, so it is a useful mental model.

The XML infoset is particularly important for schema processing because the model of a schema processor in the Schema Recommendation is that of a validator that operates on the XML infoset, not on the original XML document.

The XML infoset is made up of objects: instances of various kinds, combined in various ways. They are all called *information items*. To begin with, the root object is a *document information item*. Other information items occur as values of various properties of the document information item, or recursively of properties of those information items in turn.

## 2.2.3 The DOM

The DOM Recommendation does not exactly define a data structure; rather, it defines access methods that standardize programming access of the structured data in a document. The actual structure being queried by the access methods is left to the implementor. By defining all these access methods, the Recommendation effectively defines an implicit structure. The DOM was originally created to handle both HTML and XML documents; some of its methods apply only to one or only to the other. For more information, see http://www.w3.org/DOM/.

## 2.3 Schema Processing

Dealing with schemas involves two separate processes on two separate documents. First, the schema has to be created from one or more schema documents. Second, the document to be validated must be parsed and then validated against the schema.

### 2.3.1 Processing an XML Schema Document

An *XML schema document* (XSD) is an XML document whose document element is a *schema* and that conforms to the "Schema for Schemas" and other requirements prescribed in the Schema Recommendation. The document must be parsed, giving rise to a corresponding (abstract) infoset. The infoset, in turn, is processed by a schema processor to create a *schema*, equally abstract, that is a collection of schema *components*. (Actually, several schema documents may be processed to create one schema; the mechanisms for doing that will be discussed in Chapter 7, Sections 7.8, 7.9, and 7.11.)

The components of a schema are organized much like an infoset; there is a *schema* component and all other components are values of properties of that component or recursively of properties of already-included components. (Much like the Infoset Recommendation, the Schema Recommendation is also compatible with the "schema-as-a-set-of-components" point of view. In that case, it does not include the schema component as part of the set.) The information items in the infosets of the schema documents and the schema components in the schema created from those documents in many cases correspond rather closely. A more complete description of these components is found in Chapter 15.

> **NOTE**
>
> In practice, many of these steps may be short-circuited. The "black box" processor might read the appropriate schema document(s), configure itself internally to validate against the schema so described, and be ready to read in the XML document to be validated.

### 2.3.2 What Does a Schema Processor Add? The PSVI

A schema processor takes as input the infoset generated by an entity reference-resolving XML parser (which has parsed the XML instance) and verifies that the data in the infoset conforms to the restrictions defined by the schema. In the process, the validator also adds additional information into the infoset.

The *post-schema-validation infoset* (PSVI) is the document infoset with modifications added by the schema processor. The details of the PSVI are covered in Chapter 16; at this point only an overview is needed.

A schema processor adds a lot of information to the basic infoset, which evaluates the validity of each element and attribute (just as a DTD-based validator might if the Infoset Recommendation had been written that way). This involves an amazing amount of detail. In addition, and often more important, schema processing adds information about the structure type of each PCDATA string, which is constrained by a simple type in the schema.

# XML Namespaces

**CHAPTER**

**3**

## IN THIS CHAPTER

- 3.1 Uniform Resource Names and Uniform Resource Locators  36
- 3.2 Namespace Components  38
- 3.3 Declaring Namespaces  38
- 3.4 Qualified Names and QNames  39
- 3.5 Namespace Scoping  42
- 3.6 XML Schema and Namespaces  42

To take full advantage of XML Schema, you need to understand XML Namespaces. The W3C released the Namespaces Recommendation shortly after the XML Recommendation. Namespaces help uniquely identify attribute and element names. They also help to prevent naming collisions. They do this by associating a Uniform Resource Identifier (URI) with your XML vocabulary so that elements with the same name but associated with different namespace URIs are differentiated.

Because namespaces came out after XML, they are not the easiest to use when validating your document with a DTD. A DTD must specify the exact name of the attributes and elements that appear in the document. As you will see, because of namespaces, a name is made up of multiple parts, one of which is an optional and arbitrary prefix that must be specified in the DTD to successfully validate it. This isn't the case with XML Schema: Namespaces are an integral part of XML Schema. By its nature, a schema uses at least two Namespaces: the XML Schema namespace that identifies the XML schema vocabulary, and the target namespace for the tags you are defining.

## 3.1 Uniform Resource Names and Uniform Resource Locators

URIs identify namespaces. URIs take the form of Uniform Resource Names (URNs) or Uniform Resource Locators (URLs). URNs identify a resource by giving it a globally unique and persistent name. The following is a typical URN:

`urn:example:mytags`

in which 'urn' identifies the Uniform Resource Name scheme, which means that this URI is a URN, 'example' is a namespace identifier (NID), and 'mytags' is a namespace-specific string (NSS).

Do not confuse *namespace* in the URN syntax description with the concept of Namespace from the Namespace Recommendation. The URN specification has its own concept of namespaces.

URLs uniquely identify the location of a resource. Browsing the Web wouldn't be possible without URLs. The following is a typical URL:

`http://www.example.com/mytags`

in which 'http' identifies the scheme and '//www.example.com/mytags' is the scheme-specific part.

The scheme-specific part differs, based on the scheme used. Although you usually see URLs with the http protocol specified, URLs using other protocols are perfectly legal to use as namespace identifiers. These include `mailto`, `ftp`, and `uuid`, among others. Although no resource is required to be available when using a URL to identify an XML Namespace, people—and even applications—might try to dereference your URL, looking for resources such as an XML schema or documentation. As a best practice, you should use a URN if you have no intention of providing additional information about the XML vocabulary the XML Schema is defining. See Section 3.1.2 for ideas on what can appear at the end of a namespace URL.

## 3.1.1 Creating URIs

When generating a URI for a namespace that you plan to distribute publicly, you should follow certain protocols to ensure uniqueness. You do not want to use a common name that others might use. If you do, you risk having naming clashes with other XML vocabularies.

That is one of the reasons HTTP URLs are popular for specifying namespaces. The first part of the scheme-specific string is a domain name that you register and own. This eliminates accidental naming clashes and gives you certain rights in forbidding others to use it.

URNs have similar rules. There is a procedure to register an NID with the Internet Engineering Task Force (IETF). After you go through the registration process, you own the NID for use in creating names. You are not required to register an NID, however. There is a protocol for using unregistered names by prepending an 'x-' to the NID to identify it as *experimental*. Even so, you risk naming clashes if you choose common words for your NID, so a good practice would be to use a domain you control. For example:

```
urn:x-example-com:mytags
```

where 'example.com' is a registered domain name under the control of the author. You might have noticed that the periods used in the URL were turned into dashes in the URN. Both URLs and URNs have specific rules about which characters are allowed. For more information on creating URLs and URNs, see the IETF RFCs:

- RFC 1630, *Universal Resource Identifiers in WWW*: http://www.ietf.org/rfc/rfc1630.txt
- RFC 2141, *URN Syntax*: http://www.ietf.org/rfc/rfc2141.txt
- RFC 1738, *Uniform Resource Locators (URL)*: http://www.ietf.org/rfc/rfc1738.txt

## 3.1.2 Using RDDL with Namespace URLs

When deciding whether to use a URL or a URN, a good rule is to use a URL if something is retrievable from the identified location. This could be an XML schema, documentation for the namespace, or something else. If you don't have anything to retrieve, use a URN. When using a URL to identify a namespace, the question arises of what you get when you access the URL with a browser. There's no consensus in the XML community on this. Some in the community think it should be a DTD or schema. Others feel it should be documentation or a package of various resources related to the namespace being used.

To help solve this problem, an XML vocabulary called Resource Directory Description Language (RDDL) was developed by a group of individuals on the XML-DEV mailing list. This vocabulary uses the XLink Recommendation, *XML Linking Language (XLink) Version 1.0* (`http://www.w3org/TR/xlink`), to identify a number of resources that can be associated with a namespace. Here's an example from the XML namespace that identifies a DTD as well as a schema:

```
<rddl:resource
    xlink:title="DTD for validation"
    xlink:arcrole=
        "http://www.rddl.org/purposes#validation"
    xlink:role=
        "http://www.isi.edu/in-notes/iana/assignments
        /media-types/text/xml-dtd"
    xlink:href="XMLSchema.dtd"/>
<rddl:resource id="xmlschema"
    xlink:title="XML Schema schema document"
    xlink:role="http://www.w3.org/2001/XMLSchema"
    xlink:arcrole=
        "http://www.rddl.org/purposes#schema-validation"
    xlink:href="XMLSchema.xsd"/>
```

When processing a RDDL document, you can use the `xlink:arcrole` attribute to determine what resources are available, and then use the `xlink:href` attribute to retrieve them. This gives you the flexibility to associate a variety of resources with a document. The application that processes the document can use whichever of the resources is most appropriate. For more information on RDDL, see `http://www.rddl.org/`.

## 3.2 Namespace Components

Namespaces enable you to create unique names that appear in an XML document. You associate a URI with the names that you use in your document. When a name is associated with a URI, it is called a "qualified name" and is said to be in that namespace. You can also have names in your document that are not in any namespace. These names are called "unqualified." You associate names in your document with a namespace by using a *prefix*. A prefix is an arbitrary string of characters that acts as shorthand for the namespace URI so that names are not overly long. The prefix is also optional, because you can declare a namespace to be a default, meaning all unprefixed element names are in that namespace by default.

## 3.3 Declaring Namespaces

Namespaces are declared by using a family of reserved attributes. In XML 1.0, attributes starting with the three letters '`xml`' (including variants with capital letters) are reserved for W3C use. To declare a default namespace, you add an attribute named 'xmlns' that has a value of the URI you choose to associate the namespace with. For example:

```
<Customer xmlns="http://www.example.com/foo">
    *    *    *    *    *
</Customer>
```

In the preceding example, a default namespace is declared. All unprefixed elements will be in the namespace associated with the URI 'http://www.example.com/foo'.

> **NOTE**
>
> As specified in the Namespace Recommendation, all unprefixed *attributes* are *unqualified*—not part of any namespace.

There needs to be a way to declare multiple in-scope namespaces. This can be done by using prefixes. A prefix is a short sequence of characters that appears at the left of an element or attribute name and separated from it by a colon. To declare a namespace that is associated with a prefix, you specify an attribute whose *name* is formed by prefixing *your* prefix with the special prefix 'xmlns'.

```
<foo:Customer xmlns:foo="http://www.example.com/foo">
    *    *    *    *    *
</foo:Customer>
```

In the preceding example, we declare a namespace that has the prefix 'foo' bound to it. Any elements or attributes that have the prefix 'foo' will be in the namespace http://www.example.com/foo. Because no default namespace is declared, all unprefixed elements are not in any namespace.

It is important to remember that a prefix is arbitrary, except for any prefix that starts with the characters 'xml' (lowercase or capitals or mixed), which are reserved for W3C use. For example, when looking at schema examples in this book, you might see the prefix 'xs' or 'xsd' bound to the schema namespace and 'xsi' bound to the schema instance namespace—however, any prefixes can be used as long as they are bound to the proper namespace.

## 3.4 Qualified Names and QNames

The XML Recommendation defines a *name* as a character string that has certain restrictions as to what characters it may contain. An XML document that conforms to the Namespace

Recommendation may include "qualified names." Elements, attributes, and entities are some of the XML document components that are required to have a name.

A *qualified name* has additional namespace information and is composed of three parts and may contain one colon. If there is a colon, the character string preceding it is the optional *prefix*. If there is no colon, the prefix is an empty string. The *local part* is what follows the colon. A qualified name also has a *namespace URI* that identifies the namespace. You do not see the namespace URI as part of the name when viewing the document, because it is declared higher up in the tree. The namespace URI is associated with the qualified name through the namespace declaration, the optional *prefix*, and the namespace scoping rules.

You use a prefix when you are not using a default namespace or when you want to include names outside any default namespace. A prefix is required to specify attributes that belong to a namespace, because unprefixed attributes never belong to any namespace. Even though unprefixed attributes are not in a namespace, there is an implied association between them and the element they appear on. The prefix is an arbitrary sequence of characters that work as a shorthand notation for the namespace URI.

Schema represents qualified names with the `QName` datatype. For more information on the Schema datatype `QName`, see Section 12.4.1.

The following XML shows an example document that uses both qualified and unqualified names. The element parent declares a default namespace, one with no prefix, and another namespace that is bound to the prefix 'bar'. Because of namespace scoping rules, 'Parent' is a qualified name that is in the `http://www.example.com/foo` namespace and does not have a prefix. The element type name 'bar:Child' is a qualified name that is in the `http://www.example.com/bar` namespace and is bound to the prefix 'bar'. Last, because unprefixed attributes do not belong in any namespace, the attribute name 'attr' is not a qualified name and is not associated with any namespace.

```
<?xml version="1.0" encoding="UTF-8"?>
<Parent "xmlns=http://www.example.com/foo"
  xmlns:bar="http://www.example.com/bar">
  <bar:Child attr="abcdefg"/>
</Parent>
```

The preceding example correctly describes the lexical representation of a `QName` in a schema. However, the value space is slightly different. Because the prefix is arbitrary and is only used as a shorthand notation, it has no value in defining a `QName`. Therefore, the value space of a `QName` in a schema contains only the local part and namespace URI. See Section 12.4.1 for more details.

### 3.4.1 Qualified Names as Values

The Schema Recommendation takes the notion of qualified names further than the definition in the Namespace Recommendation. It allows attribute and element values to be qualified names, and defines a `QName` datatype. The following example schema shows how this works. This schema does not use a default namespace, so every name that is part of a namespace will contain a prefix.

```xml
<xs:schema targetNamespace="http://www.example.com/foo"
   xmlns:xs="http://www.w3.org/2001/XMLSchema"
   xmlns:foo="http://www.example.com/foo"
   elementFormDefault="qualified"
   attributeFormDefault="unqualified"
   version="1.0">
   <xs:element name="ZipCode" type="foo:ZipCodeType">
          <xs:annotation>
                 <xs:documentation>Declares an element of type
                 ZipCodeType</xs:documentation>
          </xs:annotation>
      </xs:element>
      <xs:simpleType name="ZipCodeType">
          <xs:annotation>
                 <xs:documentation>Represents a ZipCode</xs:documentation>
          </xs:annotation>
          <xs:restriction base="xs:string">
                 <xs:length value="5"/>
                 <xs:pattern value="\d{5}"/>
          </xs:restriction>
      </xs:simpleType>
</xs:schema>
```

This schema defines a simple type, `ZipCodeType`. Because this schema has a target namespace of http://www.example.com/foo that is bound to the prefix 'foo', all definitions in this schema, such as `ZipCodeType`, are in the target namespace. When you define an element to be of a certain named structure type, the `type` attribute in the defining `element` has a structure type of `QName`. As such, either its value must contain a prefix that is bound to a namespace that is in-scope, or it must be in the scope of a default namespace. In our example, the `ZipCode` element has a type of `foo:ZipCodeType`. The prefix lets a schema processor correctly identify the type being used and also prevents naming collisions if other namespaces contain different `ZipCodeType` definitions.

There is currently some debate in the W3C as to whether a default namespace will apply to QNames that are part of attribute values. By allowing the use of default namespaces, you can decrease the number of characters within an attribute value. The XML Schema Working Group takes the position that default namespace processing is used for attributes with a datatype of `QName`. However, there currently isn't consensus on this within the W3C, so a final resolution has yet to be worked out. In the meantime, always use prefixed namespaces to ensure correct results.

## 3.5 Namespace Scoping

Namespaces have scoping rules that let you have a namespace in effect for only part of your document. A namespace declaration applies to the element where it is specified and to all elements contained within it. You can also override the binding of a prefix to a namespace URI by binding it to a different namespace URI, and you can turn off default namespace processing by setting the value of the xmlns attribute to an empty string. For example:

```
<root xmlns="http://www.example.com/root">
  <inrootnamespace/>
  <child xmlns="http://www.example.com/child">
    <inchildnamespace/>
    <nonamespace xmlns="">
      *   *   *   *   *
    </nonamespace>
  </child>
</root>
```

In the preceding example, the root and inrootnamespace elements are in the http://www.example.com/root namespace. The child and inchildnamespace elements are in the www.example.com/child namespace. In addition, the nonamespace element and its subelements do not belong in any namespace. Prefixes work the same way. It is possible to redefine a prefix to be associated with a different namespace. However, this is not a good thing to do. Because a prefix is just an arbitrary character string, you should not reuse a prefix in a document. The document will be error-prone and hard to read.

## 3.6 XML Schema and Namespaces

You associate an XML Schema with a namespace by using the targetNamespace attribute. A single XML Schema document can support at most one XML Namespace. Also, you can compose an XML Schema from multiple XML Schema documents that all share the same target namespace. You can also import elements and types from other namespaces in your schema by using the import element. By importing schemas from other namespaces, you can compose schemas that combine multiple vocabularies. Chapter 7 covers use of the import element.

In XML schemas, structure types are identified by QNames. This means they either need to be prefixed, there needs to be an in scope default namespace, or there must be no target namespace for the schema. With default processing, you might use the following schema start-tag to associate all the elements you define using default namespace processing:

```
<xs:schema
targetNamespace=http://www.myserver.com/myName
xmlns="http://www.myserver.com/myName"
xmlns:xs="http://www.w3.org/2001/XMLSchema"
xml:lang="en">
```

When creating schemas, it is preferable not to set a default namespace and to always use prefixes. By doing this, you cannot accidentally associate a name with the wrong URI.

The following example uses prefixes for all namespaces:

```
<xs:schema
    targetNamespace=http://www.myserver.com/myName
    xmlns:mn="http://www.myserver.com/myName"
    xmlns:xs="http://www.w3.org/2001/XMLSchema"
    xml:lang="en">
```

# XPath and XPointer

**CHAPTER 4**

## IN THIS CHAPTER

- 4.1 XPath 46
- 4.2 XPointer 51

# XPath and XPointer

The XPath Recommendation describes a language for specifying sets of elements in an XML document. The XPath Recommendation provides the foundation for the XPointer Recommendation, *XML Pointer Language (XPointer)*, which extends the XPath language to allow for specifying any part of an XML document. XPointers specifically support incorporating fragment identifiers into URI references. The XPointer Recommendation can be found at `http://www.w3.org/TR/xptr/`.

XML schemas use a subset of the XPath location paths for identity constraints. The XPaths specified by identity constraints (see Chapter 13) serve to locate nodes (specifically elements and attributes) within a corresponding XML instance. An XML validator examines the values of these elements and attributes to ensure uniqueness or referential integrity.

An XPointer provides the location of an entire XML schema document or merely a set of schema components. An XML validator nominally assembles an entire XML schema from a collection of XML schema documents. In fact, any XML schema document may assemble individual components from a variety of XML documents (although they do not have to be XML schema documents) by using XPointers. Specifically, an XPointer can point to a set of schema components embedded in a non-schema XML document.

This chapter is not a comprehensive tutorial on XPath or XPointer. The respective Recommendations provide lots of detail and many examples. The book presents a more complete XPath tutorial—restricted to XPath usage in identity constraints—in Chapter 13. Section 4.2 presents a number of representative examples that demonstrate locating elements that represent schema components.

## 4.1 XPath

Fundamentally, an XPath is an *expression*. Evaluating an XPath expression results in one of the following:

- A node set
- A Boolean
- A floating-point number
- A string of Unicode characters

The scope of XPath is far more extensive than the constructs covered in this section. For example, many constructs are designed to support XSLT. This section covers only those portions of XPath pertinent to XML schemas. Specifically, identity constraints require the resultant node set to contain only elements or attributes. Fragment identifiers (see Section 4.2) further restrict the resultant node set to contain only elements. Therefore, the Boolean, floating-point number, and string values are mostly not relevant in the context of XML schemas (see Section 4.1.4 for a discussion of the exceptions).

Because the remainder of this chapter primarily discusses node set results, subsequent discussion focuses on the subset of an expression known as a *location path*. A location path always identifies a node set.

## 4.1.1 XPath Location Paths

Location paths nominally provide the grammar for typical XPath expressions for XML schemas. In an XML schema, all location paths are either relative to an enclosing component (for identity constraints) or relative to an entire XML document (for locating schema components). One of the general features of a location path is the ability to navigate along a number of axes. An *axis* specifies a direction of movement in the node tree. For example, you might specify a *child* node, an *attribute* node, an *ancestor* node, or a *descendant* node.

The XPath Recommendation defines 13 axes. An identity constraint is limited to containing only the axes *child*, *attribute*, and *descendant-or-self*. Furthermore, an identity constraint can only use the shortcut notation for these axes. Table 4.1 portrays these shortcuts (Table 4.3 contains the entire list of axes).

One schema document can locate another (or even parts of another) with an XPointer. An XPointer may specify any of the 13 axes in a predicate (see Sections 4.1.2 and 4.2 for more detail). Although technically feasible, not all the axes are particularly valuable with respect to schema document locations. Table 4.3 illuminates the axes with dubious merit.

## 4.1.2 Predicates

Predicates are very powerful, but slightly confusing when first encountered. A predicate is strictly a filter. A predicate filters out desired nodes from a node set.

> **TIP**
>
> In an XML schema, an XPath expression always results in a node set. An expression with a predicate also results in a node set. Specifically, an expression with a predicate results in a *subset* of the node set that corresponds to the same expression without the predicate.

The easiest way to demonstrate a predicate is to discuss two similar expressions along multiple axes. For demonstration purposes, consider a catalog consisting of several parts:

```
<catalog>
  <partNumber SKU="S1234">P1234</partNumber>
  <partNumber>P2222</partNumber>
  <partNumber SKU="Sabcd">Pabcd</partNumber>
</catalog>
```

The ensuing example returns a node set that contains all `partNumber` elements in a document:

`//partNumber`

The corresponding node set contains the `partNumber` elements whose values are 'P1234', 'P2222', and 'Pabcd'.

An addition to the location path along an *attribute* axis results in a node set that contains all `SKU` attributes of `partNumber` elements:

`//partNumber/@SKU`

The corresponding node set contains the `SKU` attributes whose values are 'S1234' and 'Sabcd'.

The predicate in the next example, on the other hand, results in a subset of the `//partNumber` node set. In particular, the subsequent example returns `partNumber` elements that *have* `SKU` attributes, *not the attributes* as in the previous example.

`//partNumber[@SKU]`

The corresponding node set contains the `partNumber` elements whose values are 'P1234' and 'Pabcd'. The `partNumber` element whose value is 'P2222' is *not* included, because this element has no `SKU` attribute.

An XPath expression, in general, can return any node set, a Boolean value, a string, or a floating-point number. In an XML schema, the results of an XPath expression (in an identity constraint), as well as the results of an XPointer expression (in a `schemaLocation` attribute value), must result in a node set. Because of this, this chapter does not go into detail describing the other result types. However, a predicate can refine a node set in an XPointer expression. Therefore, Table 4.4, which appears later in this chapter, provides a few examples of XPointers that contain predicates that return values that are not node sets. Because very few schemas contain XPointers, and even fewer contain complex XPointers, this chapter does *not* provide a comprehensive tutorial on predicates.

> **TIP**
>
> The Schema Recommendation does not support the use of predicates within identity constraints. Within an XML schema, predicates are valid only as part of an XPointer expression, which can be used only in conjunction with schema document (and part-of-document) locations.

## 4.1.3 Node IDs

An XPath expression may include any number of "functions" that either extract information from an XML document or help to restrict the resultant node set (via a predicate). Identity constraints may not contain functions. In practice, XPath pointers to (parts of) schema documents rarely contain functions. Therefore, this chapter does not include a tutorial on the XPath functions or the corresponding return types. There is one function, however, supported—and even promoted by the XPointer Recommendation—in an XPointer location path expression: the `id` function.

The XPath `id` function is a great way to locate a specific node, assuming that a node specifies an ID. Note that the XPointer Recommendation surmises that IDs are "most likely to survive document change." The thought is that the structure of the XML document might change: Elements might "move" relative to one another. Consequently, a location path may no longer find the desired element, whereas the ID of the node is much more likely to be stable.

> **NOTE**
>
> The `id` function is part of the XPath Recommendation, which is why the discussion about this function appears in Section 4.1. With respect to XML schemas, however, an XPointer (in a `schemaLocation` value) is the only expression that can access this function. The `id` function *cannot* express any part of an identity constraint.

To demonstrate the use of the `id` function, the following URI locates the `catalogEntryDescriptionType` complex type (whose ID is `'catalogEntryDescriptionType.catalog.cType'`) in the thematic catalog schema:

```
http://www.XMLSchemaReference.com/theme/catalog.xsd#xpointer
    (id("catalogEntryDescriptionType.catalog.cType"))
```

To encourage the use of IDs, the XPointer Recommendation permits an XPointer to consist of a shortcut, which is just the *bare name* of the ID:

```
http://www.XMLSchemaReference.com/theme/
    catalog.xsd#catalogEntryDescriptionType.catalog.cType
```

### 4.1.4 Using XPath with Identity Constraints

An identity constraint may reference only three of the axes specified by the XPath Recommendation: *child*, *attribute*, and *descendant-or-self*. Furthermore, an identity constraint may refer to these axes only via a shortcut. Table 4.1 lists all the shortcuts available (the three axes and a wildcard) in an identity constraint.

Table 4.2 provides a few examples that demonstrate how to locate elements in an XML document. Chapter 13, "Identity Constraints," provides a much more complete discussion.

Listing 13.3 covers the complete grammar for location paths, as pertains to identity constraints. Likewise, Table 13.2 provides a number of detailed XPath examples.

**TABLE 4.1** Identity Constraint Shortcuts

| Shortcut | Meaning | Example |
|---|---|---|
| (No axis following '/') | Implied *child* axis | /a/b |
| | | Selects a b that is a subelement of an a, which is a subelement of the document root. |
| @ | *attribute* axis | a/@b |
| | | The b attribute of the a subelement element of the current node. |
| // | *descendant-or-self* axis | a//b |
| | | Any b element that is a descendant of a. |
| * | A wildcard representing all immediate subelements | a/*/b |
| | | Any b that is a subelement of any immediate subelement of a. |

**TABLE 4.2** Identity Constraint Examples

| Example | Meaning |
|---|---|
| //bulked | This expression locates all `bulkID` elements along the *descendant-or-self* axis of the root element. Therefore, this locates all `bulkID` elements in the entire document. |
| //bulkID/description | The expression locates all `description` elements along the *child* axis of the previous example. Therefore, this locates all `description` elements that are immediate descendants of any `bulkID` element. |
| /catalog/*/partNumber | This expression locates all `partNumber` elements that are direct descendants of any (hence the '*') direct descendant of `catalog`. Note that each element reference is along the *child* axis. |
| /catalog//partNumber | This expression locates all `partNumber` elements that are descendants (but not necessarily *immediate* descendants) of `catalog`. |
| /catalog//@employeeAuthorization | This expression selects all `employeeAuthorization` attributes of *any* descendant of the `catalog` element. |

## 4.2 XPointer

XML schema documents use `schemaLocation` attributes to locate other schema documents and parts of schema documents. The value of a `schemaLocation` is always a URI, which may include an XPointer. The `schemaLocation` attribute type of `schema`, `import`, and `include` are examples of where an XPointer might locate a schema document location.

An XPointer is nominally an extension of an XPath. The XPointer Recommendation permits—even encourages—the use of the XPath `id` function. There are also several XPointer specific extensions to XPath.

The XPointer Recommendation specifies expressions for returning portions of an XML document. The expression may evaluate to a node, a set of nodes, a portion of a node, or a portion of an XML document that spans nodes. Just as XML Schema limits the use of XPath expressions, it also limits the use of XPointer expressions. In particular, an XML schema may only import individual components (nodes) or sets of components (node sets). Because a component corresponds to an entire XML element—as opposed to a portion thereof—this section covers only XPointer constructs pertinent to extracting complete nodes.

### 4.2.1 Location Sets

The previous section mentions that an XPointer expression may evaluate to a node, a set of nodes, a portion of a node, or a portion of an XML document that spans nodes. Unlike an XPath expression, which must evaluate to a node set, an XPointer expression may theoretically return results that do not conform to a node. Therefore, the XPointer infrastructure requires an XPointer to return a *location set*.

A location set is an extension of a node set that an XPath normally returns. Each location in a location set is either a point or a range. A point consists of a node and an index. The index is a character offset into the node. A range consists of two points. The concepts of both point and range exist because of the XPointer requirement that an expression might return a subset of a node or possibly a set of characters that spans nodes.

Because an XML schema can only make use of an entire node or set of nodes, the remainder of this chapter covers only the subset of location information (and location sets) specified by nodes (and node sets). The terms 'node set' and 'location set' have similar meanings in the context of XML Schema.

### 4.2.2 Namespaces

The XPointer notation permits the identification of one or more namespaces. An XPointer expression specifies a namespace with the `xmlns` function. The argument to this function resembles a namespace attribute applicable to any XML element:

```
xmlns(xsd="http://www.w3.org/2001/XMLSchema")
```

The following XPointer locates the `catalogEntryDescriptionType` complex type by name. Namespace declarations always precede the locating expression:

```
http://www.XMLSchemaReference.com/theme/catalog.xsd#
  xmlns(xsd="http://www.w3.org/2001/XMLSchema")
  xpointer(
    xsd:schema/xsd:element[@name="catalogEntryDescriptionType"]
  )
```

In general, an XPointer may specify any number of namespaces. The previous example suffices for locating most schema components. An XPointer reference in a `schemaLocation` may require multiple namespaces when an XML document that is *not* a schema document has embedded Schema elements.

## 4.2.3 Subelement Sequences

*Subelement sequences* are notations that provide a shortcut to elements in an XML document. A subelement sequence has the following grammar:

```
bareName? ('/' [1-9] [0-9]*)+
```

where the optional *bareName* is replaced by the ID name of an element, as discussed in Section 4.2.2. The numerals represent the *N*th subelement (counting from 1) at each level.

> **WARNING**
>
> Subelement sequences provide an extremely compact and convenient short notation. Unfortunately, this supported notation is highly susceptible to failure. In particular, the structure of the expected XML document (in this case, most likely an XML schema document) must be extremely stable. Any change in the element structure of the document can provide surprising results.

The following example locates the fourth subelement of the third subelement of the document root:

```
../some.xsd#/1/3/4
```

Similarly, the following example locates the fourth subelement of the third subelement of the element whose ID is 'yadayada':

```
../some.xsd#yadayada/3/4
```

## 4.2.4 XPointer Extensions to XPath

This section covers *only* those XPointer extensions applicable to XML schemas. In fact, only one extension—the `range-to` function—has any applicability with respect to XML schemas. The use of this function is not common.

The XPointer Recommendation adds the `range-to` function as an option for an XPath step. A *step* is an axis and a node. A convenient use of the `range-to` function is to locate a set of nodes to incorporate into a schema. The `range-to` function is likely to appear in conjunction with the XPath `id` function. The following example locates four schema components that appear in sequence in `pricing.xsd`: `fullPriceType`, `freePriceType`, `salePriceType`, and `clearancePriceType`.

```
http://www.XMLSchemaReference.com/theme/pricing.xsd#
   xpointer(id("fullPriceType.pricing.cType")/
      range-to(id("clearancePriceType.pricing.cType")))
```

## 4.2.5 Using XPointer and XPath to Locate Schemas

This section describes the portions of the XPath Recommendation that apply to XPointers. An XPointer may reference any of the XPath axes touched on in Section 4.1.1. Table 4.3 lists all the axes supported by the XPath Recommendation and notes where each axis applies with respect to schema document locations. Such an XPointer might contain a reference to any axis; however, validations of many of these axes are likely to fail. Table 4.3 duly notes these likely failures in the Caveats column. A '✓' indicates that an XPointer can reference the corresponding axis and expect positive results.

An XPath expression, in general, can return any node set, a Boolean value, a string, or a floating-point number. In an XML schema, the results of an XPath expression (in an identity constraint), as well as the results of an XPointer expression (in a `schemaLocation` value), must result in a node set. Because both expressions return a node set, this chapter does not go into detail describing the other result types (Boolean, string, and number). However, a predicate can refine a node set in an XPointer expression. Therefore, Table 4.4 provides a few examples of XPointers that contain predicates, which return values that are not node sets. This chapter does not provide a comprehensive tutorial on the full XPath expression options that may appear in a predicate. Note that each example is only the XPointer part of a URI. An entire URI that includes an XPointer has the following form:

```
http://www.example.com/some.xml#xpointer(exampleXPointer)
```

See Sections 4.1.3 or 4.2.4 for examples of complete URIs. The cells in the Example column of Table 4.4 provide a substitution for *exampleXPointer* in the previous code excerpt.

Table 4.4 provides a nice illustration of the power of XPointer expressions enhanced by XPath predicates. For a complete tutorial on predicates, refer to the XPath Recommendation.

**TABLE 4.3** XPath Axes Potentially Used in schemaDocument References

| Axis | Meaning | Caveats |
| --- | --- | --- |
| child | All subelements of the context node | ✓ |
| descendant | Element descendants of the context node | ✓ |
| parent | The parent of the context node | ✓ |
| ancestor | Element ancestors of the context node | An XPointer referencing this axis is technically okay, but the schema is probably bizarre at best. |
| following-sibling | All siblings of the context node that appear after the context node | Not recommended, as this will include attribute and namespace nodes (that is, undesirable nodes that are just portions of an element). Use the *following* axis instead. |
| preceding-sibling | All siblings of the context node that appear before the context node | Not recommended, as this will include attribute and namespace nodes (that is, undesirable nodes that are just portions of an element). Use the *preceding* axis instead. |
| following | Element siblings of the context node that appear after the context node | ✓ |
| preceding | Element siblings of the context node that appear before the context node | ✓ |
| attribute | Attributes of the context node | Not recommended: If the XPointer returns anything, the validation will fail. |
| namespace | Namespace nodes of the context node | Not recommended: If the XPointer returns anything, the validation will fail. |
| self | The context node | Why bother in an XPointer? |
| descendant-or-self | Descendant or self axes | ✓ |
| ancestor-or-self | Ancestor or self axes | ✓ |

**TABLE 4.4**  XPointer Examples

| Example | Meaning |
| --- | --- |
| id("foo") | The element whose ID is 'foo' (see Section 4.1.3 for a detailed example). |
| id("foo")/range-to(id("bar")) | The elements whose IDs are 'foo' and 'bar', as well as all elements in between. |
| X[position()=1] or x[1] | The first x. |
| X[position()>1] | All x elements *except* the first one. |
| X[5] | The fifth x. |
| X[last()] | The last x. |
| ./x | The x elements that are subelements of the parent of the current context. |
| X[y="hello"] | The x elements that have a subelement y whose value is 'hello'. |
| X[@y and @z] | The x elements that have both y and z attributes. |
| X[@y or @z] | The x elements that have either a y or z attribute. |
| X[@y &lt; "10"] | The x elements that have a y attribute whose value is less than '10'. Note that XPath supports '=', '!=', '<', '<=', '>', and '>='. Escape these as necessary with the standard XML entity reference, such as '&lt;' for the less-than character. |
| X[starts_with(y,"abc")] | The x elements that contain a y subelement whose value starts with 'abc'. |
| X[sum(y) &gt; 50] | The x elements that contain one or more y subelements, the sum of whose values is greater than 50. |

# The Structure of Documents and Schemas

**CHAPTER 5**

## IN THIS CHAPTER

5.1 XML Documents   58

5.2 The XML Information Set   61

5.3 Introduction to the PSVI   67

5.4 Introduction to Schemas   69

5.5 Schema Documents   70

# Chapter 5

## The Structure of Documents and Schemas

This chapter introduces XML documents and schemas, each from both the concrete and abstract points of view. When talking about documents, "concrete" means the string of characters and "abstract" means the corresponding object-oriented structure that might be constructed by a parser. That is pretty straightforward.

On the other hand, when talking about *schemas*, "concrete" means schema documents (or parts thereof) *ignoring the distinction between concrete schema document and abstract schema document*, while "abstract" means the object-structured class that might be constructed by a schema processor.

This book assumes understanding of the terminology and concepts of (concrete) XML documents as defined in the XML Recommendation. Section 5.1 relates that material to the corresponding terminology and concepts of abstract XML documents as defined in the Infoset Recommendation. Section 5.2 describes in more detail the concepts of abstract XML documents, which are *information sets* (*infosets*) or *document information items*, depending on your point of view. In this book, abstract documents are document information items.

## 5.1 XML Documents

XML documents as defined in the XML Recommendation as strings of characters, but the markup within them implies a rich structure. This structure is implied in that recommendation and defined more carefully in the Infoset Recommendation. The latter Recommendation was written after the Namespace Recommendation, so it is "namespace aware": The data structures it defines are designed to make namespace information directly available as properties of objects.

> **NOTATION NOTE**
>
> The XML Recommendation uses the term "document" solely to mean the concrete document; The Infoset Recommendation uses the terms "infoset" and "document information item" to mean the abstract document. When dealing with schemas, it is often immaterial whether the documents you think of are concrete or abstract.

A concrete XML document is a string of characters that consists of a *prolog*, an *element*, and "*misc*." ('Misc' really is an XML technical term, but you won't find it much in this book outside of this paragraph.) The prolog is typically an XML Declaration and/or a Document Type Declaration with *misc* intervening, but may be just an empty string. The element is required and is generally the important part of the document—that is where the *data characters* reside. Misc consists of incidental character strings: whitespace, processing instructions, and comments. The element's structure and content are of primary interest in this book.

An abstract XML document (an XML infoset) is made up of objects—instances of various classes—combined in various ways. These instances are all called "information items" in the Infoset Recommendation. To begin with, the topmost object is a single document information item.

> **NOTATION NOTE**
>
> *Abstract document*, *infoset*, and *document information item* are essentially the same thing. The Infoset Recommendation takes the point of view that the various information items in isolation, linked by properties, as opposed to being part of the document element, so it considers an infoset a collection of information items with links between them. This distinction is at most a matter of how you think of objects and the values of their properties—or it can be thought of as just an implementation detail.

Other information items occur as values of various properties of the document information item or (recursively) properties of those information items in turn.

Any (concrete) element must be in one of two forms. Either it consists simply of an empty-element tag, or it consists of three consecutive character strings concatenated: a start-tag, content, and an end-tag. Of these three, the simplest is the *end-tag*, which is a string consisting of '</', a type name, and '>'. A start-tag is a string consisting of '<', a type name, optional attribute value specifications, and a closing '>', with intervening whitespace where needed or desired after the type name. The type name in the start- and end-tags of an element having start- and end-tags must be the same:

**Type name:** A *name* used to name an element type.

An empty-element tag is like a start-tag except that the terminating '>' is instead a '/>'.

> **NOTE**
>
> A concrete element, thought of as an object, has no properties special to elements. Instead, it has object-valued `propertyMethods`, which return values, but these values must be defined in terms of the base string. The fact that everything devolves back to the base string is what makes it "concrete."

The content of an element is slightly more complicated. It, too, is a character string (consisting of the concatenation of data characters, complete elements, and character and entity references), which occurs between the start- and end-tags. If the element consists of an empty-element tag, the content is an empty string.

This book uses the following terms to refer to elements and parts thereof (abstract and concrete) and to connect that terminology to definitions in the various Recommendations:

*Document element:* The outermost element in an XML document.

*Element:*
1. A character string conforming to the requirements of the XML Recommendation.
2. An element information item.

*Attribute specification:* A character string conforming to the requirements of the XML Recommendation.

*Attribute:*
1. An attribute specification.
2. An attribute information item.

*Content* **of an element:**
1. The character string between the start- and end-tags of an element. (Special case: The content of an element consisting of an empty-element tag is *a priori* the empty string.)
2. The terms in the value of an element information item's *children* property (a sequence or list of various kinds of information items, especially *element* and *character* information items).

*Children* **of an element:**
1. The immediate subelements of an element.
2. The immediate subelements and data characters of an element.
3. The immediate subelements, data characters, and attributes of an element.

*Attributes* **of an element:**
1. The attribute specifications found in the start-tag or empty-element tag of the element.
2. The members of the value of the element information item's *attributes* property (a set of attribute information items).

*Subelement* **of an element:** An immediate subelement of the element or (recursively) a subelement of one of those immediate subelements.

*Immediate subelement* **of an element:** An element information item term in the element information item's *children* property's value (a sequence or list of information items) or a substring of the content of the element, which, when parsed, gives rise to such an element information item.

*Data character:*
1. A character in an XML document that an XML parser recognizes as data (rather than markup).
2. A character information item in the *children* of an element information item.
3. Such a character information item or a character in the value of an attribute.

*Metadata string:*
1. A character string recognized as markup but retained in the abstract data structure because it provides information about the abstract structure. (Example: An element's *type name* or the name of an attribute.)
2. A character string that is the value of an information item property other than the *value* property of an attribute.

*Markup punctuation:* A character string recognized as markup but which only serves to identify or delineate markup. (Examples: Whitespace and the strings '<', '</', '=', '/>', and '>' found in various tags.) Markup punctuation is typically not retained in the abstract data structure.

## 5.2 The XML Information Set

The XML Recommendation does not specify the information that a parser should deliver. That has been rectified, at least in part, by the Infoset Recommendation, which states:

> This specification defines an abstract data set called the XML Information Set (infoset). Its purpose is to provide a consistent set of definitions for use in other specifications that need to refer to the information in a well-formed XML document.

Conforming XML parsers are not *required* to implement exactly this information set, although, fortunately, many do so in one way or another. Some XML processors actually keep more detailed information about the data in an XML document than is officially in the XML infoset. Indeed, the Infoset Recommendation has an appendix listing a number of things you might expect a Recommendation to have that it does not have. In any case, the infoset is the generic abstraction used by most XML documents and many processors, so it is a useful "mental model."

XML infosets are important because the model of a schema processor used in the Schema Recommendation is that of a validator operating on an XML infoset, not on the original concrete XML document.

Each XML infoset is made up of objects—instances of various classes, combined in various ways. They are all called *information items*. To begin with, the topmost object is a document information item. Other information items occur as values of various properties of the document information item, or recursively of properties of those information items in turn.

There are two points of view toward abstract documents: One is the document information item view, which holds that the abstract document is a document information item including all the other information items that are (recursively) values of information item properties. The other is the infoset view, which holds that the abstract document is a set of information items, including a single document information item, and that information-item-valued properties' values are pointers to other members of the infoset. The Infoset Recommendation is written so as to be compatible with either point of view. This book generally takes the document information item view.

This book assumes some familiarity with the information items described in the Infoset Recommendation; it does not cover all the details of that set. A reader not at all familiar with XML infosets should consult the Recommendation after reading this section. It is not long and not difficult to read after you have it in its proper perspective. See

`http://www.w3.org/TR/xml-infoset`.

Eleven distinct classes of information items are defined in that Recommendation:

- *Document information item*
- *Element information item*
- *Attribute information item*
- *Character information item*
- *Processing instruction information item*
- *Unexpanded entity preference information item*
- *Comment information item*
- *Document type declaration information item*
- *Unparsed entity information item*
- *Notation information item*
- *Namespace information item*

Because the first four classes are most important, this chapter covers only those classes.

## 5.2.1 The *Document Information Item* Class

A document information item has a number of properties containing information pertaining to the whole document. Several are not created by a parser but are added by a validator, whose processing is "cascaded" after that of the parser. The document information item has only one property of particular interest for Schema work: the *document element* property. As you might expect from that property's name, its value is always an element information item—specifically, the one that corresponds to the document element.

Some of the properties of a document information item are related to the DTD and will only be present if the DTD is read and the document DTD-validated. These properties are not of interest for schema validation, as opposed to DTD validation. Schema validation's interest in DTDs is only to be sure that the XML infoset produced by the parser was obtained by expanding all parsable entity references.

Other properties are of interest but need not be dealt with to gain an initial understanding of schema validation. These involve processing instruction, comment, and notation information items.

One DTD-related property is of interest. For proper schema processing, all parsable entity references in the document must be resolved; therefore, it helps to know that all entity declarations have been processed. Each document information item has an *all declarations processed* Boolean-valued property. If true, the parser has asserted that it has processed all entity declarations (as well as all other declarations). For schema processing purposes, of course, related DTD validation results are irrelevant.

## 5.2.2 The *Element Information Item* Class

Element information items are very important for schema processing: Schema validation is directly concerned with the element tree structure. (We stated previously that the primary property of the document information item of interest is the *document element* property, which has an element information item as its value.) Each element information item has the following properties:

- *Namespace name*
- *Local name*
- *Prefix*
- *Children*
- *Attributes*
- *Namespace attributes*
- *In-scope namespaces*
- *Base URI*
- *Parent*

The first three properties have to do with identifying the element's type. Each element type has a name associated with it, consisting of an optional prefix and colon concatenated with a "local" name devoid of colons. The *namespace name*, if present, is the URI that identifies the namespace and is bound to the local namespace *prefix*; the remainder of the name is the *local name*. (A namespace-aware processor or application should use the namespace name, rather than the prefix, to identify the namespace.)

*Children* and *attributes* are the properties of primary interest. The *children* property has as its value an ordered list (a finite sequence) of information items that are the parsed equivalent of the content of the element. Because attributes are identified by name rather than by position, a list is not appropriate for them. Also, because an attribute can have only one attribute specification in an element's start-tag (or empty-element tag), the *attributes* property has as its value a *set* of attribute information items.

The next three properties (*namespace attributes*, *in-scope namespaces*, *base URI*) are, like several earlier ones, related to namespaces and are discussed in Chapter 3. The last property, *parent*, provides a back-link up the *children* tree, because all element information items except that of the document element are children of another element information item higher in the tree. (The parent of the document element's information item is the document's document information item.)

## 5.2.3 The *Attribute Information Item* Class

The *children* and *attributes* properties of element information items are the important ones. Children are just more element information items, and character information items. But the members of the *attributes* property's value are a new kind of object: attribute information items. Attribute information items are objects having eight properties:

- *Namespace name*
- *Local name*
- *Prefix*
- *Normalized value*
- *Specified*
- *Attribute type*
- *References*
- *Owner element*

The first three properties have to do with identifying the attribute; they function much the same as the element information item properties having the same names. *Owner element* is a backpointer to the containing element information item. *Specified* is a Boolean-valued property indicating whether the attribute was actually specified in the start-tag (or empty-element tag) of the element involved, as opposed to being inherited as the default value prescribed in the attribute list declaration of the DTD.

> **NOTE**
>
> *Schema* processing may add a default value if an attribute is not specified in an XML instance, but the indication that this has happened will be in a PSVI-added property, not in the *specified* property.

The normalized value is not always the string of characters enclosed in quotes in the attribute specification, which is the unnormalized value: Character references must be resolved and parsable general entity references should be, and whitespace must be normalized in accordance with the attribute's structure type.

If the value was not explicitly specified but was obtained as the default value prescribed by the entity's declaration, it must still be normalized to deal with parsable general entity references.

In any case, the resulting normalized value is the string of characters that is the attribute's "actual" value. (As far as DTD processing is concerned, that is—schema processing can further normalize the value. See Section 2.3, on the PSVI.)

> **NOTE**
>
> The attribute information item does *not* retain any information about the prenormalization value of an attribute.
>
> Schema processing will possibly further normalize the attribute value, but the result will be in a PSVI-added property different from the *normalized value* property. If the DTD-prescribed normalization and the schema-prescribed normalization are in conflict, unexpected results could occur, because schema normalization does not (and *cannot*) start over from the unnormalized value.

The *attribute type* property's value is the attribute's structure type as specified in the attribute's declaration in the DTD. If the attribute's structure type requires it to reference something—elements with an ID attribute, unparsed entities, or notations—the value of *references* is a list of the corresponding information items. (There are special rules for cases in which the values specified do not correspond to anything declared in the DTD; see the Infoset Recommendation for details.)

> **NOTATION NOTE**
>
> The phrase "structure type" has already been introduced in Chapter 1. In the XML Recommendation and Infoset Recommendation, this is just called the attribute's "type." This book avoids just plain 'type' because so many different kinds of types are involved when Schema enters the picture.

> **NOTE**
>
> The Infoset Recommendation does not address the form of the *attribute type* values; they are akin to values in a C or Java enumeration: named things from a finite set that can be distinguished. They are not necessarily character strings consisting of those names.

## 5.2.4 The *Character Information Item* Class

Element information items and character information items are the two most important terms in an element information item's *children* sequence. A character information item has only three properties: *character code*, *element content whitespace*, and *parent*. The *character code* is a nonnegative integer, the Unicode code for the character. The *element content whitespace* is a Boolean, necessarily FALSE if the character is not whitespace. For whitespace it may be TRUE, FALSE, UNKNOWN, or NO VALUE (see the Infoset Recommendation for details). The *parent*, of course, is a pointer back to the element information item in whose *children* property sequence the character information item occurs.

## 5.2.5 XML Information Set Summary

An abstract XML document is a document information item. For Schema purposes, the most important property is its *document element*.

An abstract element is an element information item. For Schema purposes, the important properties are those related to the element's type name, the *attributes* property, and the *children* property.

The *attributes* property's value is a set of abstract attributes (attribute information items); the *children* property's value is a list or sequence of abstract characters (character information items), abstract elements (element information items), and other less important abstract things (information items relating to processing instructions, comments, and so on).

An abstract attribute is an attribute information item. For Schema purposes, the important properties are those related to the attribute's name and the *normalized value* property.

An abstract character is a character information item. It identifies a character by its Unicode code and indicates whether that character is (known to be) a whitespace character in a position where a DTD does not permit PCDATA.

> **NOTE**
>
> A schema can also determine that a whitespace character is in a position where PCDATA is not permitted; it will indicate this in the PSVI by using a different mechanism from the abstract character property used by DTD processors.

## 5.3 Introduction to the PSVI

Schema processors do not change any values in the "basic" infoset. Instead, a schema processor provides values for new properties not defined for the basic infoset. An infoset with these additional properties is a PSVI. Chapter 16 describes the additional properties in detail; this section provides only an introduction and a partial description of the more fundamental ones.

By adding additional properties, the PSVI definitions define new classes derived from the old. They are generally known by the same names. PSVI also defines new classes, instances of which are used only as values of PSVI-added properties. For example: There are new classes of information items that mimic all of the schema component classes, so that a PSVI can include as a property value a complete "carbon copy" of the schema or any of its components.

A number of the additional properties, and properties provided by the additional classes, are optional, so a "lightweight" processor can legitimately not provide access to them (or can simply always give ABSENT as the value).

> **NOTATION NOTE**
>
> Both the Infoset Recommendation and the Schema Recommendation require that properties always have a value. Each also provides a special "designated value" that is the value of an "optional" property when that property "does not have a value." The Infoset Recommendation calls this value "NO VALUE." The Schema Recommendation calls this value "ABSENT," even when discussing the PSVI additions to the XML infoset. The divergence was probably accidental, caused by the Schema Recommendation going final while the Infoset Recommendation was still being developed. This book uses both terms, depending on context, to make correlation with material in the appropriate Recommendation easier. In point of fact, the two terms have the same meaning.

Of the various information item classes of the XML infoset, only element information items and attribute information items provide additional properties in the PSVI.

The PSVI version of element information item is derived from the original by adding 23 additional properties. They are described in more detail in Chapter 16. Seven of these properties are peculiar to element information item; the remaining 16 are also added to attribute information item. Attribute information item gets no extra properties not shared with element information item.

In this section, the following properties are mentioned and briefly discussed:

- *Schema normalized value*
- *Nil*
- *ID/IDREF table*
- *Identity-constraint table*

Of these properties, only the first applies to attributes, the first two apply to all elements, and the last two only apply to selected elements. See Chapter 16 for a more complete discussion of the properties and information items added by the PSVI, and an overview of the process by which those properties are given values.

Most of these properties serve to identify the element type or attribute type and the structure type of the attribute or element.

The *schema normalized value* property provides, for attributes and for elements with simple content, a value normalized according to the schema in much the same way that an attribute's value might be normalized according to an attribute definition in a DTD. Because elements with simple content are much like attributes, it should not be surprising that both attribute and element information items get a *schema normalized value* property. The schema normalized value is obtained by normalizing the string of characters that constitutes the content of the element concerned, with any processing instructions or comments stripped out.

> **NOTE**
>
> Schema processing is *not* required to provide the value from the value space of the datatype of an element with simple content or an attribute—only the normalized lexical representation of that value from the lexical space. No provision for attaching the "real" value is made in the PSVI. However, do not be surprised if vendors of schema processors provide a proprietary way to easily get the real value. Without such a facility, each application would have to access the lexical-space string and the information identifying the datatype, and provide its own conversion routines.

*continues*

For example, in the float datatype, all values have standard 32-bit representations prescribed by an IEEE standard (IEEE 754). The number "positive zero" has a representation consisting of 32 zero-bits. That number is named in the lexical space by the four-character string '+0.0' (among others). The four-character string may show up as a schema normalized value, but the corresponding 32-bit bit string is not required by the Schema Recommendation to be provided anywhere in the PSVI.

The *nil* property serves to indicate if an element was explicitly nulled (that is, xsi:nil specified true as well as empty content).

The *ID/IDREF table* is a collection of new kinds of information items not found in the basic infoset that are of use in checking uniqueness of IDREF references. The process of schema validation is defined in terms of actions on the *ID/IDREF table* and hence either the table must be created or equivalent computations worked out. However, upon completion of the validation process, the validator is *not* required to retain the table in the PSVI it makes visible to the receiving application. The *identity-constraint table* serves a similar role with respect to the expanded identity constraints provided by Schemas. This property is provided only by an element information item and will be absent except on the root element where schema processing is invoked (normally the document element, the root of a document's element tree).

## 5.4 Introduction to Schemas

Similar to the infoset and document information item points of view for abstract documents, there are two points of view for Schemas. The schema set point of view is that a schema is a *set* of objects generically called "schema components," with component-valued properties' values being pointers among the members of the set; the schema component view is that a schema is a particular kind of schema component and all other components of the schema are (recursively) values of component-valued properties of the components.

The Schema Recommendation generally takes the former point of view and does not include a schema schema component in the schema set; nonetheless, it defines a *schema* schema component and thus implements either point of view. This book generally takes the schema schema component point of view.

A *schema* (a schema schema component) has seven set-valued properties:

- *Type definitions*
- *Attribute declarations*
- *Element declarations*

- *Attribute group definitions*
- *Model group definitions*
- *Notation declarations*
- *Annotations*

These seven sets contain the corresponding top-level schema components; the *type definitions* set contains both simple type and complex type components. All remaining components, including all six types not accounted for in the preceding list, show up as property values of some of these components (recursively, of course—just like information items in a document information item). So a *schema* is an abstract object much like a DTD—if a DTD had ever been defined as an object.

> **NOTE**
>
> Just as a DTD does not prescribe the type of the document element (that is done only by the document type *declaration*), a schema does not prescribe the type of the document element.

The various kinds of schema components are described in Chapter 15.

## 5.5 Schema Documents

The document element of a schema document is a `schema` element. `schema`s are made up of elements of various other types; there are element types corresponding to the different schema components. An `element` element corresponds to an "element declaration schema component"—a *(Schema-defined) element type*. A `simpleType` element contains the information necessary to create a simple type (a "simple type definition schema component"). Details of the use and construction of the various types of elements in a schema document are found throughout Part II of this book.

More than one schema document may contribute to a schema for either or both of these reasons:

- Useful parts of the schema can be separated out as reusable modules.
- Different components of the schema need to be associated with different namespaces. (All of the components arising from a particular schema document must be associated with the same namespace.)

For these reasons, schema documents are able to include other schema documents, using various mechanisms:

- `include`: If a schema document describes part of the desired schema and targets that part to the same namespace as the target namespace of the schema document being written, that schema part can be included by using an `include` element in the schema document being written. An `include` element includes a pointer to the schema document to be included.

  The schema processor, while building the schema, will find and process the included schema document, placing the schema components it represents into the new, larger schema being built.

  It is also possible for an included schema document to be coerced to the target namespace of the including schema document, if the included part has no target namespace. This can make includable partial-schema documents even more reusable, but some care must be taken.

  `include` elements are described in Chapter 7.

- `redefine`: A `redefine` element is like an `include`, except that within it you can force some changes on various parts of the included schema document as it comes in. This is more controllable than simple cut-and-paste when making "one-offs."

  `redefine` elements are described in Chapter 7.

- `import`: An `import` element is again somewhat similar to an `include`, but the imported schema document is expected to have its own target namespace. This is the only mechanism for building a schema with multiple target namespaces.

  Chapter 3 provides more information on the use of namespaces with schemas. `import` elements are described in Chapter 7.

# PART II

# Creating XML Schema Documents

Part II is a tutorial that conveys how to create each element encountered in an XML schema. Part II is also a reference manual. In particular, the layout of this part of the book promotes quick location, visualization of attributes and content, and examples of specific schema elements and attributes. The chapters in this part of the book cover the following topics:

- Chapter 6 is an introduction to the layout of an XML schema document. This chapter discusses the concepts behind building an XML schema. Specifically, you should know which elements are required to build the schema you need after reading this chapter.

- Chapter 7 covers the rather complex schema element. This chapter also provides complete coverage of the `import`, `include`, and `redefine` elements that permit assembling an XML schema from multiple documents, and allow schemas to include more than one namespace. Finally, this chapter demonstrates the simple `annotation` and `notation` elements.

- Chapter 8 provides a complete discussion of element types. Elements in an XML document are instances of element types from an XML schema.

- Chapter 9 provides a complete discussion of attribute types. Attributes in an XML document are instances of attribute types from an XML schema.

- Chapter 10 covers how to derive simple types. A simple type constrains the value of an element or an attribute in an XML document.

- Chapter 11 covers how to derive complex types. A complex type constrains the structure of elements in an XML instance.
- Chapter 12 covers the built-in datatypes specified in "Part 2" of the XML Schema Recommendation. These built-in datatypes are the fundamental simple types, which provide the foundation for all other simple types.
- Chapter 13 demonstrates how to provide simple semantic validation with identity constraints. Identity constraints provide a mechanism to ensure unique values, as well as a mechanism for simple referential integrity.
- Chapter 14 provides complete coverage of the regular expression grammar for patterns. Simple types use `pattern` constraining facets to restrict data values.

# Overview of an XML Schema Document

**CHAPTER 6**

## IN THIS CHAPTER

6.1 The Enclosing schema Element  78

6.2 Namespaces  78

6.3 Scope  81

6.4 Annotating Elements  82

6.5 Constraining Elements  84

6.6 Constraining Attributes  87

6.7 Simple Types  88

6.8 Complex Types  91

6.9 Model Groups  96

6.10 Substitution Groups  99

6.11 Instantiability  100

6.12 Identity Constraint Definitions  101

6.13 Notations  102

6.14 Imports and Includes  102

6.15 Locating XML Schemas and XML Schema Components  103

6.16 Schema Element IDs  103

An XML schema is an abstract model that constrains a corresponding XML instance. An XML schema document is an XML representation of an XML schema. More precisely, multiple XML schema documents might comprise an XML schema. This chapter introduces an XML schema document. The chapter also provides terms and concepts to discuss XML schemas and XML schema documents. The goal of this chapter is to provide enough background so you can select the correct component to place in an XML schema document. Details on attribute and content options of individual components are provided in Chapter 8, Chapter 9, Chapter 10, and Chapter 11, respectively.

Listing 6.1 provides an example of a very simple, yet complete XML schema document. Listing 6.2 provides a corresponding XML instance. Both listings make up the *compact* example. These examples are discussed in enough detail to instill familiarity with the construction of an XML schema document. The goal of the chapter is to portray enough about a schema so that much of this book makes sense—even if you do not read the remaining chapters sequentially. Because of the myriad combinations possible in a schema, the compact example does not cover all schema elements and attributes; some of the sections in this chapter refer to the thematic catalog example introduced in Chapter 1 and presented in Appendix C.

**LISTING 6.1**  A Compact XML Schema Document (compact.xsd)

```
<xsd:schema xmlns:xsd="http://www.w3.org/2001/XMLSchema">

<xsd:complexType name="globalComplexType"
                abstract="true">
    <xsd:annotation>
        <xsd:documentation xml:lang="en">
            A global complex type.
        </xsd:documentation>
    </xsd:annotation>
    <xsd:sequence>
        <xsd:element name="basicTokenElement" type="xsd:token"/>
        <xsd:element name="sixToOneHundred"
                    minOccurs="0"
                    maxOccurs="unbounded">
            <xsd:simpleType>
                <xsd:restriction base="xsd:positiveInteger">
                    <xsd:minExclusive value="5"/>
                    <xsd:maxInclusive value="100"/>
                </xsd:restriction>
            </xsd:simpleType>
        </xsd:element>
        <xsd:element name="tokenElement">
            <xsd:complexType>
                <xsd:simpleContent>
                    <xsd:extension base="xsd:token">
```

```
                    <xsd:attribute name="tokenAttribute"
                                   type="xsd:token"/>
                </xsd:extension>
            </xsd:simpleContent>
        </xsd:complexType>
    </xsd:element>
    </xsd:sequence>
</xsd:complexType>

<xsd:element name="encompassingElement">
    <xsd:complexType>
        <xsd:annotation>
            <xsd:documentation xml:lang="en">
                A local complex type.
            </xsd:documentation>
        </xsd:annotation>
        <xsd:complexContent>
            <xsd:extension base="globalComplexType">
                <xsd:sequence>
                    <xsd:element
                        name="emptyContentWithAttribute">
                        <xsd:complexType>
                            <xsd:attribute
                                name="decimalAttribute"
                                type="xsd:decimal"/>
                        </xsd:complexType>
                    </xsd:element>
                </xsd:sequence>
            </xsd:extension>
        </xsd:complexContent>
    </xsd:complexType>
</xsd:element>

</xsd:schema>
```

Listing 6.2 portrays an XML instance that corresponds to the XML schema document portrayed in Listing 6.1.

**LISTING 6.2**   A Compact XML Instance (`compact.xml`)

```
<encompassingElement
 xmlns:xsi="http://www.w3.org/2001/XMLSchema-instance"
 xsi:noNamespaceSchemaLocation=
  "http://www.XMLSchemaReference.com/examples/Ch06/compact.xsd">

    <basicTokenElement>Element Value</basicTokenElement>
    <sixToOneHundred>50</sixToOneHundred>
```

*continues*

```
<sixToOneHundred>22</sixToOneHundred>
<sixToOneHundred>87</sixToOneHundred>
<sixToOneHundred>6</sixToOneHundred>
<tokenElement tokenAttribute="aValue">eValue</tokenElement>
<emptyContentWithAttribute decimalAttribute="1000"/>

</encompassingElement>
```

## 6.1 The Enclosing schema Element

Each XML schema document has exactly one schema element. The attributes of the schema element specify various defaults. Some of these attributes apply to namespaces. The content of the schema element ultimately specifies the valid set of elements and attributes, as well as the valid ranges for the element values and attribute values, permissible in a corresponding XML instance. The XML schema document disperses the specification of these elements and attributes across element types, attribute types, simple types, complex types, and other specific schema components.

Chapter 7 details the attributes and content options for a schema element. Chapter 7 also covers some miscellaneous content options (annotation, import, include, notation, and redefine). Chapters 8 through 11 cover the remainder of the specific elements that are valid content options for a schema element. Chapters 8 through 11 cover element, attribute, simpleType, and complexType, respectively. Chapter 15 covers the schema components represented by the elements in schema documents.

## 6.2 Namespaces

Specifying namespaces, default namespaces, and a target namespace takes only a few lines of code in an XML schema document, yet namespaces seem to be one of the most confusing aspects when learning about XML schemas. This section presents an overview of namespaces, including a discussion of how an XML schema applies namespaces. Chapter 3 presents a thorough discussion of namespaces.

With the exception of anonymous schema components (see Section 1.3), all schema components have a name. Each name nominally belongs to a namespace. Many schemas explicitly have no namespace. A schema specifies the value of a namespace as a URI, although the URI does not have to exist (or be accessible to the XML validator).

Although all the components nominally belong to the same namespace, each namespace has multiple partitions. Each component type has a unique partition, or *symbol space*. For example, a schema that has both a fred element type and a fred simple type is perfectly valid. This partitioning has two exceptions:

- Simple types and complex types share the same symbol space.
- Locally scoped names have no namespace. Furthermore, distinct enclosing elements can specify local elements with the same name.

Although trivial to implement, one of the most difficult tasks when planning an XML schema is determining the target and default namespaces. Frequently, initial XML schema documents do not contain any namespace information other than where to locate the schema of Schemas (see Listing 6.1). The schema documents evolve to include namespaces and target namespaces as needed. This approach is often acceptable. A schema should absolutely specify a target namespace, however, if the schema provides functionality via the Internet or in any public schema that a user might integrate with other public or proprietary schemas. Although less imperative, a public schema document should not specify a default namespace, which can lead to confusion when integrating multiple schemas with multiple namespaces.

Often an XML schema document associates a *prefix* with a namespace. The XML schema document specifies a namespace with the xmlns attribute of a schema element. The following code snippet associates the prefix 'xsd' with the namespace http://www.w3.org/2001/XMLSchema:

```
xmlns:xsd="http://www.w3.org/2001/XMLSchema"
```

Typically, a qualifier is several characters. Many of the examples in this book specify prefixes such as 'xsd', 'cat', and 'addr'. A *qualified name*, which is a prefix in conjunction with a local name, identifies a component. An *unqualified name* does not have an associated namespace. A qualified name has the form namespace:name. For example, xsd:token is a reference to the built-in datatype token in the schema for schemas namespace specified by the prefix xsd.

## 6.2.1 The Default Namespace

A schema may reference many namespaces. A schema may optionally specify a default namespace. When a schema specifies a default namespace, the default namespace is implicit for any reference to a global component that does not include a namespace qualification. For example if the default namespace is the URI associated with the prefix xsd, the name token implies the qualified name xsd:token. The default namespace applies only to references within an XML schema; the default namespace has no impact on XML instances.

The xmlns attribute of the schema element—without a namespace declaration such as xsd in the previous example—specifies a default namespace:

```
xmlns="http://www.w3.org/2001/XMLSchema"
```

> **TIP**
>
> Although not imperative, a public schema document should not specify a default namespace if the schema provides functionality via the Internet or in any public schema that a user might integrate other public or proprietary schemas. A public schema with a default namespace can lead to confusion when integrating multiple schemas with multiple namespaces.

### 6.2.2 The Target Namespace

A schema may optionally specify a target namespace. The target namespace specifies the namespace for all the schema components described in the XML schema. In other words, the names of all components must be unique within the appropriate symbol space in the target namespace. When the schema does not specify a target namespace, each component has explicitly no namespace.

The `targetNamespace` attribute of the `schema` element specifies a target namespace:

```
targetNamespace=
    "http://www.XMLSchemaReference.com/examples/theme/catalog"
```

> **TIP**
>
> A schema should absolutely specify a target namespace if the schema provides functionality via the Internet or in any public schema that a user might integrate other public or proprietary schemas. A public schema with explicitly no namespace is much more likely to have naming collisions with other schemas that also have no target namespace.

### 6.2.3 Namespaces and the XML Instance

The elements and attributes in a corresponding XML instance must reference components by name. This name is relative to the target namespace specified in the corresponding XML schema document. The XML schema document may explicitly specify no target namespace.

When the XML schema document does specify a target namespace, the XML instance can specify a qualified name to identify components. There are alternatives to qualifying every element and attribute name. The `schema` element may specify the attributes `elementFormDefault` and `attributeFormDefault`. When these attributes have a value of `unqualified` (the default value), the XML instance is globally relieved of incessantly qualifying references to global element types and attribute types, respectively. Instead, the XML validator assumes the target namespace. In addition to the `schema` element attributes, either global element types or global attribute types may specify a `form` attribute with the same effect. The only difference is that the name qualification—or lack thereof—applies only to the specific element type or attribute type.

## 6.3 Scope

Like many programming languages, scope may limit one component from referencing another. Element types, attribute types, and most of the other kinds of components in a schema may be global to the schema or local to another component.

### 6.3.1 Global Components

With some exceptions, one global component might reference global components in the same namespace or even in multiple namespaces. Global element types and attribute types also have the distinction of being generally available for use in an XML instance.

#### 6.3.1.1 Referencing Global Components from an XML Schema Document

In general, an element in an XML schema document can reference a named global component—typically with a `type` or `ref` attribute. Deriving complex types or simple types or associating an element type or attribute type with a structure type requires a `type` attribute in the representing document. For example, the following represents an element type by associating the name 'phoneNumber' with the (global) built-in `string` datatype:

```
<xsd:element name="phoneNumber" type="xsd:string"/>
```

A reference to a global element type or global attribute type requires a `ref` attribute. For example, the following is a reference to the previously defined global `phoneNumber` element type:

```
<xsd:element ref="phoneNumber"/>
```

Some components may restrict their reference within a schema via blocking. This type of blocking occurs when the component's representation has a `final` attribute with an appropriate value.

#### 6.3.1.2 Referencing Global Components from an XML Instance

An element or an attribute in an XML instance claims to be an instance of a particular element or attribute type by using that type's name: an element, by using that name as its *type name*; an attribute by using that name as its name. For example, the following element has 'phoneNumber' as its *type name*, thereby referencing the `phoneNumber` element type and claiming to be an instance of that class:

```
<phoneNumber>503-555-1212</phoneNumber>
```

Finally, an element may explicitly assert that it is to validate against a global simple or complex type with the `xsi:type` attribute:

```
<amount xsi:type="salePriceType">123.45</amount>
```

The type must be a valid derivation of the structure type of the referenced element type. In the preceding example, the structure type of `amount` is `dollarPriceType`. Furthermore, `salePriceType` derives from `dollarPriceType`. Both Chapter 10 and Chapter 11 have detailed discussions about deriving types. These chapters also cover how to invoke `xsi:type` in elements.

An XML instance may not reference a global element type or complex type if that type is not instantiable. The XML representation of a non-instantiable component has the `abstract` attribute set to 'true'. Section 6.10 has more details about component instantiability.

Certain components can prohibit direct or indirect references from an XML instance via blocking. This type of blocking occurs when the component's representation has a `block` attribute with an appropriate value (see the discussion on blocking in Section 8.2.3).

### 6.3.2 Local and Anonymous Components

A schema may reference any element type, attribute type, complex type, or simple type in the context, or scope, of another type. Element types and attribute types always have a name, because XML instances must be able to reference them using their names. *Anonymous* simple and complex types are unnamed local components. A schema may specify but not reference local components.

## 6.4 Annotating Elements

Annotations are a great way to make notes about element types, attribute types, and almost any other element in an XML schema document. An annotation provides what a developer would typically call a "comment" to the XML schema document. Comments destined for developers are stored in a `documentation` subelement. `appinfo` subelements support automated processing of annotations—a discussion beyond the scope of this chapter.

Documentation in an XML schema document comes in two forms: annotations and comments. An annotation takes the form of an `annotation` element. The following annotation, which annotates the `schema` element, comes from the XML schema document `address.xsd`:

```
<xsd:annotation>
    <xsd:documentation xml:lang="en">
        This XML Schema Document describes a customer
        address in great detail.  In particular, this
        document illuminates all of the attributes and
```

```
        content options for elements and attributes.
    </xsd:documentation>
</xsd:annotation>
```

A real comment, on the other hand, is an XML comment. An XML comment looks like this:

```
<!-- This is a comment -->
```

Annotations have the advantage that they are preserved when creating a schema from schema documents. They provide a way to document any type of component. Any element, from the all-encompassing `schema` element to a local simple type nested in a local attribute type, can contain an `annotation`. A program can easily read an `annotation` and process the contents.

> **TIP**
>
> An `annotation` element is a great way to document individual elements in an XML schema document, such as `attribute`, `complexType`, `simpleType`, and many others.

An XML comment is a way to provide documentation that might apply across elements or, perhaps, within an element. Comments have no particular format (other than the start and end punctuation characters, of course) and are not particularly associated with an element. Annotations are appropriate when describing the behavior of an element; XML comments are appropriate for providing guidance to other schema document maintainers.

Almost any element in an XML schema document may offer an annotation by specifying a nested annotation:

```
<xsd:simpleType name="partNameType"
                final="list union"
                id="catalog.partName.sType">
    <xsd:annotation>
        <xsd:documentation xml:lang="en">
            A part name can be almost anything.
            The name is a short description.
        </xsd:documentation>
    </xsd:annotation>
    <xsd:restriction base="xsd:token"
                     id="pnt-rst">
        <xsd:minLength value="1"/>
        <xsd:maxLength value="40"/>
    </xsd:restriction>
</xsd:simpleType>
```

An annotation is part of the element. Furthermore, the XML Schema Recommendation even specifies when an annotation is valid in the XML representation of an element. See the various "Content Options" sections of this book for explanations of applicability of the `annotation` subelement to each type of element is a schema.

## 6.5 Constraining Elements

Perhaps the most important goal of the XML Schema Recommendation is to provide a language for constraining XML instances. A large part of this effort is constraining elements. An element type broadly specifies either simple content or complex content. An element type bound by simple content contains only a text value. This value may be constrained by built-in datatypes or other simple types derived from those datatypes. An element type whose content is complex might specify attribute types or nested element types (or both).

### 6.5.1 Simple Content

An element type that constrains an element to contain simple content places restrictions on the text value of the element. An element type that specifies simple content may specify attribute types as well.

#### 6.5.1.1 Lexically Constrained Values

An element type lexically constrains the value of a corresponding element instance by specifying a simple type as its content type. The following two examples are elements whose structure types could be the built-in datatypes `token` and `decimal`, respectively:

```
<basicTokenElement>Element Value</basicTokenElement>
```

and

```
<sixToOneHundred>50</sixToOneHundred>
```

An element type representation may specify a built-in datatype or another global simple type with a `type` attribute:

```
<xsd:element name="basicTokenElement" type="xsd:token"/>
```

Alternatively, an element type representation may specify a local simple type with a `simpleType` element:

```
<xsd:element name="sixToOneHundred"
             minOccurs="0"
             maxOccurs="unbounded">
    <xsd:simpleType>
        <xsd:restriction base="xsd:positiveInteger">
            <xsd:minExclusive value="5"/>
            <xsd:maxInclusive value="100"/>
```

```
        </xsd:restriction>
    </xsd:simpleType>
</xsd:element>
```

### 6.5.1.2 Simple Content and Attribute Types

An element type that specifies simple content may also permit attribute types by specifying a complex type with simple content. The following example is a `tokenElement` with a `tokenAttribute` attribute.

```
<tokenElement tokenAttribute="aValue">eValue</tokenElement>
```

The corresponding element type must specify a complex type constrained to simple content:

```
<xsd:element name="tokenElement">
    <xsd:complexType>
        <xsd:simpleContent>
            <xsd:restriction base="xsd:token">
                <xsd:attribute name="tokenAttribute"
                               type="xsd:token"/>
            </xsd:restriction>
        </xsd:simpleContent>
    </xsd:complexType>
</xsd:element>
```

The XML representation of an element type can nest a local complex type, as in the previous example, or the element type can reference a global complex type using the `type` attribute.

## 6.5.2 Complex Content

An element type that constrains an element instance to contain complex content may specify subelements, empty content, mixed content, element wildcards, or attributes.

### 6.5.2.1 Nested Elements

Many XML instances require nested elements. Nested elements provide a mechanism for describing a hierarchy of data. An element type must specify a complex type that specifies a model group. The model group specifies the nested elements. Listing 6.2 is an example of an `encompassingElement`, which contains the nested elements `basicTokenElement`, `sixToOneHundred`, `elementWithAttribute`, and `emptyContentWithAttribute`.

### 6.5.2.2 Empty Content

An element that has no value—as distinct from having a value that is an empty string—has *empty content*. Typically, although not necessarily, an element type that specifies empty content also specifies one or more attribute types. The following example is an element `emptyContentWithAttribute` with a single attribute, `decimalAttribute`:

```
<emptyContentWithAttribute decimalAttribute="1000"/>
```

The corresponding element type specifies a complex type that does not provide content:

```xml
<xsd:element name="emptyContentWithAttribute">
    <xsd:complexType>
        <xsd:attribute name="decimalAttribute"
                       type="xsd:decimal"/>
    </xsd:complexType>
</xsd:element>
```

Element types that would otherwise require a value may specify that the corresponding element is nillable. The complete XML representation of `phoneNumber`, from `address.xsd`, permits a phone number to have empty content:

```xml
<xsd:element name="phoneNumber"
             type="xsd:string"
             nillable="true"/>
```

The corresponding element explicitly has empty content:

```xml
<phoneNumber xsi:nil="true"/>
```

### 6.5.2.3 Mixed Content

An element may have *mixed content*. An element with mixed content may contains text, usually interspersed with nested elements. (The text it not constrained by a simple type.) The compact example (Listing 6.1) does not demonstrate mixed content. However, the thematic catalog example specifies mixed content for an instance of `description`:

```xml
<description>
    This is made up of both
    <partList>UX002 UX003</partList>
    pieces which makes it
    better than
    <partList>ASM2000</partList>
    and better than the competition.
</description>
```

An element type must specify a complex type that permits mixed content. Either the `complexType` or the enclosed `complexContent` must specify a `mixed` attribute. The structure type that corresponds to the `description` element type specifies mixed content:

```xml
<xsd:complexType name="catalogEntryDescriptionType"
                 mixed="true"
                 id="catalogEntryDescriptionType.catalog.cType">
    <xsd:annotation>
        <xsd:documentation xml:lang="en">
            Allow the description of a part
            to include part number references.
            The "catalogEntryDescriptionType"
```

```
            is a good example of a complex type
            with "mixed" content.
                -- Shorthand Notation --
        </xsd:documentation>
    </xsd:annotation>
    <xsd:sequence minOccurs="0" maxOccurs="unbounded">
        <xsd:element name="partList" type="partNumberListType"/>
    </xsd:sequence>
</xsd:complexType>
```

For completeness, the following is the `description` element type:

```
<xsd:element name="description"
             type="catalogEntryDescriptionType"/>
```

Chapter 11 discusses how to implement mixed content.

### 6.5.2.4 Element Wildcards

An XML schema may specify element wildcards with the `any` element. An element wildcard is a mechanism for specifying a set of namespaces from which the corresponding XML instance selects element types. The compact example does not demonstrate element wildcards. Chapters 8 and 15 covers element wildcards.

### 6.5.2.5 Complex Content and Attribute Types

Like simple content, complex content may optionally specify attribute types.

## 6.6 Constraining Attributes

Constraining an attribute is similar to constraining an element. Compared to element types, attribute types are severely limited: An attribute type may only specify simple types.

## 6.6.1 Simple Attribute Values

An element may have zero or more attributes. The following example is a `tokenElement` element with a single `tokenAttribute` attribute:

```
<tokenElement tokenAttribute="aValue">eValue</tokenElement>
```

The XML representation of the `tokenAttribute` attribute type looks very much like the XML representation of an element type:

```
<xsd:attribute name="tokenAttribute" type="xsd:token"/>
```

The structure type of an element type or a complex type may specify a reference to a global attribute type or a complete local attribute type.

### 6.6.2 Named Attribute-use Groups

A schema may specify attributes as a group instead of as a list of individual attribute types. A *named attribute-use group* is little more than a set of attribute types. Like other global components, the XML schema may reference named attribute-use groups in many places.

The XML representation of a named attribute-use group is the `attributeGroup` element, which might look like the following, for `saleAttributeGroup`:

```
<xsd:attributeGroup name="saleAttributeGroup"
                    id="pricing.sale.ag">
    <xsd:annotation>
        <xsd:documentation xml:lang="en">
            Anything that is on sale (or free,
            which is a type of sale) must
            have an authorization defined.
            This is someone's name,
            initials, ID, etc.
        </xsd:documentation>
    </xsd:annotation>
    <xsd:attribute name="employeeAuthorization" type="xsd:token"/>
    <xsd:attribute name="managerAuthorization" type="xsd:token"/>
</xsd:attributeGroup>
```

When an element type or complex type specifies the `saleAttributeGroup`, the effect is the same as specifying both `employeeAuthorization` and `managerAuthorization` at the same time.

Chapters 9 and 15 cover attribute groups.

### 6.6.3 Attribute Wildcards

An XML schema may specify attribute wildcards with the `anyAttribute` element. An attribute wildcard is a mechanism for specifying a set of namespaces from which the corresponding XML instance selects attribute types. The compact example does not demonstrate attribute wildcards. Chapters 9 and 15 cover attribute wildcards.

## 6.7 Simple Types

A simple type specifies a value range. An element type or attribute type may specify a simple type to impose a range of values on a corresponding XML instance. In the simplest case, a built-in datatype imposes the value range. Frequently, a simple type derived from a built-in datatype provides further constraints. A *constraining facet* on the derived simple type specifies a restriction of the value range. Multiple constraining facets may apply to a single simple type.

### 6.7.1 Built-in Datatypes

The built-in datatypes fall mostly into three categories: strings, numbers, and dates. Each of these categories has multiple specific datatypes. For example, a date might or might not include the time. Alternatively, perhaps the only interesting part of a date is the year. Similarly, numbers can be broken into integer and floating point, positive and negative, and other subcategories. An element type, attribute type, simple type, or complex type may reference a built-in datatype. A trivial example is the XML representation of basicTokenElement, whose structure type is the built-in token datatype described in Section 6.5.1.1:

```
<xsd:element name="basicTokenElement" type="xsd:token"/>
```

Similarly, the decimalAttribute attribute type specifies a decimal number:

```
<xsd:attribute name="decimalAttribute" type="xsd:decimal"/>
```

Chapter 12 discusses all built-in datatypes.

### 6.7.2 Deriving Simple Types by Restriction

A built-in datatype does not always provide appropriate constraints. A custom simple type creates an appropriate constraint by restricting a built-in datatype or another custom simple type. The XML representation of the element type sixToOneHundred extracted from Listing 6.1 specifies a simple type that constrains the built-in datatype positiveInteger to a number between 6 and 100:

```
<xsd:element name="sixToOneHundred"
             minOccurs="0"
             maxOccurs="unbounded">
    <xsd:simpleType>
        <xsd:restriction base="xsd:positiveInteger">
            <xsd:minExclusive value="5"/>
            <xsd:maxInclusive value="100"/>
        </xsd:restriction>
    </xsd:simpleType>
</xsd:element>
```

Note that the value range is *exclusive* of the value 5 and *inclusive* of the value 100.

### 6.7.3 Constraining Facets

A simple type applies zero or more constraining facets during derivation. The constraining facets limit the range of values, as demonstrated by the use of minExclusive and maxInclusive in the element type sixToOneHundred described in the previous example. Table 6.1 introduces all the constraining facets. This introduction includes a brief description of each constraining facet.

**TABLE 6.1**  The Constraining Facets

| Element | Description |
| --- | --- |
| enumeration | The value of an `enumeration` constraining facet is a set of specific valid values for a corresponding element. Each member of the set is represented by a separate enumeration element. |
| fractionDigits | The value of a `fractionDigits` constraining facet limits the number of digits after the decimal point required to represent a decimal value. |
| length | The value of a `length` constraining facet specifies the length of a string in characters. The value of a length constraining facet may also specify the length of a list (that is, the number of items in the list). For other datatypes, the units (characters, items) may be something different, appropriate to the datatype. |
| maxExclusive | The value of a `maxExclusive` constraining facet specifies an upper bound on a numeric value. This boundary excludes the value specified. |
| maxInclusive | The value of a `maxInclusive` constraining facet specifies an upper bound on a numeric value. This boundary includes the value specified. |
| maxLength | The value of a `maxLength` constraining facet specifies the maximum number of characters in a string or the maximum number of items in a list (or the maximum "something" appropriate to the datatype constrained). |
| minExclusive | The value of a `minExclusive` constraining facet specifies a lower bound on a numeric value. This boundary excludes the value specified. |
| minInclusive | The value of a `minInclusive` constraining facet specifies a lower bound on a numeric value. This boundary includes the value specified. |
| minLength | The value of a `minLength` constraining facet specifies the minimum number of characters in a string or the minimum number of items in a list. |
| pattern | The value of a `pattern` constraining facet is a regular expression used to validate a character string. |
| totalDigits | The value of a `totalDigits` constraining facet limits the total number of digits required to represent a decimal value. |
| whiteSpace | The value of a `whiteSpace` constraining facet provides for various kinds of normalization of spaces, carriage returns, and line feeds when determining the value of an instance of a simple type. |

Each constraining facet applies to a subset of the datatypes. Chapter 12 discusses all the constraining facets.

## 6.7.4 Lists

A simple type may specify a list of values. A simple type list derives from yet another simple type that constrains each value in the list. The values in a list are space-delimited. The thematic catalog example specifies a list of part numbers. An XML instance of this part number list might look like the following:

```
<partList>UX002 UX003</partList>
```

Because of the complexity of creating a list, discussion about creating the XML representation of a list simple type is left to Section 10.8.

## 6.7.5 Unions

A simple type may specify a value space and lexical space in terms of a union of other simple types. A simple type may form a union from fundamentally different simple types. The thematic catalog example portrays the simple type `assemblyPartStatusType` that specifies a union of a date, an integer, and a string. A corresponding XML instance must be an instance of one of these three valid value classes.

Because of the complexity of creating a union, discussion about creating the XML representation of a union simple type is left to Section 10.9.

## 6.8 Complex Types

A complex type specifies the possible content of an element. A complex type specifies subelements, empty content, or mixed content, and attributes. A complex type has two flavors: a complex type that specifies simple content and a complex type that specifies complex content.

### 6.8.1 Simple Content

Complex types that specify simple content can further restrict value ranges with functionality identical to simple type restriction. Complex types with simple content provide the following functionality:

- Restricting value ranges (identical functionality to simple type restriction)
- Adding attribute types to a simple type or to a base complex type that specifies simple content
- Modifying or removing attribute types from a base complex type that specifies simple content

Section 11.7 covers simple content.

## 6.8.2 Complex Content

Complex types that specify complex content describe the content range for an element instance. Complex content provides the following functionality:

- The allowable subelement structure
- Specifying empty content
- Specifying mixed content, which includes the structure of nested elements
- Adding, modifying, or removing attribute types from a base complex type

Section 11.8 covers complex content.

## 6.8.3 Deriving Complex Types by Extension

A derived complex type may extend a base complex type by adding any of the following:

- Content (individual element types or via entire model groups)
- Attribute types (or attribute-use groups, or attribute wildcards)

Listing 6.3 demonstrates the derived complex type `assemblyCatalogEntryType` that extends `baseAssemblyCatalogEntryType` by adding two element types: `partList` and `status`.

**LISTING 6.3**   Extending a Complex Type

```
<xsd:complexType name="baseAssemblyCatalogEntryType"
                 abstract="true"
                 block="#all"
                 final="restriction"
                 id="baseAssemblyCatalogEntryType.catalog.cType">
    <xsd:annotation>
        <xsd:documentation xml:lang="en">
            An assembled item is similar to the
            other catalog entries.  The part number
            is restricted to an assembly number.
            In addition, there may be no options.
            Finally, a part list is also needed.
            Note that the "includedQuantity" has
            a default of one, but can be overridden
            in instances.
        </xsd:documentation>
    </xsd:annotation>
    <xsd:complexContent>
        <xsd:restriction base="baseCatalogEntryType"
                         id="bacet.rst">
            <xsd:sequence>
                <xsd:element ref="assemblyID"/>
```

```xml
            <xsd:element name="partName" type="partNameType"/>
            <xsd:element name="partNumber"
                    type="assemblyPartNumberType"/>
            <xsd:element name="partOption"
                    type="partOptionType"
                    minOccurs="0"
                    maxOccurs="0"/>
            <xsd:element name="description"
                    type="catalogEntryDescriptionType"/>
            <xsd:group ref="priceGroup"/>
            <xsd:element name="includedQuantity"
                    type="xsd:positiveInteger"
                    default="1"/>
            <xsd:element name="customerReview"
                    type="customerReviewType"
                    minOccurs="0"
                    maxOccurs="unbounded"/>
          </xsd:sequence>
          <xsd:attribute name="category"
                    type="categoryType"
                    fixed="assembly"/>
        </xsd:restriction>
    </xsd:complexContent>
</xsd:complexType>

<xsd:complexType name="assemblyCatalogEntryType"
            block="#all"
            final="#all"
            id="assemblyCatalogEntryType.catalog.cType">
    <xsd:annotation>
        <xsd:documentation xml:lang="en">
            The actual definition of an assembly,
            including the contained parts.
        </xsd:documentation>
    </xsd:annotation>
    <xsd:complexContent>
        <xsd:extension base="baseAssemblyCatalogEntryType"
                    id="acet.ext">
            <xsd:sequence>
                <xsd:element name="partList" type="partNumberListType"/>
                <xsd:element name="status" type="assemblyPartStatusType"/>
            </xsd:sequence>
        </xsd:extension>
    </xsd:complexContent>
</xsd:complexType>
```

Section 11.9 covers extending complex types.

### 6.8.4 Deriving Complex Types by Restriction

Many complex types derive from other complex types via restriction. A restriction is a reduction in the range of values for specific element types or attribute types—or even the elimination of element types and attribute types. Technically, the restrictions modify the "use" (as in `minOccurs` or `maxOccurs`), or the value specified by structure types. The XML representation of a restricted complex type must have element types and attribute types derived from those specified by the base complex type. A derived complex type provides the following functionality:

- Altering attributes of an element type or attribute type
- Substituting a derivation of a structure type for any structure type
- Substituting an element in the context of a substitution group
- Restricting value ranges of simple types

Derived complex types often alter the `minOccurs` and `maxOccurs` attributes of an element type: This may result in prohibiting an element in a corresponding XML instance. Similarly, a derived complex type frequently alters the `use` attribute of attribute types: This may result in prohibiting an attribute in a corresponding XML instance.

> **NOTE**
>
> Complex type specifications which use the shorthand notation (neither `restriction` nor `extension` are specified) are implicitly restrictions of `anyType`. (*Every* complex type other than `anyType` is *ultimately* a restriction of `anyType`.)

Listing 6.4, whose source is the thematic catalog example, shows that `bulkCatalogEntryType` is a restriction of `baseCatalogEntryType`. Note that both of these complex types have exactly the same nesting of element types (`sequenceID`, `partName`, `partNumber`, `partOption`, `description`, `priceGroup`, `includedQuantity`, and `customerReview`) as well as the same `category` attribute type.

**LISTING 6.4** Restricting a Complex Type

```
<xsd:complexType name="baseCatalogEntryType"
                 abstract="true"
                 id="baseCatalogEntryType.catalog.cType">
    <xsd:annotation>
        <xsd:documentation xml:lang="en">
            A catalog entry must have:
                * A database ID
                * Part Name
                * Part Number
```

```
                    * Options available
                    * Description
                    * Price
                    * Included Quantity when ordering
                      one item.
                The "baseCatalogEntryType" is
                non-instantiable:   a derived type must
                be created before a catalog
                entry can be instantiated.
                    -- Shorthand Notation--
        </xsd:documentation>
    </xsd:annotation>
    <xsd:sequence id="bacet-seq">
        <xsd:element ref="sequenceID"/>
        <xsd:element name="partName" type="partNameType"/>
        <xsd:element name="partNumber" type="partNumberType"/>
        <xsd:element name="partOption" type="partOptionType"/>
        <xsd:element name="description"
                    type="catalogEntryDescriptionType"/>
        <xsd:group ref="priceGroup"/>
        <xsd:element name="includedQuantity"
                    type="xsd:positiveInteger"/>
        <xsd:element name="customerReview"
                    type="customerReviewType"
                            minOccurs="0"
                            maxOccurs="unbounded"/>
    </xsd:sequence>
    <xsd:attribute name="category"
                    type="categoryType"
                    use="required"/>
</xsd:complexType>

<xsd:complexType name="bulkCatalogEntryType"
                block="#all"
                final="#all"
                id="bulkCatalogEntryType.catalog.cType">
    <xsd:annotation>
        <xsd:documentation xml:lang="en">
            A bulk item is just like any
            other, except that the part
            number is restricted to a
            bulk part number.
        </xsd:documentation>
    </xsd:annotation>
    <xsd:complexContent>
        <xsd:restriction base="baseCatalogEntryType">
            <xsd:sequence>
```

*continues*

```
                    <xsd:element ref="bulkID"/>
                    <xsd:element name="partName" type="partNameType"/>
                    <xsd:element name="partNumber" type="bulkPartNumberType"/>
                    <xsd:element name="partOption" type="partOptionType"/>
                    <xsd:element name="description"
                                 type="catalogEntryDescriptionType"/>
                    <xsd:group ref="priceGroup"/>
                    <xsd:element name="includedQuantity"
                                 type="xsd:positiveInteger"/>
                    <xsd:element name="customerReview"
                                 type="customerReviewType"
                                 minOccurs="0"
                                 maxOccurs="unbounded"/>
                </xsd:sequence>
                <xsd:attribute name="category"
                               type="categoryType"
                               fixed="bulk"/>
            </xsd:restriction>
        </xsd:complexContent>
</xsd:complexType>
```

In fact, `bulkCatalogEntryType` substitutes `bulkID` for `sequenceID`. Section 6.10 covers this substitution.

Section 11.10 covers restricting complex types.

### 6.8.5 Blocking Complex Types

The XML Schema Recommendation provides for blocking restriction or extension of complex types. Blocking can prevent derivations of a complex type. Blocking can also prevent substituting derived types in an XML instance via `xsi:type`. Because of the complexity of blocking, all further discussion of blocking is deferred to Chapter 11.

## 6.9 Model Groups

A model group specifies a pattern for element type instances. There are three kinds of model groups:

- An *all* model group requires instances of all members of a set of element types or other groups, in no particular order. (Each member may have occurrence restrictions.)
- A *choice* model group requires an instance of one member of a set of element types or other groups. (Each member may have occurrence restrictions.)
- A *sequence* model group requires instances of all members of a set of element types or other groups, in a specified order. (Each member may have occurrence restrictions.)

A *named model group* specifies any one of the other model groups.

### 6.9.1 The All Model Group

A complex type with complex content specifies an unordered set of element types with an all model group. The XML representation of `partOptionType` in Listing 6.5 specifies an unordered set of element types. Excluding the `minOccurs` attribute (which in this case specifies that the corresponding element instance is optional), a corresponding XML instance must include a `color` and a `size`, although these can appear in either order.

**LISTING 6.5**  An All Model Group

```
<xsd:complexType name="partOptionType"
                block="#all"
                final="#all"
                id="partOptionType.catalog.cType">
    <xsd:annotation>
        <xsd:documentation xml:lang="en">
            Appropriate parts can have a color,
            a size, or both.  Note that the use
            of the "all" element indicates that
            the "color" and "size" are unordered.
            That is, they can appear in either
            order.
                -- Shorthand Notation --
        </xsd:documentation>
    </xsd:annotation>
    <xsd:all id="pot.all">
        <xsd:element name="color"
                    type="colorOptionType"
                    minOccurs="0"
                    maxOccurs="1"/>
        <xsd:element name="size"
                    type="sizeOptionType"
                    minOccurs="0"
                    maxOccurs="1"/>
    </xsd:all>
</xsd:complexType>
```

Section 11.11 covers the all model group.

### 6.9.2 The Choice Model Group

A complex type with complex content specifies the selection of one element type from a set of element types with a choice model group. Listing 6.6 portrays a choice of pricing schemes. A corresponding XML instance must select exactly one of the pricing schemes.

**LISTING 6.6**   A Choice Model Group

```
<xsd:group name="priceGroup">
    <xsd:annotation>
        <xsd:documentation xml:lang="en">
            A price is any one of the following:
                * Full Price (with amount)
                * Sale Price (with amount and authorization)
                * Clearance Price (with amount and authorization)
                * Free (with authorization)
        </xsd:documentation>
    </xsd:annotation>
    <xsd:choice id="pg.choice">
        <xsd:element name="fullPrice"
                     type="fullPriceType"/>
        <xsd:element name="salePrice"
                     type="salePriceType"/>
        <xsd:element name="clearancePrice"
                     type="clearancePriceType"/>
        <xsd:element name="freePrice" type="freePriceType"/>
    </xsd:choice>
</xsd:group>
```

Section 11.12 covers the choice model group.

## 6.9.3 The Sequence Model Group

A complex type with complex content specifies an ordered set of element types with a sequence model group. The XML representation of `encompassingElement` in Listing 6.1 specifies an ordered set of element types. This ordering ensures that a corresponding XML instance always contains nested elements in the same order. This order may enhance readability or processing.

Section 11.13 covers the sequence model group.

## 6.9.4 The Named Model Group

A named model group takes a model group, names it, and makes it global so that it can be referenced; sequence, all, and choice model groups are always local to a complex type or a named model group. The main purpose of the named model group is to provide a reusable model group. `priceGroup` from Listing 6.5 is global. Many element types in the thematic catalog example require a price; these element types reference the global `priceGroup`.

Section 11.14 covers the named model group.

## 6.10 Substitution Groups

A substitution group consists of a set of element types. An element type associates itself with a substitution group by specifying a `substitutionGroup` attribute. The value of that attribute indicates that the new element type is a valid substitution for the referenced element type. The substitutions occur in complex type derivations or in an XML instance. Listing 6.7 is the `sequenceID` substitution group.

**LISTING 6.7** A Substitution Group

```
<xsd:element name="sequenceID"
             type="sequenceIDType"
             abstract="true">
    <xsd:annotation>
        <xsd:documentation xml:lang="en">
            This element type is
            non-instantiable:  the element
            must be replaced by a substitution
            group in either a derived type or
            an instance.
        </xsd:documentation>
    </xsd:annotation>
</xsd:element>

<xsd:element name="unitID"
             type="sequenceIDType"
             substitutionGroup="sequenceID">
    <xsd:annotation>
        <xsd:documentation xml:lang="en">
            This element represents sequence
            IDs for unit items.
            This element provides a valid
            substitution for "sequenceID".
        </xsd:documentation>
    </xsd:annotation>
</xsd:element>

<xsd:element name="bulkID"
             type="sequenceIDType"
             substitutionGroup="sequenceID">
    <xsd:annotation>
        <xsd:documentation xml:lang="en">
            This element represents sequence
            IDs for bulk items.
            This element provides a valid
```

*continues*

```
                substitution for "sequenceID".
        </xsd:documentation>
    </xsd:annotation>
</xsd:element>

<xsd:element name="assemblyID"
             type="sequenceIDType"
             substitutionGroup="sequenceID">
    <xsd:annotation>
        <xsd:documentation xml:lang="en">
            This element represents sequence
            IDs for assembled items.
            This element provides a valid
            substitution for "sequenceID".
        </xsd:documentation>
    </xsd:annotation>
</xsd:element>
```

In the context of the thematic catalog example, there are various IDs. A base complex type requires a sequenceID attribute. Derived complex types substitute a specific ID, such as a bulkID. An element type can block substitution in derived complex types or in XML instances.

Chapter 8 covers substitution groups as well as blocking substitutions.

## 6.11 Instantiability

Not all element types are instantiable in an XML instance. Element types may directly prohibit the existence of corresponding instances. Similarly, a complex type functioning as the structure type of an element type may indirectly prohibit the existence of corresponding instances. This section illuminates restrictions on instantiability of element types, attribute types, simple types, and complex types.

### 6.11.1 Element Type Instantiability

An element type is *explicitly* non-instantiable when the element type's representation specifies the abstract attribute with a value of 'true'. An element type may be *implicitly* non-instantiable due to its structure type being explicitly or implicitly non-instantiable.

Section 8.2 discusses the instantiability of element types.

### 6.11.2 Attribute Type Instantiability

An attribute type cannot derive another attribute type. Similarly, an attribute cannot be abstract. Therefore, all attribute types are instantiable.

### 6.11.3 Simple Type Instantiability

The XML Schema Recommendation does not yet permit non-instantiable simple types despite the fact that the XML schema writer might want to specify a non-instantiable base simple type. It is possible—we hope, likely—that the capability might be added in a future release of the Schema Recommendation.

### 6.11.4 Complex Type Instantiability

Complex types are *explicitly* non-instantiable when the complex type's representation specfies the `abstract` attribute with a value of 'true'. A complex type may be *implicitly* non-instantiable due to enclosed element types (that is, element types in the content model) being implicitly or explicitly non-instantiable.

Section 11.5 covers the instantiability of complex types.

## 6.12 Identity Constraint Definitions

An XML schema generally validates the structure of an XML instance in terms of element nesting and attributes. The XML schema also validates content primarily in the form of simple types. Identity constraints provide an additional mechanism to validate contents. The three types of elements for creating identity constraints are `unique`, `key`, and `keyref`.

A `unique` element specifies that repeated elements are unique given the values of one or a combination of keys. For example, Listing 6.8 demonstrates that a `partNumber` can appear only once with a particular value in the entire `completePartList`.

**LISTING 6.8**  Unique Part Numbers (sdDemo.xsd)

```
<xsd:element name="completePartList">
    <xsd:complexType>
        <xsd:sequence>
            <xsd:element name="part"
                        minOccurs="0"
                        maxOccurs="unbounded">
                <xsd:complexType>
                    <xsd:attribute name="partNumber"
                                   type="xsd:string"/>
                </xsd:complexType>
            </xsd:element>
        </xsd:sequence>
    </xsd:complexType>

<xsd:unique name="uniquePartNumbers">
        <xsd:annotation>
```

*continues*

```
                <xsd:documentation xml:lang="en">
                    Ensure unique part numbers
                </xsd:documentation>
            </xsd:annotation>
            <xsd:selector xpath="part"/>
            <xsd:field xpath="@partNumber"/>
        </xsd:unique>

</xsd:element>
```

The `key` and `unique` identity constraints interact with the `keyref` identity constraints. The set of keys specified by `keyref` must exist in the set of keys specified by `key` or `unique`. This functionality parallels foreign keys in databases.

Chapter 13 provides many examples and detailed explanations of identity constraints.

## 6.13 Notations

A notation component in an XML schema supports the XML notations documented in the XML Recommendation. They constitute information to be simply passed on to the application.

> **NOTE**
>
> The XML Recommendation states that "XML processors must provide applications with the name and external identifier(s) of any notation declared and referred to in an attribute value, attribute definition, or entity declaration. They may additionally resolve the external identifier into the system identifier, file name, or other information needed to allow the application to call a processor for data in the notation described."

The value of an element or attribute in an XML instance may refer to a notation. The corresponding element type or attribute type must have a structure type that derives from the built-in `NOTATION`.

Section 7.10 covers notations.

## 6.14 Imports and Includes

An XML schema document may reference components outside the document by importing or including these components from another XML schema document. The `include` element adds components to the current schema. In particular, the `include` element provides a mechanism to assemble an XML schema from a set of XML schema documents. An `import` element, on the other hand, permits a schema to include components in a different namespace.

Sections 7.8 and 7.9 provide details and examples of how to use `include` and `import`, respectively.

## 6.15 Locating XML Schemas and XML Schema Components

The most common mechanism for locating an XML schema document is a complete URL. The catalog schema, for example, is located at the following address:

```
xmlns:cat=
 "http://www.XMLSchemaReference.com/examples/theme/catalog.xsd"
```

An XML schema may specify a component via an XML fragment (see the W3C XML Fragment Interchange Recommendation at `http://www.w3.org/TR/xml-fragment.html`).

An XML schema may also specify components with an XPointer (see the W3C XML Pointer Language Recommendation at `http://www.w3.org/TR/WD-xptr`).

## 6.16 Schema Element IDs

In an effort to demonstrate all the features offered by the XML Schema Recommendation, many of the examples in this book specify a unique ID for each schema component. Specifically, the elements have an `id` attribute. Each ID must be unique across the entire schema, not just within an XML schema document. Unless you are using the IDs for something meaningful, such as fragment identifiers, you might prefer not to specify IDs. The IDs tend to clutter the XML schema document.

# Creating an XML Schema Document

**CHAPTER 7**

## IN THIS CHAPTER

- 7.1 A Simple XML Schema Document Example  106
- 7.2 A `schema` Element with Every Attribute  106
- 7.3 Concepts and Observations  107
- 7.4 The `schema` Element  108
- 7.5 The `annotation` Element  116
- 7.6 The `appinfo` Element  119
- 7.7 The `documentation` Element  120
- 7.8 The `include` Element  122
- 7.9 The `import` Element  124
- 7.10 The `notation` Element  128
- 7.11 The `redefine` Element  132

Every XML schema document contains a `schema` element that is the document element, which encloses all other elements. This chapter covers the attribute options and content options of a `schema` element. This chapter also discusses a few elements that pertain to XML schemas in general: `annotation`, `import`, `include`, `notation`, and `redefine`.

## 7.1 A Simple XML Schema Document Example

Listing 7.1 is a trivial XML schema document that specifies only an element type whose structure type is the built-in `string` datatype.

**LISTING 7.1**   A Trivial XML Schema Document (`simpleSchema.xsd`)

```
<xsd:schema xmlns:xsd="http://www.w3.org/2001/XMLSchema">
    <xsd:element name="stringElement" type="xsd:string"/>
</xsd:schema>
```

A few features to point out about the preceding trivial schema:

- The only attribute of the `schema` element—`xmlns:xsd`—specifies the namespace `http://www.w3.org/2001/XMLSchema`. Furthermore, the `xmlns:xsd` attribute specifies the corresponding namespace prefix, 'xsd'. The specification of the XML schema namespace implies a corresponding XML schema document `XMLSchema.xsd`, which is the Schema for Schemas.

- `xmlns:xsd` is not a `schema` attribute per se; the `xmlns:xsd` attribute applies to any XML element.

- There is explicitly no target namespace. Note that in the subsequent example, a namespace prefix does not precede the element name 'tokenElement'.

Given the XML schema document in Listing 7.1, the following is a valid XML instance:

```
<stringElement
  xmlns:xsi="http://www.w3.org/2001/XMLSchema-instance"
  xsi:schemaLocation=
   "http://www.XMLSchemaReference.com/examples/Ch07/notation.xsd"
>A String Value</stringElement>
```

Note that there is exactly one element in the XML instance: a `stringElement`. The value of that `stringElement` is 'A String Value'.

## 7.2 A schema Element with Every Attribute

Section 7.4.1 discusses all the possible XML schema attributes of the `schema` element. Listing 7.2 is a complete XML schema in which the `schema` element has all possible attributes. Many of the ensuing explanations in Section 7.4.1 refer to Listing 7.2.

**LISTING 7.2**  A schema Element with Every Attribute (`fullFeaturedSchema.xsd`)

```xml
<xsd:schema
    xmlns:xsd="http://www.w3.org/2001/XMLSchema"
    xmlns:ffs="http://www.XMLSchemaReference.com/examples/
                    Ch07/fullFeaturedSchema"
    xmlns:ra="http://www.XMLSchemaReference.com/examples/
                    Ch07/randomAttributes"
    xmlns="http://www.XMLSchemaReference.com/examples/
                    Ch07/fullFeaturedSchema"
    targetNamespace="http://www.XMLSchemaReference.com/examples/
                    Ch07/fullFeaturedSchema"
    elementFormDefault="unqualified"
    attributeFormDefault="unqualified"
    id="Full-Featured-Schema"
    blockDefault="#all"
    finalDefault="restriction"
    version="FFS:1"
    xml:lang="en-US">

<xsd:import
    namespace="http://www.XMLSchemaReference.com/examples/
                    Ch07/randomAttributes"
    schemaLocation="http://www.XMLSchemaReference.com/examples/
                    Ch07/randomAttributes.xsd"/>
<xsd:include
    schemaLocation="http://www.XMLSchemaReference.com/examples/
                    Ch07/ffs_include.xsd"/>

</xsd:schema>
```

## 7.3 Concepts and Observations

Chapter 6 has many sections that cover concepts or observations that might otherwise appear in this chapter. You should read Chapter 6 before proceeding with this chapter.

The only observation that seems worth repeating pertains to namespaces. Although trivial to implement, one of the most difficult tasks when planning an XML schema is determining the target and default namespaces. Frequently, initial XML schema documents do not contain any namespace information other than where to locate the Schema for Schemas (see Listing 7.1). The documents evolve to include namespaces and target namespaces as needed. This approach is often acceptable. A schema should absolutely specify a target namespace, however, if the schema provides functionality over the Web or in any "public" schema that a user might integrate with a proprietary schema. Section 6.2 has a more complete discussion of namespaces.

## 7.4 The schema Element

The XML representation of an XML schema is one or more XML schema documents. Each XML schema document has exactly one `schema` element that encompasses all other elements in the document. Only an XML comment may appear before or after the `schema` element.

### 7.4.1 Attributes of a schema Element

Most attributes of a `schema` element pertain to namespaces. Two attributes pertain to blocking. The remaining attributes provide minor functionality. Table 7.1 provides a summary of all of the attributes of a `schema` element.

**TABLE 7.1**  Attribute Summary for a schema Element

| Attribute | Description |
| --- | --- |
| `attributeFormDefault` | The value of the `attributeFormDefault` attribute determines the default value of the `form` attribute for all attribute types. |
| `blockDefault` | The value of the `blockDefault` attribute determines the default value of the `block` attribute for element types and complex types. |
| `elementFormDefault` | The value of the `elementFormDefault` attribute determines the default value of the `form` attribute for all element types. |
| `finalDefault` | The value of the `finalDefault` attribute determines the default value of the `final` attribute for element types, simple types, and complex types. |
| `id` | The value of an `id` attribute uniquely identifies an element within the set of schema documents that comprise an XML schema. |
| `targetNamespace` | The value of the `targetNamespace` is the namespace for any component described in the XML schema document. There may be explicitly no target namespace. |
| `version` | The `version` attribute has no special meaning. The schema writer might wish to version the XML schema or the XML schema document. |
| `xml:lang` | The value of the `xml:lang` attribute indicates the language of all human-readable information in a schema. |
| `xmlns` | The value of an `xmlns` attribute specifies an XML namespace. The `xmlns` attribute identifies existing namespaces to which qualified names might apply. Without a namespace prefix, the value of this attribute may also identify a default namespace for the XML schema document. |

### 7.4.1.1 The attributeFormDefault Attribute of a schema Element

The attributeFormDefault attribute specifies a default value for the form attribute of all attribute types. Because the form attribute of an attribute type is not required, and because the attributeFormDefault defaults to 'unqualified', the overall default is that attributes in a corresponding XML instance do not require qualification.

---
**ATTRIBUTE OVERVIEW**

**schema: attributeFormDesign**

| | |
|---:|---|
| **Value:** | 'qualified' or 'unqualified'. |
| **Default:** | 'unqualified'. |
| **Constraints:** | None. |
| **Required:** | No. |
---

The impact on a corresponding XML instance is rather complex. Section 9.5.1.3, explains qualification of attribute instances, including the impact of the schema-wide attributeFormDefault.

Listing 7.2 is an entire XML schema document. The enclosing schema element has an attributeFormDefault attribute which specifies that, without an explicit override by an individual attribute type, an attribute type reference in a corresponding XML instance does not require qualification.

### 7.4.1.2 The blockDefault Attribute of a schema Element

The blockDefault attribute specifies a default value for the block attribute of all element types and complex types. Because element types and complex types do not require a block attribute, and because blockDefault is not required, the default state for all schemas does not block extensions, restrictions, or substitutions in corresponding XML instances.

---
**ATTRIBUTE OVERVIEW**

**schema: blockDefault**

| | |
|---:|---|
| **Value:** | '#all' or a space-delimited list consisting of any or all of 'extension', 'restriction', or 'substitution'. |
| **Default:** | 'unqualified'. |
| **Constraints:** | None. |
| **Required:** | No. |
---

The impact of blocking is complicated. Section 8.3.1.2 explains blocking of element types. Section 11.6.1.2 explains blocking of complex types. Both of these explanations include the impact of the schema-wide `blockDefault`.

> **NOTE**
>
> When the value for the `blockDefault` attribute includes 'substitution', 'substitution' does not apply to complex types; any other values apply. Another way of saying this is that an XML validator ignores a value of 'substitution' in the `blockDefault` attribute when processing complex types.

Listing 7.2 is an entire XML schema document. The enclosing `schema` element has a `blockDefault` attribute which specifies that, without an explicit override, all types prohibit an XML instance from explicitly or implicitly extending, restricting, or substituting.

### 7.4.1.3 The `elementFormDefault` Attribute of a `schema` Element

The `elementFormDefault` attribute specifies a default value for the `form` attribute of all element types. Because the `form` attribute of an element type is not required, and because the `elementFormDefault` defaults to 'unqualified', the overall default is that elements in a corresponding XML instance do not require qualification.

**ATTRIBUTE OVERVIEW**

**schema: elementFormDefault**

| | |
|---:|---|
| **Value:** | 'qualified' or 'unqualified'. |
| **Default:** | 'unqualified'. |
| **Constraints:** | None. |
| **Required:** | No. |

The impact on an XML instance is rather complicated. Section 8.3.1.6 explains qualification of element instances, including the impact of the schema-wide `elementFormDefault`.

Listing 7.2 is an entire XML schema document. The enclosing `schema` element has an `elementFormDefault` attribute which specifies that, without an explicit override by an individual element type, an element type reference in a corresponding XML instance does not require qualification.

### 7.4.1.4 The `finalDefault` Attribute of a `schema` Element

The `finalDefault` attribute specifies a default value for the `final` attribute of all element types, simple types, and complex types. Because element types, simple types, and complex types do not require a `final` attribute, and because `finalDefault` is not required, the default state for all schemas is to not block extensions or restrictions in the XML schema document.

---

**ATTRIBUTE OVERVIEW**

**schema: `finalDefault`**

| | |
|---:|:---|
| **Value:** | '#all' or a space-delimited list consisting of any or all of 'extension' or 'restriction'. |
| **Default:** | 'unqualified'. |
| **Constraints:** | None. |
| **Required:** | No. |

---

The impact of blocking is complicated. Section 8.3.1.4 explains blocking of element types. Section 11.6.1.3 explains blocking of complex types. Both of these explanations include the impact of the schema-wide `finalDefault`.

Listing 7.2 is an entire XML schema document. The enclosing `schema` element has a `finalDefault` attribute which specifies that, without an explicit override, all types prohibit further restrictions (but not extensions) in the schema.

### 7.4.1.5 The `id` Attribute of a `schema` Element

The value of an `id` attribute uniquely identifies an element within the set of schema documents that comprise an XML schema.

---

**ATTRIBUTE OVERVIEW**

**schema: `id`**

| | |
|---:|:---|
| **Value:** | An ID. |
| **Default:** | None. |
| **Constraints:** | In general, the value of an ID-valued attribute must be unique within an XML document. The XML Schema Recommendation further constrains this uniqueness to the entire XML schema. |
| **Required:** | No. |

Listing 7.2 is an entire XML schema document. The enclosing `schema` element has an `id` attribute.

### 7.4.1.6 The `targetNamespace` Attribute of a `schema` Element

The target namespace is the namespace for all the components in a schema document. In particular, all component names must be appropriately unique within this namespace. The target namespace is optional. When the XML schema document does not specify a target namespace, all enclosed components explicitly have no namespace; all references to these components must be unqualified. The exception to this rule is for components that explicitly belong to another namespace because of an `import` (see Section 7.9.). Section 6.2 has a more complete discourse on the interaction of namespaces.

---

**ATTRIBUTE OVERVIEW**

**schema: targetNamespace**

| | |
|---:|---|
| **Value:** | A URI or the empty string (for example, `targetNamespace=""`), which explicitly indicates no namespace. |
| **Default:** | No namespace. |
| **Constraints:** | None; in fact, there is no requirement that the location specified by the URI can be dereferenced. |
| **Required:** | No. |

---

Listing 7.2 is an entire XML schema document. The enclosing `schema` element has a `targetNamespace` attribute.

### 7.4.1.7 The `version` Attribute of a `schema` Element

The `version` attribute of a `schema` element has no semantics. The value of the `version` attribute could represent the version of the XML schema or the XML schema document.

---

**ATTRIBUTE OVERVIEW**

**schema: version**

| | |
|---:|---|
| **Value:** | Any string that conforms to the built-in `token` datatype. |
| **Default:** | None. |
| **Constraints:** | None. |
| **Required:** | No. |

Listing 7.2 is an entire XML schema document. The enclosing `schema` element has a `version` attribute.

### 7.4.1.8 The `xml:lang` Attribute of a `schema` Element

An element in a schema document can specify various "special" attributes using the keyword 'xml', which—to the casual observer—has the appearance of an attribute. The value of `xml:lang` specifies the default human language of all text in a schema document. `xml:lang` is not defined by the XML Schema Recommendation. Rather, `xml:lang` is a reserved attribute defined by the XML Recommendation. See RFC 1766 (http://www.ietf.org/rfc/rfc1766.txt) for more information on the language choices. For the English language, the value is 'en'. The value for *United States* English is 'en-US'.

> **WARNING**
>
> Part 0 of the XML Schema Recommendation states that "you may indicate the language of all information in a schema by placing an `xml:lang` attribute on the schema element." Because multiple XML schema documents might represent an XML schema, the behavior of conflicting `xml:lang` attributes is indeterminate. The schema documents should respect other similar constraints by using the same value for `xml:lang` in all XML schema documents.

**ATTRIBUTE OVERVIEW**

**schema: xml:lang**

| | |
|---|---|
| **Value:** | Any string that conforms to the built-in `language` datatype. |
| **Default:** | None. |
| **Constraints:** | None. |
| **Required:** | No. |

Listing 7.2 is an entire XML schema document. The enclosing `schema` element has an `xml:lang` attribute that specifies United States English.

### 7.4.1.9 The `xmlns` "Attributes" of a `schema` Element

An element in a schema document can specify a namespace declaration with 'xmlns', which—to the casual observer—has the appearance of an attribute. `xmlns` provides functionality to specify namespaces, including the default namespace. `xmlns` is not defined by the XML Schema Recommendation. Rather, `xmlns` is a reserved namespace as defined by the Namespace and Infoset Recommendations.

## Creating an XML Schema Document
**CHAPTER 7**

---

**ATTRIBUTE OVERVIEW**

**schema: xmlns**

- **Value:** A URI.
- **Default:** None.
- **Constraints:** None.
- **Required:** No.

---

A namespace declaration, which starts with 'xmlns', has several functions:

- Associating a namespace prefix with a namespace
- Specifying a default namespace
- Removing a default namespace

The following example associates the namespace prefix 'cat' with the namespace http://www.XMLSchemaReference.com/examples/theme/catalog:

```
xmlns:cat=
    "http://www.XMLSchemaReference.com/examples/theme/catalog"
```

The next example specifies a default namespace, which corresponds to the catalog in the previous example:

```
xmlns=
    "http://www.XMLSchemaReference.com/examples/theme/catalog"
```

Note that the namespace prefix is missing.

Finally, when the value of xmlns is empty, there is no default namespace:

```
xmlns=""
```

> **TIP**
>
> By default, there is no default namespace for an XML schema. In addition, an element nested within the schema element can remove the default namespace with the attribute specification 'xmlns=""'.

Listing 7.2 is an entire XML schema document. The enclosing schema element has several xmlns attributes.

## 7.4.2 Content Options for a schema Element

The content options for a `schema` element pertain almost entirely to creating components that belong to the XML schema. The elements that do not represent components have to do with the details of describing an XML schema in XML schema documents, such as `include`, `import`, and `redefine`. Table 7.2 provides a summary of the numerous content options for a `schema` element.

**TABLE 7.2** Content Options for a schema Element

| Element | Description |
|---|---|
| annotation | The `annotation` element, discussed in Section 7.5, provides a way to document schema elements. |
| attribute | The XML schema document describes a global attribute type with an `attribute` element. Chapter 9 illuminates how to create XML representations of attribute types. |
| attributeGroup | The XML schema document describes a global set of attribute types with an `attributeGroup` element. Chapter 9 illuminates how to create XML representations of attribute use groups. |
| complexType | The XML schema document describes a global complex type with a `complexType` element. Chapter 11 illuminates how to create XML representations of complex types. |
| element | The XML schema document describes a global element type with an `element` element. Chapter 8 illuminates how to create XML representations of element types. |
| group | The XML schema document describes a global named model group with a `group` element. Section 11.14 illuminates how to create XML representations of named model groups. |
| include | An XML schema document can `include` components defined in the same namespace with the `include` element. The intent of the `include` element is to build a single XML schema from a set of XML schema documents. Section 7.8 illuminates how to describe an `include` element. |
| import | An XML schema document may reference components from a different or *foreign* target namespace with an `import` element. Section 7.9 illuminates how to describe an `import` element. |

*continues*

**TABLE 7.2** *(continued)*

| Element | Description |
|---|---|
| notation | A `notation` element describes XML notations (as documented in the XML Recommendation) in an XML schema document. A notation typically contains a reference to an executable program. For example, another program can refer to these notations to spawn the process identified in the notation. Section 7.10 illuminates how to create XML representations of notations. |
| redefine | An XML schema document describes a `redefine` element to replace a component. The new version of the component applies to the entire schema, not some portion thereof. Section 7.11 illuminates how to redefine existing schema components. |
| simpleType | The XML schema document describes a global simple type with a `simpleType` element. Chapter 10 illuminates how to create XML representations of simple types. |

The content pattern for the schema element follows:

```
((include | import | redefine | annotation)*
 (((simpleType |
    complexType |
    group |
    attributeGroup) |
    element |
    attribute |
    notation)
    annotation*)*)
```

## 7.5 The `annotation` Element

The `annotation` element provides a mechanism for documenting most other schema elements. Unlike an XML comment, which looks like `<!-- comment text -->`, the annotation is part of the schema component. An `annotation` provides documentation intended for human consumption in one or more languages, as well as documentation intended for programmatic consumption, such as meaningful URIs.

Listing 7.3 demonstrates the use of an annotation that describes a Private Mail Box (PMB). The following example contains an `annotation` of pmb.

## Listing 7.3  An annotation Element (address.xsd)

```xml
<xsd:element name="pmb"
             type="xsd:string"
             substitutionGroup="addressLine"
             minOccurs="1"
             maxOccurs="1">
    <xsd:annotation id="customerRecord.annotation.pmb">
        <xsd:documentation
            source="http://new.usps.com/cgi-bin/
                    uspsbv/scripts/content.jsp?D=13647"
            xml:lang="en">
            A PMB is a "Private Mail Box" that is provided
            by an entity other than the U S Postal Service.
        </xsd:documentation>
        <xsd:documentation xml:lang="en">
            Developer Note:  Someone should probably come up
            with a way to actually validate PMBs.  In fact,
            it would be great if we could validate
            every <pmb/> and <POBox/> element.
        </xsd:documentation>
        <xsd:appinfo
             source="http://www.XMLSchemaReference.com/
                     examples/java/extractJava">
            // A PMB is a "Private Mail Box" that is provided
            // by an entity other than the U S Postal Service.
            // -- create a class for the pmb
            public class pmb
                {
            *       *      *       *      *
                }
        </xsd:appinfo>
        <xsd:appinfo source="http:// www.XMLSchemaReference.com/
                     examples/perl/extractPerl">
            # A PMB is a "Private Mail Box" that is provided
            # by an entity other than the U S Postal Service.
            # -- create a variable for the PMB
            $pmb=""
        </xsd:appinfo>
    </xsd:annotation>
</xsd:element>
```

Note that XML schema document annotations do not affect the XML instances. The value of the pmb element is a Private Mail Box number; there is no annotation corollary:

```xml
<pmb>12345</pmb>
```

### 7.5.1 Attributes of an annotation Element

Since an `annotation` does not have a function with respect to XML validation, an `annotation` is limited to the `id` attribute. Table 7.3 provides an overview of the `id` attribute.

**TABLE 7.3**  Attribute Summary for an annotation Element

| Attribute | Description |
|---|---|
| id | The `id` of the current `annotation`. |

#### 7.5.1.1 The `id` Attribute of an annotation Element

The value of an `id` attribute uniquely identifies an element within the set of schema documents that comprise an XML schema.

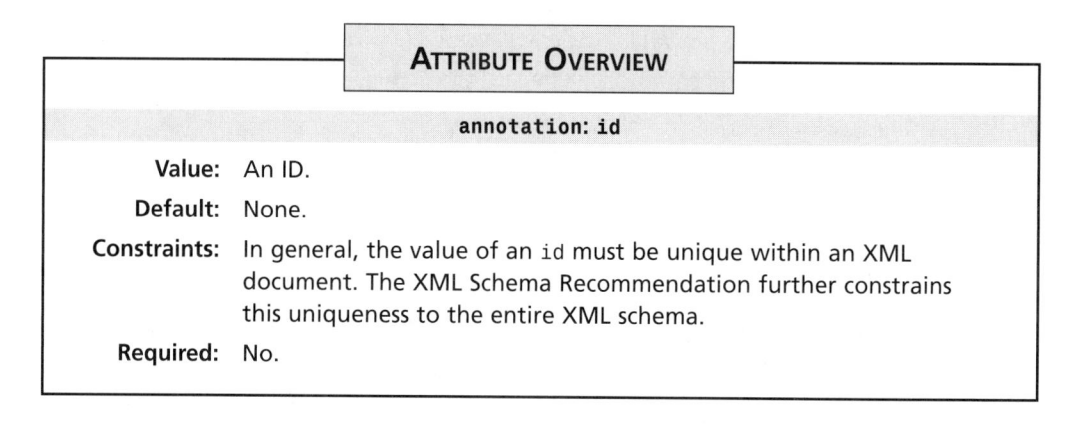

---

**ATTRIBUTE OVERVIEW**

**annotation: id**

- **Value:** An ID.
- **Default:** None.
- **Constraints:** In general, the value of an `id` must be unique within an XML document. The XML Schema Recommendation further constrains this uniqueness to the entire XML schema.
- **Required:** No.

---

See Listing 7.3, which is the XML representation of `pmb`, which has an `id` attribute.

### 7.5.2 Content Options for an annotation Element

The `annotation` element can contain human- or machine-readable documentation. Table 7.4 summarizes the content options for the `annotation` element.

**TABLE 7.4**  Content Options for an annotation Element

| Element | Description |
|---|---|
| appinfo | Provides a mechanism for specifying machine-readable documentation that pertains to the enclosing element. See Section 7.6 for details on the `appinfo` element. |
| documentation | Provides a mechanism for specifying human-readable documentation that pertains to the enclosing element. See Section 7.7 for details on the `documentation` element. |

The content pattern for the `annotation` element follows:

`(appinfo | documentation)*`

## 7.6 The `appinfo` Element

Only an `annotation` element can contain `appinfo` elements. The `appinfo` elements support automated processing of annotations—a discussion beyond the scope of this book. The following example demonstrates that the schema might support a mechanism for automatically creating source code that mirrors the XML schema document. One could, for example, create a program that extracts objects from the XML schema document in which each object mirrors a schema component. Listing 7.3 contains an `annotation` element, which encloses several `appinfo` elements. The following is a suitable excerpt:

```
<xsd:appinfo
    source=
"http://www.XMLSchemaReference.com/examples/java/extractJava">
    // A PMB is a "Private Mail Box" that is provided
    // by an entity other than the U S Postal Service.
    // -- create a class for the pmb
    public class pmb
        {
            *      *      *      *      *
        }
</xsd:appinfo>
```

### 7.6.1 Attributes of an `appinfo` Element

The `appinfo` element has only one attribute, a `source`. Table 7.5 provides an overview of the `source` attribute.

**TABLE 7.5** Attribute Summary for an `appinfo` Element

| Attribute | Description |
| --- | --- |
| source | The value of the `source` attribute is a URI. Note that an XML processor does not validate this URI (or any other values within an annotation). The URI represents any documentation deemed relevant. |

#### 7.6.1.1 The `source` Attribute of an `appinfo` Element

The `source` attribute points to a URI that could be the location of a program to run, documentation about a program, a component, or just about anything that seems pertinent.

> **ATTRIBUTE OVERVIEW**
>
> `appinfo: source`
>
> **Value:** A URI.
> **Default:** None.
> **Constraints:** None. In fact, there is no requirement that the URI can be dereferenced.
> **Required:** No.

## 7.6.2 Content Options for an `appinfo` Element

The `appinfo` element has no constraints on content. Therefore, an XML validator only ensures that an `appinfo` element is well-formed XML: The validator does not attempt to validate the contents of an `appinfo` element.

## 7.7 The `documentation` Element

Only an `annotation` element can contain a `documentation` element. The value of a `documentation` element is human-readable text that describes the element that encloses the annotation. The content, in an XML instance, of a `documentation` element is not constrained. Listing 7.3 contains an `annotation` element, which encloses several `appinfo` elements. The following is a suitable excerpt that demonstrates a `documentation` element with mixed content:

```
<xsd:documentation xml:lang="en">
    Developer Note:  Someone should probably come up
    with a way to actually validate PMBs.  In fact,
    it would be great if we could validate
    every <pmb/> and <POBox/> element.
</xsd:documentation>
```

An element that contains mixed content, as just demonstrated, may have content that intersperses elements with text. Chapter 11 provides more information about mixed content.

### 7.7.1 Attributes of a `documentation` Element

A `documentation` element may specify the language of the human-readable text. Table 7.6 provides a summary of the attributes for a `documentation` element.

## 7.7 The documentation Element

**TABLE 7.6** Attribute Summary for a documentation Element

| Attribute | Description |
|---|---|
| source | The value of the source attribute is a URI. Note that an XML processor does not validate this URI (or any other values within an annotation). The URI points to any documentation deemed relevant. |
| xml:lang | The value of the xml:lang attribute specifies the language of the documentation. Note that an annotation might contain many documentation elements. Hence, each documentation element could present redundant verbiage in a distinct language. |

### 7.7.1.1 The source Attribute of a documentation Element

The value of a source attribute is a URI that presumably assists the XML schema document reader in understanding the annotation.

---

**ATTRIBUTE OVERVIEW**

**documentation: source**

- **Value:** A URI.
- **Default:** None.
- **Constraints:** None. In fact, there is not requirement that the URI can be dereferenced.
- **Required:** No.

---

The following documentation element tells the developer what a PMB is and references a document (URI) from the United States postal service that discusses PMBs:

```
<xsd:documentation
    source="http://new.usps.com/cgi-bin/
            uspsbv/scripts/content.jsp?D=13647"
    xml:lang="en">
            PMB is a "Private Mail Box" that is provided
            by an entity other than the U S Postal Service.
</xsd:documentation>
```

#### 7.7.1.2 The `xml:lang` Attribute of a `documentation` Element

The `xml:lang` attribute indicates the human language contained within the `documentation` element. The `xml:lang` attribute is not defined by the XML Schema Recommendation. Rather, the `xml:lang` attribute is a reserved attribute defined by the XML Recommendation. See RFC 1766 for more information on the language choices. For the English language, the value is 'en'. The value for *United States* English is 'en-US'.

### 7.7.2 Content Options for a `documentation` Element

The `documentation` element has no constraints on content other than being well-formed XML. An XML validator does not validate the contents of a `documentation` element.

## 7.8 The `include` Element

Any given XML schema document may describe only a subset of an entire schema. An XML schema document may construct a larger subset of an entire schema, including the entire schema, by including other XML schema documents that contain different subsets of the components that comprise the schema. One XML schema document includes another via an `include` element.

> **TIP**
>
> An `include` element adds components from another schema, with a different namespace, to the current schema. An `import` element adds components from another schema, but associates them with the target namespace.

The schema in Listing 7.2 includes components from the file `ffs_include.xsd`:

```
<xsd:include
    schemaLocation="http://www.XMLSchemaReference.com/examples/
                    Ch07/ffs_include.xsd"/>
```

Similarly, the thematic catalog example, `catalog.xsd`, makes use of multiple `include` statements. For example, `catalog.xsd` includes `pricing.xsd`; the latter describes components for specifying the price of catalog items. The catalog XML schema document includes the pricing XML schema document via the following `include` element:

```
<xsd:include
    schemaLocation="C:\XMLSchemaExample\theme\pricing.xsd"/>
```

## 7.8.1 Attributes of an `include` Element

An `include` element specifies the location of an XML schema document. Table 7.7 provides a summary of the attributes for an `include` element.

**TABLE 7.7** Attribute Summary for an `include` Element

| Attribute | Description |
| --- | --- |
| id | The value of an `id` attribute uniquely identifies an element within the set of schema documents that comprise an XML schema. |
| schemaLocation | The value of the `schemaLocation` attribute specifies an XML schema document that contains other components for the same XML schema. |

### 7.8.1.1 The `id` Attribute of an `include` Element

The value of an `id` attribute uniquely identifies an element within the set of schema documents that comprise an XML schema.

---

**ATTRIBUTE OVERVIEW**

`include: id`

**Value:** An ID.
**Default:** None.
**Constraints:** In general, the value of an `id` must be unique within an XML document. The XML Schema Recommendation further constrains this uniqueness to the entire XML schema.
**Required:** No.

---

### 7.8.1.2 The `schemaLocation` Attribute of an `include` Element

The value of the `schemaLocation` attribute is a URI that indicates one of the following:

- The location of an XML schema document
- A fragment that indicates a part of an XML document (via an HTTP address whose "content-type" is `application/xml` or `text/xml`)
- An XPointer that resolves to a schema

---

**ATTRIBUTE OVERVIEW**

**include: schemaLocation**

| | |
|---:|---|
| **Value:** | A URI. |
| **Default:** | None. |
| **Constraints:** | The target namespace of the included document must be absent—which implies the current target namespace—or the target namespace of the included document must match the target namespace of the current document. |
| **Required:** | Yes. |

---

Unlike an `import` element, if the URI does not resolve to a valid XML schema document or an appropriate XML document, the `include` element has no effect. In other words, an XML validator ignores an `include` element whose `schemaLocation` is not valid.

### 7.8.2 Content Options for an `include` Element

Table 7.8 identifies the only content option available to an `include` element: the ubiquitous annotation element.

**TABLE 7.8**  Content Options for an `include` Element

| Element | Description |
|---|---|
| annotation | The annotation element, discussed in Section 7.5, provides a way to document schema elements. |

The content pattern for the include element follows:

annotation?

## 7.9 The `import` Element

One XML schema can appropriate components from another XML schema that has a different namespace. An `import` element identifies a schema (usually by identifying a schema document that represents it) using a different namespace, and generates equivalent components in the new schema. The components retain their original namespace in the new schema.

> **TIP**
>
> An include element adds components from another schema, with a different namespace, to the current schema. An import element adds components from another schema, but associates them with the target namespace.

Section 6.15 provides a complete discussion on how the namespace and schemaLocation attributes affect locating schema components. The following list is a brief overview of how the schema components are located and identified:

- When an import element specifies both a schemaLocation and a namespace, the XML validator builds the new components into the namespace specified by the namespace attribute, *which must be the same as that specified by the source* targetNamespace.
- When an import element specifies only a schemaLocation, the source schema must not specify a targetNamespace; the new components explicitly have no target namespace.
- When an import element specifies only a namespace, the XML validator deduces the schema location from other known schemas and namespaces when possible. The source schema must specify the same namespace as its targetNamespace; that is, the namespace of the new components.
- If an import element specifies neither a namespace nor a schema (for example, the empty element '<import />'), the XML validator is given no clues as to where to locate foreign components; if through outside means it can find that place, the source schema must not specify a targetNamespace and the new components explicitly have no target namespace.

A schema frequently infers imports by specifying a namespace as an attribute of the schema element. The following example demonstrates how to explicitly import the Schema for Schemas:

```
<import namespace="http://www.w3.org/2001/XMLSchema"
        schemaLocation="http://www.w3.org/2001/XMLSchema.xsd"
        id="import.XMLSchema"/>
```

Similarly, Listing 7.2 imports attributes defined in another namespace and another file:

```
<xsd:import
    namespace="http://www.XMLSchemaReference.com/examples/
               Ch07/randomAttributes"
    schemaLocation="http://www.XMLSchemaReference.com/examples/
                    Ch07/randomAttributes.xsd"/>
```

## 7.9.1 Attributes of an `import` Element

The attributes of an `import` element provide an XML validator clues for locating foreign components. Table 7.9 provides a summary of the attributes of an `import` element.

**TABLE 7.9**  Attribute Summary for an `import` Element

| Attribute | Description |
|---|---|
| `id` | The value of an `id` attribute uniquely identifies an element within the set of schema documents that comprise an XML schema. |
| `namespace` | The value of the `namespace` attribute specifies a target namespace for the foreign components. |
| `schemaLocation` | The value of the `schemaLocation` attribute specifies an XML schema document that contains foreign components. |

### 7.9.1.1 The `id` Attribute of an `import` Element

The value of an `id` attribute uniquely identifies an element within the set of schema documents that comprise an XML schema.

---

**ATTRIBUTE OVERVIEW**

**import: id**

- **Value:** An ID.
- **Default:** None.
- **Constraints:** In general, the value of an `id` must be unique within an XML document. The XML Schema Recommendation further constrains this uniqueness to the entire XML schema.
- **Required:** No.

---

### 7.9.1.2 The `namespace` Attribute of an `import` Element

The value of the `namespace` attribute specifies the namespace for foreign components. Specifically, subsequent elements may contain references to components in the foreign namespace—with an appropriate namespace prefix.

> **ATTRIBUTE OVERVIEW**
>
> **import: namespace**
>
> **Value:** A URI.
> **Default:** None.
> **Constraints:** Whether this attribute is present or absent, it must match the `targetNamespace` attribute on the source `schema` and be different from the target namespace of the schema being created. (If the namespace is absent then the XML validator creates the new components explicitly with no target namespace and the schema being created must have a target namespace.)
> **Required:** No.

### 7.9.1.3 The `schemaLocation` Attribute of an `import` Element

The value of the `schemaLocation` attribute is a URI that indicates the location of an XML schema document. Other permissible values are an XML document of type `application/xml` or `text/xml` that contains a fragment, or an XPointer notation that resolves to a `schema`.

> **ATTRIBUTE OVERVIEW**
>
> **import: schemaLocation**
>
> **Value:** A URI.
> **Default:** None.
> **Constraints:** An XML validator requires a valid schema location.
> **Required:** No.

Unlike an `include` element, the URI *must* resolve to a valid XML schema document or a `schema` within another document. Note, however, that the `schemaLocation` attribute is optional.

## 7.9.2 Content Options for an `import` Element

Table 7.10 identifies the only content option available to an `import` element: the ubiquitous `annotation` element.

**TABLE 7.10** Content Options for an `import` Element

| Element | Description |
|---|---|
| annotation | The annotation element, discussed in Section 7.5, provides a way to document schema elements. |

The content pattern for the `import` element follows:

annotation?

## 7.10 The `notation` Element

A notation provides a mechanism for an XML validator to locate external programs or processing instructions. An XML validator does not intrinsically validate notations. However, during validation of a corresponding XML instance, a `notation` must exist for each reference from an element or attribute whose corresponding structure type specifies an enumeration of the built-in `notation` datatype. While there are no specific requirements, the intention of a notation is that the value for a notation in an XML instance is somehow relevant to URIs specified by the notation.

Each `notation` must specify a `system` attribute, a `public` attribute, or both. The value of a `system` attribute frequently identifies a file, which might be a program. There is no requirement that the file exists on the parsing machine, or that the file exists at all. The value of a `public` attribute frequently identifies an external HTTP address. This URI might likewise represent a document or a program such as an Active Server Page (ASP) or JavaServer Page (JSP). Conversely, there is no requirement that the URI can be dereferenced. Note that "public" is relative to the current system: A URI could point to another machine accessible only within the same company.

Listing 7.4 is the XML representation of two `notation` elements, which specify the location of a Perl and a Python interpreter.

**LISTING 7.4** A `notation` Element (built-in.xsd)

```
<xsd:notation name="perlCode"
           system="/usr/bin/perl"
           public="http://www.company.com/runPerl.pl"
           id="notation.perl">
   <xsd:annotation>
      <xsd:documentation xml:lang="en">
         value of corresponding element
         should contain perl code to execute.
      </xsd:documentation>
   </xsd:annotation>
</xsd:notation>
```

```
<xsd:notation name="pythonCode"
              system="/usr/bin/python"
              public="http://www.company.com/runPython.py"
              id="notation.companyMascot">
    <xsd:annotation>
        <xsd:documentation xml:lang="en">
            value of corresponding element
            should contain python code to execute.
        </xsd:documentation>
    </xsd:annotation>
</xsd:notation>
```

Typically, the value associated with a notation is an attribute; the value of the enclosing element is a value that applies to the notation. In the next example, the demoNotation element contains a source attribute. The value of source is 'perlCode'; the value of the element is a line of Perl code:

```
<xsd:element name="demoNotation">
    <xsd:complexType>
        <xsd:simpleContent>
            <xsd:extension base="xsd:string">
                <xsd:attribute name="source">
                    <xsd:simpleType>
                        <xsd:restriction base="xsd:notation">
                            <xsd:enumeration value="perlCode"/>
                            <xsd:enumeration value="pythonCode"/>
                        </xsd:restriction>
                    </xsd:simpleType>
                </xsd:attribute>
            </xsd:extension>
        </xsd:simpleContent>
    </xsd:complexType>
</xsd:element>
```

> **NOTE**
>
> An attribute (the normal scenario) or an element cannot specify a notation as its structure type: The structure type must be a simple type that is an enumeration of other notation simple types.

Given the preceding element type, the following element is valid in a corresponding XML instance:

```
<demoNotation
  source="perlCode">print "Hello, World\n"</demoNotation>
```

## 7.10.1 Attributes of a `notation` Element

The attributes of a `notation` element must specify a name and a way to obtain the corresponding processing instructions. Table 7.11 provides a summary of the attributes for a `notation` element.

**TABLE 7.11**  Attribute Summary for a `notation` Element

| Attribute | Description |
|---|---|
| `id` | The value of an `id` attribute uniquely identifies an element within the set of schema documents that comprise an XML schema. |
| `name` | The value of the `name` attribute is the name of the `notation`. |
| `public` | The value of the `public` attribute is a character string; it may be a URI that represents the location of a corresponding document or program. While by no means a requirement, there is some expectation that the dereferenced URI is available on a system other than the one upon which the XML validator runs. |
| `system` | The value of the `system` attribute is a URI that represents the location of a corresponding document or program. While by no means a requirement, there is some expectation that the dereferenced URI is available locally—perhaps a local file. |

### 7.10.1.1 The `id` Attribute of a `notation` Element

The value of an `id` attribute uniquely identifies an element within the set of schema documents that comprise an XML schema.

---

**ATTRIBUTE OVERVIEW**

**notation: id**

- **Value:** An ID.
- **Default:** None.
- **Constraints:** In general, the value of an `id` must be unique within an XML document. The XML Schema Recommendation further constrains this uniqueness to the entire XML schema.
- **Required:** No.

### 7.10.1.2 The name Attribute of a notation Element

An XML validator places the value of the name of a notation element in the target namespace. An element or attribute in an XML instance refers to the notation with this name. The element or attribute must have a corresponding element type or attribute type whose structure type specifies an enumeration of built-in notation datatypes. An application that interacts with an XML validator may do anything—or nothing—with the data from the corresponding notation.

**ATTRIBUTE OVERVIEW**

**notation: name**

| | |
|---|---|
| **Value:** | An NCName. |
| **Default:** | None. |
| **Constraints:** | No intrinsic constraints. However, there must be a corresponding notation element for each name referenced in an XML instance. |
| **Required:** | Yes. |

### 7.10.1.3 The public Attribute of a notation Element

The value of the public attribute may be a URI that the XML validator may use as a processing instruction. For example, this URI might be the address of an HTML file or a Java servlet. The schema does not guarantee that the URI can be dereferenced.

**ATTRIBUTE OVERVIEW**

**notation: public**

| | |
|---|---|
| **Value:** | A character string; often a URI. |
| **Default:** | None. |
| **Constraints:** | None. In fact, there is no requirement that the URI can be dereferenced. |
| **Required:** | A notation element must specify either or both of the system or public attributes. |

### 7.10.1.4 The `system` Attribute of a `notation` Element

The value of a `system` attribute is a URI. For example, the path might point to a program to render a graphics file or any other executable program. The schema does not guarantee that the URI can be dereferenced, or if it can, that the dereferenced string has any meaning.

---

**ATTRIBUTE OVERVIEW**

**notation: system**

| | |
|---:|:---|
| **Value:** | A URI. |
| **Default:** | None. |
| **Constraints:** | None. In fact, the representative file may not exist or may not be accessible on the validating machine. |
| **Required:** | A `notation` element must specify either or both of the `system` or `public` attributes. |

---

## 7.10.2 Content Options for a `notation` Element

Table 7.12 identifies the only content option available to a `notation`: the ubiquitous annotation element.

**TABLE 7.12** Content Options for a `notation` Element

| Element | Description |
|---|---|
| annotation | Provides a way to document schema elements. Section 7.5 demonstrates how to apply annotations. |

The content pattern for the `notation` element follows:

annotation?

# 7.11 The `redefine` Element

An XML schema document may redefine a schema component in the current schema or in another schema by including a `redefine` element. A schema can redefine the following components: simple types, complex types, named model groups, and named attribute-use groups.

The target namespace implied by the schema location of the `redefine` element must be the same as the target namespace of the current schema. However, the `redefine` element can reference a component from another schema in which the referenced component explicitly has no namespace. In the latter case, *the components become part of the current namespace.*

> **NOTE**
>
> A redefined component is always a restriction or extension of the original component.

The following list itemizes how to redefine each kind of component:

- A redefined simple type is a restriction of the original component. This means the value of the `base` attribute must be the name of the original component.
- A redefined complex type is an extension or a restriction of the original component. This means the value of the `base` attribute *is* the name of the redefined component.
- A redefined named model group is a superset or subset of the original named model group. A superset of the original named model group must include the original named model group via a reference (that is, a `group` element that has a `ref` attribute whose value is the original named model group). A subset of the original named model group must have identical subcomponents with appropriate restrictions. An appropriate restriction of a named model group is a modification of a `minOccurs` or `maxOccurs` attribute of a contained element type.
- A redefined named attribute-use group is a superset or subset of the original named attribute-use group. A superset of the original named attribute-use group must include the original named attribute-use group via a reference (that is, an `attributeGroup` element that has a `ref` attribute whose value is the original named attribute-use group). A subset of the original group must have identical subcomponents with appropriate restrictions. An appropriate restriction is the modification of a `use` attribute for a contained attribute type.

Although XML schema documents may redefine a component many times, there is ultimately only one instance of any of the redefined components in a schema: The same schema does not have different "versions" of a component.

Finally, a redefined component may cause a schema or a corresponding XML instance to become invalid: The previous iteration of the component does not exist in the schema.

Listing 7.5 is an XML schema document that describes `aSimpleType`.

**LISTING 7.5** Defining aSimpleType

```xml
<xsd:schema xmlns:xsd="http://www.w3.org/2001/XMLSchema">
    <xsd:simpleType name="aSimpleType">
    <xsd:restriction base="xsd:token"/>
    </xsd:simpleType>
</xsd:schema>
```

Listing 7.6 redefines aSimpleType, originally defined in Listing 7.5.

**LISTING 7.6** Redefining aSimpleType

```xml
<xsd:schema xmlns:xsd="http://www.w3.org/2001/XMLSchema">
<xsd:redefine
    schemaLocation="http://www.XMLSchemaReference.com/examples/
                    Ch07/redefine1.xsd">
<xsd:simpleType name="aSimpleType">
    <xsd:restriction base="aSimpleType">
        <xsd:maxLength value="40"/>
    </xsd:restriction>
</xsd:simpleType>
</xsd:redefine>
</xsd:schema>
```

## 7.11.1 Attributes of a `redefine` Element

The attributes of a `redefine` element include the ubiquitous `id` and the `schemaLocation`, which identifies a schema document. Table 7.13 provides a summary of the attributes for a `redefine` element.

**TABLE 7.13** Attribute Summary for a `redefine` Element

| Attribute | Description |
|---|---|
| id | The value of an `id` attribute uniquely identifies an element within the set of schema documents that comprise an XML schema. |
| schemaLocation | The value of the `schemaLocation` attribute identifies a schema document that describes the original components. The target namespace of the original components must be identical to the enclosing schema document. Alternatively, there can be no target namespace for the original components, in which case the components adopt the enclosing schema's target namespace. |

### 7.11.1.1 The `id` Attribute of a `redefine` Element

The value of an `id` attribute uniquely identifies an element within the set of schema documents that comprise an XML schema.

---
**ATTRIBUTE OVERVIEW**

**redefine: id**

| | |
|---:|:---|
| **Value:** | An ID. |
| **Default:** | None. |
| **Constraints:** | In general, the value of an `id` must be unique within an XML document. The XML Schema Recommendation further constrains this uniqueness to the entire XML schema. |
| **Required:** | No. |

---

### 7.11.1.2 The `schemaLocation` Attribute for a `redefine` Element

The value of the `schemaLocation` attribute is a URI that indicates the location of an XML schema document. Another permissible value is an XML document of type `application/xml` or `text/xml` that contains a fragment or XPointer notation that resolves to a `schema`.

---
**ATTRIBUTE OVERVIEW**

**redefine: schemaLocation**

| | |
|---:|:---|
| **Value:** | A URI. |
| **Default:** | None. |
| **Constraints:** | The XML validator requires a valid URI. |
| **Required:** | Yes. |

---

## 7.11.2 Content Options for a `redefine` Element

Table 7.14 identifies the content options available to a `redefine` element. Other than the frequently seen `annotation`, the contents of a `redefine` are the redefined components.

**TABLE 7.14** Content Options for a `redefine` Element

| Element | Description |
| --- | --- |
| annotation | The annotation element, discussed in Section 7.5, provides a way to document schema elements. |
| simpleType | A restriction of a previously defined simple type. |
| complexType | A restriction or extension of a previously defined complex type. |
| group | A restriction or extension of a previously defined named model group. |
| attributeGroup | A restriction or extension of a previously defined named attribute-use group. |

The content pattern for the `redefine` element follows:

(annotation | simpleType | complexType | group | attributeGroup)*

# Element Types

**CHAPTER 8**

## IN THIS CHAPTER

8.1 An Example of a Trivial Element Type  138

8.2 Concepts and Observations  138

8.3 The `element` Element  148

8.4 The `any` Element  167

The main purpose of an *element type* is to associate an element name with a *structure type*. The structure type is a simple type or a complex type. Furthermore, the structure type may be global to the schema, or it may be local to the element type. The XML representation of an element type is an `element` element.

The simplest form of an element type is one whose only attribute is `name`. An element type that does not explicitly specify a structure type implicitly specifies `anyType` as the structure type. The content of an element in an XML instance whose structure type is `anyType` is unconstrained.

## 8.1 An Example of a Trivial Element Type

The most basic element type is one that associates an element name with a built-in datatype. The following element demonstrates the XML representation of `city`, which associates the name 'city' with the built-in `token` datatype:

```
<xsd:element name="city" type="xsd:string"/>
```

The value of a `city` element, which is an instance of the `city` element type, is a string of any length. Of course, this string is constrained by the constraining facets that specify `token` (Chapter 12 discusses all of the built-in datatypes—including `token`). Given the preceding element type, the following element is valid in an XML instance:

```
<city>New York</city>
```

> **TIP**
>
> The `city` element type example can—and probably should—cover a large percentage of the element types specified in an XML schema document. Good programming style dictates the creation of global simple and complex types with references to these types as the structure type of primarily local element types.

## 8.2 Concepts and Observations

Element types have very sophisticated, and often very confusing, capabilities. The next four sections attempt to expose some of the confusing issues surrounding element types. These sections cover global and local element types, substitution groups, blocking, `nil` elements (those with no value), and the use of namespaces vis-à-vis element types.

### 8.2.1 Global and Local Element Types

An element type is global or local. A global element type is a child of the `schema` element in the XML schema document. Otherwise, the element type is local to a complex type.

Listing 8.1 portrays the `city` element type introduced in Section 8.1 as local to the complex type `addressType`.

**LISTING 8.1**   A Local Element Type (address.xsd)

```
<xsd:complexType name="addressType">
    <xsd:sequence>
        <xsd:element ref="addressLine"
                    minOccurs="1"
                    maxOccurs="2"/>
        <xsd:element name="city" type="xsd:string"/>
        <xsd:element name="state" type="xsd:string"/>
        <xsd:element name="country"
                    type="xsd:string"
                    fixed="US"/>
        <xsd:element name="zip" type="xsd:string"/>
        <xsd:element ref="effectiveDate"/>
    </xsd:sequence>
    <xsd:attribute ref="zipPlus4" use="optional"/>
</xsd:complexType>
```

## 8.2.2 Substitution Groups

A substitution group provides functionality that parallels derivation in that appropriate element types in a substitution group replace instantiable or non-instantiable element types. The parallel is that when an instantiable-derived type replaces a base type, substitutable element types replace base element types. The substitution of element types occurs in an XML instance or in an XML schema document. Listing 8.2 is a substitution group that provides a foundation for complete addresses.

**LISTING 8.2**   The `addressLine` Substitution Group (address.xsd)

```
<xsd:element name="addressLine"
            id="customerRecord.base.addressLine"
            type="xsd:string"
            abstract="true">
    <xsd:annotation>
        <xsd:documentation xml:lang="en">
            The "addressLine" element type
            is a base non-instantiable element
            type whose structure type is
            a built-in string datatype.
        </xsd:documentation>
    </xsd:annotation>
</xsd:element>
```

*continues*

```xml
<xsd:element name="street"
            type="xsd:string"
            substitutionGroup="addressLine">
    <xsd:annotation>
        <xsd:documentation xml:lang="en">
            Street is a substitution group
            for addressLine.  This particular
            substitution only substitutes the
            name; there are no further restrictions.
        </xsd:documentation>
    </xsd:annotation>
</xsd:element>

<xsd:element name="POBox"
            substitutionGroup="addressLine">
    <xsd:simpleType>
        <xsd:annotation>
            <xsd:documentation xml:lang="en">
                The POBoxType demonstrates that
                a Substitution Group can have a
                type that is derived from the
                type used by the related
                non-instantiable base element.
            </xsd:documentation>
        </xsd:annotation>
        <xsd:restriction base="xsd:string">
            <xsd:maxLength value="10"/>
            <xsd:pattern value="[0-9]+"/>
        </xsd:restriction>
    </xsd:simpleType>
</xsd:element>

<xsd:element name="pmb"
            type="xsd:string"
            substitutionGroup="addressLine">
    <xsd:annotation id="customerRecord.annotation.pmb">
        <xsd:documentation
            source="http://new.usps.com/cgi-bin/
                    uspsbv/scripts/content.jsp?D=13647"
            xml:lang="en">
            A PMB is a "Private Mail Box" that is
            provided by an entity other than the
            U S Postal Service.
        </xsd:documentation>
        <xsd:documentation xml:lang="en">
            Developer Note:  Someone should probably
            come up with a way to actually validate PMBs.
```

```
            In fact, we should validate every <pmb/>
            and <POBox/> element.
        </xsd:documentation>
        <xsd:appinfo
            source="http://www.XMLSchemaReference.com/examples/
                                        java/extractJava">
            // A PMB is a "Private Mail Box" that is
            // provided by an entity other than the
            // U S Postal Service.
            // -- create a class for the pmb
            public class pmb
                {
        *       *       *       *       *
                }
        </xsd:appinfo>
        <xsd:appinfo
            source="http://www.XMLSchemaReference.com/examples/
                                        perl/extractPerl">
            # A PMB is a "Private Mail Box" that is provided
            # by an entity other than the U S Postal Service.
            # -- create a variable for the PMB
            $pmb=""
        </xsd:appinfo>
    </xsd:annotation>
</xsd:element>
```

Substitution groups provide quite a bit of flexibility:

- The head element type can be instantiable or non-instantiable.
- The structure types associated with the element types in a substitution group can be different from each other. Substitutable element types can specify a structure type that is a derivation of the structure type associated with the head element type.
- The structure types associated with the element types in a substitution group can be simple types or complex types. The only limitation is that the structure types are suitable derivations.

The XML representation of an element type whose structure type is the complex type addressType introduced in Listing 8.2 might look like the following element type:

```
<xsd:element name="address" type="addressType"/>
```

Given the preceding element type, any of the following elements are valid in an XML instance. Note the inline replacement of addressLine with street, POBox, and pmb, respectively:

```
<address>
    <street>123 Gravel Road</street>
    <city>Nowheresville</city>
```

*continues*

```
            <state>OR</state>
            <country>US</country>
            <zip>97000</zip>
            <effectiveDate></effectiveDate>
        </address>

        <address zipPlus4="20000-1234">
            <POBox>123</POBox>
            <city>Small Town</city>
            <state>VA</state>
            <country>US</country>
            <zip>20000</zip>
            <effectiveDate>2001-02-14</effectiveDate>
        </address>

        <address>
            <street>123 Main Street</street>
            <pmb>12345</pmb>
            <city>Metropolis</city>
            <state>CO</state>
            <country>US</country>
            <zip>80000</zip>
            <effectiveDate>2001-02-14</effectiveDate>
        </address>
```

Frequently, the substitution occurs in the XML instance. The next example shows POBox substituted for the non-instantiable addressLine:

```
        <address>
            <POBox>123</POBox>
            <city>Small Town</city>
            <state>VA</state>
            <country>US</country>
            <zip>20000</zip>
            <effectiveDate>2001-02-14</effectiveDate>
        </address>
```

Listing 8.3 provides an XML representation for POBoxAddressType. This listing demonstrates substituting POBox for addressLine in an XML schema document that specifies a derived complex type.

**LISTING 8.3**  Specifying a Substitution Group in a Derived Type (substGroup.xsd)

```
<xsd:complexType name="POBoxAddressType">
    <xsd:complexContent>
        <xsd:restriction base="addressType">
            <xsd:sequence>
                <xsd:element ref="POBox"
```

```
                            minOccurs="1"
                            maxOccurs="1"/>
            <xsd:element name="city" type="xsd:string"/>
            <xsd:element name="state" type="xsd:string"/>
            <xsd:element name="country"
                            type="xsd:string"
                            fixed="US"/>
            <xsd:element name="zip" type="xsd:string"/>
            <xsd:element ref="effectiveDate"/>
        </xsd:sequence>
        <xsd:attribute ref="zipPlus4" use="optional"/>
      </xsd:restriction>
    </xsd:complexContent>
</xsd:complexType>
```

> **TIP**
>
> Sections 8.3.1.2 and 8.3.1.4 discuss how to prevent element type substitutions by specifying the `block` and `final` attributes.

## 8.2.3 Blocking Substitution

The `block` attribute of an element type, in conjunction with the `block` attribute of a complex type, restricts the ability to substitute, in an XML instance, specific members of a substitution group. Listing 8.4 is a complex set of substitution groups. The listing includes element types and the relevant structure types. The listing sets up the discussion surrounding the `block` attribute.

> **TIP**
>
> A solid understanding of complex types (see Chapter 11), including the `block` and `final` attributes (Sections 11.6.1.2 and 11.6.1.3, respectively), is valuable before attempting to use the `block` or `final` attributes of an element type.
>
> Likewise, a solid understanding of substitution groups (see Section 8.2.2) is imperative.

There are three ways to impose blocking:

- When the head of a substitution group blocks substitution, an XML instance cannot "replace" the head with another member of the substitution group.

- When the head of a substitution group blocks extension, an XML instance cannot "replace" the head with another member of the substitution group whose structure type is an extension of the structure type associated with the head. In addition, an XML instance cannot specify a structure type, via xsi:type, that is derived—even indirectly—by extension from the structure type associated with the head.

- When the head of a substitution group blocks restriction, an XML instance cannot "replace" the head with another member of the substitution group whose structure type is a restriction of the structure type associated with the head. In addition, an XML instance cannot specify a structure type, via xsi:type, that is derived—even indirectly—by restriction from the structure type associated with the head.

> **NOTE**
>
> A complex type can also specify blocking. The blocking is transitive. That is, when an element type's structure type is a complex type, a block on that complex type effectively places a block on the element type.

In general, substitution groups are transitive. Listing 8.4 specifies two substitution groups: The first one contains the members 'A', 'B', and 'C', with 'A' being the head; the second one contains 'C' and 'D', with 'C' being the head. Transitively (through 'C'), 'B', 'C', and 'D' are valid substitutions for 'A'. Blocking, however, is *not* transitive. Specifically, a block on 'C' (or its structure type, 'T3'), does not restrict the ability of 'D' to be a valid substitution for 'A'.

**LISTING 8.4**  Multiple Substitution Groups (substGroup.xsd)

```
<xsd:element name="A" type="T1" abstract="true"
          block="restriction">
   <xsd:annotation>
      <xsd:documentation>
         Head of substitution group A.
         An A element cannot appear in an XML
         instance, since this element type is
         abstract.
      </xsd:documentation>
   </xsd:annotation>
</xsd:element>
<xsd:element name="B" type="T1" substitutionGroup="A">
```

```xml
        <xsd:annotation>
            <xsd:documentation>
            Member of substitution group A.
            </xsd:documentation>
        </xsd:annotation>
</xsd:element>
<xsd:element name="C" type="T3" substitutionGroup="A"
             block="substitution">
    <xsd:annotation>
        <xsd:documentation>
            Member of substitution group A.
            Head of substitution group C.
            Blocking 'substitution' or 'extension' on C,
            or blocking '#all' or 'extension' on T3,
            would prevent D from being a valid substitution
            for C.  D would, however, retain
            its transitive ability to be a valid
            substitution for A.
        </xsd:documentation>
    </xsd:annotation>
</xsd:element>
<xsd:element name="D" type="T4" substitutionGroup="C">
    <xsd:annotation>
        <xsd:documentation>
            Member of substitution group C.
        </xsd:documentation>
    </xsd:annotation>
</xsd:element>
<xsd:complexType name="T1">
    <xsd:sequence>
        <xsd:element name="_1" type="xsd:token"/>
    </xsd:sequence>
</xsd:complexType>
<xsd:complexType name="T2">
    <xsd:complexContent>
        <xsd:extension base="T1">
            <xsd:sequence>
                <xsd:element name="_2" type="xsd:token"/>
            </xsd:sequence>
        </xsd:extension>
    </xsd:complexContent>
</xsd:complexType>
<xsd:complexType name="T3">
    <xsd:complexContent>
        <xsd:extension base="T2">
            <xsd:sequence>
                <xsd:element name="_3" type="xsd:token"/>
            </xsd:sequence>
```

*continues*

```
            </xsd:extension>
        </xsd:complexContent>
    </xsd:complexType>
    <xsd:complexType name="T4">
        <xsd:complexContent>
            <xsd:extension base="T3">
                <xsd:sequence>
                    <xsd:element name="_4" type="xsd:token"/>
                </xsd:sequence>
            </xsd:extension>
        </xsd:complexContent>
    </xsd:complexType>
```

### 8.2.4 Element Type Instantiability

Normally, element types are instantiable. Furthermore, there is no way to "derive" one element type from another. The only utility of non-instantiable element types is in a substitution group: The head of the substitution group might be non-instantiable; the other members of the substitution group are instantiable, and can therefore "replace" the head.

Only element types and complex types can be *explicitly* non-instantiable. An XML instance cannot specify instances of an element type whose `abstract` attribute is 'false'. Some element types are *implicitly* non-instantiable: An XML instance cannot specify instances of an element type whose structure type refers to a non-instantiable complex type.

Listing 8.2 demonstrates a non-instantiable `addressLine`, along with the appropriate substitutions `street`, `POBox`, and `pmb`. Note that the structure type associated with `addressLine` is `xsd:string`. The substitution `street` has the same structure type: `xsd:string`. The structure type associated with `POBox`, on the other hand, is a derivation of `xsd:string`.

Listing 8.4 is another example. Element type `A` is non-instantiable. All of the other element types in this listing are valid instantiable substitutions for `A`.

### 8.2.5 Nillable Element Types

An element type can specify a `nillable` attribute. When this occurs, the value of an element instance can be nil. A nil value is not the same as an *empty* value. For a string, "empty" means a string of zero length; nil means no string at all. Listing 8.5 specifies the nillable `phoneNumber` element type.

**LISTING 8.5** A Nillable Element Type (address.xsd)

```
<xsd:element name="phoneNumber"
             type="xsd:string"
             nillable="true"/>
```

The XML instance must use the special `nil` attribute from the XML schema instance namespace to set the value to nil:

`<phoneNumber xsi:nil="true"/>`

For clarity, a `phoneNumber` with an empty string has just a start-tag and an end-tag, or is an empty element:

`<phoneNumber></phoneNumber>` or `</phoneNumber/>`

Note that the element that specifies the `nil` value—or an enclosing element—must declare the `http://www.w3.org/2001/XMLSchema-instance` namespace (see Chapter 7 ). The following declares this namespace tied to the 'xsi' qualifier, as used in the preceding XML instance with a nil value:

`xmlns:xsi=http://www.w3.org/2001/XMLSchema-instance`

Of course, an element whose element type permits a nil value can still have a value or content that is valid given the element type's structure type. Listing 8.5 specifies `xsd:string` as the structure type of `phoneNumber`. The following element, with a string value, is a valid instance:

`<phoneNumber>212-555-0000</phoneNumber>`

## 8.2.6 Element Types and Namespaces

This section discusses how an XML instance must specify namespaces for elements in order to locate the appropriate element types described throughout this chapter. Chapter 3 discusses how namespaces apply to the element types in the schema.

In an XML instance, the namespace of an element must match the namespace identified by the element type. Typically, element types do not specify the target namespace. Normally, the `schema` element specifies the target namespace. If a namespace is not specifically identified, and the target namespace is not specified, the element must be unqualified (that is, specified without a namespace).

In an XML instance, an element may be *qualified* (namespace specified) or *unqualified* (namespace not specified). An XML validator determines whether the namespace is required, by evaluating the following rules in order:

- The element must be appropriately qualified when the element type specifies a `form` attribute (which has a value of 'qualified' or 'unqualified').
- When the element type does not specify the `form` attribute, the `elementformDefault` attribute (which also has a value of 'qualified' or 'unqualified') of the `schema` element enclosing the element type determines whether the name of the element instance is qualified.
- When the element type does not specify the `form` attribute, and the schema does not specify the `elementformDefault` attribute, the element must be unqualified. In other words, the default value for `elementformDefault` is 'unqualified'.

Section 8.3.1.6, along with Listings 8.7 and 8.8, provides an example of how the `form` attribute of an element type works in conjunction with the `elementformDefault` attribute of the `schema` element.

## 8.3 The `element` Element

The XML representation of an element type is an `element` element. Most element types are relatively straightforward: The element type only associates a name with a structure type. Despite the fact that this simple association covers the majority of element types, element types support a wide range of functionality. Element type functionality, described in this section, includes default values, element instance cardinality, substitution groups, blocking, and more.

### 8.3.1 Attributes of an `element` Element

One of the great features about XML schemas is the ability to specify—in great detail—the structure and contents of element types. Table 8.1 summarizes the individual attributes used to constrain an `element` element.

**TABLE 8.1** Attribute Summary of an `element` Element

| Attribute | Description |
| --- | --- |
| `abstract` | The value of the Boolean `abstract` attribute deems an element type instantiable or non-instantiable. A substitution group provides functionality for inheriting from non-instantiable element types. |
| `block` | The value of the `block` attribute is a space-delimited list containing any combination of 'extension', 'restriction', and 'substitution'. These values constrain an element instance from respectively extending, restricting, or substituting the element type directly in an XML instance. The value '#all', which implies all of these values, indicates that an XML instance cannot transform the element type in any way. |
| `default` | An XML parser substitutes the value of the `default` attribute of an element type when an element instance has no value. |
| `final` | The value of the `final` attribute is a space-delimited list containing any combination of 'extension' or 'restriction'. These values restrict the schema from extension, restriction, or substitution, respectively. The value '#all', which implies all of these values, indicates that the schema cannot directly reference this element type. |

*continues*

**TABLE 8.1** *(continued)*

| Attribute | Description |
| --- | --- |
| fixed | The `fixed` attribute is similar to the default attribute. However, when an element instance does specify a value, that value must be identical to the value of the fixed attribute specified by the element type. |
| form | The `form` attribute of a local element type determines whether the element instance must—or must not—specify an appropriate namespace. |
| id | The value of an `id` attribute uniquely identifies an element within the set of schema documents that comprise an XML schema. |
| maxOccurs | The value of the `maxOccurs` attribute determines the maximum number of times that an element instance can appear in an enclosing element. Applies only to local element types. |
| minOccurs | The value of the `minOccurs` attribute determines the minimum number of times that an element instance can appear in an enclosing element. Applies only to local element types. |
| name | The value of the `name` attribute is the name used to reference an element type in the rest of the schema or in an XML instance. |
| nillable | The value of the `nillable` attribute determines if nil is a valid value for an element instance. |
| ref | The value of the `ref` attribute is a global element type. In an XML instance, this reference permits an enclosing element to contain an element whose element type is global. |
| substitutionGroup | The value of the `substitutionGroup` attribute is a global element type. Any element types in a substitution group may be substituted in the schema or in an XML instance—barring any blocks from a `final` or `block` attribute. |
| type | The value of the `type` attribute is the structure type that constrains the value or content of the element type. |

## 8.3.1.1 The abstract Attribute of an element Element

An XML instance cannot contain instances of element types whose representation sets the abstract attribute value to 'true'. However, An XML instance can replace non-instantiable element types with instantiable element types simply by refering to the name of a valid instantiable substitution. In an XML schema, complex types reference these non-instantiable element types as well as instantiable substitutions. Non-instantiable element types are only useful in the context of substitution groups. See Sections 8.2.2 and 8.3.1.14 for more information on substitution groups.

The `block` and `final` attributes of the element type control the ability to substitute element types. Sections 8.3.1.2 and 8.3.1.4 discuss the `block` attribute and the `final` attribute, respectively.

> **ATTRIBUTE OVERVIEW**
>
> **element: abstract**
>
> **Value:** A Boolean (that is, 'true' or 'false').
> **Default:** 'false'—The typical element type may be used in an XML instance.
> **Constraints:** None.
> **Required:** No.

Section 8.2.2 discusses and demonstrates how to use non-instantiable element types and their related substitution groups.

Listing 8.2 portrays the XML representation of the non-instantiable `addressLine`. Only a complex type or another element type that specifies a `substitutionGroup` attribute may reference a non-instantiable element type. The `street` element type described in Listing 8.2 is a valid reference to a non-instantiable element type.

An XML instance may not reference a non-instantiable element type. Therefore, the following element type is not valid:

```
<addressLine>123 Illegal Address</addressLine>
```

> **WARNING**
>
> Some XML parsers permit the XML schema or an XML instance to incorrectly reference non-instantiable element types.

### 8.3.1.2 The `block` Attribute of an `element` Element

The `block` attribute constrains the ability to substitute members of a substitution group. The `block` attribute can also constrain the ability to specify a derived structure type (via `xsi:type`) in an XML instance. See Section 8.2.3 for a comprehensive discussion on blocking.

> **ATTRIBUTE OVERVIEW**
>
> **element: block**
>
> **Value:** A space-delimited list containing one or more of 'extension', 'restriction', or 'substitution'. The value '#all' is analogous to a list containing all three values.
>
> **Default:** If the element type does not specify a block attribute, it inherits the value of the blockDefault attribute of the schema element.
>
> **Constraints:** None.
>
> **Required:** No.

Listing 8.4 portrays several complete substitution groups. The block on A (that is, 'block="restriction"') prevents the structure type of member element types from being restriction derivations. Specifically, the structure types of the member element types are either identical (as for B) or an extension (as for C). In addition, the XML instance cannot specify a restriction of the structure type with xsi:type.

The block on C (that is, 'block="substitution"') prevents substituting member element types (in this case, just D) from being a valid substitution for C. However, D is still, transitively, a valid substitution for A.

For clarity, note that blocking with 'substitution' is not the same as blocking with 'restriction extension', as the structure types of the member element types in a substitution group can be identical.

### 8.3.1.3 The default Attribute of an element Element

An element type can specify a default value for element instances by specifying the default attribute. An XML parser substitutes this default value when an element instance does not explicitly specify a value.

> **ATTRIBUTE OVERVIEW**
>
> **element: default**
>
> **Value:** Any string that conforms to the attribute's type.
>
> **Default:** None.
>
> **Constraints:** The default and fixed attributes are mutually exclusive.
>
> **Required:** No.

The global element type `effectiveDate` has a default value of January 01, 1900.

```
<xsd:element name="effectiveDate"
             type="xsd:date"
             default="1900-01-01"/>
```

Given the preceding element type, the following element with no explicit value is valid in an XML instance:

```
<effectiveDate></effectiveDate>
```

Of course, the XML instance can have a value:

```
<effectiveDate>1900-01-01</effectiveDate>
```

In either case, the XML parser should provide the same result: an `effectiveDate` element with the value '`1900-01-01`'.

> **WARNING**
>
> Some of the XML schema parsers do not substitute the default value; instead, the element remains empty or creates an error.

### 8.3.1.4 The `final` Attribute of an `element` Element

The `final` attribute prohibits any combination of extension, restriction, or substitution of the element type in a derived type.

> **TIP**
>
> You should have a thorough understanding of complex types (see Chapter 11) before attempting to understand element blocking. Further, you should have a comprehensive understanding of the `block` and `final` attributes of complex types (discussed in Sections 11.6.1.2 and 11.6.1.3, respectively).
>
> Likewise, you should have a thorough understanding of substitution groups, discussed in Section 8.2.2.

## 8.3 The element Element

> **ATTRIBUTE OVERVIEW**
>
> **element: final**
>
> **Value:** A space-delimited list containing one or more of 'extension', 'restriction', or 'substitution'. The value '#all' is analogous to a list containing all three values: a derivation must use the element type without any restrictions, extensions, or substitutions.
>
> **Default:** If the element type does not specify a final attribute, the element type inherits the value from the finalDefault attribute of the schema element.
>
> **Constraints:** None.
>
> **Required:** No.

Listing 8.6 is a substitution group whose base non-instantiable element type is the sequenceID element type.

**LISTING 8.6** A Substitution Group (sequence.xsd)

```
<xsd:element name="sequenceID"
             type="sequenceIDType"
             abstract="true">
    <xsd:annotation>
        <xsd:documentation xml:lang="en">
            This element type is
            abstract:  the element must be
            replaced by a substitution group
            in either a derived type or
            an instance.
        </xsd:documentation>
    </xsd:annotation>
</xsd:element>

<xsd:element name="unitID"
             type="sequenceIDType"
             substitutionGroup="sequenceID">
    <xsd:annotation>
        <xsd:documentation xml:lang="en">
            This element represents sequence
            IDs for unit items.
            This element provides a valid
            substitution for "sequenceID".
        </xsd:documentation>
    </xsd:annotation>
</xsd:element>
```

*continues*

```xml
<xsd:element name="bulkID"
            type="sequenceIDType"
            substitutionGroup="sequenceID">
    <xsd:annotation>
        <xsd:documentation xml:lang="en">
            This element represents sequence
            IDs for bulk items.
            This element provides a valid
            substitution for "sequenceID".
        </xsd:documentation>
    </xsd:annotation>
</xsd:element>

<xsd:element name="assemblyID"
            type="sequenceIDType"
            substitutionGroup="sequenceID">
    <xsd:annotation>
        <xsd:documentation xml:lang="en">
            This element represents sequence
            IDs for assembled items.
            This element provides a valid
            substitution for "sequenceID".
        </xsd:documentation>
    </xsd:annotation>
</xsd:element>

<xsd:simpleType name="sequenceIDType">
    <xsd:annotation>
        <xsd:documentation xml:lang="en">
            A Sequence ID is generated by
            the database.  Sequences are
            integers that start with "0"
        </xsd:documentation>
    </xsd:annotation>
    <xsd:restriction base="xsd:nonNegativeInteger"/>
</xsd:simpleType>
```

The baseCatalogEntryType complex type includes a reference to the non-instantiable sequenceID:

```xml
<xsd:complexType name="baseCatalogEntryType"
                abstract="true"
                id="baseCatalogEntryType.catalog.cType">
    <xsd:annotation>
        <xsd:documentation xml:lang="en">
            A catalog entry must have:
                * A database ID
                * Part Name
```

```
                    * Part Number
                    * Options available
                    * Description
                    * Price
                    * Included Quantity when ordering
                      one item.
            The "baseCatalogEntryType" is
            non-instantiable:  a derived type must
            be created before a catalog
            entry can be instantiated.
                -- Shorthand Notation --
        </xsd:documentation>
    </xsd:annotation>
    <xsd:sequence id="bacet-seq">
        <xsd:element ref="sequenceID"/>
        <xsd:element name="partName" type="partNameType"/>
        <xsd:element name="partNumber"
                    type="partNumberType"/>
        <xsd:element name="partOption"
                    type="partOptionType"
                    minOccurs="0"/>
        <xsd:element name="description"
                    type="catalogEntryDescriptionType"/>
        <xsd:group ref="priceGroup"/>
        <xsd:element name="includedQuantity"
                    type="xsd:positiveInteger"/>
        <xsd:element name="customerReview"
                    type="customerReviewType"
                    minOccurs="0"
                    maxOccurs="unbounded"/>
    </xsd:sequence>
</xsd:complexType>
```

Subsequently, the `unitCatalogEntryType` substitutes the element type `unitID`, which is a valid substitution:

```
<xsd:complexType name="unitCatalogEntryType"
                block="#all"
                final="#all"
                id="unitCatalogEntryType.catalog.cType">
    <xsd:annotation>
        <xsd:documentation xml:lang="en">
            A unit item contains nothing more
            or less than a basic catalog entry ID:
                * A database ID
                * Part Name
                * Part Number
                * Options available
```

*continues*

```
                    * Price
                    * Included Quantity when ordering
                      one item (always one for unit items).
            </xsd:documentation>
        </xsd:annotation>
        <xsd:complexContent id="ucet.cc">
            <xsd:restriction base="baseCatalogEntryType">
                <xsd:sequence>
                    <xsd:element ref="unitID"/>
                    <xsd:element name="partName"
                                 type="partNameType"/>
                    <xsd:element name="partNumber"
                                 type="unitPartNumberType"/>
                    <xsd:element name="partOption"
                                 type="partOptionType"
                                 minOccurs="1"/>
                    <xsd:element name="description
                                 type="catalogEntryDescriptionType"/>
                    <xsd:group ref="priceGroup"/>
                    <xsd:element name="includedQuantity"
                                 type="xsd:positiveInteger"
                                 fixed="1"/>
                    <xsd:element name="customerReview"
                                 type="customerReviewType"
                                 minOccurs="0"
                                 maxOccurs="unbounded"/>
                </xsd:sequence>
            </xsd:restriction>
        </xsd:complexContent>
</xsd:complexType>
```

Finally, if sequenceID had a final attribute set to 'substitution', as in the following example, the substitution in unitCatalogEntryType would have been invalid:

```
<xsd:element name="sequenceID"
             type="sequenceIDType"
             abstract="true"
             final="substitution">
    <xsd:annotation>
        <xsd:documentation xml:lang="en">
            This element type is
            abstract:  the element must be
            replaced by a substitution group
            in either a derived type or
            an instance.
        </xsd:documentation>
    </xsd:annotation>
</xsd:element>
```

## 8.3.1.5 The `fixed` Attribute of an `element` Element

The `fixed` attribute behaves very much like the `default` attribute: An XML parser substitutes the value of this attribute when the element instance has no explicit value. The only difference is that if the element specified in the XML instance has an explicit value, that value must be identical to the value specified by the `fixed` attribute.

---

**ATTRIBUTE OVERVIEW**

**element: fixed**

| | |
|---|---|
| **Value:** | Any string that conforms to the structure type of the element's element type. |
| **Default:** | None. |
| **Constraints:** | The `final` attribute is mutually exclusive with the `default` attribute. |
| **Required:** | No. |

---

The following example is the element type `country`, which has a `fixed` attribute set to 'US':

```
<xsd:element name="country" type="xsd:string" fixed="US"/>
```

Given the preceding element type, the following example with no explicit value is valid in an XML instance:

```
<country></country>
```

Of course, the XML instance can have the explicit value 'US':

```
<country>US</country>
```

In either case, the XML parser should provide the same result: a `country` element with the value 'US'.

---

**WARNING**

Some of the XML parsers do not substitute the fixed value; instead, the element remains empty or creates an error.

---

Finally, for clarity, an XML instance cannot have a value other than US. The next example is invalid in an XML instance:

```
<country>United States</country>
```

### 8.3.1.6 The `form` Attribute of an `element` Element

The `form` attribute determines if a local element type requires qualification of the start- and end-tags of an element instance. An element is *qualified* when a namespace prefix and a colon precede the respective name. For example, in Listing 8.7, `xse:nsQualified` is the *type name* of an element called 'nsQualified'; the qualifier for the related namespace is 'xse'. The subsequent examples use the `xse` namespace qualifier. The `form` attribute is not frequently used: Normally, the XML processor accesses the default value provided by the global `elementFormDefault` attribute of the `schema` element. The `form` attribute provides a mechanism to override the default qualification at the element type level. This attribute has no effect upon a global element type.

---

**ATTRIBUTE OVERVIEW**

**element: form**

| | |
|---:|:---|
| **Value:** | 'qualified' or 'unqualified'. |
| **Default:** | The element type inherits the value of the `elementFormDefault` attribute of the schema element. |
| **Constraints:** | The form attribute only applies to local element types, not global element types. |
| **Required:** | No. |

---

The interaction of namespaces, default namespaces, and target namespaces is somewhat complicated. Because of this, the subsequent two examples include an entire schema and an entire XML instance respectively. Listing 8.7 provides an XML representation for the `formElementDemo` element. The `formElementDemo` element type in turn specifies three local element types that specify the `form` attribute as 'qualified', 'unqualified', and the default value.

**LISTING 8.7** A Complete XML Schema That Demonstrates the `form` Attribute

```
<xsd:element name="formElementDemo">
    <xsd:complexType>
        <xsd:sequence>
            <xsd:element name="nsUnqualified"
                         type="xsd:string"
                         form="unqualified"/>
            <xsd:element name="nsQualified"
                         type="xsd:string"
                         form="qualified"/>
```

## 8.3 The element Element

```
        <xsd:element name="nsDefault"
                     type="xsd:string"/>
      </xsd:sequence>
   </xsd:complexType>
</xsd:element>
```

Listing 8.8 is an XML instance for the schema specified in Listing 8.7.

**LISTING 8.8** A Complete XML Instance That Demonstrates the `form` Attribute

```
<xse:formElementDemo
 xmlns:xse="http://www.XMLSchemaReference.com/examples"
 xmlns:xsi="http://www.w3.org/2001/XMLSchema-instance"
 xsi:schemaLocation="http://www.XMLSchemaReference.com/examples
                     http://www.XMLSchemaReference.com/examples/
                                           Ch08/formElement.xsd">

<nsUnqualified>abc</nsUnqualified>
<xse:nsQualified>abc</xse:nsQualified>
<nsDefault>xyz</nsDefault>

</xse:formElementDemo>
```

Note that `nsUnqualified` is not qualified, and `nsQualified` is qualified—as specified by the respective `form` attributes. `nsDefault` is not qualified, because the `elementFormDefault` attribute of `schema` element specifies a default of 'unqualified'.

### 8.3.1.7 The id Attribute of an element Element

The value of an `id` attribute uniquely identifies an element within the set of schema documents that comprise an XML schema. The example of the `city` element type in Section 8.1 provides an example of the `id` attribute.

**ATTRIBUTE OVERVIEW**

**element: id**

| | |
|---:|---|
| **Value:** | An ID. |
| **Default:** | None. |
| **Constraints:** | An `id` must be unique within an XML schema. |
| **Required:** | No. |

Most of the examples in this chapter uniquely identify each element type.

> **WARNING**
> 
> Many of the existing XML parsers do not properly enforce the uniqueness of the `id`.

### 8.3.1.8 The `maxOccurs` Attribute of an `element` Element

The `maxOccurs` attribute determines the maximum number of times that an element instance can appear in an enclosing element.

---
**ATTRIBUTE OVERVIEW**

**element: maxOccurs**

- **Value:** A non-negative integer, or 'unbounded'.
- **Default:** '1'.
- **Constraints:** The `maxOccurs` attribute applies only to local element types.
- **Required:** No.

---

Refer to Listing 8.1, which demonstrates the complex type `addressType`. An element instance of `address` (whose structure type is `addressType`) may have one or two `addressLine` elements. The following example shows an address that has a second address line (the apartment number):

```
<address>
    <street>88888 Mega Apartment Bldg</street>
    <street>Apt 5315</street>
    <city>New York</city>
    <state>NY</state>
    <country>US</country>
    <zip>10000</zip>
    <effectiveDate>2001-02-14</effectiveDate>
</address>
```

Setting the value of `maxOccurs` to 'unbounded' permits an element instance to occur an unlimited number of times with respect to the enclosing element. Listing 8.9 allows for an XML instance that specifies a `customerList` to specify any number of `customer` records.

**LISTING 8.9** Specifying the `maxOccurs` Attribute for an Unbounded List (`catalog.xsd`)

```
<xsd:element name="customerList">
    <xsd:complexType>
        <xsd:sequence>
            <xsd:element ref="customer"
                         minOccurs="0"
                         maxOccurs="unbounded"/>
        </xsd:sequence>
    </xsd:complexType>
</xsd:element>
```

> **TIP**
>
> Setting the value of the `maxOccurs` attribute to '0' is valuable when a restriction of a complex type must prohibit element instances of an element type specified in a base complex type.

Setting the value of `maxOccurs` to '0' is useful for overriding an existing `maxOccurs` value in a derived complex type. In the thematic catalog example, an assembly does not have any of the standard color or size options associated with all other types of catalog entries. Listing 8.10 specifies the `baseAssemblyCatalogEntryType` that removes the nested `partOption` element type specified by `baseCatalogEntryType`. Setting the value of the `maxOccurs` attribute to '0' prohibits an XML instance from containing a `partOption` element.

**LISTING 8.10** Removing an Element in a Derived Restricted Complex Type (`catalog.xsd`)

```
<xsd:complexType name="baseAssemblyCatalogEntryType"
                 abstract="true"
                 block="#all"
                 id="baseAssemblyCatalogEntryType.catalog.cType">
    <xsd:annotation>
        <xsd:documentation xml:lang="en">
            An assembled item is similar to the
            other catalog entries.  The part number
            is restricted to an assembly number.
            In addition, there may be no options.
            Finally, a part list is also needed.
            Note that the "includedQuantity" has
            a default of one, but can be overridden
            in instances.
        </xsd:documentation>
    </xsd:annotation>
```

*continues*

```
        <xsd:complexContent>
            <xsd:restriction base="baseCatalogEntryType"
                             id="bacet.rst">
                <xsd:sequence>
                    <xsd:element ref="assemblyID"/>
                    <xsd:element name="partName"
                                 type="partNameType"/>
                    <xsd:element name="partNumber"
                                 type="assemblyPartNumberType"/>
                    <xsd:element name="partOption"
                                 type="partOptionType"
                                 minOccurs="0"
                                 maxOccurs="0"/>
                    <xsd:element name="description"
                                 type="catalogEntryDescriptionType"/>
                    <xsd:group ref="priceGroup"/>
                    <xsd:element name="includedQuantity"
                                 type="xsd:positiveInteger"
                                 default="1"/>
                    <xsd:element name="customerReview"
                                 type="customerReviewType"
                                 minOccurs="0"
                                 maxOccurs="unbounded"/>
                </xsd:sequence>
            </xsd:restriction>
        </xsd:complexContent>
</xsd:complexType>
```

### 8.3.1.9 The `minOccurs` Attribute of an `element` Element

The value of the `minOccurs` attribute determines the minimum number of times that an element instance can appear in an enclosing element.

---

**ATTRIBUTE OVERVIEW**

**element: minOccurs**

| | |
|---:|---|
| **Value:** | A non-negative integer. |
| **Default:** | '1'. |
| **Constraints:** | The `maxOccurs` attribute applies only to local element types. |
| **Required:** | No. |

---

Listings 8.9 and 8.10 provide examples of the `minOccurs` attribute.

### 8.3.1.10 The name Attribute of an element Element

The name attribute identifies the element type. The name of an element type may be referenced in one of three ways:

- An XML instance may specify instances of global element types.
- A complex type can specify a global element type with the ref attribute.
- A complex type can specify a local element type. An XML instance can specify this element type in the context of an element whose structure type is this complex type.

---

**ATTRIBUTE OVERVIEW**

**element: name**

| | |
|---|---|
| **Value:** | An NCName. |
| **Default:** | None. |
| **Constraints:** | The name attribute is mutually exclusive with the ref attribute. |
| **Required:** | Either name or ref is required. |

---

Chapter 3 discusses namespaces. Chapter 7 describes how a schema makes use of namespaces.

### 8.3.1.11 The nillable Attribute of an element Element

When an element type specifies that an element instance is nillable, the XML parser does not require that element instances have a value. Section 8.2.5 provides a complete discussion on nillable element types.

---

**ATTRIBUTE OVERVIEW**

**element: nillable**

| | |
|---|---|
| **Value:** | A Boolean (that is, 'true' or 'false'). |
| **Default:** | 'false'. |
| **Constraints:** | None. |
| **Required:** | No. |

---

Listing 8.5 provides an example of an element type that specifies the nillable attribute.

### 8.3.1.12 The `ref` Attribute of an `element` Element

The value of a `ref` attribute is a global element type. In particular, a complex type specifies nested element types with local element types or references to global element types with the `ref` attribute.

---

**ATTRIBUTE OVERVIEW**

**element: ref**

- **Value:** A QName that refers to global element type.
- **Default:** None.
- **Constraints:** There are several constraints, itemized in the following list:
  - The qualified name must refer to a global element type.
  - The `ref` attribute is mutually exclusive with `name`.
  - Allowed: Only the `minOccurs` and `maxOccurs` attributes are permitted. Only the `annotation` element may be used as content.
  - Disallowed: The `nillable`, `default`, `fixed`, `form`, `block`, and `type` attributes. The elements `complexType`, `simpleType`, `key`, `keyref`, and `unique` are also prohibited as content.
- **Required:** Either `name` or `ref` is required.

---

The `ref` attribute provides a way to incorporate a global element type into one or more complex types. Regardless, there is only one XML representation of the element type. This is particularly useful if the element type has lots of attributes, restrictions, or other detailed functionality. The `existingCustomer` element type, specified in Listing 8.11, references the global `phoneNumber` element type, specified in Listing 8.5.

**LISTING 8.11**  Referencing a Global Element Type (`address.xsd`)

```
<xsd:element name="existingCustomer">
    <xsd:annotation>
        <xsd:documentation xml:lang="en">
            An existing customer consists of a
            name, phone number, address, and some
            keys from the database.  This element
            is restricted from further extensions.
        </xsd:documentation>
    </xsd:annotation>
    <xsd:complexType>
        <xsd:sequence>
            <xsd:element name="name" type="xsd:string"/>
```

```
            <xsd:element ref="phoneNumber"
                         minOccurs="1"
                         maxOccurs="unbounded"/>
            <xsd:element ref="address"
                         minOccurs="1"
                         maxOccurs="unbounded"/>
        </xsd:sequence>
        <xsd:attribute name="customerID"
                       type="xsd:string"
                       use="required"/>
        <xsd:attribute name="alternateKey"
                       type="xsd:string"
                       use="optional"/>
        <xsd:attribute ref="sequenceID"/>
    </xsd:complexType>
</xsd:element>
```

An element type can specify other attributes along with the `ref` attribute, as demonstrated by the use of the `minOccurs` and `maxOccurs` attributes associated with the reference to `phoneNumber` in Listing 8.11.

### 8.3.1.13 The type Attribute of an element Element

The `type` attribute determines the structure type associated with an element type. The value of the `type` attribute is a built-in datatype (such as `token` or `decimal`), a simple type derived from a built-in dataype, or a complex type.

---

**ATTRIBUTE OVERVIEW**

**element: type**

| | |
|---|---|
| **Value:** | A QName that refers to a global simple or complex type. |
| **Default:** | The built-in `anyType`—that is, no constraints on content. |
| **Constraint:** | The `type` attribute is mutually exclusive with a local `simpleType` or `complexType`. |
| **Required:** | No. |

---

There are two ways to associate a structure type with an element type. The first is to specify the structure type with a `type` attribute (most of the examples in this chapter). The other is to locally specify a simple or complex type by nesting a `simpleType` or `complexType` element. Refer to Listing 8.2, which specifies the element type `POBox` with a local simple type.

> **TIP**
>
> When an element type provides a `substitutionGroup` attribute, the type attribute is not required. When an element type that is part of a substitution group does not specify a structure type, the element type inherits the structure type from the base element type. The base element type is the element type specified by the value of the `substitutionGroup` attribute.

### 8.3.1.14 The `substitutionGroup` Attribute of an `element` Element

The `substitutionGroup` attribute specifies an element type to be substitutable for an another element type. Section 8.2.2 provides a complete discussion on the general functionality of substitution groups.

**ATTRIBUTE OVERVIEW**

**element: substitutionGroup**

| | |
|---|---|
| **Value:** | A QName that refers to a global element type. |
| **Default:** | None. |
| **Constraints:** | A `block` or `final` attribute in a base element type might prohibit substitutions. |
| **Required:** | No. |

Listing 8.2 is a complete substitution group that includes the base non-instantiable `addressLine` and the valid substitutions `POBox`, `pmb`, and `street`.

> **TIP**
>
> The use of `final` or `block` attributes on base elements might prohibit substitutions in certain circumstances.

## 8.3.2 Content Options for an `element` Element

An element type has a number of content options. Table 8.2 itemizes the valid content options. The elements representing the content options for `element` elements are also content options for many other elements. Therefore, this section provides no explicit detail on any of the options. Instead, the ensuing table references appropriate chapters of this book.

**TABLE 8.2** Content Options for an `element` Element

| Element | Description | Reference |
|---|---|---|
| annotation | The `annotation` element provides a way to document schema elements. | Section 7.5 |
| simpleType | A local simple type. Most element types have a local `simpleType` element, a local `complexType` element, or a reference to a global simple or complex type via the type attribute. | Chapter 10 |
| complexType | A local complex type. Most element types have a local `simpleType` element, a local `complexType` element, or a reference to a global simple or complex type via the type attribute. | Chapter 11 |
| key | A `key` element asserts the uniqueness of a set of elements in the XML instance. In addition, the key element asserts the existence of the elements in the XML instance. | Chapter 13 |
| keyref | A `keyref` element asserts that the values specified by a set of elements in an XML instance exist as values of elements identified by either a `key` or `unique` element. | Chapter 13 |
| unique | A `unique` element asserts uniqueness of a set of elements in the XML instance. | Chapter 13 |

The content pattern for the `element` element is:

annotation? (simpleType | complexType)? (unique | key | keyref)*

## 8.4 The any Element

The any element provides a mechanism for specifying elements with what the XML Schema Recommendation calls a wildcard. The element wildcard permits a complex type to loosely specify how an XML validator validates elements in an XML instance. This is in sharp contrast to the normal `element` element, which succinctly specifies element type.

An element wildcard generally specifies a set of namespaces against which the XML validator may validate. The XML validator searches each namespace for global element types that might correspond to the elements referenced in the XML instance.

Listing 8.12 is an element type that specifies the XML instance may contain a reference to a set of any known element types in any known namespaces. For demonstration purposes, assume that `eStrictAnyNS` is in a target namespace that is bound to the 'aeDemo' prefix. For clarity in later discussion, 'aeDemo' is bound to:

http://www.XMLSchemaReference.com/examples/Ch08/anyElementDemo

# Element Types
## CHAPTER 8

**LISTING 8.12** Specifying an any Element

```
<xsd:element name="eStrictAnyNS">
    <xsd:complexType>
        <xsd:choice minOccurs="0" maxOccurs="unbounded">
            <xsd:any id="aaStrictAny"
                     processContents="strict"
                     namespace="##any"/>
        </xsd:choice>
    </xsd:complexType>
</xsd:element>
```

To demonstrate how to use the `eStrictAnyNS` element described in Listing 8.12, suppose that the following elements are also in a namespace that is bound to the 'aeDemo' prefix:

```
<xsd:element name="e1" type="xsd:token"/>
<xsd:element name="e2" type="xsd:token"/>
<xsd:element name="e3" type="xsd:token"/>
<xsd:element name="e4" type="xsd:token"/>
<xsd:element name="e5" type="xsd:token"/>
<xsd:element name="e6" type="xsd:token"/>
```

The XML instance might contain the following element:

```
<aeDemo:eStrictAnyNS>
    <aeDemo:e1>value1</aeDemo:e1>
    <aeDemo:e2>value2</aeDemo:e2>
</aeDemo:eStrictAnyNS>
```

The remainder of this section provides detail on the attribute and content options available for the any element.

### 8.4.1 Attributes of an any Element

The attributes of an any element are complicated. Table 8.3 provides a summary of the attributes for an any element.

**TABLE 8.3** Attribute Summary for an any Element

| Attribute | Description |
| --- | --- |
| id | The value of an `id` attribute uniquely identifies an element within the set of schema documents that comprise an XML schema. |
| namespace | The value of the `namespace` attribute specifies a list of namespaces that might provide global element types for validating an element in an XML instance. |
| processContents | The value of the `processContents` attribute determines whether the XML validator validates the *typenames* of elements against element types, and the elements' content against the element types' structure types. |

### 8.4.1.1 The `id` Attribute of an any Element

The value of an `id` attribute uniquely identifies an element within the set of schema documents that comprise an XML schema.

---
**ATTRIBUTE OVERVIEW**

**any: id**

| | |
|---|---|
| **Value:** | An ID. |
| **Default:** | None. |
| **Constraints:** | An id must be unique within the set of schema documents that comprise an XML schema. |
| **Required:** | No. |

---

Listing 8.12 describes an any element that specifies an `id` attribute.

### 8.4.1.2 The `namespace` Attribute of an any Element

The value of the `namespace` attribute specifies the namespaces that an XML validator examines to determine the validity of an element in an XML instance. The element in the XML instance must correspond to a global element type specified in one of the namespaces, but only if the `processContents` attribute is `strict` (see Section 8.4.1.3).

---
**ATTRIBUTE OVERVIEW**

**any: namespace**

| | |
|---|---|
| **Value:** | '##any', '##other', or a space-delimited list containing any or all of various URIs, '##targetNamespace', or '##local'. |
| **Default:** | '##any'. |
| **Constraints:** | None. |
| **Required:** | No. |

---

An element in an XML instance must correspond to global element types specified in the namespaces that may correspond to a specified URI, or the constants defined in the following list:

- The value '##any' indicates any of the namespaces available to the XML instance.

- The value '`##targetNamespace`' indicates the namespace specified by the `targetNamespace` attribute of the `schema` element of the current schema.
- The value '`##other`' indicates a namespace that is any namespace *except* the namespace specified by the `targetNamespace` attribute of the `schema` element of the current schema.
- The value '`##local`' indicates explicitly no namespace. Of course, the element in the XML instance must be unqualified.

Note that Listing 8.12 demonstrates the use of the `namespace` attribute. Furthermore, note that the value of the `namespace` argument could be '`##targetNamespace`' or '`http://www.XMLSchemaReference.com/examples/Ch08/anyElementDemo`'—instead of '`##all`'—with the same effect, because the element `e1` exists in the target namespace.

### 8.4.1.3 The `processContents` Attribute of an `any` Element

The `processContents` attribute interacts with the `namespace` attribute. In particular, some of the values applicable to the `processContents` attribute negate the value of using the namespace attribute because the XML validator either ignores the namespace or does minimal validation against it.

---

**ATTRIBUTE OVERVIEW**

**any: processContents**

| | |
|---:|---|
| **Value:** | One of '`lax`', '`skip`', or '`strict`'. |
| **Default:** | '`strict`'. |
| **Constraints:** | None. |
| **Required:** | No. |

---

The `processContents` attribute has one of three values. These values have the following meaning:

- `strict`: The XML validator enforces that an element in an XML instance validates against an element type in one of the namespaces specified by the `namespace` attribute.
- `skip`: Other than enforcing that an element is well formed, the XML validator does not attempt to validate the element against an element type.
- `lax`: The XML validator validates the element when possible. When the validator locates a corresponding element type, the element must conform to the element type's structure type. Conversely, when there is no corresponding element type, the validator deems the element and contents valid.

Listing 8.12 demonstrates the use of the `processContents` attribute.

## 8.4.2 Content Options for an `anyAttribute` Element

Table 8.4 identifies the only content option available to a wildcard: the ubiquitous `annotation` element.

**TABLE 8.4**  Content Options for an `anyAttribute` Element

| *Element* | *Description* |
|---|---|
| annotation | The annotation element, discussed in Section 7.5, provides a way to document schema elements. |

The content pattern for the any element is:

annotation?

# Attribute Types

**CHAPTER**

**9**

## IN THIS CHAPTER

- 9.1 An Example of an Attribute Type  174
- 9.2 An Example of a Named Attribute-use Group  176
- 9.3 An Example of `anyAttribute`  177
- 9.4 Concepts and Observations Regarding Attribute Types  180
- 9.5 The `attribute` Element  182
- 9.6 The `attributeGroup` Element  193
- 9.7 The `anyAttribute` Element  196

An *attribute type* specifies constraints for corresponding attributes in an XML instance. The main purpose of an attribute type is to associate an attribute name with a structure type. The structure type of an attribute type is always a simple type. The structure type may be global, or the structure type may be local to the attribute type. The XML representation of an attribute type is an `attribute` element.

Because the structure type of an attribute is always a simple type, an attribute type cannot specify nested element types or attribute types (only a complex type—or, indirectly, an element type whose structure type is a complex type—may specify nested element types and attribute types). Other than this limitation, an attribute type is very similar to an element type.

In XML, an attribute can have only one occurrence per element; there is no notion of number of occurrences. More precisely, an element may specify at most one occurrence of an attribute.

A complex type specifies attribute uses by using an attribute group. An *attribute use* is a local attribute type, or a reference to a global attribute type. A *named attribute-use group* is nothing more than a named collection of attribute uses. Multiple complex types may reference the same named attribute-use group. However, the scope of the attribute types changes: The attribute types become local to the enclosing complex type. A named attribute-use group provides modularity: If the named attribute-use group changes, all the referencing complex types conceptually specify the new set of attribute types. The XML representation of a named attribute-use group is an `attributeGroup` element.

An *attribute wildcard* can loosely specify attributes. An attribute wildcard specifies a namespace from which the corresponding element in an XML instance selects global attribute types. The XML representation of an attribute wildcard is an `anyAttribute` element.

## 9.1 An Example of an Attribute Type

Attribute types are global or local. Listing 9.1 portrays the complex type `businessCustomer`, which incorporates the global `sequenceID` attribute type as well as local `customerID` and `primaryContact` attribute types:

**LISTING 9.1** Local and Global Attribute Types (address.xsd)

```
<xsd:complexType name="businessCustomerType">
    <xsd:sequence>
        <xsd:element name="name" type="xsd:string"/>
        <xsd:element ref="phoneNumber"
                     minOccurs="1"
                     maxOccurs="unbounded"/>
        <xsd:element name="URL"
                     type="xsd:token"
                     minOccurs="0"
```

```
                        maxOccurs="1"/>
        <xsd:element ref="address"
                        minOccurs="1"
                        maxOccurs="unbounded"/>
    </xsd:sequence>
    <xsd:attribute name="customerID"
                    type="xsd:token"
                    use="required"/>
    <xsd:attribute name="primaryContact"
                    type="xsd:token"
                    use="optional"/>
    <xsd:attribute ref="sequenceID"/>
</xsd:complexType>

<xsd:attribute name="sequenceID"
                type="sequenceIDType"
                use="optional"
                id="address.attr.sequenceID"/>
```

The XML representation of an element type whose structure type is the complex type `businessCustomerType` might look like the following:

```
<xsd:element name="businessCustomer"
            type="businessCustomerType"/>
```

The file `address.xsd` provides detail on the `address` element type. Given the preceding element type, the following is valid in an XML instance:

```
<businessCustomer customerID="SAM132E57">
    <name>Cliff Binstock</name>
    <phoneNumber>503-555-0000</phoneNumber>
    <address>
        <street>123 Gravel Road</street>
        <city>Nowheresville</city>
        <state>OR</state>
        <country>US</country>
        <zip>97000</zip>
        <effectiveDate></effectiveDate>
    </address>
</businessCustomer>
```

Because the `primaryContact` and `sequenceID` are optional, the following element, which specifies these two attributes in addition to the required `customerID`, is also valid:

```
<businessCustomer customerID="SAM132E58"
                    primaryContact="Ellie"
                    sequenceID="88742">
```

*continues*

```xml
    <name>Ellen Boxer</name>
    <phoneNumber xsi:nil="true"/>
    <address zipPlus4="20000-1234">
        <POBox>123</POBox>
        <city>Small Town</city>
        <state>VA</state>
        <country>US</country>
        <zip>20000</zip>
        <effectiveDate>2001-02-14</effectiveDate>
    </address>
</businessCustomer>
```

## 9.2 An Example of a Named Attribute-use Group

A *named attribute-use group* provides a way to specify a set of attribute types that presumably apply to multiple complex types. Listing 9.2 portrays the named attribute-use group saleAttributeGroup. In addition, the listing demonstrates the complex types freePriceType and salePriceType, both of which reference saleAttributeGroup.

**LISTING 9.2** A Named Attribute-use Group (pricing.xsd)

```xml
<xsd:attributeGroup name="saleAttributeGroup"
                    id="pricing.sale.ag">
    <xsd:annotation>
        <xsd:documentation xml:lang="en">
            Anything that is on sale (or free,
            which is a type of sale) must
            have an authorization defined.
            This is someone's name,
            initials, ID, etc.
        </xsd:documentation>
    </xsd:annotation>
    <xsd:attribute name="employeeAuthorization" type="xsd:token"/>
    <xsd:attribute name="managerAuthorization" type="xsd:token"/>
</xsd:attributeGroup>

<xsd:complexType name="freePriceType"
                 block="#all"
                 final="#all"
                 id="freePriceType.pricing.cType">
    <xsd:annotation>
        <xsd:documentation xml:lang="en">
            Anything that is free has no
            value (i.e., price), but must
            have an authorization code.
```

```
                    This is a complex type with
                    "empty" content.
                        — Shorthand Notation —
</xsd:documentation>
        </xsd:annotation>
        <xsd:attributeGroup ref="saleAttributeGroup"/>
</xsd:complexType>

<xsd:complexType name="salePriceType"
                 block="#all"
                 final="extension"
                 id="salePriceType.pricing.cType">
    <xsd:annotation>
        <xsd:documentation xml:lang="en">
            Anything on sale must have a price
            and an authorization
        </xsd:documentation>
    </xsd:annotation>
    <xsd:simpleContent>
        <xsd:extension base="dollarPriceType">
            <xsd:attributeGroup ref="saleAttributeGroup"/>
        </xsd:extension>
    </xsd:simpleContent>
</xsd:complexType>
```

The XML representation of an element type whose structure type is the complex type `freePriceType` might look like the following:

```
<xsd:element name="freePrice" type="freePriceType"/>
```

Given the preceding element type, the following is valid in an XML instance:

```
<freePrice employeeAuthorization="CB"
           managerAuthorization="ALB"/>
```

## 9.3 An Example of anyAttribute

The `anyAttribute` element provides a mechanism to loosely specify attributes. The `anyAttribute` element is analogous to the `any` element, which provides a similar mechanism for loosely specifying elements. Listing 9.3 demonstrates a simple complete schema for specifying attributes a1 through a6. The element type `eStrictAnyNS` specifies that a corresponding XML instance may reference any global attribute specified in the `http://www.XMLSchemaReference.com/examples` namespace. The entire schema is included in Listing 9.3 because the namespaces are an integral part of the attribute wildcard.

**LISTING 9.3** An Attribute Wildcard (`anyAttributeDemo.xsd`)

```xsd
<xsd:schema
    xmlns:xsd="http://www.w3.org/2001/XMLSchema"
    targetNamespace="http://www.XMLSchemaReference.com/examples/
                                Ch09/anyAttributeDemo"

    elementFormDefault="qualified"
    attributeFormDefault="qualified">

<xsd:attribute name="a1" type="xsd:token"/>
<xsd:attribute name="a2" type="xsd:token"/>
<xsd:attribute name="a3" type="xsd:token"/>
<xsd:attribute name="a4" type="xsd:token"/>
<xsd:attribute name="a5" type="xsd:token"/>
<xsd:attribute name="a6" type="xsd:token"/>

<xsd:element name="anyAttributeDemo">
    <xsd:complexType>
        <xsd:sequence>
            <xsd:element name="eStrictAnyNS">
                <xsd:complexType>
                    <xsd:anyAttribute id="aaStrictAny"
                                      processContents="strict"
                                      namespace="##any"/>
                </xsd:complexType>
            </xsd:element>
            <xsd:element name="eStrictURI">
                <xsd:complexType>
                    <xsd:anyAttribute
                        processContents="strict"
                        namespace=
  "http://www.XMLSchemaReference.com/examples/
              Ch09/anyAttributeDemo"/>
                </xsd:complexType>
            </xsd:element>
            <xsd:element name="eStrictTargetNamespace">
                <xsd:complexType>
                    <xsd:anyAttribute
                        processContents="strict"
                        namespace="##targetNamespace"/>
                </xsd:complexType>
            </xsd:element>
            <xsd:element name="eStrictOtherNS">
                <xsd:complexType>
                    <xsd:anyAttribute processContents="strict"
                                      namespace="##other"/>
```

```
            </xsd:complexType>
        </xsd:element>
        <xsd:element name="eLaxAnyNS">
            <xsd:complexType>
                <xsd:anyAttribute id="aaLaxAny"
                                  processContents="lax"
                                  namespace="##any"/>
            </xsd:complexType>
        </xsd:element>
      </xsd:sequence>
    </xsd:complexType>
</xsd:element>

</xsd:schema>
```

An entire XML instance that corresponds to the XML schema specified in Listing 9.3 might look like the following:

```
<aaDemo:anyAttributeDemo
 xmlns:aaDemo="http://www.XMLSchemaReference.com/examples/
               Ch09/anyAttributeDemo"
 xmlns:aaList="http://www.XMLSchemaReference.com/examples/
               Ch09/anyAttributeList"
 xmlns:xsi="http://www.w3.org/2001/XMLSchema-instance"
 xsi:schemaLocation="http://www.XMLSchemaReference.com/examples/
                             Ch09/anyAttributeDemo
http://www.XMLSchemaReference.com/examples/
                             Ch09/anyAttributeDemo.xsd
http://www.XMLSchemaReference.com/examples/
                             Ch09/anyAttributeList
http://www.XMLSchemaReference.com/examples/
                             Ch09/anyAttributeList.xsd">

<aaDemo:eStrictAnyNS aaDemo:a1="value1"
                     aaDemo:a2="value2"/>

<aaDemo:eStrictURI aaDemo:a3="value3"/>

<aaDemo:eStrictTargetNamespace aaDemo:a4="tns" aaDemo:a6="6"/>

<aaDemo:eStrictOtherNS aaList:o1="1"/>

<aaDemo:eLaxAnyNS aaDemo:a1="value1"
                  aaDemo:a2="value2"
                  aaDemo:totallyRandom="what?"/>

</aaDemo:anyAttributeDemo>
```

## 9.4 Concepts and Observations Regarding Attribute Types

Attribute types have fewer options than element types, simple types, or complex types. Because of the simplicity of attribute types, this section covers only three concepts: when to use an attribute type versus an element type, global and local attribute types, and how attribute types interact with namespaces in the corresponding XML instances.

### 9.4.1 When to Use an Attribute Type

In many XML schemas, the use of an attribute type versus an element type is an arbitrary choice. In the following example, the customer's ID is an attribute type:

```
<xsd:element name="customer">
    <xsd:complexType>
        <xsd:attribute name="customerID"
                       type="xsd:string"
                       use="required"/>
    </xsd:complexType>
</xsd:element>
```

Given the preceding element type, the following is valid in an XML instance:

```
<customer customerID="SAM132E57"/>
```

Alternatively, the next example shows a customer's ID specified as an element type:

```
<xsd:element name="customer">
    <xsd:complexType>
        <xsd:sequence>
            <xsd:element name="customerID" type="xsd:string"/>
        </xsd:sequence>
    </xsd:complexType>
</xsd:element>
```

When the customer's ID is an element type, as specified by the preceding `customer`, the following is valid in an XML instance:

```
<customer>
    <customerID>"SAM132E57"</customerID>
</customer>
```

Neither solution is technically superior. The following list contains some guidelines to help identify good candidates for storing data in XML attributes:

- Use attribute types when the data uniquely identifies the element. The customer ID is a good example of this.

- An element may not specify multiple occurrences of an attribute.
- Attribute types specify only simple content. If the data requires nested element types—or if nested element types are likely to become a future requirement—use an element type. Element types are much more flexible. Altering the XML instance generators to add children to elements and altering the corresponding element types is much easier than conceptually recasting attribute types as element types. The schema writer should take into consideration maintenance efforts for software developers.
- Finally, and conversely, humans are more adept at reading attributes than additional elements: The number of lines in an XML instance tends to expand when elements—not attributes—contain the data. If people frequently read or validate the XML instances, the schema writer might consider using more attribute types and fewer element types.

## 9.4.2 Global and Local Attribute Types

Attribute types can be global or local. Typically, multiple complex types reference a global attribute type. This reference to a global attribute type can be direct via the `ref` attribute or indirect via a named attribute-use group. Listing 9.1 portrays the XML representation of both global and local attribute types.

## 9.4.3 Namespaces and Attribute Types

This section discusses how the XML instance specifies namespaces for attributes (that is, how to locate, for validation purposes, the attribute types discussed in this chapter). Chapter 3 discusses how to determine which attribute types in a schema reside in which namespace.

In an XML instance, the namespace of an attribute must match the namespace identified by the attribute type. Typically, attribute types do not specify the target namespace: Normally, the `schema` element specifies the target namespace. If a namespace is not specifically identified, and the target namespace is not specified, the attribute must be unqualified (that is, specified without a namespace).

In an XML instance, an attribute may be *qualified* (namespace specified) or *unqualified* (namespace not specified). An XML validator determines whether the XML instance requires a namespace by evaluating the following rules in order:

- The attribute must be appropriately qualified when the attribute type specifies a `form` attribute (which has a value of 'qualified' or 'unqualified').
- When the attribute type does not specify the `form` attribute, the `attributeFormDefault` attribute (which also has a value of 'qualified' or 'unqualified') of the `schema` element enclosing the attribute type determines whether the name of the attribute instance is qualified.

- When the attribute type does not specify the `form` attribute, and the schema does not specify the `attributeFormDefault` attribute, the attribute must be unqualified. In other words, the default value for `attributeFormDefault` is 'unqualified'.

Section 9.5.1.3, along with the corresponding Listings 9.4 and 9.5, provides an example of how the `form` attribute of attribute types and the `attributeFormDefault` attribute of the `schema` element work.

## 9.5 The `attribute` Element

Attribute types do not have the complexity of element types, simple types, or complex types. In particular, an attribute type has many possible attributes but very few content options.

### 9.5.1 Attributes of an `attribute` Element

The XML representation of an attribute type is an `attribute` element. Table 9.1 summarizes the attributes of an `attribute` element.

**TABLE 9.1** Attribute Summary for an `attribute` Element

| Attribute | Description |
|---|---|
| `default` | The value of a `default` attribute must be a value that conforms to the structure type of the attribute type. When the XML validator encounters an element whose element type specifies this attribute type and the element does not specify the corresponding attribute, the XML validator inserts the attribute with this default value into the infoset. |
| `fixed` | This is similar to the `default` attribute, except that when the element in the corresponding XML instance does specify an attribute, the value of that attribute must match the value specified by the `fixed` attribute. |
| `form` | The value of the `form` attribute determines if a namespace prefix must or must not precede the reference to a globally defined attribute type. |
| `id` | The value of an `id` attribute uniquely identifies an element within the set of schema documents that comprise an XML schema. |
| `name` | The value of the `name` attribute is the name used to reference an attribute type in the rest of the schema or in an XML instance. |
| `type` | The value of the `type` attribute is the simple type, or structure type, that constrains an attribute type. This simple type may be a built-in datatype. |
| `use` | The value of the `use` attribute determines when an attribute is required, prohibited, or optional in an XML instance. |
| `ref` | The value of the `ref` attribute is a global attribute type. This reference permits multiple complex types to specify the same global attribute type. |

### 9.5.1.1 The `default` Attribute of an `attribute` Element

The `default` attribute of an attribute type specifies the value, in an XML instance, of a missing attribute. When an element type specifies an optional attribute type with a default value, and the element instance does not specify an attribute, the abstract element acquires the attribute along with its `default` attribute.

---

**ATTRIBUTE OVERVIEW**

**attribute: default**

| | |
|---|---|
| **Value:** | Any string that conforms to the structure type of the attribute type. |
| **Default:** | None. |
| **Constraints:** | The `default` and `fixed` attributes are mutually exclusive. In addition, when an attribute type includes both the `use` and `default` attributes, the `use` attribute must have the value 'optional'. |
| **Required:** | No. |

---

Listing 9.4 is the `customerList` element type, which specifies the attribute type `source`, which in turn specifies a default value of 'Oracle':

**LISTING 9.4** A Default Value for an Attribute Type (`catalog.xsd`)

```
<xsd:element name="customerList">
    <xsd:complexType>
        <xsd:sequence minOccurs="0"
                      maxOccurs="unbounded">
            <xsd:choice>
                <xsd:element name="businessCustomer"
                             type="businessCustomerType"/>
                <xsd:element name="privateCustomer"
                             type="privateCustomerType"/>
            </xsd:choice>
        </xsd:sequence>
        <xsd:attribute name="source"
                       type="xsd:string"
                       default="Oracle"/>
        <xsd:attribute name="deliverDataToCountry"
                       type="xsd:string"
                       fixed="US"/>
    </xsd:complexType>
</xsd:element>
```

The results of parsing the following `customerList` elements are identical:

```
<customerList>
</customerList>

<customerList source="Oracle">
</customerList>

<customerList country="US">
</customerList>

<customerList source="Oracle" country="US">
</customerList>
```

> **WARNING**
>
> Some XML validators do not create an attribute with the default value; instead, the infoset continues to not have the attribute.

In any reference to `customerList`, the XML validator creates a `source` attribute with the value 'Oracle' in the infoset.

### 9.5.1.2 The `fixed` Attribute of an `attribute` Element

The `fixed` attribute behaves very much like the `default` attribute. An XML validator creates the specified value in the infoset when the instance does not have an attribute that corresponds to the `name` attribute. The only difference between `default` and `fixed` is that if the XML instance does contain the attribute, the instance's attribute value must be identical to the value specified by the `fixed` attribute of the attribute type.

**ATTRIBUTE OVERVIEW**

**attribute: fixed**

| | |
|---:|---|
| Value: | Any string that conforms to the structure type of the attribute type. |
| Default: | None. |
| Constraints: | The `fixed` and `default` attributes are mutually exclusive. |
| Required: | No. |

Listing 9.4 demonstrates the use of the `fixed` attribute.

> **WARNING**
>
> Some XML validators incorrectly do not create an attribute when the attribute type specifies a `fixed` value; instead, the element continues to not have the attribute.

In any reference to `customerList`, the XML validator inserts the attribute `deliverDataToCountry` with the value 'US' into the infoset. If an XML instance specifies an attribute with an invalid value, the XML validator reports an error.

### 9.5.1.3 The `form` Attribute of an `attribute` Element

The `form` attribute determines if a local attribute type requires the name of an attribute instance to be qualified. An attribute name is *qualified* when a namespace prefix and a colon precede the local name. For example, in Listing 9.6, `xse:nsQualified` is the qualified name of the attribute `nsQualified`; the corresponding namespace is 'http://www.XMLSchemaReference.com/examples'. The subsequent examples bind the qualifier 'xse' to the namespace. The `form` attribute is not frequently used: The XML validator inserts the default value provided by the global `attributeFormDefault` attribute of the `schema` element. The `form` attribute provides a mechanism to override the default qualification at the attribute level. This attribute has no effect on a global attribute type.

---

**ATTRIBUTE OVERVIEW**

**attribute: form**

| | |
|---|---|
| **Value:** | 'qualified' or 'unqualified'. |
| **Default:** | The attribute type inherits the value of the `attributeFormDefault` attribute of the `schema` element. |
| **Constraints:** | The `form` attribute applies only to local attribute types, not global attribute types. |
| **Required:** | No. |

---

The interaction of namespaces, default namespaces, and target namespaces is somewhat complicated. Because of this, the subsequent two examples include an entire schema and an entire XML instance, respectively. Listing 9.5 provides an XML representation of the `abusedElement` element type. The `abusedElement` element type specifies three local attribute types that specify the `form` attribute as 'unqualified', 'qualified', and the default value.

**LISTING 9.5** An XML Schema to Demonstrate the `form` Attribute

```xml
<xsd:schema
    xmlns:xsd="http://www.w3.org/2001/XMLSchema"
    xmlns:xse="http://www.XMLSchemaReference.com/examples"
    xmlns="http://www.XMLSchemaReference.com/examples"
    targetNamespace=
        "http://www.XMLSchemaReference.com/examples"
    elementFormDefault="unqualified"
    attributeFormDefault="unqualified">

<xsd:element name="formAttributeDemo">
    <xsd:complexType>
        <xsd:sequence>
            <xsd:element name="abusedElement">
                <xsd:complexType name="abusedElementType">
                    <xsd:attribute name="nsUnqualified"
                                   type="xsd:string"
                                   form="unqualified"/>
                    <xsd:attribute name="nsQualified"
                                   type="xsd:string"
                                   form="qualified"/>
                    <xsd:attribute name="nsDefault"
                                   type="xsd:string"/>
                </xsd:complexType>
            </xsd:element>
        </xsd:sequence>
    </xsd:complexType>
</xsd:element>

</xsd:schema>
```

Listing 9.6 demonstrates an XML instance that corresponds to the schema specified in Listing 9.5.

**LISTING 9.6** An XML Instance to Demonstrate the `form` Attribute

```xml
<xse:formAttributeDemo
 xmlns:xse="http://www.XMLSchemaReference.com/examples"
 xmlns:xsi="http://www.w3.org/2001/XMLSchema-instance"
 xsi:schemaLocation="http://www.XMLSchemaReference.com/examples
                     http://www.XMLSchemaReference.com/examples/
                                                Ch09/formAttribute.xsd">
```

```
<abusedElement
    nsUnqualified="abc"
    xse:nsQualified="abc"
    nsDefault="abc"/>

</xse:formAttributeDemo>
```

Note that nsUnqualified is not qualified and nsQualified is qualified, as specified by the respective form attributes. nsDefault is not qualified because the attributeFormDefault attribute of the schema element specifies a default of 'unqualified'.

### 9.5.1.4 The id Attribute of an attribute Element

The value of an id attribute uniquely identifies an element within the set of schema documents that comprise an XML schema.

---

**ATTRIBUTE OVERVIEW**

**attribute: id**

| | |
|---|---|
| **Value:** | An ID |
| **Default:** | None. |
| **Constraints:** | Each id must be unique in an XML schema. |
| **Required:** | No. |

---

Listing 9.1 portrays an example that specifies the sequenceID attribute type, which specifies an id attribute with a value of 'address.attr.sequenceID'.

**WARNING**

Many of the validators on the market today do not properly enforce id uniqueness.

### 9.5.1.5 The name Attribute of an attribute Element

The name attribute of an attribute type is the name with which a complex type specifies an attribute type in an XML schema document. An element in an XML instance references this name when specifying attributes.

> **ATTRIBUTE OVERVIEW**
>
> **attribute: name**
>
> **Value:** An NCName.
> **Default:** None.
> **Constraints:** The `name` and `ref` attributes are mutually exclusive.
> **Required:** Either the `name` or `ref` attribute is required.

Most of the listings in this chapter contain present attribute types that specify the `name` attribute.

### 9.5.1.6 The type Attribute of an attribute Element

The value of the `type` attribute specifies the structure type of the attribute type. The structure type must be a simple type. This simple type specifies the valid values for an attribute in an XML instance that corresponds to the attribute type. An attribute type specifies the simple type that represents valid values for a corresponding XML instance with either a `type` attribute or `simpleType` content.

> **ATTRIBUTE OVERVIEW**
>
> **attribute: type**
>
> **Value:** An NCName.
> **Default:** The built-in `anyType`—that is, any (simple) content.
> **Constraints:**
> - The use of the `type` attribute is mutually exclusive with a local `simpleType` element.
> - The value of the `type` attribute must be the name of built-in datatype or the name of a custom global simple type.
>
> **Required:** No.

Listing 9.1 portrays the use of the `type` attribute with built-in datatypes (the `customerID` and `primaryContact` attribute types), as well as with a custom simple type (the `sequenceID` attribute type).

For comparison, Listing 9.8 portrays the XML representation of `addressType`, which specifies a local `zipPlus4`, which in turn specifies an anonymous `simpleType`.

### 9.5.1.7 The use Attribute of an `attribute` Element

The structure type of an element type might be a complex type. This complex type might specify an attribute type. This attribute type might specify a use attribute. The value of this use attribute determines whether an element instance (of the element type) might include an attribute instance (of the attribute type). The use options permit the attribute type to require, prohibit, or not constrain the use of the attribute instance. The use attribute has one of the following values:

- 'required': The element instance must have the attribute.
- 'optional': The element instance may or may not have the attribute.
- 'prohibited': The element instance may not have the attribute.

> **TIP**
>
> A derived complex type specifies the 'prohibited' option to remove an attribute type in a restriction of a base complex type that already specifies the attribute type as optional.

**ATTRIBUTE OVERVIEW**

**attribute: use**

| | |
|---|---|
| **Value:** | One of 'required', 'optional', or 'prohibited'. |
| **Default:** | 'optional'. |
| **Constraints:** | When an attribute type includes both the use and default attributes, the use attribute must have the value 'optional'. |
| **Required:** | No. |

In Listing 9.1, both the `primaryContact` and `sequenceID` attribute types specify the use attribute as 'optional'; `customerID` specifies the use attribute as 'required'.

Listing 9.7 portrays the complex type `privateCustomerType`, which derives from `businessCustomerType` specified in Listing 9.1. Note that `businessCustomerType` specifies the `primaryContact` attribute type as optional; `privateCustomerType` restricts this attribute type to be prohibited.

**LISTING 9.7** Prohibiting an Attribute Type

```
<xsd:complexType name="privateCustomerType">
    <xsd:complexContent>
        <xsd:restriction base="businessCustomerType">
            <xsd:sequence>
                <xsd:element name="name" type="xsd:string"/>
                <xsd:element ref="phoneNumber"
                            minOccurs="1"
                            maxOccurs="unbounded"/>
                <xsd:element name="URL"
                            type="xsd:token"
                            minOccurs="0"
                            maxOccurs="0"/>
                <xsd:element ref="address"
                            minOccurs="1"
                            maxOccurs="unbounded"/>
            </xsd:sequence>
            <xsd:attribute name="customerID"
                           type="xsd:token"
                           use="required"/>
            <xsd:attribute name="primaryContact"
                           type="xsd:token"
                           use="prohibited"/>
            <xsd:attribute ref="sequenceID"/>
        </xsd:restriction>
    </xsd:complexContent>
</xsd:complexType>
```

The XML representation of the element types whose structure type is `privateCustomerType` might look like the following:

```
<xsd:element name="privateCustomer"
             type="privateCustomerType"/>
```

Despite the fact that `privateCustomerType` is a derivation of `businessCustomerType`, a `privateCustomer` cannot specify a `primaryContact` because of the constraint on the `privateCustomer` complex type that specifies 'use="prohibited"'. Given the preceding element type, the following is a valid element in an XML instance:

```
<privateCustomer customerID="SAM01234P"
                 sequenceID="88743">
    <name>I. M. Happy</name>
    <phoneNumber>303-555-0000</phoneNumber>
    <phoneNumber>303-555-1111</phoneNumber>
    <address>
        <street>123 Main Street</street>
        <pmb>12345</pmb>
        <city>Metropolis</city>
```

```
        <state>CO</state>
        <country></country>
        <zip>80000</zip>
        <effectiveDate>2001-02-14</effectiveDate>
    </address>
</privateCustomer>
```

### 9.5.1.8 The `ref` Attribute of an `attribute` Element

A complex type specifies a global attribute type with the `ref` attribute. The XML schema specifies a global attribute type once; the XML schema references a global attribute type potentially many times.

---

**ATTRIBUTE OVERVIEW**

**attribute: ref**

| | |
|---:|:---|
| **Value:** | A `QName` name that corresponds to an attribute type. |
| **Default:** | None. |
| **Constraints:** | An attribute type may not contain any of the `name`, `form`, or `type` attributes along with the `ref` attribute. Also, only the `annotation` element is valid as a content option: The `simpleType` content option is not valid. |
| **Required:** | The `attribute` element must contain either a `name` attribute or a `ref` attribute. |

---

The `ref` attribute provides a reference to a global attribute type from within a custom complex type. Listing 9.1 portrays the custom `businessCustomerType` that references the global `sequenceID` attribute type.

## 9.5.2 Content Options for an `attribute` Element

Table 9.2 contains the content options for an `attribute` element, which are limited to `annotation` and `simpleType`.

**TABLE 9.2** Content Options for an `attribute` Element

| Element | Description |
|---|---|
| annotation | The `annotation` element, discussed in Section 7.5, provides a way to document schema elements. |
| simpleType | A local simple type. An attribute type specifies the simple type that represents valid values for an attribute instance with either a `type` attribute or `simpleType` content. |

## Attribute Types

CHAPTER 9

The content pattern for the `attribute` element is:

`annotation? simpleType?`

Listing 9.8 portrays the XML representation of the complex type `addressType`, which specifies a local `zipPlus4` attribute type, which in turn specifies an anonymous `simpleType`.

**LISTING 9.8** An Attribute Type That Specifies an Anonymous `simpleType` (address.xsd)

```
<xsd:complexType name="addressType">
    <xsd:sequence>
        <xsd:element ref="addressLine"
                     minOccurs="1"
                     maxOccurs="2"/>
        <xsd:element name="city" type="xsd:string"/>
        <xsd:element name="state" type="xsd:string"/>
        <xsd:element name="country" type="xsd:string" fixed="US"/>
        <xsd:element name="zip" type="xsd:string"/>
        <xsd:element ref="effectiveDate"/>
    </xsd:sequence>
        <xsd:attribute name="zipPlus4"
                       use="optional">
            <xsd:simpleType>
                <xsd:restriction base="xsd:string">
                    <xsd:pattern value="[0-9]{5}-[0-9]{4}"/>
                </xsd:restriction>
            </xsd:simpleType>
        </xsd:attribute>
</xsd:complexType>
```

> **TIP**
>
> Chapter 10 provides information on specifying custom simple types.

The XML representation of an element type whose structure type is the complex type `addressType` might look like the following:

`<xsd:element name="address" type="addressType"/>`

Given the preceding element type, the following is valid in an XML instance:

```
<address zipPlus4="20000-1234">
    <POBox>123</POBox>
    <city>Small Town</city>
    <state>VA</state>
```

```
<country>US</country>
<zip>20000</zip>
<effectiveDate>2001-02-14</effectiveDate>
</address>
```

## 9.6 The `attributeGroup` Element

A *named attribute-use group* specifies a set of attribute uses. An *attribute use* is either a local attribute type, or a reference to a global attribute type. The XML schema specifies a named attribute-use group once; the XML schema references the named attribute-use group potentially many times. The named attribute-use group provides a convenient mechanism for defining complex types that require the same or similar attribute types. Additionally, named attribute-use groups provide modularity: Simply modifying a named attribute-use group indirectly modifies the complex types that reference that named attribute-use group.

The XML representation of a named attribute-use group is the `attributeGroup` element. Listing 9.2 portrays the specification and the use of a named attribute-use group.

> **TIP**
>
> The scope of local attribute types—but not global attribute type references—enclosed in a named attribute-use group changes depending on context. Specifically, the attribute types become local to the enclosing complex type.

### 9.6.1 Attributes of an `attributeGroup` Element

Because a named attribute-use group is little more than a set of attribute types, there are not many attributes needed to specify a named attribute-use group. Table 9.3 summarizes the attributes of an `attributeGroup` element.

**TABLE 9.3**  Attribute Summary for an `attributeGroup` Element

| Attribute | Description |
|---|---|
| id | The value of an `id` attribute uniquely identifies an element within the set of schema documents that comprise an XML schema. |
| name | The value of the `name` attribute is the name used to reference a named attribute-use group in the rest of the schema. |
| ref | The value of the `ref` attribute is a named attribute-use group. A complex type specifies the `ref` attribute to reference a named attribute-use group. A complex type with a reference to a named attribute-use group has identical functionality to a complex type that references the individual attributes specified by the named attribute-use group. |

### 9.6.1.1 The `id` Attribute of an `attributeGroup` Element

The value of an id attribute uniquely identifies an element within the set of schema documents that comprise an XML schema.

**ATTRIBUTE OVERVIEW**

**attributeGroup: id**

| | |
|---:|---|
| Value: | An ID. |
| Default: | None. |
| Constraints: | An id must be unique within an XML schema. |
| Required: | No. |

Listing 9.2 includes the XML representation of the `saleAttributeGroup` named attribute-use group, which has an id attribute with a value set to 'pricing.sale.ag'.

**WARNING**

Many of the validators on the market today do not properly enforce id uniqueness.

### 9.6.1.2 The `name` Attribute of an `attributeGroup` Element

A complex type specifies a name to include a named attribute-use group. This name must match the value of the name attribute of a named attribute-use group.

**ATTRIBUTE OVERVIEW**

**attributeGroup: name**

| | |
|---:|---|
| Value: | An NCName. |
| Default: | None. |
| Constraints: | The name and ref attributes are mutually exclusive. |
| Required: | The attributeGroup element must contain either a name attribute or a ref attribute. |

Listing 9.2 portrays the `saleAttributeGroup`, as well as references to this named attribute-use group.

### 9.6.1.3 The `ref` Attribute of an `attributeGroup` Element

A complex type references a named attribute-use group with the `ref` attribute. An XML schema specifies a named attribute-use group once; that XML schema references a named attribute-use group potentially many times.

---

**ATTRIBUTE OVERVIEW**

**attributeGroup: ref**

| | |
|---:|---|
| **Value:** | A QName that corresponds to a named attribute-use group. |
| **Default:** | None. |
| **Constraints:** | The `name` and `ref` attributes are mutually exclusive. |
| **Required:** | The `attributeGroup` element must contain either a `name` attribute or a `ref` attribute. |

---

Listing 9.2 portrays the `saleAttributeGroup`, as well as references to this named attribute-use group.

## 9.6.2 Content Options for an `attributeGroup` Element

Other than an `annotation`, the content options for named attribute-use groups directly or indirectly specify attribute types. Table 9.4 illuminates the possible ways to specify attribute types.

**TABLE 9.4** Content Options for an `attributeGroup` Element

| Element | Description |
|---|---|
| annotation | The annotation element, discussed in Section 7.5, provides a way to document schema elements. |
| attribute | An attribute element specifies a local attribute type, or references a global attribute type. |
| attributeGroup | A named attribute-use group may reference another named attribute-use group. |
| anyAttribute | A named attribute-use group may specify attributes by identifying attribute wildcards. |

The content pattern for the `attribute` element is:

annotation? (attribute | attributeGroup)* anyAttribute?

## 9.7 The anyAttribute Element

The `anyAttribute` element provides a mechanism for specifying attributes with what the XML Schema Recommendation calls a wildcard. The attribute wildcard permits a complex type to loosely specify how an XML validator validates attributes in an XML instance. This is in sharp contrast to the normal `attribute` and `attributeGroup` elements, which succinctly specify one or a set of attribute types, respectively.

An attribute wildcard generally specifies a set of namespaces against which the XML validator may validate. The XML validator searches each namespace for global attribute types that might correspond to the attributes referenced in the XML instance.

### 9.7.1 Attributes of an anyAttribute Element

The attributes of an `anyAttribute` element are complicated. Table 9.5 provides a summary of the attributes for an `anyAttribute` element.

**TABLE 9.5**  Attribute Summary for an anyAttribute Element

| Attribute | Description |
| --- | --- |
| id | The value of an `id` attribute uniquely identifies an element within the set of schema documents that comprise an XML schema. |
| namespace | The value of the `namespace` attribute specifies a list of namespaces that might provide global attribute types for validating a corresponding attribute in an XML instance. |
| processContents | The value of the `processContents` attribute determines whether the XML validator validates the names of the attributes against attribute types, and the attribute values against the attribute types' structure types. |

#### 9.7.1.1 The id Attribute of an anyAttribute Element

The value of an `id` attribute uniquely identifies an element within the set of schema documents that comprise an XML schema.

> **ATTRIBUTE OVERVIEW**
>
> **anyAttribute: id**
>
> **Value:** An ID.
> **Default:** None.
> **Constraints:** An id must be unique within an XML schema.
> **Required:** No.

Listing 9.3 portrays an example that specifies the id attribute for an anyAttribute element.

## 9.7.1.2 The namespace Attribute of an anyAttribute Element

The value of the namespace attribute specifies the namespaces that an XML validator examines to determine the validity of an attribute in an XML instance. The attribute in the XML instance must correspond to a global attribute type specified in one of the namespaces, but only if the processContents attribute is 'strict' (see Section 9.7.1.3).

> **ATTRIBUTE OVERVIEW**
>
> **anyAttribute: namespace**
>
> **Value:** '##any', '##other', or a space-delimited list containing URIs, '##targetNamespace' or '##local'.
> **Default:** '##any'.
> **Constraints:** None.
> **Required:** No.

An attribute in an XML instance must correspond to global attribute types specified in the namespaces that may correspond to the constants defined in the following list:

- The value '##any' indicates any of the namespaces available to the XML instance.
- The value '##targetNamespace' indicates the namespace specified by the targetNamespace attribute of the schema element in the corresponding XML Schema.
- The value '##other' indicates a namespace that is any namespace *except* the namespace specified by the targetNamespace attribute of the schema element in the corresponding XML Schema.

- The value '##local' indicates that the attribute in the XML instance does not pertain to a known namespace. Furthermore, the attribute must be unqualified.

Note that Listing 9.3 demonstrates the use of the namespace attribute. Furthermore, note that the value of the namespace argument could be '##targetNamespace' or 'http://www.XMLSchemaReference.com/examples'—instead of '##all'—with the same effect, because the attribute a1 exists in the target namespace.

### 9.7.1.3 The processContents Attribute of an anyAttribute Element

The processContents attribute interacts with the namespace attribute. In particular, some of the values applicable to the processContents attribute negate the value of using the namespace attribute because the XML validator either ignores the namespace or does minimal validation.

---

**ATTRIBUTE OVERVIEW**

**anyAttribute: processContents**

| | |
|---:|:---|
| **Value:** | One of 'lax', 'skip', or 'strict'. |
| **Default:** | 'strict'. |
| **Constraints:** | None. |
| **Required:** | No. |

---

The processContents attribute has one of three values. These values have the following meaning:

- 'strict': The XML validator enforces that an element in an XML instance validates against an element type in one of the namespaces specified by the namespace attribute.
- 'skip': Other than enforcing that an element is well formed, the XML validator does not attempt to validate the element against an element type.
- 'lax': The XML validator validates the element when possible. When the validator locates a corresponding element type, the element must conform to the element type's structure type. Conversely, when there is no corresponding element type, the validator deems the element and contents valid.

Listing 9.3 demonstrates the use of the processContents attribute.

## 9.7.2 Content Options for an `anyAttribute` Element

Table 9.6 identifies the only content option available to an attribute wildcard: the ubiquitous annotation element.

**TABLE 9.6**  Content Options for an `anyAttribute` Element

| Element | Description |
| --- | --- |
| annotation | The annotation element, discussed in Section 7.5, provides a way to document schema elements. |

The content pattern for the `anyAttribute` is:

annotation?

# Simple Types

**CHAPTER 10**

## IN THIS CHAPTER

- 10.1 An Example of a Simple Type Derived from the Built-in `token` Datatype   202
- 10.2 An Example of a Pattern-constrained Simple Type   203
- 10.3 An Example of a Simple Type Derived from a User-derived Simple Type   204
- 10.4 Concepts and Observations   204
- 10.5 The `simpleType` Element   208
- 10.6 The `restriction` Element   212
- 10.7 The `list` Element   215
- 10.8 The `union` Element   221

# Simple Types

## CHAPTER 10

This chapter details how to write simple types. Simple types determine the range of possible values of an element or attribute in an XML instance. Simple types derive from either a built-in datatype or another derived simple type. The built-in datatypes fall mostly into the broad categories of strings, numbers, and dates. Chapter 12 contains more detail on the built-in datatypes.

A `simpleType` element is the XML representation of a simple type in an XML schema document. Unlike an element type or an attribute type, but like a complex type, an XML instance cannot directly contain an instance of a simple type. The simple type must be the structure type of an element type or an attribute type.

A simple type restricts the value of an element or attribute instance. A *constraining facet* specifies a restriction. Each simple type can have multiple constraining facets.

> **WARNING**
>
> Some constraining facets affect the *lexical space* of a value; some affect the *value space*. Furthermore, an XML validator transliterates every value into its *canonical representation*. In order to avoid unexpected behavior, a thorough understanding of how constraining facet perform is imperative. See Section 10.4.1 for more information.

## 10.1 An Example of a Simple Type Derived from the Built-in token Datatype

The `simpleType` element restricts the value of another simple type. Listing 10.1 demonstrates the XML representation of `partNameType`. A part name represents a short description of a part. The name is limited to 40 characters, perhaps due to database or screen real estate limitations.

**LISTING 10.1** A Simple Type Derived from a Token (`catalog.xsd`)

```
<xsd:simpleType name="partNameType"
            final="list,union"
            id="catalog.partName.sType">
    <xsd:annotation>
        <xsd:documentation xml:lang="en">
            A part name can be almost anything.
            The name is a short description.
        </xsd:documentation>
    </xsd:annotation>
    <xsd:restriction base="xsd:token"
```

```
            id="pnt-rst">
   <xsd:minLength value="1"/>
   <xsd:maxLength value="40"/>
  </xsd:restriction>
</xsd:simpleType>
```

An element type whose structure type is `partNameType` might look like the following element:

`<xsd:element name="partName" type="partNameType"/>`

Given the preceding element type, the following element is valid in an XML instance:

`<partName>Short Description of Unit 1</partName>`

## 10.2 An Example of a Pattern-Constrained Simple Type

Another example of a simple type is the `partNumberType` in Listing 10.2. The `partNumberType` contains a `pattern` that determines the valid values for a part number in a corresponding XML instance. The `annotation` provides an explanation of the pattern.

**LISTING 10.2** A Pattern-constrained Simple Type (`catalog.xsd`)

```
<xsd:simpleType name="partNumberType"
             final="union"
             id="catalog.partNumber.sType">
   <xsd:annotation>
      <xsd:documentation xml:lang="en">
         Declaration of a part number.
         Each part number consists of one to
         three alphabetic characters followed by
         one to eight digits. The following part
         numbers, for example, are valid:
            J1
            ABC32897
            ZZ22233344
      </xsd:documentation>
   </xsd:annotation>
      <xsd:restriction base="xsd:token">
         <xsd:pattern value="[A-Z]{1,3}\d{1,8}"/>
      </xsd:restriction>
</xsd:simpleType>
```

The next section demonstrates instantiating a derivation of `partNumberType`.

## 10.3 An Example of a Simple Type Derived from a User-derived Simple Type

The two previous examples demonstrate simple types derived from the built-in `token` type. Listing 10.3 portrays the `assemblyPartNumberType` derived from the `partNumberType` that is declared in Listing 10.2.

**LISTING 10.3**  Restricting a User-derived Simple Type (catalog.xsd)

```
<xsd:simpleType name="assemblyPartNumberType"
                final="#all"
                id="catalog.assemblypartNumber.sType">
    <xsd:annotation>
        <xsd:documentation xml:lang="en">
            An "assembly" represents a pre-built
            collection of unit items. The
            part number for an assembly
            always starts with "ASM."
        </xsd:documentation>
    </xsd:annotation>
    <xsd:restriction base="partNumberType">
        <xsd:pattern value="ASM\d{1,8}"/>
    </xsd:restriction>
</xsd:simpleType>
```

An element type whose structure type is `assemblyPartNumberType` might look like the following element:

```
<xsd:element name="partNumber"
             type="assemblyPartNumberType"/>
```

Given the preceding element type, the following element is valid in an XML instance:

```
<partNumber>ASM9001</partNumber>
```

## 10.4 Concepts and Observations

Creating a simple type is easy. Nonetheless, there are a few things to consider when creating a new simple type. This section covers adding constraining facets to simple types, noting the lack of non-instantiable simple types, specifying the scope of simple types, and blocking of simple types.

Each simple type has a value space and a lexical space. Furthermore, every value in the value space has a canonical lexical representation. This section covers these concepts.

## 10.4.1 Constraining Facets

The Schema Recommendation limits the use of constraining facets to simple types. Constraining facets enforce additional restrictions to a simple type derived directly or indirectly from a built-in datatype.

Listing 10.1 contains a simple example of a constraining facet associated with the `partNameType`. The `partNameType` is a restriction of the built-in `token` type. The `minLength` and `maxLength` constraining facets restrict `partNameType` to a short description of 40 characters.

The constraining facets also apply to simple types that are lists or unions of other simple types. Sections 10.5.3, 10.6.3, 10.7.3, and 10.8.3 cover the constraining facets of `simpleType`, `restriction`, `list`, and `union`, respectively.

> **TIP**
>
> The `restriction` element provides functionality for adding constraining facets to a simple type.

A `restriction` element contains constraining facets. The previously itemized sections discuss the constraining facets associated with different types. Sometimes the constraining facets occur in places that are not always obvious. Lists and unions, for example, require further derivations to add constraining facets.

## 10.4.2 The Value Space

The *value space* defines the range of permissible values. The following simple type specifies an integer between –5 and 5, inclusive, by restricting the value space:

```
<xsd:simpleType name="valueAbsoluteLessEqualFiveType">
    <xsd:annotation>
        <xsd:documentation xml:lang="en">
            This simple type specifies a range
            of integer values between -5 and 5,
            inclusive.
        </xsd:documentation>
    </xsd:annotation>
    <xsd:restriction base="xsd:integer">
        <xsd:minInclusive value="-5"/>
        <xsd:maxInclusive value="5"/>
    </xsd:restriction>
</xsd:simpleType>
```

The value space for this simple type contains the integers between –5 and 5. The lexical space automatically loses all numerals that don't name integers outside this range.

### 10.4.3 The Lexical Space

The *lexical space* defines the range of character-string representations of the values. Compare the previous example with the next example, which directly constrains the lexical space with a pattern:

```
<xsd:simpleType name="lexicalAbsoluteLessEqualFiveType">
    <xsd:annotation>
        <xsd:documentation xml:lang="en">
            This simple type specifies a range
            of integer values between -5 and 5,
            inclusive.
        </xsd:documentation>
    </xsd:annotation>
    <xsd:restriction base="xsd:integer">
        <xsd:pattern value="0|(-?[1-5])"/>
    </xsd:restriction>
</xsd:simpleType>
```

This example differs from the previous one in that it disallows "redundant leading zero" representations such as '001'.

In general, constraining facets should specify restrictions on the value space when appropriate. For example, specifying a pattern conceptually similar to the previous example, but for a *decimal* range between -5.0 and 5.0, is suspect at best.

### 10.4.4 The Canonical Lexical Representation

Each value in the value space has a canonical lexical representation. The *canonical lexical representation* of a value is the "official" *lexical* representation of a value. For example, the canonical lexical representation of the float value having representations '5', '5.0', '0005.000', and '5.0E0' is '5.0E0'. Off hand, it appears that that canonical lexical representation is of no interest to the schema writer. On the contrary, the Schema Recommendation requires that all default values adhere to the following constraint:

> If an element type or attribute type specifies a default or fixed value, that value must be valid with respect to the structure type.

This can lead to the presumably unintended situation where the canonical representation of the default value invalidates the simple type. The following scenario demonstrates this unfortunate situation. Listing 10.4 is a simple type that specifies a float value that might store dollar values.

**LISTING 10.4**   A Simple Type to Store Dollar Values (`pricing.xsd`)

```
<xsd:simpleType name="dollarType">
    <xsd:annotation>
        <xsd:documentation xml:lang="en">
            This simple type specifies decimal
            values that conform to scientific
            notation.
        </xsd:documentation>
    </xsd:annotation>
    <xsd:restriction base="xsd:float">
<xsd:pattern value="[0-9]+\.[0-9][0-9]"/>
    </xsd:restriction>
</xsd:simpleType>
```

Note that the canonical form of a float requires exactly one digit before the decimal point.

The following element type is invalid, because the canonical lexical representation of the default value (even if represented as '1.0E2' in the element type) cannot conform to the pattern specified by `dollarType`:

```
<xsd:element name="dollar"
            type="dollarType"
            default="100.00"/>
```

## 10.4.5 Non-instantiable Simple Types

Simple types are always instantiable. The XML representation of a simple type cannot specify a non-instantiable simple type. Furthermore, because a simple type does not contain element types or attribute types, there are no implicitly non-instantiable simple types. The inability to specify a simple type as non-instantiable means the XML representation of a schema cannot describe a simple type that an element cannot reference. For example, an element type is not supposed to associate the `partNumberType` in Listing 10.2 as a structure type. Instead, an element type is supposed to associate a derived type such as the `assemblyPartNumberType`. Unfortunately, there is no way to prevent an element type from directly using `partNumberType`. Conceptually, `partNumberType` is non-instantiable; in practice, `partNumberType` is always instantiable. To reiterate, the XML schema does not prohibit the ensuing element type:

```
<xsd:element name="partNumber" type="partNumberType"/>
```

Note that both complex types and element types may be non-instantiable.

> **WARNING**
>
> The inability to declare a simple type non-instantiable could lead to unintended use of what conceptually a non-instantiable base simple type. This unintended use would occur in the XML instance, such as the one portrayed in Section 10.4.2.

### 10.4.6 Global, Local, and Anonymous Simple Types

A simple type can be global or local. A local simple type can be anonymous; in other words, a local simple type does not require a name. Complex types, element types, attribute types, and other simple types can reference a global simple type. Sections 10.7 and 10.8 (which cover lists and unions, respectively) provide examples of both local and global simple types.

### 10.4.7 Blocking

The `simpleType` element can have only the `final` attribute, not the `block` attribute. In general, the `final` attribute blocks the schema from further derivations of a simple type; the `block` attribute blocks a corresponding XML instance from specifying further derivations of a simple type. Presumably, because all simple types are instantiable, the World Wide Web Consortium (W3C) Schema Working Group found little value in supporting the `block` attribute.

## 10.5 The `simpleType` Element

The XML representation of a simple type is a `simpleType` element. A `simpleType` must contain exactly one of the following elements: `restriction`, `list`, or `union`. Because all three of the aforementioned elements are moderately complex, this chapter includes a section for each element. The `simpleType` and `restriction` elements cover the majority of simple types, which are frequently easy derivations of built-in datatypes.

### 10.5.1 Attributes of a `simpleType` Element

The `simpleType` element has only three attributes: `final`, `id`, and `name`. All three of these attributes behave similarly to the identically named attributes for the `element` element. Chapter 8 provides details on the `element` element. Table 10.1 provides an overview of the simple type attributes.

**TABLE 10.1** Attribute Summary of a `simpleType` Element

| Attribute | Description |
|---|---|
| final | The value of the `final` attribute is a space-delimited list containing any combination of 'list', 'union', or 'restriction'. This further restricts derivations of simple types specifically `list`, `union`, or `restriction`, respectively. The value '#all' indicates that no further derivations are possible. |
| id | The value of the `id` attribute uniquely identifies an element. |
| name | The value of the `name` attribute is the name of a simple type. A derived simple type references this name as the base simple type. An element type references this name to associate a structure type. |

### 10.5.1.1 The `final` Attribute of a `simpleType` Element

The `final` attribute restricts the ability to derive other types. Its values are defined as follows:

- 'list': prevents a derived type from creating a list of the restricted type.
- 'union': prevents a derived type from using the restricted type in a union.
- 'restriction': prevents a derived type from using constraining facets to further restrict the restricted type.
- '#all': prohibits all further derivations.

---

**ATTRIBUTE OVERVIEW**

**simpleType: final**

- **Value:** Any or all of 'list', 'union', or 'restriction'. The value '#all' can be used as a shortcut for a list containing all three values.
- **Default:** In general, there is no default. However, a `schema` element can set a global default by setting the `finalDefault` attribute.
- **Constraints:** None.
- **Required:** No.

The `partNumberType` in Listing 10.2 has the `final` attribute set to `union`. Another simple type cannot be a union that contains `partNumberType` as a member type. Similarly, the `assemblyPartNumberType` in Listing 10.2 cannot have any derived classes, including those that might further restrict the value of an element in a corresponding XML instance. Listings 10.1, 10.3, 10.6, 10.8, and 10.9 also contain examples that incorporate the `final` attribute.

> **WARNING**
>
> Many existing XML parsers do not respect the `final` attribute of simple types or complex types.

### 10.5.1.2 The `id` Attribute of a `simpleType` Element

The value of an `id` attribute uniquely identifies an element within the set of schema documents that comprise an XML schema. Listing 10.1 provides an example that associates an `id` attribute with a `simpleType` element.

**ATTRIBUTE OVERVIEW**

**simpleType: id**

| | |
|---|---|
| **Value:** | An ID. |
| **Default:** | None. |
| **Constraints:** | An `id` must be unique within an XML schema. |
| **Required:** | No. |

Most of the examples in this chapter uniquely identify the type.

> **WARNING**
>
> Many of the existing XML parsers to not enforce the uniqueness of an `id`.

### 10.5.1.3 The `name` Attribute of a `simpleType` Element

The value of `name` is the name used in the schema to reference a `simpleType`.

## 10.5 The simpleType Element

---

**ATTRIBUTE OVERVIEW**

**simpleType: name**

- **Value:** An NCName.
- **Default:** None.
- **Constraints:** None.
- **Required:** Yes, unless the `simpleType` is local to an element type, another simple type, or a complex type—in which case the name is prohibited. A `simpleType` without a name is *anonymous*.

---

Section 10.4.3 discusses the usage and requirements of the name attribute. Listing 10.1 provides an example that associates the name attribute with a `simpleType` element.

### 10.5.2 Content Options for a simpleType Element

This section itemizes the possible child elements of a `simpleType` element. Table 10.2 provides a quick summary of all the content options.

**TABLE 10.2** Content Options for a `simpleType` Element

| Element | Description |
| --- | --- |
| annotation | The annotation element, discussed in Section 7.5, provides a way to document schema elements. |
| restriction | The restriction element provides functionality for adding constraining facets to a derived simple type. |
| list | The list element provides functionality for creating a simple type that specifies a list of simple type values. |
| union | The union element provides functionality for creating a simple type that specifies a selection from a set of simple type values. |

The content pattern for a `simpleType` element is:

annotation? (restriction | list | union)

### 10.5.3 Constraining Facets of a simpleType Element

Constraining facets can be associated with a simple type for three reasons:

- The user-derived simple type further restricts a built-in datatype or another, atomic user-derived simple type ultimately derived from a built-in datatype.

- The user-derived simple type restricts a list containing simple type values.
- The user-derived simple type restricts a union whose member types are other simple types.

For simple types ultimately derived as a restriction of a built-in datatype—as opposed to a list or union—the constraining facets apply to the base datatype. A constraining facet limits the values that are permissible in an XML instance. These limits are in addition to those constraining facets already associated with the base simple type. For example, the `partNameType` introduced in Listing 10.1 is a refinement, or restriction, of the built-in `token` type. Similarly, the values permissible for the `assemblyPartNumberType` presented in Listing 10.3 are constrained further than the `partNumberType` in Listing 10.2. Chapter 12 discusses constraining facets in detail.

Sections 10.7.3 and 10.8.3 illuminate the constraining facets of the `list` and `union` elements, respectively.

## 10.6 The `restriction` Element

The `restriction` element provides the functionality to add constraining facets to a simple type. For all simple types except those that represent lists and unions, the `simpleType` contains a `restriction`. In the case of a list or a union, a simple type derived from the list or union must add the restrictions.

### 10.6.1 Attributes of a `restriction` Element

A `restriction` has two attributes: `base` and `id` Table 10.3 provides a brief summary of the `base` and `id` attributes. The subsequent two sections discuss these attributes in detail.

**TABLE 10.3**  Attribute Summary for a `restriction` Element

| Attribute | Description |
|---|---|
| base | The value of the `base` attribute identifies the base simple type, which is often a built-in datatype, of the current derived simple type. |
| id | The value of an `id` attribute uniquely identifies an element within the set of schema documents that comprise an XML schema. |

#### 10.6.1.1 The `base` Attribute of a `restriction` Element

The value of a `base` attribute indicates the global base type. The base type must be a global simple type. The new simple type typically restricts the base simple type by adding constraining facets.

> **ATTRIBUTE OVERVIEW**
>
> **restriction: base**
>
> **Value:** A QName.
> **Default:** None.
> **Constraints:** The base type must refer to a global simple type in the XML schema. The specification of the `base` attribute and the specification of a local simple type are mutually exclusive.
> **Required:** No.

Most of the listings in this chapter use the `base` attribute. In fact, most simple types, except for those specifying lists or unions, make use of the `base` attribute.

### 10.6.1.2 The `id` Attribute of a `restriction` Element

The value of an `id` attribute uniquely identifies an element within the set of schema documents that comprise an XML schema.

> **ATTRIBUTE OVERVIEW**
>
> **restriction: id**
>
> **Value:** An ID.
> **Default:** None.
> **Constraints:** An id must be unique within an XML schema.
> **Required:** No.

Listing 10.1 contains an example of a `restriction` that specifies an `id` attribute.

## 10.6.2 Content Options for a `restriction` Element

The content options for a `restriction` element, when nested within a `simpleType` element, are limited to an `annotation`, a `simpleType`, and a set of appropriate constraining facets. The base built-in datatype determines the appropriate constraining facets. Table 10.4 provides a summary of content options. Note that the entire chapter illuminates the limitations of an embedded `simpleType`. The sections on constraining facets portray multiple ways for applying constraining facets to restrictions, lists, and unions.

**TABLE 10.4** Content Options for a `restriction` Element

| Element | Description |
| --- | --- |
| annotation | The `annotation` element, discussed in Section 7.5, provides a way to document schema elements. |
| enumeration | The value of an `enumeration` constraining facet specifies a possible (constant) value. |
| fractionDigits | The value of a `fractionDigits` constraining facet determines the number of digits after the decimal point in a decimal number. |
| length | The value of a `length` constraining facet specifies the exact length of a string of characters that must appear in an element instance, after normalization. This constraining facet also specifies the number of items in a list (see the caveats regarding `hexBinary` and `base64binary` datatypes in Section 12.4.3). |
| maxExclusive | The value of the `maxExclusive` constraining facet specifies an upper bound on a numeric value. This boundary excludes the value specified. |
| maxInclusive | The value of the `minInclusive` constraining facet specifies an upper bound on a numeric value. This boundary includes the value specified. |
| maxLength | The value of the `maxLength` constraining facet specifies the maximum number of characters in a string, after normalization or the maximum number of items in a list (see caveats on `hexBinary` and `base64Binary` in Section 12.4.3). |
| minExclusive | The value of the `minExclusive` constraining facet specifies a lower bound on a numeric value. This boundary excludes the value specified. |
| minInclusive | The value of a `minInclusive` constraining facet specifies a lower bound on a numeric value. This boundary includes the value specified. |
| minLength | The value of a `minLength` constraining facet specifies the minimum number of characters in a string, after normalization or the minimum number of items in a list. |
| pattern | The value of a `pattern` constraining facet specifies a regular expression often used to validate a character string. Specifically, the pattern constrains lexical representations. |
| totalDigits | The value of a `totalDigits` constraining facet specifies the total number of digits in a decimal number. |
| simpleType | The `simpleType` element specifies a local simple type. |
| whiteSpace | The value of a `whiteSpace` constraining facet determines the normalization of spaces, carriage returns, and line feeds in a string. This normalization frequently removes undesirable white space. |

The content pattern for a restriction element is:

```
annotation? simpleType? (minExclusive |
                         minInclusive |
                         maxExclusive |
                         maxInclusive |
                         totalDigits |
                         fractionDigits |
                         length |
                         minLength |
                         maxLength |
                         enumeration |
                         whiteSpace |
                         pattern)*
```

The content options for simple types vary according to which element includes the restriction element. Refer to Sections 10.7.3 and 10.8.3 for further clarification: These sections illuminate the constraining facets that apply to list and union elements, respectively. Chapter 12 portrays the applicability of constraining facets to each built-in datatype.

### 10.6.3 Constraining Facets of a restriction Element

The base built-in datatype associated with the simple type determines appropriate constraining facets of a restriction element. Chapter 12 provides a discussion on which constraining facets are applicable to which built-in datatype.

## 10.7 The list Element

A simple type can specify a space-delimited list consisting of values specified by other global or local simple types. An instance of a list declared in the context of a simple type has all the values contained within a single element:

```
<listElement>value1 value2 value3</listElement>
```

> **TIP**
>
> The list element does *not* support the notion of a list comprised of repeating elements:
>
> ```
> <element>value1</element>
> <element>value2</element>
> <element>value3</element>
> ```
>
> Both the element element (covered in Chapter 8) and the complexType element (covered in Chapter 11) support repeating elements.

Listing 10.5 shows the XML representation of `partNumberListType`, which contains a list of `partNumberType`. Listing 10.2 portrays the `partNumberType` referenced by the `itemType` attribute of `partNumberListType`.

**LISTING 10.5**  Specifying a List of Simple Types (`catalog.xsd`)

```
<xsd:simpleType name="partNumberListType"
            id="catalog.partNumber.list.sType">
    <xsd:annotation>
        <xsd:documentation xml:lang="en">
            The "partNumberListType" describes the value
            for an element that contains a set of part
            numbers.  Given that a part number might look
            like any of the following:
                J1
                ABC32897
                ZZ22233344
            A list of these part numbers might look like:
                J1 ABC32897 ZZ22233344
        </xsd:documentation>
    </xsd:annotation>
    <xsd:list id="transaction.partNumberList"
            itemType="partNumberType">
    </xsd:list>
</xsd:simpleType>
```

An element type whose structure type is `partNumberListType` might look like the following element:

```
<xsd:element name="partNumberList" type="partNumberListType"/>
```

Given the preceding element type, the following element specifying the requisite space-delimited list is valid in an XML instance:

```
<partNumberList>J1 ABC32897 ZZ22233344</partNumberList>
```

## 10.7.1 Attributes of a `list` Element

The `list` element has two optional attributes. The first is the ubiquitous `id` attribute. The other is the `itemType` attribute that specifies the valid simple type of values that are acceptable in the list. Table 10.5 provides an overview of the attributes appropriate for a `list` element.

> **TIP**
>
> A list of values is always space delimited. Therefore, the value specified by the `itemType` attribute or `simpleType` element must not specify values that contain a space.

## 10.7 The list Element

**TABLE 10.5** Attribute Summary for a `list` Element

| Attribute | Description |
|---|---|
| id | The value of an `id` attribute uniquely identifies an element within the set of schema documents that comprise an XML schema. |
| itemType | The value of an `itemType` attribute is a global simple type. A value permitted by the simple type specified by the `itemType` is a valid item value in the list. |

The space character (' ') delimits a list of values: A value in a list may not contain embedded spaces besides the delimiter. A list could contain the colors 'cyan', 'magenta', 'yellow', and 'black'. The resultant list might look like the following instance:

`<colors>yellow cyan</colors>`

The list could *not* contain 'Ocean', 'Pink Grapefruit', 'Sunshine', and 'Midnight'. The theoretical resultant list might look like the following invalid instance, which, examined carefully, appears to have *five* values:

`<colors>Ocean Pink Grapefruit Sunshine Midnight<colors>`

The Schema recommendation does not require or allow that the XML parsers distinguish that the previous example has four, not five, values in the list specified by the `colors` element.

### 10.7.1.1 The id Attribute of a list Element

The value of an `id` attribute uniquely identifies an element within the set of schema documents that comprise an XML schema.

---
**ATTRIBUTE OVERVIEW**

**list: id**

- **Value:** An ID.
- **Default:** None.
- **Constraints:** An `id` attribute must be unique within an XML schema.
- **Required:** No.
---

Listing 10.4 demonstrates the use of the `id` attribute in conjunction with a `list` element.

### 10.7.1.2 The `itemType` Attribute of a `list` Element

The value of the `itemType` attribute references a global simple type. The simple type referenced by the `itemType` specifies the value of individual items in the list.

---

**ATTRIBUTE OVERVIEW**

**list: itemType**

- **Value:** A QName.
- **Default:** None.
- **Constraints:** The value must be the name of a global simple type.
- **Required:** No. Either the `itemType` attribute or a local `simpleType` element is required; they are mutually exclusive.

---

Listing 10.4 demonstrates the use of the `itemType` attribute in conjunction with a `list` element.

## 10.7.2 Content Options for a `list` Element

The `list` element has two optional content options: `annotation` and `simpleType`. The `annotation` element documents the `list`. The `simpleType` element specifies the valid individual values that may be contained in an XML instance of the list. The syntax for the `simpleType` element is recursive in the sense that virtually anything in this chapter might appear within the local `simpleType`. Table 10.6 provides an overview of the content options for the `list` element.

**TABLE 10.6** Content Options for a `list` Element

| Element | Description |
| --- | --- |
| annotation | The annotation element, discussed in Section 7.5, provides a way to document schema elements. |
| simpleType | The valid contents of the list are determined either by this local `simpleType`, or by the simple type referenced in the value of an `itemType` attribute. |

The content pattern for a `list` element is:

`annotation? simpleType?`

The XML representation of a list might contain local simple types. Listing 10.6 is a rewrite of the `partNumberListType` presented in Listing 10.5. The only difference is that `partNumberType` is anonymous in Listing 10.6.

**LISTING 10.6** A Simple Type with an Anonymous List Item Simple Type (`listExamples.xsd`)

```xml
<xsd:simpleType name="partNumberListType"
                final="list">
    <xsd:annotation>
        <xsd:documentation xml:lang="en">
            A transaction consists of an order (or return)
            of a list of parts.  Each part number consists
            of 1 to 3 alpha characters followed by 1 to 8
            numeric characters.  The following part numbers,
            for example, are valid:
                J1
                ABC32897
                ZZ22233344
            Note that the "list" of these part numbers
            might look like:
                J1 ABC32897 ZZ22233344
        </xsd:documentation>
    </xsd:annotation>
        <xsd:list id="transaction.partNumberList">
        <xsd:simpleType>
            <xsd:annotation>
                <xsd:documentation xml:lang="en">
                    Anonymous declaration of a part number.
                    Each part number consists of 1 to 3 alpha
                    characters followed by 1 to 8 numerics.
                    The following part numbers, for
                    example, are valid:
                        J1
                        ABC32897
                        ZZ22233344
                </xsd:documentation>
            </xsd:annotation>
            <xsd:restriction base="xsd:token">
                <xsd:pattern value="[A-Z]{1,3}\d{1,8}"/>
            </xsd:restriction>
        </xsd:simpleType>
    </xsd:list>
</xsd:simpleType>
```

Note that the XML representation of the element type is the same as when the simple type describing the list is global:

```xml
<xsd:element name="partNumberList" type="partNumberListType"/>
```

Not surprisingly, the same XML instance works too:

```xml
<partNumberList>J1 ABC32897 ZZ22233344</partNumberList>
```

### 10.7.3 Constraining Facets of a `list` Element

The values in a list are constrained by either the `itemType` attribute or a nested `simpleType`. The list, however, may be further constrained by constraining facets that apply to the list—not the list items. Like most simple types, only certain constraining facets apply to lists. Table 10.7 provides a summary of the constraining facets applicable to a `list`.

> **WARNING**
>
> Part 1 of the W3C XML Schema specification incorrectly states, "Only length, minLength, maxLength, pattern and enumeration facet components are allowed among the {facets}." Part 2, however, correctly specifies that the `whiteSpace` attribute is applicable. Part 2 also specifies that `whiteSpace` is fixed to 'collapse' making the difference largely academic. However, because of the discrepancy between these two documents, XML parsers may or may not accept the `whiteSpace` attribute.

**TABLE 10.7** Constraining Facets of a `list`

| Constraining Facet | Description |
| --- | --- |
| `length` | The value of the `length` constraining facet specifies the number of elements that may be contained in the list. |
| `maxLength` | The value of the `maxLength` constraining facet specifies the maximum number of elements that may be contained in the list. |
| `minLength` | The value of the `minLength` constraining facet specifies the minimum number of elements that may be contained in the list. |
| `enumeration` | The value of the `enumeration` constraining facet specifies the actual values of the entire list that are valid in the corresponding XML instance. These values are additional to the constraining facets specified by the list's type. |
| `pattern` | The value of the `pattern` constraining facet contains a regular expression of values that may appear in a corresponding XML instance. This pattern specifies the value of the entire list. These values are additional to the constraining facets specified by the list's type. |
| `whiteSpace` | The value of the `whiteSpace` constraining facet specifies the validity of spaces, carriage returns, and line feeds in a string. The `whiteSpace` constraining facet is redundant for a list because the value of the `whiteSpace` constraining facet must be COLLAPSE. |

Listing 10.7 demonstrates a `list` whose `length` is constrained to contain only one item.

**LISTING 10.7**  A Constrained `list` (`listExamples.xsd`)

```
<xsd:simpleType name="oneItemPartNumberListType">
    <xsd:annotation>
        <xsd:documentation xml:lang="en">
            In some cases the list of part numbers
            must be restricted to just one item.
        </xsd:documentation>
    </xsd:annotation>
    <xsd:restriction base="partNumberListType">
        <xsd:length value="1"/>
    </xsd:restriction>
</xsd:simpleType>
```

## 10.8 The union Element

A simple type can specify a union of other simple types. The contents in the XML instance of an element constructed from a union can be any of the valid types. A union can be thought of as an "or" construct. That is, "a union b union c" is the conceptual representation of "a or b or c."

> **TIP**
>
> A `union` may contain member types that have completely distinct base types, as demonstrated in Listing 10.8.

Listing 10.8 demonstrates the XML representation of the `colorOptionType`, which is a union of the anonymously declared `standardColorOptionType`, `fancifulColorOptionType`, and `codedColorOptionType` enumerations.

**LISTING 10.8**  A `union` Specifying Local `simpleType` Elements (`catalog.xsd`)

```
<xsd:simpleType name="colorOptionType"
            id="catalog.colorOption.union.sType">
    <xsd:annotation>
        <xsd:documentation xml:lang="en">
            A part has one of the following color definitions:
                - a standard name (cyan, yellow, etc.),
                - a fanciful name (Ocean, Sunshine, etc.), or
```

*continues*

## Simple Types
### CHAPTER 10

```xml
                    - an internal code 1..n
             </xsd:documentation>
        </xsd:annotation>
        <xsd:union id="colorOptionType.union">

<xsd:simpleType name="standardColorOptionType"
                final="restriction"
                id="catalog.standardColorOption.sType">
        <xsd:annotation>
            <xsd:documentation xml:lang="en">
                Color selection is limited.
                The colors apply to unit and
                bulk items.
            </xsd:documentation>
        </xsd:annotation>
        <xsd:restriction base="xsd:token">
            <xsd:enumeration value="cyan"/>
            <xsd:enumeration value="magenta"/>
            <xsd:enumeration value="yellow"/>
            <xsd:enumeration value="black"/>
        </xsd:restriction>
    </xsd:simpleType>

<xsd:simpleType name="fancifulColorOptionType"
                final="restriction"
                id="catalog.fancifulColorOption.sType">
        <xsd:annotation>
            <xsd:documentation xml:lang="en">
                Color selection is limited.
                The colors apply to unit and
                bulk items.
            </xsd:documentation>
        </xsd:annotation>
        <xsd:restriction base="xsd:token">
            <xsd:enumeration value="Ocean"/>
            <xsd:enumeration value="Pink Grapefruit"/>
            <xsd:enumeration value="Sunshine"/>
            <xsd:enumeration value="Midnight"/>
        </xsd:restriction>
    </xsd:simpleType>

<xsd:simpleType name="codedColorOptionType"
                id="catalog.codedColorOption.sType">
        <xsd:annotation>
            <xsd:documentation xml:lang="en">
                A color can be defined by an
                internal integer that maps
```

```
                    directly to a standard or
                    fanciful color
                    1 = cyan = Ocean
                    2 = magenta = Pink Grapefruit
                    etc.
                </xsd:documentation>
            </xsd:annotation>
            <xsd:restriction base="xsd:positiveInteger">
                <xsd:maxInclusive value="4"/>
            </xsd:restriction>
        </xsd:simpleType>
    </xsd:union>
</xsd:simpleType>
```

An element type whose structure type is colorOptionType might look like the following element:

`<xsd:element name="color" type="colorOptionType"/>`

Given the preceding element type, the following color element containing the standard color 'magenta' is valid in an XML instance:

`<color>magenta</color>`

A fanciful name is also valid as a color:

`<color>Pink Grapefruit</color>`

Finally, a coded integer can determine the color:

`<color>2</color>`

## 10.8.1 Attributes of a union Element

The union element has two optional attributes. The first is the ubiquitous id attribute. The other is the memberTypes attribute that specifies the set of simple type from whose conceptual values form a union. Table 10.8 provides an overview of the attributes associated with a union element.

TABLE 10.8    Attribute Summary for a union Element

| Attribute | Description |
| --- | --- |
| id | The value of an id attribute uniquely identifies an element within the set of schema documents that comprise an XML schema. |
| memberTypes | The value of a memberTypes attribute is a list of global simple type names. Each member type specifies an acceptable set of values in the union. |

### 10.8.1.1 The `id` Attribute of a `union` Element

The value of an `id` attribute uniquely identifies an element within the set of schema documents that comprise an XML schema.

---
**ATTRIBUTE OVERVIEW**

**union: id**

- **Value:** An ID.
- **Default:** None.
- **Constraints:** An id must be unique within an XML schema.
- **Required:** No.

---

Listing 10.8 demonstrates the use of the `id` attribute in conjunction with a `union` element.

### 10.8.1.2 The `memberTypes` Attribute of a `union` Element

The `memberTypes` attribute specifies a set of simple types. The union is the set of all values represented by these types. The `union` element can specify `simpleType` elements locally in addition to, or instead of, the simple types associated with the `memberTypes` attribute.

---
**ATTRIBUTE OVERVIEW**

**union: memberTypes**

- **Value:** A list of QNames.
- **Default:** None.
- **Constraints:** Each QName in the value-list must refer to a global simple type.
- **Required:** No. The simple type can specify the `memberTypes` attribute, local simple types, or both.

---

The primary example for this section—Listing 10.8—shows the `colorOptionType` with anonymous member types. Listing 10.9 is a rewrite of Listing 10.8, demonstrating references to global member types; the `memberTypes` attribute references the global simple types that enumerate the color selections.

**LISTING 10.9** A union Specifying the memberTypes Attribute (unionExamples.xsd)

```xsd
<xsd:simpleType name="standardColorOptionType"
                final="restriction">
    <xsd:annotation>
        <xsd:documentation xml:lang="en">
            Color selection is limited.
            The colors apply to unit and
            bulk items.
        </xsd:documentation>
    </xsd:annotation>
    <xsd:restriction base="xsd:token">
        <xsd:enumeration value="cyan"/>
        <xsd:enumeration value="magenta"/>
        <xsd:enumeration value="yellow"/>
        <xsd:enumeration value="black"/>
    </xsd:restriction>
</xsd:simpleType>

<xsd:simpleType name="fancifulColorOptionType"
                final="restriction">
    <xsd:annotation>
        <xsd:documentation xml:lang="en">
            Color selection is limited.
            The colors apply to unit and
            bulk items.
        </xsd:documentation>
    </xsd:annotation>
    <xsd:restriction base="xsd:token">
        <xsd:enumeration value="Ocean"/>
        <xsd:enumeration value="Pink Grapefruit"/>
        <xsd:enumeration value="Sunshine"/>
        <xsd:enumeration value="Midnight"/>
    </xsd:restriction>
</xsd:simpleType>

<xsd:simpleType name="codedColorOptionType">
    <xsd:annotation>
        <xsd:documentation xml:lang="en">
            A color can be defined by an
            internal integer that maps
            directly to a standard or
            fanciful color
            1 = cyan = Ocean
            2 = magenta = Pink Grapefruit
            etc.
        </xsd:documentation>
```

*continues*

```xml
        </xsd:annotation>
        <xsd:restriction base="xsd:positiveInteger">
            <xsd:maxInclusive value="4"/>
        </xsd:restriction>
</xsd:simpleType>

<xsd:simpleType name="colorOptionType">
    <xsd:annotation>
        <xsd:documentation xml:lang="en">
            A part has one of the following color definitions:
            - a standard name (cyan, yellow, etc.),
            - a fanciful name (Ocean, Sunshine, etc.), or
            - an internal code 1..n
        </xsd:documentation>
    </xsd:annotation>
    <xsd:union id="colorOptionType.union"
               memberTypes="standardColorOptionType
                            fancifulColorOptionType
                            codedColorOptionType"/>
</xsd:simpleType>
```

## 10.8.2 Content Options for a union Element

The union element has only two options for associated content: an optional annotation and an optional simple type. The syntax for the simple type is recursive in the sense that virtually anything in this chapter might appear within the local simple type. Table 10.9 provides a quick summary of the available content options for union.

**TABLE 10.9** Content Options for a union Element

| Element | Description |
| --- | --- |
| annotation | The annotation element, discussed in Section 7.5, provides a way to document schema elements. |
| simpleType | The values specified by any local simpleType elements are acceptable values in the union. These values are in addition to those specified by the memberTypes attribute. |

The content pattern for a union element is:

annotation? simpleType*

A union might contain multiple member types. Any or all of these member types can be anonymous. Listing 10.8 demonstrates anonymous member types.

## 10.8.3 Constraining Facets of a union Element

Only the enumeration and pattern constraining facets listed in Table 10.10 are applicable to the union element. Chapter 12 discusses constraining facets in detail.

**TABLE 10.10** Constraining Facets of a union Element

| Constraining | Facet Description |
|---|---|
| enumeration | The value of the enumeration constraining facet is one of perhaps many values that are valid in an XML instance that corresponds to the union element. Any enumerated value is a further restriction of the constraining facets associated with the member types that comprise the union. |
| pattern | The value of the pattern constraining facet is a regular expression representing the valid values in an XML instance that corresponds to the union element. Any pattern is a further restriction of the constraining facets associated with the member types that make up the union. |

Listing 10.10 demonstrates a rather nonsensical restriction of the colorOptionType declared in Listing 10.8. The result of adding the pattern '.*c.*' to the new cColorUnionRestrictionType is that only values in the union that contain a 'c' are valid. Therefore, only 'Ocean' and 'cyan' are valid values of cColorUnionRestrictionType.

**LISTING 10.10** Adding Constraining Facets of a union Element (unionExamples.xsd)

```
<xsd:simpleType name="cColorUnionRestrictionType">
    <xsd:annotation>
        <xsd:documentation xml:lang="en">
            A restriction of all valid colors.
            In particular, the pattern only
            allows colors with the character 'c.'
            This limits the valid values to
            "cyan" and "Ocean."
        </xsd:documentation>
    </xsd:annotation>
    <xsd:restriction base="colorOptionType">
        <xsd:pattern value=".*c.*"/>
    </xsd:restriction>
</xsd:simpleType>
```

# Complex Types

**CHAPTER 11**

## IN THIS CHAPTER

- 11.1 An Example of a Complex Type Specifying Empty Content   230
- 11.2 An Example of a Complex Type That Adds Attributes to a Simple Type   231
- 11.3 An Example of a Complex Type Specifying Nested Element Types   234
- 11.4 An Example of a Complex Type Specifying Mixed Content   237
- 11.5 Concepts and Observations   238
- 11.6 The `complexType` Element   246
- 11.7 The `simpleContent` Element   255
- 11.8 The `complexContent` Element   258
- 11.9 The `extension` Element   260
- 11.10 The `restriction` Element   265
- 11.11 The `all` Element   271
- 11.12 The `choice` Element   274
- 11.13 The `sequence` Element   278
- 11.14 The `group` Element   281

Complex types provide sophisticated groupings of element types. Complex types specify the following functionality:

- Adding attribute types to simple types.
- Requiring *empty content*: An XML instance has no text or embedded elements. A complex type that specifies empty content may have attributes.
- Nesting element types.
- Permitting *mixed content*: An XML instance may contain text interspersed with elements.

A `complexType` element is the XML representation of a complex type in an XML schema document. Unlike an element type or an attribute type, but like a simple type, a complex type cannot be directly instantiated in an XML instance. The complex type must be associated with an element type (that is, the complex type must be the structure type of an element type).

## 11.1 An Example of a Complex Type Specifying Empty Content

A complex type can specify empty content. In other words, an XML instance that contains an element that is an instance of an element type whose structure type is this complex type does not contain any text or any other elements. The `freePriceType` complex type presented in Listing 11.1 is used to "price" items in the catalog that have no cost associated with them. Any discount catalog item has an `authorization` attribute. The complex type `freePriceType` has no content (that is, no base simple type or nested element types):

**LISTING 11.1**  A Complex Type Specifying Empty Content (`pricing.xsd`)

```
<xsd:complexType name="freePriceType"
                 block="#all"
                 final="#all"
                 id="freePriceType.pricing.cType">
    <xsd:annotation>
        <xsd:documentation xml:lang="en">
            Anything that is free has no
            value (i.e., price), but must
            have an authorization code.
            This is a complex type with
            "empty" content.
                -- Shorthand Notation --
        </xsd:documentation>
    </xsd:annotation>
    <xsd:attributeGroup ref="saleAttributeGroup"/>
</xsd:complexType>
```

```
<xsd:attributeGroup name="saleAttributeGroup">
    <xsd:annotation>
        <xsd:documentation xml:lang="en">
            Anything that is on sale (or free,
            which is a type of sale), must
            have an authorization defined.
            This is someone's name,
            initials, ID, etc.
        </xsd:documentation>
    </xsd:annotation>
    <xsd:attribute name="authorization" type="xsd:token"/>
</xsd:attributeGroup>
```

An element type whose structure type is `freePriceType` might look like the following element:

```
<xsd:element name="freePrice" type="freePriceType"/>
```

Given the preceding element type, the following element is valid in an XML instance:

```
<freePrice authorization="CB"/>
```

## 11.2 An Example of a Complex Type That Adds Attributes to a Simple Type

A complex type can add attribute types to a simple type. Listing 11.2 is the complex type `salePriceType`. `salePriceType` extends the globally described `dollarPriceType` simple type by adding the `saleAttributeGroup` attribute group. Note that the `simpleContent` element provides the functionality to extend simple types into complex types.

**LISTING 11.2**  Adding an Attribute to a Simple Type (`pricing.xsd`)

```
<xsd:complexType name="salePriceType"
                 block="#all"
                 final="extension"
                 id="salePriceType.pricing.cType">
    <xsd:annotation>
        <xsd:documentation xml:lang="en">
            Anything on sale must have a price
            and an authorization.
        </xsd:documentation>
    </xsd:annotation>
    <xsd:simpleContent>
        <xsd:extension base="dollarPriceType">
            <xsd:attributeGroup ref="saleAttributeGroup"/>
        </xsd:extension>
```

*continues*

## Complex Types
### CHAPTER 11

```xsd
            </xsd:simpleContent>
</xsd:complexType>

<xsd:attribute name="currency"
               type="xsd:token"
               fixed="U S Dollars">
    <xsd:annotation>
        <xsd:documentation xml:lang="en">
            U S Dollars are the only currency
            currently allowed.  This attribute
            is a great example of using "ref"
            (elsewhere), but is not set up well
            for extending to other currencies
            later.  This should really be a
            type that keeps getting restricted.
        </xsd:documentation>
    </xsd:annotation>
</xsd:attribute>

<xsd:simpleType name="currencyAmountType"
                id="pricing.currencyAmount.sType">
    <xsd:annotation>
        <xsd:documentation xml:lang="en">
            Limit all transactions to less than
            500,000.00 of any currency
            This can be represented as NNNNNN.NN
            or eight total digits, two of which are
            after the decimal point.

            ***********************************************
                Note that the W3C XML Schema
                Recommendation does not support
                non-instantiable simple types.

                This simple type is conceptually
                not instantiable.  This type is not
                intended to be used directly, only
                indirectly, such as via the ...DollarType
                simple types.
            ***********************************************
        </xsd:documentation>
    </xsd:annotation>
    <xsd:restriction base="xsd:decimal">
        <xsd:totalDigits value="8" fixed="true"/>
        <xsd:fractionDigits value="2" fixed="true"/>
        <xsd:minExclusive value="0.00" fixed="true"/>
        <xsd:maxInclusive value="500000.00" fixed="true"/>
```

```
        </xsd:restriction>
</xsd:simpleType>

<xsd:simpleType name="restrictedDollarAmountType"
                id="pricing.restrictedDollarAmount.sType">
    <xsd:annotation>
        <xsd:documentation xml:lang="en">
            Nothing sells for less than $1 or
            greater than or equal to $10,000.00.
        </xsd:documentation>
    </xsd:annotation>
    <xsd:restriction base="currencyAmountType">
        <xsd:minInclusive value="1.00"
                          fixed="true"/>
        <xsd:maxExclusive value="10000.00"
                          fixed="true"/>
    </xsd:restriction>
</xsd:simpleType>

<xsd:complexType name="dollarPriceType"
                 final="restriction"
                 block="restriction"
                 abstract="true"
                 id="dollarPriceType.pricing.cType">
    <xsd:annotation>
        <xsd:documentation xml:lang="en">
            Currently, currency is limited to
            U S Dollars. Note that this type is
            non-instantiable.  A derived type must be
            defined that sets the range.
        </xsd:documentation>
    </xsd:annotation>
    <xsd:simpleContent>
        <xsd:extension base="restrictedDollarAmountType">
            <xsd:attribute ref="currency"/>
        </xsd:extension>
    </xsd:simpleContent>
</xsd:simpleType>
```

The XML representation of an element type whose structure type is `salePriceType` might look like the following element:

```
<xsd:element name="salePrice" type="salePriceType"/>
```

Given the preceding element type, the following element is valid in an XML instance:

```
<salePrice>123.45</salePrice>
```

## 11.3 An Example of a Complex Type Specifying Nested Element Types

A complex type can specify multiple element types. An XML instance might contain an element whose element type's structure type is this complex type; the XML instance contains nested elements. Listing 11.3 demonstrates how to create an XML representation of a complex type that contains nested element types. The thematic catalog example has a `partOptionType` complex type. This `partOptionType` permits a catalog entry to have a nested `color`, `size`, or both.

**LISTING 11.3**  A Complex Type Specifying Nested Element Types (`catalog.xsd`)

```
<xsd:complexType name="partOptionType"
                 block="#all"
                 final="#all"
                 id="partOptionType.catalog.cType">
    <xsd:annotation>
        <xsd:documentation xml:lang="en">
            Appropriate parts can have a color,
            a size, or both.  Note that the use
            of the "all" element indicates that
            the "color" and "size" are unordered.
            That is, they can appear in either
            order.
                -- Shorthand Notation --
        </xsd:documentation>
    </xsd:annotation>
    <xsd:all id="pot.all">
        <xsd:element name="color"
                     type="colorOptionType"
                     minOccurs="0"
                     maxOccurs="1"/>
        <xsd:element name="size"
                     type="sizeOptionType"
                     minOccurs="0"
                     maxOccurs="1"/>
    </xsd:all>
</xsd:complexType>

<xsd:simpleType name="colorOptionType"
                id="catalog.colorOption.union.sType">
    <xsd:annotation>
        <xsd:documentation xml:lang="en">
            A part has one of the following color definitions:
                - a standard name (cyan, yellow, etc.),
```

## 11.3 An Example of a Complex Type Specifying Nested Element Types

```xml
              - a fanciful name (Ocean, Sunshine, etc.), or
              - an internal code 1..n
        </xsd:documentation>
    </xsd:annotation>
    <xsd:union id="colorOptionType.union">

        <xsd:simpleType name="standardColorOptionType"
                        final="restriction"
                        id="catalog.standardColorOption.sType">
            <xsd:annotation>
                <xsd:documentation xml:lang="en">
                    Color selection is limited.
                    The colors apply to unit and
                    bulk items.
                </xsd:documentation>
            </xsd:annotation>
            <xsd:restriction base="xsd:token">
                <xsd:enumeration value="cyan"/>
                <xsd:enumeration value="magenta"/>
                <xsd:enumeration value="yellow"/>
                <xsd:enumeration value="black"/>
            </xsd:restriction>
        </xsd:simpleType>

        <xsd:simpleType name="fancifulColorOptionType"
                        final="restriction"
                        id="catalog.fancifulColorOption.sType">
            <xsd:annotation>
                <xsd:documentation xml:lang="en">
                    Color selection is limited.
                    The colors apply to unit and
                    bulk items.
                </xsd:documentation>
            </xsd:annotation>
            <xsd:restriction base="xsd:token">
                <xsd:enumeration value="Ocean"/>
                <xsd:enumeration value="Pink Grapefruit"/>
                <xsd:enumeration value="Sunshine"/>
                <xsd:enumeration value="Midnight"/>
            </xsd:restriction>
        </xsd:simpleType>

        <xsd:simpleType name="codedColorOptionType"
                        id="catalog.codedColorOption.sType">
            <xsd:annotation>
                <xsd:documentation xml:lang="en">
```

*continues*

```
                        A color can be defined by an
                        internal integer that maps
                        directly to a standard or
                        fanciful color
                        1 = cyan = Ocean
                        2 = magenta = Pink Grapefruit
                        etc.
                    </xsd:documentation>
                </xsd:annotation>
                <xsd:restriction base="xsd:positiveInteger">
                    <xsd:maxInclusive value="4"/>
                </xsd:restriction>
            </xsd:simpleType>

        </xsd:union>
    </xsd:simpleType>

    <xsd:simpleType name="sizeOptionType"
                    final="#all"
                    id="catalog.sizeOption.sType">
        <xsd:annotation>
            <xsd:documentation xml:lang="en">
                Size selection is limited.
                The sizes apply to unit and
                bulk items.
            </xsd:documentation>
        </xsd:annotation>
        <xsd:restriction base="xsd:token">
            <xsd:enumeration value="tiny"/>
            <xsd:enumeration value="small"/>
            <xsd:enumeration value="medium"/>
            <xsd:enumeration value="large"/>
            <xsd:enumeration value="grandiose"/>
        </xsd:restriction>
    </xsd:simpleType>
```

The XML representation of an element type whose structure type is partOptionType might look like the following element:

```
<xsd:element name="partOption" type="partOptionType"/>
```

Given the preceding element type, the following partOption element, with nested size and color elements, is valid in an XML instance:

```
<partOption>
    <size>grandiose</size>
    <color>cyan</color>
</partOption>
```

For clarity, note that an XML instance of partOption can contain just one of the size or color elements because of the minOccurs attribute of the respective element type:

```
<partOption>
    <color>cyan</color>
</partOption>
```

## 11.4 An Example of a Complex Type Specifying Mixed Content

A complex type can specify mixed content. Mixed content means that an element whose element type's structure type is this complex type can contain text interspersed with elements. The text is always free form (there is no way to specify constraints on the text). The elements are typically partially confined. Listing 11.4 is catalogEntryDescriptionType, which permits valid lists of part numbers to be interspersed with text.

**LISTING 11.4**  A Complex Type Specifying Mixed Content (catalog.xsd)

```
<xsd:complexType name="catalogEntryDescriptionType"
                 mixed="true"
                 id="catalogEntryDescriptionType.catalog.cType">
    <xsd:annotation>
        <xsd:documentation xml:lang="en">
            Allow the description of a part
            to include part number references.
            The "catalogEntryDescriptionType"
            is a good example of a complex type
            with "mixed" content.
                -- Shorthand Notation --
        </xsd:documentation>
    </xsd:annotation>
    <xsd:sequence minOccurs="0" maxOccurs="unbounded">
        <xsd:element name="partList" type="partNumberListType"/>
    </xsd:sequence>
</xsd:complexType>
```

The XML representation of an element type whose structure type is catalogEntryDescription might look like the following element:

```
<xsd:element name="description"
             type="catalogEntryDescriptionType"/>
```

Given the preceding element type, the following description element is valid in an XML instance:

```
<description>
    This is made up of both
    <partList>UX002 UX003</partList>
    pieces which makes this assembly
    better than
    <partList>ASM2000</partList>
    and better than the competition.
</description>
```

## 11.5 Concepts and Observations

A complex type has many options. Accordingly, the XML representation of a complex type has many possible attributes and many choices for content. Because of the capabilities of a complex type, this section highlights quite a few observations about the Schema Recommendation.

### 11.5.1 Explicitly Non-instantiable Complex Types

Only complex types and element types can be explicitly non-instantiable. A complex type that specifies the `abstract` attribute with the value 'false' cannot have instances. Listing 11.5 is the explicitly non-instantiable `dollarPriceType` complex type.

> **WARNING**
>
> Read the discussion about terminology in Section 1.8 before reading about abstraction and instantiation. The Schema Recommendation uses the term *abstract* to mean both a conceptual data model and a non-instantiable complex or element type.

**LISTING 11.5**   An Explicitly Non-instantiable Complex Type (`pricing.xsd`)

```
<xsd:complexType name="dollarPriceType"
                 final="restriction"
                 block="restriction"
                 abstract="true"
                 id="dollarPriceType.pricing.cType">
    <xsd:annotation>
<xsd:documentation xml:lang="en">
        Currently, currency is limited to
        U S Dollars.  Note that this type is
        non-instantiable.  A derived type must be
        defined that sets the range.
</xsd:documentation>
    </xsd:annotation>
    <xsd:simpleContent>
```

```
            <xsd:extension base="restrictedDollarAmountType">
                <xsd:attribute ref="currency"/>
            </xsd:extension>
        </xsd:simpleContent>
</xsd:complexType>
```

If the complex type is explicitly non-instantiable, a derivation might be instantiable. Listing 11.6 has several instantiable complex types, which are derivations of the non-instantiable `dollarPriceType`.

**LISTING 11.6**  An Instantiable Complex Type Derived from a Non-instantiable Complex Type (pricing.xsd)

```
<xsd:complexType name="fullPriceType"
                 block="#all"
                 final="#all"
                 id="fullPriceType.pricing.cType">
    <xsd:annotation>
        <xsd:documentation xml:lang="en">
            The pricing element for all items
            sold at full price have no elements
            or attributes.  The price is simply
            the amount, stored in the value
            of the element.
        </xsd:documentation>
    </xsd:annotation>
    <xsd:simpleContent>
        <xsd:extension base="dollarPriceType"/>
    </xsd:simpleContent>
</xsd:complexType>

<xsd:complexType name="salePriceType"
                 block="#all"
                 final="extension"
                 id="salePriceType.pricing.cType">
    <xsd:annotation>
        <xsd:documentation xml:lang="en">
            Anything on sale must have a price
            and an authorization
        </xsd:documentation>
    </xsd:annotation>
    <xsd:simpleContent>
        <xsd:extension base="dollarPriceType">
            <xsd:attributeGroup ref="saleAttributeGroup"/>
        </xsd:extension>
    </xsd:simpleContent>
</xsd:complexType>
```

An element type whose structure type is `fullPriceType` might look like the following element:

```
<xsd:element name="fullPrice" type="fullPriceType"/>
```

Given the preceding element type, the following element is valid in an XML instance:

```
<fullPrice>32.00</fullPrice>
```

An instance can specify an instantiable derivation by using the `xsi:type` attribute. An element type whose structure type is `dollarPriceType` might look like the following element:

```
<xsd:element name="amount" type="dollarPriceType"/>
```

Given the preceding element type, the following element is valid in an XML instance:

```
<amount xsi:type="salePriceType">123.45</amount>
```

Note that `salePriceType`, described in Listing 11.6, is a valid instantiable derivation of `dollarPriceType`.

### 11.5.2 Implicitly Non-instantiable Complex Types

A complex type can be implicitly non-instantiable because of a nested non-instantiable element type. Transitively, the element type can be non-instantiable either because the element type is explicitly non-instantiable or because the structure type associated with the element type is non-instantiable.

The `baseCatalogEntryType` in Listing 11.7 is explicitly non-instantiable (it has an `abstract` attribute whose value is 'true'). The `baseCatalogEntryType` is also implicitly non-instantiable: It contains a reference to the global `sequenceID` element type, which is non-instantiable.

> **TIP**
>
> In theory, describing `basecatalogEntryType` as non-instantiable is redundant. This explicit attribute may be—in practice—required. The Recommendation mandates that a complex type must be explicitly defined as non-instantiable when the intent is that the XML instance—not the schema—specifies the structure type (see various discussions on the use of `xsi:type` in this book). This tip applies only to complex types; a simple type is always instantiable.

**LISTING 11.7** An Implicitly Non-instantiable Complex Type (`catalog.xsd`)

```
<xsd:complexType name="baseCatalogEntryType"
                abstract="true"
                id="baseCatalogEntryType.catalog.cType">
    <xsd:annotation>
```

```xml
        <xsd:documentation xml:lang="en">
            A catalog entry must have:
               * A database ID
               * Part Name
               * Part Number
               * Options available
               * Description
               * Price
               * Included Quantity when ordering
                 one item.
            The "baseCatalogEntryType" is
            non-instantiable:   a derived type must
            be created before a catalog
            entry can be instantiated.
                -- Shorthand Notation --
        </xsd:documentation>
    </xsd:annotation>
    <xsd:sequence id="bacet-seq">
        <xsd:element ref="sequenceID"/>
        <xsd:element name="partName" type="partNameType"/>
        <xsd:element name="partNumber" type="partNumberType"/>
        <xsd:element name="partOption" type="partOptionType"/>
        <xsd:element name="description"
                     type="catalogEntryDescriptionType"/>
        <xsd:group ref="priceGroup"/>
        <xsd:element name="includedQuantity"
                     type="xsd:positiveInteger"/>
    </xsd:sequence>
    <xsd:attribute name="category"
                   type="categoryType"
                   use="required"/>
</xsd:complexType>
```

The baseCatalogEntryType in Listing 11.7 requires the database sequence types from Listing 11.8.

**LISTING 11.8** Database Sequence Types (sequence.xsd)

```xml
<xsd:simpleType name="sequenceIDType">
    <xsd:annotation>
        <xsd:documentation xml:lang="en">
            A Sequence ID is generated by
            the database.   Sequences are
            integers that start with "0"
        </xsd:documentation>
    </xsd:annotation>
```

*continues*

## Complex Types
### Chapter 11

```
            <xsd:restriction base="xsd:nonNegativeInteger"/>
</xsd:simpleType>

<xsd:element name="sequenceID"
             type="sequenceIDType"
             abstract="true"
             block="substitution">
    <xsd:annotation>
        <xsd:documentation xml:lang="en">
            This element is
            non-instantiable:  the element
            must be replaced by a substitution
            group in either a derived type or
            an instance.
        </xsd:documentation>
    </xsd:annotation>
</xsd:element>

<xsd:element name="unitID"
             type="sequenceIDType"
             substitutionGroup="sequenceID">
    <xsd:annotation>
        <xsd:documentation xml:lang="en">
            This element represents sequence
            IDs for unit items.
            This element provides a valid
            substitution for "sequenceID".
        </xsd:documentation>
    </xsd:annotation>
</xsd:element>

<xsd:element name="bulkID"
             type="sequenceIDType"
             substitutionGroup="sequenceID">
    <xsd:annotation>
        <xsd:documentation xml:lang="en">
            This element represents sequence
            IDs for bulk items.
            This element provides a valid
            substitution for "sequenceID".
        </xsd:documentation>
    </xsd:annotation>
</xsd:element>

<xsd:element name="assemblyID"
             type="sequenceIDType"
             substitutionGroup="sequenceID">
```

```
    <xsd:annotation>
        <xsd:documentation xml:lang="en">
            This element represents sequence
            IDs for assembled items.
            This element provides a valid
            substitution for "sequenceID".
        </xsd:documentation>
    </xsd:annotation>
</xsd:element>
```

Listing 11.9 is the `unitCatalogEntryType`, which is a derivation of the `baseCatalogEntryType` described in Listing 11.7. The `restriction` element specifies the base complex type. In addition, the instantiable `unitID` replaces the non-instantiable `sequenceID`.

**LISTING 11.9**  An Instantiable Derivation of an Implicitly Non-instantiable Complex Type (catalog.xsd)

```
<xsd:complexType name="unitCatalogEntryType"
                block="#all"
                final="#all"
                id="unitCatalogEntryType.catalog.cType">
    <xsd:annotation>
        <xsd:documentation xml:lang="en">
            A unit item contains nothing more
            or less than a basic catalog entry ID:
                * A database ID
                * Part Name
                * Part Number
                * Options available
                * Price
                * Included Quantity when ordering
                    one item (always one for unit items).
        </xsd:documentation>
    </xsd:annotation>
    <xsd:complexContent id="ucet.cc">
        <xsd:restriction base="baseCatalogEntryType">
            <xsd:sequence>
                <xsd:element ref="unitID"/>
                <xsd:element name="partName" type="partNameType"/>
                <xsd:element name="partNumber"
                            type="unitPartNumberType"/>
                <xsd:element name="partOption" type="partOptionType"/>
                <xsd:element name="description"
                            type="catalogEntryDescriptionType"/>
                <xsd:group ref="priceGroup"/>
                <xsd:element name="includedQuantity"
```

*continues*

```
                              type="xsd:positiveInteger"
                              fixed="1"/>
            </xsd:sequence>
            <xsd:attribute name="category"
                           type="categoryType"
                           fixed="unit"/>
        </xsd:restriction>
    </xsd:complexContent>
</xsd:complexType>
```

> **TIP**
>
> Some complex types are implicitly non-instantiable because they contain a reference to a global non-instantiable element type; an element in the XML instance can determine the instantiable element type by specifying an appropriate substitution group as its typename, or by specifying an instantiable structure type via `xsi:type`.

### 11.5.3 Adding Element Types or Attribute Types to a Derived Complex Type

A complex type can specify attribute types for simple or complex types. A `complexType` element, along with a nested `simpleContent` element, provides the functionality necessary to add attribute types to simple types. Similarly, a `complexType` element, along with a nested `complexContent` element, provides the functionality necessary to add element types—or attribute types—to complex types.

Listing 11.2 portrays a complex type that specifies a `simpleContent` element. Listing 11.9 portrays an XML representation of a complex type derivation that specifies a `complexContent` element.

### 11.5.4 Removing Element Types or Attribute Types from a Derived Complex Type

A derived complex type can remove element types or attribute types from a base complex type. A derived complex type removes a nested element type by setting the `maxOccurs` attribute of the appropriate element type to have a value of '0'. A derived complex type removes an attribute type by setting the `use` attribute of the appropriate attribute type to 'prohibited'. Listing 8.13 portrays removing an element type from a complex type. Listing 9.7 portrays removing an attribute type from a complex type.

## 11.5.5 Prohibiting Extension or Restriction of a Complex Type

The `final` attribute prohibits further derivations of a complex type. In other words, when a complex type specifies a `final` attribute, the schema cannot contain derived complex types. In fact, the `final` attribute has a number of values that permit the complex type to limit only certain derivations. See Section 11.6.1.3 for more details.

The effects of the `block` attribute are convoluted. The `block` attribute affects substitution groups. The `block` attribute can also affect specifying a derived complex type in an XML instance. Both complex types and element types can specify a `block` attribute: There are complicated interactions. In order to avoid reiterating a lengthy discussion, please refer to Section 8.2.3 (Chapter 8 covers element types in general). Section 11.6.1.2 covers the options for specifying a `block` attribute for a complex type.

## 11.5.6 Shorthand Notation of a Complex Type

A complex type always has associated content (even empty content classifies as content). The complex type specifies its content as either simple or complex. The corollary XML representation is a `simpleContent` or a `complexContent`.

The XML Schema syntax permits a shorthand notation where a `complexType` element does not explicitly contain either a `simpleContent` or a `complexContent` element. The shorthand notation specifies that when the content type is not explicit, the processor infers complex content that restricts a base of `anyType`.

The XML representation of `longhandPartOptionType` in Listing 11.10 is functionally equivalent to the XML representation of `partOptionType` in Listing 11.3.

LISTING 11.10   Longhand Notation of a Complex Type

```
<xsd:complexType name="longhandPartOptionType"
              block="#all"
              final="#all">
   <xsd:annotation>
      <xsd:documentation xml:lang="en">
         The "partOptionType" is defined
         using the shorthand notation for
         complex types.  This element
         demonstrates the equivalence
         using the normal notation.
      </xsd:documentation>
   </xsd:annotation>
   <xsd:complexContent>
      <xsd:restriction base="xsd:anyType">
```

*continues*

```
            <xsd:all>
                <xsd:element name="color"
                             type="colorOptionType"
                             minOccurs="0"
                             maxOccurs="1"/>
                <xsd:element name="size"
                             type="sizeOptionType"
                             minOccurs="0"
                             maxOccurs="1"/>
            </xsd:all>
        </xsd:restriction>
    </xsd:complexContent>
</xsd:complexType>
```

> **TIP**
>
> The shorthand notation used in Listing 11.10 restricts anyType, which permits any combination of elements and attributes.

Note that the shorthand notation permits the following subelements of a complexType:

- all
- anyAttribute
- attribute
- attributeGroup
- choice
- group
- sequence

Sections 11.11–11.14 discuss the all, choice, sequence, and group elements, respectively. Sections 9.5–9.7 cover the attribute, attributeGroup, and anyAttribute elements, respectively.

## 11.6 The complexType Element

Complex types provide a wide range of functionality. This wide range includes, but is not limited to, extending simple types and restricting or extending complex types, empty content, and mixed content. Most of the listings in this chapter, especially Listings 11.1–11.4, contain examples of complex types.

## 11.6.1 Attributes of a `complexType` Element

A `complexType` element can specify the `name` and `id` attributes that are also applicable to many other elements. The attributes `abstract`, `block`, and `final` provide the capability to derive instantiable complex types. The `mixed` attribute determines when a complex type permits or prohibits mixed content. Table 11.1 provides a summary of all of the attributes applicable to a `complexType`.

**TABLE 11.1**  Attribute Summary for a `complexType` Element

| Attribute | Description |
| --- | --- |
| abstract | The value of the `abstract` attribute is a Boolean value that determines if a complex type is explicitly non-instantiable. An XML instance may not contain data corresponding directly to a non-instantiable complex type. |
| block | The value of the `block` attribute determines the capability of an XML instance to specify an instantiable derivation of a non-instantiable complex type. The `block` attribute also limits the ability to substitute member element types of a substitution group—when the structure type of the head of the substitution group is this complex type. |
| final | The value of the `final` attribute determines the capability of an XML schema to specify an instantiable derivation of a non-instantiable complex type. |
| id | The value of an `id` attribute uniquely identifies an element within the set of schema documents that comprise an XML schema. |
| mixed | The value of the `mixed` attribute controls whether an XML instance can intersperse text between elements in the contents of a complex type. |
| name | The value of the `name` attribute is the name of a complex type. A derived complex type references this name as the base complex type. An element type references this name to specify a structure type. |

### 11.6.1.1 The abstract Attribute of a `complexType` Element

The value of the `abstract` attribute is a Boolean value that determines if a complex type is explicitly non-instantiable. An XML instance may not contain data corresponding directly to a non-instantiable complex type.

Listing 11.5 contains sample code that creates a non-instantiable complex type.

> **ATTRIBUTE OVERVIEW**
>
> complexType: abstract
>
> **Value:** A Boolean value (that is, 'true' or 'false').
> **Default:** 'false'.
> **Constraints:** None.
> **Required:** No.

### 11.6.1.2 The block Attribute of a complexType Element

Conveying how complex types block is extremely complicated. The block attribute determines the capability of an XML instance to substitute a derived complex type. The XML instance can substitute a derived type in one of two ways:

- The XML instance can request element validation against an instantiable derivation of a non-instantiable complex type by specifying xsi:type as an attribute to an element. The requested complex type must be a valid derivation of the element's element type's structure type.

- When an element type is a member of a substitution group (see Section 8.2.2), the XML instance can refer to an element type that is a valid substitution for the element type specified by the structure type. Note that a substitution group requires that the structure type of a substitutable element type is a derived structure type (or the same structure type) as the root (of the substitution group) element type.

The block attribute can disallow either or both of the substitutions just discussed. Furthermore, the block attribute can prohibit substitutions based on the kind of derivation. For example, a complex type could prohibit an XML instance from substituting elements whose element type's structure type is a restriction of itself, but allow the XML instance to substitute elements whose element type's structure type is an extension.

> **TIP**
>
> A solid understanding of extending and restricting complex types (that is, the use of the extension and restriction elements) is valuable before attempting to use the block or final attributes.

> **ATTRIBUTE OVERVIEW**
>
> **complexType: block**
>
> **Value:** An enumeration that consists of '#all', or a space-delimited list of any or all of 'extension' and 'restriction'.
>
> **Default:** In general, there is no default. However, the schema element can create a global default using the blockDefault attribute.
>
> **Constraints:** None.
>
> **Required:** No.

Listing 11.11 revisits the dollarPriceType described in Listing 11.5. This time dollarPriceType has the block attribute set to 'restriction'. Note that for complex types 'block="#all"' provides the same functionality as 'block="restriction extension"'.

**LISTING 11.11**  Blocking Restrictions or Extensions of a Complex Type

```
<xsd:complexType name="dollarPriceType"
                 final="restriction"
                 block="restriction"
                 abstract="true">
    <xsd:annotation>
        <xsd:documentation xml:lang="en">
            Currently, currency is limited to
            U S Dollars.  Note that this type is
            non-instantiable.  A derived type must be defined
            that sets the range.
        </xsd:documentation>
    </xsd:annotation>
    <xsd:simpleContent>
        <xsd:extension base="restrictedDollarAmountType">
            <xsd:attribute ref="currency"/>
        </xsd:extension>
    </xsd:simpleContent>
</xsd:complexType>
```

The global amount element is now not so valuable; an XML instance cannot substitute an instantiable derivation of the dollarPriceType structure type:

```
<xsd:element name="amount" type="dollarPriceType"/>
```

Note that another complex type could reference the amount element type.

The previously defined `dollarPriceType` prohibits an instance from extending the type; therefore, the following is not valid:

```
<amount xsi:type="salePriceType">123.45</amount>
```

Limitations on extension work similarly when the `block` attribute includes 'extension'. Finally, the value of the `block` attribute can be set to '#all', which blocks both restriction and extension in XML instances.

> **WARNING**
>
> Many of the existing XML validators do not properly respect the `block` attribute of complex types.

Blocking is not inherited. Because of this limitation, derived types—in most cases—repeat the `block` attribute (e.g., a hierarchy of complex types derived by extension might all have a 'block="restriction"' attribute). The same is true for the `final` attribute.

### 11.6.1.3 The `final` Attribute of a `complexType` Element

The `final` attribute prohibits extending or restricting a complex type. In other words, the `final` attribute prohibits derived complex types. When the value of the `final` attribute is 'extension', there can be no complex types derived by extension. The `final` attribute can similarly prohibit restrictions.

**ATTRIBUTE OVERVIEW**

**complexType: final**

| | |
|---|---|
| **Value:** | An enumeration that consists of '#all', or a space-delimited list of any or all of 'extension' and 'restriction'. |
| **Default:** | In general, there is no default. However, the `schema` element can create a global default using the `finalDefault` attribute. |
| **Constraints:** | None. |
| **Required:** | No. |

> **TIP**
>
> A solid understanding of extending and restricting complex types (that is, the use of the `extension` and `restriction` elements) is valuable before attempting to use the `block` or `final` attributes.

Listing 11.11 assumes the original `dollarPriceType` described in 11.5; the `final` attribute has the value 'restriction'. Because the value of the `final` attribute is 'restriction', `fullPriceType` is a valid derivation by extension.

> **NOTE**
>
> The Schema Recommendation states that a complex type that does not allow restrictions or extensions is "final". The complex type `fullPriceType` described in Listing 11.11 is "final".

**LISTING 11.12**   A Final Complex Type

```
<xsd:complexType name="fullPriceType"
                 block="#all"
                 final="#all">
   <xsd:annotation>
       <xsd:documentation xml:lang="en">
           The pricing element for all items
           sold at full price have no elements
           or attributes.  The price is simply
           the amount, stored in the value
           of the element.
       </xsd:documentation>
   </xsd:annotation>
   <xsd:simpleContent>
       <xsd:extension base="dollarPriceType"/>
   </xsd:simpleContent>
</xsd:complexType>
```

This `fullPriceType` described in Listing 11.12 does not permit any restrictions or extensions. For example, there cannot be a derivation that restricts the dollar amount.

Like the `block` attribute, the `final` attribute can be set to 'restriction' to prevent derivations by restriction, 'extension' to prevent derivations by extension, or '#all' to prevent any further derivations.

> **WARNING**
>
> Many of the existing XML validators do not properly respect the `final` attribute of complex type definitions.

> **WARNING**
>
> The following excerpt is from the Schema Recommendation: "Finality is not inherited, that is, a type definition derived by restriction from a type definition which is final for extension is not itself, in the absence of any explicit final attribute of its own, final for anything."

Finality is not inherited. Because of this limitation on finality, derived types—in most cases—repeat the `final` attribute (e.g., a hierarchy of complex types derived by extension might all have a 'final="restriction"' attribute). The same is true for the `block` attribute.

### 11.6.1.4 The `id` Attribute of a `complexType` Element

The value of an id attribute uniquely identifies an element within the set of schema documents that comprise an XML schema.

**ATTRIBUTE OVERVIEW**

**complexType: id**

| | |
|---:|:---|
| **Value:** | An ID. |
| **Default:** | None. |
| **Constraints:** | An id must be unique within an XML schema. |
| **Required:** | No. |

Many of the listings in this chapter contain examples of complex types that specify an id.

### 11.6.1.5 The mixed Attribute of a complexType Element

Having mixed content is useful when the XML is less structured. A good use of mixed content is embedding style in documents; highly structured XML schemas do not typically specify complex types that permit mixed content.

---
**ATTRIBUTE OVERVIEW**

**complexType: mixed**

| | |
|---:|:---|
| **Value:** | A Boolean value (that is, 'true' or 'false'). |
| **Default:** | 'false'. |
| **Constraints:** | None. |
| **Required:** | No. |

---

The mixed attribute applies to either the complexType element or the complexContent element (when the shorthand notation is not used). Listing 11.4 demonstrates the use of the mixed attribute associated with the catalogEntryDescriptionType element.

The mixed attribute of a complexContent element is redundant with the mixed attribute of a complexType element. Regardless, the attribute applies to the content (that is, complexContent). The attribute appears on the complexType element primarily to allow the shorthand notation (see Section 11.5.6). If a base complexContent element sets the mixed attribute to 'false', a complexType that permits mixed content is not a valid derivation.

### 11.6.1.6 The name Attribute of a complexType Element

The name identifies a complex type. Another complex type can reference this name to create a derived complex type. An element type can use this name to associate a structure type. An XML instance can reference this name to specify a derivation of a non-instantiable complex type.

---
**ATTRIBUTE OVERVIEW**

**complexType: name**

| | |
|---:|:---|
| **Value:** | An NCName. |
| **Default:** | None. |
| **Constraints:** | None. |
| **Required:** | Yes, unless describing a local, or anonymous, complexType within the context of another element or complex type in which case the name attribute is prohibited. |

---

All of the examples in this chapter have a name.

## 11.6.2 Content Options for a `complexType` Element

Complex types provide a wide range of functionality. This wide range includes, but is not limited to, extending simple types and restricting or extending complex types, permitting empty content, and permitting mixed content. Because of this complexity, there is a correspondingly large range of content options. Table 11.2 summarizes these content options.

**TABLE 11.2** Content Options for a `complexType` Element

| Element | Description |
| --- | --- |
| annotation | The `annotation` element, discussed in Section 7.5, provides a way to document schema elements. |
| all | The `all` element, discussed in Section 11.11, specifies a model group that indicates an unordered set of element types; an XML instance must reference all the nested element types in any order. |
|  | A `complexType` element containing an immediate `all` subelement is a form of the shorthand notation. See Section 11.5.6 for a clarification of the shorthand notation. |
| anyAttribute | The `anyAttribute` element, discussed in Section 9.7, specifies a set of namespaces, each of which may provide global attribute types; the XML instance may reference any of these attribute types. |
|  | A `complexType` element directly containing an `anyAttribute` element is a form of the shorthand notation. See Section 11.5.6 for a clarification of the shorthand notation. |
| attribute | The `attribute` element, discussed in Section 9.5, specifies a local attribute type or refers to a global attribute type; the XML instance must reference this attribute, unless the attribute is optional or prohibited. |
|  | A `complexType` element directly containing an `attribute` element is a form of the shorthand notation. See Section 11.5.6 for a clarification of the shorthand notation. |
| attributeGroup | The `attributeGroup` element, discussed in Section 9.6, specifies a reference to a named attribute-use group. An XML instance must reference each attribute type according to the appropriate nested model group. |
|  | A `complexType` element directly containing an `attributeGroup` element is a form of the shorthand notation. See Section 11.5.6 for a clarification of the shorthand notation. |

*continues*

**TABLE 11.2** *(continued)*

| Element | Description |
|---|---|
| choice | The `choice` element, discussed in Section 11.12, specifies a model group that indicates a selection of one element type from a set of element types; an XML instance must reference only one of the element types.<br><br>A `complexType` element directly containing a `choice` element is a form of the shorthand notation. See Section 11.5.6 for a clarification of the shorthand notation. |
| complexContent | The `complexContent` element provides functionality for restricting or extending global complex types. The `complexContent` element also provides functionality for describing empty content, mixed content, and nested element types. See Section 11.8 for details and examples. |
| group | The `group` element, discussed in Section 11.14, specifies a reference to a named model group. The named model group specifies another model group (that is, `all`, `choice`, or `sequence`).<br><br>A `complexType` element directly containing a `group` element is a form of the shorthand notation. See Section 11.5.6 for a clarification of the shorthand notation. |
| sequence | The `sequence` element, covered in Section 11.13, specifies a model group that indicates an ordered set of element types; an XML instance must reference all the nested element types in the schema order.<br><br>A `complexType` element directly containing a `sequence` element is a form of the shorthand notation. See Section 11.5.6 for a clarification of the shorthand notation. |
| simpleContent | The `simpleContent` element provides functionality for adding attribute types to a global simple type. See Section 11.7 for details and examples. |

The content pattern for a `complexType` element is:

```
annotation?
(simpleContent |
 complexContent |
 ((group | all | choice | sequence)?
  (attribute | attributeGroup)* anyAttribute?)))
```

## 11.7 The `simpleContent` Element

The `simpleContent` element can specify attributes for simple types. This element can also extend or restrict attribute types on other complex types with simple content. Listing 11.2 provides an example of adding attribute types to a simple type.

## 11.7.1 Attributes of a `simpleContent` Element

The only attribute of the `simpleContent` element is the ubiquitous `id` attribute (see Table 11.3).

**TABLE 11.3** Attribute Summary of a `simpleContent` Element

| Attribute | Description |
| --- | --- |
| id | The value of an `id` attribute uniquely identifies an element within the set of schema documents that comprise an XML schema. |

### 11.7.1.1 The `id` Attribute of a `simpleContent` Element

The value of an `id` attribute uniquely identifies an element within the set of schema documents that comprise an XML schema.

---

**ATTRIBUTE OVERVIEW**

**simpleContent: id**

- **Value:** An ID.
- **Default:** None.
- **Constraints:** An `id` must be unique within an XML schema.
- **Required:** No.

---

Listing 11.12 demonstrates the use of the `id` attribute of a `simpleContent` element in the XML representation of `clearancePriceType`.

## 11.7.2 Content Options for a `simpleContent` Element

The `simpleContent` can specify attribute types (via extensions) and it can restrict existing attribute types (via restrictions). Table 11.4 provides an overview of the content options of a `simpleContent` element.

The content pattern for a `simpleContent` element is:

annotation? (restriction | extension)

The `extension` element, nested within a `simpleContent` element, provides functionality for adding attribute types to simple types or to complex types with simple content. Listing 11.2 portrays adding attribute types to a simple type.

**TABLE 11.4** Content Options for a `simpleContent` Element

| Element | Description |
| --- | --- |
| annotation | The `annotation` element, discussed in Section 7.5, provides a way to document schema elements. |
| extension | The `extension` element provides functionality to add attribute types to a complex type. See Section 11.9, which covers the `extension` element, and Section 11.2, which provides a more thorough description and example. |
| restriction | The `restriction` element provides functionality to restrict the values of attributes already associated with a base complex type. See Section 11.10 for more detail. |

The `extension` element also provides functionality for creating instantiable derivations of non-instantiable complex types with simple content. Listing 11.6 provides an example that demonstrates how to create the instantiable complex type `fullPriceType`. The complex type `fullPriceType` is a derivation of the non-instantiable complex type `dollarPriceType`.

> **TIP**
>
> The use of the `final` attribute on the base complex type may prohibit the extension of that complex type. In addition, the use of a `fixed` attribute on a constraining facet of the base complex type may prohibit further modification of that constraining facet.

Much like simple types, the `restriction` element, nested within a `simpleContent` element, provides functionality to add or modify constraining facets that apply to the simple type. The `salePriceType` component has simple content; the XML representation of `salePriceType` associates attribute types but not element types. The complex type `clearancePriceType` described in Listing 11.13 restricts the complex type `salePriceType` (described in Listing 11.2) to have a value of no more than $10.00.

**LISTING 11.13** Adding Restrictions to a Complex Type with Simple Content (`pricing.xsd`)

```
<xsd:complexType name="clearancePriceType"
                 block="#all"
                 final="#all">
    <xsd:annotation>
        <xsd:documentation xml:lang="en">
            Anything on sale must have a price
            and an authorization
        </xsd:documentation>
```

*continues*

```
            </xsd:annotation>
            <xsd:simpleContent>
                <xsd:restriction base="salePriceType">
                    <xsd:maxInclusive value="10.00"/>
                </xsd:restriction>
            </xsd:simpleContent>
</xsd:complexType>
```

## 11.8 The `complexContent` Element

A `complexContent` element can specify nested element types. This includes the special case of zero elements, also known as "empty content." The `complexContent` element also provides functionality that permits text interspersed with elements, known as "mixed content." Listings 11.1 and 11.4 portray empty content and mixed content, respectively.

### 11.8.1 Attributes of a `complexContent` Element

Table 11.5 details the limited attributes available for use with a `complexContent` element.

**TABLE 11.5** Attribute Summary of a `complexContent` Element

| Attribute | Description |
| --- | --- |
| id | The value of an id attribute uniquely identifies an element within the set of schema documents that comprise an XML schema. |
| mixed | The value of the mixed attribute determines the capability of the complex type to contain mixed content. Mixed content is usually a rigid element structure (like the majority of complex types) that has free-form text interspersed between the elements. |

#### 11.8.1.1 The `id` Attribute of a `complexContent` Element

The value of an `id` attribute uniquely identifies an element within the set of schema documents that comprise an XML schema.

---

**ATTRIBUTE OVERVIEW**

**complexContent: id**

- **Value:** An ID.
- **Default:** None.
- **Constraints:** An `id` must be unique within an XML schema.
- **Required:** No.

Listing 11.9 demonstrates a `complexContent` element with an associated `id` attribute.

### 11.8.1.2 The `mixed` Attribute of a `complexContent` Element

The `mixed` attribute controls whether a complex type contains only elements (`mixed="false"`) or embedded text and elements (`mixed="true"`).

---

**ATTRIBUTE OVERVIEW**

**complexContent: mixed**

| | |
|---:|:---|
| **Value:** | A Boolean value (that is, 'true' or 'false'). |
| **Default:** | 'false'. |
| **Constraints:** | None. |
| **Required:** | No. |

---

Having mixed content is useful when the XML is less structured. A good use of mixed content is embedding style in documents; highly structured XML schemas do not typically define complex types that allow mixed content. The `mixed` attribute applies to either the `complexType` element or the `complexContent` element (if the shorthand notation is not used). Listing 11.4 demonstrates the use of the `mixed` attribute.

---

**WARNING**

The `mixed` attribute on the `complexContent` element is redundant with the `mixed` attribute on the `complexType` element. If a base `complexContent` element set the `mixed` to 'false', a derived `complexType` that permits mixed content is not valid.

---

## 11.8.2 Content Options for a `complexContent` Element

Complex types that contain complex content are either extensions or restrictions of other base complex types. Note that even the shorthand notation—which does not explicitly describe extension or restriction—is a restriction of `anyType`. Table 11.6 provides a brief description of the content options for a `complexContent` element.

The content pattern for the `complexContent` element is:

annotation? (attribute | attributeGroup)* anyAttribute?

**TABLE 11.6** Content Options for a `complexContent` Element

| Element | Description |
| --- | --- |
| annotation | The annotation element, discussed in Section 7.5, provides a way to document schema elements. |
| extension | The extension element provides functionality for deriving complex types that add attribute types or elements to an existing base `complexType`. |
| restriction | The restriction element provides functionality for deriving complex types that restrict attributes or constraining facets of attributes or elements associated with an existing base `complexType`. |

## 11.9 The `extension` Element

The `extension` element applies to complex types that contain simple content as well as complex types that contain complex content. The `extension` element provides functionality for adding attribute types to simple content. For complex content, the `extension` element provides functionality for adding either attributes or nested element types. Finally, with respect to simple content, the base type can be either a simple type or a complex type that contains simple content.

> **TIP**
>
> The use of the `final` attribute on the base complex type may prohibit the extension of that complex type. In addition, the use of a `fixed` attribute on a constraining facet of the base complex type may prohibit further modification of that constraining facet.

In the following example, an *assembly* represents an orderable item made of many smaller parts. Listing 11.14 demonstrates deriving a complex type that specifies this assembly—assemblyCatalogEntryType—from the base baseAssemblyCatalogEntryType by adding a list of part numbers. The simple type partNumberListType represents the list of part numbers.

**LISTING 11.14** Extending a Complex Type That Contains Complex Content (`catalog.xsd`)

```
<xsd:complexType name="assemblyCatalogEntryType"
                 block="#all"
                 final="#all"
                 id="assemblyCatalogEntryType.catalog.cType">
    <xsd:annotation>
```

## 11.9 The extension Element

```
            <xsd:documentation xml:lang="en">
                The actual definition of an assembly,
                including the contained parts.
            </xsd:documentation>
        </xsd:annotation>
        <xsd:complexContent>
            <xsd:extension base="baseAssemblyCatalogEntryType"
                           id="acet.ext">
                <xsd:sequence>
                    <xsd:element name="partList"
                                 type="partNumberListType"/>
                    <xsd:element name="status"
                                 type="assemblyPartStatusType"/>
                </xsd:sequence>
            </xsd:extension>
        </xsd:complexContent>
    </xsd:complexType>
    <xsd:complexType name="baseAssemblyCatalogEntryType"
                     abstract="true"
                     block="#all"
                     id="baseAssemblyCatalogEntryType.catalog.cType">
        <xsd:annotation>
            <xsd:documentation xml:lang="en">
                An assembled item is similar to the
                other catalog entries.  The part number
                is restricted to an assembly number.
                In addition, there may be no options.
                Finally, a part list is also needed.
                Note that the "includedQuantity" has
                a default of one, but can be overridden
                in instances.
            </xsd:documentation>
        </xsd:annotation>
        <xsd:complexContent>
            <xsd:restriction base="baseCatalogEntryType"
                             id="bacet.rst">
                <xsd:sequence>
                    <xsd:element ref="assemblyID"/>
                    <xsd:element name="partName"
                                 type="partNameType"/>
                    <xsd:element name="partNumber"
                                 type="assemblyPartNumberType"/>
                    <xsd:element name="partOption"
                                 type="partOptionType"
                                 minOccurs="0"
                                 maxOccurs="0"/>
                    <xsd:element name="description"
```

*continues*

```
                                type="catalogEntryDescriptionType"/>
                <xsd:group ref="priceGroup"/>
                <xsd:element name="includedQuantity"
                                type="xsd:positiveInteger"
                                default="1"/>
                <xsd:element name="customerReview"
                                type="customerReviewType"
                                minOccurs="0"
                                maxOccurs="unbounded"/>
            </xsd:sequence>
        </xsd:restriction>
    </xsd:complexContent>
</xsd:complexType>

<xsd:simpleType name="partNumberListType"
            id="catalog.partNumber.list.sType">
    <xsd:annotation>
        <xsd:documentation xml:lang="en">
            The "partNumberListType" describes the value
            for an element that contains a set of part
            numbers.  Given that a part number might look
            like any of the following:
                J1
                ABC32897
                ZZ22233344
            A list of these part numbers might look like:
                J1 ABC32897 ZZ22233344
        </xsd:documentation>
    </xsd:annotation>
    <xsd:list id="transaction.partNumberList"
            itemType="partNumberType">
    </xsd:list>
</xsd:simpleType>
```

> **TIP**
>
> Use an extension to create an instantiable derivation of an otherwise non-instantiable complex type. Simply do not add any attributes or elements. Listing 11.6 provides an example of using extension in this manner.

## 11.9.1 Attributes of an extension Element

The only attributes applicable to the `extension` element are the ubiquitous `base` attribute and the `id` attribute. Table 11.7 identifies these two attributes.

**TABLE 11.7**  Attribute Summary of an `extension` Element

| Attribute | Description |
|---|---|
| base | The value of the `base` attribute identifies the base simple or complex type of the current derived complex type. |
| id | The value of an `id` attribute uniquely identifies an element within the set of schema documents that comprise an XML schema. |

### 11.9.1.1 The base Attribute of an extension Element

The value of a `base` attribute indicates the global base type. For an extension of simple content, the base type can be either a simple type or a complex type with simple content. Otherwise, the derived complex type is an extension of complex content, which means that the value of the `base` attribute must refer to a global complex type.

**ATTRIBUTE OVERVIEW**

**extension: base**

- **Value:** A QName.
- **Default:** None.
- **Constraints:** The base type must refer to a global simple or complex type in the XML schema.
- **Required:** No.

### 11.9.1.2 The id Attribute of an extension Element

The value of an `id` attribute uniquely identifies an element within the set of schema documents that comprise an XML schema.

## Complex Types
### CHAPTER 11

---

**ATTRIBUTE OVERVIEW**

**extension: id**

**Value:** An ID.
**Default:** None.
**Constraints:** An `id` must be unique within an XML schema.
**Required:** No.

---

Listing 11.13 portrays an `extension` element with an associated `id` attribute.

### 11.9.2 Content Options for an extension Element

Both the `complexContent` and the `simpleContent` elements may contain an `extension` element. Some of the content options described in this section apply to the `complexContent` element, some to the `simpleContent` element, and some to both. The description of each element in Table 11.8 identifies the appropriate applicability.

Note the Applies To column in Table 11.8. The Applies To column indicates whether the element applies to simple content (the cell value is 'S'), complex content (the cell value is 'C'), or both (the cell value is 'S/C').

**TABLE 11.8** Content Options for an extension Element

| Element | Description | Applies To |
|---|---|---|
| all | The `all` element, discussed in Section 11.11, specifies a model group that indicates an unordered set of element types; an XML instance must reference all the nested element types in any order. | C |
| annotation | The `annotation` element, discussed in Section 7.5, provides a way to document schema elements. | S/C |
| anyAttribute | The `anyAttribute` element, discussed in Section 9.7, specifies a set of namespaces, each of which may provide global attribute types; the XML instance may reference any of these attribute types. | S/C |
| attribute | The `attribute` element, discussed in Section 9.5, specifies a local attribute type or refers to a global attribute type; the XML instance must reference this attribute, unless the attribute is optional or prohibited. | S/C |

*continues*

**TABLE 11.8** *(continued)*

| Element | Description | Applies To |
|---|---|---|
| attributeGroup | The `attributeGroup` element, discussed in Section 9.6, specifies a reference to a named attribute-use group. An XML instance must reference each attribute type according to the appropriate nested model group. | S/C |
| choice | The `choice` element, discussed in Section 11.12, specifies a model group that indicates a selection of one element type from a set of element types; an XML instance must reference only one of the element types. | C |
| group | The `group` element, discussed in Section 11.14, references to a named model group. The named model group specifies another model group (that is, `all`, `choice`, or `sequence`). | C |
| sequence | The `sequence` element, covered in Section 11.13, specifies a model group that indicates an ordered set of element types; an XML instance must reference all the nested element types in the schema order. | C |

The content pattern for an `extension` element nested within a `simpleContent` element is:

annotation? (attribute | attributeGroup)* anyAttribute?

The content pattern for the `extension` element nested within a `complexContent` element is:

annotation?
(group | all | choice | sequence)?
(attribute | attributeGroup)* anyAttribute?

## 11.10 The restriction Element

The `restriction` element provides functionality for deriving a complex type that restricts a base complex type. For simple content, these restrictions may only specify constraining facets that apply to simple content. For complex content, the restriction permits altering attributes of nested element or attribute types.

> **TIP**
>
> The use of the `final` attribute on the base complex type may prohibit the restriction of that complex type. In addition, the use of a `fixed` attribute on a constraining facet of the base complex type may prohibit further modification of that constraining facet.

Listing 11.15 demonstrates how to use a `restriction` element for complex content. The `baseAssemblyCatalogEntryType` is a derivation of `baseCatalogEntryType`. In particular, note that the `assemblyPartNumberType` is a derivation of `partNumberType`. In addition, the `partOptionType` cannot appear in an XML instance, because the value of the `maxOccurs` attribute is '0'.

**LISTING 11.15**   Restricting a Complex Type That Contains Complex Content (`catalog.xsd`)

```
<xsd:complexType
      name="baseAssemblyCatalogEntryType"
      abstract="true"
      block="#all"
      final="restriction"
      id="baseAssemblyCatalogEntryType.catalog.cType">
   <xsd:annotation>
      <xsd:documentation xml:lang="en">
         An assembled item is similar to the
         other catalog entries.  The part number
         is restricted to an assembly number.
         In addition, there may be no options.
         Finally, a part list is also needed.
         Note that the "includedQuantity" has
         a default of one, but can be overridden
         in instances.
      </xsd:documentation>
   </xsd:annotation>
   <xsd:complexContent>
      <xsd:restriction base="baseCatalogEntryType"
                  id="bacet.rst">
         <xsd:sequence>
            <xsd:element ref="assemblyID"/>
            <xsd:element name="partName"
                     type="partNameType"/>
            <xsd:element name="partNumber"
                     type="assemblyPartNumberType"/>
            <xsd:element name="partOption"
                     type="partOptionType"
                     minOccurs="0"
                     maxOccurs="0"/>
            <xsd:element
               name="description"
               type="catalogEntryDescriptionType"/>
            <xsd:group ref="priceGroup"/>
            <xsd:element name="includedQuantity"
                     type="xsd:positiveInteger"
                     default="1"/>
```

```
            <xsd:element name="customerReview"
                         type="customerReviewType"
                         minOccurs="0"
                         maxOccurs="unbounded"/>
        </xsd:sequence>
        <xsd:attribute name="category"
                       type="categoryType"
                       fixed="assembly"/>
      </xsd:restriction>
    </xsd:complexContent>
</xsd:complexType>
```

## 11.10.1 Attributes of a restriction Element

The attributes applicable to a `restriction` element are identical to the attributes applicable to an `extension` element: the base attribute and the `id` attribute. Table 11.9 identifies these two attributes.

**TABLE 11.9**  Attribute Summary of a `restriction` Element

| Attribute | Description |
|---|---|
| base | The value of the base attribute identifies the base simple or complex type of the current derived complex type. |
| id | The value of an `id` attribute uniquely identifies an element within the set of schema documents that comprise an XML schema. |

### 11.10.1.1 The base Attribute of a restriction Element

The value of a base attribute indicates the global base structure type. For an extension of simple content, the base type can be either a simple type or a complex type with simple content. Otherwise, the derived complex type is an extension of complex content, which means that base structure type is a complex type.

---

**ATTRIBUTE OVERVIEW**

**restriction: base**

- **Value:** A QName.
- **Default:** None.
- **Constraints:** The base type must refer to a global simple or a complex type in the XML schema.
- **Required:** No.

---

### 11.10.1.2 The `id` Attribute of a `restriction` Element

The value of an `id` attribute uniquely identifies an element within the set of schema documents that comprise an XML schema.

---

**ATTRIBUTE OVERVIEW**

**restriction: id**

- **Value:** An ID.
- **Default:** None.
- **Constraints:** An id must be unique within an XML schema.
- **Required:** No.

---

Listing 11.14 portrays a `restriction` element with an associated `id` attribute.

## 11.10.2 Content Options for a `restriction` Element

Both the `complexContent` and the `simpleContent` elements may contain a `restriction` element. Some of the content options described later in this section apply to the `complexContent` element, some to the `simpleContent` element, and some to both. The description of each element identifies the appropriate applicability.

Note the Applies To column in Table 11.10. The Applies To column indicates whether the element applies to simple content (the cell value is 'S'), complex content (the cell value is 'C'), or both (the cell value is 'S/C').

**TABLE 11.10** Content Options for a `restriction` Element

| Element | Description | Applies To |
| --- | --- | --- |
| `all` | The all element, discussed in Section 11.11, specifies a model group that indicates an unordered set of element types; an XML instance must reference all the nested element types in any order. | C |
| `annotation` | The `annotation` element, discussed in Section 7.5, provides a way to document schema elements. | S/C |
| `anyAttribute` | The `anyAttribute` element, discussed in Section 9.7, specifies a set of namespaces, each of which may provide global attribute types; the XML instance may reference any of these attribute types. | S/C |

*continues*

**TABLE 11.10**   *(continued)*

| Element | Description | Applies To |
|---|---|---|
| attribute | The `attribute` element, discussed in Section 9.5, specifies a local attribute type or refers to a global attribute type; the XML instance must reference this attribute, unless the attribute is optional or prohibited. | S/C |
| attributeGroup | The `attributeGroup` element, discussed in Section 9.6, specifies a reference to a named attribute-use group. An XML instance must reference each attribute type according to the appropriate nested model group. | S/C |
| choice | The `choice` element, discussed in Section 11.12, specifies a model group that indicates a selection of one element type from a set of element types; an XML instance must reference only one of the element types. | C |
| group | The `group` element, discussed in Section 11.14, references to a named model group. The named model group specifies another model group (that is, `all`, `choice`, or `sequence`). | C |
| enumeration | The value of an `enumeration` constraining facet specifies a possible (constant) value. | S |
| fractionDigits | The value of a `fractionDigits` constraining facet determines the number of digits after the decimal point in a decimal number. | S |
| length | The value of a `length` constraining facet specifies the exact length of a string of characters that must appear in an element instance after normalization. This constraining facet also specifies the number of items in a list (see the caveats regarding `hexBinary` and `base64binary` datatypes in Section 12.4.3). | S |
| maxExclusive | The value of the `maxExclusive` constraining facet specifies an upper bound on a numeric value. This boundary excludes the value specified. | S |
| maxInclusive | The value of the `minInclusive` constraining facet specifies an upper bound on a numeric value. This boundary includes the value specified. | S |
| maxLength | The value of the `maxLength` constraining facet specifies the maximum number of characters in a string after normalization or the maximum number of items in a list (see caveats on `hexBinary` and `base64Binary` in Section 12.4.3). | S |

*continues*

**TABLE 11.10**   *(continued)*

| Element | Description | Applies To |
|---|---|---|
| `minExclusive` | The value of the `minExclusive` constraining facet specifies a lower bound on a numeric value. This boundary excludes the value specified. | S |
| `minInclusive` | The value of a `minInclusive` constraining facet specifies a lower bound on a numeric value. This boundary includes the value specified. | S |
| `minLength` | The value of a `minLength` constraining facet specifies the minimum number of characters in a string after normalization, or the minimum number of items in a list (see caveats on `hexBinary` and `base64Binary` in Section 12.4.3). | S |
| `pattern` | The value of a `pattern` constraining facet specifies a regular expression often used to validate a character string. Specifically, the pattern constrains lexical representations. | S |
| `totalDigits` | The value of a `totalDigits` constraining facet specifies the total number of digits in a decimal number. | S |
| `simpleType` | The `simpleType` element specifies a local simple type. | S |
| `whiteSpace` | The value of a `whiteSpace` constraining facet determines the normalization of spaces, carriage returns, and line feeds in a string. In certain cases, the value also specifies implied transformations. This normalization frequently removes undesirable white space. | S |
| `sequence` | The sequence element, covered in Section 11.13, specifies a model group that indicates an ordered set of element types; an XML instance must reference all the nested element types in the schema order. | C |

The content pattern for `restriction` is similar to the content pattern for the `extension` element, with one huge difference. When the restriction applies to simple content, the restriction may contain constraining facets that apply to the base (or locally described) `simpleType` element. Chapter 10 covers simple types. Chapter 12 covers built-in datatypes.

The content pattern for a `restriction` element nested within a `simpleContent` element is:

```
annotation?
(simpleType? (minExclusive |
              minInclusive |
              maxExclusive |
```

```
                maxInclusive |
                totalDigits |
                fractionDigits |
                length |
                minLength |
                maxLength |
                enumeration |
                whiteSpace |
                pattern)*)?
(attribute | attributeGroup)* anyAttribute?
```

The content pattern for the `restriction` element nested within a `complexContent` element is

```
annotation?
(group | all | choice | sequence)?
(attribute | attributeGroup)* anyAttribute?
```

## 11.11 The all Element

The `all` element specifies an unordered set of element types. For each element type associated with an `all` element in an XML schema document, there must be an element in the XML instance. However, they may appear in any order. In fact, there may be zero or many elements for each type, depending on the values of the `minOccurs` and `maxOccurs` attributes associated with the appropriate element type.

> **TIP**
>
> The Schema Recommendation generally permits XML elements that represent a model group to contain an element representing another model group. This nesting typically excludes the `all` element.

Listing 11.3 provides an example of the `partOptionType` that describes a complex type containing an `all` element.

### 11.11.1 Attributes of an all Element

Other than the ubiquitous `id` attribute, the attributes of the `all` element describe whether the entire model group is optional or required. Table 11.11 details the attributes of the `all` element.

**TABLE 11.11** Attribute Summary of an `all` Element

| Attribute | Description |
| --- | --- |
| id | The value of an `id` attribute uniquely identifies an element within the set of schema documents that comprise an XML schema. |
| maxOccurs | The value of the `maxOccurs` attribute determines the maximum number of occurrences of this model group. The attribute is irrelevant, because `maxOccurs` is fixed to the value '1'. |
| minOccurs | The value of the `minOccurs` attribute determines the minimum number of occurrences of this model group. In fact, the `minOccurs` attribute determines whether the entire model group is optional or required as the value is limited to '0' or '1'. |

#### 11.11.1.1 The `id` Attribute of an `all` Element

The value of an `id` attribute uniquely identifies an element within the set of schema documents that comprise an XML schema.

---
**ATTRIBUTE OVERVIEW**

**all: id**

- **Value:** An ID.
- **Default:** None.
- **Constraints:** An `id` must be unique within an XML schema.
- **Required:** No.
---

Listing 11.3 portrays an `all` element with an associated `id` attribute.

#### 11.11.1.2 The `maxOccurs` Attribute of an `all` Element

The `maxOccurs` attribute determines the maximum number of occurrences in the XML instance of elements whose element types are the set specified by the `all` element. Because the value of the `maxOccurs` attribute is fixed to '1', there can be at most one occurrence of the entire set of elements.

## ATTRIBUTE OVERVIEW

### all: maxOccurs

**Value:** '1'.
**Default:** '1'.
**Constraints:** Fixed; redundant if specified.
**Required:** No.

### 11.11.1.3 The `minOccurs` Attribute of an `all` Element

The `minOccurs` attribute determines the minimum number of occurrences in the XML instance of elements whose element types are the entire set specified by the `all` Element. When the value of the `minOccurs` attribute is set to '0', the entire set of elements is optional.

## ATTRIBUTE OVERVIEW

### all: minOccurs

**Value:** '0' or '1'.
**Default:** '1'.
**Constraints:** None.
**Required:** No.

## 11.11.2 Content Options for an `all` Element

An `all` element may contain an annotation and any number of elements. Table 11.12 details these content options.

**TABLE 11.12** Content Options for an `all` Element

| Element | Description |
| --- | --- |
| annotation | The `annotation` element, discussed in Section 7.5, provides a way to document schema elements. |
| element | Each nested `element` describes an element type, zero or more instances of which might appear in an XML instance (as controlled by each element's `minOccur` and `maxOccur` attribute values). However, the elements may appear in any order. |

The content pattern for an `all` element is:

annotation? element*

## 11.12 The choice Element

The `choice` element provides an XML representation for describing a selection from a set of element types. An XML instance contains elements whose element types are the set specified by the `choice` element in an XML schema document. The `minOccurs` and `maxOccurs` attributes may permit the XML instance to select several (for example, between two and four) occurrences of element types from the set. Listing 11.16 demonstrates the use of a `choice` element whose description is part of the global `priceGroup`. A XML instance must contain one of the following: a `fullPrice` element, a `salePrice` element, a `clearancePrice` element, or a `freePrice` element.

**LISTING 11.16** Selecting from a Set of Elements (pricing.xsd)

```
<xsd:group name="priceGroup" id="priceGroup.group">
    <xsd:annotation>
        <xsd:documentation xml:lang="en">
            A price is any one of the following:
                * Full Price (with amount)
                * Sale Price (with amount and authorization)
                * Clearance Price (with amount and
                  authorization)
                * Free (with authorization)
        </xsd:documentation>
    </xsd:annotation>
    <xsd:choice id="pg.choice">
        <xsd:element name="fullPrice"
                    type="fullPriceType"/>
        <xsd:element name="salePrice"
                    type="salePriceType"/>
        <xsd:element name="clearancePrice"
                    type="clearancePriceType"/>
        <xsd:element name="freePrice" type="freePriceType"/>
    </xsd:choice>
</xsd:group>
```

The XML representation of an element type that ultimately contains the `priceGroup` from Listing 11.16 might look like the following element:

```
<xsd:element name="price">
    <xsd:complexType>
        <xsd:group ref="priceGroup"/>
    </xsd:complexType>
</xsd:element>
```

Given the preceding element type, the following is valid in an XML instance:

```
<price>
    <freePrice authorization="CB"/>
</price>
```

Because of the `choice` element, an alternative to the previous element is to use `<fullPrice>` instead of `<freePrice>` in an XML instance:

```
<price>
    <fullPrice>32.00</fullPrice>
</price>
```

### 11.12.1 Attributes of a `choice` Element

Other than the ubiquitous `id` attribute, the attributes of the `choice` element describe the number of times each element type may occur. Table 11.13 details the attributes of the `choice` element.

> **NOTE**
>
> A `choice` element with no contents is invalid.

**TABLE 11.13**   Attribute Summary of a `choice` Element

| Attribute | Description |
| --- | --- |
| id | The value of an `id` attribute uniquely identifies an element within the set of schema documents that comprise an XML schema. |
| maxOccurs | The value of the `maxOccurs` attribute determines the maximum number of occurrences of the element types represented in an XML instance. Each element in an XML instance must reference an element type that is a member of the set of element types defined by the `choice` element. Furthermore, the maximum number of occurrences of each element type is the product of the `maxOccurs` attribute of the `choice` element and the `maxOccurs` attribute of the element type. |
| minOccurs | The value of the `minOccurs` attribute determines the minimum number of occurrences of the element types represented in an XML instance. Each element in an XML instance must reference an element type that is a member of the set of element types defined by the `choice` element. Furthermore, the minimum number of occurrences of each element type is the product of the `minOccurs` attribute of the `choice` element and the `minOccurs` attribute of the element type. |

> **CAUTION**
>
> The quantity of elements that may appear in an XML instance is constrained by the `minOccurs` and `maxOccurs` attributes of the `choice` element as well as the `minOccurs` and `maxOccurs` attributes of the particular element type.

### 11.12.1.1 The `id` Attribute of a `choice` Element

The value of an `id` attribute uniquely identifies an element within the set of schema documents that comprise an XML schema.

**ATTRIBUTE OVERVIEW**

**choice: id**

| | |
|---:|---|
| **Value:** | An ID. |
| **Default:** | None. |
| **Constraints:** | An `id` must be unique within an XML schema. |
| **Required:** | No. |

Listing 11.16 demonstrates a `choice` element with an associated `id` attribute.

### 11.12.1.2 The `maxOccurs` Attribute of a `choice` Element

The `maxOccurs` attribute determines the maximum number of occurrences in the XML instance of elements whose element types are the set specified by the `choice` element. Note that—as described in Table 11.13—the maximum number of elements associated with each element type cannot be more than the product of the value of the `maxOccurs` attribute of the `choice` element and the value of the `maxOccurs` attribute on the element type.

**ATTRIBUTE OVERVIEW**

**choice: maxOccurs**

| | |
|---:|---|
| **Value:** | A non-negative integer or 'unbounded'. |
| **Default:** | '1'. |
| **Constraints:** | None. |
| **Required:** | No. |

### 11.12.1.3 The `minOccurs` Attribute of a `choice` Element

The `minOccurs` attribute determines the minimum number of occurrences in the XML instance of elements whose element types are the set specified by the `choice` element. Note that—as described in Table 11.13—the minimum number of elements associated with each element type cannot be more than the product of the value of the `minOccurs` attribute of the `choice` element and the value of the `minOccurs` attribute on the element type.

**ATTRIBUTE OVERVIEW**

**choice: minOccurs**

| | |
|---:|:---|
| **Value:** | A non-negative integer. |
| **Default:** | '1'. |
| **Constraints:** | None. |
| **Required:** | No. |

## 11.12.2 Content Options for a `choice` Element

Excluding annotations, the content options for the `choice` element must ultimately resolve to a set of element types. Table 11.14 portrays the options available for a `choice` element.

**TABLE 11.14** Content Options for a `choice` Element

| Element | Description |
|---|---|
| annotation | The `annotation` element, discussed in Section 7.5, provides a way to document schema elements. |
| any | When a `choice` element contains an immediate `any` subelement, the XML instance might contain any set of global element types from the namespaces that the `any` element specifies. Section 8.4 covers the `any` element. |
| choice | When a `choice` element contains another immediate `choice` subelement, the XML instance might contain one of the elements that correspond to an appropriate "selection" from the enclosed `choice`. |
| element | Normally a `choice` element contains a number of element types, each of whose XML representation is an `element`. |
| group | When a `choice` element contains an immediate `group` subelement, the XML instance might contain a set of elements whose element types are the set constrained by the referenced named model group. The contents of the group determines the valid elements. |
| sequence | When a `choice` element contains an immediate `sequence` subelement, the XML instance might contain an ordered set of elements whose element types are the set specified by the enclosed `sequence`. |

The content pattern for a `choice` element is:

annotation? (element | group | choice | sequence | any)*

> **WARNING**
>
> A `choice` element may not contain an immediate `all` subelement. However, the `group` element may contain an `all` subelement. The transitive relationship that might make a `choice` indirectly contain an `all` is invalid, an XML validator might not be able to determine veracity.

## 11.13 The sequence Element

The `sequence` element provides an XML representation of an ordered set of element types. For each element type associated with a `sequence` element in an XML schema document, there must be an element in the XML instance, in the same order. In fact, there may be zero or many elements for each type, depending on the values of the `minOccurs` and `maxOccurs` attributes associated with the element types.

The `baseCatalogEntryType` described in Listing 11.7 contains a `sequence` describing an ordered set of element types.

### 11.13.1 Attributes of a sequence Element

Other than the ubiquitous `id` attribute, the attributes of the `sequence` element describe the number of times each element type must occur. Table 11.15 details the attributes of the `sequence` element.

**TABLE 11.15** Attribute Summary of a `sequence` Element

| Attribute | Description |
| --- | --- |
| id | The value of an `id` attribute uniquely identifies an element within the set of schema documents that comprise an XML schema. |
| maxOccurs | The value of the `maxOccurs` attribute determines the maximum number of occurrences of the element types represented in an XML instance. Each element in an XML instance must reference an element type that is a member of the set of element types defined by the `sequence` element. Furthermore, the maximum number of occurrences of each element type is the product of the `maxOccurs` attribute of the `choice` element and the `maxOccurs` attribute of the element type. |

*continues*

**TABLE 11.15**  *(continued)*

| Attribute | Description |
|---|---|
| minOccurs | The value of the `minOccurs` attribute determines the minimum number of occurrences of the element types represented in an XML instance. Each element in an XML instance must reference each element type, in order, that is a member of the set of element types defined by the `sequence` element. Furthermore, the minimum number of occurrences of each element type is the product of the `minOccurs` attribute of the `choice` element and the `minOccurs` attribute of the element type. |

> **CAUTION**
>
> The quantity of elements that may appear in an XML instance is constrained by the `minOccurs` and `maxOccurs` attributes of the `sequence` element as well as the `minOccurs` and `maxOccurs` attributes of the particular element type.

### 11.13.1.1 The `id` Attribute of a `sequence` Element

The value of an `id` attribute uniquely identifies an element within the set of schema documents that comprise an XML schema.

---

**ATTRIBUTE OVERVIEW**

**sequence: id**

  **Value:** An ID.
  **Default:** None.
  **Constraints:** An `id` must be unique within an XML schema.
  **Required:** No.

---

Listing 11.7 demonstrates a `sequence` element with an associated `id` attribute.

### 11.13.1.2 The `maxOccurs` Attribute of a sequence Element

The `maxOccurs` attribute determines the maximum number of times an XML instance may reference the entire set of element types.

**ATTRIBUTE OVERVIEW**

**sequence: maxOccurs**

| | |
|---:|---|
| Value: | A non-negative integer or 'unbounded'. |
| Default: | '1'. |
| Constraints: | None. |
| Required: | No. |

### 11.13.1.3 The `minOccurs` Attribute of a sequence Element

The `minOccurs` attribute determines the minimum number of times an XML instance may reference the entire set of element types.

**ATTRIBUTE OVERVIEW**

**sequence: minOccurs**

| | |
|---:|---|
| Value: | A non-negative integer or 'unbounded'. |
| Default: | '1'. |
| Constraints: | None. |
| Required: | No. |

## 11.13.2 Content Options for a sequence Element

Excluding annotations, the content options for the sequence element must ultimately resolve to a set of element types. Table 11.16 portrays the options available for a sequence element.

The content pattern for a sequence element is:

```
annotation? (element | group | choice | sequence | any)*
```

TABLE 11.16  Content Options for a sequence Element

| Element | Description |
| --- | --- |
| annotation | The annotation element, discussed in Section 7.5, provides a way to document schema elements. |
| any | When a sequence element contains an immediate any subelement, the XML instance might contain any set of global element types from the namespaces that the any element specifies. Section 8.4 covers the any element. |
| choice | When a sequence element contains an immediate choice subelement, the XML instance might contain the sequence of elements that correspond to an appropriate "selection" from the enclosed choice. |
| element | Normally a sequence element contains a number of element types, each of whose XML representation is an element. |
| group | When a sequence element contains an immediate group subelement, the XML instance might contain a set of elements whose element types are the set specified by the referenced named model group. The contents of the group determines the valid elements. |
| sequence | When a sequence element contains another immediate sequence sub-element, the XML instance might contain an ordered set of elements whose element types are the set specified by the enclosed sequence. |

**WARNING**

A sequence element may not contain an immediate all subelement. However, the sequence element may contain an all subelement. The transitive relationship that might make a sequence indirectly contain an all is invalid, an XML validator might not be able to determine veracity.

## 11.14 The group Element

The group element describes a named model group. A named model group encapsulates an all element, a choice element, or a sequence element. When a complex type incorporates a named model group (via the ref attribute), the scope of the enclosed components change: The namespace for these components becomes local to the parent element type. Note that there might be many different parent element types when the complex type is global, and the complex type is the structure type of multiple element types.

Listing 11.17 repeats the XML representation of `priceGroup`. In addition, Listing 11.17 portrays the utility of this group by repeatedly including `priceGroup` in various catalog entry types.

**LISTING 11.17**  Reuse of a group Element (`pricing.xsd` and `catalog.xsd`)

```xsd
<xsd:group name="priceGroup" id="priceGroup.group">
    <xsd:annotation>
        <xsd:documentation xml:lang="en">
            A price is any one of the following:
                * Full Price (with amount)
                * Sale Price (with amount and authorization)
                * Clearance Price (with amount and
                  authorization)
                * Free (with authorization)
        </xsd:documentation>
    </xsd:annotation>
    <xsd:choice>
        <xsd:element name="fullPrice"
                     type="fullPriceType"/>
        <xsd:element name="salePrice"
                     type="salePriceType"/>
        <xsd:element name="clearancePrice"
                     type="clearancePriceType"/>
        <xsd:element name="freePrice" type="freePriceType"/>
    </xsd:choice>
</xsd:group>

<xsd:complexType name="baseCatalogEntryType"
                 abstract="true"
                 id="baseCatalogEntryType.catalog.cType">
    <xsd:annotation>
        <xsd:documentation xml:lang="en">
            A catalog entry must have:
                * A database ID
                * Part Name
                * Part Number
                * Options available
                * Description
                * Price
                * Included Quantity when ordering
                  one item.
            The "baseCatalogEntryType" is
            non-instantiable: a derived type must
            be created before a catalog
            entry can be instantiated.
                -- Shorthand Notation --
```

```xml
        </xsd:documentation>
    </xsd:annotation>
    <xsd:sequence id="bacet-seq">
        <xsd:element ref="sequenceID"/>
        <xsd:element name="partName" type="partNameType"/>
        <xsd:element name="partNumber" type="partNumberType"/>
        <xsd:element name="partOption" type="partOptionType"/>
        <xsd:element name="description"
                    type="catalogEntryDescriptionType"/>
        <xsd:group ref="priceGroup"/>
        <xsd:element name="includedQuantity"
                    type="xsd:positiveInteger"/>
        <xsd:element name="customerReview"
                    type="customerReviewType"
                            minOccurs="0"
                            maxOccurs="unbounded"/>
    </xsd:sequence>
    <xsd:attribute name="category"
                type="categoryType"
                use="required"/>
</xsd:complexType>

<xsd:complexType name="unitCatalogEntryType"
                block="#all"
                final="#all"
                id="unitCatalogEntryType.catalog.cType">
    <xsd:annotation>
        <xsd:documentation xml:lang="en">
            A unit item contains nothing more
            or less than a basic catalog entry ID:
                * A database ID
                * Part Name
                * Part Number
                * Options available
                * Price
                * Included Quantity when ordering
                    one item (always one for unit items).
        </xsd:documentation>
    </xsd:annotation>
    <xsd:complexContent>
        <xsd:restriction base="baseCatalogEntryType">
            <xsd:sequence>
                <xsd:element ref="unitID"/>
                <xsd:element name="partName"
                            type="partNameType"/>
                <xsd:element name="partNumber"
                            type="unitPartNumberType"/>
```

*continues*

## Complex Types
### Chapter 11

```xml
                    <xsd:element name="partOption"
                                 type="partOptionType"/>
                    <xsd:element name="description"
                                 type="catalogEntryDescriptionType"/>
                    <xsd:group ref="priceGroup"/>
                    <xsd:element name="includedQuantity"
                                 type="xsd:positiveInteger"
                                 fixed="1"/>
                    <xsd:element name="customerReview"
                                 type="customerReviewType"
                                 minOccurs="0"
                                 maxOccurs="unbounded"/>
                </xsd:sequence>
                <xsd:attribute name="category"
                               type="categoryType"
                               fixed="unit"/>
            </xsd:restriction>
        </xsd:complexContent>
    </xsd:complexType>

    <xsd:complexType name="bulkCatalogEntryType"
                     block="#all"
                     final="#all"
                     id="bulkCatalogEntryType.catalog.cType">
        <xsd:annotation>
            <xsd:documentation xml:lang="en">
                A bulk item is just like any
                other, except that the part
                number is restricted to a
                bulk part number.
            </xsd:documentation>
        </xsd:annotation>
        <xsd:complexContent>
            <xsd:restriction base="baseCatalogEntryType">
                <xsd:sequence>
                    <xsd:element ref="bulkID"/>
                    <xsd:element name="partName"
                                 type="partNameType"/>
                    <xsd:element name="partNumber"
                                 type="bulkPartNumberType"/>
                    <xsd:element name="partOption"
                                 type="partOptionType"/>
                    <xsd:element name="description"
                                 type="catalogEntryDescriptionType"/>
                    <xsd:group ref="priceGroup"/>
                    <xsd:element name="includedQuantity"
                                 type="xsd:positiveInteger"/>
```

```xml
            <xsd:element name="customerReview"
                         type="customerReviewType"
                         minOccurs="0"
                         maxOccurs="unbounded"/>
        </xsd:sequence>
        <xsd:attribute name="category"
                       type="categoryType"
                       fixed="bulk"/>
      </xsd:restriction>
    </xsd:complexContent>
</xsd:complexType>

<xsd:complexType
        name="baseAssemblyCatalogEntryType"
        abstract="true"
        block="#all"
        final="restriction"
        id="baseAssemblyCatalogEntryType.catalog.cType">
    <xsd:annotation>
        <xsd:documentation xml:lang="en">
            An assembled item is similar to the
            other catalog entries.  The part number
            is restricted to an assembly number.
            In addition, there may be no options.
            Finally, a part list is also needed.
            Note that the "includedQuantity" has
            a default of one, but can be overridden
            in instances.
        </xsd:documentation>
    </xsd:annotation>
    <xsd:complexContent>
        <xsd:restriction base="baseCatalogEntryType"
                         id="bacet.rst">
            <xsd:sequence>
                <xsd:element ref="assemblyID"/>
                <xsd:element name="partName"
                             type="partNameType"/>
                <xsd:element name="partNumber"
                             type="assemblyPartNumberType"/>
                <xsd:element name="partOption"
                             type="partOptionType"
                             minOccurs="0"
                             maxOccurs="0"/>
                <xsd:element name="description"
                             type="catalogEntryDescriptionType"/>
                <xsd:group ref="priceGroup"/>
                <xsd:element name="includedQuantity"
```

*continues*

```xml
                        type="xsd:positiveInteger"
                        default="1"/>
            <xsd:element name="customerReview"
                        type="customerReviewType"
                        minOccurs="0"
                        maxOccurs="unbounded"/>
        </xsd:sequence>
        <xsd:attribute name="category"
                       type="categoryType"
                       fixed="assembly"/>
      </xsd:restriction>
    </xsd:complexContent>
</xsd:complexType>

<xsd:complexType name="assemblyCatalogEntryType"
                 block="#all"
                 final="#all"
                 id="assemblyCatalogEntryType.catalog.cType">
    <xsd:annotation>
       <xsd:documentation xml:lang="en">
          The actual definition of an assembly,
          including the contained parts.
       </xsd:documentation>
    </xsd:annotation>
    <xsd:complexContent>
       <xsd:extension base="baseAssemblyCatalogEntryType"
                      id="acet.ext">
          <xsd:sequence>
             <xsd:element name="partList"
                          type="partNumberListType"/>
          </xsd:sequence>
       </xsd:extension>
    </xsd:complexContent>
</xsd:complexType>

<xsd:complexType name="catalogType"
                 id="catalogType.catalog.cType">
    <xsd:annotation>
       <xsd:documentation xml:lang="en">
          This catalog type must be altered
          every time a new catalog entry
          type is created.  The
          "catalogType2" complex type refers
          only instantiable derived classes.
                -- Shorthand Notation --
       </xsd:documentation>
    </xsd:annotation>
```

```
    <xsd:choice minOccurs="1"
                maxOccurs="unbounded">
        <xsd:element name="unitPart"
                     type="unitCatalogEntryType"
                     block="restricion extension"/>
        <xsd:element name="bulkPart"
                     type="bulkCatalogEntryType"
                     block="restricion extension"/>
        <xsd:element name="assemblyPart"
                     type="assemblyCatalogEntryType"
                     block="restricion extension"/>
    </xsd:choice>
</xsd:complexType>
```

A `catalog` element whose structure type is the preceding element type might look like the following:

```
<xsd:element name="catalog" type="catalogType"/>
```

Given the preceding element, the following is a valid `catalog` XML instance:

```
<catalog>
    <unitPart>
        <unitID>10327</unitID>
        <partName>Unit 1</partName>
        <partNumber>UX001</partNumber>
        <partOption>
            <color>magenta</color>
        </partOption>
        <description>Unit 1 is the thing to buy</description>
        <fullPrice>28.00</fullPrice>
        <includedQuantity>1</includedQuantity>
    </unitPart>
    <unitPart>
        <unitID>10329</unitID>
        <partName>Unit 2</partName>
        <partNumber>UX002</partNumber>
        <partOption>
            <color>Pink Grapefruit</color>
        </partOption>
        <description>Unit 2 lasts longer than Unit 1</description>
        <fullPrice>28.01</fullPrice>
        <includedQuantity>1</includedQuantity>
    </unitPart>
    <bulkPart>
        <bulkID>40000397</bulkID>
        <partName>Bulk 1</partName>
        <partNumber>BLK2088</partNumber>
```

*continues*

```xml
            <partOption />
            <description>
                This includes 1,000
                <partList>UX002</partList>
                pieces.
            </description>
            <fullPrice>1700.00</fullPrice>
            <includedQuantity>200</includedQuantity>
        </bulkPart>
        <unitPart>
            <unitID>40004787</unitID>
            <partName>Unit 3</partName>
            <partNumber>UX003</partNumber>
            <partOption />
            <description>
                This is obsolete ... on sale
            </description>
            <salePrice employeeAuthorization="MWS"
                    managerAuthorization="ALB">28.03</salePrice>
            <includedQuantity>1</includedQuantity>
        </unitPart>
        <unitPart>
            <unitID>40004787</unitID>
            <partName>Unit 4</partName>
            <partNumber>UX004</partNumber>
            <partOption />
            <description>
                This is also obsolete ... on clearance
            </description>
            <clearancePrice employeeAuthorization="MWS"
                    managerAuthorization="ALB">8.57</clearancePrice>
            <includedQuantity>1</includedQuantity>
        </unitPart>
        <assemblyPart>
            <assemblyID>40004788</assemblyID>
            <partName>Assembly 1</partName>
            <partNumber>ASM9001</partNumber>
            <description>
                This is made up of both
                <partList>UX002 UX003</partList>
                pieces which makes assembly 1
                better than the competition.
            </description>
            <fullPrice>3200.00</fullPrice>
            <includedQuantity>1</includedQuantity>
            <customerReview>
                <customerName>I. M. Happy</customerName>
```

```
            <customerFeedback>This is the most
awesome phat product in the entire
    world.</customerFeedback>
        </customerReview>
        <partList>UX002 UX003</partList>
    </assemblyPart>
</catalog>
```

## 11.14.1  Attributes of a group Element

Named model groups have a name. A local group element must contain a reference to a global named model group. The other attributes of a named model group are similar to other tyes of groups. Table 11.17 describes the attributes for a named model group.

**TABLE 11.17**   Attribute Summary of a group Element

| Attribute | Description |
| --- | --- |
| id | The value of an id attribute uniquely identifies an element within the set of schema documents that comprise an XML schema. |
| maxOccurs | The value of the maxOccurs attribute determines the maximum number of occurrences of the model group represented in an XML instance. The XML instance must reference element types in accordance with the rules of the enclosed model group. Furthermore, the maximum number of occurrences of each element type at most is the product of the maxOccurs attribute of the group element and the maxOccurs attribute of the element type. |
| minOccurs | The value of the minOccurs attribute determines the minimum number of occurrences of the model group represented in an XML instance. The XML instance must reference element types in accordance with the rules of the enclosed model group. Furthermore, the minimum number of occurrences of each element type is the product of the minOccurs attribute of the group element and the minOccurs attribute of the element type, assuming that the element is selected at all. |
| name | The value of the name attribute is the name of the named model group. One or more complex types might reference this named model group. |
| ref | The value of a ref attribute is a reference to a named model group. |

### 11.14.1.1 The `id` Attribute of a group Element

The value of an id attribute uniquely identifies an element within the set of schema documents that comprise an XML schema.

**ATTRIBUTE OVERVIEW**

**group: id**

| | |
|---|---|
| **Value:** | An ID. |
| **Default:** | None. |
| **Constraints:** | An id must be unique within an XML schema. |
| **Required:** | No. |

Listing 11.16 demonstrates a group element with an associated id attribute.

### 11.14.1.2 The `maxOccurs` Attribute of a group Element

The maxOccurs attribute determines the maximum number of times an XML instance may reference the entire set of element types. This attribute is not valid for the global group: This attribute is only valid when the group element is enclosed within a complexType.

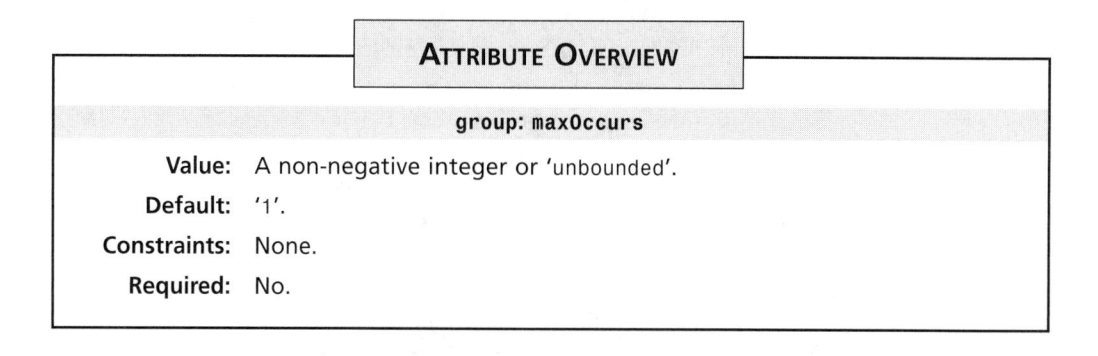

**ATTRIBUTE OVERVIEW**

**group: maxOccurs**

| | |
|---|---|
| **Value:** | A non-negative integer or 'unbounded'. |
| **Default:** | '1'. |
| **Constraints:** | None. |
| **Required:** | No. |

### 11.14.1.3 The `minOccurs` Attribute of a group Element

The minOccurs attribute determines the minimum number of times an XML instance may reference the entire set of element types. This attribute is not valid for a global group: This attribute is only valid when the group element is enclosed within a complexType.

> **ATTRIBUTE OVERVIEW**
>
> **group: minOccurs**
>
> **Value:** A non-negative integer.
> **Default:** '1'.
> **Constraints:** None.
> **Required:** No.

### 11.14.1.4 The name Attribute of a group Element

The value of the name attribute is the name of a global model group. A complex type specifies a global named model group by referring to this name.

> **ATTRIBUTE OVERVIEW**
>
> **group: name**
>
> **Value:** An NCName.
> **Default:** None.
> **Constraints:** None.
> **Required:** No.

### 11.14.1.5 The ref Attribute of a group Element

The ref attribute references a global group.

> **ATTRIBUTE OVERVIEW**
>
> **group: ref**
>
> **Value:** A QName.
> **Default:** None.
> **Constraints:** The name must refer to a named model group (that is, a group element).
> **Required:** No.

## 11.14.2 Content Options for a group Element

Excluding annotations, the content options for the group element must ultimately resolve to a set of element types. Table 11.18 contains the options available for a group element.

**TABLE 11.18** Content Options for a group Element

| Element | Description |
| --- | --- |
| annotation | The annotation element, discussed in Section 7.5, provides a way to document schema elements. |
| all | An all element is the representation of an all model group. |
| choice | A choice element is the XML representation of a choice model group Schema component. |
| sequence | A sequence element is the XML representation of a sequence model group. |

The content pattern for a group element is:

annotation? (all | choice | sequence)

# Built-in Datatypes

CHAPTER
**12**

## IN THIS CHAPTER

12.1 Numeric Datatypes  295

12.2 Date, Time, and Duration Datatypes  304

12.3 String Datatypes  316

12.4 Oddball Datatypes  322

A datatype has two primary components, plus "facets" that are used to describe derived datatypes. The two primary components are a value space and a lexical space. The character strings in the lexical space serve as names for the abstract objects in the value space. There must, of course be a prescribed mapping from lexical-space character strings to value-space values. It's the lexical-space strings that actually occur in XML documents.

On the other hand, most restriction derivations involve restrictions on permitted values in the value space, so when defining restrictions (via an appropriate `simpleType` element in a schema document), you should be aware of the interrelationship between the two. Apart from this, *values* occur at only one point in schema processing. When a default value is prescribed in the schema, the abstract value is recorded in the appropriate place; when the default is placed into an information item, it is converted back to one of the strings in the lexical space that "names" that value.

Specifically, the name to be selected—if there is more than one candidate—is also prescribed as part of the datatype's definition. Every value in the value space is expected to have a distinguished name in the lexical space; that name is the *canonical representation*. The canonical representation is sometimes also used by applications that deal directly with the values when they need to create an XML representation of a result.

> **WARNING**
>
> Derived datatypes normally use the same canonical representation as the base type. However, it is possible, by using a *pattern* facet, to create a derived type that does not have canonical representations from the base type remaining in the lexical space. No way is provided for users to define new canonical representations. Therefore, users should be very careful when using pattern facets; carelessness could produce a datatype with no canonical representations for some or all values, and the defaulting mechanism of schemas is broken for such a datatype. This is a known problem in the current Schema Recommendation, and will undoubtedly be addressed in a subsequent revision.
>
> Also, note that the `integer` datatype is derived by restriction from `decimal`; it too suffers from this problem. The Schema Recommendation solves the problem for `integer` "by fiat"—by simply prescribing in the text a different canonical representation algorithm. This avenue is not available to users.

The remainder of this chapter includes brief descriptions of all the built-in datatypes.

## 12.1 Numeric Datatypes

Datatypes are *numeric* if their value space consists primarily of real numbers. Of the built-in numeric datatypes, all except two have value spaces containing only numbers. The two exceptions, `float` and `double`, have three additional values: POSITIVE INFINITY, NEGATIVE INFINITY, and NOT A NUMBER. (These two datatypes were inspired by IEEE 754, a standard for "floating point" arithmetic.)

Recall that the *natural numbers*—or *nonnegative integers*—are all real numbers, the *integers* are the natural numbers and their negatives, and the *rational numbers* are those real numbers that can be obtained by dividing one integer by another. As it happens, all the built-in numeric datatypes have data spaces that contain only rational numbers. In fact, the largest such value space is that of `decimal`; it consists of those rational numbers that can be expressed as the quotient of an integer and a *power of ten*. (Such numbers are often called "decimal numbers," or simply "decimals" when it is not important to distinguish between numbers and their names.) All other built-in numeric datatypes have value spaces that are subsets of `decimal`'s value space (not counting the three special values in `float` and `double`). (This ignores the fact that the value spaces of primitive datatypes are artificially made disjoint.)

*Numerals*, the character strings in the lexical space of numeric datatypes that serve as "names" for the numbers, are another story. The `float` and `double` datatypes have the largest lexical spaces.

*Base ten Arabic numerals* are the standard names for natural numbers. From them are built other numerals that ultimately name all the decimal numbers. To name the integers, an Arabic numeral can be prefixed with a *sign*, either '+' or '−'. To name the decimal numbers, a *decimal point* may be added to signify division by an appropriate power of ten. Signed Arabic numerals with an internal decimal point are called "decimal numerals," or just "decimals" when it isn't important to distinguish numbers and their names. Finally, a variant is obtained by concatenating a decimal numeral, the letter 'E' (or 'e'), and an Arabic numeral. This complicated numeral names a decimal number that is the result of multiplying the first-named decimal number by ten raised to the power of the named integer. For example, '1.3E3', '0.013E5', and '1300' all name the same number. These more complicated numerals, collectively called "scientific notation," simply add more (and often *more convenient*) names for the same numbers. (For example, the number 1E100 is a "googol"; to name it by using a simple Arabic numeral would require one hundred and one digits.)

`decimal` does not include "scientific notation" numerals in its lexical space, but `float` and `double` both do. However, the latter two are unusual in their treatment of the numeral-to-number mapping. See Section 12.1.2.

## 12.1.1 The Built-in `decimal` Datatype

When a schema component specifies a `decimal` datatype, a valid XML instance must contain a value (character string) that is a decimal numeral—one with no "exponent" ('E') part but possibly a decimal point. The matching abstract value must be a decimal number, as just defined.

The Schema Recommendation currently requires that a schema implementation handle at least 18 decimal digits (`totalDigits`). Some implementations will handle more and more digits until they run out of real and virtual memory; others may have real limits, but the limits must be at least 18 digits.

> **CAUTION**
>
> The Schema Recommendation does not exactly specify how an implementation is to react when presented with a lexical representation of a value it does not implement. It should not silently round to a value it implements; rather it should behave like it might if it ran out of memory—however that is. This may change in a subsequent revision of the Recommendation.

The following two `element` elements are each a representation of an element type with `decimal` (or `decimal`-derived) simple content. The simple version is:

```
<xsd:element name="demoDecimal" type="xsd:decimal"/>
```

A version with some constraining facets is:

```
<xsd:element name="demoDecimal">
    <xsd:simpleType>
        <xsd:restriction base="xsd:decimal">
            <xsd:totalDigits value="8"/>
            <xsd:fractionDigits value="2"/>
        </xsd:restriction>
    </xsd:simpleType>
</xsd:element>
```

Given either of the preceding element types, the following are both valid instances:

```
<demoDecimal>-32.81</demoDecimal>
<demoDecimal>-32</demoDecimal>
```

> **TIP**
>
> Restricting `fractionDigits` to 2 nonetheless allows
>
> `<demoDecimal>-32.8100</demoDecimal>`
>
> and
>
> `<demoDecimal>-32</demoDecimal>`
>
> as valid instances because the restriction applies to the value, not the lexical representation. To restrict the lexical representations directly, a `pattern` restriction is required. But see the warning near the beginning of this chapter regarding the possible deleterious impact on canonical representations.

### 12.1.1.1 `decimal` Constraining Facets

The following constraining facets apply when deriving from the built-in `decimal` datatype:

- `fractionDigits`
- `totalDigits`
- `maxExclusive`
- `maxInclusive`
- `minExclusive`
- `minInclusive`
- `pattern`
- `enumeration`
- `whiteSpace`

`fractionDigits` and `totalDigits` are unique to `decimal` and the other datatypes derived from `decimal`. `whiteSpace` is fixed to COLLAPSE and therefore cannot be further restricted.

Note that constraining with `totalDigits` or `fractionDigits` does not constrain the lexical space to prohibit numerals that appear to have excessive redundant '`0`' digits.

### 12.1.1.2 `decimal` Derivation Relationships

The `decimal` datatype is primitive. The `integer` datatype is the only built-in that is directly derived from `decimal`, but `nonNegativeInteger`, `nonPositiveInteger`, `int`, `long`, `short`, `byte`, `unsignedInt`, `unsignedLong`, and `unsignedShort` are all "ultimately" derived from `decimal`.

### 12.1.1.3 `decimal` Alternatives

If you need values that conveniently support very large and very small numbers (up to a point), and you don't need to deal with arbitrary accuracy, use `float` or `double` instead. On the other hand, if you need only integers, use `integer` or—to closely match the restrictions inherent in most computer implementations—`byte`, `long`, or one of the other size-restricted integer datatypes. Don't derive your own version of `integer` from `float` unless you choose to permit redundant decimal points and fractional zeros in lexical representations—the `decimal` canonical representations that you will inherit must have a decimal point and one fractional zero digit following it.

## 12.1.2 The Built-in Floating-point Datatypes: `float` and `double`

The special characteristic about `float` and `double` is their handling of the numeral-to-number (lexical space to value space) mapping. The usual mapping, derived directly from the basic Arabic numerals and described earlier in Section 12.1, provides names for every decimal number. However, the `float` and `double` datatypes have finite value spaces. Rather than eliminating the numerals that name numbers not in the value space, they *remap* the numerals to the closest remaining value. Numerals nominally naming very large or very negative decimal numbers well beyond the maximum or minimum of the data space are mapped to the appropriate signed infinity.

When a schema component specifies a `float` datatype, a valid XML instance may contain any "scientific notation" numeral, as defined earlier. It may also contain any of the four strings 'Inf', '+Inf', '-Inf', and 'NaN'. `float` is designed to work with floating-point computational systems that comply with IEEE 754; that standard prescribes these additional "numerals." (See *ANSI/IEEE Std 754-1985, IEEE Standard for Binary Floating-point Arithmetic*, for more information.)

Values in the value space for `float`, other than the special values POSITIVE INFINITY, NEGATIVE INFINITY, and NOT A NUMBER, are constrained to those that can be obtained by computing $m \cdot 2^e$, where $m$ is an integer whose absolute value is less than $2^{24}$, and $e$ is an integer between $-149$ and $104$, inclusive. The value space for `double` is the same, except that $m$ must have an absolute value less than $2^{53}$, and $e$ must be between $-1075$ and $970$. These ranges are prescribed by IEEE 754.

> **CAUTION**
>
> The data space of `float` is a subset of the data space of `double` that could be described as a derivation if the appropriate facet were provided. The problem with such an attempt is that doing so destroys the mapping; numerals mapping to numbers in the base space but not in the derived space disappear from the lexical space instead of being mapped to other remaining numbers.
>
> The writers of the Schema Recommendation therefore made `float` independent of `double`. Users do not have this option and must be wary of making restrictions to `float` or `double` lest they get unexpected results.

The following two element elements are representations of element types with `float` (or `float`-derived) simple content. The simple version is

```
<xsd:element name="demoFloat" type="xsd:float"/>
```

A version with some constraining facets is

```
<xsd:element name="demoFloat">
    <xsd:simpleType>
        <xsd:restriction base="xsd:float">
            <xsd:pattern value="[0-9].[0-9]{5}E[0-9]+"/>
        </xsd:restriction>
    </xsd:simpleType>
</xsd:element>
```

Given either of the preceding element types, the following is a valid instance:

```
<demoFloat>3.14159E0</demoFloat>
```

Replace 'xsd:float' with 'xsd:double' and you have an example using `double`.

> **CAUTION**
>
> Lest you be misled, be aware that, for example, the number 3.14159 is not in the `float` datatype's data space: It cannot be obtained as $m \cdot 2^e$. The actual `float` value of the numeral '3.14159E0' is a number that *can* be so represented and is the closest such to 3.14159.

### 12.1.2.1 Floating-point Constraining Facets

The following constraining facets apply when deriving from the built-in `float` and `double` datatypes:

- maxExclusive
- maxInclusive
- minExclusive
- minInclusive
- pattern
- enumeration
- whiteSpace

`whiteSpace` is COLLAPSE and therefore cannot be further restricted.

### 12.1.2.2 Floating-point Derivation Relationships

The `float` and `double` datatypes are primitive, and no built-in datatypes are derived from them.

### 12.1.2.3 Floating-point Alternatives

If the XML instances will not contain exponents, consider using `decimal`. If you need numbers larger than those supported by `float`, use `double`; if you need numbers larger than those supported by `double`, you must use `decimal`. You must then be prepared for *huge* numerals in the XML representations, and be sure your implementation can handle the number of digits you require. If you need exact representations of decimal numbers (such as 0.1, 3.14159, or very large integers) that cannot be *exactly* represented by float or double, you must use `decimal` and have an implementation that supports very large total digits.

## 12.1.3 The Built-in Infinite Integer Datatypes: `integer`, `positiveInteger`, `negativeInteger`, `nonPositiveInteger`, and `nonNegativeInteger`

When a schema component specifies an `integer` datatype, a valid XML instance must contain an integer numeral—one with no decimal point or "exponent part" but possibly a sign. The matching value in the value space must be a negative or positive integer (number, not numeral) or zero. (The derivation is by `fractionDigits` to zero *and* a pattern prohibiting the decimal point in the lexical representation.) The remaining datatypes, `positiveInteger`, `negativeInteger`, `nonPositiveInteger`, and `nonNegativeInteger`, cut off at zero, using respectively the `minExclusive`, `maxExclusive`, `maxInclusive`, and `minInclusive` facets with value zero. The corresponding restrictions of their lexical spaces are obvious.

The canonical representations of `integer` values are the same as their canonical representations as `decimal` values, but with the decimal point and trailing fractional zero digit removed. See the note in Section 12.1.3.2.

The following two `element` elements are each a representation of an element type with `integer` (or integer-derived) simple content. The simple version is:

```
<xsd:element name="demoInteger" type="xsd:integer"/>
```

A version with some constraining facets is:

```
<xsd:element name="demoInteger">
    <xsd:simpleType>
        <xsd:restriction base="xsd:integer">
            <xsd:minInclusive value="3"/>
            <xsd:maxInclusive value="5"/>
        </xsd:restriction>
    </xsd:simpleType>
</xsd:element>
```

Given either of the preceding element types, the following is a valid instance:

```
<demoInteger>4</demoInteger>
```

The same element would be valid when using `positiveInteger` or `nonNegativeInteger`, but obviously not when using `negativeInteger` or `nonPositiveInteger`.

### 12.1.3.1 Infinite Integer Constraining Facets

The following constraining facets apply when deriving from the built-in `integer`, `positiveInteger`, `negativeInteger`, `nonPositiveInteger`, and `nonNegativeInteger` datatypes:

- `fractionDigits`
- `totalDigits`
- `maxExclusive`
- `maxInclusive`
- `minExclusive`
- `minInclusive`
- `pattern`
- `enumeration`
- `whiteSpace`

`fractionDigits` and `totalDigits` are unique to `decimal` and the other datatypes derived from it. `whiteSpace` is COLLAPSE and `fractionDigits` is zero; therefore, neither can be further restricted.

> **CAUTION**
>
> Constraining with `totalDigits` constrains the *value space*; it does *not* constrain the lexical space to prohibit numerals that have apparently excessive redundant leading '0' digits. A pattern is required to prohibit redundant '0' digits.

### 12.1.3.2 Infinite Integer Derivation Relationships

The `integer` datatype is directly derived from `decimal`, which is primitive. `nonNegativeInteger` and `nonPositiveInteger` are the built-in infinite datatypes directly derived from `integer`; `positiveInteger` and `negativeInteger` derive respectively from those two. Of the finite derived datatypes, `long` directly derives from `integer`, and `unsignedLong` from `nonNegativeInteger`. `int`, `short`, and `byte` derive through `long`; `unsignedInt`, `unsignedShort`, and `unsignedByte` derive through `unsignedLong`. Hence, all are "ultimately" derived from `decimal`.

> **NOTE**
>
> In deriving the `integer` datatype from `decimal`, a pattern facet is used to eliminate such strings as '3.000' from the lexical space. This actually makes the restriction of `fractionDigits` to zero redundant. It also has the effect of removing the canonical representations from the lexical space. A user has no means of defining new canonical representations, which can cause trouble with schema-provided default values. Because `integer` is built in, it gets new canonical representations "by fiat" in the Schema Recommendation; this avenue is not available for user-defined derivations.

### 12.1.3.3 Infinite Integer Alternatives

If you need a datatype that conveniently supports very large integers (up to a point), and you don't need to deal with arbitrary accuracy, consider using `float` or `double` instead. If you want to restrict to a commonly used range of integers such as you might find in programming systems, consider `int`, `long`, `short`, or `byte` or their nonnegative-only counterparts `unsignedInt`, `unsignedLong`, `unsignedShort`, or `unsignedbyte`. If you specifically want to constrain values to positive or negative (including or excluding zero), use `positiveInteger`, `negativeInteger`, `nonPositiveInteger`, or `nonNegativeInteger`.

## 12.1.4 The Built-in Finite Integer Datatypes: `long`, `int`, `short`, `byte`, `unsignedLong`, `unsignedInt`, `unsignedShort`, and `unsignedByte`

When a schema component specifies any `integer`-derived datatype, a valid XML instance must contain an integer numeral—one with no decimal point or "exponent part" but possibly a sign. The matching value in the value space must be a negative or positive integer (number, not numeral) or zero. The finite derivatives are sized so that they will store (as binary Arabic numerals with one-bit digits, using twos-complement for the signed versions) in 32, 16, and 8 bits, respectively.

The following two `element` elements are representations of element types with `long` (or `long`-derived) simple content. The simple version is

```
<xsd:element name="demoLong" type="xsd:long"/>
```

A version with some constraining facets is:

```
<xsd:element name="demoLong">
    <xsd:simpleType>
        <xsd:restriction base="xsd:long">
            <xsd:minInclusive value="3"/>
            <xsd:maxInclusive value="5"/>
        </xsd:restriction>
    </xsd:simpleType>
</xsd:element>
```

Given either of the preceding element types, the following is a valid instance:

```
<demoLong>4</demoLong>
```

If any other of the built-in finite integer datatypes is used instead of `long`, the instance would still be valid.

### 12.1.4.1 Finite Integer Constraining Facets

The following constraining facets apply when deriving from the built-in `long`, `int`, `short`, `byte`, `unsignedLong`, `unsignedInt`, `unsignedShort`, and `unsignedByte` datatypes:

- fractionDigits
- totalDigits
- maxExclusive
- maxInclusive
- minExclusive
- minInclusive
- pattern

- enumeration
- whiteSpace

`fractionDigits` and `totalDigits` are unique to `decimal` and the other datatypes derived from it. `whiteSpace` is COLLAPSE and `fractionDigits` is zero; therefore, neither can be further restricted.

> **CAUTION**
>
> Constraining with `totalDigits` constrains the *value space*; it does *not* constrain the lexical space to prohibit numerals that have apparently excessive redundant leading '0' digits.

### 12.1.4.2 Finite Integer Derivation Relationships

The `long` datatype directly derives from `integer`, and `unsignedLong` from `nonNegativeInteger`. `int` is a derivative of `long`, `short` of `int`, and `byte` of `int`; `unsignedInt` is a derivative of `unsignedLong`, `unsignedShort` of `unsignedInt`, and `unsignedByte` of `unsignedInt`. Hence, all are "ultimately" derived from `decimal`. All are derived using appropriate `maxInclusive` limits (and `minInclusive` limits, for the signed versions) so that they will store (as binary Arabic numerals with one-bit digits, using twos-complement for the signed versions) in 32, 16, and 8 bits, respectively.

### 12.1.4.3 Finite Integer Alternatives

If you want to restrict to a commonly used range of integers such as you might find in programming systems, consider `int`, `long`, `short`, or `byte`, or their nonnegative-only counterparts `unsignedInt`, `unsignedLong`, `unsignedShort`, or `unsignedbyte`. If you need a datatype that conveniently supports very large integers (up to a point), and you don't need to deal with arbitrary accuracy, consider using `float` or `double` instead. If you specifically want to constrain values to positive or negative (including or excluding zero), use `positiveInteger`, `negativeInteger`, `nonPositiveInteger`, or `nonNegativeInteger`.

## 12.2  Date, Time, and Duration Datatypes

The Schema Recommendation introduces a number of datatypes related to dates and times. They can be partitioned naturally into three groups:

- Individual points on the "*time line*": dates, with and without times
- Lengths of intervals on the *time line*: durations
- Sets of points on the *time line*, modulo some interval: repeating times

In this respect, the *time line* is much like the "number line" used to describe real numbers (and Schema's `decimal`, for that matter).

Think of a continuous number line: One point is the origin; another is "one year" to the right. Think of the origin as the moment at the boundary of the year A.D. 1 and the year 1 B.C. and the other point as the moment at the boundary of A.D. 1 and A.D. 2. From there on, you can divide years into months, months into days, days into hours, hours into minutes, and minutes into seconds, and then have arbitrary fractional seconds between the whole seconds. This is the *time line*.

Start with the value space of decimal; treat it as counting time in seconds. Zero is the boundary between 1 C.E. ("Common Era," often called "A.D.") and 1 B.C.E. ("Before Common Era," often called "B.C."). Every so many seconds there is a *minute*: usually 60 seconds, occasionally 61, and there are a few other weird "minutes" on the time line. Yes, not all minutes have 60 seconds, only most of them. Now look at the minutes; every so many (usually but not *always* 60) minutes there is an *hour*. Every (usually) 24 hours there is a *day*. Every so many (28, 29, 30, 31; even this list has an exception or two) days there is a *month*. Almost always every 12 months there is a year. The anomalies, of course, arise from leap years, "leap seconds," various sizes of months, and an arbitrary fix or two when someone decided that the calendar had gotten too far out of sync with the earth's rotation around the sun.

Seconds are very smooth; all else is somewhat chaotic—but we have a time line. However, it is clear that you cannot exactly say, for example, how many seconds there are in a month, at least until you specify *which* month. The same for a year, a day, a week, an hour, a minute, or a century. 5:00 A.M. on 15 April 1998 is a specific number of seconds from zero, but it is pretty tricky to figure out exactly how many.

More complication arises because times can be "absolute" (tied to a time zone) or "generic" (not tied to a time zone). No problem comparing time points when both are in the same category, but the generic noon, 12:00:00, can be any time during the day on the "absolute" time line (which is explicitly tied to Coordinated Universal Time ("Z," formerly Greenwich Mean Time, "GMT").

> **CAUTION**
>
> The ISO Standard for which the various date, time, and duration datatypes were designed permits a year 0000, which seems to be generally interpreted, at least in computer-based systems, as 1 B.C.E., the year before the year 0001, which is 1 C.E. So –0001 is 2 B.C.E., and so forth.

## 12.2.1 The Built-in *Time-line*-based Datatypes: dateTime, date, gYearMonth, and gYear

When a schema component specifies a `dateTime` datatype, a valid XML instance must contain a value (character string) that corresponds to the date and time components specified in ISO 8601. The lexical values of the `dateTime` datatype are nominally of the form

```
cctt-mm-ddThh:mm:ss
```

in which the date and time are represented as follows:

- *cc* represents the century.
- *yy* represents the year within the century.
- '-' is a separator between parts of the date portion.
- the first *mm* represents the month.
- *dd* represents the day.
- 'T' is a separator indicating that time-of-day follows (compare `date` and `time`, Section 12.2.3).
- *hh* represents the hour.
- ':' is a separator between parts of the time-of-day portion.
- The second *mm* represents the minutes.
- *ss* represents the seconds.

The preceding lexical values must all be positive integer numerals with exactly two digits (which might require a leading zero), with two exceptions. One exception is the century (*cc*), which may have '+' or '-' prefixed and may have more than two digits (in which case, no leading zero digits permitted). A negative century indicates years B.C.E. (Before Common Era, often called B.C.). The other exception is the seconds (*ss*), which may be an unsigned decimal numeral (denoting fractions of a second)—but must still have exactly two leading integer digits.

The following two `element` elements are representations of element types with `dateTime` (or `dateTime`-derived) simple content. The simple version is

```
<xsd:element name="demoDateTime" type="xsd:dateTime"/>
```

A version with some constraining facets that constrain corresponding instances to a date and time between 1970 and 2050, inclusive, is:

```
<xsd:element name="demoDateTime">
    <xsd:simpleType>
        <xsd:restriction base="xsd:dateTime">
            <xsd:minInclusive value="1970-01-01T00:00:00"/>
            <xsd:maxExclusive value="2051-01-01T00:00:00"/>
```

```
        </xsd:restriction>
    </xsd:simpleType>
</xsd:element>
```

The upper bound is given via a `maxExclusive` attribute to ensure that all fractional-second values, no matter how close to the end of the last day, are included.

Given either of the preceding element types, the following is a valid instance:

```
<demoDateTime>2000-04-01T16:58:03.22</demoDateTime>
```

On the other hand, the following is a valid instance only of the "simple" datatype, because the derived datatype does not permit years before 1970 (–2000 is well before 1970):

```
<demoDateTime>-2000-04-01T16:58:03.22</demoDateTime>
```

> **CAUTION**
>
> Implementations are not required to handle centuries of more than two digits. They must handle fractional seconds to six fraction digits (microseconds), and must round if more digits are presented in a representation.

> **WARNING**
>
> ISO 8601 permits year 0000, and the Schema Recommendation makes 0000 valid and prescribes that, in conformity with a common current practice, 0000 be the year 1 B.C.E.—the year before 1 C.E., which is 0001. (This wasn't always the case; a prohibition against using year 0000 was removed by an Erratum to the Recommendation.)

### 12.2.1.1 Discrete Times: The "Integers" of the *Time Line*

It would be easy to "integerize" the *time line* at many different granularities. For example, you could ignore fractions of a second. You could ignore seconds—or minutes—or hours or days or months or years (leaving centuries or millennia). These would all appear to be relatively easy to derive from `dateTime` by using a `pattern` facet restriction.

However, removing any of these parts of the lexical representation results in a character string that is not a valid representation of a `dateTime`. Therefore, the Schema Recommendation has chosen to provide three discrete date/time datatypes—`date`, `gYearMonth`, and `gYear`—and makes them all primitive with their own lexical representations. They represent ignoring time-of-day, day-within-month, and month-within-year, respectively.

When a schema component specifies a `date` datatype, a valid XML instance must contain a value (character string) that corresponds to the date components specified in ISO 8601. The lexical values of the `date`, `gYearMonth`, and `gYear` datatypes are nominally of the forms

```
cctt-mm-dd
cctt-mm
cctt
```

respectively (with optional sign), where the date is represented exactly the same way as for `dateTime` just described.

The following two `element` elements are each a representation of an element type whose structure type is `date` (or derived from `date`). The simple version is:

```
<xsd:element name="demoDate" type="xsd:date"/>
```

A version with constraining facets that constrain corresponding instances to a date between 1970 and 2050, inclusive, is:

```
<xsd:element name="demoDate">
    <xsd:simple>
        <xsd:restriction base="xsd:date">
            <xsd:minInclusive value="1970-01-01"/>
            <xsd:maxInclusive value="2050-01-01"/>
        </xsd:restriction>
    </xsd:simpleType>
</xsd:element>
```

Given either of the preceding element types, the following is a valid instance:

```
<demoDate>2000-04-01</demoDate>
```

On the other hand, the following is a valid instance only of the "simple" datatype, because the derived datatype does not permit years before 1970 (–2000 is well before 1970):

```
<demoDateTime>-2000-04-01</demoDate>
```

To illustrate the other datatypes, here are two examples, with values:

'`2000-04`': April 2000

'`2000`': the year 2000

### 12.2.1.2 Time Zones

The generic points in time just described have no associated time zone, not even Coordinated Universal Time, which is the correct modern term for what is often called Greenwich Mean Time. It is possible to pin a time zone to a point in time, still using any of the *time-line*-based datatypes.

## 12.2 Date, Time, and Duration Datatypes

Any of the lexical values described for the *time-line*-based datatypes may have a time zone suffix attached.

The universal suffix consists of

    +hh:mm

or

    -hh:mm

to indicate the time to add or subtract to indicate a specific time zone. The simple suffix 'Z' has the same meaning as '+00:00': "Coordinated Universal Time."

To illustrate, here are a few examples:

- '2000-04-01T13:58:03.22': April 1, 2000 13:58:03.22, generic—no time zone
- '2000-04-01T13:58:03.22Z': April 1, 2000 13:58:03.22, Coordinated Universal Time
- '2000-04-01T13:58:03.22-07:00': April 1, 2000 13:58:03.22, (US) Mountain Standard Time
- '-0004-04-01T13:58:03.22Z': April 1, 5 B.C.E. 13:58:03.22, Coordinated Universal Time
- '2000-04-01': April 1, 2000, generic—no time zone
- '2000-04-01Z': April 1, 2000, Coordinated Universal Time
- '2000-04': April 2000, generic—no time zone
- '-0004-04-01Z': April 1, 3 B.C.E., Coordinated Universal Time

(In these examples we have assumed that 1 B.C.E. is 0000, not –0001.)

> **NOTE**
>
> 2000-04-01T13:58:03.22Z is eight hours before 2000-04-01T13:58:03.22-08:00; thus the former is less than the latter. 2000-04-01T13:58:03.22-08:00 is the same as 2000-04-01T21:58:03.22Z.
>
> 2000-04-01T16:58:03.22 is a generic time that is not comparable with either of the other two.

> **NOTE**
>
> No distinction is made between Standard Time and Daylight Saving Time, nor between *which* time zone is indicated—all are effectively converted to Coordinated Universal Time. 2000-04-01T13:58:03.22-07:00 is also 13:58:03.22 April 1, 2000, *Pacific Daylight Saving Time*—and is also 2000-04-01T20:58:03.22Z.
>
> This conversion to Coordinated Universal Time gives the *canonical* representation for all date/time datatype values that are not generic (that *have* an attached time zone), using the 'Z' suffix.

### 12.2.1.3 *Time-line*-based Constraining Facets

The following constraining facets apply when deriving from the built-in `dateTime` or `date` datatypes:

- `maxExclusive`
- `maxInclusive`
- `minExclusive`
- `minInclusive`
- `pattern`
- `enumeration`
- `whiteSpace`

`whiteSpace` is COLLAPSE and therefore cannot be further restricted.

> **WARNING**
>
> *Time-line*-based datatypes are only partially ordered. Generic points in time can be thought of as having an unknown time zone. Because of this, comparing (in the sense of ordering from earlier times to later times) a generic `dateTime` or `date` value with a corresponding `dateTime` or `date` value tied to a time zone can have unexpected results: some are not comparable! You cannot tell whether 2000-04-01T16:58:03.22 is before or after—or the same as—2000-04-01T16:58:03.22Z. Because they are not comparable, specifying either in setting a max or min limit will disallow the other.

> **TIP**
>
> If *all* values are tied to time zones, or *all* values are generic, the ordering is total. You should derive datatypes that either require or prohibit time zones if a total order is important. This is most easily done by using a `pattern` facet restriction.

### 12.2.1.4 *Time-line*-based Derivation Relationships

The `dateTime`, `date`, `gMonthYear`, and `gYear` datatypes are primitive. There are no built-in derivations of `dateTime`, `date`, `gMonthYear`, and `gYear`. `date` cannot be derived from `dateTime` as `integer` is derived from `decimal`, for two reasons:

- Although the value space is a subset, no facets are provided that will furnish the precise restriction needed.
- The lexical values for the `date` datatype are not available in the lexical space of `dateTime`.

The others cannot be derived one from another for much the same reasons.

### 12.2.1.5 *Time-line*-based Alternatives

There are no reasonable built-in alternatives to `dateTime`, `date`, `gMonthYear`, and `gYear` datatypes—other than each other, depending on the value granularity you need.

## 12.2.2 The Built-in `duration` Datatype

"Time-line" dates and times cannot be added one to another. The "arithmetic" of dates and times is carried out using *durations*. Durations can be added and subtracted one from another *ad infinitum*. A duration also can be added or subtracted from a time-line date or time; the result is another date or time.

That said, you should be aware that Schema does not care about the arithmetic of dates, times, and durations, with only one exception: The time zone suffix is effectively a duration added to the date or time indicated to get the Coordinated Universal Time point on the time line.

When a schema component specifies a `duration` datatype, a valid XML instance must contain a value (character string) that corresponds to the date and time components specified in ISO 8601. The lexical values of the `duration` datatype are nominally of the form

    P*y*Y*m*M*d*DT*h*H*m*M*s*S

in which the date and time are broken up as follows:

- 'P' is a prefix indicating that this is a `duration` (required by ISO 8601).
- *y* represents the number of years.

- 'Y' is a terminator indicating the preceding digits represent years.
- The first *m* represents the number of months.
- The first 'M' is a terminator indicating the preceding digits represent months.
- *d* represents the number of days.
- 'D' is a terminator indicating the preceding digits represent months; 'T' is a separator indicating that time-of-day follows (compare `dateTime` in Section 12.2.1).
- *h* represents the number of hours.
- 'H' is a terminator indicating the preceding digits represent hours.
- The second *m* represents the number of minutes.
- The second 'M' is a terminator indicating the preceding digits represent minutes.
- *s* represents the number of seconds.
- 'S' is a terminator indicating the preceding unsigned decimal numeral represents seconds.

All of the preceding numerals must be positive integer numerals, with one exception: the seconds(*s*), which may be an unsigned decimal numeral (denoting fractions of a second). Fractions finer than microseconds are rounded to microseconds. A negative sign preceding the `'P'` indicates a negative duration.

The combination of a numeral (*y*, *m*, *d*, *h*, *m*, *s*) and its following terminator is called (just for this discussion) a "component." Any of the components may be omitted, as long as one remains; the 'T' separator must occur if any time components occur, but otherwise must not. The initial 'P' is always required.

The following two `element` elements are representations of element types whose structure type is `duration` (or derived from `duration`). The simple version is

```
<xsd:element name="demoDuration" type="xsd:duration"/>
```

A version with some constraining facets that constrain corresponding instances to durations of at least one month is

```
<xsd:element name="demoDuration">
    <xsd:simpleType>
        <xsd:restriction base="xsd:duration">
            <xsd:minInclusive value="P1M"/>
        </xsd:restriction>
    </xsd:simpleType>
</xsd:element>
```

Given either of the preceding element types, the following is a valid instance:

```
<demoDuration>P1M3DT6H</demoDuration>
```

On the other hand, the following is a valid instance only of the simple datatype, because the derived datatype requires values greater than or equal to P1M, and P30D is incomparable with P1M:

```
<demoDuration>P30D</demoDuration>
```

> **TIP**
>
> To avoid problems with incomparable values, consider using a `pattern` facet restriction to permit only one duration component—or warn your users about the problems and enjoin them to avoid edge cases.

To illustrate other possibilities, here are a few examples, with corresponding values:

- `'P80D'`: 80 days
- `'P2Y3M'`: Two years and three months
- `'P1DT6H32M7.544S'`: One day, six hours, 32 minutes, 7.544 seconds
- `'-P5D'`: Five days, *negative*

> **NOTE**
>
> `duration`s cannot carry a time zone.

### 12.2.2.1 `duration` Constraining Facets

The following constraining facets apply when deriving from the built-in `duration` datatype:

- `maxExclusive`
- `maxInclusive`
- `minExclusive`
- `minInclusive`
- `pattern`
- `enumeration`
- `whiteSpace`

`whiteSpace` is COLLAPSE and therefore cannot be further restricted.

> **WARNING**
>
> The duration value space is only partially ordered. For example, one month is not comparable to 30 days. Specifying a maxInclusive of one month eliminates not only durations of 32 days and more but also 29 through 31 days. Similar possibly unexpected edge cases occur when years compare with days and years or months compare with hours, minutes, and seconds. All days are exactly 24 hours; leap seconds are ignored. Multiple duration components in one value (months, days, seconds, and so on) can make edge cases even more fuzzy.
>
> These comparisons apply to Schema uses only; if an application chooses to compare differently, it may do so.

> **TIP**
>
> To avoid comparison problems with durations, consider using a pattern facet to derive datatypes that permit only one of the possible duration components.

### 12.2.2.2 duration Derivation Relationships

duration is a primitive datatype, and no built-in datatypes are derived from it.

### 12.2.2.3 duration Alternatives

There are no useful alternatives to duration. Make sure, however, that what you need is a *duration* and not a repeating time period (time, gMonthDay, gDay, or gMonth). Specifically, a duration is a *time interval*, whereas a repeating date or time is a *recurring event*. For example, to indicate a report date on the first of each month, do not specify a duration of one month—rather, specify a gDay of "first day of the month."

## 12.2.3 The Built-in Repeating Dates and Times Datatypes: time, gMonthDay, gDay, and gMonth

Repeating dates and times are effectively dates and/or times modulo an appropriate time interval. time is modulo day (so that 24:00:00 *is the same value* as 00:00:00), gMonthDay is modulo years and "integerized" to "day precision", gDay is modulo months and integerized to day precision, and gMonth is modulo years and integerized to month precision.

When a schema component specifies a repeating time datatype, a valid XML instance must contain a value lexical representation that corresponds to the components specified in ISO

8601. The lexical values of the `time`, `gMonthDay`, `gDay`, and `gMonth` datatypes are nominally of the form

*hh:mm:ss*

*--mm-dd*

*---dd*

*--mm*

respectively, where the date is represented exactly the same way as for `dateTime` (described in Section 12.2.1).

Appropriate `element` elements for these element types should be obvious. To illustrate lexical representations and corresponding values, here are a few examples:

- '`--04`': The month of April, recurring each year, generic—no time zone
- '`---04`': The fourth day of the month, recurring each month, generic—no time zone
- '`--04-04`': The fourth day of April, recurring each year, generic—no time zone
- '`16:58:03-05:00`': Fifty-eight minutes and three seconds after 4 P.M., recurring each day, Eastern Standard Time or Central Daylight Saving Time—or after 9 P.M. Coordinated Universal Time

### 12.2.3.1 Repeating Dates and Times Constraining Facets

The following constraining facets apply when deriving from any of the built-in repeating dates and times datatypes:

- `maxExclusive`
- `maxInclusive`
- `minExclusive`
- `minInclusive`
- `pattern`
- `enumeration`
- `whiteSpace`

`whiteSpace` is COLLAPSE and therefore cannot be further restricted.

### 12.2.3.2 Repeating Dates and Times Derivation Relationships

All of the repeating dates and times datatypes are primitive datatypes, and no built-in datatypes are derived from them.

### 12.2.3.3 Repeating Dates and Times Alternatives

There are no serious alternatives to the repeating time period datatypes. Make sure, however, that what you need is a repeating time point and not a duration. Specifically, a duration is a *time interval*, whereas a repeating date or time is a *recurring event*. See the description of durations at the beginning of Section 12.2.2.

## 12.3 String Datatypes

The `string` datatype is the archetype for all string-oriented datatypes. It is effectively completely defined by these facts:

- The mapping from the lexical space to the value space is the identity function.
- Both spaces consist of all possible strings of characters of finite length.

As a result, all derived types are completely defined by restrictions on the space. Because the mapping between them is the identity, any restriction on either space automatically induces the same restriction on the other.

A few datatypes nominally derived from `string` have aspects that do not follow from their derivation. We discuss them separately in Section 12.3.3.

### 12.3.1 The Built-in `string` Datatype

When a schema component specifies a `string` datatype, a valid XML instance must contain a character string; any Unicode characters permitted in XML documents are allowed. The matching value in the value space must be identical. (You can always get arbitrary characters in by using character references in the document; they are resolved in the character strings that occur in the infoset, which is what schema processors see.)

The following two `element` elements each represent element types whose structure type is `string`. The simple version is:

```
<xsd:element name="demoString" type="xsd:string"/>
```

A version with some constraining facets is

```
<xsd:element name="demoString">
    <xsd:simpleType>
        <xsd:restriction base="xsd:string">
            <xsd:maxLength value="40"/>
            <xsd:whiteSpace value="preserve"/>
        </xsd:restriction>
    </xsd:simpleType>
</xsd:element>
```

Given either of the preceding element types, the following are valid instances:

```
<demoString>Note embedded
line break</demoString>
<demoString>Note embedded&#0D;&#0A;line break</demoString>
```

Because of the preprocessing done by parsers, the first element's information item will always contain a line feed but no carriage return, whereas the second's will always contain both—regardless of the line-break conventions of the host computer system in either case. (Macintosh systems use only a CR, Unix systems use only an LF, and Windows systems use both.)

### 12.3.1.1 `string` Constraining Facets

The following constraining facets apply when deriving from the built-in `string` datatype:

- `maxLength`
- `minLength`
- `length`
- `pattern`
- `enumeration`
- `whiteSpace`

Only for `string` and its derived datatypes is `whiteSpace` not COLLAPSE. For `string`, `whiteSpace` is PRESERVE. Derivation from `string` might restrict the `whiteSpace` to REPLACE or COLLAPSE (except list derivation, which always forces COLLAPSE). When restriction is by any of the length facets, the length involved is the number of characters in the value space string.

> **NOTE**
>
> A `whiteSpace` restriction impacts "normalization" done *before the lexical representation is checked*. It has *no impact* on the lexical or value space of a datatype. If the restriction is REPLACE or COLLAPSE, any offending whitespace will be removed or replaced as appropriate before the lexical representation is checked for validity.

### 12.3.1.2 `string` Derivation Relationships

The `string` datatype is primitive. `normalizedString` is the only built-in datatype directly derived from `string`. `token`, `NMTOKEN`, `NMTOKENS`, `Name`, and `NCName` are ultimately derived from `string` (Section 12.3.2). `ID`, `IDREF`, `IDREFS`, `ENTITY`, and `ENTITIES` are "magic" datatypes that are nominally ultimately derived from `string` (Section 12.3.3).

### 12.3.1.3 `string` Alternatives

Because of the many derivations of `string`, you should assess your needs against all the string-derived datatypes. The `token` datatype conforms to the needs of many schemas. A `token` does not permit leading or trailing spaces, two or more adjacent spaces, or any other whitespace characters. `ID`, `IDREF`, and `IDREFS` are included only for backward compatibility with DTDs; in a schema environment, it is generally better to use `QName` or `NCName`—or any other convenient marker combination—with the Schema identity-constraint mechanism (see Chapter 13). language is a specialized datatype for specifying languages and sublanguages by using codes prescribed in RFC 1766: *Tags for the Identification of Languages* 1995, www.ietf.org/rfc/rfc1766.txt. ENTITY and ENTITIES are to be used to point to non-XML datasets.

When dealing with names and namespaces, QName is the appropriate datatype; if namespaces are not involved, NCName is probably appropriate. For URIs, use anyURI. Generally, Name should be avoided.

## 12.3.2 Ordinary string-derived Datatypes: normalizedString, token, language, NMTOKEN, NMTOKENS, Name, and NCName

normalizedString is derived from string, token from normalizedString, NMTOKEN and language from token, NMTOKENS and Name from NMTOKEN, and NCName from Name. Amost all of these derivations are derived by pattern (except normalizedString and token, which are derived by whiteSpace from string and normalizedString respectively, and NMTOKENS, which is derived by list from NMTOKEN). The effect of derivation by pattern is that the lexical spaces shrink right along with the value spaces.

The effect of whiteSpace restriction to REPLACE or COLLAPSE is to cause the processor to change all whitespace to space characters and, in the case of COLLAPSE, to further remove leading and trailing whitespace completely and shrink other substrings of contiguous whitespace characters to a single space character; all of this is done before the resulting string is considered as a potential lexical representation.

> **NOTATION NOTE**
>
> The REPLACE process is prescribed by the XML Recommendation for "normalizing" the values of attributes, from whence the name 'normalizedString' was created. Values of various tokenized attribute types (such as NMTOKEN and NMTOKENS) are obtained by the COLLAPSE process, also as prescribed in the XML Recommendation; from this we get the name 'token'.

The derivations previously mentioned are done with pattern facets, except for normalizedString and token, which are derived using whiteSpace. The effect in each datatype is as follows:

- `normalizedString`: The strings in either the lexical space or the value space may not contain whitespace other than the space character. (Any excess whitespace will have been removed by the normalization process.)
- `token`: The strings in either the lexical space or the value space may not contain whitespace other than single-space characters flanked by other-than-space characters. (Any excess whitespace will have been removed by the normalization process.)
- `NMTOKEN`: The strings in either the lexical space or the value space may not contain whitespace. The characters permitted are those allowed by the *NameChar* production in the XML Recommendation.
- `language`: The strings in either the lexical space or the value space are restricted to those specified in RFC 1766: *Tags for the Identification of Languages* 1995, `http://www.ietf.org/rfc/rfc1766.txt`. (They should be used only to specify languages.)
- `NMTOKENS`: The strings in either the lexical space or the value space must contain one or more strings from `NMTOKEN`, separated by single-space characters. (`NMTOKENS` is derived as a list of `NMTOKEN`s.)
- `Name`: The strings in either the lexical space or the value space may contain only those characters permitted for `NMTOKEN`, with the additional restriction that the first character must be allowed by the *Letter* production in the XML Recommendation, *XML Schema*. (Many characters qualify as *Letters* that are not ordinary ASCII Roman-alphabet letters.)
- `NCName`: The strings in either the lexical space or the value space are those allowed for `Name`, with the further restriction that they may not contain the colon character, as prescribed by the *NCName* production in the Namespace Recommendation, *Namespaces in XML*. ('NCName' is derived from 'no-colon name'.)

The following two `element` elements are representations of element types whose structure type is `language` (or derived from `language`). The simple version is:

```
<xsd:element name="demoLanguage" type="xsd:language"/>
```

A version with a constraining facet that restricts the value to prescribed language designators designating variants of English is:

```
<xsd:element name="demoLanguage">
    <xsd:simpleType>
        <xsd:restriction base="xsd:language">
            <xsd:pattern value="en.*"/>
        </xsd:restriction>
    </xsd:simpleType>
</xsd:element>
```

Given either of the preceding element types, the following is a valid instance:

```
<demoLanguage>en-US</demoLanguage>
```

The remainder of the ordinary `string`-derived datatypes have value and lexical spaces whose constraints are obvious. You should be able to construct your own examples.

### 12.3.2.1 Ordinary `string`-derived Constraining Facets

The following constraining facets apply when deriving from any of the built-in `string`-derived datatypes:

- `maxLength`
- `minLength`
- `length`
- `pattern`
- `enumeration`
- `whiteSpace`

For all of the *built-in* `string`-derived datatypes except `normalizedString`, `whiteSpace` is COLLAPSE and therefore cannot be further restricted. `normalizedString`-derived derivations can further restrict `whiteSpace` to COLLAPSE. When restriction is by any of the length facets, the length involved is the number of characters in the string in the value space.

### 12.3.2.2 Ordinary `string`-derived Derivation Relationships

`normalizedString` is the only built-in datatype directly derived from `string`. `token` is derived from `normalizedString`, `NMTOKEN` and `language` from `token`, `NMTOKENS` and `Name` from `NMTOKEN`, and `NCName` from `Name`. Thus all of these are ultimately derived from `string`.

### 12.3.2.3 Ordinary `string`-derived Alternatives

Because of the many derivations of `string`, you should assess your needs against all the `string`-derived datatypes. Note that the `token` datatype conforms to the needs of many schemas. A `token` does not permit leading or trailing spaces, two or more adjacent spaces, or any other whitespace characters. (All different whitespace characters will be converted to space; all extra whitespace characters will be removed.) `ID`, `IDREF`, and `IDREFS` are included only for backward compatibility with DTDs; in a schema environment it is generally better to use `NCName`—or any other convenient marker combination—with the Schema identity-constraint mechanism (see Chapter 13). `language` is a specialized datatype for specifying languages and sublanguages by using codes prescribed in RFC 1766: *Tags for the Identification of Languages* 1995, http://www.ietf.org/rfc/rfc1766.txt. `ENTITY` and `ENTITIES` are to be used to point to non-XML datasets.

When dealing with names and namespaces, `QName` is the appropriate datatype; if namespaces are not involved, `NCName` is probably appropriate. Generally, `Name` should be avoided. For URIs, use `anyURI`.

## 12.3.3 "Magic" string-derived Datatypes: ID, IDREF, IDREFS, ENTITY, and ENTITIES

We call several string-derived datatypes "magic" because the validity of potential instances is context-dependent. As usual, the lexical representation that is the XML character data string involved needs to conform to the requirements of the datatype. The magic is that there are also context-dependent constraints on its interpretation as a value or that determine whether it is actually a valid instance or not. The magic string-derived datatypes are ID, IDREF, IDREFS, ENTITY, and ENTITIES.

All the magic string-derived datatypes are derived from NCName and add no lexical restrictions to the values.

ID instances are required to occur at most once in any element's attributes and content combined. They are also required to have values that are unique within any one XML document. IDREF instances are each required to have a value identical to some ID value in the document. IDREFS is list-derived from IDREF and inherits its restrictions on each item in the list.

ENTITY instances' values are required to be names declared in the document's DTD to be unparsed entities. ENTITIES is list-derived from ENTITY and inherits its restrictions.

> **WARNING**
>
> Referencing entities is the only situation in which schema validation requires the presence of a DTD. There is talk about not requiring schema processors to check this validity rule. There is also talk that entities might in general be replaced by other mechanisms for pointing at non-XML datasets.

The following element element represents an element type whose structure type is ENTITY:

```
<xsd:element name="demoEntity" type="xsd:ENTITY"/>
```

A valid ENTITY instance must be in the scope of an *unparsed entity declaration* in a DTD, such as the following; there must also be an appropriate notation declaration (which we do not show) for the local name 'EPS'.

```
<!ENTITY CorporateLogo SYSTEM
    "http://www.aw.com/TheXMLSchemaCompleteReference/EntityDemo"
    NDATA EPS>
```

Given the preceding element type and entity declaration, the following is a valid instance:

```
<demoEntity>CorporateLogo</demoEntity>
```

#### 12.3.3.1 Magic `string`-derived Constraining Facets

The following constraining facets apply when deriving from the built-in magic `string`-derived datatypes:

- `maxLength`
- `minLength`
- `length`
- `pattern`
- `enumeration`
- `whiteSpace`

`whiteSpace` is COLLAPSE and therefore cannot be further restricted. When restriction is by any of the length facets, the length involved is the length of the character string in the value space.

#### 12.3.3.2 Magic `string`-derived Derivation Relationships

All magic `string`-derived datatypes are primitive, and no built-in datatypes are derived from them.

#### 12.3.3.3 Magic `string`-derived Alternatives

There are no alternatives to `ENTITY` and `ENTITIES`. In a schema-aware environment, the schema-based identity-constraint mechanisms are preferable to `ID`, `IDREF`, and `IDREFS`, which exist to support backward compatibility with DTDs.

## 12.4 Oddball Datatypes

Several datatypes do not fit well into the foregoing partitioning:

- `QName`'s lexical space is related to that of `Name`, but `QName` values are not strings. `QName` is a "magic" datatype, in the sense of Section 12.3.3.
- `boolean` is the only mathematical datatype that is not numerical.
- `hexBinary` and `base64Binary` are both popular methods of encoding multiple-octet bit strings into printable ASCII character strings.
- `anyURI` is very much like a `string`-derived datatype, but uses a different mapping from its lexical space to its value space.
- `notation` is even more of an oddball: each application gets to define what a *notation* is. As far as XML is concerned, a *notation* is simply "something" that is identified by a system or public identifier. The identification is passed on to the application, to do with as it wishes. `notation` is also a "magic" datatype, in the sense of Section 12.3.3.

## 12.4.1 The Built-in QName Datatype

The lexical space of QName is that of Name with only the requirement that there be at most one colon present and that the characters following the colon, if there is one, must conform to the lexical requirements of NCName. However, the value space is quite different from that of Name.

When a schema component specifies a QName datatype, a valid XML instance must contain a *Name* with the further restrictions just described. The matching value in the value space is a pair consisting not of the *prefix* and *local part*, but rather of a URI and the *local part*. (The *local part* is the *NCName* following the colon, if there is one; otherwise the *local part* is the entire *Name*.) The URI is always the *namespace name* associated by a "namespace declaration" attribute in whose scope the QName instance occurs. *If a claimed instance of a QName is not in the scope of such a namespace declaration attribute, it is not valid—not a QName.* This context-dependency makes QName a magic datatype in the same sense as those described in Section 12.3.3.

The following two element elements are representations of element types whose structure type is QName (or derived from QName). The simple version is:

```
<xsd:element name="demoQName1" type="xsd:QName"/>
```

A version with some constraining facets that constrain corresponding instances to a character string that specifies a QName whose *local part* starts with the string 'demo' is:

```
<xsd:element name="demoQName1"/>
    <xsd:simpleType>
        <xsd:restriction base="xsd:xsd:QName">
            <xsd:pattern value="demo.*"/>
            <xsd:pattern value=".*:demo.*"/>
        </xsd:restriction>
    </xsd:simpleType>
</xsd:element>
```

Note that two patterns specified in the same restriction are effectively "or"ed together.

Given either of the preceding element types, the following is a valid instance:

```
<demoQName
   xmlns:demo=
      "http://www.aw.com/TheXMLSchemaCompleteReference/QNameDemo"
   >demo:demoDouble</demoQName>
```

The value of the QName is the ordered pair of two strings:

> ('http://www.aw.com/TheXMLSchemaCompleteReference/QNameDemo','demoDouble')

#### 12.4.1.1 QName Constraining Facets

The following constraining facets apply when deriving from the built-in QName datatype:

- pattern
- enumeration
- whiteSpace

whiteSpace is COLLAPSE and therefore cannot be further restricted.

#### 12.4.1.2 QName Derivation Relationships

QName is a primitive datatype, and no built-in datatypes are derived from it.

#### 12.4.1.3 QName Alternatives

When dealing with names and namespaces, QName is the appropriate datatype; if namespaces are not involved, NCName is probably appropriate. Generally, Name should be avoided.

### 12.4.2 The Built-in boolean Datatype

Boolean values (TRUE and FALSE) are mathematical but not numerical. The boolean datatype is the only mathematical but nonnumeric built-in datatype.

When a schema component specifies boolean, a valid XML instance must contain one of 'true', 'false', '1', or '0'. The corresponding values are in the value space TRUE, FALSE, TRUE, and FALSE, respectively.

The following two element elements represent element types whose structure type is boolean. The simple version is

```
<xsd:element name="demoBoolean" type="xsd:boolean"/>
```

A version with a constraining facet is

```
<xsd:element name="demoBoolean">
    <xsd:simpleType>
        <xsd:restriction base="xsd:boolean">
            <xsd:pattern value="0|1"/>
        </xsd:restriction>
    </xsd:simpleType>
</xsd:element>
```

Given either of the preceding element types, the following is a valid instance:

```
<demoBoolean>0</demoBoolean>
```

> **WARNING**
>
> Although '`<xsd:pattern value="0|1"/>`' produces an interesting example, the canonical representations for `boolean` are 'true' and 'false'. Therefore, this derived type has no canonical representations for its values, and trouble will ensue if defaults are declared and used. A user creating a user-defined datatype has no means of defining new canonical representations.

#### 12.4.2.1 `boolean` Constraining Facets

The following constraining facets apply when deriving from the built-in `boolean` datatype:

- `pattern`
- `whiteSpace`

`whiteSpace` is COLLAPSE and therefore cannot be further restricted.

#### 12.4.2.2 `boolean` Derivation Relationships

`boolean` is a primitive datatype, and no built-in datatypes are derived from it.

#### 12.4.2.3 `boolean` Alternatives

If a Boolean is what you need, `boolean` is your only reasonable choice.

### 12.4.3 The Built-in `hexBinary` and `base64Binary` Datatypes

Inserting arbitrary bit strings into XML character strings is notoriously difficult—too much chance exists that some bit pattern will look like a markup character. Therefore you need to transform arbitrary bit strings into character strings that will not be mistaken for markup—and will not have any "illegal characters" embedded. (Not every 16-bit bit-pattern is a legal Unicode character, and even some legal Unicode characters are prohibited in XML.)

The simplest "encoding" is to treat the bit string as a base-two Arabic numeral and encode it as a string of '`0`' and '`1`' digits. But this is expensive: The resulting bit-string representation of the binary numeral will be 8 or 16 times as long as the original. There are reasonably straightforward ways to get more compressed encodings of bit strings, however. Two methods are implemented as built-in datatypes: `hexBinary` and `base64Binary`. Both of these assume the bit strings are multiples of eight bits—a reasonable assumption, given the universality of eight-bit-chunk memory in modern computers. (Said eight-bit chunks are properly called "octets" and are often called "bytes," although technically bytes are not necessarily eight bits.)

`hexBinary` is simple enough that most people can learn it and directly write encoded strings; it simply means grouping the bits into groups of four and encoding each group as a hexadecimal (base 16) digit ('`0`' through '`9`' followed by '`A`' through '`F`', possibly lowercase). The result, with eight-bit character representations, is only a 2:1 expansion in bit-stream size—much better than 8:1 or 16:1.

`base64Binary` is more complicated, but most conversions of bit strings to character strings are done by computers, anyhow. Once the algorithm is implemented, the subroutine does the job as needed. The idea behind base-64 representation is similar: Group the bit stream into groups of six bits each. Each such group can be encoded into one base-64 digit; it takes four such digits to encode three octets. A special convention is needed for bit strings that are not multiples of three octets—a mechanism for indicating that not all the bits are used. The net result is an expansion ratio of just over 4:3. If compression better than that is needed, the best bet is to first compress the bit string by using a standard compression algorithm and then use `base64Binary` to encode the result.

The choice of characters used as digits and the mechanism for handling odd-length octet strings are fully described in the IETF "Request for Comment" (yet another way to say "Standard") *RFC 2045: Multipurpose Internet Mail Extensions (MIME) Part One: Format of Internet Message Bodies* 1996, `http://www.ietf.org/rfc/rfc2045.txt`. Because `base64Binary` lexical strings are complex and will essentially never be created or read directly by unaided humans, we will not bother to go into the details of the algorithm in this book. There is no need for a schema writer to care.

The data space of both `hexBinary` and `base64Binary` is the set of all bit strings that are multiples of eight bits.

The lexical space of `hexBinary` consists of all strings made up only of hexadecimal digits, as described earlier in this section. The mapping is almost one-to-one: The only redundancy is that uppercase or lowercase letters may be used for the higher digits. The canonical representation uses uppercase only.

On the other hand, the lexical space of `base64Binary` consists of almost all arbitrary strings of characters—the same space as `string`. Characters that are not meaningful in the calculations described in RFC 2045 are simply ignored. This is in conformance with RFC 2045.

The following two `element` elements are representations of element types whose structure type is `hexBinary` (or derived from `hexBinary`). The simple version is

```
<xsd:element name="demoHexBinary" type="xsd:hexBinary"/>
```

With a constraining facet that constrains corresponding instances to a length of exactly four binary octets, it is

```
<xsd:element name="demoHexBinary">
<xsd:simpleType>
```

```
<xsd:restriction base="xsd:hexBinary">
 <xsd:length value="4"/>
</xsd:restriction>
</xsd:simpleType>
</xsd:element>
```

Because each octet encodes into two hexadecimal digits (characters), there must be eight characters in the lexical representation.

Given either of the preceding element types, the following is a valid instance:

`<demoHexBinary>3CEFA25B</demoHexBinary>`

### 12.4.3.1 hexBinary and base64Binary Constraining Facets

The following constraining facets apply when deriving from the built-in `hexBinary` and `base64Binary` datatype:

- maxLength
- minLength
- length
- pattern
- enumeration
- whiteSpace

`whiteSpace` is COLLAPSE and therefore cannot be further restricted. When restriction is by any of the length facets, the length involved is the number of octets in the value.

### 12.4.3.2 hexBinary and base64Binary Derivation Relationships

`hexBinary` and `base64Binary` are both primitive datatypes, and no built-in datatypes are derived from them. They have the same value space, but their lexical spaces and the mappings from lexical space to value space are quite different.

### 12.4.3.3 hexBinary and base64Binary Alternatives

If you need to encode bit-string data into an XML document, there are no other reasonable alternatives. Choose between the two, basing your choice on the standard practice in the context of the kind of data you are encoding. If there is no standard practice, consider whether mostly short or mostly long bit strings will be encoded and whether an implementation of `base64Binary` is available.

## 12.4.4 The Built-in anyURI Datatype

When a schema component specifies an `anyURI` datatype, a valid XML instance must contain a character string such that when URI-invalid characters are escaped, the result is a valid URI according to the rules of RFC 2396 as modified by RFC 2732. The lexical-to-value-space conversion is required to escape any URI-invalid characters so that the resulting string is a valid URI. The escaping is to be done by using the algorithm provided in Section 5.4 of the W3C XLink Recommendation, *XML Linking Language (XLink) Version 1.0*, `http://www.w3.org/TR/xlink`. Note, however, that a schema processor is not required to validate that the result is in fact a valid URI, since generally protocols place additional protocol-specific constraints on what may follow the protocol indicator. The schema processor only makes the escape conversion and accepts the result.

> **TIP**
>
> Use already-escaped strings that are valid URIs as values in the lexical space. The result is easier to read and less likely to give unexpected results.

The following two `element` elements are representations of element types whose structure type is `anyURI` (or derived from `anyURI`). The simple version is:

```
<xsd:element name="demoAnyURI" type="xsd:anyURI"/>
```

A version with a constraining facet that constrains corresponding instances to values that are locations on the Addison-Wesley Web site (`http://www.aw.com/`) is:

```
<xsd:element name="demoAnyURI">
    <xsd:simpleType>
        <xsd:restriction base="xsd:anyURI">
            <xsd:pattern value="http://www\.aw\.com/.*"/>
        </xsd:restriction>
    </xsd:simpleType>
</xsd:element>
```

Given either of the preceding element types, the following is a valid instance:

```
<demoAnyURI>http://www.aw.com/XMLSchemaCompleteReference</demoAnyURI>
```

### 12.4.4.1 anyURI Constraining Facets

The following constraining facets apply when deriving from the built-in `anyURI` datatype:

- `maxLength`
- `minLength`
- `length`
- `pattern`
- `enumeration`
- `whiteSpace`

`whiteSpace` is COLLAPSE and therefore cannot be further restricted. When restriction is by any of the length facets, the length involved is the number of characters in the *value*, not the *lexical representation*.

### 12.4.4.2 anyURI Derivation Relationships
`anyURI` is a primitive datatype, and no built-in datatypes are derived from it.

### 12.4.4.3 anyURI Alternatives
If you are not intending the data to be URIs as defined in RFCs 2396 and 2732, you should probably use `token` instead, unless for some reason you need the specialized lexical-to-value-space map used by `anyURI`.

## 12.4.5 The Built-in `notation` Datatype

When a schema component specifies a `notation` datatype, a valid XML instance must contain a value (character string) that is a valid `QName`. The matching abstract value is also that of `QName`. The only difference between `QName` and `notation` is that `notation` has extra "magic": Any `notation` instances must be in the scope of a matching *notation* schema component.

Each application gets to define what a *notation* is. As far as XML is concerned, a *notation* is simply "something" that is identified by a system or public identifier. The identification is passed on to the application, to do with as it wishes.

> **CAUTION**
>
> `notation` is *non-instantiable*—you cannot validate an element directly against `notation`. Not only must you use a derived datatype; the Schema Recommendation also requires that the datatype must be derived by enumeration. This is in addition to the requirement that any notation values must be in the scope of a matching schema notation component (which automatically limits you to an implied "enumeration" of all the notations defined in the schema).

The following `element` element represents an element type whose structure type is appropriately derived from `notation`:

```
<xsd:element name="demoNotation">
    <xsd:simpleType>
        <xsd:restriction base="xsd:NOTATION">
            <xsd:enumeration value="EPS"/>
        </xsd:restriction>
    </xsd:simpleType>
</xsd:element>
```

*continues*

```
<xsd:notation name="EPS"
          system="file:C:\company\EPS\eps.exe">
    <xsd:annotation>
        <xsd:documentation>
            Local copy of the Encapsulated PostScript
            processor
        </xsd:documentation>
    </xsd:annotation>
</xsd:notation>
```

Given the preceding element type and notation, the following is a valid instance:

`<demoNotation>EPS</demoNotation>`

You will be more likely to use `notation` values for attributes than elements.

### 12.4.5.1 notation Constraining Facets
The following constraining facets apply when deriving from the built-in `boolean` datatype:

- pattern
- enumeration
- whiteSpace

`whiteSpace` is COLLAPSE and therefore cannot be further restricted.

### 12.4.5.2 notation Derivation Relationships
`notation` is a primitive datatype, and no built-in datatypes are derived from it.

### 12.4.5.3 notation Alternatives
If you need a notation, there is no alternative. If you don't, use something different—perhaps `QName` or one of the other `Name`-derived built-in datatypes.

# Identity Constraints

**CHAPTER**

**13**

## IN THIS CHAPTER

**13.1** Identity Constraint Example  332

**13.2** Concepts and Observations  338

**13.3** The `unique` Element  343

**13.4** The `key` Element  346

**13.5** The `keyref` Element  349

**13.6** The `selector` Element  353

**13.7** The `field` Element  354

Identity Constraints

CHAPTER 13

Chapter 1 defines an XML validator as an XML parser layer that validates an XML instance against an XML schema. An XML validator is effectively the front end of a compiler. Specifically, a "vanilla" XML parser understands XML lexical tokens and parses against a simple XML grammar. Most of the features of a DTD place further constraints on the grammar. The newer XML Schema provides an even more complete grammar definition.

When a compiler has finished parsing, the next step is typically semantic validation. Semantic validation assures the veracity of the *meaning* of the data, whereas the aforementioned parsing assures the veracity of the *structure* of the data.

Identity constraints provide for some limited semantic validation. In particular, the unique and key elements enforce data uniqueness; the keyref element enforces referential integrity.

The last step in a compiler (barring optional steps like optimization) is code generation. XSLT arguably provides a rudimentary mechanism for specifying code generation.

## 13.1 Identity Constraint Example

The examples in this section provide a fairly condensed, but complete XML schema and a corresponding XML instance. Listing 13.1 demonstrates more than one example of each type of identity constraint (unique, key, and keyref). The remaining sections of this chapter reiterate excerpts from this schema to emphasize specific characteristics of the identity constraints.

LISTING 13.1   Compressed Order Data Schema (idConstraintDemo.xsd)

```
<xsd:complexType name="compressedOrderType">
    <xsd:sequence>
        <xsd:element name="order"
                    minOccurs="1"
                    maxOccurs="unbounded">
            <xsd:complexType>
                <xsd:sequence>
                    <xsd:element name="customerID"
                                type="xsd:token"/>
                    <xsd:element name="item"
                                minOccurs="1"
                                maxOccurs="unbounded">
                        <xsd:complexType>
                            <xsd:sequence minOccurs="1"
                                    maxOccurs="unbounded">
                                <xsd:element
                                    name="partNumber"
                                    type="partNumberType"/>
                                <xsd:element name="quantity"
                                        type="xsd:positiveInteger"/>
```

```xml
                    </xsd:sequence>
                </xsd:complexType>
            </xsd:element>
        </xsd:sequence>
        <xsd:attribute name="totalQuantity"
                       type="xsd:positiveInteger"
                       use="required"/>
        <xsd:attribute name="orderID"
                       type="xsd:token"
                       use="required"/>
        <xsd:attribute name="shipmentID"
                       type="xsd:token"
                       use="optional"/>
    </xsd:complexType>

    <xsd:key name="orderPartNumberKey">
        <xsd:annotation>
            <xsd:documentation xml:lang="en">
                The part number must be unique
                within the order, but NOT
                across orders.
            </xsd:documentation>
        </xsd:annotation>
        <xsd:selector xpath="item"/>
        <xsd:field xpath="partNumber"/>
    </xsd:key>

        </xsd:element>
    </xsd:sequence>
</xsd:complexType>

<xsd:complexType name="shippedOrderSummaryType">
    <xsd:sequence>
        <xsd:element name="shipped"
                     minOccurs="1"
                     maxOccurs="unbounded">
            <xsd:complexType>
                <xsd:attribute name="shipmentID"
                               type="xsd:token"/>
                <xsd:attribute name="custID"
                               type="xsd:token"/>
                <xsd:attribute name="qty"
                               type="xsd:positiveInteger"/>
            </xsd:complexType>
        </xsd:element>
    </xsd:sequence>
</xsd:complexType>
```

*continues*

## Identity Constraints
### CHAPTER 13

```xml
<xsd:element name="idConstraintDemo">
    <xsd:complexType>
        <xsd:sequence>

            <xsd:element name="compressedOrder"
                         type="compressedOrderType">

                <xsd:key name="orderKey"
                         id="orderKey.key">
                    <xsd:annotation>
                        <xsd:documentation xml:lang="en">
                            The customerID uniquely identifies
                            each customer.
                        </xsd:documentation>
                    </xsd:annotation>
                    <xsd:selector xpath="order"
                                  id="orderKey.key.selector"/>
                    <xsd:field xpath="@orderID"
                               id="orderKey.key.field"/>
                </xsd:key>

                <xsd:unique name="orderShippedUnique"
                            id="orderShippedUnique.unique">
                    <xsd:annotation>
                        <xsd:documentation xml:lang="en">
                            The customerID uniquely identifies
                            each customer.
                        </xsd:documentation>
                    </xsd:annotation>
                    <xsd:selector xpath="order"/>
                    <xsd:field xpath="@shipmentID"/>
                </xsd:unique>

            </xsd:element>

            <xsd:element name="shippedOrderSummary"
                         type="shippedOrderSummaryType"/>

            <xsd:element ref="customerList"/>
            <xsd:element name="catalog" type="catalogType"/>

        </xsd:sequence>

    </xsd:complexType>

    <xsd:key name="customerKey">
        <xsd:annotation>
```

```xml
        <xsd:documentation xml:lang="en">
            The customerID uniquely identifies
            each customer.
        </xsd:documentation>
    </xsd:annotation>
    <xsd:selector xpath="customerList/*"/>
    <xsd:field xpath="@customerID"/>
</xsd:key>

<xsd:keyref name="customerRef" refer="customerKey">
    <xsd:annotation>
        <xsd:documentation xml:lang="en">
            Each order must refer to a known customer.
        </xsd:documentation>
    </xsd:annotation>
    <xsd:selector xpath="compessedOrder/order"/>
    <xsd:field xpath="customerID"/>
</xsd:keyref>

<xsd:key name="partNumberKey"
         id="partNumberKey.key">
    <xsd:annotation>
        <xsd:documentation xml:lang="en">
            The part number uniquely identifies
            each orderable item.
        </xsd:documentation>
    </xsd:annotation>
    <xsd:selector xpath="catalog/*"/>
    <xsd:field xpath="partNumber"/>
</xsd:key>

<xsd:keyref name="partNumberRef"
            id="partNumberRef.keyref"
            refer="partNumberKey">
    <xsd:annotation>
        <xsd:documentation xml:lang="en">
            Each order must refer to a known part number.
        </xsd:documentation>
    </xsd:annotation>
    <xsd:selector xpath="compressedOrder/order/item"/>
    <xsd:field xpath="partNumber"/>
</xsd:keyref>

<xsd:key name="orderedItemsKey"
         id="orderedItemsKey.key">
    <xsd:annotation>
        <xsd:documentation xml:lang="en">
```

*continues*

```xml
                    Identify ordered customers and
                    shipping quantities.  Note that
                    while schema already enforces
                    the following constraint, the
                    'key' also assures that there *is*
                    a customerID and a shippingQuantity
                    identified for each order
                </xsd:documentation>
            </xsd:annotation>
            <xsd:selector xpath="compressedOrder/order"/>
            <xsd:field xpath="@totalQuantity"/>
            <xsd:field xpath="customerID"/>
        </xsd:key>

        <xsd:keyref name="shippedItemsRef"
                    id="shippedItems.keyref"
                    refer="orderedItemsKey">
            <xsd:annotation>
                <xsd:documentation xml:lang="en">
                    Ensure a shipped customer/qty
                    for each ordered customer/qty
                </xsd:documentation>
            </xsd:annotation>
            <xsd:selector xpath="shippedOrderSummary/shipped"/>
            <xsd:field xpath="@qty"/>
            <xsd:field xpath="@custID"/>
        </xsd:keyref>

</xsd:element>
```

Listing 13.2 provides an XML instance that corresponds to the XML schema introduced in Listing 13.1.

**LISTING 13.2** Compressed Order Data Instance (`idConstraintDemo.xml`)

```xml
<idConstraintDemo>

<compressedOrder>
    <order orderID="X012532"
           shipmentID="X012432-S"
           totalQuantity="3">
        <customerID>AW132E57</customerID>
        <item>
            <partNumber>ASM9001</partNumber>
            <quantity>3</quantity>
        </item>
    </order>
```

```xml
    <order orderID="X012533"
           totalQuantity="2">
        <customerID>AW220A38</customerID>
        <item>
            <partNumber>UX001</partNumber>
            <quantity>1</quantity>
        </item>
        <item>
            <partNumber>UX002</partNumber>
            <quantity>1</quantity>
        </item>
    </order>
</compressedOrder>

<shippedOrderSummary>
    <shipped shipmentID="X012432-S" custID="AW132E57" qty="3"/>
</shippedOrderSummary>

<customerList>
    <businessCustomer customerID="SAM132E57">
        <name>Cliff Binstock</name>
        <phoneNumber>503-555-0000</phoneNumber>
        <address>
            <street>123 Gravel Road</street>
            <city>Nowheresville</city>
            <state>OR</state>
            <country>US</country>
            <zip>97000</zip>
            <effectiveDate>2001-11-08</effectiveDate>
        </address>
    </businessCustomer>
</customerList>

<catalog>
    <unitPart>
        <unitID>10327</unitID>
        <partName>Unit 1</partName>
        <partNumber>UX001</partNumber>
        <partOption>
            <color>magenta</color>
        </partOption>
        <description>Unit 1 is the thing to buy</description>
        <fullPrice>28.00</fullPrice>
        <includedQuantity>1</includedQuantity>
    </unitPart>
    <unitPart>
        <unitID>10329</unitID>
```

*continues*

```xml
            <partName>Unit 2</partName>
            <partNumber>UX002</partNumber>
            <partOption>
                <color>Pink Grapefruit</color>
            </partOption>
     <description>Unit 2 lasts longer than Unit 1</description>
            <fullPrice>28.01</fullPrice>
            <includedQuantity>1</includedQuantity>
     </unitPart>
     <assemblyPart>
            <assemblyID>40004788</assemblyID>
            <partName>Assembly 1</partName>
            <partNumber>ASM9001</partNumber>
            <description>
                This is made up of both
                <partList>UX002 UX003</partList>
                pieces which makes this assembly
                better than the competition.
            </description>
            <fullPrice>3200.00</fullPrice>
            <includedQuantity>1</includedQuantity>
            <customerReview>
                <customerName>I. M. Happy</customerName>
                <customerFeedback>This is the most
awesome phat product in the entire.
    world.</customerFeedback>
            </customerReview>
            <partList>UX002 UX003</partList>
            <status>3</status>
     </assemblyPart>
</catalog>

</idConstraintDemo>
```

## 13.2 Concepts and Observations

This section covers terminology unique to identity constraints. Furthermore, this section expounds upon two of the new terms: *selector* and *field*. Every identity constraint specifies a selector and one or more fields.

### 13.2.1 Identity Constraint Terminology

Identity constraints are a very small part of the Schema Recommendation. There is some terminology specific to identity constraints. The following list provides the terminology that is the foundation of the text in this chapter:

*Node:* The PSVI describes a tree that represents an XML instance. The tree is made up of a set of nodes (See Chapter 2). Some of these nodes, particularly those associated with elements and attributes, provide the infrastructure for the validation provided by identity constraints.

*Selector:* In an XML schema, each identity constraint specifies a selector. Technically, the value of a selector is an XPath that identifies an element. From the perspective of writing the schema, the XPath identifies an element type. The XPath must specify an element type that is a descendant of the element type enclosing the identity constraint.

*Field:* In an XML schema, each identity constraint specifies one or more fields. Technically, the value of each field is an XPath that identifies a child element or an attribute of the element identified by the XPath of the corresponding selector. From the perspective of writing the schema, the XPath identifies an element type or attribute type. The XPath must specify an element type or attribute type that is the element type—or is a descendant of the element type—that encloses the identity constraint.

*Target node set:* During XML instance validation, the target node set is the set of nodes identified by the selector of an identity constraint.

*Key sequence:* During XML instance validation, the key sequence is the set of values associated with the elements and attributes identified by the fields of an identity constraint. There is one key sequence for each node in the target node set.

## 13.2.2 Selectors and Fields

Each identity constraint identifies a set of nodes that must be unique or that require referential integrity. The grammar for locating these nodes is a subset of XPath (see Chapter 4). Each identity constraint has a specific scope, which is the enclosing element type: Any element type may provide any number of identity constraints.

Each identity constraint specifies a selector and one or more fields. The value of the XPath of each selector ultimately identifies a target node set in a corresponding XML instance. Each field, which is slightly more complicated, identifies one of the following:

- The value of an element corresponding to a node in the target node set
- The value of an attribute of the element corresponding to a node in the target node set
- The value of a descendant of the element corresponding to a node in the target node set
- The value of an attribute of a descendant of the element corresponding to a node in the target node set

Like a selector, a field ultimately identifies an element or an attribute. The XPath specified by the field is relative to the XPath specified by the selector. A key sequence is the set of values for a specific node in the target set that correspond to the set of fields specified by an identity constraint.

## 13.2.3 Limited XPath Support

Element types provide the context for identity constraints. The XPath for each selector is relative to the enclosing element type. Furthermore, the XPath for each field is relative to the XPath for each selector.

Listing 13.3 is the grammar for the XPath expressions for selectors and fields.

**LISTING 13.3** Selector and Field XPath Grammar

```
<selector> ::= <path> |
               <selector> '|' <path>

<field>    ::= <path> |
               <attributeStep> |
               <path> <attributeStep>

<path>     ::= './/' |
               <path> |
               './/' <path>

<path> ::= <elementStep> |
           <path> '/' <elementStep>

<elementStep> ::= '.' | <nameTest>

<attributeStep> ::= '@' <nameTest>

<nameTest> ::= <qName> | '*' | <ncName> ':*'
```

Note that a selector may specify multiple XPaths.

Table 13.1 provides some sample XPath values. Note that each XPath for a selector locates a particular element. Each field locates the value of a particular element or attribute.

**TABLE 13.1** Sample Selector and Field XPaths

| XPath | Description | Structure |
|---|---|---|
| . | The current element | `<current>foo</current>` |
| xyz | The xyz child element of the current element | `<current>`<br>`  <xyz>foo</xyz>`<br>`  <xyz>bar</xyz>`<br>`</current>` |

*continues*

**TABLE 13.1** *(continued)*

| XPath | Description | Structure |
|---|---|---|
| abc/xyz | The xyz child elements of the abc child elements of the current element | `<current>`<br>  `<abc>`<br>    `<xyz>foo</xyz>`<br>  `</abc>`<br>  `<abc>`<br>    `<xyz>bar</xyz>`<br>  `</abc>`<br>`</current>` |
| .//xyz | Any xyz descendant element of the current element | `<current>`<br>  `<xyz>foo</xyz>`<br>  `<abc>`<br>    `<xyz>bar</xyz>`<br>  `<abc/>`<br>`<current>` |
| */xyz | The xyz child elements of all child elements of the current element | `<current>`<br>  `<abc>`<br>    `<xyz>foo</xyz>`<br>  `</abc>`<br>  `<def>`<br>    `<xyz>bar</xyz>`<br>  `</def>`<br>`</current>` |
| @attr | The attr attribute of the current element | `<current attr="1"/>` |
| xyz/@attr | The attr attribute of the xyz child element | `<current>`<br>  `<xyz @attr="1">`<br>  `<xyz @attr="2"/>`<br>`</current>` |
| .//@attr | The attr attributes of any descendant element of the current element | `<current>`<br>  `<xyz @attr="1"/>`<br>  `<abc @attr="2">`<br>    `<xyz @attr="3"/>`<br>  `<abc/>`<br>`<current>` |
| */@attr | The attr attributes of all immediate child elements of the current element | `<current>`<br>  `<abc @attr="1">`<br>  `<def @attr="2"/>`<br>`</current>` |

## 13.2.4 Value Equality

The foundation of identity constraints is a test for equality. Each key sequence specified by a `unique` or `key` identity constraint must be distinct: The test is equality (or more correctly, lack of equality). Additionally, each key sequence specified by a `keyref` identity constraint must exist as a key sequence in the target node set to which the `keyref` refers: Again, the test is equality. In an XML schema, two (simple type) values are *equal* when

- The simple types for the two values are identical, or they both have a common derivation ancestor. The derived simple types may be built-in derived datatypes or user-derived. (The idea is that value spaces in primitive datatypes are disjoint "by fiat" even if, for example, they both are numeric and have value spaces one of which is a nominal subset of the other.)
- The values in the value space are equal (identical).

For example, none of the `string` '3', the `integer` 3, the `float` 3, or the `double` 3 are equal. Conversely, any of the following with the value 3 are equal: an `unsignedInt`, an `unsignedLong`, a `nonNegativeInteger`, an `integer`, or a `decimal`. Logically, the representations in the lexical space do not have to be identical. For example, the `float` value represented by '3.0' is equal to (the same as) the `float` value represented by '3'.

## 13.2.5 Enforcing Uniqueness

Both the `unique` and `key` identity constraints assure the uniqueness of each set of values—the key sequence—in a corresponding target node set. The `key` identity constraint adds an additional constraint: For each node in the target node set, there *must be* a corresponding key. The `unique` identity constraint, however, assures uniqueness *only when the keys exist*.

This section demonstrates the difference between `unique` and `key`. In Listing 13.2, each order has a required order identifier and an optional shipment identifier. Each order identifier is unique. Each shipment identifier is also unique, although the company has not yet shipped all orders. The `key` element is appropriate for enforcing uniqueness on the order identifier, because each order has a *required* unique order identifier. On the other hand, the `unique` element is appropriate for enforcing uniqueness on the shipment identifier, because each `order` has an *optional*, yet unique shipment identifier.

> **NOTE**
>
> The uniqueness of the key sequence specified by the set of `field` elements is relative to the element specified by the `selector` element. For example, in Listing 13.1, the `compressedOrder` contains an `order`, which contains (ultimately) a `partNumber`. Note that the `orderPartNumberKey` ensures that an order has only one reference to any part number. On the other hand, many customers, with distinct orders, might order the same part number. Therefore, the selector specifies the `orderPartNumberKey`, not `compressedOrder`.

## 13.2.6 Enforcing Referential Integrity

Enforcing referential integrity is one easy step beyond creating a key, which was portrayed in the previous section. The `keyref` element specifies a target node set and a corresponding key sequence in the same manner as the `unique` and `key` elements. In addition, the `keyref` element specifies a reference identity constraint, which is the name of a `unique` or `key` identity constraint. The values for each key sequence specified by the `keyref` element must "equal" the corresponding set of values in any key sequence specified by the reference key.

> **TIP**
>
> An XML validator can test the values of a set of elements or attributes identified by a `keyref` element against a set of presumably corresponding values specified by either a `key` identity constraint or a `unique` identity constraint.

## 13.3 The unique Element

The `unique` identity constraint assures that each key sequence—the set of values specified by the XPath expressions of the nested `field` elements—is unique. A key sequence is unique if no two key sequences have "equal" values for all keys. Unlike the `key` element, the key sequence does not have to exist for each node in the target node set. The `unique` identity constraint is appropriate, for example, for optional elements or attributes.

> **NOTE**
>
> The uniqueness of the key sequence specified by the set of `field` elements is relative to the element specified by the `selector` element.

The uniqueness of the keys is dependent on the selector. In the example for this chapter, an identity constraint confines an order to have no more than one part number. However, the XML instance that contains a set of orders might have multiple part numbers; different customers might order the same part.

Listing 13.4 is the XML representation of the `orderShippedUnique` identity constraint. Each order (a node in the target node set) must have a unique shipping ID (the key sequence). Because this is a `unique` element, the order is not required to have a shipping ID.

**LISTING 13.4**  Example of unique

```
<xsd:unique name="orderShippedUnique"
            id="orderShippedUnique.unique">
    <xsd:annotation>
        <xsd:documentation xml:lang="en">
            The customerID uniquely identifies
            each customer.
        </xsd:documentation>
    </xsd:annotation>
    <xsd:selector xpath="order"/>
    <xsd:field xpath="@shipmentID"/>
</xsd:unique>
```

## 13.3.1 The Attributes of a unique Element

The `unique` element has only two attributes: the ubiquitous `id`, and the `name` of the identity constraint. Table 13.2 itemizes the attributes of a `unique` element.

**TABLE 13.2**  Attribute Summary for a unique Element

| Attribute | Description |
| --- | --- |
| id | The value of an `id` attribute uniquely identifies an element within the set of schema documents that comprise an XML schema. |
| name | The value of the `name` attribute uniquely identifies an identity constraint. A `keyref` may optionally reference this name to enforce referential integrity against the set of keys specified by this identity constraint. |

### 13.3.1.1 The `id` Attribute of a `unique` Element

The value of an `id` attribute uniquely identifies an element within the set of schema documents that comprise an XML schema.

**ATTRIBUTE OVERVIEW**

**unique: id**

| | |
|---|---|
| **Value:** | An ID. |
| **Default:** | None. |
| **Constraints:** | An `id` must be unique within an XML schema. |
| **Required:** | No. |

Listing 13.3 is a `unique` element that has an `id` attribute.

### 13.3.1.2 The `name` Attribute of a `unique` Element

The value of a `name` uniquely identifies an identity constraint. A `keyref` may optionally reference this name to enforce referential integrity against the set of keys specified by this identity constraint.

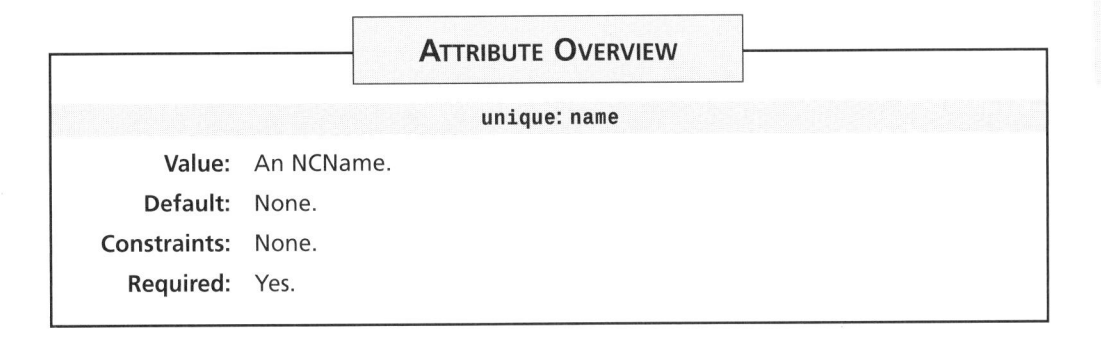

**ATTRIBUTE OVERVIEW**

**unique: name**

| | |
|---|---|
| **Value:** | An NCName. |
| **Default:** | None. |
| **Constraints:** | None. |
| **Required:** | Yes. |

Listing 13.3 is a `unique` element that has a `name` attribute.

## 13.3.2 Content Options for a `unique` Element

All of the identity constraints have the same attributes. Other than the `annotation`, the attributes locate a set of nodes. Table 13.3 itemizes these attributes.

**TABLE 13.3** Content Options for a unique Element

| Element | Description |
| --- | --- |
| annotation | The annotation element, discussed in Section 7.5, provides a way to document schema elements. |
| selector | The value of the selector attribute is an abbreviated XPath that determines the target node set in a corresponding XML instance. |
| field | The value of the field attribute is an abbreviated XPath that determines the key sequence for each node in the target node set. |

The content pattern for the unique element is:

annotation? selector field+

## 13.4 The key Element

The key identity constraint assures that each key sequence—the set of values specified by the XPath expressions of the nested field elements—is unique. A key sequence is unique if no two key sequences have "equal" values for all keys. Unlike the unique element, a key sequence *must* exist for each node in the target node set. The key identity constraint is appropriate, for example, for required elements or attributes.

> **NOTE**
>
> The uniqueness of the key sequence specified by the set of field elements is relative to the element specified by the selector element.

The uniqueness of the keys is dependent on the selector. In the example for this chapter, an identity constraint confines an order to no more than one part number. However, the XML instance that contains a set of orders might have multiple part numbers; different customers might order the same part.

Listing 13.5 is the XML representation of the orderKey identity constraint. Each order (a node in the target node set) must have a unique order ID (the key sequence). Because this is a key element, the order is required to have an order ID.

**LISTING 13.5** Example of key

```
<xsd:key name="orderKey"
         id="orderKey.key">
    <xsd:annotation>
```

```
        <xsd:documentation xml:lang="en">
            The customerID uniquely identifies
            each customer.
        </xsd:documentation>
    </xsd:annotation>
    <xsd:selector xpath="order"
                  id="orderKey.key.selector"/>
    <xsd:field xpath="@orderID"
               id="orderKey.key.field"/>
</xsd:key>
```

## 13.4.1 The Attributes of a key Element

The key element has only two attributes: the ubiquitous id, and the name of the identity constraint. Table 13.4 itemizes the attributes of a key element.

**TABLE 13.4**  Attribute Summary for a key Element

| Attribute | Description |
| --- | --- |
| id | The value of an id attribute uniquely identifies an element within the set of schema documents that comprise an XML schema. |
| name | Uniquely identifies the identity constraint. A keyref may optionally reference this name to enforce referential integrity against the set of keys specified by this identity constraint. |

### 13.4.1.1 The id Attribute of a key Element

The value of an id attribute uniquely identifies an element within the set of schema documents that comprise an XML schema.

**ATTRIBUTE OVERVIEW**

**key: id**

| | |
| --- | --- |
| **Value:** | An ID. |
| **Default:** | None. |
| **Constraints:** | An id must be unique within an XML schema. |
| **Required:** | No. |

Listing 13.5 is a key element that has an id attribute.

### 13.4.1.2 The name Attribute of a key Element

The value of a `name` uniquely identifies an identity constraint. A `keyref` may optionally reference this name to enforce referential integrity against the set of keys specified by this identity constraint.

**ATTRIBUTE OVERVIEW**

**key: name**

| | |
|---:|:---|
| **Value:** | An NCName. |
| **Default:** | None. |
| **Constraints:** | None. |
| **Required:** | Yes. |

Listing 13.5 is a `key` element that has a `name` attribute.

## 13.4.2 Content Options for a key Element

All of the identity constraints have the same elements. Other than the `annotation`, the elements locate a set of nodes. Table 13.5 itemizes these elements.

The content pattern for the `key` element is:

`annotation? selector field+`

**TABLE 13.5** Content Options for a key Element

| Element | Description |
|---|---|
| annotation | The annotation element, discussed in Section 7.5, provides a way to document schema elements. |
| selector | The value of the `selector` attribute is an abbreviated XPath that determines the target node set in a corresponding XML instance. |
| field | The value of the `field` attribute is an abbreviated XPath that determines the key sequence for each node in the target node set. |

## 13.5 The keyref Element

The `keyref` identity constraint assures that each key sequence specified by the `keyref` exists, by virtue of equality, as a key sequence in the reference identity constraint. The reference identity constraint is always a `unique` or `key` identity constraint. Because the `keyref` identity constraints are slightly more complicated, this section includes two examples. Note that Listing 13.6 is not complicated: It is one key comprised of an element instance value. Listing 13.7 demonstrates the use of two keys. Listing 13.7 also demonstrates mixing key values comprised of element and attribute instance values.

Listing 13.6 portrays both the `partNumberKey` and a corresponding `partNumberRef`. The `partNumberKey` enforces unique part numbers in a catalog. The `partNumberRef` ensures that orders contain only part numbers in the catalog.

**LISTING 13.6**  Example of keyref

```
<xsd:key name="partNumberKey"
         id="partNumberKey.key">
    <xsd:annotation>
        <xsd:documentation xml:lang="en">
            The part number uniquely identifies
            each orderable item.
        </xsd:documentation>
    </xsd:annotation>
    <xsd:selector xpath="catalog/*"/>
    <xsd:field xpath="partNumber"/>
</xsd:key>

<xsd:keyref name="partNumberRef"
            id="partNumberRef.keyref"
            refer="partNumberKey">
    <xsd:annotation>
        <xsd:documentation xml:lang="en">
            Each order must refer to a known part number.
        </xsd:documentation>
    </xsd:annotation>
    <xsd:selector xpath="compressedOrder/order/item"/>
    <xsd:field xpath="partNumber"/>
</xsd:keyref>
```

Listing 13.7 portrays both the `orderItemsKey` and a corresponding `shippedItemsRef`. The `orderItemsKey` specifies a unique customer ID and the total quantity of parts ordered. The `shippedItemsRef` ensures that each customer receives the appropriate number of parts. This example has a two-part key (customer ID and quantity). In addition, this example demonstrates the use of attributes as keys.

**LISTING 13.7**   Multi-part Key Sequences

```
<xsd:key name="orderedItemsKey"
         id="orderedItemsKey.key">
    <xsd:annotation>
        <xsd:documentation xml:lang="en">
            Identify ordered customers and
            shipping quantities.  Note that
            while schema already enforces
            the following constraint, the
            'key' also assures that there *is*
            a customerID and a shippingQuantity
            identified for each order
        </xsd:documentation>
    </xsd:annotation>
    <xsd:selector xpath="compressedOrder/order"/>
    <xsd:field xpath="@totalQuantity"/>
    <xsd:field xpath="customerID"/>
</xsd:key>

<xsd:keyref name="shippedItemsRef"
            id="shippedItems.keyref"
            refer="orderedItemsKey">
    <xsd:annotation>
        <xsd:documentation xml:lang="en">
            Ensure a shipped customer/qty
            for each ordered customer/qty
        </xsd:documentation>
    </xsd:annotation>
    <xsd:selector xpath="shippedOrderSummary/shipped"/>
    <xsd:field xpath="@qty"/>
    <xsd:field xpath="@custID"/>

</xsd:keyref>
```

## 13.5.1 The Attributes of a `keyref` Element

In addition to the `id` and `name` attributes which apply to all identity constraints, the `keyref` element has the `refer` attribute, which points to the reference against which to validate. Table 13.6 itemizes the attributes of a `keyref` element.

**TABLE 13.6**  Attribute Summary for a `keyref` Element

| Attribute | Description |
|---|---|
| `id` | The value of an `id` attribute uniquely identifies an element within the set of schema documents that comprise an XML schema. |
| `name` | The value of the `name` attribute uniquely identifies the identity constraint. |
| `refer` | Each key sequence specified by this identity constraint must equal any key sequence in the target node set specified by the reference identity constraint. |

### 13.5.1.1  The `id` Attribute of a `keyref` Element

The value of an `id` attribute uniquely identifies an element within the set of schema documents that comprise an XML schema.

---
**ATTRIBUTE OVERVIEW**

**keyref: id**

- **Value:** An ID.
- **Default:** None.
- **Constraints:** The value of an `id` must be unique within an XML schema.
- **Required:** No.

---

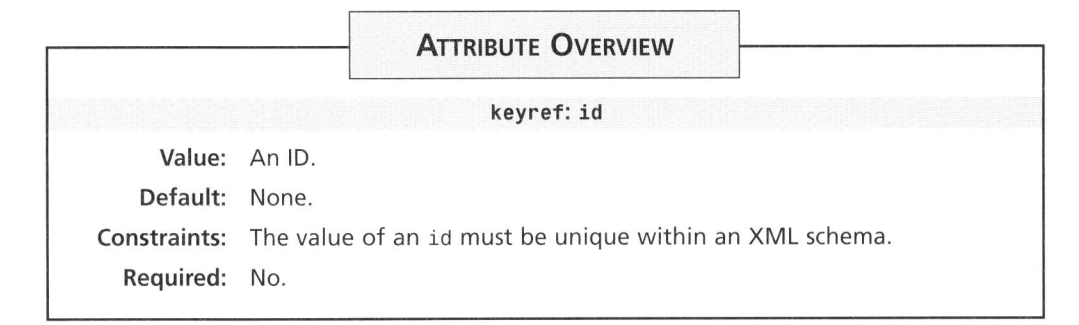

Listing 13.6 portrays a `keyref` element that has an `id` attribute.

### 13.5.1.2  The `name` Attribute of a `keyref` Element

The value of a `name` uniquely identifies an identity constraint.

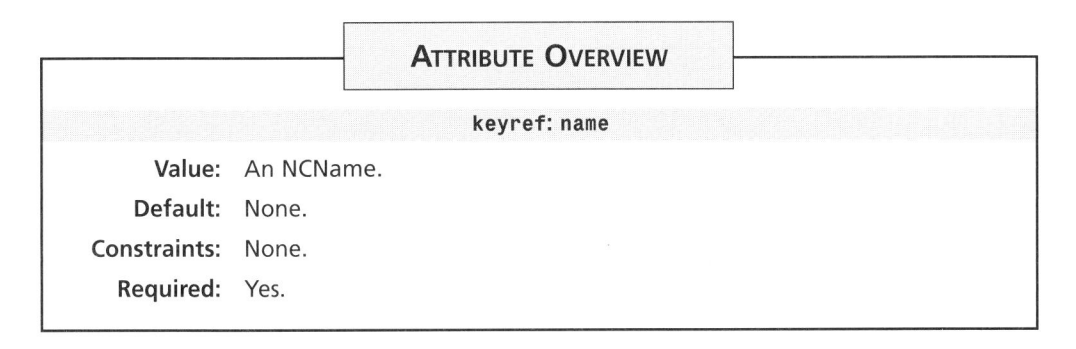

---
**ATTRIBUTE OVERVIEW**

**keyref: name**

- **Value:** An NCName.
- **Default:** None.
- **Constraints:** None.
- **Required:** Yes.

---

Listing 13.6 portrays a `keyref` element that has a `name` attribute.

### 13.5.1.3 The `refer` Attribute of a `keyref` Element

The value of a `refer` attribute is the name of a `unique` or `key` identity constraint. During XML validation, each key sequence specified by the `keyref` element must equal a key sequence specified by the reference identity constraint.

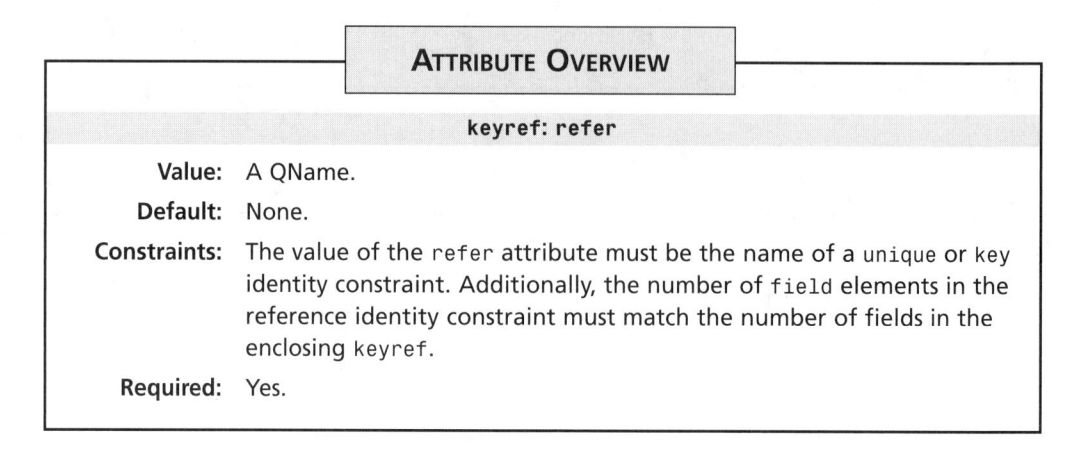

**ATTRIBUTE OVERVIEW**

**keyref: refer**

| | |
|---|---|
| **Value:** | A QName. |
| **Default:** | None. |
| **Constraints:** | The value of the `refer` attribute must be the name of a `unique` or `key` identity constraint. Additionally, the number of `field` elements in the reference identity constraint must match the number of fields in the enclosing `keyref`. |
| **Required:** | Yes. |

Listing 13.6 portrays a `keyref` element that has a `refer` attribute.

## 13.5.2 Content Options for a `keyref` Element

All of the identity constraints have the same attributes. Other than the `annotation`, the attributes locate a set of nodes. Table 13.7 itemizes these attributes.

**TABLE 13.7** Content Options for a `keyref` Element

| Element | Description |
|---|---|
| annotation | The annotation element, discussed in Section 7.5, provides a way to document schema elements. |
| selector | The value of the `selector` attribute is an abbreviated XPath that determines the target node set in a corresponding XML instance. |
| field | The value of the `field` attribute is an abbreviated XPath that determines the key sequence for each node in the target node set. |

The content pattern for the `keyref` element is:

```
annotation? selector field+
```

## 13.6 The selector Element

The value of the xpath attribute of a selector element specifies a target node set for any type of identity constraint. See any listing in this chapter for an example of the selector element.

### 13.6.1 The Attributes of a selector Element

In addition to the ubiquitous id attribute, the selector element must specify an xpath, which selects a set of nodes. Table 13.8 itemizes the attributes of a selector element.

**TABLE 13.8**  Attribute Summary for a selector Element

| Attribute | Description |
| --- | --- |
| id | The value of an id attribute uniquely identifies an element within the set of schema documents that comprise an XML schema. |
| xpath | The value of the xpath attribute determines the target node set of a corresponding XML instance. |

#### 13.6.1.1 The id Attribute of a selector Element

The value of an id attribute uniquely identifies an element within the set of schema documents that comprise an XML schema.

---
**ATTRIBUTE OVERVIEW**

**selector: id**

- **Value:** An ID.
- **Default:** None.
- **Constraints:** The value of an id must be unique within an XML schema.
- **Required:** No.
---

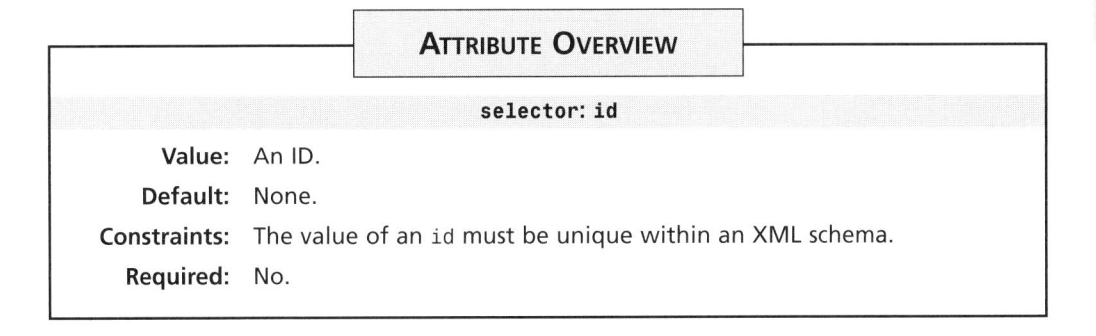

Listing 13.5 portrays a selector element that has an id attribute.

#### 13.6.1.2 The xpath Attribute of a selector Element

The value of the xpath attribute determines the target node set of a corresponding XML instance. Although there are no specific constraints on the value of the xpath attribute, the appropriate element type containment should mirror the XPath.

## ATTRIBUTE OVERVIEW

**selector: xpath**

| | |
|---:|:---|
| **Value:** | An appropriate subset of an XPath expression. |
| **Default:** | None. |
| **Constraints:** | None. |
| **Required:** | Yes. |

All listings in this chapter portray `selector` elements that have an `xpath` attribute.

### 13.6.2 Content Options for a `selector` Element

Table 13.9 shows that an `annotation` is the only content option available for the `selector` element.

**TABLE 13.9**  Content Options for a `selector` Element

| Element | Description |
|---|---|
| annotation | The annotation element, discussed in Section 7.5, provides a way to document schema elements. |

The content pattern for the `selector` element is:

annotation?

## 13.7 The `field` Element

The value of the `xpath` attribute of a `field` element specifies a key for any type of identity constraint. In an XML instance, a key sequence is the set of keys that correspond to the set of fields for an identity constraint. See any listing in this chapter for an example of the `field` element.

### 13.7.1 The Attributes of a `field` Element

The `field` element has the same attributes as the `selector` element. Table 13.10 itemizes these attributes.

TABLE 13.10   Attribute Summary for a `field` Element

| Attribute | Description |
|---|---|
| id | The value of an `id` attribute uniquely identifies an element within the set of schema documents that comprise an XML schema. |
| xpath | The value of the `xpath` attribute determines one key value from the target node set of a corresponding XML instance. The set of `xpath` attributes corresponding to the set of `field` elements associated with an identity constraint determines the entire key sequence. |

### 13.7.1.1 The `id` Attribute of a `field` Element

The value of an `id` attribute uniquely identifies an element within the set of schema documents that comprise an XML schema.

**ATTRIBUTE OVERVIEW**

**field: id**

- **Value:** An ID.
- **Default:** None.
- **Constraints:** The value of an `id` must be unique within an XML schema.
- **Required:** No.

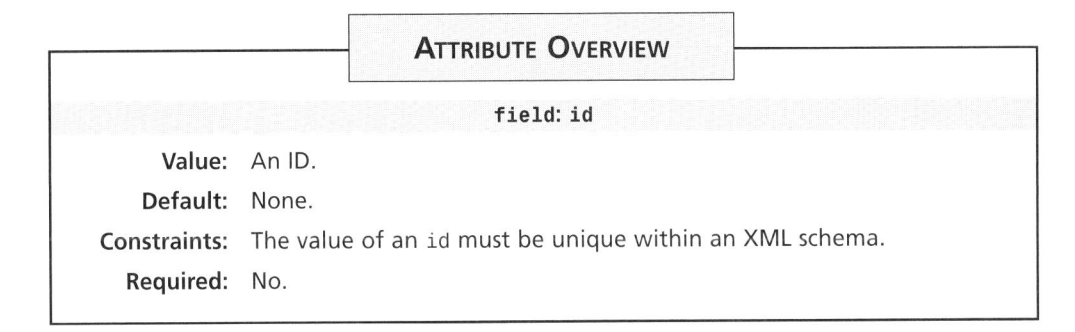

Listing 13.5 portrays a `field` element that has an `id` attribute.

### 13.7.1.2 The `xpath` Attribute of a `field` Element

The value of the `xpath` attribute determines a specific key. The key may be one of many that comprise a key sequence. Although there are no specific constraints on the value of the `xpath` attribute, the appropriate element type (or attribute type) containment should mirror the XPath.

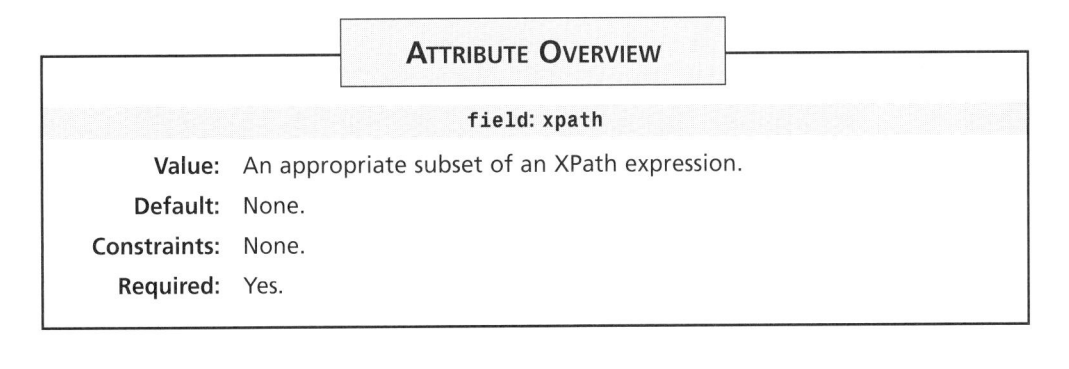

**ATTRIBUTE OVERVIEW**

**field: xpath**

- **Value:** An appropriate subset of an XPath expression.
- **Default:** None.
- **Constraints:** None.
- **Required:** Yes.

All listings in this chapter portray `field` elements that have an `xpath` attribute.

## 13.7.2 Content Options for a `field` Element

Table 13.11 shows that an `annotation` is the only content option available for the `selector` element.

**TABLE 13.11** Content Options for a `field` Element

| Element | Description |
| --- | --- |
| annotation | The annotation element, discussed in Section 7.5, provides a way to document schema elements. |

The content pattern for the `field` element is:

annotation?

# Regular Expressions

**CHAPTER 14**

## IN THIS CHAPTER

14.1 Concepts and Observations   359

14.2 Regular Expression Syntax   361

14.3 Constraining Simple Content   381

# Regular Expressions
## Chapter 14

A *regular expression* is a pattern for identifying a range of string values. This pattern conforms to a specific grammar. The Schema Recommendation suggests that an XML validator should implement "Level 1" regular expressions as defined in the *Unicode Regular Expression Guidelines*. These guidelines reside at http://unicode.org/unicode/reports/tr18/.

An *expression* (without "regular") is a regular expression snippet, or a part of a regular expression. An expression may match one or many characters. An expression may comprise an entire regular expression.

> **NOTATION NOTE**
>
> In this chapter, all strings that might appear in an XML instance appear in double quotes (for example, "a sample value"). This is different from most of the rest of book. There are so many quoted regular expressions (for example, 'reg.*exp?') and corresponding instance values, that the visual distinction between schema values and instance values is valuable. Occasionally, the instance value contains line delimiters, such as:
>
>     "this string contains
>     a line break"
>
> Additionally, some instance values contain meaningful spaces (unlike elements in an XML schema document), that would be difficult to see if no quotes were presented.

A simple type in an XML schema (or a complex type constrained to simple content) specifies a regular expression with a `restriction` element that contains a `pattern` element. Section 14.4 demonstrates generally how to specify simple types that incorporate regular expressions to constrain element instance values. Chapter 10 provides detail on the `pattern` element.

An XML validator can validate appropriate values in an XML instance against a regular expression specified by a simple type. The validation assures that each string value in the XML instance conforms to the appropriate set of regular expressions.

This chapter assumes an understanding of XML schemas in general (specifically any chapter before this one). Furthermore, for simplicity, most of this chapter discusses *only* the regular expressions, not the simple or complex types that incorporate the regular expression. All of the XML schema examples in this chapter describe a regular expression and a set of strings that validate against that regular expression. This chapter skips discussion of element types, element instances, attribute types, and attribute instances, although an XML validator requires these to create and validate an XML instance.

All the regular expressions described in this chapter come from `regexpDemo.xsd`. Similarly, `regexpDemo.xml` contains the strings that purport to be valid in a corresponding XML instance. Both of these files are online at `http://www.XMLSchemaReference.com/examples/Ch14`.

## 14.1 Concepts and Observations

*The Unicode Standard* is the basis of the character set for XML. Further, most software in the United States makes use of the Latin character subset. The following sections contain guidelines for regular expressions. They also provide a comparison to regular expressions in the Perl language, because many programmers are familiar with Perl. Finally, there is a brief overview of how regular expressions integrate into base and derived types in an XML schema.

### 14.1.1 Unicode Regular Expression Guidelines

The *Unicode Regular Expression Guidelines* is a technical report associated with *The Unicode Standard*. The Schema Recommendation suggests that an XML validator should implement "Level 1" regular expressions as defined in the *Unicode Regular Expression Guidelines*. There are a few global differences between the Schema Recommendation and the *Unicode Regular Expression Guidelines*:

- The Schema Recommendation specifies that the XML hex notation provides the capability to specify Unicode characters. The XML hex notation, which looks like '`&#x`*nnnn*`;`', is a valid substitution of the '`\u`*nnnn*' notation, according to the *Unicode Regular Expression Guidelines*. Note that *nnnn* represents a specific Unicode character.

- The *Unicode Regular Expression Guidelines* suggests—but does not go as far as recommending—that many regular expression engines support line or paragraph separators; the Schema Recommendation does not provide support for these separators.

Otherwise, the Schema Recommendation is consistent with the *Unicode Regular Expression Guidelines* except where explicitly noted in the subsequent sections of this chapter.

### 14.1.2 The Latin Character Set

The English language is a derivation of Latin. Similarly, the foundation of many programming languages, as well as data, comes from the 'BasicLatin' character block defined by *The Unicode Standard* (see Section 14.2.5.6). Note that this particular character block overlaps with ASCII characters.

In general, a discussion regarding character sets is superfluous. Regular expressions, however, require extra care. Many single-character patterns (such as '`\p{Lu}`', which matches uppercase characters, and '`\w`', which matches a word—a sequence of selected non-whitespace characters) match characters from many character sets. The result is that what seems like an innocuous regular expression might match many strings that a program or part of a program is probably not ready to handle. Suppose, for example, that an XML schema contains the regular expression 'the \w word'. Many developers would expect—in the XML instance—to see Latin-based strings that conform to this pattern, such as perhaps "the green word" or "the automobile word" (where "green" and "automobile" are valid pattern matches with '\w'). In all probability, the XML instance contains the expected Latin-based strings. However the regular expression also matches strings that contain, say, Greek or Arabic characters. Such a string might look like "the ΩπΔ word".

### 14.1.3 Perl Regular Expressions

Many software developers are familiar with regular expressions from the Perl programming language. The regular expressions for XML schemas are similar to regular expressions in Perl, with two important differences:

- There is no support in XML schema regular expressions for line separators. Perl provides line separators such as '^' to match the beginning of a line and '$' to match the end of a line.
- The XML schema regular expressions do not support the notion of a "lookahead" anchor or a "lookbehind" anchor, both of which match a pattern, but do not become part of the result—a concept not particularly relevant to XML schemas.

Finally, for those perhaps familiar with other sophisticated string-processing languages, XML schemas do not support the notion of a "fence", where the regular expression prohibits backtracking.

### 14.1.4 XML Schemas

Section 14.3 goes into detail about creating simple types that validate values in XML instances against regular expressions. Two overriding—and opposing—rules are worth noting here:

- When a simple type specifies multiple regular expression patterns, the value in an XML instance must be a legal value for *at least one* of the regular expressions.
- When both the base and derived simple types specify regular expressions, the value in an XML instance must be a legal value for at least one of the regular expressions in the base type *and* at least one of the regular expressions in the derived type.

> **CAUTION**
>
> The interaction between two pattern constraining facets specified by the same simple type is different than the interaction between two pattern constraining facets when one is specified by the base type and one by the derived type. See this section and Section 14.3 for clarification.

## 14.2 Regular Expression Syntax

A regular expression is a set of characters that represents a pattern. Many instance strings may match the pattern identified by the regular expression. Any set of characters in a regular expression may be required, repeated, optional, or otherwise controlled. Because of this flexibility, the number of strings that match a regular expression is potentially unbounded.

### 14.2.1 Metacharacters

A regular expression has a number of special characters, or *metacharacters*, that generally denote groupings or repetition. Table 14.1 describes these metacharacters.

**TABLE 14.1**  Metacharacter Examples

| Metacharacter | Description | Sample Regular Expression | Sample Match |
|---|---|---|---|
| . | Match any character as defined by *The Unicode Standard*. | a.c | "aXc" "a9c" |
| \ | Precedes a metacharacter (to specify that character) or specifies a single- or multiple-character escape sequence. | \*\d*\* | "*1234*" |
| ? | Zero or one occurrences. | ab?c | "ac" "abc" |
| * | Zero or more occurrences. | ab*c | "ac" "abc" "abbbbbc" |
| + | One or more occurrences. | ab+c | "abc" "abbbbbc" |
| \| | The "or" operator. | ab\|cd | "ab" "cd" |
| ( | Start grouping. | a(b\|c)d | "abd" "acd" |
| ) | End grouping. | a(b\|c)d | "abd" "acd" |
| { | Start repetition. | a{2,4} | "aaa" |
| } | End repetition. | a{2,4} | "aaa" |
| [ | Start range. | xx[A-Z]*xx | "xxABCDxx" |
| ] | End range. | xx[A-Z]*xx | "xxABCDxx" |

The subsequent sections of this chapter cover all the metacharacters in greater detail. This "metacharacters" section is early in the chapter because the metacharacters modify the regular expression and sometimes create boundary conditions. Most of the sections in this chapter discuss boundary conditions that pertain to the metacharacters pertinent to that section.

## 14.2.2 Concatenation

*Concatenation* is the implicit foundation of a regular expression. All other forms of combining expressions require metacharacters. Furthermore, expressions that contain metacharacters may be concatenated. Despite the fact that this chapter has not yet covered each metacharacter in detail, Table 14.2 portrays concatenation of expressions, some of which include metacharacters.

**TABLE 14.2**  Concatenation Examples

| Regular Expression | Comment | Matching Strings |
|---|---|---|
| abc | Concatenation of the expressions 'a', 'b', 'c' | "abc" |
| abc?d*e | Concatenation of the expressions 'a', 'b', 'c?', 'd*', and 'e' | "abcde" "abdddde" "abce" "abe" |
| BLK\d{1,8} | Concatenation of the expressions 'B', 'L', 'K', and '\d{1,8}' | "BLK1" "BLK3333" "BLK87" |

## 14.2.3 Alternatives

A regular expression provides alternative patterns by specifying the '|' character (which is the "or" operator). Table 14.3 demonstrates expressions that contain alternatives.

**TABLE 14.3**  Alternative Examples

| Regular Expression | Comment | Matching Strings |
|---|---|---|
| ab\|cd | The concatenated string 'ab' or the concatenated string 'cd' | "ab" "cd" |
| \d\|[A-Z]+ | A decimal digit or a sequence of uppercase Latin letters | "3" "B" "CAT" |

## 14.2.4 Grouping

Expressions can be "grouped" with the '(' and ')' characters; entire expressions can be optional, required, or otherwise embedded. Table 14.4 demonstrates expressions that contain grouping

**TABLE 14.4** Grouping Examples

| Regular Expression | Comment | Matching Strings |
|---|---|---|
| a(b\|c)d | The concatenation of 'a', 'b' or 'c', and 'd' | "abd" <br> "acd" |
| (\d\|[A-Z])+ | A sequence of one or more decimal digits or uppercase Latin letters | "3" <br> "B" <br> "CAT" <br> "B4U" <br> "WE8DINNER" <br> "8887" |

## 14.2.5 Individual Characters

Regular expressions provide numerous ways to match a set of characters (ranges, groupings, cardinality, and such). Regular expressions also provide many ways to match a single character. A regular expression may match a single character from any of the following groupings:

- Normal Character
- Character Category
- Single Character Escape
- Multiple Character Escape
- Character Block
- XML Character

The following sections explain these individual character expressions.

### 14.2.5.1 Normal Character

A regular expression can match a *normal* character. A normal character is any XML character that is not a metacharacter (that is, not '.', '\', '?', '*', '+', '|', '{', '}', '(', ')', '[', or ']'). See Section 14.2.1 for further clarification regarding metacharacters. With the noted previous exceptions, a normal character might appear in an XML schema.

> **WARNING**
>
> The Schema Recommendation does not consistently represent the set of metacharacters. See Section 14.2.1 for more details.

Table 14.5 demonstrates normal characters by portraying some regular expressions as well as some corresponding matching strings.

**TABLE 14.5** Character Examples

| Regular Expression | Comment | Matching Strings |
|---|---|---|
| abc?d*e | 'a', 'b', 'c', 'd', and 'e' are normal characters. | "abcde"<br>"abdddde"<br>"abce"<br>"abe" |
| BLK[0-9]{1,8} | 'B', 'L', and 'K', and '0' through '9' are normal characters. | "BLK1"<br>"BLK3333"<br>"BLK87" |

### 14.2.5.2 Character Categories

A regular expression can match a character by using a *character category*. The expression can be inclusive or exclusive of the character category. A regular expression must escape a character category. An inclusive character category that represents any lowercase letter looks like the following:

\p{Lu}

An exclusive category that represents any character *except* a lowercase letter looks like the following:

\P{Lu}

Note that inclusive requires a lowercase 'p', whereas exclusive requires an uppercase 'P'.

Table 14.6 itemizes the many character categories.

**TABLE 14.6** Regular Expression Character Categories

| Category | Description | Notes |
|---|---|---|
| L | Letter, Any | |
| Lu | Letter, Uppercase | |
| Ll | Letter, Lowercase | |
| Lt | Letter, Titlecase | |
| Lm | Letter, Modifier | |
| Lo | Letter, Other | |
| L& | Letter, uppercase, lowercase, and titlecase letters (Lu, Ll, and Lt) | Optional in *The Unicode Standard*; not supported by the Schema Recommendation |

*continues*

**TABLE 14.6**   *(continued)*

| Category | Description | Notes |
|---|---|---|
| M | Mark, Any | |
| Mn | Mark, Nonspacing | |
| Mc | Mark, Spacing Combining | |
| Me | Mark, Enclosing | |
| N | Number, Any | |
| Nd | Number, Decimal Digit | |
| Nl | Number, Letter | |
| No | Number, Other | |
| P | Punctuation, Any | |
| Pc | Punctuation, Connector | |
| Pd | Punctuation, Dash | |
| Ps | Punctuation, Open | |
| Pe | Punctuation, Close | |
| Pi | Punctuation, Initial quote (may behave like 'Ps' or 'Pe,' depending on usage) | |
| Pf | Punctuation, Final quote (may behave like 'Ps' or 'Pe,' depending on usage) | |
| Po | Punctuation, Other | |
| S | Symbol, Any | |
| Sm | Symbol, Math | |
| Sc | Symbol, Currency | |
| Sk | Symbol, Modifier | |
| So | Symbol, Other | |
| Z | Separator, Any | |
| Zs | Separator, Space | |
| Zl | Separator, Line | |
| Zp | Separator, Paragraph | |
| C | Other, Any | |
| Cc | Other, Control | |
| Cf | Other, Format | |
| Cs | Other, Surrogate | Explicitly not supported by Schema Recommendation. |
| Co | Other, Private Use | |
| Cn | Other, Not Assigned (No characters in the file have this property.) | |

Table 14.7 demonstrates a character category by portraying some regular expressions as well as some corresponding matching strings.

**TABLE 14.7** Character Category Examples

| Regular Expression | Comment | Matching Strings |
|---|---|---|
| `upper\p{Lu}case` | '`\p{Lu}`' matches any uppercase character—in any Unicode language. | "`upperAcase`" "`upperDcase`" |
| `\P{Lu}*` | '`\P{Lu}`' matches any character *except* an uppercase character. | "`012aa7c`" "" (empty string) "`strange regexp`" |
| `\p{Nd}+` | '`\p{Nd}`' matches any decimal number. Note that the single character escape '`\d`' is a shortcut for '`\p{Nd}`'. | "`9`" "`1234`" |

### 14.2.5.3 Single Character Escape

A regular expression can match distinct characters with a *single character escape*. Most of these special characters are characters that would otherwise be meaningful in a regular expression.

Table 14.8 itemizes the entire list of single character escapes that a regular expression may contain.

**TABLE 14.8** Regular Expression Single Character Escape

| Single Character Escape | Description |
|---|---|
| `\n` | New line character (&#xA;): line feed |
| `\r` | Return character (&#xD;): carriage return |
| `\t` | Tab character (&#x9;) |
| `\\` | \ |
| `\|` | \| |
| `\.` | . |
| `\-` | - |
| `\^` | ^ |
| `\?` | ? |
| `\*` | * |

*continues*

## TABLE 14.8 (continued)

| Single Character Escape | Description |
|---|---|
| \+ | + |
| \{ | { |
| \} | } |
| \( | ( |
| \) | ) |
| \{ | { |
| \} | } |
| \[ | [ |
| \] | ] |

Table 14.9 demonstrates the single character escape by portraying some regular expressions as well as some corresponding matching strings.

## TABLE 14.9  Single Character Escape Examples

| Regular Expression | Comments | Matching Strings |
|---|---|---|
| [0-9]+\.[0-9]+ | '\.' is a single character escape that matches the '.' character, as opposed to the normal meaning of '.' which matches any normal character. | "1.3"<br>"55.7"<br>"768.444444" |
| \p{Ll}*[\r\n]*\p{Ll}* | '\r' is a single character escape that matches a return; '\n' matches a new line. | "note<br>return" |

### 14.2.5.4 Multiple Character Escape

A regular expression matches a set of characters with a *multiple character escape*. The characters matched by each multiple character escape are often meaningful to human documentation, such as whitespace.

Table 14.10 itemizes the entire list of multiple character escapes that a regular expression may contain.

**TABLE 14.10** Regular Expression Multiple Character Escape

| Multiple Character Escape | Description |
|---|---|
| . | Any character except '\n' (new line) and '\r' (return). |
| \s | Whitespace, specifically '&#x20;' (space), '\t' (tab), '\n' (new line), and '\r' (return). |
| \S | Any character except those matched by '\s'. |
| \i | The first character in an XML identifier. Specifically, any *letter*, the character '_', or the character ':'. See the XML Recommendation for the complex specification of a *letter*. This character represents a subset of *letter* that might appear in '\c'. |
| \I | Any character except those matched by '\i'. |
| \c | Any character that might appear in the built-in NMTOKEN datatype. See the XML Recommendation for the complex specification of a *NameChar*. |
| \C | Any character except those matched by '\c'. |
| \d | Any decimal digit. A shortcut for '\p{Nd}'. |
| \D | Any character except those matched by '\d'. |
| \w | Any character that might appear in a word. Specifically, '[#x0000-#x10FFFF]-[\p{P}\p{Z}\p{C}]' (all characters except the set of "punctuation", "separator", and "other" characters). |
| \W | Any character except those matched by '\w'. |

Table 14.11 demonstrates the multiple character escape by portraying some regular expressions as well as some corresponding matching strings.

**TABLE 14.11** Multiple Character Escape Examples

| Regular Expression | Comments | Matching Strings |
|---|---|---|
| h\dwdy | '\d' is a multiple character escape that matches any decimal digit. | "h0wdy" "h8wdy" |
| \w*\s*\w* | '\w' is a multiple character escape that nominally matches a word. \s is a multiple character escape that matches whitespace. | "two words" "8 dinner" |
| \p{Lu}\.\S* | '\S' is a multiple character escape that matches any character *except* whitespace. | "X.25" "U.rCrazy8" |

## 14.2.5.5 Wildcard Escape

The '.' character is the wildcard escape. This wildcard escape matches any character except new line ('\n') and carriage return ('\r'). The wildcard escape is identical in functionality to the expression '[^\r\n]'.

> **NOTE**
>
> The W3C XML Schema 1.0 Specification Errata introduces the wildcard escape.

Table 14.12 demonstrates the wildcard escape by portraying some regular expressions as well as some corresponding matching strings.

**TABLE 14.12** Wildcard Escape Examples

| Regular Expression | Comments | Matching Strings |
|---|---|---|
| .* | Any sequence of characters, except the end-of-line characters | "Anything goes!" |
| \p{Lu}.*\. | An uppercase character followed by any sequence of characters except end-of-line characters, followed by a period | "A sentence." "Really? Sure." |

### 14.2.5.6 Character Blocks

*The Unicode Standard* supports character blocks. A *block* is a range of characters set aside for a specific purpose. Some examples of these blocks are the characters for a language (such as Greek), the Braille character set, and various drawing symbols.

The Schema Recommendation provides a regular expression mechanism for identifying characters that belong to a specific block of interest. The syntax for identifying a block is '`\p{Is`*BlockName*`}`', where '*BlockName*' is a name from Table 14.13. Like the character categories, an uppercase 'P' (as in '`\P{Is`*BlockName*`}`') excludes the characters in that block.

Table 14.13 provides a list of all block names, as well as the Unicode character ranges.

**TABLE 14.13**  Block Names

| Block Name | Start Code | End Code |
| --- | --- | --- |
| BasicLatin | #x0000 | #x007F |
| Latin-1Supplement | #x0080 | #x00FF |
| LatinExtended-A | #x0100 | #x017F |
| LatinExtended-B | #x0180 | #x024F |
| IPAExtensions | #x0250 | #x02AF |
| SpacingModifierLetters | #x02B0 | #x02FF |
| CombiningDiacriticalMarks | #x0300 | #x036F |
| Greek | #x0370 | #x03FF |
| Cyrillic | #x0400 | #x04FF |
| Armenian | #x0530 | #x058F |
| Hebrew | #x0590 | #x05FF |
| Arabic | #x0600 | #x06FF |
| Syriac | #x0700 | #x074F |
| Thaana | #x0780 | #x07BF |
| Devanagari | #x0900 | #x097F |
| Bengali | #x0980 | #x09FF |
| Gurmukhi | #x0A00 | #x0A7F |
| Gujarati | #x0A80 | #x0AFF |
| Oriya | #x0B00 | #x0B7F |
| Tamil | #x0B80 | #x0BFF |
| Telugu | #x0C00 | #x0C7F |

*continues*

**TABLE 14.13**   *(continued)*

| Block Name | Start Code | End Code |
|---|---|---|
| Kannada | #x0C80 | #x0CFF |
| Malayalam | #x0D00 | #x0D7F |
| Sinhala | #x0D80 | #x0DFF |
| Thai | #x0E00 | #x0E7F |
| Lao | #x0E80 | #x0EFF |
| Tibetan | #x0F00 | #x0FFF |
| Myanmar | #x1000 | #x109F |
| Georgian | #x10A0 | #x10FF |
| HangulJamo | #x1100 | #x11FF |
| Ethiopic | #x1200 | #x137F |
| Cherokee | #x13A0 | #x13FF |
| UnifiedCanadianAboriginalSyllabics | #x1400 | #x167F |
| Ogham | #x1680 | #x169F |
| Runic | #x16A0 | #x16FF |
| Khmer | #x1780 | #x17FF |
| Mongolian | #x1800 | #x18AF |
| LatinExtendedAdditional | #x1E00 | #x1EFF |
| GreekExtended | #x1F00 | #x1FFF |
| GeneralPunctuation | #x2000 | #x206F |
| SuperscriptsandSubscripts | #x2070 | #x209F |
| CurrencySymbols | #x20A0 | #x20CF |
| CombiningMarksforSymbols | #x20D0 | #x20FF |
| LetterlikeSymbols | #x2100 | #x214F |
| NumberForms | #x2150 | #x218F |
| Arrows | #x2190 | #x21FF |
| MathematicalOperators | #x2200 | #x22FF |
| MiscellaneousTechnical | #x2300 | #x23FF |
| ControlPictures | #x2400 | #x243F |
| OpticalCharacterRecognition | #x2440 | #x245F |
| EnclosedAlphanumerics | #x2460 | #x24FF |
| BoxDrawing | #x2500 | #x257F |

*continues*

**TABLE 14.13**   *(continued)*

| Block Name | Start Code | End Code |
|---|---|---|
| BlockElements | #x2580 | #x259F |
| GeometricShapes | #x25A0 | #x25FF |
| MiscellaneousSymbols | #x2600 | #x26FF |
| Dingbats | #x2700 | #x27BF |
| BraillePatterns | #x2800 | #x28FF |
| CJKRadicalsSupplement | #x2E80 | #x2EFF |
| KangxiRadicals | #x2F00 | #x2FDF |
| IdeographicDescriptionCharacters | #x2FF0 | #x2FFF |
| CJKSymbolsandPunctuation | #x3000 | #x303F |
| Hiragana | #x3040 | #x309F |
| Katakana | #x30A0 | #x30FF |
| Bopomofo | #x3100 | #x312F |
| HangulCompatibilityJamo | #x3130 | #x318F |
| Kanbun | #x3190 | #x319F |
| BopomofoExtended | #x31A0 | #x31BF |
| EnclosedCJKLettersandMonths | #x3200 | #x32FF |
| CJKCompatibility | #x3300 | #x33FF |
| CJKUnifiedIdeographsExtensionA | #x3400 | #x4DB5 |
| CJKUnifiedIdeographs | #x4E00 | #x9FFF |
| YiSyllables | #xA000 | #xA48F |
| YiRadicals | #xA490 | #xA4CF |
| HangulSyllables | #xAC00 | #xD7A3 |
| HighSurrogates | #xD800 | #xDB7F |
| HighPrivateUseSurrogates | #xDB80 | #xDBFF |
| LowSurrogates | #xDC00 | #xDFFF |
| PrivateUse | #xE000 | #xF8FF |
| CJKCompatibilityIdeographs | #xF900 | #xFAFF |
| AlphabeticPresentationForms | #xFB00 | #xFB4F |
| ArabicPresentationForms-A | #xFB50 | #xFDFF |
| CombiningHalfMarks | #xFE20 | #xFE2F |
| CJKCompatibilityForms | #xFE30 | #xFE4F |

*continues*

## TABLE 14.13   (continued)

| Block Name | Start Code | End Code |
|---|---|---|
| SmallFormVariants | #xFE50 | #xFE6F |
| ArabicPresentationForms-B | #xFE70 | #xFEFE |
| Specials | #xFEFF | #xFEFF |
| HalfwidthandFullwidthForms | #xFF00 | #xFFEF |
| Specials | #xFFF0 | #xFFFD |
| OldItalic | #x10300 | #x1032F |
| Gothic | #x10330 | #x1034F |
| Deseret | #x10400 | #x1044F |
| ByzantineMusicalSymbols | #x1D000 | #x1D0FF |
| MusicalSymbols | #x1D100 | #x1D1FF |
| MathematicalAlphanumericSymbols | #x1D400 | #x1D7FF |
| CJKUnifiedIdeographsExtensionB | #x20000 | #x2A6D6 |
| CJKCompatibilityIdeographsSupplement | #x2F800 | #x2FA1F |
| Tags | #xE0000 | #xE007F |
| PrivateUse | #xF0000 | #x10FFFD |

Table 14.14 demonstrates the block name escape by portraying some regular expressions as well as some corresponding matching strings.

### TABLE 14.14   Block Name Escape Examples

| Regular Expression | Comments | Matching Strings |
|---|---|---|
| Greek \p{IsGreek}*! | '\p{IsGreek}' matches any character in the Greek alphabet. | "Greek &#x03B3;!" <br> "Greek !" <br> "Greek &#x03A5;&#x03B3;!" |
| xx\p{IsBasicLatin}*xx | '\p{IsBasicLatin}' matches any character in the Latin alphabet. This book uses primarily the Latin alphabet. | "xx~word~xx" |
| xx\P{IsGreek}*xx | '\P{IsGreek}' matches any character *except* for those in the Greek alphabet. | "xx~word~xx" |

### 14.2.5.7 XML Character References

An expression may match a character by using the common XML character reference, which is a decimal number delimited by '&#' and ';', or hex number delimited by '&#x' and ';'. For example, the uppercase letter 'Z' is referenced by the decimal representation '&#90;' and the hex representation '&#x5A;'. These numbers correspond directly to the characters documented in *The Unicode Standard*.

Table 14.15 demonstrates the block name escape by portraying some regular expressions as well as some corresponding matching strings.

**TABLE 14.15** XML Character Examples

| Regular Expression | Comments | Matching Strings |
| --- | --- | --- |
| `Why [&#x5A;] not\?` | '&#x5A;' is the hex representation of the Latin uppercase 'Z'. | "Why Z not?" |
| `Why[&#x20;&#x5A;]+` | '&#x20;' is the hex representation of a space; '&#x5A;' is the hex representation of the character 'Z'. | "Why ZZZ" |
| `Why[&#32;]not\?` | '&#32;' is the decimal representation of a space. | "Why not?" |

## 14.2.6 Cardinality Quantifiers

An expression can define cardinality, or number of occurrences, of a character sequence with a *quantifier*. Without any quantifier, the default cardinality is always one. A quantifier can be one of the metacharacters (specifically '?', '*', or '+'). A quantifier can also be an explicit numeric range that looks like '{n,m}', where n represents the minimum number of occurrences and m represents the maximum number of occurrences.

### 14.2.6.1 One Occurrence

Without a quantifier, an expression matches exactly one occurrence of the character sequence. Table 14.16 demonstrates several relatively simple expressions.

**TABLE 14.16** No Quantifier Examples

| Regular Expression | Comments | Matching Strings |
| --- | --- | --- |
| `abc` | An exact match. | "abc" |
| `a(b|c)d` | The string that matches this expression must contain exactly one occurrence of 'a' or 'b'. | "abd" "acd" |
| `a(XYZ)b` | The subexpression 'XYZ' must appear exactly once. | "aXYZb" |

### 14.2.6.2 Zero or One Occurrences

The metacharacter '?' indicates that an expression is optional. Table 14.17 demonstrates optional character sequences.

**TABLE 14.17** Optional Quantifier Examples

| Regular Expression | Comments | Matching Strings |
|---|---|---|
| ab?c | The character 'b' is optional. | "abc" <br> "ac" |
| a(b\|c)?d | A matching string may optionally include 'b' or 'c'. | "ad" <br> "abd" <br> "acd" |
| a(XYZ)?b | The entire subexpression 'XYZ' is optional. | "ab" <br> "aXYZb" |

### 14.2.6.3 Zero or More Occurrences

The metacharacter '*' indicates that an expression is optional. Furthermore, the expression may be repeated any number of times. Table 14.18 demonstrates how to use the optional repeatable expressions.

**TABLE 14.18** Optional Repeating Quantifier Examples

| Regular Expression | Comments | Matching Strings |
|---|---|---|
| ab*c | The character 'b' may appear any number of times, including never. | "abc" <br> "ac" <br> "abbbbbc" |
| a(b\|c)*d | The characters 'b' or 'c' may appear any number of times, including never. | "abd" <br> "acd" <br> "ad" <br> "accccd" <br> "abbbbd" <br> "acbcbcbd" |
| a(XYZ)*b | The string 'XYZ' may appear any number of times, including never. | "ab" <br> "aXYZb" <br> "aXYZXYZb" |

### 14.2.6.4 One or More Occurrences

The metacharacter '+' indicates that an expression is required. Furthermore, the expression may be repeated any number of times. Table 14.19 demonstrates repeatable required expressions.

**TABLE 14.19** Required Repeating Quantifier Examples

| Regular Expression | Comments | Matching Strings |
|---|---|---|
| ab+c | The character 'b' may appear any number of times, but must appear once. | "abc"<br>"abbbbbc" |
| a(b\|c)+d | The characters 'b' or 'c' may appear any number of times, but at least one of them must appear once. | "abd"<br>"acd"<br>"accccd"<br>"abbbbd"<br>"acbcbcbd" |
| a(XYZ)+b | The string 'XYZ' may appear any number of times, but must appear once. | "aXYZb"<br>"aXYZXYZb" |

### 14.2.6.5 Explicit Numeric Range

A regular expression matches strings that have an exact number or a range of occurrences of a character sequence. The syntax for a numeric range quantifier is nominally '$\{n,m\}$', where $n$ is a required lower bound and $m$ is an optional upper bound. Table 14.20 demonstrates how to use the numeric range quantifier.

**TABLE 14.20** Numeric Range Quantifier Examples

| Regular Expression | Comments | Matching Strings |
|---|---|---|
| ab{3,5}c | The character 'b' must appear at least three times and no more than five times. | "abbbc"<br>"abbbbc"<br>"abbbbbc" |
| ab{0,0}c | The character 'b' must never appear. | "ac" |
| a(b\|c){0,2}d | The characters 'b' or 'c' may never appear or can appear a maximum of two times. | "ad"<br>"abd"<br>"abbd"<br>"acbd"<br>"accd" |
| a(b\|c){3}d<br>or<br>a(b\|c){3,3}d | The characters 'b' or 'c' must appear exactly three times. | "abbbd"<br>"acccd"<br>"abcbd"<br>"accbd"<br>"abbcd" |
| a(XYZ){3,}b | The string 'XYZ' must appear at least three times but is otherwise unbounded. | "aXYZXYZXYZb"<br>"aXYZXYZXYZXYZb" |

## 14.2.7 Character Classes Expressions

*Character class expressions* provide a way to match a range of characters. A character class expression, barring a quantifier, matches exactly one character. A character class expression may contain positive character groups (inclusive) or negative character groups (exclusive). In addition, an expression may subtract one character class expression (which is a set of characters) from another. The result is a mathematical set subtraction. The characters '[' and ']' delimit a character class expression.

> **WARNING**
>
> The *W3C XML Schema 1.0 Specification Errata* introduces the wildcard escape. A character class expression never contains a wildcard escape. The expression '[.]' is equivalent to the unique character perhaps better represented as '\.', *not* the wildcard character as would be the case in most other expressions. Specifically, the expression '[.]*' matches a sequence of '.' (for example, "........"), not a sequence of wildcards (for example, "Anything goes!").

### 14.2.7.1 Positive Character Groups

A *positive character group* is one or more character ranges. A character range is either a single character or the range of characters between two other characters, inclusive, although there are exceptions. The '-' character is the range delimiter. With a few exceptions noted later in this section, a character range consists of one of the following:

- Any two XML characters or single escape characters, or any combination thereof, with an intervening '-'. This notation provides many obvious ranges, such as 'A-Z'. Another way to think of the endpoints of the range is that both the beginning and end characters must resolve to a single character. Therefore, the following are invalid endpoints: a multiple character escape, a character category, or a character block.
- One XML character (for example, 'A' or 'Z')
- One single escape character (for example, '\t' or '\r')
- One multiple character escape (for example, '\w' or '\s')
- One XML character reference (for example, '&#32;' or '&#x20;')
- One character category (for example, '\p{Lu}' or '\P{D}')
- One character block (for example, '\p{IsGreek}' or '\P{IsBasicLatin}')

A positive character group consists of one or more concatenated character ranges. For example, '[A-Za-z\s]*' matches an unbounded sequence (because of the '*' quantifier) of all uppercase Latin characters, lowercase Latin characters, and whitespace.

Because of the power of the character ranges, there are a few invalid boundary conditions. In particular, all XML characters are valid character ranges, with the following exceptions:

- The characters '[', ']', and '\' are not valid character ranges.
- The '^' character is valid at the beginning of a positive character group only if a negative character group subsumes the positive character group.
- The '-' character is a valid single character range only at the beginning or end of a positive character group.

When a character range is truly a range, written in the form 'start-end' (where 'start' represents the start of the range and 'end' represents the end of the range), the following constraints also apply:

- '\' is an invalid value for 'start'.
- In a positive character group, '^' is an invalid value for 'start'.
- '\' and '[' are invalid values for 'end'.
- The Unicode character value for 'start' must be less than or equal to the Unicode character value for 'end'.

Table 14.21 provides some examples of positive character ranges.

**TABLE 14.21**  Positive Character Range Examples

| Regular Expression | Comments | Matching Strings |
| --- | --- | --- |
| [A-Z] | Any character between 'A' and 'Z', inclusive. | "A" <br> "F" <br> "Z" |
| [A-Za-z\s]* | An unbounded sequence of characters, all of which are uppercase Latin characters, lowercase Latin characters, or whitespace characters. | "" <br> "Sentence fragment" <br> "w ACKY    sTRI NG" |
| [\p{Nd}x]{3} | Exactly three characters, all of which are decimal digits or the letter 'x'. | "3xx" <br> "222" <br> "xxx" <br> "xx2" |
| a\|c([d-r]\|[3-9]*)z | One of 'a' or 'c', followed by either a character between 'd' and 'r' or an optional sequence of characters between '3' and '9', followed by the character 'z'. | "aez" <br> "crz" <br> "c7z" <br> "a63779z" <br> "cz" |

*continues*

**TABLE 14.21**  *(continued)*

| Regular Expression | Comments | Matching Strings |
|---|---|---|
| [A-Z^]* | An unbounded sequence of any uppercase Latin character or a caret. | "^^^^^"<br>"HELLO"<br>"HI^DUDE" |

### 14.2.7.2 Negative Character Ranges

A *negative character range* is the inverse of a positive character range. For character ranges that consist of a single character, a string that matches the expression must not contain that character. For a true range, the matching string must not contain the two range-defining characters or anything in between. Essentially, a negative character range is a positive character range preceded by a caret ('^').

Although all boundary conditions described in the previous section apply, one boundary condition seems worth reiterating because this section defines negative character ranges. The '^' character is valid at the beginning of a positive character group only if a negative character group subsumes the positive character group. For example, '[^^-z]' matches every character *except* those between '^' and 'z', inclusive. Table 14.22 demonstrates how to use negative character ranges.

**TABLE 14.22**  Negative Character Range Examples

| Regular Expression | Comments | Matching Strings |
|---|---|---|
| [^A-Z] | Any character except for those between 'A' and 'Z', inclusive. | "a"<br>"9" |
| [^A-Za-z\s]* | An unbounded sequence of characters, none of which may be uppercase Latin characters, lowercase Latin characters, or whitespace characters. | ""<br>"88!*88" |
| [^\p{Nd}x]{3} | Exactly three characters, none of which is a decimal digit or the letter 'x'. | "Hey"<br>"Oh!" |
| (a\|c)([^d-r3-9]*)z | One of 'a' or 'c', followed by any number of characters that are not in the range 'd' through 'r' or the range '3' through '9', followed by the character 'z'. | "aaa22z"<br>"cDUDE!z"<br>"cz"<br>"a&amp;12tuvz" |
| [^^-z]+ | An unbounded sequence of characters, each of which is any character *except* those between '^' and 'z', inclusive. | "FRED"<br>"(CRAZY)~{8}" |

### 14.2.7.3 Character Class Subtraction

A regular expression may match a set that corresponds to a character class expression subtracted from a positive or negative character group. Table 14.23 demonstrates character class expressions that match these constrained character ranges.

**TABLE 14.23** Character Class Subtraction Examples

| Regular Expression | Comments | Matching Strings |
| --- | --- | --- |
| [A-Z-[G-L]] | Any character between 'A' and 'Z', inclusive, except any character between 'G' and 'L', inclusive. | "B" "F" "P" "Z" |
| [\p{IsBasicLatin}-[\d]]* | At least one, but an otherwise unbounded sequence of Latin characters except a decimal digit. | "We be jammin" "Whatever!" |
| X\|([^\d-[A-Z]]{2,3}) or X\|([^\dA-Z]{2,3}) | Either the character 'X' or a sequence of two or three characters that are not decimal digits or between 'A' and 'Z', inclusive. | "X" "why" "oh!" "no" |
| [\p{IsBasicLatin}-[0-3]] | Any Latin character except the digits '0' through '3', inclusive. | "X" "a" "(" "8" |
| [^\p{IsGreek}-[^\p{Lu}]] or [\P{IsGreek}-[\P{Lu}]] | Not (that is, all characters except) the set of uppercase characters removed from the set of Greek characters. That is, any uppercase letter *except* a Greek uppercase letter. | "M" |

## 14.2.8 Precedence

The precedence of operators in the language derives from the grammar in Appendix B. Because of the dearth of operators for regular expressions, precedence is easy to remember. The following list itemizes the operators from highest to lowest precedence:

- Quantifiers ('?', '*', '+', and '{n,m}')
- Concatenation
- Alternatives ('|')

Of course, grouping with '(' and ')' overrides precedence, as in almost any programming language.

Table 14.24 provides examples that demonstrate precedence.

**TABLE 14.24** Precedence Examples

| Regular Expression | Comments | Matching Strings |
|---|---|---|
| X\|abc? | Either the character 'X', or the sequence 'ab' followed by an optional 'c' | "X" "ab" "abc" |
| ab+c\|de+f | The sequence 'abc' (with one or more 'b') or the sequence 'def' (with one or more 'e') | "abbbc" "deeef" |
| (X\|a?)bc | 'Xbc' or 'abc', 'a' being optional on the latter string | "Xbc" "abc" "bc" |
| ab\|c{1,2}\|de | 'ab', or one or two 'c', or 'de' | "ab" "c" "cc" "de" |
| a(xyz)? | 'a' followed by zero or one 'xyz' | "a" "axyz" |

## 14.3 Constraining Simple Content

Most of this chapter discusses the syntax of a regular expression. The link to XML schemas is that either a simple type or a complex type constrained to simple content may specify a regular expression. The value of a `pattern` constraining facet is a regular expression. Note that the `pattern` constraining facet applies only to certain base types (see the discussion on built-in datatypes in Chapter 12).

> **CAUTION**
>
> The interaction between two `pattern` constraining facets specified by the same simple type is different than the interaction between two `pattern` constraining facets when one is specified by the base type and one by the derived type. See this section and Section 14.3 for clarification.

The remainder of this chapter contains simple type examples, although the examples conceptually apply to complex types constrained to simple content. The simplest case is a simple type with a single `pattern` constraining facet. The other examples demonstrate the interactions of multiple `pattern` constraining facets, as well as the distinct behavior for derived types.

### 14.3.1 The `pattern` Constraining Facet

The XML representation of a simple type that has one pattern restriction is trivial. The following `xmlRE` constrains a corresponding value in an XML instance to a string that starts with "XML":

```
<xsd:simpleType name="xmlRE">
    <xsd:restriction base="xsd:string">
        <xsd:pattern value="XML.*"/>
    </xsd:restriction>
</xsd:simpleType>
```

In the pattern value, note that '.' means any character and '*' means unbounded occurrences. Therefore, the regular expression 'XML.*' matches the string "XML" followed by any number of arbitrary characters. The following strings are all valid values in a corresponding XML instance:

- "XML"
- "XML string"
- "XML1234"
- "XML is lame, at least without a corresponding XML schema"

### 14.3.2 Multiple `pattern` Constraining Facets (or)

A simple type that has multiple pattern restrictions is not much more difficult: The patterns are "ored" together. In other words, an XML validator considers a corresponding value valid when the value matches the regular expression described by any one pattern. The following `xmlSchemaRE` constrains a corresponding value to a string that starts with "XML" *or* contains the string "schema":

```
<xsd:simpleType name="xmlSchemaRE">
    <xsd:restriction base="xsd:string">
        <xsd:pattern value="XML.*"/>
        <xsd:pattern value=".*schema.*"/>
    </xsd:restriction>
</xsd:simpleType>
```

All of the following strings are valid values in a corresponding XML instance:

- "XML"
- "schema"
- "Write an XML schema in XML"
- "XML is great"
- "What about SQL schemas"
- "XMLschema"
- "schemaXML"
- "XML schema document"
- "XML is lame, at least without a corresponding XML schema"

## 14.3.3 Constraining Derived Types (and)

Simple type derivations are slightly more complicated to conceptualize. The patterns of the derived type are "anded" together with the patterns in the base type; the corresponding value must validate against both sets of patterns *concurrently*. The following xmlSchemaDocumentRE constrains a value corresponding to the values specified in the previous section. In addition, the string must contain the string "document":

```
<xsd:simpleType name="xmlSchemaDocumentRE">
    <xsd:restriction base="xmlSchemaRE">
        <xsd:pattern value=".*document.*"/>
    </xsd:restriction>
</xsd:simpleType>
```

All of the following strings are valid values in a corresponding XML instance:

- "XMLdocument"
- "schemadocument"
- "documentSchema"
- "XML schema document"
- "Is there a document for SQL schemas?"

Note that the corresponding value must contain "document" *and* either "XML" *or* "schema". Furthermore, if the value matches the 'XML.*' pattern, "XML" must appear at the beginning of the string.

The most confusing type of derivation occurs when both the base and derived types have multiple patterns. The following example derives xmlSchemaDocumentGreatRE, which has two patterns. The base xmlSchemaRE also has two patterns:

```xml
<xsd:simpleType name="xmlSchemaDocumentGreatRE">
    <xsd:restriction base="xmlSchemaRE">
        <xsd:pattern value=".*document.*"/>
        <xsd:pattern value=".*great.*"/>
    </xsd:restriction>
</xsd:simpleType>
```

Now the corresponding value must contain either "XML" *or* "schema" *and* either "document" *or* "great". Note the emphasis in the previous sentence on 'or' and 'and', as the preceding example demonstrates simple types with multiple patterns as well as derivations of simple types. All the following strings are valid values in a corresponding XML instance:

- "XMLdocument"
- "greatschema"
- "schemagreat"
- "XMLgreat"
- "XML is great"
- "An XML schema is great"
- "XML can be in a document?"

# Validation

**PART III**

Part III has two functions. The first is to discuss the abstract representation of an XML schema. The second is to demonstrate how to access this abstract representation programmatically.

- Chapter 15 is a detailed discussion on the abstract representation of XML schemas. This discussion includes each of the schema components, as well as how these components constrain XML instances.
- Chapter 16 covers the post-schema-validation infoset (PSVI). The PSVI includes properties that extend the functionality of a basic infoset. A basic infoset provides the data necessary to validate XML instances. The PSVI provides additional properties for intermediate calculations and final results.
- Chapter 17 is a tutorial on how to use the Apache XML Project with Java. Specifically, this chapter covers Xerces2. The tutorial provides examples on how to validate an XML instance. The chapter also covers how to use DOM and SAX to locate data in the XML instance, which is often the primary goal for programmers accessing XML.
- Chapter 18 is a tutorial on how to use XML in a Microsoft environment. Specifically, this chapter covers MSXML 4.0. The code examples provided in this chapter are Visual Basic 6.0, but because of the nature of COM and MSXML the examples translate easily to other languages that support the COM, .NET, and MSXML infrastructures.

# XML Schema Component Detail

## CHAPTER 15

### IN THIS CHAPTER

- 15.1 Schemas: The Basic Idea  388
- 15.2 Schema (Schema Schema Component)  391
- 15.3 Attribute Types  392
- 15.4 Element Types  396
- 15.5 Annotation (Annotation Schema Component)  411
- 15.6 Notation (Notation Declaration Schema Component)  411

The first section of this chapter talks about XML schemas in general and discusses a few properties that are provided by many of the component classes. The remainder of the chapter describes separately each of the component classes.

> **NOTATION NOTE**
>
> For some component classes, we use different names from those used in the Schema Recommendation; our terminology choices are discussed in more detail in Section 1.5. In this chapter, each component class has one section devoted specifically to describing the components it provides. Each such section has a title consisting of the name we use in this book, followed in parentheses by the name used in the Recommendation, as in "Element Type (Element Declaration Schema Component)." This format is used even when this book and the Schema Recommendation use essentially the same name, as in "Attribute Use (Attribute Use Schema Component)."

## 15.1 Schemas: The Basic Idea

A schema is like a DTD; each describes a set of element types and notations that can be used to validate an XML document. (A DTD also describes the document's entity structure, which a schema cannot do.)

A schema is an object with properties that are sets of other objects, which in turn have properties that may be yet other objects (or sets of or sequences or lists of yet other objects). The new classes of objects used to build schemas are called "schema components." Even *schema* itself is a schema component class: the "*schema* schema component."

> **NOTE**
>
> An abstract DTD could also be built as an object similar to a schema, but no one has chosen to define the classes that would be DTD components. Under most circumstances, a utility that reads a DTD could be made to construct a schema from that DTD. Such a schema could not contain the DTD's entity information. Validation against the schema would yield results almost identical to validation against the original DTD; there are only a few exotic cases in which they are not identical.

Element types, attribute types, and notations are special schema components because they have names that are expected to be mentioned in the XML instance being validated against the schema. Element and attribute types are *types* in the object-oriented (OO) sense that the word is used in this book; they are objects having properties and are classes having restrictors that accept certain elements and attributes as instances. An element or attribute is required to claim that it is an instance of the appropriate type by giving that type's name as its *type name*. *Validation* is the process of verifying that claim.

Notations, on the other hand, are primarily information for applications. They can be referenced by notation-valued attributes in elements whose element types permit them and by notation-valued elements with simple content whose structure types permit them; it is up to the application to decide what effect they should have.

Basically, an element type associates its name with a content model, an attribute set model, and possibly a substitution group. Element types are mentioned within content models, where their presence indicates that subelements that are instances of that element type can validly occur where indicated. See Section 15.4.4 for more information on content models.

An attribute type associates its name with a *value model*, that is, a simple type and possibly a value constraint (that serves to provide a default value and possibly to prohibit any other values). Attribute types are mentioned indirectly within element types, where their presence indicates that attributes that are instances of those attribute types can validly occur. See Sections 15.3 and 15.4.3.1 for more information on the use of attribute types.

These and the remaining schema components are described in the sections that follow, organized in a way that should clarify their interrelationships. The remainder of this section discusses some properties common to many kinds of components.

> **NOTATION NOTE**
>
> The Schema Recommendation calls schema components "declarations" if they establish a name that is to be used in the XML instance being validated: the names of element and attribute types, and of notations. Other schema components that have name properties are called "definitions" in the Recommendation. The components that cannot be named (schema, particle, model group, and wildcard) get neither appellation. This book does not make a distinction between declarations and definitions. It also uses totally different terms for element types (element definition schema components) and attribute types (attribute definition schema components), for reasons given in Section 1.5.1.

### 15.1.1 Names

In addition to element type, attribute type, and notation, there are five other schema component classes that provide name-related properties. Because schemas are XML-namespace-aware, these eight schema component classes provide the following two properties, which together yield a name unique within an appropriate context:

- *Name*

    The basic name without any namespace prefix. (The *local part* of the corresponding *qualified name* occurring in a schema document.)

- *Target namespace*

    Either ABSENT or a *namespace name* (a URI, not the local prefix associated with that URI) that identifies the namespace in which the basic name resides. Must be ABSENT for unqualified names and must not be ABSENT for namespace-qualified names. Unqualified names are used on nonglobal element types whose name applies only within the content models of which they are a part, and other named components that are local to them.

> **NOTE**
>
> Unlike information items, which carry the basic name and both the target namespace name *and* the local namespace prefix, schema components do not carry the prefix. This is because schema processors *must* be namespace-aware, and the Infoset Recommendation recommends that namespace-aware applications access the namespace URI rather than the local prefix.

All the nameable components may be referred to by name in the schema documents from which the schema is constructed. Element and attribute types and notations must always be named so they can be referred to in the XML instance documents being validated against the schema. The names of the others are involved only during the process of building the schema; during validation they are irrelevant.

### 15.1.2 Annotations

An *annotation* is a component whose properties are just lists of element and attribute information items taken from the content of `annotations` in the schema document. They have no impact on schema validation or processing. They are primarily human- or machine-readable documentation. See Sections 7.5 and 15.5 for more details.

Ten of the component classes provide an *annotation* property; its value must always be an annotation component (see Section 15.5) or, because the *annotation* property is always optional, ABSENT.

## 15.2 Schema (Schema Schema Component)

A schema component is represented in an XML schema document by a `schema` element.

A schema is an object having the following set-valued properties:

- *Element declarations*

    A set containing the global element types. (All element types are named.) See Section 15.4.

- *Type definitions*

    A set containing the global (hence named) structure types (simple and complex types). See Sections 15.3.2 and 15.4.2.

- *Attribute declarations*

    A set containing the global (hence named) attribute types. See Section 15.3.

- *Attribute group definitions*

    A set containing the *named attribute-use groups*. (All *named attribute-use groups* are global and named.) See Section 15.4.6.1.

- *Model group definitions*

    A set containing the *named model groups*. (All *named model groups* are global and named.) See Section 15.4.6.2.

- *Notation declarations*

    A set containing the notations. (All notations are global and named.) See Section 15.6.

- *Annotations*

    A set containing annotations from schema documents that are immediate subelements of the `schema` element and hence not associated with one particular component. See Section 15.5.

These seven sets contain all the global schema components, selected by kind (with both simple type and complex type components in one set). All remaining components, including all those of the six types not accounted for in the preceding list, show up as property values of some of these components (recursively, of course, just like information items in a document information item). A *schema* is an abstract object much like an "abstract DTD"—if a DTD had ever been defined as an object.

> **NOTE**
>
> Just as a DTD does not specify the type of the document element (that is done only by the document type *declaration*), a schema also does not specify the type of the document element.

## 15.3 Attribute Types

Attributes are part of elements. Each attribute has a name and a value. The name serves both to identify the value (as when querying values in the PSVI) and to identify its type: a class of which the attribute claims to be an instance. Because attributes are specified within elements, the attribute type corresponding to a particular name may be dependent on the type of the element. Accordingly, attribute types are ultimately buried in the structure of an element type. See Section 15.4.3 for details.

The structure of attributes and their types is simpler than the structure of elements and *their* types. An attribute type has a name (see Section 15.1.1), a value model (which plays a role similar to that of a content model), a scope, and possibly an annotation. A portion of the value model—the *simple type*—is separated out into a separate component because it has a complicated structure of its own. It is also used to restrict the content of elements, and it is potentially reusable.

### 15.3.1 Attribute Type (Attribute Declaration Schema Component)

An attribute type is represented in an XML schema document by an `attribute` element. (If the `attribute` is within a `complexType`, it also represents an attribute use component that has this attribute type as the value of its *attribute declaration* property.)

A schema-defined attribute type is an object having the following properties:

- *Names:* All schema-component classes whose instances have names, have the following two properties:
    - *Name*
    - *Target namespace*

    Attribute types must have names: ABSENT is not an acceptable value. See Section 15.1.1 for details about the names of schema components.

- *Structure restrictions:* The only things about an attribute that can be constrained are its *name* (just covered) and its *value* (covered here). The structure type constraint for an attribute must be a simple type; see Section 15.3.2 for details about simple types.
    - *Type definition*

        A simple type. Instances of an attribute type are constrained to be instances of this structure type.

        *Type definition*'s value corresponds to the *attribute type* part of an *attribute definition* in a DTD. (The *value constraint* property can also provide a further restriction on the permitted values of an attribute.)

- *Value constraint*

    Either ABSENT or a pair consisting of a value and either DEFAULT or FIXED. This property's value corresponds to part of the *attribute default* part of an *attribute definition* in a DTD. (The *value constraint* does *not* specify optionality, as does an *attribute default*. That's handled by an *attribute use* component—allowing the same attribute type to be used optionally with some element types and required with others.)

    An attribute with a value constraint (other than ABSENT) can never be truly optional—it will always have a value in the PSVI, either because one was specified in the containing element's start-tag or empty-element tag or because the default value in the value constraint was placed there during schema processing.

    If the *value constraint* is marked DEFAULT, it *only* affects attributes that are expected but not specified in an element's start-tag or empty-element tag, where it provides a value for the attribute. The value constraint can provide a further restriction beyond that provided by the structure type: If it is marked FIXED, the value constraint's value is the only value permitted for the attribute if a value is specified.

- *Miscellaneous:* Attribute types (and element types) may be global or local; this is called their "scope." Such components have a *scope* property that specifies their scope. Attribute types (and most schema components) may have an annotation.

    - *Scope*

        Either ABSENT or GLOBAL or a complex type. Some attribute types are global; others are directly contained in a complex type and are local to that complex type. Still others occur buried in named attribute-use groups; their scope is ABSENT—separately determined by the scope of each complex type into which they are copied. (Such attribute types must be copied—you cannot implement them by using a pointer back to the original in the named attribute-use group, because each copy will have a different scope.) See Sections 9.6 and 15.4.6.1 for details about the use of named attribute-use groups.

    - *Annotation*

        See Section 15.1.2 for details about the use of the annotation property. See Section 15.5 for details about the structure of annotation components.

**NOTATION NOTE**

In this book, the simple type that is the value of the *type definition* property of an attribute type is called the attribute type's "structure type"; in the Schema Recommendation, it's just the "type." (The Schema Recommendation does not use the phrase 'structure type'.)

## 15.3.2 Simple Type (Simple Type Definition Schema Component)

A simple type is represented in an XML schema document by a `simpleType` element.

A simple type is an object having the following properties:

- *Names:* All schema-component classes whose instances have names, have the following two properties:
    - Name
    - *Target namespace*

    Simple types must have names if they are global; otherwise the name must be ABSENT. See Section 15.1.1 for details about the names of schema components.

- *Derivation data:* Simple types used in schemas are necessarily derived from other base types; primitive simple types are considered to be derived from a special "simple ur-type," so that all simple types in a schema form a derivation tree with the simple ur-type at its root. The derivation mechanism uses *constraining facets* and a derivation technique (the *variety* of the simple type) to prescribe how the derivation from the base simple type is accomplished.

    The simple ur-type is the value of the *primitive type definition* and *base type definition* properties of a simple type if—and only if—that simple type is primitive. No simple types not defined in the Schema Recommendation may be directly derived from the simple ur-type.

> **NOTE**
>
> Some simple types are types *de facto* derived from the simple ur-type. Their derivation from the simple ur-type cannot be simply by the standard mechanisms of derivation; each is described from scratch in the Schema Recommendation. These simple types are called "primitive simple types." Other truly derived types also are defined in the Schema Recommendation. All simple types defined in the Schema Recommendation are called "built-in simple types." Simple types (necessarily derived) not defined in the Schema Recommendation are called "user-defined simple types."

- *Base type definition*

    A simple type, which may be the simple ur-type. The base type is the simple type from which this type is directly derived. Only primitive simple types are derived directly from the simple ur-type. A simple type is primitive if it is defined in the

Schema Recommendation, and not defined there as being derived from another simple type also defined there.

- *Facets*

  A set of constraining facet components. See discussion of constraining facets in Section 15.3.3.

- *Fundamental facets*

  A set of fundamental facet components. For the purposes of this book, fundamental facets are irrelevant—and hence are not discussed. For example, we care whether a simple type is ordered, because that determines whether a *max inclusive* constraining facet is permitted—but only ordered simple types have a *max inclusive* property; we don't need to check the value of an *ordered* facet to determine whether it would be useful. The user has no control over the values of fundamental facets, and no reason other than curiosity to ascertain their values.

- *Final*

  A subset of EXTENSION, LIST, RESTRICTION, and UNION. This property permits a simple type to prevent itself from being used as the base class of further derivations. In this context, EXTENSION means creating a complex type with this simple type as its content type.

- *Variety*

  One of ATOMIC, LIST, and UNION. Each simple type must be one of these three varieties. These varieties identify the three techniques for deriving a new simple type from an existing one. See the discussion of derivation in Chapter 10.

  Depending on the variety, one of three additional properties must have a value:

  - *Primitive type definition*

    A primitive simple type or the simple ur-type—in any case, the primitive simple type from which this one ultimately derives if this simple type's variety is atomic; otherwise ABSENT. The value may only be the simple ur-type if *this* simple type is itself primitive.

  - *Item type definition*

    Another simple type, if *this* simple type is a list; otherwise ABSENT. If not ABSENT, each member of the list must be of this type.

  - *Member type definitions*

    A nonempty sequence of simple types, if *this* simple type is a union; otherwise ABSENT. The sequence is the sequence of simple types of which this union is made. For some purposes, the order is relevant.

- *Miscellaneous:* Simple types (and most schema components) may have an *annotation*.

  - Annotation

    See Section 15.1.2 for details about the use of the *annotation* property; see Section 15.5 for details about the structure of annotation components.

### 15.3.3 Constraining Facets

There are 12 kinds of constraining facet classes: length, minLength, maxLength, pattern, enumeration, whiteSpace, maxInclusive, maxExclusive, minExclusive, minInclusive, totalDigits, and fractionDigits. The Schema Recommendation defines each kind separately, but they all provide essentially the same collection of properties (some do not provide a *fixed* property). Since instances of the various kinds might occur in one set, we have added a "*kind*" property so that one kind of facet may be distinguished from another in the same set. This extra property is not explicitly provided in the Schema Recommendation definitions, but it is clearly necessary; we have simply given a name to it.

Constraining facet components are represented in an XML schema document by various attributes of `simpleType` elements.

A constraining facet is an object having the following properties:

- "Kind"

  One of LENGTH, MINLENGTH, MAXLENGTH, PATTERN, ENUMERATION, WHITESPACE, MAXINCLUSIVE, MAXEXCLUSIVE, MINEXCLUSIVE, MININCLUSIVE, TOTALDIGITS, and FRACTIONDIGITS.

- *Value*

  A value appropriate to the kind of facet. For example, a pattern facet's *value* is a character string; a maxInclusive facet's *value* is a number.

- *Fixed*

  A Boolean value. If TRUE, subsequent derivations cannot change this facet's value.

  The *fixed* property is not provided by *pattern facet* and *enumeration facet*—not just that it must have a value of ABSENT; the property is simply not there.

- Annotation

  See Section 15.1.2 for details about the use of the *annotation* property; see Section 15.5 for details about the structure of annotation components.

## 15.4 Element Types

Elements are the primary components of XML documents. Each element has a *type name*, a set of attributes, and content. The *type name* serves to identify its element type: a class, of which the element claims to be an instance.

The structure of elements and their types is more complicated than the structure of attributes and *their* types. Instead of just a value model, an element type has both an attribute set model and a content model and substitution information. Like an attribute type, an element type has a name, a scope, and possibly an annotation. Most of the attribute set and content models—the *structure type*—is separated out into a separate component because it has a complicated structure of its own and is potentially reusable.

## 15.4.1 Element Type (Element Declaration Schema Component)

An element type is represented in an XML schema document by an `element` element. (If the `element` is within a `complexType`, it also represents a particle component that has this element type as the value of its *term* property.)

A (schema-defined) element type is an object having the following properties.

- *Names:* All schema-component classes whose instances have names have the following two properties:
    - *Name*
    - *Target namespace*

    Element types must have names: ABSENT is not an acceptable value. See Section 15.1.1 for details about the names of schema components.

- *Structure restrictions:* An *attribute* can be constrained only in its type name and its value. An element can similarly be constrained in its *type name* (just covered), but its structure constraints are more complex. In fact, the typical structure type for elements is called a "complex type." (There is a mechanism whereby a simple type can stand in for a complex type as the structure type of an element type. See Section 15.4.5 for details.)

    A complex type constrains both the *content* and *attributes* of an element. If a simple type is specified as the *type definition* value, it is effectively shorthand for a complex type permitting no attributes and having this simple type for its *content type* property.

> **NOTATION NOTE**
>
> An element type whose structure type is either a simple type or a complex type that has a simple type as its *content type* has *simple content*.

- The structure of an element's content and attributes is controlled by several properties of the element type:

- *Type definition*

    Either a simple type or a complex type. Instances of an element type are constrained to be instances of this structure type.

    In this book, the simple or complex type that is the value of the type definition property of an element type is called the element type's structure type; in the Schema Recommendation, it's just the type. Instances of an element type are constrained to be instances of the structure type.

- *Value constraint*

    Either ABSENT or a pair consisting of a value and either DEFAULT or FIXED. *Must* be ABSENT if no default or fixed value is specified or if the structure type does not provide simple content; otherwise, *may* be ABSENT.

    Attributes are like elements with simple content; just as an attribute type may have a value constraint, so may an element type that prescribes simple content.

- *Nillable*

    TRUE or FALSE, depending on whether elements of this element type are permitted to use the special `xsi:nil` attribute.

    Elements that use `xsi:nil` are required to ignore their structure type and have empty content if they specify `xsi:nil` to be 'true'.

- *Substitutability:* DTDs do not provide for one type of element to be substituted for another. This is unlike instances of a derived class, which are automatically instances of the base class and may be used wherever instances of the base class are prescribed. Schemas do provide such a mechanism. It works as follows:

    A *substitution group* is associated with each global element type. It is a set of global element types (itself and possibly others) whose instances may occur and satisfy a content model specifying an instance of this global element type at a given point. Each global element type is *de facto* a member of its own substitution group; it is the *head* of the group.

    The easiest way to define substitution group is to first define a related set, the "potential substitution group."

> **NOTATION NOTE**
>
> In the Schema Recommendation of 2001, what we call here the "potential substitution group" was called the "substitution group"; members of the substitution group were simply *substitutable*. In an Erratum to the Recommendation, 'substitution group' now has the meaning we are using. Our term 'potential substitution group' is local to this book, at least as we go to press.

Nominally, any other element type can unilaterally specify that it is substitutable for a given global element type, by making that global type the value of its substitution group affiliation. In reality, this is only the beginning. This element type has two hurdles to jump to get into the potential substitution group, and a third to be a member of the substitution group itself.

- This element type must have attributes and content models consistent with those of the group head it specifies. Specifically, its content type must be either the same as or derived from the content type of the group head. If it is not, the schema is broken.
- The group head must not prohibit, by use of its *substitution group exclusions* property, this element type from being a member of its potential substitution group. If this happens, the schema is not broken—this element type is simply not a member of the potential substitution group.

If these two hurdles are passed, this element type becomes a member of the potential substitution group of the group head, and also of any potential substitution groups of which the group head is a member.

The substitution group of a global element type is the set of that element type itself plus all members of its potential substitution group that pass the third hurdle:

- The group head must not prohibit, by use of its disallowed substitutions property, the potential substitution group member from being a member of its substitution group.

An element type can also effectively take *itself* out of its own substitution group by specifying that it is non-instantiable.

These are the properties involved in substitutability:

- *Substitution group affiliation*

  Either ABSENT or a global element type. Must be ABSENT unless this element type is a member of another element type's substitution group; if it is, the head of the group is the value of this property.

- *Substitution group exclusions*

  A subset of EXTENSION and RESTRICTION. This property provides the capability to block other element types from membership even in the *potential* substitution group of which this element type is the head.

- *Disallowed substitutions*

  A subset of SUBSTITUTION, EXTENSION, and RESTRICTION. This property provides the capability to block other element types of various kinds from being in the substitution group it heads, without preventing them from being members of substitution "supergroups" of which this group is a member, because of the transitive nature of the *potential substitution groups* involved.

- *Abstract*

    TRUE or FALSE, depending on whether instances of this element type are valid. If TRUE, the element type is *non-instantiable*—in other words, elements whose *type name* is the name of this element type are not valid, regardless of whether they satisfy the usual constraints. A non-instantiable element type is primarily useful serving as the head of a substitution group.

- *Miscellaneous:* Schemas can provide enhanced reference capabilities intended to subsume most uses of ID/IDREF. In particular, rather than having all references be unique-throughout-the-document IDs, the reference can be made unique throughout some smaller region of the document. Thus, an element type has an *identity-constraint definitions* property that tracks the necessary uniqueness constraints. See Section 15.4.5 for more information on the structure of identity constraint components; see Chapter 13 for more information on the reference capabilities available when using schemas.

Element types (and attribute types) may be global or local; this is called their "scope"; such components have a *scope* property that specifies their scope. All schema components may have an *annotation* containing component-specific human-readable documentation or machine-readable application-specific information:

- *Identity-constraint definitions*

    A set of identity-constraint definition schema components.

- *Scope*

    Either ABSENT or GLOBAL or a complex type. Some element types are global; others are directly contained in a complex type and are local to that complex type. Still others occur buried in named model groups; their *scope* is ABSENT—their scope is separately determined by the scope of each complex type into which they are copied. (Such element types must be *copied*—you cannot implement them by using a pointer back to the original in the named model group, because each copy will have a different scope.) See Sections 11.14 and 15.4.6.2 for details about the use of named model groups.

- *Annotation*

    See Section 15.1.2 for details about the use of the *annotation* property; see Section 15.5 for details about the structure of annotation components.

### 15.4.2 Complex Type (Complex Type Definition Schema Component)

A complex type is represented in an XML schema document by a `complexType` element.

A complex type is an object having the following properties:

- *Names:* All schema-component classes whose instances have names, have the following two properties:
  - *Name*
  - *Target namespace*

  Complex types must have names if they are global; otherwise they must be ABSENT. See Section 15.1.1 for details about the names of schema components.

- *Structure restrictions:* A complex type constrains both the *content* and *attributes* of an element. The structure of an element's content and attributes is controlled by the following properties of the complex type.

  The attribute set model drives the constraints on the set of attributes of an element that is an instance of this complex type. It is the combination of the value of two properties: *attribute uses* and *attribute wildcard*.

  The content model drives the constraints on the content of instances of this complex type; it is the value of the *content type* property.

  (See Section 15.4.3 for more information about attribute set models; see Section 15.4.4 for more information about content models.)

  - *Attribute uses*

    A set of attribute uses. An *attribute use* is a special schema component that plays a role similar to that of a *particle* in a content model; it prescribes optionality and default values and points to an attribute type.

    See Section 15.4.3.1 for more information on attribute uses.

  - *Attribute wildcard*

    Either ABSENT or a wildcard. A wildcard is a special component that permits validation of many or all attributes without specifying their names explicitly.

    See Section 15.4.3.2 for more information on wildcards.

  - *Content type*

    Either EMPTY, a simple type, or a pair consisting of a particle (which is the *content model* when subelements are permitted) and either MIXED and ELEMENT-ONLY. Thus a complex type can prescribe that the content of an element must be empty, must have only character data (no subelements) conforming to a specified simple type, or may have subelements. In the last case (may have subelements), a complex type may further prescribe whether data characters may also occur in the content.

- *Derivation data:* Complex types used in schemas are necessarily derived from other base types; primitive complex types are considered to be derived from a special "ur-type," so that all the complex types in a schema form a derivation tree with the ur-type at its root. The *derivation method* tells which derivation technique was used to derive this complex type from its base complex type.

- *Base type definition*

  Either a simple type or a complex type. Every complex type is derived from some other structure type; the ultimate root of the structure type tree is a special content type called the "ur-type."

- *Derivation method*

  Either EXTENSION or RESTRICTION. The method by which this complex type is derived from its base type (which is the value of *base type definition*). Note that derivation for complex types is not exactly OO derivation treating the complex types simply as classes, but it is sufficiently analogous to make the term appropriate.

- *Final*

  A subset of EXTENSION and RESTRICTION. This property permits complex types to prohibit their use as base classes for further derivation.

- *Abstract*

  TRUE or FALSE, depending on whether elements may be validated directly against this complex type. If TRUE, then instances must be instances of an element type that has a derived structure type that is *not* abstract.

- *Miscellaneous:* There is a somewhat tricky "escape hatch" in Schema that under some circumstances permits an element to assert that it satisfies a specific structure type other than that which is specified by its element type.

  Complex types (and most schema components) may have an *annotation*.

  - *Prohibited substitutions*

    A subset of EXTENSION and RESTRICTION. This property permits a complex type to disallow validating elements by using the "forced in the instance" escape hatch.

  - *Annotation*

    See Section 15.1.2 for details about the use of the *annotation* property; see Section 15.5 for details about the structure of annotation components.

### 15.4.3 Attribute Set Models

For an element's attributes, an "attribute set model" is the equivalent of a content model for that element's content. The attribute set model constrains the attributes (name and value) that can be included in an element. The structure of the attribute set of an element is simpler than that of its content—the attributes are not ordered, and only one attribute with a given name can be in the set. This means that the attribute's *type name* serves as a unique name for the attribute within the context of an element. (Contrast this with subelements in content, for which there may be many with the same *type name*. Most elements are not given unique names, and are referenced by location within the content of their containing element.)

The attribute set model of a given complex type is a set of attribute uses (attribute types with optionality and default/fixed information attached) plus an optional wildcard, which, if present, contains information about allowing other attributes not individually prescribed by name in the set of attribute uses.

> **NOTATION NOTE**
>
> The term 'attribute use' originated in the Schema Recommendation. It is not terribly descriptive, but then it doesn't get used much either. An attribute use corresponds to a particle in a content model, when that particle is applied to a single element type.

### 15.4.3.1 Attribute Use (Attribute Use Schema Component)

An attribute use component exists solely to put optionality and default/fixed information on an attribute type. This is separated out so that attributes of the same type can be optional in some types of elements and required (or defaulted) in others—an aid to reuse by reference rather than copy-and-paste in the source. Because an attribute use has no name, it cannot be global and cannot be used by reference itself.

An attribute use is represented in an XML schema document by an `attribute` element within a `complexType`; it is always created with the represented or referenced attribute type as its *attribute declaration* value.

An attribute use is an object having the following properties:

- *Required*

  Either TRUE or FALSE. Because attributes cannot occur more than once in an element, *required* subsumes the roles of both *min occurs* and *max occurs* as used on particles.

- *Attribute declaration*

  An attribute type.

- *Value constraint*

  Either ABSENT or a pair consisting of a value and either DEFAULT or FIXED.

(An attribute use does not have an *annotation* property.)

### 15.4.3.2 Wildcard (Wildcard Schema Component)

An attribute type wildcard is represented in an XML schema document by an `anyAttribute` element; it is always created as the *attribute declaration* of an attribute use. (An element type wildcard is represented by an any element; it is always created as the *term* of a particle in a content model.)

A wildcard is used in an attribute set model to allow attributes in addition to those singled out by name. You can allow absolutely all attributes, all attributes whose names fall in one or several given namespaces, or all attributes except those falling in one given namespace. In this context, a "given namespace" can also be all those that are not namespace-qualified. (The given namespaces are specified in the describing schema document, by the document author.)

A wildcard is an object having the following properties:

- *Namespace constraint*

    Either ANY, a pair consisting of NOT and either a namespace name or ABSENT, or a set whose members are either namespace names or ABSENT.

    ABSENT is used for the collection of names that are *not* namespace-qualified.

- *Process contents*

    Either SKIP, LAX, or STRICT.

    Because an attribute made acceptable by a wildcard (as opposed to an attribute use) does not have an associated attribute type (or element type, when the wildcard is used in a content model; see Section 15.4.4.3), you can specify what values are considered valid via one of three validation algorithms:

    - SKIP means no constraints (including subelements when used to constrain content).
    - STRICT means there must be a top-level attribute type (or element type, as appropriate) whose name is the *type name* of the attribute (or element), and the attribute (or element) must be validated with respect to this attribute type (or element type).
    - LAX means if there is a top-level attribute (or element) type whose name matches the *type name* of the attribute (or element), then the attribute (or element) must be validated against that type; otherwise it is automatically valid. (The same applies separately to subelements recursively when applied to elements. Subelements of automatically validated elements get LAX validation, not automatic acceptance.)

- *Annotation*

    See Section 15.1.2 for details about the use of the *annotation* property; see Section 15.5 for details about the structure of annotation components.

## 15.4.4 Content Models

Content models are different from attribute set models because content can be more complicated. A *content model* restrains the structure of an element's content. There are several options, all controlled by the value of a complex type's content type property:

- Content can be forced empty, although even this permits comments or processing instructions in the content (unlike with a DTD, where 'EMPTY' disallows even comments and processing instructions). The *content type* is EMPTY.
- Content can consist of subelements allowed in various sequences, with interstitial comments and/or processing instructions. The *content type* is a particle paired with ELEMENT–ONLY.
- The same as just described, with interstitial data characters also allowed. The *content type* is a particle paired with MIXED.
- Content can be data characters only, in which case the lexical structure and interpretation can be controlled in the same way as the value of an attribute, using a simple type. The content type is a simple type, or a complex type with simple content. (This case is different from the previous case with a top-level particle having *max occurs* equal to zero; in this case, the character string content is associated with a datatype.)

> **NOTATION NOTE**
>
> An element type whose structure type is either a simple type or a complex type with a simple type as its content type is said to have "simple content."

> **NOTE**
>
> When the content type of a complex type is a simple type, the rest of the content model is carried in the value constraint of the element type having this complex type as its structure type.

> **NOTE**
>
> When interstitial data characters are allowed, a schema can restrict the structure of the subelement sequence as fully as it can without interstitial data, which an XML DTD cannot do. On the other hand, a schema cannot restrict the structure of the sequence of interstitial data strings, which an SGML DTD can do. (An SGML DTD can specify that interstitial data strings, called "PCDATA," can occur at some places in the content model but not at others. In SGML there is no control over the lexical structure or interpretation of each individual PCDATA string.)

### 15.4.4.1 Particle (Particle Schema Component)

In the part of a DTD's element type declarations that specifies content models, DTD model groups and individual names of element types can both have repetition indicators attached. Particles are the equivalent in schemas; they attach repetition information to a schema model group, wildcard, or element type.

Every model group, wildcard, or element type in a schema content model occurs as the *term* of a particle. If no repetition information is specified in the part of a schema document that corresponds to the model group, wildcard, or element type, a particle still is constructed to hold the *term*, with *min occurs* and *max occurs* both equal to 1.

The top level of a content model allowing subelements in a DTD is required to be a group, even if that group has only one member. There are syntactic reasons for this, for DTDs. On the other hand, in a schema the top level must be a particle, but its *term* does not have to be a model group.

A particle is represented in an XML schema document by an `all`, `sequence`, or `choice` element (in which case its *term* is a model group), or by an `element` element (in which case its *term* is an element type), or by an `any` element (in which case its *term* is a wildcard).

A particle is an object having the following properties:

- *Min occurs*

    A nonnegative integer.

- *Max occurs*

    Either a nonnegative integer not less than *min occurs*, or UNBOUNDED.

- *Term*

    One of a model group, a wildcard, or an element type.

(A particle does not have an *annotation* property.)

### 15.4.4.2 Model Group (Model Group Schema Component)

A (schema) model group corresponds to a content model group in a DTD: everything in a DTD content model between a matching pair of parentheses. A model group can represent a point in the model where an element of any of several element types may be legal (CHOICE) or where elements of all of several element types may occur (ALL or, when the order is prescribed, SEQUENCE). Model groups can apply the same options to smaller subgroups as well as to individual element types: Their list is a list of particles.

A *model group* is represented in an XML schema document by an `all`, `sequence`, or `choice` element; it is always created as the *term* of a particle.

A model group is an object having the following properties:

- *Compositor*

  Either ALL, CHOICE, or SEQUENCE.

- *Particles*

  A list of particles. The list may be empty (but not ABSENT).

- *Annotation*

  See Section 15.1.2 for details about the use of the *annotation* property; see Section 15.5 for details about the structure of annotation components.

### 15.4.4.3 Wildcard (Wildcard Schema Component) *Reprise*

Wildcards are used in content models to permit subelements of types not explicitly named to occur at various points in the content of elements. See Section 15.4.3.2 for details about the structure of wildcards.

An element type wildcard is represented by an `any` element; it is always created as the *term* of a particle in a content model.

### 15.4.4.4 Element Type (Element Type Schema Component) *Reprise*

Element types are used in content models to permit subelements of explicitly named types to occur at various points in the content of elements. See Section 15.4.1 for details about the structure of element types.

### 15.4.5 Simple Type (Simple Type Definition Schema Component) *Reprise*

A simple type can occur as an element type's *type definition* in lieu of a complex type; the effect is exactly as though there were a complex type permitting no attributes and having this simple type as its *content type*. See Section 15.3.2 for details about the structure of simple types.

> **NOTATION NOTE**
>
> An element type whose structure type is either a simple type or a complex type that has a simple type as its content type is said to have "simple content."

Schemas can provide enhanced reference capabilities intended to subsume most uses of ID/IDREF. Rather than having all references be unique-throughout-the-document IDs, the reference can be made unique throughout other regions. A reference may be uniquely identified not only by the value of a particular attribute but also by the value of a particular simple-content subelement—or by some combination of the values of several attributes or subelements. An identity constraint contains the information needed to track the correct use of these capabilities when validating an XML instance. See Chapter 13 for more information on the reference capabilities available when using schemas.

An identity constraint is represented in an XML schema document by a `key`, `unique`, or `keyref` element.

An identity constraint is an object with the following properties:

- *Names:* All schema-component classes whose instances have names, have the following two properties:
    - *Name*
    - *Target namespace*

   Identity constraints are necessarily global and hence must have names. See Section 15.1.1 for details about the names of schema components.

- *Constraint data:* Each identity constraint contains data about one "namespace" in which elements can be given unique identifiers. It is a generalization of the only such "namespace" provided by DTDs, where the unique identifiers are the values of attributes whose content type is ID and which are required to be unique over all of the document, and not every element is required to have a unique identifier.

    - *Identity-constraint category*

      Either KEY, KEYREF, or UNIQUE. This is always the type name of the element in the schema document from which this identity constraint is constructed.

      KEY and UNIQUE specify that this identity constraint should define a constraint. If UNIQUE, every element falling under the purview of the identity constraint must have a "unique identifier."

      KEYREF, on the other hand, makes this an identity constraint that associates itself with another KEY or UNIQUE identity constraint. KEYREF is used to create links similar to IDREF links to IDs. See Chapter 13 for details on how KEYREF identity constraints relate to KEY or UNIQUE identity constraints.

- *Selector*

    A restricted XPath expression. See Chapter 4 for information about XPath expressions; see Chapter 13 for details on how identity constraints are constructed and used.

- *Fields*

    A nonempty list of restricted XPath expressions. See Chapter 4 for information about XPath expressions; see Chapter 13 for details on how identity constraints are constructed and used.

- *Referenced key*

    An identity-constraint definition whose identity-constraint category is KEY or UNIQUE if identity-constraint category is KEYREF; otherwise ABSENT.

- *Miscellaneous:* Identity constraints (and most schema components) may have an *annotation*.

    - *Annotation*

        See Section 15.1.1 for details about the use of the *annotation* property; see Section 15.5 for details about the structure of annotation components.

## 15.4.6 Reusability

An "attribute-use group" is a set of attribute uses and possibly a wildcard. Each complex type has an attribute-use group as the combined values of its attribute uses and attribute wildcard properties. There is no special component defined for attribute-use groups. However, an attribute-use group is a candidate for reuse; thus there is a mechanism for separating them out and associating a name with the group so that the group may be subsumed into the attribute uses of various complex types. This is not quite simple incorporation by reference, because when the group is subsumed by several different complex types, its attribute types inherit a possibly different scope from each complex type.

The same is true for model groups, except that in their case, a component is defined. Their named equivalents work the same way as for attribute-use groups.

### 15.4.6.1 Named Attribute-use Group (Attribute Group Definition Schema Component)

A named attribute-use group (an "attribute group definition schema component") corresponds closely to an *attribute (definition) list declaration* in a DTD: It collects a group of attribute uses (and possibly a wildcard) so they can be associated with possibly more than one element type. However, unlike with DTDs, where an attribute list declaration is the *only* mechanism for such associating, a schema is not required to use named attribute-use groups.

As a result, a named attribute-use group exists only so that its components can be subsumed into the *attribute uses* collection of one or more complex types. The subsuming complex type does not contain a pointer back to the named attribute-use group from which the attribute uses came.

A named attribute-use group is represented in an XML schema document by an `attributeGroup` element. (An `attributeGroup`, necessarily without a `name` attribute, may occur within a `complexType` or another `attributeGroup`; these `attributeGroups` do not represent separate components.)

A named attribute-use group is an object having the following properties:

- *Names:* All schema-component classes whose instances have names, have the following two properties:
    - *Name*
    - *Target namespace*

    Named attribute-use groups are necessarily global and hence must have names. See Section 15.1.1 for details about the names of schema components.

- *Attribute-use group:* The following properties together form an "attribute-use group", more or less comparable to a model group.
    - *Attribute uses*

        A set of attribute uses.

    - *Attribute wildcard*

        Either ABSENT or a wildcard.

- *Miscellaneous:* Named attribute-use groups (and most schema components) may have an *annotation*.
    - *Annotation*

        See Section 15.1.2 for details about the use of the *annotation* property; see Section 15.5 for details about the structure of annotation components.

### 15.4.6.2 Named Model Group (Model Group Definition Schema Component)

A named model group is literally a model group tied to a name. A named model group exists only so that its component model group can be subsumed into the content model of one or more complex types.

A named model group is represented in an XML schema document by a `group` element. (A `group`, necessarily without a `name` attribute, may occur within a content model representation, in which case it references a named model group and represents a particle component.)

A named model group is an object having the following properties:

- *Names:* All schema-component classes whose instances have names, have the following two properties:
  - *Name*
  - *Target namespace*

  Named model groups are necessarily global and hence must have names. See Section 15.1.1 for details about the names of schema components.
- *Model group:* This is the important property of a named model group.
  - *Model group*

    A model group.
- *Miscellaneous:* Named model groups (and most schema components) may have an *annotation*.
  - *Annotation*

    See Section 15.1.2 for details about the use of the *annotation* property; see Section 15.5 for details about the structure of annotation components.

## 15.5 Annotation (Annotation Schema Component)

An annotation component consists of the important information items from the corresponding `annotation` element in the corresponding schema document.

An annotation component is represented in an XML schema document by an `annotation` element.

An annotation is an object having the following properties:

- *Application information*

  A sequence of `appinfo` element information items.
- *User information*

  A sequence of `documentation` element information items.
- *Attributes*

  A sequence of attribute information items that may be permitted on the `annotation` element whose names are not in the schema namespace.

## 15.6 Notation (Notation Declaration Schema Component)

"Notation" is not something that is ever accurately defined, in XML or SGML. There are allusions to the idea that notations identify a markup language; various markup languages for text and graphics have all been called "notations." But as far as XML is concerned, a notation is just a "something" identified by a system or public identifier (or both). XML processing just passes the identifier(s) on to the application, which has to be programmed to recognize them and implement them properly for its purposes.

A notation component is simply a mechanism for tying a referenceable name to a system and/or public identifier, so that the identifiers can be passed to the application wherever the name is encountered.

A notation component is represented in an XML schema document by a `notation` element.

A notation component is an object having the following properties:

- *Names:* All schema-component classes whose instances have names, have the following two properties:
  - *Name*
  - *Target namespace*
  
  Notations are necessarily global and hence must have names. See Section 15.1.1 for details about the names of schema components.

- *Miscellaneous:* A notation must have either a system or public identifier. (System identifiers must be URIs; public identifiers are less constrained but may be URNs.)
  
  Notations (and most schema components) may have an *annotation*.
  
  - *System identifier*
    
    A URI. May be ABSENT if *public identifier* is not.
  
  - *Public identifier*
    
    A public identifier, as defined in the XML Recommendation. May be ABSENT if *system identifier* is not.
  
  - *Annotation*
    
    See Section 15.1.2 for details.

# PSVI Detail

**CHAPTER 16**

## IN THIS CHAPTER

16.1 Schema Validation and Schema Processing   414

16.2 The PSVI   416

We think of elements as objects and of element types as classes that have these objects as instances. Similarly, attribute types are classes that have attributes as instances. We also consider the structure types of attribute and element types to be classes. Unlike element and attribute types, they do not require their instances to have any particular *type name*. Thus, structure types may have instances that are instances of many different attribute or element types.

We generally think of instances of any of these four kinds of classes as those attributes or elements that are *valid* under those types. Unfortunately, the process of determining *validity* under a schema is somewhat complicated. The primary purposes of this chapter are to give you a reasonable understanding of how *validity* is determined and to provide an idea of what new properties and new kinds of information items can be found in the *post-schema-validation infoset* (PSVI).

## 16.1 Schema Validation and Schema Processing

For processing a document against a schema, the schema must normally first be built from one or more schema documents. The resulting (abstract) schema is described in Chapter 15. Also, the document to be processed against that schema must first be parsed and an information set for the (concrete) document built, as described in Section 2.2. At least this must appear to happen; as long as the results are correct, the internals of the processor are up to the processor writer.

The point, for the purposes of this chapter, is that schema processing is described in the Schema Recommendation as validation of abstract information items (which we call the "XML instance") with respect to an abstract schema. We have used that processing model in this book. In the rest of the chapter we will usually not emphasize this point by adding the phrase 'information item'.

Actually, while you're validating a document, the document information item itself is not involved. To validate a document, the schema processor only looks at the *element* information item that is the *document element* of the *document* information item. In fact, it is perfectly possible to begin validating at *any* element in the document; the Schema Recommendation imposes no requirement that only entire documents can be validated. The element where validation begins is called the "validation root"; necessarily all subelements (recursively) will also be validated.

### 16.1.1 Kinds of Validation

One of the interesting aspects of validation is that there is more than one kind of validation. XML does not require that all elements' *type names* name element types defined in a DTD, and neither does XML Schema require that all elements' *type names* name element types defined in a schema. In particular, by virtue of the ANY and NOT wildcard options, a schema can explicitly permit elements whose *type names* do not name element types in the schema.

A wildcard can specify how elements matching it are to be validated:

***Strict* validation:** The element's *type name* must name a global element type, and the element is validated against that element type. If no such global type exists, the element is invalid. Subelements in the content are validated strictly, and may be valid even though this ancestor is not.

***Lax* validation:** If the element's *type name* names a global element type, the element is validated against that element type. If no such global type exists, the element is automatically valid. All subelements are also validated laxly.

***Skip* validation:** The element *and all of its subelements (recursively)* are automatically valid, without inspection.

(All of these validation methods are recursive; it is mentioned specifically for skip validation because their recursion is not automatic. For the other validation mechanisms, the requirement that the immediate children be validated forces recursion.)

In either strict or lax validation, an element that has an `xsi:type`-mandated structure type is validated against *that* structure type.

A robust schema processor should also permit the user to specify the kind of validation to start out with on the *validation root*. There is, of course, no point in starting out with skip validation; *everything* would automatically validate. Lax validation might make sense if the document is expected to have elements whose types are not accounted for in the schema, while strict validation would be appropriate if the document is expected to avoid having any such elements. Validation always continues deeper into the subelement tree in the same mode unless a wildcard forces a different mode.

## 16.1.2 The Steps of Schema Processing

Schema processing consists of validating each element and its attributes and content, doing some global validation, and building a PSVI. In the Schema Recommendation these steps are described separately, but the distinctions are irrelevant for the purposes of this book. It is difficult to validate the elements without tracking most of the information put into the PSVI; it is impossible to correctly build a PSVI without validating elements in the process. Our use of the terms 'schema processing' and 'schema validating' reflects only whether we want to emphasize the building of the PSVI or the validation of the elements and attributes in the XML instance.

Schema processing includes a preprocess: that of building a schema from one or more schema documents. The schema documents must be validated against the Schema for Schemas and a schema component built in order to have a schema against which the XML instance can be validated. For the record, in this book we never use 'schema processing' to mean just this process of building a schema from schema documents.

### 16.1.3 The Results of Validation

With different kinds of validation coming into play at different points, a Boolean "valid or not valid" result is often not enough information. To quote the Schema Recommendation: "The architecture of schema-aware processing allows for a rich characterization of XML documents: schema validity is not a binary predicate." Many of the PSVI additions to the basic infoset provide places to record the results of schema validation. Some add "real information" about default values or cross-reference values (as in ID/IDREF and Schema-specific cross-references). Still others provide links to (or copies of) the actual types from the schema. These additions are all described in the remainder of this chapter.

## 16.2 The PSVI

The various kinds of infoset classes defined in the Infoset Recommendation are specific classes providing specific properties. If you consider additional properties, what you have is no longer that infoset but something else. In the case of schema processing, what we have is just that: properties added to the infoset classes and new classes added. The result is the PSVI (the "*post-schema-validation* infoset"). In this book, the infoset structure defined in the Infoset Recommendation is called the "*basic* infoset."

A qualitative difference exists between the PSVI and the basic infoset. Specifically, the basic infoset contains almost no information about the results of validation against a DTD other than attribute values that are implied because they have defaults and are not specified in the start-tag or empty-element tag of the element involved. Most of the additions in the PSVI, on the other hand, make available in the infoset a lot of information determined during schema processing.

> **WARNING**
>
> The Schema Recommendation describes the PSVI and recommends that the information in it be made accessible to the application. But it does not define a standard programming interface for that access, nor does it make that recommendation mandatory for conformance. Until standard APIs are defined and supporting products become available, be sure to carefully check the information that is made available by each schema processor you consider using. Watch for a future DOM revision, perhaps (http://www.w3.org/DOM/).

## 16.2.1 The Basic Infoset

Eleven distinct information item classes are defined in the Infoset Recommendation:

- *Document information item*
- *Element information item*
- *Attribute information item*
- *Character information item*
- *Processing instruction information item*
- *Unexpanded entity reference information item*
- *Comment information item*
- *Document type declaration information item*
- *Unparsed entity information item*
- *Notation information item*
- *Namespace information item*

Of these, only element, attribute, character, and notation information items have anything at all to do with the PSVI; the latter two only marginally. All but notation information items are described in Section 5.2.

A notation information item plays the same role as a notation component in a schema: it's just some information to be passed on to the application. Schema processing does nothing with notations except check that the local notation name is in fact associated with a notation. (Compare the description of notation components in Section 15.6; for more information about handling notations, see Section 7.10.)

> **NOTE**
>
> "Notation" is not something that is ever accurately defined. There are allusions to the idea that it identifies a markup language; various markup languages for text and graphics have all been called "notations." But as far as XML is concerned, a notation is just a "something" identified by a system or public identifier (or both). XML processing passes the identifier(s) on to the application, which has to be programmed to recognize them and implement them properly for its purposes.
>
> Schema processing (or DTD processing, for that matter) does only one thing with notations: It ensures that any QName used as the value of a `notation`-datatyped element or attribute matches a `notation` component that associates the local QName with the system and/or public identifier the application is expected to be able to recognize and act upon.

## 16.2.2 PSVI-added Properties

The PSVI adds properties to only two basic-infoset information items: element and attribute. All else is added via these properties, some of which have new PSVI-added information items as values.

### 16.2.2.1 The PSVI Element Information Item

These are the properties of basic *element* information items:

- *Namespace name*
- *Local name*
- *Prefix*
- *Children*
- *Attributes*
- *Namespace attribute*
- *In-scope namespaces*
- *Base URI*
- *Parent*

These properties are discussed in Section 5.2.2.

Twenty-four more properties of element information items are added for the PSVI:

- Properties applicable only to the *validation root* element:
    - *ID/IDREF table*
    - A set of ID/IDREF bindings. (These information items are discussed in Section 16.2.4.)
    - *Identity-constraint table*
    - A set of identity-constraint bindings. (These information items are discussed in Section 16.2.4.)
    - *Schema information*
    - A set of namespace schema information information items. (These information items are discussed in Section 16.2.4.)
- "Real information": If the element has a valid attribute whose structure type specifies the *notation* datatype, there will be *either* a *notation* property or a *system identifier* and/or *public identifier* on the *element* information item. The value of *notation* is a notation component (see Sections 16.2.4 and 15.6); the value of either identifier is a character string. Specifically, these are the possible properties; either the first or the other two must be present:

- *Notation*
- *Notation public*
- *Notation system*

If the element has *simple content*, the datatype specifies one of several normalization algorithms (involving whitespace modification) to be applied to the raw character string. The schema-normalized value is the value of this property. For elements, schema normalization begins with the raw data character string that is the element's content; for attributes, the starting value has already been normalized according to rules in the XML Recommendation.

- *Schema normalized value*

  The normalized data: a character string, or ABSENT if the element does not have simple content or does have an `xsi:nil` attribute whose value is 'true').

- *Schema specified*

  Either SCHEMA or INFOSET. SCHEMA specifies that the *schema normalized value*'s value came from a schema-specified default rather than from raw data present in the basic infoset.

(Some might consider the *nil* property to be real information, but the Schema Recommendation considers it to be parallel to the *element declaration* property, which is clearly type information. You'll find *nil* described under "type information", following.)

- Validity information:
  - *Validity*

    One of VALID, INVALID, or NOTKNOWN.

  - *Schema error code*

    A list of outcomes as prescribed in Appendix C of the Schema Recommendation; ABSENT unless *validity* is INVALID.

  - *Validation attempted*

    One of FULL, PARTIAL, or NONE.

  - *Validation context*

    A back-pointer to the *validation root*.

- Type information:
  - *Schema default*

    The canonical lexical representation of the default value, if the governing element type provides one.

There are two options: Either schema processing provides full copies of the structure type components or it provides name information identifying the structure type.

Providing full structure type components will give values to these properties:

- *Element declaration*

    The element type component (or "*element declaration* schema component") against which this element was validated, if any. (It may have been validated only against a content type specified by the xsi:type "escape hatch.")

- *Type definition*

    The structure type prescribed by the element type (or the structure type specified in the element itself by using the xsi:type "escape hatch").

- *Member type definition*

    If the structure type is a simple type that is a union, the string that is the content matches a string in the lexical space of this member of the union (otherwise ABSENT).

Providing only name information identifying the structure type will give values to these properties:

- *nil*

    TRUE if the element was explicitly nilled by specifying xsi:nil to be 'true'; otherwise, FALSE. (The attribute is also reflected in the *attributes* set.)

    The Schema Recommendation considers *nil* to be parallel to *element declaration*.

- *Type definition anonymous*

    A Boolean; FALSE if the type definition has a name.

- *Type definition name*

    The *name* of the applicable structure type, if the *type definition anonymous* property value is FALSE; otherwise, ABSENT or a system-generated unique identifier that distinguishes between distinct unnamed structure types.

- *Type definition namespace*

    A namespace name (a URI) or ABSENT; the *target namespace* of the applicable structure type.

- *Type definition type*
- Either SIMPLE or COMPLEX.

If the content type is a simple type that is a union, the following three additional properties provide information about the member type of the union that gave rise to the element, similar to that provided by the three similarly-named properties just described:

- *Member type definition anonymous*
- *Member type definition name*
- *Member type definition namespace*

### 16.2.2.2 The PSVI Attribute Information Item

These are the properties of basic *attribute* information items:

- *Namespace name*
- *Local name*
- *Prefix*
- *Normalized value*
- *Specified*
- *Attribute type*
- *References*
- *Owner element*

These properties are discussed in Section 5.2.3.

> **NOTE**
>
> Unlike elements, which get no direct indication of their structure type in the basic infoset, attributes do get an indication of their DTD-prescribed structure type. When schema processing occurs, much more information is made directly available in the PSVI, as it is for elements.

Seventeen more properties of *attribute* information items are added for the PSVI:

- "Real information": The (simple) structure type of the attribute specifies a datatype to which it must conform. That datatype specifies one of several normalization algorithms (mostly involving whitespace modification) to be applied to the raw character string. This schema-normalized value is the value of this property. For elements, schema normalization begins with the raw data character string that is the element's content. For attributes, the value has already been normalized according to rules in the XML Recommendation; it is this already-normalized value (the only available value from the basic infoset) that is further normalized according to the datatype requirements. (For elements, the only prior normalization is the replacement of character references by the characters referenced.)
    - *Schema normalized value*
      
      The normalized data (a character string, even if the attribute's structure type specifies a non-string datatype).
    - *Schema specified:* Either SCHEMA or INFOSET. SCHEMA specifies that the *schema normalized value*'s value came from a schema-specified default rather than from a *specified* attribute.

- Validity information:
  - *Validity*

    One of VALID, INVALID, or NOTKNOWN.
  - *Schema error code*

    A list of outcomes as prescribed in Appendix C of the Schema Recommendation; ABSENT unless validity is INVALID.
  - *Validation attempted*

    One of FULL or NONE.
  - *Validation context*

    A back-pointer to the validation root.
- Type information:
  - *Schema default*

    The canonical lexical representation of the default value, if the governing attribute type provides one.

There are two options: Either schema processing provides full copies of the structure type components or it provides name information identifying the type.

Providing full structure type components will give values to these properties:

- *Attribute declaration*

  The attribute type component against which this attribute was validated, if any.
- *Type definition*

  The structure type prescribed by the attribute type.
- *Member type definition*

  If the content type is a union, the string that is the value matches a string in the lexical space of this member of the union (otherwise ABSENT).

Providing only name information identifying the structure type will give values to these properties:

- *Type definition anonymous*

  A Boolean; FALSE if the structure type has a name.
- *Type definition name*

  The *name* of the applicable structure type if the *type definition anonymous* property value is FALSE; if not, may be ABSENT or a system-generated unique identifier that distinguishes between distinct unnamed structure types.
- *Type definition namespace*

  A namespace name (a URI) or ABSENT; the target namespace of the applicable structure type.

- *Type definition type*

    Always SIMPLE for attributes.

If the content type is a simple type that is a union, the following three additional properties provide information about the member type of the union that gave rise to the element, similar to that provided by the three similarly-named properties just described:

- *Member type definition anonymous*
- *Member type definition name*
- *Member type definition namespace*

## 16.2.3 PSVI-added Information Items

A number of new kinds of information items are added in the PSVI. They occur as values of added properties on the element and attribute information items.

Unlike the basic infoset, the PSVI loads in a lot of information about the results of processing the XML instance against the schema. This includes pointers to (or copies of) components of the schema, Booleans, and other indications of whether particular elements and attributes were validated, which validation algorithm (strict, lax or skip) was used, how validation failed (if it did), what schema was used, what particular structure type was used for each element and attribute, where validation was attempted, and so on.

The PSVI not only includes the *name* of the structure type—it can also include the entire structure type component and any other components that might be appended to it via values of properties. As a result, many kinds of schema components can wind up in any given PSVI.

> **NOTATION NOTE**
>
> The Schema Recommendation does not want to call schema components "information items" and does not want to pollute infosets with specialized objects that are not information items. Accordingly, the Recommendation introduces the notion of information items "isomorphic to" schema components: objects with the same properties and values thereof, except that all of the values that are themselves schema components are replaced by corresponding "isomorphic" information items. It's as though you took a schema, painted all the components green, and declared that the green components (with green child components) are really *information items* suitable for inclusion in information sets. There's really no difference between the two.
>
> In this book, they're called "components," even when they're used as information items. The Schema Recommendation's isomorphism is, at least for this book's purposes, the identity.

Four brand-new kinds of information items are also added by the PSVI:

- *ID/IDREF binding*
- *Identity-constraint binding*
- *Namespace schema information*
- *Schema document*

Of these, the first two play similar roles with respect to the ID/IDREF binding capabilities of DTDs mimicked by schemas and the more complex binding capabilities available only via schemas. The third and fourth serve to identify the various schema documents that make up the schema, and are collected by the target namespace. In fact, one property (to be given a value "if available") has as its value the document information item: the entire schema document in "abstract" form.

## 16.2.4 The New PSVI Information Items

In addition to the information items considered isomorphic to schema components, four totally new kinds of information items are used in schema processing. Two relate to binding by ID/IDREF constraints and schema-specific identity constraints. The other two relate to identifying relevant schema parts by target namespace and schema-document source. All occur only at the *validation root* element, as members of the *ID/IDREF table*, *identity-constraint table*, and *schema information* properties' values (each of which are sets).

ID/IDREF bindings provide information linking IDs with IDREFs. Identity-constraint bindings provide similar information for links determined by schema-based identity constraints (discussed in Chapter 13).

Both ID/IDREF bindings and identity-constraint bindings are used during validation to determine the existence and uniqueness of targets for corresponding pointers. Neither is required to be made visible by the processor to the using application. Accordingly, their structure is not important. The structure of ID/IDREF bindings is described here because it is relatively simple; the structure of identity-constraint bindings is not. For any details of the identity-constraint binding mechanism's structure not available in Chapter 13, see the Schema Recommendation itself.

Here follow descriptions of each new information item's properties.

- The *ID/IDREF binding* information item

These two properties are provided by *ID/IDREF binding*:

- *id*

    A name used somewhere as an ID *or IDREF*.

- *binding*

    The set of all element information items given that ID. (Validation will require this set to have exactly one member. The set will be empty if the name is used as an IDREF but never as an ID; it will have more than one member if two elements are given the same ID.)

- The *identity-constraint binding* information item

    These two properties are provided by *identity-constraint binding*:

    - *Definition*
    - *Node table*

*Namespace schema information* information items give information about that part of a schema that relates to one namespace. They occur only as members of the *schema information* property (of the *validation root*); that entire set ultimately contains information from the entire schema, sorted by target namespace.

Schema document information items in turn occur only as members of the *schema documents* property of namespace schema information items.

- The *namespace schema information* information item

    These three properties are provided by *namespace schema information*:

    - *Schema namespace*

        A namespace name (a URI), naming the namespace about which this information item provides information.

    - *Schema components*

        A set of schema components; all the components whose *target namespace* is this object's *schema namespace*.

    - *Schema documents*

        A set of schema document information items, one for each schema document that contributed components to the *schema components* set.

> **NOTE**
>
> A schema can in theory be created by some means other than being built from schema documents, in which case the *schema documents* property will be an empty set.

- The *schema document* information item:

  These two properties are provided by *schema document*:
  - *Document location*
  
    A URI pointing to the schema document.
  - *Document*
  
    The document information item that is the abstract version of the schema document.

# Java and the Apache XML Project

CHAPTER

# 17

## IN THIS CHAPTER

- **17.1** Apache Background  428
- **17.2** Java Xerces on Your Computer  430
- **17.3** "Hello Apache"  435
- **17.4** Critical Xerces Packages  442
- **17.5** Xerces Java DOM In-depth  447
- **17.6** Java Xerces SAX In-depth  459

# Chapter 17

This chapter is a tour through the emerging world of Apache, specifically the Xerces Java XML parser. The chapter introduces the Xerces download component, its integrated parser, documentation, and samples. Then it focuses on the critical packages and shows how to construct working applications, using both the Document Object Model (DOM) and Simple API for XML (SAX) models. You may use these samples as frameworks for further development. Along the way, the chapter introduces every important class and interface, so that by the end of the chapter, you will be adept in the construction of XML applications.

We assume that you have at least an intermediate comfort level with Java, that you understand the concepts of paths and classpaths, that you have utilized Java packages, classes, and interfaces, and that you have experience writing, compiling, and running applications. If you meet these requirements, and are comfortable with previous chapters, then hop on board.

## 17.1 Apache Background

Apache is a story that warms the hearts of Internet traditionalists. Sometimes confused with IBM (thanks to the influential corporation's mass acceptance of its software), Apache is actually a pure not-for-profit, open-source endeavor. Formed in 1995 by a half dozen Webmasters to consciously develop "a cog for the Internet," Apache emerged as the most widely accepted HTTP server—possibly the most successful piece of shareware ever released in terms of market share. Their triumph has ensured that at least one standard, the HTTP protocol, remains simple and approachable, safeguarded from proprietary interests.

The Apache Software Foundation (at http://www.apache.org) now boasts 60+ members whose open-source vision has embraced emerging standards to provide practical, zero-cost implementations for technologies ranging from Perl to PHP to XML. This chapter, of course, focuses on the XML technologies (and trust us, all the others are just as fun as this one!).

The Apache project features the Xerces XML parsers (available in Java and C++) but also hosts a broad realm of XML technologies. Developers can access additional tools that assist Web publishing, SOAP development, and formatting. The following is a brief list of XML subprojects, taken from the Apache XML Web site (http://xml.apache.org).

> **Xerces:** XML parsers in Java, C++ (with Perl and COM bindings)
> **Xang:** Rapid development of dynamic server pages, in JavaScript
> **Xalan:** XSLT stylesheet processors, in Java and C++
> **SOAP:** Simple Object Access Protocol
> **FOP:** XSL formatting objects, in Java
> **Crimson:** Java XML parser derived from the Sun Project X Parser
> **Cocoon:** XML-based Web publishing, in Java
> **Batik:** Java-based toolkit for Scalable Vector Graphics (SVG)
> **AxKit:** XML-based Web publishing, in mod_perl

Many of these projects support recent additions to the XML set of standards. The Apache-Xerces parser, for instance, has provided XML Schema functionality since early in its inception; Xerces version 1.1 (released in May 2000) supported the working draft specification and has been updated regularly. Xerces has been fully XML Schema-compliant since Xerces version 1.1.3 (save for minor limitations, which are well documented at `http://xml.apache.org/xerces-j/releases.html`).

Note that we have referred to a singular parser, but a visit to `http://xml.apache.org` reveals links to *two* different parsers: Xerces Java 1 and Xerces Java 2. Xerces Java 2, or simply Xerces2, is much more recent, a complete rewrite of the existing version 1 codebase. Xerces2 has a custom Xerces Native Interface (XNI), and its source code is said to be "much cleaner, more modular, and easier to maintain" than Xerces1. Xerces2 also implements the latest W3 XML Schema standards. Table 17.1 contains a matrix of implemented standards for both parsers.

Because the features are nearly parallel, your choice between the two parsers rests primarily on your desire for customization. Will you need access to code for adjustment or extension (possibly to implement late W3 features yourself)? Xerces2 might be your best choice; but extend your test schedule appropriately because Xerces2 might be a bit less stable and reliable (and check back to the `http://xml.apache.org` Web site often for updates). Xerces2 now receives the majority of attention from Apache developers. For purposes of this chapter,

**TABLE 17.1** A Comparison of Xerces Parsers

| *Supported Standards* | *Xerces Java 1* | *Xerces Java 2* |
|---|---|---|
| Current Version (8/2002) | 1.4.4 | 2.0.2 |
| XML Recommendation | 1.0 Recommendation | 1.0, Second Edition |
| XML Namespaces | Recommendation | Recommendation |
| Document Object Model | DOM Level 1 and 2 | DOM Level 2 Core, Events, Traversal, and Range Recommendations |
|  |  | DOM Level 3 Core, Abstract Schemas, Load, and Save Working Drafts |
| Simple API for XML (SAX) | SAX Level 1 and 2 | SAX Level 2 Core, Extension |
| Java APIs for XML Processing (JAXP) | JAXP 1.1 | JAXP 1.1 |
| XML Schema | 1.0 | 1.0, Structures and Datatypes Recommendation, DOM Level 3 revalidation |

we use Xerces2. When we refer to Xerces or "the parser," understand that we explicitly mean Xerces2.

## 17.2 Java Xerces on Your Computer

We will now take you through the process of downloading and exploring the Xerces2 package. By the end of this section, you should know the basic layout of the package and have successfully run several Xerces example applications.

### 17.2.1 Downloading Java Xerces 2 Parser

The download location for the Java Xerces2 parser is at

`http://xml.apache.org/dist/xerces-j/`

or you can click Xerces Java 2 on `http://xml.apache.org`, then click Download. A menu of options appears as shown in Figure 17.1.

Figuring out which file to download is easy. The working parser, packaged with supporting API documentation, is found in `bin` packages (`bin` being short for binaries or executables). Next, match the version you want to employ. There should be one 1.x.x version and one 2.x.x version. Only the latest of each parser version is available through this main page; older versions can be found at the bottom of the page (or with a little digging, if this page has changed).

The `bin` package is only one of three options. `src` packages contain the full source code for each version. The `tools` package includes the `ant` source-code compiler, the `junit` test package, and `xerces` and `xalan` JAR files. If you intend to customize code (by downloading the `src` package), you might find these tools quite helpful. Again, the version numbering applies, just as for the `bin` packages.

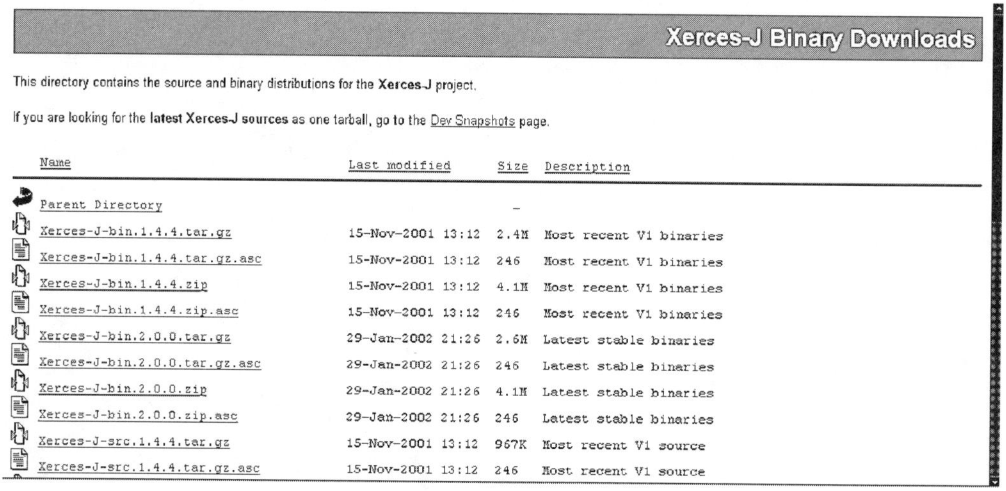

**FIGURE 17.1** *The Xerces download page.*

## Tip

There are many download options once you have selected your type and version of Xerces. The two of interest end with '.zip' and '.tar.gz'. Windows users recognize '.zip', just as Unix users know well the tared, "GunZipped" format. The latter format is actually a *double-compressed* file and almost always smaller (and quicker to download) than its .zip counterpart. What many Windows users do not realize is that *they too* can open .tar.gz files, using the familiar WinZip utility, so there is no reason not to download the smallest package for your version.

### 17.2.2 Exploring the Xerces Package

After you have downloaded and unzipped your Xerces package, you will see a top-level layout of files and folders (Xerces version 2.0) as in Figure 17.2.

Table 17.2 contains a brief summary of contents. Explore these folders and files for a few minutes.

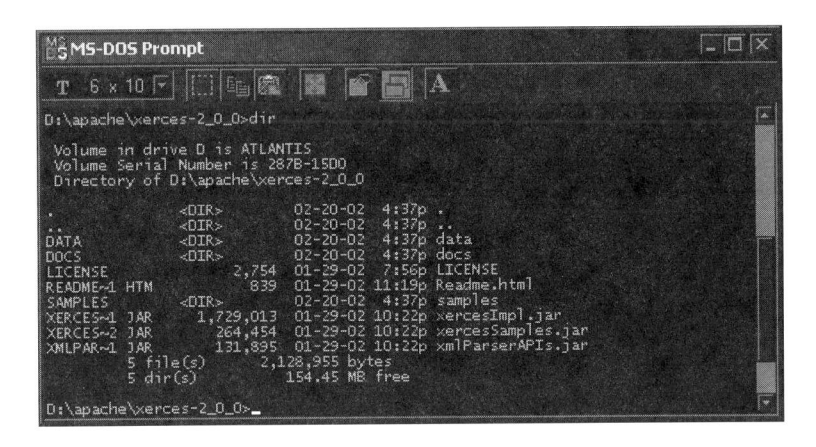

**FIGURE 17.2**   *The Xerces2 project folder.*

**TABLE 17.2**   Xerces2 Download Package, Top-level Files and Folders

| Xerces2 Top-level Files and Directories | Contents |
| --- | --- |
| docs/ | Contains the API documentation, including Javadocs |
| samples/ | A plethora of source code samples demonstrating DOM and SAX as well as XML UI and IO and the custom XNI Xerces features |

*continues*

**TABLE 17.2** *(continued)*

| Xerces2 Top-level Files and Directories | Contents |
| --- | --- |
| `data/` | Contains XML, Document Type Definition (DTD), and XML schema document files for the sample apps |
| `License` | The Apache-Xerces license |
| `Readme.html` | Links to the official API documentation |
| `xercesImpl.jar` | All the parser class files |
| `xmlParserAPIs.jar` | Implementation for all the standard APIs (DOM Level 2, SAX 2.0 R2 PR1, and the javax.xml.parsers of JAXP 1.1) |
| `xercesSamples.jar` | Compiled samples (class files) from the samples/folder |

> **NOTE**
>
> For experienced users of Xerces who might have expected to see a `xerces.jar` file (from the official documentation): "Xerces formerly came with a file called `xerces.jar`. This file contained all of the parser's functionality. Two files are now included: `xercesImpl.jar`, our implementation of various APIs, and `xmlParserAPIs.jar`, the APIs themselves. This was done so that, if your XSLT [XSL Transformations] processor ships with APIs at the same level as those supported by Xerces-J, you can avoid putting `xmlParserAPIs.jar` on your classpath."

### 17.2.3 Running the Samples

Installation and execution of Java applications has always been a breeze. Certainly you know by now that you must have Java installed on your system, which simply means that a virtual machine is accessible on your path. Visit `http://java.sun.com` to locate and download a Java virtual machine/Java Runtime Environment (JRE) or a full Java Development Kit (JDK); most packages have an extractor or installation program to take care of all details. After you have Java installed, running Xerces samples is a piece of cake.

> **NOTE**
>
> Xerces Java samples run in JDK 1.x and Java 2 (Java 1.2.x, 1.3, and later) except those with a user interface (the samples in the `samples\ui` folder), which require Java 2 because they were written in Swing 1.1.

The Xerces parser includes over a dozen complete code samples. This is code you can reuse immediately to see quick results, and these samples reveal techniques that go even beyond this chapter. The following list contains some of the more useful sample classes, with brief descriptions summarized from the official documentation:

- `dom.Counter`: Shows the duration and count of elements, attributes, ignorable whitespaces, and characters appearing in the document. Three durations are shown: the parse time, the first traversal of the document, and the second traversal of the tree.
- `dom.DOMAddLines`: Illustrates how to add lines to the DOM `Node` and override methods from `DocumentHandler`, how to turn off ignorable whitespaces by overriding `ignorableWhitespace`, how to use the SAX `Locator` to return row position (line number of DOM element), and how to attach user-defined objects to `Nodes` by using the `setUserData` method.
- `dom.GetElementsByTagName`: Illustrates how to use the `Document#getElementsByTagName()` method to quickly and easily locate elements by name. This sample is also a DOM filter.
- `dom.Writer`: Illustrates how to traverse a DOM tree to print a document that is parsed.
- `dom.ASBuilder`: Illustrates how to preparse XML schema documents and build schemas, and how to validate XML instances against those schemas, using DOM Level 3 classes.
- `sax.Counter`: Illustrates how to register a SAX2 `ContentHandler` and receive the callbacks to print information about the document. The output of this program shows the time and count of elements, attributes, ignorable whitespaces, and characters appearing in the document.
- `sax.DocumentTracer`: Provides a complete trace of SAX2 events for files parsed. This is useful for making sure a SAX parser implementation faithfully communicates all information in the document to the SAX handlers.
- `sax.Writer`: Illustrates how to register a SAX2 `ContentHandler` and receive the callbacks to print a document that is parsed.
- `socket.DelayedInput`: Delays the input to the SAX parser to simulate reading data from a socket where data is not always immediately available.
- `socket.KeepSocketOpen`: Provides a solution to the problems of sending multiple XML documents over a single socket connection or sending other types of data after the XML document without closing the socket connection.
- `ui.TreeView`: Allows exploration of XML nodes via a tree panel in a Java Swing application. This sample also reveals document messages sent as the tree is traversed.

The names of the samples in the preceding list are used to invoke the corresponding code in the `xercesSamples.jar` package. If all three Xerces JAR files are placed in the classpath, running the `sax.DocumentTracer` sample, for example, is as simple as typing the following anywhere on the command line:

```
java sax.DocumentTracer my.xml
```

in which `my.xml` is any XML file (in the current path). If you do not want to add all three JAR files to your classpath, use the `-cp` option, with each JAR file listed afterward (separated by semicolons), as shown in Figure 17.3.

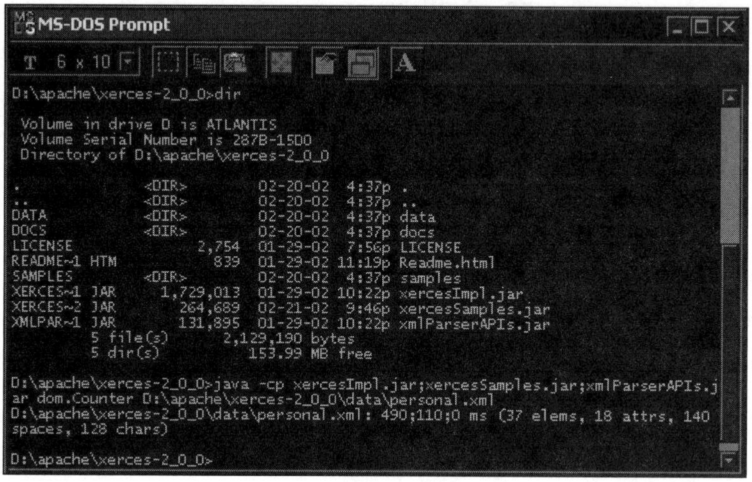

**FIGURE 17.3** *Execution and output of first Xerces samples.*

> **NOTE**
>
> If you have a Java virtual machine version 1.3 or later, find the `ext` folder. For Windows users, this is typically:
>
> ```
> C:\Program Files\JavaSoft\JRE\1.4\lib\ext\
> ```
>
> Here you can place JAR files for global access, just as if you had placed each JAR file in your classpath. This makes using the `-cp` option unnecessary.

We conclude this section with one more sample, just for fun (and also because it might come in useful for message tracing in the future). This is the UI example from the sample set, called

"TreeView," which we are going to feed our `address.xml` file (make sure the `address.xsd` file is also in the current path). At the command line, enter the following line (presuming, this time, that you *do not* have the Xerces JAR files in the classpath):

```
java -cp xercesImpl.jar;xmlParserAPIs.jar;xercesSamples.jar
    ui.TreeView address.xml
```

Within a few seconds, a brand-new window appears, similar to the window shown in Figure 17.4.

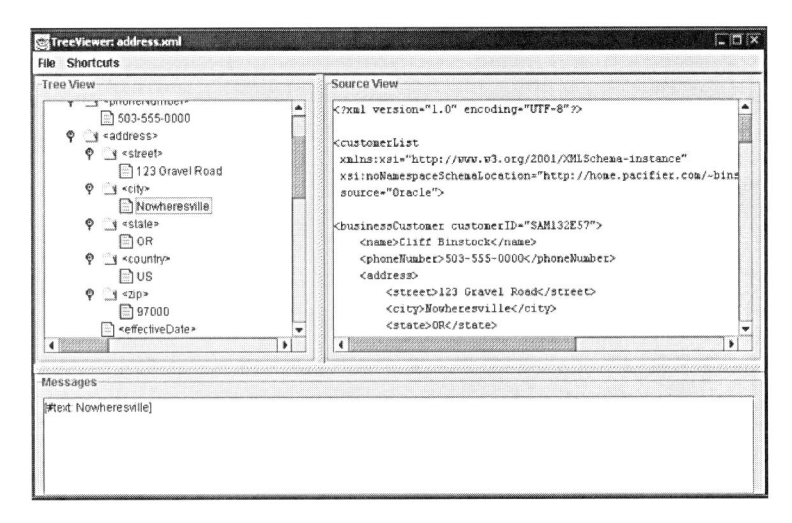

**FIGURE 17.4**  *Output of Xerces* `TreeView` *sample.*

In this window, you can expand the entire tree, refresh the view, and load new documents. (You *must* load an XML file from the command line initially, though; otherwise, the window will not appear.)

## 17.3 "Hello Apache"

In this section, you gain a little momentum, and a success or two, before digging into the nitty-gritty of Xerces. You use basic DOM methods to create a simple XML document, and then you reverse the process and parse an existing XML document.

### 17.3.1 Your First Parser

Listing 17.1 is a complete program that creates a few XML elements and then displays the serialized XML. The name of the file is `HelloApache.java`.

**LISTING 17.1** HelloApache Example

```java
import java.io.StringWriter;
import org.w3c.dom.Document;
import org.w3c.dom.Element;
import org.apache.xerces.dom.DocumentImpl;
import org.apache.xerces.dom.DOMImplementationImpl;
import org.apache.xml.serialize.OutputFormat;
import org.apache.xml.serialize.Serializer;
import org.apache.xml.serialize.XMLSerializer;

public class HelloApache
{
  public static void main (String[] args)
  {
    try
    {
      Document doc = new DocumentImpl();

      // Create Root Element
      Element root = doc.createElement("BOOK");

      // Create 2nd level Element and attach to the Root Element
      Element item = doc.createElement("AUTHOR");
      item.appendChild(doc.createTextNode("Bachelard.Gaston"));
      root.appendChild(item);

      // Create one more Element
      item = doc.createElement("TITLE");
      item.appendChild(doc.createTextNode
                      ("The Poetics of Reverie"));
      root.appendChild(item);

      item = doc.createElement("TRANSLATOR");
      item.appendChild(doc.createTextNode("Daniel Russell"));
      root.appendChild(item);

      // Add the Root Element to Document
      doc.appendChild(root);

      //Serialize DOM
      OutputFormat    format  = new OutputFormat (doc);
      // as a String
      StringWriter  stringOut = new StringWriter ();
      XMLSerializer    serial = new XMLSerializer (stringOut,
                                                    format);
```

```
      serial.serialize(doc);

      // Display the XML
      System.out.println(stringOut.toString());
    }
    catch (Exception e)
    {
      e.printStackTrace();
    }
  }
}
```

Naturally, you could shorten the number of import statements, but type these out at first to get comfortable with the locations of important classes.

To compile and execute this example, type these statements at the command line:

```
javac -classpath xercesImpl.jar;xmlParserAPIs.jar;.
    HelloApache.java
java -cp xercesImpl.jar;xmlParserAPIs.jar;.HelloApache
```

Hopefully, your results match the screen shown in Figure 17.5.

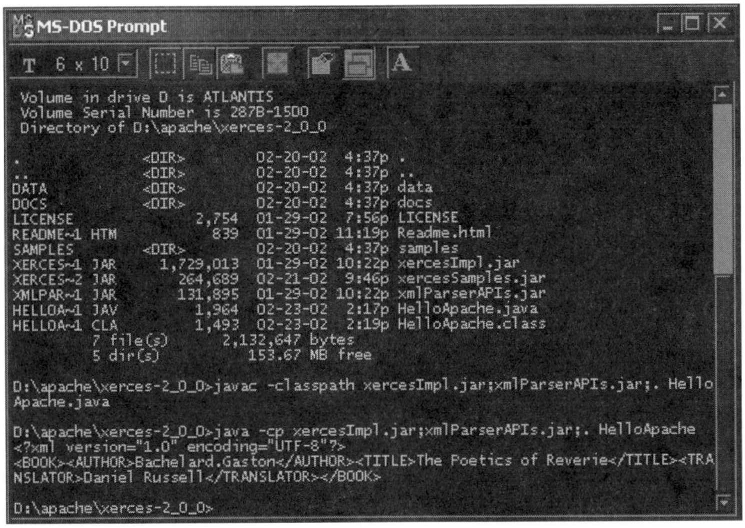

**FIGURE 17.5** *Output of* HelloApache *example.*

> **WARNING**
>
> Be sure to check that no other XML parsers or packages are located on your classpath (which is why explicit definition of the classpath is used in our example) or in your JRE/JDK's `lib/ext` folder (which is another virtual classpath). Because Xerces2 uses `org.w3.*`-defined interfaces and permits use of other XML packages (such as JAXP), conflicts are possible. If compilation or execution fails, this should be the first thing that you verify. Know thy classpath.

Those familiar with other XML APIs recognize the `Document` and `Element` interfaces (mini-API references for both can be found in Section 17.5). Both interfaces permit calls of `appendChild` to attach DOM elements, and the `Document` interface is most often used to create new DOM elements (that is, `createElement`, `createTextNode`).

But first you must create the DOM Document. The easiest way to do this is by following the example code:

```
Document doc = new org.apache.xerces.dom.DocumentImpl();
```

This might be considered cheating by purists because, theoretically, specific implementation classes should not be created directly. Instead, they would prefer indirect creation via factory classes and interfaces. Xerces2 provides these as well:

```
javax.xml.parsers.DocumentBuilderFactory dbf =
    javax.xml.parsers.DocumentBuilderFactory.newInstance();
javax.xml.parsers.DocumentBuilder db = dbf.newDocumentBuilder();
Document doc = db.newDocument();
```

> **WARNING**
>
> Beware: If you have installed more than one XML parser implementation, *you are not guaranteed to receive a Xerces2 Document in the* `javax.xml.parsers.DocumentBuilder`'s `newDocument` *call*. If you can be certain that the Xerces parser is the only XML parser accessible by your virtual machine, all should go well. But if you must have multiple XML parsers installed, use the Xerces-specific `Document` instantiator call. (There are also other workarounds—see the Xerces DOM samples for more hints.)

Also, notice the four lines of I/O calls that create the XML output string. You can find the `XMLSerializer` class in the `org.apache.xml.serialize` package (this, along with other utility classes, is introduced in Tables 17.3 through 17.10), which also includes HTML, XHTML, and simple text serializers. These serializer classes can output to either `java.io.OutputStreams` or `java.io.Writers` (designated by the first parameter to the `*Serializer` constructor). The second parameter of the `XMLSerializer` constructor is an `org.apache.xml.serialize.OutputFormat` object, which typically takes an entire `Document` object (this is a very interesting class—you can take great control of the style and content of the output). See the API documentation for the classes referenced here to see your range of I/O options.

## 17.3.2 Parsing "Hello Apache"

So now that you have seen how to build a simple XML document in Xerces2, take a brief look at how to load and parse an existing XML document. Listing 17.2 is a small program that takes an XML document's file name as a command-line argument and outputs the file's contents.

**LISTING 17.2**  HelloApache2 Example

```java
import java.io.StringWriter;
import java.io.IOException;
import javax.xml.parsers.DocumentBuilder;
import javax.xml.parsers.DocumentBuilderFactory;
import javax.xml.parsers.FactoryConfigurationError;
import javax.xml.parsers.ParserConfigurationException;
import org.w3c.dom.Document;
import org.xml.sax.SAXException;
import org.apache.xml.serialize.OutputFormat;
import org.apache.xml.serialize.Serializer;
import org.apache.xml.serialize.DOMSerializer;
import org.apache.xml.serialize.SerializerFactory;
import org.apache.xml.serialize.XMLSerializer;

public class HelloApache2
{
  public static void main (String[] args)
  {
    try
    {
      DocumentBuilderFactory factory =
          DocumentBuilderFactory.newInstance();
      DocumentBuilder builder = factory.newDocumentBuilder();
      Document doc = builder.parse(args[0]);

      OutputFormat format = new OutputFormat (doc);
      StringWriter stringOut = new StringWriter ();
      XMLSerializer serial = new XMLSerializer (stringOut,
                                                format);
      serial.serialize(doc);
```

*continues*

```
        System.out.println(stringOut.toString());
      }
      catch (FactoryConfigurationError e)
      {
        System.out.println
            ("Unable to get a document builder factory: " + e);
      }
      catch (ParserConfigurationException e)
      {
        System.out.println("Parser was unable to be configured: "
                            + e);
      }
      catch (SAXException e)
      {
        System.out.println("Parsing error: " + e);
      }
      catch (IOException e)
      {
        System.out.println("I/O error: " + e);
      }
    }
}
```

Compile `HelloApache2.java` exactly as before, with the explicit classpath specified (or set as you prefer—just do not forget that there are two Xerces JAR files that must be made available to the compiler).

If you run your `address.xml` file through `HelloApache2`, remembering that `address.xsd` must be in the same path, you get the somewhat cluttered output shown in Figure 17.6.

You can tell that all your content is present, and if you save this output to a different file, Web browsers or other XML interpreters can read this output. However, if you want a cleaner output, you can use the `IndentPrinter` class from the `org.apache.xml.serialize` package (and a full example is in the included sample class xerces-2_0_0\samples\xni\PSVIWriter.java) for some helpful hints. As of Xerces2 version 2.0.0, the only way to output XML cleanly with line breaks and tabs is to write your own serializer; several of the samples do this.

The code specifically responsible for the parsing is found in these three lines:

```
DocumentBuilderFactory factory = DocumentBuilderFactory.newInstance();
DocumentBuilder builder = factory.newDocumentBuilder();
Document doc = builder.parse(args[0]);
```

This should look familiar, because it uses the `DocumentBuilder` and `Factory` classes. But whereas you used the `Document` object to *create* XML elements, you now *receive* a whole XML document, using the parse function in `DocumentBuilder`. `DocumentBuilder`'s parse

**FIGURE 17.6**  *Output of* `HelloApache2` *example.*

method can receive either a `java.io.File` or an `org.xml.sax.InputSource` object (the latter can itself accept `java.io.InputStream`s or `java.io.Reader`s).

In addition, take note of the four types of exceptions that can be thrown. The first two in Listing 17.2, `javax.xml.parsers.FactoryConfigurationError` and `javax.xml.parsers.ParserConfigurationException`, alert you to major setup or configuration problems; you can then alert the system administrator to verify that only the correct Xerces JAR and class files are fed into the virtual machine. These exceptions might only need to be caught in the initialization stages. After the first successful parse, you probably only need to worry about the other, more common parsing exceptions: `org.xml.sax.SAXException` and `java.io.IOException` (which you should catch in *every* instance of XML document construction and parsing).

> **WARNING**
>
> The DOM parser encapsulates an inner SAX parser, so be prepared to catch SAX exceptions even in pure DOM applications.

## 17.4 Critical Xerces Packages

You have seen a decent handful of new classes so far, in several different packages. Before going deeper, we want to try to wrap up what you have seen and what you are about to see with a summarized subset of the Xerces API.

Listed in Tables 17.3 through 17.10 are the critical packages, classes, interfaces, and exceptions of the Java Xerces2 parser (with descriptions extracted from the API documentation). Take a look at these names and read the table a few times—if you become familiar with these types, you will soon feel comfortable building applications with Java Xerces. (Note that this is not an exhaustive list, so see the official API reference for a full package, class, interface, and exception list.)

The `java.xml.parsers` package lets you construct and access the actual parsers and document builders.

The `org.w3c.dom` package includes all the DOM Level 2 XML elements, which are listed in Table 17.4.

**TABLE 17.3** The `java.xml.parsers` Package

| Class | Descriptions |
| --- | --- |
| DocumentBuilder | Defines the API to obtain DOM `Document` instances from an XML document or to create a new DOM `Document` |
| DocumentBuilderFactory | Enables applications to obtain a parser that produces DOM object trees from XML documents |
| SAXParser | Defines the API that wraps an `XMLReader` implementation class |
| SAXParserFactory | Enables applications to configure and obtain a SAX-based parser to parse XML documents |
| *Exception* | *Description* |
| ParserConfigurationException | Indicates a serious configuration error |
| *Error* | *Description* |
| FactoryConfigurationError | Thrown when a problem with configuration of the parser factories exists |

**TABLE 17.4** The org.w3c.dom Package

| Interface | Description |
|---|---|
| Attr | Represents an attribute in an Element object. |
| CDATASection | Used to escape blocks of text containing characters that would otherwise be regarded as markup. |
| CharacterData | Extends Node with a set of attributes and methods for accessing character data in the DOM. |
| Comment | Inherits from CharacterData and represents the content of a comment, that is, all the characters between the starting '<!--' and ending '-->'. |
| Document | Represents the entire HTML or XML document. |
| DocumentFragment | A lightweight or minimal Document object used to represent portions of an XML Document larger than a single node. |
| DocumentType | Each document has a doctype attribute whose value is either null or a DocumentType object ("DocumentType" as in DTD). |
| DOMImplementation | Provides methods for performing operations independent of a particular document object model instance. |
| Element | The majority of objects (apart from text) in a document are Element nodes. |
| Entity | Represents an entity, either parsed or unparsed, in a XML document. |
| EntityReference | May be inserted into the structure model when an entity reference is in the source document or when the user wants to insert an entity reference. |
| NamedNodeMap | Objects implementing the NamedNodeMap interface are used to represent collections of nodes that can be accessed by name. |
| Node | The primary datatype for the entire Document Object Model and each of its constituent elements. |
| NodeList | Provides the abstraction of an ordered collection of nodes. |
| Notation | Represents notation declared in the DTD. |
| ProcessingInstruction | Used to place processor-specific information in the text of the document. |
| Text | Inherits from CharacterData and represents the textual content (called "character data" in XML) of an Element or Attr. |

| Exception | Description |
|---|---|
| DOMException | Encapsulates a DOM error. |

Use the DOM helper classes in org.w3c.dom.traversal in Table 17.5 to perform advanced iteration down your XML trees.

The essence of XML processing with SAX is to create an object that implements special interfaces (which receive SAX messages) and handle only the XML elements that interest you. Table 17.6 lists the primary interfaces you can implement.

**TABLE 17.5** The org.w3c.dom.traversal Package

| Interface | Description |
|---|---|
| DocumentTraversal | Contains methods that create Iterators to traverse a node and its children. |
| NodeFilter | Filters are objects that know how to filter out nodes (very useful, because the DOM does not provide any filters. These are quite easy to write, as well). |
| NodeIterator | Used for stepping through a set of nodes. |
| TreeWalker | Used to navigate a document tree or subtree using the view of the document. |

**TABLE 17.6** The org.w3c.sax Package

| Interface | Description |
|---|---|
| Attributes | Interface for a list of XML attributes. |
| ContentHandler | Receives notification of the logical content of a document. |
| DTDHandler | Receives notification of basic DTD-related events. |
| EntityResolver | Basic interface for resolving entities. |
| ErrorHandler | Basic interface for SAX error handlers. |
| Locator | Interface for associating a SAX event with a document location. |
| XMLFilter | Interface for an XML SAX filter—used to build an additional bridge between an XMLReader parser and an event-handling client. |
| XMLReader | Interface for reading an XML document by using callbacks. |
| *Class* | *Description* |
| InputSource | A single input source for an XML entity |

*continues*

**TABLE 17.6** *(continued)*

| Exception | Description |
|---|---|
| SAXException | Encapsulates a general SAX error or warning. |
| SAXNotRecognizedException | Exception class for an unrecognized identifier. |
| SAXNotSupportedException | Exception class for an unsupported operation. |
| SAXParseException | Encapsulates an XML parse error or warning. |

The classes in Table 17.7 help ease the burden of building Java XML SAX applications. Feel free to use them. Because they are part of the standard API, they are supported by all recent Java XML implementations (which means that if you move from Apache-Xerces to something else, your code hardly needs to change).

Use the classes and interfaces in `org.apache.xml.serialize`, shown in Table 17.8, to construct or utilize output facilities.

**TABLE 17.7** The `org.w3c.sax.helpers` Package

| Class | Description |
|---|---|
| AttributesImpl | Default implementation of the `Attributes` interface. |
| DefaultHandler | Default base class for SAX2 event handlers. |
| LocatorImpl | Optional convenience implementation of `Locator`. |
| NamespaceSupport | Encapsulates namespace logic for use by SAX drivers. |
| ParserAdaptor | Adapts a SAX1 parser as a SAX2 `XMLReader`. |
| XMLFilterImpl | Base class for deriving an XML filter (to sit between an `XMLReader` parser and an event-handling client). |
| XMLReaderAdaptor | Adapts a SAX2 `XMLReader` as a SAX1 parser. |
| XMLReaderFactory | Factory for creating an XML reader. |

**TABLE 17.8** The `org.apache.xml.serialize` Package

| Interface | Description |
|---|---|
| DOMSerializer | Interface for a DOM serializer implementation |
| Serializer | Interface for a DOM serializer implementation, factory for DOM and SAX serializers, and static methods for serializing DOM documents |

*continues*

**TABLE 17.8** *(continued)*

| Class | Description |
|---|---|
| HTMLSerializer | Implements an HTML/XHTML serializer supporting both DOM and SAX pretty serializing. |
| IndentPrinter | Extends printer and adds support for indentation and line-wrapping. |
| OutputFormat | Specifies an output format to control the serializer. |
| Printer | Responsible for sending text to the output stream or writer. |
| TextSerializer | Implements a text serializer supporting both DOM and SAX serializing. |
| XHTMLSerializer | Implements an XHTML serializer supporting both DOM and SAX pretty serializing. |
| XMLSerializer | Implements an XML serializer supporting both DOM and SAX pretty serializing. |

Additional useful classes are listed in Table 17.9.

If you need direct access to Xerces parsers, study the API for the org.apache.xerces.parsers package to access the classes listed in Table 17.10.

**TABLE 17.9** The org.apache.xerces Package

| Class | Description |
|---|---|
| DOMUtil | Very useful helper functions—can get the first or last child elements; given a org.w3c.dom.Node, can get the name for a Node, a Node's siblings, and much more |
| EncodingMap | A convenience class that handles conversions between Internet Assigned Numbers Authority (IANA) encoding names and Java encoding names, and vice versa |
| URI | A class to represent a Uniform Resource Identifier (URI)—designed to handle the parsing of URIs and provide access to the various constituent components (scheme, host, port, userinfo, path, query string, and fragment) |

**TABLE 17.10** The org.apache.xerces.parsers Package

| Class | Description |
|---|---|
| AbstractDOMParser | The base class of all DOM parsers |
| AbstractSAXParser | The base class of all SAX parsers |

*continues*

## TABLE 17.10  (continued)

| Class | Description |
| --- | --- |
| DOMASBuilderImpl | The Abstract Schema DOM builder class |
| DOMBuilderImpl | The Xerces DOM builder class |
| DOMParser | The main Xerces DOM parser class |
| SAXParser | The main Xerces SAX parser class |

## 17.5  Xerces Java DOM In-depth

This section plunges into the Java DOM, using Xerces to construct a couple of larger applications. It also presents the critical packages and classes you will most likely use while building XML DOM applications. Included are APIs for the three most important DOM interfaces, along with sample code that explores many of their interesting methods.

### 17.5.1  The Document Interface

Xerces2 implements the DOM Level 2 API, which builds on the original Level 1 core. As you know, DOM is most useful when a new XML document must be created from scratch or when a parsed document must be saved in memory, presumably to be manipulated at a later time. The common Xerces DOM API elements are found in the package org.w3.dom and its subpackages.

The org.w3.dom package (whose interfaces are described in the previous section) is the starting point from which to construct Java DOM code. Look through Table 17.4, which describes the package org.w3c.dom, and see if you can locate which three interfaces *you* think are most important to your task of building DOM applications.

As you saw in Listing 17.2, an object that implements the Document interface is returned from the DocumentBuilder object via a call to either the newDocument or parse method. Once you have an object of type Document, you may call any of the methods in Table 17.11 to create actual XML elements (the create* methods) or access elements (the get* methods).

## TABLE 17.11  The org.w3c.dom.Document Interface

| Return Value | Method Name (parameters)<br>Explanation |
| --- | --- |
| Attr | createAttribute(String name)<br>'Attr' is short for 'Attribute'—here you can create an Attr with a name of your choice and then set the value of the Attr with a call to setValue(String). |

*continues*

**TABLE 17.11**  *(continued)*

| Return Value | Method Name (parameters) / Explanation |
|---|---|
| Attr | createAttributeNS(String namespaceURI, String qualifiedName)<br>If you want to qualify the Attribute with a particular namespace URI, use this method. |
| CDATASection | createCDATASection(String data)<br>Create a CDATASection and set the value of its data by using this method. |
| Comment | createComment(String data)<br>Create a Comment and set the value of its data by using this method. |
| DocumentFragment | createDocumentFragment()<br>A DocumentFragment object is a lightweight version of an XML document. If you want to move portions of a document around, you can use a DocumentFragment object to designate this purpose instead of using just a general Node object. |
| Element | createElement(String tagName)<br>Here is how we commonly create XML document elements, which you can manipulate with one of many method calls. (Remember, Element extends the node interface, so all these methods are available.) |
| Element | createElementNS(String namespaceURI, String qualifiedName)<br>If you want to qualify the Element's *type name* with a particular namespace URI, use this method. |
| EntityReference | createEntityReference(String name)<br>An EntityReference object points to another Entity somewhere in the XML document. Think of it as a shortcut. |
| ProcessingInstruction | createProcessingInstruction(String target, String data)<br>Processing instructions are parser-specific commands (in XML documents, they are wrapped between '<?' and '?>'). Create them and set their target and data here. |
| Text | createTextNode(String data)<br>An Element can have one Text node. Create and set data here. |
| DocumentType | getDoctype()<br>This returns the Document Type Declaration associated with this document. |

*continues*

**TABLE 17.11**   *(continued)*

| Return Value | Method Name (parameters) / Explanation |
|---|---|
| Element | getDocumentElement() <br> This returns the root Element of the document, which you can then access. |
| Element | getElementById(String elementId) <br> This returns an Element based on its ID (ID is a specific XML type). |
| NodeList | getElementsByTagName(String tagname) <br> All Elements with a given tag name are returned in a NodeList, in the order in which they are encountered in a pre-order traversal of the Document tree. |
| NodeList | getElementsByTagNameNS(String namespaceURI, String localName) <br> Same as getElementsByTagName, except only Elements with a matching namespace are returned in the NodeList. |
| DOMImplementation | getImplementation() <br> Returns the DOMImplementation object that handles this document. Useful for testing whether the DOM implementation supports certain features through the returned interface's hasFeature (String feature, String version) method. |
| Node | importNode(Node importedNode, boolean deep) <br> Imports a Node from another document to this document. The source node is not altered, and the node returned from this call has no parent node. |
| Plus all methods from org.w3c.dom.Node. | |

The last line in Table 17.11 is important. The Document interface also extends a lower interface: Node. As you have probably guessed, Node is the second of the three critical org.w3c.dom interfaces. Before you get overwhelmed with the APIs, however, practice with a little bit of code by creating a more interesting XML document, with many of the features described in the Document interface in Table 17.11.

## 17.5.2 Creating DOM Documents

In this section, you create your first XML elements. You do this by using a Document object that is returned from the DocumentBuilder (just like HelloApache2). Once you have the Document object, you can use that object to create most XML nodes, such as Text, CDATA, and of course Elements themselves.

Every XML node has a corresponding method in the `Document` object. For example, to create a `Comment`, you call `createComment`, with the parameter being the actual comment text. (There is a caveat, with `Attributes`. See Listing 17.3, and we will explain afterward.)

When instantiated, all XML components must be attached to one another; because they are separate objects, they must be able to refer to one another. For instance, once you have created an `Element` and then a `Text` node for that `Element`, you must link them together. You do this by using the `appendChild` method, available in each object. Eventually the root `Element` itself must be attached to something: the `Document`. Then you can serialize out the `Document` object, as in Listing 17.2.

To add a twist, the code also specifies a namespace for this `Element`; you will see the effects after you compile and run the example. Also, instead of using a `StringWriter`, as in HelloApache2, you use a `FileOutputStream`. This lets you persist the finalized DOM document out to an XML file, which you can then access and transmit as you prefer (see the `XMLSerializer` class API in the official documentation to discover all the output options you have available).

**LISTING 17.3** HelloApacheDOM Example

```java
import org.w3c.dom.Document;
import org.w3c.dom.Element;
import org.w3c.dom.Attr;
import org.w3c.dom.Comment;
import org.w3c.dom.CDATASection;
import org.w3c.dom.Text;
import org.apache.xml.serialize.OutputFormat;
import org.apache.xml.serialize.Serializer;
import org.apache.xml.serialize.XMLSerializer;
import java.io.FileOutputStream;

public class HelloApacheDOM
{
  public static void main (String[] args)
  {
    try
    {
      javax.xml.parsers.DocumentBuilderFactory dbf =
        javax.xml.parsers.DocumentBuilderFactory.newInstance();
      javax.xml.parsers.DocumentBuilder db =
        dbf.newDocumentBuilder();
      Document doc = db.newDocument();

      // Create the parent Element object, and add a Comment
      Element root = doc.createElementNS
          ("http://www.galtenberg.net", "books:BOOK");
```

```
        Comment comment = doc.createComment
            ("Publisher 'Beacon Press' address is unknown");
        root.appendChild(comment);

        // Create a child Element with its own Text
        Element item =
            doc.createElementNS("http://www.galtenberg.net",
                                "books:AUTHOR");
        Text text = doc.createTextNode("Bachelard.Gaston");
        item.appendChild(text);
        root.appendChild(item);

        // Do the same as above, but this time add Attributes
        item = doc.createElementNS("http://www.galtenberg.net",
            "books:TITLE");
        text = doc.createTextNode("The Poetics of Reverie");
        Attr attrib = doc.createAttributeNS
            ("http://www.galtenberg.net", "books:ISBN");
        attrib.setValue("0-8070-6413-0");
        // Attributes are attached differently
        item.setAttributeNodeNS(attrib);
        item.appendChild(text);
        root.appendChild(item);

        item = doc.createElementNS("http://www.galtenberg.net",
            "books:TRANSLATOR");
        attrib = doc.createAttributeNS("http://www.galtenberg.net"
            ,"books:ORIGINAL-LANGUAGE");
        attrib.setValue("French");
        item.setAttributeNodeNS(attrib);
        item.appendChild(doc.createTextNode("Daniel Russell"));
        root.appendChild(item);

        item = doc.createElementNS("http://www.galtenberg.net",
            "books:EXCERPT");
        CDATASection cdata = doc.createCDATASection
            ("One does not dream with taught ideas.");
        item.appendChild(cdata);
        root.appendChild(item);

        doc.appendChild(root);
        OutputFormat format  = new OutputFormat (doc);
        FileOutputStream fs  = new FileOutputStream
          ("d:\\helloapache.xml");
        XMLSerializer serial = new XMLSerializer (fs, format);
        serial.serialize(doc);
    }
    catch (Exception e)
```

*continues*

```
    {
      e.printStackTrace();
    }
  }
}
```

When you get into this example, you will see that the fundamentals of building XML DOM applications are pretty straightforward. Decide which XML node you would like to utilize, import that interface, declare a type, use the `Document` object to create the node, fill in its data, and attach it to the appropriate `Element`, like this:

```
Element root = doc.createElementNS ("http://www.galtenberg.net",
    "books:BOOK");
Comment comment = doc.createComment
    ("Publisher 'Beacon Press' address is unknown");
root.appendChild(comment);
```

How else could you have created this `Element` (maybe without the namespace)? Look back to Table 17.11, which describes the `Document` interface. Yes, you could call `doc.createElement("BOOK");`.

Now compile and execute your sample. Out on your `D:` drive (make sure to change the code if this is not what you want), you now see the file `helloapache.xml`. When you open it in a Web browser, it should look like Figure 17.7.

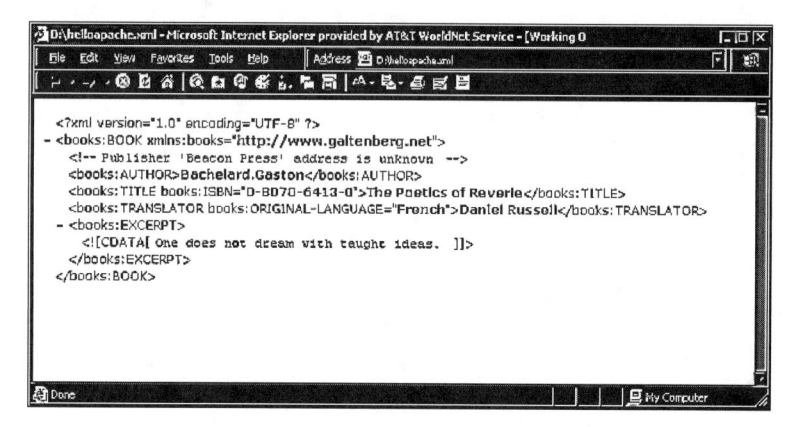

**FIGURE 17.7** *Viewing output of* `HelloApacheDOM` *example in Web browser.*

### 17.5.3 The Element Interface

As mentioned earlier, there is one caveat in the `HelloApacheDOM` example, which is a good lesson if you are new to the XML APIs. When you created an XML attribute (using the `Attr` interface), you did the normal things: You asked the `Document` to return you an `Attr` object and then you filled in the attribute's value. But unlike with other XML components, you did not call `appendChild` on an `Element` as follows:

```
Element item = doc.createElementNS("http://www.galtenberg.net",
     "books:TRANSLATOR");
Attr attrib = doc.createAttributeNS("http://www.galtenberg.net",
     "books:ORIGINAL-LANGUAGE");
attrib.setValue("French");
item.setAttributeNodeNS(attrib);
```

Instead of calling `appendChild` on `item`, you called `setAttributeNodeNS` with your `Attr` object. `Elements` have their own interface, which deals primarily with XML attributes. Table 17.12 contains `org.w3c.dom.Element`, which is the other critical interface with which you should become acquainted.

**TABLE 17.12**  The `org.w3c.dom.Element` Interface

| Return Value | Method Name (parameters) |
| --- | --- |
| String | getAttribute(String name) |
| Attr | getAttributeNode(String name) |
| Attr | getAttributeNodeNS(String namespaceURI, String localName) |
| String | getAttributeNS(String namespaceURI, String localName) |
| NodeList | getElementsByTagName(String name) |
| NodeList | getElementsByTagNameNS(String namespaceURI, String localName) |
| String | getTagName() |
| boolean | hasAttribute(String name) |
| boolean | hasAttributeNS(String namespaceURI, String localName) |
| void | removeAttribute(String name) |
| Attr | removeAttributeNode(Attr oldAttr) |
| void | removeAttributeNS(String namespaceURI, String localName) |
| void | setAttribute(String name, String value) |
| Attr | setAttributeNode(Attr newAttr) |
| Attr | setAttributeNodeNS(Attr newAttr) |
| void | setAttributeNS(String namespaceURI, String qualifiedName, String value) |
| Plus all methods from `org.w3c.dom.Node` | |

## NOTE

We omitted the explanation for the methods in Table 17.12 because the naming and parameter patterns are pretty basic. If you want to explore these methods in detail, see the official API documentation.

### 17.5.4 The Node Interface

That leaves one more critical DOM interface to master. Nearly all the XML types returned from the methods in `Document` (`Attr`, `CDATASection`, `CharacterData`, `Comment`, `DocumentFragment`, `DocumentType`, `Element`, `Entity`, `EntityReference`, `ProcessingInstruction`, `Text`) extend the interface node. You already know the first method well. The rest of the interface methods (from the API documentation) are listed in Table 17.13.

**TABLE 17.13** The `org.w3c.dom.Node` Interface

| Return Value | Method Name (parameters) Explanation |
|---|---|
| Node | `appendChild(Node newChild)` Adds the node `newChild` to the end of the list of children of this node. |
| Node | `cloneNode(boolean deep)` Returns a duplicate of this node; that is, serves as a generic copy constructor for nodes. |
| NamedNodeMap | `getAttributes()` A `NamedNodeMap` containing the attributes of this node (if an `Element`), or `null` otherwise. |
| NodeList | `getChildNodes()` A `NodeList` that contains all children of this node. |
| Node | `getFirstChild()` The first child of this node. |
| Node | `getLastChild()` The last child of this node. |
| String | `getLocalName()` Returns the local part of the qualified name of this node. |
| String | `getNamespaceURI()` The namespace URI of this node, or `null` if unspecified. |

*continues*

**TABLE 17.13** *(continued)*

| Return Value | Method Name (parameters) Explanation |
|---|---|
| Node | getNextSibling() <br> The node immediately following this node. |
| String | getNodeName() <br> The name of this node, depending on its type. |
| short | getNodeType() <br> A code representing the type of the underlying object. (See the official API documentation for a listing of the potential types.) |
| String | getNodeValue() <br> The value of this node, depending on its type. |
| Document | getOwnerDocument() <br> The `Document` object associated with this node. |
| Node | getParentNode() <br> The parent of this node. |
| String | getPrefix() <br> The namespace prefix of this node, or `null` if unspecified. |
| Node | getPreviousSibling() <br> The node immediately preceding this node. |
| boolean | hasAttributes() <br> Returns whether this node (if an element) has any attributes. |
| boolean | hasChildNodes() <br> Returns whether this node has any children. |
| Node | insertBefore(Node newChild, Node refChild) <br> Inserts the node `newChild` before the existing child node `refChild`. |
| boolean | isSupported(String feature, String version) <br> Tests whether the DOM implementation implements a specific feature and that feature is supported by this node. |
| void | normalize() <br> Puts all text nodes in the full depth of the subtree underneath this node, including attribute nodes, into a "normal" form where only structure (for example, elements, comments, processing instructions, CDATA sections, and entity references) separates text nodes. That is, there are neither adjacent text nodes nor empty text nodes. |

*continues*

**TABLE 17.13**  *(continued)*

| Return Value | Method Name (parameters) Explanation |
|---|---|
| Node | removeChild(Node oldChild)<br>Removes the child node indicated by oldChild from the list of children and returns it. |
| Node | replaceChild(Node newChild, Node oldChild)<br>Replaces the child node oldChild with newChild in the list of children and returns the oldChild node. |
| void<br>void | setNodeValue(String nodeValue)<br>setPrefix(String prefix) |

Note how the Node interface only deals with "its own kind" (other Nodes and Node-utility classes). Because it is the base XML DOM interface, this makes sense. All of the methods listed in Table 17.13 are available in the XML node classes, so we highly recommend that you get comfortable with Node.

### 17.5.5 An Advanced DOM Example

There is one more DOM example in this chapter to demonstrate the accessing, parsing, and traversing of an XML document. But this time, you generate your own custom report.

In this example, instead of outputting everything you find in the document, you sort through the Document object to find the components that interest you. To do this, you use the NamedNodeMap and NodeList utility classes.

Think of these as their java.util counterparts. Maps, which are hashtables, have a key and value (use the key to *retrieve* the value). Lists are just linked lists of objects (traverse them until there are no more objects). The NamedNodeMap and NodeList interfaces are quite simple; see the API documentation for the org.w3c.dom package.

One other thing to remember: The specific XML objects such as those of type Text and Comments and CDATA were attached as *children* to their parent Element. They must be accessed in the same way. The NamedNodeMap and NodeList hold Elements; you must go one level deeper to access your data. Also, you can check the *type* of the Node with a call to getNodeType (a list of the possible types can be found in the Node interface API) to confirm that the child you have accessed is the correct one.

Listing 17.4 shows one possible implementation of a program that generates a report using the XML data created from Listing 17.3.

**LISTING 17.4**   HelloApacheDOM2 Example

```java
import org.w3c.dom.Document;
import org.w3c.dom.Element;
import org.w3c.dom.Node;
import org.w3c.dom.NodeList;
import org.w3c.dom.NamedNodeMap;

public class HelloApacheDOM2
{
  public static void main (String[] args)
  {
    try
    {
      javax.xml.parsers.DocumentBuilderFactory dbf =
        javax.xml.parsers.DocumentBuilderFactory.newInstance();
      javax.xml.parsers.DocumentBuilder db =
        dbf.newDocumentBuilder();
      Document doc = db.parse(args[0]);

      // Display the root Element
      Element root = doc.getDocumentElement();
      System.out.println("\nDocument Element: Name = " +
        root.getNodeName() +", Value = "+ root.getNodeValue());

      // Traverse through list of the root Element's Attributes
      NamedNodeMap nnm = root.getAttributes();
      System.out.println("# of Attributes: " + nnm.getLength());
      for (int x = 0; x < nnm.getLength(); x++)
      {
        Node n = nnm.item(0);
        System.out.println("Attribute: Name = "
          + n.getNodeName() + ", Value = " + n.getNodeValue());
      }

      // Retrieve author name (Text is a child!)
      NodeList elementList = root.getElementsByTagName
        ("books:AUTHOR");
      String authorName =
          elementList.item(0).getFirstChild().getNodeValue();

      // Do the same for the title
      elementList = root.getElementsByTagName("books:TITLE");
      String bookName =
          elementList.item(0).getFirstChild().getNodeValue();

      // Pull the quote out
      elementList = doc.getElementsByTagName("books:EXCERPT");
```

*continues*

```java
      for (int x = 0; x < elementList.getLength(); x++)
      {
        // This node is books:EXCERPT
        Node node = elementList.item(x);

        // Access CDATA underneath (remember, it's a child)
        Node childNode = node.getFirstChild();
        if (childNode.getNodeType() != Node.CDATA_SECTION_NODE)
          throw new Exception ("This element is not CDATA!");
        System.out.println("\nBook excerpt:");

        String value = childNode.getNodeValue();
        System.out.println(value);
        System.out.println("   —" +authorName+ ", " + bookName);
      }
    }
    catch (Exception e)
    {
      e.printStackTrace();
    }
  }
}
```

Compiling and executing this code should result in the information shown in Figure 17.8 (make sure to add the path to the XML file as an argument).

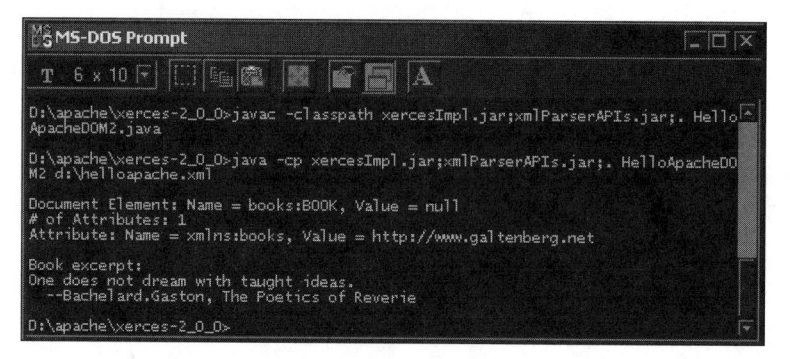

**FIGURE 17.8**  *Viewing output of* `HelloApacheDOM2` *example.*

## 17.5.6  DOM Helpers and DOM Level 3

Before moving on from DOM, know that there are also subpackages that provide advanced DOM Level 2 functionality. Take a look at the packages listed in Table 17.14 when you are comfortable with the previous samples and interfaces.

**TABLE 17.14** Java Packages for Advanced DOM Functionality

| Advanced DOM Package | Functionality |
|---|---|
| org.w3c.dom.events | Contains five interfaces (DocumentEvent, Event, EventListener, EventTarget, MutationEvent) to provide a generic event system. Useful for defining specific parsing and traversal functionality. |
| org.w3c.dom.html | Contains dozens of interfaces that let you build an HTML document just as you would an XML document; this functionality not only supports the DOM Level 0 specification but may also simplify common and frequent HTML operations. |
| org.w3.dom.ranges | Contains two interfaces (DocumentRange, Range) that let you identify and manipulate a range of document content. |
| org.w3.dom.traversal | Contains four interfaces (DocumentTraversal, NodeFilter, NodeIterator, TreeWalker) that let you dynamically identify, traverse, and filter a selected range of document content. |

Also, if you want to explore DOM Level 3 functionality, see the org.apache.xerces.dom3 package (and its subpackages) for the latest interfaces and behaviors. Note that this is a parser-specific package whose APIs might change, but if you require the abstract schema and load-and-save features described in the DOM Level 3 working drafts, at least you have this foothold. Make sure to keep current with new Xerces updates. (There are two Xerces discussion groups you can join to receive the latest news, bug reports, fixes, and releases. Click Mailing Lists on the main panel at http://xml.apache.org for subscription instructions.)

## 17.6 Java Xerces SAX In-depth

In this section, we switch over to the SAX XML mindset and write more Java code to explore this new paradigm. By the end of this section, you will have nearly completed your tour of the Xerces parser's XML capabilities, and you will be ready to build complete XML applications on your own.

### 17.6.1 The ContentHandler Interface

The premise of Java SAX is quite simple, but people marvel at the richness of its features. SAX is the epitome of interface- or contract-based development via events. Simply implement one or more of the SAX interfaces, tell the parser you want to be notified when certain XML nodes are found, and designate an XML document. As the document is parsed, your methods are called: one call, or event, for each new XML node discovered. And Apache-Xerces makes it as simple as it sounds.

The SAX paradigm has crystal-clear advantages and disadvantages you need to be aware of before you write your code. Most prominently, in SAX, the XML document's components are not *stored* anywhere (whereas in DOM, *everything* is stored—and accessible via a `Document`-derived object). When a new `Element` is reached, you are handed its name and `Attributes` (if you have requested this behavior of the parser). Store the data, set a flag, skip it—do whatever you want. But when a new `Element` is found and your method is called again, the old `Element` has been completely forgotten (unless your code has taken the data and copied it elsewhere, such as in a report or database).

So remember the fundamentals: Implement one or more SAX interfaces and write code for the XML components you are interested in. Take a look at the most important of the SAX interfaces: `org.w3c.sax.ContentHandler`. Study the methods in Table 17.15, because they are the events that occur as an XML document is parsed.

**TABLE 17.15**  The `org.w3c.sax.ContentHandler` Interface

| Method | Description |
| --- | --- |
| void | `characters(char[] ch, int start, int length)`<br>Here is where you are notified of the content of `Elements` if you implement this method. Caution: Test this event well—sometimes only partial chunks are sent. And *make sure you use the start and length parameters*—often the character buffer contains the whole document (or a large part). |
| void | `endDocument()`<br>When the end of the document has been reached, you receive this event. You receive this event only once, and no other events will follow—this is a good place to do clean-up or finalization. |
| void | `endElement(String namespaceURI, String localName, String qualifiedName)`<br>You receive one of these notifications when the end of the `Element` being parsed is reached. There is one `endElement` call for every `startElement` call. |
| void | `endPrefixMapping(String prefix)`<br>This corresponds to the `startPrefixMapping` call. This event (if appropriate) happens after the `Element`'s `endElement` event. |
| void | `ignorableWhitespace(char[] ch, int start, int length)`<br>If you want to be notified when the parser hits unnecessary whitespace (for custom behavior or error-handling), implement this method. |
| void | `processingInstruction(String target, String data)`<br>Every time a processing instruction (other than an XML or text declaration) is reached, you are notified. (Remember that processing instructions are commands between '<?' and '?>'.) |

*continues*

**TABLE 17.15** *(continued)*

| Method | Description |
|---|---|
| void | setDocumentLocator(Locator locator)<br>Use this method to receive a handy object for locating the origin of SAX document events. |
| void | skippedEntity(String name)<br>The parser must notify you if it could not locate a particular DTD (or if the parser doesn't do validation). |
| void | startDocument()<br>You receive this notification when parsing begins. This is a good place to do initialization. |
| void | startElement(String namespaceURI, String localName, String qualifiedName, Attributes atts)<br>This is an important method to implement. Here you are given the namespace and name and all attributes associated with the Element. |
| void | startPrefixMapping(String prefix, String uri)<br>If you want to implement custom behavior when new prefixes are discovered, implement this method. In the example case of<br><br>`<books:BOOK xmlns:books = "http://www.galtenberg.net">`<br><br>prefix would equal 'books' and uri would equal 'http://www.galtenberg.net'. |

Remember that when you implement an interface in Java, you must provide at least a body for every single method. We will show you how to work around this in Listing 17.6, but for now, send your very own `ContentHandler` through the SAX parser and see what comes out.

In Listing 17.5, we are simply going to report when parse events occur, with a `println` statement. Observe where each of the important types is imported from. Note that the `characters` and `ignorableWhitespace` events are handled differently (because their parameters are `char[]`s instead of `String`s). Also pay attention to the parameters passed to each method; some methods have no parameters and thus are essentially pure events.

**LISTING 17.5**  HelloApacheSAX Example

```java
import org.xml.sax.ContentHandler;
import org.xml.sax.Locator;
import org.xml.sax.Attributes;
import org.xml.sax.XMLReader;
import org.xml.sax.helpers.XMLReaderFactory;

public class HelloApacheSAX implements ContentHandler
{
  public void characters (char[] ch, int start, int length)
  {
    System.out.print("New Characters: ");
    for (int i = 0; i < length; i++)
      System.out.print(ch[start + i]);
    System.out.print("\n");
  }
  public void endDocument ()
  {
    System.out.println("End Document");
  }
  public void endElement (String namespaceURI, String localName,
                          String qualifiedName)
  {
    System.out.println("End Element:  Name = " + localName);
  }
  public void endPrefixMapping (String prefix)
  {
    System.out.println("End Prefix Mapping:  Prefix = "
                       + prefix);
  }
  public void ignorableWhitespace (char[] ch, int start,
                                   int length)
  {
    System.out.print("Ignorable Whitespace: ");
    for (int i = 0; i < length; i++)
      System.out.print(ch[start + i]);
    System.out.print("\n");
  }
  public void processingInstruction (String target, String data)
  {
    System.out.println("Processing Instruction:  Target = "
        + target + ", Data = " + data);
  }
  public void setDocumentLocator (Locator l)
  {
    System.out.println("\nSet Document Locator");
```

```java
}
public void skippedEntity (String name)
{
  System.out.println("Skipped entity:  Name = " + name);
}
public void startDocument ()
{
  System.out.println("Start Document");
}
public void startElement (String namespace, String localName,
                 String qualifiedName, Attributes attribs)
{
  System.out.println("Start Element:  Name = " + localName);
}
public void startPrefixMapping (String prefix, String uri)
{
  System.out.println("Start Prefix Mapping:  Prefix = " +
      prefix + ", URI = " + uri);
}
public static void main (String[] args)
{
  try
  {
    XMLReader parser;
    parser = XMLReaderFactory.createXMLReader();

    parser.setContentHandler(new HelloApacheSAX());

    parser.parse(args[0]);
  }
  catch (Exception e)
  {
    e.printStackTrace();
  }
}
}
```

After a new parser is created, you simply inform it that *your class* handles notifications with the following call. (It could have been *any* class as long as it implemented the ContentHandler interface.)

```java
parser.setContentHandler(new HelloApacheSAX());
```

The XMLReader is the actual SAX parser. If you are wondering why we did not use the parser and factory from the javax.xml.parsers package, the short answer is that the SAXParser type does not accept a basic ContentHandler-derived object. It expects a DefaultHandler-derived object (explained in Listing 17.6). But this is still the same parser: The SAXParser object actually *contains* an XMLReader object. You will use the SAXParser in the next sample. Simply know that the XMLReader can accept any one (or more) of the critical SAX interfaces.

If you compile and run our faithful helloapache.xml file through your new parser, the output should look like the screen shown in Figure 17.9.

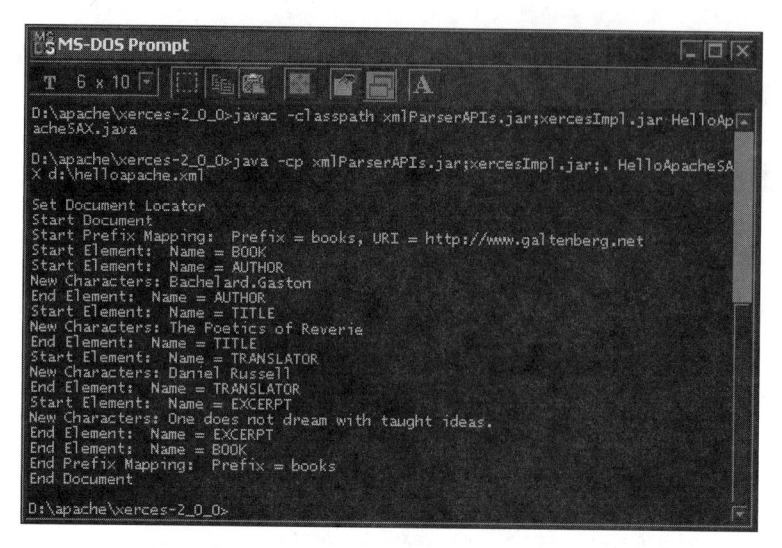

**FIGURE 17.9** *Output of the* HelloApacheSAX *Example.*

We only want to display element content, so as soon as the AUTHOR element is handled, it is discarded and the parser moves right on to TITLE, and so on. Execution is extremely rapid, and very little memory is used. With SAX and Xerces, you can write a full XML application in mere minutes.

Can we make this any easier? You bet! Instead of implementing the full menu of ContentHandler methods, you can simply extend a class, DefaultHandler (in the org.xml.sax.helpers package), which already implements these methods (although they do not do anything). Now implement methods only for events that interest you. If you only care about catching processingInstructions, for example, you need implement only that single method.

org.xml.sax.helpers.DefaultHandler implements four SAX interfaces, ContentHandler, DTDHandler, EntityResolver, and ErrorHandler, described in Table 17.6 when we introduced the critical SAX packages. You have seen ContentHandler—the other three interfaces have only a couple of methods each, for performing lower-level handling (see the API documentation for details). You might be interested in examining org.xml.sax.ErrorHandler, because it can also be used in DOM parsing applications. Just add code similar to the following:

```
ErrorHandler handler = object that implements ErrorHandler;
DocumentBuilder builder = object that implements DocumentBuilder;
builder.setErrorHandler(handler);
```

For nearly all SAX applications, `DefaultHandler` is your base class of choice. In Listing 17.6, we use `DefaultHandler` in collaboration with the SAXParser class from the `javax.xml.parsers` package. (Remember, in the future, if you want to specify exact SAX interface-implementations, access the `XMLReader` within the SAX parser.)

Also, you will be catching the full complement of parser exceptions. These should look familiar, because you used them in the `HelloApache2` sample in Listing 17.6.

To make this final example more challenging, there are two additional assigned tasks:

- Use the `address.xml` document to print a report, but this time, only display names and ID information.
- Validate the document's XML schema (found in `address.xsd`).

The first task should be a piece of cake. You need to write just a bit of logic for the `startElement`, `endElement`, and `characters` methods. (And now, because you are using `DefaultHandler`, you do not have to write code for methods you will not use.)

Validating the XML schema is a bit more complicated. But the ride has been pretty smooth to this point, and Xerces makes schemas a breeze, too.

Xerces introduces the notion of properties and features, which are very similar to Java and Visual Basic properties. There is a key and value for each one. Simply set the data for whichever property or feature you care about. The only difference between properties and features is that features are Boolean, like on and off switches: Turn features on or off as you choose. Features can be of any type and are useful for both setting and retrieving specific parser settings.

To set features or properties for SAX processing, access the `XMLReader` object and call either `setFeature` or `setProperty`, with the appropriate key and value. You will find these calls in the `main` function block.

**LISTING 17.6** `HelloApacheSAX2` Example

```
import javax.xml.parsers.FactoryConfigurationError;
import javax.xml.parsers.ParserConfigurationException;
import javax.xml.parsers.SAXParser;
import javax.xml.parsers.SAXParserFactory;
import org.xml.sax.Attributes;
import org.xml.sax.XMLReader;
import org.xml.sax.SAXException;
import org.xml.sax.SAXParseException;
```

*continues*

```java
import org.xml.sax.helpers.DefaultHandler;
import org.xml.sax.helpers.XMLReaderFactory;
import java.io.IOException;

public class HelloApacheSAX2 extends DefaultHandler
{
  // A flag which indicates we've reached the Element
  //   we're interested in
  private boolean bName = false;

  // The three methods of the ErrorHandler interface
  public void error (SAXParseException e)
  {
    System.out.println("\n***Error*** " + e);
  }
  public void warning (SAXParseException e)
  {
    System.out.println("\n***Warning*** " + e);
  }
  public void fatalError (SAXParseException e)
  {
    System.out.println("\n***Fatal Error*** " + e);
  }

  public void startDocument ()
  {
    System.out.println("\n***Start Document***");
  }
  public void endDocument ()
  {
    System.out.println("\n***End Document***");
  }

  // There are many ways to filter out Elements -
  //   this is an elementary example
  public void startElement (String namespace, String localName,
                     String qualifiedName, Attributes attribs)

  {
    if (qualifiedName == "privateCustomer" ||
        qualifiedName == "businessCustomer")
    {
      System.out.println ("\nNew " + qualifiedName + " Entry:");

      for (int i = 0; i < attribs.getLength(); i++)
      {
        System.out.println(attribs.getQName(i) + ": " +
            attribs.getValue(i));
```

```
      }
    }
    else if (qualifiedName == "name")
    {
      bName = true;
    }
}

// Only print characters from the 'name' elements
public void characters (char[] ch, int start, int length)
{
  if (bName == true)
  {
    System.out.print("Name: ");
       for (int i = 0; i < length; i++)
      System.out.print(ch[start + i]);
       System.out.print("\n");
  }
}

// Regardless of what Element we're on, we're done with 'name'
public void endElement (String namespaceURI, String localName,
                        String qualifiedName)
{
  bName = false;
}

public static void main (String[] args)
{
  try
  {
    SAXParserFactory factory = SAXParserFactory.newInstance();
    SAXParser parser = factory.newSAXParser();

    DefaultHandler handler = new HelloApacheSAX2();
    XMLReader reader = parser.getXMLReader();

    // set parser features
    try
    {
      reader.setFeature
          ("http://xml.org/sax/features/validation", true);
      reader.setFeature
          ("http://apache.org/xml/features/validation/schema",
           true);
      reader.setFeature ("http://apache.org/xml/features/
        validation/warn-on-undeclared-elemdef", true);
```

*continues*

```
          reader.setProperty
          ("http://apache.org/xml/properties/schema/external-
          noNamespaceSchemaLocation", "address.xsd");
        }
        catch (SAXException e)
        {
          System.out.println
          ("Warning: Parser does not support schema validation");
        }

        parser.parse(args[0], handler);

    }
    catch (FactoryConfigurationError e)
    {
      System.out.println("Factory configuration error: " + e);
    }
    catch (ParserConfigurationException e)
    {
      System.out.println("Parser configuration error: " + e);
    }
    catch (SAXException e)
    {
      System.out.println("Parsing error: " + e);
    }
    catch (IOException e)
    {
      System.out.println("I/O error: " + e);
    }
  }
}
```

You can see that you are using a different method to retrieve your SAX parser, but XMLReader is there too (and vital for setting features and properties).

Make sure that both address.xml and address.xsd are available in your current path as you compile and run the example. Output should look similar to the screen shown in Figure 17.10.

You also need a socket open to the Internet, because address.xsd references another XSD document from the book.

Did you notice that execution took longer this time? Maybe you even saw the lag between the '***StartDocument***' message and the actual parsing. XML schema validation is time-consuming. Performance should improve over time as later Xerces parsers are released, but there is always a fair amount of overhead (just as there is overhead in using Java rather than a compiled language).

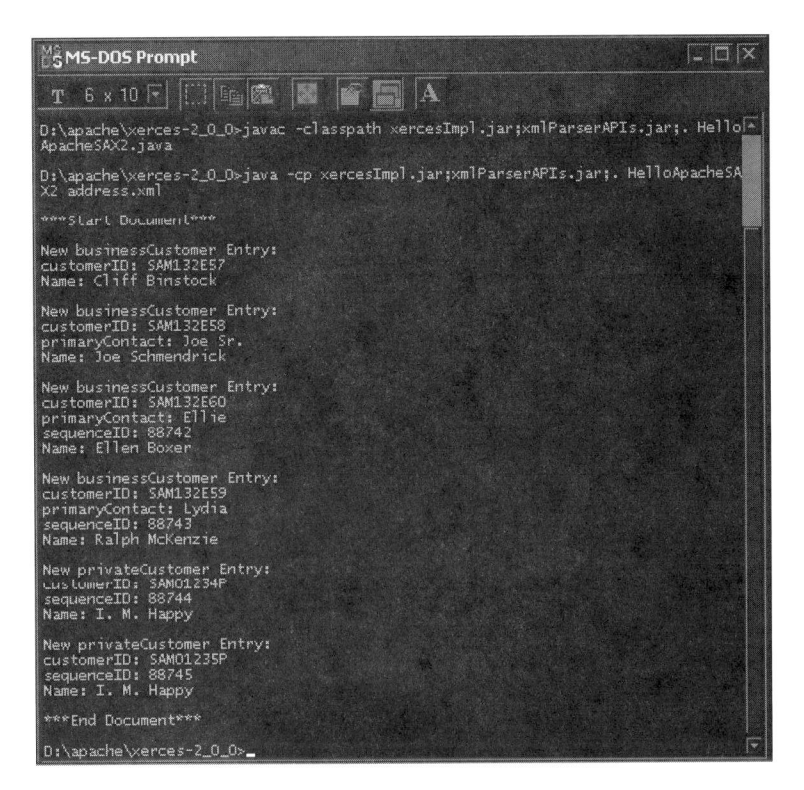

**FIGURE 17.10**   *Viewing output of* HelloApacheSAX2 *example.*

But you succeeded in both your tasks. You will of course want to implement a more robust method of filtering Elements, and you will not want to hard-code schema locations in your reader.setProperty calls.

There are multiple ways to specify Schema functionality and file locations (in DOM as well as SAX—the code is virtually the same). In fact, entire sections in the API documentation are devoted to the dozens of properties and features. Study these well, and remember that they are subject to updates over time, so keep up with the latest Xerces releases.

# MSXML and the Schema Object Model (SOM)

**CHAPTER 18**

## IN THIS CHAPTER

18.1 Introducing MSXML    472

18.2 Concepts and Observations    473

18.3 XML Schema Examples    474

18.4 MSXML Fundamentals    474

18.5 Schema Object Model (SOM)    483

18.6 Validation    488

18.7 Example: XML Schema Tree    493

This chapter describes how to build applications that work with XML schemas by using MSXML, the Microsoft XML Core Services. The components that make up MSXML support the established APIs as well as such languages like XSLT and XPath. In the latest version of MSXML, Microsoft has also provided full support for XML schemas through the addition of the Schema Object Model (SOM). By using both the standard XML components of MSXML and the XML schema-specific SOM, developers can create and examine XML schemas in addition to performing validation of XML documents.

## 18.1 Introducing MSXML

For those who have not worked with MSXML in the past, it might help to understand what MSXML is and what it can be used for. The Microsoft XML Core Services, or MSXML, is a COM-based library of components that consume and (or) generate XML. This library is free and downloadable from the Microsoft Web site. The most recent release of MSXML is version 4.0. The components are contained in the application extension file `msxml4.dll`.

> **TIP**
>
> The most recent version of the Microsoft XML Core Services can be found at the Microsoft Developer Network Site, specifically at:
>
> `http://msdn.microsoft.com/downloads/sample.asp?url=/MSDN-FILES/027/`
> `001/766/msdncompositedoc.xml`
>
> In addition to MSXML, Microsoft has a variety of other XML-related downloads that are free. Be aware that a preview version of MSXML 4.0 was released, and that version must be uninstalled prior to installing this final release.

MSXML 4.0 contains a variety of components and interfaces that can be used to work with XML. For parsing documents, MSXML contains implementations of both the Document Object Model (DOM) Level 2 and SAX2 feature sets. For performing transformations, there is an XSLT processor. XPath queries are supported throughout the tools as well, and there are even components to simplify access to XML documents over HTTP. Figure 18.1 lists the APIs and standards supported in MSXML.

With such a large number of components and a depth of features, covering MSXML in any detail would take more than this chapter. This chapter focuses just on the features of MSXML 4.0 that relate specifically to XML schemas. These include the capability to examine and create XML schemas and to validate XML documents by using XML schemas. To do this, we examine some of the basic features of MSXML, and then we examine the Schema Object Model in detail.

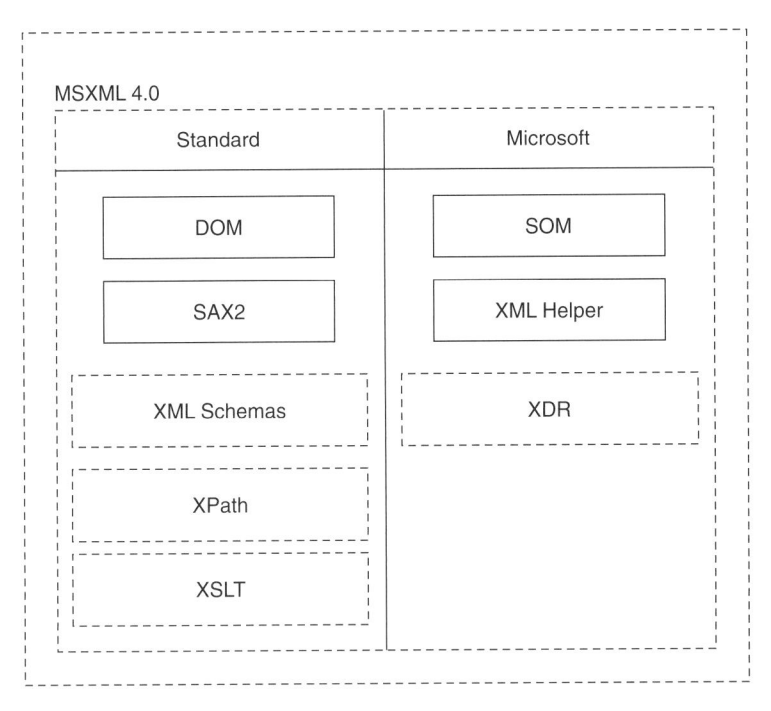

**FIGURE 18.1** *MSXML overview.*

> **TIP**
>
> Version 4.0 of MSXML is contained in the file `msxml4.dll`. As in previous versions of MSXML, version 4.0 can exist on the same machine as previous versions of MSXML in a side-by-side compatibility mode. This is possible because the components made available in 4.0 are registered with identifiers (CLSIDs) different from those of their older counterparts. To make sure you are working with version 4.0, be sure to use components such as `DOMDocument40` whose CLSIDs end with '40'.

## 18.2 Concepts and Observations

The content of this chapter is slanted heavily toward the interests of application developers. Although most of the content of this book is applicable to any work involving XML schemas, either design or application, this chapter is most useful for software developers who need programmatic access to XML schemas. For those developers, it helps to remember that…

### 18.2.1 ...MS Stands for Microsoft

This chapter is, of course, vendor specific, which differs greatly from the majority of the content of this book. Because the focus is on application development using MSXML and the Schema Object Model, this assumes that the reader is developing for Windows platforms. To work with the Microsoft XML Parser and other tools included in MSXML, you need access to a development tool that can consume a COM-based API such as MSXML. Most development environments for Windows platforms support such an API. The examples provided in this chapter were written in Visual Basic 6.0, but because of the nature of COM and MSXML, the examples should translate easily to other languages that support the tools.

### 18.2.2 Proprietary versus Standard

MSXML support for XML schemas is a new feature, in large part because the specification has been a work in progress. While the specification was still evolving, Microsoft created its own language, called XML Data Reduced (XDR). Version 4.0 of MSXML supports both XDR and XML schemas. It appears that Microsoft will favor XML Schema over its own language in the future.

It should be noted, however, that the Schema Object Model (SOM) introduced in version 4.0 is a proprietary API for working with XML schemas. It is modeled directly after the XML Schema structure, so the learning curve for those familiar with XML schemas is gentle. Aside from the general XML APIs such as DOM and SAX, there is no standard API for accessing XML schemas, and they provide no access to the schema components themselves. The SOM is just Microsoft's way of simplifying access to XML schemas. Code written against this model will currently have no counterpart on other platforms.

## 18.3 XML Schema Examples

Several examples of code using MSXML are in this chapter, but to build reasonable examples of code, we need some XML to work with. In this case, we need three documents: an XML schema document from which to generate a schema, a document that validates against that schema, and a document that does not validate against it.

In previous chapters, we worked with an XML schema that represents the address of a customer. This schema document, `address.xsd`, is shown in Listing C.2. The address schema is used in this chapter in the sample code to illustrate how the SOM and MSXML behave. The sample documents used for validation are shown in Listings 18.10 and 18.11 later in the chapter.

## 18.4 MSXML Fundamentals

DOM and SAX were mentioned in Chapter 2. DOM Level 2 and SAX2 are both standard APIs for parsing XML, and MSXML supports both standards. In fact, it is possible to use both the DOM and SAX with MSXML to validate XML instances.

## 18.4.1 Using MSXML from Visual Basic

The first step in using MSXML in Visual Basic is referencing the MSXML components. Like any other COM components you need to use from Visual Basic, you can add a reference to MSXML from your project file. Inside the Visual Basic IDE, you use the Projects menu to add or remove components of the project. One of these project components is a reference to a library. Selecting the Project menu and then the References item from that menu launches the References dialog box. This dialog box provides a checklist of all COM-type libraries on your machine. Checking one of these libraries, such as MSXML 4.0, includes the type information about those components in your project and enables you to create instances of those components and refer to them through early binding. Figure 18.2 shows the References dialog box with MSXML 4.0 loaded.

Throughout the chapter, it is assumed that the Visual Basic examples are included in a project that has referenced MSXML 4.0. Any of the stand-alone code samples listed will function in any Visual Basic project that has referenced the MSXML 4.0 components.

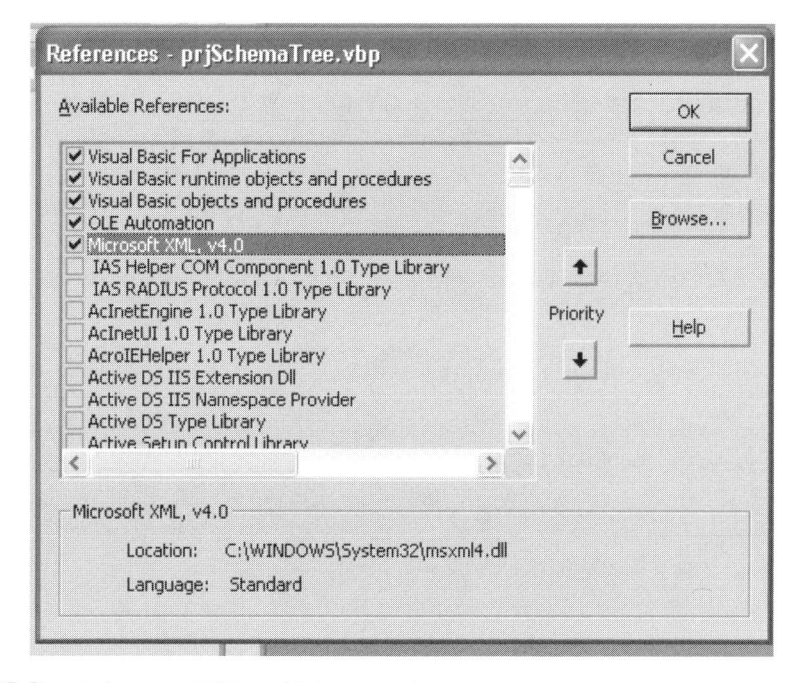

**FIGURE 18.2**  *Referencing MSXML 4.0 from Visual Basic.*

## 18.4.2 Using the DOM

When you are using the MSXML implementation of the DOM Level 2 feature set, the component that represents the DOM Document node is a `DOMDocument40` component. Through `DOMDocument40`, we have complete access to the contents of an XML document.

### 18.4.2.1 `DOMDocument40`

`DOMDocument40` is the starting point for using the MSXML DOM implementation. The '40' suffix of the component indicates its version. Earlier versions of MSXML included `DOMDocument` components, and it is possible to declare and use `DOMDocument` components if you are not concerned with the version of the component you will be using. Because the behavior and feature set of the `DOMDocument` component has grown over each of the versions, it is often necessary to specifically reference the version you need to guarantee that the functionality you need is available.

To work with a `DOMDocument40` component, you need to instantiate an instance of `DOMDocument40`. Listing 18.1 shows the code required in Visual Basic to create an instance of a `DOMDocument40` component if the reference to the MSXML 4.0 library has been added.

**LISTING 18.1** Creating a `DOMDocument40` (early binding)

```
Dim doc As DOMDocument40
Set doc = New DOMDocument40
```

If you are working from a scripting language or other language that only provides for late binding to COM objects, you can create the `DOMDocument40` instance by using its PROGID, its user-friendly object identifier. The PROGID for the `DOMDocument40` component is 'MSXML2.DOMDocument.4.0'. An example of late binding in VBScript is shown in Listing 18.2.

**LISTING 18.2** Creating a `DOMDocument40` (late binding for scripting)

```
Dim doc
Set doc = CreateObject("MSXML2.DOMDocument.4.0")
```

For the purposes of this chapter, assume that we are working inside the Visual Basic or similar IDE and have access to early binding to the MSXML components. This is just to simplify the sample code. The only difference between the two sets of code would be the instantiation code shown in Listings 18.1 and 18.2. As with any COM object, you gain performance at runtime through the use of early binding to the MSXML library.

> **TIP**
>
> PROGIDs can be used to create instances of any of the MSXML components. If you need to create an object instance from a scripting language such as VBScript or ECMAScript, use the PROGID of the object. The PROGIDs will follow the same form:
>
> MSXML2.<object name>.4.0
>
> For example, the XMLSchemaCache40 object has a PROGID of 'MSXML2.XMLSchemaCache.4.0'.

### 18.4.2.2 Reading XML with DOMDocument40

Using DOMDocument40, we can load an XML document and examine its contents after they are loaded into the DOM tree. Two methods of the DOMDocument40 can be used to load an XML document: load and loadXML. The load method, shown in Listing 18.3, accepts a URL that points to an XML document file. Alternatively, the loadXML method accepts the XML content directly, either as a string or as an IStream.

**LISTING 18.3** Loading an XML Document Using DOMDocument40

```
Dim doc As DOMDocument40
Set doc = New DOMDocument40

doc.async = False
doc.validateOnParse = False

If (doc.Load("c:\test\address.xml")) Then
    MsgBox "Document is well-formed"
Else
    Dim docError As IXMLDOMParseError
    Set docError = doc.parseError
    MsgBox docError.reason, vbCritical
End If
```

Listing 18.3 shows two properties of the DOMDocument40 component that greatly impact the parsing behavior. The first is the async property, which is a Boolean flag indicating whether the document should be loaded synchronously or asynchronously. In the preceding code, we have set it to FALSE so the code will block on the Load method until the document is fully parsed or an error occurs. The default value for this property is TRUE, in which case the application must wait until the DOMDocument40 fires an onreadystatechange event or until the readystate property has changed to indicate a successful load.

The second property is `validateOnParse`, which is also a Boolean flag. The `validateOnParse` property defines the behavior you might expect; when TRUE, the parser attempts to validate the document against any XML schemas or XDR. When FALSE, the parser only verifies that the document is well-formed XML. The default value for this property is also TRUE.

> **NOTE**
>
> The `async` and `validateOnParse` properties are not part of the DOM Level 2 feature set; they are specific to the MSXML implementation.

Once we have a DOM tree that can be traversed, which occurs after a successful load, we can use other MSXML components to perform a traversal.

#### 18.4.2.3 DOM Parsing Errors

Whenever the `DOMDocument40` is used to parse an XML document, there is always a chance of error. The variety of errors that could be experienced during parsing varies from the obvious (not well-formed XML) to the complicated (the document did not conform to one of the associated XML schemas). To understand what went wrong during the parsing process and try to rectify it, we need to check the error generated by the parser.

The `DOMDocument` interface provides access to error information after parsing. Error information is provided through another, separate interface called `IXMLDOMParseError`. This interface returns information about the error type, the reason, and the location in the document where the error occurred. If validation were to fail, this information would be provided through the `parseError` property of the `DOMDocument` interface. The sample code that reads an XML document using `DOMDocument40` accesses the `parseError` property to determine whether or not the document was loaded successfully.

### 18.4.3 Using SAX2

The SAX and DOM parsers take a very different approach to working with an XML document. When working with the DOM, we load the XML document using a single object and then examine the tree that is built from the document contents. When working with SAX, we are notified through events whenever the parser encounters a particular element or a particular action occurs. Applications working with the SAX parser must implement handlers for each of these events and connect them to the parser.

Because MSXML is a COM-based API, the notification that comes from the MSXML SAX implementation comes through COM. This means that to create a handler, we must implement the COM interfaces that MSXML expects a SAX handler to implement.

Table 18.1 lists the three handler interfaces currently supported by the MSXML 4.0 SAX implementation, with the types of notifications they receive.

**TABLE 18.1**  SAX Handler Interfaces

| Interface | Type of Notification |
| --- | --- |
| `IVBSAXContentHandler` | Document and elements |
| `IVBSAXDeclHandler` | DTD declarations |
| `IVBSAXDTDHandler` | DTD-related events |
| `IVBSAXErrorHandler` | Errors and warnings |
| `IVBSAXLexicalHandler` | Comments and CDATA |
| `IMXSchemaDeclHandler` | XML schema declarations |

Any handler component can implement as many of these interfaces as needed, and that handler will receive notification about all events related to that category.

### 18.4.3.1 `SAXXMLReader40`

The `SAXXMLReader40` component is responsible for parsing an XML document and triggering the notifications to the SAX handlers that have registered with it. Triggering the parsing of an XML document takes about as much code as using the DOM and `DOMDocument40`. The major difference is that in addition to this code, the application must also create any handlers it needs.

### 18.4.3.2 Reading XML with `SAXXMLReader40`

The most basic use of the SAX handler would be to sink the events related to content, so a handler interested in those events would need to implement the `IVBSAXContentHandler` interface. After that handler instance exists, it can be attached to the `SAXXMLReader40` component and the parsing can occur.

Listing 18.4 defines a Visual Basic class whose instances function as content handlers. This class is defined as `SAXContent`, and it implements the `IVBSAXContentHandler` interface. Whenever an element is parsed, the class checks the local name and conditionally outputs the qualified name of the element by using the `Debug.Print` statement, the equivalent of a trace statement in other languages.

> **TIP**
>
> The code for the handler has a number of empty methods; in fact, it is almost completely empty. The methods are necessary, however, because to implement an interface, you must implement all its methods, even if they are just stubbed out.

**LISTING 18.4**   Content Handler Class

```
'SAXContent.cls
Implements IVBSAXContentHandler

Private Sub IVBSAXContentHandler_characters( _
  strChars As String)

End Sub

Private Property Set IVBSAXContentHandler_documentLocator( _
  ByVal RHS As MSXML2.IVBSAXLocator)

End Property

Private Sub IVBSAXContentHandler_endDocument()

End Sub

Private Sub IVBSAXContentHandler_endElement(_
  strNamespaceURI As String, strLocalName As String, _
  strQName As String)

End Sub

Private Sub IVBSAXContentHandler_endPrefixMapping(_
  strPrefix As String)

End Sub

Private Sub IVBSAXContentHandler_ignorableWhitespace(_
  strChars As String)

End Sub

Private Sub IVBSAXContentHandler_processingInstruction(_
  strTarget As String, strData As String)

End Sub

Private Sub IVBSAXContentHandler_skippedEntity(_
  strName As String)

End Sub

Private Sub IVBSAXContentHandler_startDocument()

End Sub
```

```
Private Sub IVBSAXContentHandler_startElement(_
 strNamespaceURI As String, strLocalName As String, _
 strQName As String, _
 ByVal oAttributes As MSXML2.IVBSAXAttributes)

    If strLocalName = "businessCustomer" Then
        Debug.Print "element found: " & strQName
    End If

End Sub

Private Sub IVBSAXContentHandler_startPrefixMapping(_
 strPrefix As String, strURI As String)

End Sub
```

To use the handler, you need to instantiate an instance of the reader. The `SAXXMLReader40`, when instantiated, is used to parse the document. The handlers are attached to the reader, using the appropriate property. Several properties of the `SAXXMLReader40` are used to attach handlers, as listed in Table 18.2.

**TABLE 18.2**   `SAXXMLReader40` Handler Properties

| Property | Related Handler Interface |
| --- | --- |
| contentHandler | IVBSAXContentHandler |
| dtdHandler | IVBSAXDTDHandler |
| errorHandler | IVBSAXErrorHandler |

The code in Listing 18.5 shows how to use your handler class, `SAXContent`, and `SAXXMLReader40` to read the document. The `parseURL` method of the reader accepts a path to a local XML document file just as the `load` method of the `DOMDocument40` did in Listing 18.3.

**LISTING 18.5**   Using `SAXXMLReader40` with the Content Handler

```
Dim sax As SAXXMLReader40
Set sax = New SAXXMLReader40
Set sax.contentHandler = New SAXContent
sax.parseURL "c:\temp\address.xml"
```

Unlike with the DOM, you do not need to traverse a tree to find what you are looking for. The call to `parseURL` begins the parsing; after that, it is up to the event handlers to get the information they need. The `SAXXMLReader40` component informs you via a callback to your handler interface whenever a particular event occurs. When loading the thematic `address.xml` document, the output generated by the code appears as shown in Listing 18.6.

**LISTING 18.6**   Debug Output of the Content Handler from `address.xml`

```
element found: businessCustomer
element found: businessCustomer
element found: businessCustomer
element found: businessCustomer
```

### 18.4.3.3. SAXXMLReader40 Configuration

In SAX, there are defined procedures for modifying the XMLReader component. These methods allow the application to set two types of values of the XMLReader: properties and features. Properties are named values that can be set on the reader, and features are Boolean properties. MSXML follows the SAX standard and implements these methods for the SAXXMLReader40.

The XMLReader properties and features are accessed by four methods: getFeature, putFeature, getProperty, and putProperty. SAX defines a set of standard features and properties to be implemented, but these are not the only ones that can be used. This approach means a particular SAX implementation can define its own properties and features that may be proprietary and the standard can grow over time without a change to the interface for every new configuration setting. For example, handlers for content or errors have fixed COM properties that are part of the reader, whereas declaration handlers need to use the getProperty and putProperty to work with the reader. Listing 18.7 illustrates how to set the declaration handler of the SAXXMLReader40 using the putProperty method.

**LISTING 18.7**   Using `putProperty` for `XMLReader` Configuration

```
Dim sax As SAXXMLReader40
Set sax = New SAXXMLReader40

' Assume we have a declHandler that implements
' IVBSAXDeclHandler
sax.putProperty _
 "http://xml.org/sax/properties/declaration-handler", _
 declHandler
```

Whenever you use the SAXXMLReader40 to validate against a specific XML schema, you must use the configuration methods discussed here.

### 18.4.3.4 SAX2 Parsing Errors

To handle parsing errors in a SAX application, the application must implement a handler for errors that are fired by the SAX parser. As stated earlier, components that are MSXML SAX error handlers implement the IVBSAXErrorHandler interface. If your application needs to know when the validation of an XML document fails, a component must implement `IVBSAXErrorHandler` and include code in the `fatalerror` handler to respond to the failed validation. The XML Schema Tree example at the end of this chapter uses SAX2 and the error handler interface to validate an XML document against an XML schema.

## 18.5 Schema Object Model (SOM)

So far, this chapter has focused on the generic approach that MSXML provides for accessing XML schemas. This consists of accessing the XML schema documents directly as ordinary XML documents. In this manner, you can work with them programmatically, using the same DOM you use for any other document. This approach is limited, however, because you are working with the least common denominator. XML schemas have a higher structure that has already been defined for us, so it makes sense to use a higher level API to access them if one is available.

Beginning with version 4.0 of MSXML, this higher level API is available and is called the "Schema Object Model" (SOM). The SOM is a set of components and interfaces that represent the compiled structure of an XML schema rather than just the structure of its XML.

### 18.5.1 SOM Fundamentals

The SOM can be used to load an XML schema document, and that document is then loaded into a tree structure that closely models the relationships of an XML schema document. Rather than a DOM-based tree that treats the elements of the schema document as normal XML, the SOM understands the Schema-based relationships between the parts of a schema document and models those relationships in the SOM structure. For example, XML schema document `element` elements are represented by the `ISchemaElement`, which has a `type` property. That property corresponds to an XML Schema document `simpleType` or `complexType` element, and that is represented in the SOM by the `ISchemaType` interface. This compiled model makes the SOM much more attractive than the DOM for developers that need to examine XML schemas. Table 18.3 describes how each interface in the model relates to an XML schema, but it does not illustrate how some of the interfaces relate.

**TABLE 18.3** Schema Object Model Interfaces

| Interface | Description |
| --- | --- |
| `ISchema` | schema element |
| `ISchemaAny` | any element |
| `ISchemaAttribute` | attribute element |
| `ISchemaAttributeGroup` | attributeGroup element |

*continues*

**TABLE 18.3**   *(continued)*

| Interface | Description |
| --- | --- |
| ISchemaComplexType | complexType element |
| ISchemaElement | element element |
| ISchemaIdentityConstraint | complexType element |
| ISchemaItem | Base interface |
| ISchemaItemCollection | Collection of SOM objects |
| ISchemaModelGroup | modelGroup element |
| ISchemaNotation | notation element |
| ISchemaParticle | Piece of a modelGroup element |
| ISchemaStringCollection | Collection of strings in the SOM |
| ISchemaType | simpleType element or complexType element |

Many of the SOM interfaces inherit from other SOM interfaces. Figure 18.3 shows where that inheritance occurs.

To help explain the SOM, we can take a look at some of the principal interfaces that make up the SOM. The first of those interfaces is ISchemaItem, the foundation of all the SOM interfaces.

> **TIP**
>
> This chapter does not provide a complete reference to all the properties and methods of the Schema Object Model. For a complete list, see the documentation provided with the MSXML 4.0 SDK.

## 18.5.2 The ISchemaItem Interface

In most object models, you will find some root class or interface from which all the objects in the system inherit. In Java, this root is the Object class. In the .NET Framework, the same is true: A root class called "Object" exists for all object classes. Within the framework of the SOM, all interfaces inherit from the ISchemaItem interface. Through the common properties of the ISchemaItem interface, you can learn a great deal about any of the component instances in the model. Table 18.4 lists the properties of the ISchemaItem interface.

## 18.5 Schema Object Model (SOM)

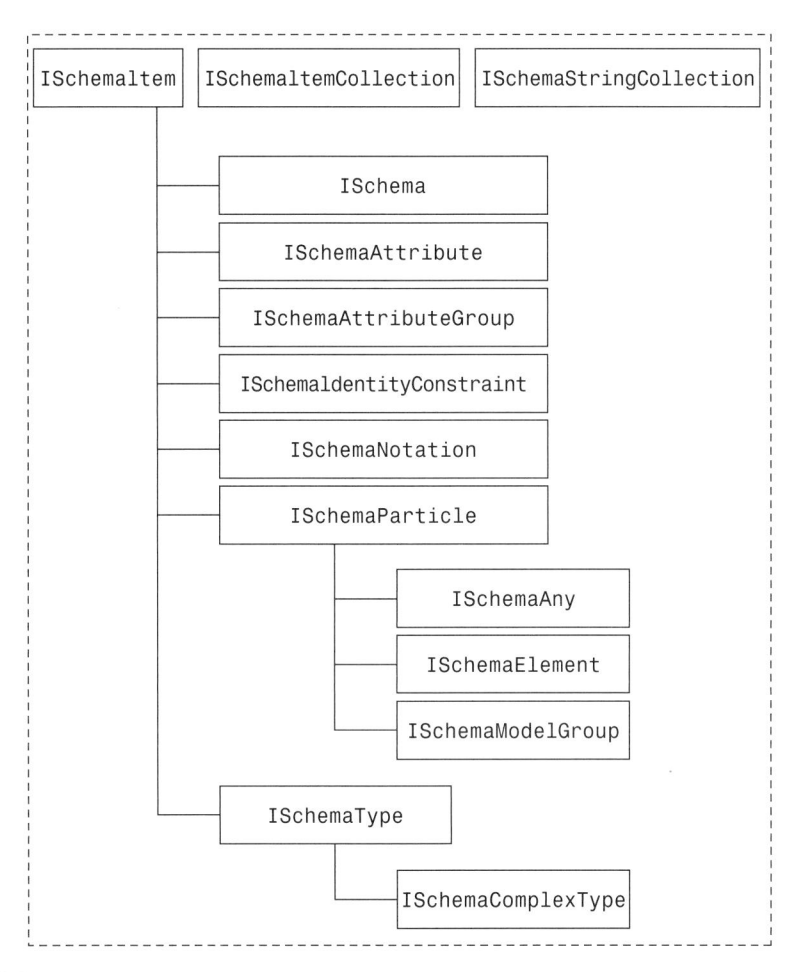

**FIGURE 18.3** *SOM diagram.*

**TABLE 18.4** Property Summary of the `ISchemaItem` Interface

| Property | Description |
| --- | --- |
| Id | Value of id attribute of the element |
| itemType | Constant defining the type of the object. |
| Name | Item name. |
| namespaceURI | URI of associated namespace. |
| Schema | `ISchema` of this model. |
| writeAnnotation | Writes top-level annotations into an output document. |
| unhandledAttributes | Any attributes not defined in the XML Schema Recommendation. |

The `ISchemaItem` interface provides two properties you might find yourself relying upon. The first is the `Schema` property, which returns the `ISchema` interface for the XML schema of which this particular item is a part. This means that from any item in the SOM, you can reach the root. This is not true, however, for built-in types and the `ISchema` interface itself (to avoid a circular reference problem).

The second property is the `itemType` property, which returns one of a list of constants provided in the SOM. These constants define the type of item this instance of `ISchemaItem` represents (for example, built-in type, complex type, attribute, notation). These constants are contained in the `SOMITEM_TYPE` enumeration.

Some of the `SOMITEM_TYPE` constants are used alone to indicate the type of the object in question, whereas others are combined to create new values that determine the type. For example, `SOMITEM_SCHEMA` indicates that an item is a schema and therefore is also an `ISchema` interface. On the other hand, `SOMITEM_DATATYPE` and `SOMITEM_DATATYPE_BOOLEAN` are combined in a bitmask to indicate a built-in Boolean datatype. With one or more of these constants, all the types can be expressed.

### 18.5.3 The `ISchema` Interface

While the `ISchemaItem` is the foundation of the SOM, the `ISchema` interface is at the root of the schema model itself. The `ISchema` interface of the Schema Object Model directly corresponds to the `schema` element of the XML schema. Through the `ISchema` interface, you have access to all the other elements that make up the schema.

To get an `ISchema` interface from an XML document, you use a utility component included in MSXML, `XMLSchemaCache40`. `XMLSchemaCache40` functions as a map of target namespaces to valid XML schemas. When the `add` method of `XMLSchemaCache40` is called, as shown in Listing 18.8, the XML schema document is read to make sure it conforms to the XML Schema Recommendation. If it does, it is loaded into the cache. If it does not, an error is thrown by the `add` method.

**LISTING 18.8** Getting the `ISchema` Interface

```
Dim schemaCache As XMLSchemaCache40
Set schemaCache = New XMLSchemaCache40

schemaCache.Add "http://www.XMLSchemaReference.com/examples/theme/addr", _
 "c:\temp\address.xsd"

Dim schema As ISchema
Set schema = schemaCache.getSchema(_
 "http://www.XMLSchemaReference.com/examples/theme/addr")
```

The add method in the preceding code takes two parameters: the namespace to associate with the XML schema and the XML schema itself (either as a URL or as a DOMDocument). Typically, the namespace you would associate with the XML schema would be the targetNamespace of the XML schema document, but the SOM does not enforce this relationship. Once we have an ISchema interface, we have access to all the parts that make up an XML Schema. These are provided as properties of the ISchema interface, as listed in Table 18.5.

Some of the properties listed in Table 18.5 have values that are nothing more than strings that provide access to information such as the version or namespace. However, properties that allow programmatic access to the remainder of the XML schema's components are more complex than that. All the other seven properties represent collections of objects, such as the attributes or structure types. Because the SOM is implemented as a COM programming interface, these are COM collections that are easily traversed by using just a few lines of Visual Basic code. Each of these collections is represented as an ISchemaItemCollection interface.

Listing 18.9 illustrates how to traverse one of the collections provided by the ISchema interface. In this instance, a For . . . Each loop cycles through all the elements in the XML schema and prints the output to the debugger.

**LISTING 18.9**  Walking the SOM Elements Collection

```
Dim elem As ISchemaElement
For Each elem In schema.elements
    Debug.Print elem.Name
Next elem
```

**TABLE 18.5**  Property Summary of the ISchema Interface

| Property | Description |
| --- | --- |
| attributeGroups | Collection of ISchemaAttributeGroup |
| attributes | Collection of ISchemaAttribute |
| elements | Collection of ISchemaElement |
| modelGroups | Collection of ISchemaModelGroup |
| notations | Collection of ISchemaNotation |
| schemaLocations | Location of linked schemas |
| targetNamespace | String, target namespace for the XML schema |
| types | Collection of ISchemaType |
| version | String version of the XML schema |

### 18.5.4 DOM versus SOM

We have worked with XML documents by using both the DOM and the Schema Object Model (SOM), and each model has limitations. Because of their tight integration in the MSXML components, separating the core MSXML components from SOM components and deciding which approach is needed for a particular problem is difficult.

Obviously, the SOM is designed to read XML schema documents—and only XML schema documents. The DOM, on the other hand, works with any well-formed XML document. In cases where an application must examine an XML schema document, it makes sense to use the SOM, the higher-level API, to determine the components of the schema.

This advantage of the SOM, however, applies only to the reading of an XML schema. As mentioned earlier, the SOM is a read-only representation of an XML schema, loaded from a document. *The SOM cannot be used to create or modify an XML schema document, only to examine it.* If your application must create an XML schema document or modify an existing XML schema document, the application should use the DOM or SAX, or perhaps even a transformation for that purpose.

### 18.5.5 Creating XML Schemas

From an application, you are most likely going to programmatically access an XML schema to read its contents. XML schema documents are typically written to function as a binding contract; as such, their creation typically involves collaboration between developers and designers and even outside parties. That creating or modifying a schema programmatically is the exception—and reading a schema is the rule—is evident in that the SOM provides no mechanism for performing either creation or modification. The SOM is only a tool for reading XML schemas and using them to validate an XML instance.

Of course, we can still create an XML schema document with MSXML. There are cases where creating or modifying an XML schema might be necessary. For example, an application that exports a database schema to an XML schema document needs to create an XML schema document. In those cases, developers must return to the standard APIs for XML. The DOMDocument40 component provides not only the capability to read an XML document and traverse the tree, but also to create and modify documents.

## 18.6 Validation

Whenever the MSXML parser loads an XML document, some level of validation must occur. Unless a particular document is a valid XML document, applications will not want to treat it as such. With MSXML, you can validate XML documents at different levels depending on the needs of your application. Specifically, you can use the methods of the DOMDocument40 or

`SAXXMLReader40` to validate an XML document against an XML schema. In both cases, you follow the same steps. Using the SOM to load an XML schema, you inform the parser about the specified schema documents and allow it to validate against the XML schema during parsing.

> **TIP**
>
> If your application already uses either the DOM or SAX2 to access XML documents, and you want to use the SOM from the same application, you can refer to the code in Listing 18.14. If you need to choose between adding either DOM or SAX2 code to your application to perform validation, validation using the DOM requires less code to achieve the same effect.

## 18.6.1 XML Document Samples

The sample address documents are shown in Listings 18.10 and 18.11. As you might expect, the document `address.xml` (18.10) conforms to the earlier XML schema, whereas `badaddress.xml` (18.11) does not. In particular, `badaddress.xml` does not contain the required `customerID` attribute on one of the `businessCustomer` elements.

**LISTING 18.10** Sample document (`address.xml`)

```xml
<?xml version="1.0"?>
<customerList
 xmlns:xsi="http://www.w3.org/2001/XMLSchema-instance"
 xmlns:cat=
 "http://www.XMLSchemaReference.com/Examples/Ch18"
 xsi:schemaLocation=
 "http://www.XMLSchemaReference.com/Examples/Ch18address.xsd">
<businessCustomer customerID="SAM132E57">
    <name>Cliff Binstock</name>
    <phoneNumber>503-555-0000</phoneNumber>
    <address>
        <street>123 Gravel Road</street>
        <city>Nowheresville</city>
        <state>OR</state>
        <country>US</country>
        <zip>97000</zip>
        <effectiveDate>2001-02-14</effectiveDate>
    </address>
</businessCustomer>
<businessCustomer customerID="SAM132E58"
 primaryContact="Joe Sr.">
```

*continues*

```xml
            <name>Joe Schmendrick</name>
            <phoneNumber>212-555-0000</phoneNumber>
            <phoneNumber>212-555-1111</phoneNumber>
            <URL>http://www.Joe.Schmendrick.name</URL>
            <address>
                <street>88888 Mega Apartment Bldg</street>
                <street>Apt 5315</street>
                <city>New York</city>
                <state>NY</state>
                <country>US</country>
                <zip>10000</zip>
                <effectiveDate>2001-02-14</effectiveDate>
            </address>
        </businessCustomer>
        <businessCustomer customerID="SAM132E58"
         primaryContact="Ellie"
         sequenceID="88742">
            <name>Ellen Boxer</name>
            <phoneNumber xsi:nil="true"/>
            <address zipPlus4="20000-1234">
                <POBox>123</POBox>
                <city>Small Town</city>
                <state>VA</state>
                <country>US</country>
                <zip>20000</zip>
                <effectiveDate>2001-02-14</effectiveDate>
            </address>
        </businessCustomer>
        <businessCustomer customerID="SAM132E59"
         primaryContact="Lydia"
         sequenceID="88743">
            <name>Ralph McKenzie</name>
            <phoneNumber xsi:nil="true"/>
            <address>
                <street>123 Main Street</street>
                <pmb>12345</pmb>
                <city>Metropolis</city>
                <state>CO</state>
                <country>US</country>
                <zip>80000</zip>
                <effectiveDate>2001-02-14</effectiveDate>
            </address>
        </businessCustomer>
        <privateCustomer customerID="SAM01234P"
         sequenceID="88743">
            <name>I. M. Happy</name>
            <phoneNumber>303-555-0000</phoneNumber>
```

```
        <phoneNumber>303-555-1111</phoneNumber>
        <address>
            <street>123 Main Street</street>
            <pmb>12345</pmb>
            <city>Metropolis</city>
            <state>CO</state>
            <country>US</country>
            <zip>80000</zip>
            <effectiveDate>2001-02-14</effectiveDate>
        </address>
    </privateCustomer>
</customerList>>
```

**LISTING 18.11** Sample document with errors (badaddress.xml)

```
<?xml version="1.0"?>
<customerList
 xmlns:xsi="http://www.w3.org/2001/XMLSchema-instance"
 xmlns:cat=
 "http://www.XMLSchemaReference.com/Examples/Ch18"
 xsi:schemaLocation=
 "http://www.XMLSchemaReference.com/Examples/Ch18address.xsd">
<businessCustomer >
    <name>Cliff Binstock</name>
    <phoneNumber>503-555-0000</phoneNumber>
    <address>
        <street>123 Gravel Road</street>
        <city>Nowheresville</city>
        <state>OR</state>
        <country>US</country>
        <zip>97000</zip>
        <effectiveDate>2001-02-14</effectiveDate>
    </address>
</businessCustomer>
<businessCustomer customerID="SAM132E58"
 primaryContact="Joe Sr.">
    <name>Joe Schmendrick</name>
    <phoneNumber>212-555-0000</phoneNumber>
    <phoneNumber>212-555-1111</phoneNumber>
    <URL>http://www.Joe.Schmendrick.name</URL>
    <address>
        <street>88888 Mega Apartment Bldg</street>
        <street>Apt 5315</street>
        <city>New York</city>
        <state>NY</state>
        <country>US</country>
```

*continues*

```xml
            <zip>10000</zip>
            <effectiveDate>2001-02-14</effectiveDate>
        </address>
    </businessCustomer>
    <privateCustomer customerID="SAM01234P"
     sequenceID="88743">
        <name>I. M. Happy</name>
        <phoneNumber>303-555-0000</phoneNumber>
        <phoneNumber>303-555-1111</phoneNumber>
        <address>
            <street>123 Main Street</street>
            <pmb>12345</pmb>
            <city>Metropolis</city>
            <state>CO</state>
            <country>US</country>
            <zip>80000</zip>
            <effectiveDate>2001-02-14</effectiveDate>
        </address>
    </privateCustomer>
</customerList>
```

## 18.6.2 Validation by Using the DOM

To validate an XML document against an XML schema, all that is required is to load that document with knowledge of the XML schema in question. To do that, it is first necessary to load the schema into the cache used by that `DOMDocument40` component.

The cache in question is represented by the `XMLSchemaCache40` component. The `DOMDocument40` uses the cache of schemas located in its `schemas` property during parsing, so prior to loading the document you want to validate, set the `schemas` property to your already loaded `XMLSchemaCache40`. If the DOM is able to load the document and validate it, it is valid against all the schemas in the cache. The example in the next section shows how the DOM can be used to perform validation.

## 18.6.3 Validation by Using SAX2

Validation with the `DOMDocument40` component is simple and requires very little code. To use the SAX2 API to perform similar validation, additional code is required, but the complexity does not increase. All that is required to validate by using SAX2 is to define a relationship between the reader and the schema cache and to have content and error handlers in place during the parsing.

To use the schema cache with SAX, you must use the configuration methods of the SAX API. There is one property associated with XML schema validation, and one feature as well. The property is `schemas`, which must be set to the schema cache. The feature is `schema-validation`, which must be set to TRUE. When these are configured properly and the reader initiates a parse, the parser will validate against all the XML schemas in the cache. If the validation succeeds, the endDocument method of ContentHandler is fired. If validation fails, the error method of the ErrorHandler is fired.

The example application that follows uses SAX and DOM for validation, and provides sample code for those operations.

## 18.7 Example: XML Schema Tree

Now that we have examined some of the features of the Microsoft XML Core Services, we can pull these concepts together in a single application. To illustrate the XML Schema features of MSXML, you can build a simple tool in Visual Basic to examine an XML schema document and validate documents against it.

Before building the project, you must have already installed the MSXML 4.0 components on the development machine. You can find these components, which are both free and redistributable, at the Microsoft Developer Network site, specifically at:

```
http://msdn.microsoft.com/downloads/sample.asp?url=/MSDN-FILES/027/
    001/766/msdncompositedoc.xml
```

After you have downloaded and executed the installation, you can develop applications by using MSXML.

The XML Schema Tree sample was created in Visual Basic 6.0 as a Standard Executable project. The project has a single form, SchemaTreeForm, that provides menus and displays the schema information. The sample code can be downloaded from

```
http://www.XMLSchemaReference.com/examples/Ch18.
```

Figure 18.4 shows the design-time view of the SchemaTreeForm. It consists of a menu, a tree view, an image list, and a common dialog control.

To create this project, first select a new Standard Executable. Next you must include the necessary components to build the project. The project requires three additional libraries: MSXML 4.0, the Microsoft Common Dialog Control, and the Microsoft Windows Common Controls. The Microsoft Common Dialog Control contains the common file Open/Save dialog box used in Windows applications, and the Common Controls library holds both the tree view and the image list controls. To load these into your application, you must configure the project file to use them. You can add MSXML support to this project just as shown in Figure 18.2. Under the Visual Basic menu, select the Project menu, and then select References to add the MSXML 4.0 components. Add the other two libraries in a similar fashion: From the Project\Components check list, select both the Microsoft Common Dialog Control and the Microsoft Windows Common Controls.

### Tip

Depending on the system you are running, you might have different versions of the Common Dialog and Common Controls libraries. The feature set used in this application is common to all versions of these libraries, so just select the ones available on your machine.

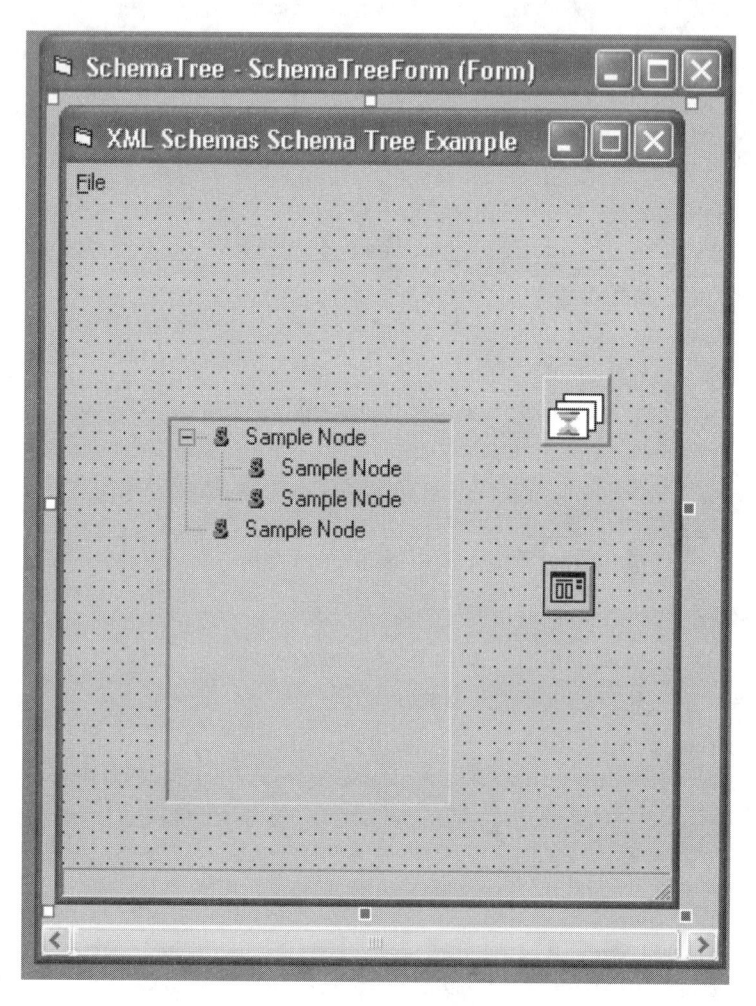

**FIGURE 18.4** *XML Schema Tree form at design time.*

Now that you have configured your project to use all the necessary libraries, you can examine the application. The tree view, treeSchema, displays the schema contents whenever the File\Open Schema menu item is selected. The application fills the tree with items for the various element types, attribute types, and other parts of the XML schema. The other menu items let users select an XML document to be validated against the loaded schema, by using either the DOM or SAX2 features. The common dialog box allows users to browse for files, and the image list provides icons for the tree view items.

The code for the Schema Tree application is shown in the following listings. Listing 18.12 begins the code for the form shown in Figure 18.4. Loading and selecting an XML schema file and resizing the windows are handled here in code.

**LISTING 18.12**  SchemaTreeForm.frm Code Part 1

```
'SchemaTreeForm.frm
'
'Tree view representation of an XML schema using MSXML and SOM

Private m_schemaCache As XMLSchemaCache40

Private Sub Form_Load()
    status.SimpleText = "No schema"
    Set m_schemaCache = Nothing
End Sub

Private Sub Form_Resize()
    treeSchema.Move 0, 0, Me.ScaleWidth, Me.ScaleHeight
End Sub

Private Sub IDM_FILEEXIT_Click()
    Set m_schemaCache = Nothing
    Unload Me
End Sub

Private Sub IDM_FILEOPEN_Click()
On Error GoTo OpenErr
    status.SimpleText = "Working.."
    treeSchema.Nodes.Clear
    Set m_schemaCache = New XMLSchemaCache40
    Dim docSchema As DOMDocument40
    Dim schema As ISchema
    Dim strTargetNS As String
    Set docSchema = New DOMDocument40
    docSchema.async = False
    docSchema.validateOnParse = False
```

*continues*

## MSXML and the Schema Object Model (SOM)
### CHAPTER 18

```
        Dim strFile As String
        filedlg.ShowOpen
        If filedlg.FileName = "" Then Exit Sub
        strFile = filedlg.FileName
        If (docSchema.Load(strFile)) Then
            status.SimpleText = "Loaded " & strFile
        Else
            Dim docError As IXMLDOMParseError
            MsgBox docError.reason, vbCritical, "Schema Tree"
            Exit Sub
        End If
        Dim elemDoc As IXMLDOMElement
        Dim attr As IXMLDOMAttribute
        Set elemDoc = docSchema.documentElement
        Set attr = elemDoc.getAttributeNode("targetNamespace")
        strTargetNS = ""
        If attr Is Nothing = False Then
            strTargetNS = attr.Value
        End If
        m_schemaCache.Add strTargetNS, docSchema
        Set schema = m_schemaCache.getSchema(strTargetNS)
        FillSchemaTree schema, treeSchema
        Exit Sub
OpenErr:
        MsgBox Err.Description, vbCritical, "Schema Tree"
        status.SimpleText = "No schema"
        Set m_schemaCache = Nothing
        Exit Sub
End Sub
```

Listing 18.13 continues the form code. The subroutine `FillSchemaTree` uses the SOM to traverse the contents of the XML schema and load each set of parts into the tree view. Beginning with the `ISchema` interface, this routine accesses the properties of `ISchema` and walks the returned `ISchemaItemCollection` interfaces.

**LISTING 18.13** SchemaTreeForm.frm Code Part 2

```
'Fill a standard TreeView with a tree representation of an XML
' Schema as returned by the MSXML SOM ISchema interface
'This code currently only loads the list of elements,
' attributes, and types
Public Sub FillSchemaTree(schema As ISchema, tree As TreeView)
    If schema Is Nothing Then Exit Sub
    If tree Is Nothing Then Exit Sub
    tree.Nodes.Clear
    Dim nodeRoot As Node
```

```
Dim nodeCurr As Node
Dim strRoot As String
strRoot = schema.Name
If strRoot = "" Then strRoot = "<schema>"
Set nodeRoot = tree.Nodes.Add(,,, strRoot, 1)
'Elements
Dim nodeElemGroup As Node
Set nodeElemGroup = tree.Nodes.Add(nodeRoot.Index, _
 tvwChild, , "<elements>", 2)
Dim elem As ISchemaElement
For Each elem In schema.elements
    Dim nodeElem As Node
    Set nodeElem = tree.Nodes.Add(nodeElemGroup.Index, _
      tvwChild,, elem.Name, 2)
Next elem

'Attributes
Dim nodeAttrGroup As Node
Set nodeAttrGroup = tree.Nodes.Add(nodeRoot.Index, _
 tvwChild,, "<attributes>", 3)

Dim attr As ISchemaAttribute
For Each attr In schema.Attributes
Dim nodeAttr As Node
Set nodeAttr = tree.Nodes.Add(nodeAttrGroup.Index, _
 tvwChild,, attr.Name, 3)
Next attr

'Types
Dim nodeTypeGroup As Node
Set nodeTypeGroup = tree.Nodes.Add(nodeRoot.Index, _
 tvwChild,, "all types", 5)

Dim nodeSimpleTypeGroup As Node
Set nodeSimpleTypeGroup = tree.Nodes.Add(_
 nodeTypeGroup.Index, tvwChild,, "simple types", 5)

Dim nodeComplexTypeGroup As Node
Set nodeComplexTypeGroup = tree.Nodes.Add(_
 nodeTypeGroup.Index, tvwChild,, "complex types", 4)

Dim t As ISchemaType
For Each t In schema.types
    Dim nodeType As Node
    If t.itemType = SOMITEM_COMPLEXTYPE Then
        Dim ct As ISchemaComplexType
        Set ct = Nothing
```

*continues*

## MSXML and the Schema Object Model (SOM)
### CHAPTER 18

```
                Set ct = t
                Set nodeType = tree.Nodes.Add( _
                  nodeComplexTypeGroup.Index, tvwChild,, _
                  t.Name, 4)
            End If

            If t.itemType = SOMITEM_SIMPLETYPE Then
                Set nodeType = tree.Nodes.Add( _
                  nodeSimpleTypeGroup.Index, tvwChild,, t.Name, 5)
            End If
        Next t

        'Expand the schema element
        nodeRoot.Expanded = True
End Sub
```

Listing 18.14 shows the last portion of form code: the menu handlers for the validation. These routines handle the validation by DOM or SAX, respectively. For both validations, the `XMLSchemaCache40` is used to select the schemas in question. The DOM validation uses the schemas property of the `DOMDocument40`, whereas the SAX2 validation uses the `getProperty` method of `SAXXMLReader40`. In addition, in both cases you must make sure validation is active. When using the DOM, you activate validation using the `validateOnParse` property, and when using SAX, the `getFeature` method is used.

**LISTING 18.14**   SchemaTreeForm.frm Code Part 3

```
Private Sub IDM_FILEVALIDATEDOM_Click()
    Dim doc As DOMDocument40
    Dim docError As IXMLDOMParseError
    If m_schemaCache Is Nothing Then
        MsgBox "No schema is loaded", vbCritical, "Schema Tree"
        Exit Sub
    End If
    Set doc = New DOMDocument40
    doc.async = False
    doc.validateOnParse = True
    Set doc.schemas = m_schemaCache
    Dim strFile As String
    filedlg.ShowOpen
    If filedlg.FileName = "" Then Exit Sub
    strFile = filedlg.FileName
    Dim b As Boolean
    b = doc.Load(strFile)
    Set docError = doc.parseError
```

## 18.7 Example: XML Schema Tree

```
    If (docError.errorCode = 0) Then
        MsgBox _
          "The document is valid according to the schema.", _
          vbOKOnly, "Schema Tree"
    Else
        MsgBox docError.reason, vbCritical, "Schema Tree"
    End If
    Set doc = Nothing
End Sub

Private Sub IDM_FILEVALIDATESAX_Click()
On Error GoTo SaxErr
    Dim sax As SAXXMLReader40
    If m_schemaCache Is Nothing Then
        MsgBox "No schema is loaded", vbCritical, "Schema Tree"
        Exit Sub
    End If
    Set sax = New SAXXMLReader40
    Dim handler As SAXTest
    Set handler = New SAXTest
    Dim strFile As String
    filedlg.ShowOpen
    If filedlg.FileName = "" Then Exit Sub
    strFile = filedlg.FileName
    sax.putFeature "schema-validation", True
    sax.putProperty "schemas", m_schemaCache
    Set sax.contentHandler = handler
    Set sax.errorHandler = handler
    sax.parseURL strFile
    Exit Sub
SaxErr:
    MsgBox Err.Description
    Exit Sub
End Sub
```

The validation is determined by the errors—or lack thereof—that occur during parsing. Once again, DOM code just checks the `parseError`, whereas SAX2 relies on the handlers being used. The handler for the Schema Tree application is a Visual Basic class defined in Listing 18.15. This class, `SAXTest`, resembles the handler shown in Listing 18.4. With both content and error handling combined in the `SAXTest` class, the `SAXTest` class receives all the notifications needed to validate with SAX. Just as in Listing 18.4, the handler has a number of empty methods that exist only to make sure you fully implement the interfaces you support.

**LISTING 18.15** SAXTest.cls (SAX Validation Handler)

```
'SAXTest
'SAX Handler for XML Schema Validation

Implements IVBSAXContentHandler
Implements IVBSAXErrorHandler

Private Sub IVBSAXContentHandler_characters(strChars As String)

End Sub

Private Property Set IVBSAXContentHandler_documentLocator(_
  ByVal RHS As MSXML2.IVBSAXLocator)

End Property

' Document is validated against the XML Schema
Private Sub IVBSAXContentHandler_endDocument()
    MsgBox "The document is valid according to the schema.", _
      vbOKOnly, "Schema Tree"
End Sub

Private Sub IVBSAXContentHandler_endElement(_
  strNamespaceURI As String, strLocalName As String,
  strQName As String)

End Sub

Private Sub IVBSAXContentHandler_endPrefixMapping(_
  strPrefix As String)

End Sub

Private Sub IVBSAXContentHandler_ignorableWhitespace(_
  strChars As String)

End Sub

Private Sub IVBSAXContentHandler_processingInstruction(_
  strTarget As String, strData As String)

End Sub

Private Sub IVBSAXContentHandler_skippedEntity(_
  strName As String)

End Sub
```

```
Private Sub IVBSAXContentHandler_startDocument()

End Sub

Private Sub IVBSAXContentHandler_startElement(_
 strNamespaceURI As String, strLocalName As String, _
 strQName As String, _
 ByVal oAttributes As MSXML2.IVBSAXAttributes)

End Sub

Private Sub IVBSAXContentHandler_startPrefixMapping(_
 strPrefix As String, strURI As String)

End Sub

' Validation failed for the reason indicated by parameters
Private Sub IVBSAXErrorHandler_error(_
 ByVal oLocator As MSXML2.IVBSAXLocator, _
 strErrorMessage As String, ByVal nErrorCode As Long)
    MsgBox strErrorMessage, vbCritical, "Schema Tree"
End Sub

Private Sub IVBSAXErrorHandler_fatalError(_
 ByVal oLocator As MSXML2.IVBSAXLocator, _
 strErrorMessage As String, ByVal nErrorCode As Long)
    MsgBox strErrorMessage, vbCritical, "Schema Tree"
End Sub

Private Sub IVBSAXErrorHandler_ignorableWarning(_
 ByVal oLocator As MSXML2.IVBSAXLocator, _
 strErrorMessage As String, ByVal nErrorCode As Long)

End Sub
```

With this code, we have a minimal XML schema explorer and document validator. Figures 18.5 and 18.6 show the XML Schema Tree loading an XML schema. Items in the tree are given different locations and icons depending on their types. This user interface provides a view of the schema hierarchy.

When you load the XML document badaddress.xml, the validation code fails because of the missing customerID attribute in that document. Figure 18.6 shows the message box displayed by the XML Schema Tree application when badaddress.xsd fails to validate against the address schema. This error is caught using the same error-checking code shown in Listing 18.15.

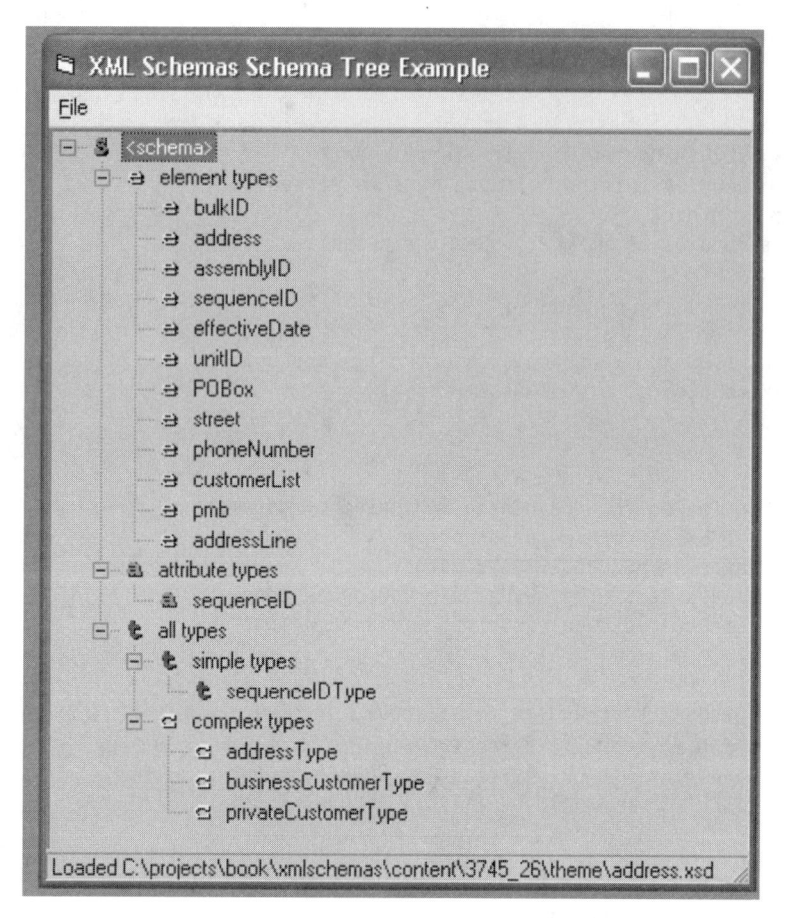

**FIGURE 18.5** *XML Schema Tree in action.*

18.7 Example: XML Schema Tree

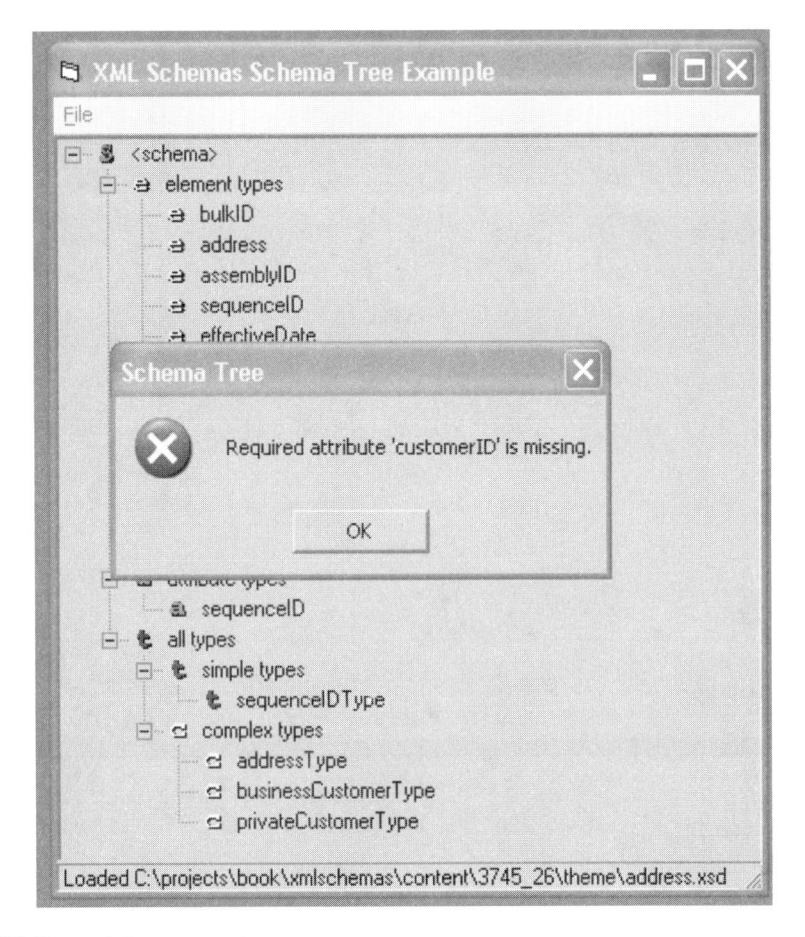

**FIGURE 18.6**  *Validation error for* `badaddress.xml`.

# Result-oriented Schemas

**PART IV**

Most of this book teaches you how to write an XML schema. However, an XML schema is only valuable in the context of a deployed system. Part IV covers the broader issues of how to design software, documents, and even entire systems around XML schemas. Specifically, this part provides analysis suggestions, design hints, and code examples:

- Chapter 19 demonstrates how to integrate XML schemas with object-oriented technology. The chapter contains an overview of object inheritance. The code examples in this chapter, which demonstrate integration with the .NET Framework, cover Visual Basic, C#, and C++.

- Chapter 20 is a discussion on how to analyze requirements for, and design XML schemas destined for, human-readable documents. Much of the chapter covers identifying document components, uncoupling content and layout, and considerations for stylesheet formatting.

- Chapter 21 covers how to design an application around XML and XML schemas. In particular, a good design focuses on "contracts," or programmatic interfaces. XML schemas are the newest and best mechanism for defining this contract. The examples demonstrate how to specify input parameters, output parameters, and even methods to call, simply by creating an XML schema.

# Object-oriented Schemas

**CHAPTER**

**19**

## IN THIS CHAPTER

- **19.1 Concepts and Observations** 508
- **19.2 Object-oriented Concepts** 509
- **19.3 XML Schemas and Objects** 510
- **19.4 Mapping XML Schemas to Object-oriented Languages** 511
- **19.5 Sample Schema: `party.xsd`** 521
- **19.6. Design Patterns** 527
- **19.7 Language Examples** 529

… This chapter discusses how XML schemas can be used in conjunction with object-oriented (OO) concepts and languages. In particular, the chapter examines how XML schemas can be used to model data that is stored in objects.

## 19.1 Concepts and Observations

Because this chapter discusses object-oriented design and development, there is a need to discuss the choice of both methodology and language. The content of the chapter focuses on the relationship between object-oriented code and XML schemas. As such, it is intended for developers who have experience working with an object-oriented language. Developers with different backgrounds—or readers new to development—might have a more difficult time with the content of this chapter.

### 19.1.1 Fundamentals of Object-oriented Development

Any developer who has worked in an object-oriented language for some time has a particular approach or slant to the questions of OO methodology. Countless tools, books, philosophies, and methods have been built for object-oriented development. This chapter touches only on concepts at the heart of object-oriented development and how those concepts can be related to XML schemas. The concepts considered here are encapsulation, inheritance, and polymorphism. Some approaches disagree about whether inheritance is a fundamental component of an object-oriented language. Inheritance is an approach; reuse is the goal. Reuse can be attained through other approaches, such as aggregation of objects, but because inheritance is a method of reuse common to most object-oriented development (as well as XML Schema), we will examine it in this chapter.

### 19.1.2 Use of Languages

Throughout this chapter are examples of mapping XML schemas to object-oriented language constructs, and vice-versa. There is probably some question about which languages are object-oriented, and as with methodologies, everyone has a favorite. In fact, the only issue that creates more division and newsgroup traffic than object-oriented methodology is the language to which it should be applied. This chapter includes examples in C++, Java, Visual Basic, and C#. Each language has strengths and weaknesses, and the best language, of course, is the one that will help you as a developer be most productive and solve the problem at hand.

Because this chapter provides examples in several languages, there is not enough space for an explanation of the syntax of the languages used. The best approach for readers is to focus on the examples in languages that are familiar to them and then compare those to the other language examples. Some examples only illustrate the mapping between XML schemas and objects. For the examples that specifically use an XML validator, a validator suitable for that language has been selected, but an explanation of how that validator should be used has not been included. For information on how to use these tools, refer to Chapters 17 and 18, which explain how to use validation components in both Java and COM respectively.

## 19.2 Object-oriented Concepts

Before discussing object-oriented XML schemas, we must first define "object-oriented." *Object-oriented* means "dealing with objects," which in software development means solving problems by using software constructs to model real-world objects. This approach provides several advantages. First, software that models the real world is easier to understand. Creating an object that represents an employee within a system and then manipulating that Employee object and its properties, simplifies development because it is intuitive. People know what an employee is. Second, objects provide a unit of reuse for software. An object can be used as a "black box" that developers can take advantage of without needing to know the details of its implementation.

The advantages of object-oriented software development are best realized, of course, through the use of object-oriented languages. Like politics and religion, discussions of what makes an object-oriented language are best avoided among friends. At the heart of object-oriented languages, however, three key concepts are implemented to varying degrees. Those concepts are encapsulation, inheritance, and polymorphism.

### 19.2.1 Encapsulation

*Encapsulation* is the hiding of detail about the internal structure of an object from the users of that object. For example, a calculator provides an interface through which mathematical calculations can be performed. How those calculations occur is irrelevant, and the user of the calculator would probably prefer not to know the details of the implementation. The buttons and screen interface of the calculator encapsulate the functionality and data of the calculator. Similarly, an object in software that performs calculations encapsulates the logic involved behind the public methods of that class.

### 19.2.2 Inheritance

In object-oriented languages, *inheritance* is a method of describing common characteristics of classes by using a single class. That class is considered the base, and all classes built from that base are said to have inherited or to be derived (or subclassed) from that base. By inheriting from a base class, a new class gains the characteristics of that base class in addition to any of its own. For example, consider a base class called "Vehicle" that has properties and methods to represent characteristics common to all vehicles: maximum speed, number of occupants, fuel type, and so on. Any class that represents a specific form of vehicle, such as a train, can then derive from the Vehicle base class and inherit all those properties and methods.

### 19.2.3 Polymorphism

*Polymorphism* is similar to inheritance and builds on that concept. If two objects share a base type that expresses some common functionality, those two objects can be represented by using the base without a need to know their derived type. Inheritance is a common method of implementing polymorphism. In our previous example, both a car and a helicopter are vehicles. Although they have many different properties (altitude hopefully being one), they share the characteristics common to all vehicles. Both a car and a helicopter would be polymorphic through the vehicle base class, and one can examine either a car or a helicopter for fuel capacity, for example.

## 19.3 XML Schemas and Objects

Now that we have reviewed some of the concepts associated with object-oriented development, we can examine how those concepts apply to XML schemas. For each concept—encapsulation, inheritance, and polymorphism—Section 19.4 describes how it is used in XML schemas. For now, let's just consider to what extent they are available in an XML schema.

### 19.3.1 The Good

XML schemas have methods for expressing inheritance and polymorphism. Structure types can be derived from other structure types and thus inherit the properties of the base. Structure types defined in an XML schema are polymorphic about any base class they share. XML schemas provide a rich substitution mechanism that allows for polymorphic behavior between structure types. In both cases, the object-oriented concepts related to inheritance and polymorphism are fully available in XML schemas. In fact, as shown in Section 19.4.1, some measure of inheritance is available in XML schemas that is not available in a language such as C++. The methods for specifying inheritance and—through inheritance—polymorphism are details associated with the structure type components of an XML schema.

### 19.3.2 The Bad

The concept of encapsulation is basically foreign to XML Schema. XML schemas are all about describing data, not hiding it. There are no facilities for describing hidden data or methods for an object. When you model an object in an XML schema, you are essentially modeling only its data and not its capabilities.

### 19.3.3 The Answer

XML schemas have facilities for inheritance and polymorphism but not encapsulation. Because of this, XML schemas are good tools for modeling the data of an object for purposes such as serialization. Despite the lack of encapsulation, XML schemas provide a very useful method for data representation and have advantages because of this.

Now that we have considered the object-oriented features of XML schemas, we can draw some guidelines for combining XML schemas and object-oriented languages. Any object described in an XML schema is defined solely by its data. When mapping between objects and XML schemas, you must decide how the data of an object should be modeled. The best approach is to assume that all data defined as part of the object is describing public properties of that object. These properties can, however, be provided to the outside world through a pair of accessor methods and represented as protected members of the object. This allows some degree of encapsulation of data. There is still, however, no method for defining a private data member of an object.

## 19.4 Mapping XML Schemas to Object-oriented Languages

Development tools are now adding support for XML and XML schemas, and code generators are becoming available to perform the translation between XML schemas and classes in programming languages. Such a tool might create an XML schema based on an existing class, or it might generate source code to match an XML schema that was already designed. In any case, tools such as code generators are not foolproof, especially when they are used for such complicated tasks as mapping between these two syntaxes. It is important for developers to understand how to map between XML schemas and objects before they begin to alter generated code. Let's take a look at how an XML schema can be mapped to an object-oriented language.

### 19.4.1 Complex Types

In the process of mapping XML schemas to objects, the `complexType` element deserves the most attention. `complexType` elements are the parts of an XML schema document that most obviously resemble the definition of a class. In object-oriented terms, the `complexType` defines an object type. The elements and attributes associated with that `complexType` describe the properties and/or data members of the object. Table 19.1 shows the mapping of `complexType` elements to object definitions in each of the languages examined in this chapter. Coincidentally, all four languages use 'class' as a keyword to indicate an object type definition, although in Visual Basic the meaning is somewhat different than in the other languages.

**TABLE 19.1**  Mapping the `complexType` Element

| Language | `<complexType/>` Corresponds To |
| --- | --- |
| C++ | class |
| Java | class |
| Visual Basic | Class |
| C# | class |

### 19.4.1.1 Non-instantiable versus Instantiable

As shown in Table 19.1, the `complexType` element can be used to describe a class, but in each case that class can be defined as either instantiable or non-instantiable. The `complexType` element is the representation for either instantiable or non-instantiable classes, and the differentiation is made through use of the `abstract` attribute.

The `abstract` attribute indicates whether or not the `complexType` element it appears on can be used in an XML instance. If the attribute is specified 'false', elements of this type can appear in an instance document. If the attribute is specified 'true', an element type specifying this complex type directly cannot have instances. Consider Listing 19.1, where a `complexType` element is defined as non-instantiable.

**LISTING 19.1**  Abstract Complex Type Schema Fragment

```
<xsd:complexType name="Room" abstract="true">
    <xsd:sequence>
        <xsd:element name="number" type="xsd:decimal" />
        <xsd:element name="description" type="xsd:string" />
    </xsd:sequence>
</xsd:complexType>
```

This complex type represents a non-instantiable `Room` class that would serve as a base class for distinct room complex types such as `Office`, `Closet`, and so on. This complex type can be represented in C# with the source code in Listing 19.2.

**LISTING 19.2**  Mapping the Non-instantiable `Room` Complex Type in C#

```
abstract class Room
{
    public int number;
    public string description;
}
```

The same code in Java looks almost identical, but in C++ you must use a different approach. In C++, you can create a non-instantiable class by defining one or more pure virtual functions as members of that class. Listing 19.3 adds a single pure virtual method to our class that would need to be implemented in any derived classes. When this code is used, the `Room` class becomes non-instantiable. The method `concreteRoom` must be implemented in `Office` or another derived class, indicating that the derived `Room` type is instantiable.

**LISTING 19.3**   Mapping the Non-instantiable Room Type in C++

```
class Room
{
    public:
        int   number;
        char* description;
    public:
        virtual void concreteRoom( void ) = 0;
};
```

> **TIP**
>
> In C++, when a pure virtual method of a class is defined for the purpose of making that class non-instantiable, the name of the method is not important. What is significant is the fact that such a method is defined. Some developers even use a pure virtual destructor in order to make a class non-instantiable.

Some discretion can be exercised as to the mapping of abstract `complexType` elements to object constructs. For example, in C# and many other languages, there exists the concept of a non-instantiable class as well as an interface. A non-instantiable class is an class with potentially both data and methods that cannot be directly instantiated, whereas an interface is a set of related methods that must be implemented in a derived class. An abstract `complexType` element could be modeled as a non-instantiable class, or it could be modeled as an interface with get/set accessor methods for each of the properties. Because XML schemas model the data of an object, a better approach is to map an abstract `complexType` element to a non-instantiable class and thereby capture the data members of the base class.

Table 19.2 lists the language mappings for the `abstract` attribute. You might notice the lack of a corresponding language feature in Visual Basic. The object features of Visual Basic 6.0 are built on the Component Object Model (COM), which does not have any facilities for implementation inheritance. It would be possible, as previously discussed, to map to an interface in this case, which in Visual Basic is represented as a `Class` with an `Instancing` property of `PublicNotCreatable`. This is as close as you can come to a non-instantiable base class in Visual Basic 6.0. Visual Basic .NET, however, is built on the .NET Common Language Runtime and supports the same object constructs as C# but with different syntax. Table 19.2 shows a map between the `abstract` attribute and the corresponding conventions in each programming language.

**TABLE 19.2** Mapping the abstract Attribute

| Language | abstract TRUE Corresponds To |
|---|---|
| C++ | Pure virtual method |
| Java | abstract class |
| Visual Basic | N/A (`PublicNotCreatable` class) |
| C# | abstract class |

### 19.4.1.2 Inheritance and Polymorphism

Because the `complexType` element corresponds to object types, any degree of inheritance you apply to objects must be expressed by using the `complexType` element. XML schemas provide mechanisms for expressing inheritance or restricting it, depending on your needs.

Inheritance is expressed in XML schemas by using two different elements: the `extension` element and the `restriction` element. Their names suggest their usage. When a derived structure type wants to extend the capabilities of the base structure type, it derives by extension. When the derived structure type wants to restrict the capabilities of the base structure type, derivation by restriction is used. The `extension` element can be used with either the `simpleContent` or `complexContent` elements, and the `restriction` element can be used with either of those as well as with the `simpleType` element.

The best way to examine inheritance in XML schemas is to look at a couple of examples. Consider the C# listing that follows, which defines a set of classes that model rooms of a building. The non-instantiable base class, `Room`, defines the common characteristics, and the derived classes `Office` and `Closet` inherit those characteristics from `Room`. Listing 19.4 shows a quick set of class definitions for the `Room` classes.

**LISTING 19.4** C# Code for `Room` and Derived Classes

```
abstract class Room
{
    public int number;
    public string description;
    public int maxOccupancy;
}

class Office : Room
{
    public int cubes;
}

class Closet : Room
{
```

```
    Closet()
    {
        maxOccupancy = 0;
    }
}
```

If you want to model these classes in an XML schema, you need to be able to express the inheritance that exists between the classes. In the case of Office, you want to add an additional member, cubes, that represents the number of cubicles in the office. For the Closet class, you do not need any new members, but you do want to force the maxOccupancy field to be equal to 0. These relationships define two different types of inheritance. In one case, you want to add to the capabilities of a type, and in the other case, you want to limit the original type. These two relationships represent instances of inheritance by extension and inheritance by restriction, respectively.

For developers of C# and other object-oriented languages, the concept of inheritance by extension is a familiar one. Inheritance by restriction is slightly more difficult to express in such languages, as shown in Listing 19.4. In that case, you must take measures to fix the value of the property. Restriction can take many forms, but whatever the restriction, the relationship between objects is the same. The schema fragment shown in Listing 19.5 models the three Room classes and their inheritance. By using the extension and restriction elements, you can express in an XML schema the same inheritance that was expressed in C#.

**LISTING 19.5** Room Schema Fragment

```
<xsd:complexType name="Room" abstract="true">
    <xsd:sequence>
        <xsd:element name="number"      type="xsd:decimal" />
        <xsd:element name="description" type="xsd:string" />
        <xsd:element name="maxOccupancy" type="xsd:decimal" />
    </xsd:sequence>
</xsd:complexType>

<xsd:complexType name="Office">
    <xsd:complexContent>
        <xsd:extension base="Room">
            <xsd:sequence>
                <xsd:element name="cubes" type="xsd:decimal" />
            </xsd:sequence>
        </xsd:extension>
    </xsd:complexContent>
</xsd:complexType>

<xsd:complexType name="Closet">
    <xsd:complexContent>
```

*continues*

```
            <xsd:restriction base="Room">
                <xsd:sequence>
                    <xsd:element name="number" type="xsd:decimal" />
                    <xsd:element name="description"
                     type="xsd:string" />
                    <xsd:element name="maxOccurs"
                     type="xsd:decimal" fixed="0" />
                </xsd:sequence>
            </xsd:restriction>
        </xsd:complexContent>
</xsd:complexType>
```

The inheritance between XML Schema structure types allows for polymorphic behavior between derived structure types. For example, an element whose element type specifies a structure type of Room can be substituted for an element whose structure type is Office. This replacement can be accomplished by using the xsi:type attribute in the instance document. To demonstrate this, you can add a new type called Employee to your XML schema, as shown in Listing 19.6.

**LISTING 19.6** Employee Schema Fragment

```
<xsd:complexType name="Employee">
    <xsd:sequence>
        <xsd:element name="name" type="xsd:string"/>
        <xsd:element name="location" type="Room"/>
    </xsd:sequence>
</xsd:complexType>
```

The Employee complex type's content model contains an element type, location, of type Room, but in the XML instance, the location element can be of any structure type that is derived from Room and is part of the substitution group of location. The substitution will validate when the xsi:type attribute of the location element defines a structure type that derives from Room. The instance document shown in Listing 19.7 uses the xsi:type attribute to specify a location that has an instantiable Office structure type.

**LISTING 19.7** Employee Instance Document

```
<Employee>
    <name>John Stewart</name>
        <location xsi:type='Office'>
        <number>101</number>
        <description>Development</description>
        <maxOccupancy>3</maxOccupancy>
    </location>
</Employee>
```

The polymorphic behavior of XML schemas mimics that of traditional object-oriented languages enough that you can model complex object relationships by using inheritance and the `xsi:type` attribute.

### 19.4.1.3 Order

With XML schemas, you have the ability to express type definitions in several different ways. Consider Listing 19.8, which is a schema fragment for a simple address.

**LISTING 19.8**  Schema Fragment for address #1

```
<xsd:complexType name="addressType">
    <xsd:sequence>
        <xsd:element name="street" type="xsd:string" />
        <xsd:element name="city" type="xsd:string" />
        <xsd:element name="state" type="xsd:string" />
        <xsd:element name="zip"   type="xsd:decimal" />
    </xsd:sequence>
</xsd:complexType>
<xsd:element name="organization" type="party:organizationType"/>
<xsd:element name="address" type="party:addressType"/>
```

This element type can also be expressed as shown in Listing 19.9.

**LISTING 19.9**  Schema Fragment for address #2

```
<xsd:element name="address">
    <xsd:complexType>
        <xsd:sequence>
            <xsd:element name="street" type="xsd:string" />
            <xsd:element name="city" type="xsd:string" />
            <xsd:element name="state" type="xsd:string" />
            <xsd:element name="zip"   type="xsd:decimal" />
        </xsd:sequence>
    </xsd:complexType>
</xsd:element>
```

The two type definitions are the same, but the restriction placed on other structure types is different. In the first example, a structure type has been defined with which you can associate multiple element types in the XML schema. In the second example, the `address` element is associated with the `complexType` element it contains, and that structure type cannot be used again to define another element in the schema. This syntax is difficult to reproduce in an object-oriented language, where the class definition and the variable definition are more clearly separated. When modeling objects in an XML schema, following the syntax of Listing 19.8 results in a more accurate model.

### 19.4.2 Element Types

If we model a complex type as a definition of a class in object-oriented languages, then an element type can also be modeled as a declaration of a class, for the purpose of having instances that correspond to elements of those types. On the other hand, an element type is also used in a content model to indicate where elements of specific types can or must occur, and this usage can be modeled differently. Consider the complex type shown in Listing 19.1. In the content model of the complex type Room, element types appear for both room number and description. In Listing 19.2, we show how those element types can be modeled as variables. Element types are used to build a content model, and every element type has a content type. If an element type has simple content (as in Listing 19.1), then that element type should be modeled as a scalar variable. If an element type has complex content, then that element type should be modeled as an object variable. Element types that are part of the content model of a complex type should be modeled as member variables of the corresponding class (also as in Listing 19.1).

### 19.4.3 Attributes

When modeling objects in XML schemas, an attribute is slightly more difficult to map than some of the other elements. Attribute types that appear as part of a complex type should be mapped to properties of the object being modeled, just as the element is treated. Attributes that appear in other places in the XML schema do not contribute to the object type and therefore are not part of our model.

Alternatively, attribute elements that appear as children of a complexType element can be mapped to something other than a class property. In the .NET Framework, for example, there are class attributes that can be placed on a class definition to define additional characteristics such as Help text or Web Service mappings. This approach is very language-specific, but because the role of properties is already fulfilled by the element element, mapping attribute elements to class attributes might be a useful approach in these cases.

### 19.4.4 Schemas

The schema element of an XML schema document maps to a namespace, or group of related objects, in the corresponding language. Although many languages do not use the term namespace to describe object groups, the concept exists in most object-oriented languages. Table 19.3 shows a map between the schema element of an XML schema document and the corresponding convention in each programming language.

Using these groupings, you can achieve the same results as by using namespaces within your XML documents. In particular, you can avoid naming collisions through the use of this mapping. The most difficult aspect of mapping a schema element to a namespace-level language construct is the choice of name for the namespace. In XML schemas, the schema element is best defined by its targetNamespace attribute. This value, however, is a URI (Uniform

## 19.4 Mapping XML Schemas to Object-oriented Languages

**TABLE 19.3** Mapping the schema Element

| Language | A schema Corresponds To |
| --- | --- |
| C++ | Namespace |
| Java | Package |
| Visual Basic | Project |
| C# | Namespace |

Resource Identifier), which in all likelihood violates the naming conventions of the target language. A close mapping might be created between namespace/package and URI: For example, the URI 'http://www.example.com/foo/bar' might map to the package com.example.foo.bar. Alternatively, the id attribute could be used to define the mapped name. The id attribute of a schema element is not normally used, but utilities that generate source code from an XML schema document might use it in this fashion. This would allow schema authors to select a descriptive name that would only be used in a place in the schema document that is not used in ordinary processing. This identifier is less likely to be unique in a given instance document but might conform better to the naming conventions of programming languages.

In Listing 19.10, a brief XML schema redefines the Employee type first defined in Listing 19.6. The schema element that appears in the example is given an id of "HR," a fictional company's human resources department. The source code in C# that models the same Employee object appears in Listing 19.11, which immediately follows the example schema document, and it maps the schema element to the C# namespace.

**LISTING 19.10** Sample Employee Schema

```
<xsd:schema
 xmlns:xsd="http://www.w3.org/2001/XMLSchema"
 targetNamespace=" http://www.schemacompany.com/hr"
 id="HR"
 xmlns="http://www.schemacompany.com/hr"
 xmlns:hr="http://www.schemacompany.com/hr"
 elementFormDefault="qualified">
    <xsd:element name="employee" type="m:employee"/>
    <xsd:complexType name="employeeType">
        <xsd:sequence>
            <xsd:element name="name" type="xsd:string" />
            <xsd:element name="job" type="xsd:string" />
        </xsd:sequence>
    </xsd:complexType>
</xsd:schema>
```

**LISTING 19.11**   C# Code for HR Namespace

```
namespace HR
{
    class Employee
    {
        public string name;
        public string job;
    }

}
```

## 19.4.5 Simple Types

Simple types are not of primary concern when mapping objects, because they do not represent objects. Simple types are, as the Schema Recommendation defines it, to be mapped to the simple or scalar data types of the language in question. Strings map to strings, integers to integers, and so on. Simple types found as part of a complex content definition (elements of a `complexType` element, for example) become the properties of the object being described. From an object-oriented standpoint, we are really concerned about simple types only because they may represent types used as object properties. The exception to this rule would be simple types with restrictions.

In the case of simple types with restrictions, we can map the simple type in different ways depending on its use. In the case of a simple type that is to be mapped to an object property, we can implement restrictions using code inside the accessor methods of the object. For example, a simple type that represented age might restrict the range of numbers it would accept to integers between 0 and 130. If this simple type is defined as a part of a complex type that represents an employee, then we could restrict the valid range inside the `getAge` method of the Employee object.

Alternatively, we could map a restricted simple type to an object that we create for the sole purpose of implementing the restriction. The age simple type mentioned in the previous paragraph could be represented as an `Age` class, which had a value property that included the restrictive code in the accessor method. This `Age` class could then be used by any other code in the system, with the restrictive logic in one place that could be easily modified if the schema were to change.

> **NOTE**
>
> The Schema Recommendation *does not require* that the PSVI provide the value space of datatypes: The PSVI is only required to provide the canonical representation of values named by any particular lexical representation. Implementations obviously *can*—and probably should—provide the values in an appropriate internal representation. For example, accessing the value of each `float` or `date` would be quite annoying if software referencing a value had to reparse and convert to an internal representation.

### 19.4.6 Annotation

In XML schemas, `annotation` elements can appear anywhere to help document the parts of the schema. Annotation and other forms of documentation are not directly related to any object-oriented concepts. Object-oriented code, like any other code, is easier to work with when documented, and so it can be helpful to translate between XML Schema annotation and documentation in our objects. The exact syntax for comments in each language differs, but the principle is the same. (With annotation, some information can be provided for human readability, and some information can be provided for machines processing a schema.)

The question of how to map an annotation is answered by its content and its location in the XML schema. The level on which the annotation appears should be the same level on which it is placed in the source code. For example, annotations that appear at the `schema` element level should be associated with the namespace or package, and annotations that appear on a `complexType` element should be mapped to comments for that class.

### 19.4.7 Putting It Together

Starting with complex types and using many of the other parts of an XML schema, it is possible to model complex objects. With the inherently hierarchical structure of XML and XML schemas, modeling an entire graph of objects is only slightly more difficult than modeling a single class. XML schemas already provide all the syntax to express the data associated with objects and the relationships between object types.

Now that we have examined how the mapping could be approached, we will introduce an example schema and take a look at one object-oriented approach to constructing objects from XML.

## 19.5 Sample Schema: `party.xsd`

Many applications require business entities such as employees and organizations to be modeled as objects. Over time, it becomes apparent that there are similarities between the information stored about individuals and the information stored about groups. In particular, contact information is often stored about both, but perhaps that information is stored in different ways. In *Analysis Patterns: Reusable Object Models*, Addison-Wesley, 1996, Martin Fowler models this relationship as a single business entity known as a 'Party'. The Party is an entity that has a name, location, and contact information stored about it. In this pattern, Party becomes an abstract base class of both the Person class and the Organization class. For the purposes of our example, a Person is simply a Party with a Social Security number, and an Organization is a Party that contains a member list of other parties. Figure 19.1 diagrams the relationship between the object types modeled in `party.xsd`.

# Chapter 19
## Object-oriented Schemas

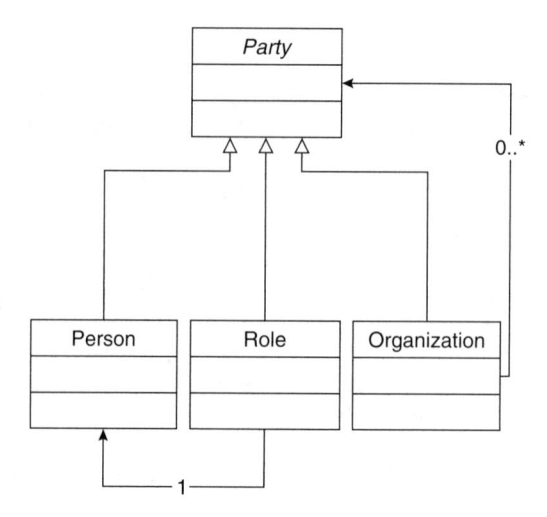

**FIGURE 19.1** *Model of the Party types.*

The sample XML schema in Listing 19.12 models this pattern as well, but it represents the relationships between Party and its derived types by using the facilities of XML Schema rather than an object model. In this example, we have added another type to the model, called Role. The Role type is represented in the XML schema by the `roleType` complex type. A Role represents a business title or position. Such a role might be filled over time by different individuals, but it maintains its own contact information. For example, System Administrator is a role with an e-mail address of 'sysadmin@mycompany.com'.

**LISTING 19.12** Sample XML Schema (`party.xsd`)

```
<xsd:schema
 xmlns:xsd="http://www.w3.org/2001/XMLSchema"
 targetNamespace=
  "http://www.XMLSchemaReference.com/Examples/Ch19/"
 xmlns="http://www.XMLSchemaReference.com/Examples/Ch19/"
 xmlns:party="http://www.XMLSchemaReference.com/Examples/Ch19/"
 elementFormDefault="qualified">
    <xsd:annotation>
        <xsd:documentation xml:lang="en">
            This XML Schema Document describes the components
            that represent parties and organizations in an
            OO fashion.  It is derived from Martin Fowler's
            Party pattern in "Analysis Patterns" by
                Addison-Wesley.
        </xsd:documentation>
    </xsd:annotation>
```

```xml
<xsd:element name="organization"
 type="party:organizationType"/>
<xsd:complexType name="addressType">
    <xsd:annotation>
        <xsd:documentation xml:lang="en">
          A mailing address for a party.
        </xsd:documentation>
    </xsd:annotation>
    <xsd:sequence>
        <xsd:element name="street" type="xsd:string" />
        <xsd:element name="city" type="xsd:string" />
        <xsd:element name="state" type="xsd:string" />
        <xsd:element name="zip"   type="xsd:decimal" />
    </xsd:sequence>
</xsd:complexType>
<xsd:complexType name="partyType" abstract="true">
    <xsd:annotation>
        <xsd:documentation xml:lang="en">
          Abstract data type for a business entity with
          a name, location, and contact information.
        </xsd:documentation>
    </xsd:annotation>
        <xsd:sequence>
        <xsd:element name="name" type="xsd:string" />
        <xsd:element name="address"
         type="party:addressType" />
        <xsd:element name="email" type="xsd:string" />
        <xsd:element name="phone" type="xsd:string" />
    </xsd:sequence>
</xsd:complexType>
<xsd:complexType name="partiesType">
    <xsd:annotation>
        <xsd:documentation xml:lang="en">
          This is a list of parties, whatever their
          true type might be.
        </xsd:documentation>
    </xsd:annotation>
    <xsd:sequence>
        <xsd:element name="party"
         type="party:partyType" minOccurs="0"
         maxOccurs="unbounded" />
    </xsd:sequence>
</xsd:complexType>
<xsd:complexType name="personType">
   <xsd:annotation>
       <xsd:documentation xml:lang="en">
         This type represents a person or individual.
```

*continues*

## Object-oriented Schemas
### CHAPTER 19

```xml
            </xsd:documentation>
        </xsd:annotation>
        <xsd:complexContent>
            <xsd:extension base="party:partyType">
                <xsd:sequence>
                    <xsd:element name="ssn" type="xsd:string" />
                </xsd:sequence>
            </xsd:extension>
        </xsd:complexContent>
    </xsd:complexType>
    <xsd:complexType name="roleType">
        <xsd:annotation>
            <xsd:documentation xml:lang="en">
             This type represents a role in an organization
             (ex. CEO).
            </xsd:documentation>
        </xsd:annotation>
        <xsd:complexContent>
            <xsd:extension base="party:partyType">
                <xsd:sequence>
                    <xsd:element name="description"
                      type="xsd:string" />
                    <xsd:element name="person"
                      type="party:personType" />
                </xsd:sequence>
            </xsd:extension>
        </xsd:complexContent>
    </xsd:complexType>
    <xsd:complexType name="organizationType" >
        <xsd:annotation>
            <xsd:documentation xml:lang="en">
             This type represents an organization
             within a company, including its employees
             and units.
            </xsd:documentation>
        </xsd:annotation>
        <xsd:complexContent>
            <xsd:extension base="party:partyType">
                <xsd:sequence>
                    <xsd:element name="members"
                      type="party:partiesType" />
                </xsd:sequence>
            </xsd:extension>
        </xsd:complexContent>
    </xsd:complexType>
</xsd:schema>
```

Using this XML schema, we can model an Organization object by using an instance document like the one in Listing 19.13. In this example, you are representing the Quality Assurance organization within a company. This organization happens to conveniently include one person, one role, and one unit or suborganization. That unit also includes a person.

**LISTING 19.13**  Organization Example Document (org.xml)

```xml
<?xml version="1.0"?>
<organization
 xmlns:xsi="http://www.w3.org/2001/XMLSchema-instance"
 xmlns="://www.XMLSchemaReference.com/Examples/Ch19/" >
    <name>Quality Assurance</name>
    <address>
        <street>2000 Main St.</street>
        <city>San Rafael</city>
        <state>CA</state>
        <zip>94903</zip>
    </address>
    <email>bugs@schemacompany.com</email>
    <phone>555-5000</phone>
    <members>
        <party xsi:type="personType" >
            <name>Jennifer Dix</name>
            <address>
                <street>11 Oak St.</street>
                <city>San Rafael</city>
                <state>CA</state>
                <zip>94903</zip>
            </address>
            <email>cdix@schemacompany.com</email>
            <phone>555-8888</phone>
            <ssn>333-33-3333</ssn>
        </party>
        <party xsi:type="roleType" >
            <name>Webmaster</name>
            <address>
                <street>45 Meadow Lane</street>
                <city>San Rafael</city>
                <state>CA</state>
                <zip>94903</zip>
            </address>
            <email>web@schemacompany.com</email>
            <phone>555-9000</phone>
            <description>System Administrator for the
             QA Web Site</description>
            <person >
```

*continues*

```xml
                    <name>Alexander Dix</name>
                    <address>
                        <street>45 Meadow Lane</street>
                        <city>San Rafael</city>
                        <state>CA</state>
                        <zip>94903</zip>
                    </address>
                    <email>lex@schemacompany.com</email>
                    <phone>555-9000</phone>
                    <ssn>444-44-4444</ssn>
                </person>
            </party>
            <party xsi:type="organizationType">
                <name>QA Documentation</name>
                <address>
                    <street>2000 Main St.</street>
                    <city>San Rafael</city>
                    <state>CA</state>
                    <zip>94903</zip>
                </address>
                <email>qadocs@schemacompany.com</email>
                <phone>555-5000</phone>
                <members>
                    <party xsi:type="personType" >
                        <name>Peter Parker</name>
                        <address>
                            <street>55 Pine Dr.</street>
                            <city>San Rafael</city>
                            <state>CA</state>
                            <zip>94903</zip>
                        </address>
                        <email>peterp@schemacompany.com</email>
                        <phone>555-2121</phone>
                        <ssn>999-99-9999</ssn>
                    </party>
                </members>
            </party>
        </members>
</organization>
```

Alternatively, you can create an XML instance document that does not validate against our new Organization schema. The instance document in Listing 19.14 does not match the Organization object you have defined because the xsi:type attribute of our organization member is not a type that derives from the partyType base.

**LISTING 19.14** Organization Example Document 2 (badorg.xml)

```xml
<organization
 xmlns:xsi="http://www.w3.org/2001/XMLSchema-instance"
 xmlns="://www.XMLSchemaReference.com/Examples/Ch19/" >
    <name>Quality Assurance</name>
    <address>
        <street>2000 Main St.</street>
        <city>San Rafael</city>
        <state>CA</state>
        <zip>94903</zip>
    </address>
    <email>bugs@schemacompany.com</email>
    <phone>555-5000</phone>
    <members>
        <party xsi:type="addressType">
            <street>11 Oak St.</street>
            <city>San Rafael</city>
            <state>CA</state>
            <zip>94903</zip>
        </party>
    </members>
</organization>
```

Using the example XML schema and the org.xml instance document, the following sections consider the problem of creating objects from this model.

## 19.6 Design Patterns

No discussion of object-oriented concepts would be complete without mentioning design patterns. Design patterns are one of the most powerful applications of object-oriented design. Object-oriented design patterns describe a common problem and describe the basis for an object-oriented solution to that problem. Design patterns are valuable because they describe a method of reuse that can be applied to a variety of applications. The concept of design patterns has been around for some time, but it might be best associated with the work of Gamma, Helm, Johnson, and Vlissides in their book *Design Patterns: Elements of Reusable Object-oriented Software* (Addison-Wesley, 1995). In this book, the authors collected some of the key patterns they had identified from their experiences as object-oriented designers.

### 19.6.1 Builder Pattern and XML Schemas

One of the design patterns used to construct objects is the Builder pattern. The Builder pattern provides an interface for creating complex objects whose construction process varies. In cases where an application must construct a tree of objects, the algorithm for construction can be complicated, and the objects that make up the tree can change depending on some state of the application.

The Builder pattern can be used very successfully in relation to XML schemas and XML serialization of objects. Many vendors and developers have looked at XML as a format on which to standardize object serialization, which requires software that would generate XML documents that contain the serialized representation of an object or set of objects. Much of the work in serialization involves verifying the format of the serialized state against the object structure. Using a validating parser, polymorphism, and XML schemas, this construction is easy to perform. This process can occur inside the Builder object, allowing creation of a class based on an instance document.

To use this pattern with an XML schema, you must pass in a path to an XML instance document. This is passed to the Builder object, which then loads the instance document and validates it against the correct XML schema. If the document is valid, the Builder object parses the instance to determine the structure type of each node. For a given derived type, the Builder object implements a Create<type> method that accepts a node of that type.

The Builder pattern described above fits well with the Party XML schema shown in Listing 19.12. In party.xsd, you have a non-instantiable class (Party) that in its derived classes can represent either an individual or a group. To construct such an object from a serialized state, you can use recursion to convert the XML representation into the objects. This construction process is somewhat complicated, however, so you can take advantage of the Builder pattern to encapsulate some of that complexity. The complexity is encapsulated inside a Builder object, which in this case is the PartyBuilder class. This class is responsible for creating any objects that derive from the Party non-instantiable class. PartyBuilder validates instance documents against party.xsd, parses the nodes of a valid document to find their structure types, and converts each node to an object that derives from the Party class. The object that corresponds to the document node is then returned as the newly created Party. Figure 19.2 illustrates the use of the Builder pattern with the Party object model.

The rest of this chapter provides some additional sample code for different languages. All the examples use the XML schema document party.xsd shown in Listing 19.12 to define a set of polymorphic business entities. In each language, we show source code that maps to the objects described in the XML schema.

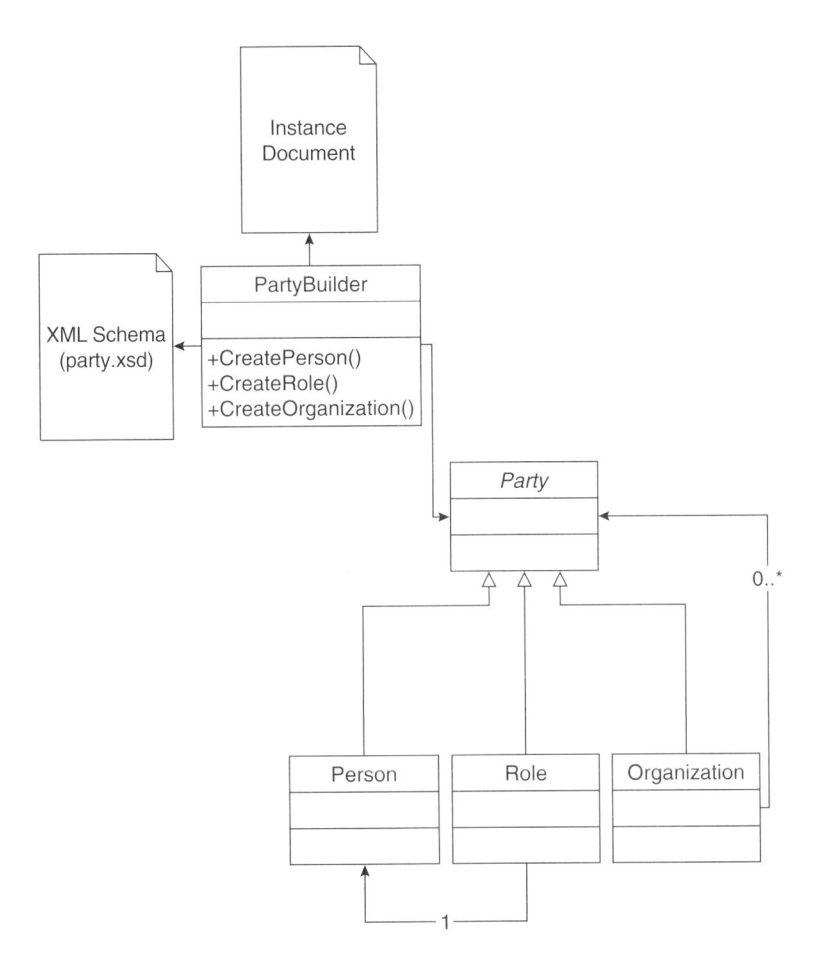

**FIGURE 19.2** *Party model with Builder pattern.*

## 19.7 Language Examples

In each of the examples that follow, we show a method for implementing the object structure of the Party schema in a particular language. We then explain how you might go about creating an Organization object from an XML document that conforms to your schema. In any of these examples, the Builder design pattern would let you create objects from an instance document. Describing how to implement this pattern with each of the languages in question and covering all the technologies needed (parsers, validation processes using those parsers, and so on) is too large a topic for this chapter. Assume for each example that a Builder object called "PartyBuilder" exists and that it can take a path to an instance document and return a reference to the created object.

## 19.7.1 Visual Basic

The implementation of the address type defined in our XML schema is straightforward. You can create a single class, `Address`, that models the structure of the `addressType` element of `party.xsd`. In Visual Basic 6.0, a class is created by going to the Project menu and selecting Add Class Module. This results in the addition of a new file to the project, with a .cls extension. Listing 19.15 shows the source code for the `Address` class, which would be stored in `Address.cls`.

**LISTING 19.15**  Address Class in Visual Basic 6.0 (Address.cls)

```
' Address
'
' A mailing address for a party.
'
Public street As String

Public city As String

Public state As String

Public zip As Integer
```

As stated earlier, there is no mechanism for implementation inheritance in Visual Basic 6.0. To create your `Party` base type, you must instead map it to an interface. This means you can only define the methods that will be required to provide the data that was modeled in the `partyType` type. Classes that derive from this type are required to implement each of these methods in order to be treated polymorphically as a party. Listing 19.16 shows the source code for `Party` class in Visual Basic 6.0.

**LISTING 19.16**  Party Class in Visual Basic 6.0 (Party.cls)

```
' Party
'
' Abstract data type for a business entity with a name,
' location, and contact information.
'
Public Property Get Name() As String

End Property

Public Property Let Name(rhs As String)

End Property
```

```
Public Property Get Address() As Address

End Property

Public Property Let Address(rhs As Address)

End Property

Public Property Get Email() As String

End Property

Public Property Let Email(rhs As String)

End Property

Public Property Get Phone() As String

End Property

Public Property Let Phone(rhs As String)

End Property
```

Now that you have defined your base type, you can derive from it in another class. In Visual Basic 6.0, interface inheritance is realized by using the 'Implements' keyword. For your Organization class, you must implement the Party interface so you can use polymorphism between all the Party objects. Listing 19.17 shows the source for the Organization class, as defined in Org.cls.

**LISTING 19.17**   Organization Class in Visual Basic 6.0 (Org.cls)

```
' Organization
'
' Abstract data type for a business entity with a name,
' location, and contact information.
'
Private m_name As String
Private m_address As Address
Private m_email As String
Private m_phone As String
Private m_ssn As String

Public Property Get Name() As String
    Name = m_name
End Property
```

*continues*

```
Public Property Let Name(rhs As String)
    m_name = rhs
End Property

Public Property Get Address() As Address
    Address = m_address
End Property

Public Property Let Address(rhs As Address)
    m_address = rhs
End Property

Public Property Get Email() As String
    Email = m_email
End Property

Public Property Let Email(rhs As String)
    m_email = rhs
End Property

Public Property Get Phone() As String
    Phone = m_phone
End Property

Public Property Let Phone(rhs As String)
    m_phone = rhs
End Property

Public Property Get Members() As Collection
    Members = m_members
End Property

Public Property Let Members(rhs As Collection)
    m_members = rhs
End Property
```

For the sake of brevity, we are not providing full listings for each of the objects. Every class that derives from the Party interface looks almost exactly like the Organization class, because it too must fill out each of the methods. The only difference between the classes is in the specific fields: Person adds the Social Security number, whereas Role adds a description and a person. Instead of repeating that code, look at the code in Listing 19.18, which is required to use these classes in Visual Basic 6.0.

**LISTING 19.18** Using VB 6.0 Party Classes

```
Public Sub PartyTest()
    Dim builder as New PartyBuilder
```

```
    Dim p as Party

    Set p = builder.CreateParty 'org.xml'

    Debug.Print p.name

    Dim org As Organization
    Set org = p

     ' Was p actually pointing to an Org?
    If org Is Nothing Then Exit Sub

    Dim member As Party

    For Each member In p.Members
        Debug.Print member.Name
    Next member
End Sub
```

In this example, the instance document `org.xml` is loaded by the Builder and returned as a Party interface reference. Because that reference actually points to an instance of the Organization class, you can set the two to equal and then check the value of the org variable to see if the coercion was possible.

## 19.7.2 C++

In C++, it is simple to implement the objects we have modeled inside `party.xsd`. All of the classes modeled in that XML schema are defined in Listing 19.19, `party.h`. In those C++ classes, we are using arrays for any variable-length datatypes and assuming reasonable lengths for the constants used. All the classes are contained in a namespace called `PartySchema`. The source code for the namespace and class definitions, `party.h`, is in Listing 19.19. Because we are only modeling the data of these classes in this code, the listing of the header will suffice.

**LISTING 19.19** Party Types in C++ (party.h)

```
namespace PartySchema
{
    class Address
    {
        public:
            char street[MAX_STREET_LEN];
            char city[MAX_CITY_LEN];
            char state[MAX_STATE_LEN];
            int zip;
    };
```

*continues*

```cpp
class Party
{
    public:
        char name[MAX_NAME_LEN];
        Address address;
        char email[MAX_EMAIL_LEN];
        char phone[MAX_PHONE_LEN];
    public:
        virtual void concreteParty( void ) = 0;
};

class Person : public Party
{
    public:
        char ssn[MAX_SSN_LEN];
    public:
        virtual void concreteParty( void ) {}
};

class Role : public Party
{
    public:
        char description[MAX_DESC_LEN];
        Person* person;
    public:
        virtual void concreteParty( void ) {}
};

class Organization : public Party
{
    public:
        Party* members[MAX_ORG_SIZE];
    public:
        virtual void concreteParty( void ) {}
};

};
```

> **TIP**
>
> In a real-world scenario, it is a good idea to use some kind of string classes for string data, and the members list of the Organization class shown in Listing 19.19 would be better implemented as a collection using STL (Standard Template Library) or some other class library.

Given these classes, you can create instances of the `Person`, `Role`, or `Organization` classes and use them in your code. Through the non-instantiable base class `Party`, you are able to treat any of these three classes polymorphically. In that case, the code in Listing 19.20 can be used.

**LISTING 19.20**  Polymorphism of C++ Party Classes

```
PartyBuilder builder;

Party* p = builder.CreateParty( 'org.xml' );

// Builder actually created an instance of Organization
// This will output the string 'Quality Assurance'
stdout << p->name;
```

### 19.7.3 C# and the .NET Framework

The code for C# resembles the C++ code shown in Listing 19.19. In C#, there is no separation of source code between headers and other source-code files. All source code is listed in a single .cs file. The source code that maps to the `Party` types is shown in Listing 19.21 for `party.cs`. As you can see, the source code is much cleaner because of the addition of the non-instantiable class type used to define `Party`.

**LISTING 19.21**  Party Types in C# (party.cs)

```
namespace PartySchema
{
    class Address
    {
        public string street;
        public string city;
        public string state;
        public int zip;
    }

    abstract class Party
    {
        public string name;
        public Address address;
        public string email;
        public string phone;
    }

    class Person : Party
    {
        public string ssn;
    }
```

*continues*

```
    class Role : Party
    {
        public string description;
        public Person person;
    }

    class Organization : Party
    {
        public Party members;
    }
}
```

With C# and the .NET Framework, developers reap the benefits of a language and development platform designed around XML. Because of this, much of the work of bridging the gap between objects and XML has been taken care of by the platform itself. The `System.Xml` namespace of the .NET Framework contains a number of classes and interfaces that simplify the use of XML and XML schemas. Another example of the advantages of the platform is the .NET XML Schema Definition Tool, or `xsd.exe`.

### 19.7.3.1 NET XML Schema Definition Tool

The .NET Framework is tightly integrated with XML, and that support extends to XML schemas. For example, a utility ships with the release of the .NET Framework to help with mapping XML schemas to objects. This utility is the XML Schema Definition Tool, or `xsd.exe`. The XML Schema Definition Tool is able to automatically perform the manual process described in this chapter: It can process an XML schema or document and generate class definitions that match. This utility is just one of the first of many code generators that will be compatible with XML schemas, so we examine its capabilities here to see how the mapping between objects and XML schemas will be realized by development tools.

The XML Schema Definition Tool can be executed using the arguments listed in Listing 19.22.

**LISTING 19.22**  `xsd.exe` Usage

```
xsd file.xsd {/classes | /dataset} [/element:element]
  [/language:language] [/namespace:namespace]
  [/outputdir:directory] [URI:uri]
```

The parameters to `xsd.exe` let you specify what should be generated from an XML schema, where it should be placed, what language in the .NET Framework should be used for code generation, and how the related namespace should be mapped. Mapping the namespace by using parameters helps work around the issues we saw in Section 19.4.4 with mapping the schema element to a namespace-level language construct.

To get an idea of how the XML Schema Definition Tool works, we can execute it against our Party schema. The usage in that case would be as follows:

xsd party.xsd /classes /language:CS /namespace:PartySchema

From this call, the XML Schema Definition Tool generates the file `party.cs`, which is shown in Listing 19.23.

**LISTING 19.23**  Party Types in C# (party.cs) Generated By xsd.exe

```
//------------------------------
// <autogenerated>
//     This code was generated by a tool.
//     Runtime Version: 1.0.3705.0
//
//     Changes to this file may cause incorrect behavior and
//     will be lost if the code is regenerated.
// </autogenerated>
//------------------------------

//
// This source code was auto-generated by xsd,
// Version=1.0.3705.0.
//
namespace PartySchema {

    using System.Xml.Serialization;

    /// <remarks/>
    [System.Xml.Serialization.XmlTypeAttribute(
     Namespace=
     "http://www.XMLSchemaReference.com/Examples/Ch19/")]
    [System.Xml.Serialization.XmlRootAttribute("organization",
     Namespace=
     "http://www.XMLSchemaReference.com/Examples/Ch19/",
     IsNullable=false)]
    public class organizationType : partyType {

        /// <remarks/>
        [System.Xml.Serialization.XmlArrayItemAttribute(
         "party", IsNullable=false)]
        public partyType[] members;
    }

    /// <remarks/>
    [System.Xml.Serialization.XmlTypeAttribute(
     Namespace=
```

*continues*

```
    "http://www.XMLSchemaReference.com/Examples/Ch19/")]
[System.Xml.Serialization.XmlIncludeAttribute(
 typeof(organizationType))]
[System.Xml.Serialization.XmlIncludeAttribute(
 typeof(roleType))]
[System.Xml.Serialization.XmlIncludeAttribute(
 typeof(personType))]
public abstract class partyType {

    /// <remarks/>
    public string name;

    /// <remarks/>
    public addressType address;

    /// <remarks/>
    public string email;

    /// <remarks/>
    public string phone;
}

/// <remarks/>
[System.Xml.Serialization.XmlTypeAttribute(
 Namespace=
 "http://www.XMLSchemaReference.com/Examples/Ch19/")]
public class addressType {

    /// <remarks/>
    public string street;

    /// <remarks/>
    public string city;

    /// <remarks/>
    public string state;

    /// <remarks/>
    public System.Decimal zip;
}

/// <remarks/>
[System.Xml.Serialization.XmlTypeAttribute(
 Namespace="
 http://www.XMLSchemaReference.com/Examples/Ch19/")]
public class roleType : partyType {
```

```
        /// <remarks/>
        public string description;

        /// <remarks/>
        public personType person;
    }

    /// <remarks/>
    [System.Xml.Serialization.XmlTypeAttribute(
     Namespace=
     "http://www.XMLSchemaReference.com/Examples/Ch19/")]
    public class personType : partyType {

        /// <remarks/>
        public string ssn;
    }
}
```

The executable has generated a file that maps the XML schema to classes in much the same way you did manually, but with one obvious addition. The class attributes that appear before each class in the source listing are used by the .NET Framework to allow direct serialization between XML and objects. By tagging each class type in the namespace with the `XmlTypeAttribute`, the Framework is able to use XML schemas to validate against the serialized state contained in an instance document. This is similar to the approach used earlier with the Builder pattern, but in this case the development platform takes on that responsibility. As XML schemas are adopted more widely in development tools, this type of functionality will be available for a variety of platforms.

# Document-oriented Schemas

**CHAPTER**
# 20

## IN THIS CHAPTER

**20.1** Why Use XML for Documents? 542

**20.2** Creating a Schema for a Set of Documents: Document Analysis 544

**20.3** Implementing Document Processing 548

An XML document is always a tree-structured data set. For applications involving ordinary relational databases, selecting the appropriate tree structure to match the data is fairly straightforward. The tricky part is ensuring that the datatypes used can be implemented in the database and vice versa.

On the other hand, when XML is used to structure "real documents" (technical books, novels, textbooks, catalogs, mathematical and chemical papers—the list goes on and on), figuring out the structure can be difficult because of the sheer number of variations.

Schemas for documents tend to use the structuring capabilities of XML Schema more heavily, rather than its datatyping capabilities.

This chapter provides an overview of each half of the problem. But first, "Why bother?"

## 20.1 Why Use XML for Documents?

You gain several advantages when your primary-source documents are XML.

- Authors gain control over correct display of content without being style specialists (or even having to know the styles to be used).

    Authors are content experts; editors are style experts. Unfortunately, the traditional mechanism of communication between the two is a display style that might be called "manuscript"; it is traditionally very limited, and—for technical work especially—conveying all the necessary content distinctions is difficult.

    Editors are not content experts. Given the restrictions of the manuscript display style, they must sometimes guess which final display a given phrase should have because they aren't sure of the semantics the author intends (and probably don't understand the esoteric distinctions). This leads to the classic complaint

    > That's a *wodget*, not a *widget*! You've completely destroyed the meaning by making that *wodget* look like a *widget*!

    followed rapidly by insistence that the author must have absolute control over the formatting. Unfortunately, many authors are poor style designers.

    With content-based XML markup, authors can specify precisely the semantic intent of each phrase that might need special handling, without having to know—or be trusted to implement—the final display style, and they can be confident that their intended semantics will not be (from their point of view) "butchered by an ignorant editor."

- Editors can ensure that display conventions are followed.

    After a document style has been designed and implemented in the software that produces display-oriented material from the source XML documents, the editor can be confident that when the content expert (the author) indicates particular semantics for a phrase, the system will translate it into correct markup.

Editors can spend their time worrying about authors' grammar and organization and—at the other end of the process—about organization of the document's component parts and the overall appearance of the material. (The latter is most common in magazines rather than books, but is also important for some kinds of books.)

- Display conventions can be changed without requiring any "fixing" of primary-source documents.

   New styles come in vogue; books are transferred from one division of a publisher to another while they are being written; books are republished at a later date. There are many reasons a display style might change.

- Documents can be displayed in multiple ways without revision. For example, they can be produced as printed documents, as Web-based "documents," or as spoken word. Each display medium has different capabilities, shortcomings, and conventions, so the styles must be tailored to each medium and might not be the same.

   For example, with Web-based display, color is usually available, but variations in font, font variant (italic, slant, upright, bold, and so on), and size are not as easily controlled. (And they shouldn't be—people with visual handicaps need to control the size and font themselves.)

   Comparing between the conventions of the traditional written and spoken word illustrates the utility of content-based markup even when the only intent is to "publish" the material. For example, *semantic emphasis* is generally indicated in written text by switching to an italic font, but in spoken text it is indicated by a rise in pitch and volume. Technical terms might also be italicized but spoken with a slight pause before and after, along with a slight "push" of raised volume (but not pitch) at the beginning of each word. Phrases used with unusual or special meanings might be enclosed in double quotes in print but spoken in an manner similar to technical terms—possibly even accompanied with a two-hand gesture drawing quotation marks in the air. Text-to-speech is already here, and XML-based schemes are being worked up to facilitate text-to-speech conversion with more natural-sounding presentation. Content-based markup plus the markup-conversion capabilities of XSLT (see Section 20.3) make it possible to utilize these new presentation mechanisms as they arise. (One can easily imagine a virtual speaker implementing gestures as well as sound in the future.)

   Content-based markup enables the display conventions to be adapted to new media much more readily.

- Documents can more easily be "data-mined," and can be excerpted for use in other documents.

   As just one example of the latter, consider the possibility of a general-purpose, multi-volume encyclopedia with articles on many subjects. If, for example, all the sports-related articles could be easily identified, they could be extracted and compiled into another document, which could be given a different, "sporty" format and published as a one-volume sports encyclopedia at a relatively small cost.

- Standard parts of documents can be automatically generated: lists of figures, tables of contents, indexes, cross-references to other chapters and sections, and references to floating tables, figures, or code listings.

## 20.2 Creating a Schema for a Set of Documents: Document Analysis

The process of examining a collection of documents and describing its "shape" by using a DTD or schema is called "document analysis." The process works best when a schema specialist works with a cadre of people already dealing with the documents whose structure is to be analyzed (rather than doing it alone, with just sample documents, or rather than having some untrained person doing the analysis without a schema specialist). In this section, we call the cadre plus the specialist the "team."

In the following sections, we cover a sample scenario showing how a document analysis might proceed and a few examples of things a document analyst must look for.

### 20.2.1 Scenario: A Document Analysis

The following kinds of people should be in the document analysis cadre. It generally works best if there are two or three from each group, except perhaps the senior editor, resulting in a cadre of about ten people.

- Those who have been responsible for writing or rewriting the documents to be analyzed. They might be called "authors," "writers," or "editors," depending on the corporate culture. They will have a good, albeit possibly subconscious, understanding of the kinds of content found in various parts of the documents.

- Those who have been responsible for formatting and publishing the documents to be analyzed. They will complement the authors and will have different insights into the real structure of the documents. Two subgroups should be represented: *editors*, who make decisions about style, and *compositors*, who implement those decisions and make sure the final output is formatted correctly. (Sometimes *composition* is called "production".)

- A manager, possibly called a "senior editor" or "executive editor" (again, depending on the corporate culture) who is familiar with the documents and has the authority to make decisions when structure anomalies are found.

- Those who will be responsible for maintaining the schema as it evolves over time and/or will be responsible for configuring the various XML processing products to be used. They might not yet be content/structure experts but will have to become so. Participation in the document analysis is the best and fastest way to immerse them in this area.

### 20.2.1.1 The First Meeting: Roughing Out the Structure

The first meeting is scheduled for an entire week but probably terminates by the fourth day. Two things are done during this first meeting:

- During the first day and a half or so, the team engages in a structured XML exercise. The purpose of this exercise is to quickly familiarize everyone with some common terminology and—most important—help them understand the "XML point of view" toward textual data. This often involves quite a shift of mental gears—a "paradigm shift."

  The information will come too fast and too furiously—like drinking from a fire hose, some say—but the attendees don't need to get all the details consciously sorted out right away. Only the schema maintainers have to worry about the details, and they will get extra help and training down the road. What is important is that attendees start to pick up the new paradigm intuitively. Reinforcement comes during the rest of the week.

- Sometime during the second day, the exercise ends and the real document analysis begins. The specialist helps find the various parts of the documents and get descriptions of those parts on paper (or PC file). Within a couple of days, all will have a good understanding and description of what the cadre members (the subject-matter experts) *believe* is the structure of the documents. Together, the team will also have found, by then, a number of anomalies: things that are in existing documents that don't fit the structure cadre members originally thought the documents were following. (Anomalies *will* be found. It has never failed yet.)

This terminates the first week's effort for most of the cadre. The schema-maintainers-in-training, at least one of whom serves as the scribe for the team, will get some extra help from the specialist to correctly cast their notes in the form of a good schema (or possibly, to begin with, a good DTD, since that will be easier to input without fancy tools).

### 20.2.1.2 Between Meetings: The Anomaly Search

By now the cadre members need a chance to sort out what's been done, let their heads clear, and take care of all the other work that piled up on their desks while they were meeting all day, every day. The schema specialist is available by phone if anything needs clarification, but stays out of the way for two to four weeks.

There is work to be done before the next formal meeting of the team, however. Specifically, the cadre members now make a page-by-page, document-by-document search for more kinds of anomalies. This search can be done part time and be spread over several weeks.

### 20.2.1.3 The Second Meeting: "Sorting Sheep"

The second team meeting probably occurs two to four weeks after the first one ends. It might be scheduled for a week, just to be safe, but more likely takes about three days. The team must work through the collection of anomalies and separate the sheep from the goats—decide which anomalies are useful and should be accounted for in the schema and which are just the result of a writer's "getting the bit in his teeth" and deviating unnecessarily from the way other writers handle similar material.

It's important to remember at this time that similar material should have similar presentations, especially when the material is technical. Otherwise, readers will waste time trying to figure out how the differently presented material is different when it isn't different at all. This is why a manager with decision-making authority should already be involved in the analysis. If not involved, that person probably won't have picked up the "XML point of view" and is liable not to understand the decisions that must be made.

### 20.2.1.4 Moving Onward

At the end of the second meeting, a pretty good schema emerges. It won't anticipate every unusual situation that might come down the pike in the future, but it can be used as is. That's the object of a document analysis: a schema that is usable. A well-designed schema can be extended, normally without requiring any modification of existing documents, when new requirements come to light.

> **CAUTION**
>
> Peterson's Maxim: "A cast-in-concrete schema is an obsolete schema." Always plan your schema *and your processes that use that schema* to be easily extended.

What is next? With a usable schema in hand, you can get on with developing your applications. And you can begin conversion of legacy data: all the existing documents that have to be converted to XML and to the newly developed schema. In most cases there is legacy data to be converted; these documents are the foundations on which revised and republished documents will be built. The schema specialist initially helps make the choices and develop applications. You might decide to convert your legacy data yourself, but more likely you will decide to have a conversion-specialist firm convert it for you. You need a DTD or schema to begin that effort, because that is what defines the form the documents must have after conversion. You can now begin converting—or start up your conversion contractor.

## 20.2.2 Structures to Look For

Some structures are obvious—especially because the structure of SGML documents (and hence of XML) was originally designed to capture the structure of "real, published documents." Nonetheless, some structures seem to be well hidden, at least at first glance. Discerning hidden but important structures can make the difference between a mediocre document analysis and a useful one.

### 20.2.2.1 Big Pieces

Most documents are logically hierarchical: A book has front matter, a body, and back matter. The body has parts, which have chapters, which have sections, which have subsections, . . . . There might be differences in the terminology within a corporate culture—for example, some might call the large parts "sections" and the small sections "numbered paragraphs." Some of the levels (such as parts) might be omitted. Some or all of these levels will begin with a title, sometimes called a "heading." Most writing, at least in most Western European languages, winds up in paragraphs. But it's all hierarchical: Each part is made up of some smaller parts. Ultimately, some parts are just plain raw text characters.

### 20.2.2.2 Specialized Pieces

Certain kinds of documents have structure elements that have specific semantics: Each chapter might have an *introduction* or a *summary*. There might be other special-purpose sections, such as in this book's Chapter 12, where each section that describes one or more specific datatypes has a subsection listing the facets available for derivations, a subsection telling about the datatypes derived from the subject datatypes and the datatypes from which they are derived, and a subsection that suggests when another datatype might be more appropriate. If many documents—or even chapters or sections in a document—have the same structure, you can ensure that nothing is overlooked by creating special element types for those specific-topic subsections and creating content models that require them.

### 20.2.2.3 Paragraphs and Things That Break Them

Paragraphs typically include running text and things that break running text. Running text includes phrases that need *emphasis* in one form or another: foreign phrases, titles, new terms being introduced, short quotations, or words being used with weird, unusual, or special meanings—let your imagination run! Then there are the subject-matter-dependent, specialized words and phrases. For example, some parts of this book were originally authored in XML: We separately tracked element type names, attribute type names, XML samples, names of facets, and a number of other XML- and Schema-specific phrases. When we began authoring, we didn't know what display format would be used for all of them. And we didn't have to. (That is a big advantage of XML-based authoring.)

What breaks running text? Displayed formulas, long quotations, lists, small tables, code listings, . . . . (You can have fun debating whether lists and tables occur *within* paragraphs or *between* paragraphs. But it is particularly easy to make up examples where, say, an equation should be displayed for emphasis but is grammatically part of a sentence that extends both fore and aft of the equation. If the equation is part of the sentence, it must be part of the paragraph—sentences do not span across paragraph boundaries.)

Some things clearly do not belong to paragraphs. The Notes, Tips, and Warnings you find in this book clearly occur *between* paragraphs (and occasionally "float"). Other things, usually for appearance reasons, regularly float when published: figures, large tables, long listings, footnotes or endnotes, and "sidebars" (separate mini-articles closely attached to a primary article in a magazine) are all examples. They are usually printed near where they are first referenced but may be moved to the top of the page, or even to another page. Such things are *referenced* by number or title in the text, and provision for a number or title must be made in the content model of corresponding element types.

### 20.2.2.4 Specialized and Non-obvious Structures

Accommodating automatic table-of-contents generation is quite easy when every chapter, section, and subsection is marked and its title identified. Automatic indexing requires additional markup and a specialized processor to generate the index, as does automatic generation of cross-references (identifying chapter and section numbers and/or titles and then automatically generating copies where the reference occurs). This is especially useful when titles and sequence of chapters and sections have not been locked in when the reference was written. You can use the capabilities of ID/IDREF or the more flexible capabilities of schema-based identity constraints and a special post-processor that can generate the copies automatically.

Recognizing logical structure, rather than just physical appearance, can be tricky. Some years ago, the U.S. Department of Defense CALS documentation included a table that actually had eight entries for each thing that it had data about: Each thing had eight "properties" whose values were given in the table, but the physical display in the book used a three-column table, with five pieces of data listed in each cell in the last column. If you look, you can find even more interesting logical-structure-versus-display examples. Find a copy of the Alaska Fish and Game Regulations—or just get the owner's manual for your car and try to figure out the logical structure (not just the display structure). With many car brands, the latter is an excellent exercise. Catching all these unexpected structures in your documents is one reason it pays to have an experienced document analyst help with your document analysis.

## 20.2.3 More Detail

The problem of correctly finding an appropriate description of the structure of a set of books or magazines is complex—it warrants an entire book. Fortunately, an excellent text, *Developing SGML DTDs*[1], covers the process. Although it was written for SGML, the processes it describes are the same; XML and SGML were cut from the same mold.

## 20.3 Implementing Document Processing

Without a good system to make use of the resulting schemas, a document analysis is of little value. Following are some advantages (described more detail in Section 20.1) that can accrue with XML-based authoring, editing, and publishing:

---

[1] Maler, Eve and Jeanne El Andaloussi. *Developing SGML DTDs: From Text to Model to Markup.* Englewood Cliffs, NJ: Prentice Hall, 1995.

- Authors gain control over correct display of content without being style specialists (or even having to know the styles to be used).
- Editors can ensure that display conventions are followed.
- Display conventions can be changed without requiring any "fixing" of primary-source documents.
- Content-based markup allows the display conventions to be adapted to new media much more easily.
- Documents can more easily be "data-mined" and excerpted for use in other documents.
- Standard parts of documents can be automatically generated: lists of figures, tables of contents, indexes, cross-references to other chapters and sections, and references to floating tables, figures, or code listings.

## 20.3.1 Help for the Author

Experience shows that documents written in a non-XML-aware environment (for example, by using a typical word processor program) are difficult to convert to XML that contains content-based markup. If the author doesn't indicate why something is italic or quoted or whatever, it takes *very* smart artificial intelligence capability to automatically discern the reason for using the special display. And it is even more difficult, if the style is such that there is nothing special about the display, to detect special terms that should be identified for later data-mining.

Accordingly, the best implementation provides XML-smart authoring tools for the author. There are quite a few on the market; the market is evolving rapidly, so we will not try to recommend specific tools. Attend one of the many XML trade shows and see what's available when you are ready to make a selection.

A good authoring tool provides several features:

- The capability to see the XML structure via representations of the tags embedded in the document.
- The capability to suppress representations of the tags embedded in the document.
- The capability to see the current editing location in the XML structure via a separate display area.
- The capability to display different types of elements (and elements of the same type in different contexts or with different attributes) differently. The options should include font and type style (underlining, strike-through, slant-versus-upright, small caps, weight, and so on), size, glyph color, background color, and affixed text.

It turns out that carefully marked-up text sometimes has deeply nested markup—enough that displaying all the markup makes understanding the interrupted text impossible. Hence the requirement to be able to hide the markup itself.

On the other hand, authoring involves a lot of rereading of already written material. If the author has no indication of what markup has been put in place, it is very difficult to check whether markup is correct and to ensure that parallel constructs are marked up in the same manner. Hence the requirement to be able to display the markup, at least in some iconic form.

Most people have learned many common display conventions. There are the "everybody does this" conventions, such as displaying paragraphs as blocks of running text and running on (and word-wrapping) most of the text within the paragraph. Titles of chapters and sections are typically in a different font, height, and/or weight, with some indication of how deeply nested in the subsection hierarchy they are. Quotations are enclosed in quotation marks. Some display conventions vary quite a bit, such as the convention for indicating "use" versus "mention"—in this book, we either display the material on a separate line or enclose it in *single* quotation marks. Various writers use various conventions and often choose between different conventions in the same document. The important point is that if an authoring tool can select different display styles, it can cue the author as to what the underlying markup is even when the markup is being suppressed. This is often the easiest mode for authors to write and reread in.

> **NOTE**
>
> It is *not* necessary to provide WYSIWYG display in the sense of accurately showing the same fonts, layouts, line-wraps, and page-breaks that will occur in the final publication. Indeed, as more and more material is prepared that is intended for display using disparate media with conflicting styles, WYSIWYG is impossible. And for well-designed XML markup schemas, authors will likely need to track the accuracy of their markup in details that don't differentiate in the final product, once a particular display medium and matching style are selected.
>
> This is why control over text color, background color, and such are useful: They can be used to differentiate between different types of elements. Then authors need only occasionally make the markup visible, when they need to refresh their memory as to which colors mean what element types or they need to see just where their cursors are within strings of contiguous markup.
>
> This approach to text display is sometimes called "what you see is what you *need*," or "WYSIWYN," a term coined by one of the authors in 1994. "What you see is what you get" was popularized by the comedian Flip Wilson, with his character Geraldine, decades ago.

## 20.3.2 Help for the Editor

Programs designed to facilitate the input and subsequent modification of textual data are often called editors. Authors should have a good *editor program*, but in this section we are talking about what helps the human editor.

Human editors have two jobs: reviewing and correcting text submitted by authors and ensuring adherence to the display style selected for the material. For the first job, you need a good *editor program*; for the second, you need good *production software*. The former is discussed in the preceding section, the latter in the following section.

Some WYSIWYG editing programs have specialized facilities for tracking changes. With a good XML-based *WYSIWYN* editor, specialized facilities might not be necessary; mechanisms for tracking changes can be built into the schema. An XML editor that can lock certain parts from change facilitates the process; the state of the art is getting there.

With a versatile formatting and composition system, most of the style decisions can be implemented in software, rather than relying on "wetware" (humans). When style is in software, the same things get formatted the same way every time. If the formatter is wrong, it is wrong every time, and the wrongness is usually obvious.

## 20.3.3 Automating Production

When you have a process in place that provides well-marked-up, carefully edited documents in an XML format, you still have to publish them somehow. The structure- and content-based XML markup does not itself include any instructions on how to format and display the material, in print or otherwise.

### 20.3.3.1 Stylesheet-based Formatting

The ideal formatting system for XML-marked-up input is stylesheet-based. A *stylesheet* is a separate document (or dataset) that describes how each type of element should be formatted—much like the best editor programs but with different options. For example, the stylesheet might specify that a section title gets:

- An automatically generated number prefixed to the title text
- Helvetica bold 18-point formatting
- "Poured" into a display area providing 30 points of vertical separation from the preceding display area, unless this display area is at the top of a page (which is also a display area), in which the title display area is nested

Display-area models such as just described are currently in vogue for describing the relative placement of text glyphs. Specifying font characteristics is quite standard. Providing enough flexibility to cover oddball situations and worldwide writing, text-flow, and formatting conventions is not so trivial. Careful development of this sort of formatting model was begun in the

SGML community and resulted in the DSSSL Standard, ISO/IEC 10179: 1996, *Document Style Semantics and Specification Language (DSSSL)*.

Many of the same developers have recently finished the W3C XML XSL Recommendation, *Extensible Stylesheet Language (XSL) Version 1.0*, http://www.w3.org/TR/xsl/. This defines a similar model, using XML as its syntax and designed to work with XML, and implementations should be available soon. Until then, proprietary formatting stylesheet implementations are available and adequate for many situations.

For many simple documents, this is all you need. But for more complex formatting situations, the order of presentation of the material might not be the same as the order in which it logically occurs in the XML document. Or perhaps specifying a stylesheet where instances of element types in different contexts have different *type names* is easier. In such situations, it would be very useful to be able to translate elements of a given type in a given context into elements with a different *type name* or in a different location in the document. DSSSL devised a language for describing such transformations; the W3C XSL Working Group earlier designed an XML-based transformation language in the XSLT Recommendation, *XSL Transformations (XSLT)*, http://w3.org/TR/xslt. XSLT transformation processors already exist and can be used with proprietary stylesheet- or XSL-based systems.

For more information about XSL and XSLT, see http://w3.org/Style/XSL.

### 20.3.3.2 Formatting-markup-based Formatting

Many proprietary and essentially public-domain systems for formatting already exist. Indeed, for Web-based presentation, HTML is often the markup of choice. There are several advantages to using HTML:

- The markup is very close to XML.
- Many available presentation systems accept HTML input. (They're called "web browsers.")
- XSLT-based transformers can transform XML documents directly into HTML documents that display properly.

Unfortunately, HTML and Web browsers do not provide adequate formatting control for printed documents. (Even for Web display of things like mathematics, they are inadequate at present.) For print, at least, there are existing proprietary and near-public-domain systems that do very good jobs of formatting—even word processors do an adequate job for undemanding applications.

Most of these systems have a proprietary means of input of ASCII text with appropriate markup in the form of escape sequences for special characters and formatting instructions. Two such examples are $T_{E}X$-based systems and systems that understand the *Rich Text Format* (RTF) markup language promulgated by Microsoft. Many other proprietary system-specific markup languages exist as well.

(Some parts of this book were originally authored in XML and then translated into RTF.)

In order to use a T$_E$X-, RTF-, or proprietary-markup-based system, you need to translate the XML markup into the appropriate non-XML-based markup for the system being used. A number of SGML- and XML-aware translators are available; all the fancy ones are proprietary. Some programmers have successfully built Perl- and Python-based translators. Many generic text-manipulation languages such as Perl have XML-aware extensions; some are available in the public domain. Such translators complete the chain of processing necessary to get from XML to formatted-for-print output. If the translation process requires it, the combination of a transformation (to a specialized XML vocabulary designed to assist the process), followed by a translation into the markup language of the formatter, followed by the formatting itself gets you from an XML document to ready-to-print Postscript files.

Look for implementations of the new XSL Recommendation (*Extensible Stylesheet Language (XSL) Version 1.0,* `http://www.w3.org/TR/xsl/`) over and above XSLT to provide standard ways of dealing with the document layout process in the future.

Unfortunately, sometimes the formatting rules you want (such as placement of floating figures and tables when there are a lot of them) are more complicated than can be handled by the system you have—or can afford. Or you might have layout problems that are almost artistic in nature. At this point, you must turn from software to "wetware": human layout artists. This is often the case with magazines. Blending articles and advertisements, and deciding where to cut articles and continue them further on in the issue is indeed an art that must be done by humans.

# Application-oriented Schemas

**CHAPTER 21**

## IN THIS CHAPTER

- 21.1 XML Applications    556
- 21.2 Role of XML Schemas    558
- 21.3 Describing Applications    560
- 21.4 Application Structure    561
- 21.5 Transporting XML    563
- 21.6 Describing Applications    569
- 21.7 Example Application    572

# Application-oriented Schemas
## CHAPTER 21

This chapter discusses how XML schemas can be used to define the structure of an XML application. An XML application is a program or system that accepts XML as input, returns XML as output, or both. XML schemas give us the opportunity to define what XML should look like and to describe the data we use in our applications. Because we can describe our data in detail, schemas make a powerful tool for not only validating the data we work with, but also for describing the arguments of the system and the operations it is capable of performing. This chapter looks at how we can put XML schemas to work both inside and outside our XML applications.

## 21.1 XML Applications

The uses to which XML schemas can be applied within an application are too numerous to list. When discussing application-oriented schemas, we are addressing a specific subset of the potential applications that use XML schemas. Specifically, we are focusing on applications that utilize XML as their mechanism for data transfer. These applications define one or more simple and complex types in an XML schema. These simple and complex types are mapped to application types and application arguments that are manipulated by the business logic.

### 21.1.1 Fundamentals of XML Applications

The basic architecture of an XML application is shown in Figure 21.1. The application consumes and produces XML. That XML is transported between the input source, business logic, and output target, using an identified transport protocol.

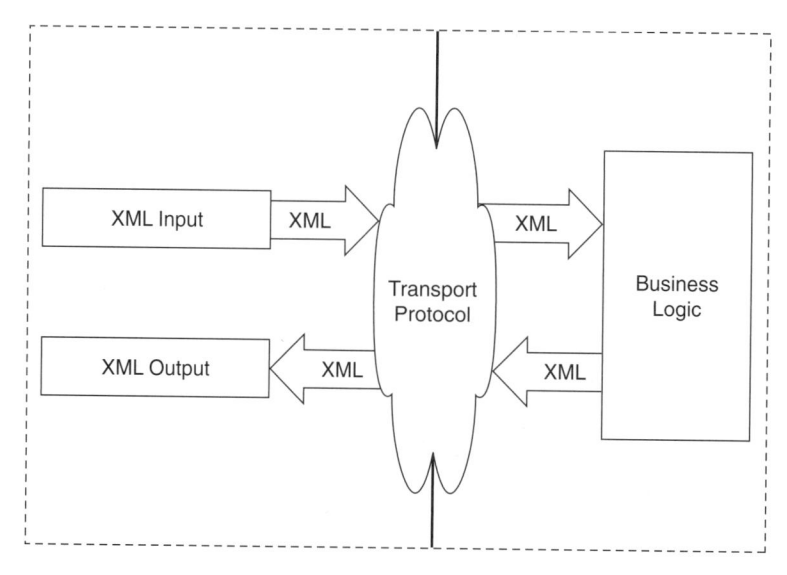

**FIGURE 21.1**  *Generic XML application structure.*

## 21.1.2 XML Input and Output

We can begin to understand the structure of the application by examining its inputs and outputs. In an XML application, any inputs and outputs are XML instances. The complexity of the XML instances differ greatly, depending on the needs of the application. It is even possible that depending on the operation, multiple input XML instance documents or output documents might be involved.

In addition, depending on the model and the transport involved, the actor (a user of a system) that invokes the application and passes the input XML might not be the eventual recipient of the output XML. For example, an application might simply implement a remote procedure call that would return information in XML format based on a database lookup. In that case, the call would probably be handled in a request-response style; within the request-response convention, the sender and recipient would be the same. In another case, you might want to add some additional information to the input XML and route it to another application for processing. In that case, you have still implemented an XML application, but you have implemented one with a communications pattern other than request-response.

## 21.1.3 Transport Protocol

In a traditional application, the transport protocol for inputs and outputs could be thought of as the call stack. Inputs are placed on the stack and popped off for manipulation by the logic of the application, and the outputs are then pushed onto the stack. In a similar fashion, the transport protocol of an XML application functions as the means of moving values into and out of operations that occur at the business logic level.

## 21.1.4 Business Logic

At the heart of any application is the business logic, and XML applications are no different. The business logic of an application defines its operations. Based on the input XML as provided by the transport, the business logic generates some output XML that is then returned to the transport protocol for delivery.

The method in which the business logic can be implemented varies, depending on the application or framework used. In .NET, remote communication can occur by using XML and the Simple Object Access Protocol (SOAP), but that communication is transparent to the developer because the framework is responsible for converting XML into arguments, method calls, and return values. The business logic has been abstracted from both the transport protocol and the XML data. Alternatively, an application could be written using a scripting language such as Active Server Pages (ASP) or JavaServer Pages (JSP) and an XML parser or transformation engine. In that case, the application has business logic that is aware of both the transport and the true format of the XML input and output.

## 21.2 Role of XML Schemas

At the foundation of any application, XML or otherwise, lies the type system on which that application is built. Any application is limited in what it can do by the types of available data. Before XML schemas, the structure of an XML application was difficult to define. The best method for defining the XML used in an application was a DTD, which was unfortunately very difficult to work with programmatically. With XML schemas, you can generate and manipulate type information for your applications with the same ease that you have in using XML for data. XML schemas also allow for a much more descriptive set of type information to be defined than a DTD. With XML as both your type system and your data, you can create applications that are flexible and open.

In creating applications, you can also create an XML schema that defines the structure and content passed into and out of the system. Creating such an XML schema provides three key benefits:

- You can describe to the outside world the data format your application accepts.
- You can take advantage of schema validation to programmatically validate the data passing through the application.
- The XML schema you create can help describe the structure of the application itself.

### 21.2.1 Validation of Data

As we have seen throughout this book, XML schemas can be used to perform a validity test against an XML instance. There are several parsers and tools that can be used to programmatically validate an instance document against an XML schema. In relation to the applications we are describing, this validation process becomes an important step in the data transfer between *tiers*, partitions of the application that are separated by process or machine boundaries.

The validation of data we are describing is something most developers take for granted in a high-level language. For example, in many languages, if a function requires a numeric argument and receives a string, an error results. This error (hopefully) occurs at compile time or, in a language with a more relaxed data type system, it might be a run-time error. This error describes some kind of type mismatch that helps the developer locate the erroneous function call. In the case of XML, without a type validation system such as XML schemas, the developer needs to manually parse and examine each entity of the input XML document to ensure that it conforms to the expected format.

### 21.2.2 Describing Arguments

We have established that XML serves as the data transfer mechanism for the applications we are discussing. Typically, you can think of this XML as a source document and a target document. The source and target have a defined structure, and if an XML schema exists that defines this structure for validation purposes, it also functions as a method of publishing a description of the structure in question.

Just as an XML schema can be used to define what an XML instance must contain, it can also define what you would like that XML instance to become as a result of your application execution. In your applications, the XML data in question is analogous to the arguments passed to and values returned from a function. Consider the function signature shown in Listing 21.1. Listing 21.1 describes a simple operation and the arguments and return values involved in that operation. Given a Social Security number, the method FindEmployee returns the data for an employee.

**LISTING 21.1**  Employee Lookup (C#)

```
class Employee
{
    public string name;
    public string ssn;
    public string job;
}

class Application
{
    public Employee FindEmployee( string ssn )
    {
        *   *   *   *   *
    }
}
```

The arguments and return values define the basic units of the operation: A string identifier is the input argument and the output is a complex type representing an employee. The schema fragment shown in Listing 21.2 defines the same data. In this case, we have used an XML schema to describe the input and output associated with the application. The ssn element type describes the input argument, and the employee element type describes the output. In addition to describing the data with these elements, we can also use XML schemas to describe the application itself.

**LISTING 21.2**  Example Employee Schema Fragment

```
<xsd:element name="employee" type="employeeType"/>
<xsd:element name="ssn" type="xsd:string"/>
<xsd:complexType name="employeeType">
    <xsd:sequence>
        <xsd:element name="name" type="xsd:string" />
        <xsd:element name="ssn"  type="xsd:string" />
        <xsd:element name="job"  type="xsd:string" />
```

*continues*

```
        </xsd:sequence>
</xsd:complexType>
```

## 21.3 Describing Applications

As we stated earlier, you can use an XML schema to describe the results you expect from an operation. The method by which that operation is implemented is not important. It is possible to look at the method signature and determine what inputs and outputs are required to perform the operation. Those argument types are relatively easy to express in an XML schema, either as built-in types or as some additional simple or complex type that you define. From a simple string to a complex complete XML instance, the facilities in an XML schema give you all the power you need to describe the arguments to an XML application.

With the example shown in Listings 21.1 and 21.2, it was not difficult to map the application arguments used in the code to the structure defined in the XML schema. However, if you were to continue this process and try to reverse-engineer the code from the XML schema fragment, you would produce something like the code in Listing 21.3.

**LISTING 21.3** Employee Lookup Code Revisited (C#)

```
class Employee
{
    public string name;
    public string ssn;
    public string job;
}

// Assuming there is an application, what does it do???
class Application
{
    // No code defined
}
```

Just from reading the structure of the XML schema fragment in Listing 21.2, we do not have enough information to identify the inputs and outputs for the application. That is why in the schema fragment shown in Listing 21.3, we are missing one key component: the method itself. It is important that we have defined the parts that make up an operation, but without any glue to combine them, they do not describe a functional piece of business logic. The schema document that contains those application arguments does not describe the manner in which the operation can be triggered. Using XML schemas, you can create a simple description of your application that provides this information.

## 21.4 Application Structure

The basic structure of an XML application, shown in Figure 21.1, remains the same, but specific applications define additional behavior that can shape the flow of data in the application. The needs of the application decide where input XML comes from, how it is transported to the application for execution, and how and where the output XML is delivered. There are many different kinds of XML applications, differentiated by their input and output handling. Three common kinds are the *sovereign application*, the *request-response application*, and the *routing application*.

### 21.4.1 Sovereign

Although it is often the first scenario that comes to mind, XML applications are not necessarily distributed applications. An XML application could be a single process running on a single machine that does batch transformations of XML instances. Alternatively, the XML application in question could be a local process that encapsulates an XML data store, such as a database. In both of these situations, the application is not distributed; it is a single local process that expects its arguments to be XML. This type of application—a sovereign application—does not have some of the transport complexities of a distributed application, but in many cases it cannot accomplish what you need. In these cases, a distributed application that moves XML data between tiers is required to solve a problem.

### 21.4.2 Request-Response

The most common model for an XML application, and the one most commonly found on the Web, is the request-response model. Figure 21.2 illustrates the data flow that occurs in an application that uses the request-response model.

In the request-response model, the client process creates an XML document and uses the transport protocol to deliver that document as a request to the server process. The server process then executes some block of logic based on the request. During the execution, the client process is waiting for the response. Once the server has generated a response, it is delivered through the transport protocol back to the client process. This is the model a Web browser uses to request a Web page. In that case, the transport protocol is Hypertext Transfer Protocol (HTTP), which itself uses a request-response model. As you will see in Section 21.5.1, HTTP is a good choice for the transport protocol in a request-response model XML application.

### 21.4.3 Routing

In the request-response model, the input XML and output XML are related to a single client. Multiple clients may exist, but each client node is unaware of the others with regard to a specific operation. For many applications, this model will suffice. For others, however, there is a need to have the XML data flow through multiple nodes that operate based on the XML input. In this type of application, the data is routed through a series of nodes as shown in Figure 21.3.

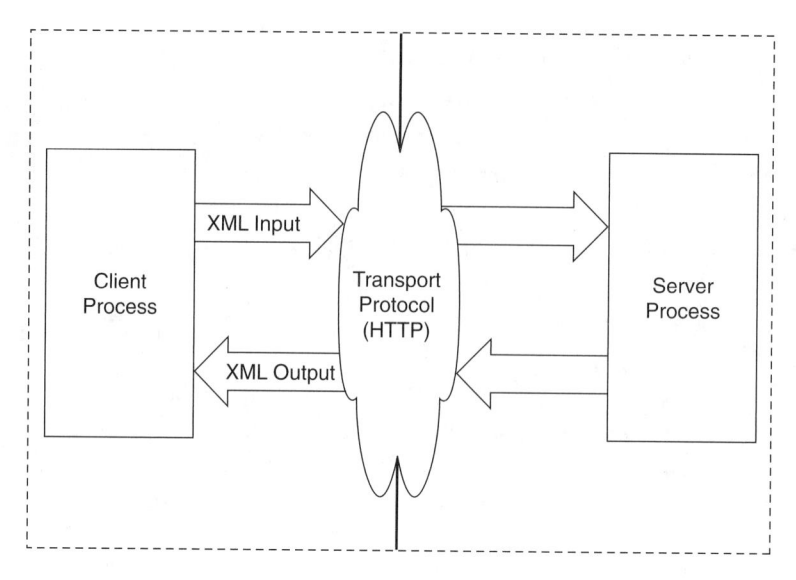

**FIGURE 21.2** *Request-response structure.*

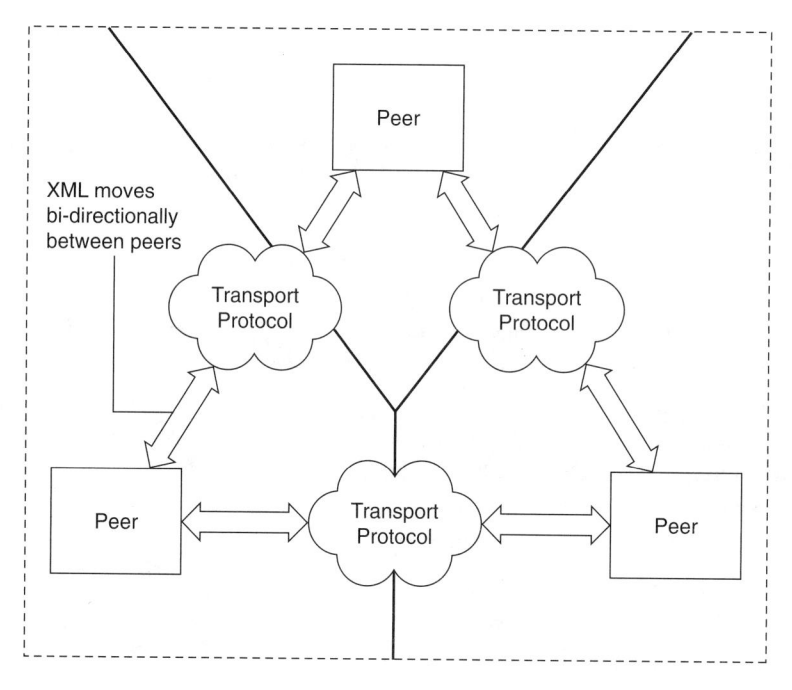

**FIGURE 21.3** *Routing structure.*

In a peer model, any peer or node can either send or receive data. This is a more open approach than the request-response model, but it is also considerably more complicated. These nodes can communicate directly, one to another, as in a peer-to-peer (P2P) architecture. Alternatively, you can use this model to construct an architecture that handles transactions or workflow by chaining nodes together for processing.

## 21.5 Transporting XML

In the distributed XML applications we have described, there is a need to move data between the tiers of the application. In the request-response model, there is a need for communication between the two. For routing, it might be necessary to broadcast or route data between entities. In either case, the need for transporting XML across a network is apparent. XML is the data transfer mechanism, but that only defines the semantics of how the data is expressed. We must look beyond XML for methods of transporting that data.

### 21.5.1 Transport Protocols

As Figure 21.1 shows, some sort of transport protocol is needed in an XML application. The transport protocol to choose for your application depends on two factors: the degree to which you want your application to be accessible, and the framework you are using to create the application.

The first factor to consider when choosing a transport protocol is accessibility. Different applications need to transport data in different ways, depending on the application's requirements. For a Web application that imports data nightly from another site, a request-response model using HTTP would be a good choice. Alternatively, a self-contained application that processes XML documents might only need access to the local file system to input and output data. In that case, the local file system is the transport protocol.

Once you have determined the transport protocol requirements, you should consider the development framework: the languages, platforms, and tools that will be used to create the application. The requirements of the application may dictate the choice of framework, but you can choose from many different frameworks and still gain the functionality that you require.

When considering the transport protocol, examine two development paths at opposite ends of the spectrum: an application built by using an enterprise-level framework and a scripting application that transforms XML by using an XSLT stylesheet. Consider the choices available in these two situations. If you want to take full advantage of an enterprise-level framework such as the .NET Framework or J2EE, the choice of transport protocols is limited to the protocols that have been implemented (although they might be numerous). The format for XML data is already selected by the framework, and the XML schemas related to this format are likely to be generated automatically. In contrast, with raw transformations using scripting, both the format for data and the transport protocol are in the application's control. Developers might write substantially more code to accomplish a task, but the control over XML within the application is fine-grained.

## 21.5.2 HTTP

A good candidate for transporting XML through a distributed application is HTTP: an application-level protocol used to transmit text over a TCP/IP connection. The HTTP protocol is used by Web browsers to query a Web server and return content such as an HTML page. In the case of browsers and Web servers, HTTP traffic usually occurs over the TCP/IP port 80. Figure 21.4 shows the request-response model as implemented with an HTTP transport protocol.

As stated in our discussion of application architecture in Section 21.4, HTTP uses the request-response model. A client issues an HTTP request, and the server returns an HTTP response. Each request contains a verb and headers, and each response contains a status code, headers, and content. Listing 21.4 provides an example of a simple HTTP request. This request was issued by Internet Explorer 6.0, requesting an HTML page, 'hello.htm' from a location on a local Web server.

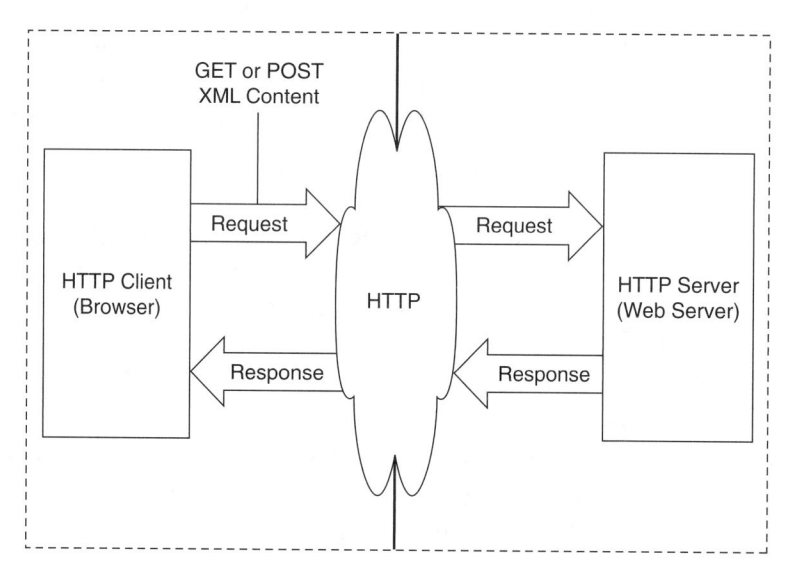

**FIGURE 21.4** *HTTP request-response structure.*

**LISTING 21.4**   Sample HTTP Request

```
GET /appschemas/hello.htm HTTP/1.1
Accept: image/gif, image/x-xbitmap, image/jpeg, image/pjpeg,
 application/vnd.ms-excel, application/vnd.ms-powerpoint,
 application/msword, */*
Accept-Language: en-us
Accept-Encoding: gzip, deflate
User-Agent: Mozilla/4.0 (compatible; MSIE 6.0; Windows NT 5.1;
 Q312461; .NET CLR 1.0.3705)
Host: localhost
Connection: Keep-Alive
```

In the preceding example, the verb used for the request was 'GET'. HTTP uses only a handful of verbs or commands to issue requests. Table 21.1 lists those verbs and their meanings. Although all of the verbs are listed, the majority of HTTP requests are GET, HEAD, or POST.

Listing 21.5 shows an HTTP response to our previous request. In the case of the HTTP response, we first receive a status code. Status codes are integers that indicate the success or failure of the client request; a value of 200 (200–299) indicates success. Other headers of the response contain information about the server, date, and time the request was handled. Two of the headers contained in the response indicate information about the type of content returned by the response and the size of that content. These are the Content-Type and Content-Length headers, respectively. Content-Type is a string representing the MIME type of the content returned in the response. Content-Length is the number of bytes of content returned.

**TABLE 21.1**   HTTP Verbs

| Verb | Description |
| --- | --- |
| GET | Requests the content and headers associated with the indicated location. |
| HEAD | Requests only the headers associated with the indicated location. |
| POST | Submits content to the server at the indicated location to be executed upon. |
| PUT | Replaces the content at the indicated location with the content submitted with this request. |
| DELETE | Deletes the content associated with the indicated location. |
| OPTIONS | Requests the settings and options of the server. |
| TRACE | Requests detailed information about request receipt and processing. |

**LISTING 21.5** Sample HTTP Response

```
HTTP/1.1 200 OK
Server: Microsoft-IIS/5.1
Date: Fri, 08 Mar 2002 15:06:19 GMT
Content-Type: text/html
Accept-Ranges: bytes
Last-Modified: Fri, 08 Mar 2002 15:03:48 GMT
ETag: "0508273b2c6c11:90f"
Content-Length: 148

<html>
    <head>
        <title>Hello XML Schemas</title>
    </head>
    <body>
        <p><b>Hello XML Schemas</b></p>
    </body>
</html>
```

## 21.5.3 XML and HTTP

HTTP works very well as a transport protocol for XML data because XML is text. Most of the difficulties that arise in using HTTP as a transport protocol occur when arguments of binary data (images, code, and so on) are transmitted. In that case, the binary data must first be converted to text and encoded by using MIME. Transmission of XML is no more complicated than transmission of HTML. The difference between transmitting XML over HTTP as opposed to other textual data is the Content-Type header. Whenever XML is transmitted over HTTP, the Content-Type header should have a value of text/xml. This indicates to the components of the application that the content is in fact XML and can be treated as such programmatically.

Listings 21.6 and 21.7 provide an example of a request-response pair for retrieving an XML document, hello.xml. The content for hello.xml is contained in the HTTP response, and the Content-Type header indicates that the content is XML.

**LISTING 21.6** Sample GET HTTP Request for hello.xml

```
GET /appschemas/hello.xml HTTP/1.1
Accept: image/gif, image/x-xbitmap, image/jpeg, image/pjpeg,
 application/vnd.ms-excel, application/vnd.ms-powerpoint,
 application/msword, */*
Accept-Language: en-us
Accept-Encoding: gzip, deflate
User-Agent: Mozilla/4.0 (compatible; MSIE 6.0; Windows NT 5.1;
```

```
Q312461; .NET CLR 1.0.3705)
Host: localhost
Connection: Keep-Alive
```

**LISTING 21.7**  Sample HTTP Response for `hello.xml`

```
HTTP/1.1 200 OK
Server: Microsoft-IIS/5.1
Date: Fri, 08 Mar 2002 15:31:18 GMT
Content-Type: text/xml
Accept-Ranges: bytes
Last-Modified: Fri, 08 Mar 2002 15:31:11 GMT
ETag: "20dfa846b6c6c11:90f"
Content-Length: 74

<?xml version='1.0'?>
<hello>Hello XML Schemas</hello>
```

Using a GET, you can retrieve an XML document by using HTTP. This is useful when the client needs to receive data from the server, but in many cases, the client needs to send data to the server for the application to process. Without yet going into the details of how a POST is handled on the server, let's consider an XML application that processes XML data. In Section 21.2.2, we discussed an application that would accept a Social Security number and return employee information. The schema fragment used to define those types is provided in Listing 21.8.

**LISTING 21.8**  Example Employee Schema Fragment

```
<xsd:element name="employee" type="employeeType"/>

<xsd:element name="ssn" type="xsd:string"/>

<xsd:complexType name="employeeType">
    <xsd:sequence>
        <xsd:element name="name" type="xsd:string" />
        <xsd:element name="ssn"  type="xsd:string" />
        <xsd:element name="job"  type="xsd:string" />
    </xsd:sequence>
</xsd:complexType>
```

Assume we have an application that uses HTTP as its transport protocol and that it can accept input at the relative URI location `appschemas/lookup.asp`. In that case, we can define a sample request-response pair that shows what a call to that application would look like over HTTP.

The sample request is provided in Listing 21.9, and the corresponding response is shown in Listing 21.10.

**LISTING 21.9**   Sample POST HTTP Request for `hello.xml`

```
POST /appschemas/lookup.asp HTTP/1.1
Content-Type: text/xml
Content-Length: nnn

<?xml version='1.0'?>
<ssn>007</ssn>
```

**LISTING 21.10**   Sample POST HTTP Response for `hello.xml`

```
HTTP/1.1 200 OK
Server: Microsoft-IIS/5.1
Date: Fri, 08 Mar 2002 15:59:17 GMT
Content-Type: text/xml
Accept-Ranges: bytes
Last-Modified: Fri, 08 Mar 2002 15:59:11 GMT
ETag: "1092e30bac6c11:90f"
Content-Length: 196

<?xml version='1.0'?>
<employee>
    <name>Sean Connery</name>
    <ssn>007</ssn>
    <job>Agent in Her Majesty&apos;s Secret Service</job>
</employee>
```

These examples show how you can use HTTP as a transport protocol to pass XML data into an application and receive XML output as a response. On both sides of the application, you can use the XML schema represented by the schema fragment in Listing 21.7 to validate your data. The server can validate input against the schema, and the client can validate the output after it receives a response.

In these examples, we are transporting XML instances of a specific XML schema. The request describes the input argument, and the response describes the output message. The entire document is made up of application arguments, and only the arguments are contained in the XML. We could take extra steps to make the XML data we are transporting more standard by using an application protocol such as SOAP or XML-RPC (XML Remote Procedure Calls), but the use of those protocols does not change the architecture we are describing. Regardless of the specific content of the XML data for the application, XML data is being passed in the form of input and output messages. The question once again becomes how we can determine what the inputs and outputs to the application should be. This is where we can use XML schemas to describe the application itself.

## 21.6 Describing Applications

In many cases, the applications we create as developers exist in a box, unaware that any other applications exist. The only communication that such applications are aware of might be the initially defined communication between client and server. This communication occurs over a set protocol and possibly with a fixed set of data and time requirements. If an application never needs to communicate with the world outside its box, it does not necessarily need to publish its operations.

Increasingly, the applications we develop do not exist in a box. When successful, these applications rapidly become units of functionality that other processes or systems might wish to access. This is the concept of Web Services, creating reusable components that can be accessed by using protocols like XML and HTTP. To make applications accessible to the world, we must describe our applications in a way that other applications can understand. The starting point for such a description is an XML schema.

### 21.6.1 Using XML Schemas

Using an XML schema to describe the features of our application fails for one key reason. Although we can describe everything about our application by using an XML schema, that information is described in a manner that is specific to our implementation. In that sense, despite the fact that we are using a standard such as an XML schema to describe our application data, the structure that we define using the schema is proprietary. Another application that wanted to communicate with ours would be able to do so only based on documentation or the less exact "word of mouth" description of the API.

To describe applications in a way that allows outside developers and systems to interact with them, we must create an XML schema that is clear and unlikely to be misinterpreted. We can use namespaces to accomplish part of this requirement. Using namespaces in this case prevents the possibility that an application reading our description schema document will confuse all or part of it with one of its own descriptions. Beyond collision problems, we still face problems in creating a clear description of our application structure. This is the same problem faced by individual industries that have supported the widespread use of XML for business-to-business communications. In those instances, working groups have formed to define one or more XML schemas that are industry-specific. This adoption of a common vocabulary makes it possible for the companies concerned to communicate in a meaningful way. The same solution has been adopted by developers of XML applications. In their case, the common vocabulary for describing an application is Web Services Definition Language (WSDL).

### 21.6.2 WSDL and XML Schemas

WSDL is a proposed industry standard for describing the programmatic interface to a Web Service. WSDL is comparable to IDL (Interface Definition Language) for both CORBA (Common Object Request Broker Architecture) and COM (Component Object Model) in that it allows an application to describe the methods and types that an application exposes.

> **TIP**
>
> Detailed information about WSDL and the WSDL specification can be obtained at http://www.w3.org/TR/wsdl.

Each WSDL document has as its root a `definitions` element. This definition contains all the structure for defining an application interface. Within the `definitions` element are elements to define what operations are supported, what protocols they are supported on, and what particular address those operations are implemented on. Below the operation level, however, the WSDL document defines messages. These messages are represented by the `message` element, and `message` elements are combined to define an operation using the `operation` element. Each `message` element is defined by either an element name or a type name (simple or complex type). Listing 21.11 shows a fragment of a WSDL document that defines a pair of messages and the operation they are grouped into. Portions of the WSDL have been excluded for brevity. The fragment refers to a complex type defined in the schema fragment in Listing 21.2.

**LISTING 21.11** WSDL Fragment for Messages

```
<definitions...>
    <message name="GetEmployeeRequest">
        <part name="ssn" type="xsd:string" />
    </message>
    <message name="GetEmployeeResponse">
        <part name="emp" type="emp:employeeType" />
    </message>
    <portType name="EmployeeOps">
        <operation name="GetEmployee">
            <input message="tns:GetEmployeeRequest" />
            <input message="tns:GetEmployeeResponse" />
        </operation>
    </portType>
</definitions>
```

Rather than develop a type system to go along with the syntax for describing messages, the authors of the WSDL specification have wisely adopted XML schemas as the method of choice for describing messages (and therefore application types) within a WSDL document. In fact, unless specifically defined as using something other than the XML schemas definition, all type definitions that appear in a WSDL document are assumed to use the types of XML schemas. Either an XML schema can be embedded into the `types` section of a WSDL document, or the WSDL can refer to an external XML schema by using the `import` element.

With the first approach, the simple and complex types used in messages are embedded within the WSDL document. This embedded XML schema is contained inside the `types` element of the WSDL. The `types` element has as a child element a `schema` element, so an entire XML schema document can appear as a child of the `types` element. Listing 21.12 shows this embedded schema approach inside a WSDL fragment.

**LISTING 21.12**   WSDL Fragment Using types

```xml
<definitions...>
    <types>
        <schema xmlns="http://www.w3.org/2001/XMLSchema"
            xmlns:emp="http://www.schemabook.com/employee"
            targetNamespace="http://www.schemabook.com/employee">
            <complexType name="employeeType">
                <sequence>
                    <element name="name" type="xsd:string" />
                    <element name="ssn"  type="xsd:string" />
                    <element name="job"  type="xsd:string" />
                </sequence>
            </complexType>
        </schema>
    </types>
    <message name="GetEmployeeRequest">
        <part name="ssn" type="xsd:string" />
    </message>
    <message name="GetEmployeeResponse">
        <part name="emp" type="emp:employeeType" />
    </message>
    <portType name="EmployeeOps">
        <operation name="GetEmployee">
            <input message="tns:GetEmployeeRequest" />
            <input message="tns:GetEmployeeResponse" />
        </operation>
    </portType>
</definitions>
```

The alternative to the embedded XML schema is the `import` element. Using the `import` element, a WSDL document can refer to an XML schema that exists in a separate XML instance. Listing 21.13 provides the same functionality in WSDL, but it uses the `import` element instead of the embedded schema. This approach allows for industry-standard schemas to be included in an application definition.

**LISTING 21.13**  WSDL Fragment Using `import`

```
<definitions...>
    <import namespace="http://www.schemabook.com/employee"
            location="http://www.schemabook.com/employee.xsd" />
    <message name="GetEmployeeRequest">
        <part name="ssn" type="xsd:string" />
    </message>
    <message name="GetEmployeeResponse">
        <part name="emp" type="emp:employeeType" />
    </message>
    <portType name="EmployeeOps">
        <operation name="GetEmployee">
            <input message="tns:GetEmployeeRequest" />
            <input message="tns:GetEmployeeResponse" />
        </operation>
    </portType>
</definitions>
```

Although WSDL provides an extensive vocabulary for describing a Web Service, using WSDL to describe a simple XML application can be overkill. Our earlier examples described an operation that our application might perform using only a few elements, but even the tersest WSDL document contains several parts. We eliminated much of the boilerplate WSDL for the examples included in this chapter just to keep them short for readability. The significance of WSDL, however, is that it is a standard, and standards such as this one must support both simple and complex cases. The idea of a standard for describing an application would fall apart if there were one standard for simple applications and a separate standard for enterprise-level applications.

The reality of WSDL is that for simple applications, much of the content is boilerplate. Organizations could standardize internally on a subset of WSDL or their own proprietary syntax for application metadata and could use XSLT (Extensible Stylesheet Language Transformations) or a similar method to generate full WSDL documents to allow for greater interoperability.

## 21.7 Example Application

With the concept of a distributed XML application in mind, we can create an example application that uses XML to communicate between a client and server. This example provides a simple XML application for testing the position of a given point in relation to a potentially bounding polygon. Given point A, defined by two coordinates, and polygon B, defined by a list of points that indicate vertices, the application determines whether point A lies inside polygon B. Figure 21.5 shows the concept—one that comes up often in computer graphics but that also has applications in other areas. For example, in location-based services, the same algorithms can be used to determine if a GPS-enabled device has entered a particular region defined by coordinates of latitude and longitude.

Our application is a Web application, so it relies on HTTP as the transport protocol. On the client, which is browser-based, the application can trigger a polygon test based on an input XML document displayed in the browser. The client code is contained in a single HTML file, pptest.htm. On the server, an ASP page contains the logic that processes the input XML document and returns a response. The structure for this application is illustrated in Figure 21.6.

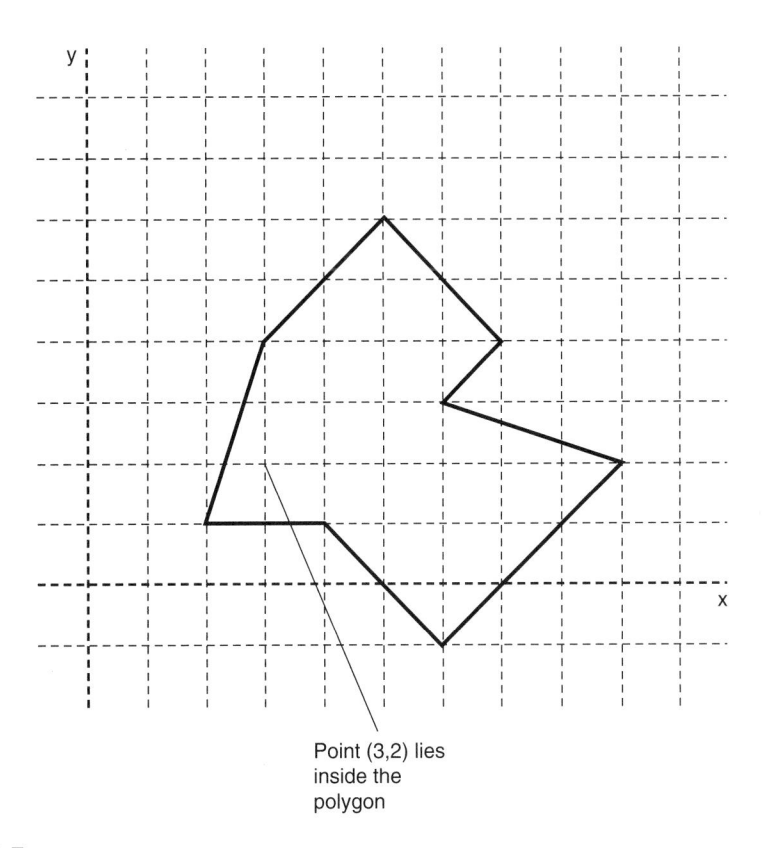

Point (3,2) lies inside the polygon

**FIGURE 21.5**  *Point-in-polygon test.*

## Application-oriented Schemas
### CHAPTER 21

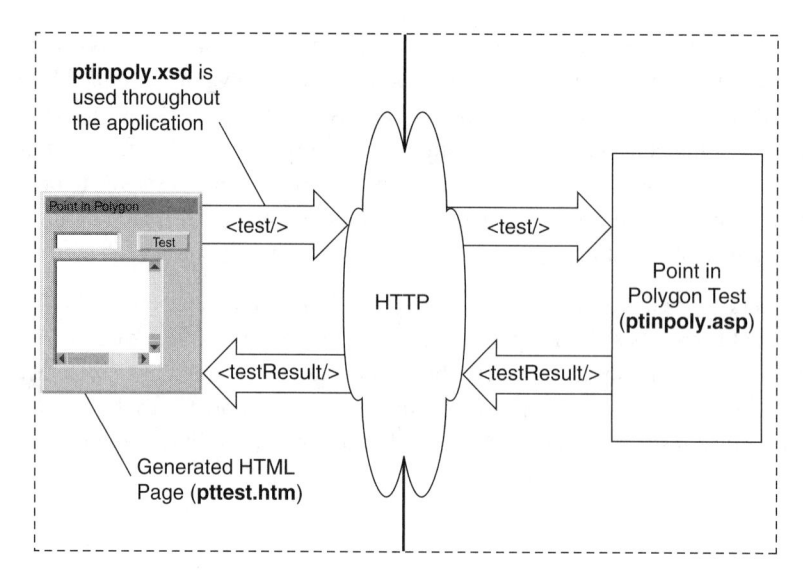

**FIGURE 21.6** *Point-in-polygon application structure.*

We can define an XML Schema, `ptinpoly.xsd`, to represent the types we will be passing between the client and server. Listing 21.14 shows this schema document, which contains types for representing points and polygons, as well as the application requests and responses.

**LISTING 21.14** Schema Document for Example Application `ptinpoly.xsd`

```
<xsd:schema xmlns:xsd="http://www.w3.org/2001/XMLSchema"
      targetNamespace=
        "http://www.XMLSchemaReference.com/Examples/Ch21"
      xmlns=
        "http://www.XMLSchemaReference.com/Examples/Ch21"
      xmlns:pt=
        "http://www.XMLSchemaReference.com/Examples/Ch21"
      elementFormDefault="qualified">
   <xsd:annotation>
      <xsd:documentation xml:lang="en">
         This XML Schema Document describes the components
         used to determine whether a given 2D point lies
         within a given polygon.
      </xsd:documentation>
   </xsd:annotation>
   <xsd:element name="point" type="pt:pointType"/>
   <xsd:element name="polygon" type="pt:polygonType"/>
   <xsd:element name="test" type="pt:testType"/>
   <xsd:element name="testResult" type="xsd:string"/>
```

```
<xsd:complexType name="testType">
    <xsd:sequence>
        <xsd:element name="point"    type="pt:pointType" />
        <xsd:element name="polygon"  type="pt:polygonType" />
    </xsd:sequence>
</xsd:complexType>
<xsd:complexType name="pointType">
    <xsd:annotation>
        <xsd:documentation xml:lang="en">
            2D point.
        </xsd:documentation>
    </xsd:annotation>
    <xsd:sequence>
        <xsd:element name="x" type="xsd:int" />
        <xsd:element name="y" type="xsd:int" />
    </xsd:sequence>
</xsd:complexType>
<xsd:complexType name="pointsType">
    <xsd:annotation>
        <xsd:documentation xml:lang="en">
            This is a list of points.
        </xsd:documentation>
    </xsd:annotation>
    <xsd:sequence>
        <xsd:element name="point"   type="pt:pointType"
                    minOccurs="0" maxOccurs="unbounded" />
    </xsd:sequence>
</xsd:complexType>
<xsd:complexType name="polygonType">
    <xsd:annotation>
        <xsd:documentation xml:lang="en">
            Data type for a polygon.
        </xsd:documentation>
    </xsd:annotation>
    <xsd:sequence>
        <xsd:element name="name"    type="xsd:string" />
        <xsd:element name="polypts" type="pt:pointsType" />
    </xsd:sequence>
</xsd:complexType>
</xsd:schema>
```

## 21.7.1 Client

The client code in our XML application is contained an HTML page with only a few lines of JavaScript that transmit the request to the server. The page loads an XML instance into a text area for display, and it provides a button that when clicked submits that XML instance as input to the server application by using HTTP. Once the server has processed the request and returned a response, the page displays the XML of the response in another text area at the bottom of the page. Figure 21.7 shows a screenshot of the client page in action.

On the client as well as the server, this application uses the Microsoft XML Parser 4.0 to handle the XML instances. For this page, very little has to be done with the XML other than loading and displaying the content in text areas. The real use of the MSXML components on the client side is to transport the request to the server. The MSXML components contain an object called the XMLHTTP object. This object provides a set of methods for transmitting XML instances over HTTP.

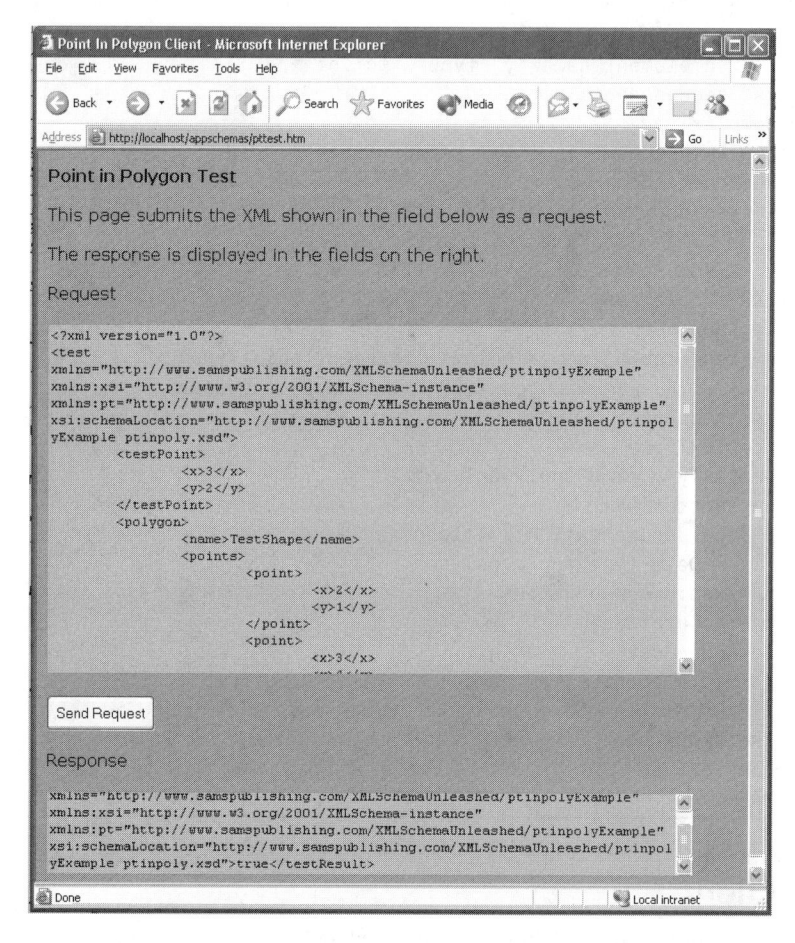

**FIGURE 21.7** *Client screen shot for* `pttest.htm`.

The XMLHTTP object exposes two methods that can be used together to transport XML over HTTP. The first method is the open method, which accepts as arguments the HTTP verb to use for the request (such as 'POST' or 'GET') and the URL of the request. The second method is the send method, which actually forms the request and transmits it by using sockets. For a POST operation, the send method can be passed an XML instance as a argument that will be the contents of the POST. Once the send method returns, the contents of a successful HTTP response will be contained in the responseXML property of the XMLHTTP object. The responseXML property is an instance of a DOMDocument object, so it can be traversed and can use an XML schema for validation.

> **TIP**
>
> For more information about the Microsoft XML Core Services, MSXML 4.0, refer to Chapter 18.

The source for the client page is shown in Listing 21.15. As you can see, the web object is created as an instance of the XMLHTTP component. Using the instance of XMLHTTP, the client opens a connection to the server page and performs a POST of the XML instance contained in the XML data island request. This XML is then sent to the server, and the call blocks further activity until the response is returned. The response XML is placed back into the text area at the bottom of the page for display.

**LISTING 21.15**   pttest.htm Source Code

```
<html>
    <head>
        <title>Point In Polygon Client</title>
        <script>
            function Send_onclick()
              {
                var web;
                web = new ActiveXObject(
                   "MSXML2.XMLHTTP.4.0");
                // Point this at your server URL
                web.open("POST",
                   "http://localhost/appschemas/ptinpoly.asp",
                   false);
                web.send(request.XMLDocument.xml);
                ResponseXml.innerText = web.responseXML.xml;
              }
```

*continues*

**578** Application-oriented Schemas

**CHAPTER 21**

```
        </script>
        <script event="onload" for="window">
            RequestXml.innerText = request.XMLDocument.xml;
        </script>
        <XML id="request" src="testshapetrue.xml"></XML>
    </head>
    <body style="COLOR: black; FONT-FAMILY: Verdana"
            bgColor="#cc9900">
        <P><STRONG>Point in Polygon Test</STRONG></P>
        <P></P>
        <P>This page submits the XML shown in the field below
         as a request.</P>
        <P>The response is displayed in the fields on the
         right.</P>
        <P></P>
        <P>Request</P>
        <P><TEXTAREA id="RequestXml"
            style="WIDTH: 633px; HEIGHT: 331px" name="RequestXml"
            rows="20" readOnly wrap="soft" cols="76">
            </TEXTAREA> </P>
        <P><INPUT language="javascript"
            id="Button" style="WIDTH: 106px; HEIGHT: 34px"
            onclick="Send_onclick()" type="button"
            value="Send Request" name="SendButton"></P>
        <P>Response</P>
        <P><TEXTAREA id="ResponseXml"
            style="WIDTH: 632px; HEIGHT: 79px" name="ResponseXml"
            rows="5" readOnly cols="76"></TEXTAREA> </P>
    </body>
</html>
```

The XML tag in `pttest.htm` refers to a document on the server that functions as the input to the application. That document, `testshapetrue.xml`, is an XML instance that contains a test point and a polygon for the server to process. Listing 21.16 shows the content of that document. The resulting point and polygon described by this instance define the point and polygon shown in Figure 21.5. In this case, the point (3,2) we are testing does lie inside the polygon. Therefore, the server would return 'true' in response to this request. If the `testPoint` element described the point (–1,0), the server would return 'false'.

**LISTING 21.16**   TestShapeTrue.xml Instance Document for an Application Request

```
<?xml version="1.0"?>
<test
     xmlns="http://www.XMLSchemaReference.com/Examples/Ch21/"
     xmlns:xsi="http://www.w3.org/2001/XMLSchema-instance"
```

```xml
        xmlns:pt=
            "http   http://www.XMLSchemaReference.com/Examples/Ch21"
        xsi:schemaLocation=
            "http://www.XMLSchemaReference.com/Examples/Ch21/ptinpoly.xsd">
    <testPoint>
        <x>3</x>
        <y>2</y>
    </testPoint>
    <polygon>
        <name>TestShape</name>
        <points>
            <point>
                <x>2</x>
                <y>1</y>
            </point>
            <point>
                <x>3</x>
                <y>4</y>
            </point>
            <point>
                <x>5</x>
                <y>6</y>
            </point>
            <point>
                <x>7</x>
                <y>4</y>
            </point>
            <point>
                <x>6</x>
                <y>3</y>
            </point>
            <point>
                <x>9</x>
                <y>2</y>
            </point>
            <point>
                <x>6</x>
                <y>-1</y>
            </point>
            <point>
                <x>4</x>
                <y>1</y>
            </point>
        </points>
    </polygon>
</test>
```

## 21.7.2 Server

The server shown in Listing 21.17 is written using ASP and the Microsoft XML Parser 4.0. On the server, we do not need the capabilities of the XMLHTTP component. Instead, we need to use the DOM implementation of the MSXML components to parse the input XML instance and return a response.

The crossing algorithm determines whether the point in question is within the polygon. It is one of the simplest algorithms to implement for the point-in-polygon problem, although it is just one of many possible solutions. From the point in question, the application projects a line parallel to the *x*-axis. If that line crosses the polygon an even number of times, it is not in the polygon; if it crosses an odd number of times, it is inside the polygon.

> **NOTE**
>
> For more information about the point-in-polygon problem and its various solutions, read the article "Point in Polygon Strategies" by Eric Haines, which can be found at http://www.acm.org/pubs/tog/editors/erich/ptinpoly/.

Listing 21.17 shows the ASP code, written in VBScript, that processes the request and returns the response. The ASP page first checks to make sure a POST was performed on this page, as opposed to a GET. If the POST occurred, the server page reads the XML instance from the ASP Request object and parses it, using the MSXML DOM implementation. The page reads the test point and the polygon data passed to it and then uses the crossing algorithm to determine if the point is within the polygon. The variable strResponse contains the XML response returned to the client.

> **NOTE**
>
> Instead of generating the XML response in a string variable, an application can create a new DOMDocument object and use it to generate the XML. In the case of a single simple type, it is just as easy to use a string. For complex responses, a better approach would be to generate XML by using a component like the MSXML DOMDocument40.

**LISTING 21.17** PtInPoly.asp Source Code

```vbscript
<%@Language="VBSCRIPT"%>
<%
    Response.Expires = 0
    On Error Resume Next

    Response.ContentType = "text/xml"
    Dim objRequest
    Dim strMethod

    strMethod = Request.ServerVariables( "REQUEST_METHOD" )

    Dim strResponse
    Dim strAnswer

    strAnswer = "false"
    strResponse = "<testResult " & _
      " xmlns='http://www.XMLSchemaReference.com/" & _
      "Examples/Ch21' "
    strResponse = strResponse & _
        "xmlns:xsi='http://www.w3.org/2001/XMLSchema-instance' "
    strResponse = strResponse & _
      "xmlns:pt=' http://www.XMLSchemaReference.com/" & _
      "Examples/Ch21' "
    strResponse = strResponse & _
      "xsi:schemaLocation='http://www.XMLSchemaReference.com/" & _
      "Examples/Ch21 ptinpoly.xsd'>"

    If ( strMethod = "POST" ) Then
        Set objRequest = _
          Server.CreateObject( "MSXML2.DOMDocument.4.0" )
        objRequest.ValidateOnParse = True
        Dim bRequestLoaded
        bRequestLoaded = objRequest.load( Request )
        Dim nodeTest
        Set nodeTest = objRequest.documentElement
        Dim nodePoint
        Set nodePoint = nodeTest.firstChild
        Dim ptX
        ptX = CInt(nodePoint.firstChild.Text)
        Dim ptY
        ptY = CInt(nodePoint.lastChild.Text)
        Dim nodeTemp
        Set nodeTemp = nodeTest.lastChild
        Dim nodePoints
        Set nodePoints = nodeTemp.lastChild
        Dim nodePointList
```

*continues*

# Application-oriented Schemas
## CHAPTER 21

```
Set nodePointList = nodePoints.childNodes
Dim numVerts
numVerts = nodePointList.length
Dim vertexXi
Dim vertexYi
Dim vertexXj
Dim vertexYj
vertexXi = 0
vertexYi = 0
vertexXj = 0
vertexYj = 0

Dim yflag0
Dim yflag1
Dim xflag0
Dim xflag1
xflag0 = 0
xflag1 = 0
yflag0 = 0
yflag1 = 0

Dim i
Dim j
Dim c
i = 0
j = 0
c = False

j = numVerts - 1
' Walk the list of vertices
While (i < numVerts)
    Set nodePoint = nodePointList.Item(i)
    vertexXi = CInt(nodePoint.firstChild.Text)
    vertexYi = CInt(nodePoint.lastChild.Text)
    Set nodePoint = nodePointList.Item(j)
    vertexXj = CInt(nodePoint.firstChild.Text)
    vertexYj = CInt(nodePoint.lastChild.Text)

    Dim intersect
    intersect = 0

    ' Calculation to test the intersection
    If (ptX < (vertexXj - vertexXi) * _
      (ptY - vertexYi) / (vertexYj - vertexYi) _
      + vertexXi) Then
        intersect = 1
    End If
```

```
            ' Test to see if the point falls inside the y
            ' coords and intersects the line
            If ((((vertexYi <= ptY) And (ptY < vertexYj)) Or _
                ((vertexYj <= ptY) And (ptY < vertexYi))) And _
                (intersect)) Then
                c = Not c
            End If

            j = i
            i = i + 1
        Wend

        If ( c = True ) Then
            strAnswer = "true"
        End If
    End If

    strResponse = strResponse & strAnswer
    strResponse = strResponse & "</testResult>"

    Response.Write strResponse
    Response.End
    Response.Flush

%>
```

This example shows a distributed XML application with its most basic and most common architecture. A client process sends an HTTP request containing an XML document, and a server process consumes the request and generates an HTTP response containing an XML document. Throughout the application, the documents that are being passed are validated against a single schema that defines what the application supports.

# Data-oriented Schemas

**PART V**

Many development efforts require a database to store or retrieve data. Most databases today are relational. Part V discusses mapping an XML schema to a relational (SQL) schema. The examples in this part pertain specifically to Oracle9*i*. However, the concepts generally apply to any SQL database.

- Chapter 22 covers storing the values associated with built-in XML schema datatypes in Oracle. Moreover, this chapter discusses how and when to apply the constraining facets in the database. Appendix D portrays the differences between Oracle8*i* and Oracle9*i*.

- Chapter 23 discusses how to store values associated with these simple types, as well as the pros and cons of using specific constraining facets. In an XML schema, all simple types are ultimately restrictions of the built-in datatypes.

- Chapter 24 provides suggestions on how to create tables with SQL that correspond to complex types. Unlike simple types, whose XML Schema values map to table column values, complex types tend to map to entire relational tables.

# Data-oriented Schemas: Datatypes

**CHAPTER 22**

## IN THIS CHAPTER

- 22.1 XML Schema Design Considerations   588
- 22.2 General Discussion of Facet Restrictions   590
- 22.3 Check Constraints versus Triggers   598
- 22.4 Datatypes   598

# Chapter 22

## Data-oriented Schemas: Datatypes

This chapter covers the mapping of XML Schema datatypes to an Oracle9*i* relational database. Whereas XML Schema datatypes are numerous and have a wide range of facets, database schema columns have a small subset and have little built-in support for datatype facets. Representing datatype types is complex and requires numerous design and implementation trade-offs.

Because much of this chapter is meant for a database designer and implementer, the chapter begins with some issues an XML schema designer should be aware of when designing an XML schema that will be represented in a relational database. In some cases, small XML schema decisions have major database implications and the "gotchas" are presented here.

This chapter then continues with a general discussion of constraining facets, because much of the discussion is germane to nearly all the datatypes. This includes the design decision of implementing constraining facets with check constraints or triggers. The chapter then covers each datatype, showing multiple implementations, if appropriate, and discussing the design trade-offs of each.

> **NOTE**
>
> The database code implementing each datatype is meant to be a set of contrived, albeit working, examples. The hard-coded values in many of the examples would be changed or set to PL/SQL package constants in real-world scenarios.
>
> All code examples have been tested on Oracle 9.0.1.0.1 running under Windows 2000.

## 22.1 XML Schema Design Considerations

When creating an XML schema document whose XML instances will be stored in a relational database (in non-XML form), the XML schema designer needs to consider the impacts that design decisions might have on the database representation. In addition, certain decisions need to be made explicitly that would not normally affect an XML schema document. This section lists the major considerations and provides recommendations and discussion around each of them.

### 22.1.1 Patterns

When patterns are used, determine whether the database needs to enforce the pattern or whether the enforcement can be left solely to the XML schema processor. If database enforcement is required, be aware that SQL does not perform regular expression pattern matching but only wildcard and single character matching. Patterns such as 'ab{2,}x' simply cannot be represented in SQL and would require significant effort using Java stored procedures to enforce.

However, simple patterns and most real-world examples are representable. Refer to Section 22.2.1 for more detail. This section also provides working examples of some simpler patterns.

## 22.1.2 Whitespace

Whitespace can be preserved, trimmed, or collapsed. Although the database can trim and collapse whitespace for every database insert and update, this should be preprocessed before the database is involved. From a design pattern perspective, this would be done using a decorating filter. Otherwise, triggers would need to convert every insert and update for every character datatype column in every table where trim or collapse is explicitly or implicitly specified.

## 22.1.3 Strings

The length of a string is of critical importance to a database designer. Different string lengths force substantially different implementations in the database and affect the size and performance of the RDBMS. In addition, know what languages need to be supported. These again force substantially different implementations.

## 22.1.4 Decimals

For the `decimal` datatype and all its datatypes derived by restriction, specifying an appropriate combination of the number of `totalDigits`, `fractionDigits`, `minInclusive`, `maxInclusive`, `minExclusive`, and `maxExclusive` is critically important. Databases allocate a fixed amount of space for numbers; not specifying these constraining facets leads to wasted disk space and/or XML instance values that cannot be represented in the database.

## 22.1.5 Floats and Doubles

The `float` and `double` datatypes are described by IEEE 754-1985, *IEEE Standard for Binary Floating-Point Arithmetic*. Oracle does not support this standard directly; as a result, certain numbers cannot be represented easily and some operations require special support. The annotation associated with the use of these datatypes should be clear as to whether full support is required. This support is rarely needed in most business software systems. The XML schema designer should seriously consider using the `decimal` datatype or one of the datatypes derived from it by restriction, if possible.

## 22.1.6 Boolean

For the `boolean` datatype, maintaining all four possible literals in the database ('true', 'false', '1', and '0') is problematic because a `boolean` has two values in the value space but four in the database. Either use a pattern to restrict the values to two literals or have the database insert and update only two of the literals.

### 22.1.7 Time Zones and Their Interaction with gMonth, gYear, and gDay

For the `gMonth`, `gYear`, and `gDay` datatypes, consider whether a time zone is necessary or whether all values can be represented in UST. If not, these can be implemented as though they were `integer` datatypes. With a time zone, the implementation becomes complex and somewhat baroque.

### 22.1.8 Time Zones and Their Interaction with Other Date/Time Datatypes

For the `time`, `date`, `dateTime`, `gYearMonth`, and `gMonthDay` datatypes, considering the value of a time zone is important or whether all values can be represented in UST. In Oracle, a different database column datatype is chosen that is easier to use when a time zone is not necessary.

### 22.1.9 IDREFS and NMTOKENS Datatypes

The `IDREFS` and `NMTOKENS` datatypes allow multiple values by definition. The database can support multiple representations and can support full or partial validation. Determine whether the individual values need to be accessed separately or only together and whether database validation is necessary.

## 22.2 General Discussion of Facet Restrictions

This section details the general design issues and possible implementations of facet restrictions that vary little with respect to the XML Schema datatype. Each of the constraining facets can be implemented as either table check constraints or triggers (detailed in Section 22.4 later in this chapter).

### 22.2.1 pattern Constraining Facet

`pattern` constraints, in general, cannot be represented in SQL or PL/SQL. SQL has a built-in operator for single-character and multiple-character wildcards. In addition, SQL has functions that can be used to determine whether some patterns have been violated. You can add more general mechanisms by using Java stored procedures.

SQL has the `LIKE` operator that can be used for wildcard matching. Single characters can be matched with a '?' character and multiple characters can be represented with a '%' operator. For example, the `assemblyPartNumberType` in `catalog.xsd` has a pattern constraint of `'ASM\d{1,8}'`. This can be partially fulfilled with the following SQL fragment:

```
CatalogItem.assemblyPartNumber LIKE 'ASM%'
```

and more completely fulfilled by checking for minimum and maximum length with the following SQL fragment:

```
LENGTH(CatalogItem.assemblyPartNumber) BETWEEN 4 AND 12
```

To represent the digit portion of the `pattern` constraint, the following SQL fragment can be used:

```
CAST(SUBSTR((CatalogItem.assemblyPartNumber, 4, 8) AS NUMBER) IS NOT NULL
```

This use of SQL and PL/SQL functions works for simple patterns, but more complex patterns become more difficult to represent. In the case of a `partNumberType` in `catalog.xsd`, the restriction pattern is '`[A-Z]{1,3}\d{1,8}`'. In this case, TRANSLATE could be used to determine that the part number had one to three characters and one to eight digits, but not that the alphabetic characters precede the numeric characters.

Listing 22.1 contains a SQL statement that checks for a simple pattern using the LENGTH, SUBSTR, TRANSLATE, and UPPER SQL and PL/SQL functions.

**LISTING 22.1**   A SQL Statement That Checks for a Simple `pattern`

```
SELECT 1
FROM DUAL
WHERE LENGTH(?value) >= 2 AND
   -- There are between 1 and 3 alphabetic characters
   -- in the first 3 characters.
   LENGTH(TRANSLATE(SUBSTR(UPPER(?value), 1, 3),
          'ABCDEFGHIJKLMNOPQRSTUVWXYZ0123456789',
          'ABCDEFGHIJKLMNOPQRSTUVWXYZ'))
     BETWEEN 1 AND 3 AND
   -- There are no more alphabetic characters after
   -- the first 3.
   LENGTH(TRANSLATE(SUBSTR(UPPER(?value), 1, 3),
          'ABCDEFGHIJKLMNOPQRSTUVWXYZ0123456789',
          'ABCDEFGHIJKLMNOPQRSTUVWXYZ')) =
   LENGTH(TRANSLATE(UPPER(?value),
          'ABCDEFGHIJKLMNOPQRSTUVWXYZ0123456789',
          'ABCDEFGHIJKLMNOPQRSTUVWXYZ')) AND
   -- There are between 1 and 8 numeric characters after
   -- the first character.
   LENGTH(TRANSLATE(SUBSTR(UPPER(?value), 2,
             LENGTH(UPPER(?value)) - 1),
          '0123456789ABCDEFGHIJKLMNOPQRSTUVWXYZ',
          '0123456789'))
     BETWEEN 1 AND 8 AND
   -- The first character is not numeric
   SUBSTR(?value, 1, 1) NOT IN ('0', '1', '2', '3', '4',
              '5', '6', '7', '8', '9');
```

This code example returns the value '1' when the ?value bind variable is replaced with a string that matches the pattern '[A-Z]{1,3}\d{1,8}' and no rows when it does not. This code makes the assumption that only alphabetic and numeric characters are present in the bind variable.

As this example demonstrates, this more complicated pattern can be translated by writing more SQL. The representation in the XML schema document and the PL/SQL become further and further apart as the amount of PL/SQL grows because the XML schema document representation is declarative and the PL/SQL is procedural.

One possible solution to this and the patterns that cannot be handled is to use the pattern-matching functionality built into the JDK1.4 through the classes in the `java.util.regex` package. Although the Oracle JVM's version is 1.3, specific 1.4 classes can be loaded into the Oracle JVM and then wrapped in a PL/SQL function. This approach involves three major issues:

- The XML Schema `pattern` language and the Java pattern language are not identical but are both based on Perl regular expressions. This means that XML Schema regular expressions *must be translated* into Java regular expressions.
- There is a large, potentially significant one-time loading cost. Oracle will load a JVM into the database session for this trigger assuming that the application does not use Java stored procedures elsewhere.
- Although Oracle has made large strides in reducing the performance gap between PL/SQL procedures and Java procedures, the gap still exists. Instantiating Java classes and performing pattern matching is likely to be an expensive operation compared to using the built-in PL/SQL functions.
- Installing the `java.util.regex` classes involves significant effort because they rely on other Java V1.4 classes. Some amount of refactoring of these classes is probably necessary.

Java pattern matching is probably best avoided by using check constraints or triggers in production databases unless it is critical that the database verify that the `pattern` constraint is not violated. This need is ameliorated when the software systems(s) communicating with the database can be assumed to have already performed this function or when the pattern enforcement is not critical to the business systems.

## 22.2.2 enumeration Constraining Facet

The `enumeration` constraining facet restricts a valid XML document to a fixed set of choices. Enumerations can be represented in the database in the following ways:

- Hard-coded values—appropriate if the number of values is small, fixed, unlikely to change, and there is no requirement for an application to retrieve these values.

- A separate table with the domain values—appropriate if the number of values is likely to change, there are few enumerations, and referential integrity is required.
- A "picklist" table with the domain values for all enumerations—appropriate if the number of values is likely to change, there are numerous enumerations, and referential integrity is not required. The word "picklist" is used because in many applications the picklist values form the basis for combo boxes, drop-down menus, and so on.

### 22.2.2.1 Hard-coded Values

The most straightforward representation of hard-coded values is with a database constraint to block insert or update from succeeding.

For example, `catalog.xsd` includes a simple type named `colorOptionType` that has four options: CYAN, MAGENTA, YELLOW, and BLACK. These four choices can be represented as either strings or numbers. Listing 22.2 is a table-creation script with a column constraint.

**LISTING 22.2**   Create the Hard-coded Picklist Values Table

```
CREATE TABLE HardcodedPicklistExample (
value VARCHAR2(30) CHECK (value IN ('cyan', 'magenta',
                 'yellow', 'black'))
);
```

### 22.2.2.2 Separate Table

A separate table is created to hold the values of the domain and other tables that need this domain. Simply create a foreign key relationship to guarantee referential integrity. Listing 22.3 contains a SQL statement that creates the `ColorOptionType` table and other SQL statements that insert the initial values.

**LISTING 22.3**   Create a Separate `ColorOptionType` Table and Insert Initial Values

```
CREATE TABLE ColorOptionType (
colorOptionTypeID NUMBER(4) NOT NULL,
name     VARCHAR2(30) NOT NULL,
description    VARCHAR2(255) NULL,
PRIMARY KEY(colorOptionTypeID));

INSERT INTO ColorOptionType
(colorOptionTypeID, name, description)
VALUES
(1, 'cyan', 'test');

INSERT INTO ColorOptionType
(colorOptionTypeID, name, description)
VALUES
```

*continues*

```
(2, 'magenta', 'test');

INSERT INTO ColorOptionType
(colorOptionTypeID, name, description)
VALUES
(3, 'yellow', 'test');

INSERT INTO ColorOptionType
(colorOptionTypeID, name, description)
VALUES
(4, 'black', 'test');
COMMIT;
```

The choice of a NUMBER(4) for the primary key allows this table to hold 9,999 colors (assuming that the key values are positive and one-based). The name and description have 30 and 255 characters, respectively, allowing for long names and descriptions.

Here is an example table creation script to use the ColorOptionType table:

```
CREATE TABLE SeparateTableExample (
value NUMBER(4) NOT NULL,
FOREIGN KEY (value)
REFERENCES ColorOptionType);
```

This table now has a referential integrity constraint to the ColorOptionType that restricts the appropriate values.

### 22.2.2.3 Picklist Table

The picklist table contains all the values for each enumeration in the schema. Each enumeration type is represented as a separate picklist domain associated with a picklist value. enumeration types are also represented as tables to which the picklist table refers. Listing 22.4 shows how to create a picklist domain and picklist table and create an alternate key on the picklist table to prevent duplicate values. Listing 22.5 shows the SQL statements that insert the initial values into the PicklistDomain and Picklist tables.

**LISTING 22.4**  Create the PicklistDomain and Picklist Tables

```
CREATE TABLE PicklistDomain (
picklistDomainID NUMBER(3) NOT NULL,
name     VARCHAR2(30) NOT NULL,
description  VARCHAR2(255) NULL,
PRIMARY KEY(picklistDomainID));

CREATE TABLE Picklist (
picklistID   NUMBER(4) NOT NULL,
```

```
picklistDomainID NUMBER(3) NOT NULL,
name        VARCHAR2(30) NOT NULL,
description  VARCHAR2(255) NULL,
PRIMARY KEY(picklistID),
FOREIGN KEY (picklistDomainID) REFERENCES PicklistDomain);

CREATE UNIQUE INDEX XAK1Picklist ON Picklist
(
picklistDomainID, name
);
```

**LISTING 22.5**  Insert the Initial Values into the `PicklistDomain` and `Picklist` Tables

```
INSERT INTO PicklistDomain
(picklistDomainID, name, description)
VALUES
(1, 'ColorOptionType',
'There is a limited selection of color choices. As defined, [ccc]
*any* part could have any one of these colors.');

INSERT INTO Picklist
(picklistID, picklistDomainID, name)
VALUES
(1, 1, 'cyan');

INSERT INTO Picklist
(picklistID, picklistDomainID, name)
VALUES
(2, 1, ' magenta');

INSERT INTO Picklist
(picklistID, picklistDomainID, name)
VALUES
(3, 1, ' yellow');

INSERT INTO Picklist
(picklistID, picklistDomainID, name)
VALUES
(4, 1, 'black');
COMMIT;
```

In Listing 22.6, an example table is created to use the `Picklist` table, and two triggers are created to enforce referential integrity programmatically. Before-insert and before-update triggers are used to prevent the data from being inserted or updated when an error occurs.

**LISTING 22.6**  Example Table using Picklists and Triggers

```
CREATE TABLE PicklistTableExample (
value NUMBER(4) NOT NULL
);

CREATE OR REPLACE TRIGGER InsertPicklistTableExample
BEFORE INSERT
ON PicklistTableExample
FOR EACH ROW
DECLARE
 I PLS_INTEGER;
BEGIN
 I := 0;
 SELECT COUNT(1)
 INTO I
 FROM Picklist
 WHERE picklistDomainID = 1 AND -- 1 = colorOptionType
    picklistID = :new.value;

 IF I = 0 THEN
   RAISE_APPLICATION_ERROR(-20000,
            'Not good colorOptionType');
 END IF;
END;

CREATE OR REPLACE TRIGGER UpdatePicklistTableExample
BEFORE UPDATE
ON PicklistTableExample
FOR EACH ROW
DECLARE
 I PLS_INTEGER;
BEGIN
 I := 0;
 SELECT COUNT(1)
 INTO I
 FROM Picklist
 WHERE picklistDomainID = 1 AND -- 1 = colorOptionType
    picklistID = :new.value;
 IF I = 0 THEN
   RAISE_APPLICATION_ERROR(-20000,
            'Not good colorOptionType');
 END IF;
END;
```

> **NOTE**
>
> Triggers for picklists are frequently not created. Because a picklist is most useful when there are numerous enumerations, this would cause a proliferation of triggers. If they are created, they are sometimes used in development and dropped or disabled in the test and production environments. Essentially, the triggers mimic referential integrity but at a much greater run-time cost.

### 22.2.3 whiteSpace Constraining Facet

The whiteSpace constraining facet is implicitly specified for most datatypes and cannot be changed by the XML schema designer. Whitespace is collapsed for all non-string datatypes as well as list datatypes (that is, IDREFS, ENTITIES, and NMTOKENS). It is always preserved for the string datatype and can be preserved, replaced, or collapsed for all datatypes derived by restriction from the string datatype. Whitespace is always REPLACE for the normalized string datatype, and can be REPLACE or COLLAPSE for all datatypes derived by restriction from the normalizedString datatype.

Database designers need to understand whether an XML instance will contain extra space that needs to be collapsed automatically. For most datatypes, this is inconsequential because mapping a decimal datatype to a database NUMBER column datatype automatically removes extraneous whitespace. However, for XML Schema datatypes that are mapped to a database character column datatype, this becomes important.

When whitespace is to be replaced, the tab, line feed, and carriage return characters need to be replaced by a space. The following SQL fragment can accomplish this:

```
TRANSLATE(?replaceWhitespaceValue,
    UNISTR('\0009') || UNISTR('\000A') || UNISTR('\000D'),
    ' ')
```

where the ?replaceWhitespaceValue bind variable is replaced by the appropriate string.

When whitespace is to be collapsed, the tab, line feed, and carriage return characters need to be replaced by a space. The following SQL fragment can accomplish this:

```
REPLACE(TRIM(TRANSLATE(?collapseWhitespaceValue,
        UNISTR('\0009') || UNISTR('\000A') ||
        UNISTR('\000D'), ' ')),
   ' ', ' ')
```

where the ?collapseWhitespaceValue bind variable is replaced by the appropriate string.

## 22.3 Check Constraints versus Triggers

For each of the individual datatypes, this chapter presents examples using both check constraints in table creation and insert and update triggers. Which is best depends on the datatype being implemented and other system considerations. Here are some considerations:

- Check constraints are far less verbose than triggers in terms of code.
- Check constraints are not PL/SQL procedures and thus have limited functionality.
- Other parts of the database may rely on triggers already or may have no triggers and already use check constraints.
- Besides the validation work required against the XML schema document, other validations may be required for the system. Triggers are a more natural fit because multiple triggers can be defined for the same event.
- The users/developers who will actually get the database error or need to easily interpret the error. Unlike check constraints, triggers are allowed to define the error message. Oracle provides a PL/SQL procedure RAISE_APPLICATION_ERROR to allow application-defined error messages and error numbers.

The important point is to decide on a set of guidelines during the database design process and enforce it during implementation. The examples in this chapter demonstrate the use of both, when applicable.

## 22.4 Datatypes

This section covers each of the XML Schema built-in datatypes and provides design issues, implementation considerations, and warnings when implementing an XML Schema datatype as a database column datatype. Both check constraints and triggers are listed, when appropriate, as both implementations are applicable in many cases.

### 22.4.1 `string` Datatype

The `string` datatype in XML Schema is defined to support, at a minimum, UTF-8 and UTF-16 representations. Oracle9*i* is the first version of the Oracle database to fully support these representations (Oracle8*i* has partial support for UTF-8). Oracle9*i* also supports 8-bit character sets such as ISO-Latin-8859-1 that might be appropriate if full international support is not required. Oraclea9*i* supports the following character column datatypes (each with a maximum length):

- CHAR: 2000 characters
- NCHAR: 2000 bytes
- VARCHAR2: 4000 characters
- NVARCHAR2: 4000 bytes

- `CLOB`: 4 gigabytes
- `NCLOB`: 4 gigabytes

in which the "N" versions of the character column datatypes are used for UTF-8 and UTF-16 representations. Depending on the maximum length specified and whether the text is of a variable length, different character datatypes should be used.

### 22.4.1.1 `CLOB` Support in Oracle

A `CLOB` should not be used lightly, because a `VARCHAR2` is more space- and time-efficient. However, `CLOB` support in Oracle9*i* has greatly increased over Oracle8*i*. The PL/SQL functions in Oracle8*i* that support `VARCHAR2` now support a `CLOB` as well. Unfortunately, PL/SQL limits the size of character variables to 32,767 characters or fewer. Above this size, `DBMS_LOB` package functions must be used. Table 22.1 lists the mapping when `DBMS_LOB` package functions must be used.

**TABLE 22.1**  Mapping of Typical PL/SQL Functions to `DBMS_LOB` Package Functions for a Large CLOB

| Typical PL/SQL | DBMS_LOB *Package Functions* |
|---|---|
| INSTR | DBMS_LOB.INSTR |
| LENGTH | DBMS_LOB.GET_LENGTH |
| SUBSTR | DBMS_LOB.SUBSTR |

Implementations for the `minLength` constraining facet in this section cover both sets of functions.

Finally, the use of a before trigger for a `CLOB` is disallowed by Oracle because the :new value is not available. In addition, table check constraints are not allowed. As a result, using an after trigger forces application developers to roll back the insert or update statement manually.

### 22.4.1.2 `length` Constraining Facet

The database `CHAR` or `NCHAR` column datatypes are appropriate if there is a `length` constraining facet. Unlike their variable equivalents, space for these database column datatypes is allocated on a fixed basis rather than on a variable basis.

There is no built-in database support for the `length` constraining facet, but this can be added as a column constraint in table creation or as a trigger. See Section 22.4.1.3 for details.

### 22.4.1.3 `minLength` Constraining Facet

There is no built-in database support for the `minLength` constraining facet, but this can be added as a column constraint in table creation or as a trigger. Using the `VARCHAR2` column datatype, Listing 22.7 implements this as a column constraint, and Listing 22.8 implements this as a trigger. Listing 22.9 implements the `minLength`, using a `CLOB` column datatype. Refer to Section 22.3 regarding the decision to use column constraints or triggers.

> **NOTE**
>
> If the database table column is specified as an NCHAR, an NVARCHAR2, or an NCLOB, then use the LENGTHC function instead of the LENGTH function, as LENGTHC counts the number of octets in the value.

**LISTING 22.7** StringExample Table Creation with a Column Constraint by Using VARCHAR2

```
CREATE TABLE StringExample (
value VARCHAR2(30) CHECK (LENGTH(value) >= 5)
);
```

**LISTING 22.8** StringExample Table Creation with Insert and Update Triggers by Using VARCHAR2

```
CREATE TABLE StringExample (
value VARCHAR2(30)
);

CREATE OR REPLACE TRIGGER InsertStringExample
BEFORE INSERT
ON StringExample
FOR EACH ROW
WHEN (LENGTH(new.value) < 5)
BEGIN
RAISE_APPLICATION_ERROR(-20000, 'String too small');
END;

CREATE OR REPLACE TRIGGER UpdateStringExample
BEFORE UPDATE
ON StringExample
FOR EACH ROW
WHEN (LENGTH(new.value) < 5)
BEGIN
RAISE_APPLICATION_ERROR(-20000, 'String too small');

END;
```

**LISTING 22.9** CLOBStringExample Table Creation with Insert and Update Triggers by Using a CLOB

```
CREATE TABLE CLOBStringExample (
value CLOB
);
```

```
CREATE OR REPLACE TRIGGER InsertCLOBStringExample
AFTER INSERT
ON CLOBStringExample
FOR EACH ROW
BEGIN
IF DBMS_LOB.GETLENGTH(:new.value) < 5 THEN
 RAISE_APPLICATION_ERROR(-20000, 'String too small');
END IF;
END;

CREATE OR REPLACE TRIGGER UpdateCLOBStringExample
BEFORE UPDATE
ON CLOBStringExample
FOR EACH ROW
BEGIN
IF DBMS_LOB.GETLENGTH(:new.value) < 5 THEN
 RAISE_APPLICATION_ERROR(-20000, 'String too small');
END IF;
END;
```

### 22.4.1.4 `maxLength` Constraining Facet

This facet is directly supported in the database because the maximum character length is specified at column creation. If the XML schema designer did not place a `maxLength` constraining facet, it is best to make the designer do so. If this is not possible, it is best to determine whether 4,000 characters/bytes are enough or whether a `CLOB` is required.

### 22.4.1.5 `pattern` Constraining Facet

Refer to Section 22.2.1 for design and implementation issues.

### 22.4.1.6 `enumeration` Constraining Facet

Refer to Section 22.2.2 for design and implementation issues.

### 22.4.1.7 `whiteSpace` Constraining Facet

Refer to Section 22.2.3 for design and implementation issues.

## 22.4.2 `normalizedString` Datatype

The `normalizedString` datatype is derived from `string` by restricting the allowable characters. To validate that a string is a `normalizedString`, a constraint or trigger may be created. The `normalizedString` datatype may not contain a carriage return (#xD), line feed (#xA), or tab (#x9). Listing 22.10 implements this datatype as a column constraint, and Listing 22.11 implements this as a trigger. Refer to Section 22.3 regarding the decision to use column constraints or triggers.

**LISTING 22.10** NormalizedStringExample Table Creation with a Column Constraint

```
CREATE TABLE NormalizedStringExample (
value VARCHAR2(30)
    CHECK (INSTR(value, UNISTR('\000D')) = 0 AND
        INSTR(value, UNISTR('\000A')) = 0 AND
        INSTR(value, UNISTR('\0009')) = 0)
);
```

**LISTING 22.11** NormalizedStringExample Table Creation with Insert and Update Triggers

```
CREATE TABLE NormalizedStringExample (
value VARCHAR2(30)
);

CREATE OR REPLACE TRIGGER InsertNormalizedStringExample
BEFORE INSERT
ON NormalizedStringExample
FOR EACH ROW
WHEN (INSTR(new.value, UNISTR('\000D')) <> 0 OR
  INSTR(new.value, UNISTR('\000A')) <> 0 OR
  INSTR(new.value, UNISTR('\0009')) <> 0)
BEGIN
RAISE_APPLICATION_ERROR(-20000, 'Not normalizedString');
END;

CREATE OR REPLACE TRIGGER UpdateNormalizedStringExample
BEFORE UPDATE
ON NormalizedStringExample
FOR EACH ROW
WHEN (INSTR(new.value, UNISTR('\000D')) <> 0 OR
  INSTR(new.value, UNISTR('\000A')) <> 0 OR
  INSTR(new.value, UNISTR('\0009')) <> 0)
BEGIN
RAISE_APPLICATION_ERROR(-20000, 'Not normalizedString');
END;
```

### 22.4.2.1 pattern Constraining Facet
Refer to Section 22.2.1 for design and implementation issues.

### 22.4.2.2 enumeration Constraining Facet
Refer to Section 22.2.2 for design and implementation issues.

### 22.4.2.3 whiteSpace Constraining Facet
Refer to Section 22.2.3 for design and implementation issues.

### 22.4.2.4 `length` Constraining Facet
Refer to Section 22.4.1.2 for design and implementation issues.

### 22.4.2.5 `minLength` Constraining Facet
Refer to Section 22.4.1.3 for design and implementation issues.

### 22.4.2.6 `maxLength` Constraining Facet
Refer to Section 22.4.1.4 for design and implementation issues.

## 22.4.3 `token` Datatype

The `token` datatype is derived from `string` by restricting the allowable characters. To validate that a string is a `token`, a constraint or trigger may be created. The `token` datatype may not contain a carriage return (#xD), line feed (#xA), tab (#x9), two space characters in a row, or spaces surrounding the `token`. Listing 22.12 implements this datatype as a column constraint, and Listing 22.13 implements this as a trigger. Refer to Section 22.3 regarding the decision to use column constraints or triggers.

**LISTING 22.12**  TokenExample Table Creation with a Column Constraint

```
CREATE TABLE TokenExample (
value VARCHAR2(30)
   CHECK (INSTR(value, UNISTR('\000D')) = 0 AND
      INSTR(value, UNISTR('\000A')) = 0 AND
      INSTR(value, UNISTR('\0009')) = 0 AND
      LENGTH(value) = LENGTH(TRIM(value)) AND
      INSTR(value, '  ') = 0)
);
```

**LISTING 22.13**  TokenExample Table Creation with Insert and Update Triggers

```
CREATE TABLE TokenExample (
value VARCHAR2(30)
);

CREATE OR REPLACE TRIGGER InsertTokenExample
BEFORE INSERT
ON TokenExample
FOR EACH ROW
WHEN (INSTR(new.value, UNISTR('\000D')) <> 0 OR
  INSTR(new.value, UNISTR('\000A')) <> 0 OR
  INSTR(new.value, UNISTR('\0009')) <> 0 OR
  LENGTH(new.value) <> LENGTH(TRIM(new.value)) OR
  INSTR(new.value, '  ') <> 0)
BEGIN
```

*continues*

```
RAISE_APPLICATION_ERROR(-20000, 'Not token');
END;

CREATE OR REPLACE TRIGGER UpdateTokenExample
BEFORE UPDATE
ON TokenExample
FOR EACH ROW
WHEN (INSTR(new.value, UNISTR('\000D')) <> 0 OR
  INSTR(new.value, UNISTR('\000A')) <> 0 OR
  INSTR(new.value, UNISTR('\0009')) <> 0 OR
  LENGTH(new.value) <> LENGTH(TRIM(new.value)) OR
  INSTR(new.value, '  ') <> 0)
BEGIN
RAISE_APPLICATION_ERROR(-20000, 'Not token');
END;
```

#### 22.4.3.1 `pattern` Constraining Facet
Refer to Section 22.2.1 for design and implementation issues.

#### 22.4.3.2 `enumeration` Constraining Facet
Refer to Section 22.2.2 for design and implementation issues.

#### 22.4.3.3 `whiteSpace` Constraining Facet
Refer to Section 22.2.3 for design and implementation issues.

#### 22.4.3.4 `length` Constraining Facet
Refer to Section 22.4.1.2 for design and implementation issues.

#### 22.4.3.5 `minLength` Constraining Facet
Refer to Section 22.4.1.3 for design and implementation issues.

#### 22.4.3.6 `maxLength` Constraining Facet
Refer to Section 22.4.1.4 for design and implementation issues.

### 22.4.4 `language` Datatype

Restricting a database schema to valid language identifiers requires some work to set up and maintain. Refer to *RFC 1766: Tags for the Identification of Languages 1995*, `http://www.ietf.org/rfc/rfc1766.txt` for specific details. As a quick summary, a langcode may be any of the following:

- A two-letter language code as defined by ISO 639.
- A language identifier beginning with the prefix 'i-' (or 'I-'); these are registered with the Internet Assigned Numbers Authority (IANA).
- A country code beginning with the prefixes as defined by ISO 3166.

- A language identifier beginning with the prefix 'x-' (or 'X-'); these are assigned for private use.

For more complete, accurate, and up-to-date information, review the RFC.

To partially ensure that valid language values are the only ones used, the values from ISO 639, the IANA, and ISO 3166 must be inserted into the database and checked for each entry. Because these are enumerations that will change over time, a picklist implementation is used. Because the constraints listed for languages are too complex for check constraints, triggers will be created instead.

Listing 22.14 adds the language code domains to the `PicklistDomain` table and some of the entries required to the `Picklist` table. Listing 22.15 creates a contrived table that uses the language domains with triggers to enforce the XML Recommendation, *Extensible Markup Language (XML) 1.0 (Second Edition)* on languages.

**LISTING 22.14**  `PicklistDomain` and `Picklist` Table Entries for Language Codes

```
INSERT INTO PicklistDomain
(picklistDomainID, name, description)
VALUES
(2, 'TwoLanguageLetterCodes',
'The two-letter language code as defined by [ISO 639],[ccc]
Codes for the representation of names of languages');

INSERT INTO PicklistDomain
(picklistDomainID, name, description)
VALUES
(3, 'IANACodes',
'A language identifier registered with the Internet Assigned [ccc]
Numbers Authority [IANA]; these begin with the prefix i- (or I-)');

INSERT INTO PicklistDomain
(picklistDomainID, name, description)
VALUES
(4, 'TwoLanguageCountryCodes',
'The country code from [ISO 3166], [ccc]
Codes for the representation of names of countries.');

INSERT INTO Picklist
(picklistID, picklistDomainID, name, description)
VALUES
(5, 2, 'en', 'English');

INSERT INTO Picklist
(picklistID, picklistDomainID, name, description)
VALUES
(6, 3, 'I-', '');
```

*continues*

```
INSERT INTO Picklist
(picklistID, picklistDomainID, name, description)
VALUES
(7, 4, 'US', 'United States');

INSERT INTO Picklist
(picklistID, picklistDomainID, name, description)
VALUES
(8, 4, 'GB', 'Great Britain');
COMMIT;
```

**LISTING 22.15** Use of the Language Domains in a Table with Trigger Enforcement

```
CREATE TABLE LanguageExample (
value VARCHAR2(255)
);

CREATE OR REPLACE TRIGGER InsertLanguageExample
BEFORE INSERT
ON LanguageExample
FOR EACH ROW
DECLARE
 I PLS_INTEGER;
BEGIN
I := 0;

SELECT COUNT(1)
INTO I
FROM Picklist TwoLanguageLetterCodes, Picklist IANACodes,
     Picklist TwoLanguageCountryCodes
WHERE --Match up the appropriate picklist domains to get
    --the right values.
    TwoLanguageLetterCodes.picklistDomainID = 2 AND
    IANACodes.picklistDomainID = 3 AND
    TwoLanguageCountryCodes.picklistDomainID = 4 AND
    (TwoLanguageLetterCodes.name = :new.value OR
    IANACodes.name = :new.value OR
    -- The language is private and starts with X- or x-
    INSTR(UPPER(:new.value), 'X-') = 1 OR
      -- The language is more than two characters and
      -- therefore must be followed by a country code
      -- subcode.
      (TwoLanguageLetterCodes.name =
         SUBSTR(:new.value, 1, 2) AND
      TwoLanguageCountryCodes.name =
         SUBSTR(:new.value, 4, 2)));
IF I = 0 THEN
```

```
 RAISE_APPLICATION_ERROR(-20000, 'Not a language');
END IF;
END;

CREATE OR REPLACE TRIGGER UpdateLanguageExample BEFORE INSERT
ON LanguageExample
FOR EACH ROW
WHEN (new.value <> old.value)
DECLARE
I PLS_INTEGER;
BEGIN
SELECT COUNT(1)
INTO I
FROM Picklist TwoLanguageLetterCodes, Picklist IANACodes,
    Picklist TwoLanguageCountryCodes
WHERE --Match up the appropriate picklist domains to get
    --the right values.
    TwoLanguageLetterCodes.picklistDomainID = 2 AND
    IANACodes.picklistDomainID = 3 AND
    TwoLanguageCountryCodes.picklistDomainID = 4 AND
    (TwoLanguageLetterCodes.name = :new.value OR
    IANACodes.name = :new.value OR
    -- The language is private and starts with X- or x-
    INSTR(UPPER(:new.value), 'X-') = 1 OR
     -- The language is more than two characters and
     -- therefore must be followed by a country code
     -- subcode.
    (TwoLanguageLetterCodes.name =
      SUBSTR(:new.value, 1, 2) AND
     TwoLanguageCountryCodes.name =
      SUBSTR(:new.value, 4, 2)));
IF I = 0 THEN
 RAISE_APPLICATION_ERROR(-20000, 'Not a language');
END IF;
END;
```

The two triggers could be refactored to call the same stored procedure.

## 22.4.4.1 pattern Constraining Facet
Refer to Section 22.2.1 for design and implementation issues.

## 22.4.4.2 enumeration Constraining Facet
Refer to Section 22.2.2 for design and implementation issues.

## 22.4.4.3 whiteSpace Constraining Facet
Refer to Section 22.2.3 for design and implementation issues.

### 22.4.4.4 `length` Constraining Facet
Refer to Section 22.4.1.2 for design and implementation issues.

### 22.4.4.5 `minLength` Constraining Facet
Refer to Section 22.4.1.3 for design and implementation issues.

### 22.4.4.6 `maxLength` Constraining Facet
Refer to Section 22.4.1.4 for design and implementation issues.

## 22.4.5 Name Datatype

The `Name` datatype is derived from `token` by restricting the first character to a letter or underscore or colon. Unfortunately, the allowable characters are over 250 ranges of Unicode characters that would be tedious to implement in Oracle9*i*.

An alternative is to determine the characters in the `Name` datatype required for your application, and use this set for compliance checking. If this set is small, enforcing this datatype is easier to implement. For example, if the character set is United States English, the list of allowable characters is 'A' to 'Z', '0' to '9', underscore, colon, period, and ASCII hyphen. Listing 22.16 implements this datatype as a column constraint, and Listing 22.17 implements this as a trigger. Refer to Section 22.3 regarding the decision to use column constraints or triggers.

**LISTING 22.16** `NameExample` Table Creation with a Column Constraint

```
CREATE TABLE NameExample (
value VARCHAR2(30)
    CHECK (LENGTH(TRANSLATE(UPPER(value),
        '_:.-ABCDEFGHIJKLMNOPQRSTUVWXYZ0123456789,/;''[]\<>?"{}|~!@#$%^&*()+=',
        '_:.-ABCDEFGHIJKLMNOPQRSTUVWXYZ0123456789'))
     = LENGTH(value) AND
    (UPPER(SUBSTR(value, 1, 1))
       BETWEEN 'A' AND 'Z' OR
     SUBSTR(value, 1, 1) IN ('_', ':')) AND
    INSTR(value, UNISTR('\000D')) = 0 AND
    INSTR(value, UNISTR('\000A')) = 0 AND
    INSTR(value, UNISTR('\0009')) = 0 AND
    LENGTH(value) = LENGTH(TRIM(value)) AND
    INSTR(value, ' ') = 0)
);
```

**LISTING 22.17** `NameExample` Table Creation with Insert and Update Triggers

```
CREATE TABLE NameExample (
value VARCHAR2(30)
);
```

```
CREATE OR REPLACE TRIGGER InsertNameExample
BEFORE INSERT
ON NameExample
FOR EACH ROW
WHEN (LENGTH(TRANSLATE(UPPER(new.value),
       '_:.-ABCDEFGHIJKLMNOPQRSTUVWXYZ0123456789,/;''[]\<>?"{}|~!@#$%^&*()+=',
       '_:.-ABCDEFGHIJKLMNOPQRSTUVWXYZ0123456789')) <>
   LENGTH(new.value) OR
  NOT (UPPER(SUBSTR(new.value, 1, 1))
    BETWEEN 'A' AND 'Z' OR
  SUBSTR(new.value, 1, 1) IN ('_', ':')) OR
  INSTR(new.value, UNISTR('\000D')) <> 0 OR
  INSTR(new.value, UNISTR('\000A')) <> 0 OR
  INSTR(new.value, UNISTR('\0009')) <> 0 OR
  LENGTH(new.value) <> LENGTH(TRIM(new.value)) OR
  INSTR(new.value, '  ') <> 0)
BEGIN
RAISE_APPLICATION_ERROR(-20000, 'Not Name');
END;

CREATE OR REPLACE TRIGGER UpdateNameExample
BEFORE UPDATE
ON NameExample
FOR EACH ROW
WHEN (LENGTH(TRANSLATE(UPPER(new.value),
       '_:.-ABCDEFGHIJKLMNOPQRSTUVWXYZ0123456789,/;''[]\<>?"{}|~!@#$%^&*()+=',
       '_:.-ABCDEFGHIJKLMNOPQRSTUVWXYZ0123456789')) <>
   LENGTH(new.value) OR
  NOT (UPPER(SUBSTR(new.value, 1, 1))
    BETWEEN 'A' AND 'Z' OR
  SUBSTR(new.value, 1, 1) IN ('_', ':')) OR
  INSTR(new.value, UNISTR('\000D')) <> 0 OR
  INSTR(new.value, UNISTR('\000A')) <> 0 OR
  INSTR(new.value, UNISTR('\0009')) <> 0 OR
  LENGTH(new.value) <> LENGTH(TRIM(new.value)) OR
  INSTR(new.value, '  ') <> 0)
BEGIN
RAISE_APPLICATION_ERROR(-20000, 'Not Name');
END;
```

### 22.4.5.1 pattern Constraining Facet
Refer to Section 22.2.1 for design and implementation issues.

### 22.4.5.2 enumeration Constraining Facet
Refer to Section 22.2.2 for design and implementation issues.

### 22.4.5.3 `whiteSpace` Constraining Facet
Refer to Section 22.2.3 for design and implementation issues.

### 22.4.5.4 `length` Constraining Facet
Refer to Section 22.4.1.2 for design and implementation issues.

### 22.4.5.5 `minLength` Constraining Facet
Refer to Section 22.4.1.3 for design and implementation issues.

### 22.4.5.6 `maxLength` Constraining Facet
Refer to Section 22.4.1.4 for design and implementation issues.

## 22.4.6 NCName Datatype

The `NCName` datatype is derived from the `Name` datatype by restricting the first character to a letter or underscore. Unfortunately, the allowable characters are over 250 ranges of Unicode characters that would be tedious to implement in Oracle9*i*. `NCName` differs from the `Name` datatype in that the colon character is disallowed.

An alternative is to determine the characters in the `NCName` datatype required for your application, and use this set for compliance checking. If this set is small, enforcing this datatype is easier to implement. For example, if the character set is United States English, the list of allowable characters is 'A' to 'Z', '0' to '9', underscore, period, and ASCII hyphen. Listing 22.18 implements this datatype as a column constraint, and Listing 22.19 implements this as a trigger. Refer to Section 22.3 regarding the decision to use column constraints or triggers.

**LISTING 22.18**  `NCNameExample` Table Creation with a Column Constraint

```
CREATE TABLE NCNameExample (
value VARCHAR2(30)
   CHECK (LENGTH(TRANSLATE(UPPER(value),
       '.-_ABCDEFGHIJKLMNOPQRSTUVWXYZ0123456789,/;''[]\<>?"{}|~!@#$%^&*()+=:',
       '.-_ABCDEFGHIJKLMNOPQRSTUVWXYZ0123456789')) =
     LENGTH(value) AND
     (UPPER(SUBSTR(value, 1, 1))
       BETWEEN 'A' AND 'Z' OR
      SUBSTR(value, 1, 1) = '_') AND
     INSTR(value, UNISTR('\000D')) = 0 AND
     INSTR(value, UNISTR('\000A')) = 0 AND
     INSTR(value, UNISTR('\0009')) = 0 AND
     LENGTH(value) = LENGTH(TRIM(value)) AND
     INSTR(value, ' ') = 0)
);
```

**LISTING 22.19**  NCNameExample Table Creation with Insert and Update Triggers

```
CREATE TABLE NCNameExample (
value VARCHAR2(30)
);

CREATE OR REPLACE TRIGGER InsertNCNameExample
BEFORE INSERT
ON NCNameExample
FOR EACH ROW
WHEN (LENGTH(TRANSLATE(UPPER(new.value),
      '.-_ABCDEFGHIJKLMNOPQRSTUVWXYZ0123456789,/;''[]\<>?"{}|~!@#$%^&*()+=:',
      '.-_ABCDEFGHIJKLMNOPQRSTUVWXYZ0123456789')) <>
   LENGTH(new.value) OR
  NOT (UPPER(SUBSTR(new.value, 1, 1))
      BETWEEN 'A' AND 'Z' OR
    SUBSTR(new.value, 1, 1) = '_') OR
  INSTR(new.value, UNISTR('\000D')) <> 0 OR
  INSTR(new.value, UNISTR('\000A')) <> 0 OR
  INSTR(new.value, UNISTR('\0009')) <> 0 OR
  LENGTH(new.value) <> LENGTH(TRIM(new.value)) OR
  INSTR(new.value, ' ') <> 0)
BEGIN
RAISE_APPLICATION_ERROR(-20000, 'Not NCName');
END;

CREATE OR REPLACE TRIGGER UpdateNCNameExample
BEFORE UPDATE
ON NCNameExample
FOR EACH ROW
WHEN (LENGTH(TRANSLATE(UPPER(new.value),
      '.-_ABCDEFGHIJKLMNOPQRSTUVWXYZ0123456789,/;''[]\<>?"{}|~!@#$%^&*()+=:',
      '.-_ABCDEFGHIJKLMNOPQRSTUVWXYZ0123456789')) <>
   LENGTH(new.value) OR
  NOT (UPPER(SUBSTR(new.value, 1, 1))
      BETWEEN 'A' AND 'Z' OR
    SUBSTR(new.value, 1, 1) = '_') OR
  INSTR(new.value, UNISTR('\000D')) <> 0 OR
  INSTR(new.value, UNISTR('\000A')) <> 0 OR
  INSTR(new.value, UNISTR('\0009')) <> 0 OR
  LENGTH(new.value) <> LENGTH(TRIM(new.value)) OR
  INSTR(new.value, ' ') <> 0)
BEGIN
RAISE_APPLICATION_ERROR(-20000, 'Not NCName');
END;
```

### 22.4.6.1 `pattern` Constraining Facet
Refer to Section 22.2.1 for design and implementation issues.

### 22.4.6.2 `enumeration` Constraining Facet
Refer to Section 22.2.2 for design and implementation issues.

### 22.4.6.3 `whiteSpace` Constraining Facet
Refer to Section 22.2.3 for design and implementation issues.

### 22.4.6.4 `length` Constraining Facet
Refer to Section 22.4.1.2 for design and implementation issues.

### 22.4.6.5 `minLength` Constraining Facet
Refer to Section 22.4.1.3 for design and implementation issues.

### 22.4.6.6 `maxLength` Constraining Facet
Refer to Section 22.4.1.4 for design and implementation issues.

## 22.4.7 ID Datatype

Although the `ID` datatype is derived from `NCName`, it has the same value space as `NCName`. Refer to Section 22.4.6 for details on how to implement this type.

## 22.4.8 IDREF Datatype

Although the `IDREF` datatype is derived from `NCName`, it has the same value space as `NCName`. Refer to Section 22.4.6 for details on how to implement this type.

## 22.4.9 IDREFS Datatype

Because the `IDREFS` datatype is a list of `IDREF` datatypes, the same constraints that apply to `IDREF` (which essentially is an `NCName`) are applicable. Refer to Section 22.4.6 for details on how to implement this type. Unlike `NCName`, however, there are three distinct ways to implement the `IDREFS` datatype:

- Create a single column to hold the list of `IDREFS` as a set of characters.
- Create a table to hold the `IDREFS` that are associated with a primary table.
- Create a single column of type `VARRAY` to hold the list of `IDREFS`.

Each of these approaches has its own merits. The first places little burden on the application developer or database designer and is applicable if the sole purpose is to insert, update, delete, and select the values in their entirety. The second requires more work from both the application developer and the database designer, but allows individual `IDREF` values that are part of the list to be easily inserted, updated, deleted, and selected. The third requires the most work from both the application developer and database designer and provides little benefit beyond the first approach. Its implementation will not be detailed.

In either the first or second approach, IDREFS is derived from the NCName datatype by restricting the first character to a letter or underscore. Unfortunately, the allowable characters are over 250 ranges of Unicode characters that would be tedious to implement in Oracle9*i*. An alternative is to determine the characters in the IDREFS datatype required for your application, and use this set for compliance checking. If this set is small, enforcing this datatype is easier to implement. For example, if the character set is United States English, the list of allowable characters is 'A' to 'Z', '0' to '9', space, period, ASCII hyphen, and underscore.

### 22.4.9.1 Single Column

In a single column scenario, the IDREFS datatype is essentially a multivalued NCNAME datatype where the values are maintained as a single string. Listing 22.20 implements IDREFS datatype as a column constraint, and Listing 22.21 implements this as a trigger. Refer to Section 22.3 regarding the decision to use column constraints or triggers.

**LISTING 22.20**  IDREFSExample Single Column Table Creation with a Column Constraint

```
CREATE TABLE IDREFSExample (
value VARCHAR2(30)
   CHECK (LENGTH(TRANSLATE(UPPER(value),
       '.-_ABCDEFGHIJKLMNOPQRSTUVWXYZ0123456789,/;''[]\<>?"{}|~!@#$%^&*()+=:',
       '.-_ABCDEFGHIJKLMNOPQRSTUVWXYZ0123456789')) =
     LENGTH(value) AND
     (UPPER(SUBSTR(value, 1, 1))
       BETWEEN 'A' AND 'Z' OR
      SUBSTR(value, 1, 1) = '_') AND
     INSTR(value, UNISTR('\000D')) = 0 AND
     INSTR(value, UNISTR('\000A')) = 0 AND
     INSTR(value, UNISTR('\0009')) = 0 AND
     LENGTH(value) = LENGTH(TRIM(value)) AND
     INSTR(value, ' ') = 0)
);
```

**LISTING 22.21**  IDREFSExample Single Column Table Creation with Insert and Update Triggers

```
CREATE TABLE IDREFSExample (
value VARCHAR2(30)
);

CREATE OR REPLACE TRIGGER InsertIDREFSExample
BEFORE INSERT
ON IDREFSExample
FOR EACH ROW
```

*continues*

```
       WHEN (LENGTH(TRANSLATE(UPPER(new.value),
              '.-_ABCDEFGHIJKLMNOPQRSTUVWXYZ0123456789,/;''[]\<>?"{}|~!@#$%^&*()+=:',
              '.-_ABCDEFGHIJKLMNOPQRSTUVWXYZ0123456789')) <>
           LENGTH(new.value) OR
          NOT (UPPER(SUBSTR(new.value, 1, 1))
              BETWEEN 'A' AND 'Z' OR
              SUBSTR(new.value, 1, 1) = '_') OR
          INSTR(new.value, UNISTR('\000D')) <> 0 OR
          INSTR(new.value, UNISTR('\000A')) <> 0 OR
          INSTR(new.value, UNISTR('\0009')) <> 0 OR
          LENGTH(new.value) <> LENGTH(TRIM(new.value)) OR
          INSTR(new.value, ' ') <> 0)
       BEGIN
       RAISE_APPLICATION_ERROR(-20000, 'Not IDREFS');
       END;

       CREATE OR REPLACE TRIGGER UpdateIDREFSExample
       BEFORE UPDATE
       ON IDREFSExample
       FOR EACH ROW
       WHEN (LENGTH(TRANSLATE(UPPER(new.value),
              '.-_ABCDEFGHIJKLMNOPQRSTUVWXYZ0123456789,/;''[]\<>?"{}|~!@#$%^&*()+=:',
              '.-_ABCDEFGHIJKLMNOPQRSTUVWXYZ0123456789')) <>
           LENGTH(new.value) OR
          NOT (UPPER(SUBSTR(new.value, 1, 1))
              BETWEEN 'A' AND 'Z' OR
              SUBSTR(new.value, 1, 1) = '_') OR
          INSTR(new.value, UNISTR('\000D')) <> 0 OR
          INSTR(new.value, UNISTR('\000A')) <> 0 OR
          INSTR(new.value, UNISTR('\0009')) <> 0 OR
          LENGTH(new.value) <> LENGTH(TRIM(new.value)) OR
          INSTR(new.value, ' ') <> 0)
       BEGIN
       RAISE_APPLICATION_ERROR(-20000, 'Not IDREFS');
       END;
```

### 22.4.9.2 Separate Table

In a separate table scenario, the IDREFS datatype is essentially a multivalued NCNAME datatype where each value is stored separately in a table row. In Listing 22.22 and Listing 22.23, a sequence, primary keys, and a foreign key are created. A sequence provides the unique values for the primary key of the IDREFSExample table. The sole column of the IDREFSExample table, IDREFSExampleID, is a foreign key to the IDREFSInternalExample table that also has listOrder as the second part of the primary key. The IDREFSInternalExample table holds the IDREF value. Listing 22.24 shows how an IDREFS example of 'a b c' would be inserted into the database.

22.4 Datatypes
CHAPTER 22

Listing 22.22 implements IDREFS datatype as a column constraint, and Listing 22.23 implements this as a trigger. Refer to Section 22.3 regarding the decision to use column constraints or triggers.

**LISTING 22.22**  IDREFS Example Tables Creation with a Column Constraint

```
--Start the sequence at 1, don't let it cycle, and have
--the numbers in the sequence ordered.
CREATE SEQUENCE Seq_IDREFS INCREMENT BY 1 START
 WITH 1 MAXVALUE 999999999 MINVALUE 1 NOCYCLE ORDER;

CREATE TABLE IDREFSExample (
IDREFSExampleID NUMBER(9) NOT NULL,
PRIMARY KEY (IDREFSExampleID)
);

CREATE TABLE IDREFSInternalExample (
IDREFSInternalExampleID NUMBER(9) NOT NULL,
listOrder       NUMBER(3) NOT NULL,
value           VARCHAR2(30)
 CHECK (LENGTH(TRANSLATE(UPPER(value),
      '.-_ABCDEFGHIJKLMNOPQRSTUVWXYZ0123456789,/;''[]\<>?"{}|~!@#$%^&*()+=:',
      '.-_ABCDEFGHIJKLMNOPQRSTUVWXYZ0123456789')) =
    LENGTH(value) AND
    (UPPER(SUBSTR(value, 1, 1))
     BETWEEN 'A' AND 'Z' OR
    SUBSTR(value, 1, 1) = '_') AND
    INSTR(value, UNISTR('\000D')) = 0 AND
    INSTR(value, UNISTR('\000A')) = 0 AND
    INSTR(value, UNISTR('\0009')) = 0 AND
    LENGTH(value) = LENGTH(TRIM(value)) AND
    INSTR(value, ' ') = 0),
PRIMARY KEY (IDREFSInternalExampleID, listOrder),
FOREIGN KEY (IDREFSInternalExampleID)
REFERENCES IDREFSExample
);
```

**LISTING 22.23**  IDREFS Example Tables Creation with Insert and Update Triggers

```
--Start the sequence at 1, don't let it cycle, and have
--the numbers in the sequence ordered.
CREATE SEQUENCE Seq_IDREFS INCREMENT BY 1 START
 WITH 1 MAXVALUE 999999999 MINVALUE 1 NOCYCLE ORDER;

CREATE TABLE IDREFSExample (
IDREFSExampleID NUMBER(9) NOT NULL,
```

*continues*

```
  PRIMARY KEY (IDREFSExampleID)
);

CREATE TABLE IDREFSInternalExample (
IDREFSInternalExampleID  NUMBER(9) NOT NULL,
listOrder      NUMBER(3) NOT NULL,
value          VARCHAR2(30),
PRIMARY KEY (IDREFSInternalExampleID, listOrder),
FOREIGN KEY (IDREFSInternalExampleID)
REFERENCES IDREFSExample
);

CREATE OR REPLACE TRIGGER InsertIDREFSInternalExample
BEFORE INSERT
ON IDREFSInternalExample
FOR EACH ROW
WHEN (LENGTH(TRANSLATE(UPPER(new.value),
        '.-_ABCDEFGHIJKLMNOPQRSTUVWXYZ0123456789,/;''[]\<>?"{}|~!@#$%^&*()+=:',
        '.-_ABCDEFGHIJKLMNOPQRSTUVWXYZ0123456789')) <>
   LENGTH(new.value) OR
  NOT (UPPER(SUBSTR(new.value, 1, 1))
      BETWEEN 'A' AND 'Z' OR
      SUBSTR(new.value, 1, 1) = '_') OR
  INSTR(new.value, UNISTR('\000D')) <> 0 OR
  INSTR(new.value, UNISTR('\000A')) <> 0 OR
  INSTR(new.value, UNISTR('\0009')) <> 0 OR
  LENGTH(new.value) <> LENGTH(TRIM(new.value)) OR
  INSTR(new.value, ' ') <> 0)
BEGIN
RAISE_APPLICATION_ERROR(-20000, 'Not IDREFS');
END;

CREATE OR REPLACE TRIGGER UpdateIDREFSInternalExample
BEFORE UPDATE
ON IDREFSInternalExample
FOR EACH ROW
WHEN (LENGTH(TRANSLATE(UPPER(new.value),
      '.-_ABCDEFGHIJKLMNOPQRSTUVWXYZ0123456789,/;''[]\<>?"{}|~!@#$%^&*()+=:',
      '.-_ABCDEFGHIJKLMNOPQRSTUVWXYZ0123456789')) <>
   LENGTH(new.value) OR
  NOT (UPPER(SUBSTR(new.value, 1, 1))
      BETWEEN 'A' AND 'Z' OR
      SUBSTR(new.value, 1, 1) = '_') OR
  INSTR(new.value, UNISTR('\000D')) <> 0 OR
  INSTR(new.value, UNISTR('\000A')) <> 0 OR
  INSTR(new.value, UNISTR('\0009')) <> 0 OR
  LENGTH(new.value) <> LENGTH(TRIM(new.value)) OR
  INSTR(new.value, ' ') <> 0)
```

```
BEGIN
RAISE_APPLICATION_ERROR(-20000, 'Not IDREFS');
END;
```

**LISTING 22.24**   IDREFS Example Values Insertion

```
INSERT INTO IDREFSExample
VALUES
(Seq_IDREFS.NEXTVAL);

INSERT INTO IDREFSInternalExample
VALUES
(Seq_IDREFS.CURRVAL, 1, 'a');

INSERT INTO IDREFSInternalExample
VALUES
(Seq_IDREFS.CURRVAL, 2, 'b');

INSERT INTO IDREFSInternalExample
VALUES
(Seq_IDREFS.CURRVAL, 3, 'c');
```

### 22.4.9.3 `pattern` Constraining Facet
Refer to Section 22.2.1 for design and implementation issues.

### 22.4.9.4 `enumeration` Constraining Facet
Refer to Section 22.2.2 for design and implementation issues.

### 22.4.9.5 `whiteSpace` Constraining Facet
Refer to Section 22.2.3 for design and implementation issues.

### 22.4.9.6 `length` Constraining Facet
Refer to Section 22.4.1.2 for design and implementation issues.

### 22.4.9.7 `minLength` Constraining Facet
Refer to Section 22.4.1.3 for design and implementation issues.

### 22.4.9.8 `maxLength` Constraining Facet
Refer to Section 22.4.1.4 for design and implementation issues.

## 22.4.10 ENTITY Datatype
Although the ENTITY datatype is derived from NCName, it has the same value space as NCName. Refer to Section 22.4.6 for details on how to implement this datatype.

## 22.4.11 ENTITIES Datatype

Although the ENTITIES datatype is a not derived from IDREFS, it has the same value space as IDREFS. Refer to Section 22.4.9 for details on how to implement this datatype.

## 22.4.12 NMTOKEN Datatype

The NMTOKEN datatype is derived from the token datatype and restricts the allowable characters. Unfortunately, the allowable characters are over 250 ranges of Unicode characters that would be tedious to implement in Oracle9*i*.

An alternative is to determine the characters in the NMTOKEN datatype for required for your application, and use this set for compliance checking. If this set is small, enforcing this datatype is easier to implement. For example, if the character set is United States English, the list of allowable characters is 'A' to 'Z', '0' to '9', underscore, colon, period, and ASCII hyphen. Listing 22.25 implements NMTOKEN as a column constraint, and Listing 22.26 implements it as a trigger. Refer to Section 22.3 regarding the decision to use column constraints or triggers.

**LISTING 22.25**  NMTOKENExample Table Creation with a Column Constraint

```
CREATE TABLE NMTOKENExample (
value VARCHAR2(30)
    CHECK (LENGTH(TRANSLATE(UPPER(value),
        '.-_:ABCDEFGHIJKLMNOPQRSTUVWXYZ0123456789,/;''[]\<>?"{}|~!@#$%^&*()+=',
        '.-_:ABCDEFGHIJKLMNOPQRSTUVWXYZ0123456789')) =
      LENGTH(value) AND
      INSTR(value, UNISTR('\000D')) = 0 AND
      INSTR(value, UNISTR('\000A')) = 0 AND
      INSTR(value, UNISTR('\0009')) = 0 AND
      LENGTH(value) = LENGTH(TRIM(value)) AND
      INSTR(value, ' ') = 0)
);
```

**LISTING 22.26**  NMTOKENExample Table Creation with Insert and Update Triggers

```
CREATE TABLE NMTOKENExample (
value VARCHAR2(30)
);

CREATE OR REPLACE TRIGGER InsertNMTOKENExample
BEFORE INSERT
ON NMTokenExample
FOR EACH ROW
WHEN (LENGTH(TRANSLATE(UPPER(new.value),
        '.-_:ABCDEFGHIJKLMNOPQRSTUVWXYZ0123456789,/;''[]\<>?"{}|~!@#$%^&*()+=',
```

```
         '.-_:ABCDEFGHIJKLMNOPQRSTUVWXYZ0123456789'))  <>
    LENGTH(new.value) OR
  INSTR(new.value, UNISTR('\000D')) <> 0 OR
  INSTR(new.value, UNISTR('\000A')) <> 0 OR
  INSTR(new.value, UNISTR('\0009')) <> 0 OR
  LENGTH(new.value) <> LENGTH(TRIM(new.value)) OR
  INSTR(new.value, ' ') <> 0)
BEGIN
RAISE_APPLICATION_ERROR(-20000, 'Not NMTOKEN');
END;

CREATE OR REPLACE TRIGGER UpdateNMTOKENExample
BEFORE UPDATE
ON NMTokenExample
FOR EACH ROW
WHEN (LENGTH(TRANSLATE(UPPER(new.value),
         '.-_:ABCDEFGHIJKLMNOPQRSTUVWXYZ0123456789,/;''[]\<>?"{}|~!@#$%^&*()+=',
         '.-_:ABCDEFGHIJKLMNOPQRSTUVWXYZ0123456789'))  <>
    LENGTH(new.value) OR
  INSTR(new.value, UNISTR('\000D')) <> 0 OR
  INSTR(new.value, UNISTR('\000A')) <> 0 OR
  INSTR(new.value, UNISTR('\0009')) <> 0 OR
  LENGTH(new.value) <> LENGTH(TRIM(new.value)) OR
  INSTR(new.value, ' ') <> 0)
BEGIN
RAISE_APPLICATION_ERROR(-20000, 'Not NMTOKEN');
END;
```

### 22.4.12.1 `pattern` Constraining Facet
Refer to Section 22.2.1 for design and implementation issues.

### 22.4.12.2 `enumeration` Constraining Facet
Refer to Section 22.2.2 for design and implementation issues.

### 22.4.12.3 `whiteSpace` Constraining Facet
Refer to Section 22.2.3 for design and implementation issues.

### 22.4.12.4 `length` Constraining Facet
Refer to Section 22.4.1.2 for design and implementation issues.

### 22.4.12.5 `minLength` Constraining Facet
Refer to Section 22.4.1.3 for design and implementation issues.

### 22.4.12.6 `maxLength` Constraining Facet
Refer to Section 22.4.1.4 for design and implementation issues.

## 22.4.13 NMTOKENS Datatype

Because the NMTOKENS datatype is a list of NMTOKEN, the same constraints that apply to NMTOKEN are applicable. Refer to Section 22.4.12 for details on how to implement this datatype. Unlike NMTOKEN, however, there are three distinct ways to implement this datatype:

- Create a single column to hold the list of NMTOKENS as a set of characters.
- Create a table to hold the NMTOKENS that are associated with a primary table.
- Create a single column of type VARRAY to hold the list of NMTOKENS.

Each of these approaches has its own merits. The first places little burden on the application developer or database designer and is applicable if the sole purpose is to insert, update, delete, and select the values in their entirety. The second requires more work from both the application developer and database designer, but allows individual NMTOKEN values that are part of the list to be easily inserted, updated, deleted, and selected. The third requires the most work from both the application developer and database designer and provides little benefit beyond the first approach. Its implementation will not be detailed.

In either the first or second approach, NMTOKENS is derived from the NMTOKEN datatype by restricting the first character to a letter or underscore. Unfortunately, the allowable characters are over 250 ranges of Unicode characters that would be tedious to implement in Oracle9*i*. An alternative is to determine the characters in the NMTOKENS datatype required for your application, and use this set for compliance checking. If this set is small, enforcing this datatype is easier to implement. For example, if the character set is United States English, the list of allowable characters is 'A' to 'Z', '0' to '9', space, period, ASCII hyphen, underscore, and colon.

### 22.4.13.1 Single Column

In a single column scenario, the NMTOKENS datatype is essentially a multivalued NMTOKEN datatype where the values are maintained as a single string. Listing 22.27 implements this datatype as a column constraint, and Listing 22.28 implements this as a trigger. Refer to Section 22.3 regarding the decision to use column constraints or triggers.

**LISTING 22.27** NMTOKENSExample Single-Column Table Creation with a Column Constraint

```
CREATE TABLE NMTOKENSExample (
value VARCHAR2(30)
    CHECK (LENGTH(TRANSLATE(UPPER(value),
        '.-_:ABCDEFGHIJKLMNOPQRSTUVWXYZ0123456789,/;''[]\<>?"{}|~!@#$%^&*()+=',
        '.-_:ABCDEFGHIJKLMNOPQRSTUVWXYZ0123456789')) =
      LENGTH(value) AND
     INSTR(value, UNISTR('\000D')) = 0 AND
     INSTR(value, UNISTR('\000A')) = 0 AND
     INSTR(value, UNISTR('\0009')) = 0 AND
```

```
      LENGTH(value) = LENGTH(TRIM(value)) AND
      INSTR(value, ' ') = 0)
);
```

**LISTING 22.28** NMTOKENSExample Single-Column Table Creation with Insert and Update Triggers

```
CREATE TABLE NMTOKENSExample (
value VARCHAR2(30)
);

CREATE OR REPLACE TRIGGER InsertNMTOKENSExample
BEFORE INSERT
ON NMTOKENSExample
FOR EACH ROW
WHEN (LENGTH(TRANSLATE(UPPER(new.value),
      '.-_:ABCDEFGHIJKLMNOPQRSTUVWXYZ0123456789,/;''[]\<>?"{}|~!@#$%^&*()+=',
      '.-_:ABCDEFGHIJKLMNOPQRSTUVWXYZ0123456789')) <>
   LENGTH(new.value) OR
  INSTR(new.value, UNISTR('\000D')) <> 0 OR
  INSTR(new.value, UNISTR('\000A')) <> 0 OR
  INSTR(new.value, UNISTR('\0009')) <> 0 OR
  LENGTH(new.value) <> LENGTH(TRIM(new.value)) OR
  INSTR(new.value, ' ') <> 0)
BEGIN
RAISE_APPLICATION_ERROR(-20000, 'Not NMTOKENS');
END;

CREATE OR REPLACE TRIGGER UpdateNMTOKENSExample
BEFORE UPDATE
ON NMTOKENSExample
FOR EACH ROW
WHEN (LENGTH(TRANSLATE(UPPER(new.value),
      '.-_:ABCDEFGHIJKLMNOPQRSTUVWXYZ0123456789,/;''[]\<>?"{}|~!@#$%^&*()+=',
      '.-_:ABCDEFGHIJKLMNOPQRSTUVWXYZ0123456789')) <>
   LENGTH(new.value) OR
  INSTR(new.value, UNISTR('\000D')) <> 0 OR
  INSTR(new.value, UNISTR('\000A')) <> 0 OR
  INSTR(new.value, UNISTR('\0009')) <> 0 OR
  LENGTH(new.value) <> LENGTH(TRIM(new.value)) OR
  INSTR(new.value, ' ') <> 0)
BEGIN
RAISE_APPLICATION_ERROR(-20000, 'Not NMTOKENS');
END;
```

### 22.4.13.2 Separate Table

In a separate table scenario, the NMTOKENS datatype is essentially a multivalued NMTOKEN datatype where each value is stored separately in a table row. In Listing 22.29 and Listing 22.30, a sequence, primary keys, and a foreign key are created. A sequence provides the unique values for the primary key of the NMTOKENSExample table. The sole column of the NMTOKENSExample table, NMTOKENSExampleID, is a foreign key to the NMTOKENSInternalExample table that also has listOrder as the second part of the primary key. The NMTOKENSInternalExample table holds the NMTOKEN value. Listing 22.31 shows how a NMTOKENS example of 'a b c' would be inserted into the database.

Listing 22.29 implements this datatype as a column constraint, and Listing 22.30 implements this as a trigger. Refer to Section 22.3 regarding the decision to use column constraints or triggers.

**LISTING 22.29**  NMTOKENS Example Tables Creation with a Column Constraint

```
--Start the sequence at 1, don't let it cycle, and have
--the numbers in the sequence ordered.
CREATE SEQUENCE Seq_NMTOKENS INCREMENT BY 1 START
 WITH 1 MAXVALUE 999999999 MINVALUE 1 NOCYCLE ORDER;

CREATE TABLE NMTOKENSExample (
NMTOKENSExampleID NUMBER(9) NOT NULL,
PRIMARY KEY (NMTOKENSExampleID)
);

CREATE TABLE NMTOKENSInternalExample (
NMTOKENSInternalExampleID NUMBER(9) NOT NULL,
listOrder         NUMBER(3) NOT NULL,
value             VARCHAR2(30)
CHECK (LENGTH(TRANSLATE(UPPER(value),
       '.-_:ABCDEFGHIJKLMNOPQRSTUVWXYZ0123456789,/;''[]\<>?"{}|~!@#$%^&*()+=',
       '.-_:ABCDEFGHIJKLMNOPQRSTUVWXYZ0123456789')) =
    LENGTH(value) AND
   INSTR(value, UNISTR('\000D')) = 0 AND
   INSTR(value, UNISTR('\000A')) = 0 AND
   INSTR(value, UNISTR('\0009')) = 0 AND
   LENGTH(value) = LENGTH(TRIM(value)) AND
   INSTR(value, ' ') = 0),
PRIMARY KEY (NMTOKENSInternalExampleID, listOrder),
FOREIGN KEY (NMTOKENSInternalExampleID)
REFERENCES NMTOKENSExample
);
```

**LISTING 22.30** NMTOKENS Example Tables Creation with Insert and Update Triggers

```
--Start the sequence at 1, don't let it cycle, and have
--the numbers in the sequence ordered.
CREATE SEQUENCE Seq_NMTOKENS INCREMENT BY 1 START
 WITH 1 MAXVALUE 999999999 MINVALUE 1 NOCYCLE ORDER;

CREATE TABLE NMTOKENSExample (
NMTOKENSExampleID NUMBER(9) NOT NULL,
PRIMARY KEY (NMTOKENSExampleID)
);

CREATE TABLE NMTOKENSInternalExample (
NMTOKENSInternalExampleID NUMBER(9) NOT NULL,
listOrder         NUMBER(3) NOT NULL,
value             VARCHAR2(30),
PRIMARY KEY (NMTOKENSInternalExampleID, listOrder),
FOREIGN KEY (NMTOKENSInternalExampleID)
REFERENCES NMTOKENSExample
);

CREATE OR REPLACE TRIGGER InsertNMTOKENSInternalExample
BEFORE INSERT
ON NMTOKENSInternalExample
FOR EACH ROW
WHEN (LENGTH(TRANSLATE(UPPER(new.value),
      '.-_:ABCDEFGHIJKLMNOPQRSTUVWXYZ0123456789,/;''[]\<>?"{}|~!@#$%^&*()+=',
      '.-_:ABCDEFGHIJKLMNOPQRSTUVWXYZ0123456789')) <>
   LENGTH(new.value) OR
  INSTR(new.value, UNISTR('\000D')) <> 0 OR
  INSTR(new.value, UNISTR('\000A')) <> 0 OR
  INSTR(new.value, UNISTR('\0009')) <> 0 OR
  LENGTH(new.value) <> LENGTH(TRIM(new.value)) OR
  INSTR(new.value, ' ') <> 0)
BEGIN
RAISE_APPLICATION_ERROR(-20000, 'Not NMTOKENS');
END;

CREATE OR REPLACE TRIGGER UpdateNMTOKENSInternalExample
BEFORE UPDATE
ON NMTOKENSInternalExample
FOR EACH ROW
WHEN (LENGTH(TRANSLATE(UPPER(new.value),
      '.-_:ABCDEFGHIJKLMNOPQRSTUVWXYZ0123456789,/;''[]\<>?"{}|~!@#$%^&*()+=',
      '.-_:ABCDEFGHIJKLMNOPQRSTUVWXYZ0123456789')) <>
   LENGTH(new.value) OR
```

*continues*

```
    INSTR(new.value, UNISTR('\000D')) <> 0 OR
    INSTR(new.value, UNISTR('\000A')) <> 0 OR
    INSTR(new.value, UNISTR('\0009')) <> 0 OR
    LENGTH(new.value) <> LENGTH(TRIM(new.value)) OR
    INSTR(new.value, '  ') <> 0)
BEGIN
RAISE_APPLICATION_ERROR(-20000, 'Not NMTOKENS');
END;
```

**LISTING 22.31**  NMTOKENS Example Values Insertion

```
INSERT INTO NMTOKENSExample
VALUES
(Seq_NMTOKENS.NEXTVAL);

INSERT INTO NMTOKENSInternalExample
VALUES
(Seq_NMTOKENS.CURRVAL, 1, 'a');

INSERT INTO NMTOKENSInternalExample
VALUES
(Seq_NMTOKENS.CURRVAL, 2, 'b');

INSERT INTO NMTOKENSInternalExample
VALUES
(Seq_NMTOKENS.CURRVAL, 3, 'c');
```

### 22.4.13.3 `pattern` Constraining Facet
Refer to Section 22.2.1 for design and implementation issues.

### 22.4.13.4 `enumeration` Constraining Facet
Refer to Section 22.2.2 for design and implementation issues.

### 22.4.13.5 `whiteSpace` Constraining Facet
Refer to Section 22.2.3 for design and implementation issues.

### 22.4.13.6 `length` Constraining Facet
Refer to Section 22.4.1.2 for design and implementation issues.

### 22.4.13.7 `minLength` Constraining Facet
Refer to Section 22.4.1.3 for design and implementation issues.

### 22.4.13.8 `maxLength` Constraining Facet
Refer to Section 22.4.1.4 for design and implementation issues.

## 22.4.14 `decimal` Datatype

The `decimal` datatype can be represented as an Oracle `NUMBER` datatype. Oracle guarantees portability of numbers that have a precision of up to 38 total digits. Numbers that have more digits should be avoided, if possible. Also note that XML schema processors are only required to support 18 total digits.

> **WARNING**
>
> XML schema validators might round a decimal value with greater than 18 total digits, *or* generate an error, or do anything else as this portion of the Schema Recommendation is not clear. The database designer should determine—with the XML schema designer— whether this precise level of validation needs to occur, and if so, which choice is appropriate. This issue will most likely be resolved in an XML Schema errata document.

Database designers should avoid having an XML schema document with `decimal`-derived datatypes that have neither `totalDigits` nor min/max exclusive/inclusive constraining facets defined. These might already be implicit if the development language is Java, Visual Basic, and so on, because language datatypes have an upper and lower bound. If the constraining facets are not explicitly or implicitly defined, determining the intention of the XML schema designer avoids having potential decimal values dependent on the instance of the XML schema processor, incredibly large or small numbers, and so on.

### 22.4.14.1 `totalDigits` Constraining Facet

Listing 22.32 creates the `TotalDigitsExample` table with a `value` column with 18 total digits.

**LISTING 22.32** `totalDigits` Constraining Facet Example Table Creation

```
CREATE TABLE TotalDigitsExample (
value    NUMBER(18)
);
```

### 22.4.14.2 `fractionDigits` Constraining Facet

Listing 22.33 creates the `FractionDigitsExample` table with a `value` column having 18 total digits and 2 fractional digits.

**LISTING 22.33** `fractionDigits` Constraining Facet Example Table Creation

```
CREATE TABLE FractionDigitsExample (
value    NUMBER(18, 2)
);
```

### 22.4.14.3 `pattern` Constraining Facet
Refer to Section 22.2.1 for design and implementation issues.

### 22.4.14.4 `whiteSpace` Constraining Facet
Refer to Section 22.2.3 for design and implementation issues.

### 22.4.14.5 `enumeration` Constraining Facet
Refer to Section 22.2.2 for design and implementation issues.

### 22.4.14.6 `maxInclusive` Constraining Facet
There is no built-in database support for the `maxInclusive` constraining facet, but this can be added as a column constraint in table creation or as a trigger. Listing 22.34 implements the `maxInclusive` constraining facet in a column constraint, and Listing 22.35 implements it as a trigger. Refer to Section 22.3 regarding the decision to use column constraints or triggers.

**LISTING 22.34** `maxInclusive` Constraining Facet Example Table Creation with a Column Constraint

```
CREATE TABLE MaxInclusiveExample (
value NUMBER(3, 2) CHECK (value <= 5)
);
```

**LISTING 22.35** `maxInclusive` Constraining Facet Example Table Creation with Insert and Update Triggers

```
CREATE TABLE MaxInclusiveExample (
value  NUMBER(3, 2)
);

CREATE OR REPLACE TRIGGER InsertMaxInclusiveExample
BEFORE INSERT
ON MaxInclusiveExample
FOR EACH ROW
WHEN (new.value > 5)
BEGIN
RAISE_APPLICATION_ERROR(-20000, 'Number too large');
END;

CREATE OR REPLACE TRIGGER UpdateMaxInclusiveExample
BEFORE UPDATE
ON MaxInclusiveExample
FOR EACH ROW
WHEN (new.value > 5)
BEGIN
```

```
RAISE_APPLICATION_ERROR(-20000, 'Number too large');
END;
```

### 22.4.14.7 `maxExclusive` Constraining Facet

There is no built-in database support for the `maxExclusive` constraining facet, but this can be added as a column constraint in table creation or as a trigger. Listing 22.36 implements the `maxExclusive` constraining facet in a column constraint, and Listing 22.37 implements it as a trigger. Refer to Section 22.3 regarding the decision to use column constraints or triggers.

**LISTING 22.36**   `maxExclusive` Constraining Facet Example Table Creation with a Column Constraint

```
CREATE TABLE MaxExclusiveExample (
value NUMBER(3, 2) CHECK (value < 5)
);
```

**LISTING 22.37**   `maxExclusive` Constraining Facet Example Table Creation with Insert and Update Triggers

```
CREATE TABLE MaxExclusiveExample (
value   NUMBER(3, 2)
);

CREATE OR REPLACE TRIGGER InsertMaxExclusiveExample
BEFORE INSERT
ON MaxExclusiveExample
FOR EACH ROW
WHEN (new.value > 4)
BEGIN
RAISE_APPLICATION_ERROR(-20000, 'Number too large');
END;

CREATE OR REPLACE TRIGGER UpdateMaxExclusiveExample
BEFORE UPDATE
ON MaxExclusiveExample
FOR EACH ROW
WHEN (new.value > 4)
BEGIN
RAISE_APPLICATION_ERROR(-20000, ' Number too large');
END;
```

### 22.4.14.8 `minInclusive` Constraining Facet

There is no built-in database support for the `minInclusive` constraining facet, but this can be added as a column constraint in table creation or as a trigger. Listing 22.38 implements the minInclusive constraining facet in a column constraint, and Listing 22.39 implements it as a trigger. Refer to Section 22.3 regarding the decision to use column constraints or triggers.

**LISTING 22.38** minInclusive Constraining Facet Example Table Creation with a Column Constraint

```
CREATE TABLE MinInclusiveExample (
value   NUMBER(18, 2) CHECK (value >= 5)
);
```

**LISTING 22.39** minInclusive Constraining Facet Example Table Creation with Insert and Update Triggers

```
CREATE TABLE MinInclusiveExample (
value   NUMBER(18, 2)
);

CREATE OR REPLACE TRIGGER InsertMinInclusiveExample BEFORE INSERT
ON MinInclusiveExample
FOR EACH ROW
WHEN (new.value > 5)
BEGIN
RAISE_APPLICATION_ERROR(-20000, 'Number too small');
END;

CREATE OR REPLACE TRIGGER UpdateMinInclusiveExample BEFORE UPDATE
ON MinInclusiveExample
FOR EACH ROW
WHEN (new.value > 5)
BEGIN
RAISE_APPLICATION_ERROR(-20000, ' Number too small');
END;
```

### 22.4.14.9 minExclusive Constraining Facet

There is no built-in database support for the minExclusive constraining facet, but this can be added as a column constraint in table creation or as a trigger. Listing 22.40 implements the minExclusive constraining facet in a column constraint, and Listing 22.41 implements it as a trigger. Refer to Section 22.3 regarding the decision to use column constraints or triggers.

**LISTING 22.40** minExclusive Constraining Facet Example Table Creation with a Column Constraint

```
CREATE TABLE MinExclusiveExample (
value   NUMBER(18, 2) CHECK (value < 5)
);
```

**LISTING 22.41**  minExclusive Constraining Facet Example Table Creation with Insert and Update Triggers

```
CREATE TABLE MinExclusiveExample (
value   NUMBER(18, 2)
);

CREATE OR REPLACE TRIGGER InsertMinExclusiveExample
BEFORE INSERT
ON MinExclusiveExample
FOR EACH ROW
WHEN (new.value > 4)
BEGIN
RAISE_APPLICATION_ERROR(-20000, 'Number too small');
END;

CREATE OR REPLACE TRIGGER UpdateMinExclusiveExample
BEFORE UPDATE
ON MinExclusiveExample
FOR EACH ROW
WHEN (new.value > 4)
BEGIN
RAISE_APPLICATION_ERROR(-20000, ' Number too small');
END;
```

## 22.4.15 `integer` Datatype

The `integer` datatype is derived from the `decimal` datatype by restricting the values to have 0 `fractionDigits`. Refer to Section 22.4.14 for design and implementation issues of this datatype.

## 22.4.16 `nonPositiveInteger` Datatype

The `nonPositiveInteger` datatype is derived by restriction from the `integer` datatype with a `maxInclusive` of 0. Refer to Section 22.4.14 for design and implementation issues of this type.

## 22.4.17 `negativeInteger` Datatype

The `negativeInteger` datatype is derived by restriction from the `nonPositiveInteger` number with a `maxInclusive` of −1. Refer to Section 22.4.14 for design and implementation issues of this type.

## 22.4.18 `long` Datatype

The `long` datatype is derived by restriction from the `integer` datatype with a `maxInclusive` of 9223372036854775807 and a `minInclusive` of −9223372036854775808. Refer to Section 22.4.14 for design and implementation issues of this type.

## 22.4.19 `int` Datatype

The `int` datatype is derived by restriction from the `long` datatype with a `maxInclusive` of 2147483647 and a `minInclusive` of −2147483648. Refer to Section 22.4.14 for design and implementation issues of this type.

## 22.4.20 `short` Datatype

The `short` datatype is derived by restriction from the `int` datatype with a `maxInclusive` of 32767 and a `minInclusive` of −32768. Refer to Section 22.4.14 for design and implementation issues of this type.

## 22.4.21 `byte` Datatype

The `byte` datatype is derived by restriction from the `short` datatype with a `maxInclusive` of 127 and a `minInclusive` of −128. Refer to Section 22.4.14 for design and implementation issues of this type.

## 22.4.22 `nonNegativeInteger` Datatype

The `nonNegativeInteger` datatype is derived by restriction from the `integer` datatype with a `minInclusive` of 0. Refer to Section 22.4.14 for design and implementation issues of this type.

## 22.4.23 `unsignedLong` Datatype

The `unsignedLong` datatype is derived by restriction from the `nonNegativeInteger` datatype with a `maxInclusive` of 18446744073709551615 and a `minInclusive` of 0. Refer to Section 22.4.14 for design and implementation issues of this type.

## 22.4.24 `unsignedInt` Datatype

The `unsignedInt` datatype is derived by restriction from the `unsignedLong` number with a `maxInclusive` of 4294967295 and a `minInclusive` of 0. Refer to Section 22.4.14 for design and implementation issues of this type.

## 22.4.25 `unsignedShort` Datatype

The `unsignedShort` datatype is derived by restriction from the `unsignedInt` datatype with a `maxInclusive` of 65535 and a `minInclusive` of 0. Refer to Section 22.4.14 for design and implementation issues of this type.

### 22.4.26 `unsignedByte` Datatype

The `unsignedByte` datatype is derived by restriction from the `unsignedShort` datatype with a `maxInclusive` of 255 and a `minInclusive` of 0. Refer to Section 22.4.14 for design and implementation issues of this type.

### 22.4.27 `positiveInteger` Datatype

The `positiveInteger` datatype is derived by restriction from the `integer` datatype with a `minInclusive` of 1. Refer to Section 22.4.14 for design and implementation issues of this type.

### 22.4.28 `float` Datatype

Oracle does not support the IEEE 754-1985 specification for numbers on which this datatype is based. The values NOT-A-NUMBER, POSITIVE INFINITY, and NEGATIVE INFINITY simply cannot be represented directly. Refer to Section 22.4.14 on approximating the implementation of the `float` datatype. This representation accurately represent floats for most business applications.

If a complete representation is required, a number of solutions are possible:

- Use one of the character column datatypes instead—a good solution when the data only needs to be stored and retrieved.
- Use a set of numbers outside the min/max inclusion/exclusion range to signify each of the possible unrepresentable values—a good solution when the floats need to be manipulated inside the database, but requires implementation of IEEE 754-1985 rules for addition of NOT-A-NUMBER and POSITIVE INFINITY, and so on.
- Create database columns for each of the possible unrepresentable values—a good solution when the floats need to be manipulated inside the database and the IEEE 754-1985 value needs to be made explicit (by creating a separate column), but requires implementation of IEEE 754-1985 rules for addition of NOT-A-NUMBER and POSITIVE INFINITY, and so on.

For each of these solutions, you can create Java stored procedures that take floats or floats represented by characters and perform the arithmetic operations in Java. The Java stored procedure then returns an appropriate float or an appropriate float represented by characters.

> **TIP**
>
> Java did not support the IEEE 754-1985 standard for floats until the introduction of the 'strict' keyword. To get full IEEE 754-1985 support, this keyword needs to be used when creating a class.

## 22.4.29 double Datatype

Oracle does not support the IEEE 754-1985 specification for numbers on which this datatype is based. The values NOT-A-NUMBER, POSITIVE INFINITY, and NEGATIVE INFINITY simply cannot be represented directly. Refer to Section 22.4.14 on approximating the implementation of the `double` datatype. This representation accurately represent floats for most business applications.

If a complete representation is required, refer to Section 22.4.28 for a series of options.

## 22.4.30 hexBinary Datatype

The `hexBinary` datatype can be represented naturally in one of three ways: as a VARCHAR2, CLOB, or BLOB. When the `minLength` or `length` has been specified at fewer than 4,000 characters, VARCHAR2 has significant performance and ease-of-use advantages over a CLOB or BLOB from an application development perspective. At over 4,000 characters, a CLOB or BLOB must be used. A BLOB is much more compact; constraining facets are more difficult to implement. A CLOB is space inefficient, but allows a straightforward implementation of the constraining facets.

> **WARNING**
>
> The length of the `hexBinary` datatype is measured in 8-bit octets.

A BLOB is not recommended when a constraining facet occurs. Unfortunately, a BLOB value must be decoded to check the constraint in after-insert and after-update triggers. A before trigger is not allowed. The result is slow performance and the requirement for the application to manually rollback any errors. When there are no constraining facets, a BLOB is a good implementation. To convert a `hexBinary` value to a BLOB, call the UTL_ENCODE.UUENCODE PL/SQL procedure. To convert a BLOB to a `hexBinary` value, call the UTL_ENCODE.UUDECODE PL/SQL procedure.

### 22.4.30.1 length Constraining Facet
Refer to Section 22.4.1.2 for design and implementation issues.

### 22.4.30.2 minLength Constraining Facet
Refer to Section 22.4.1.3 for design and implementation issues.

### 22.4.30.3 maxLength Constraining Facet
Refer to Section 22.4.1.4 for design and implementation issues.

### 22.4.30.4 `pattern` Constraining Facet

Refer to Section 22.2.1 for design and implementation issues.

### 22.4.30.5 `enumeration` Constraining Facet

Refer to Section 22.2.2 for design and implementation issues.

### 22.4.30.6 `whiteSpace` Constraining Facet

Refer to Section 22.2.3 for design and implementation issues.

## 22.4.31 `base64Binary` Datatype

Although `base64Binary` is not derived by restriction from the `hexBinary` datatype, it has almost identical design issues and implementation details. Review Section 22.4.30 for design and implementation issues of this datatype. Note that a `base64Binary` value can be converted to a `BLOB` by using the `UTL_ENCODE.BASE64_UUENCODE` procedure. To convert a `BLOB` to a `base64Binary` value, call the `UTL_ENCODE.BASE64_UUDECODE` procedure.

## 22.4.32 `QName` Datatype

The `QName` datatype is a combination of the `anyURI` datatype and the `NCName` datatype. `QName` is probably best represented as two columns in a table. Refer to Sections 22.4.33 and 22.4.6 for design and implementation issues of this type.

## 22.4.33 `anyURI` Datatype

The `anyURI` datatype can now be implemented directly in Oracle9*i*. The PL/SQL `SYS` package includes a `UriType` type and a URI factory class. However, from an XML schema perspective, there is little to recommend the use of the `SYS.UriType` over the `VARCHAR2` datatype, because Oracle performs little or no syntax checking of the URI. In addition, many of the older—but still widely used—database drivers do not support Oracle objects. The `anyURI` datatype is probably best treated as a `string` datatype, because it has the same constraining facets. Refer to Section 22.4.1 for information on designing and implementing the `anyURI` datatype.

Using the `SYS.UriType` column datatype in Oracle has potential benefits for an application. Oracle supports functionality with respect to URLs and internal database URIs that can aid in application development as the location of data within the database can now be specified with a URI.

## 22.4.34 `NOTATION` Datatype

Although `NOTATION` datatype is not derived by restriction from the `QName` datatype, it has the same value space. Refer to Section 22.4.32 for design and implementation issues of this type.

## 22.4.35 boolean Datatype

Oracle does not yet support the `boolean` datatype as defined in the SQL-92 standard. As a result, a `boolean` datatype should be mapped to either a database `NUMBER` or `VARCHAR` column datatype.

The `boolean` datatype has the following legal literals: 'true', 'false', '1', and '0'. Having all four literals in the database is problematic because there are only two values in the value space. The database designer should communicate with the XML schema designer to determine if all four literals will exist in XML instances. If all four literals are possible, then consider using a database `NUMBER` column datatype to store the value and using a `DECODE` statement to map 'true' to 1 and 'false' to 0. The following SQL fragment can accomplish this:

```
DECODE(?booleanValue, 'true', 1, 'false', 0, 1, 1, 0, 0)
```

where the `?booleanValue` bind variable is replaced by the appropriate Boolean value.

### 22.4.35.1 Representation of the boolean Datatype as True and False

In this scenario, the `boolean` datatype is represented by the strings of 'true' and 'false'. Listing 22.42 implements this as a column constraint, and Listing 22.43 implements this as a trigger. Refer to Section 22.3 regarding the decision to use column constraints or triggers.

**LISTING 22.42**  BooleanStringExample Table Creation with a Column Constraint

```
CREATE TABLE BooleanStringExample (
value   VARCHAR(5) CHECK (value = 'true' OR value = 'false')
);
```

**LISTING 22.43**  BooleanStringExample Table Creation with Insert and Update Triggers

```
CREATE TABLE BooleanStringExample (
value   VARCHAR(5)
);

CREATE OR REPLACE TRIGGER InsertBooleanStringExample
BEFORE INSERT
ON BooleanStringExample
FOR EACH ROW
WHEN (new.value <> 'true' AND new.value <> 'false')
BEGIN
RAISE_APPLICATION_ERROR(-20000, 'Not a boolean');
END;

CREATE OR REPLACE TRIGGER UpdateBooleanStringExample
BEFORE UPDATE
ON BooleanStringExample
```

```
FOR EACH ROW
WHEN (new.value <> 'true' AND new.value <> 'false')
BEGIN
RAISE_APPLICATION_ERROR(-20000, 'Not a boolean');
END;
```

### 22.4.35.2 Representation of the boolean Datatype as 1 and 0

In this scenario, the boolean datatype is represented by the numbers 0 and 1. Listing 22.44 implements this as a column constraint, and Listing 22.45 implements this as a trigger. Refer to Section 22.3 regarding the decision to use column constraints or triggers.

**LISTING 22.44** BooleanNumberExample Table Creation with a Column Constraint

```
CREATE TABLE BooleanNumberExample (
value  NUMBER(1) CHECK (value IN (0, 1))
);
```

**LISTING 22.45** BooleanNumberExample Table Creation with Insert and Update Triggers

```
CREATE TABLE BooleanNumberExample (
value  NUMBER(1)
);

CREATE OR REPLACE TRIGGER InsertBooleanNumberExample
BEFORE INSERT
ON BooleanNumberExample
FOR EACH ROW
WHEN (new.value NOT IN (0, 1))
BEGIN
RAISE_APPLICATION_ERROR(-20000, 'Not boolean');
END;

CREATE OR REPLACE TRIGGER UpdateBooleanNumberExample
BEFORE UPDATE
ON BooleanNumberExample
FOR EACH ROW
WHEN (new.value NOT IN (0, 1))
BEGIN
RAISE_APPLICATION_ERROR(-20000, 'Not boolean');
END;
```

### 22.4.35.3 pattern Constraining Facet

Refer to Section 22.2.1 for design and implementation issues.

#### 22.4.35.4 `whiteSpace` Constraining Facet
Refer to Section 22.2.3 for design and implementation issues.

## 22.4.36 `duration` Datatype

The `duration` datatype represents a duration of time that is either positive or negative and may include years, months, hours, minutes, seconds, and fractional seconds. The `duration` value space is partially ordered. For example, one year is greater than 364 days, not comparable with 365 days, not comparable with 366 days, and less than 367 days (because some years are equal to 365 days and others are equal to 366 days).

Validating a `duration` requires pattern matching through the Java JVM in Oracle or a significant effort in hand-coded PL/SQL. Validating the `minimum` and `maximum` constraining facets requires a significant amount of hand-coded PL/SQL, again because `duration` values are only partially ordered.

If the database designer can determine that the XML instances will be constrained to one `duration` components ('Y', 'M', 'D', and so on), then the durations are totally ordered and can be represented as a `decimal` datatype or `integer` datatype. Refer to Sections 22.4.14 and 22.4.15 for design and implementation issues of the `duration` subtypes.

The `duration` datatype is probably best treated as a `string` datatype, with validation left to the application developer. If validation is required by the database, refer to Section 22.2.1.

#### 22.4.36.1 `pattern` Constraining Facet
Refer to Section 22.2.1 for design and implementation issues.

#### 22.4.36.2 `enumeration` Constraining Facet
Refer to Section 22.2.2 for design and implementation issues.

#### 22.4.36.3 `whiteSpace` Constraining Facet
Refer to Section 22.2.3 for design and implementation issues.

#### 22.4.36.4 `maxInclusive` Constraining Facet
Refer to Section 22.4.14.6 for design and implementation issues.

#### 22.4.36.5 `maxInclusive` Constraining Facet
Refer to Section 22.4.14.7 for design and implementation issues.

#### 22.4.36.6 `minInclusive` Constraining Facet
Refer to Section 22.4.14.8 for design and implementation issues.

#### 22.4.36.7 `minExclusive` Constraining Facet
Refer to Section 22.4.14.9 for design and implementation issues.

## 22.4.37 dateTime Datatype

The `dateTime` datatype represents a specific instance in time. Oracle9*i* now has a TIMESTAMP column datatype that represents a date, time of day, and an optional time zone. A `dateTime` value may or may not include a time zone. The database designer should confer with the XML schema designer to determine if time-zone values will exist in XML instances and, if so, whether the values need to be preserved or the `dateTime` values can be reduced to their canonical form. This section on the `dateTime` datatype assumes that they exist in the XML instance and must be preserved.

> **WARNING**
>
> Mixing `datetime` values that have time zones with those that do not in the same database table column is problematic. From an XML schema perspective, the values are only partially ordered since the time zone is not specified in some cases. However, when using a database TIMESTAMP WITH TIME ZONE column datatype, Oracle9*i* will *default* the time zone to the time zone of the database server that results in a complete ordering. Separating `datetime` values that have time zones with those that do not into two database columns is advisable.

Listing 22.46 implements a `dateTime` table creation.

**LISTING 22.46** DateTimeExample Table Creation

```
CREATE TABLE DateTimeExample (
value   TIMESTAMP WITH TIME ZONE
);
```

To insert a row into the table with a `dateTime` datatype, Oracle needs to convert a value from its ISO 8601 standard format to an internal Oracle representation.

> **WARNING**
>
> The database TIMESTAMP column datatype does not support the time value of '24:00:00', but does support its value space equivalent '00:00:00'.

Listing 22.47 is a SQL statement that inserts a `dateTime` into the `DateTimeExample` table (`?datetimeValue` is the `dateTime` bind variable).

**LISTING 22.47**  DateTimeExample Example Insert

```
INSERT INTO DateTimeExample
(value)
SELECT TO_TIMESTAMP_TZ('2001-12-21T12:45:30Z+05:00',
          'YYYY-MM-DD"T"HH24:MI:SS"Z"TZH:TZM')
FROM dual;
```

Listing 22.48 is a SQL statement that retrieves all of the values from the DateTimeExample table.

**LISTING 22.48**  DateTimeExample Values Retrieval via a Select Statement

```
SELECT TO_CHAR(value, 'YYYY-MM-DD"T"HH24:MI:SS"Z"TZH:TZM')
FROM DateTimeExample;
```

### 22.4.37.1 `pattern` Constraining Facet
Refer to Section 22.2.1 for design and implementation issues.

### 22.4.37.2 `enumeration` Constraining Facet
Refer to Section 22.2.2 for design and implementation issues.

### 22.4.37.3 `whiteSpace` Constraining Facet
Refer to Section 22.2.3 for design and implementation issues.

### 22.4.37.4 `maxInclusive` Constraining Facet
There is no built-in database support for the `maxInclusive` constraining facet, but Listing 22.49 shows how this can be enforced as a trigger. Note that Oracle limits the values of the check clause to constant values and does not allow calling of PL/SQL conversion functions.

**LISTING 22.49**  DatetimeMaxInclusiveExample Table Creation with Insert and Update Triggers

```
CREATE TABLE DatetimeMaxInclusiveExample (
value   TIMESTAMP WITH TIME ZONE
);

CREATE OR REPLACE TRIGGER InsertDatetimeMaxInclusive
BEFORE INSERT
ON DatetimeMaxInclusiveExample
FOR EACH ROW
WHEN (new.value >
  TO_TIMESTAMP_TZ('2001-12-21T12:45:30Z+05:00',
         'YYYY-MM-DD"T"HH24:MI:SS"Z"TZH:TZM'))
```

```
BEGIN
RAISE_APPLICATION_ERROR(-20000, 'Datetime too late');
END;

CREATE OR REPLACE TRIGGER UpdateDatetimeMaxInclusive BEFORE UPDATE
ON DatetimeMaxInclusiveExample
FOR EACH ROW
WHEN (new.value >
    TO_TIMESTAMP_TZ('2001-12-21T12:45:30Z+05:00',
        'YYYY-MM-DD"T"HH24:MI:SS"Z"TZH:TZM'))
BEGIN
RAISE_APPLICATION_ERROR(-20000, 'Datetime too late');
END;
```

### 22.4.37.5 maxExclusive Constraining Facet

There is no built-in database support for the maxExclusive constraining facet, but Listing 22.50 shows how this can be enforced as a trigger. Note that Oracle limits the values of the check clause to constant values and does not allow calling of PL/SQL conversion functions.

**LISTING 22.50** DatetimeMaxExclusiveExample Table Creation with Insert and Update Triggers

```
CREATE TABLE DatetimeMaxExclusiveExample (
value   TIMESTAMP WITH TIME ZONE
);

CREATE OR REPLACE TRIGGER InsertDatetimeMaxExclusive
BEFORE INSERT
ON DatetimeMaxExclusiveExample
FOR EACH ROW
WHEN (new.value >=
    TO_TIMESTAMP_TZ('2001-12-21T12:45:30Z+05:00',
        'YYYY-MM-DD"T"HH24:MI:SS"Z"TZH:TZM'))
BEGIN
RAISE_APPLICATION_ERROR(-20000, 'Datetime too late');
END;

CREATE OR REPLACE TRIGGER UpdateDatetimeMaxExclusive
BEFORE UPDATE
ON DatetimeMaxExclusiveExample
FOR EACH ROW
WHEN (new.value >=
    TO_TIMESTAMP_TZ('2001-12-21T12:45:30Z+05:00',
        'YYYY-MM-DD"T"HH24:MI:SS"Z"TZH:TZM'))
BEGIN
RAISE_APPLICATION_ERROR(-20000, 'Datetime too late');
END;
```

### 22.4.37.6 `minInclusive` Constraining Facet

There is no built-in database support for the `minInclusive` constraining facet, but Listing 22.51 shows how this can be enforced as a trigger. Note that Oracle limits the values of the check clause to constant values and does not allow calling of PL/SQL conversion functions.

**LISTING 22.51** `DatetimeMinInclusiveExample` Table Creation with Insert and Update Triggers

```
CREATE TABLE DatetimeMinInclusiveExample (
value   TIMESTAMP WITH TIME ZONE
);

CREATE OR REPLACE TRIGGER InsertDatetimeMinInclusive BEFORE INSERT
ON DatetimeMinInclusiveExample
FOR EACH ROW
WHEN (new.value <
  TO_TIMESTAMP_TZ('2001-12-21T12:45:30Z+05:00',
        'YYYY-MM-DD"T"HH24:MI:SS"Z"TZH:TZM'))
BEGIN
RAISE_APPLICATION_ERROR(-20000, 'Datetime too early');
END;

CREATE OR REPLACE TRIGGER UpdateDatetimeMinInclusive BEFORE UPDATE
ON DatetimeMinInclusiveExample
FOR EACH ROW
WHEN (new.value <
  TO_TIMESTAMP_TZ('2001-12-21T12:45:30Z+05:00',
        'YYYY-MM-DD"T"HH24:MI:SS"Z"TZH:TZM'))
BEGIN
RAISE_APPLICATION_ERROR(-20000, 'Datetime too early');
END;
```

### 22.4.37.7 `minExclusive` Constraining Facet

There is no built-in database support for the `minExclusive` constraining facet, but Listing 22.52 shows how this can be enforced as a trigger. Note that Oracle limits the values of the check clause to constant values and does not allow calling of PL/SQL conversion functions.

**LISTING 22.52** `DatetimeMinExclusiveExample` Table Creation with Insert and Update Triggers

```
CREATE TABLE DatetimeMinExclusiveExample (
value   TIMESTAMP WITH TIME ZONE
);
```

```
CREATE OR REPLACE TRIGGER InsertDatetimeMinExclusive
BEFORE INSERT
ON DatetimeMinExclusiveExample
FOR EACH ROW
WHEN (new.value <=
  TO_TIMESTAMP_TZ('2001-12-21T12:45:30Z+05:00',
          'YYYY-MM-DD"T"HH24:MI:SS"Z"TZH:TZM'))
BEGIN
RAISE_APPLICATION_ERROR(-20000, 'Datetime too early');
END;

CREATE OR REPLACE TRIGGER UpdateDatetimeMinExclusive
BEFORE UPDATE
ON DatetimeMinExclusiveExample
FOR EACH ROW
WHEN (new.value <=
  TO_TIMESTAMP_TZ('2001-12-21T12:45:30Z+05:00',
          'YYYY-MM-DD"T"HH24:MI:SS"Z"TZH:TZM'))
BEGIN
RAISE_APPLICATION_ERROR(-20000, 'Datetime too early');
END;
```

## 22.4.38 date Datatype

The date datatype represents a Gregorian calendar date. Oracle has a DATE column datatype that represents a date and time without a time-zone offset and a TIMESTAMP column datatype that represents both date and time with a time-zone offset. The database designer should confer with the XML schema designer to determine if time-zone values will exist in the XML instances because implementations using the DATE column datatype are simpler. This section on the date datatype assumes that time zones exist in the XML instances and must be preserved.

> **WARNING**
>
> Mixing date values that have time zones with those that do not in the same database table column is problematic. From an XML schema perspective, the values are only partially ordered since the time zone is not specified in some cases. However, when using a database TIMESTAMP WITH TIME ZONE column datatype, Oracle9*i* will *default* the time zone to the time zone of the database server that results in a complete ordering. Separating date values that have time zones and those that do not into two database columns is advisable.

Listing 22.53 implements a date table creation.

**LISTING 22.53**   DateExample Table Creation

```
CREATE TABLE DateExample (
value   TIMESTAMP WITH TIME ZONE
);
```

To insert a row into the table with a date datatype, Oracle needs to convert it from its ISO 8601 standard format to an internal Oracle representation. Listing 22.54 is a SQL statement that inserts a date into the DateExample table (?dateValue is the date bind variable).

**LISTING 22.54**   DateExample Example Insert

```
INSERT INTO DateExample
(value)
SELECT TO_TIMESTAMP_TZ(?dateValue, 'YYYY-MM-DD"Z"TZH:TZM')
FROM dual;
```

Listing 22.55 is a SQL statement that retrieves all of the values from the DateExample table.

**LISTING 22.55**   DateExample Values Retrieval via a Select Statement

```
SELECT TO_CHAR(value, 'YYYY-MM-DD"Z"TZH:TZM')
FROM DateExample;
```

### 22.4.38.1 pattern Constraining Facet
Refer to Section 22.2.1 for design and implementation issues.

### 22.4.38.2 enumeration Constraining Facet
Refer to Section 22.2.2 for design and implementation issues.

### 22.4.38.3 whiteSpace Constraining Facet
Refer to Section 22.2.3 for design and implementation issues.

### 22.4.38.4 maxInclusive Constraining Facet
There is no built-in database support for the maxInclusive constraining facet, but Listing 22.56 shows how this can be enforced as a trigger. Note that Oracle limits the values of the check clause to constant values and does not allow calling PL/SQL conversion functions.

**LISTING 22.56**  `DateMaxInclusiveExample` Table Creation with Insert and Update Triggers

```
CREATE TABLE DateMaxInclusiveExample (
value   TIMESTAMP WITH TIME ZONE
);

CREATE OR REPLACE TRIGGER InsertDateMaxInclusiveExample
BEFORE INSERT
ON DateMaxInclusiveExample
FOR EACH ROW
WHEN (new.value >
  TO_TIMESTAMP_TZ('2001-12-24Z05:00',
          'YYYY-MM-DD"Z"TZH:TZM'))
BEGIN
RAISE_APPLICATION_ERROR(-20000, 'Date too late');
END;

CREATE OR REPLACE TRIGGER UpdateDateMaxInclusiveExample
BEFORE UPDATE
ON DateMaxInclusiveExample
FOR EACH ROW
WHEN (new.value >
  TO_TIMESTAMP_TZ('2001-12-24Z05:00',
          'YYYY-MM-DD"Z"TZH:TZM'))
BEGIN
RAISE_APPLICATION_ERROR(-20000, 'Date too late');
END;
```

## 22.4.38.5 `maxExclusive` Constraining Facet

There is no built-in database support for the `maxExclusive` constraining facet, but Listing 22.57 shows how this can be enforced as a trigger. Note that Oracle limits the values of the check clause to constant values and does not allow calling PL/SQL conversion functions.

**LISTING 22.57**  `DateMaxExclusiveExample` Table Creation with Insert and Update Triggers

```
CREATE TABLE DateMaxExclusiveExample (
value   TIMESTAMP WITH TIME ZONE
);

CREATE OR REPLACE TRIGGER InsertDateMaxExclusiveExample
BEFORE INSERT
ON DateMaxExclusiveExample
FOR EACH ROW
WHEN (new.value >=
  TO_TIMESTAMP_TZ('2001-12-24Z05:00',
          'YYYY-MM-DD"Z"TZH:TZM'))
```

```
BEGIN
RAISE_APPLICATION_ERROR(-20000, 'Date too late');
END;

CREATE OR REPLACE TRIGGER UpdateDateMaxExclusiveExample
BEFORE UPDATE
ON DateMaxExclusiveExample
FOR EACH ROW
WHEN (new.value >=
  TO_TIMESTAMP_TZ('2001-12-24Z05:00',
          'YYYY-MM-DD"Z"TZH:TZM'))
BEGIN
RAISE_APPLICATION_ERROR(-20000, 'Date too late');
END;
```

### 22.4.38.6 minInclusive Constraining Facet

There is no built-in database support for the `minInclusive` constraining facet, but Listing 22.58 shows how this can be enforced as a trigger. Note that Oracle limits the values of the check clause to constant values and does not allow calling PL/SQL conversion functions.

**LISTING 22.58** DateMinInclusiveExample Table Creation with Insert and Update Triggers

```
CREATE TABLE DateMinInclusiveExample (
value   TIMESTAMP WITH TIME ZONE
);

CREATE OR REPLACE TRIGGER InsertDateMinInclusiveExample
BEFORE INSERT
ON DateMinInclusiveExample
FOR EACH ROW
WHEN (new.value <
  TO_TIMESTAMP_TZ('2001-12-24Z05:00',
          'YYYY-MM-DD"Z"TZH:TZM'))
BEGIN
RAISE_APPLICATION_ERROR(-20000, 'Date too early');
END;

CREATE OR REPLACE TRIGGER UpdateDateMinInclusiveExample
BEFORE UPDATE
ON DateMinInclusiveExample
FOR EACH ROW
WHEN (new.value <
  TO_TIMESTAMP_TZ('2001-12-24Z05:00',
          'YYYY-MM-DD"Z"TZH:TZM'))
BEGIN
```

```
RAISE_APPLICATION_ERROR(-20000, 'Date too early');
END;
```

### 22.4.38.7 `minExclusive` Constraining Facet

There is no built-in database support for the `minExclusive` constraining facet, but Listing 22.59 shows how this can be enforced as a trigger. Note that Oracle limits the values of the check clause to constant values and does not allow calling PL/SQL conversion functions.

**LISTING 22.59**  DateMinExclusiveExample Table Creation with Insert and Update Triggers

```
CREATE TABLE DateMinExclusiveExample (
value   TIMESTAMP WITH TIME ZONE
);

CREATE OR REPLACE TRIGGER InsertDateMinExclusiveExample
BEFORE INSERT
ON DateMinExclusiveExample
FOR EACH ROW
WHEN (new.value <=
  TO_TIMESTAMP_TZ('2001-12-24Z05:00',
        'YYYY-MM-DD"Z"TZH:TZM'))
BEGIN
RAISE_APPLICATION_ERROR(-20000, 'Date too early');
END;

CREATE OR REPLACE TRIGGER UpdateDateMinExclusiveExample
BEFORE UPDATE
ON DateMinExclusiveExample
FOR EACH ROW
WHEN (new.value <=
  TO_TIMESTAMP_TZ('2001-12-24Z05:00',
        'YYYY-MM-DD"Z"TZH:TZM'))
BEGIN
RAISE_APPLICATION_ERROR(-20000, 'Date too early');
END;
```

## 22.4.39 gYear Datatype

The gYear datatype represents a Gregorian calendar year. Without the optional time zone, gYear is essentially an integer datatype. Refer to Sections 22.4.14 and 22.4.15 for details implementing gYear when no time-zone offsets are required.

If time-zone offsets are required, the representation becomes much more complex. Oracle9*i* now has a TIMESTAMP column datatype that represents both date and time with a time-zone offset. The database designer should confer with the XML schema designer to determine if time-zone values will exist in XML instances and, if so, whether the values need to be preserved or the gYear values can be reduced to their canonical form.

> **WARNING**
>
> Mixing gYear values that have time zones with those that do not in the same database table column is problematic. From an XML schema perspective, the values are only partially ordered since the time zone is not specified in some cases. However, when using a database TIMESTAMP WITH TIME ZONE column datatype, Oracle9*i* will *default* the time zone to the time zone of the database server that results in a complete ordering. Separating gYear values that have time zones and those that do not into two database columns is advisable.

Listing 22.60 implements a gYear table creation.

**LISTING 22.60**   GYearExample Table Creation

```
CREATE TABLE GYearExample (
value   TIMESTAMP WITH TIME ZONE
);
```

To insert a row into the table with a gYear datatype, Oracle needs to convert the datatype from its XML Schema format to an internal Oracle representation. Listing 22.59 is a SQL statement that inserts a gYear into the GYearExample table (?gYearValue is the gYear bind variable). Note that January 1st was arbitrarily chosen as the day of the year.

**LISTING 22.61**   GYearExample Example Insert

```
INSERT INTO gYearExample
(value)
SELECT TO_TIMESTAMP_TZ(?gYearValue || '-01-01',
            'YYYY"Z"TZH:TZM MM-DD')
FROM dual;
```

Listing 22.62 is a SQL statement that retrieves all of the values from the GYearExample table.

**LISTING 22.62**   GYearExample Values Retrieval via a Select Statement

```
SELECT TO_CHAR(value, 'YYYY"Z"TZH:TZM')
FROM GYearExample;
```

### 22.4.39.1 `pattern` Constraining Facet
Refer to Section 22.2.1 for design and implementation issues.

### 22.4.39.2 `enumeration` Constraining Facet
Refer to Section 22.2.2 for design and implementation issues.

### 22.4.39.3 `whiteSpace` Constraining Facet
Refer to Section 22.2.3 for design and implementation issues.

### 22.4.39.4 `maxInclusive` Constraining Facet
There is no built-in database support for the `maxInclusive` constraining facet, but Listing 22.63 shows how this can be enforced as a trigger. Note that Oracle limits the values of the check clause to constant values and does not allow calling of PL/SQL conversion functions. This could be obviated in this case by not using the ISO 8601 `dateTime` format and using the default Oracle external `date` format, but this is not shown here.

**LISTING 22.63** `GYearMaxInclusiveExample` Table Creation with Insert and Update Triggers

```
CREATE TABLE GYearMaxInclusiveExample (
value   TIMESTAMP WITH TIME ZONE
);

CREATE OR REPLACE TRIGGER InsertGYearMaxInclusive
BEFORE INSERT
ON GYearMaxInclusiveExample
FOR EACH ROW
WHEN (new.value >
  TO_TIMESTAMP_TZ('2001-01-01Z+05:00',
        'YYYY-MM-DD"Z"TZH:TZM'))
BEGIN
RAISE_APPLICATION_ERROR(-20000, 'GYear too late');
END;

CREATE OR REPLACE TRIGGER UpdateGYearMaxInclusive
BEFORE UPDATE
ON GYearMaxInclusiveExample
FOR EACH ROW
WHEN (new.value >
  TO_TIMESTAMP_TZ('2001-01-01Z+05:00',
        'YYYY-MM-DD"Z"TZH:TZM'))
BEGIN
RAISE_APPLICATION_ERROR(-20000, 'Date too late');
END;
```

### 22.4.39.5 `maxExclusive` Constraining Facet

There is no built-in database support for the `maxExclusive` constraining facet, but Listing 22.64 shows how this can be enforced as a trigger. Note that Oracle limits the values of the check clause to constant values and does not allow calling of PL/SQL conversion functions. This could be obviated in this case by not using the ISO 8601 `dateTime` format and using the default Oracle external `date` format, but this is not shown here.

**LISTING 22.64**  `GYearMaxExclusiveExample` Table Creation with Insert and Update Triggers

```
CREATE TABLE GYearMaxExclusiveExample (
value   TIMESTAMP WITH TIME ZONE
);

CREATE OR REPLACE TRIGGER InsertGYearMaxExclusive
BEFORE INSERT
ON GYearMaxExclusiveExample
FOR EACH ROW
WHEN (new.value >=
  TO_TIMESTAMP_TZ('2001-01-01Z+05:00',
      'YYYY-MM-DD"Z"TZH:TZM'))
BEGIN
RAISE_APPLICATION_ERROR(-20000, 'GYear too late');
END;

CREATE OR REPLACE TRIGGER UpdateGYearMaxExclusive
BEFORE UPDATE
ON GYearMaxExclusiveExample
FOR EACH ROW
WHEN (new.value >=
  TO_TIMESTAMP_TZ('2001-01-01Z+05:00',
      'YYYY-MM-DD"Z"TZH:TZM'))
BEGIN
RAISE_APPLICATION_ERROR(-20000, 'GYear too late');
END;
```

### 22.4.39.6 `minInclusive` Constraining Facet

There is no built-in database support for the `minInclusive` constraining facet, but Listing 22.65 shows how this can be enforced as a trigger. Note that Oracle limits the values of the check clause to constant values and does not allow calling of PL/SQL conversion functions. This could be obviated in this case by not using the ISO 8601 `dateTime` format and using the default Oracle external `date` format, but this is not shown here.

**LISTING 22.65** GYearMinInclusiveExample Table Creation with Insert and Update Triggers

```
CREATE TABLE GYearMinInclusiveExample (
value   TIMESTAMP WITH TIME ZONE
);

CREATE OR REPLACE TRIGGER InsertGYearMinInclusive BEFORE INSERT
ON GYearMinInclusiveExample
FOR EACH ROW
WHEN (new.value <
   TO_TIMESTAMP_TZ('2001-01-01Z+05:00',
          'YYYY-MM-DD"Z"TZH:TZM'))
BEGIN
RAISE_APPLICATION_ERROR(-20000, 'GYear too early');
END;

CREATE OR REPLACE TRIGGER UpdateGYearMinInclusive BEFORE UPDATE
ON GYearMinInclusiveExample
FOR EACH ROW
WHEN (new.value <
   TO_TIMESTAMP_TZ('2001-01-01Z+05:00',
          'YYYY-MM-DD"Z"TZH:TZM'))
BEGIN
RAISE_APPLICATION_ERROR(-20000, 'GYear too early');
END;
```

### 22.4.39.7 minExclusive Constraining Facet

There is no built-in database support for the minExclusive constraining facet, but Listing 22.66 shows how this can be enforced as a trigger. Note that Oracle limits the values of the check clause to constant values and does not allow calling of PL/SQL conversion functions. This could be obviated in this case by not using the ISO 8601 dateTime format and using the default Oracle external date format, but this is not shown here.

**LISTING 22.66** GYearMinExclusiveExample Table Creation with Insert and Update Triggers

```
CREATE TABLE GYearMinExclusiveExample (
value   TIMESTAMP WITH TIME ZONE
);

CREATE OR REPLACE TRIGGER InsertGYearMinExclusive
BEFORE INSERT
ON GYearMinExclusiveExample
FOR EACH ROW
WHEN (new.value <=
   TO_TIMESTAMP_TZ('2001-01-01Z+05:00',
```

*continues*

```
          'YYYY-MM-DD"Z"TZH:TZM'))
BEGIN
RAISE_APPLICATION_ERROR(-20000, 'GYear too early');
END;

CREATE OR REPLACE TRIGGER UpdateGYearMinExclusive
BEFORE UPDATE
ON GYearMinExclusiveExample
FOR EACH ROW
WHEN (new.value <=
   TO_TIMESTAMP_TZ('2001-01-01Z+05:00',
          'YYYY-MM-DD"Z"TZH:TZM'))
BEGIN
RAISE_APPLICATION_ERROR(-20000, 'GYear too early');
END;
```

## 22.4.40 gYearMonth Datatype

The gYearMonth datatype represents a Gregorian calendar month. Oracle9*i* now has a TIMESTAMP column datatype that represents both date and time with a time-zone offset. The database designer should confer with the XML schema designer to determine if time-zone values will exist in XML instances and, if so, whether the values need to be preserved or the gYearMonth values can be reduced to their canonical form. Listing 22.67 implements a gYearMonth table creation.

**LISTING 22.67**  GYearMonthExample Table Creation

```
CREATE TABLE GYearMonthExample (
value TIMESTAMP WITH TIME ZONE
);
```

To insert a row into the table with a gYearMonth datatype, Oracle needs to convert it from its XML Schema format to an internal Oracle representation. Listing 22.68 is a SQL statement that inserts a gYearMonth into the GYearMonthExample table (?gYearMonthValue is the gYearMonth bind variable). Note that the 1st was arbitrarily chosen as the day of the month.

**LISTING 22.68**  GYearMonthExample Example Insert

```
INSERT INTO gYearMonthExample
(value)
SELECT TO_TIMESTAMP_TZ(?gYearMonthValue || '01',
          'YYYY-MM"Z"TZH:TZM DD')
FROM dual;
```

Listing 22.69 is a SQL statement that retrieves all of the values from the `GYearMonthExample` table.

**LISTING 22.69**  `GYearMonthExample` Values Retrieval via a Select Statement

```
SELECT TO_CHAR(value, 'YYYY-MM"Z"TZH:TZM')
FROM GYearMonthExample;
```

### 22.4.40.1 `pattern` Constraining Facet
Refer to Section 22.2.1 for design and implementation issues.

### 22.4.40.2 `enumeration` Constraining Facet
Refer to Section 22.2.2 for design and implementation issues.

### 22.4.40.3 `whiteSpace` Constraining Facet
Refer to Section 22.2.3 for design and implementation issues.

### 22.4.40.4 `maxInclusive` Constraining Facet
There is no built-in database support for the `maxInclusive` constraining facet, but Listing 22.70 shows how this can be enforced as a trigger. Note that Oracle limits the values of the check clause to constant values and does not allow calling PL/SQL conversion functions. This could be obviated in this case by not using the ISO 8601 `dateTime` format and using the default Oracle external `date` format, but this is not shown here.

**LISTING 22.70**  `GYearMonthMaxInclusiveExample` Table Creation with Insert and Update Triggers

```
CREATE TABLE GYearMonthMaxInclusiveExample (
value    TIMESTAMP WITH TIME ZONE
);

CREATE OR REPLACE TRIGGER InsertGYearMonthMaxInclusive
BEFORE INSERT
ON GYearMonthMaxInclusiveExample
FOR EACH ROW
WHEN (new.value >
  TO_TIMESTAMP_TZ('1999-01-01Z+05:00',
         'YYYY-MM-DD"Z"TZH:TZM'))
BEGIN
RAISE_APPLICATION_ERROR(-20000, 'GYearMonth too late');
END;

CREATE OR REPLACE TRIGGER UpdateGYearMonthMaxInclusive
BEFORE UPDATE
```

*continues*

```
ON GYearMonthMaxInclusiveExample
FOR EACH ROW
WHEN (new.value >
  TO_TIMESTAMP_TZ('1999-01-01Z+05:00',
         'YYYY-MM-DD"Z"TZH:TZM'))
BEGIN
RAISE_APPLICATION_ERROR(-20000, 'GYearMonth too late');
END;
```

### 22.4.40.5 `maxExclusive` Constraining Facet

There is no built-in database support for the `maxExclusive` constraining facet, but Listing 22.71 shows how this can be enforced as a trigger. Note that Oracle limits the values of the check clause to constant values and does not allow calling PL/SQL conversion functions. This could be obviated in this case by not using the ISO 8601 `dateTime` format and using the default Oracle external `date` format, but this is not shown here.

**LISTING 22.71**  `GYearMonthMaxExclusiveExample` Table Creation with Insert and Update Triggers

```
CREATE TABLE GYearMonthMaxExclusiveExample (
value   TIMESTAMP WITH TIME ZONE
);

CREATE OR REPLACE TRIGGER InsertGYearMonthMaxExclusive
BEFORE INSERT
ON GYearMonthMaxExclusiveExample
FOR EACH ROW
WHEN (new.value >=
  TO_TIMESTAMP_TZ('1999-01-01Z+05:00',
         'YYYY-MM-DD"Z"TZH:TZM'))
BEGIN
RAISE_APPLICATION_ERROR(-20000, 'GYearMonth too late');
END;

CREATE OR REPLACE TRIGGER UpdateGYearMonthMaxExclusive
BEFORE UPDATE
ON GYearMonthMaxExclusiveExample
FOR EACH ROW
WHEN (new.value >=
  TO_TIMESTAMP_TZ('1999-01-01Z+05:00',
         'YYYY-MM-DD"Z"TZH:TZM'))
BEGIN
RAISE_APPLICATION_ERROR(-20000, 'GYearMonth too late');
END;
```

### 22.4.40.6 minInclusive Constraining Facet

There is no built-in database support for the `minInclusive` constraining facet, but Listing 22.72 shows how this can be enforced as a trigger. Note that Oracle limits the values of the check clause to constant values and does not allow calling PL/SQL conversion functions. This could be obviated in this case by not using the ISO 8601 `dateTime` format and using the default Oracle external `date` format, but this is not shown here.

**LISTING 22.72** GYearMonthMinInclusiveExample Table Creation with Insert and Update Triggers

```
CREATE TABLE GYearMonthMinInclusiveExample (
value   TIMESTAMP WITH TIME ZONE
);

CREATE OR REPLACE TRIGGER InsertGYearMonthMinInclusive
BEFORE INSERT
ON GYearMonthMinInclusiveExample
FOR EACH ROW
WHEN (new.value <
   TO_TIMESTAMP_TZ('1999-01-01Z+05:00',
           'YYYY-MM-DD"Z"TZH:TZM'))
BEGIN
RAISE_APPLICATION_ERROR(-20000, 'GYearMonth too early');
END;

CREATE OR REPLACE TRIGGER UpdateGYearMonthMinInclusive
BEFORE UPDATE
ON GYearMonthMinInclusiveExample
FOR EACH ROW
WHEN (new.value <
   TO_TIMESTAMP_TZ('1999-01-01Z+05:00',
           'YYYY-MM-DD"Z"TZH:TZM'))
BEGIN
RAISE_APPLICATION_ERROR(-20000, 'GYearMonth too early');
END;
```

### 22.4.40.7 minExclusive Constraining Facet

There is no built-in database support for the `minExclusive` constraining facet, but Listing 22.73 shows how this can be enforced as a trigger. Note that Oracle limits the values of the check clause to constant values and does not allow calling PL/SQL conversion functions. This could be obviated in this case by not using the ISO 8601 `dateTime` format and using the default Oracle external `date` format, but this is not shown here.

**LISTING 22.73** GYearMonthMinExclusiveExample Table Creation with Insert and Update Triggers

```
CREATE TABLE GYearMonthMinExclusiveExample (
value   TIMESTAMP WITH TIME ZONE
);

CREATE OR REPLACE TRIGGER InsertGYearMonthMinExclusive
BEFORE INSERT
ON GYearMonthMinExclusiveExample
FOR EACH ROW
WHEN (new.value <=
   TO_TIMESTAMP_TZ('1999-01-01Z+05:00',
         'YYYY-MM-DD"Z"TZH:TZM'))
BEGIN
RAISE_APPLICATION_ERROR(-20000, 'GYearMonth too early');
END;

CREATE OR REPLACE TRIGGER UpdateGYearMonthMinExclusive
BEFORE UPDATE
ON GYearMonthMinExclusiveExample
FOR EACH ROW
WHEN (new.value <=
   TO_TIMESTAMP_TZ('1999-01-01Z+05:00',
         'YYYY-MM-DD"Z"TZH:TZM'))
BEGIN
RAISE_APPLICATION_ERROR(-20000, 'GYearMonth too early');
END;
```

## 22.4.41 time Datatype

The time datatype represents an instance of time that recurs every day. A time value may or may not include a time zone. Oracle9*i* now has a TIMESTAMP column datatype that represents a date, time of day, and an optional time zone. The database designer should confer with the XML schema designer to determine if time-zone values will exist in XML instances and, if so, whether the values need to be preserved or the time values can be reduced to their canonical form. Listing 22.74 implements a time table creation.

**LISTING 22.74** TimeExample Table Creation

```
CREATE TABLE TimeExample (
value TIMESTAMP WITH TIME ZONE
);
```

To insert a row into the table with a time datatype, Oracle needs to convert it from its XML Schema format to an internal Oracle representation. In addition, because Oracle needs a date for the insert, it is appropriate to use a date that indicates that no date was specified. Oracle has a minimum date of January 1, 4712 B.C. It is represented by the number 1 and is translated into January 1, 4712 B.C. by the 'J' datetime format element. A hard-coded date is especially useful when min/max inclusion/exclusion facets have been specified.

> **WARNING**
>
> The database `TIMESTAMP` column datatype does not support the time value of '`24:00:00`', but does support its value space equivalent '`00:00:00`'.

Listing 22.75 is a SQL statement that inserts a time into the `TimeExample` table (`?timeValue` is the time bind variable).

**LISTING 22.75** `TimeExample` Example Insert

```
INSERT INTO TimeExample
(value)
SELECT TO_TIMESTAMP_TZ('1 ' || ?timeValue,
        'J HH24:MI:SS"Z"TZH:TZM')
FROM dual;
```

Listing 22.76 is a SQL statement that retrieves all of the values from the `TimeExample` table.

**LISTING 22.76** `TimeExample` Values Retrieval via a Select Statement

```
SELECT TO_CHAR(value, 'HH24:MI:SS"Z"TZH:TZM')
FROM TimeExample;
```

### 22.4.41.1 `pattern` Constraining Facet
Refer to Section 22.2.1 for design and implementation issues.

### 22.4.41.2 `enumeration` Constraining Facet
Refer to Section 22.2.2 for design and implementation issues.

### 22.4.41.3 `whiteSpace` Constraining Facet
Refer to Section 22.2.3 for design and implementation issues.

### 22.4.41.4 `maxInclusive` Constraining Facet
There is no built-in database support for the `maxInclusive` constraining facet, but Listing 22.77 shows how this can be enforced with a trigger. Note that Oracle limits the values of

the check clause to constant values and does not allow calling of PL/SQL conversion functions.

**LISTING 22.77** TimeMaxInclusiveExample Table Creation with Insert and Update Triggers

```
CREATE TABLE TimeMaxInclusiveExample (
value TIMESTAMP WITH TIME ZONE
);

CREATE OR REPLACE TRIGGER InsertTimeMaxInclusiveExample
BEFORE INSERT
ON TimeMaxInclusiveExample
FOR EACH ROW
WHEN (new.value > TO_TIMESTAMP_TZ('1 12:45:30Z+05:00',
                 'J HH24:MI:SS"Z"TZH:TZM'))
BEGIN
RAISE_APPLICATION_ERROR(-20000, 'Time too late');
END;

CREATE OR REPLACE TRIGGER UpdateTimeMaxInclusiveExample
BEFORE UPDATE
ON TimeMaxInclusiveExample
FOR EACH ROW
WHEN (new.value > TO_TIMESTAMP_TZ('1 12:45:30Z+05:00',
                 'J HH24:MI:SS"Z"TZH:TZM'))
BEGIN
RAISE_APPLICATION_ERROR(-20000, 'Time too late');
END;
```

### 22.4.41.5 maxExclusive Constraining Facet

There is no built-in database support for the maxExclusive constraining facet, but Listing 22.78 shows how this can be enforced with a trigger. Note that Oracle limits the values of the check clause to constant values and does not allow calling of PL/SQL conversion functions.

**LISTING 22.78** TimeMaxExclusiveExample Table Creation with Insert and Update Triggers

```
CREATE TABLE TimeMaxExclusiveExample (
value TIMESTAMP WITH TIME ZONE
);

CREATE OR REPLACE TRIGGER InsertTimeMaxExclusiveExample
BEFORE INSERT
ON TimeMaxExclusiveExample
FOR EACH ROW
WHEN (new.value >= TO_TIMESTAMP_TZ('1 12:45:30Z+05:00',
```

```
                'J HH24:MI:SS"Z"TZH:TZM'))
BEGIN
RAISE_APPLICATION_ERROR(-20000, 'Time too late');
END;

CREATE OR REPLACE TRIGGER UpdateTimeMaxExclusiveExample
BEFORE UPDATE
ON TimeMaxExclusiveExample
FOR EACH ROW
WHEN (new.value >= TO_TIMESTAMP_TZ('1 12:45:30Z+05:00',
                'J HH24:MI:SS"Z"TZH:TZM'))
BEGIN
RAISE_APPLICATION_ERROR(-20000, 'Time too late');
END;
```

### 22.4.41.6 `minInclusive` Constraining Facet

There is no built-in database support for the `minInclusive` constraining facet, but Listing 22.79 shows how this can be enforced with a trigger. Note that Oracle limits the values of the check clause to constant values and does not allow calling of PL/SQL conversion functions.

**LISTING 22.79** `TimeMinInclusiveExample` Table Creation with Insert and Update Triggers

```
CREATE TABLE TimeMinInclusiveExample (
value TIMESTAMP WITH TIME ZONE
);

CREATE OR REPLACE TRIGGER InsertTimeMinInclusiveExample
BEFORE INSERT
ON TimeMinInclusiveExample
FOR EACH ROW
WHEN (new.value < TO_ TIMEZONE_TZ('1 12:45:30Z+05:00',
                'J HH24:MI:SS"Z"TZH:TZM'))
BEGIN
RAISE_APPLICATION_ERROR(-20000, 'Time too early');
END;

CREATE OR REPLACE TRIGGER UpdateTimeMinInclusiveExample
BEFORE UPDATE
ON TimeMinInclusiveExample
FOR EACH ROW
WHEN (new.value < TO_ TIMEZONE_TZ('1 12:45:30Z+05:00',
                'J HH24:MI:SS"Z"TZH:TZM'))
BEGIN
RAISE_APPLICATION_ERROR(-20000, 'Time too early');
END;
```

### 22.4.41.7 `minExclusive` Constraining Facet

There is no built-in database support for the `minExclusive` constraining facet, but Listing 22.80 shows how this can be enforced with a trigger. Note that Oracle limits the values of he check clause to constant values and does not allow calling of PL/SQL conversion functions.

**LISTING 22.80**   TimeMinExclusiveExample Table Creation with Insert and Update Triggers

```
CREATE TABLE TimeMinExclusiveExample (
value TIMESTAMP WITH TIME ZONE
);

CREATE OR REPLACE TRIGGER InsertTimeMinExclusiveExample
BEFORE INSERT
ON TimeMinExclusiveExample
FOR EACH ROW
WHEN (new.value <= TO_TIMEZONE_TZ('1 12:45:30Z+05:00',
                 'J HH24:MI:SS"Z"TZH:TZM'))
BEGIN
RAISE_APPLICATION_ERROR(-20000, 'Time too early');
END;

CREATE OR REPLACE TRIGGER UpdateTimeMinExclusiveExample
BEFORE UPDATE
ON TimeMinExclusiveExample
FOR EACH ROW
WHEN (new.value <= TO_TIMEZONE_TZ('1 12:45:30Z+05:00',
                 'J HH24:MI:SS"Z"TZH:TZM'))
BEGIN
RAISE_APPLICATION_ERROR(-20000, 'Time too early');
END;
```

## 22.4.42  `gMonth` Datatype

The `gMonth` datatype represents a Gregorian calendar month that recurs every year. Without the optional time zone, `gMonth` is essentially an `integer` datatype with a `minInclusive` of 0 and a `maxInclusive` of 11. Refer to Sections 22.4.14 and 22.4.15 for details implementing `gMonth` when no time-zone offsets are required.

If time-zone offsets are required, the representation becomes much more complex. Oracle9*i* now has a `TIMESTAMP` column datatype that represents both date and time with a time-zone offset. The database designer should confer with the XML schema designer to determine if time-zone values will exist in XML instances and, if so, whether the values need to be preserved or the `gMonth` values can be reduced to their canonical form.

## WARNING

Mixing gMonth values that have time zones with those that do not in the same database table column is problematic. From an XML schema perspective, the values are only partially ordered since the time zone is not specified in some cases. However, when using a database TIMESTAMP WITH TIME ZONE column datatype, Oracle9*i* will *default* the time zone to the time zone of the database server that results in a complete ordering. Separating gMonth values that have time zones and those that do not into two database columns is advisable.

Listing 22.81 implements a gMonth table creation.

**LISTING 22.81** GMonthExample Table Creation

```
CREATE TABLE GMonthExample (
value TIMESTAMP WITH TIME ZONE
);
```

To insert a row into the table with a gMonth datatype, Oracle needs to convert the datatype from its XML Schema format to an internal Oracle representation. In addition, because Oracle needs a date for the insert, it is appropriate to use a date that indicates that no date was specified. Oracle has a minimum date of January 1, 4712 B.C. It is represented by the number 1 and is translated into January 1, 4712 B.C. by the 'J' dateTime format element. A hard-coded date is especially useful when min/max inclusion/exclusion facets have been specified. Listing 22.82 is a SQL statement that inserts a gMonth into the GMonthExample table (?gMonthValue is a gMonth bind variable without the time zone and ?timezoneValue is the time-zone bind variable). FROM_TZ converts a time zone without a time-zone indicator to one with a time-zone indicator.

**LISTING 22.82** GMonthExample Example Insert

```
INSERT INTO gMonthExample
(value)
SELECT FROM_TZ(CAST(ADD_MONTHS(TO_DATE('1', 'J'),
            ?gMonthValue - 1)
      AS TIMESTAMP), ?timezoneValue)
FROM dual;
```

Listing 22.83 is a SQL statement that retrieves all of the values from the GMonthExample table.

**LISTING 22.83** GMonthExample Values Retrieval via a Select Statement

```
SELECT TO_CHAR(value, 'MM"Z"TZH:TZM')
FROM GMonthExample;
```

### 22.4.42.1 `pattern` Constraining Facet
Refer to Section 22.2.1 for design and implementation issues.

### 22.4.42.2 `enumeration` Constraining Facet
Refer to Section 22.2.2 for design and implementation issues.

### 22.4.42.3 `whiteSpace` Constraining Facet
Refer to Section 22.2.3 for design and implementation issues.

### 22.4.42.4 `maxInclusive` Constraining Facet
There is no built-in database support for the `maxInclusive` constraining facet, but Listing 22.84 shows how this can be enforced as a trigger. Note that Oracle limits the values of the check clause to constant values and does not allow calling PL/SQL conversion functions.

**LISTING 22.84** GMonthMaxInclusiveExample Table Creation with Insert and Update Triggers

```
CREATE TABLE GMonthMaxInclusiveExample (
value   TIMESTAMP WITH TIME ZONE
);

CREATE OR REPLACE TRIGGER InsertGMonthMaxInclusive
BEFORE INSERT
ON GMonthMaxInclusiveExample
FOR EACH ROW
WHEN (new.value >
   FROM_TZ(CAST(ADD_MONTHS(TO_DATE('1', 'J'), 10)
      AS TIMESTAMP), '+05:00'))
BEGIN
RAISE_APPLICATION_ERROR(-20000, 'GMonth too late');
END;

CREATE OR REPLACE TRIGGER UpdateGMonthMaxInclusive
BEFORE UPDATE
ON GMonthMaxInclusiveExample
FOR EACH ROW
WHEN (new.value >
   FROM_TZ(CAST(ADD_MONTHS(TO_DATE('1', 'J'), 10)
      AS TIMESTAMP), '+05:00'))
BEGIN
RAISE_APPLICATION_ERROR(-20000, ''GMonth too late');
END;
```

### 22.4.42.5 `maxExclusive` Constraining Facet

There is no built-in database support for the `maxExclusive` constraining facet, but Listing 22.85 shows how this can be enforced as a trigger. Note that Oracle limits the values of the check clause to constant values and does not allow calling PL/SQL conversion functions.

**LISTING 22.85** `GMonthMaxExclusiveExample` Table Creation with Insert and Update Triggers

```
CREATE TABLE GMonthMaxExclusiveExample (
value   TIMESTAMP WITH TIME ZONE
);

CREATE OR REPLACE TRIGGER InsertGMonthMaxExclusive
BEFORE INSERT
ON GMonthMaxExclusiveExample
FOR EACH ROW
WHEN (new.value >=
  FROM_TZ(CAST(ADD_MONTHS(TO_DATE('1', 'J'), 10)
      AS TIMESTAMP), '+05:00'))
BEGIN
RAISE_APPLICATION_ERROR(-20000, 'GMonth too late');
END;

CREATE OR REPLACE TRIGGER UpdateGMonthMaxExclusive
BEFORE UPDATE
ON GMonthMaxExclusiveExample
FOR EACH ROW
WHEN (new.value >=
  FROM_TZ(CAST(ADD_MONTHS(TO_DATE('1', 'J'), 10)
      AS TIMESTAMP), '+05:00'))
BEGIN
RAISE_APPLICATION_ERROR(-20000, 'GMonth too late');
END;
```

### 22.4.42.6 `minInclusive` Constraining Facet

There is no built-in database support for the `minInclusive` constraining facet, but Listing 22.86 shows how this can be enforced as a trigger. Note that Oracle limits the values of the check clause to constant values and does not allow calling PL/SQL conversion functions.

**LISTING 22.86** `GMonthMinInclusiveExample` Table Creation with Insert and Update Triggers

```
CREATE TABLE GMonthMinInclusiveExample (
value   TIMESTAMP WITH TIME ZONE
);
```

*continues*

```
CREATE OR REPLACE TRIGGER InsertGMonthMinInclusive
BEFORE INSERT
ON GMonthMinInclusiveExample
FOR EACH ROW
WHEN (new.value <
  FROM_TZ(CAST(ADD_MONTHS(TO_DATE('1', 'J'), 10)
      AS TIMESTAMP), '+05:00'))
BEGIN
RAISE_APPLICATION_ERROR(-20000, 'GMonth too early');
END;

CREATE OR REPLACE TRIGGER UpdateGMonthMinInclusive
BEFORE UPDATE
ON GMonthMinInclusiveExample
FOR EACH ROW
WHEN (new.value <
  FROM_TZ(CAST(ADD_MONTHS(TO_DATE('1', 'J'), 10)
      AS TIMESTAMP), '+05:00'))
BEGIN
RAISE_APPLICATION_ERROR(-20000, 'GMonth too early');
END;
```

### 22.4.42.7 `minExclusive` Constraining Facet

There is no built-in database support for the `minExclusive` constraining facet, but Listing 22.87 shows how this can be enforced as a trigger. Note that Oracle limits the values of the check clause to constant values and does not allow calling PL/SQL conversion functions.

**LISTING 22.87** `GmonthMinExclusiveExample` Table Creation with Insert and Update Triggers

```
CREATE TABLE GMonthMinExclusiveExample (
value   TIMESTAMP WITH TIME ZONE
);

CREATE OR REPLACE TRIGGER InsertGMonthMinExclusive
BEFORE INSERT
ON GMonthMinExclusiveExample
FOR EACH ROW
WHEN (new.value <=
  FROM_TZ(CAST(ADD_MONTHS(TO_DATE('1', 'J'), 10)
      AS TIMESTAMP), '+05:00'))
BEGIN
RAISE_APPLICATION_ERROR(-20000, 'GMonth too early');
END;
```

```
CREATE OR REPLACE TRIGGER UpdateGMonthMinExclusive
BEFORE UPDATE
ON GMonthMinExclusiveExample
FOR EACH ROW
WHEN (new.value <=
  FROM_TZ(CAST(ADD_MONTHS(TO_DATE('1', 'J'), 10)
      AS TIMESTAMP), '+05:00'))
BEGIN
RAISE_APPLICATION_ERROR(-20000, 'GMonth too early');
END;
```

## 22.4.43 gDay Datatype

The gDay datatype represents a Gregorian calendar day of the month. Without the optional time zone, gDay is essentially an `integer` datatype that has a `minInclusive` of 1 and a `maxExclusive` of 31. Refer to Sections 22.4.14 and 22.4.15 for details implementing gDay when no time-zone offsets are required.

If time-zone offsets are required, the representation becomes much more complex. Oracle9*i* now has a `TIMESTAMP` column datatype that represents both date and time with a time zone. The database designer should confer with the XML schema designer to determine if time-zone values will exist in XML instances and, if so, whether the values need to be preserved or the gDay values can be reduced to their canonical form. Listing 22.88 implements a gDay table creation.

**LISTING 22.88**   GDayExample Table Creation

```
CREATE TABLE GDayExample (
value TIMESTAMP WITH TIME ZONE
);
```

To insert a row into the table with a gDay datatype, Oracle needs to convert the datatype from its XML Schema format to an internal Oracle representation. Listing 22.89 is a SQL statement that inserts a gDay into the GDayExample table (?gDayValue is a gDay bind variable).

**LISTING 22.89**   GDayExample Example Insert

```
INSERT INTO gDayExample
(value)
BEGIN
SELECT TO_TIMESTAMP_TZ(?gDayValue, 'J"Z"TZH:TZM')
FROM dual;
```

Listing 22.90 is a SQL statement that retrieves all of the values from the `GDayExample` table.

**LISTING 22.90**  `GDayExample` Values Retrieval via a Select Statement

```
SELECT TO_CHAR(value, 'DD"Z"TZH:TZM')
FROM GDayExample;
```

### 22.4.43.1 `pattern` Constraining Facet
Refer to Section 22.2.1 for design and implementation issues.

### 22.4.43.2 `enumeration` Constraining Facet
Refer to Section 22.2.2 for design and implementation issues.

### 22.4.43.3 `whiteSpace` Constraining Facet
Refer to Section 22.2.3 for design and implementation issues.

### 22.4.43.4 `maxInclusive` Constraining Facet
There is no built-in database support for the `maxInclusive` constraining facet, but Listing 22.91 shows how this can be enforced as a trigger. Note that Oracle limits the values of the check clause to constant values and does not allow calling PL/SQL conversion functions.

**LISTING 22.91**  `GDayMaxInclusiveExample` Table Creation with Insert and Update Triggers

```
CREATE TABLE GDayMaxInclusiveExample (
value   TIMESTAMP WITH TIME ZONE
);

CREATE OR REPLACE TRIGGER InsertGDayMaxInclusive
BEFORE INSERT
ON GDayMaxInclusiveExample
FOR EACH ROW
WHEN (new.value > TO_TIMESTAMP_TZ('20Z05:00', 'J"Z"TZH:TZM'))
BEGIN
RAISE_APPLICATION_ERROR(-20000, 'GDay too late');
END;

CREATE OR REPLACE TRIGGER UpdateGDayMaxInclusive
BEFORE UPDATE
ON GDayMaxInclusiveExample
FOR EACH ROW
WHEN (new.value > TO_TIMESTAMP_TZ('20Z05:00', 'J"Z"TZH:TZM'))
BEGIN
RAISE_APPLICATION_ERROR(-20000, 'Date too late');
END;
```

### 22.4.43.5 `maxExclusive` Constraining Facet

There is no built-in database support for the `maxExclusive` constraining facet, but Listing 22.92 shows how this can be enforced as a trigger. Note that Oracle limits the values of the check clause to constant values and does not allow calling PL/SQL conversion functions.

**LISTING 22.92**   `GDayMaxExclusiveExample` Table Creation with Insert and Update Triggers

```
CREATE TABLE GDayMaxExclusiveExample (
value   TIMESTAMP WITH TIME ZONE
);

CREATE OR REPLACE TRIGGER InsertGDayMaxExclusive
BEFORE INSERT
ON GDayMaxExclusiveExample
FOR EACH ROW
WHEN (new.value >= TO_TIMESTAMP_TZ('20Z05:00', 'J"Z"TZH:TZM'))
BEGIN
RAISE_APPLICATION_ERROR(-20000, 'GDay too late');
END;

CREATE OR REPLACE TRIGGER UpdateGDayMaxExclusive
BEFORE UPDATE
ON GDayMaxExclusiveExample
FOR EACH ROW
WHEN (new.value >= TO_TIMESTAMP_TZ('20Z05:00', 'J"Z"TZH:TZM'))
BEGIN
RAISE_APPLICATION_ERROR(-20000, 'GDay too late');
END;
```

### 22.4.43.6 `minInclusive` Constraining Facet

There is no built-in database support for the `minInclusive` constraining facet, but Listing 22.93 shows how this can be enforced as a trigger. Note that Oracle limits the values of the check clause to constant values and does not allow calling PL/SQL conversion functions.

**LISTING 22.93**   `GDayMinInclusiveExample` Table Creation with Insert and Update Triggers

```
CREATE TABLE GDayMinInclusiveExample (
value   TIMESTAMP WITH TIME ZONE
);

CREATE OR REPLACE TRIGGER InsertGDayMinInclusive
BEFORE INSERT
ON GDayMinInclusiveExample
FOR EACH ROW
WHEN (new.value < TO_TIMESTAMP_TZ('20Z05:00', 'J"Z"TZH:TZM'))
```

*continues*

```
BEGIN
RAISE_APPLICATION_ERROR(-20000, 'GDay too early');
END;

CREATE OR REPLACE TRIGGER UpdateGDayMinInclusive
BEFORE UPDATE
ON GDayMinInclusiveExample
FOR EACH ROW
WHEN (new.value < TO_TIMESTAMP_TZ('20Z05:00', 'J"Z"TZH:TZM'))
BEGIN
RAISE_APPLICATION_ERROR(-20000, 'GDay too early');
END;
```

### 22.4.43.7 `minExclusive` Constraining Facet

There is no built-in database support for the `minExclusive` constraining facet, but Listing 22.94 shows how this can be enforced as a trigger. Note that Oracle limits the values of the check clause to constant values and does not allow calling PL/SQL conversion functions.

**LISTING 22.94** GDayMinInclusiveExample Table Creation with Insert and Update Triggers

```
CREATE TABLE GDayMinExclusiveExample (
value   TIMESTAMP WITH TIME ZONE
);

CREATE OR REPLACE TRIGGER InsertGDayMinExclusive
BEFORE INSERT
ON GDayMinExclusiveExample
FOR EACH ROW
WHEN (new.value <= TO_TIMESTAMP_TZ('20Z05:00', 'J"Z"TZH:TZM'))
BEGIN
RAISE_APPLICATION_ERROR(-20000, 'GDay too early');
END;

CREATE OR REPLACE TRIGGER UpdateGDayMinExclusive
BEFORE UPDATE
ON GDayMinExclusiveExample
FOR EACH ROW
WHEN (new.value <= TO_TIMESTAMP_TZ('20Z05:00', 'J"Z"TZH:TZM'))
BEGIN
RAISE_APPLICATION_ERROR(-20000, 'GDay too early');
END;
```

## 22.4.44 gMonthDay Datatype

The gMonthDay datatype represents a Gregorian calendar day in a year. Oracle9*i* now has a TIMESTAMP column datatype that represents both date and time with a time-zone offset. The database designer should confer with the XML schema designer to determine if time-zone values will exist in XML instances and, if so, whether the values need to be preserved or the gMonthDay values can be reduced to their canonical form. Listing 22.95 implements a gMonthDay table creation.

**LISTING 22.95** GMonthDayExample Table Creation

```
CREATE TABLE GMonthDayExample (
value   TIMESTAMP WITH TIME ZONE
);
```

To insert a row into the table with a gMonthDay datatype, Oracle needs to convert the datatype from its XML Schema format to an internal Oracle representation.

Listing 22.96 is a SQL statement that inserts a gMonthDay into the GMonthDayExample table, including offsetting for the time-zone indicator. In addition, because Oracle automatically uses today's year for the insert by default, it is appropriate to use a date that indicates that no date was specified. Oracle has a minimum date of January 1, 4712 B.C. It is represented by the number 1 and is translated into January 1, 4712 B.C. by the 'J' dateTime format element.

**LISTING 22.96** GMonthDayExample Example Insert

```
INSERT INTO GMonthDayExample
(value)
SELECT FROM_TZ(CAST(ADD_MONTHS(TO_DATE(?dayValue, 'J'),
         ?monthValue - 1)
    AS TIMESTAMP), ?timezoneValue)
FROM dual;
```

The ?dayValue bind variable is the day portion of a gMonthDay, the ?monthValue bind variable is the month portion of a gMonthDay, and the ?timeZone bind variable is the time-zone portion in a gMonthDay.

Listing 22.97 is a SQL statement that retrieves all of the values from the GMonthDayExample table.

**LISTING 22.97** GMonthDayExample Values Retrieval via a Select Statement

```
SELECT TO_CHAR(value, 'MM-DD"Z"TZH:TZM')
FROM GMonthDayExample;
```

### 22.4.44.1 `pattern` Constraining Facet
Refer to Section 22.2.1 for design and implementation issues.

### 22.4.44.2 `enumeration` Constraining Facet
Refer to Section 22.2.2 for design and implementation issues.

### 22.4.44.3 `whiteSpace` Constraining Facet
Refer to Section 22.2.3 for design and implementation issues.

### 22.4.44.4 `maxInclusive` Constraining Facet
There is no built-in database support for the `maxInclusive` constraining facet, but Listing 22.98 shows how this can be enforced as a trigger. Note that Oracle limits the values of the check clause to constant values and does not allow calling PL/SQL conversion functions.

**LISTING 22.98** GMonthDayMaxInclusiveExample Table Creation with Insert and Update Triggers

```
CREATE TABLE GMonthDayMaxInclusiveExample (
value   TIMESTAMP WITH TIME ZONE
);

CREATE OR REPLACE TRIGGER InsertGMonthDayMaxInclusive
BEFORE INSERT
ON GMonthDayMaxInclusiveExample
FOR EACH ROW
WHEN (new.value >
  FROM_TZ(CAST(ADD_MONTHS(TO_DATE(5, 'J'), 8)
      AS TIMESTAMP), '+05:00'))
BEGIN
RAISE_APPLICATION_ERROR(-20000, 'GMonthDay too late');
END;

CREATE OR REPLACE TRIGGER UpdateGMonthDayMaxInclusive
BEFORE UPDATE
ON GMonthDayMaxInclusiveExample
FOR EACH ROW
WHEN (new.value >
  FROM_TZ(CAST(ADD_MONTHS(TO_DATE(5, 'J'), 8)
    AS TIMESTAMP), '+05:00'))
BEGIN
RAISE_APPLICATION_ERROR(-20000, 'Date too late');
END;
```

### 22.4.44.5 `maxExclusive` Constraining Facet

There is no built-in database support for the `maxExclusive` constraining facet, but Listing 22.99 shows how this can be enforced as a trigger. Note that Oracle limits the values of the check clause to constant values and does not allow calling PL/SQL conversion functions.

**LISTING 22.99**  `GMonthDayMaxExclusiveExample` Table Creation with Insert and Update Triggers

```
CREATE TABLE GMonthDayMaxExclusiveExample (
value TIMESTAMP WITH TIME ZONE
);

CREATE OR REPLACE TRIGGER InsertGMonthDayMaxExclusive
BEFORE INSERT
ON GMonthDayMaxExclusiveExample
FOR EACH ROW
WHEN (new.value >=
 FROM_TZ(CAST(ADD_MONTHS(TO_DATE(5, 'J'), 8)
    AS TIMESTAMP), '+05:00'))
BEGIN
RAISE_APPLICATION_ERROR(-20000, 'GMonthDay too late');
END;

CREATE OR REPLACE TRIGGER UpdateGMonthDayMaxExclusive
BEFORE UPDATE
ON GMonthDayMaxExclusiveExample
FOR EACH ROW
WHEN (new.value >=
 FROM_TZ(CAST(ADD_MONTHS(TO_DATE(5, 'J'), 8)
      AS TIMESTAMP), '+05:00'))
BEGIN
RAISE_APPLICATION_ERROR(-20000, 'GMonthDay too late');
END;
```

### 22.4.44.6 `minInclusive` Constraining Facet

There is no built-in database support for the `minInclusive` constraining facet, but Listing 22.100 shows how this can be enforced as a trigger. Note that Oracle limits the values of the check clause to constant values and does not allow calling PL/SQL conversion functions.

**LISTING 22.100**  `GMonthDayMinInclusiveExample` Table Creation with Insert and Update Triggers

```
CREATE TABLE GMonthDayMinInclusiveExample (
value  TIMESTAMP WITH TIME ZONE
);
```

*continues*

```
CREATE OR REPLACE TRIGGER InsertGMonthDayMinInclusive
BEFORE INSERT
ON GMonthDayMinInclusiveExample
FOR EACH ROW
WHEN (new.value <
  FROM_TZ(CAST(ADD_MONTHS(TO_DATE(5, 'J'), 8)
      AS TIMESTAMP), '+05:00'))
BEGIN
RAISE_APPLICATION_ERROR(-20000, 'GMonthDay too early');
END;

CREATE OR REPLACE TRIGGER UpdateGMonthDayMinInclusive
BEFORE UPDATE
ON GMonthDayMinInclusiveExample
FOR EACH ROW
WHEN (new.value <
  FROM_TZ(CAST(ADD_MONTHS(TO_DATE(5, 'J'), 8)
      AS TIMESTAMP), '+05:00'))
BEGIN
RAISE_APPLICATION_ERROR(-20000, 'GMonthDay too early');
END;
```

### 22.4.44.7 minExclusive Constraining Facet

There is no built-in database support for the minExclusive constraining facet, but Listing 22.101 shows how this can be enforced as a trigger. Note that Oracle limits the values of the check clause to constant values and does not allow calling PL/SQL conversion functions.

**LISTING 22.101** GMonthDayMinExclusiveExample Table Creation with Insert and Update Triggers

```
CREATE TABLE GMonthDayMinExclusiveExample (
value   TIMESTAMP WITH TIME ZONE
);

CREATE OR REPLACE TRIGGER InsertGMonthDayMinExclusive
BEFORE INSERT
ON GMonthDayMinExclusiveExample
FOR EACH ROW
WHEN (new.value <=
  FROM_TZ(CAST(ADD_MONTHS(TO_DATE(5, 'J'), 8)
      AS TIMESTAMP), '+05:00'))
BEGIN
RAISE_APPLICATION_ERROR(-20000, 'GMonthDay too early');
END;
```

```
CREATE OR REPLACE TRIGGER UpdateGMonthDayMinExclusive
BEFORE UPDATE
ON GMonthDayMinExclusiveExample
FOR EACH ROW
WHEN (new.value <=
  FROM_TZ(CAST(ADD_MONTHS(TO_DATE(5, 'J'), 8)
       AS TIMESTAMP), '+05:00'))
BEGIN
RAISE_APPLICATION_ERROR(-20000, 'GMonthDay too early');
END;
```

# Data-oriented Schemas: Simple Types

**CHAPTER 23**

## IN THIS CHAPTER

- 23.1 XML Schema Design Considerations  674
- 23.2 An Example of a Simple Type Mapping to a Database Schema  675
- 23.3 Concepts and Observations  678
- 23.4 The `list` Element  678
- 23.5 The `union` Element  690

This chapter details how to map XML Schema simple types to a relational database. Representing simple types is fairly straightforward but requires some consideration of design and implementation trade-offs. This chapter loosely follows Chapter 10 and builds on its examples. This chapter also builds on Chapter 22, which covers the database implementation of XML built-in datatypes and their constraining facets.

Because much of this chapter is meant for a database designer and implementer, the chapter begins with some issues of which an XML schema designer should be aware when designing XML Schema simple types that will be represented in a relational database. In some cases, small XML schema decisions have major database implications.

This chapter continues with a few examples of simple types and then moves on to represent list elements and union elements in a relational database. The database implementations of simple types, except for the list and union derivations, are covered in Chapter 22.

> **NOTE**
>
> The database code implementing each simple type is meant to be a set of contrived, albeit working, examples. The hard-coded values in many of the examples would be changed or set to PL/SQL package constants in real-world scenarios.
> All code examples have been tested in Oracle 9.0.1.0.1 running in Windows 2000.

## 23.1 XML Schema Design Considerations

When creating an XML schema document that contains list or union elements whose XML instances will be stored in a relational database (in non-XML form), the XML schema designer needs to consider the effect of design decisions on the database representation. In addition, certain decisions need to be made explicitly that would not normally affect an XML schema document. This section lists the major considerations and provides recommendations and discussion around each of them.

### 23.1.1 list Element Design Considerations

When using the list element, determine if the items in the list need to be stored separately in a relational database or can be maintained in a single string. Will the members of the list be accessed or updated separately? Will reports be run that need to count or reference the individual items in the list? If the answer is no, a single string may suffice. Document the intended use of the list element in the annotation.

Maintaining a length constraining facet or a minLength constraining facet is nontrivial in the database. Determine if these are needed and, if so, whether the database needs to enforce these constraining facets.

### 23.1.2 union Element Design Considerations

From a database design perspective, `union`s should be avoided, if possible, due to their design and implementation complexity. If the `union` is, for example, a `union` of lists, a `union` of `IDREFS`, or a `union` of `NMTOKENS`, the database schema to support these is complex.

If a `union` element is required, determine if the item of the `union` needs to be stored in separate columns in a relational database (by `memberType`) or can be maintained in a single string. Will reports be run that need to count or reference the item of the `union` by type? If the answer is no, a single string may suffice. Document the intended use of the `union` element in the annotation.

## 23.2 An Example of a Simple Type Mapping to a Database Schema

Listing 23.1 shows the simple type `partNameType`, first seen in Listing 10.1.

**LISTING 23.1**  A Simple Type Derived from a Token (catalog.xsd)

```
<xsd:simpleType name="partNameType"
                final="list,union"
                id="catalog.partName.sType">
    <xsd:annotation>
        <xsd:documentation xml:lang="en">
            A part name can be almost anything.
            The name is a short description.
        </xsd:documentation>
    </xsd:annotation>
    <xsd:restriction base="xsd:token"
                     id="pnt-rst">
        <xsd:minLength value="1"/>
        <xsd:maxLength value="40"/>
    </xsd:restriction>
</xsd:simpleType>
```

Mapping this to a database schema involves creating a database column of type token, entering a description of the column, and enforcing the `minLength` and `maxLength` constraining facets. Listing 23.2 creates the `PartNameTypeExample` table, using a check constraint.

**LISTING 23.2**  Mapping a Simple Type Derived from a Token to a Database Representation (catalog.xsd)

```
CREATE TABLE PartNameTypeExample (
partNameType VARCHAR2(40) NOT NULL
     CHECK (INSTR(partNameType, UNISTR('\000D')) = 0 AND
            INSTR(partNameType, UNISTR('\000A')) = 0 AND
```

*continues*

```
              INSTR(partNameType, UNISTR('\0009')) = 0 AND
              LENGTH(partNameType) =
                LENGTH(TRIM(partNameType)) AND
              INSTR(partNameType, ' ') = 0 AND
              LENGTH(partNameType) >= 1)
);

--Add a column comment to match the annotation.
COMMENT ON COLUMN PartNameTypeExample.partNameType IS
' A part name can be almost anything.
The name is a short description.';
```

Given the preceding table declaration, the following is a valid insert statement:

```
INSERT INTO PartNameTypeExample
VALUES
('Short Description of Unit 1');
```

Listing 23.3 iterates Listings 10.2 and 10.3 and shows the XML schema document representation of `partNumberType` and an `assemblyPartNumberType`.

**LISTING 23.3**  Restricting a Custom Simple Type (catalog.xsd)

```
<xsd:simpleType name="partNumberType"
                final="union"
                id="catalog.partNumber.sType">
    <xsd:annotation>
        <xsd:documentation xml:lang="en">
            Declaration of a part number.
            Each part number consists of one to
            three alphabetic characters followed by
            one to eight digits. The following part
            numbers, for example, are valid:
                J1
                ABC32897
                ZZ22233344
        </xsd:documentation>
    </xsd:annotation>
        <xsd:restriction base="xsd:token">
            <xsd:pattern value="[A-Z]{1,3}\d{1,8}"/>
        </xsd:restriction>
</xsd:simpleType>

<xsd:simpleType name="assemblyPartNumberType"
                final="#all"
                id="catalog.assemblypartNumber.sType">
    <xsd:annotation>
        <xsd:documentation xml:lang="en">
```

```
                An "assembly" represents a pre-built
                collection of unit items. The
                part number for an assembly
                always starts with "ASM."
            </xsd:documentation>
        </xsd:annotation>
        <xsd:restriction base="partNumberType">
            <xsd:pattern value="ASM\d{1,8}"/>
        </xsd:restriction>
</xsd:simpleType>
```

Mapping assemblyPartNumberType to a database schema involves creating a database column of type token, entering a description of the column, enforcing the minLength and maxLength constraining facets, and enforcing the pattern facet. Listing 23.4 creates an AssemblyPartNumberTypeExample table, using a check constraint.

**LISTING 23.4** Mapping a Pattern Simple Type Derived from a Token to a Database Representation (catalog.xsd)

```
CREATE TABLE AssemblyPartNumberTypeExample (
assemblyPartNumberType VARCHAR2(40) NOT NULL
  CHECK (INSTR(assemblyPartNumberType, UNISTR('\000D')) = 0 AND
         INSTR(assemblyPartNumberType, UNISTR('\000A')) = 0 AND
         INSTR(assemblyPartNumberType, UNISTR('\0009')) = 0 AND
         LENGTH(assemblyPartNumberType) =
            LENGTH(TRIM(assemblyPartNumberType)) AND
         INSTR(assemblyPartNumberType, ' ') = 0 AND
         LENGTH(assemblyPartNumberType) BETWEEN 4 AND 11 AND
     SUBSTR(assemblyPartNumberType, 1, 3) = 'ASM' AND
         -- If the value is not a number, then an
         -- error will be thrown. IS NOT NULL makes
         -- this valid SQL, but is meaningless.
         CAST(SUBSTR(assemblyPartNumberType, 4, 8) AS NUMBER)
            IS NOT NULL)
);

COMMENT ON COLUMN
AssemblyPartNumberTypeExample.assemblyPartNumberType IS
'An "assembly" represents a pre-built collection of unit items.[ccc]
The part number for an assembly always starts with "ASM."';
```

Given the preceding table declaration, the following is a valid insert statement:

```
INSERT INTO AssemblyPartNumberTypeExample
VALUES
('ASM4534');
```

## 23.3 Concepts and Observations

Creating a database schema representation of an XML schema document is fairly straightforward but requires some knowledge of the database column datatypes and Oracle PL/SQL functions. In addition, the following portions of the XML schema document were *not* translated in Listing 23.4:

- There is no translation of the `id` attribute into the database schema.
- There is no easy general programmatic enforcement of the `final` attribute. An XML schema processor would have already accomplished this. Otherwise, it needs to be done manually by the database designer.
- The language of the documentation annotation was specified as 'en', but the database column documentation does not reflect this.
- The `partNumberType` simple type was not translated into a database representation. Although in theory all simple types can be instantiated, this one will never be, because it is intended to be abstract.
- The `assemblyPartNumberType` is a subtype of `partNumberType`, but this is not represented in the database schema. Instead, the restriction of token in `partNumberType` is represented directly in the check constraint in the `AssemblyPartNumberTypeExample` table.
- The restriction `pattern` of `assemblyPartNumberType` requires strings to satisfy both '[A-Z]{1,3}\d{1,8}' and 'ASM\d{1,8}'. The database schema check constraint was written to satisfy the `pattern` 'ASM\d{1,8}'. Satisfying the `pattern` '[A-Z]{1,3}\d{1,8}' would have been substantially more difficult.

Each of these points could have been addressed, but database schemas do not have this functionality built in. What is more important is that valid values are allowed into the database and an error is thrown for invalid values. It is far less important for the XML schema document *itself* to have a database schema representation.

## 23.4 The `list` Element

The `list` element declares an ordered series of items of any atomic type. An instance of a list contains all the items within a single element. There are four distinct ways to implement the `list` element:

- Create a single column to hold the list of values as a set of characters.
- Create a table to hold the values associated with a primary table.
- Create a single column of type `VARRAY` to hold the list of values.
- Create a single column of type `SYS.ANYDATASET` to hold the list of values.

Each of these approaches has merits and drawbacks with respect to ease of use, functionality, and ease of implementing the constraining facets. With respect to ease of use and functionality, the first approach places little burden on the application developer or database designer and is applicable if the sole purpose is to insert, update, delete, and select the values in their entirety. The second approach requires more work from both the application developer and database designer, but allows individual values that are part of the list to be easily inserted, updated, deleted, and selected. The third and fourth approaches require significant effort from both the application developer and the database designer and provide little benefit beyond the first approach. They are not implemented in this section. With respect to the ease of implementing constraining facets, refer to Sections 23.4.3, 23.4.4, 23.4.5, 23.4.6, and 23.4.7.

Listing 23.5 provides an XML schema example to demonstrate the single column and separate table approaches.

**LISTING 23.5**  An XML Schema Document Fragment of a Simple Type Supporting a List of Values (catalog.xsd)

```
<xsd:simpleType name="assemblyPartNumberListType"
            id="catalog.assemblyPartNumber.list.sType">
   <xsd:annotation>
      <xsd:documentation xml:lang="en">
         The "assemblyPartNumberListType" describes the
         value for an element that contains a set of part
         numbers. Given that a part number might look
         like any of the following:
            ASM1
            ASM32897
            ASM2233344
         A list of these part numbers might look like:
            ASM1 ASM32897 ASM2233344
      </xsd:documentation>
   </xsd:annotation>
   <xsd:list id="transaction.assemblyPartNumberList"
           itemType="assemblyPartNumberType">
   </xsd:list>
</xsd:simpleType>
```

## 23.4.1 Single Column

In this scenario, the assemblyPartNumberListType simple type is comprised of a series of assemblyPartNumberType simple types where the items are represented as a single string. Listing 23.6 shows this as a column constraint. Note that the pattern constraining facet of 'ASM\d{1,8}' is not enforced because it would require additional user-defined PL/SQL procedures to parse the string into individual asemblyPartNumberTypes and validate each one separately. The example uses a database column datatype of VARCHAR2 with a length of 300. To determine the best database column datatype, refer to Section 22.4.1.

**LISTING 23.6** AssPartNumberListTypeSC Single Column Table Creation with a Column Constraint

```
CREATE TABLE AssPartNumberListTypeSC (
assPartNumberListTypeSCID VARCHAR2(300) NOT NULL
  CHECK (INSTR(assPartNumberListTypeSCID,
              UNISTR('\000D')) = 0 AND
         INSTR(assPartNumberListTypeSCID,
              UNISTR('\000A')) = 0 AND
         INSTR(assPartNumberListTypeSCID,
              UNISTR('\0009')) = 0 AND
         LENGTH(assPartNumberListTypeSCID) =
           LENGTH(TRIM(assPartNumberListTypeSCID)) AND
         INSTR(assPartNumberListTypeSCID, ' ') = 0)
);
```

Listing 23.7 shows how an AssPartNumberListTypeSC element, which specifies the list of 'ASM1 ASM32897 ASM2233344', would be inserted into the database.

**LISTING 23.7** AssPartNumberListTypeSC Example Values Insertion

```
INSERT INTO AssPartNumberListTypeSC
VALUES
('ASM1 ASM32897 ASM2233344');
```

## 23.4.2 Separate Table

In this scenario, the assemblyPartNumberListType simple type is essentially a multivalued assemblyPartNumberType simple type where each value is stored separately in a table row. In Listing 23.8, a sequence, primary keys, and a foreign key are created. A sequence provides the unique values for the primary key of the AssPartNumberListTypeMT table. The sole column of the AssPartNumberListTypeMT table, assPartNumberListTypeMTID, is a foreign key to the AssPartNumberTypeMT table that also has listOrder as the second part of the primary key. The AssPartNumberTypeMT table holds the assemblyPartNumberType value.

**LISTING 23.8** AssemblyPartNumberListType Example Tables Creation with a Column Constraint

```
--Start the sequence at 1, don't let it cycle, and have
--the numbers in the sequence ordered.
CREATE SEQUENCE Seq_AssPartNumberListType INCREMENT BY 1 START
    WITH 1 MAXVALUE 999999999 MINVALUE 1 NOCYCLE ORDER;
```

```
CREATE TABLE AssPartNumberListTypeMT (
assPartNumberListTypeMTID NUMBER(9) NOT NULL,
PRIMARY KEY (AssPartNumberListTypeMTID)
);

CREATE TABLE AssPartNumberTypeMT (
assPartNumberTypeMTID   NUMBER(9) NOT NULL,
listOrder               NUMBER(3) NOT NULL,
partNumberType          VARCHAR2(11) NOT NULL
  CHECK (INSTR(partNumberType, UNISTR('\000D')) = 0 AND
         INSTR(partNumberType, UNISTR('\000A')) = 0 AND
         INSTR(partNumberType, UNISTR('\0009')) = 0 AND
         LENGTH(partNumberType) =
           LENGTH(TRIM(partNumberType)) AND
         INSTR(partNumberType, ' ') = 0 AND
         LENGTH(partNumberType) BETWEEN 4 AND 11 AND
         SUBSTR(partNumberType, 1, 3) = 'ASM' AND
         -- If the value is not a number, then an
         -- error will be thrown. IS NOT NULL makes
         -- this valid SQL, but is meaningless.
         CAST(SUBSTR(partNumberType, 4, 8) AS NUMBER)
           IS NOT NULL),
PRIMARY KEY (assPartNumberTypeMTID, listOrder),
FOREIGN KEY (assPartNumberTypeMTID)
REFERENCES AssPartNumberListTypeMT
);
```

Listing 23.9 shows how an `AssPartNumberListTypeMT` element, which specifies the list of 'ASM1 ASM32897 ASM2233344', would be inserted into the database.

**LISTING 23.9**  `AssPartNumberListTypeMT` Example Values Insertion

```
INSERT INTO AssPartNumberListTypeMT
VALUES
(Seq_AssPartNumberListType.NEXTVAL);

INSERT INTO AssPartNumberTypeMT
(assPartNumberTypeMTID, listOrder, partNumberType)
VALUES
(Seq_AssPartNumberListType.CURRVAL, 1, 'ASM1');

INSERT INTO AssPartNumberTypeMT
(assPartNumberTypeMTID, listOrder, partNumberType)
VALUES
(Seq_AssPartNumberListType.CURRVAL, 2, 'ASM32897');
```

*continues*

```
INSERT INTO AssPartNumberTypeMT
(assPartNumberTypeMTID, listOrder, partNumberType)
VALUES
(Seq_AssPartNumberListType.CURRVAL, 3, 'ASM2233344');
```

### 23.4.3 length Constraining Facet

The `length` constraining facet determines the number of items in the list and *not* the length of each item in the list. Implementing this facet when either a single column or separate table approach is chosen requires some coding and design trade-offs.

#### 23.4.3.1 Single Column

With the single column approach, the string would need to be examined to determine the number of tokens. Listing 23.10 creates an `AssPartNumberListTypeSC` table using a check constraint that counts the number of space characters, assuming a length of three has been specified. Note that, to simplify the code, the `pattern` constraining facet on `assemblyPartNumberType` is not verified.

**LISTING 23.10** Mapping an `AssemblyPartNumberListTypeSC` in a Single Column Implementing the `length` Constraining Facet to a Database Representation

```
CREATE TABLE AssPartNumberListTypeSC (
assPartNumberListTypeSCID VARCHAR2(300) NOT NULL
  CHECK (INSTR(assPartNumberListTypeSCID,
           UNISTR('\000D')) = 0 AND
         INSTR(assPartNumberListTypeSCID,
           UNISTR('\000A')) = 0 AND
         INSTR(assPartNumberListTypeSCID,
           UNISTR('\0009')) = 0 AND
        LENGTH(assPartNumberListTypeSCID) =
          LENGTH(TRIM(assPartNumberListTypeSCID)) AND
        INSTR(assPartNumberListTypeSCID, ' ') = 0 AND
        --Check to see if enough remaining tokens.
        --If there are three spaces, then there are too
        --many tokens. It there are not two, then there
        --are too few.
        INSTR(assPartNumberListTypeSCID, ' ', 1, 3) = 0 AND
        INSTR(assPartNumberListTypeSCID, ' ', 1, 2) <> 0)
);
```

#### 23.4.3.2 Separate Table

With the separate table approach, the number of items cannot be counted until all of the items have been inserted. What is needed is a before-commit trigger, but such a trigger does not exist. In this case, there are three options:

- Create a column in the table that tells the database this is the last entry, and have a trigger run to validate the length at that point.
- Create a validation PL/SQL procedure that the application developer can explicitly call.
- Have the system call the validation procedure periodically and write any issues to an error log.

The first two options, which rely on the application to inform the database that the validation can occur, are prone to error. The last option handles this automatically but allows for incorrect data in the database and then creates the need for manual inspection and correction. However, the first and second options do not preclude the addition of the third option. All three options are explored further in the following sections. Note that, to simplify the code, the `pattern` constraining facet on `assemblyPartNumberType` is not verified in any of these options.

#### 23.4.3.2.1 Create a Last Entry Column

Creating a last entry column involves adding an extra database column solely for use by the validation trigger. This is unfortunate, but functional. It will throw an error so that the last entry will not be inserted, but because previous rows will have already been inserted, the application code will need to perform a rollback. Listings 23.11, 23.12, and 23.13 create the `assemblyPartNumberType` table and an insert trigger, and test the trigger with some sample data.

**LISTING 23.11**  AssPartNumberTypeMT Example Table Creation with a `length` Constraining Facet and Last Entry Column

```
--Start the sequence at 1, don't let it cycle, and have
--the numbers in the sequence ordered.
CREATE SEQUENCE Seq_AssPartNumberListType INCREMENT BY 1 START
    WITH 1 MAXVALUE 999999999 MINVALUE 1 NOCYCLE ORDER;

CREATE TABLE AssPartNumberTypeMT (
assPartNumberTypeMTID NUMBER(9) NOT NULL,
listOrder             NUMBER(3) NOT NULL,
partNumberType        VARCHAR2(11) NOT NULL .
  CHECK (INSTR(partNumberType, UNISTR('\000D')) = 0 AND
         INSTR(partNumberType, UNISTR('\000A')) = 0 AND
         INSTR(partNumberType, UNISTR('\0009')) = 0 AND
         LENGTH(partNumberType) =
           LENGTH(TRIM(partNumberType)) AND
         INSTR(partNumberType, ' ') = 0 AND
         LENGTH(partNumberType) BETWEEN 4 AND 11 AND
         SUBSTR(partNumberType, 1, 3) = 'ASM' AND
         -- If the value is not a number, then an
         -- error will be thrown. IS NOT NULL makes
         -- this valid SQL, but is meaningless.
```

*continues*

```
            CAST(SUBSTR(partNumberType, 4, 8) AS NUMBER)
                IS NOT NULL),
    isLastPartNumberOfOrder NUMBER(1) NOT NULL,
    PRIMARY KEY (assPartNumberTypeMTID, listOrder),
    FOREIGN KEY (assPartNumberTypeMTID )
    REFERENCES AssPartNumberListTypeMT
);
```

Listing 23.12 shows a SQL statement that creates a before-insert trigger to ensure that the length of the list is three.

**LISTING 23.12**  Before-Insert Trigger on `AssPartNumberTypeMT` Implementing the `length` Constraining Facet

```
CREATE OR REPLACE TRIGGER InsertAssPartNumberTypeMT
BEFORE INSERT
ON AssPartNumberTypeMT
FOR EACH ROW
WHEN (new.isLastPartNumberOfOrder = 1)
DECLARE
I PLS_INTEGER;
BEGIN
  I := 0;
  SELECT COUNT(1)
  INTO   I
  FROM   AssPartNumberTypeMT
  WHERE  assPartNumberTypeMTID = :new.assPartNumberTypeMTID;

  -- Check to see if enough rows. Since this a before trigger,
  -- the last row has not yet been inserted.
  IF I <> 2 THEN
    RAISE_APPLICATION_ERROR(-20000, 'Not length of 3.');
  END IF;
END;
```

Listing 23.13 shows a few SQL statements that insert some sample valid data to demonstrate use of the tables.

**LISTING 23.13**  `AssPartNumberListTypeMT` Example Values Insertion with a Last Entry Column

```
INSERT INTO AssPartNumberListTypeMT
VALUES
(Seq_AssPartNumberListType.NEXTVAL);
```

```sql
INSERT INTO AssPartNumberTypeMT
(assPartNumberTypeMTID, listOrder, partNumberType, isLastPartNumberOfOrder)
VALUES
(Seq_AssPartNumberListType.CURRVAL, 1, 'ASM1', 0);

INSERT INTO AssPartNumberTypeMT
(assPartNumberTypeMTID, listOrder, partNumberType, isLastPartNumberOfOrder)
VALUES
(Seq_AssPartNumberListType.CURRVAL, 2, 'ASM32897', 0);

INSERT INTO AssPartNumberTypeMT
(assPartNumberTypeMTID, listOrder, partNumberType, isLastPartNumberOfOrder)
VALUES
(Seq_AssPartNumberListType.CURRVAL, 3, 'ASM2233344', 1);
```

#### 23.4.3.2.2 Create a Validation Procedure

Creating a validation procedure involves developing a PL/SQL procedure that the application needs to call manually before a commit to the database. The application will need to perform a rollback in case the validation fails. Listings 23.8 and 23.9 are still applicable; Listing 23.14 shows the validation procedure for assemblyPartNumberTypes.

**LISTING 23.14**   Validation Procedure Implementing the length Constraining Facet

```sql
CREATE OR REPLACE FUNCTION ValidateAssPartNumberTypeMTLen
  (assPartNumberID IN
     AssPartNumberTypeMT.assPartNumberTypeMTID%TYPE)
RETURN BOOLEAN IS
  I PLS_INTEGER;
BEGIN
  I := 0;
  SELECT COUNT(1)
  INTO   I
  FROM   AssPartNumberTypeMT
  WHERE  assPartNumberTypeMTID = assPartNumberID;

  IF I <> 3 THEN
    RETURN FALSE;
  END IF;

  RETURN TRUE;
END;
```

### 23.4.3.2.3 Create a System-Called Validation Procedure

Creating a system-called validation procedure involves developing a PL/SQL procedure that is called automatically by the system at specified intervals. The results need to be reviewed by the database administrator and application administrator, and then manually corrected. Listings 23.8 and 23.9 are still applicable; Listing 23.15 shows the validation procedure and Listing 23.16 creates a cron job to run it at midnight to validate assemblyPartNumberTypes.

**LISTING 23.15** Validation Procedure Implementing the length Constraining Facet for the AssPartNumberTypeMT Table

```
CREATE OR REPLACE PROCEDURE ValidateAllAssPartNumberLen IS
  CURSOR AllInvalidIDS IS
    SELECT assPartNumberTypeMTID
    FROM   AssPartNumberTypeMT
    HAVING COUNT(assPartNumberTypeMTID) <> 3
    GROUP BY assPartNumberTypeMTID;
BEGIN
  FOR ID IN AllInvalidIDS LOOP
    --This line needs to be replaced with a logfile
    --using the UTL_FILE package, with a queue entry,
    --using DBMS_AQ package, etc.
    DBMS_OUTPUT.PUT_LINE(ID.assPartNumberTypeMTID);
  END LOOP;
END;
```

To run this procedure manually, leaving in the call to DBMS_OUTPUT.PUT_LINE, run the following code snippet:

```
SET serveroutput ON;
BEGIN
  DBMS_OUTPUT.ENABLE;
  ValidateAllAssPartNumberLen;
END;
```

Listing 23.16 is an anonymous PL/SQL block that creates a cron job using the DBMS_JOB package in Oracle. This one first runs at midnight and then every midnight thereafter.

**LISTING 23.16** Creating a Cron Job to Run the Validation Procedure Nightly

```
DECLARE
  jobNo PLS_NUMBER;
BEGIN
  DBMS_JOB.SUBMIT(:jobNo,' ValidateAllAssPartNumberLen;'
                  TRUNC(SYSDATE), 'TRUNC(SYSDATE) + 1');
  COMMIT;
END;
```

## 23.4.4 `minLength` Constraining Facet

The `minLength` constraining facet determines the minimum number of items in the list and *not* the minimum length of each item in the list. Implementing this facet when either a single column or separate table approach is chosen requires some coding and design trade-offs. The same discussion concerning the `length` constraining facet in 23.4.3 applies to the `minLength` constraining facet.

## 23.4.5 `maxLength` Constraining Facet

The `maxLength` constraining facet determines the maximum number of items in the list and *not* the maximum length of each item in the list. Implementing these when either a single column or separate table approach is chosen requires some coding and design trade-offs.

### 23.4.5.1 Single Column

With the single column approach, the string would need to be examined to determine the number of tokens. Listing 23.17 creates an `AssPartNumberListTypeSCML` table using a check constraint that counts the number of space characters, assuming a maximum length of three has been specified. Note that, to simplify the code, the `pattern` constraining facet on `assemblyPartNumberType` is not verified.

**LISTING 23.17** A Mapping of an `AssemblyPartNumberListTypeSCML` in a Single Column Implementing the `maxLength` Constraining Facet to a Database Representation

```
CREATE TABLE AssPartNumberListTypeSCML (
assPartNumberListTypeSCMLID VARCHAR2(300) NOT NULL
  CHECK (INSTR(assPartNumberListTypeSCMLID,
             UNISTR('\000D')) = 0 AND
         INSTR(assPartNumberListTypeSCMLID,
             UNISTR('\000A')) = 0 AND
         INSTR(assPartNumberListTypeSCMLID,
             UNISTR('\0009')) = 0 AND
         LENGTH(assPartNumberListTypeSCMLID) =
           LENGTH(TRIM(assPartNumberListTypeSCMLID)) AND
         INSTR(assPartNumberListTypeSCMLID, '  ') = 0 AND
         --Check to see if enough remaining tokens.
         --If there are three spaces, then there are too
         --many tokens. It there are not two, then there
         --are too few.
         INSTR(assPartNumberListTypeSCMLID, ' ', 1, 3) = 0)
);
```

### 23.4.5.2 Separate Table

With the separate table approach, unlike the `length` and `minLength` constraining facets, counting the number of maximum items can be validated as each element is inserted. Listings 23.18

and 23.19 are the SQL statements that create the `assemblyPartNumberTypeMTML` table and an insert trigger to implement the `maxLength` constraining facet.

**LISTING 23.18** `AssemblyPartNumberListTypeMTML` Example Tables Creation with a `maxLength` Constraining Facet

```
--Start the sequence at 1, don't let it cycle, and have
--the numbers in the sequence ordered.
CREATE SEQUENCE Seq_AssPartNumberListType INCREMENT BY 1 START
  WITH 1 MAXVALUE 999999999 MINVALUE 1 NOCYCLE ORDER;

CREATE TABLE AssPartNumberTypeMTML (
assPartNumberTypeMTMLID  NUMBER(9) NOT NULL,
listOrder                NUMBER(3) NOT NULL,
partNumberType           VARCHAR2(11) NOT NULL
  CHECK (INSTR(partNumberType, UNISTR('\000D')) = 0 AND
         INSTR(partNumberType, UNISTR('\000A')) = 0 AND
         INSTR(partNumberType, UNISTR('\0009')) = 0 AND
         LENGTH(partNumberType) =
           LENGTH(TRIM(partNumberType)) AND
         INSTR(partNumberType, ' ') = 0 AND
         LENGTH(partNumberType) BETWEEN 4 AND 11 AND
         SUBSTR(partNumberType, 1, 3) = 'ASM' AND
         -- If the value is not a number, then an
         -- error will be thrown. IS NOT NULL makes
         -- this valid SQL, but is meaningless.
         CAST(SUBSTR(partNumberType, 4, 8) AS NUMBER)
           IS NOT NULL),
PRIMARY KEY (assPartNumberTypeMTMLID, listOrder),
FOREIGN KEY (assPartNumberTypeMTMLID)
REFERENCES AssPartNumberListTypeMT
);
```

Listing 23.19 shows a SQL statement that creates a before-insert trigger to ensure that the length of the maximum number of items is three.

**LISTING 23.19** Before-Insert Trigger on `AssPartNumberTypeMTML` Implementing the `maxLength` Constraining Facet

```
CREATE OR REPLACE TRIGGER InsertAssPartNumberTypeMTML
BEFORE INSERT
ON AssPartNumberTypeMTML
FOR EACH ROW
DECLARE
I PLS_INTEGER;
```

```
BEGIN
  I := 0;
  SELECT COUNT(1)
  INTO   I
  FROM   AssPartNumberTypeMTML
  WHERE assPartNumberTypeMTMLID = :new.assPartNumberTypeMTMLID;
  -- Check to see if enough rows. Since this a before trigger,
  -- the last row has not yet been inserted.
  IF I > 2 THEN
    RAISE_APPLICATION_ERROR(-20000, 'Not length of 3.');
  END IF;
END;
```

## 23.4.6 pattern Constraining Facet

The pattern constraining facet determines the pattern for the *entire* list and *not* the pattern of each item in the list. Implementing this facet when a single column approach has been chosen is simply a string pattern match. Refer to Section 22.1.1 for design decisions and implementation details and to Listing 23.4, which details the implementation of the constraint in the assemblyPartNumberType example.

Implementing a pattern constraining facet when a separate table approach has been chosen is more difficult. This issue is similar to the length constraining facet in that all the values need to be inserted before the pattern matching can be checked. Instead of summing up the number of values, they need to be concatenated with one space between adjacent values. There is one additional wrinkle: Updating a value can invalidate the pattern. Refer to Section 22.1.1 for design decisions and implementation details and to Listing 23.4, which details the implementation of the constraint in the assemblyPartNumberType example.

## 23.4.7 enumeration Constraining Facet

The enumeration constraining facet determines the value for the *entire* list and *not* the enumerations of each item in the list. Refer to Section 22.2.2 for design decisions and implementation details.

Implementing an enumeration constraining facet when a separate table approach has been chosen is more difficult. This is similar to the length constraining facet in that all the values need to be inserted before the enumeration can be checked. Instead of summing up the number of values, they need to be concatenated with a space between the values. There is one additional wrinkle: Updating a value can invalidate the enumeration. Refer to the Section 22.2.2 for design decisions and implementation details.

## 23.5 The union Element

A union is a simple type that specifies a series of allowable other simple types as possible values. It is implemented in C and C++ as a union and in Oracle as the SYS.AnyData type. From a database design perspective, unions should be avoided, if possible, due to their design and implementation complexity. This section details a number of possible implementations for two fairly straightforward cases.

> **WARNING**
>
> The complex cases of the union element such as a union of lists or a union of IDREFS and NMTOKENS are problematic to properly design and implement in a relational database. Clear representation, easy inserts, updates, and deletes, and proper datatype validation of the union value (which itself is composed of a series of values), are all significant issues. These complex cases are not implemented.

### 23.5.1 A Simple Example of a union of Enumerations

Listing 23.20 iterates Listing 10.8 and demonstrates the XML schema document representation of the colorOptionType, which is a union of the declared standardColorOptionType, fancifulColorOptionType, and codedColorOptionType enumerations.

**LISTING 23.20**  An XML Schema Document Fragment of a Simple Type Supporting a union (catalog.xsd)

```
<xsd:simpleType name="colorOptionType"
            id="catalog.colorOption.union.sType">
    <xsd:annotation>
        <xsd:documentation xml:lang="en">
            A part has one of the following color definitions:
                - a standard name (cyan, yellow, etc.),
                - a fanciful name (Ocean, Sunshine, etc.), or
                - an internal code 1..n
        </xsd:documentation>
    </xsd:annotation>
    <xsd:union id="colorOptionType.union">

        <xsd:simpleType name="standardColorOptionType"
                    final="restriction"
                    id="catalog.standardColorOption.sType">
            <xsd:annotation>
                <xsd:documentation xml:lang="en">
```

## 23.5 The union Element

```
                Color selection is limited.
                The colors apply to unit and
                bulk items.
            </xsd:documentation>
        </xsd:annotation>
        <xsd:restriction base="xsd:token">
            <xsd:enumeration value="cyan"/>
            <xsd:enumeration value="magenta"/>
            <xsd:enumeration value="yellow"/>
            <xsd:enumeration value="black"/>
        </xsd:restriction>
</xsd:simpleType>

<xsd:simpleType name="fancifulColorOptionType"
                final="restriction"
                id="catalog.fancifulColorOption.sType">
    <xsd:annotation>
        <xsd:documentation xml:lang="en">
            Color selection is limited.
            The colors apply to unit and
            bulk items.
        </xsd:documentation>
    </xsd:annotation>
    <xsd:restriction base="xsd:token">
        <xsd:enumeration value="Ocean"/>
        <xsd:enumeration value="Pink Grapefruit"/>
        <xsd:enumeration value="Sunshine"/>
        <xsd:enumeration value="Midnight"/>
    </xsd:restriction>
</xsd:simpleType>

<xsd:simpleType name="codedColorOptionType"
                id="catalog.codedColorOption.sType">
    <xsd:annotation>
        <xsd:documentation xml:lang="en">
            A color can be defined by an
            internal integer that maps
            directly to a standard or
            fanciful color
            1 = cyan = Ocean
            2 = magenta = Pink Grapefruit
            etc.
        </xsd:documentation>
    </xsd:annotation>
    <xsd:restriction base="xsd:positiveInteger">
        <xsd:maxInclusive value="4"/>
    </xsd:restriction>
```

*continues*

```
        </xsd:simpleType>

    </xsd:union>
</xsd:simpleType>
```

Listing 23.21 demonstrates the mapping of the XML schema document to a database representation by using a picklist as described in Section 22.2.2.3.

**LISTING 23.21**    Mapping a Simple Type Supporting a union to a Database Representation (catalog.xsd)

```
--Insert the standardColorOptionType
INSERT INTO PicklistDomain
(picklistDomainID, name, description)
VALUES
(5, 'standardColorOptionType',
 'Color selection is limited.
The colors apply to unit and bulk items.');

INSERT INTO Picklist
(picklistID, picklistDomainID, name)
VALUES
(9, 5, 'cyan');

INSERT INTO Picklist
(picklistID, picklistDomainID, name)
VALUES
(10, 5, 'magenta');

INSERT INTO Picklist
(picklistID, picklistDomainID, name)
VALUES
(11, 5, 'yellow');

INSERT INTO Picklist
(picklistID, picklistDomainID, name)
VALUES
(12, 5, 'black');

--Insert the fancifulColorOptionType
INSERT INTO PicklistDomain
(picklistDomainID, name, description)
VALUES
(6, 'fancifulColorOptionType',
 'Color selection is limited.
The colors apply to unit and bulk items.');
```

```sql
INSERT INTO Picklist
(picklistID, picklistDomainID, name)
VALUES
(13, 6, 'Ocean');

INSERT INTO Picklist
(picklistID, picklistDomainID, name)
VALUES
(14, 6, 'Pink Grapefruit');

INSERT INTO Picklist
(picklistID, picklistDomainID, name)
VALUES
(15, 6, 'Sunshine');

INSERT INTO Picklist
(picklistID, picklistDomainID, name)
VALUES
(16, 6, 'Midnight');

--Insert the codedColorOptionType
INSERT INTO PicklistDomain
(picklistDomainID, name, description)
VALUES
(7, 'codedColorOptionType',
 'A color can be defined by an internal integer that maps[ccc]
 directly to a standard or fanciful color.');

INSERT INTO Picklist
(picklistID, picklistDomainID, name, description)
VALUES
(17, 7, '1', 'cyan or Ocean');

INSERT INTO Picklist
(picklistID, picklistDomainID, name, description)
VALUES
(18, 7, '2', 'magenta or Pink Grapefruit');

INSERT INTO Picklist
(picklistID, picklistDomainID, name, description)
VALUES
(19, 7, '3', 'yellow or Sunshine');

INSERT INTO Picklist
(picklistID, picklistDomainID, name, description)
VALUES
(20, 7, '4', 'black or Midnight');
COMMIT;
```

Listing 23.22 demonstrates an example table that uses the newly created union.

**LISTING 23.22** ColorOptionTypeExample Table using Picklists

```
CREATE TABLE ColorOptionTypeExample (
colorOptionTypeID NUMBER(4) NOT NULL
);
```

Triggers can be created to enforce this union. Refer to Listing 22.6 for more details.

## 23.5.2 A Complex Example of a union of Single-Valued Simple Types

Listing 23.23 is assemblyPartStatusType, which is a union of the anonymously declared preProductionStatusType, assemblyPartNumberType, and lastDateManufacturedType. The union allows one field to contain a status code in preproduction, the part number in production, and the date the item was no longer manufactured.

**LISTING 23.23** An XML Schema Document Fragment of assemblyPartStatusType Simple Type Supporting a union of simpleType Elements (catalog.xsd)

```
<xsd:simpleType name="assemblyPartStatusType"
            id="catalog.assemblyPartStatusType.union.sType">
   <xsd:annotation>
      <xsd:documentation xml:lang="en">
         A part status depends upon whether it is
         pre-production, in production, or no longer
         being manufactured.
      </xsd:documentation>
   </xsd:annotation>
   <xsd:union id="assemblyPartStatusType.union">

      <xsd:simpleType name="preProductionStatusType"
                  final="restriction"
                  id="catalog.preProductionStatusType.sType">
         <xsd:annotation>
            <xsd:documentation xml:lang="en">
               The pre-production status is an
               enumeration of the statuses prior
               to manufacturing.
               1 = roughed
               2 = designed
               3 = prototyped
               4 = approved
            </xsd:documentation>
```

```
            </xsd:annotation>
            <xsd:restriction base="xsd:positiveInteger">
                <xsd:maxInclusive value="4"/>
            </xsd:restriction>
        </xsd:simpleType>

        <xsd:simpleType name="assemblyPartNumberType"
                    final="#all"
                    id="catalog.assemblypartNumber.sType">
            <xsd:annotation>
                <xsd:documentation xml:lang="en">
                    An "assembly" represents a pre-built
                    collection of unit items. The
                    the part number for an assembly
                    always starts with "ASM."
                </xsd:documentation>
            </xsd:annotation>
            <xsd:restriction base="partNumberType">
                <xsd:pattern value="ASM\d{1,8}"/>
            </xsd:restriction>
        </xsd:simpleType>

        <xsd:simpleType name="lastDateManufacturedType"
                    id="catalog.lastDateManufactured.sType">
            <xsd:annotation>
                <xsd:documentation xml:lang="en">
                    The date the part was last manufactured.
                    The company first manufactured a part on
                    2000-01-01.
                </xsd:documentation>
            </xsd:annotation>
            <xsd:restriction base="xsd:date">
                <xsd:minInclusive value="2000-01-01"/>
            </xsd:restriction>
        </xsd:simpleType>

    </xsd:union>
</xsd:simpleType>
```

## 23.5.3  Mapping a union of Single-Valued Simple Types to a Database Representation

In Listing 23.23, the possible values for the assembly part status are essentially a number with a low and high range, a string with a pattern, and a date with a minimum. There are three potential mappings of the possible values to a database representation:

- Single Column—Represent everything as a database character column datatype and a check constraint to enforce the constraints on inserts and updates.
- Multiple Columns—Represent everything as a database character column datatype and a separate column for each different datatype. Use triggers to enforce the constraints on inserts and updates.
- SYS.AnyData Type—Use the new Oracle9*i* features to represent a union in a single column and maintain its datatype as well.

The single column option is straightforward for the application developer and is best used when the `simpletype` database column datatype does not really matter—when just validating it is enough. The single column option is sufficient when the data is inserted and directly retrieved. The multiple column option is straightforward for the application developer and can be used when the resulting type does matter, such as in analytic reports of the number of parts in a particular preproduction status or the distribution of dates over which parts were no longer manufactured. The SYS.AnyData type option allows the type and data to exist in a single column. This option is applicable in situations where the application already knows the type of the data and will retrieve it based on type.

### 23.5.3.1 Single Column Database Mapping of a `union`

In a single column database mapping of a `union`, a single character column is created and the value is validated with a check constraint. Listing 23.24 shows the create table script with a check constraint. The check constraint clauses are ordered so that errors are thrown only when other possible types have been excluded.

**LISTING 23.24** Mapping a union to a Single Column Database Representation

```
CREATE TABLE AssemblyPartStatusSCExample (
assemblyPartStatus   VARCHAR2(100) NOT NULL
  CHECK (--First check for the pre-production statuses
         assemblyPartStatus IN ('1', '2', '3', '4') OR
      --Next check for the date. TO_DATE will throw
      --an error if the value is not a date. Verify
      --that it should be a date first.
      (INSTR(assemblyPartStatus, '-') <> 0 AND
       TO_DATE(assemblyPartStatus, 'YYYY-MM-DD') >
         TO_DATE('2000-01-01', 'YYYY-MM-DD')) OR
      --Finally verify that it is an assembly part.
      (INSTR(assemblyPartStatus, UNISTR('\000A')) = 0 AND
       INSTR(assemblyPartStatus, UNISTR('\0009')) = 0 AND
       LENGTH(assemblyPartStatus) =
         LENGTH(TRIM(assemblyPartStatus)) AND
       INSTR(assemblyPartStatus, ' ') = 0 AND
       LENGTH(assemblyPartStatus) BETWEEN 4 AND 11 AND
```

```
            SUBSTR(assemblyPartStatus, 1, 3) = 'ASM' AND
            -- If the value is not a number, then an
            -- error will be thrown. IS NOT NULL makes
            -- this valid SQL, but is meaningless.
            CAST(SUBSTR(assemblyPartStatus, 4, 8) AS NUMBER)
              IS NOT NULL))
);

COMMENT ON COLUMN
AssemblyPartStatusSCExample.assemblyPartStatus IS
'A part status depends upon whether it is pre-production,
in production, or no longer being manufactured.';
```

Given the preceding table declaration, the following are valid insert statements:

```
INSERT INTO AssemblyPartStatusSCExample
VALUES
('ASM4534');

INSERT INTO AssemblyPartStatusSCExample
VALUES
('1');

INSERT INTO AssemblyPartStatusSCExample
VALUES
('2001-12-23');
COMMIT;
```

### 23.5.3.2 Multiple Column Database Mapping of a union

In a multiple column database mapping of a union, the initial value is stored in a character column, but other columns are created to hold the value in its native type. Thus, a number column, a character column, and a date column are also created. The value being inserted is validated by a trigger that also inserts the value into another column. Listing 23.25 shows the create table script and the triggers that keep the values in sync and throw errors in invalid cases. There is no enforcement in Listing 23.25 to ensure that the additional columns are not updated independently. This could be enforced via triggers or grants.

**LISTING 23.25**   Mapping a union to a Multi-Column Database Representation

```
CREATE TABLE AssemblyPartStatusMCExample (
assemblyPartStatus   VARCHAR2(100) NOT NULL,
preProductionStatus   NUMBER(1) NULL,
assemblyPartNumberType VARCHAR2(100) NULL,
lastManufacturedDate  DATE NULL
);
```

*continues*

```sql
COMMENT ON COLUMN
AssemblyPartStatusMCExample.assemblyPartStatus IS
'A part status depends upon whether it is pre-production,
in production, or no longer being manufactured.';

COMMENT ON COLUMN
AssemblyPartStatusMCExample.preProductionStatus IS
'The pre-production status is an enumeration of the
statuses prior to manufacturing.
   1 = roughed
   2 = designed
   3 = prototyped
   4 = approved';

COMMENT ON COLUMN
AssemblyPartStatusMCExample.assemblyPartNumberType IS
'An """assembly""" represents a pre-built collection of
unit items. The the part number for an assembly
always starts with """ASM""".';

COMMENT ON COLUMN
AssemblyPartStatusMCExample.lastManufacturedDate IS
'The date the part was last manufactured.
The company first manufactured a part on 2000-01-01.';

--A trigger to insert the pre-production status.
CREATE OR REPLACE TRIGGER InsertAssPartPreProdStatus
BEFORE INSERT
ON AssemblyPartStatusMCExample
FOR EACH ROW
WHEN (new.assemblyPartStatus IN ('1', '2', '3', '4'))
BEGIN
   :new.preProductionStatus := :new.assemblyPartStatus;
END;

--A trigger to update the pre-production status.
CREATE OR REPLACE TRIGGER UpdateAssPartPreProdStatus
BEFORE UPDATE
ON AssemblyPartStatusMCExample
FOR EACH ROW
WHEN (new.assemblyPartStatus IN ('1', '2', '3', '4'))
BEGIN
  :new.preProductionStatus := :new.assemblyPartStatus;
  :new.assemblyPartNumberType := NULL;
  :new.lastManufacturedDate := NULL;
END;
```

```sql
--A trigger to insert the last production date.
CREATE OR REPLACE TRIGGER InsertAssPartLastDate
BEFORE INSERT
ON AssemblyPartStatusMCExample
FOR EACH ROW
WHEN (INSTR(new.assemblyPartStatus, '-') <> 0 AND
      TO_DATE(new.assemblyPartStatus, 'YYYY-MM-DD') >
         TO_DATE('2000-01-01', 'YYYY-MM-DD'))
BEGIN
  :new.lastManufacturedDate :=
    TO_DATE(:new.assemblyPartStatus, 'YYYY-MM-DD');
END;

--A trigger to update the last production date.
CREATE OR REPLACE TRIGGER UpdateAssPartLastDate
BEFORE UPDATE
ON AssemblyPartStatusMCExample
FOR EACH ROW
WHEN (INSTR(new.assemblyPartStatus, '-') <> 0 AND
      TO_DATE(new.assemblyPartStatus, 'YYYY-MM-DD') >
         TO_DATE('2000-01-01', 'YYYY-MM-DD'))
BEGIN
  :new.lastManufacturedDate :=
    TO_DATE(:new.assemblyPartStatus, 'YYYY-MM-DD');
  :new.assemblyPartNumberType := NULL;
  :new.preProductionStatus := NULL;
END;

--A trigger to insert the assemblyPartType.
CREATE OR REPLACE TRIGGER InsertAssemblyPartType
BEFORE INSERT
ON AssemblyPartStatusMCExample
FOR EACH ROW
WHEN (INSTR(new.assemblyPartStatus, UNISTR('\000A')) = 0 AND
      INSTR(new.assemblyPartStatus, UNISTR('\0009')) = 0 AND
      LENGTH(new.assemblyPartStatus) =
         LENGTH(TRIM(new.assemblyPartStatus)) AND
      INSTR(new.assemblyPartStatus, ' ') = 0 AND
      LENGTH(new.assemblyPartStatus) BETWEEN 4 AND 11 AND
      SUBSTR(new.assemblyPartStatus, 1, 3) = 'ASM' AND
        -- If the value is not a number, then an
        -- error will be thrown. IS NOT NULL makes
        -- this valid SQL, but is meaningless.
        CAST(SUBSTR(new.assemblyPartStatus, 4, 8) AS NUMBER)
          IS NOT NULL)
DECLARE
I PLS_INTEGER;
```

*continues*

```
BEGIN
 :new.assemblyPartNumberType := :new.assemblyPartStatus;
END;

--A trigger to update the assemblyPartType.
CREATE OR REPLACE TRIGGER UpdateAssemblyPartType
BEFORE UPDATE
ON AssemblyPartStatusMCExample
FOR EACH ROW
WHEN (INSTR(new.assemblyPartStatus, UNISTR('\000A')) = 0 AND
      INSTR(new.assemblyPartStatus, UNISTR('\0009')) = 0 AND
      LENGTH(new.assemblyPartStatus) =
        LENGTH(TRIM(new.assemblyPartStatus)) AND
      INSTR(new.assemblyPartStatus, ' ') = 0 AND
      LENGTH(new.assemblyPartStatus) BETWEEN 4 AND 11 AND
      SUBSTR(new.assemblyPartStatus, 1, 3) = 'ASM' AND
        -- If the value is not a number, then an
        -- error will be thrown. IS NOT NULL makes
        -- this valid SQL, but is meaningless.
        CAST(SUBSTR(new.assemblyPartStatus, 4, 8) AS NUMBER)
          IS NOT NULL)
DECLARE
I PLS_INTEGER;
BEGIN
  :new.assemblyPartNumberType:= :new.assemblyPartStatus;
  :new.lastManufacturedDate := NULL;
  :new.preProductionStatus := NULL;
END;

--A trigger to throw errors when the assemblyPartStatus
--is invalid during an insert.
CREATE OR REPLACE TRIGGER InsertAssemblyPartStatusError
BEFORE INSERT
ON AssemblyPartStatusMCExample
FOR EACH ROW
WHEN
  --Negate the positive check for assemblyPartStatus
  (NOT (--First check for the pre-production statuses
        new.assemblyPartStatus IN ('1', '2', '3', '4') OR
        --Next check for the date. TO_DATE will throw
        --an error if the value is not a date. Verify
        --that it should be a date first.
        (INSTR(new.assemblyPartStatus, '-') <> 0 AND
         TO_DATE(new.assemblyPartStatus, 'YYYY-MM-DD') >
           TO_DATE('2000-01-01', 'YYYY-MM-DD')) OR
        --Finally verify that it is an assembly part.
        (INSTR(new.assemblyPartStatus,
```

```
                UNISTR('\000A')) = 0 AND
        INSTR(new.assemblyPartStatus,
                UNISTR('\0009')) = 0 AND
        LENGTH(new.assemblyPartStatus) =
          LENGTH(TRIM(new.assemblyPartStatus)) AND
        INSTR(new.assemblyPartStatus, ' ') = 0 AND
        LENGTH(new.assemblyPartStatus) BETWEEN 4 AND 11 AND
        SUBSTR(new.assemblyPartStatus, 1, 3) = 'ASM' AND
        -- If the value is not a number, then an
        -- error will be thrown. IS NOT NULL makes
        -- this valid SQL, but is meaningless.
        CAST(SUBSTR(new.assemblyPartStatus, 4, 8) AS NUMBER)
          IS NOT NULL)))
BEGIN
 RAISE_APPLICATION_ERROR(-20000, 'Not an assemblyPartStatus.');
END;

--A trigger to throw errors when the assemblyPartStatus
--is invalid during an update.
CREATE OR REPLACE TRIGGER UpdateAssemblyPartStatusError
BEFORE UPDATE
ON AssemblyPartStatusMCExample
FOR EACH ROW
WHEN
  --Negate the positive check for assemblyPartStatus
  (NOT (--First check for the pre-production statuses
        new.assemblyPartStatus IN ('1', '2', '3', '4') OR
        --Next check for the date. TO_DATE will throw
        --an error if the value is not a date. Verify
        --that it should be a date first.
        (INSTR(new.assemblyPartStatus, '-') <> 0 AND
         TO_DATE(new.assemblyPartStatus, 'YYYY-MM-DD') >
           TO_DATE('2000-01-01', 'YYYY-MM-DD')) OR
        --Finally verify that it is an assembly part.
        (INSTR(new.assemblyPartStatus,
                UNISTR('\000A')) = 0 AND
        INSTR(new.assemblyPartStatus,
                UNISTR('\0009')) = 0 AND
        LENGTH(new.assemblyPartStatus) =
          LENGTH(TRIM(new.assemblyPartStatus)) AND
        INSTR(new.assemblyPartStatus, ' ') = 0 AND
        LENGTH(new.assemblyPartStatus) BETWEEN 4 AND 11 AND
        SUBSTR(new.assemblyPartStatus, 1, 3) = 'ASM' AND
        -- If the value is not a number, then an
        -- error will be thrown. IS NOT NULL makes
        -- this valid SQL, but is meaningless.
        CAST(SUBSTR(new.assemblyPartStatus, 4, 8) AS NUMBER)
```

*continues*

```
           IS NOT NULL)))
BEGIN
 RAISE_APPLICATION_ERROR(-20000, 'Not an assemblyPartStatus.');
END;
```

### 23.5.3.3 Oracle SYS.AnyData Type Mapping of a union

In an Oracle SYS.AnyData type database mapping of a union, a single SYS.AnyData column datatype is created and the value is validated with triggers. Note that the SYS.AnyData column does not support the timestamp column datatype, which limits the number of XML Schema datatypes it can support. Listing 23.26 shows the create table script and the triggers to validate the inserts and updates.

**LISTING 23.26** SYS.AnyData Column Database Representation Mapping a union

```
CREATE TABLE AssemblyPartStatusAnyExample (
assemblyPartStatus   SYS.ANYDATA NOT NULL
);

COMMENT ON COLUMN
AssemblyPartStatusSCExample.assemblyPartStatus IS
'A part status depends upon whether it is pre-production,
in production, or no longer being manufactured.';

--A trigger to throw errors when the assemblyPartStatus
--is invalid during an insert.
CREATE OR REPLACE TRIGGER InsertAssPartAnyPreProdError
BEFORE INSERT
ON AssemblyPartStatusAnyExample
FOR EACH ROW
DECLARE
  anyInt PLS_INTEGER;
  status PLS_INTEGER;
  anyDate DATE;
  anyString VARCHAR2(11);
BEGIN
  IF :new.assemblyPartStatus.GETTYPENAME() = 'SYS.NUMBER' THEN
    -- return status not used.
    status := :new.assemblyPartStatus.GETNUMBER(anyInt);
    IF anyInt NOT BETWEEN 1 AND 4 THEN
      RAISE_APPLICATION_ERROR(-20000,
                     'Not an assemblyPartStatus.');
    END IF;
  ELSIF :new.assemblyPartStatus.GETTYPENAME() = 'SYS.DATE' THEN
    -- return status not used.
    status := :new.assemblyPartStatus.GETDATE(anyDate);
```

```
      IF anyDate <= TO_DATE('2000-01-01', 'YYYY-MM-DD') THEN
        RAISE_APPLICATION_ERROR(-20000,
                                'Not an assemblyPartStatus.');
      END IF;
    ELSIF :new.assemblyPartStatus.GETTYPENAME() = 'SYS.VARCHAR2' THEN
      -- return status not used.
      status := :new.assemblyPartStatus.GETVARCHAR2(anyString);
      IF NOT(INSTR(anyString, UNISTR('\000A')) = 0 AND
             INSTR(anyString, UNISTR('\0009')) = 0 AND
             LENGTH(anyString) =
               LENGTH(TRIM(anyString)) AND
             INSTR(anyString, ' ') = 0 AND
             LENGTH(anyString) BETWEEN 4 AND 11 AND
             SUBSTR(anyString, 1, 3) = 'ASM' AND
             -- If the value is not a number, then an
             -- error will be thrown. IS NOT NULL makes
             -- this valid SQL, but is meaningless.
             CAST(SUBSTR(anyString, 4, 8) AS NUMBER)
               IS NOT NULL) THEN
        RAISE_APPLICATION_ERROR(-20000,
                'Not an assemblyPartStatus.');
      END IF;
    ELSE
      RAISE_APPLICATION_ERROR(-20000,
                              'Not an assemblyPartStatus.');
    END IF;
END;

--A trigger to throw errors when the assemblyPartStatus
--is invalid during an update.
CREATE OR REPLACE TRIGGER UpdateAssPartAnyPreProdError
BEFORE UPDATE
ON AssemblyPartStatusAnyExample
FOR EACH ROW
DECLARE
  anyInt PLS_INTEGER;
  status PLS_INTEGER;
  anyDate DATE;
  anyString VARCHAR2(11);
BEGIN
  IF :new.assemblyPartStatus.GETTYPENAME() = 'SYS.NUMBER' THEN
    -- return status not used.
    status := :new.assemblyPartStatus.GETNUMBER(anyInt);
    IF anyInt NOT BETWEEN 1 AND 4 THEN
      RAISE_APPLICATION_ERROR(-20000,
                              'Not an assemblyPartStatus.');
    END IF;
```

*continues*

```
      ELSIF :new.assemblyPartStatus.GETTYPENAME() = 'SYS.DATE' THEN
        -- return status not used.
        status := :new.assemblyPartStatus.GETDATE(anyDate);
        IF anyDate <= TO_DATE('2000-01-01', 'YYYY-MM-DD') THEN
          RAISE_APPLICATION_ERROR(-20000,
                          'Not an assemblyPartStatus.');
        END IF;
      ELSIF :new.assemblyPartStatus.GETTYPENAME() = 'SYS.VARCHAR2' THEN
        -- return status not used.
        status := :new.assemblyPartStatus.GETVARCHAR2(anyString);
        IF NOT(INSTR(anyString, UNISTR('\000A')) = 0 AND
            INSTR(anyString, UNISTR('\0009')) = 0 AND
            LENGTH(anyString) =
              LENGTH(TRIM(anyString)) AND
            INSTR(anyString, ' ') = 0 AND
            LENGTH(anyString) BETWEEN 4 AND 11 AND
            SUBSTR(anyString, 1, 3) = 'ASM' AND
            -- If the value is not a number, then an
            -- error will be thrown. IS NOT NULL makes
            -- this valid SQL, but is meaningless.
            CAST(SUBSTR(anyString, 4, 8) AS NUMBER)
              IS NOT NULL) THEN
          RAISE_APPLICATION_ERROR(-20000,
                          'Not an assemblyPartStatus.');
        END IF;
      ELSE
        RAISE_APPLICATION_ERROR(-20000,
                          'Not an assemblyPartStatus.');
      END IF;
END;
```

Listing 23.27 shows the insert statements to get SYS.AnyData data values into the database. Notice the use of specialized conversion routines to convert the data to the proper SYS.AnyData values into a representation that the database can accept.

**LISTING 23.27**  SYS.AnyData Column Inserts into the Database

```
INSERT INTO AssemblyPartStatusAnyExample
VALUES
(SYS.ANYDATA.CONVERTVARCHAR2('ASM4534'));

INSERT INTO AssemblyPartStatusAnyExample
VALUES
(SYS.ANYDATA.CONVERTNUMBER(1));

INSERT INTO AssemblyPartStatusAnyExample
```

```
VALUES
(SYS.ANYDATA.CONVERTDATE(TO_DATE('2001-12-23', 'YYYY-MM-DD')));
COMMIT;
```

Listing 23.28 demonstrates how SYS.AnyData values can be retrieved from the database by using an anonymous PL/SQL block. When calling Listing 23.28 from Java, Visual Basic, etc., the anyInt, anyDate, and anyString variables would be replaced with bind variables. And in a real-world example, the table key or alternate key(s) would replace ROWNUM.

**LISTING 23.28**   SYS.AnyData Column Retrieval from the Database

```
SET serveroutput ON;
DECLARE
  anyInt PLS_INTEGER;
  status PLS_INTEGER;
  anyDate DATE;
  anyString VARCHAR2(11);
  anyAny SYS.ANYDATA;
BEGIN
  DBMS_OUTPUT.ENABLE;

  SELECT assemblyPartStatus
  INTO   anyAny
  FROM   AssemblyPartStatusAnyExample
  WHERE ROWNUM = 1;

  IF anyAny.GETTYPENAME() = 'SYS.NUMBER' THEN
    -- return status not used.
    status := anyAny.GETNUMBER(anyInt);
  ELSIF anyAny.GETTYPENAME() = 'SYS.DATE' THEN
    -- return status not used.
    status := anyAny.GETDATE(anyDate);
  ELSIF anyAny.GETTYPENAME() = 'SYS.VARCHAR2' THEN
    -- return status not used.
    status := anyAny.GETVARCHAR2(anyString);
  END IF;

  DBMS_OUTPUT.PUT_LINE(anyAny.GETTYPENAME());
  DBMS_OUTPUT.PUT_LINE(anyInt);
  DBMS_OUTPUT.PUT_LINE(anyDate);
  DBMS_OUTPUT.PUT_LINE(anyString);
END;
```

### 23.5.4 `pattern` Constraining Facet

The `pattern` constraining facet determines the pattern for all the simple types that make up the `union`. Because the `pattern` constraining facet is represented as a string, its implementation needs a character datatype with which to perform validation. Using a character column datatype in the database or converting the `SYS.AnyData` column datatype to an appropriate string representation and validating against that would accomplish this. Refer to Section 22.1.1 for design decisions and implementation details. All the `union` element examples in this section implement the `pattern` constraining facet of 'ASM\d{1,8}'.

### 23.5.5 `enumeration` Constraining Facet

The `enumeration` constraining facet determines the enumeration for all the simple types that make up the `union` element. Because the value of an `enumeration` constraining facet is a string, its implementation needs a character datatype with which to perform validation. This could be accomplished by using a database character column datatype or converting the `SYS.AnyData` column datatype to an appropriate string representation and performing validation. Refer to Section 22.2.2 for design decisions and implementation details. All the `union` element examples in Section 23.5.5 implement the `enumeration` constraining facet as specified in the `preProductionStatusType`.

# Data-oriented Schemas: Complex Types

**CHAPTER**

**24**

## IN THIS CHAPTER

- **24.1** XML Schema Design Considerations 708
- **24.2** An Example of a Complex Type Mapping to a Database Schema 709
- **24.3** An Example of a Complex Type Mapping Supporting Mixed Content to a Database Schema 713
- **24.4** Concepts and Observations 718
- **24.5** `complexType` Element 719
- **24.6** `all` Element 720
- **24.7** `annotation` Element 722
- **24.8** `any` Element 722
- **24.9** `anyAttribute` Element 723
- **24.10** `attributeGroup` Element 724
- **24.11** `choice` Element 724
- **24.12** `complexContent` Element 727
- **24.13** `group` Element 727
- **24.14** `sequence` Element 731
- **24.15** `simpleContent` Element 738
- **24.16** `restriction` Element 738
- **24.17** `extension` Element 745

This chapter details how to map XML schema document complex types to relational database schema tables and columns. Representing complex types requires numerous design and implementation trade-offs. This chapter loosely follows Chapter 11 and builds on its examples. The chapter also builds on Chapters 22 and 23.

Because much of this chapter is meant for database designers and implementers, it begins with some issues an XML schema designer should be aware of when designing an XML schema document that will be represented in a relational database. In some cases, small XML schema document decisions have major database implications.

The chapter continues with a couple of examples and derives some concepts and observations. It then covers each attribute of a `complexType` element and all the elements that a `complexType` element can contain directly or indirectly. Whenever appropriate, multiple implementations are given, with discussion of the design trade-offs of each.

> **NOTE**
>
> The database code implementing each `complexType` element and the elements it can contain, directly or indirectly, is meant to be a set of contrived, albeit working examples. Some of the examples are close to real-world examples as a `complexType` element can be mapped to numerous database tables. Note that there are hard-coded values in many of the examples that would be changed or set to PL/SQL package constants in real-world scenarios. All code examples have been tested on Oracle 9.0.1.0.1 running under Windows 2000.

## 24.1 XML Schema Design Considerations

When creating an XML schema document whose XML instances will be stored in a relational database (in non-XML form), the XML schema designer needs to consider the effects that design decisions might have on the database representation. In addition, certain decisions need to be made explicitly that would not normally affect an XML schema document. This section lists major considerations and provides recommendations and discussion for each of them.

The `processContents` attribute is problematic unless 'strict' is specified. If 'lax' or 'skip' is chosen, content that has not been defined in the XML schema document may appear in an XML instance. As a result, part of the XML instance may not be stored in the database because there is no structure for its representation. Determine if the 'lax' or 'skip' values are necessary for the XML schema document.

### 24.1.1 `mixed` Attribute

For the `mixed` attribute, determine whether the element types will be queried independent of the content in which they are embedded. From a database design perspective, an XML instance of `mixed` attribute could be simply stored as a string. In addition, each embedded element could be stored separately as well.

### 24.1.2 `any` and `anyAttribute` Elements

Document which of the any element types and `anyAttribute` attribute types will actually be referenced in an XML instance. When an existing database schema implements the target namespace, document the value of using the existing tables and data. In other words, is only the database structure important or is the data valuable as well?

### 24.1.3 `attributeGroup` and `group` Elements

For the `attributeGroup` and `group` elements, be sure to understand whether these elements will be queried independent of the `complexType` that refers to them or dependent on the `complexType` that refers to them. In Unified Modeling Language (UML) terms, one would be an association and the other would be a composition. From a database design perspective, the former more likely leads to separate tables, whereas the latter leads to additional database columns.

### 24.1.4 `annotation` Element

The `annotation` element is a great way to provide the intention of the element type to the database designer.

## 24.2 An Example of a Complex Type Mapping to a Database Schema

Listing 24.1 iterates Listing 11.3 and demonstrates the XML schema document representation of `partOptionType`. `partOptionType` requires content of two elements, which are `colorOptionType` and `sizeOptionType`.

**LISTING 24.1** An XML Schema Document Fragment of a Complex Type That Supports Nested Elements (`catalog.xsd`)

```
<xsd:complexType name="partOptionType"
        block="#all"
        final="#all"
        id="partOptionType.catalog.cType">
  <xsd:annotation>
```

*continues*

```xml
      <xsd:documentation xml:lang="en">
        Appropriate parts can have a color,
        a size, or both. Note that the use
        of the "all" element indicates that
        the "color" and "size" are unordered.
        That is, they can appear in either
        order.
            -- Shorthand Notation --
      </xsd:documentation>
    </xsd:annotation>
    <xsd:all id="pot.all">
      <xsd:element name="color"
            type="colorOptionType"
            minOccurs="0"
            maxOccurs="1"/>
      <xsd:element name="size"
            type="sizeOptionType"
            minOccurs="0"
            maxOccurs="1"/>
    </xsd:all>
  </xsd:complexType>

  <xsd:simpleType name="colorOptionType"
          id="catalog.colorOption.union.sType">
    <xsd:annotation>
      <xsd:documentation xml:lang="en">
        A part has one of the following color definitions:
          - a standard name (cyan, yellow, etc.),
          - a fanciful name (Ocean, Sunshine, etc.), or
          - an internal code 1.n
      </xsd:documentation>
    </xsd:annotation>
    <xsd:union id="colorOptionType.union">

      <xsd:simpleType name="standardColorOptionType"
              final="restriction"
              id="catalog.standardColorOption.sType">
        <xsd:annotation>
          <xsd:documentation xml:lang="en">
            Color selection is limited.
            The colors apply to unit and
            bulk items.
          </xsd:documentation>
        </xsd:annotation>
        <xsd:restriction base="xsd:token">
          <xsd:enumeration value="cyan"/>
          <xsd:enumeration value="magenta"/>
          <xsd:enumeration value="yellow"/>
```

## 24.2 An Example of a Complex Type Mapping to a Database Schema

```xml
        <xsd:enumeration value="black"/>
      </xsd:restriction>
    </xsd:simpleType>

    <xsd:simpleType name="fancifulColorOptionType"
            final="restriction"
            id="catalog.fancifulColorOption.sType">
      <xsd:annotation>
        <xsd:documentation xml:lang="en">
          Color selection is limited.
          The colors apply to unit and
          bulk items.
        </xsd:documentation>
      </xsd:annotation>
      <xsd:restriction base="xsd:token">
        <xsd:enumeration value="Ocean"/>
        <xsd:enumeration value="Pink Grapefruit"/>
        <xsd:enumeration value="Sunshine"/>
        <xsd:enumeration value="Midnight"/>
      </xsd:restriction>
    </xsd:simpleType>

    <xsd:simpleType name="codedColorOptionType"
            id="catalog.codedColorOption.sType">
      <xsd:annotation>
        <xsd:documentation xml:lang="en">
          A color can be defined by an
          internal integer that maps
          directly to a standard or
          fanciful color
          1 = cyan = Ocean
          2 = magenta = Pink Grapefruit
          etc.
        </xsd:documentation>
      </xsd:annotation>
      <xsd:restriction base="xsd:positiveInteger">
        <xsd:maxInclusive value="4"/>
      </xsd:restriction>
    </xsd:simpleType>

  </xsd:union>
</xsd:simpleType>

<xsd:simpleType name="sizeOptionType"
        final="#all"
        id="catalog.sizeOption.sType">
```

*continues*

```
<xsd:annotation>
  <xsd:documentation xml:lang="en">
    Size selection is limited.
    The sizes apply to unit and
    bulk items.
  </xsd:documentation>
</xsd:annotation>
<xsd:restriction base="xsd:token">
  <xsd:enumeration value="tiny"/>
  <xsd:enumeration value="small"/>
  <xsd:enumeration value="medium"/>
  <xsd:enumeration value="large"/>
  <xsd:enumeration value="grandiose"/>
</xsd:restriction>
</xsd:simpleType>
```

The partOptionType could be represented as its own table. However, given that it is essentially two enumeration simple types with a minOccurs of 0 and a maxOccurs of 1, a more natural representation is two columns in a table. Listing 24.2 implements the mapping of sizeOptionType to a database by using a picklist, as described in Section 22.2.2.3.

**LISTING 24.2**  Mapping of sizeOptionType to a Database Representation (catalog.xsd)

```
--Insert the sizeOptionType
INSERT INTO PicklistDomain
(picklistDomainID, name, description)
VALUES
(8, 'sizeOptionType',
'Size selection is limited. The sizes apply to unit and
bulk items.');

INSERT INTO Picklist
(picklistID, picklistDomainID, name)
VALUES
(21, 8, 'tiny');

INSERT INTO Picklist
(picklistID, picklistDomainID, name)
VALUES
(22, 8, 'small');

INSERT INTO Picklist
(picklistID, picklistDomainID, name)
VALUES
(23, 8, 'medium');
```

```
INSERT INTO Picklist
(picklistID, picklistDomainID, name)
VALUES
(24, 8, 'large');

INSERT INTO Picklist
(picklistID, picklistDomainID, name)
VALUES
(25, 8, 'grandiose');
COMMIT;
```

Listing 24.3 demonstrates an example table that uses the new created `partOptionType`.

**LISTING 24.3** Mapping `partOptionType` to the `PartOptionTypeExample` Database Table

```
CREATE TABLE PartOptionTypeExample (
colorOptionTypeID NUMBER(4) NULL,
sizeOptionTypeID NUMBER(4) NULL
);

--Add a column comment to match the annotation.
COMMENT ON TABLE PartOptionTypeExample IS
'Appropriate parts can have a color, a size, or both.
Note that the use of the "all" element indicates that
the "color" and "size" are unordered. That is, they can
appear in either order.';
```

Triggers can be created to enforce the `union` in `colorOptionType`. Refer to Listing 22.6 for more details.

Given the preceding table declaration, the following is a valid insert statement:

```
INSERT INTO PartOptionTypeExample
VALUES
(9, 25);
```

where 9 is the `picklistID` of 'cyan' and 25 is the `picklistID` of 'grandiose'.

## 24.3 An Example of a Complex Type Mapping Supporting Mixed Content to a Database Schema

Mixed content allows free-form text interspersed with elements. Listing 24.4 demonstrates an XML representation of `assemblyCatalogEntryDescriptionType` that permits valid lists of part numbers to be interspersed with text. This listing is similar to Listing 11.4 and differs only in the type that forms the element type and the addition of an attribute for the manufacturer.

**LISTING 24.4** An XML Document Fragment of a Complex Type That Supports Mixed Content

```
<xsd:complexType name="assemblyCatalogEntryDescriptionType"
        mixed="true"
        id="assemblyCatalogEntryDescriptionType.[ccc]
catalog.cType">
 <xsd:annotation>
   <xsd:documentation xml:lang="en">
     Allow the description of a part
     to include assembly part number references.
   </xsd:documentation>
 </xsd:annotation>
 <xsd:sequence minOccurs="0" maxOccurs="unbounded">
   <xsd:element name="assemblypartList"
           type="assemblypartNumberListType"/>
 </xsd:sequence>
 <xsd:attribute name="manufacturer" type="xsd:string"/>
</xsd:complexType>
```

The XML document representation of an element type whose structure type is `assemblyCatalogEntryDescriptionType` might look like the following:

```
<xsd:element name="description"
       type="assemblyCatalogEntryDescriptionType"/>
```

Given the preceding element type, the following `description` element is valid in an XML instance:

```
<description>
 Our product line in this area, the
 <assemblypartList>ASM2000 ASM2002</assemblypartList>
 are far superior to our competitors' products, the
 <assemblypartList manufacturer="Acme">ASM020 ASM030
 </assemblypartList> which are manufactured in Elbonia.
 Even our last generation products
 <assemblypartList>ASM0200 ASM0202</assemblypartList>
 are far superior to our competitors' existing products.
</description>
```

In mapping this to a relational database, it is important to understand the usage requirements of the `description` element. If the sole need is to simply insert the entire `description` without validation and retrieve it later on, a character database column datatype is sufficient. Otherwise, all the `assemblyPartList` items must be stored individually. In addition, a charac-

## 24.3 An Example of a Complex Type Mapping Supporting Mixed Content to a Database Schema

ter database column is needed for storing the entire mixed content string. First, Listing 24.5 maps an `assemblyPartNumberListType` to a database representation. Second, Listing 24.6 maps a `description` to a database representation.

**LISTING 24.5**  Mapping `assemblyPartNumberListType` to the Database Tables `AssPartNumberListType` and `AssPartNumberType` with a Column Constraint

```
--Start the sequence at 1, don't let it cycle, and have
--the numbers in the sequence ordered.
CREATE SEQUENCE Seq_AssPartNumberListType INCREMENT BY 1 START
 WITH 1 MAXVALUE 999999999 MINVALUE 1 NOCYCLE ORDER;

CREATE TABLE AssPartNumberListType (
assPartNumberListTypeID NUMBER(9) NOT NULL,
PRIMARY KEY (assPartNumberListTypeID)
);

CREATE TABLE AssPartNumberType (
assPartNumberTypeID NUMBER(9) NOT NULL,
listOrder       NUMBER(3) NOT NULL,
partNumberType    VARCHAR2(11) NOT NULL
CHECK (INSTR(partNumberType, UNISTR('\000D')) = 0 AND
    INSTR(partNumberType, UNISTR('\000A')) = 0 AND
    INSTR(partNumberType, UNISTR('\0009')) = 0 AND
    LENGTH(partNumberType) =
     LENGTH(TRIM(partNumberType)) AND
    INSTR(partNumberType, ' ') = 0 AND
    LENGTH(partNumberType) BETWEEN 4 AND 11 AND
    SUBSTR(partNumberType, 1, 3) = 'ASM' AND
    -- If the value is not a number, then an
    -- error will be thrown. IS NOT NULL makes
    -- this valid SQL, but is meaningless.
    CAST(SUBSTR(partNumberType, 4, 8) AS NUMBER)
     IS NOT NULL),
manufacturer    VARCHAR2(100),
PRIMARY KEY (assPartNumberTypeID, listOrder),
FOREIGN KEY (assPartNumberTypeID)
REFERENCES AssPartNumberListType
);
```

Simply storing a list of lists of part numbers for a `description` is probably insufficient in this case, because the context of the part numbers would not be represented. In the XML instance example, it appears that some of the parts are manufactured by this company but others are manufactured by competitors. It would be difficult to determine which is which without representing the context. Listing 24.6 maps a `description` to a database representation with the following five columns:

- This manufacturer's `assemblypartNumberListType`
- The competitor's `assemblypartNumberListType`
- The mixed content text
- An order (because the type specifies a sequence)
- A surrogate primary key (because the type does not specify that there is any content or that the content is unique)

Parsing the description into these five columns is beyond the scope of this chapter.

**LISTING 24.6** DescriptionExample Tables Creation with a Column Constraint

```
--Start the sequence at 1, don't let it cycle, and have
--the numbers in the sequence ordered.
CREATE SEQUENCE Seq_AssCatalogEntryDescType INCREMENT BY 1
START WITH 1 MAXVALUE 999999999 MINVALUE 1 NOCYCLE ORDER;

CREATE TABLE DescriptionExample (
ourAssPartNumberListTypeID    NUMBER(9),
theirAssPartNumberListTypeID  NUMBER(9),
assCatalogEntryDescType       VARCHAR2(1000),
sequenceOrder                 NUMBER(3) NOT NULL,
assCatalogEntryDescTypeID     NUMBER(9) NOT NULL,
PRIMARY KEY (assCatalogEntryDescTypeID, sequenceOrder),
FOREIGN KEY (ourAssPartNumberListTypeID)
REFERENCES AssPartNumberListType,
FOREIGN KEY (theirAssPartNumberListTypeID)
REFERENCES AssPartNumberListType
);
```

Listing 24.7 inserts the `description` element type into the database by using an anonymous PL/SQL block to maintain the primary keys between insert statements.

**LISTING 24.7** Inserting a Description Element Type into the Database

```
--Since there is one sequence for the primary key in
--AssPartNumberListType and multiple keys are needed
--for the insert into DescriptionExample,
--create an anonymous PL/SQL block.

DECLARE
val1 PLS_INTEGER;
val2 PLS_INTEGER;
BEGIN
```

## 24.3 An Example of a Complex Type Mapping Supporting Mixed Content to a Database Schema

```
SELECT Seq_AssPartNumberListType.NEXTVAL
INTO   val1
FROM   dual;

SELECT Seq_AssPartNumberListType.NEXTVAL
INTO   val2
FROM   dual;

INSERT INTO AssPartNumberListType
VALUES
(val1);

INSERT INTO AssPartNumberType
(assPartNumberTypeID, listOrder, partNumberType)
VALUES
(val1, 1, 'ASM2000');

INSERT INTO AssPartNumberType
(assPartNumberTypeID, listOrder, partNumberType)
VALUES
(val1, 2, 'ASM2002');

INSERT INTO AssPartNumberListType
VALUES
(val2);

INSERT INTO AssPartNumberType
(assPartNumberTypeID, listOrder, partNumberType,
manufacturer)
VALUES
(val2, 1, 'ASM0020', 'Acme');

INSERT INTO AssPartNumberType
(assPartNumberTypeID, listOrder, partNumberType)
VALUES
(val2, 2, 'ASM0030');

INSERT INTO DescriptionExample
(ourAssPartNumberListTypeID, theirAssPartNumberListTypeID,
assCatalogEntryDescType, sequenceOrder,
assCatalogEntryDescTypeID)
VALUES
(val1, val2,
'Our product line in this area, the
<assemblypartList>ASM2000 ASM2002</assemblypartList>
are far superior to our competitors' products, the
<assemblypartList manufacturer="Acme">ASM020 ASM030
```

*continues*

```
</assemblypartList> which are manufactured in Elbonia.
Even our last generation products
<assemblypartList>ASM0200 ASM0202</assemblypartList>
are far superior to our competitors' existing products.', 1,
Seq_AssCatalogEntryDescType.NEXTVAL);

COMMIT;

END;
```

## 24.4 Concepts and Observations

Complex types are more expressive than simple types and require more effort from the database designer. Creating a database schema representation of complex types is fairly straightforward but requires attention to detail, some knowledge of the datatypes, and Oracle PL/SQL functions.

Similar to simple types, the following portions of the XML schema document fragments in listings 24.1 and 24.4 were *not* translated:

- There is no translation of the `id` attribute into the database schema.
- There is no easy general programmatic enforcement of the `final` and `block` attributes. An XML schema validation program would have already validated the attributes. Otherwise, the enforcement needs to be done manually by the database designer.
- The language of the documentation annotation was specified as 'en', but the database column documentation does not reflect this.
- The `assemblyCatalogEntryDescriptionType` complex type is used in the element type named `description`. The element type is then mapped to the `DescriptionExample` database table. The name of the database table could have been mapped to the complex type `assemblyCatalogEntryDescriptionType` instead, but mapping to both is not possible. If the complex type is used in multiple element types, using the name of the complex type for the database table is more appropriate.
- The `xsd:string` simple type is used in the `manufacturer` attribute type. The attribute type is then mapped to the `manufacturer` database column. The name of the database table could have been mapped to the simple type `xsd:string` instead, but `string` as a name is uninformative. If the simple type name were more informative, it could be used instead of the attribute type name.

Each one of these points could have been addressed, but database schemas do not have this functionality built in. What is important is that valid values are allowed into the database and that an error is thrown for invalid values. For every aspect of the XML schema document *itself* to have a database representation is far less important.

## 24.5 `complexType` Element

Complex types provide a wide range of functionality, and their mapping to a database schema has a wide range of design options. In this section, each of the `complexType` attributes is briefly reviewed. The sections that follow discuss the content options available for a `complexType`, with database design options and implementations. The content options are the following element types:

- `all`
- `any`
- `anyAttribute`
- `attributeGroup`
- `choice`
- `complexContent`
- `group`
- `sequence`
- `simpleContent`
- `restriction`
- `extension`

Examples are demonstrated, where appropriate.

### 24.5.1 Attributes of a `complexType` Element

`complexType` elements may contain the following attributes:

- `abstract`
- `block`
- `final`
- `id`
- `mixed`
- `name`

#### 24.5.1.1 `abstract` Attribute

The `abstract` attribute specifies that the type is explicitly noninstantiable; hence, there is no database implementation of this attribute. This concept is typically used when there are multiple derivations of a `complexType` that *are* instantiable. Sections 24.16 and 24.17 on the `restriction` element and the `extension` element, respectively, describe implementations of multiple derivations of a `complexType`. Although the discussion is not specifically about non-instantiable complex types, it is about derivations in general.

### 24.5.1.2 `block` Attribute

The `block` attribute is important in database design because using it either prevents or allows an XML instance to substitute an instantiable derivation of a `complexType`. When the `block` attribute does not have a value of '#all', the type of the `complexType` can differ for each XML instance. Section 24.17 on `extension` elements describes implementations of multiple derivations.

### 24.5.1.3 `final` Attribute

The `final` attribute is important in XML schema design, but it is not significant to a database schema design. It eliminates the potential for substitution of an instantiable derivation, limiting the number of database schema design possibilities.

### 24.5.1.4 `id` Attribute

The `id` attribute is important in XML schema design but has little importance to a database schema design. It could be used to help determine the database table and column names and may be added to the database table and column comments.

### 24.5.1.5 `mixed` Attribute

The `mixed` attribute was described in Section 24.3.

### 24.5.1.6 `name` Attribute

The `name` attribute is typically used in formulating the names of the database tables and columns. Use of the `name` attribute in a database schema, whenever possible, diminishes the "cognitive distance" between an XML schema document and its corresponding database implementation.

## 24.6 `all` Element

Now that the attributes of a `complexType` element have been discussed, the elements of a `complexType` follow in the next sections. The `all` element requires that every element type in a set of element types must exist. Listing 24.1 and 24.3 demonstrate the mapping from XML schema document to a database schema in a case where implementation of the element types is straightforward, the `minOccurs` is 0, and the `maxOccurs` is 1. As a result, the table columns are nullable. If both element types are required, the `all` element has a `minOccurs` attribute of 1. Listing 24.8 demonstrates the XML representation of `requiredPartOptionType`. `requiredPartOptionType` is made up of two required elements: `colorOptionType` and `sizeOptionType`.

**LISTING 24.8** An XML Representation of the `all` Complex Type Where the Elements Are Required

```
<xsd:complexType name="requiredPartOptionType"
        block="#all"
        final="#all"
```

```
        id="requiredPartOptionType.catalog.cType">
<xsd:annotation>
  <xsd:documentation xml:lang="en">
    Appropriate parts must have a color
    and can have a size. Note that the use
    of the "all" element indicates that
    the "color" and "size" are unordered.
    That is, they can appear in either
    order.
       -- Shorthand Notation --
  </xsd:documentation>
</xsd:annotation>
<xsd:all id="pot.all" minOccurs="1">
  <xsd:element name="color"
        type="colorOptionType"/>
  <xsd:element name="size"
        type="sizeOptionType"/>
</xsd:all>
</xsd:complexType>
```

Listing 24.9 maps `requiredPartOptionType` to a database table.

**LISTING 24.9**  Mapping the `requiredPartOptionType` to a Database RequiredPartOptionTypeExample Table

```
CREATE TABLE RequiredPartOptionTypeExample (
colorOptionTypeID NUMBER(4) NOT NULL,
sizeOptionTypeID NUMBER(4) NOT NULL
);

--Add a column comment to match the annotation.
COMMENT ON TABLE RequiredPartOptionTypeExample IS
'Appropriate parts must have a color and can have a size.
Note that the use of the "all" element indicates that
the "color" and "size" are unordered. That is, they can
appear in either order.';
```

Triggers can be created to enforce the union in `colorOptionType`. Refer to Listing 22.6 for more details.

Given the preceding table declaration, the following is a valid insert statement:

```
INSERT INTO RequiredPartOptionTypeExample
VALUES
(9, 25);
```

where 9 is the `picklistID` of 'cyan' and 25 is the `picklistID` of 'grandiose'.

In cases where the `all` element types cannot be expressed simply as column attributes, separate tables and foreign key relationships are required.

### 24.6.1 `id` Attribute

Refer to Section 24.5.1.4 for design and implementation issues.

### 24.6.2 `minOccurs` Attribute

The `minOccurs` attribute is either the value 0 or 1 and forces database columns and foreign keys to be nullable or not nullable, respectively. In certain cases, the minimum range of a complex type contained in an `all` element can be greater than 1. If this occurs, a separate table, as described in Section 24.14, is appropriate.

### 24.6.3 `maxOccurs` Attribute

The `maxOccurs` attribute is fixed to 1 and forces database columns and foreign keys to be not nullable. In certain cases, the maximum range of a complex type contained in an `all` element can be greater than 1. If this occurs, a separate table, as described in Section 24.14, is appropriate.

## 24.7 `annotation` Element

The `annotation` element can be represented by either a column or a table comment. Refer to Listing 24.3 for an example. Note that a comment is limited to 4,000 characters and its datatype is `VARCHAR2`. This implies that the language cannot be specified in the comment (unless added to the comment itself) and the comment is restricted to 8-bit character sets such as ISO-Latin-8859-1.

## 24.8 `any` Element

The any element allows element types from different namespaces to be valid for an XML instance using the namespace attribute. A database designer needs to understand which element types, in practice, will be used. Otherwise, the database schema needs to be designed to handle any of the possible element types in the `namespace`. The `complexType`, which forms the basis for an element type, has been discussed extensively in this chapter.

If the allowable element types are complex in nature from a database perspective, it may be appropriate to link to a remote database. For example, the XML schema document representation of an element type whose structure type is `siDBBusinessType` in Listing 24.15 might look like the following element:

```
<xsd:element name="siDBBusiness" type="siDBBusinessType"/>
```

If this element type were already mapped to a database schema, the `siDBCatalogEntryType` could refer to it by using the any element. From a database perspective, the following SQL command links the `SiDBBusiness` table to the current database schema:

```
CREATE SYNONYM SiDBBusiness FOR business.SiDBBusiness;
```

This allows the `SiDBCatalogEntry` table to reference it locally as though it were part of its database. Obviously, the `SiDBBusiness` table could be copied into the database schema in this simple example. If a business were truly represented in the other database schema, copying it into the current schema would not be advisable.

### 24.8.1 `id` Attribute

Refer to Section 24.5.1.4 for design and implementation issues.

### 24.8.2 `minOccurs` Attribute

Refer to Section 24.14 for design and implementation issues on the `minOccurs` attribute.

### 24.8.3 `maxOccurs` Attribute

Refer to Section 24.14 for design and implementation issues on the `maxOccurs` attribute.

### 24.8.4 `namespace` Attribute

The `namespace` attribute has been discussed at the beginning of Section 24.8.

### 24.8.5 `processContents` Attribute

The `processContents` attribute is problematic unless 'strict' is chosen. If 'lax' or 'skip' is chosen, content that has not been defined in the XML schema document may appear in an XML instance. As a result, part of the XML instance may not be stored in the database because there is no structure for its representation. The database designer should discuss this with the XML schema designer and try to have the value of the `processContents` attribute set to 'strict'. If this is not possible, the appropriate solution is to use the Oracle `XMLType` column datatype, which essentially stores all XML instance data as a `CLOB`.

## 24.9 `anyAttribute` Element

The `anyAttribute` element allows attribute types from different namespaces to be valid for an XML instance using the `namespace` attribute. A database designer needs to understand which attribute types, in practice, will be used. Otherwise, the database schema needs to be designed to handle any of the possible attribute types in the `namespace`.

Because attributes correspond to attribute types whose structure type is just a simple type, refer to Chapter 23 to understand the design issues and example implementations. Most simple types are mapped to a single database table column; for those that map to tables, the tables should be created in a local database rather than linked to existing tables in a remote database. Linking to a remote database for attributes internal to a `complexType` creates performance penalties with very few, if any, gains in database cohesion.

### 24.9.1 `id` Attribute

Refer to Section 24.5.1.4 for design and implementation issues.

### 24.9.2 `namespace` Attribute

The `namespace` attribute has been discussed at the beginning of Section 24.9.

### 24.9.3 `processContents` Attribute

Refer to Section 24.8.5 for design and implementation issues.

## 24.10 `attributeGroup` Element

The `attributeGroup` element typically allows a global `attributeGroup` to be used in a `complexType` through the `ref` attribute. Because attributes correspond to attribute types whose structure type is just a simple type, refer to Chapter 23 to understand the design issues and example implementations.

The `attributeGroup` is best subsumed into the database table that refers to this `attributeGroup`, unless the `attributeGroup` is used in numerous places in the XML schema document and the `attributeGroup` is the subject of numerous queries that are *independent* of the complex types in which the `attributeGroup` is contained. Refer to Section 24.13 if the `attributeGroup` should not be subsumed.

### 24.10.1 `id` Attribute

Refer to Section 24.5.1.4 for design and implementation issues.

### 24.10.2 `name` Attribute

Refer to Section 24.5.1.6 for design and implementation issues.

### 24.10.3 `ref` Attribute

The `ref` attribute has been discussed at the beginning of Section 24.10.

## 24.11 `choice` Element

The `choice` element restricts an XML instance to choose one element type from a set of element types. From a database schema perspective, this restricts a set of columns to have one non-null value. This is similar to how `union`s are implemented in Section 23.5.3.2. Choices, by default, have one element type but can have a `minOccurs` attribute and a `maxOccurs` attribute. Listing 24.10 creates a `colorSizeChoicesType` setting the `minOccurs` to 0 and `maxOccurs` to 4. The `colorSizeChoicesType` allows up to four choices, and they can be of `color` and/or `size`.

**LISTING 24.10**  A Complex `colorSizeChoicesType` XML Document Fragment

```
<xsd:complexType name="colorSizeChoicesType"
        block="#all"
        final="#all"
        id="colorSizeChoicesType.catalog.cType">
 <xsd:annotation>
   <xsd:documentation xml:lang="en">
     Consumers can design their options based upon
     size and color. They can choose up to a total
     of four different sizes and colors.
   </xsd:documentation>
 </xsd:annotation>
 <xsd:choice id="csct.all"
        minOccurs="0"
        maxOccurs="4">
   <xsd:element name="color"
         type="colorOptionType"/>
   <xsd:element name="size"
         type="sizeOptionType"/>
 </xsd:choice>
</xsd:complexType>
```

Listing 24.11 maps the `colorSizeChoicesType` to an example table.

**LISTING 24.11**  Mapping the `colorSizeChoicesType` to a `ColorSizeChoicesTypeExample` Database Table

```
--Start the sequence at 1, don't let it cycle, and have
--the numbers in the sequence ordered.
CREATE SEQUENCE Seq_ColorSizeChoicesType INCREMENT BY 1 START
 WITH 1 MAXVALUE 999999999 MINVALUE 1 NOCYCLE ORDER;

--Part of this table's primary key is from the sequence.
CREATE TABLE ColorSizeChoicesTypeExample (
colorSizeChoicesTypeExampleID   NUMBER(9) NOT NULL,
--The order this element appeared in the choice.
--Not necessary from an XML Schema perspective, but
--creates part of a unique primary key.
setOrder              NUMBER(1) NOT NULL,
colorOptionTypeID     NUMBER(4) NULL,
sizeOptionTypeID      NUMBER(4) NULL,
```

*continues*

```
  PRIMARY KEY (colorSizeChoicesTypeExampleID, setOrder),
  CHECK (colorOptionTypeID IS NOT NULL OR
     sizeOptionTypeID IS NOT NULL)
);

--Add a table comment to match the annotation.
COMMENT ON TABLE ColorSizeChoicesTypeExample IS
'Consumers can design their options based upon
size and color. They can choose up to a total
of four different sizes and colors.';
```

This table ensures that there is at least one `colorOptionType` and `sizeOptionType` per row, because both are non-nullable. Triggers can be created to enforce the union in `colorOptionType`. Refer to Listing 22.6 for more details. Listing 24.12 is a SQL statement that creates a before insert trigger to ensure that the length of the maximum number of elements is four.

**LISTING 24.12** A Before-Insert Trigger on `ColorSizeChoicesTypeExample` Implementing the `maxOccurs` Content Option

```
CREATE OR REPLACE TRIGGER InsertColorSizeChoicesTypeEx
BEFORE INSERT
ON ColorSizeChoicesTypeExample
FOR EACH ROW
DECLARE
I PLS_INTEGER;
BEGIN
I := 0;
SELECT COUNT(1)
INTO  I
FROM  ColorSizeChoicesTypeExample
WHERE colorSizeChoicesTypeExampleID = :new.colorSizeChoicesTypeExampleID;

-- Check to see if enough rows. Since this is a before trigger,
-- the last row has not yet been inserted.
IF I > 3 THEN
 RAISE_APPLICATION_ERROR(-20000, 'Max length of 4.');
END IF;
END;
```

Given the preceding table declaration, the following are valid insert statements:

```
INSERT INTO ColorSizeChoicesTypeExample
(colorSizeChoicesTypeExampleID,
setOrder, colorOptionTypeID, sizeOptionTypeID)
VALUES
(Seq_ColorSizeChoicesType.NEXTVAL, 1, 9, NULL);
```

```
INSERT INTO ColorSizeChoicesTypeExample
(colorSizeChoicesTypeExampleID,
setOrder, colorOptionTypeID, sizeOptionTypeID)
VALUES
(Seq_ColorSizeChoicesType.CURRVAL, 2, NULL, 25);
```

in which 9 is the `picklistID` of 'cyan' and 25 is the `picklistID` of 'grandiose'.

### 24.11.1 `id` Attribute

Refer to Section 24.5.1.4 for design and implementation issues.

### 24.11.2 `minOccurs` Attribute

The `minOccurs` attribute has been discussed at the beginning of Section 24.11.

### 24.11.3 `maxOccurs` Attribute

The `maxOccurs` attribute has been discussed at the beginning of Section 24.11.

## 24.12 `complexContent` Element

The `complexContent` element is an XML Schema construct for extending or restricting a global `complexType`. Refer to Sections 24.16 and 24.17 for design and implementation issues and examples.

### 24.12.1 `id` Attribute

Refer to Section 24.5.1.4 for design and implementation issues.

### 24.12.2 `mixed` Attribute

The `mixed` attribute was described in Section 24.3.

## 24.13 `group` Element

The `group` element typically allows a global model group to be used in a `complexType` through the `ref` attribute. The global `group` is a `choice` element, `sequence` element, or `all` element that can be used in numerous complex types. A database designer has two major options in designing a schema for using a `group`:

- Subsume the `group` into the table(s) that refer to the `group`.
- Create a separate table or series of tables to represent the `group` and refer to the `group` when needed through a foreign key relationship.

Each of these approaches has merits. The first approach is best when the group can be mapped directly to a series of table columns and the group itself is not the source of numerous queries. For example, Listing 24.13 demonstrates a group that has four choices, each of which can be mapped to a single database column (for example, fullPrice, salePrice, clearancePrice, and freePrice) or two database columns (one for the price category and the other for the value). In either case, the database column(s) are best incorporated directly into the table that refers to the group unless the group is used in numerous places in the XML schema document and the group is the subject of numerous queries that are independent of the complex types in which the group is contained. This means that unless a query such as "What were the number of salePrice items sold in the last month?" is required and priceGroup is used in numerous places, the preference is for incorporating priceGroup into a table.

**LISTING 24.13**  group with Four Elements (pricing.xsd)

```
<xsd:group name="priceGroup">
 <xsd:annotation>
   <xsd:documentation xml:lang="en">
     A price is any one of the following:
       * Full Price (with amount)
       * Sale Price (with amount and authorization)
       * Clearance Price (with amount and authorization)
       * Free (with authorization)
   </xsd:documentation>
 </xsd:annotation>
 <xsd:choice id="pg.choice">
   <xsd:element name="fullPrice"
         type="fullPriceType"/>
   <xsd:element name="salePrice"
         type="salePriceType"/>
   <xsd:element name="clearancePrice"
         type="clearancePriceType"/>
   <xsd:element name="freePrice" type="freePriceType"/>
 </xsd:choice>
</xsd:group>
```

On the other hand, if the group simply cannot be mapped to a series of table columns or will be queried independent of the complex types in which the group is contained, a separate table or series of tables is appropriate. The referencing table would simply have a foreign key relationship to the group table's primary key. Listing 24.14 demonstrates some transaction types in the anyTransactionType. Each of the types is a sequence of choices, some derived by extension, that also add additional attributes. For a complete listing of anyTransactionType, refer to order.xsd.

**LISTING 24.14**  Complex group That Requires Separate Tables (order.xsd)

```xsd
<xsd:group name="anyTransactionType">
 <xsd:choice>
   <xsd:element name="cash" type="baseTransactionType"/>
   <xsd:element name="check" type="checkTransactionType"/>
   <xsd:element name="charge" type="chargeTransactionType"/>
 </xsd:choice>
</xsd:group>

<xsd:complexType name="baseTransactionType">
 <xsd:annotation>
   <xsd:documentation xml:lang="en">
     This defines the abstract type for all transactions.
     Each transaction includes:
        * Clerk identification
        * Date stamp
        * type (purchase or return)
        * An amount of the transaction
        * A list of part numbers.
   </xsd:documentation>
 </xsd:annotation>
 <xsd:sequence>
   <xsd:element name="clerk" type="clerkType"/>
   <xsd:choice>
     <xsd:element ref="existingCustomer"/>
     <xsd:element ref="newCustomer"/>
   </xsd:choice>
   <xsd:element name="dateStamp" type="xsd:dateTime"/>
   <xsd:element name="transactionType">
     <xsd:simpleType>
       <xsd:restriction base="xsd:token">
         <xsd:enumeration value="purchase"/>
         <xsd:enumeration value="return"/>
       </xsd:restriction>
     </xsd:simpleType>
   </xsd:element>
   <xsd:element name="amount" type="positiveDollarAmountType"/>
   <xsd:element name="partNumberList" type="partNumberListType"/>
 </xsd:sequence>
</xsd:complexType>

<xsd:complexType name="checkTransactionType"
        abstract="false"
        block="extension"
        final="extension">
 <xsd:annotation>
```

*continues*

```xml
      <xsd:documentation xml:lang="en">
        A check transaction is a transaction
        (i.e., baseTransactionType), but with
        an attribute that defines the check.
      </xsd:documentation>
    </xsd:annotation>
    <xsd:complexContent id = "transaction.checkTransactionType.cc">
      <xsd:extension base="baseTransactionType">
        <xsd:attribute name="transitNumber"
               type="xsd:positiveInteger"
               use="required"/>
        <xsd:attribute name="accountNumber"
               type="xsd:positiveInteger"
               use="required"/>
        <xsd:attribute name="checkNumber"
               type="xsd:positiveInteger"
               use="required"/>
      </xsd:extension>
    </xsd:complexContent>
</xsd:complexType>

<xsd:complexType name="chargeTransactionType">
  <xsd:annotation>
    <xsd:documentation xml:lang="en">
      A charge transaction is a transaction
      (i.e., baseTransactionType), but with
      a number of attributes that are necessary
      when a charge card is used.
    </xsd:documentation>
  </xsd:annotation>
  <xsd:complexContent>
    <xsd:extension base="baseTransactionType">
      <xsd:attributeGroup ref="creditCardTransactionAttributeGroup"/>
    </xsd:extension>
  </xsd:complexContent>
</xsd:complexType>
```

## 24.13.1 `name` Attribute

Refer to Section 24.5.1.6 for design and implementation issues.

## 24.13.2 `ref` Attribute

The `ref` attribute has been discussed at the beginning of Section 24.13.

## 24.14 sequence Element

The `sequence` element describes a required ordered set of element types. From a database schema perspective, if the `minOccurs` and `maxOccurs` are both 1 for the `sequence` and for each element type, the database representation maps to a table with a series of columns that are all required. If an underlying element type is complex, it requires a foreign key relationship. If the `minOccurs` is 0, the column becomes optional; if the `maxOccurs` is greater than 1, a separate table is required. Listing 24.15 implements the `siDBCatalogEntryType` to illustrate a number of these possibilities.

**LISTING 24.15** A `siDBCatalogEntryType` XML Schema Document Fragment That Is a Simplification of `catalogEntryType`

```xml
<xsd:complexType name="siDBBusinessType"
        id="siDBBusinessType.catalog.cType">
 <xsd:annotation>
   <xsd:documentation xml:lang="en">
     A very simple entry for a business that
     provides enough catalog entry information.
        -- Shorthand Notation --
   </xsd:documentation>
 </xsd:annotation>
 <xsd:sequence id="manu-seq">
   <xsd:element name="name" type="xsd:string"/>
   <xsd:element name="telephoneNumber" type="xsd:string"/>
   <xsd:element name="contact" type="xsd:string"/>
 </xsd:sequence>
</xsd:complexType>

<xsd:complexType name="siDBCatalogEntryType"
        id="siDBCatalogEntryType.catalog.cType">
 <xsd:annotation>
   <xsd:documentation xml:lang="en">
     A catalog entry must have:
       * A database ID
       * Part Name
       * Part Number
       * Description (optional)
       * 0 to 4 colors
       * 1 to 2 sizes
       * Price
       * Included Quantity when ordering
         one item.
        -- Shorthand Notation --
   </xsd:documentation>
 </xsd:annotation>
```

*continues*

## 732 | Data-oriented Schemas: Complex Types
### CHAPTER 24

```
<xsd:sequence id="siDB-cat-entry-type-seq">
  <xsd:element name="partName" type="xsd:string"/>
  <xsd:element name="partNumber" type="xsd:token"/>
  <xsd:element name="description"
        type="xsd:string"
        minOccurs="0"
        maxOccurs="1"/>
  <xsd:element name="color"
        type="colorOptionType"
        minOccurs="1"
        maxOccurs="4"/>
  <xsd:element name="size"
        type="sizeOptionType"
        minOccurs="1"
        maxOccurs="2"/>
  <xsd:element name="manufacturerInfo"
        type="siDBBusinessType"/>
  <xsd:element name="price" >
    <xsd:simpleType>
      <xsd:restriction base="xsd:decimal">
        <xsd:minInclusive value="0.00"/>
        <xsd:totalDigits value="6"/>
        <xsd:fractionDigits value="2"/>
      </xsd:restriction>
    </xsd:simpleType>
  </xsd:element>
  <xsd:element name="includedQuantity"
        type="xsd:nonNegativeInteger"/>
</xsd:sequence>
</xsd:complexType>
```

Listing 24.16 maps siDBBusinessType and siDBCatalogEntryType to a database implementation that involves four tables. siDBBusinessType maps to the SiDBBusiness table. siDBCatalogEntryType maps to SiDBCatalogEntry and to two child tables: SiDBCatalogEntryColor and SiDBCatalogEntrySize. These child tables allow multiple colors and sizes. The SiDBCatalogEntry table also has a foreign key relationship to the SiDBBusiness table to show that the manufacturer is independent of a particular catalog entry. The foreign key constraints in the SiDBCatalogEntryColor table and the SiDBCatalogEntrySize table are deferred to allow the foreign key constraint to be checked only when a commit is being attempted.

**LISTING 24.16** Mapping siDBBusinessType and siDBCatalogEntryType to SiDBBusiness and SiDBCatalogEntry Database Tables

```
--Start the sequence at 1, don't let it cycle, and have
--the numbers in the sequence ordered.
```

```sql
CREATE SEQUENCE Seq_SiDBBusiness INCREMENT BY 1 START
 WITH 1 MAXVALUE 999999999 MINVALUE 1 NOCYCLE ORDER;

--The table's primary key is from the sequence.
CREATE TABLE SiDBBusiness (
siDBBusinessID   NUMBER(9)    NOT NULL,
name             VARCHAR2(100) NOT NULL,
telephoneNumber  VARCHAR2(30) NOT NULL,
contact          VARCHAR2(100) NOT NULL,
PRIMARY KEY (siDBBusinessID)
);

--Add a table comment to match the annotation.
COMMENT ON TABLE SiDBBusiness IS
'A very simple entry for a business that
provides enough catalog entry information.';

--Start the sequence at 1, don't let it cycle, and have
--the numbers in the sequence ordered.
CREATE SEQUENCE Seq_siDBCatalogEntry INCREMENT BY 1 START
 WITH 1 MAXVALUE 999999999 MINVALUE 1 NOCYCLE ORDER;

--The table's primary key is from the sequence.
CREATE TABLE SiDBCatalogEntry (
siDBCatalogEntryID    NUMBER(9) NOT NULL,
partName              VARCHAR2(100) NOT NULL,
partNumber            VARCHAR2(30) NOT NULL
--partNumber is a token.
CHECK (INSTR(partNumber, UNISTR('\000D')) = 0 AND
    INSTR(partNumber, UNISTR('\000A')) = 0 AND
    INSTR(partNumber, UNISTR('\0009')) = 0 AND
    LENGTH(partNumber) =
      LENGTH(TRIM(partNumber)) AND
    INSTR(partNumber, ' ') = 0),
description           VARCHAR2(255) NULL,
manufacturerID        NUMBER(9) NOT NULL,
price                 NUMBER(6,2) NOT NULL
CHECK(price >= 0),
includedQuantity      NUMBER(3) NOT NULL
CHECK(includedQuantity >= 0),
PRIMARY KEY (siDBCatalogEntryID),
FOREIGN KEY (manufacturerID)
REFERENCES SiDBBusiness
);

--Add a table comment to match the annotation.
COMMENT ON TABLE SiDBCatalogEntry IS
'A catalog entry must have:
```

*continues*

```
* A database ID
* Part Name
* Part Number
* Description (optional)
* 0 to 4 colors
* 1 to 2 sizes
* Price
* Included Quantity when ordering one item.';

--This makes the assumption that colors are unique
--for a catalog entry.
CREATE TABLE SiDBCatalogEntryColor (
siDBCatalogEntryColorID NUMBER(9) NOT NULL,
colorID         NUMBER(4) NOT NULL,
PRIMARY KEY (siDBCatalogEntryColorID, colorID),
FOREIGN KEY (siDBCatalogEntryColorID)
REFERENCES SiDBCatalogEntry
--Defer the constraint until the commit.
INITIALLY DEFERRED DEFERRABLE
);

--This makes the assumption that sizes are unique
--for a catalog entry.
CREATE TABLE SiDBCatalogEntrySize (
siDBCatalogEntrySizeID NUMBER(9) NOT NULL,
sizeID         NUMBER(4) NOT NULL,
PRIMARY KEY (siDBCatalogEntrySizeID, sizeID),
FOREIGN KEY (siDBCatalogEntrySizeID)
REFERENCES SiDBCatalogEntry
--Defer the constraint until the commit.
INITIALLY DEFERRED DEFERRABLE
);
```

Listing 24.17 enforces the maxOccurs constraining facet for color and size using insert triggers.

**LISTING 24.17** maxOccurs Constraining Facet Enforcement via Before-Insert Triggers

```
CREATE OR REPLACE TRIGGER InsertSiDBCatalogEntryColor
BEFORE INSERT
ON SiDBCatalogEntryColor
FOR EACH ROW
DECLARE
I PLS_INTEGER;
BEGIN
I := 0;
SELECT COUNT(1)
INTO   I
```

```
FROM  SiDBCatalogEntryColor
WHERE siDBCatalogEntryColorID = :new.siDBCatalogEntryColorID;

-- Check to see if enough rows. Since this is a before trigger,
-- the last row has not yet been inserted.
IF I > 3 THEN
 RAISE_APPLICATION_ERROR(-20000, 'Max occurence of 4.');
END IF;
END;

CREATE OR REPLACE TRIGGER InsertSiDBCatalogEntrySize
BEFORE INSERT
ON SiDBCatalogEntrySize
FOR EACH ROW
DECLARE
I PLS_INTEGER;
BEGIN
I := 0;
SELECT COUNT(1)
INTO  I
FROM  SiDBCatalogEntrySize
WHERE siDBCatalogEntrySizeID = :new.siDBCatalogEntrySizeID;

-- Check to see if enough rows. Since this is a before trigger,
-- the last row has not yet been inserted.
IF I > 1 THEN
 RAISE_APPLICATION_ERROR(-20000, 'Max occurence of 2.');
END IF;
END;
```

Listing 24.18 enforces the minOccurs constraining facet for color and size by using two insert triggers. The triggers make the assumption that the colors and sizes are inserted before an insert is made into the SiDBCatalogEntry table. If this assumption cannot be made, the database schema could be refactored so that color and size have foreign keys in the SiDBCatalogEntry table. The consequence of this is that the part-of relationship between the SiDBCatalogEntry table and SiDBCatalogEntryColor and SiDBCatalogEntrySize tables would no longer be enforced because the same set of colors and sizes *could* appear in multiple tables. The other possibility is to not enforce the minOccurs constraint.

**LISTING 24.18**  minOccurs Constraining Facet Enforcement via Before-Insert Triggers

```
CREATE OR REPLACE TRIGGER InsertSiDBCatalogEntryCheck1
AFTER INSERT
ON SiDBCatalogEntry
FOR EACH ROW
```

*continues*

```
DECLARE
I PLS_INTEGER;
BEGIN
I := 0;
SELECT COUNT(1)
INTO   I
FROM   SiDBCatalogEntryColor
WHERE siDBCatalogEntryColorID = :new.siDBCatalogEntryID;

IF I = 0 THEN
 RAISE_APPLICATION_ERROR(-20000, 'Need at least one color');
END IF;
END;

CREATE OR REPLACE TRIGGER InsertSiDBCatalogEntryCheck2
AFTER INSERT
ON SiDBCatalogEntry
FOR EACH ROW
DECLARE
I PLS_INTEGER;
BEGIN
I := 0;
SELECT COUNT(1)
INTO   I
FROM   SiDBCatalogEntrySize
WHERE siDBCatalogEntrySizeID = :new.siDBCatalogEntryID;

IF I = 0 THEN
 RAISE_APPLICATION_ERROR(-20000, 'Need at least one size');
END IF;
END;
```

The XML representation of an element type whose structure type is `siDBCatalogEntryType` might look like the following element:

```
<xsd:element name="siDBCatalogEntry" type="siDBCatalogEntryType"/>
```

Given the preceding element type, the following element is valid in a corresponding XML instance:

```
<siDBCatalogEntry>
 <partName>Shovel</partName>
 <partNumber>AB1204</partNumber>
 <color>black</color>
 <color>magenta</color>
 <size>large</size>
 <manufacturerInfo>
```

```
     <name>Elbonia Industries</name>
     <telephoneNumber>303-555-1212</telephoneNumber>
     <contact>Mr. Anderson</contact>
  </manufacturerInfo>
  <price>20.45</price>
  <includedQuantity>1</includedQuantity>
</siDBCatalogEntry>
```

Listing 24.19 maps the preceding XML instance to a database representation.

**LISTING 24.19**  Inserting a Catalog Entry XML Instance into the Database

```
SET CONSTRAINTS ALL deferred;

INSERT INTO SiDBCatalogEntryColor
(siDBCatalogEntryColorID, colorID)
VALUES
(Seq_siDBCatalogEntry.NEXTVAL, 12);

INSERT INTO SiDBCatalogEntryColor
(siDBCatalogEntryColorID, colorID)
VALUES
(Seq_siDBCatalogEntry.CURRVAL, 10);

INSERT INTO SiDBCatalogEntrySize
(siDBCatalogEntrySizeID, sizeID)
VALUES
(Seq_siDBCatalogEntry.CURRVAL, 24);

INSERT INTO SiDBBusiness
(siDBBusinessID, name, telephoneNumber, contact)
VALUES
(Seq_SiDBBusiness.NEXTVAL, 'Elbonia Industries',
'303-555-1212', 'Mr. Anderson');

INSERT INTO SiDBCatalogEntry
(siDBCatalogEntryID, partName, partNumber, description,
manufacturerID, price, includedQuantity)
VALUES
(Seq_siDBCatalogEntry.CURRVAL, 'Shovel', 'AB1204', NULL,
Seq_SiDBBusiness.CURRVAL, 20.45, 1);

COMMIT;
```

## 24.14.1 `id` Attribute

Refer to Section 24.5.1.4 for design and implementation issues.

### 24.14.2 `minOccurs` Attribute

The `minOccurs` attribute has been discussed at the beginning of Section 24.14.

### 24.14.3 `maxOccurs` Attribute

The `maxOccurs` attribute has been discussed at the beginning of Section 24.14.

## 24.15 `simpleContent` Element

The `simpleContent` element is an XML Schema construct for adding an attribute to a global `simpleType`. Because attributes are just simple types, refer to Chapter 23 to understand the design issues and example implementations.

### 24.15.1 `id` Attribute

Refer to Section 24.5.1.4 for design and implementation issues.

## 24.16 `restriction` Element

The `restriction` element is used to derive a `complexType` from another by restricting constraining facets for simple content and altering attribution and substitutions for complex content. A database designer has two major options in designing a schema to create a `restriction`:

- Add a type column to a table and handle the restrictions in check clauses and triggers that key off of the type column. In other words, add the type to the existing set of tables.
- Create a (partially) separate set of tables to handle the new type.

Each of these approaches has trade-offs. The first approach is best when the `restriction` element type is associated with content that is mapped to database columns and not relationships; it best handles the simple cases of `restriction` element types. If the `restriction` element type is mapped to the elimination of database columns (by setting a `maxOccurs` to 0), an adjunct table that contains the unneeded columns might be appropriate.

If the new type, on the other hand, removes significant relationships from the original `complexType`, the second approach—using a (partially) separate set of tables—is probably appropriate. Depending on the restrictions, it might even be appropriate to make the original `complexType` an extension of the restricting `complexType`. This would occur if the `complexType` derived by restriction were to eliminate database attribute columns and relationships. Instead of eliminating them, they could simply be added. Demonstrating such trade-offs is, unfortunately, outside the scope of this chapter because it would require near real-world examples spanning numerous pages to list and explain. Refer to Section 24.17 if a `restriction` element type is best refactored as an `extension` element type.

Listing 24.20 implements the `siDBPriceyCatalogEntryType`, which is derived by restriction from the `siDBCatalogEntryType`. The following set of examples is derived from the examples in Section 24.14.

**LISTING 24.20**  A `siDBPriceyCatalogEntryType` XML Schema Document Fragment Derived by Restriction from `siDBCatalogEntryType`

```
<xsd:complexType name="siDBBusinessType"
        id="siDBBusinessType.catalog.cType">
 <xsd:annotation>
   <xsd:documentation xml:lang="en">
     A very simple entry for a business that
     provides enough catalog entry information.
        -- Shorthand Notation --
   </xsd:documentation>
 </xsd:annotation>
 <xsd:sequence id="manu-seq">
   <xsd:element name="name" type="xsd:string"/>
   <xsd:element name="telephoneNumber" type="xsd:string"/>
   <xsd:element name="contact" type="xsd:string"/>
 </xsd:sequence>
</xsd:complexType>

<xsd:complexType name="siDBCatalogEntryType"
        id="siDBCatalogEntryType.catalog.cType">
 <xsd:annotation>
   <xsd:documentation xml:lang="en">
     A catalog entry must have:
        * A database ID
        * Part Name
        * Part Number
        * Description (optional)
        * 0 to 4 colors
        * 1 to 2 sizes
        * Price
        * Included Quantity when ordering
          one item.
        -- Shorthand Notation --
   </xsd:documentation>
 </xsd:annotation>
 <xsd:sequence id="siDB-cat-entry-type-seq">
   <xsd:element name="partName" type="xsd:string"/>
   <xsd:element name="partNumber" type="xsd:token"/>
   <xsd:element name="description"
          type="xsd:string"
          minOccurs="0"
```

*continues*

```xml
                    maxOccurs="1"/>
    <xsd:element name="color"
            type="colorOptionType"
            minOccurs="1"
            maxOccurs="4"/>
    <xsd:element name="size"
            type="sizeOptionType"
            minOccurs="1"
            maxOccurs="2"/>
    <xsd:element name="manufacturerInfo"
            type="siDBBusinessType"/>
    <xsd:element name="price" >
      <xsd:simpleType>
        <xsd:restriction base="xsd:decimal">
          <xsd:minInclusive value="0.00"/>
          <xsd:totalDigits value="6"/>
          <xsd:fractionDigits value="2"/>
        </xsd:restriction>
      </xsd:simpleType>
    </xsd:element>
    <xsd:element name="includedQuantity"
            type="xsd:nonNegativeInteger"/>
  </xsd:sequence>
</xsd:complexType>

<xsd:complexType name="siDBPriceyCatalogEntryType"
        id="siDBPriceyCatalogEntryType.catalog.cType">
  <xsd:annotation>
    <xsd:documentation xml:lang="en">
      A pricey catalog entry must have:
        * A database ID
        * Part Name
        * Part Number
        * Description (optional)
        * 0 to 4 colors
        * 1 to 2 sizes
        * Price greater than 1000
        * Included Quantity when ordering
          one item.
        -- Shorthand Notation --
    </xsd:documentation>
  </xsd:annotation>
  <xsd:complexContent id="spcet.cc">
    <xsd:restriction base="siDBCatalogEntryType">
      <xsd:sequence id="siDB-cat-res-entry-type-seq">
        <xsd:element name="partName"
```

```
                    type="xsd:string"/>
        <xsd:element name="partNumber"
                    type="xsd:token"/>
        <xsd:element name="description"
                    type="xsd:string"
                    minOccurs="0"
                    maxOccurs="1"/>
        <xsd:element name="color"
                    type="colorOptionType"
                    minOccurs="1"
                    maxOccurs="4"/>
        <xsd:element name="size"
                    type="sizeOptionType"
                    minOccurs="1"
                    maxOccurs="2"/>
        <xsd:element name="manufacturerInfo"
                    type="siDBBusinessType"/>
        <xsd:element name="price" >
          <xsd:simpleType>
            <xsd:restriction base="xsd:decimal">
              <xsd:minInclusive value="1000.00"/>
              <xsd:totalDigits value="6"/>
              <xsd:fractionDigits value="2"/>
            </xsd:restriction>
          </xsd:simpleType>
        </xsd:element>
        <xsd:element name="includedQuantity"
                    type="xsd:nonNegativeInteger"/>
      </xsd:sequence>
    </xsd:restriction>
  </xsd:complexContent>
</xsd:complexType>
```

Listing 24.21 maps siDBBusinessType, siDBPriceyCatalogEntryType, and siDBCatalogEntryType to a database implementation that involves four tables. siDBBusinessType maps to the SiDBBusiness table. siDBPriceyCatalogEntryType and siDBCatalogEntryType both map to SiDBCatalogEntry and to two child tables: SiDBCatalogEntryColor and SiDBCatalogEntrySize. These child tables allow multiple colors and sizes. The SiDBCatalogEntry table also has a foreign key relationship to the SiDBBusiness table to show that the manufacturer is independent of a particular catalog entry. The foreign key constraints in the SiDBCatalogEntryColor table and the SiDBCatalogEntrySize table are deferred to allow the foreign key constraint to be checked only when a commit is being attempted. The siDBPriceyCatalogEntryType creates the need for a siDBCatalogEntryTypeID column and a check on the SiDBCatalogEntry table.

**LISTING 24.21** Mapping the `siDBBusinessType`, `siDBCatalogEntryType`, and `siDBPriceyCatalogEntryType` Types to `SiDBBusiness` and `SiDBCatalogEntry` Database Tables

```sql
--Start the sequence at 1, don't let it cycle, and have
--the numbers in the sequence ordered.
CREATE SEQUENCE Seq_SiDBBusiness INCREMENT BY 1 START
 WITH 1 MAXVALUE 999999999 MINVALUE 1 NOCYCLE ORDER;

--The table's primary key is from the sequence.
CREATE TABLE SiDBBusiness (
siDBBusinessID   NUMBER(9)    NOT NULL,
name             VARCHAR2(100) NOT NULL,
telephoneNumber  VARCHAR2(30) NOT NULL,
contact          VARCHAR2(100) NOT NULL,
PRIMARY KEY (siDBBusinessID)
);

--Add a table comment to match the annotation.
COMMENT ON TABLE SiDBBusiness IS
'A very simple entry for a business that
provides enough catalog entry information.';

--Start the sequence at 1, don't let it cycle, and have
--the numbers in the sequence ordered.
CREATE SEQUENCE Seq_siDBCatalogEntry INCREMENT BY 1 START
 WITH 1 MAXVALUE 999999999 MINVALUE 1 NOCYCLE ORDER;

--The table's primary key is from the sequence.
CREATE TABLE SiDBCatalogEntry (
siDBCatalogEntryID    NUMBER(9) NOT NULL,
--new type column which is a picklist entry.
siDBCatalogEntryTypeID NUMBER(4) NOT NULL,
partName         VARCHAR2(100) NOT NULL,
partNumber       VARCHAR2(30) NOT NULL
--partNumber is a token.
CHECK (INSTR(partNumber, UNISTR('\000D')) = 0 AND
    INSTR(partNumber, UNISTR('\000A')) = 0 AND
    INSTR(partNumber, UNISTR('\0009')) = 0 AND
    LENGTH(partNumber) =
     LENGTH(TRIM(partNumber)) AND
    INSTR(partNumber, ' ') = 0),
description      VARCHAR2(255) NULL,
manufacturerID   NUMBER(9) NOT NULL,
price            NUMBER(6,2) NOT NULL
CHECK(price >= 0),
includedQuantity    NUMBER(3) NOT NULL
CHECK(includedQuantity >= 0),
```

```
PRIMARY KEY (siDBCatalogEntryID),
FOREIGN KEY (manufacturerID)
REFERENCES SiDBBusiness,
--Add a new check to ensure that the pricey
--price is enforced.
-- 27 = 'siDBPriceyCatalogEntryTypeID'
CHECK((siDBCatalogEntryTypeID = 27 AND
    price >= 1000) OR
    siDBCatalogEntryTypeID <> 27)
);

--Add a table comment to match the annotation.
COMMENT ON TABLE SiDBCatalogEntry IS
'A catalog entry must have:
* A database ID
* Part Name
* Part Number
* Description (optional)
* 0 to 4 colors
* 1 to 2 sizes
* Price (greater than 1000 if pricey)
* Included Quantity when ordering one item.';

--This makes the assumption that colors are unique
--for a catalog entry.
CREATE TABLE SiDBCatalogEntryColor (
siDBCatalogEntryColorID NUMBER(9) NOT NULL,
colorID         NUMBER(4) NOT NULL,
PRIMARY KEY (siDBCatalogEntryColorID, colorID),
FOREIGN KEY (siDBCatalogEntryColorID)
REFERENCES SiDBCatalogEntry
--Defer the constraint until the commit.
INITIALLY DEFERRED DEFERRABLE
);

--This makes the assumption that sizes are unique
--for a catalog entry.
CREATE TABLE SiDBCatalogEntrySize (
siDBCatalogEntrySizeID NUMBER(9) NOT NULL,
sizeID          NUMBER(4) NOT NULL,
PRIMARY KEY (siDBCatalogEntrySizeID, sizeID),
FOREIGN KEY (siDBCatalogEntrySizeID)
REFERENCES SiDBCatalogEntry
--Defer the constraint until the commit.
INITIALLY DEFERRED DEFERRABLE
);
```

Listing 24.22 implements the `siDBCatalogEntryTypeID` column values as two picklist values. Picklists are described in Section 22.2.2.3.

**LISTING 24.22**  An Implementation of the `siDBCatalogEntryTypeID` Value Space

```
--Insert the siDBCatalogEntryType
INSERT INTO PicklistDomain
(picklistDomainID, name, description)
VALUES
(9, 'SiDBCatalogEntryType',
'The type of siDBCatalogEntryType this represents.');

INSERT INTO Picklist
(picklistID, picklistDomainID, name)
VALUES
(26, 9, 'siDBCatalogEntryType');

INSERT INTO Picklist
(picklistID, picklistDomainID, name)
VALUES
(27, 9, 'siDBPriceyCatalogEntryType');
COMMIT;
```

The triggers in Listings 24.17 and 24.18 and the discussion about them remain unchanged.

The XML representation of an element type whose structure type is `siDBPriceyCatalogEntryType` might look like the following element:

```
<xsd:element name="siDBPriceyCatalogEntry" type="siDBPriceyCatalogEntryType"/>
```

Given the preceding element type, the following element is valid in a corresponding XML instance:

```
<siDBPriceyCatalogEntry>
 <partName>Diamond Studded Shovel</partName>
 <partNumber>AB1205</partNumber>
 <color>black</color>
 <size>large</size>
 <manufacturerInfo>
   <name>Elbonia Industries</name>
   <telephoneNumber>303-555-1212</telephoneNumber>
   <contact>Mr. Anderson</contact>
 </manufacturerInfo>
 <price>4995.00</price>
 <includedQuantity>1</includedQuantity>
</siDBPriceyCatalogEntry>
```

Listing 24.23 maps the preceding XML instance to a database representation.

**LISTING 24.23** Inserting a Restricted Catalog Entry XML Instance into the Database

```
SET CONSTRAINTS ALL deferred;

INSERT INTO SiDBCatalogEntryColor
(siDBCatalogEntryColorID, colorID)
VALUES
(Seq_siDBCatalogEntry.NEXTVAL, 12);

INSERT INTO SiDBCatalogEntrySize
(siDBCatalogEntrySizeID, sizeID)
VALUES
(Seq_siDBCatalogEntry.CURRVAL, 24);

INSERT INTO SiDBBusiness
(siDBBusinessID, name, telephoneNumber, contact)
VALUES
(Seq_SiDBBusiness.NEXTVAL, 'Elbonia Industries',
'303-555-1212', 'Mr. Anderson');

INSERT INTO SiDBCatalogEntry
(siDBCatalogEntryID, siDBCatalogEntryTypeID, partName,
partNumber, description, manufacturerID, price,
includedQuantity)
VALUES
(Seq_siDBCatalogEntry.CURRVAL, 27, ' Diamond Studded Shovel',
'AB1204', NULL, Seq_SiDBBusiness.CURRVAL, 4995.00,
1);

COMMIT;
```

### 24.16.1 base Attribute
The base attribute specifies the complexType that is being restricted.

### 24.16.2 id Attribute
Refer to Section 24.5.1.4 for design and implementation issues.

## 24.17 extension Element

The extension element is used to derive a complexType from another by adding attribute types for simple content and element types for complex content. A database designer has two major options in designing a schema to create an extension:

- Add a type column to a table and handle the extensions in check clauses and triggers that key off of the type column. In other words, add the type to the existing set of tables.
- Create a new table (or tables) to handle the new type.

Each of these approaches has trade-offs. The first approach is best when the `extension` element type is associated with content that is mapped to a couple of database columns and not relationships. It best handles the simple cases of `extension` element types. The second approach is best when there are more than a couple of additional columns or an additional relationship is required to another table. It is an easy way to extend an existing database with minimal effect on the existing applications that do not use the `extension` element type.

Listing 24.24 implements `siDBExtendedBusinessType`, which is derived by extension from `siDBBusinessType`. It also implements the `siDBExtendedCatalogEntryType`, which is meant to be used in conjunction with `siDBCatalogEntryType` to provide additional element types. The following set of examples is derived from the examples in Section 24.14.

**LISTING 24.24** A `siDBExtendedCatalogEntryType` XML Schema Document Fragment and `siDBExtendedBusinessType` XML Schema Document Fragment Derived by Extension from `siDBBusinessType`

```
<xsd:complexType name="siDBBusinessType"
        id="siDBBusinessType.catalog.cType">
 <xsd:annotation>
   <xsd:documentation xml:lang="en">
     A very simple entry for a business that
     provides enough catalog entry information.
        -- Shorthand Notation --
   </xsd:documentation>
 </xsd:annotation>
 <xsd:sequence id="manu-seq">
   <xsd:element name="name" type="xsd:string"/>
   <xsd:element name="telephoneNumber" type="xsd:string"/>
   <xsd:element name="contact" type="xsd:string"/>
 </xsd:sequence>
</xsd:complexType>

<xsd:complexType name="siDBExtendedBusinessType"
        id="siDBExtBusinessType.catalog.cType">
 <xsd:annotation>
   <xsd:documentation xml:lang="en">
     A very simple add-on to siDBBusinessType
     that provides a fax and email.
        -- Shorthand Notation --
   </xsd:documentation>
 </xsd:annotation>
```

```xml
<xsd:sequence id="manu-seq">
  <xsd:element name="faxNumber" type="xsd:string"/>
  <xsd:element name="emailaddress" type="xsd:anyURI"/>
</xsd:sequence>
</xsd:complexType>

<xsd:complexType name="siDBCatalogEntryType"
        id="siDBCatalogEntryType.catalog.cType">
  <xsd:annotation>
    <xsd:documentation xml:lang="en">
      A catalog entry must have:
        * A database ID
        * Part Name
        * Part Number
        * Description (optional)
        * 0 to 4 colors
        * 1 to 2 sizes
        * Price
        * Included Quantity when ordering
          one item.
        -- Shorthand Notation --
    </xsd:documentation>
  </xsd:annotation>
  <xsd:sequence id="siDB-cat-entry-type-seq">
    <xsd:element name="partName" type="xsd:string"/>
    <xsd:element name="partNumber" type="xsd:token"/>
    <xsd:element name="description"
          type="xsd:string"
          minOccurs="0"
          maxOccurs="1"/>
    <xsd:element name="color"
          type="colorOptionType"
          minOccurs="1"
          maxOccurs="4"/>
    <xsd:element name="size"
          type="sizeOptionType"
          minOccurs="1"
          maxOccurs="2"/>
    <xsd:element name="manufacturerInfo"
          type="siDBBusinessType"/>
    <xsd:element name="price" >
      <xsd:simpleType>
        <xsd:restriction base="xsd:decimal">
          <xsd:minInclusive value="0.00"/>
          <xsd:totalDigits value="6"/>
          <xsd:fractionDigits value="2"/>
        </xsd:restriction>
```

*continues*

```
          </xsd:simpleType>
        </xsd:element>
        <xsd:element name="includedQuantity"
              type="xsd:nonNegativeInteger"/>
    </xsd:sequence>
</xsd:complexType>

<xsd:complexType name="siDBExtendedCatalogEntryType"
      id="siDBExtendedCatalogEntryType.catalog.cType">
  <xsd:annotation>
    <xsd:documentation xml:lang="en">
      An extended catalog entry must have:
        * A database ID
        * Part Name
        * Part Number
        * Description (optional)
        * 0 to 4 colors
        * 1 to 2 sizes
        * Price
        * Included Quantity when ordering
          one item.
      AND
        * JPEG Photo (no lossiness)
        * MP3 Movie
        * URL for catalog entry
        * an extended business description.
    </xsd:documentation>
  </xsd:annotation>
  <xsd:complexContent id="secet.cc">
    <xsd:extension base="siDBCatalogEntryType">
      <xsd:sequence id="siDB-ext-cat-entry-type-seq">
        <xsd:element name="extendedManufacturerInfo"
             type="siDBExtendedBusinessType"/>
        <xsd:element name="JPEGPicture"
                type="xsd:hexBinary"/>
        <xsd:element name="MP3Movie"
                type="xsd:hexBinary"/>
        <xsd:element name="partURL"
                type="xsd:anyURI"/>
      </xsd:sequence>
    </xsd:extension>
  </xsd:complexContent>
</xsd:complexType>
```

Listing 24.25 maps `siDBBusinessType`, `siDBExtendedBusinessType`, `siDBCatalogEntryType`, and `siDBExtendedCatalogEntryType` to a database implementation that involves five tables.

siDBBusinessType and siDBExtendedBusinessType both map to the SiDBBusiness table. siDBCatalogEntryType maps to SiDBCatalogEntry and to two child tables: SiDBCatalogEntryColor and SiDBCatalogEntrySize. siDBExtendedCatalogEntryType maps to the SiDBExtendedCatalogEntry table.

The child tables of SiDBCatalogEntry allow multiple colors and sizes. The SiDBCatalogEntry table also has a foreign key relationship to the SiDBBusiness table to show that the manufacturer is independent of a particular catalog entry. The foreign key constraints in the SiDBCatalogEntryColor table and the SiDBCatalogEntrySize table are deferred to allow the foreign key constraint to be checked only when a commit is being attempted. The SiDBExtendedCatalogEntry table has a foreign primary key from the SiDBCatalogEntry table.

**LISTING 24.25**  DatabaseTables Implementing the siDBBusinessType, siDBCatalogEntryType, and siDBExtendedCatalogEntryType Types

```
--Start the sequence at 1, don't let it cycle, and have
--the numbers in the sequence ordered.
CREATE SEQUENCE Seq_SiDBBusiness INCREMENT BY 1 START
 WITH 1 MAXVALUE 999999999 MINVALUE 1 NOCYCLE ORDER;

--The table's primary key is from the sequence.
CREATE TABLE SiDBBusiness (
siDBBusinessID    NUMBER(9)     NOT NULL,
--new type column which is a picklist entry.
siDBBusinessTypeID NUMBER(4)    NOT NULL,
name              VARCHAR2(100) NOT NULL,
telephoneNumber   VARCHAR2(30)  NOT NULL,
contact           VARCHAR2(100) NOT NULL,
faxNumber         VARCHAR2(30)  NULL,
emailaddress      VARCHAR2(255) NULL,
PRIMARY KEY (siDBBusinessID),
--Add a new check to ensure that the
--faxNumber and emailAddress are required
--when this is an extended business type.
-- 30 = 'siDBExtendedBusinessType'
CHECK((siDBBusinessTypeID = 30 AND
    faxNumber IS NOT NULL AND
    emailaddress IS NOT NULL) OR
    siDBBusinessTypeID <> 30)
);

--Add a table comment to match the annotation.
COMMENT ON TABLE SiDBBusiness IS
'A very simple entry for a business that
provides enough catalog entry information.';
```

*continues*

## Data-oriented Schemas: Complex Types
### CHAPTER 24

```sql
--Start the sequence at 1, don't let it cycle, and have
--the numbers in the sequence ordered.
CREATE SEQUENCE Seq_siDBCatalogEntry INCREMENT BY 1 START
  WITH 1 MAXVALUE 999999999 MINVALUE 1 NOCYCLE ORDER;

--The table's primary key is from the sequence.
CREATE TABLE SiDBCatalogEntry (
siDBCatalogEntryID    NUMBER(9) NOT NULL,
--new type column which is a picklist entry.
siDBCatalogEntryTypeID NUMBER(4) NOT NULL,
partName              VARCHAR2(100) NOT NULL,
partNumber            VARCHAR2(30) NOT NULL
--partNumber is a token.
CHECK (INSTR(partNumber, UNISTR('\000D')) = 0 AND
    INSTR(partNumber, UNISTR('\000A')) = 0 AND
    INSTR(partNumber, UNISTR('\0009')) = 0 AND
    LENGTH(partNumber) =
      LENGTH(TRIM(partNumber)) AND
    INSTR(partNumber, ' ') = 0),
description           VARCHAR2(255) NULL,
manufacturerID        NUMBER(9) NOT NULL,
price                 NUMBER(6,2) NOT NULL
CHECK(price >= 0),
includedQuantity      NUMBER(3) NOT NULL
CHECK(includedQuantity >= 0),
PRIMARY KEY (siDBCatalogEntryID),
FOREIGN KEY (manufacturerID)
REFERENCES SiDBBusiness
);

--Add a table comment to match the annotation.
COMMENT ON TABLE SiDBCatalogEntry IS
'A catalog entry must have:
* A database ID
* Part Name
* Part Number
* Description (optional)
* 0 to 4 colors
* 1 to 2 sizes
* Price
* Included Quantity when ordering one item.
* an extended business description.';

CREATE TABLE SiDBExtendedCatalogEntry (
siDBExtCatalogEntryID NUMBER(9) NOT NULL,
JPEGPicture           CLOB NOT NULL,
MP3Movie              CLOB NOT NULL,
partURL               VARCHAR2(2000) NOT NULL,
```

```
PRIMARY KEY (siDBExtCatalogEntryID),
FOREIGN KEY (siDBExtCatalogEntryID)
REFERENCES SiDBCatalogEntry
);

--Add a table comment to match the annotation.
COMMENT ON TABLE SiDBExtendedCatalogEntry IS
'An extended catalog entry must have:
* JPEG Photo
* MP3 Movie
* URL for catalog entry';

--This makes the assumption that colors are unique
--for a catalog entry.
CREATE TABLE SiDBCatalogEntryColor (
siDBCatalogEntryColorID NUMBER(9) NOT NULL,
colorID         NUMBER(4) NOT NULL,
PRIMARY KEY (siDBCatalogEntryColorID, colorID),
FOREIGN KEY (siDBCatalogEntryColorID)
REFERENCES SiDBCatalogEntry
--Defer the constraint until the commit.
INITIALLY DEFERRED DEFERRABLE
);

--This makes the assumption that sizes are unique
--for a catalog entry.
CREATE TABLE SiDBCatalogEntrySize (
siDBCatalogEntrySizeID NUMBER(9) NOT NULL,
sizeID          NUMBER(4) NOT NULL,
PRIMARY KEY (siDBCatalogEntrySizeID, sizeID),
FOREIGN KEY (siDBCatalogEntrySizeID)
REFERENCES SiDBCatalogEntry
--Defer the constraint until the commit.
INITIALLY DEFERRED DEFERRABLE
);
```

Listing 24.26 implements the `siDBCatalogEntryTypeID` column values as two picklist values and the `siDBBusinessTypeID` column values as two picklist values as well. Picklists are described in Section 22.2.2.3.

**LISTING 24.26** An Implementation of the `siDBCatalogEntryTypeID` and `siDBBusinessTypeID` Value Space

```
--Insert the siDBCatalogEntryType
INSERT INTO PicklistDomain
(picklistDomainID, name, description)
VALUES
```

*continues*

```
(9, 'SiDBCatalogEntryType',
'The type of siDBCatalogEntryType this represents.');

INSERT INTO Picklist
(picklistID, picklistDomainID, name)
VALUES
(26, 9, 'siDBCatalogEntryType');

INSERT INTO Picklist
(picklistID, picklistDomainID, name)
VALUES
(28, 9, 'siDBExtendedCatalogEntryType');

--Insert the siDBBusinessType
INSERT INTO PicklistDomain
(picklistDomainID, name, description)
VALUES
(10, 'SiDBBusinessType',
'The type of siDBBusinessType this represents.');

INSERT INTO Picklist
(picklistID, picklistDomainID, name)
VALUES
(29, 10, 'siDBBusinessType');

INSERT INTO Picklist
(picklistID, picklistDomainID, name)
VALUES
(30, 10, 'siDBExtendedBusinessType');
COMMIT;
```

The triggers in Listings 24.17 and 24.18 and the discussion about them remain unchanged.

The XML representation of an element type whose structure type is `siDBExtendedCatalogEntryType` might look like the following element:

```
<xsd:element name="siDBExtendedCatalogEntry"
type="siDBExtendedCatalogEntryType"/>
```

Given the preceding element type, the following element is valid in a corresponding XML instance:

```
<siDBExtendedCatalogEntry>
 <partName>Diamond Studded Shovel</partName>
 <partNumber>AB1205</partNumber>
 <color>black</color>
 <size>large</size>
 <manufacturerInfo>
```

```
  <name>Elbonia Industries</name>
  <telephoneNumber>303-555-1212</telephoneNumber>
  <contact>Mr. Anderson</contact>
</manufacturerInfo>
<extendedManufacturerInfo>
  <faxNumber>303-555-0000</faxNumber>
  <emailaddress>anderson@elboniaindustries.com</emailaddress>
</extendedManufacturerInfo>
<price>4995.00</price>
<includedQuantity>1</includedQuantity>
<JPEGPicture>DE12CE90</JPEGPicture>
<MP3Movie>AB12CD80</MP3Movie>
<partURL>www.elboniaindustries.com?partNumber=AB1205</partURL>
</siDBExtendedCatalogEntry>
```

Listing 24.27 maps the preceding XML instance to a database representation.

**LISTING 24.27** Inserting a Catalog Entry XML Instance into the Database

```
SET CONSTRAINTS ALL deferred;

INSERT INTO SiDBCatalogEntryColor
(siDBCatalogEntryColorID, colorID)
VALUES
(Seq_siDBCatalogEntry.NEXTVAL, 12);

INSERT INTO SiDBCatalogEntrySize
(siDBCatalogEntrySizeID, sizeID)
VALUES
(Seq_siDBCatalogEntry.CURRVAL, 24);

INSERT INTO SiDBBusiness
(siDBBusinessID, siDBBusinessTypeID, name,
telephoneNumber, contact, faxNumber, emailaddress)
VALUES
(Seq_SiDBBusiness.NEXTVAL, 30, 'Elbonia Industries',
'303-555-1212', 'Mr. Anderson', '303-555-0000',
'anderson@elboniaindustries.com');

INSERT INTO SiDBCatalogEntry
(siDBCatalogEntryID, siDBCatalogEntryTypeID, partName,
partNumber, description, manufacturerID, price,
includedQuantity)
VALUES
(Seq_siDBCatalogEntry.CURRVAL, 28, ' Diamond Studded Shovel',
'AB1204', NULL, Seq_SiDBBusiness.CURRVAL, 4995.00,
1);
```

*continues*

```
INSERT INTO SiDBExtendedCatalogEntry
(siDBExtCatalogEntryID, JPEGPicture, MP3Movie, partURL)
VALUES
(Seq_siDBCatalogEntry.CURRVAL, 'DE12CE90',
'AB12CD80', 'www.elboniaindustries.com?partNumber=AB1205');

COMMIT;
```

### 24.17.1  base Attribute

The base attribute specifies the complexType that is being extended.

### 24.17.2  id Attribute

Refer to Section 24.5.1.4 for design and implementation issues.

# A Case Study: The Campus Resource and Scheduling System (CRSS)

## PART VI

Part VI is a complete case study. The case study is the Campus Resource and Scheduling System (CRSS). XML, and of course the supporting XML schema, is the transport to query a server. XML is also the transport to serialize the response. The case study uses Microsoft technology: SQL 2000, the .NET Framework, XDR Schemas, IIS, and VB.

- Chapter 25 introduces the requirements. In addition, this chapter suggests some possible approaches at a granular level (e.g., Java/Apache versus a Microsoft solution). This chapter provides a rationale for the selected framework, while noting that any framework easily supports the requirements.

- Chapter 26 discusses the specific approach to implementing CRSS. This discussion includes which technologies implement the client and server tiers. This chapter also provides the XML Schemas that are the contractual interfaces for the software.

- Chapter 27 covers creation of database tables in SQL 2000 using an XDR schema.

- Chapter 28 provides detailed examples of the very simple VB code that implements CRSS. This chapter also has a number of figures that demonstrate the integrated solution.

# The Business Case

**CHAPTER 25**

## IN THIS CHAPTER

25.1 Basic CRSS Flow    758

25.2 CRSS Requirements    759

25.3 System Users    759

25.4 Extensible Style Language Transform (XSLT)    764

25.5 SQL 2000 XML Capabilities    767

25.6 CRSS Technical Architecture    770

25.7 Summary    771

You have looked at specific features of the Schema Recommendation. This section focuses on applying XML schemas in an actual case study. Obviously a case study involves the integration of many technologies. No one book could hope to cover all the tools and technologies you need to use. The focus here is on using XML schemas in designing a complete system. The purpose of the case study is to provide an opportunity to weave the discrete pieces of knowledge into an integrated tapestry.

This chapter shows how to use XML schemas in the design of a system, building a campus resource and scheduling system (CRSS). This system should meet several criteria:

- Users should be able to access the system by using the Web.
- The system easily adapts to PDAs and other wireless technologies.
- XML schemas should be used to validate all user interaction with the system.
- Database interaction should occur by using XML schemas to map XML data to relational tables automatically.

## 25.1 Basic CRSS Flow

Creating the CRSS system requires that you understand the workflow. The workflow is usually derived from sequence diagrams. The following steps outline the basic workflow that the CRSS system will use.

1. User requests various actions from the system.
2. Requester is validated via a security component.
3. Request is fulfilled by a database query.
4. Response is formatted to render correctly on user's Web device.

The system uses XML technologies extensively. The user's request is converted to XML. Required processing from that point forward is conducted by using XML messages. Obviously you need to apply XML schemas to the messages and database interface to validate the input message and provide correct results.

The CRSS application illustrates the following techniques:

- Using XML messaging between all three tiers
- Using XML schemas to validate the data at each tier
- Mapping XML hierarchical data into relational tables by using Microsoft's SQL 2000
- Using XSLT to dynamically render the client views
- Creating Web Services that can be called from ASP.NET or directly from XML-compliant devices

## 25.2 CRSS Requirements

Establishing requirements can be done using many different techniques. The CRSS application requirements are captured using UML sequence diagrams. Sequence diagrams provide an industry standard way to capture messages between objects. Identifying messages between the client and server tier is essential. Each message represents an XML message with various datatypes that will need to be validated using schemas.

### 25.2.1 Frameworks

Frameworks provide class libraries that allow applications to be developed faster. Most Web-based applications use either the Java framework or Microsoft's .NET Framework. Using a framework allows software developers to focus an application's business logic rather than its plumbing.

You could begin designing the CRSS system and determine what framework to use later. In general, this is a good approach; however, only two choices exist:

- Microsoft's .NET Framework
- Sun's J2EE Java-based framework

Both frameworks have pros and cons. Many books and articles have been written debating these points, but this one bypasses the entire discussion and uses Microsoft's .NET Framework, for two reasons. First, Microsoft has completely replaced its core technology (Component Object Model, COM) with .NET, which uses XML as its foundation. Second, Microsoft SQL Server has some interesting support for XML schemas that you will use.

> **NOTE**
>
> The techniques you learn in this case study can be easily applied by using Sun's J2EE framework. Virtually all database vendors are adding XML support. That is the beauty of XML: Using XML technologies minimizes dependencies on a specific vendor's implementation. All vendors can deliver XML solutions.

## 25.3 System Users

Profiling a system's users before jumping into the code is always a good idea. Several types of users want to use this system. Certainly the administration and staff members need to be able to request resource reservations. Only a few people have the right to actually place a confirmation for a reservation. You also want to allow the school community to view resource availability at any time, from any Web-enabled device. Other users need to be authenticated only when they request a reservation. A production application should include internationalization features allowing each user a view that is specific to his or her culture. Our sample application is designed for this contingency but does not implement it.

### 25.3.1 CRSS Scalability

You need to design this system to easily scale for use with small elementary schools and large universities. The same system should run on a single server or on a Web farm. You might even think about selling system usage as a Web Service instead of a stand-alone application. Web Services clearly have significant appeal for smaller schools that have difficulty just keeping their PCs running. Certainly you want to keep all your options open during the initial design.

Web-based applications can scale nicely when using Web farms, assuming that several key design issues are addressed up front. The primary issues are

- State management (sometimes referred to as session management)
- Component-based architecture allowing software to run on one or more servers
- Minimizing of database access

### 25.3.2 CRSS Technologies

Several technologies are needed for creating the CRSS. You first need to model the application and look for common features. All Web-enabled devices connecting with the CRSS have one thing in common: They all pass messages. Your application needs to convert the messages to XML, and your components will all use XML as the common message substrate. You will model the CRSS with use cases and sequence diagrams.

> **NOTE**
>
> The Unified Modeling Language (UML) is an ANSI standard language used to model all phases of a software application. This project focuses on a small subset of the model elements supported by UML. For more information on UML, see *Teach Yourself UML in 24 Hours, Second Edition*.[1]

Use cases provide a simple way to model what the system will do. Use cases have no input about how the system will accomplish its requirements. Figure 25.1 shows an example of a use case.

You might be wondering what UML diagrams have to do with XML schemas. The answer is simple: All user interaction must be regarded as error-prone. These errors have to be trapped and dealt with. One of the biggest challenges to producing reliable software systems has been user input validation and error testing. After all, what is the worst place to have an error in

---

[1] Schmuller, Joseph. *Teach Yourself UML in 24 Hours, Second Edition*. Indianapolis, IN: Sams, 2001.

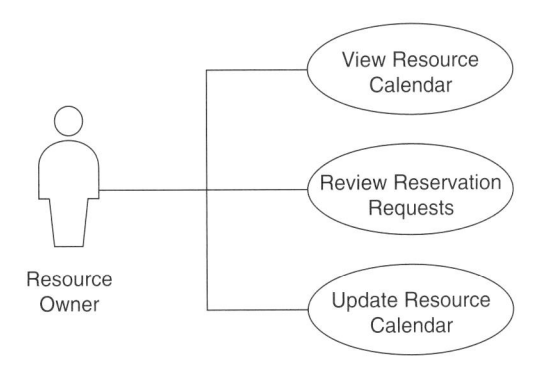

**FIGURE 25.1**  *Resource Owner use case.*

your program? How about in the error handler? That is an easy way to overflow the stack and cause the application to "hang."

### 25.3.2.1 XML Schemas and Testing

The most important reason to use XML schemas is to provide guaranteed results. Certainly a significant trend in software applications today is the emergence of XML-based Web Services. When you are designing a new system architecture that will use Web Services, you are really defining interfaces. XML schemas are the essential ingredient required to guarantee that all consumers of the service are abiding by the interface definition.

Imagine that you are building a system that is only a piece of the total system. You might build a Web Service that simply provides a calendar function for the CRSS system to use. How do you stipulate what your interface requirements are? The need to specify interfaces using standards is a requirement when using Web Services. Each interface must be defined using an XML schema. Prior to XML Schema, the following popular protocols relied on custom interfaces:

- Java's Remote Method Invocation (RMI)
- Microsoft's Distributed Component Object Model (DCOM/COM) conventions
- A custom application programming interface (API)
- Common Object Request Broker Architecture (CORBA)
- The protocols mentioned are all popular, but over the next few years the Simple Object Access Protocol (SOAP) will grow in popularity and become the dominant approach to multi-tier, component-based software architecture. SOAP messages require validation for components to properly process them. SOAP services must also be advertised using Internet standards. Again, XML Schema is used to create the Web Services Description Language (WSDL).
- An example of a SOAP message is shown in Listing 25.1. Note the use of the XML Schema namespace. This listing is provided to illustrate the importance of XML Schema

to Web Services. When designing the CRSS application it is helpful to think of each component as a small Web Service.

**LISTING 25.1**  SOAP Message to Return Calendar Range

```xml
<?xml version="1.0" encoding="utf-8"?>
<soap:Envelope
xmlns:xsi="http://www.w3.org/2001/XMLSchema-instance"
xmlns:xsd="http://www.w3.org/2001/XMLSchema"
xmlns:soap="http://schemas.xmlsoap.org/soap/envelope/">
<soap:Body>
    <showSchedule xmlns="http://www.sams.com/schemasUnleased/">
        <xRange>
            <getCalendar>
                <resource id="201" name="Main Gymnasium">
                    <range startMonth="1" endMonth="1"
                     startDate="2" endDate="5" />
                </resource>
            </getCalendar>
        </xRange>
    </showSchedule>
</soap:Body>
</soap:Envelope>
```

> **NOTE**
>
> The Simple Object Access Protocol (SOAP) standard allows object methods to be accessed regardless of the platform they are on. The key requirement is to format the message by using XML. A full discussion of SOAP is beyond the scope of this book. Some excellent references are *Building Web Services with Java: Making Sense of XML, SOAP, WSDL and UDDI*[2] or *Microsoft .NET XML Web Services*.[3]

Listing 25.1 shows the use of the XML Schema namespace in the SOAP message. When the message is received, the input can be validated by using a custom XML schema to ensure that the rules you stipulate for your calendar method input messages are followed so that your service will always respond successfully to a service request. Success in this case means returning

---

[2] Graham, Steve, et al. *Building Web Services with Java: Making Sense of XML, SOAP, WSDL and UDDI*. Indianapolis, IN: Sams, 2001.

[3] Tabor, Robert. *Microsoft .NET XML Web Services*. Indianapolis, IN: Sams, 2002.

the desired date range or a message indicating that the range is not available. Web Services using schemas can provide the same level of reliability as database transactions.

Using the SOAP message shown in Listing 25.1, we can take this discussion one step further. You might think, "I am not going to make a simple calendar service—I am building complete systems." If you are using any of the frameworks popular today, you will be creating your system from components. Depending on the framework, each piece is called a *bean* or a component—but that is insignificant. Odds are good that you are not doing all the work yourself, so how do you make sure other developers create components that meet your requirements? You guessed it: by using an XML schema to describe and validate the inputs and outputs. This lets you interoperate on software development projects and guarantee the outcome. That is something you rarely hear in software engineering: *guarantee*!

Each message from the client can be easily converted to XML. Converting the message from HTTP or WAP to XML provides a standard interface to all business components. Listing 25.2 illustrates a typical reservation message converted to XML.

**LISTING 25.2** XML Message to Return Calendar Range

```
<?xml version="1.0" encoding="utf-8"?>
<getCalendar>
    <resource id="201" name="Main Gymnasium">
        <range startMonth="1" endMonth="1"
               startDate="2" endDate="5"/>
    </resource>
</getCalendar>
```

It's easy to see that Listing 25.2 is simply a subset of Listing 25.1. This technique works great when you are calling custom components within your own application. When component *A* calls component *B* within the same application, no SOAP overhead is required. However, you still might want to test and validate each component by using an XML schema. In fact, you need the XML schema defined before you can code the component successfully.

Listing 25.3 is a simple XML schema document that describes the `getCalendar` XML message shown in Listing 25.2.

**LISTING 25.3** XML Schema to Validate `getCalendar` Inputs

```
<?xml version="1.0" encoding="UTF-8"?>
<xsd:schema xmlns:xsd="http://www.w3.org/2001/XMLSchema"
                        elementFormDefault="qualified">
    <xsd:element name="getCalendar">
        <xsd:complexType>
            <xsd:sequence>
```

```
                <xsd:element name="resource"
                             type="resourceType"/>
            </xsd:sequence>
        </xsd:complexType>
    </xsd:element>
    <xsd:complexType name="rangeType">
        <xsd:attribute name="startMonth" type="xsd:int"
                       use="required"/>
        <xsd:attribute name="endMonth" type="xsd:int"
                       use="required"/>
        <xsd:attribute name="startDate" type="xsd:int"
                       use="required"/>
        <xsd:attribute name="endDate" type="xsd:int"
                       use="required"/>
    </xsd:complexType>
    <xsd:complexType name="resourceType">
        <xsd:sequence>
            <xsd:element name="range" type="rangeType"/>
        </xsd:sequence>
        <xsd:attribute name="id" type="xsd:int"
                       use="required"/>
        <xsd:attribute name="name" type="xsd:string"
                       use="required"/>
    </xsd:complexType>
</xsd:schema>
```

The root element type, `getCalendar`, must contain one subelement, a `resource`, which has its structure type specified as `resourceType`. As you can see the `resourceType` complex type prescribes a `rangeType` child and two attributes. The `rangeType` complex type is then fully specified by the two complex types. You will apply additional constraints in the actual application as you build it. Further restrictions can be applied by using the regular expression syntax discussed in Chapter 14. Listing 25.3 simply illustrates how you can separate validation logic from code logic.

Testing is paramount when developing component-based, distributed software systems. Until now it has always been done with embedded software that itself was potentially the source of the error. By using XML schemas, you can now easily separate the code from the test case. Designing distributed components using XML for the input argument and XML as the return data type allows you to use XML schemas to develop component test cases.

## 25.4 Extensible Style Language Transform (XSLT)

Another important technology is XSLT. XSLT uses XML to introduce its own processing language. For the CRSS application to work with a myriad of display devices, you obviously need to separate the data from the presentation. XSLT is a vast subject itself, but our CRSS application will certainly require its use.

The advantage of XSLT is that it cleanly separates the data from the view. When designing your application, you can have a graphics artist create the views and then you can simply create the data representation. Obviously, someone must convert the graphics artist's inputs to XSLT. Figure 25.2 provides an architectural example similar to what the CRSS system will use.

As Figure 25.2 shows, the application consists of a user interface broker (`UIBroker`) that processes all Web-based user interaction. The application itself has a broker (`ScheduleBroker`) that receives the incoming requests as XML messages. Extending the system to work with different front ends can be accomplished in one of two ways:

- Create a list of stylesheets for each view. Apply the view by using the `UIBroker`.
- Create a functional mirror of the `UIBroker` for whatever other protocol you need.

The important thing to realize with this approach is that you can easily adapt to changing user-device configurations. This will simplify your needs as you move to support wireless devices.

As you can see in Figure 25.3, the `UIBroker` can easily choose whichever view is correct.

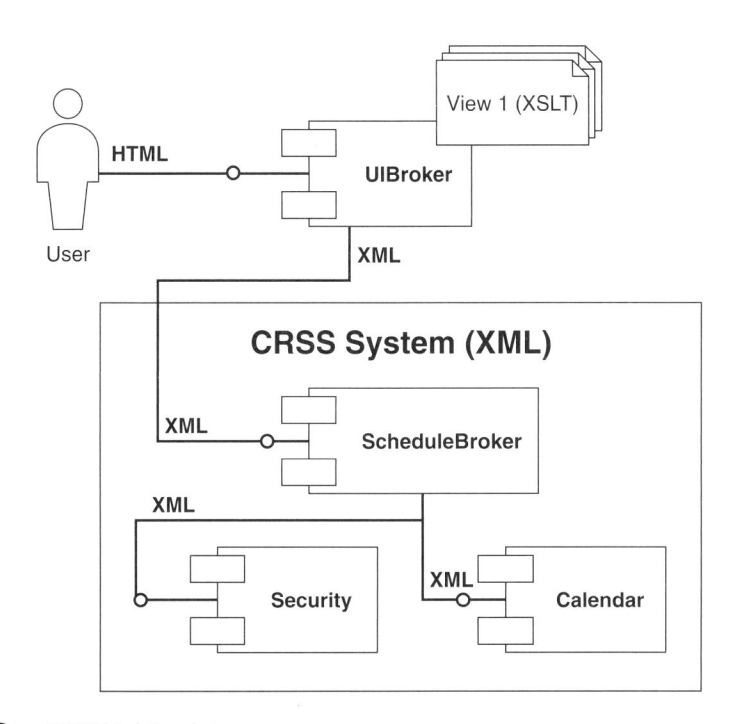

**FIGURE 25.2**  *CRSS high-level view.*

## The Business Case
### Chapter 25

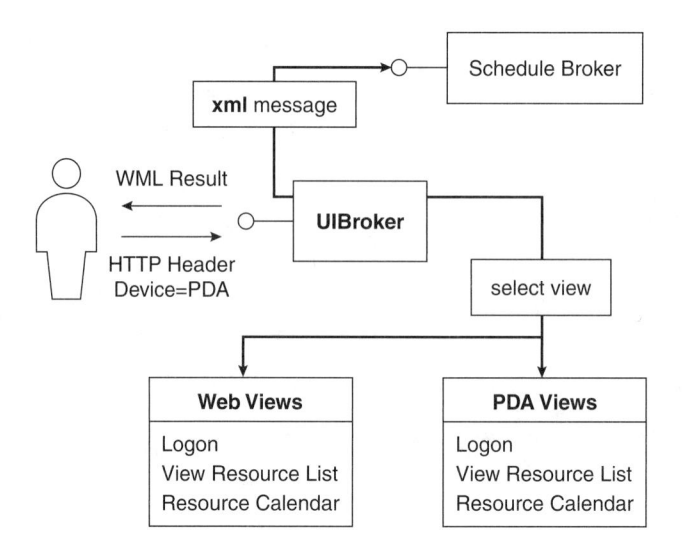

**Figure 25.3** *UIBroker supporting multiple views.*

Obviously, the view is dependent on the user's device type and the application state. You could also extend this architecture to handle multiple languages. You will use XSLT for all views that you provide.

## 25.4.1 Business Uses for XSLT

One area in which XSLT and XML schemas need to work together is transforming XML from one business system to another (Figure 25.4). For example, perhaps you developed the CRSS system to list all resources in use by date and some accounting system needs to use this for billing information later. The accounting system would be developed independently, with its own schema. XSLT is a powerful technology that can be used to transform the CRSS XML schema to meet the requirements of the new accounting XML schema. Microsoft's BizTalk system is a good example. It makes extensive use of XSLT to map schemas from one business system to another.

The other area in which XSLT is extremely important is converting XML hierarchical data to relational data (Figure 25.5). XML schemas are used to map the datatypes, but obviously the flat file structure used by XML must be mapped to the relational structure of databases. This is an important technical conversion because XML data does not replace databases. Relational databases are here to stay and handle concurrency, security, and transactional processes that XML is not designed for.

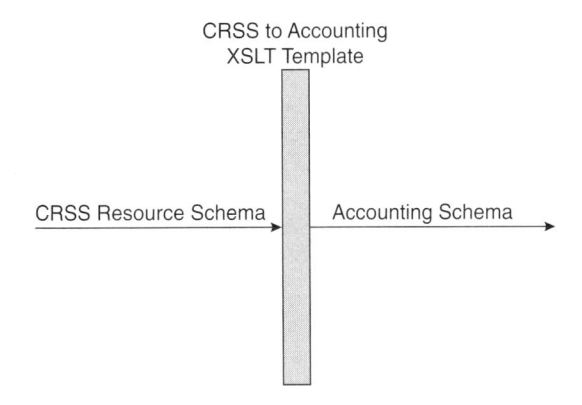

**FIGURE 25.4**  *XSLT business-to-business transformation.*

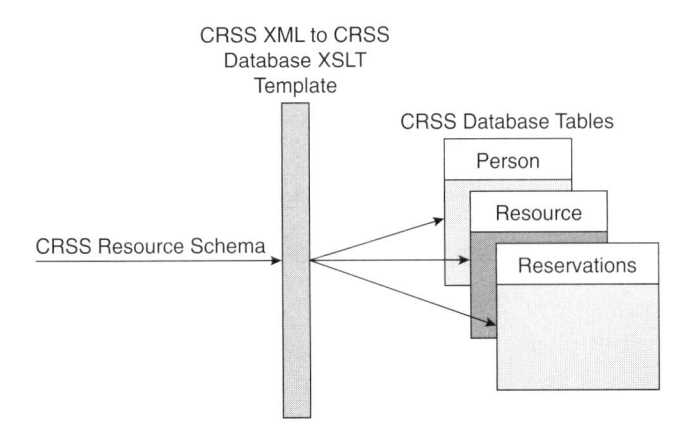

**FIGURE 25.5**  *XSLT database transformation.*

## 25.5 SQL 2000 XML Capabilities

Ultimately, all the CRSS data will reside in a SQL 2000 database. You might wonder why you want to bother with XML at all if the data is still in the database. Using XML in the middle tier allows each of your business components to be completely tested by XML schemas as discussed earlier. Another advantage of XML is performance. Many Web sites require users to access the database server for every request. XML can be queried by using XPath, which often removes the need to contact the database. Obviously, the database will always be needed for transactions or any issue requiring synchronization.

**The Business Case**

**CHAPTER 25**

Microsoft released many XML enhancements with its preview release of SQL version 7. These enhancements, and others, have been incorporated directly into SQL 2000. Specifically, SQL 2000 has the following XML-related features:

- Native XML support
- HTTP accessibility to the database
- Excellent performance for XML template based queries
- Mapping support for XML schemas
- XPath query support
- SOAP-based queries

Now step back and think about the XML integration for a minute. Typically people look at a new feature and think that it must result in a performance hit or be terribly difficult to use. After using SQL 2000's XML features, most people wonder why database access hasn't always been this simple. If you have had experience with Microsoft's Active Server Pages (ASP) or Sun's Java Server Pages (JSP), the design pattern in Figure 25.6 will look familiar.

The approach shown in Figure 25.6 is typical. Developers write a good deal of code that simply converts database data to HTML. Receiving the data as XML allows you to provide whatever view you'd like using XSLT.

Using SQL 2000's XML capabilities can circumvent the process shown in Figure 25.6. SQL 2000 supports a number of XML query types. The simplest way to verify that you have configured your system to allow XML queries is to execute a URL-based query. In general, these queries are not as useful as template queries, but they do allow you to do a quick test by using an XML-enabled browser to verify your setup. Notice the URL shown in Figure 25.7. A simple SQL query is added as a suffix to the URL where the SQL virtual directory for a specific database has been configured.

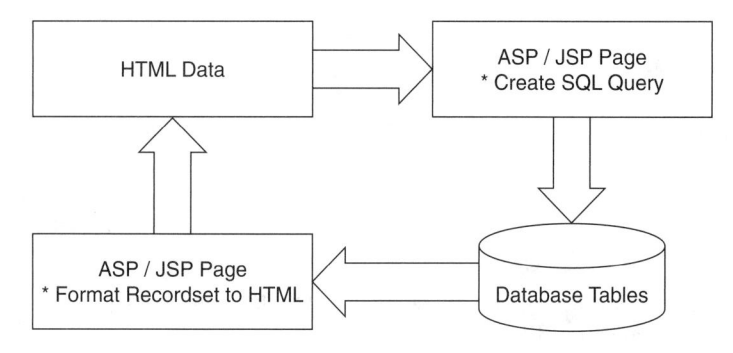

**FIGURE 25.6** *Web-based database access.*

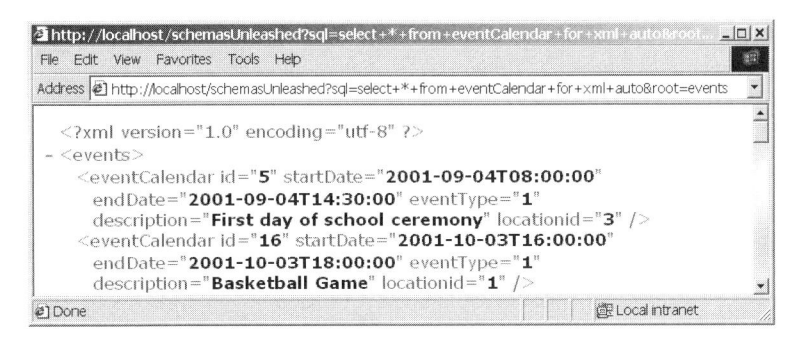

**FIGURE 25.7** *SQL 2000 URL query.*

Template-based queries are more powerful and easier to use. SQL queries can be used in a template-based query—template queries can execute stored procedures, perform parameterized inserts, or simply execute *ad hoc* queries. You can follow these seven simple steps to execute a template-based query:

1. Create a virtual directory accessible to SQL Server by launching the IIS Virtual Directory Management for SQL Server tool. Right-click on the Default Web site and select New Virtual Directory.
2. Add a name for the virtual directory in the dialog box and then browse to the directory where your templates will be stored and set the Local Path.
3. Select the Security tab and enter your logon credentials.
4. Select the Data Source tab, choose the location of your SQL server, and enter the name of the database your templates will be acting on.
5. Select the Settings tab and select the types of URL queries you will allow. Template, XPath, and POST queries are typically selected, although URL queries can be useful for testing.
6. Select the Virtual Names tab and click the New button. Enter a name that will be used to access the template folder, and change the Type to 'template'. Set the path to point to your templates.
7. Apply the settings and close the tool.

After SQL Server is configured you can create a template query and test it. Figure 25.8 shows an example of the template. Place this template in the directory that you created in step 6 above.

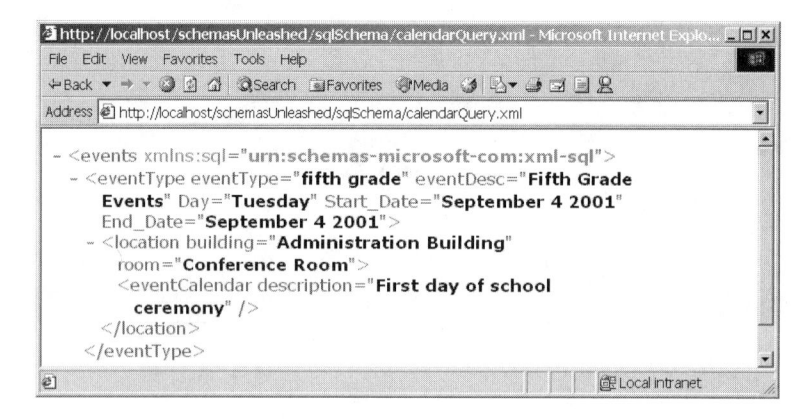

**FIGURE 25.8**  *SQL 2000 template query.*

## 25.6 CRSS Technical Architecture

From a tools perspective, you should add a few additional requirements. Ideally, develop and maintain the application in a team environment. This implies the use of some existing tools and a few new ones. The development environment will use the following tools:

- Visual Studio .NET: http://www.microsoft.com/net/
- XML Spy: http://www.xmlspy.com/
- eXcelon Stylus Studio: http://www.stylusStudio.com
- Schema Validation Service: http://www.w3.org/2001/03/webdata/xsv
- SQL Server 2000: http://www.microsoft.com/sql

These are a few tools that you can use to create the CRSS application. There are other products that can provide the same capabilities.

We have not yet discussed most of these tools. In the next chapter you will begin using some of them as you build the CRSS model and move toward developing the XML schema structure. A quick word about each of these tools is in order at this point.

### 25.6.1 Visual Studio .NET

Visual Studio .NET is Microsoft's premiere software development product. The .NET platform, which relies heavily on XML technologies, can be viewed as a replacement for COM. Think of .NET as a language-independent, platform-dependent development environment, and you will see how to use it as you develop this application. The CRSS application uses Visual Basic .NET, although any language compliant with Microsoft's Common Language Specification (CLS) would work fine.

## 25.6.2 XML Spy

XML Spy is a useful tool for creating XML schemas and test documents. It has the capability to automatically generate sample data from XML schemas, which is useful when testing components.

## 25.6.3 eXcelon Stylus Studio

XSLT templates are not easy to develop or debug. Not many tools are available that feature an integrated debugger and preview mode. eXcelon's Stylus Studio does, and it allows you to test by using whatever XSLT processor you'd like.

## 25.6.4 SQL Validation Service

The URL Schema Validation Service (http://www.w3.org/2001/03/webdata/xsv) lets you test your XML schemas to verify compliance with the final World Wide Web Consortium recommendation. This is useful because many tools on the market today, including those in the preceding list, have compliance problems.

## 25.7 Summary

Now that you've taken a quick look at the various pieces of the puzzle, it's time to look at how to assemble it. You've contrasted existing architectural design patterns with an XML-based approach. Several tools and frameworks have been introduced that will be required for creating the application.

In the next chapter you will begin building the components and look at modeling each of them in further detail.

Here is a review of the high-level system requirements. The CRSS system must allow users to

- Request a resource reservation
- View existing reservations on a per resource basis
- Access the site by using multiple Web-enabled devices

# The Architecture

**CHAPTER 26**

## IN THIS CHAPTER

- 26.1 System Architecture  774
- 26.2 Creating HTML Pages by Using XSLT  795
- 26.3 Sending Form Data  800
- 26.4 Summary  807

In the previous chapter, we introduced a number of technologies that need to work together to create the Campus Resource Scheduling System (CRSS). Now you need to model the pieces of the CRSS system and design an XML-based solution. As you develop this solution, you will integrate the use of XML schemas. Our solution involves components distributed across the three logical tiers, with particular emphasis on the role of XML schemas within each tier.

This chapter covers how to model elements of CRSS. You will use the Unified Modeling Language (UML) to model the system and the interfaces required. Using this information, you will be able to develop the XML schemas required to ensure high-integrity integration across all three tiers. Let us review the CRSS requirements:

- Users can access the system by using the Web.
- The system easily adapts to PDAs and other wireless technologies.
- XML schemas validate all user interaction with the system.
- Database interaction occurs by using XML schemas to map XML data automatically to relational tables.

In this chapter we work with the following technologies:

- Unified Modeling Language (UML)
- Extensible Markup Language (XML)
- XML Schema

## 26.1 System Architecture

Most distributed architectures discuss three tiers in the development of Web-based applications, but the Web Server tier should really be thought of as a separate layer. In fact, as we move closer and closer to Web services this layer might be replaced altogether. Therefore, the layers modeled for the CRSS are:

- Client tier
- Web Server tier
- Application tier
- Database tier

Let's look at each tier and the technologies used today. The Client tier typically consists of HTML and JavaScript for computers and Wireless Markup Language (WML) for PDAs. It is possible to embed many other controls (Shockwave, applets, ActiveX), but we will exclude these plug-in technologies from our application.

The simplest way to model the application is to start with high-level architectural diagrams and then model the tiers one at a time.

The architecture shown in Figure 26.1 has been used in many applications for quite a few years now. In fact, the success of this architecture has accelerated the acceptance and emergence of XML standards.

You might wonder why XML Schema and the other XML concepts should be introduced to the mix illustrated in Figure 26.1. We certainly have enough acronyms without introducing all the X-based ones. You should not start to use all these X technologies without a good justification. Properly justifying the use of XML-based technologies will seem simple if you have already been dealing with some of the following issues:

- HTML browsers do not comply with rigid standards. This might not be a stunning revelation to any Web developer who has been up all night sorting out a Netscape versus Internet Explorer issue. Use XML with XSLT to produce well-formed HTML—or better yet, XHTML.

- The Web Server tier in Figure 26.1 has many competing technologies. Learning all of them is difficult. They are all trying to do the same thing: accept user inputs as HTTP messages and format the output results as HTML or WML. Many applications have misused the Web server layer and placed far too much validation and business logic in it. Maintaining these projects is extremely difficult. The technologies are simplified dramatically if you switch to XML-based technologies and use XML schemas to perform the validation.

- The Component tier is certainly the most interesting. You have the never-ending debate about Java versus anything else. What is frequently lost in this debate is the real purpose of this tier, which is to provide business logic. Business logic is based on data, and XML is tailor-made for manipulating data. By using XML, you can simplify your components by passing XML nodes back and forth. Each node can use an XML schema for its test

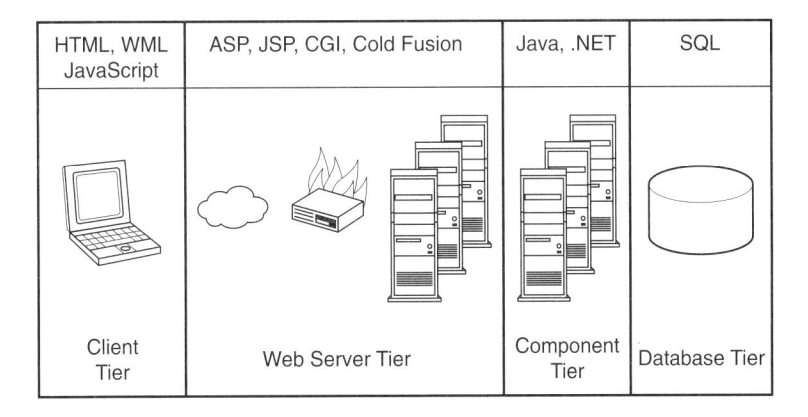

**FIGURE 26.1** *n-Tier architecture.*

case. This eliminates the need to write software to test software—a classic Catch-22. If you ask Web developers how they test an application, they're likely to say they open Netscape and Internet Explorer and verify that the application works. Could you imagine testing a new aircraft wing by installing it on a plane and taking it up for a flight? If it works once, will it work every time? Will it work with all revisions? Obviously, much better test methodology is required.

- The Database tier is a moving target right now. Both Microsoft and Oracle are rapidly adding XML capabilities to their databases. These capabilities enable you to use XML messages to request database actions, eliminating all the formatting required in an Active Server Page/Active Data Object (ASP/ADO) solution or corresponding Java Server Page/Java Database Connectivity (JSP/JDBC) scenario.

> **NOTE**
>
> Microsoft and Oracle are not the only vendors using XML in their database products. IBM, Informix, Sybase, and others are adding similar capabilities.

Our Campus Resource and Schedule System (CRSS) case study uses XML as its foundation, which is illustrated in Figure 26.2. When comparing Figure 26.2 to Figure 26.1, the most striking difference is the reliance on XML across all the tiers.

As you can see from Figure 26.2, XML technologies do not replace HTML, JavaScript, .NET, Java, or SQL. XML simply is used by these technologies to increase their reliability and robustness.

In the model in Figure 26.2, XML schemas are used in two ways:

- Defining interfaces between different processes or tiers
- Validating data

Figure 26.2 shows that the Web tier converts an incoming HTTP request into an XML message. This message is validated against an XML schema. Once you have valid user input, the message is sent to the Component tier where business logic is applied. Database access is also accomplished with XML messages.

The challenge at the database interface is different than at the user interface. You can ensure that your components are producing valid XML in the design of the components, but you need to map the data from an XML source to a relational database format and vice versa. XML schemas can provide the hierarchical to relational mapping, as you will see a bit later.

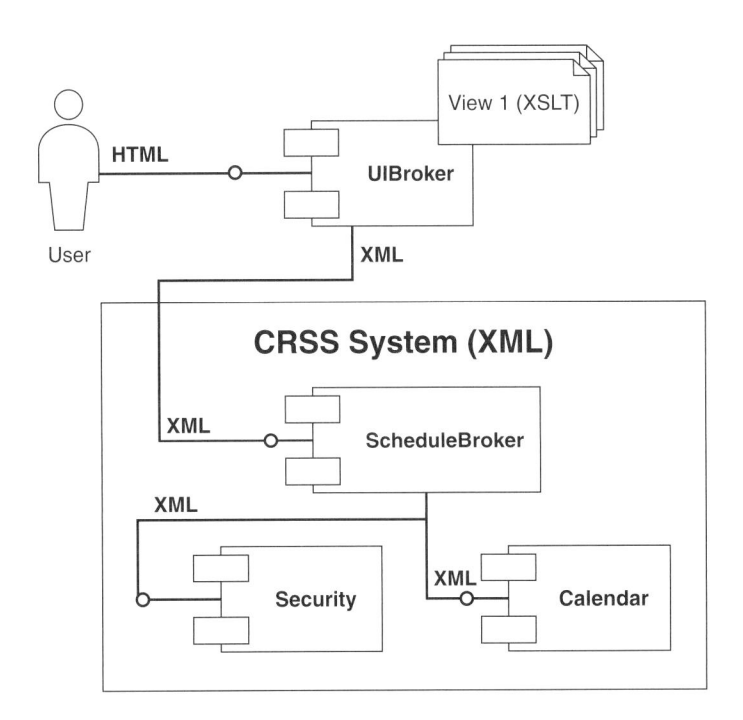

**FIGURE 26.2**  *n-Tier XML architecture.*

Interfaces between all three tiers are simplified when using XML. Testing at all interfaces is accomplished using XML schemas. This ability to test the interfaces declaratively allows software projects to be worked on by teams more easily.

You will begin the CRSS application by modeling the Client tier to the Web Server tier. You will model each requirement by using UML sequence diagrams. Then you will convert each of these sequence diagrams into XML messages. These messages define the workflow of the application.

Let's start by modeling the following requirement: View existing reservations on a per resource basis.

Obviously, user input will be required. You need to support multiple devices, but let's start by assuming a browser interface. As you will see later, implementing the support for any other Web-enabled device is easy. The sequence diagram in Figure 26.3 models the first requirement.

You can see from the sequence diagram in Figure 26.3 that each tier is modeled by an interface. There is a Web interface that can be implemented by using Active Server Pages (ASP), Java Server Pages (JSP), Common Gateway Interface (CGI), or any other Web-server-based

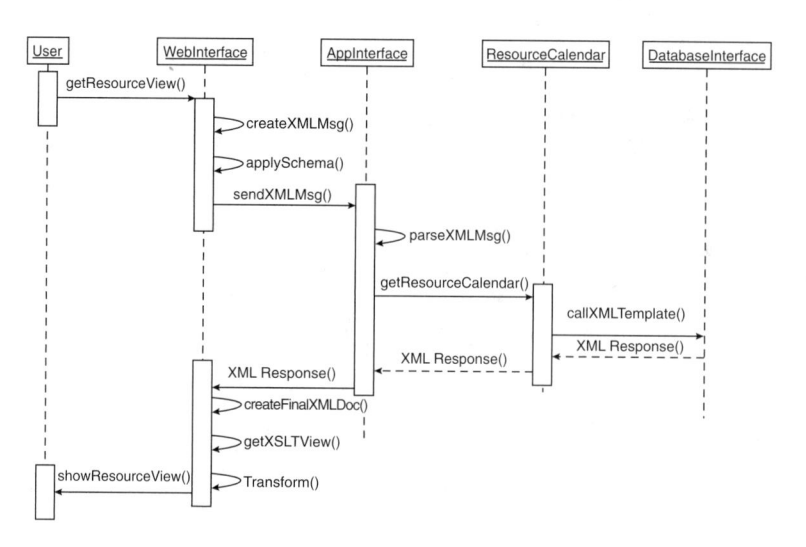

**FIGURE 26.3**  *View Resource Reservation sequence diagram.*

framework. The Web interface does not do any significant processing; its purpose is to support user interaction. This is exactly what you intend. Keep the code in ASP or JSP to an absolute minimum to increase the maintainability of your applications. Simply applying an XML schema provides user-input validation. The parser will throw any validation errors in the repackaged XML data.

You have enough information at this point to decide on the contents of the XML message. The XML message used to request the resource calendar view is shown in Listing 26.1.

**LISTING 26.1**   XML Message to Get Resource Calendar

```xml
<?xml version="1.0" encoding="utf-8"?>
<getResourceCalendar>
        <resource name="bigBuilding">
                <range startMonth="1" endMonth="3" startDay="13"
            endDay="16"/>
        </resource>
</getResourceCalendar>
```

As you can see, the preceding code is a simple XML message created in the Web Client tier. You can use an XML schema to validate this message. The schema provides the contract you have with the input device. Using this model enables us to support Web-based clients or XML-enabled devices. You can use schemas to open your service to the Internet by creating a Web service.

> **NOTE**
>
> The ability to publish schemas on the Internet so your services can be made available to anyone is the basis for Web services. Web Services Description Language (WSDL) uses XML schemas and has been submitted as a possible standard to the W3C. WSDL uses XML schemas to describe your application interfaces and interface definitions.

You need to create the XML schema by using the XML message created in Listing 26.1. You have several ways you could go about creating the XML schema. There are quite a few tools that do a reasonable job; however, no tool can know your business application requirements. Most tools that automatically generate XML schemas produce something similar to the example in Listing 26.2, produced by XML Spy.

**LISTING 26.2**  XML Schema for Resource Calendar Message

```xml
<?xml version="1.0" encoding="UTF-8"?>
<xsd:schema
targetNamespace=
  "http://www.XMLSchemaReference.com/examples/CRSS/
   resourceCalendar"
xmlns:xsd="http://www.w3.org/2001/XMLSchema"
xmlns=
  "http://www.XMLSchemaReference.com/examples/CRSS/
   resourceCalendar"
elementFormDefault="qualified"
attributeFormDefault="unqualified">
  <xsd:element name="getResourceCalendar">
    <xsd:complexType>
      <xsd:sequence>
        <xsd:element ref="resource"/>
      </xsd:sequence>
    </xsd:complexType>
  </xsd:element>
  <xsd:element name="range">
    <xsd:complexType>
      <xsd:attribute name="startMonth" type="xs:int"
            use="required"/>
      <xsd:attribute name="endMonth" type="xs:int"
            use="required"/>
      <xsd:attribute name="startDay" type="xs:int"
            use="required"/>
      <xsd:attribute name="endDay" type="xs:int"
            use="required"/>
```

*continues*

```
      </xs:complexType>
    </xsd:element>
    <xsd:element name="resource">
      <xsd:complexType>
        <xsd:sequence>
          <xsd:element ref="range"/>
        </xsd:sequence>
        <xsd:attribute name="name" type="xs:string"
                  use="required"/>
      </xsd:complexType>
    </xsd:element>
</xsd:schema>
```

Now you have a schema to validate your input message against. You can test this schema by using a plug-in (http://msdn.microsoft.com/downloads) for Internet Explorer that lets you simply right-click on a file and select Validate. You could also use any validating XML parser for this operation. Before you can do any testing, however, you have to associate the XML source with its corresponding schema. You can do that as shown in Listing 26.3.

**LISTING 26.3** Schema Reference Added to Get Resource Calendar Message

```
<?xml version="1.0" encoding="utf-8"?>
<getResourceCalendar
xmlns=
 "http://www.XMLSchemaReference.com/examples/CRSS/calendar"
xmlns:xsi="http://www.w3.org/2001/XMLSchema-instance"
xsi:schemaLocation=
"http://www.XMLSchemaReference.com/examples/CRSS/calendar.xsd">
  <resource name="bigBuilding">
    <range startMonth="1" endMonth="3" startDay="13"
        endDay="16"/>
  </resource>
</getResourceCalendar>
```

Note the custom namespace on the third line. This is a good practice because namespaces provide scope to XML documents. Listing 26.2 defined the namespace, and you use it within XML documents that will be validated by schemas with the same namespace. More information on namespaces can be found in Chapter 3.

Testing the XML schema is very straightforward. You can use any validating parser to load the document. If the document loads with no errors, the XML message is valid relative to the XML schema. Naturally we must make the assumption that the validating parser does not have errors. There are many tools you can use to provide validation. Some of the popular tools are

- XML Spy by Altova (http://www.xmlspy.com)
- Xerces (http://xml.apache.org/xerces-c/)
- .NET from Microsoft (http://msdn.microsoft.com/vstudio)
- IBM's parsers (http://www.alphaworks.ibm.com)

When just doing quick tests, the Internet Explorer plug-in is convenient. Microsoft has a download called `iexmltls.exe` that can be found by following the links at the http://msdn.microsoft.com/xml site. After installing iexmltls.exe you can just add the reference to our XML schema into the XML document and then open the XML document in Internet Explorer. Right-clicking within the document in Internet Explorer provides a menu item to validate. Let's test our document using this test right now.

Performing validation tests using Internet Explorer's plug-in is simple, as shown in Figure 26.4 below. You can see that the document is valid. You can make changes to the XML and verify that the XML schema functions as expected. You should test all the permutations possible, so feel free to experiment.

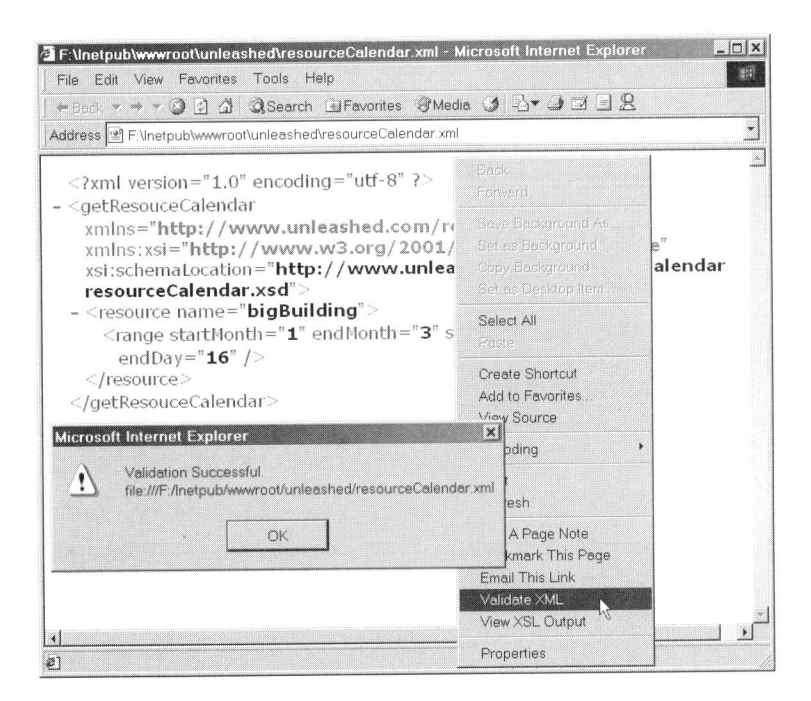

**FIGURE 26.4** *Validation test.*

> **TIP**
>
> The Schema Recommendation is very recent and some areas can be interpreted in different ways. When testing your schemas, you should use the validating parser that will be used in your production environment. Test by using several validating parsers to ensure that the schema design is robust. Check at www.w3.org for additional tools that test XML schema compliance.

## 26.1.1 Client Tier Model Revisited

Technically there is certainly nothing wrong with the XML schema generated in Listing 26.2. In fact, the tools do a great job of getting you started. Unfortunately, that's too often as far as anyone gets with the XML schema design. For XML schemas to provide real power to your projects, you need to take a step back and think about all the datatypes your client application is likely to send. You should then create simple datatypes and include them as needed to create flexible XML schemas. This way you build small, easily tested elements and their corresponding schemas and then aggregate them as needed into a governing document schema on a per document basis.

The following section shows how to

- Identify reusable datatypes
- Create modular XML schemas
- Test modular schemas
- Aggregate the modules into a master XML schema to allow resource reservations

### 26.1.1.1 XML Schema Support for Reusable Datatypes

Obviously the question is how to modularize your schemas to provide a more production-worthy solution. Fortunately, the Schema Recommendation provides techniques to achieve this modularity. The three techniques are

- `include`: Used to include other schema documents that have the same target namespace.
- `import`: Used to refer to components from other namespaces.
- `redefine`: Similar to `include` with the additional option that you can provide new definitions for some or all of the types in the redefined schema document.

Below is an example of the `include` element:

```
<xsd:include schemaLocation= "mySchemaModule.xsd"/>
```

Sometimes you need to override an element definition in an included schema. In object-oriented (OO) programming environments, you would simply inherit from the base class and override the base class's implementation of a specific method. XML schemas borrow from this popular approach through the use of `redefine` elements. Listing 26.4 demonstrates the use of `redefine`. Redefining schemas is useful when you are including large libraries and need to change one or two types. In many cases you will find it more useful to just alter the schema rather than using `redefine`.

**LISTING 26.4** Redefining the `rangeType` Simple Type

```
<xsd:redefine schemaLocation="mySchemaModule.xsd">
<xsd:simpleType name="rangeType">
<xsd:restriction base="xsd:string">
<xsd:maxLength="30"/>
</xsd:restriction>
</xsd:simpleType>
</xsd:redefine>
```

### 26.1.1.2 Identifying Reusable Datatypes

You know how XML Schema lets you reuse and redefine datatypes. Now you need to determine what reusable simple types you need. Modeling each message by using the UML techniques discussed in this chapter identifies your application's required datatypes. The complete design processes required to properly model the application are beyond the scope of this book; however, we do review the sequence diagram you will use to create the XML schema.

You use the desired reservation request XML message to identify the datatypes you would like to create. This approach lets us focus on the XML Schema techniques and illustrate how to create reusable XML schemas. Typically, you start with the UML sequence diagram and then create a sample XML message representing the data required to accomplish the task. The sequence diagram for reserving a resource is shown in Figure 26.5.

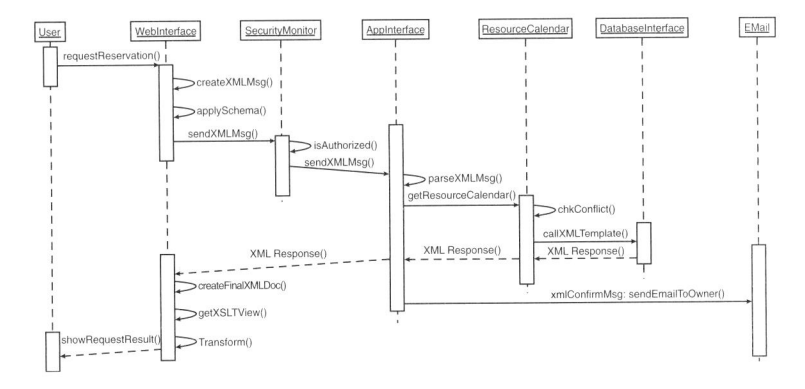

**FIGURE 26.5** *CRSS Reservation Request Sequence diagram.*

In a real system, the sequence diagram would have far more complexity. For our CRSS application, a simple diagram illustrates how the diagrams can assist in creating XML schemas.

Using the sequence diagram in Figure 26.5, you can create a sample XML message that assists in determining the data required to satisfy the request. The sample is in Listing 26.5.

**LISTING 26.5** Reservation Request XML Message

```xml
<?xml version="1.0" encoding="utf-8"?>
<reservation_request>
  <reservation building="Linden Hall" room="Gymnasium"
        start_date="2001-02-23"
        start_time="22:30:00"
        duration="5"
        description="Varsity basketball practice"
        configuration="basketball"/>
  <security>
    <requestor first="Paul"
        last="Lamere"
        email="plamere@bball.com"
        type="coach"/>
  </security>
  <building id="1" name="Linden Hall"
      location="images/linden.gif">
    <room name="Gymnasium" capacity="100">
      <form id="201" name="legal"
          url="forms/legal.html"/>
      <form id="202" name="rental_contract"
          url="forms/rental.html"/>
      <form id="203" name="cost_contract"
          url="forms/costContract.html"/>
      <resource_owner first="Ed" last="Agenda"
            email="ed@reserveThis.com"
            type="administration"/>
    </room>
  </building>
  <workflow>
    <request view="xslt/request.xslt" status="false"/>
    <approval view="xslt/approval.xslt" status="false"/>
    <viewCalendar view="xslt/viewCalendar.xslt"
          status="false"/>
    <viewPending view="xslt/viewPending.xslt"
          status="false"/>
  </workflow>
</reservation_request>
```

## 26.1 System Architecture

**CHAPTER 26**

The reservation request shown in Figure 26.5 can be broken down into several important steps. The `reservation` element contains the information a user is going to provide by using a browser or some other Web interface device. The 'security' element is used to attach security information to the incoming message. The `workflow` element is used to track the status of the reservation request. The `building` element contains response data that will be sent to the user with room capacity information, required forms, the room's contact person and more. The application will fill in the user's security information, supply the user with the required forms to fill in, and keep track of the user's status in completing the workflow.

Let's use the message in Listing 26.6 to create a matrix of datatypes and the constraints we would like to apply. The matrix information in Table 26.1 is a reasonable start.

**TABLE 26.1**  Datatypes and Required Constraints

| Item | Element Type | Attribute Type | Base Datatype | Desired Constraints |
|---|---|---|---|---|
| 1 | reservation | building | string | Enumerated list of possible buildings |
| 2 | | room | string | Apply a min and max size |
| 3 | | start_date | date | Constrain value to a valid date format |
| 4 | | start_time | time | Constrain value to a valid time format |
| 5 | | duration | int | Value between 1 and 23 hours inclusive |
| 6 | | configuration | string | Enumerated list of room configurations |
| 7 | requestor | first | string | Apply a min and max size (2, 24) |
| 8 | | last | string | Apply a min and max size (2, 24) |
| 9 | | email | string | Constrain to e-mail W3C Recommendations |
| 10 | | type | string | Enumerated list |
| 11 | building | id | int | Number assigned to each building |
| 12 | | location | anyURI | Constrain to W3C specs for URLs |
| 13 | room | name | string | Same rule as reservation\room |

*continues*

## TABLE 26.1 (continued)

| Item | Element Type | Attribute Type | Base Datatype | Desired Constraints |
|------|--------------|----------------|---------------|---------------------|
| 14   |              | capacity       | int           | Constrain with minInclusive and maxInclusive |
| 15   | request      | status         | boolean       | Enumerated value equal to TRUE or FALSE |
| 16   | approval     | status         | boolean       | Same as line 15 |
| 17   | viewCalendar | status         | boolean       | Same as line 15 |
| 18   | viewPending  | status         | boolean       | Same as line 15 |

You can see in Table 26.1 that each XML message has a number of datatypes and desired constraints. Several of these datatypes will be very reusable on many messages. Specifically, constraints on user's names, e-mail formatting, date, time, and status will be usable across many XML schemas. You always want to achieve the highest reusable rate from your work. Developing many small XML schemas that can be tested independently and then included in your project will help achieve the goal of reusability.

### 26.1.1.3 Creating XML Schema Reusable Datatypes

You should identify the datatypes you think will be reusable in this and future applications from those in Table 26.1. Many datatypes can be reused frequently.

Start by creating an XML Schema simple type to model `start_date`. The Schema Recommendation has a `date` datatype as one of the primitive datatypes. The CRSS application needs to be restricted to allow reservation requests to be placed only between 2001 and 2099. In a production application you might not want to create a Y2.1K problem, but you will in the CRSS application to demonstrate XML Schema restrictions.

Creating a simple type to constrain the attribute date can be done as shown in Figure 26.2. Notice that a pattern is used to constrain the value range and the format that the date must be submitted in. If you just needed to constrain the values to range, the `minInclusive` and `maxInclusive` constraints could have been applied.

**LISTING 26.6**  CRSS Start Date Constrained

```
<?xml version="1.0" encoding="utf-8" ?>
<xsd:schema id="dateType"
   xmlns:xsd="http://www.w3.org/2001/XMLSchema">
<xsd:annotation>
  <xsd:documentation>
    Format date range to CCYY-MM-DD w/range 2001 to 2009
  </xsd:documentation>
```

```
    </xsd:annotation>
    <xsd:simpleType name="dateType">
    <xsd:restriction base="xsd:date">
    <xsd:pattern
       value="([2][0][0][1-9])-((0[1-9])|(1[0-2]))-\d{1,31}"/>
    </xsd:restriction>
</xsd:simpleType>
</xsd:schema>
```

Documenting your XML schemas is always a good idea. The `restriction` element specifies that the base datatype you will derive from is the XML Schema `date`. The next line derives a new date type by adding additional restrictions. You have chosen to name the newly derived type 'dateType'. The new `dateType` datatype has all the properties of the XML Schema `date` datatype and our additional restrictions.

The `pattern` value must be an XML Schema regular expression. For more information, refer to Chapter 14.

Now that you have created a simple datatype, `dateType`, the question is how to test it. One technique is to create another XML schema with a very simple structure and just use the XML Schema `include` element to reference the datatype you have created. In the test case in Listing 26.7, a test XML schema is created that has a root element named `root` with one additional element called `test`. The `test` element takes one attribute, `dateTest`, which uses our new `dateType`. Listing 26.7 is the test case.

**LISTING 26.7**  Schema for Testing dateType

```
1. <?xml version="1.0" encoding="utf-8" ?>
2. <xsd:schema id="dateTypeTest" elementFormDefault="qualified"
3. targetNamespace="http://www.XMLSchemaReference.com/
4.              examples/CRSS/dateTypeTest.xsd"
5. xmlns="http://www.XMLSchemaReference.com/
6.              examples/CRSS/dateTypeTest.xsd"
7. xmlns:xsd="http://www.w3.org/2001/XMLSchema">
8. <xsd:include schemaLocation="dateType.xsd" />
9. <xsd:element name="root">
     <xsd:complexType>
       <xsd:sequence minOccurs="1" maxOccurs="1">
         <xsd:element name="test">
           <xsd:complexType>
             <xsd:attribute name="dateTest"
                     type="dateType"/>
           </xsd:complexType>
         </xsd:element>
       </xsd:sequence>
```

*continues*

```
    </xsd:complexType>
  </xsd:element>
</xsd:schema>
```

The `include` element in Listing 26.7 includes our new `dateType` simple type. The `dateTest` attribute uses the custom datatype that you defined. You need to test this by creating a XML document that adheres to the XML schema in Listing 26.7 and then validating by using one of any number of tools. For our purposes, use Microsoft's .NET Framework to perform the test. If you do not have Visual Studio .NET then use the validation plug-in for Internet Explorer mentioned earlier.

Use any text editor to create the code shown in Listing 26.8. This listing references the `dateTypeTest` schema that includes the `dateType` simple type created first. This provides a very simple test to verify that the simple type is correct.

**LISTING 26.8**   XML Test Case for dateType Simple Type

```
1. <?xml version="1.0" encoding="utf-8" ?>
2. <root xmlns="http://www.XMLSchemaReference.com/
          examples/CRSS/dateTypeTest.xsd">
3. <test dateTest="2001-02-26"/>
4. </root>
```

You can experiment with the XML document in Listing 26.8 and verify that your new `dateType` XML schema is working. Changing the `dateTest` attribute in Listing 26.8 to 2000-02-26 results in an error in the .NET Framework, as shown in Figure 26.6.

Testing the schema in .NET is simple. Add the listings shown in Listings 26.6, 26.7, and 26.8. Next, open the file containing Listing 26.8. Then open the XML menu and choose Validate. Note the status messages displayed in the output pane of the .NET windows.

Just to be thorough, also test the `dateType` by using XML Spy. With XML Spy, you can use whatever validating parser you prefer. Using XML Spy, simply load your XML document and assign the desired schema to validate with. XML Spy displays errors if your XML source violates the governing schema's rules, as shown in Figure 26.7.

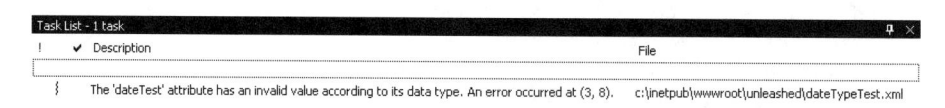

**FIGURE 26.6**   *Failed validation result.*

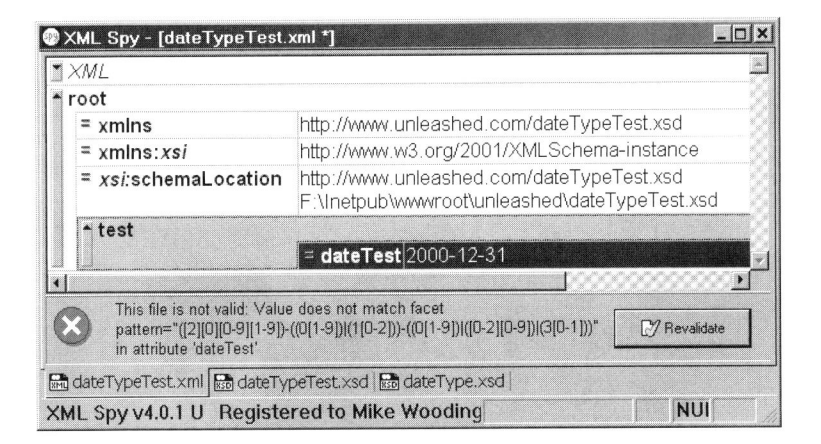

**FIGURE 26.7** *Failed validation result when using XML Spy.*

The failed result in Figure 26.7 is not due to the XML schema date format. The 2000-12-31 format works well with the XML schema primitive `date` datatype. The pattern you used constrained the date range to the years 2001 through 2099. Properly restricting your datatypes by using XML Schema facets reduces the amount of validation code typically required by the application.

> **NOTE**
>
> In addition to Chapter 14, a good source for regular expressions is `http://regxlib.com/`. Beware that XML Schema regular expressions are not the same as Perl regular expressions. A good place to test regular expressions for compliance with the XML Schema version is Daniel Potter's site at `http://www.xfront.org/xml-schema/`. This site features a Java applet that can be used to test your Schema patterns online interactively.

### 26.1.1.4 Reusable Datatype Review

This is a good point to review what we've done so far in creating reusable datatypes. The process is outlined below:

1. Create a UML sequence diagram for a specific action.
2. Use the sequence diagram to create a sample XML message.
3. Determine the datatypes required to fulfill the action modeled by the sequence diagram.
4. Identify the reusable datatypes.

5. Create a separate XML schema with the proper restrictions for each reusable datatype.
6. Test each XML schema module.
7. Aggregate your tested XML schema modules into a master for the action modeled by your sequence diagram.

There are many different ways to restrict data by using XML schemas. You have seen several examples in previous chapters of the book. The CRSS application XML schemas restrict the data by using many XML Schema techniques, including the following:

- `pattern`: Entries must match the pattern specified
- `minOccurs`: Minimum number of repetitions allowed
- `maxOccurs`: Maximum number of repetitions allowed
- `minLength`: Minimum string length
- `enumeration`: List of allowed entries
- `minInclusive`: Minimum integer value allowed
- `maxInclusive`: Maximum integer value allowed

Each XML simple type will not be reviewed in detail. The final code listing for our reservation request is in Listing 26.9. Listing 26.9 can be applied to Listing 26.7 to provide validation to the completed reservation request.

**LISTING 26.9** XML Schema for Completed Reservation Request

```xml
<?xml version="1.0" encoding="utf-8" ?>
<xsd:schema id="resRequest" elementFormDefault="qualified"
targetNamespace=
"http://www.XMLSchemaReference.com/examples/CRSS"
xmlns="http://XMLSchemaReference.com/examples/CRSS"
xmlns:xsd="http://www.w3.org/2001/XMLSchema">
<xsd:include schemaLocation="dateType.xsd"/>
<xsd:include schemaLocation="buildingType.xsd" />
<xsd:include schemaLocation="roomType.xsd" />
<xsd:include schemaLocation="configType.xsd" />
<xsd:include schemaLocation="durationType.xsd" />
<xsd:include schemaLocation="emailType.xsd" />
<xsd:include schemaLocation="requestorType.xsd" />
<xsd:include schemaLocation="locationType.xsd" />
<xsd:include schemaLocation="nameType.xsd" />
<xsd:include schemaLocation="urlFormType.xsd" />
<xsd:element name="reservation_request">
  <xsd:complexType>
    <xsd:sequence minOccurs="1" maxOccurs="1">
      <xsd:element name="reservation" minOccurs="1"
```

```xml
            maxOccurs="1">
<xsd:complexType>
  <xsd:attribute name="building" use="required"
        type="buildingType" />
  <xsd:attribute name="room" use="required"
        type="roomType" />
  <xsd:attribute name="start_date"
        use="required"
        type="dateType" />
  <xsd:attribute name="start_time"
        use="required"
        type="xs:time" />
  <xsd:attribute name="duration"
        use="required"
        type="durationType" />
  <xsd:attribute name="description"
        use="required"
        type="xs:string" />
  <xsd:attribute name="configuration"
        use="required"
        type="configType" />
</xsd:complexType>
</xsd:element>
<xsd:element name="security">
<xsd:complexType>
  <xsd:sequence minOccurs="1" maxOccurs="1">
    <xsd:element name="requestor">
    <xsd:complexType>
    <xsd:attributeGroup ref="userAttGroup"/>
    </xsd:complexType>
    </xsd:element>
  </xsd:sequence>
</xsd:complexType>
</xsd:element>
<xsd:element name="building">
<xsd:complexType>
  <xsd:sequence minOccurs="1" maxOccurs="1">
    <xsd:element name="room">
    <xsd:complexType>
    <xsd:sequence>
      <xsd:element name="form"
            minOccurs="0"
            maxOccurs="unbounded">
    <xsd:complexType>
    <xsd:attribute name="id" use="required"
          type="xs:int" />
```

*continues*

```xml
            <xsd:attribute name="name" use="required"
                   type="nameType" />
            <xsd:attribute name="urlForm"
                   use="optional"
                   type="urlFormType"/>
           </xsd:complexType>
          </xsd:element>
          <xsd:element name="resource_
                  owner" minOccurs="1"
                  maxOccurs="2">
           <xsd:complexType>
            <xsd:attributeGroup ref="userAttGroup"/>
           </xsd:complexType>
          </xsd:element>
         </xsd:sequence>
         <xsd:attribute use="required" name="name"
                 type="nameType"/>
         <xsd:attribute use="required"
                 name="capacity">
            <xsd:simpleType id="capLimits">
            <xsd:restriction base="xs:int">
              <xsd:minInclusive value="5"/>
              <xsd:maxInclusive value="200"/>
            </xsd:restriction>
            </xsd:simpleType>
         </xsd:attribute>
        </xsd:complexType>
       </xsd:element>
    </xsd:sequence>
    <xsd:attribute name="id" use="required"
            type="xs:int" />
    <xsd:attribute name="name" use="required"
            type="nameType" />
    <xsd:attribute name="location" use="required"
    type="locationType" />
   </xsd:complexType>
</xsd:element>
<xsd:element name="workflow">
<xsd:complexType>
  <xsd:sequence>
    <xsd:element name="workFlowItem"
          minOccurs="1"
          maxOccurs="10">
    <xsd:complexType>
    <xsd:sequence />
    <xsd:attribute name="action"
            use="required">
```

```xml
          <xsd:simpleType>
           <xsd:restriction base="xs:string">
            <xsd:enumeration value="request"/>
            <xsd:enumeration value="approval"/>
            <xsd:enumeration
               value="viewCalendar"/>
            <xsd:enumeration
               value="viewPendingRequests"/>
           </xsd:restriction>
          </xsd:simpleType>
         </xsd:attribute>
         <xsd:attribute name="view">
         <xsd:simpleType>
          <xsd:restriction base="xs:string">
           <xsd:enumeration
              value="xslt/request.xslt"/>
           <xsd:enumeration
              value="xslt/approval.xslt"/>
           <xsd:enumeration
              value="xslt/viewCalendar.xslt"/>
           <xsd:enumeration
              value="xslt/viewPending.xslt"/>
          </xsd:restriction>
         </xsd:simpleType>
         </xsd:attribute>
         <xsd:attribute name="status"
                 type="xs:boolean"/>
        </xsd:complexType>
        </xsd:element>
      </xsd:sequence>
     </xsd:complexType>
      </xsd:element>
    </xsd:sequence>
  </xsd:complexType>
</xsd:element>
<xsd:attributeGroup name="userAttGroup">
<xsd:attribute name="first" type="nameType" use="required"/>
<xsd:attribute name="last" type="nameType" use="required"/>
<xsd:attribute name="email" type="emailType" use="required"/>
<xsd:attribute name="type" type="requestorType"
         use="required"/>
</xsd:attributeGroup>
</xsd:schema>
```

You can see from the preceding code listing that we have achieved a modular XML schema. The xsd:include elements reference simple XML schemas that have been created and tested independently. The userAttGroup element near the end of the listing creates a named attribute group that includes the `first`, `last`, `email`, and `type` attributes. Named attribute groups maximize reuse by consolidating the definition of a group of frequently occurring attributes. The final XML schema is an aggregation of the various modules. This expedites future XML schema developments.

You need to test the final XML schema to verify that the conformant XML documents match your expectations. Fortunately, tools can assist quite a bit in this area. XML Spy has an option for generating an XML sample document from the XML schema. Listing 26.10 shows an output from XML Spy, using its sample document facility.

**LISTING 26.10**  XML Spy Auto-Generated Sample XML

```xml
<?xml version="1.0" encoding="UTF-8"?>
<!-- generated by XML Spy v4.0.1 U (http://www.xmlspy.com)-->
<reservation_request
 xmlns="http://XMLSchemaReference.com/examples/resRequest.xsd"
 xmlns:xsi="http://www.w3.org/2001/XMLSchema-instance"
 xsi:schemaLocation=
 "http://XMLSchemaReference.com/examples/CRSS/resRequest.xsd">
<reservation building="Library" room="class room"
        start_date="2001-01-01"
        start_time="00:00:00" duration="8"
        description="String" configuration="lecture"/>
 <security>
    <requestor first="abc" last="abc" email="aa@a.aaa"
         type="student"/>
 </security>
 <building id="0" name="a" location="images/a.gif">
   <room name="a" capacity="200">
      <form id="0" name="abc" urlForm="forms/a.html"/>
      <form id="0" name="abc" urlForm="forms/a.html"/>
      <form id="0" name="abc" urlForm="forms/a.html"/>
      <form id="0" name="abc" urlForm="forms/a.html"/>
      <form id="0" name="abc" urlForm="forms/a.html"/>
      <resource_owner first="abc" last="abc"
         email="aa@a.aaa" type="administration"/>
   </room>
 </building>
 <workflow>
   <workFlowItem action="request"
         view="xslt/request.xslt" status="1"/>
   <workFlowItem action="request"
         view="xslt/request.xslt" status="1"/>
   <workFlowItem action="request"
         view="xslt/request.xslt" status="1"/>
   <workFlowItem action="request"
         view="xslt/request.xslt" status="1"/>
```

```
        <workFlowItem action="request"
                view="xslt/request.xslt" status="1"/>
    </workflow>
</reservation_request>
```

XML Spy's automatically generated XML document provides an easy way to identify problems with your schema. If you are satisfied with the output, you can continue. If other constraints are needed, you should continue working with the XML schema until you are satisfied.

## 26.2 Creating HTML Pages by Using XSLT

You have enough information to begin creating the views for your application. This section illustrates how the XML schema you have created is going to facilitate the creation of the views. Using the sequence diagram shown in Figure 26.3, you know that the end user requires two views. The first view is the reservation request itself, and the second view is the response.

The CRSS applications HTML page is a composite of header, footer, menu, and application-specific sections of data. Obviously, the page must also have various background images, fonts, and other styles. In our CRSS application, we use Internet standards to deliver the page to the user. Start by creating an XSLT view that is modular in nature. The illustration in Figure 26.8 indicates the various modules in the view. Each view module needs a corresponding XML data file.

To create the XSLT view, several pieces of data must come together.

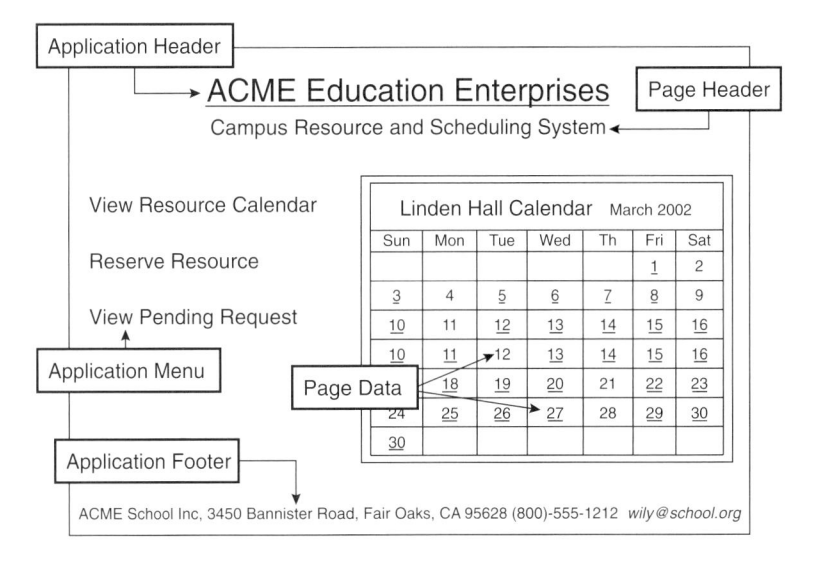

**FIGURE 26.8**  *XSLT modules.*

> **NOTE**
>
> XSLT is a W3C Recommendation that focuses on how to convert one XML-compliant tree structure to another tree structure—for example, HTML and WML. You are dealing with XML data, so it makes sense to use XSLT to provide the views. Using XSLT lets you easily accommodate PDAs and other emerging Internet access devices. For more information on XSLT, see *Teach Yourself XSLT in 21 Days*[1] and http://www.w3.org/TR/XSLT.

The user's selection results in changes in the data section of the page in Figure 26.8. The remainder of the page is static in nature. The background colors, fonts, and other styles are specified by using a cascading style sheet (CSS). Cascading style sheets provide a separation of style from content and enhance reusability.

> **NOTE**
>
> Cascading style sheets are a W3C Recommendation. The latest Recommendation can be found at www.w3.org/TR/REC-CSS2/. A good reference is *Teach Yourself Web Publishing with HTML and XHTML in 21 Days*.[2]

The static sections of the page are easily modeled as XML files containing the data. This data, along with the application data, can be merged at runtime into a final data representation of the page. This final representation may then have the XSLT template applied to provide the view. The pseudocode shown in Listing 26.11 should reinforce this concept.

**LISTING 26.11**   Pseudocode XML Data for XSLT Template

```
<crss>
  <appHeader>Application Header Data goes here</appHeader>
  <pageHeader>Page header data goes here</pageHeader>
  <appMenu>Application menu data goes here</appMenu>
  <pageData>Unique page data goes here </pageData>
  <appFooter>Application footer goes here</appFooter>
</crss>
```

---

[1] van Otegen, Michiel. *Teach Yourself XSLT in 21 Days*. Indianapolis, IN: Sams, 2002.

[2] Lemay, Laura, Denise Tyler, and Rafe Colburn. *Teach Yourself Web Publishing with HTML and XHTML in 21 Days*. Indianapolis, IN: Sams, 2001.

Your application will be very portable if you use XSLT to render the view. By using Internet standards, the portion of the code that is vendor-specific can be minimized. Your final application will create the final XML data on the Web Server tier. You will then apply the XSLT template to render the user's view. Listing 26.11 illustrates the idea behind this application design. The `pageData` section of the document changes frequently. The rest of the page is static.

During development, it is simple to achieve the document outline shown in Listing 26.11. You can simply open a text editor and add the static data to your dynamic data for a final XML document. You can then construct the XSLT template by using the final XML document, as in Listing 26.12.

**LISTING 26.12**  Final Data to Transform by Using XSLT

```
<crss>
  <appHeader>
    <title>ACME Education Enterprises</title>
  </appHeader>
  <pageHeader>
    <title>Campus Resource and Scheduling System</title>
  </pageHeader>
  <appMenu>
    <menuItem
link="http://www.sams.com/default.aspx?view=resourceCalendar"
      altText="View Resource Calendar"/>
    <menuItem
link="http://www.sams.com/default.aspx?view=reserveResource"
      altText="Request a resource reservation"/>
    <menuItem
link="http://www.sams.com/default.aspx?view=pending"
      altText="View Pending Requests"/>
  </appMenu>
  <pageData>
   <reservation_request>
   <reservation building="Linden Hall"
     room="Gymnasium" start_date="2001-02-23"
     start_time="22:30:00" duration="5"
     description="Varsity basketball practice"
     configuration="basketball"/>
   <security>
    <requestor first="Paul" last="Lamere"
          email="plamere@bball.com" type="coach"/>
   </security>
   <building id="1" name="Linden Hall"
         location="images/linden.gif">
    <room name="Gymnasium" capacity="100">
```

*continues*

```
      <form id="201" name="legal"
          url="forms/legal.html"/>
      <form id="202" name="rental_contract"
          url="forms/rental.html"/>
      <form id="203" name="cost_contract"
          url="forms/costContract.html"/>
      <resource_owner first="Ed" last="Agenda"
            email="ed@reserveThis.com"
            type="administration"/>
     </room>
    </building>
    <workflow>
     <request view="xslt/request.xslt" status="false"/>
     <approval view="xslt/approval.xslt" status="false"/>
     <viewCalendar view="xslt/viewCalendar.xslt"
            status="false"/>
     <viewPending view="xslt/viewPending.xslt"
            status="false"/>
    </workflow>
   </reservation_request>
  </pageData>
  <appFooter>
   <footer street="3450 Bannister Rd." city="Fair Oaks"
     state="CA" zip="95628" phone="(800) 555-1212"
     email="wily@school.org"/>
  </appFooter>
</crss>
```

Now that you have the final document, you simply have to construct the XSLT template. You construct the template the same way you did the XML schema template: by using tested modules. Listing 26.13 is an XSLT template that transforms Listing 26.12 into the view you want the user to see. Listing 26.13 omits a number of useful XSLT constructs for the sake of simplicity.

**LISTING 26.13**  Partial XSLT Template for Reservation Request

```
<xsl:stylesheet version="1.0"
xmlns:xsl="http://www.w3.org/1999/XSL/Transform">
 <xsl:import href="appStyle.xslt"/>
 <xsl:import href="appHeader.xslt"/>
 <xsl:import href="pageHeader.xslt"/>
 <xsl:import href="appMenu.xslt"/>
 <xsl:import href="appFooter.xslt"/>
 <xsl:output method="html" encoding="UTF-16"
    media-type="screen"/>
 <xsl:strip-space elements="*"/>
```

## 26.2 Creating HTML Pages by Using XSLT

```xml
<xsl:template match="/">
<html>
<xsl:apply-templates select="crss/appStyle"/>
<body bgcolor="white" marginwidth="0" marginheight="0"
   topmargin="0" leftmargin="0">
<!--========= OUTER WRAPPER TABLE - START ===========-->
<form name="frmAction" id="frmAction"
   action="default.aspx" method="get">
<table cellspacing="4" cellpadding="3" border="0"
   width="800">
<tr>
 <xsl:apply-templates select="crss/appHeader"/>
 <xsl:apply-templates select="crss/pageHeader"/>
 <table border="1">
 <tr><xsl:apply-templates select="crss/appMenu"/><td>
  <table border="0">
   <tr><xsl:apply-templates select="crss/pageData"/></tr>
  </table>
  </td>
 </tr>
 </table>
 <xsl:apply-templates select="crss/appFooter"/>
</tr>
</table>
<input type="hidden" name="req" id="req">
<xsl:attribute name="value">
<xsl:value-of select="crss/workflow/workFlowItem/@action"/>
</xsl:attribute>
</input>
</form>
</body>
</html>
</xsl:template>
<xsl:template match="pageData">
INSERT PAGE DATA HTML HERE
</xsl:template>

</xsl:stylesheet>
```

In Listing 26.13, you can see the modular approach. Several XSLT import elements are used to import XSLT templates that apply the correct formatting. The dynamic page data that will change often has its own template, '`<xsl:template match="pageData">`'. Inside this template, HTML is required to display the view. After you insert the pageData template, the HTML view illustrated in Figure 26.9 is rendered in the user's browser.

All that remains to do now is dynamically create this page on the Web Server tier so that your application remains browser-independent. All the views required by our sequence diagram,

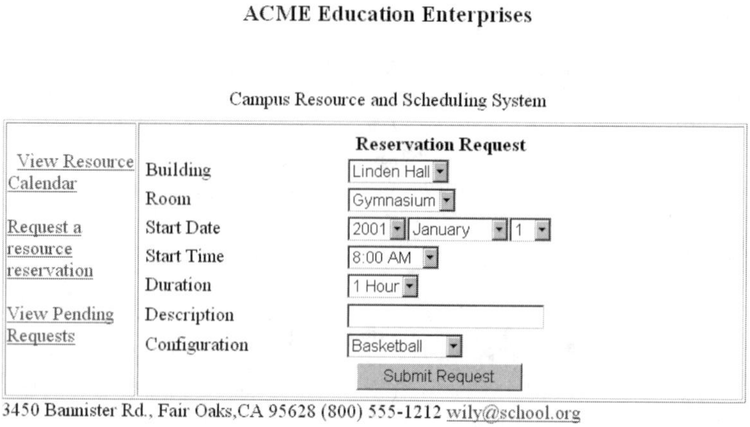

**FIGURE 26.9** *HTML rendered from XSLT and XML.*

Figure 26.3, can be constructed in a manner similar to that shown in Listing 26.13. You will not be working with additional XSLT templates; that discussion is beyond the scope of this book.

> **TIP**
>
> XSLT is an Internet standard. More information can be found at www.w3.org/TR/xslt. There are several useful tools for creating XSLT templates. Stylus by Excelon is a good choice. More information on this tool can be found at www.stylusstudio.com/. Stylus and XML Spy both have the capability to use whichever XML parser you prefer. Testing with multiple parsers helps ensure that your XSLT behaves as expected.

You might be wondering how using an XML schema assisted in the XSLT template creation. Several XSLT tools use XML schemas to assist in mapping the XML fields into the XSLT template. Stylus, XML Spy, and Microsoft's BizTalk all provide this capability.

## 26.3 Sending Form Data

The XSLT document you created in the previous section created HTML that works with any HTML-3.2-compliant browser. You will transmit the form data as usual, by using the browser's HTTP capabilities. New capabilities in Microsoft's Internet Explorer version 5.0+ and Netscape version 6.2+ allow the XML to be sent directly to and from the browser. These capabilities are certainly the direction that Internet devices should take in the future.

Unfortunately, you cannot be certain that all users will be using XML-compliant browsers, so you will continue to send the data by using HTML standards in our case study.

After you send the data, you must commit to a server development framework. The CRSS case study is going to use Microsoft's .NET Framework. This section looks at how to receive the client request by using ASP.NET. You should carefully consider certain features when choosing a framework. Defining what you are looking for in a Web application development framework will help. Ideal Web applications should have the following characteristics:

- No broken links
- No business logic in the Web tier
- No database logic in the Web tier
- Easy deployment from development to test to production
- Ability to scale by using the selected framework
- Ability to respond to any type of Web-enabled device
- Ability to respond by using the correct cultural settings

Achieving all the characteristics in the preceding list is a bit beyond the scope of this case study. However, you will achieve the first five items, with the ability to do the sixth item readily apparent. We do not attempt to deal with the last item in this case study.

Accepting a client request assumes that you have installed the Microsoft .NET Framework on your Web server. Specifically, the following configuration is suggested:

- Windows 2000 Professional or Server
- IIS version 5 or later
- .NET Framework installed
- Visual Studio .NET is optional but quite useful

> **NOTE**
>
> Choosing a language for programming the .NET Framework is a matter of individual preference. The .NET Framework works with any language that is compliant with the Common Language Specification (CLS). Microsoft has submitted the specifications of C#, the runtime, the metadata, and the other parts of the .NET development platform to the European Computer Manufacturers Association (ECMA) for standardization. The specifications submitted to ECMA are available at http://www.dotnetexperts.com/ecma. ECMA is an international industry association founded in 1961 and dedicated to the standardization of information and communication systems. More information on ECMA is available at http://www.ecma.ch.

You develop the CRSS application by using Visual Basic .NET.

Assuming that you have successfully installed the framework as noted previously, you can now create your Web application. The steps are

1. Open Visual Studio.NET.
2. Create a VB.NET Web application.
3. Open `default.aspx` and add one line of code.
4. Test.

Start by creating a Visual Basic ASP.NET Web application called CRSS. Figure 26.10 shows how you can create a Visual Basic .NET Web project.

You then create a new page called `default.aspx` as shown in Figure 26.11.

Open the default.aspx page. There are two tabs to choose from for viewing the page. Choose the HTML tab at the bottom of the screen. Delete all content except the first line, as shown in Figure 26.12.

You will not be using any Microsoft-specific client controls in your application. The application uses XSLT for all views, so no HTML is required on the page.

Now you need to add content to your Web application. Drag the XML and XSL files into folders created under the CRSS project, as shown in Figure 26.13.

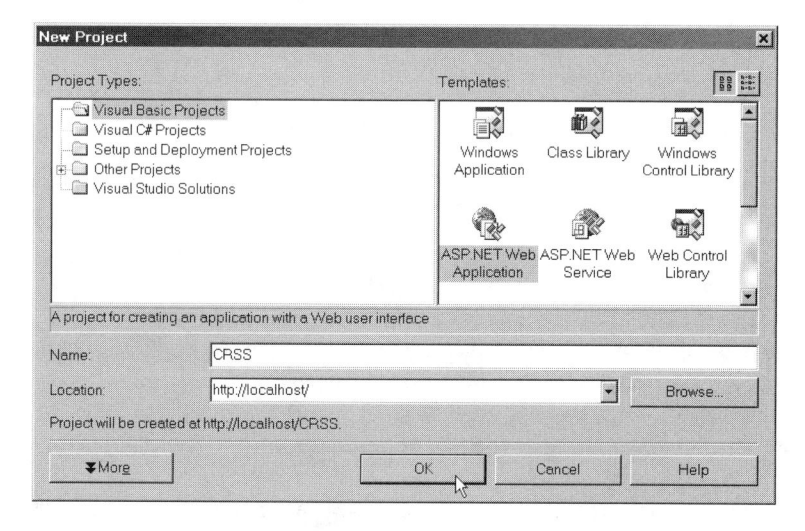

**FIGURE 26.10**  *Creating a Web project in .NET.*

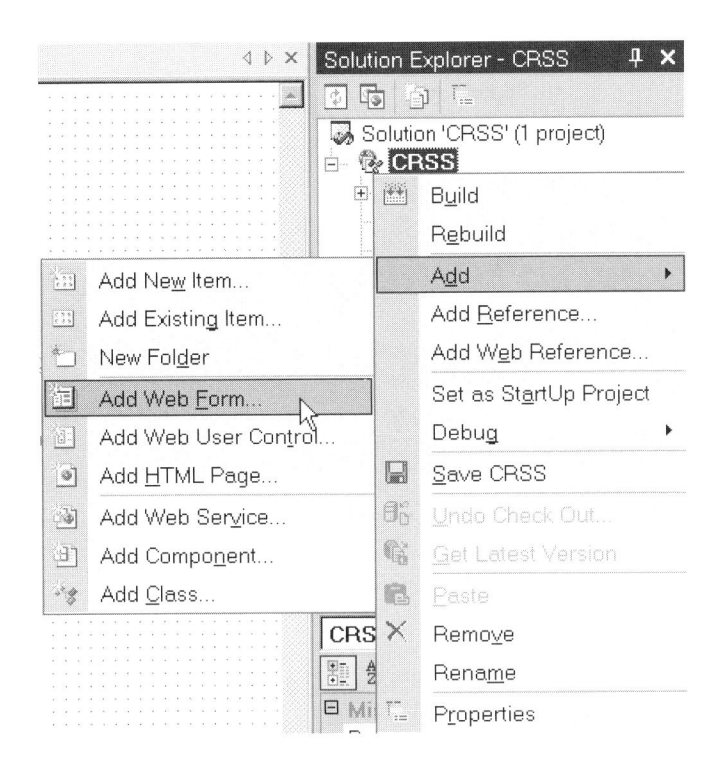

**FIGURE 26.11**  *Adding default.aspx.*

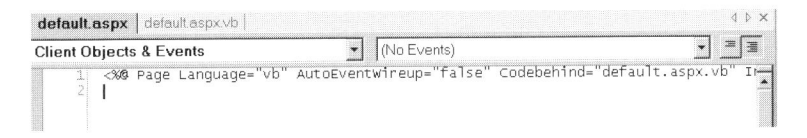

**FIGURE 26.12**  *Default.aspx HTML view.*

> **NOTE**
>
> You will want to download the files shown from `http://www.XMLSchemaReference.com/examples/CRSS`. Set up the folder structure as shown in Figure 26.13.

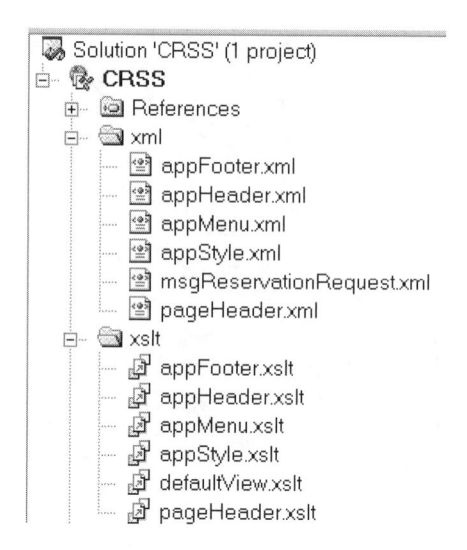

**FIGURE 26.13** *Folder structure in CRSS Web project.*

Next you need to add some code to the `Page_Load` event. Open the `default.aspx.vb` page by right-clicking on the `default.aspx` page and choosing `View | Code`. The code to begin testing your site is in Listing 26.14.

**LISTING 26.14** ASP.NET Listing for Default Page

```
Option Explicit On
Option Strict On
Imports System.Xml
Imports System.Xml.Xsl
Imports System.Xml.XPath

Public Class Cdefault
    Inherits System.Web.UI.Page
'AUTO GENERATED CODE REMOVED FROM THIS LISTING FOR BREVITY
'Holds the final XML - UI XML and page data XML
    Private o_FinalDoc As New XmlDocument()
'Contains the application footer XML
    Private o_appFooter As New XmlDocument()
'Contains the application header XML
    Private o_appHeader As New XmlDocument()
'Contains the application menu XML
    Private o_appMenu As New XmlDocument()
'Contains the application style XML
    Private o_appStyle As New XmlDocument()
'Contains the page header XML
```

```vb
    Private o_pageHeader As New XmlDocument()
'Contains empty reservation request XML
    Private o_msgReservationRequest As New XmlDocument()

'Initialize the xslt objects you will need
'used to hold the request reservation XSLT template
    Private o_requestView As New XslTransform()
'used to hold the approval XSLT template
    Private o_approvalView As New XslTransform()
'used to hold the calendar XSLT template
    Private o_viewCalendarView As New XslTransform()
'used to hold the pending requests XSLT template
    Private o_viewPendingView As New XslTransform()
'XSLT template to be used in final transformation
    Private o_FinalView As New XslTransform()

'Initialize fully qualified path to this web site
    Private sServerPath As String
    Private Sub Page_Load(ByVal sender As System.Object, _
            ByVal e As System.EventArgs) _
            Handles MyBase.Load
    Try
'get the fully qualified URL path to server root
    sServerPath = "http://" & _
            Request.ServerVariables("SERVER_NAME") _
            & Request.ApplicationPath & "/"

'Load the xml documents
        o_appFooter.Load(sServerPath & "xml/appFooter.xml")
        o_appHeader.Load(sServerPath & "xml/appHeader.xml")
        o_appMenu.Load(sServerPath & "xml/appMenu.xml")
        o_appStyle.Load(sServerPath & "xml/appStyle.xml
'Put user code to initialize the page here
        Dim req As String
        req = Request.QueryString("req")
        Select Case req
          Case "request"
            'do stuff
          Case "approval"
            'do pending work
          Case "viewCalendar"
            'show Calendar
          Case "viewPending"
            'view the Pending Work
          Case Else
            'create the final doc
            o_FinalDoc.LoadXml("<crss><pageData/></crss>")
```

*continues*

## The Architecture
### CHAPTER 26

```vb
        Dim oFinalNode As XmlNode = _
          o_FinalDoc.DocumentElement
        'Update oFinalDoc with page data inputs
        FinalNode.FirstChild.AppendChild _
          (o_FinalDoc.ImportNode( _
          o_msgReservationRequest.DocumentElement,
          True))
        'Update oFinalDoc with inputs UI nodes
        oFinalNode.AppendChild(o_FinalDoc.ImportNode
            (o_appStyle.DocumentElement,True))
        oFinalNode.AppendChild(o_FinalDoc.ImportNode _
            (o_appHeader.DocumentElement,True))
        oFinalNode.AppendChild(o_FinalDoc.ImportNode _
            (o_pageHeader.DocumentElement,True))
        oFinalNode.AppendChild(o_FinalDoc.ImportNode _
            (o_appMenu.DocumentElement,True))
        oFinalNode.AppendChild(o_FinalDoc.ImportNode _
            (o_appFooter.DocumentElement,True))
        'Set the XSLT template to use
        o_FinalView.Load(sServerPath & _
                "xslt/defaultView.xslt")
        showPage()
      End Select
    Catch ex As Exception
      'should log the exception
      Response.AppendToLog(ex.Message)
    Finally
      'Cleanup any resources open
    End Try
  End Sub

  Private Sub showPage()
    Dim parmList As New XsltArgumentList()
    Dim xWriter As New XmlTextWriter(Response.Output)
    xWriter.Formatting = Formatting.Indented
    xWriter.Indentation = 4
    o_FinalView.Transform(o_FinalDoc, parmList, xWriter)
  End Sub
End Class
```

Listing 26.14 creates the basic framework for the CRSS application. Let's review what this code is doing and then examine the pros and cons of this approach. The Page_Load event is called by the ASP.NET framework whenever the page is called. The XML CRSS user interface data is loaded using the load methods for each XML document. Remember, we chose to construct the final XML document programmatically, so you must load each of the XML documents and then create a final XML document that includes the UI XML data and the CRSS application XML data. The final data representation of the page is created by using the `appendChild` methods to concatenate the user interface data and dynamic data.

Each XSLT template contains a hidden form field with the next action to take in a variable, `req`. The case statement is used when the page is accessed. Each case statement will take action depending on the requested action. Finally, all case statements call the `showPage` subroutine, which writes the transformed result back to the client browser by using the ASP.NET Response object's output stream.

The code in Listing 26.14 is more than we would like to see in the production CRSS application. All of this code can be moved into components. This is what you will be doing in the next chapter so the application will begin to comply with the design in our sequence diagram (see Figure 26.3).

## 26.4 Summary

You have covered a lot of ground in this chapter. You started with a UML sequence diagram and saw how to decompose it into XML messages with corresponding XML schemas. You have seen how to create modular XML schemas by using the Visual Studio .NET framework. You have also seen how you can test your XML schemas in a modular way, providing a high degree of reuse. Next, we looked at using the XML schemas to create an XSLT template for rendering the HTML view. Finally, you learned how to use the ASP.NET framework to receive the HTML form submission, build the final XML document from your UI and page data, and transform it by using XSLT. In the next chapter you are going to develop the business logic and database code to create the functioning application.

# The Server Tier

**CHAPTER 27**

## IN THIS CHAPTER

- 27.1 Database Design with XML Schemas  810
- 27.2 SQL IIS Configuration  823
- 27.3 CRSS Application Requirements  831
- 27.4 Updategrams  832
- 27.5 Summary  833

In Chapter 26 we worked our way from the Campus Resource and Scheduling System (CRSS) design to the Client tier issuing a request. Now we need to model and construct the Web Server tier. The server architecture includes the business components and the database structure. You will see how XML schemas assist in all phases of the middle and Database tier design and implementation.

When we first looked at the CRSS requirements, we had four primary requirements. As a review, here are the CRSS requirements again:

- Users should be able to access the system by using the Web.
- The system should easily adapt to PDAs and other wireless technologies.
- XML schemas should be used to validate all user interaction with the system.
- Database interaction should occur by using XML schemas to map XML data automatically to relational tables.

In this chapter you will work with the following technologies:

- SQL Server XML View Mapper
- Microsoft SQL 2000
- Visual Studio .NET

## 27.1 Database Design with XML Schemas

You have already looked extensively at the Client tier. This chapter will focus on the Database and Component tiers. Our goal is to complete the development of the CRSS to the point where you can add and view the reservation requests. Therefore, this chapter will model the database tier and the application tier.

Many existing applications add significant business logic in Active Server Page (ASP) or JavaServer Page (JSP) pages. In Chapter 26, we added some workflow logic to our user interface (UI) logic. This illustrated how to send and receive the XSLT-generated data to the Web tier. You will be simplifying the Web tier considerably as you further develop your business components.

Prior to working on the business components, you need to develop a database for the CRSS application. In Chapter 26 you developed a complete XML schema that models the reservation request. This XML schema was created by using the sequence diagram that is shown in Figure 26.3. You will now use this XML schema to assist in the creation of the database.

The fundamental difficulty in working with XML and relational databases is mapping the database tables and fields to the XML elements and attributes. A number of tools and competing standards are emerging to assist in this work.

## Note

Microsoft created a schema dialect called XDR, (XML Data Reduced), to work with Internet Explorer prior to the W3C development of the XML Schema Recommendation by the W3C. This format is still used by some tools to provide integration to databases. Other initiatives are aimed at integrating XML schemas with relational databases. Two of the more notable open-source initiatives are Schematron and RELAX NG.

Perhaps the quickest way to use our XML schema to create a database is to open the schema by using Visual Studio .NET. Visual Studio .NET provides a view of the XML schema that looks like a relational database structure. The partial view in Figure 27.1 is of the reservation request schema created in the Chapter 26.

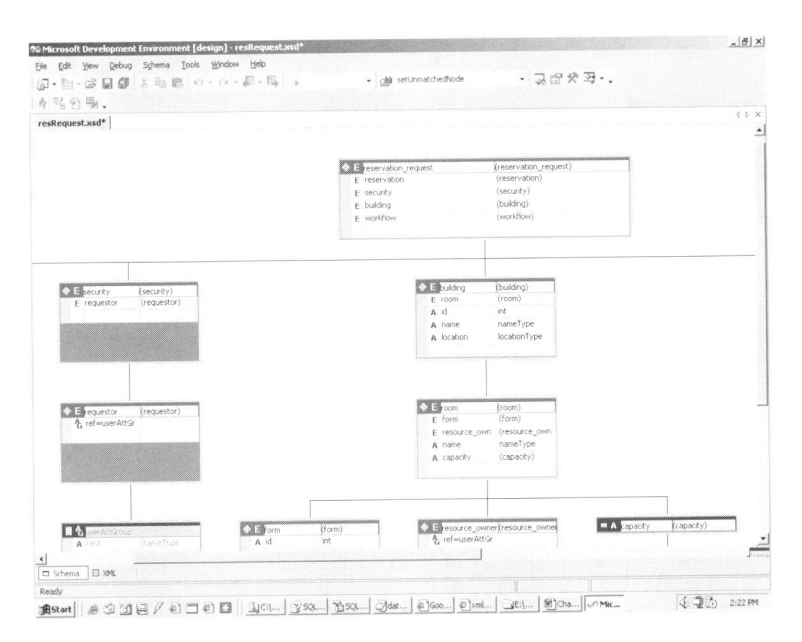

**FIGURE 27.1** *CRSS reservation request schema in Visual Studio .NET.*

You can modify this view by right-clicking and selecting Preview Dataset. Voila, you are looking at the start of a database table structure, as shown in Figure 27.2.

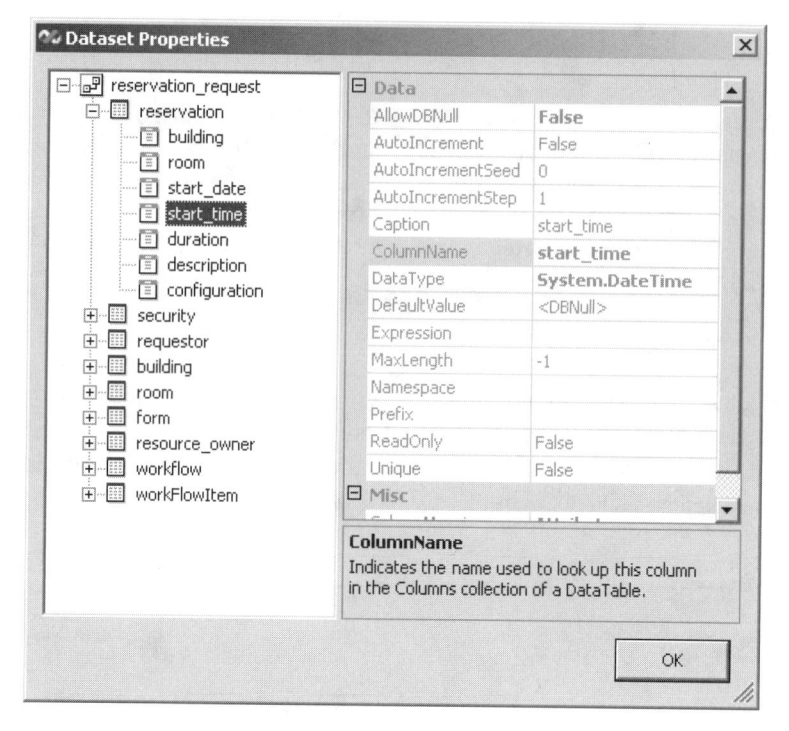

**FIGURE 27.2** *Dataset Properties from Visual Studio .NET.*

Naturally, no database design will ever be completed automatically. Proper database design entails a good model, normalization, security, and so on, but it never hurts to have a little help from good tools. Using the dataset in .NET, you could write code to loop through the Tables collection and create a new table on the database. Although this is a valid approach, it is not too useful because you would end up making changes to the database design anyway.

Another approach is to use XML Spy (http://www.xmlspy.com) and load the schema. After the schema has been loaded, you can use XML Spy to automatically generate a valid XML document that can be used to create a database structure.

The Visual Studio .NET view of a schema is shown in Figure 27.3.

After you have created the XML structure for the database as shown in Figure 27.3, you simply select the elements that will become tables. Several options exist for mapping attributes to columns, determining the depth within the XML document you will traverse, and more. The XML Spy documentation and tutorial cover these options in detail. Figure 27.4 illustrates how you create the tables using XML Spy.

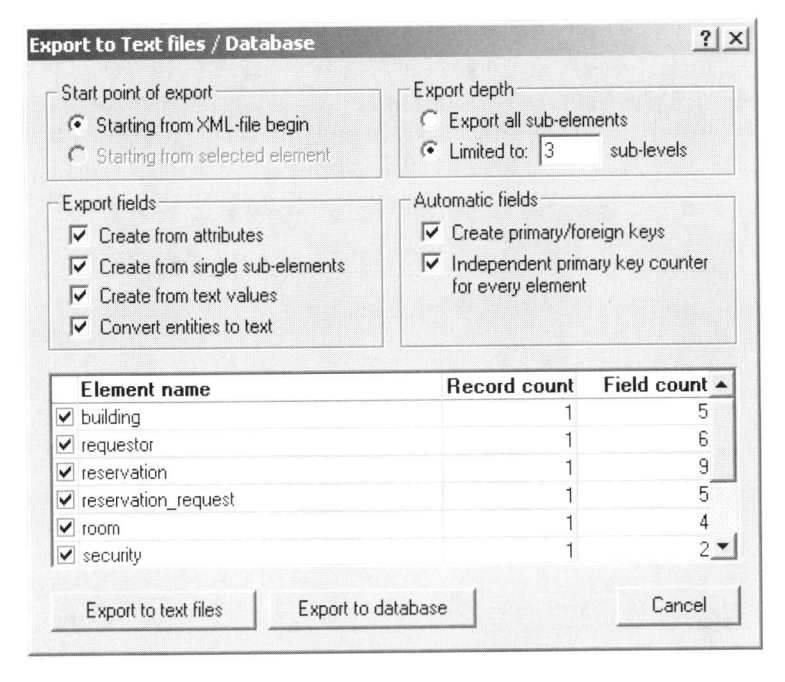

**FIGURE 27.3**  *Dataset preview from Visual Studio .NET.*

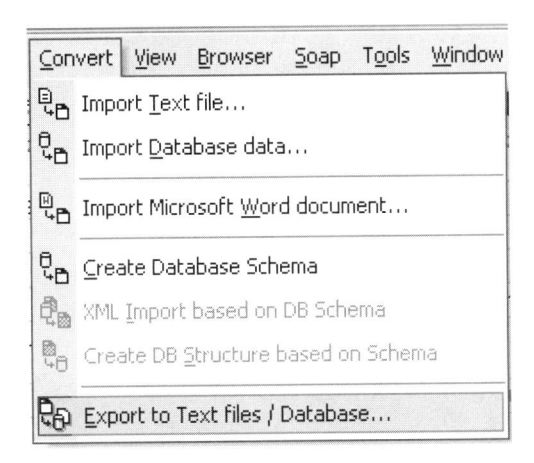

**FIGURE 27.4**  *XML Spy table creation.*

After using XML Spy, you have tables in your database, but you still have quite a bit of work to do. The database conversion has not made any relationships, the names of primary keys should conform to your naming standards, and other relationship constraints need to be applied. In the future you should see significant improvements in moving from XML Schema to relational databases. Most of the tools today do a better job by using an existing database to create an XML schema. The final table structure produced using XML Spy is shown in Figure 27.5.

> **CAUTION**
>
> XML Spy will throw an error if your XML sample document has attribute or element names that conflict with SQL's reserved names. If this occurs, you should simply rename the element or attribute and allow XML Spy to succeed. Afterward, change the guilty attribute or element back to your preferred name.

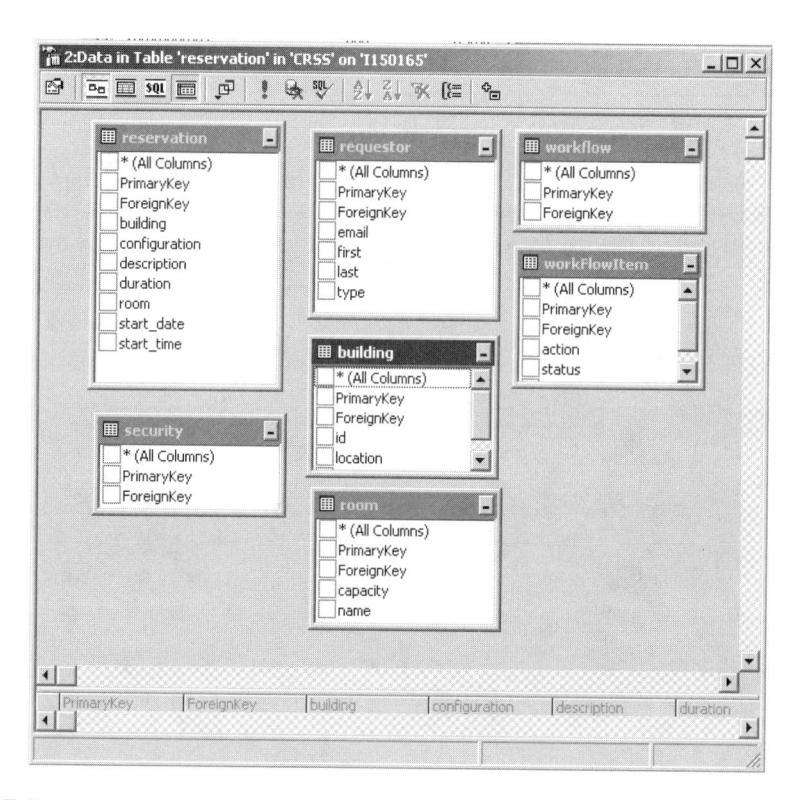

**FIGURE 27.5**  *Final table design from XML Spy.*

You will clean up the database schema manually and use the table structure illustrated in Figure 27.6 for the remainder of your work in the CRSS application. As you can see, the relational structure of the CRSS database is radically different from the XML hierarchical structure.

## 27.1.1 Mapping XML to Relational Databases

Mapping hierarchical XML schemas to relational database structures is inherently difficult. Consequently, maintaining this mapping is equally difficult. Many vendors are working on solutions for this problem. Microsoft, Oracle, IBM, Sun, and others have been XML-enabling their databases for the past few years. XML schemas have been the key ingredient that was missing to allow a simple integration between the XML hierarchical structure and the relational structure.

Microsoft updates SQL 2000 with more XML capabilities periodically. The CRSS case study uses SQLXML3, which was released in March 2002. If SQL 2000 is your database environment, watch for more tools at `http://www.microsoft.com/sql/techinfo/xml`. Oracle has a wealth of information on its Web site at `http://www.oracle.com/` regarding tools for mapping XML to Oracle data.

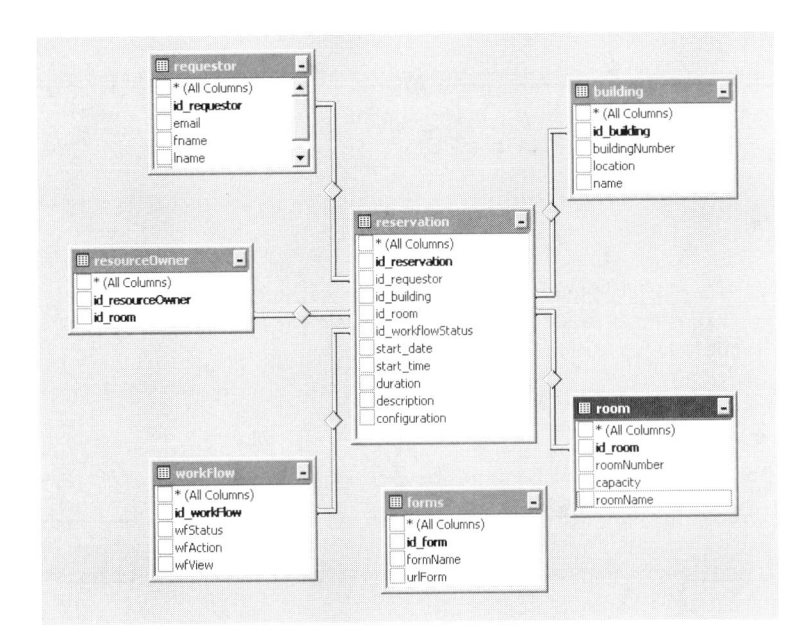

**FIGURE 27.6**  *CRSS database model.*

You are going to map the XML reservation request message that you saw in the previous chapter (reprinted in Listing 27.1) by using a Microsoft tool called the SQL XML View Mapper, available online at http://www.microsoft.com/sql.

**LISTING 27.1**  Reservation Request XML Message Reprinted

```xml
<?xml version="1.0" encoding="utf-8" ?>
<reservation_request>
  <reservation building="Linden Hall" room="Gymnasium"
        start_date="2001-02-23" start_time="22:30:00"
        duration="5" description="Varsity basketball"
        configuration="basketball"/>
  <security>
    <requestor first="Paul" last="Lamere"
          email="plamere@bball.com" type="coach"/>
  </security>
  <building id="1" name="Linden Hall"
      location="images/linden.gif">
    <room name="Gymnasium" capacity="100">
      <form id="201" name="legal"
          url="forms/legal.html"/>
      <form id="202" name="rental_contract"
          url="forms/rental.html"/>
      <form id="203" name="cost_contract"
          url="forms/costContract.html"/>
      <resource_owner first="Ed" last="Agenda"
            email="ed@reserveThis.com"
            type="administration"/>
    </room>
  </building>
  <workflow>
    <request view="xslt/request.xslt" status="false"/>
    <approval view="xslt/approval.xslt" status="false"/>
    <viewCalendar view="xslt/viewCalendar.xslt"
          status="false"/>
    <viewPending view="xslt/viewPending.xslt"
          status="false"/>
  </workflow>
</reservation_request>
```

With the SQL XML View Mapper, you can graphically create a mapping schema between your XML message and the database tables.

The following software must be installed as a prerequisite to the use of SQL XML View Mapper:

- SQL 2000

- Microsoft Windows 2000 (any edition)
- Microsoft Installer v2.0+

After correctly installing the XML View Mapper, you can launch it and start working on your mapping schema, as shown in Figure 27.7.

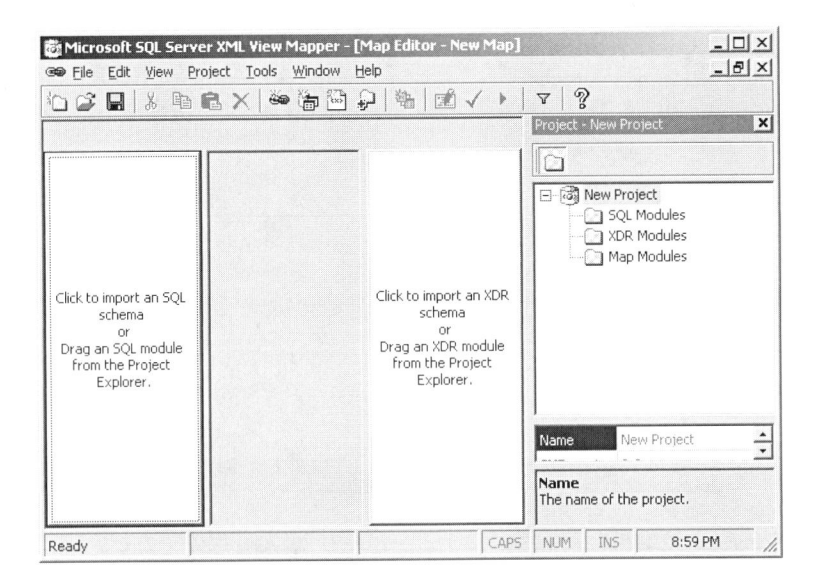

**FIGURE 27.7**  *CRSS database model.*

The SQL XML View Mapper only accepts Microsoft-specific XDR schemas: SQL XML View Mapper does *not* accept Schema-Recommendation-compliant schemas. XML Spy has the capability to perform the translation; after translating, you can load the reservation request XDR schema. Microsoft uses its proprietary XDR schemas to map SQL 2000 databases to XML. XDR schemas are not an Internet standard. Figure 27.8 shows the initial view that is presented when the SQL XML View Mapper is launched.

```
<?xml version="1.0" encoding="UTF-8"?>
<!--XML-Data generated by XML Spy v4.3 U (http://www.xmlspy.com)-->
<Schema name="Untitled-schema" xmlns="urn:schemas-microsoft-com:xml-data" xmlns:dt="urn:schemas-microsoft-com:datatypes">
    <ElementType name="reservation_request" model="closed" content="eltOnly" order="seq">
        <AttributeType name="xmlns" dt:type="string"/>
        <attribute type="xmlns"/>
        <group minOccurs="1" maxOccurs="1" order="seq">
            <element type="reservation" minOccurs="1" maxOccurs="1"/>
            <element type="security" minOccurs="1" maxOccurs="1"/>
            <element type="building" minOccurs="1" maxOccurs="1"/>
            <element type="workflow" minOccurs="1" maxOccurs="1"/>
        </group>
```

**FIGURE 27.8**  *XDR Schema (partial).*

> **NOTE**
>
> Microsoft's SQLXML3 does support XML schemas and has a tool to assist in converting XDR schemas to W3C-compliant XML schemas. Unfortunately, the SQL XML View Mapper tool only uses XDR schemas. You will use the SQL XML View Mapper tool to learn about mapping XML hierarchical data to relational database data. You will then return to using Schema-Recommendation-compliant schemas. You can also create the XDR mapping schemas using XML Spy if you find that using the SQL XML View Mapper is cumbersome. The tool is quite powerful but also quite difficult to master.

It's easy to see that XDR schemas have similiarities to the Schema-Recommendation-compliant schemas. Microsoft has stated that they will be updating their tools to conform to the XML Schema Recommendation, so perhaps this step will not be required in the future.

Now that you have an XDR schema, you can take another look at the XML Mapper tool. Figure 27.9 shows a partial listing of the XDR schema that the SQL XML View Mapper created.

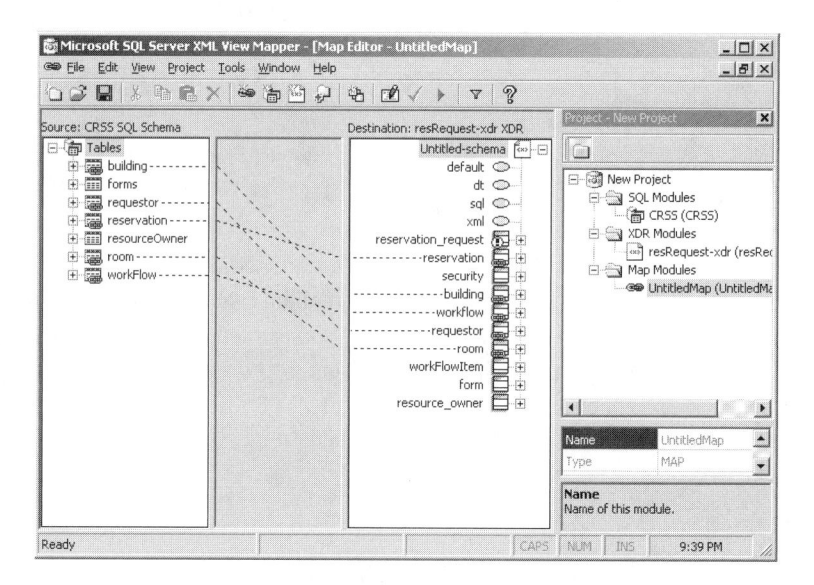

**FIGURE 27.9** *XML Mapper loaded with XDR schema.*

You can see from Figure 27.9 that the SQL XML View Mapper has automatically found several matches between our SQL schema and the reservation request XDR schema. The only action required for the XML Mapping tool to get started was connecting to the CRSS database and the XDR schema. Now you must manually set some matches and accept or reject others.

27.1 Database Design with XML Schemas   819

The first step in creating a successful mapping is to map the element types to their corresponding tables. Then you map the attribute types to their respective fields. Finally, you look at mapping attribute types across tables, resulting in implicit join operations. Figure 27.10 illustrates the mapping results thus far.

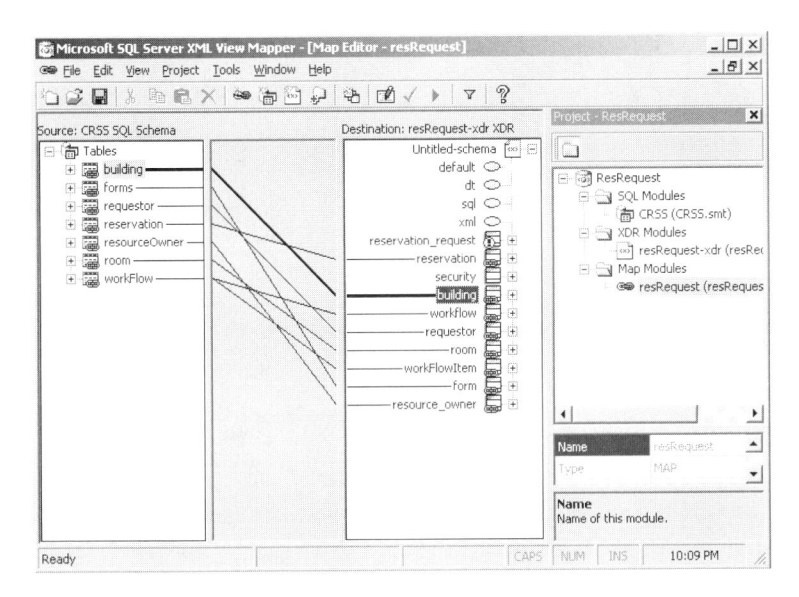

**FIGURE 27.10**   *XML Mapper with tables mapped to elements.*

Notice what occurs when you map one of the elements to its respective table. Additional information is added to the mapping XDR schema, using the `sql` namespace. The mapping information is shown in Listing 27.2.

**LISTING 27.2**   Reservation Element XDR After Mapping

```
<ElementType name="reservation"
    model="closed"
    content="empty"
    order="many"
    sql:relation="reservation">
```

You can see the newly added relationship in the last step of Listing 27.2. This is how Microsoft uses XML schemas to provide additional mapping information. These additions allow XML technologies to be used from anywhere. In fact, Microsoft's latest SQLXML3 release allows us to expose any database query as a Simple Object Access Protocol (SOAP)-based Web service. This is beyond the scope of this chapter; however, it will be an exciting area as business-to-business partnerships grow, using HTTP and HTTPS for data transport.

> **NOTE**
>
> The XML Mapping tool allows objects other than tables to be mapped. Tables, views, and columns can be mapped to XDR element types and attribute types.

The best way to ensure that you have mapped all of your XDR elements and attributes is to right-click anywhere on one of the XDR elements. This opens a context-sensitive menu where you can select the Show Pending Mappings menu item. You can then continue mapping until all XDR mappings are completed. You can appreciate the tool more after viewing the complete mapping shown in Figure 27.11.

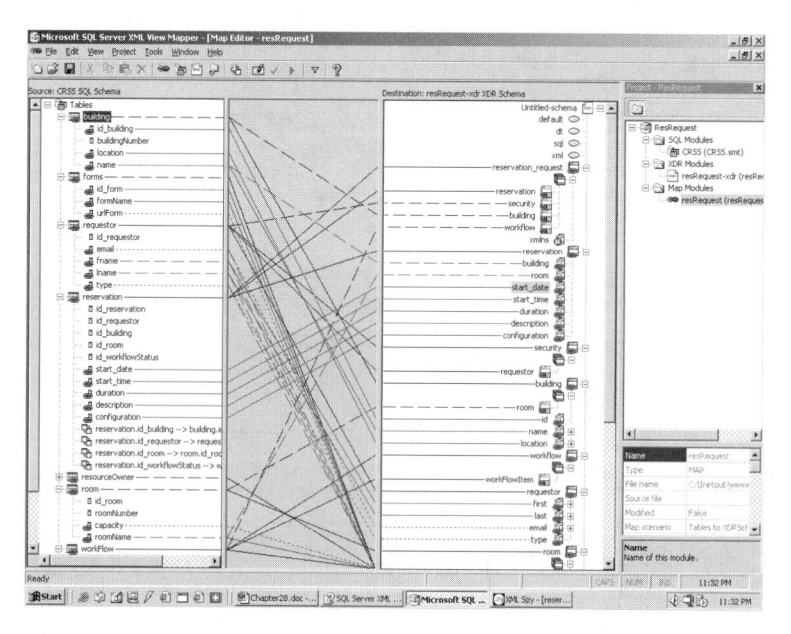

**FIGURE 27.11**  *Completed mapping of XDR to SQL.*

The XML Mapping tool has created all the necessary relationships to let you deal with SQL tables as if they were XML, and vice versa. You can examine one of the relationships in more detail to understand what the tool is doing behind the scenes.

If you look at a partial mapping of the reservation `ElementType` element shown in Listing 27.3, you can see several uses of the `sql` namespace. The 'sql' prefix applies only to one namespace in the document's root element namespace declaration. The declaration was left out for the sake of brevity. You are only going to look at the building and room fields within the XDR mapping. Each of these represents a mapping that was done by the SQL XML View Mapper tool.

**LISTING 27.3**  Partial XDR-to-SQL Mapping Result

```
<attribute type="building"
    required="yes"
    sql:relation="building"
    sql:field="name" >
 <sql:relationship key-relation="reservation"
    key="id_building"
    foreign-relation="building"
    foreign-key="id_building" >
 </sql:relationship>
</attribute>
<attribute type="room"
    required="yes"
    sql:relation="room"
    sql:field="roomName" >
 <sql:relationship key-relation="reservation"
    key="id_room"
    foreign-relation="room"
    foreign-key="id_room" >
 </sql:relationship>
</attribute>
```

When you examine the results shown in Listing 27.3, the purpose of the tool becomes clearer. You can see that the `building` attribute type's relationships are being defined. The attribute type `building` is mapped to the building table's `name` column. Looking a bit further down in the listing you can see that the reservation table is joined to the building table using the `id_building` foreign key. The XDR schema enables SQL server to enforce referential integrity rules when data is being added, deleted, or updated using a XML source.

The latter half of Listing 27.3 illustrates another relationship. This time the `room` attribute type is mapped to the `roomName` column in the `room` table. The foreign key relationship is specified showing that the `id_room` column in the reservation table is acting as a foreign key linking the reservation and the room tables.

The `sql:relation` annotation is added to map an element in the XML schema document to a column in a database table. The name of a table (view) is specified as the value of the `sql:relation` annotation.

Microsoft refers to attributes like `sql:relation` and `sql:field` as annotations in their documentation. This term should not be confused with XML schema annotation elements that are used to provide documentation within a schema. To be consistent with Microsoft's documentation on XDR schemas this chapter will use the term "annotate" when referring to XDR mapping attributes.

When `sql:relation` is specified on an element type, the scope of this annotation applies to all attributes and subelements described in the complex type definition of that element, providing a shortcut in writing annotations.

The `sql:relation` annotation is also useful when identifiers that are valid in Microsoft SQL Server are not valid in XML. For example, say you have a table named Reservation Request. This is a valid table name in SQL Server but not in XML. In these instances, the `sql:relation` annotation can be used to specify the mapping, as in this example:

```
<xsd:element name="resRequest"
   sql:relation="[Reservation Request]">
```

The `sql:field` annotation is added to map an XML attribute type or element type in the schema to a database column. You cannot specify `sql:field` on an empty content element.

## 27.1.2 Testing the SQL Mapping

Now that you have mapped your reservation request to the SQL tables, what can you do with it? You can load some data into the database tables and begin to execute XPath queries against the database. All you have to do is select the XPath Query tool from within the XML Mapping program by pressing F5 and begin entering queries. If you issue a simple XPath query as shown in Figure 27.12, you will get the result displayed.

Notice that the XPath query is configured as if you were querying the XML data. Remember that you do not even have any XML data in the tool—you only supplied the XDR schema. The

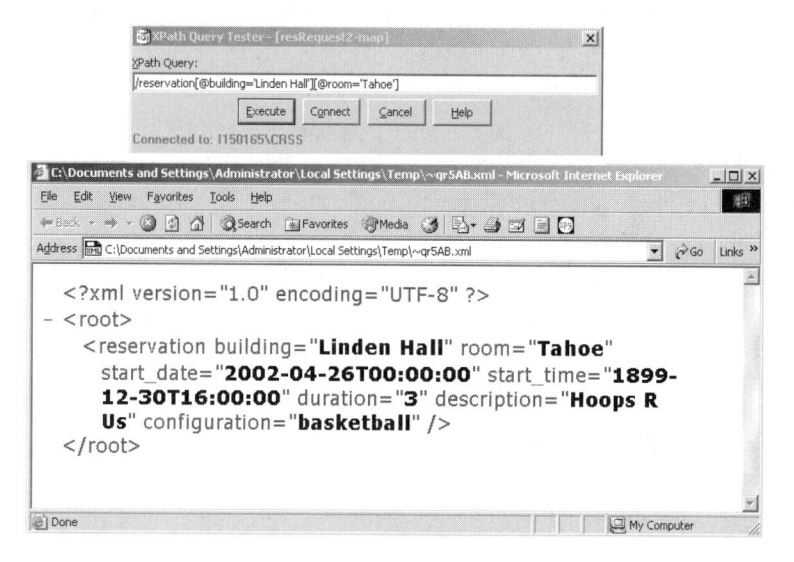

**FIGURE 27.12** *XPath query example.*

result of the XPath query is a well-formed XML document that conforms to your XDR schema. You now can query, using XPath for all reservations, for a particular room in a certain date range and get the results as XML.

You might be wondering why you should bother with getting the data as XML. You could simply continue to deal with the database and get data back and deal with it as before. The advantage of XML over traditional database techniques is that it provides structure for data that is inherently unstructured. As a result, you have a way to manipulate data and use frameworks such as Microsoft's .NET or Sun's J2EE.

You also can expose certain data as Web services that will facilitate many capabilities. Imagine not having to completely redo the security module at your company for each new application. Simply create one server-based security module by using the database and expose the login as a Web service. All developers anywhere in the world can use it. If scalability is required, add more servers to the Web farm. XML provides extensibility that makes these new database capabilities exciting.

### 27.1.3 Database Mapping Summary

You now have a basis for working with the database. You have seen how to use the SQL XML View Mapper with XDR schemas to create the illusion that the SQL Server is merely a large XML document. You finish your work with the SQL XML View Mapper by exporting your XDR mapping schema so you can reuse it in your application later.

You know from the work you did in the previous chapter that you can receive data from the Web browser into your ASP.NET page. Now you can take this data and insert the request into the database, using the mapping schema you just created. To accomplish this, you need to create custom code using Visual Basic .NET to do the following:

- Receive HTML form data
- Package the form data into an XML message
- Validate the XML message using your XML schema
- Insert the reservation request into the database using the mapping schema

## 27.2 SQL IIS Configuration

To use the mapping schema from the previous section, you need to configure SQL Server to allow for XML queries. Using HTTP to access SQL Server requires that you set up an appropriate virtual directory. You can use the IIS Virtual Directory Management for SQL Server utility to define and register a new virtual directory, also known as the *virtual root*, on the computer that is running Microsoft Internet Information Services (IIS). This utility instructs IIS to create an association between the new virtual directory and an instance of Microsoft SQL Server.

The name of the IIS server and the virtual directory must be specified as part of the URI. The information in the virtual directory is used to establish a connection to a specific database and execute the query. Administrators can use this tool to establish security information, including login, password, and access permissions.

You have several possible actions to take after you create the virtual directory:

- Execute template files.
- Execute XPath queries.
- Access database objects (such as tables) directly.
- Access a Web Services Description Language (WSDL) file.

Template files are valid XML documents that contain one or more SQL statements as values. Templates use a Microsoft-specified namespace and several specified elements and attributes to allow the SQL query to execute.

The XPath queries are executed against an XDR mapping schema that is specified as part of the URI. This is what you just did when testing your XDR mapping in Section 27.1.3.

Accessing database objects directly can be done by setting up a virtual name of dbobject type. This can lead to security issues and should be considered carefully before implementing. Rarely will you want your database objects, tables, stored procedures, and such available via HTTP.

Finally, you can access a WSDL file by using a URI that includes a virtual directory path specified as a soap type in the SQL IIS configuration tool. WSDL provides a description of the services offered by a Web service. A client application can access the WSDL file and then send SOAP requests to SQL 2000 using the SQLXML3 functionality.

You need to perform several steps to begin using any XML interfaces to the CRSS database:

1. Create the virtual directory.
2. Set the virtual directory access permissions.
3. Establish the name you will use to access template files.

> **TIP**
>
> Previous versions of the Configure IIS Support Tool are not completely backward-compatible with the one included with SQLXML3. To guarantee successful results, you should remove previous versions of SQLXML before installing the most recent version.

## 27.2 SQL IIS Configuration

### CHAPTER 27

Creating the virtual directory is accomplished by launching the Configure IIS Support tool located in the SQLXML3 program group. Figure 27.13 illustrates the default dialog you will see after launching the tool.

After you have the tool launched, you can create the virtual directory to the CRSS database as shown in Figure 27.14.

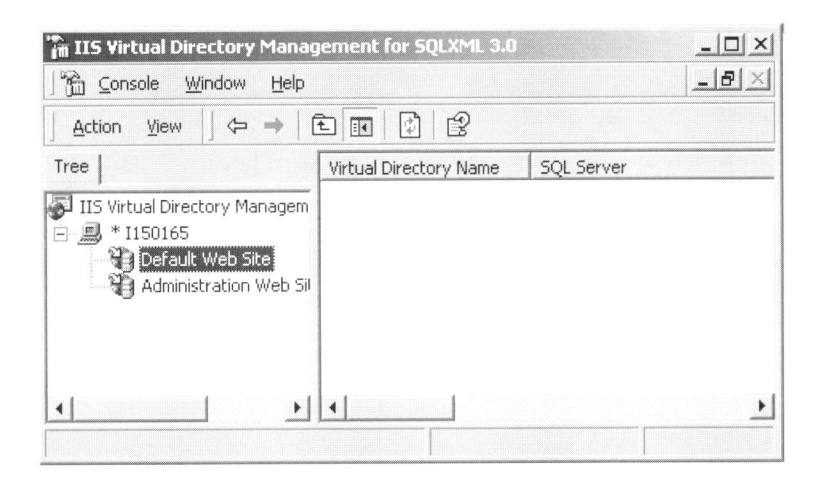

**FIGURE 27.13** *Configuring IIS virtual directory support for SQL Server.*

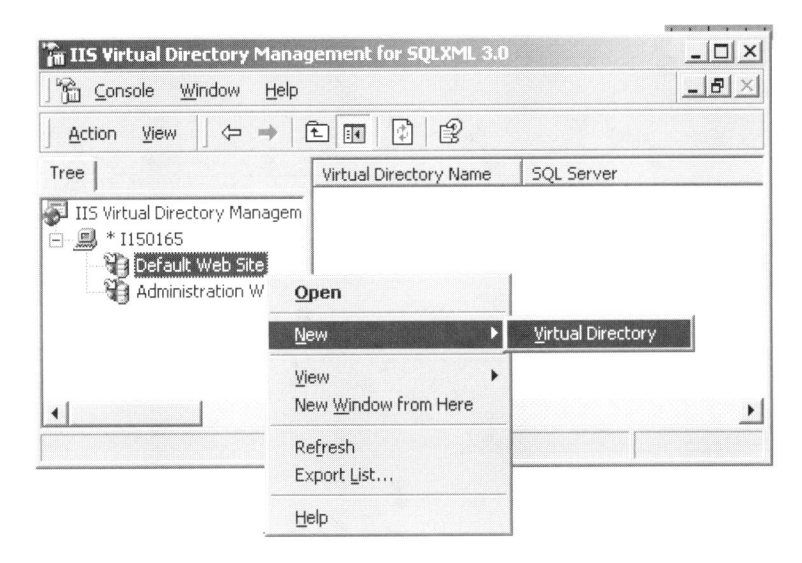

**FIGURE 27.14** *Creating a SQL virtual directory.*

Name the virtual directory CRSS and provide a physical path of `c:\crss`. Next, set the security by providing the user account name that will be executing the templates. A full discussion of security is beyond the scope of this book; however, you should defer to the database administrator to configure security for the application. You have several choices for security settings, including 'Windows Integrated', 'Basic', and the one we have chosen: 'Always log on as'. Using the policy of least privilege is always a good idea. Configure the security using the dialog shown in Figure 27.15.

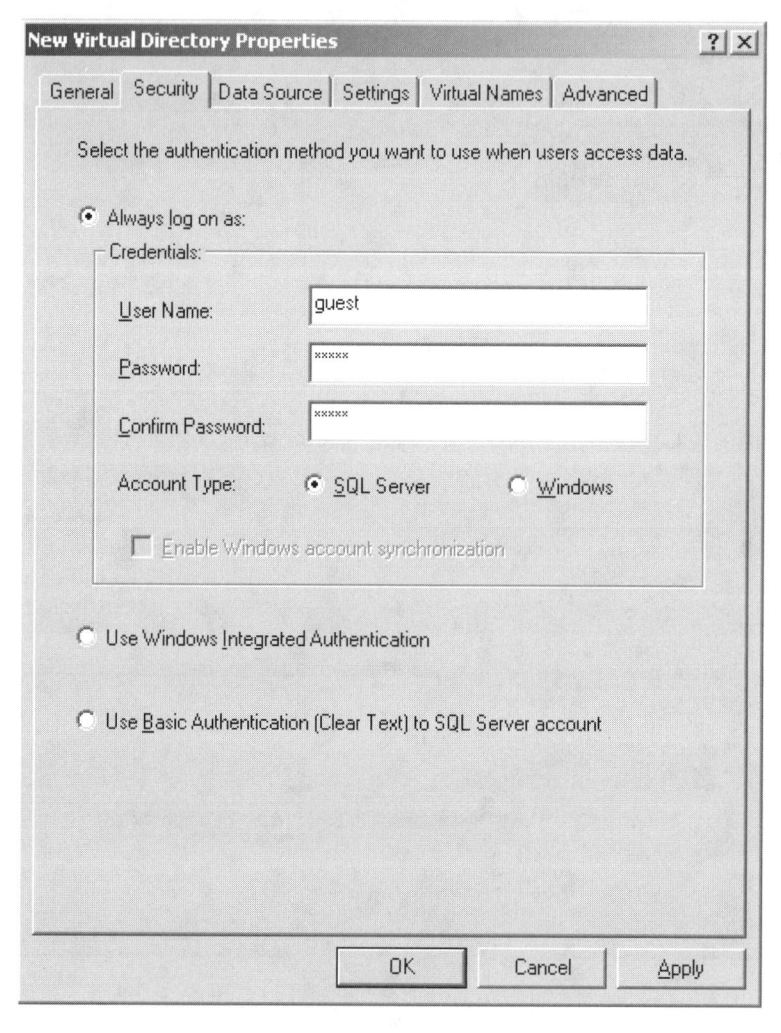

**FIGURE 27.15** *Configuring IIS virtual directory security.*

Next you need to set the data source settings. Select the server that the database is on and then select the name of the database you will be working against. The settings shown in Figure 27.16 will work for the CRSS application.

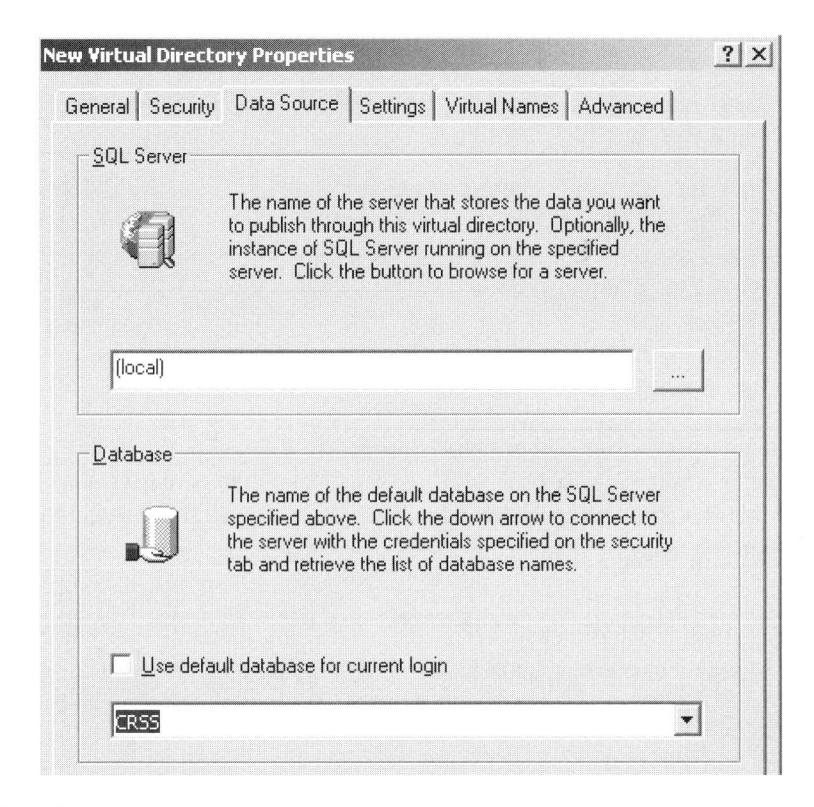

**FIGURE 27.16**  *Data source settings.*

Now you have to set the access capabilities by using the 'Settings' tab. During development and testing, enabling all the options is fine. However, you need to understand what these options mean so that you can set them properly for the production release.

By default, only template-based queries are allowed. The first options available are the 'Allow sql=' or 'template=' queries. These allow anyone with HTTP access to perform ad hoc queries against the database. Obviously this is not a very secure approach and should be used only when there are no security concerns.

The next option, 'Allow Posted Updategrams', allows only XML templates using XML updategrams to be posted to the URI. This further restricts access by disallowing SQL and XPath queries from being performed. However, a malicious person with access could write a script to update the database millions of times, so caution is always advised.

The next option, 'Allow Template Queries', is enabled by default and is the most secure choice. This choice allows the execution of template files in the URI. Templates are valid XML documents that consist of one or more SQL and XPath queries and Updategrams.

The Allow XPath option allows the execution of XPath queries against the XML schema files located at the URI. Again, this is what you did by using the SQL XML View Mapper tool. During testing, allowing URL access has the advantage of verifying that the mapping schema you have created is correct.

The 'Allow Post' option is required if you create virtual directories of SOAP type. Typically, HTTP's GET and HEAD methods are allowed by default; however, they are limited in the amount of data they can send. The data size limit is equal to the maximum size of the URI, typically about 1K. Enabling POST allows POST requests to be sent to any virtual name defined in this directory. For security and performance reasons, it is a good idea to create a separate virtual directory for SOAP requests. Setting the maximum size for POST queries specifies the maximum amount of data (in KB) that can be posted per HTTP request.

The 'Running on the Client' option simply specifies that the XML formatting is done on the client. The 'Expos runtime errors as HTTP errors' option throws any errors to the HTTP client. Again this is useful during development but more of a distraction for end users running production applications.

The next tab is the Virtual Names tab. This is where you can create virtual names that will be specified as part of the URI to execute template files, perform XPath queries against a mapping schema, access database objects directly (if allowed), and POST SOAP requests. Only the virtual names are exposed. This abstracts any knowledge of the physical paths, thereby enhancing security and providing a mechanism for assisting in portability.

An XML template can include SQL queries, XPath queries, or Updategrams or DiffGrams. For example, in the CRSS application, you can access templates as follows:

```
http://localhost/crss/query/myTemplate.xml
```

You must have a template named myTemplate.xml located at the c:\crss physical path for the query to succeed. Figure 27.17 illustrates the dialog settings required for the URL template query above to succeed.

You can create multiple virtual names that can point to the same or different physical directories. For example, you can create another virtual name, 'xpath', that also points to c:\crss. The c:\crss physical path would then be the location for your mapping schemas and your template XML query documents.

Creating a 'soap' virtual name creates the associated WSDL file and allows stored procedures to be accessed using SOAP requests. The Web Service name in the WSDL file associates a

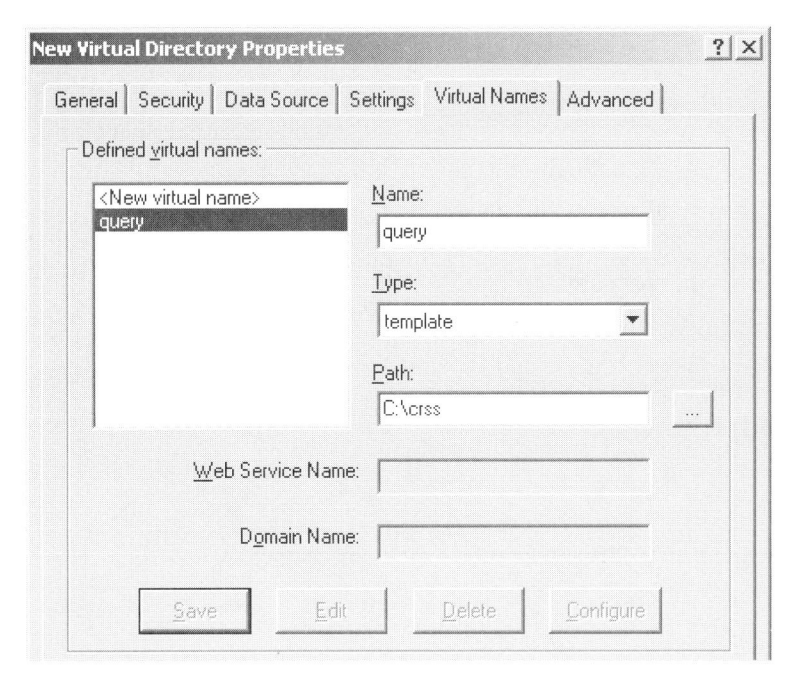

**FIGURE 27.17**  *Virtual Names tab.*

"SOAP virtual name" with a physical path name. SOAP requests require a domain name so that the URI can be located. Within intranets, the default name—also known as a NetBIOS name—works, but a fully qualified DNS name is needed for Internet SOAP services.

## 27.2.1 Testing the SQL IIS Configuration

Now that you have configured SQL 2000 to work with IIS, it's time to perform some quick tests to verify that your configuration is functioning. The simplest test is to execute a query by using Internet Explorer v5+, as shown in Figure 27.18.

Notice that you have not yet put any template queries into your physical path (c:\crss). You are simply performing an ad hoc query from the command line. You can modify this query as you would any SQL query and view the results. You need to take into account that all the queries must comply with HTTP address rules. Spaces, for example, are not allowed and must be encoded with a '%'. Similarly, the '+' symbol concatenates the strings that comprise the SQL query.

You can also test by using a simple template. Create the template in Listing 27.4 and place it in the c:\crss physical directory.

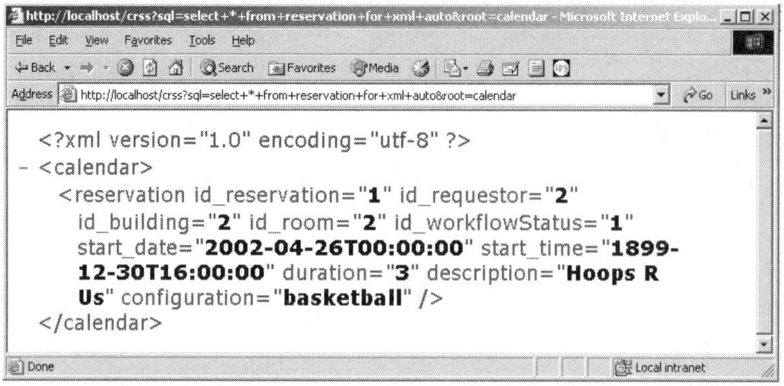

[Screenshot of Internet Explorer showing XML output from URL query]

**FIGURE 27.18**  *URL query test.*

**LISTING 27.4**  Template Query

```
<events xmlns:sql="urn:schemas-microsoft-com:xml-sql">
<sql:query>
 SELECT *
 FROM reservation
 FOR XML AUTO
</sql:query>
</events>
```

Now execute the query shown in Figure 27.19 and view the results.

You are on your way to using some very powerful XML SQL features. You must simply create the SQL queries that will be used by the CRSS application, wrap them as template queries, and place them in the c:\crss folder. You will then use your mapping schema from earlier in this chapter to update the database. This will allow you to test the data tier integration.

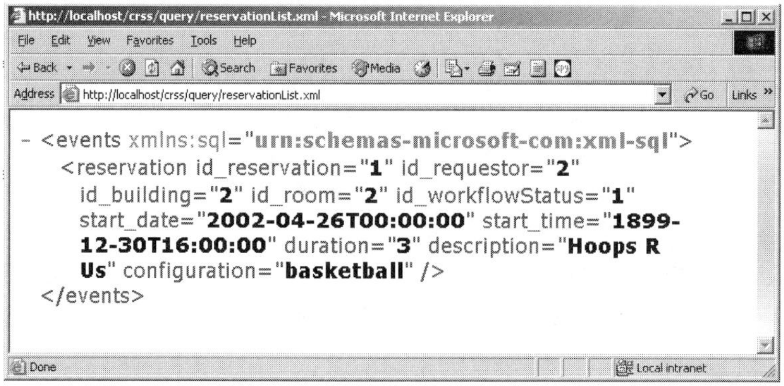

[Screenshot of Internet Explorer showing template query XML output]

**FIGURE 27.19**  *Template test.*

## 27.3 CRSS Application Requirements

Now that you have configured SQL 2000 to work with XML templates and XPath queries, it's time to look at the CRSS application requirements. You need the following database queries from the sequence diagram at the start of Chapter 26:

1. View all reservations by resource.
2. Insert a new pending reservation request.
3. Approve a specific reservation.

You can create and test the queries one at a time. The first query, Viewing Reservations by Resource, is simple enough, as shown in Listing 27.5.

**LISTING 27.5**  Parameter-Based Template Query

```
<viewReservations
 xmlns:sql='urn:schemas-microsoft-com:xml-sql'>
<sql:header>
   <sql:param name='room'>Tahoe</sql:param>
   <sql:param name='bdlg'>Linden Hall</sql:param>
</sql:header>
<sql:query >
SELECT reservation.start_date, reservation.start_time,
    reservation.duration, reservation.description,
    reservation.configuration
FROM reservation
INNER JOIN building ON
  reservation.id_building = building.id_building
INNER JOIN room ON
  reservation.id_room = room.id_room
WHERE (building.name = @bdlg) AND (room.roomName = @room)
ORDER BY reservation.start_date
FOR XML AUTO
</sql:query>
</viewReservations>
```

As you can see, this query receives two input parameters. These can be passed as part of the URI. In this case you have predefined some default values, 'Tahoe' and 'Linden Hall'. Again, you can test this parameter-base by using the browser as shown in Figure 27.20.

As Figure 27.20 shows, the parameters can be passed in the URI. Simply use a '?' to separate the name of the template query from the parameter names. Concatenate parameters using the ampersand symbol ('&'). Remember that spaces are not allowed, so URI-encode these by using the '+' symbol.

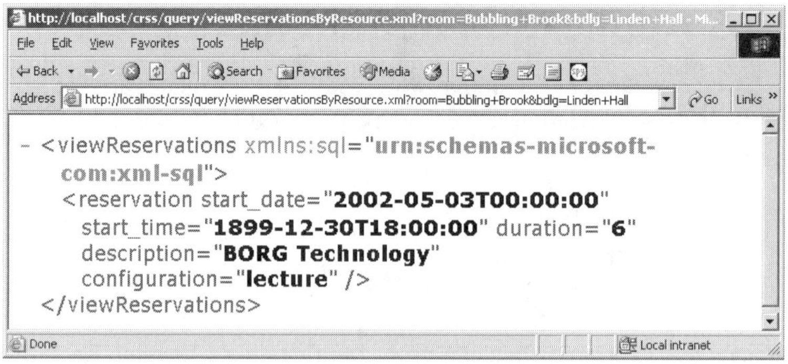

**FIGURE 27.20** *Passing parameters to template queries.*

## 27.4 Updategrams

Database data can be modified using Updategrams. Suppose you want to delete a reservation that was previously created. You use an Updategram to accomplish this. Updategrams can be used to insert, edit, or delete data from the database. Listing 27.6 shows an example of an Updategram. In the listing the `before` element has data but the `after` has none. The result is the deletion of the row specified.

**LISTING 27.6** Removing a Reservation

```
<removeReservation
  xmlns:updg="urn:schemas-microsoft-com:xml-updategram">
  <updg:header>
    <updg:param name="rid"/>
  </updg:header>
  <updg:sync>
    <updg:before updg:returnid="record">
      <reservation updg:at-identity="record"
            id_reservation="$rid"/>
    </updg:before>
    <updg:after/>
  </updg:sync>
</removeReservation>
```

The third line uses a parameter to choose which reservation to delete. By filling in a value for the parameter with the same type of URI as before, you can easily delete any reservation. Figure 27.21 demonstrates this, using the parameter named 'rid' for the reservation ID.

Inserting a reservation is the opposite of deleting one. Simply fill in the `updg:after` element and leave the `updg:before` element empty. You update data by filling in both elements.

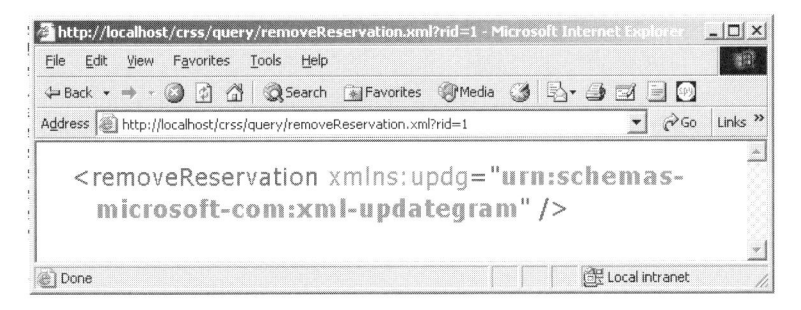

**FIGURE 27.21** *Delete data with parameterized Updategrams.*

The remainder of the stored procedures and the template queries required for the CRSS application can be downloaded from `http://www.XMLSchemaReference.com/examples/CRSS`.

## 27.5 Summary

In this chapter you investigated how to integrate relational data with hierarchical data. Our focus has been on Microsoft's SQL 2000 and the tools available to support that product. The techniques described in this chapter are very similar to the techniques used to work with Oracle's tools. You now have all the tools for assembling a working application.

You have seen two uses for XML schemas in the past two chapters. Chapter 26 focused on the use of XML schemas in validating user data. This chapter used XML schemas to provide a mapping between two completely different data structures. Many business-to-business applications use XSLT to convert from one form of XML schema to another. Microsoft's BizTalk is a good example of a product that uses XML technologies to automate the Business to Business Schema mapping.

In Chapter 28, you will use the XML schemas covered in Chapter 26 for validation and the XML schemas used for database mapping in this chapter to create the final CRSS application.

# The Integrated Solution

**CHAPTER 28**

## IN THIS CHAPTER

- 28.1 CRSS Design Review  836
- 28.2 Web Tier Construction  838
- 28.3 UI Broker Component Construction  842
- 28.4 Security Broker Component Construction  846
- 28.5 CRSS Broker Component Construction  847
- 28.6 Template Query  851
- 28.7 CRSS Review  853

In the previous two chapters you created pieces of the Campus Resource and Scheduling System (CRSS) architecture. You learned how to use XML schemas for three purposes:

- Validating client requests
- Creating XSLT transformations to provide the HTML view
- Mapping XML hierarchical data to the relational database

Now you need to combine this work into a functioning application. Until this point, the majority of the work has been dependent on XML technologies only. You have been able to remain relatively vendor-independent—with the exception of the SQL 2000 mapping in Chapter 27. The advantage of this approach is that you have several key pieces of your design already tested without committing to a vendor, allowing you to more easily move between vendor frameworks in the future. However, assembling the final application does require you to commit to a vendor framework. You will use Microsoft's .NET Framework to create the final application.

When you first looked at the CRSS requirements in Chapter 25, you had four primary goals. Here they are again:

- Users should be able to access the system by using the Web.
- The system easily adapts to PDAs and other wireless technologies.
- XML schemas should be used to validate all user interaction with the system.
- Database interaction should occur by using XML schemas to map XML data to relational tables automatically.

In Chapter 26, you validated user inputs with schemas and created the XSLT templates required to meet the first three goals. Chapter 27 focused solely on meeting the fourth goal. At this point you have an XML framework with XML schema validation that will meet all four goals. Although you did not create the XSLT template to work with PDAs, the framework certainly allows this.

In this chapter you work with the following technologies:

- Microsoft's Visual Studio .NET
- Visual Basic .NET language
- ASP.NET for the Web interface
- SQL 2000 for database access

## 28.1 CRSS Design Review

The CRSS design allows a user to view existing reservations on a per-resource basis and request a new reservation. Architecturally, the design satisfies the sequence diagram previously

## 28.1 CRSS Design Review

reviewed in Figure 26.3. Physically, the flow of code resembles a state machine with the following states:

1. User requests to view a list of resources.
2. Web tier converts user request to an XML message.
3. XML message is validated according to an XML schema.
4. Business components receive valid XML message and process request.
5. Database interactions occur, using XML and mapping XML schemas.
6. Business components apply the correct view to the output message.
7. User receives HTML result.

> **NOTE**
>
> Microsoft's .NET Framework includes many tools and features. You will not be covering all these features. In fact, you will be avoiding all components that create a strong dependence on non-Internet standard features.

Take a look at Figure 28.1 to understand exactly what you build in this chapter. The diagram shows the UML component model required to process the user's requests through the seven states previously mentioned. You are ready now to begin constructing each of these pieces.

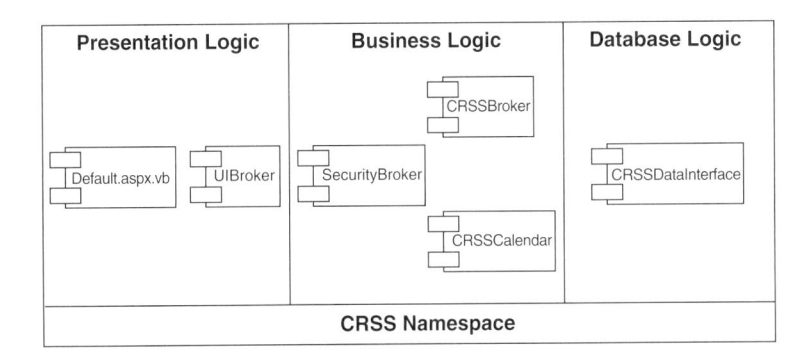

**FIGURE 28.1** *CRSS final design component diagram.*

## 28.2 Web Tier Construction

Creating the Web tier requires that you understand the incoming messages provided by the Web-enabled device. First, a review the two messages your CRSS case study will implement. Listing 28.1 is the Calendar Request Message, and Listing 28.2 is the Client Reservation Request.

**LISTING 28.1** Calendar Request Message

```xml
<?xml version="1.0" encoding="utf-8"?>
<getResouceCalendar
  xmlns="http://www.XMLSchemaReference.com/examples/CRSS"
  xmlns:xsi="http://www.w3.org/2001/XMLSchema-instance"
  xsi:schemaLocation="http://sams/msgCalendarRequest.xsd">
  <resource name="">
    <range startDate="" endDate=""/>
  </resource>
</getResouceCalendar>
```

**LISTING 28.2** Client Reservation Request

```xml
<?xml version="1.0" encoding="utf-8"?>
<reservation_request
  xmlns="http://www.XMLSchemaReference.com/examples/CRSS"
  xmlns:xsi="http://www.w3.org/2001/XMLSchema-instance"
  xsi:schemaLocation="http://localhost/sams/resRequest.xsd">
  <reservation building="" room="" start_date=""
        start_time="" duration=""
        description="" configuration="" user=""/>
</reservation_request>
```

> **NOTE**
>
> Listing 28.2 is the portion of the resource reservation message supplied by the user. The complete request is shown in Figure 26.5. The user name has been added to simplify the security portion of the final code. You will not go into security details in the CRSS application.

Listings 28.1 and 28.2 are blank templates that your application populates by using the HTML form data submitted by the client. Obviously, user input data to your system cannot be trusted to be valid. You will use the XML schemas shown in the `schemaLocation` attribute in Listing 28.2 above. Listing 28.3 is the XML schema used to validate the user's input.

**LISTING 28.3**  Reservation Request Schema

```xml
<?xml version="1.0" encoding="UTF-8"?>
<xsd:schema
targetNamespace=
  "http://www.XMLSchemaReference.com/examples/CRSS"
xmlns:xsd="http://www.w3.org/2001/XMLSchema"
xmlns="http://XMLSchemaReference.com/examples"
elementFormDefault="qualified"
attributeFormDefault="unqualified" id="msgResRequest">
 <xsd:include schemaLocation="dateType.xsd"
    id="dateType"/>
 <xsd:include schemaLocation="timeType.xsd"
    id="timeType"/>
 <xsd:include schemaLocation="configType.xsd"
    id="configType"/>
 <xsd:include schemaLocation="buildingType.xsd"
    id="buildingType"/>
 <xsd:include schemaLocation="durationType.xsd"
    id="durationType"/>
 <xsd:include schemaLocation="roomType.xsd"
    id="roomType"/>
 <xsd:complexType name="reservationType">
   <xsd:attribute name="building" type="buildingType"
      use="required"/>
   <xsd:attribute name="room" type="roomType"
      use="required"/>
   <xsd:attribute name="start_date" type="dateType"
      use="required"/>
   <xsd:attribute name="start_time" type="timeType"
      use="required"/>
            <xsd:attribute name="duration" type="durationType"
      use="required"/>
            <xsd:attribute name="configuration" type="configType"
      use="required"/>
    <xsd:attribute name="description" use="required">
      <xsd:simpleType>
        <xsd:restriction base="xsd:string">
          <xsd:minLength value="4"/>
            <xsd:maxLength value="64"/>
        </xsd:restriction>
      </xsd:simpleType>
    </xsd:attribute>
    <xsd:attribute name="user" use="required">
      <xsd:simpleType>
        <xsd:restriction base="xsd:string">
          <xsd:minLength value="2"/>
          <xsd:maxLength value="12"/>
```

*continues*

```
            <xsd:whiteSpace value="collapse"/>
          </xsd:restriction>
        </xsd:simpleType>
      </xsd:attribute>
    </xsd:complexType>
    <xsd:element name="reservation_request">
      <xsd:complexType>
        <xsd:sequence>
          <xsd:element name="reservation"
                  type="reservationType"/>
        </xsd:sequence>
      </xsd:complexType>
    </xsd:element>
</xsd:schema>
```

Listing 28.3 illustrates how you can create one logical application schema from many schema documents. You created several of the schema documents that the application schema in Listing 28.3 is using in Chapter 26. Notice the use of the include type for the dateType, timeType, and others. Using include maximizes reuse of existing schema documents.

You can now create the ASP.NET page that receives the two empty messages identified in Listings 28.1 and 28.2. Launch Visual Studio and create a VB.NET Web project named CRSS. Add a Web form page named default.aspx.

In Visual Studio .NET a Web page has several different views. One view represents the HTML, another view represents the programming logic. Microsoft made this change to logically remove programming code from presentation markup. In this next section you will need to modify the same page using two different views.

Open the default.aspx page by double-clicking on it in the Solution Explorer view. Switch to the HTML view by selecting the HTML tab shown at the bottom of Figure 28.2. Delete the HTML added by Visual Studio as shown in Figure 28.2. The text highlighted in Figure 28.2 is to be deleted. The line beginning with '<%@ Page...' is the only line that should remain.

You will not be using any of the Web form features, so the HTML is not required. Now open default.aspx again, but this time you will use the code view. You open the code view by right-clicking on the default.aspx page in the Solution Explorer view and selecting View | Code. You are going to add exactly one line of code to complete this page. Add the line shown in Figure 28.3 to complete the ASP.NET Web tier implementation.

This is the total amount of code that you will be using in the ASP.NET tier. Not bad—only a single line of code added. The entire Web site will consist of this page and nothing more. You can say good-bye to broken links.

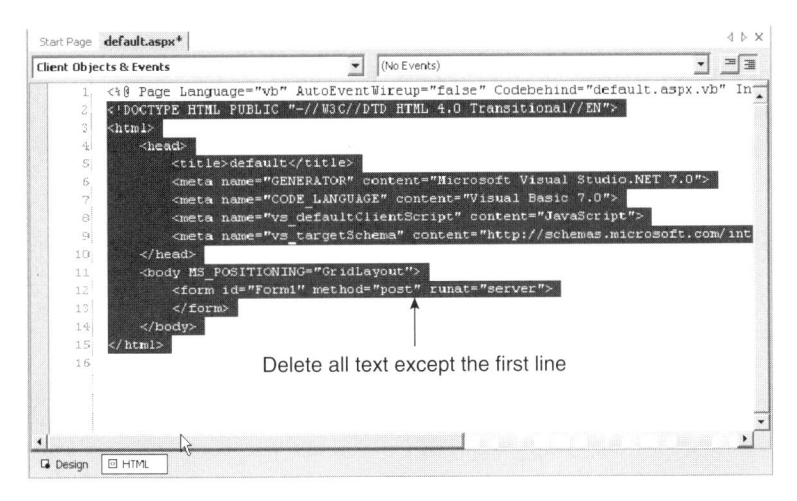

**FIGURE 28.2** *Default.aspx in CRSS Web project.*

**FIGURE 28.3** *Final Default.aspx page.*

Notice that the business object that receives the HTTP request and response object is the CRSS.UIBroker. Microsoft uses namespaces to qualify component names. In the case of your CRSS.UIBroker component, 'CRSS' is the namespace and 'UIBroker' is the name of the component. The namespaces used to qualify your component names have nothing to do with the namespaces used by your XML schemas.

Using a single page to receive and respond to the incoming data stream simplifies the architecture and removes a number of common Web problems. No broken links, no dependencies on vendor "features," and so on. It also forces you to completely separate the business logic from the user interface logic.

Now that you have a way to receive and respond to the Web-enabled device, you need to build a component. The default.aspx page that you created shown in Figure 28.3 is sending the HTTP request and response object to another component. This component will be called the UIBroker component. The UIBroker component receives incoming data from Web-enabled devices, translates the incoming requests to XML, calls the business components, receives the results of the business component data transformations, and applies the correct XSLT document to provide the view. You will construct the `CRSS` component using VB.NET.

## 28.3 UI Broker Component Construction

The primary purpose of the `UIBroker` component is to determine what action was requested by the Web-enabled device. After determining the requested action, the `UIBroker` does the following:

1. Loads the appropriate XML message template.
2. Fills the template with the HTML data submitted by the user.
3. Sends the message to the `SecurityBroker` component.
4. Receives the final XML result.
5. Applies the XSLT template.
6. Sends the HTML response to the user.

You will create the code to implement the processing requirements. First you should add your empty XML messages to the Web site. Name these empty messages '`msgCalendarRequest.xml`' and '`msgReservationRequest.xml`' and place them in a folder named '`XML`' under your `CRSS` Web application root. You need to also add your XML schemas into the same folder.

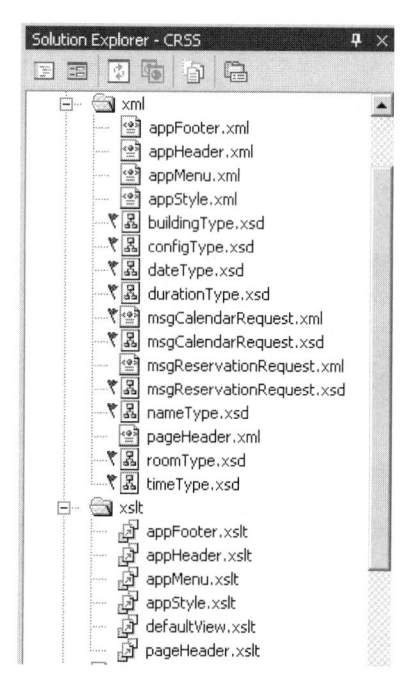

**FIGURE 28.4**  *CRSS project XML/XSLT files.*

## 28.3 UI Broker Component Construction

Note that in Figure 28.4, a number of XML and XML schema (*.xsd) files have been added to the project. These validate the inputs you receive from the user. Now that you have the files added to the project, you can use these in your VB.NET component, using the code in Listing 28.4.

**LISTING 28.4**  Partial VB.NET UIBroker Code Listing

```
Public Sub doAction()
Try
Dim oXmlResult As XmlDocument
'Call for a view the application default view
Select Case sAction
Case "viewResourceCalendar"
'Extract form data and pack the message
Dim sBuilding As String = request.QueryString("building")
Dim sStartDate As String = request.QueryString("startMonth")
Dim sEndDate As String = request.QueryString("endMonth")
'Pack the xml message with the HTML form data
o_requestCalendarMsg.SelectSingleNode("//@name").Value _
   = sBuilding
o_requestCalendarMsg.SelectSingleNode("//@startDate").Value _
   = sStartDate
o_requestCalendarMsg.SelectSingleNode("//@endDate").Value _
   = sEndDate
'Send Message to SecurityBroker
oXmlResult = o_SecurityBroker.CanUserDo(o_requestCalendarMsg)
Case "requestResourceReservation"
'Extract form data and pack the message
Dim sBuilding As String = request.QueryString("building")
Dim sRoom As String = request.QueryString("room")
Dim sStartDate As String = request.QueryString("start_date")
Dim sStartTime As String = request.QueryString("start_time")
Dim sDuration As String = request.QueryString("duration")
Dim sDescription As String = _
  request.QueryString("description")
Dim sConfiguration As String = _
  request.QueryString("configuration")
Dim sUser As String = request.QueryString("user")
'Pack the xml message with the HTML form data
o_requestReservationMsg.SelectSingleNode _
   ("//@building").Value = sBuilding
o_requestReservationMsg.SelectSingleNode _
   ("//@room").Value = sRoom
o_requestReservationMsg.SelectSingleNode _
   ("//@start_date").Value = sStartDate
o_requestReservationMsg.SelectSingleNode _
```

*continues*

```
    ("//@start_time").Value = sStartTime
o_requestReservationMsg.SelectSingleNode _
    ("//@duration").Value = sDuration
 o_requestReservationMsg.SelectSingleNode _
    ("//@description").Value = sDescription
o_requestReservationMsg.SelectSingleNode _
    ("//@configuration").Value = sConfiguration
o_requestReservationMsg.SelectSingleNode _
    ("//@user").Value = sUser
'Send Message to SecurityBroker
oXmlResult = o_SecurityBroker.CanUserDo(o_requestCalendarMsg)
End Select
'Add UI Data to create final document
Dim oFinalNode As XmlNode = o_FinalDoc.DocumentElement
oFinalNode.AppendChild
    (o_FinalDoc.ImportNode(oXmlResult.DocumentElement, True))
        oFinalNode.AppendChild
    (o_FinalDoc.ImportNode(o_appHeader.DocumentElement, True))
        oFinalNode.AppendChild
    (o_FinalDoc.ImportNode(o_pageHeader.DocumentElement, True))
     oFinalNode.AppendChild
    (o_FinalDoc.ImportNode(o_pageStyle.DocumentElement, True))
        oFinalNode.AppendChild _
    (o_FinalDoc.ImportNode(o_appMenu.DocumentElement, True))
        oFinalNode.AppendChild
    (o_FinalDoc.ImportNode(o_appFooter.DocumentElement, True))
'Display result to user
Me.showView()
  Catch ex As Exception
    logException(ex)
  Finally
    'Cleanup
  End Try
End Sub
```

> **NOTE**
>
> Listing 28.4 is a partial listing. We will focus on specific features of the message flow as we move forward.

In Listing 28.4, the `UIBroker` is simply extracting HTML data and populating the reservation request or calendar view message. You use the `QueryString` collection to extract the form data. The bolded lines are performing this type of action for the two messages you are modeling. If you focus on the `viewResourceCalendar Case` statement only, you will see that the `requestResourceReservation Case` statement has the exactly same flow—the only difference is the form data that is submitted.

The following is the flow you want to achieve:

1. *Load the appropriate XML message template.*

   This was accomplished in the constructor. `sServerPath` is a variable that gets the name of the server you are running on and the virtual path, that is, `http://myserver/CRSS/`. This was done to improve portability of the application.

   ```
   'initialize all the messages
   o_requestCalendarMsg.Load _
     (sServerPath & "XML/msgCalendarRequest.xml")
   o_requestReservationMsg.Load _
     (sServerPath & "XML/msgReservationRequest.xml")
   ```

2. *Fill the template with the HTML data submitted by the user.*

   The `viewResourceCalendar Case` shown in Listing 28.4 show the HTML data being extracted using the ASP.NET `request.QueryString` method. The `SelectSingleNode` method is then used to pack the data into your XML message.

3. *Send the message to the `SecurityBroker` component.*

   This is done using the `o_SecurityBroker.CanUserDo(o_requestCalendarMsg)` method call. The XML message that the `UIBroker` component created is passed to the `SecurityBroker` to determine whether the user has the required privileges.

4. *Receive the final XML result.*

   The object variable, `oXmlResult`, contains the result of the business logic. `oXmlResult` is an XML document object variable allowing it to be easily transformed to HTML or WML using XSLT.

5. *Apply the XSLT template.*

   When the `Select Case` statement concludes, a call is made to `showView` shown in Listing 28.5. This uses the .NET Framework's `XslTransform` class to render the HTML. The `o_FinalView` object is initialized as follows in the constructor:

   `Private o_FinalView As New XslTransform()`

   The code for `showView` is shown in Listing 28.5.

**LISTING 28.5** XSLT Transform Using System.XML Classes

```
Private Sub showView()
Try
  Dim parmList As New XsltArgumentList()
  Dim xWriter As New XmlTextWriter(resp.Output)
  xWriter.Formatting = Formatting.Indented
  xWriter.Indentation = 4
  o_FinalView.Transform(o_FinalDoc, parmList, xWriter)
  Catch ex As Exception
    logException(ex)
  End Try
End Sub
```

6. *Send the response to the user.*

   Listing 28.5 sends the response to the user. The response steam is initialized by passing the `resp.Output` stream as an argument to the `XmlTextWriter` constructor. The transform method of the `XsltTransform` class performs the XML to HTML transformation and delivers the final view.

## 28.4 Security Broker Component Construction

The security broker can be designed in many ways. One of the best techniques is to expose the authentication service as a Web service and use this Web service for all of your applications. A more integrated approach is to use the Active Directory service and Microsoft's role-based security model. Each approach has pros and cons. The integrated approach uses existing tools but incurs licensing fees and possible update issues. The custom security Web service requires a unique security design for each company. The CRSS application would be overly complicated if you implemented a full security model: A stub is provided that simply passes the request through. Listing 28.6 is the stub that fulfills the architecture and provides a placeholder for work that you should complete, based on the unique security concerns of your environment:

**LISTING 28.6** Security Broker Stub

```
Option Explicit On
Option Strict On

Imports System
Imports System.XML
Imports System.Configuration
Imports Microsoft.VisualBasic.DateAndTime
Namespace CRSS
  Public Class SecurityBroker
```

```
    Private o_objConfigNode As Xml.XmlNode
    Private Property ConfigNode() As Xml.XmlNode
      Set(ByVal Value As Xml.XmlNode)
        o_objConfigNode = Value
      End Set
      Get
        Return o_objConfigNode
      End Get
    End Property
    Public Function CanUserDo _
      (ByVal p_objSubXml As XmlDocument) As XmlDocument
        Dim objCRSSXML As New XmlDocument()
        Dim objCRSSBroker As New CRSS.CRSSBroker()
        Dim objSecurityNode As XmlNode
'IF USER CAN DO THEN
        objCRSSXML = objCRSSBroker.initialize(p_objSubXml)
'ELSE
        'ERROR Details put in XML Response
' END IF
        Return objCRSSXML
      End Function
  End Class
End Namespace
```

## 28.5 CRSS Broker Component Construction

The `CRSSBroker` is responsible for all the business logic. It receives requests from a `SecurityBroker` object. The `CRSSBroker` assumes that if it receives a request, the user has been authenticated and has permissions. Following receipt of the request, the `CRSSBroker` performs the following actions:

1. Validates the XML incoming document, using its associated schema.
2. Extracts the action requested from the incoming message.
3. Applies whatever business rules are required, using the `CRSSCalendar` component if necessary.
4. Retrieves data using XML template-based queries.
5. Returns the completed XML document to the `UIBroker`.

The code for each action is quite similar. The differences are at the database tier. Let's look at retrieving a resource calendar first. You will follow each of the aforementioned steps in your subsequent code.

Listing 28.7 is the `Case` statement dealing with the resource calendar. Recall that the security broker sent the user input XML message to the `CRSSBroker` without validating the XML data against a schema. In this case you need to start by validating the incoming XML message using the applicable schema document. You will throw validation errors that are written to the NT Event Viewer's Application log.

Listing 28.7 shows the processing required for the resource calendar view. The basic flow is as follows:

1. *Specify the schema location that will be used to validate the XML input.*

   The variable `sSchema` contains the hard-coded path to the appropriate schema document. In a production application, use the `Web.config` file to avoid having to recompile when you move the physical locations of these files.

2. *Validate the incoming data against the XML schema.*

   The `validate(p_objSubXml, sSchema)` method performs the validation work, which you will examine in detail.

3. *Parse the incoming message for data.*

   XPath expressions are used to extract the user data from the XML message. This message requires the user to supply the building, a start date, and an end date so that a list of reservations for the specified building can be returned.

4. *Create the URI which invokes the SQL template query.*

5. *The parameterized template executes and returns the XML result to the variable* `o_FinalDoc`.

**LISTING 28.7** Resource Calendar View Code Snippet

```
Case "calendar_view"
 sSchema = "http://localhost/crss/xml/msgCalendarRequest.xsd"
'Validate incoming data
 validate(p_objSubXml, sSchema)
'No validation errors so execute business logic
'Get user information
 Dim strBuilding As String
 Dim strStartDate As String
 Dim strEndDate As String
 strBuilding = p_objSubXml.SelectSingleNode("//@name").Value
 strStartDate = _
  p_objSubXml.SelectSingleNode("//@startDate").Value
 strEndDate = _
  p_objSubXml.SelectSingleNode("//@endDate").Value
'Execute template based SQL Query using valid date
 o_FinalDoc.Load _
   ("http://localhost/crssDb/qry/showView?pBldg=" _
    & strBuilding & "&pSDate=" & strStartDate & " & _
```

```
&pEndDate=" & strEndDate)
'Return the final document to UIBroker
Return o_FinalDoc
```

Microsoft's .NET Framework presently supports W3C schemas, Microsoft's proprietary XDR schemas, and W3C DTDs. Programmatically validating an XML instance is not simple using the .NET Framework. You must first programmatically associate the XML schema with the XML document instance.

Microsoft's .NET Framework deals with XML validation a bit differently than most parser-based environments. Typically you associate an XML schema with an XML document instance by adding the `schemaLocation` attribute into the XML document to be validated—as in Listing 28.2. Unfortunately, this common approach does not conform to the .NET implementation. Microsoft opted for a more flexible approach in its `System.Xml` packages, which allow schemas to be added dynamically at runtime. Therefore, you must strip the XML schema information from the root element attributes in your XML messages and then perform the validation.

The `validate` subroutine has three arguments: the XML instance to validate and the schema to use for the validation. The third input is the name of a namespace to use. This input is not passed in as an argument, because it is a class level string variable. The variable 'ns' contains the namespace name and has the value 'http://www.XMLSchemaReference.com'. A non-validating TextReader object is required to translate the XML document object to an `XMLTextReader`. Once you have a nonvalidating `XMLTextReader`, you can use this as an input to create an `XmlValidatingReader`, which is exactly what is shown in Listing 28.8. Microsoft's .NET Framework allows the use of many types of Schema documents. You must specify that you are using the W3C Recommended Schema by setting the `ValidationType` property equal to `ValidationType.Schema` as shown in Listing 28.8.

Creating a validating reader method requires the software to perform the following steps:

1. Create a non-validating `XmlTextReader` from the XML document instance.
2. Specify the type of Schema that you are using.
3. Add the schema document and the namespace name used by your document instance to the `XmlSchemaCollection` instance.
4. Specify an event handler for the validating reader to call when validation errors occur using an event type of `ValidationEventHandler`.
5. Use the `XmlValidatingReader` instance's `read` method to raise any validation error events.

Listing 28.8 illustrates the validation logic.

**LISTING 28.8**  .NET Validation of the XML Instance

```vb
Private Sub validate(ByVal xDoc As XmlDocument, _
          ByVal sSchema As String)
Try
'.NET validating reader requires XmlDocument conversion to
'XMLTextReader
Dim o_sReader As New StringReader _
   (xDoc.DocumentElement.InnerXml)
Dim o_nvXmlReader As New XmlTextReader(o_sReader)
'create validating reader
Dim o_vXmlReader As New XmlValidatingReader(o_nvXmlReader)
o_vXmlReader.ValidationType = ValidationType.Schema
'create schema collection
Dim oSchemaCollection As New XmlSchemaCollection()
'ns declared elsewhere as a string
oSchemaCollection.Add(ns, sSchema)
'Associate our validating reader with the schema
o_vXmlReader.Schemas.Add(oSchemaCollection)
'Set the validation event handler.
AddHandler o_vXmlReader.ValidationEventHandler, _
     AddressOf ValidationCallBack
'Read and validate the XML data.
While o_vXmlReader.Read()
End While
Catch ex As Exception
logException(ex.ToString)
End Try
End Sub
```

Validation errors must be trapped and reported to the user so action can be taken to correct the problem. You will create an XML error document that contains all the errors. This error document can be transformed by using XSLT and then displayed to the end user.

Listing 28.8 declared an event handler to manage all `ValidationEventHandler` type events. The `ValidationCallback` error handler shown in Listing 28.9 is called each time the validating reader encounters a validation error. The error handler creates a new `errorItem` element each time a validation error occurs. This element is stored in the XML error document instance. The `errorItem` element contains an `errorMsg` attribute and is returned to the `UIBroker` component and rendered with XSLT to display all validation errors.

The event handler code is shown in Listing 28.9.

**LISTING 28.9**  Catching Validation Errors

```
Public Sub ValidationCallBack
  (ByVal sender As Object, ByVal args As ValidationEventArgs)
Try
  Dim eNode As XmlElement
  eNode = o_ErrorDoc.CreateElement("errorItem")
  eNode.SetAttribute("errorMsg", args.Message)
  o_ErrorDoc.DocumentElement.AppendChild(eNode)
  m_status = False  'failed validation
Catch ex As Exception
  logException(ex.Message)
End Try
End Sub 'ValidationCallBack
```

## 28.6 Template Query

We looked at template queries in Chapter 27 in detail. In this chapter all you need to use is the template query, shown in Listing 28.10, to retrieve all reservations for a specific resource between two date ranges. The template query for looking up your resource calendar is in Listing 28.10.

**LISTING 28.10**  XML Template Query

```
<viewReservations
  xmlns:sql='urn:schemas-microsoft-com:xml-sql'>
  <sql:header>
    <sql:param name='pBldg'>Linden Hall</sql:param>
    <sql:param name='pSDate'>05-01-2001</sql:param>
    <sql:param name='pEndDate'>06-01-2003</sql:param>
  </sql:header>
  <sql:query >
SELECT building.name AS Building, room.roomName AS Room,
room.roomNumber AS [Room Number],
reservation.start_date AS Date,reservation.start_time AS Time,
```

*continues*

```
reservation.duration AS Duration,
reservation.description AS [Desc], room.capacity AS Capacity
FROM building INNER JOIN reservation ON
building.id_building = reservation.id_building
INNER JOIN room ON reservation.id_room = room.id_room
WHERE (building.name = @pBldg) AND
    (reservation.start_date BETWEEN @pSDate AND @pEndDate)
FOR XML AUTO
  </sql:query>
</viewReservations>
```

The template query in Listing 28.10 is placed in the directory established by the database administrator and configured by using the SQLXML3 tool discussed in Chapter 27. Default values for the building, start date, and end date have been added to simplify testing. These parameters are used in the WHERE clause shown in Listing 28.10 and are executed using the template query shown in Listing 28.11. Parameters passed in the URL will override the default parameters you supplied. The XML document in Listing 28.11 is returned when the template in Listing 28.10 is executed.

**LISTING 28.11**    XML Template Query Result

```
<viewReservations
  xmlns:sql="urn:schemas-microsoft-com:xml-sql">
  <building Building="Linden Hall">
    <room Room="Bubbling Brook" Room_x0020_Number="322"
        Capacity="100">
    <reservation Date="2002-05-03T00:00:00"
          Time="1899-12-30T18:00:00"
          Duration="6" Desc="BORG Technology"/>
    </room>
  </building>
</viewReservations>
```

You now have satisfied the requirement to review a list of calendar events occurring within a specified date range. You now have to render the result, using XSLT as discussed in Chapter 26. The final view of this rendering is shown in Figure 28.5.

The code for adding a reservation is analogous to what we have just reviewed for viewing a reservation. The best way to continue with this case study is for you to load the code into Visual Studio .NET and create the application yourself. This will give you the opportunity to walk through the code, set break points, and experiment. The code for the CRSS application can be downloaded from http://www.XMLSchemaReference.com/examples/CRSS.

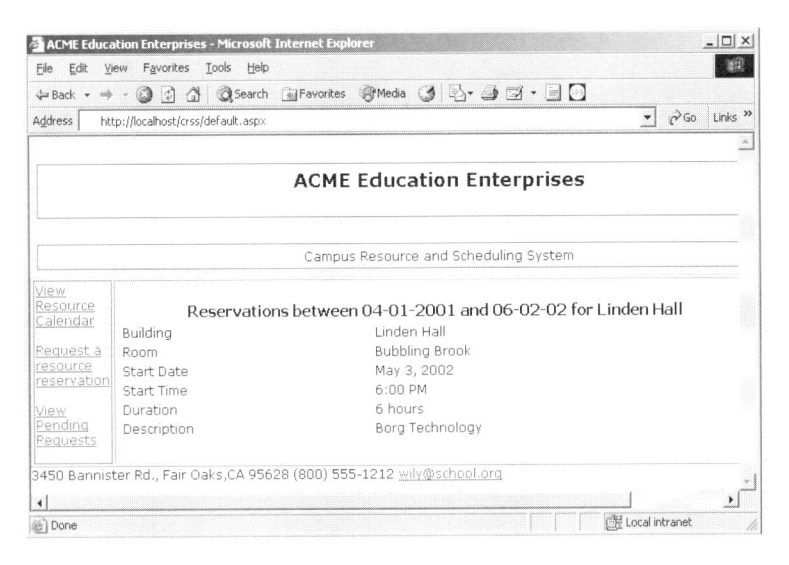

**FIGURE 28.5**  *CRSS calendar view.*

## 28.7 CRSS Review

You have integrated several technologies in the CRSS application. You started by looking at how to use UML diagrams to map HTML form input to XML messages. From there you created the XSLT templates for viewing the results. You also examined how to map XML structures to relational databases by using XPath queries. The Visual Studio .NET Framework was used to create the application logic to integrate the XML schemas, XSLT templates, XPath expressions, and SQL 2000 template queries.

The techniques shown in this case study focus on creating reusable modules. The XML schemas you created were reused within the CRSS application at several points and will also be useful on future projects. The XSLT templates were created in small modules and again aggregated into a master application specific template, providing flexibility for the various views you might wish to have your application perform. You did not need to use ODBC, JDBC, ADO, or any other lower-level database-access technology. All of your work was performed by using XML.

In addition, you only have a single Web page, which displays many views, in the entire application. It's very difficult to have broken links when you have one page. You can extend the CRSS application a number of ways, including:

- Adding the XSLT templates to render WML output for wireless devices
- Providing international capabilities with a combination of XSLT and XML schemas

# Appendixes

**PART VII**

The appendixes in Part VII cover a broad range of material that supports the rest of this book. This range includes reference material, examples, Oracle8*i*, and a glossary.

- Appendix A is a compact representation of all of the schema document elements and attributes thereof. Appendix A supports the experienced user who may have forgotten the specific needed syntax.
- Appendix B is a formal representation of the regular expression grammar. The value of a `pattern` constraining facet is a regular expression.
- Appendix C contains a listing of important XML schema documents that comprise the "catalog" example, which is prevalent throughout the book.
- Appendix D points out the unique features of Oracle8*i*, which does not as comprehensively support the XML datatypes as does Oracle9*i*.
- Appendix E is a compilation of terms that are used throughout this book.

# XML Schema Quick Reference

**APPENDIX A**

# XML Schema Quick Reference
## Appendix A

This appendix provides a quick reference for assembling an XML schema document. Specifically, this reference summarizes the Schema for Schemas.

Each element in an XML schema document has one or more attributes; most are optional. Similarly, each element may contain nested elements; most of these are optional as well.

Each attribute option has the following form:

*attributeName*? (='*defaultValue*') : *type*

The *attributeName* is the name of the attribute type. When the name has a '?' suffix, the attribute is optional. Most attributes are optional. If there is a default value when the attribute is not explicit, that value appears in quotes and in parentheses. Finally, the *type* describes the structure type of that attribute type. In many cases, the structure type is a built-in datatype. Occasionally, *type* is an enumeration of specific values, or an English description of an unusual datatype.

Each content option has one of the following forms:

*elementName*

*elementName*?

*elementName**

*elementName*+

*elementName* / ... / *elementName*

(*elementName* | ... | *elementName*)?

Each *elementName* is the name of an element type. The suffixes '?', '*', and '+' correspond to the regular expression meaning of "optional", "zero or more", and "one or more", respectively. '|' means that the encompassing element may contain one from a set of choices. Finally, the parentheses with '?' mean that choosing from the set of choices is optional.

Each row in Table A.1 corresponds to an element type whose instances can occur in an XML schema document. This reference lists every such element type.

**TABLE A.1** XML Schema Document Quick Reference

| Type of Element | Attribute Types | Subelement Types |
|---|---|---|
| all | id? : ID<br>minOccurs? (='1') : '1'<br>maxOccurs? (='1') : '0' or '1' | annotation?<br>element* |
| annotation | id? : ID | appinfo*<br>documentation* |
| any | id? : ID<br>maxOccurs? (='1') : a nonNegativeInteger or 'unbounded'<br>minOccurs? (='1') : nonNegativeInteger<br>namespace? : '##any', '##other', or a list containing any of anyURI, '##targetNamespace', '##local'<br>processContents? : 'lax', 'skip', or 'strict' | annotation? |
| anyAttribute | id? : ID<br>namespace? : '##any', '##other', or a list containing any of an anyURI, '##targetNamespace', '##local'<br>processContents? : 'lax', 'skip', or 'strict' | annotation? |
| appinfo | source? : anyURI | appinfo may contain any well-formed XML. |
| attribute | default? : string<br>fixed? : string<br>form? : 'qualified' or 'unqualified'<br>id? : ID<br>name? : NCName<br>ref? : QName<br>type? : QName<br>use? : 'optional', 'prohibited', or 'required' | annotation?<br>simpleType? |

*continues*

**TABLE A.1** *(continued)*

| Type of Element | Attribute Types | Subelement Types |
|---|---|---|
| attributeGroup | id? : ID<br>name? : NCName<br>ref? : QName | annotation?<br>anyAttribute?<br>attribute*<br>attributeGroup* |
| choice | id? : ID<br>maxOccurs? (='1') : nonNegativeInteger or 'unbounded'<br>minOccurs? (='1') : nonNegativeInteger | annotation?<br>any*<br>choice*<br>element*<br>group*<br>sequence* |
| complexContent | id? : ID<br>mixed? : boolean | annotation?<br>extension?<br>restriction? |
| complexType | abstract? (='false') : boolean<br>block? : '#all', or a list containing any of 'extension', 'restriction'<br>final? : '#all', or a list containing any of 'extension', 'restriction'<br>id? : ID<br>mixed? (='false') : boolean<br>name? : NCName | annotation?<br>anyAttribute?<br>attribute*<br>attributeGroup?<br>(simpleContent \|<br>complexContent \| group \| all \|<br>choice \| sequence)? |
| documentation | source? : anyURI<br>xml:lang : language | Documentation may contain any well-formed XML. |

*continues*

# XML Schema Quick Reference

**APPENDIX A**

**TABLE A.1** *(continued)*

| Type of Element | Attribute Types | Subelement Types |
|---|---|---|
| element | abstract? (='false') : boolean<br>block? : '#all', or a list containing any of 'extension', 'restriction', 'substitution'<br>final? : '#all', or a list containing any of 'extension', 'restriction'<br>default? : string<br>final? : '#all', or a list containing any of 'extension', 'restriction'<br>fixed? : string<br>form? : 'qualified' or 'unqualified'<br>id? : ID<br>maxOccurs? (='1') : a nonNegativeInteger or 'unbounded'<br>minOccurs? (='1') : nonNegativeInteger<br>name? : NCName<br>nillable? (='false') : boolean<br>ref? : QName<br>substitutionGroup? : QName<br>type? = QName | annotation?<br>(simpleType \| complexType)?<br>key*<br>keyref*<br>unique* |
| extension (complexContent) | base : QName<br>id? : ID | annotation?<br>attribute*<br>attributeGroup*<br>anyAttribute?<br>(group \| all \| choice \| sequence)? |
| extension (simpleContent) | base : QName<br>id? : ID | annotation?<br>attribute*<br>attributeGroup*<br>anyAttribute? |

*continues*

## Appendix A

**TABLE A.1** *(continued)*

| Type of Element | Attribute Types | Subelement Types |
| --- | --- | --- |
| field | id? : ID<br>xpath : string conforming to an appropriate subset of XPath | annotation? |
| group | name : NCName | annotation?<br>all \| choice \| sequence |
| import | id? : ID<br>namespace? : anyURI<br>schemaLocation? : anyURI | annotation? |
| include | id? : ID<br>schemaLocation : anyURI | annotation? |
| key | id? : ID<br>name : NCName | annotation?<br>field+<br>selector |
| keyref | id? : ID<br>name : NCName<br>refer : QName | annotation?<br>field+<br>selector |
| list | id? : ID<br>itemType? : QName | annotation?<br>simpleType? |
| notation | id? : ID<br>name : NCName<br>public : anyURI<br>system? : anyURI | annotation? |
| redefine | id? : ID<br>schemaLocation : anyURI | annotation*<br>attributeGroup*<br>complexType*<br>group*<br>simpleType* |

*continues*

**TABLE A.1** *(continued)*

| Type of Element | Attribute Types | Subelement Types |
|---|---|---|
| restriction (complexContent) | base : QName<br>id? : ID | annotation?<br>(group \| all \| choice \| sequence)?<br>attribute*<br>attributeGroup*<br>anyAttribute? |
| restriction (simpleContent) | base? : QName<br>id? : ID | annotation?<br>anyAttribute?<br>attribute*<br>attributeGroup*<br>enumeration*<br>fractionDigits*<br>length*<br>minExclusive*<br>minInclusive*<br>minLength*<br>maxExclusive*<br>maxInclusive*<br>maxLength*<br>pattern*<br>simpleType?<br>totalDigits*<br>whiteSpace* |

*continues*

# XML Schema Quick Reference

## APPENDIX A

**TABLE A.1** *(continued)*

| Type of Element | Attribute Types | Subelement Types |
|---|---|---|
| restriction (simpleType) | base? : QName<br>id? : ID | annotation?<br>enumeration*<br>fractionDigits*<br>length*<br>minExclusive*<br>minInclusive*<br>minLength*<br>maxExclusive*<br>maxInclusive*<br>maxLength*<br>pattern*<br>simpleType?<br>totalDigits*<br>whiteSpace* |
| schema | attributeFormDefault? (='unqualified') : 'qualified' or 'unqualified'<br>blockDefault? : '#all' or a list containing any of 'extension', 'restriction', 'substitution'<br>elementFormDefault? (='unqualified') : 'qualified' or 'unqualified'<br>finalDefault? : '#all' or a list containing any of 'extension', 'restriction'<br>id? : = ID | annotation*<br>attribute*<br>attributeGroup*<br>complexType*<br>element*<br>group*<br>include*<br>import*<br>notation*<br>redefine*<br>simpleType* |

*continues*

TABLE A.1  (continued)

| Type of Element | Attribute Types | Subelement Types |
| --- | --- | --- |
| selector | id? : ID<br>xpath : string conforming to an appropriate subset of XPath | annotation? |
| sequence | maxOccurs? (='1') : a nonNegativeInteger or 'unbounded'<br>minOccurs? (='1') : nonNegativeInteger | annotation?<br>any*<br>choice*<br>element*<br>group*<br>sequence* |
| simpleContent | id? : ID | annotation?<br>restriction \| extension |
| simpleType | final? : '#all', 'list', 'union', or 'restriction'<br>id? : ID<br>name? : NCName | annotation?<br>restriction \| list \| union |
| unique | id? : ID<br>name : NCName | annotation?<br>field+<br>selector |
| union | id? : ID<br>memberTypes : A list of QNames | annotation?<br>simpleType* |

# XML Schema Regular Expression Grammar

APPENDIX B

# XML Schema Regular Expression Grammar
## Appendix B

Listing B.1 provides a complete grammar for XML Schema regular expressions. A *regular expression* is the value for a `pattern` constraining facet. Refer to Chapter 14 for a detailed discussion of how to write and incorporate regular expressions.

The file `regexp.grammar` in Listing B.1 contains detailed comments. This appendix contains no discussion other than the running commentary in the listing.

**LISTING B.1** The XML Schema Regular Expression Grammar (`regexp.grammar`)

```
;;;==========================================================
;;;==========================================================
;;;
;;; regexp.grammar
;;;
;;; The grammar in this file represents the XML Schema
;;; interpretation of a regular expression.
;;; This grammar takes the form of standard BNF, not
;;; the rarely used ISO-EBNF or the pseudo Extended BNF
;;; in the W3C XML Schema Recommendation
;;;
;;; Note the following:
;;;
;;;    * Comments start with ';' and end at the line break.
;;;
;;;    * Regular expressions are whitespace sensitive:
;;;      This grammar actually specifies a complete lexical
;;;      token that matches a regular expression.
;;;      Typically, a grammar represents a language where
;;;      whitespace is relatively meaningless.
;;;
;;;    * The '..' notation specifies a range of characters
;;;      For example, 'a' .. 'z' identifies a range of
;;;      characters between 'a' and 'z', inclusive.
;;;      This is a shortcut for 'a' | 'b' | ... | 'z'
;;;
;;;
;;;==========================================================
;;;==========================================================


;;;----------------------------------------------------------
;;;
;;; A regular expression is fundamentally a set of 'atom'.
;;; The atoms can be modified with a 'quantifier' and or
;;; concatenated into a 'sequence'.  Finally, a regular
;;; expression may match alternative sequences (via the
;;; '|' operator).
```

```
;;;
;;;-----------------------------------------------------

<regularExpression> ::= |                  ; Nothing is okay
         <sequence> |
         <regularExpression> '|' <sequence>

<sequence> ::= <piece> |
               <sequence> <piece>

<piece> ::= <atom> |
            <atom> <quantifier>

;;;-----------------------------------------------------
;;; An 'atom' is:
;;;      * Any character that is not a metacharacter
;;;      * A character class
;;;      * Any regular expression grouped with parentheses.
;;;-----------------------------------------------------

<atom> ::= <notMetaCharacter> |
           <characterClass> |
           '(' <regularExpression> ')'

;;;-----------------------------------------------------
;;; A 'quantifier' identifies the number of possible
;;; occurrences of an atom.  Specifically one of:
;;;      ? ==> Zero or one
;;;      + ==> One or more
;;;      * ==> Zero or more
;;;      {n} ==> Exactly n occurrences
;;;      {n,m} ==> Between n and m occurrences - n <= m
;;;      {n,} ==> n or more occurrences
;;;-----------------------------------------------------

<quantifier> ::= '?' |
                 '+' |
                 '*' |
                 '{' <quantifierRange> '}'

<quantifierRange> ::= decimalDigit |
                      decimalDigit ',' |
                      decimalDigit ',' decimalDigit

;;;-----------------------------------------------------
;;;
;;; A 'character class' is one of:
```

*continues*

```
;;;
;;;        * A 'character class escape'
;;;          (A '\' followed by a set of tokens; these
;;;           escape match one or more characters)
;;;
;;;        * A 'character class expression'
;;;          (A range delimited by [...])
;;;
;;;        * A 'wildcard escape'
;;;
;;;-------------------------------------------------------
<characterClass> ::= <characterClassEscape> |
                     <characterClassExpression> |
                     <wildcardEscape>


;;;-------------------------------------------------------
;;;
;;; A 'character class expression' is a range, which can
;;; be positive (inlusive, looks like "[...]") or
;;; negative (exclusive, looks like "[^...]").
;;; Furthermore, one set of ranges can subtract another
;;; (Subtraction looks like "[...-[...]]"; the effect
;;; is a mathematical set subtraction
;;;
;;;-------------------------------------------------------

<characterClassExpression> ::= '[' <characterGroup> ']'

<characterGroup> ::= <positiveCharacterGroup> |
                     <negativeCharacterGroup> |
                     <characterClassSubtraction>

<positiveCharacterGroup> ::= <characterGroupContents> |
    <positiveCharacterGroup> <characterGroupContents>

<negativeCharacterGroup> ::= '^' <positiveCharacterGroup>

<characterClassSubtraction> ::= ( <positiveCharacterGroup> |
                                  <negativeCaracterGroup> )
                                '-' <characterClassExpression>



;;;-------------------------------------------------------
;;;
;;; The contents of a character group expression is
;;; generally one of the following:
;;;      * A range (like "A-Z")
;;;      * An XML character reference
```

```
;;;         ("&#nnnn;" or "&#xnnnn;")
;;;       * Any character generally valid in an XML document
;;;       * Any escape sequence (starts with '\')
;;;
;;;-------------------------------------------------------

<characterGroupContents> ::= <characterRange> |
                             <characterClassEscape>

<characterRange> ::= <startEndRange> |
                     <xmlCharacterReference> |
                     <xmlCharacterIncludingDash>

<startEndRange> ::= <singleCharacterMaybeEscaped> '-' <singleCharacterMaybeEscaped>

<characterClassEscape> ::= <singleCharacterEscape> |
                           <multipleCharacterEscape> |
                           <categoryOrBlockEscape>

<xmlCharacterReference> ::= ( '&#' <decimalDigitList> ';' ) |
                            ( '&#x' <hexDigitList> ';' )

<singleCharacterMaybeEscaped> ::= <xmlCharacterNoDash> |
<singleCharacterEscape>

<xmlCharacterNoDash> ::= [^\#x2D#x5B#x5D]

<xmlCharacterIncludingDash> ::= [^\#x5B#x5D]

<wildcardEscape> ::= '.'

;;;-------------------------------------------------------
;;;
;;; <notMetaCharacter> represents any Unicode character
;;; except for the meta characters.  The meta characters
;;; consist of the following characters:
;;; . + ? * \ ( ) [ ]
;;;
;;; So, for example, <asciiNotMetaChar> represents any
;;; character, such as the letter 'c' or the number '7'
;;;
;;;
;;;-------------------------------------------------------

<notMetaCharacter> ::= ( \0 .. \10FFFF ) -
                       '.' -
```

*continues*

## Appendix B

```
                            '+' -
                            '\' -
                            '?' -
                            '*' -
                            '+' -
                            '(' -
                            ')' -
                            '[' -
                            ']' -
                            '|'

;;;-------------------------------------------------------
;;;
;;;-------------------------------------------------------

<decimalDigit> ::= '0' | '1' | '2' | '3' | '4' |
                   '5' | '6' | '7' | '8' | '9'

<decimalDigitList> ::= <decimalDigit> |
                 ( <decimalDigitList> <decimalDigit> )

<hexDigit> ::= <decimalDigit> |
               'A' | 'B' | 'C' | 'D' | 'E' | 'F' |
               'a' | 'b' | 'c' | 'd' | 'e' | 'f'

<hexDigitList> ::= <hexDigit> |
                 ( <hexDigitList> <hexDigit> )

;;;-------------------------------------------------------
;;; Each 'single character escape' matches exactly one
;;; character.
;;;-------------------------------------------------------

<singleCharacterEscape> ::=
    '\' (
        'n'             ; the newline character (#xA)
        'r'             ; the return character (#xD)
        't'             ; the tab character (#x9)
        '\'             ; \
        '|'             ; |
        '.'             ; .
        '-'             ; -
        '^'             ; ^
        '?'             ; ?
        '*'             ; *
        '+'             ; +
        '{'             ; {
        '}'             ; }
```

```
              '('              ; (
              ')'              ; )
              '['              ; [
              ']'              ; ]
     )

;;;-------------------------------------------------------
;;; Each 'multiple character escape' matches one occurence of
;;; a variety of characters.
;;;-------------------------------------------------------

<multipleCharacterEscape> ::=
     '.' |                ; [^\r\n]
     ('\' (
          's' |           ; [#x20\t\n\r]
          'S' |           ; [^s]
          'i' |           ; A letter or ':' or '_'
          'I' |           ; [^\i]
          'c' |           ; NameChar from the XML Recommendation
          'C' |           ; [^\c]
          'd' |           ; \p{Nd}
          'D' |           ; [^\d]
          'w' |           ; [#x0000-#x10FFFF]- [\p{P}\p{Z}\p{C}]
                          ;    (all characters except the set of
                          ;    "punctuation", "separator" and
                          ;    "other" characters)
          'W'             ; [^\w]
     ) )

;;;-------------------------------------------------------
;;; \p{x} means a character specified by 'x'
;;; \P{x} means any character NOT specified by 'x'
;;;-------------------------------------------------------

<categoryOrBlockEscape> ::= ( '\\p{' | '\\P{' )
                            ( <category> | 'Is' <block> ) '}'

;;;-------------------------------------------------------
;;; The Unicode Standard defines these categories
;;;-------------------------------------------------------

<category> ::= 'L'  |        ; Any Letter
               'Lu' |        ; Letter, Uppercase
               'Ll' |        ; Letter, Lowercase
               'Lt' |        ; Letter, Titlecase
               'Lm' |        ; Letter, Modifier
               'Lo' |        ; Letter, Other
```

*continues*

# XML Schema Regular Expression Grammar

## APPENDIX B

```
                      'M'  |        ; Any Mark
                      'Mn' |        ; Mark, Non-Spacing
                      'Mc' |        ; Mark, Spacing Combining
                      'Me' |        ; Mark, Enclosing
                      'N'  |        ; Any Number
                      'Nd' |        ; Number, Decimal Digit
                      'Nl' |        ; Number, Letter
                      'No' |        ; Number, Other
                      'P'  |        ; Any Punctuation
                      'Pc' |        ; Punctuation, Connector
                      'Pd' |        ; Punctuation, Dash
                      'Ps' |        ; Punctuation, Open
                      'Pe' |        ; Punctuation, Close
                      'Pi' |        ; Punctuation, Initial quote
                                    ;     (may behave like Ps or
                                    ;      Pe depending on usage)
                      'Pf' |        ; Punctuation, Final quote
                                    ;     (may behave like Ps or
                                    ;      Pe depending on usage)
                      'Po' |        ; Punctuation, Other
                      'S'  |        ; Any Symbol
                      'Sm' |        ; Symbol, Math
                      'Sc' |        ; Symbol, Currency
                      'Sk' |        ; Symbol, Modifier
                      'So' |        ; Symbol, Other
                      'Z'  |        ; Any Separator
                      'Zs' |        ; Separator, Space
                      'Zl' |        ; Separator, Line
                      'Zp' |        ; Separator, Paragraph
                      'C'  |        ; Any Other
                      'Cf' |        ; Other, Format
                      'Cs' |        ; Other, Surrogate
                      'Co' |        ; Other, Private Use
                      'Cn'          ; Other, Not Assigned
                                    ;    (no characters in the
                                    ;     file have this
                                    ;     property)

;;;------------------------------------------------------------
;;; The Unicode Standard defines these blocks
;;;------------------------------------------------------------

<block> ::= 'BasicLatin' |
            'Latin-1Supplement' |
            'LatinExtended-A' |
            'LatinExtended-B' |
            'IPAExtensions' |
            'SpacingModifierLetters' |
```

```
'CombiningDiacriticalMarks' |
'Greek' |
'Cyrillic' |
'Armenian' |
'Hebrew' |
'Arabic' |
'Syriac' |
'Thaana' |
'Devanagari' |
'Bengali' |
'Gurmukhi' |
'Gujarati' |
'Oriya' |
'Tamil' |
'Telugu' |
'Kannada' |
'Malayalam' |
'Sinhala' |
'Thai' |
'Lao' |
'Tibetan' |
'Myanmar' |
'Georgian' |
'HangulJamo' |
'Ethiopic' |
'Cherokee' |
'UnifiedCanadianAboriginalSyllabics' |
'Ogham' |
'Runic' |
'Khmer' |
'Mongolian' |
'LatinExtendedAdditional' |
'GreekExtended' |
'GeneralPunctuation' |
'SuperscriptsandSubscripts' |
'CurrencySymbols' |
'CombiningMarksforSymbols' |
'LetterlikeSymbols' |
'NumberForms' |
'Arrows' |
'MathematicalOperators' |
'MiscellaneousTechnical' |
'ControlPictures' |
'OpticalCharacterRecognition' |
'EnclosedAlphanumerics' |
'BoxDrawing' |
'BlockElements' |
```

*continues*

## APPENDIX B
# XML Schema Regular Expression Grammar

```
                    'GeometricShapes' |
                    'MiscellaneousSymbols' |
                    'Dingbats' |
                    'BraillePatterns' |
                    'CJKRadicalsSupplement' |
                    'KangxiRadicals' |
                    'IdeographicDescriptionCharacters' |
                    'CJKSymbolsandPunctuation' |
                    'Hiragana' |
                    'Katakana' |
                    'Bopomofo' |
                    'HangulCompatibilityJamo' |
                    'Kanbun' |
                    'BopomofoExtended' |
                    'EnclosedCJKLettersandMonths' |
                    'CJKCompatibility' |
                    'CJKUnifiedIdeographsExtensionA' |
                    'CJKUnifiedIdeographs' |
                    'YiSyllables' |
                    'YiRadicals' |
                    'HangulSyllables' |
                    'HighSurrogates' |
                    'HighPrivateUseSurrogates' |
                    'LowSurrogates' |
                    'PrivateUse' |
                    'CJKCompatibilityIdeographs' |
                    'AlphabeticPresentationForms' |
                    'ArabicPresentationForms-A' |
                    'CombiningHalfMarks' |
                    'CJKCompatibilityForms' |
                    'SmallFormVariants' |
                    'ArabicPresentationForms-B' |
                    'Specials' |
                    'HalfwidthandFullwidthForms' |
                    'Specials' |
                    'OldItalic' |
                    'Gothic' |
                    'Deseret' |
                    'ByzantineMusicalSymbols' |
                    'MusicalSymbols' |
                    'MathematicalAlphanumericSymbols' |
                    'CJKUnifiedIdeographsExtensionB' |
                    'CJKCompatibilityIdeographsSupplement' |
                    'Tags' |
                    'PrivateUse'
```

# The Thematic Catalog XML Schema

APPENDIX C

# Appendix C
## The Thematic Catalog XML Schema

Many of the chapters in this book provide examples that stem from either a "catalog" or an "address" schema. The catalog schema primarily demonstrates simple types and complex types. The address schema primarily demonstrates element types and attribute types. Of course, both schemas include many types, due to the nature of building a schema.

This appendix provides a complete listing for the thematic catalog and address XML schema examples. The following four XML schema documents comprise the two complete XML schema examples:

- Thematic Catalog Schema Document (`catalog.xsd`)
- Thematic Address Schema Document (`address.xsd`)
- Supporting Pricing Schema (`pricing.xsd`)
- Supporting Database Sequence Schema (`sequence.xsd`)

These, and all of the other "mini-schemas" used to test all the examples in this book, are online at `http://www.XMLSchemaReference.com/examples`.

Listing C.1 is the thematic catalog schema document. The catalog represents a number of orderable items. These items include unit orderable items, bulk groupings of items, and entire assemblies (comprised of unit items).

**LISTING C.1** Thematic Catalog Schema Document (`catalog.xsd`)

```xml
<xsd:schema xmlns:xsd="http://www.w3.org/2001/XMLSchema">

<xsd:include schemaLocation=
    "http://www.XMLSchemaReference.com/examples/theme/pricing.xsd"/>
<xsd:include schemaLocation=
    "http://www.XMLSchemaReference.com/examples/theme/sequence.xsd"/>

<xsd:simpleType name="partNameType"
                final="#all"
                id="catalog.partName.sType">
    <xsd:annotation>
        <xsd:documentation xml:lang="en">
            A part name can be almost anything.
            The name is a short description.
        </xsd:documentation>
    </xsd:annotation>
    <xsd:restriction base="xsd:token"
                     id="pnt-rst">
        <xsd:minLength value="1"/>
        <xsd:maxLength value="40"/>
    </xsd:restriction>
</xsd:simpleType>
```

```
<xsd:simpleType name="partNumberType"
                final="union"
                id="catalog.partNumber.sType">
    <xsd:annotation>
        <xsd:documentation xml:lang="en">
            Declaration of a part number.
            Each part number consists of one to
            three alphabetic characters followed by
            one to eight digits. The following part
            numbers, for example, are valid:
                J1
                ABC32897
                ZZ22233344
        </xsd:documentation>
    </xsd:annotation>
        <xsd:restriction base="xsd:token">
            <xsd:pattern value="[A-Z]{1,3}\d{1,8}"/>
        </xsd:restriction>
</xsd:simpleType>

<xsd:simpleType name="unitPartNumberType"
                final="#all"
                id="catalog.unitpartNumber.sType">
    <xsd:annotation>
        <xsd:documentation xml:lang="en">
            A "unit" part defines small parts,
            not bulk items or assemblies.
            The "unitPartNumberType" describes the
            pattern for unit items.
        </xsd:documentation>
    </xsd:annotation>
    <xsd:restriction base="partNumberType">
        <xsd:pattern
  value="(([^AB])|(B[^L])|(BL[^K])|(A[^S])|(AS[^M])).*"/>
    </xsd:restriction>
</xsd:simpleType>

<xsd:simpleType name="bulkPartNumberType"
                final="#all"
                id="catalog.bulkpartNumber.sType">
    <xsd:annotation>
        <xsd:documentation xml:lang="en">
            A "bulk" part represents a quantity
            of "unit" parts.  The
            "bulkPartNumberType" describes the
            part number for bulk items.
        </xsd:documentation>
    </xsd:annotation>
```

*continues*

```xml
        <xsd:restriction base="partNumberType">
            <xsd:length value="7" fixed="true"/>
            <xsd:pattern value="BLK.*"/>
            <xsd:enumeration value="BLK2088"/>
            <xsd:enumeration value="BLK2089"/>
        </xsd:restriction>
    </xsd:simpleType>

    <xsd:simpleType name="assemblyPartNumberType"
                    final="restriction"
                    id="catalog.assemblypartNumber.sType">
        <xsd:annotation>
            <xsd:documentation xml:lang="en">
                An "assembly" represents a pre-built
                collection of unit items.  The
                part number for an assembly
                always starts with "ASM."
            </xsd:documentation>
        </xsd:annotation>
        <xsd:restriction base="partNumberType">
            <xsd:pattern value="ASM\d{1,8}"/>
        </xsd:restriction>
    </xsd:simpleType>

    <xsd:simpleType name="partNumberListType"
                    id="catalog.partNumber.list.sType">
        <xsd:annotation>
            <xsd:documentation xml:lang="en">
                The "partNumberListType" describes the value
                for an element that contains a set of part
                numbers.  Given that a part number might look
                like any of the following:
                    J1
                    ABC32897
                    ZZ22233344
                A list of these part numbers might look like:
                    J1 ABC32897 ZZ22233344
            </xsd:documentation>
        </xsd:annotation>
        <xsd:list id="transaction.partNumberList"
                  itemType="partNumberType">
        </xsd:list>
    </xsd:simpleType>

    <xsd:simpleType name="colorOptionType"
                    id="catalog.colorOption.union.sType">
        <xsd:annotation>
            <xsd:documentation xml:lang="en">
```

```
            A part has one of the following color definitions:
                - a standard name (cyan, yellow, etc.),
                - a fanciful name (Ocean, Sunshine, etc.), or
                - an internal code 1..n
        </xsd:documentation>
    </xsd:annotation>
    <xsd:union id="colorOptionType.union">

        <xsd:simpleType>
            <xsd:annotation>
                <xsd:documentation xml:lang="en">
                    Color selection is limited.
                    The colors apply to unit and
                    bulk items.
                </xsd:documentation>
            </xsd:annotation>
            <xsd:restriction base="xsd:token">
                <xsd:enumeration value="cyan"/>
                <xsd:enumeration value="magenta"/>
                <xsd:enumeration value="yellow"/>
                <xsd:enumeration value="black"/>
            </xsd:restriction>
        </xsd:simpleType>

        <xsd:simpleType>
            <xsd:annotation>
                <xsd:documentation xml:lang="en">
                    Color selection is limited.
                    The colors apply to unit and
                    bulk items.
                </xsd:documentation>
            </xsd:annotation>
            <xsd:restriction base="xsd:token">
                <xsd:enumeration value="Ocean"/>
                <xsd:enumeration value="Pink Grapefruit"/>
                <xsd:enumeration value="Sunshine"/>
                <xsd:enumeration value="Midnight"/>
            </xsd:restriction>
        </xsd:simpleType>

        <xsd:simpleType>
            <xsd:annotation>
                <xsd:documentation xml:lang="en">
                    A color can be defined by an
                    internal integer that maps
                    directly to a standard or
                    fanciful color
                    1 = cyan = Ocean
```

*continues*

## The Thematic Catalog XML Schema
### APPENDIX C

```
                    2 = magenta = Pink Grapefruit
                        etc.
                </xsd:documentation>
            </xsd:annotation>
            <xsd:restriction base="xsd:positiveInteger">
                <xsd:maxInclusive value="4"/>
            </xsd:restriction>
        </xsd:simpleType>

    </xsd:union>
</xsd:simpleType>

<xsd:simpleType name="sizeOptionType"
                final="#all"
                id="catalog.sizeOption.sType">
    <xsd:annotation>
        <xsd:documentation xml:lang="en">
            Size selection is limited.
            The sizes apply to unit and
            bulk items.
        </xsd:documentation>
    </xsd:annotation>
    <xsd:restriction base="xsd:token">
        <xsd:enumeration value="tiny"/>
        <xsd:enumeration value="small"/>
        <xsd:enumeration value="medium"/>
        <xsd:enumeration value="large"/>
        <xsd:enumeration value="grandiose"/>
    </xsd:restriction>
</xsd:simpleType>

<xsd:complexType name="partOptionType"
                 block="#all"
                 final="#all"
                 id="partOptionType.catalog.cType">
    <xsd:annotation>
        <xsd:documentation xml:lang="en">
            Appropriate parts can have a color,
            a size, or both.  Note that the use
            of the "all" element indicates that
            the "color" and "size" are unordered.
            That is, they can appear in either
            order.
                -- Shorthand Notation --
        </xsd:documentation>
    </xsd:annotation>
    <xsd:all id="pot.all">
        <xsd:element name="color"
```

```xml
                        type="colorOptionType"
                        minOccurs="0"
                        maxOccurs="1"/>
        <xsd:element name="size"
                        type="sizeOptionType"
                        minOccurs="0"
                        maxOccurs="1"/>
    </xsd:all>
</xsd:complexType>

<xsd:complexType name="customerReviewType">
    <xsd:annotation>
        <xsd:documentation xml:lang="en">
            The customer review provides a place to
            attach customer feedback to catalog items.
                -- Shorthand Notation --
        </xsd:documentation>
    </xsd:annotation>
    <xsd:sequence>
        <xsd:element name="customerName">
            <xsd:simpleType>
                <xsd:restriction base="xsd:string">
                    <xsd:whiteSpace value="collapse"/>
                </xsd:restriction>
            </xsd:simpleType>
        </xsd:element>
        <xsd:element name="customerFeedback">
            <xsd:simpleType>
                <xsd:restriction base="xsd:string">
                    <xsd:whiteSpace value="preserve"/>
                </xsd:restriction>
            </xsd:simpleType>
        </xsd:element>
    </xsd:sequence>
</xsd:complexType>

<xsd:complexType name="catalogEntryDescriptionType"
                    mixed="true"
                    id="catalogEntryDescriptionType.catalog.cType">
    <xsd:annotation>
        <xsd:documentation xml:lang="en">
            Allow the description of a part
            to include part number references.
            The "catalogEntryDescriptionType"
            is a good example of a complex type
            with "mixed" content.
                -- Shorthand Notation --
        </xsd:documentation>
```

*continues*

# Appendix C

## The Thematic Catalog XML Schema

```xml
        </xsd:annotation>
        <xsd:sequence minOccurs="0" maxOccurs="unbounded">
            <xsd:element name="partList"
                         type="partNumberListType"/>
        </xsd:sequence>
    </xsd:complexType>

    <xsd:complexType name="baseCatalogEntryType"
                     abstract="true"
                     id="baseCatalogEntryType.catalog.cType">
        <xsd:annotation>
            <xsd:documentation xml:lang="en">
                A catalog entry must have:
                    * A database ID
                    * Part Name
                    * Part Number
                    * Options available
                    * Description
                    * Price
                    * Included Quantity when ordering
                      one item.
                The "baseCatalogEntryType" is
                non-instantiable:  a derived type must
                be created before a catalog
                entry can be instantiated.
                    -- Shorthand Notation --
            </xsd:documentation>
        </xsd:annotation>
        <xsd:sequence id="bacet-seq">
            <xsd:element ref="sequenceID"/>
            <xsd:element name="partName" type="partNameType"/>
            <xsd:element name="partNumber" type="partNumberType"/>
            <xsd:element name="partOption" type="partOptionType" minOccurs="0"/>
            <xsd:element name="description"
                         type="catalogEntryDescriptionType"/>
            <xsd:group ref="priceGroup"/>
            <xsd:element name="includedQuantity"
                         type="xsd:positiveInteger"/>
            <xsd:element name="customerReview"
                         type="customerReviewType"
                             minOccurs="0"
                             maxOccurs="unbounded"/>
        </xsd:sequence>
    </xsd:complexType>

    <xsd:complexType name="unitCatalogEntryType"
                     block="#all"
                     final="#all"
```

```xml
                        id="unitCatalogEntryType.catalog.cType">
    <xsd:annotation>
        <xsd:documentation xml:lang="en">
            A unit item contains nothing more
            or less than a basic catalog entry ID:
                * A database ID
                * Part Name
                * Part Number
                * Options available
                * Price
                * Included Quantity when ordering
                  one item (always one for unit items).
        </xsd:documentation>
    </xsd:annotation>
    <xsd:complexContent id="ucet.cc">
        <xsd:restriction base="baseCatalogEntryType">
            <xsd:sequence>
                <xsd:element ref="unitID"/>
                <xsd:element name="partName"
                            type="partNameType"/>
                <xsd:element name="partNumber"
                            type="unitPartNumberType"/>
                <xsd:element name="partOption"
                            type="partOptionType"
                            minOccurs="1"/>
                <xsd:element name="description"
                            type="catalogEntryDescriptionType"/>
                <xsd:group ref="priceGroup"/>
                <xsd:element name="includedQuantity"
                            type="xsd:positiveInteger"
                            fixed="1"/>
                <xsd:element name="customerReview"
                            type="customerReviewType"
                            minOccurs="0"
                            maxOccurs="unbounded"/>
            </xsd:sequence>
        </xsd:restriction>
    </xsd:complexContent>
</xsd:complexType>

<xsd:complexType name="bulkCatalogEntryType"
                block="#all"
                final="#all"
                id="bulkCatalogEntryType.catalog.cType">
    <xsd:annotation>
        <xsd:documentation xml:lang="en">
            A bulk item is just like any
            other, except that the part
```

*continues*

```
                    number is restricted to a
                    bulk part number.
                </xsd:documentation>
            </xsd:annotation>
            <xsd:complexContent>
                <xsd:restriction base="baseCatalogEntryType">
                    <xsd:sequence>
                        <xsd:element ref="bulkID"/>
                        <xsd:element name="partName"
                                    type="partNameType"/>
                        <xsd:element name="partNumber"
                                    type="bulkPartNumberType"/>
                        <xsd:element name="partOption"
                                    type="partOptionType"
                                    minOccurs="1"/>
                        <xsd:element name="description"
                                type="catalogEntryDescriptionType"/>
                        <xsd:group ref="priceGroup"/>
                        <xsd:element name="includedQuantity"
                                    type="xsd:positiveInteger"/>
                        <xsd:element name="customerReview"
                                    type="customerReviewType"
                                    minOccurs="0"
                                    maxOccurs="unbounded"/>
                    </xsd:sequence>
                </xsd:restriction>
            </xsd:complexContent>
    </xsd:complexType>

    <xsd:complexType name="baseAssemblyCatalogEntryType"
                    abstract="true"
                    block="#all"
                id="baseAssemblyCatalogEntryType.catalog.cType">
        <xsd:annotation>
            <xsd:documentation xml:lang="en">
                An assembled item is similar to the
                other catalog entries.  The part number
                is restricted to an assembly number.
                In addition, there may be no options.
                Finally, a part list is also needed.
                Note that the "includedQuantity" has
                a default of one, but can be overridden
                in instances.
            </xsd:documentation>
        </xsd:annotation>
        <xsd:complexContent>
            <xsd:restriction base="baseCatalogEntryType"
                            id="bacet.rst">
```

```xml
            <xsd:sequence>
                <xsd:element ref="assemblyID"/>
                <xsd:element name="partName"
                             type="partNameType"/>
                <xsd:element name="partNumber"
                             type="assemblyPartNumberType"/>
                <xsd:element name="partOption"
                             type="partOptionType"
                             minOccurs="0"
                             maxOccurs="0"/>
                <xsd:element name="description"
                            type="catalogEntryDescriptionType"/>
                <xsd:group ref="priceGroup"/>
                <xsd:element name="includedQuantity"
                             type="xsd:positiveInteger"
                             default="1"/>
                <xsd:element name="customerReview"
                             type="customerReviewType"
                             minOccurs="0"
                             maxOccurs="unbounded"/>
            </xsd:sequence>
        </xsd:restriction>
    </xsd:complexContent>
</xsd:complexType>

<xsd:complexType name="assemblyCatalogEntryType"
                 block="#all"
                 final="#all"
                 id="assemblyCatalogEntryType.catalog.cType">
    <xsd:annotation>
        <xsd:documentation xml:lang="en">
            The actual definition of an assembly,
            including the contained parts.
        </xsd:documentation>
    </xsd:annotation>
    <xsd:complexContent>
        <xsd:extension base="baseAssemblyCatalogEntryType"
                       id="acet.ext">
            <xsd:sequence>
                <xsd:element name="partList" type="partNumberListType"/>
                <xsd:element name="status" type="assemblyPartStatusType"/>
            </xsd:sequence>
        </xsd:extension>
    </xsd:complexContent>
</xsd:complexType>

<xsd:simpleType name="assemblyPartStatusType"
                id="catalog.assemblyPartStatusType.union.sType">
```

*continues*

```xml
<xsd:annotation>
    <xsd:documentation xml:lang="en">
        A part status depends upon whether it is
        pre-production, in production, or no longer
        being manufactured.
    </xsd:documentation>
</xsd:annotation>
<xsd:union id="assemblyPartStatus.union"
           memberTypes="assemblyPartNumberType">

    <xsd:simpleType>
        <xsd:annotation>
            <xsd:documentation xml:lang="en">
                The pre-production status is an
                enumeration of the statuses prior
                to manufacturing.
                1 = roughed
                2 = designed
                3 = prototyped
                4 = approved
            </xsd:documentation>
        </xsd:annotation>
        <xsd:restriction base="xsd:positiveInteger">
            <xsd:maxInclusive value="4"/>
        </xsd:restriction>
    </xsd:simpleType>

    <xsd:simpleType>
        <xsd:annotation>
            <xsd:documentation xml:lang="en">
                The date the part was last manufactured.
                The company first manufactured a part on
                2000-01-01.
            </xsd:documentation>
        </xsd:annotation>
        <xsd:restriction base="xsd:date">
            <xsd:minInclusive value="2000-01-01"/>
        </xsd:restriction>
    </xsd:simpleType>

</xsd:union>
</xsd:simpleType>

<xsd:complexType name="finalCatalogType"
                 id="finalCatalogType.catalog.cType">
    <xsd:annotation>
        <xsd:documentation xml:lang="en">
            This catalog type permits catalog
```

```
                entry types to be created without
                making any changes to this type.
                These additions are possible since
                "finalCatalogType" contains only the
                non-instantiable base class.
                      -- Shorthand Notation --
            </xsd:documentation>
        </xsd:annotation>
        <xsd:sequence minOccurs="1"
                      maxOccurs="unbounded">
            <xsd:element name="part"
                         type="baseCatalogEntryType"/>
        </xsd:sequence>
    </xsd:complexType>

    <xsd:complexType name="blockedCatalogType"
                     id="blockedCatalogType.catalog.cType">
        <xsd:annotation>
            <xsd:documentation xml:lang="en">
                This catalog type permits catalog
                entry types to be created without
                making any changes to this type.
                These additions are possible since
                "catalogType1" contains only the
                non-instantiable base class.
                      -- Shorthand Notation --
            </xsd:documentation>
        </xsd:annotation>
        <xsd:sequence minOccurs="1"
                      maxOccurs="unbounded">
            <xsd:element name="part"
                         type="baseCatalogEntryType"
                         block="#all"/>
        </xsd:sequence>
    </xsd:complexType>

    <xsd:complexType name="catalogType"
                     id="catalogType.catalog.cType">
        <xsd:annotation>
            <xsd:documentation xml:lang="en">
                This catalog type must be altered
                every time a new catalog entry
                type is created.  The
                "catalogType2" complex type refers
                only instantiable derived classes.
                      -- Shorthand Notation --
            </xsd:documentation>
        </xsd:annotation>
```

*continues*

# The Thematic Catalog XML Schema
## APPENDIX C

```
            <xsd:choice minOccurs="1"
                        maxOccurs="unbounded">
                <xsd:element name="unitPart"
                             type="unitCatalogEntryType"
                             block="restriction extension"/>
                <xsd:element name="bulkPart"
                             type="bulkCatalogEntryType"
                             block="restriction extension"/>
                <xsd:element name="assemblyPart"
                             type="assemblyCatalogEntryType"
                             block="restriction extension"/>
            </xsd:choice>
        </xsd:complexType>

</xsd:schema>
```

Listing C.2 is the thematic address schema document. An address includes, not surprisingly, such information as name, street address, city, state, and zip code. A number of other properties, such as `primaryContact`, help demonstrate prohibiting element types and attribute types in derivations.

**LISTING C.2** Thematic Address Schema Document (address.xsd)

```
<xsd:schema xmlns:xsd="http://www.w3.org/2001/XMLSchema">

<xsd:annotation>
    <xsd:documentation xml:lang="en">
        This XML Schema Document describes a customer
        address in great detail.  In particular, this
        document illuminates all of the attributes and
        content options for elements and attributes.
    </xsd:documentation>
</xsd:annotation>

<xsd:include schemaLocation=
"http://www.XMLSchemaReference.com/examples/theme/sequence.xsd"
/>

<xsd:element name="addressLine"
             id="customerRecord.base.addressLine"
             type="xsd:string"
             abstract="true">
    <xsd:annotation>
        <xsd:documentation xml:lang="en">
            The "addressLine" element type
            is a base non-instantiable element
            type whose (structure) type is
```

```xml
            a built-in string datatype.
        </xsd:documentation>
    </xsd:annotation>
</xsd:element>

<xsd:element name="street"
             type="xsd:string"
             substitutionGroup="addressLine">
    <xsd:annotation>
        <xsd:documentation xml:lang="en">
            Street is a substitution group
            for addressLine.  This particular
            substitution only substitutes the
            name; there are no further restrictions.
        </xsd:documentation>
    </xsd:annotation>
</xsd:element>

<xsd:element name="POBox"
             substitutionGroup="addressLine">
    <xsd:simpleType>
        <xsd:annotation>
            <xsd:documentation xml:lang="en">
                The POBoxType demonstrates that
                a Substitution Group can have a
                type that is derived from the
                type used by the related
                non-instantiable base element.
            </xsd:documentation>
        </xsd:annotation>
        <xsd:restriction base="xsd:string">
            <xsd:maxLength value="10"/>
            <xsd:pattern value="[0-9]+"/>
        </xsd:restriction>
    </xsd:simpleType>
</xsd:element>

<xsd:element name="pmb"
             type="xsd:string"
             substitutionGroup="addressLine">
    <xsd:annotation id="customerRecord.annotation.pmb">
        <xsd:documentation source=
"http://new.usps.com/cgi-bin/uspsbv/scripts/content.jsp?D=13647"
                           xml:lang="en">
            A PMB is a "Private Mail Box" that is
            provided by an entity other than the
            U S Postal Service.
        </xsd:documentation>
```

*continues*

```xml
            <xsd:documentation xml:lang="en">
                Developer Note:  Someone should probably
                come up with a way to actually validate PMBs.
                In fact, we should validate every <pmb/>
                and <POBox/> element.
            </xsd:documentation>
            <xsd:appinfo source=
              "http://www.XMLSchemaReference.com/java/extractJava">
                // A PMB is a "Private Mail Box" that is
                // provided by an entity other than the
                // U S Postal Service.
                // -- create a class for the pmb
                public class pmb
                    {
                    ...
                    }
            </xsd:appinfo>
            <xsd:appinfo source=
              "http://www.XMLSchemaReference.com/perl/extractPerl">
                # A PMB is a "Private Mail Box" that is provided
                # by an entity other than the U S Postal Service.
                # -- create a variable for the PMB
                $pmb=""
            </xsd:appinfo>
        </xsd:annotation>
 </xsd:element>

 <xsd:attribute name="sequenceID"
                type="sequenceIDType"
                id="address.attr.sequenceID"/>

 <xsd:complexType name="businessCustomerType">
     <xsd:sequence>
         <xsd:element name="name" type="xsd:string"/>
         <xsd:element ref="phoneNumber"
                      minOccurs="1"
                      maxOccurs="unbounded"/>
         <xsd:element name="URL"
                      type="xsd:token"
                      minOccurs="0"
                      maxOccurs="1"/>
         <xsd:element ref="address"
                      minOccurs="1"
                      maxOccurs="unbounded"/>
     </xsd:sequence>
     <xsd:attribute name="customerID"
                    type="xsd:token"
```

```xml
                            use="required"/>
    <xsd:attribute name="primaryContact"
                   type="xsd:token"
                   use="optional"/>
    <xsd:attribute ref="sequenceID"/>
</xsd:complexType>

<xsd:complexType name="privateCustomerType">
    <xsd:complexContent>
        <xsd:restriction base="businessCustomerType">
            <xsd:sequence>
                <xsd:element name="name" type="xsd:string"/>
                <xsd:element ref="phoneNumber"
                             minOccurs="1"
                             maxOccurs="unbounded"/>
                <xsd:element name="URL"
                             type="xsd:token"
                             minOccurs="0"
                             maxOccurs="0"/>
                <xsd:element ref="address"
                             minOccurs="1"
                             maxOccurs="unbounded"/>
            </xsd:sequence>
            <xsd:attribute name="customerID"
                           type="xsd:token"
                           use="required"/>
            <xsd:attribute name="primaryContact"
                           type="xsd:token"
                           use="prohibited"/>
            <xsd:attribute ref="sequenceID"/>
        </xsd:restriction>
    </xsd:complexContent>
</xsd:complexType>

<xsd:element name="phoneNumber"
             type="xsd:string"
             nillable="true"/>

<xsd:element name="effectiveDate"
             type="xsd:date"
             default="1900-01-01"/>

<xsd:complexType name="addressType">
    <xsd:sequence>
        <xsd:element ref="addressLine"
                     minOccurs="1"
                     maxOccurs="2"/>
```

*continues*

## APPENDIX C · The Thematic Catalog XML Schema

```xml
            <xsd:element name="city" type="xsd:string"/>
            <xsd:element name="state" type="xsd:string"/>
            <xsd:element name="country"
                         type="xsd:string"
                         fixed="US"/>
            <xsd:element name="zip" type="xsd:string"/>
            <xsd:element ref="effectiveDate"/>
        </xsd:sequence>
        <xsd:attribute name="zipPlus4"
                       use="optional">
            <xsd:simpleType>
                <xsd:restriction base="xsd:string">
                    <xsd:pattern value="[0-9]{5}-[0-9]{4}"/>
                </xsd:restriction>
            </xsd:simpleType>
        </xsd:attribute>
</xsd:complexType>

<xsd:element name="address" type="addressType"/>

<xsd:element name="businessCustomer"
             type="businessCustomerType"/>

<xsd:element name="privateCustomer"
             type="privateCustomerType"/>

<xsd:element name="customerList">

    <xsd:complexType>
        <xsd:sequence minOccurs="0"
                      maxOccurs="unbounded">
            <xsd:choice>
                <xsd:element ref="businessCustomer"/>
                <xsd:element ref="privateCustomer"/>
            </xsd:choice>
        </xsd:sequence>
        <xsd:attribute name="source"
                       type="xsd:string"
                       default="Oracle"/>
        <xsd:attribute name="deliverDataToCountry"
                       type="xsd:string"
                       fixed="US"/>
    </xsd:complexType>

    <xsd:unique name="uniqueCustomerID">
        <xsd:selector xpath="*"/>
        <xsd:field xpath="@customerID"/>
    </xsd:unique>
```

```
        </xsd:element>

</xsd:schema>
```

The pricing schema document, Listing C.3, has a reusable group that provides a mechanism for assigning various pricing schemes to items in the catalog. In particular, there is a standard `fullPriceType`. There are also three discounted pricing schemes, all of which require an attribute that denotes authorization.

**LISTING C.3**  Supporting Pricing Schema (`pricing.xsd`)

```
<xsd:schema xmlns:xsd="http://www.w3.org/2001/XMLSchema">

<xsd:attribute name="currency"
               type="xsd:token"
               fixed="U S Dollars">
    <xsd:annotation>
        <xsd:documentation xml:lang="en">
            U S Dollars are the only currency
            currently allowed.  This attribute
            is a great example of using "ref"
            (elsewhere), but is not set up well
            for extending to other currencies
            later.  This should really be a
            type that keeps getting restricted.
        </xsd:documentation>
    </xsd:annotation>
</xsd:attribute>

<xsd:attributeGroup name="saleAttributeGroup"
                    id="pricing.sale.ag">
    <xsd:annotation>
        <xsd:documentation xml:lang="en">
            Anything that is on sale (or free,
            which is a type of sale) must
            have an authorization defined.
            This is someone's name,
            initials, ID, etc.
        </xsd:documentation>
    </xsd:annotation>
    <xsd:attribute name="employeeAuthorization"
                   type="xsd:token"/>
    <xsd:attribute name="managerAuthorization"
                   type="xsd:token"/>
</xsd:attributeGroup>
```

*continues*

## Appendix C

## The Thematic Catalog XML Schema

```xml
<xsd:simpleType name="currencyAmountType"
            id="pricing.currencyAmount.sType">
    <xsd:annotation>
        <xsd:documentation xml:lang="en">
            Limit all transactions to less than
            500,000.00 of any currency
            This can be represented as NNNNNN.NN
            or eight total digits, two of which are
            after the decimal point.

            ***********************************************
                Note that the W3C XML Schema
                Recommendation does not support
                non-instantiable simple types.

                This simple type is conceptually
                not instantiable.  This type is not
                intended to be used directly, only
                indirectly, such as via the ...DollarType
                simple types.
            ***********************************************
        </xsd:documentation>
    </xsd:annotation>
    <xsd:restriction base="xsd:decimal">
        <xsd:totalDigits value="8" fixed="true"/>
        <xsd:fractionDigits value="2" fixed="true"/>
        <xsd:minExclusive value="0.00" fixed="true"/>
        <xsd:maxInclusive value="500000.00" fixed="true"/>
    </xsd:restriction>
</xsd:simpleType>

<xsd:simpleType name="restrictedDollarAmountType"
            id="pricing.restrictedDollarAmount.sType">
    <xsd:annotation>
        <xsd:documentation xml:lang="en">
            Nothing sells for less than $1 or
            greater than or equal to $10,000.00.
        </xsd:documentation>
    </xsd:annotation>
    <xsd:restriction base="currencyAmountType">
        <xsd:minInclusive value="1.00"
                        fixed="true"/>
        <xsd:maxExclusive value="10000.00"
                        fixed="true"/>
    </xsd:restriction>
</xsd:simpleType>
```

## Appendix C — The Thematic Catalog XML Schema

```xml
<xsd:complexType name="dollarPriceType"
                 final="restriction"
                 block="restriction"
                 abstract="true"
                 id="dollarPriceType.pricing.cType">
    <xsd:annotation>
        <xsd:documentation xml:lang="en">
            Currently, currency is limited to
            U S Dollars.  Note that this type defined
            non-instantiable.  A derived type must be
            defined that sets the range.
        </xsd:documentation>
    </xsd:annotation>
    <xsd:simpleContent>
        <xsd:extension base="restrictedDollarAmountType">
            <xsd:attribute ref="currency"/>
        </xsd:extension>
    </xsd:simpleContent>
</xsd:complexType>

<xsd:complexType name="fullPriceType"
                 block="#all"
                 final="#all"
                 id="fullPriceType.pricing.cType">
    <xsd:annotation>
        <xsd:documentation xml:lang="en">
            The pricing element for all items
            sold at full price have no elements
            or attributes.  The price is simply
            the amount, stored in the value
            of the element.
        </xsd:documentation>
    </xsd:annotation>
    <xsd:simpleContent>
        <xsd:extension base="dollarPriceType"/>
    </xsd:simpleContent>
</xsd:complexType>

<xsd:complexType name="freePriceType"
                 block="#all"
                 final="#all"
                 id="freePriceType.pricing.cType">
    <xsd:annotation>
        <xsd:documentation xml:lang="en">
            Anything that is free has no
            value (i.e., price), but must
            have an authorization code.
```

*continues*

```
                    This is a complex type with
                    "empty" content.
                        -- Shorthand Notation --
            </xsd:documentation>
        </xsd:annotation>
        <xsd:attributeGroup ref="saleAttributeGroup"/>
    </xsd:complexType>

    <xsd:complexType name="salePriceType"
                     block="#all"
                     final="extension"
                     id="salePriceType.pricing.cType">
        <xsd:annotation>
            <xsd:documentation xml:lang="en">
                Anything on sale must have a price
                and an authorization
            </xsd:documentation>
        </xsd:annotation>
        <xsd:simpleContent>
            <xsd:extension base="dollarPriceType">
                <xsd:attributeGroup ref="saleAttributeGroup"/>
            </xsd:extension>
        </xsd:simpleContent>
    </xsd:complexType>

    <xsd:complexType name="clearancePriceType"
                     block="#all"
                     final="#all"
                     id="clearancePriceType.pricing.cType">
        <xsd:annotation>
            <xsd:documentation xml:lang="en">
                Anything on sale must have a price
                and an authorization
            </xsd:documentation>
        </xsd:annotation>
        <xsd:simpleContent id="cpt.simpleContent">
            <xsd:restriction base="salePriceType">
                <xsd:maxInclusive value="10.00"/>
            </xsd:restriction>
        </xsd:simpleContent>
    </xsd:complexType>

    <xsd:group name="priceGroup">
        <xsd:annotation>
            <xsd:documentation xml:lang="en">
                A price is any one of the following:
                    * Full Price (with amount)
```

```
                * Sale Price (with amount and authorization)
                * Clearance Price (with amount and
                  authorization)
                * Free (with authorization)
        </xsd:documentation>
    </xsd:annotation>
    <xsd:choice id="pg.choice">
        <xsd:element name="fullPrice"
                    type="fullPriceType"/>
        <xsd:element name="salePrice"
                    type="salePriceType"/>
        <xsd:element name="clearancePrice"
                    type="clearancePriceType"/>
        <xsd:element name="freePrice" type="freePriceType"/>
    </xsd:choice>
</xsd:group>

</xsd:schema>
```

Listing C.4 is a small schema document that supports database sequence identifiers. The main purpose of this schema document, in conjunction with both thematic schema documents, is to demonstrate substitution groups.

**LISTING C.4**  Supporting Database Sequence Schema (sequence.xsd)

```
<xsd:schema xmlns:xsd="http://www.w3.org/2001/XMLSchema">

<xsd:simpleType name="sequenceIDType">
    <xsd:annotation>
        <xsd:documentation xml:lang="en">
            A Sequence ID is generated by
            the database.  Sequences are
            integers that start with "0"
        </xsd:documentation>
    </xsd:annotation>
    <xsd:restriction base="xsd:nonNegativeInteger"/>
</xsd:simpleType>

<xsd:element name="sequenceID"
             type="sequenceIDType"
             abstract="true"
             block="substitution">
    <xsd:annotation>
        <xsd:documentation xml:lang="en">
            This element type is
            non-instantiable:  the element
```

*continues*

```xml
            must be replaced by a substitution
            group in either a derived type or
            an instance.
        </xsd:documentation>
    </xsd:annotation>
</xsd:element>

<xsd:element name="unitID"
             type="sequenceIDType"
             substitutionGroup="sequenceID">
    <xsd:annotation>
        <xsd:documentation xml:lang="en">
            This element represents sequence
            IDs for unit items.
            This element provides a valid
            substitution for "sequenceID".
        </xsd:documentation>
    </xsd:annotation>
</xsd:element>

<xsd:element name="bulkID"
             type="sequenceIDType"
             substitutionGroup="sequenceID">
    <xsd:annotation>
        <xsd:documentation xml:lang="en">
            This element represents sequence
            IDs for bulk items.
            This element provides a valid
            substitution for "sequenceID".
        </xsd:documentation>
    </xsd:annotation>
</xsd:element>

<xsd:element name="assemblyID"
             type="sequenceIDType"
             substitutionGroup="sequenceID">
    <xsd:annotation>
        <xsd:documentation xml:lang="en">
            This element represents sequence
            IDs for assembled items.
            This element provides a valid
            substitution for "sequenceID".
        </xsd:documentation>
    </xsd:annotation>
</xsd:element>

</xsd:schema>
```

# Data-oriented Schemas: Oracle8*i* Datatypes

APPENDIX D

This appendix covers the differences in mapping XML Schema datatypes between Oracle8*i* and Oracle9*i*. Oracle9*i* is a signifcant improvement over Oracle8*i* in terms of XML Schema datatype support. Database designers should determine if the differences are sufficient for their projects to warrant the upgrade. New projects should start out in Oracle9*i*, if possible.

This appendix is divided into two parts: a general overview of the functionality missing in Oracle8*i* and an appropriate, specific discussion of the consequences with implementations.

## D.1 General Overview

Oracle9*i* was developed to take nearly full advantage of the current and upcoming XML Recommendations. Oracle8*i* was released long before XML was widely used, and much of the XML work in Oracle8*i* was added *onto* the database rather than being supported *in* the database. As a result, some functionality simply cannot be represented and other functionality requires extra effort to design and implement.

### D.1.1 UTF-16 Support

Oracle8*i* does not support UTF-16, but does have partial UTF-8 support. As a result, Oracle8*i* does not support Unicode 3.0, on which the new XML Recommendations are based. In addition, many of the PL/SQL functions do not exist for Unicode support.

### D.1.2 TIMESTAMP and Time-zone Support

Oracle8*i* does not have the TIMESTAMP column datatype and time-zone support. As a result, the constraining facets of many of the XML Schema date/time/calendar datatypes must be represented differently, with either less fidelity or greater development effort.

### D.1.3 CLOB and NCLOB Support

The PL/SQL functions of Oracle8*i* were not written to take either a VARCHAR2 column datatype or a CLOB column datatype, but Oracle9*i* has overloaded the functions. In addition, Oracle9*i* has a CAST function to easily map between VARCHAR2 and a CLOB, but Oracle8*i* does not. As a result, the special CLOB functions in the DBMS_LOB package must be used for a small CLOB (fewer than 32,767 characters).

This same discussion applies to an NCLOB column datatype, because the NVARCHAR2 PL/SQL functions in Oracle9*i* were also overloaded. The CAST function works on an NCLOB column datatype and a NVARCHAR2 column datatype as well as a CLOB column datatype and a VARCHAR2 column datatype .

### D.1.4 UTL_ENCODE PL/SQL Package Not Implemented

Oracle8*i* does not have the UTL_ENCODE PL/SQL package built in. As a result, the hexBinary datatype and the base64Binary datatype cannot be easily converted to a database BLOB column datatype to minimize storage requirements. These XML Schema datatypes could be represented as database `VARCHAR2` column datatype or a database `CLOB` column datatype to take up more space, or you could convert them to a `BLOB` column datatype by using a hand-coded PL/SQL package.

### D.1.5 `SYS.UriType` Oracle Datatype Not Implemented

The `SYS.UriTyp` Oracle type does not exist in Oracle8*i*. This might affect the implementation of the `anyURI` datatype.

### D.1.6 `SYS.AnyData` Oracle Datatype Not Implemented

The `SYS.AnyData` Oracle type does not exist in Oracle8*i*. This does not affect any particular XML Schema datatype but does eliminate native support for one of the `union` simple type implementations. Hand-coding the `SYS.AnyData` type by using Oracle's object extensions is possible, if desired.

## D.2 Discussion of the Consequences

The database representation and validation for XML Schema datatypes is affected by using Oracle8*i*. In particular, the `normalizedString` datatype and all the subtypes derived by restriction are affected, as well as the `time` datatype, `dateTime` datatype, `date` datatype, `gMonth` datatype, `gYear` datatype, `gYearMonth` datatype, `gDay` datatype, and `gMonthDay` datatype. `gMonth`, `gYear`, and `gDay` are unaffected if time-zone offsets are not required, because they can simply be represented as `positiveInteger` datatypes with `minInclusive` and `maxInclusive` facet restrictions. Refer to Section 22.4.37 for more information about the need to implement time-zone offsets.

Each of these XML Schema datatypes is discussed in this section, with various implementation options, when applicable.

### D.2.1 `normalizedString` Datatype and Subtypes Derived by Restriction

Without the support for Unicode strings in Oracle9*i*, the PL/SQL function `UNISTR` is not implemented. To validate that a set of characters is a `normalizedString` datatype, the `CHR` function must be used instead. Unfortunately, the `CHR` function is based on the type of machine used (ASCII, EBCDIC, and so on) and on the character set defined for the database. Listing D.1 iterates Listing 22.10 in Oracle9*i*, and Listing D.2 maps it to Oracle8*i* when the character set is defined as `'WE8ISO8859P1'`.

**LISTING D.1**   Oracle9*i* `NormalizedStringExample` Table Creation with a Column Constraint

```
CREATE TABLE NormalizedStringExample (
 value   VARCHAR2(30)
```

*continues*

```
        CHECK (INSTR(value, UNISTR('\000D')) = 0 AND
            INSTR(value, UNISTR('\000A')) = 0 AND
            INSTR(value, UNISTR('\0009')) = 0)
);
```

**LISTING D.2**  Oracle8*i* `NormalizedStringExample` Table Creation with a Column Constraint

```
CREATE TABLE NormalizedStringExample (
value   VARCHAR2(30)
    CHECK (INSTR(value, CHR(13)) = 0 AND
        INSTR(value, CHR(10)) = 0 AND
        INSTR(value, CHR(9)) = 0)
);
```

### D.2.2 `dateTime` Datatype

Without native time-zone support, the XML Schema `dateTime` datatype can be represented as a database `DATE` column datatype with an `INTERVAL` offset. This does not maintain the time zone of the original `dateTime` value. Listing D.3 implements a `dateTime` datatype table creation.

**LISTING D.3**  `DateTimeExample` Table Creation

```
CREATE TABLE DateTimeExample (
value   DATE
);
```

To insert a row into the table with a `dateTime` datatype, Oracle needs to convert a value from its ISO 8601 standard format to an internal Oracle representation. Listing D.4 is a SQL statement that inserts a `dateTime` value into the `DateTimeExample` table excluding offsetting for the time-zone indicator. When the SQL executes, the `?datetimeValue` bind variable is the `dateTime` value.

**LISTING D.4**  `DateTimeExample` Example Insert with No Time-Zone Offset

```
INSERT INTO DateTimeExample
(value)
SELECT TO_DATE(SUBSTR(?datetimeValue, 1, 19),
       'YYYY-MM-DD"T"HH24:MI:SS')
FROM   dual;
```

Listing D.5 is a SQL statement that inserts a `dateTime` into the `DateTimeExample` table, including the offset for the time-zone indicator. When the SQL executes, the `?timeZoneSign` bind variable is the twentieth character in a `dateTime` value, the `?datetimeValue` bind variable is the first 19 characters in a `dateTime` value, and the `?timeZone` bind variable is the last 4 characters in a `dateTime` value.

**LISTING D.5**   `DateTimeExample` Table Insert with a Time-Zone Offset

```
INSERT INTO DateTimeExample
(value)
SELECT (CASE WHEN ?timeZoneSign= '-'
      THEN TO_DATE(?datetimeValue, 'YYYY-MM-DD"T"HH24:MI:SS')
        - INTERVAL ?timeZone HOUR TO MINUTE
      ELSE TO_DATE(?datetimeValue, 'YYYY-MM-DD"T"HH24:MI:SS')
        + INTERVAL ?timeZone HOUR TO MINUTE
   END)
FROM  dual;
```

Listing D.6 is a SQL statement that retrieves all of the values from the `DateTimeExample` table.

**LISTING D.6**   `DateTimeExample` Values Retrieval via a Select Statement

```
SELECT TO_CHAR(value, 'YYYY-MM-DD"T"HH24:MI:SS')
FROM  DateTimeExample;
```

### D.2.2.1 `maxInclusive` Constraining Facet

There is no built-in database support for the `maxInclusive` constraining facet, but Listing D.7 shows how this can be enforced as a column constraint.

**LISTING D.7**   `DatetimeMaxInclusiveExample` Table Creation with a Column Constraint

```
CREATE TABLE DatetimeMaxInclusiveExample (
value DATE
CHECK (value <= TO_DATE('2001-12-24T12:23:45',
          'YYYY-MM-DD"T"HH24:MI:SS')
    + INTERVAL '05:00' HOUR TO MINUTE)
);
```

### D.2.2.2 `maxExclusive` Constraining Facet

There is no built-in database support for the `maxExclusive` constraining facet, but Listing D.8 shows how this can be enforced as a column constraint.

**LISTING D.8**   `DatetimeMaxExclusiveExample` Table Creation with a Column Constraint

```
CREATE TABLE DatetimeMaxExclusiveExample (
value DATE
```

*continues*

```
        CHECK (value < TO_DATE('2001-12-24T12:23:45',
                  'YYYY-MM-DD"T"HH24:MI:SS')
            + INTERVAL '05:00' HOUR TO MINUTE)
);
```

### D.2.2.3 `minInclusive` Constraining Facet

There is no built-in database support for the `minInclusive` constraining facet, but Listing D.9 shows how this can be enforced as a column constraint.

**LISTING D.9**    `DatetimeMinInclusiveExample` Table Creation with a Column Constraint

```
CREATE TABLE DatetimeMinInclusiveExample (
value DATE
CHECK (value >= TO_DATE('2001-12-24T12:23:45',
                  'YYYY-MM-DD"T"HH24:MI:SS')
            + INTERVAL '05:00' HOUR TO MINUTE)
);
```

### D.2.2.4 `minExclusive` Constraining Facet

There is no built-in database support for the `minExclusive` constraining facet, but Listing D.10 shows how this can be enforced as a column constraint.

**LISTING D.10**    `DatetimeMinExclusiveExample` Table Creation with a Column Constraint

```
CREATE TABLE DatetimeMinExclusiveExample (
value DATE
CHECK (value > TO_DATE('2001-12-24T12:23:45',
                  'YYYY-MM-DD"T"HH24:MI:SS')
            + INTERVAL '05:00' HOUR TO MINUTE)
);
```

## D.2.3 `date` Datatype

Without native time-zone support, the XML Schema `date` datatype can be represented as a database `DATE` column datatype with an `INTERVAL` offset. This does not maintain the time-zone of the original `date` value. Listing D.11 implements a `date` datatype table creation.

**LISTING D.11**    `DateExample` Table Creation

```
CREATE TABLE DateExample (
value   DATE
);
```

To insert a row into the table with a date datatype, Oracle needs to convert a value from its ISO 8601 standard format to an internal Oracle representation. Listing D.12 is a SQL statement that inserts a date into the DateExample table, excluding offsetting for the time-zone indicator. When the SQL executes, the ?dateValue bind variable is the date value.

**LISTING D.12**   DateExample Example Insert with No Time-Zone Offset

```
INSERT INTO DateExample
(value)
SELECT TO_DATE(SUBSTR(?dateValue, 1, 10), 'YYYY-MM-DD')
FROM   dual;
```

Listing D.13 is a SQL statement that inserts a date into the DateExample table, including the offset for the time-zone indicator. When the SQL executes, the ?timeZoneSign bind variable is the eleventh character in a date value, the ?dateValue bind variable is the first 10 characters in a date value, and the ?timeZone bind variable is the last 4 characters in a date value.

**LISTING D.13**   DateExample Table Insert with a Time-Zone Offset

```
INSERT INTO DateExample
(value)
SELECT (CASE WHEN ?timeZoneSign= '-'
       THEN TO_DATE(?dateValue, 'YYYY-MM-DD')
          - INTERVAL ?timeZone HOUR TO MINUTE
       ELSE TO_DATE(?dateValue, 'YYYY-MM-DD')
          + INTERVAL ?timeZone HOUR TO MINUTE
    END)
FROM   dual;
```

Listing D.14 is a SQL statement that retrieves of the values from the DateExample table.

**LISTING D.14**   DateExample Values Retrieval via a Select Statement

```
SELECT TO_CHAR(value, 'YYYY-MM-DD"T"HH24:MI:SS')
FROM   DateTimeExample;
```

### D.2.3.1 maxInclusive Constraining Facet

There is no built-in database support for the maxInclusive constraining facet, but Listing D.15 shows how this can be enforced as a column constraint.

**LISTING D.15**  DateMaxInclusiveExample Table Creation with a Column Constraint

```
CREATE TABLE DateMaxInclusiveExample (
value DATE
CHECK (value <= TO_DATE('2001-12-24T12:23:45',
         'YYYY-MM-DD"T"HH24:MI:SS')
   + INTERVAL '05:00' HOUR TO MINUTE)
);
```

### D.2.3.2 maxExclusive Constraining Facet

There is no built-in database support for the maxExclusive constraining facet, but Listing D.16 shows how this can be enforced as a column constraint.

**LISTING D.16**  DateMaxExclusiveExample Table Creation with a Column Constraint

```
CREATE TABLE DateMaxExclusiveExample (
value DATE
CHECK (value < TO_DATE('2001-12-24T12:23:45',
         'YYYY-MM-DD"T"HH24:MI:SS')
   + INTERVAL '05:00' HOUR TO MINUTE)
);
```

### D.2.3.3 minInclusive Constraining Facet

There is no built-in database support for the minInclusive constraining facet, but Listing D.17 shows how this can be enforced as a column constraint.

**LISTING D.17**  DateMinInclusiveExample Table Creation with a Column Constraint

```
CREATE TABLE DateMinInclusiveExample (
value DATE
CHECK (value >= TO_DATE('2001-12-24T12:23:45',
         'YYYY-MM-DD"T"HH24:MI:SS')
   + INTERVAL '05:00' HOUR TO MINUTE)
);
```

### D.2.3.4 minExclusive Constraining Facet

There is no built-in database support for the minExclusive constraining facet, but Listing D.18 shows how this can be enforced as a column constraint.

**LISTING D.18**  DateMinExclusiveExample Table Creation with a Column Constraint

```
CREATE TABLE DateMinExclusiveExample (
value DATE
CHECK (value > TO_DATE('2001-12-24T12:23:45',
```

```
            'YYYY-MM-DD"T"HH24:MI:SS')
      + INTERVAL '05:00' HOUR TO MINUTE)
);
```

## D.2.4 gYear Datatype

Without native time-zone support, the gYear datatype can be represented as a DATE column datatype with an INTERVAL offset. This does not maintain the time zone of the original gYear value. Listing D.19 implements a gYear table creation.

**LISTING D.19** GYearExample Table Creation

```
CREATE TABLE GYearExample (
value   DATE
);
```

To insert a row into the table with a gYear datatype, Oracle needs to convert a value from its XML Schema format to an internal Oracle representation. Listing D.20 is a SQL statement that inserts a gYear into the GYearExample table. When the SQL executes, the ?timeZoneSign bind variable is the third character in a gYear value, the ?gYearValue bind variable is the first 4 characters in a gYear value, and the ?timeZone bind variable is the last 4 characters in a gYear value. Note that when a month is not specified, Oracle chooses the current month. However, Oracle defaults to the first day of the month if the day is not specified.

**LISTING D.20** GYearExample Example Insert

```
INSERT INTO gYearExample
SELECT (CASE WHEN ?timeZoneSign= '-'
      THEN TO_DATE(?gYearValue || '-01', 'YYYY-MM')
        - INTERVAL ?timeZone HOUR TO MINUTE
      ELSE TO_DATE(?gYearValue || '-01', 'YYYY-MM')
        + INTERVAL ?timeZone HOUR TO MINUTE
    END)
FROM  dual;
```

Listing D.21 is a SQL statement that retrieves of the values from the GYearExample table.

**LISTING D.21** GYearExample Values Retrieval via a Select Statement

```
SELECT TO_CHAR(value, 'IYYY-MM-DD"T"HH24:MI:SS')
FROM   GYearExample;
```

### D.2.4.1 `maxInclusive` Constraining Facet

There is no built-in database support for the `maxInclusive` constraining facet, but Listing D.22 shows how this can be enforced as a column constraint.

**LISTING D.22**   GYearMaxInclusiveExample Table Creation with a Column Constraint

```
CREATE TABLE GYearMaxInclusiveExample (
value DATE
CHECK (value <= TO_DATE(1999 || '-01', 'YYYY-MM')
    - INTERVAL '05:00' HOUR TO MINUTE)
);
```

### D.2.4.2 `maxExclusive` Constraining Facet

There is no built-in database support for the `maxExclusive` constraining facet, but Listing D.23 shows how this can be enforced as a column constraint.

**LISTING D.23**   GYearMaxExclusiveExample Table Creation with a Column Constraint

```
CREATE TABLE GYearMaxExclusiveExample (
value DATE
CHECK (value < TO_DATE(1999 || '-01', 'YYYY-MM')
    - INTERVAL '05:00' HOUR TO MINUTE)
);
```

### D.2.4.3 `minInclusive` Constraining Facet

There is no built-in database support for the `minInclusive` constraining facet, but Listing D.24 shows how this can be enforced as a column constraint.

**LISTING D.24**   GYearMinInclusiveExample Table Creation with a Column Constraint

```
CREATE TABLE GYearMinInclusiveExample (
value DATE
CHECK (value >= TO_DATE(1999 || '-01', 'YYYY-MM')
    - INTERVAL '05:00' HOUR TO MINUTE)
);
```

### D.2.4.4 `minExclusive` Constraining Facet

There is no built-in database support for the `minExclusive` constraining facet, but Listing D.25 shows how this can be enforced as a column constraint.

**LISTING D.25**   GYearMinExclusiveExample Table Creation with a Column Constraint

```
CREATE TABLE GYearMinExclusiveExample (
value DATE
```

```
    CHECK (value > TO_DATE(1999 || '-01', 'YYYY-MM')
        - INTERVAL '05:00' HOUR TO MINUTE)
);
```

## D.2.5 gYearMonth Datatype

Without native time-zone support, the gYearMonth datatype can be represented as a DATE column datatype with an INTERVAL offset. This does not maintain the time zone of the original gYearMonth value. Listing D.26 implements a gYearMonth table creation.

**LISTING D.26**   GYearMonthExample Table Creation

```
CREATE TABLE GYearMonthExample (
value   DATE
);
```

To insert a row into the table with a gYearMonth datatype, Oracle needs to convert a value from its ISO 8601 standard format to an internal Oracle representation. Listing D.27 inserts a gYearMonth into the GYearMonthExample table, excluding offsetting for the time-zone indicator. When the SQL executes, the ?gYearMonthValue bind variable is the gYearMonth value.

**LISTING D.27**   GYearMonthExample Example Insert with No Time-Zone Offset

```
INSERT INTO GYearMonthExample
(value)
SELECT TO_DATE(SUBSTR(?gYearMonthValue, 1, 7), 'YYYY-MM')
FROM   dual;
```

Listing D.28 inserts a gYearMonth into the GYearMonthExample table, including the offset for the time-zone indicator. When the SQL executes, the ?timeZoneSign bind variable is the eighth character in a gYearMonth value, the ?gYearMonthValue bind variable is the first 7 characters in a gYearMonth value, and the ?timeZone bind variable is the last 4 characters in a gYearMonth value.

**LISTING D.28**   GYearMonthExample Table Insert with a Time-Zone Offset

```
INSERT INTO GYearMonthExample
SELECT (CASE WHEN ?timeZoneSign= '-'
        THEN TO_DATE(?gYearMonthValue, 'YYYY-MM')
           - INTERVAL ?timeZone HOUR TO MINUTE
        ELSE TO_DATE(?gYearMonthValue, 'YYYY-MM')
           + INTERVAL ?timeZone HOUR TO MINUTE
    END)
FROM   dual;
```

To insert a row into the table with a `gYearMonth` datatype, Oracle needs to convert a value from its XML Schema format to an internal Oracle representation. Listing D.29 is a SQL statement that inserts a `gYearMonth` into the `GYearMonthExample` table.

**LISTING D.29**  `GYearMonthExample` Example Insert

```
INSERT INTO GYearMonthExample
SELECT (CASE WHEN ?timeZoneSign= '-'
             THEN TO_DATE(?gYearMonthValue, 'YYYY-MM')
                  - INTERVAL ?timeZone HOUR TO MINUTE
             ELSE TO_DATE(?gYearMonthValue, 'YYYY-MM')
                  + INTERVAL ?timeZone HOUR TO MINUTE
        END)
FROM   dual;
```

Listing D.30 is a SQL statement that retrieves all of the values from the `GYearMonthExample` table.

**LISTING D.30**  `GYearMonthExample` Values Retrieval via a Select Statement

```
SELECT TO_CHAR(value, 'IYYY-MM-DD"T"HH24:MI:SS')
FROM   GYearMonthExample;
```

### D.2.5.1 `maxInclusive` Constraining Facet

There is no built-in database support for the `maxInclusive` constraining facet, but Listing D.31 shows how this can be enforced as a column constraint.

**LISTING D.31**  `GYearMonthMaxInclusiveExample` Table Creation with a Column Constraint

```
CREATE TABLE GYearMonthMaxInclusiveExample (
value DATE
CHECK (value <= TO_DATE('2001-12', 'YYYY-MM')
    + INTERVAL '05:00' HOUR TO MINUTE)
);
```

### D.2.5.2 `maxExclusive` Constraining Facet

There is no built-in database support for the `maxExclusive` constraining facet, but Listing D.32 shows how this can be enforced as a column constraint.

## Data-oriented Schemas: Oracle8*i* Datatypes
### APPENDIX D

**LISTING D.32**  GYearMonthMaxExclusiveExample Table Creation with a Column Constraint

```
CREATE TABLE GYearMonthMaxExclusiveExample (
value DATE
CHECK (value < TO_DATE('2001-12', 'YYYY-MM')
    + INTERVAL '05:00' HOUR TO MINUTE)
);
```

### D.2.5.3 `minInclusive` Constraining Facet

There is no built-in database support for the `minInclusive` constraining facet, but Listing D.33 shows how this can be enforced as a column constraint.

**LISTING D.33**  GYearMonthMinInclusiveExample Table Creation with a Column Constraint

```
CREATE TABLE GYearMonthMinInclusiveExample (
value DATE
CHECK (value >= TO_DATE('2001-12', 'YYYY-MM')
    + INTERVAL '05:00' HOUR TO MINUTE)
);
```

### D.2.5.4 `minExclusive` Constraining Facet

There is no built-in database support for the `minExclusive` constraining facet, but Listing D.34 shows how this can be enforced as a column constraint.

**LISTING D.34**  GYearMonthMinExclusiveExample Table Creation with a Column Constraint

```
CREATE TABLE GYearMonthMinExclusiveExample (
value DATE
CHECK (value > TO_DATE('2001-12', 'YYYY-MM')
    + INTERVAL '05:00' HOUR TO MINUTE)
);
```

## D.2.6 `time` Datatype

Without native time-zone support, the XML Schema `time` datatype can be represented as a database `DATE` column datatype with an `INTERVAL` offset. This does not maintain the time zone of the original `time` value. Listing D.35 implements a `time` datatype table creation.

**LISTING D.35**  TimeExample Table Creation

```
CREATE TABLE TimeExample (
value   DATE
);
```

To insert a row into the table with a `time` datatype, Oracle needs to convert a value from its XML Schema format to an internal Oracle representation. In addition, because Oracle needs a date for the insert, it is appropriate to use a date that indicates that no date was specified. Oracle has a minimum date of January 1, 4712 B.C. It is represented by the number 1 and is translated into January 1, 4712 B.C. by the 'J' datetime format element. A hard-coded date is especially useful when min/max inclusion/exclusion facets have been specified. Listing D.36 is a SQL statement that inserts a time into the `TimeExample` table, excluding offsetting for the time-zone indicator. When the SQL executes, the `?timeValue` bind variable is the `time` value.

**LISTING D.36**  `TimeExample` Table Insert with No Time-Zone Offset

```
INSERT INTO TimeExample
(value)
SELECT TO_DATE('1 ' || SUBSTR(?timeValue, 1, 8), 'J HH24:MI:SS')
FROM   dual;
```

Listing D.37 is a SQL statement that inserts a `time` into the `TimeExample` table, including the offset for the time-zone indicator. When the SQL executes, the `?timeZoneSign` bind variable is the ninth character in a `time` value, the `?timeValue` bind variable is the first 8 characters in a `time` value, and the `?timeZone` bind variable is the last 4 characters in a `time` value.

**LISTING D.37**  `TimeExample` Table Insert with a TimeZone Offset

```
INSERT INTO TimeExample
(value)
SELECT (CASE WHEN ?timeZoneSign = '-'
      THEN TO_DATE('1 ' || ?timeValue, 'J HH24:MI:SS')
         - INTERVAL ?timeZone HOUR TO MINUTE
      ELSE TO_DATE('1 ' || ?timeValue, 'J HH24:MI:SS')
         + INTERVAL ?timeZone HOUR TO MINUTE
   END)
FROM   dual;
```

Listing D.38 is a SQL statement that retrieves all of the values from the `TimeExample` table.

**LISTING D.38**  `TimeExample` Values Retrieval via a Select Statement

```
SELECT TO_CHAR(value, 'HH24:MI:SS')
FROM   TimeExample;
```

### D.2.6.1 `maxInclusive` Constraining Facet

There is no built-in database support for the `maxInclusive` constraining facet, but Listing D.39 shows how this can be enforced as a column constraint.

**LISTING D.39**  TimeMaxInclusiveExample Table Creation with a Column Constraint

```
CREATE TABLE TimeMaxInclusiveExample (
value DATE
CHECK (value <= TO_DATE('1 12:45:30', 'J HH24:MI:SS')
    + INTERVAL '05:00' HOUR TO MINUTE)
);
```

### D.2.6.2 maxExclusive Constraining Facet

There is no built-in database support for the maxExclusive constraining facet, but Listing D.40 shows how this can be enforced as a column constraint.

**LISTING D.40**  TimeMaxExclusiveExample Table Creation with a Column Constraint

```
CREATE TABLE TimeMaxExclusiveExample (
value DATE
CHECK (value < TO_DATE('1 12:45:30', 'J HH24:MI:SS')
    + INTERVAL '05:00' HOUR TO MINUTE)
);
```

### D.2.6.3 minInclusive Constraining Facet

There is no built-in database support for the minInclusive constraining facet, but Listing D.41 shows how this can be enforced as a column constraint.

**LISTING D.41**  TimeMinInclusiveExample Table Creation with a Column Constraint

```
CREATE TABLE TimeMinInclusiveExample (
value DATE
CHECK (value >= TO_DATE('1 12:45:30', 'J HH24:MI:SS')
    + INTERVAL '05:00' HOUR TO MINUTE)
);
```

### D.2.6.4 minExclusive Constraining Facet

There is no built-in database support for the minExclusive constraining facet, but Listing D.42 shows how this can be enforced as a column constraint.

**LISTING D.42**  TimeMinExclusiveExample Table Creation with a Column Constraint

```
CREATE TABLE TimeMinExclusiveExample (
value DATE
CHECK (value > TO_DATE('1 12:45:30', 'J HH24:MI:SS')
    + INTERVAL '05:00' HOUR TO MINUTE)
);
```

## D.2.7 gMonth Datatype

Without native time-zone support, the XML Schema gMonth datatype can be represented as a database DATE column datatype with an INTERVAL offset. This does not maintain the time zone of the original gMonth value. Listing D.43 implements a gMonth table creation.

**LISTING D.43** GMonthExample Table Creation

```
CREATE TABLE GMonthExample (
value   DATE
);
```

To insert a row into the table with a gMonth datatype, Oracle needs to convert a value from its XML Schema format to an internal Oracle representation. Listing D.44 is a SQL statement that inserts a gMonth into the GMonthExample table. When the SQL executes, the ?timeZoneSign bind variable is the third character in a gMonth value, the ?gMonthValue bind variable is the first 2 characters in a gMonth value, and the ?timeZone bind variable is the last 4 characters in a gMonth value.

**LISTING D.44** GMonthExample Example Insert

```
INSERT INTO gMonthExample
SELECT (CASE WHEN ?timeZoneSign= '-'
        THEN ADD_MONTHS(TO_DATE('1', 'J'), ?gMonthValue - 1)
          - INTERVAL ?timeZone HOUR TO MINUTE
        ELSE ADD_MONTHS(TO_DATE('1', 'J'), ?gMonthValue - 1)
          + INTERVAL ?timeZone HOUR TO MINUTE
    END)
FROM dual;
```

Listing D.45 is a SQL statement that retrieves of the values from the GMonthExample table.

**LISTING D.45** GMonthExample Values Retrieval via a Select Statement

```
SELECT TO_CHAR(value, 'IYYY-MM-DD"T"HH24:MI:SS')
FROM GMonthExample;
```

### D.2.7.1 maxInclusive Constraining Facet

There is no built-in database support for the maxInclusive constraining facet, but Listing D.46 shows how this can be enforced as a column constraint.

**LISTING D.46** GMonthMaxInclusiveExample Table Creation with a Column Constraint

```
CREATE TABLE GMonthMaxInclusiveExample (
value DATE
CHECK (value <= ADD_MONTHS(TO_DATE('1', 'J'), 10)
    - INTERVAL '05:00' HOUR TO MINUTE)
);
```

### D.2.7.2 `maxExclusive` Constraining Facet

There is no built-in database support for the `maxExclusive` constraining facet, but Listing D.47 shows how this can be enforced as a column constraint.

**LISTING D.47** GMonthMaxExclusiveExample Table Creation with a Column Constraint

```
CREATE TABLE GMonthMaxExclusiveExample (
value DATE
CHECK (value < ADD_MONTHS(TO_DATE('1', 'J'), 10)
    - INTERVAL '05:00' HOUR TO MINUTE)
);
```

### D.2.7.3 `minInclusive` Constraining Facet

There is no built-in database support for the `minInclusive` constraining facet, but Listing D.48 shows how this can be enforced as a column constraint.

**LISTING D.48** GMonthMinInclusiveExample Table Creation with a Column Constraint

```
CREATE TABLE GMonthMinInclusiveExample (
value DATE
CHECK (value >= ADD_MONTHS(TO_DATE('1', 'J'), 10)
    - INTERVAL '05:00' HOUR TO MINUTE)
);
```

### D.2.7.4 `minExclusive` Constraining Facet

There is no built-in database support for the `minExclusive` constraining facet, but Listing D.49 shows how this can be enforced as a column constraint.

**LISTING D.49** GMonthMinExclusiveExample Table Creation with a Column Constraint

```
CREATE TABLE GMonthMinExclusiveExample (
value DATE
CHECK (value > ADD_MONTHS(TO_DATE('1', 'J'), 10)
    - INTERVAL '05:00' HOUR TO MINUTE)
);
```

## D.2.8 gDay Datatype

Without native time-zone support, the gDay datatype can be represented as a DATE column datatype with an INTERVAL offset. This does not maintain the time zone of the original gDay value. Listing D.50 implements a gDay table creation.

**LISTING D.50**  GDayExample Table Creation

```
CREATE TABLE GDayExample (
value   DATE
);
```

To insert a row into the table with a gDay datatype, Oracle needs to convert a value from its XML Schema format to an internal Oracle representation. Listing D.51 is a SQL statement that inserts a gDay into the GDayExample table. When the SQL executes, the ?timeZoneSign bind variable is the sixth character in a gDay value, the ?gDayValue bind variable is the fourth and fifth characters in a gDay value, and the ?timeZone bind variable is the last 4 characters in a gDay value.

**LISTING D.51**  GDayExample Example Insert

```
INSERT INTO gDayExample
SELECT (CASE WHEN ?timeZoneSign= '-'
        THEN TO_DATE('1', 'J') + ?gDayValue
           - INTERVAL ?timeZone HOUR TO MINUTE
        ELSE TO_DATE('1', 'J') + ?gDayValue
           + INTERVAL ?timeZone HOUR TO MINUTE
    END)
FROM  dual;
```

Listing D.52 is a SQL statement that retrieves all of the values from the GDayExample table.

**LISTING D.52**  GDayExample Values Retrieval via a Select Statement

```
SELECT TO_CHAR(value, 'IYYY-MM-DD"T"HH24:MI:SS')
FROM   GDayExample;
```

### D.2.8.1 maxInclusive Constraining Facet

There is no built-in database support for the maxInclusive constraining facet, but Listing D.53 shows how this can be enforced as a column constraint.

### LISTING D.53  `GDayMaxInclusiveExample` Table Creation with a Column Constraint

```
CREATE TABLE GDayMaxInclusiveExample (
value DATE
CHECK (value <= TO_DATE('1', 'J') + 5
    - INTERVAL '05:00' HOUR TO MINUTE)
);
```

#### D.2.8.2 `maxExclusive` Constraining Facet

There is no built-in database support for the `maxExclusive` constraining facet, but Listing D.54 shows how this can be enforced as a column constraint.

### LISTING D.54  `GDayMaxExclusiveExample` Table Creation with a Column Constraint

```
CREATE TABLE GDayMaxExclusiveExample (
value DATE
CHECK (value < TO_DATE('1', 'J') + 5
    - INTERVAL '05:00' HOUR TO MINUTE)
);
```

#### D.2.8.3 `minInclusive` Constraining Facet

There is no built-in database support for the `minInclusive` constraining facet, but Listing D.55 shows how this can be enforced as a column constraint.

### LISTING D.55  `GDayMinInclusiveExample` Table Creation with a Column Constraint

```
CREATE TABLE GDayMinInclusiveExample (
value DATE
CHECK (value >= TO_DATE('1', 'J') + 5
    - INTERVAL '05:00' HOUR TO MINUTE)
);
```

#### D.2.8.4 `minExclusive` Constraining Facet

There is no built-in database support for the `minExclusive` constraining facet, but Listing D.56 shows how this can be enforced as a column constraint.

### LISTING D.56  `GDayMinExclusiveExample` Table Creation with a Column Constraint

```
CREATE TABLE GDayMinExclusiveExample (
value DATE
CHECK (value > TO_DATE('1', 'J') +
    5 - INTERVAL '05:00' HOUR TO MINUTE)
);
```

### D.2.9 gMonthDay Datatype

Without native time-zone support, the gMonthDay datatype can be represented as a DATE column datatype with an INTERVAL offset. This does not maintain the time zone of the original gMonthDay value. Listing D.57 implements a gMonthDay table creation.

**LISTING D.57**   GMonthDayExample Table Creation

```
CREATE TABLE GMonthDayExample (
value    DATE
);
```

To insert a row into the table with a gMonthDay datatype, Oracle needs to convert a value from its XML Schema format to an internal Oracle representation. Listing D.58 is a SQL statement that inserts a gMonthDay into the GMonthDayExample table. When the SQL executes, the ?timeZoneSign bind variable is the eighth character in a GMonthDay value, the ?GMonthDayValue bind variable is the first 7 characters in a GMonthDay value, and the ?timeZone bind variable is the last 4 characters in a GMonthDay value.

**LISTING D.58**   GMonthDayExample Example Insert

```
INSERT INTO GMonthDayExample
SELECT (CASE WHEN ?timeZoneSign = '-'
    THEN ADD_MONTHS(TO_DATE('1', 'J'),
       SUBSTR(?GMonthDayValue, 3, 2) - 1) +
       SUBSTR(?GMonthDayValue, 6, 2) -
     INTERVAL ?timeZone HOUR TO MINUTE
    ELSE ADD_MONTHS(TO_DATE('1', 'J'),
       SUBSTR(?GMonthDayValue, 3, 2) - 1) +
       SUBSTR(?GMonthDayValue, 6, 2) +
     INTERVAL ?timeZone HOUR TO MINUTE
   END)
FROM dual;
```

Listing D.59 is a SQL statement that retrieves of the values from the GMonthDayExample table.

**LISTING D.59**   GMonthDayExample Values Retrieval via a Select Statement

```
SELECT TO_CHAR(value, 'IYYY-MM-DD"T"HH24:MI:SS')
FROM GMonthDayExample;
```

#### D.2.9.1 maxInclusive Constraining Facet

There is no built-in database support for the maxInclusive constraining facet, but Listing D.60 shows how this can be enforced as a column constraint.

**LISTING D.60**  GMonthDayMaxInclusiveExample Table Creation with a Column Constraint

```
CREATE TABLE GMonthDayMaxInclusiveExample (
value DATE
CHECK (value <= TO_DATE('1', 'J') + 5
    - INTERVAL '05:00' HOUR TO MINUTE)
);
```

### D.2.9.2 maxExclusive Constraining Facet

There is no built-in database support for the maxExclusive constraining facet, but Listing D.61 shows how this can be enforced as a column constraint.

**LISTING D.61**  GMonthDayMaxExclusiveExample Table Creation with a Column Constraint

```
CREATE TABLE GMonthDayMaxExclusiveExample (
value DATE
CHECK (value < ADD_MONTHS(TO_DATE('1', 'J'), 5) + 5
    - INTERVAL '05:00' HOUR TO MINUTE)
);
```

### D.2.9.3 minInclusive Constraining Facet

There is no built-in database support for the minInclusive constraining facet, but Listing D.62 shows how this can be enforced as a column constraint.

**LISTING D.62**  GMonthDayMinInclusiveExample Table Creation with a Column Constraint

```
CREATE TABLE GMonthDayMinInclusiveExample (
value DATE
CHECK (value >= ADD_MONTHS(TO_DATE('1', 'J'), 5) + 5
    - INTERVAL '05:00' HOUR TO MINUTE)
);
```

### D.2.9.4 minExclusive Constraining Facet

There is no built-in database support for the minExclusive constraining facet, but Listing D.63 shows how this can be enforced as a column constraint.

**LISTING D.63**  GMonthDayMinExclusiveExample Table Creation with a Column Constraint

```
CREATE TABLE GMonthDayMinExclusiveExample (
value DATE
CHECK (value > ADD_MONTHS(TO_DATE('1', 'J'), 5) + 5
    - INTERVAL '05:00' HOUR TO MINUTE)
);
```

# Glossary

APPENDIX E

# Glossary

## APPENDIX E

Throughout this glossary, terms being defined occur in **bold italic**; if the definition requires context, the context is in upright **bold**.

The glossary is arranged by topic, not just alphabetically. This is so that the glossary can be read as a quick refresher on the various topics, and so that when you are reading one definition the definitions of related terms are close at hand. Accordingly, the definitions may not read exactly the same as those found in the text itself; it each case, the context of the definition was considered. Selected terms that are used only occasionally in this book but may be common elsewhere are included, but the bold definienda of their definitions are grey instead of black.

At the end is a concise alphabetic index for the reader who is not sure of the topic under which a particular term will be found.

## E.1 Objects, Classes, and Instances

*object-oriented (OO):* The point of view that considers things to be objects, in the technical sense defined here. This point of view may be either *intensional* or *extensional*. Objects have *properties* and *methods*, and are instances of *classes*; all of the instances of a given class have the same properties and methods.

*extensional* **OO:** A description of things as objects, instances of classes, in which objects become instances of classes by virtue of satisfying the restrictions the class places on the object's properties, propertyMethods, and methods (and "restrictors").

*intensional* **OO:** A description of things as objects, instances of classes, in which objects become instances of classes by virtue of being so created; because of this, their satisfying the restrictions of the class is automatic. A *class* is derived from another only if it is declared to be so as part of *its* instantiation. Intensional OO is the usual way OO programming is understood.

*object*: Everything of interest is an object. Objects have various aspects: properties, propertyMethods, methods, and/or "restrictors".

*aspect* **of an object:** A property, propertyMethod, method, or restrictor.

*property* **of an object:** An aspect of an object that has a name and a value; the name identifies the property, the value is another object.

*method* **of an object:** An aspect of an object that has a name and an algorithm; the name identifies the property, the algorithm describes a process that "changes the world"— for example, it might change the value of one of that object's properties. The algorithm is akin to a programming *procedure*.

*propertyMethod* **of an object:** An aspect of an object that has a name and an algorithm. The name identifies the property; the algorithm returns as a value an object and may change the world as well. The algorithm is akin to a programming *function*.

Some people call propertyMethods "properties," because both provide a value when queried. Others call them "methods," because they are not independently assigned values but rather are values computed from those of the "real" properties (and because that computation may have side effects that change the world). Whichever point of view is chosen, the additional distinction imposed by the other is sometimes useful. This glossary straddles the fence.

*restrictor* **of an object:** An aspect of an object that is a Boolean-valued algorithm used to determine whether another object satisfies a restriction. A restrictor may require that the other object have a property (or method, etc.) with a particular name, and may place restrictions on the values of properties (or methods, etc.). Restrictors are not generally named, and only referred to in the aggregate—all of the restrictors of a class. See *class*.

*class:* An object that has restrictors. Classes *provide* the properties (and other aspects), which they require of objects that satisfy their restrictors.

Instances of a class must satisfy *all* of that class's restrictors. If an object has no restrictors, one could consider it a class, but *every object* would be an instance—not very interesting!

It is common for classes' restrictors to require that the algorithms of propertyMethods and the methods they require must be constant for all objects satisfying the restrictors—in other words, all such objects must have the same algorithms. (This does not preclude the algorithms from using properties of the instance to produce different results with different instances.) Alternatively, common classes may permit alternate algorithms as long as the propertyMethods take the same arguments and produce the same class of results; this is a useful way of dealing with derivations which change the algorithms. These are useful kinds of classes and are typical of the classes common in object-oriented programming.

A class is sometimes called a "type," but in this book we use 'type' in a slightly more restrictive way (except where we are describing things with respect to a particular programming language for which 'type' is the standard term).

*instance* **of a class:** An object that satisfies all of the restrictors of the class.

**an object** *has* **aspects:** (In this book we consider 'have' to be a technical term when applied to objects, and try to avoid other terms for this relationship—especially 'provides'. Compare *provides* with respect to classes.)

**a class** *provides* **aspects:** A class requires of (or permits and places restrictions on) various aspects of its instances. (In this book we consider 'provide' to be a technical term when applied to objects, and classes in particular; we try to avoid other terms—especially 'have'—for this relationship. Compare *has* with respect to objects.) A class *provides* the aspects that its instances *have*. It is important to maintain this distinction since a class is itself an object; a class may *have* certain aspects as an object and *provide* different (or occasionally the same) aspects for its instances.

**a class is *derived from* another:** The derived class requires all of the properties (etc.) which the other requires, prohibits all that the other prohibits, and its restrictors place the same or more restrictive requirements on its instances than does the other class. (The result is that any instance of the derived class is necessarily an instance of the original.) When one class is derived from another, the original (other) class is the *base class*. A derived class is analogous to what some might call a "subclass."

***base class* of a derived class:** The class from which the derived class is derived. A base type is analogous to what some might call a "superclass" or "archetype."

***instantiable* class:** A class that can directly have instances. (See also *instantiable type*.)

***non-instantiable* class:** A class that can only have instances by virtue of them being instances of another class derived from this class. (Sometimes called "abstract" in OO scenarios, but we reserve that term for a different meaning in this book. See also *non-instantiable type*, Section E.4.)

***class generator:*** A class whose instances are classes.

***type generator:*** A class generator which provides fixed algorithms for its instances' restrictors which these class instances may vary only by having different values for their properties, which serve as parameters to the algorithms.

***type:***

1. A class that is an instance of a type generator. A class is called a "type" only in the context of various other classes that are instances of the same type generator. For example, the many assorted *element types* are all instances of the same type generator; the same is true of *attribute types*, *simple types*, and *complex types*.

   The various DTD-defined or schema-defined element types are classes whose instances are elements; the primary properties of the element types (considered as objects themselves) provide the name, content model, and attribute definitions. The restrictors of the classes use these objects as parameters to their algorithms; all element types use the same restrictor algorithms, but a different value for name or content model (for example) will cause the restrictor to accept different elements as instances of the element type. Therefore we view *element type* as a type generator; *an* element type is an instance of the class *element type*, and hence a type; *its* instances are elements "of that [element] type." The same holds for the other four XML Schema *types*. Care must be taken when talking about an element or attribute's *type*; the context must make it clear whether the element or attribute type is meant, or the content type is meant.

2. Any class. (This meaning is not used in this book except when discussing OO programming systems for which this is the standard terminology.)

## E.2 Markup

A marked-up character string includes some characters that are *markup* and some that are *data*. One job of a parser is to separate the two.

*markup:* characters added into a string of data characters to identify and provide information about the data. It can be divided into *metadata* and *punctuation*.

*data character:*
  1. A character in an XML document that an XML parser recognizes as data (rather than markup).
  2. A character information item in the *children* of an element information item.
  3. Such a character information item or a character in the value of an attribute.

*metadata string:*
  1. A character string recognized as markup but retained in the abstract data structure because it provides information about the abstract structure. (Example: An element's or attribute's *type name*.)
  2. A character string that is the value of an information item property other than the *value* property of an attribute.

*markup punctuation:* A character string recognized as markup but which only serves to identify or delineate markup. (Examples: Whitespace and the strings '<', '</', '/>', and '>' found in various tags; whitespace, '=', '"', and ''' found in attribute specifications.) Markup punctuation is typically not retained in the abstract data structure.

## E.3 XML Documents

### E.3.1 Whole Documents

*XML document:*
  1. A character string conforming to the grammar of the XML Recommendation; it might be in the form of an input stream, a buffer, a disk file, or any other form.
  2. Either an XML document (definition 1) or a document information element, which is the product of parsing an XML document. Commonly used when there is no need to distinguish between the two.

*XML instance:* An XML document—or even part of a document—whose validity is being determined. Specifically, the validity of this document depends on examining an XML schema specified by the XML instance, or possibly a different schema selected using information not in the document.

The term 'XML instance' as used in this book is not generic: XML is not a class of which these character strings are instances. An XML document (or a fragment of one) is called an "XML instance" only when we intend the connotation of a candidate for validation in the context where the term is used.

**XML information set (infoset):** A collection of *information items* including a *document information item* and all of the other information items that are (recursively) property values of the document information item (abbreviated 'infoset').

*Abstract document*, *infoset*, and *document information item* are essentially the same thing. The Infoset Recommendation takes the point of view that the various information items in isolation, linked by properties, as opposed to being part of the document information item, so it considers an infoset a collection of information items with links between them. This distinction is at most a matter of how you think of objects and the values of their properties—or it can be thought of as just an implementation detail.

In the context of a post-schema-validation infoset, an ordinary infoset is called a "basic infoset."

*information item:* An instance of any of 11 classes defined in the Infoset Recommendation:

- Document information item
- Element information item
- Attribute information item
- Character information item
- Processing instruction information item
- Unexpanded entity reference information item
- Comment information item
- Document type declaration information item
- Unparsed entity information item
- Notation information item
- Namespace information item

Of these, only the document, element, attribute, character, namespace, and notation information items are of interest for the purposes of this book. An information item is the "abstract" (post-parser-processing) version of a part or all of a (concrete) document.

**post-schema-validation infoset (PSVI):** An infoset augmented by causing element and attribute information items to have additional properties. Some of whose values are new kinds of information items, as defined in the Schema Recommendation. See Chapter 16.

*basic* **infoset:** An infoset as defined in the Infoset Recommendation; used when contrasting with a PSVI.

*well-formed* **XML document:** An XML document. (A document purported to be an XML document that does not conform to the grammatical requirements of the XML Recommendation fails to be an XML document; the adjective 'well-formed' is redundant, but useful when documents are discussed without knowing whether they so conform. (Compare *valid XML document* in Section E.4.)

*namespace:* An abstraction defined by the Namespace Recommendation that is used to differentiate between what would otherwise be incompatibly identical names in XML markup. XML NCNames can be differentiated by being associated with different namespaces, either by being in the context of an explicit default namespace or by having a default namespace prescribed by a schema. If the defaults do not get the correct namespace, an NCName can be forced into a particular namespace by making it the *local name* of a QName.

*namespace declaration:* An attribute specification specifying an attribute whose name begins with 'xmlns', as prescribed in the Namespace Recommendation. A namespace declaration is not treated as a normal attribute specification by namespace-aware processors. (All schema processors are namespace-aware.)

A namespace declaration's purpose is to associate a local *prefix* with a namespace name (a URI). The lexical form of a namespace is like any attribute specification: The attribute name is normally a QName lexically (but with a different interpretation of the parts) where the prefix 'xmlns' and the "local name" is the new *prefix* being established; The attribute value is the associated namespace name. As a special case, if the QName is simply 'xmlns', the namespace name is associated with other QNames having no prefix.

*scope* of a **namespace declaration:** The element in which a namespace is declared, and all of its subelements and their attributes (except those elements which are shielded by having the same prefix redeclared).

*namespace name:* A URI used or intended to be used as the "name" of a namespace.

## E.3.2 Parts of Documents

*element:*
1. A character string that conforms to the requirements of being an element, as found in the XML Recommendation. (An element consists of a start-tag, content, and an end-tag, or it is an empty-element tag.)
2. Either an element (definition 1) or an element information item. Used when the distinction is irrelevant to the discussion in context.

*element information item:* An object created from a (concrete) element by a parser, which reflects explicitly the structure, data, and metadata recognized by the parser while parsing the element.

*type name* **of an element:** A *name* used in an element's tags to name an element type. Since there can be many subelements of a given type in the content of a single element, the *type name* cannot serve to identify the subelement, even in the context of that parent element; most elements do not have unique identifiers, and when one is needed, an ID-valued attribute is normally used. (This is in contrast to the attributes of an element, which are uniquely identified by their *type name* because there can be only one instance of an attribute type in the attribute set of any one element. In the SGML community, a *type name* was originally called a "generic identifier.")

*generic identifier*: The *type name* of an element; the name of an element type. (A terminological holdover from early SGML.)

*start-tag:* A character string concatenated from '<', a name (the *type name*), zero or more attribute specifications and/or namespace declarations (which may be intermixed), and a terminal '>'. Additional whitespace is permitted between any of the parts except between the initial '<' and the *type name*. A start-tag marks the beginning of an element that ends with an end-tag.

*empty-element tag:* A character string of the same form as a start-tag except that its terminal punctuation is '/>'. An empty-element tag is a complete element whose content is empty.

*end-tag:* A character string concatenated from '</', a name, and a terminal '>'. Additional whitespace is permitted after the name. The name must be the *type name* of the element introduced in the start-tag which begins the element ending with this end-tag.

*content* **of an element:**
1. The character string between the start- and end-tags of an element. (Special case: The content of an element consisting of an empty-element tag is *a priori* the empty string.)
2. The terms in the value of an element information item's *children* property (a sequence or list of various kinds of information items, especially *element* and *character* information items).

*immediate subelement* **of an element:** An element information item term in the element information item's *children* property's value (a sequence or list of information items) or a substring of the content of the element, which, when parsed, gives rise to such an element information item.

*subelement* **of an element:** An immediate subelement of the element or (recursively) a subelement of one of those immediate subelements.

*children of an element:* (used only rarely in this book)
1. The immediate subelements of an element.
2. The immediate subelements and data characters of an element.
3. The immediate subelements, data characters, and attributes of an element.

***attributes* of an element:**
1. The attribute specifications found in the start-tag or empty-element tag of the element.
2. The members of the value of the element information item's *attributes* property (a set of attribute information items)

*document element:* The outermost element in an XML document.

*attribute specification:* A character string conforming to the requirements of the XML Recommendation. It consists of a name, an equal sign, and a quoted string, with intervening optional whitespace. The quoted string, when normalized, provides the *value*. (An attribute specification that is a *namespace declaration* is treated specially by namespace-aware processors—which includes all schema processors.)

*attribute information item:* An object created from an attribute specification by a parser, which reflects explicitly the data and metadata recognized by the parser while parsing the element, as defined in the Infoset Recommendation.

*attribute:* An *attribute specification* or an *attribute information item*. (Used when the distinction is irrelevant to the discussion, or cannot be misunderstood.)

***type name* of an attribute:** The *name* used in an attribute (specification) to name an attribute type. Since there can be only one attribute of a given type in the set of attributes of a single element, the *type name* serves to identify the attribute in the context of that element, and is often simply called the "name" of the attribute. (This is in contrast to the immediate subelements of an element, which are not in general uniquely identified by their *type name*; most elements do not have unique identifiers, and when one is needed, the value of an ID-valued attribute is normally used.)

***value* of an attribute or element:** The character string obtained by normalizing the quoted string of an attribute specification, or by normalizing the character string made of the characters in the content of an element which has *simple content*. Normalization is a process defined in the XML and Schema Recommendations and primarily involves resolving character references and, depending on the particular simple type, possibly removing or modifying some or all of the whitespace characters under the control of the `whiteSpace` facet of the simple type.

*abstract:* Pertaining to the post-parser-processing "infoset" form of an XML document. For example, an *abstract element* is an element information item. In general, 'abstract' when applied to a document or part of a document means the corresponding information item. Used only when emphasizing the comparison with *concrete*.

*(concrete):* Pertaining to the pre-parser-processing "flat" character stream form of an XML document or any of its parts, as compared with *abstract* parts of an *abstract* document. Used only to emphasize the comparison with *abstract*.

***notation* information item:** An information item containing either or both of a system identifier and a public identifier (which are described in the XML Recommendation) and identified as a notation.

*Notation* is not well defined in XML or SGML: Its semantics are determined by the application. The original intended use, and still one current use, is to identify character streams not in XML (or SGML), such as EPS graphics. In fact, a notation information item simply conveys to the application a system identifier or public identifier, which the application must interpret.

***processing instruction:*** A character string in an XML document beginning with '<?' and ending with '?>'. All processing-instruction-format *declarations* (declaration ) begin with the characters 'xml' after the initial '<?'. Their use is application-specific; those whose interior string begins with 'xml' (or any case-changed variants) are reserved for use by W3C Recommendations pertaining to XML; some are currently used as declarations (see Section E.4).

***comment declaration:*** A declaration in an XML document beginning with '<!--' and ending with '-->'.

## E.4  XML DTDs and Schemas

***document type declaration:*** A declaration that may occur near the beginning of an XML document which prescribes the *type name* of the document element, sets up the information needed for the parser to handle the documents entity structure, and includes—directly or by reference—a DTD.

***document type definition (DTD):*** A part of an XML document contained in the document type declaration either directly or by reference, which provides a much weaker but similar capability in prescribing allowable types of attributes and elements at various points in the document.

*Validity with respect to a DTD* is defined by the XML Recommendation.

***declaration:***
1. A character string beginning with '<!' and ending with '>', typically making up a comment, a document type declaration, or a part of a DTD, whose internal substring conforms to the requirements prescribed by the SGML Standard (ISO 8879) or the

XML Recommendation. Not all XML declarations have this form, which is the prescribed form for SGML declarations. During the creation of XML, the creators tried to remain as compatible with SGML as possible and so used another form of declaration (definition 2) for those that were not SGML declarations.

2. A processing instruction designated by the XML Recommendation to be a declaration. In SGML, processing instructions are reasonably used for nonstandard (not prescribed by the SGML Standard) declarations; for compatibility, XML uses them for some declarations.

3. An attribute specification beginning with 'xmlns'; namespace-aware processors will not treat such a specification as a normal attribute specification. (See *namespace declaration* in Section 12.4.1.)

4. A schema component that can be referenced by name in an XML document: an element type, attribute type, or notation component. We do not use the term in this sense regularly in this book because in most of the SGML and XML community *declarations* are character strings that occur in the concrete representations of abstract classes (rather than *being* the abstract classes), and because we do not see any reason to restrict the terms 'element type' and 'attribute type' to those types only when defined by declarations in a DTD.

*definition:* A schema component other than a declaration (definition 4) which can be given a name and referenced elsewhere in a schema. This terminology is used in the Schema Recommendation but not in this book.

**schema component:** An instance of one of the classes defined and so designated in the Schema Recommendation.

***element type:***

1. A class whose instances are elements. Each element type requires that its instances all have the same type name and all satisfy the same constraints on their content and attributes. An element type may originate from an element type declaration in a DTD or from an `element` element in a schema document.

2. An *element type* specifically defined by an element type declaration in a DTD. (This meaning is common, but this book uses "*DTD-defined* element type.")

3. An element type (definition 1) specifically defined by an `element` in a schema document; one kind of schema component. It primarily binds a structure type to a name.

4. An element type, as an object but not a class, also serves as a component in a *content model*, indicating that at that point in the model an element of that type is permitted. A few of the properties provided by *element type* are to enhance this purpose.

5. Either an element type (definition 1) or the corresponding element type declaration or `element`. Used only when the distinction is irrelevant to the discussion in context.

*element type declaration:* A declaration in a DTD used to define an element type: the XML representation of a DTD-defined element type. (In the early days of SGML, an element type declaration was called an "element declaration.")

`element`: A type of element in a schema document used to define an element type: the XML representation of a (schema-defined) element type.

*attribute type:*
1. A class whose instances are attributes. Each attribute type requires that its instances all have the same type name and all satisfy the same constraints on their values. An attribute type may originate from an attribute definition in a DTD or from an `attribute` element in a schema document.
2. An attribute type (definition 1) specifically defined by an `attribute` in a schema document; one kind of schema component. It primarily binds a structure type to a name.

*attribute type declaration:* A declaration in a DTD used to define an attribute type: the XML representation of a DTD-defined attribute type.

`attribute`: The element type of elements in a schema document used to define attribute types: the XML representation of a (schema-defined) attribute type.

***DTD-defined* element type or attribute type:** An element type whose XML representation is an element type declaration in a DTD (element type, definition 2), or an attribute definition in a DTD.

***schema-defined* element type or attribute type:** An element type or attribute type whose XML representation is an `element` or `attribute`, respectively, in a schema document.

*concrete element type or attribute type:* An element type declaration or an attribute definition in a DTD, or an `element` or `attribute`: The XML representation of an (abstract) element type or attribute type. Used only when necessary to emphasize the parallel with (abstract) element types and (abstract) attribute types.

*(abstract) element type or attribute type:* Element type (definition 1 or 2), or attribute type. Used only when necessary to emphasize the parallel with concrete element types or concrete attribute types.

*element declaration schema component:* Schema-defined element type.

The standard notation in the Schema Recommendation; used in this book only when necessary to correlate with material from that source. (The Schema Recommendation does not adopt the "classes are special kinds of objects" approach; the *class* is only closely related to the element declaration schema component, which is the *object*. The Recommendation focuses on the object, and its terminology is in terms of *validity with respect to the object*, rather than of *being an instance of the class*.) The Schema

Recommendation prefers to use the term 'element type' solely for what we call "DTD-defined element type."

*attribute declaration schema component:* Schema-defined attribute type.

This is the standard notation in the Schema Recommendation; used in this book only when necessary to correlate with material from that source. (The Schema Recommendation does not adopt the "classes are special kinds of objects" approach; the *class* is only closely related to the attribute declaration schema component, which is the *object*. The Recommendation focuses on the object and its terminology is in terms of *validity with respect to the object*, rather than of *being an instance of the class*.)

*simple type:* A component of a schema; a class whose instances are elements and attributes; it restricts the value of its instances according to rules set forth in the Schema Recommendation. See *datatype* in Section E.5 for a more complete discussion. (In the Schema Recommendation, a simple type is called a "simple type definition schema component.")

*complex type:* A component of a schema; a class whose instances are elements. It restricts the content and attribute set of its instances according to rules set forth in the Schema Recommendation. (In the Schema Recommendation, a complex type is called a "complex type definition schema component.")

*structure type* **of an element type or attribute type:** The simple type or complex type which is the value of the *type* property of an element type; the simple type which is the value of the *type* property of an attribute type.

*instantiable* **type:** A complex type or element type that does not require a derivation or substitution to instantiate directly in an XML instance. (See also *instantiable class*.) All attribute types and simple types are instantiable.

*non-instantiable* **type:** A complex type or element type that requires a derivation or substitution to instantiate directly in an XML instance. Explicitly non-instantiable complex types and element types have their *abstract* property TRUE; an element type can be *implicitly* noninstantiable by having a noninstantiable structure type. (See also *non-instantiable class*.) No attribute types or simple types are non-instantiable.

*base* **(simple or complex) type:** Simple types and complex types benefit from object-oriented class inheritance. A *base type* is the simple type or complex type from which another is derived.

*derived* **(simple or complex) type:** A derived type is a simple type or complex type derived from a base type. In an XML schema, derivation occurs by *extension* or *restriction*. Chapter 10 and Chapter 11 discuss extension and restriction in detail. A derived type is analogous to what some might call a *subclass*.

***content pattern:*** A content pattern specifies a set of content options available for a specific element in an XML Schema. The content pattern loosely follows a simplistic regular expression. Appendix A includes a brief discussion regarding the grammar, or format, of a content pattern. This is a notation adopted for this book because of its conciseness.

***notation* declaration or component:** An association of a name with either or both of a system identifier and a public identifier, which are described in the XML Recommendation. Used during DTD or schema processing to create notation information items as needed in an infoset in response to identifying an appropriate name in a (concrete) XML instance.

*Notation* is not well defined in XML or SGML: Its semantics are determined by the application. The original intended use, and still one current use, is to identify character streams not in XML (or SGML), such as EPS graphics. In fact, a notation information item simply conveys to the application a system identifier or public identifier, which the application must interpret.

***DTD-valid* XML document:** An XML document that satisfies the validity constraints of its DTD. In the XML Recommendation, this is called simply "valid"; at the time of its publication, this was the only kind of validity defined.

***schema-valid* XML document:** An XML document that satisfies the validity constraints of a schema.

***valid* XML document:** An XML document that is DTD- or schema-valid. Usually used when the context makes it obvious which is intended. In this book, usually *schema-valid*.

***XML validator:*** An XML validator is a program—or a module in a program—that examines XML purported to be an XML instance and validates that XML against an XML schema or DTD.

# E.5 Selected Datatypes Used in Schema Documents

***datatype:*** A class defined as a simple type. A simple type (or datatype) is, on the one hand, a class that restricts character strings, and, on the other hand, a mapping of those character strings to objects such as numbers or dates or strings. See Chapter 12 for a discussion of all of the datatypes defined in the Schema Recommendation, and Chapter 10 for a discussion of the mechanisms for deriving *user-defined* simple types from the *built-in* datatypes.

'Datatype' and 'simple type' are essentially synonyms. Often in this book we use datatype when talking about the *built-in* datatypes defined in the Schema Recommendation and 'simple type' when talking about *user-defined* datatypes. Alternatively you may find 'simple type' used when discussing the classes that constrain character-string values in an XML document, and 'datatype' when discussing those lexical representations and the abstract values they represent.

*name:* A character string that conforms to the *Name* production in the Schema Recommendation; it consists of "name characters—letters, digits, colon, underscore, ASCII hyphen, and various Unicode combining and extending characters." The first character is required to be a letter, underscore, or colon.

*NCName:* A *name* that does not contain a colon character. (The etymology of 'NCName' is from "no-colon name" or "non-colonized name"; however, neither of these terms is in common use. NCName is embodied in the NCName datatype, Section 12.3.2.)

*QName:* A "qualified name"—the combination of a *prefix* (an NCName that in the scope of an appropriate namespace declaration determines a namespace), a colon character, and a *local name* (another NCName). Note that a default namespace might *imply* a namespace for a QName, in which case the prefix and colon is omitted and the QName *is* the local name, an NCName. (QName is embodied in the QName datatype, Section 12.4.1. The lexical space of QName consists of QNames; the value space consists of ordered pairs: the corresponding namespace paired with the *local name*. If the QName is not in the scope of an appropriate namespace declaration, it is necessarily *invalid*.) Chapter 3 has more to say about namespaces.

For example, a QName might refer to a global element type. Attributes of various schema elements are constrained to have a value that is a QName.

*qualified name:* A QName. (In the Namespace Recommendation, 'qualified name' is used in text; 'QName' is a production nonterminal for the lexical constraint that makes a character string a qualified name. In this book, the Schema Recommendation, and many other texts, the two terms are used interchangeably in text.)

*ID:* An NCName that must be unique among all attribute (and element, when schema processing) values asserted to be IDs in an XML document. (ID is a DTD-prescribable attribute structure type, and it is embodied in the ID datatype, Section 12.3.3.)

# E.6 Miscellaneous

*application:* A program that accepts as input the output of a parser (often with some additional intervening processing, such as by a validator); *this is a special use of the word 'application'.*

*XML application:* A program that accepts XML as input and/or emits XML as output.

*XPath:* A grammar and attached semantics for specifying locations in XML documents, defined in the XPath Recommendation.

# About the Authors

**Cliff Binstock** has more than twenty years of software development experience. His current roles range from hands-on architecture and code development to mentoring and managing large groups of developers. Cliff's object-oriented experience began with relatively unknown languages in the 1980s and culminated in years of development in the extremely popular C++ and Java languages. Cliff has also spent many years working with multiple SQL databases. In 2000 and 2001, Cliff helped deliver shrink-wrap software for a biotech firm. The software used multiple XML schemas to provide the software contracts for various modules. XML, along with appropriate supporting XML schemas, provided a programmatic pipeline. The pipeline architecture not only supplanted many lines of Java, but it turned many "code changes" into trivial XML edits. The expertise acquired during this development effort led to the writing of this book. Cliff is the owner of the consulting firm Robust Software.

**Dave Peterson** is principal consultant with his own firm, SGML*Works!*, providing SGML and XML solutions for publishing and database systems worldwide. Dave has been working with SGML since before the ISO Standard was published in 1986, and with XML since it was just a gleam in a few people's eyes. He's been programming and architecting systems professionally since 1967. He helped design the system that produces and processes the largest SGML document in the world—more than three billion characters, markup, and text in one document (not counting graphics). He ran the document analysis that ultimately defined the document structure used by the New Zealand Parliament for legal publications, and has done the same for other legal and pharmaceutical publishers, as well as for publishers of journals and military and civilian technical documents. Dave's first job with SGML in 1986 involved using SGML (XML was not around yet) to transfer data from one database to another. He has designed and programmed numerous SGML and XML processing systems. Dave served on the ISO committee that oversaw the continuing development from 1990 through 1998. Since then, he has served on the W3C Schema Working Group, which produced the XML Schema Recommendation in 2001 and is now working on the 1.1 version. He has given numerous presentations and tutorials at SGML and XML conferences, and has written about forty articles on various SGML and XML topics. He was on the editorial board of the journal *Markup Languages: Theory and Practice*.

**Mitchell Smith** is Chief Software Architect at Array BioPharma Inc., in Boulder, Colorado. He has seventeen years of experience developing software solutions and has been working with relational databases for more than twelve years. He is currently developing rapid software solutions to integrate chemists' processes, integrating hardware/software products with the existing chemo-infomatics infrastructure, and assisting chemists (in a small way) to produce breakthrough drug candidates. Prior to joining Array BioPharma Inc., Mitch worked for Rational Software Corporation, where he co-architected a next-generation requirements management system using J2EE and XML technologies. Mitch holds an A.B. from Harvard College and an M.S. in computer science from the University of Colorado, Boulder. Mitch is a member of the ACM and senior member of the IEEE. He votes on IEEE software standards and is currently secretary of the IEEE Denver/Boulder Computer Society chapter. Mitch is a co-inventor on patent number 6,199,047, entitled "Apparatus and method for an event rating engine." Outside work, Mitch is an avid year-round mountain biker; he also enjoys camping and overseas vacations.

**Mike Wooding** has been in the computer industry for twenty years. He has authored several courses for Learning Tree International, including Enterprise Active Server Pages and Microsoft Transaction Server. He was involved with the ActiveServerPages.com site and speaks regularly at industry conferences. As a partner at Kiefer Consulting, Mike focuses on delivering advanced architectures using Internet standards and leveraging Microsoft's .NET Framework using many tools, including COM+, .NET, Visual Studio .NET, and .NET Web Services. Prior to joining Kiefer Consulting, Mike developed products with Intel, Baxter Healthcare, and several smaller Silicon Valley start-up companies. Mike holds two patents for work in robotics and DNA probe analysis. In his spare time, Mike enjoys snow skiing, wind surfing, basketball, and automating his house with a combination of custom and off-the-shelf hardware.

**Chris Dix** has been developing software for fun since he was ten years old, and doing it for a living for the past eight years. Chris recently made the transition from C++ and COM to C# and .NET and is finding he likes it better than he expected. He's written magazine articles on SOAP and Windows development, and he has contributed to two books on XML and Web Services. Chris is lead developer for Navtrak, where he designs and develops products for mobile data access and asset tracking.

**Chris Galtenberg** is a writer, inventor, and methodologist. His interests lie in the realms of extending human intelligence through philosophy and software. Galtenberg poetry, which explores this philosophy, can be found at http://www.deiforming.com.

# INDEX

# Index

## Regular Expression Symbols

. escape character, 368, 369
. metacharacter, 361
? metacharacter, 361, 375
( metacharacter, 361
) metacharacter, 361
{ metacharacter, 361
} metacharacter, 361
+ metacharacter, 361, 375
* metacharacter, 361, 375
^ metacharacter, 379
\ metacharacter, 361
| metacharacter, 361
\. escape character, 366
\? escape character, 366
\( escape character, 367
\) escape character, 367
\{ escape character, 367
\} escape character, 367
\+ escape character, 367
\- escape character, 366
\* escape character, 366
\^ escape character, 366
\\ escape character, 366
\| escape character, 366
\c escape character, 368
\C escape character, 368
\d escape character, 368
\D escape character, 368
\i escape character, 368
\I escape character, 368
\n escape character, 366
\r escape character, 366
\s escape character, 368
\S escape character, 368
\t escape character, 366
\w escape character, 368
\W escape character, 368
\[ escape character, 367
\] escape character, 367
- metacharacter, 377
[ metacharacter, 361
] metacharacter, 361

## A

ABSENT value, 67
abstract attribute, 62, 64–66
 of complexType element, 247–248, 512, 719
 of element element, 148–149
 mapping to object-oriented language, 513–514
Abstract
 attribute type, 934
 defined, 58
 element type, 16, 17, 18, 934
 object, corresponding to document, 14
 uses of term, 238, 931–932
Abstract character, 67
Abstract document
 document information item view of, 62
 infoset view of, 62
 makeup of, 59
 properties of, 66
Abstract element, 14–15
 properties of, 66
AbstractDOMParser class (DOM), 446
AbstractSAXParser class (SAX), 446
Active Server Page (ASP), 810
address.xml example file, 489–491
address.xsd explanation, 117, 139–141, 164–165, 174–176, 192
 complete listing, 890–895
all element, 254, 859
 attributes of, 271–273, 722
 content options for, 273–274
 function of, 271
 and relational database, 709, 720–722
All model group, 96, 97
AlphabeticPresentationForms Unicode character block, 372

Alternatives, 362
Analysis Patterns: Reusable Object Models, 521
ancestor (XPath axis), 54
ancestor-or-self (XPath axis), 54
Annotation, 82
 defined, 390
 mapping to object-oriented language, 521
 Microsoft use of term, 821–822
 properties of, 411
annotation content option for schema element, 115
annotation element, 82, 83, 254, 260, 722, 859
 attributes of, 118
 content options for, 118–119
 example of use of, 117
 function of, 116, 124, 128
 nested, 83–84
Anonymous component, 82
any element, 859
 attributes of, 168–171
 content options for, 171
 function of, 167
 and relational database, 722–723
 specification of, 168
anyAttribute element, 177–179, 254, 391, 859
 attributes of, 196–198
 content options for, 199
 function of, 196
 and relational database, 709, 723–724
anyAttributeDemo.xsd example file, 178–179
anyURI datatype, 318
 alternatives to, 329
 constraining facets of, 328–329
 and relational database, 633
 unique features of, 322
 use of, 320, 327–328

# Index

**Apache**
  history of, 428
  projects of, 428–429
  *See also* Xerces.
**appinfo element, 82, 859**
  attributes of, 119
  content options for, 120
  function of, 119
**Application, defined, 31, 937**
**Arabic Unicode character block, 370**
**ArabicPresentationForms-A Unicode character block, 372**
**ArabicPresentationForms-B Unicode character block, 373**
**Archetype, 12**
**Argument description, schemas for, 558–559**
**Armenian Unicode character block, 370**
**Arrows Unicode character block, 371**
**ASBuilder Xerces sample class (DOM), 433**
**ASP (Active Server Page), 810**
**ASP code, 580**
**ASP.NET, receiving data through, 801–807**
**async property, in DOMDocument40, 477**
**Attr interface (DOM), 443**
**Attribute, 48**
  adding to simple type, 231–233
  constraint of, 87–88
  defined, 60, 931
  mapping to object-oriented language, 519
  type name of, 931
  value of, 931–932
**attribute (XPath axis), 48, 54**
**attribute content option for schema element, 115**

**attribute element, 182, 254, 859, 934**
  attributes of, 182–191
  content options for, 191–193
  and relational database, 709
**Attribute declaration, 403**
  of schema, 391, 935
**Attribute group definitions, of schema, 391**
**Attribute information item, 62, 64–66, 931**
  basic, 421
  default value of, 65
  PSVI, 68, 421–423
  normalization of, 65
**Attribute set model, 389, 401**
  components in, 403–404
  described, 402–403
**Attribute specification, defined, 60, 931**
**Attribute type, 11, 88**
  abstract *vs.* concrete, 934
  associations of, 389
  DTD-defined, 934
  defined, 934
  example of, 174–176
  function of, 174
  indications for use of, 180–181
  instantiability of, 101
  name of, 392
  namespaces and, 181–182
  prohibiting, 189–191
  properties of, 392–393
  qualified *vs.* unqualified, 181
  schema-defined, 934
  structure of, 392
  structure restrictions on, 392
  structure type of, 935
  value constraints on, 393
**Attribute type declaration, 934**
**Attribute type property, of attribute information item, 64, 65**

form of values of, 66
**Attribute use, 174, 193, 401**
  properties of, 403
**Attribute wildcard, 88, 174, 401, 404**
**Attribute-use group**
  named, 409–410
  reuse of, 409
**attributeFormDefault attribute, 80**
  of schema element, 108, 109
**attributeGroup content option for schema element, 115**
**attributeGroup element, 88, 193, 254, 724, 860**
  attributes of, 193–195
  content options for, 195–196
  and relational database, 709
**Attributes interface (SAX), 444**
**Attributes property, of element information item, 63, 64, 66**
**AttributesImpl class (SAX), 445**
**Axis (XPath), 47**
  types of, 54
**AxKit, Apache XML subproject, 428**

# B

**base attribute**
  of extension element, 263
  of restriction element, 212, 213, 267
**Base class, 926**
**Base ten, 295**
**Base type, 12, 935**
**Base type definition, 394**
**Base URI property, of element information item, 63, 64**

base64Binary datatype, 322
  compatibility issues, 902–903
  constraining facets of, 327
  and relational database, 633
  use of, 326–327
Basic infoset, 929
  distinguished from PSVI, 416
  information items in, 417
BasicLatin Unicode character block, 370
Batik, Apache XML subproject, 428
Bengali Unicode character block, 370
BLOB, SQL datatype, advantages of, 632
Block (Unicode character), defined, 370
block attribute, 143, 166
  of complexType element, 247, 248–250, 720
  of element element, 148, 150–151
blockDefault attribute, of schema element, 108, 109–110
BlockElements Unicode character block, 372
Blocking
  of complex type, 96, 245
  impact of, 111
  methods of, 144
  non-inheritance of, 250
  of simple type, 208
  of substitution, 143–146
boolean datatype, 322
  constraining facets of, 325
  in relational database, 589, 634
  representation of, 634–635
  using, 324
Bopomofo Unicode character block, 372
BopomofoExtended Unicode character block, 372

BoxDrawing Unicode character block, 371
BraillePatterns Unicode character block, 372
Builder pattern, 528
Building Web Services with Java, 762
Built-in datatypes, 89
  date, time, and duration, 304–316
  numeric, 295–304
  oddball, 322–330
  and relational database, 598
  string, 316–322
  time-line-based, 306–311
built-in.xsd example file, 128–129
byte datatype, 297
  constraining facets of, 303–304
  derivation relationships of, 304
  and relational database, 630
  use of, 302, 303, 304
ByzantineMusicalSymbols Unicode character block, 373

## C

C Unicode character category, 365
C++
  class polymorphism in, 535
  XML implementation using, 533–535
C#
  and .NET Framework, 536
  XML implementation using, 535–539
Campus Resource and Scheduling System (CRSS) case study, 758

  application requirements of, 831
  architecture of, 770–771, 836–837
  business logic of, 847–851
  creating views of, 795–800
  database design for, 810–823
  high-level view of, 765
  requirements of, 759
  scalability issues, 760
  SecurityBroker component construction, 846–847
  sending form data in, 800–807
  system architecture for, 774–795
  system users in, 759–764
  technologies for, 760–764
  template queries in, 851–852
  UIBroker component construction, 842–846
  Web tier construction of, 838–842
  XML/XSLT files of, 842
Canonical lexical representation, 202, 206–207
Canonical representation, 294
Cardinality quantifiers, 374–377
Cascading style sheets, 796
catalog.xsd explanation, 161–162, 183, 202–204, 216, 221–223, 234–238, 240–241, 243–244, 260–262, 266–267, 282–289, 675–677, 679, 690–695, 709–713
  complete listing, 878–890
Cc Unicode character category, 365
CDATASection interface (DOM), 443
Cf Unicode character category, 365
CHAR datatype, 598
Character categories, 364

# Index

Character class, 869–870
Character class expressions, 377, 870
　subtraction, 380
Character code property, of character information item, 66
Character information item, 62, 66
Character set, 359–360
CharacterData interface (DOM), 443
Check constraints (SQL), 598
child (XPath axis), 54
Children, of element, defined, 60, 931
Children property, 15
　of element information item, 63, 64, 66
choice element, 255, 860
　attributes of, 275–277
　content options for, 277–278
　function of, 274–275
　and relational database, 724–727
　restrictions on, 278, 281
Choice model group, 96, 97–98
CJKCompatibility Unicode character block, 372
CJKCompatibilityForms Unicode character block, 372
CJKCompatibilityIdeographs Unicode character block, 372
CJKCompatibilityIdeographsSupplement Unicode character block, 373
CJKIdeographs Unicode character block, 372
CJKIdeographsExtensionA Unicode character block, 372

CJKIdeographsExtensionB Unicode character block, 373
CJKRadicalsSupplement Unicode character block, 372
CJKSymbolsandPunctuation Unicode character block, 372
Class, 14
　characteristics of, 925–926
　derivation of, 926
　instantiable vs. non-instantiable, 12, 926
　provision of aspects by, 925
Class generator, 926
Client tier, 774, 782
　reusable datatypes in, 782–795
CLOB, SQL datatype, 902
　drawbacks of, 632
　Oracle support of, 599
CLSIDs, 473
Cn Unicode character category, 365
Co Unicode character category, 365
Cocoon, Apache XML subproject, 428
Code generation, 332
COLLAPSE process, 318
COM (Component Object Model), 570
CombiningDiacriticalMarks Unicode character block, 370
CombiningHalfMarks Unicode character block, 372
CombiningMarksforSymbols Unicode character block, 371
Comment, 83
Comment information item, 62

Comment declaration, 932
Comment interface (DOM), 443
Common Object Request Broker Architecture (CORBA), 570
compact.xml example file, 77–78
compact.xsd example file, 76–77
Company catalog example, 20–22
Complex content
　empty content, 85
　mixed, 86–87
　nested elements, 85
　wildcards in, 87
Complex type, 11, 79
　adding attributes to simple type, 231–233
　annotations in, 402
　blocking, 96
　with complex content, 92
　defined, 935
　derivation data for, 401–402
　derivation by extension, 92–93
　derivation by restriction, 94–96
　explicitly non-instantiable, 238–240
　function of, 230
　implicitly non-instantiable, 240–244
　instantiability of, 101
　longhand notation of, 245–246
　mapping to database schema, 709–713, 718
　mapping to object-oriented language, 511–517
　mapping supporting mixed content to database schema, 713–718
　name of, 401
　prohibiting extension of, 245
　redefined, 133

# Index

**Complex type** *(continued)*
  and relational databases, 708–718
  restriction of, 245, 249–250, 257–258
  shorthand notation of, 245, 246
  with simple content, 91
  specifying attribute types, 244
  specifying empty content, 230–231
  specifying mixed content, 237–238
  specifying nested element types, 234–237
  structure restrictions on, 401
  substitution restrictions on, 402
  use in content models, 407
**complexContent element, 245, 255, 860**
  attributes of, 258–260
  content options for, 259–260
  and relational database, 727
**complexType content option for schema element, 115**
**complexType element, 230, 246, 860**
  attributes of, 247–253, 719–720
  content options for, 254–255
  and relational database, 719–720
**Component Object Model (COM), 570**
**Component tier, 775–776**
**Components, of schema, 34**
**Concatenation, of expressions, 362, 363**
**Concrete**
  attribute type, 934
  defined, 58
  element, 14, 15
  element type, 17, 18, 934
  uses of term, 932

**Constraining**
  of attributes, 87–88
  of derived types, 383–384
  of elements, 84–87
  of simple content, 381–383
**Constraining facets**
  described, 396
  listed, 90
  of restriction element, 215
  of simpleType element, 212
  and relational databases, 590–597
  of simple type, 88–89, 91, 202, 205
**Content**
  complex, 85–87
  of element, 59, 60, 930
  mixed, 86–87
  simple, 84–85
**Content model, 389, 401**
  options for, 405
**Content pattern, 12, 935**
**Content type, 401, 405**
**Content-Length header, HTTP, 565**
**Content-Type header, HTTP, 565**
**ContentHandler interface (SAX), 444, 459–460**
**ControlPictures Unicode character block, 371**
**Coordinated Universal Time, 308, 310**
**CORBA (Common Object Request Broker Architecture), 570**
**Correspond, defined, 15, 19**
**Counter Xerces sample class (DOM), 433**
**Crimson, XML subproject, 428**
**Cs Unicode character category, 365**
**CurrencySymbols Unicode character block, 371**

**Customer list example, 22–24**
**Cyrillic Unicode character block, 370**

# D

**Data character, defined, 61, 927**
**Data-oriented schemas**
  complex types, 708–754
  datatypes, 588–671
  simple types, 674–706
**Database**
  check constraints *vs.* triggers in, 598
  design of, using XML schemas, 810–815
  facet restrictions and, 590–597
  mapping complex types to, 708–754
  mapping schemas to, 815–823
  mapping simple types to, 674–706
  Oracle PL/SQL functions and, 678
  XML datatypes and, 598–671
  XML schema design considerations regarding, 588–590, 674–675, 708–709
**Database data**
  direct access of, 824
  updategrams and, 832–833
**Database sequence identifiers, support for, 899–900**
**Database tier, 776**
**Datatypes**
  built-in, 89
  date, time, and duration, 304–316
  defined, 936
  derived, 294
  numeric, 295–304
  oddball, 322–330
  Oracle, 902–921
  and relational databases, 598

reusable, 782–795
string, 316–322
time-line-based, 306–311
types of, 936
user-defined, 936
**date datatype, 89, 308**
  constraining facets of, 642–645
  Oracle8*i* compatibility issues, 906–909
  and relational database, 641–645
  time zones and, 641
**dateTime datatype, 306, 307**
  constraining facets of, 638–641
  Oracle8*i* compatibility issues, 904–906
  and relational database, 637–641
**Daylight Savings Time, 310**
**decimal datatype, 84, 294, 295**
  alternatives to, 298
  constraining facets of, 297, 625–629
  derivation relationships of, 297, 302
  level of validation and, 625
  in relational database, 589, 625
  use of, 296–297, 300
**Decimal point, 295**
**Declaration**
  defined, 932–933
  entity, 29
  schema component as, 389
**default attribute**
  of attribute element, 182, 183
  of element element, 148, 151–152
**Default namespace, 40**
  declaring, 39
  using, 41, 43

**DefaultHandler class (SAX), 445, 465**
**Definition**
  defined, 933
  schema component as, 389
**definitions element, in WDSL document, 570**
**DelayedInput Xerces sample class (SAX), 433**
**DELETE, HTTP verb, 565**
**Derived complex type**
  adding element types or attribute types to, 244
  instantiability of, 239
  removing element types or attribute types from, 244
**Derived datatypes, 294**
**Derived type, 12, 935**
**descendant (XPath axis), 54**
**descendant-or-self (XPath axis), 54**
**Describe, defined, 19**
**Deseret Unicode character block, 373**
**Design patterns, 527**
  Builder pattern, 528
**Design Patterns: Elements of Reusable Object-Oriented Software, 527**
**Designated value, of optional property, 67**
**Devanagari Unicode character block, 370**
**Developing SGML DTDs, 548**
**Dingbats Unicode character block, 372**
**Document**
  abstract *vs.* concrete, 58
  display of, 543
  display conventions for, 550
  editing of, 542–543
  as flat character string, 13
  parsing of, 13
  parts of, 929–932
**Document analysis**

  personnel for, 544
  procedures for, 545–546
  schema arising from, 546
**Document element, 66**
  defined, 60, 931
**Document element property, of document information item, 63**
**Document information item, 33, 59, 62–63**
**Document interface (DOM), 438, 443**
**Document Object Model (DOM), 428**
  advanced example of, 456–458
  advanced functionality in, 458–459
  advantages and disadvantages of, 488
  APIs based on, 28
  creating documents, 449–452
  example file, 450–452
  Level 3 functionality, 459
  recommendation for, 33
  validation using, 492
**Document processing**
  editor programs for, 551
  importance of, 549
  production software for, 551–553
  XML-smart authoring tools for, 549–550
**Document structure**
  finding, 546
  major divisions, 547
  paragraphs, 547–548
  specialized pieces, 547
  specialized structures, 548
**Document Style Semantics and Specification Language (DSSSL), 552**
**Document type declaration information item, 62, 932**

# Index

Document Type Definitions.
    *See* DTDs.
**documentation element**
    attributes of, 120–122
    content options for, 122
    function of, 120
**documentation subelement, 82, 860**
**DocumentBuilder class (DOM), 440, 442**
**DocumentBuilderFactory class (DOM), 442**
**DocumentFragment interface (DOM), 443**
**DocumentTracer Xerces sample class (SAX), 433**
**DocumentTraversal interface (DOM), 444**
**DocumentType interface (DOM), 443**
**DOM.** *See* Document Object Model (DOM).
**DOMAddLines Xerces sample class (DOM), 433**
**DOMASBuilderImpl class (DOM), 447**
**DOMBuilderImpl class (DOM), 447**
**DOMDocument40 (Microsoft), 476**
    creating document with, 476
    loading document with, 477
    parsing errors in, 478
    reading XML with, 477–478
    unique properties of, 477–478
    validation using, 492
**DOMException (DOM), 443**
**DOMImplementation interface (DOM), 443**
**DOMParser class (DOM), 447**
**DOMSerializer interface (DOM), 445**
**DOMUtil class (DOM), 446**
**double datatype, 295**
    alternatives to, 300

constraining facets of, 300
in relational database, 589, 632
use of, 298, 302
**DSSSL (Document Style Semantics and Specification Language), 552**
**DTD (Document Type Definition), 8**
    abstract, 388
    attribute type defined by, 934
    compared with schema, 14, 388
    defined, 932
    element type defined by, 16–17, 18, 934
    entity-declarations-only, 31
    validating against, 30
**DTDHandler interface (SAX), 444**
**DTD-valid document, 936**
**duration datatype**
    constraining facets of, 313
    ordering of, 314
    and relational database, 636
    use of, 311–313
    database validation of, 636
**Durations, 311, 315–316**

# E

**Editing programs, 549–550**
**Element(s), 15, 18**
    abstract, 14–15
    annotation of, 82–85
    attributes of, 931
    children of, 60, 931
    components of, 14
    concrete, 14, 15
    constraint of, 84–87
    content of, 59, 60, 930
    defined, 60, 929
    form of, 59

listed, 858–865
overriding definition of, 782–783
qualified *vs.* unqualified, 147
removing, 161–162
terminology of, 15
type name of, 14, 15, 16, 81, 389, 930
value of, 931
in XML document, 58
**element content option for schema element, 115**
**Element content whitespace property, of character information item, 66**
**Element declaration, 17**
    of schema, 391
**Element declaration schema component, 17, 934**
**element element, 147, 861, 934**
    attributes of, 148–166
    content options for, 166–167
**Element IDs, 103**
**Element information item, 15, 62, 63–64**
    basic, 418
    defined, 930
    PSVI, 68, 418–420
**Element interface (DOM), 438, 443**
**Element type, 11, 15–16, 389**
    abstract, 16, 17, 18
    annotations in, 400
    associations of, 389
    concrete, 17, 18
    DTD-defined, 16–17, 18, 934
    example of, 138
    function of, 138
    global *vs.* local, 138–139
    instantiability of, 101, 146–147
    mapping to object-oriented language, 518
    and namespace, 147–148

# Index

nillable value of, 398
properties of, 398
referencing of, 164–165
schema-defined, 17, 18, 934
scope of, 400
structure of, 396–397
structure type of, 935
substitutability of, 398, 399–400
terminology of, 18, 933
type definition of, 397, 398
value constraint on, 398
**Element type declaration, 18, 934**
**Element wildcard, 87**
**elementFormDefault attribute, 80**
of schema element, 108, 109
**Empty content, 85–86**
specification of, 230–231
**Empty-element tag, 14, 59, 930**
**Encapsulation, 509, 510**
**EnclosedAlphanumerics Unicode character block, 371**
**EnclosedCJKLettersandMonths Unicode character block, 372**
**EncodingMap class (Xerces), 446**
**End-tag, 14, 29**
of concrete element, 59
**ENTITIES datatype, 317**
constraining facets of, 322
derivation of, 321
and relational database, 618
**ENTITY datatype, 317**
constraining facets of, 322
derivation of, 321
and relational database, 617
**Entity interface (DOM), 443**
**Entity manager, 28, 29**
**Entity-declarations-only DTD, 31**

**EntityReference interface (DOM), 443**
**EntityResolver interface (SAX), 444**
**enumeration constraining facet, 90, 220**
hard-coded values in, 593
picklist table for, 594–597
and relational database, 592–593, 689, 706
separate table for, 593–594
**Equality, testing identity constraints for, 342**
**ErrorHandler interface (SAX), 444**
**Ethiopic Unicode character block, 371**
**Event, 28**
**Event-token emitting parser, 31–32**
validation by, 32
**eXcelon Stylus Studio, 771**
**Expressions, 358**
**Extensible Style Language Transform (XSLT), 552**
advantages of, 765
business uses for, 766, 767
characteristics of, 764–766, 800
conversion of XML to relational data, 766, 767
debugging templates in, 771
HTML creation in, 795–800
using System.XML classes, 846
**Extensible Stylesheet Language (XSL), 552, 553**
**Extension, of complex type, 92–93**
**extension element, 260, 514, 861**
attributes of, 263–264
content options for, 264–265
examples of use of, 746–754
function of, 745–746

and object-oriented languages, 515
and relational database, 745–754
use of, 260
**Extensional objects, 10**
**Extensional OO, 924**
**Extensions, in XML, 10**

# F

**Facets, 395**
described, 294
**Factory class (Xerces), 440**
**FactoryConfigurationError (SAX), 442**
**field element, 862**
attributes of, 354–355
content options for, 356
**Field, in XML schema, 339**
XPaths for, 340–341
**Final, 395**
**final attribute**
of complexType element, 245, 247, 250–252, 265, 720
of element element, 148, 152–153, 166
of simpleType element, 208, 209–210
**finalDefault attribute, of schema element, 108, 109**
**Finality, non-inheritance of, 252**
**fixed attribute**
of attribute element, 182, 184–185
of element element, 149, 157
**float datatype, 69, 295**
alternatives to, 300
constraining facets of, 300
data space of, 299
in relational database, 589, 631–632
use of, 298–299, 302
values of, 298

# Index

following (XPath axis), 54
following-sibling (XPath axis), 54
Fonts, 551
FOP, XML subproject, 428
form attribute
    of attribute element, 182, 185–187
    of element element, 149, 158–159
Form data, sending, 800–807
Formal grammar, 30
formElementDefault attribute, 147
Fowler, Martin, 521
fractionDigits constraining facet, 90, 625
Frameworks, types of, 759
fullFeaturedSchema.xsd example file, 107
Fundamental facets, 395

## G

Gamma, Erich, 527
gDay datatype, 314, 315
    Oracle8i compatibility issues, 918–919
    in relational database, 590, 663–666
GeneralPunctuation Unicode character block, 371
Generic identifier, 14, 930
GeometricShapes Unicode character block, 372
Georgian Unicode character block, 371
GET, HTTP verb, 565, 567
GetElementsByTagName Xerces sample class (DOM), 433
getFeature method, 482
getProperty method, 482
Global component, 81

XML instance and, 81–82
XML schema document and, 81
Global element type, 138
    referencing, 164–165
gMonth datatype, 314, 315
    constraining facets of, 660–663
    Oracle8i compatibility issues, 916–917
    in relational database, 590, 658–663
gMonthDay datatype, 314, 315
    constraining facets of, 668–671
    Oracle8i compatibility issues, 920–921
    and relational database, 667–671
Googol, 295
Gothic Unicode character block, 373
Grammar, formal, 30
Greek Unicode character block, 370
GreekExtended Unicode character block, 371
Greenwich Mean Time, 308
group content option for schema element, 115
group element, 255, 862
    advanced use of, 729–730
    attributes of, 289–291
    content options for, 292
    function of, 281
    and relational database, 727–730
    reuse of, 282–289
    use of, 728
Groupings, of expressions, 363
Gujarati Unicode character block, 370

Gurmukhi Unicode character block, 370
gYear datatype, 308
    constraining facets of, 647–650
    Oracle8i compatibility issues, 909–911
    and relational database, 590, 645–650
    and time zones, 646
gYearMonth datatype, 308
    constraining facets of, 651–654
    Oracle8i compatibility issues, 911–913
    and relational database, 650–654

## H

Haines, Eric, 580
HalfwidthandFullwidthForms Unicode character block, 373
HangulCompatibilityJamo Unicode character block, 372
HangulJamo Unicode character block, 371
HangulSyllables Unicode character block, 372
HEAD, HTTP verb, 565
Hebrew Unicode character block, 370
hello.xml, 566, 567, 568
HelloApache.java, 435–437
    parsing, 439–441
HelloApacheDOM example file, 450–452
HelloApacheDOM2 example file, 457–458
HelloApacheSAX example file, 462–463

# Index

**HelloApacheSAX2 example file**, 465–468
**Helm, Richard**, 527
**hexBinary datatype**, 322
   compatibility issues, 902–903
   constraining facets of, 327
   and relational database, 632–633
   use of, 325–327
**HighPrivateUseSurrogates Unicode character block**, 372
**HighSurrogates Unicode character block**, 372
**Hiragana Unicode character block**, 372
**HTML**
   advantages of, 552
   creating using XSLT, 795–800
   shortcomings of, 775
**HTMLSerializer class (DOM and SAX)**, 446
**HTTP (Hypertext Transfer Protocol)**, 561, 563
   actions in, 565
   request-response structure for, 564–566
   sample request in, 565
   sample response in, 566
   transmission of XML instances through, 576
   XML and, 566–569

# I

**IBM, parsers from**, 781
**id attribute**, 13
   of all element, 272, 722
   of complexType element, 247, 252, 720
   of annotation element, 118
   of any element, 168, 169
   of anyAttribute element, 196–197
   of attribute element, 182, 187
   of attributeGroup element, 194
   of choice element, 275, 276
   of complexContent element, 258–259
   of element element, 149, 159–160
   of extension element, 263–264
   of field element, 355
   of group element, 289, 290
   of import element, 126
   of include element, 123
   of key element, 347
   of keyref element, 351
   of list element, 217
   of notation element, 130
   of redefine element, 134, 135
   of restriction element, 212, 213, 267, 268
   of schema element, 108, 111
   of sequence element, 278, 279
   of simpleContent element, 256
   of simpleType element, 209, 210
   of union element, 224
   of unique element, 344, 345
**id function (XPointer)**, 49
**ID datatype**, 317
   constraining facets of, 322
   defined, 13, 937
   derivation of, 321
   and relational database, 612
   use of, 320
**ID/IDREF binding**, 68, 69
   properties added by, 424–425
   schema reference capabilities substituted for, 408
**Identity constraint(s)**, 49, 101
   binding, 424, 425
   definitions, 400
   enforcing uniqueness, 342
   examples of, 59, 332–338
   fields in, 339
   properties of, 408–409
   and referential integrity, 343
   representation of, 408
   selectors in, 339
   shortcuts for, 59
   terminology of, 339
   value equality and, 342
   and XPath support, 340–341
**Identity-constraint table property**, 68, 69
**IdeographicDescriptionCharacters Unicode character block**, 372
**IDL (Interface Definition Language)**, 570
**IDREF datatype**, 317
   constraining facets of, 322
   derivation of, 321
   and relational database, 612
   use of, 320
**IDREFS datatype**, 317
   constraining facets of, 322, 612
   derivation of, 321
   in relational database, 590, 612–617
   single-column implementation of, 612, 613–614
   table implementation of, 612, 614–617
   use of, 320
   VARRAY implementation of, 612
**iexmltls.exe**, 781
**IIS (Internet Information Services)(Microsoft)**, 823
   configuration of SQL 2000 to work with, 823–829
   testing of configuration, 829–830
   using, 823–824
**IIS Support tool, configuration**, 824–829

# Index

Immediate subelement, defined, 60, 930
import content option for schema element, 115
import element, 71, 103, 571, 862
  attributes of, 126
  content options for, 127–128
  purpose of, 124–125
  using, 572
include content option for schema element, 115
include element, 71, 102–103, 862
  attributes of, 123
  content options for, 124
  purpose of, 122
IndentPrinter class (DOM and SAX), 446
Individual character (regular) expressions, 363
Inf (infinity), 295, 298
Infinite integers, representing, 302
Information item, 33
  attribute, 62, 64–66, 68, 421–423
  element, 15, 62, 63–64, 68, 418–420
  terminology issues, 423
  types of, 62–66, 928
  XML, 31
Information set (infoset), 28, 31, 59
Infoset Recommendation, of W3C, 8–9, 58, 59, 61
Inheritance, 509, 510
  in intensional technologies, 10
  mapping to object-oriented language, 514–515
Input, 557
Input controller, 28
InputSource class (SAX), 444

In-scope namespaces property, of element information item, 63, 64
Instance, 14, 925
Instantiability, 935
  of attribute type, 100
  of complex type, 101, 146
  of derived type, 239–240
  of element type, 100, 146–147
  of simple type, 101
Instantiable class, 12, 926
int datatype, 297
  constraining facets of, 303–304
  derivation relationships of, 304
  and relational database, 630
  use of, 302, 303, 304
integer datatype
  constraining facets of, 301–302
  derivation of, 294, 297
  derivation relationships of, 302
  and relational database, 629
  use of, 298, 301
Intensional objects, 10
Intensional OO, 924
Interface Definition Language (IDL), 570
Internet Explorer (Microsoft), XML compatibility of, 800
Internet Information Services (Microsoft), 823
  configuration of SQL 2000 to work with, 823–829
  testing of configuration, 829–830
  using, 823–824
IPAExtensions Unicode character block, 370
ISchema interface, 486–487
  getting, 486
  properties of, 487
ISchemaItem interface, 484–486

properties of, 484
Item type definition, 395
itemType attribute, of list element, 217, 218
IVBSAXContentHandler interface, 479

## J

J2EE, 759
  transport protocols for, 563
Java Development Kit (JDK), 432
Java Runtime Environment (JRE), 432
java.xml.parsers package, 442
JavaServer Page (JSP), 810
Johnson, Ralph, 527

## K

Kanbun Unicode character block, 372
KangxiRadicals Unicode character block, 372
Kannada Unicode character block, 371
Katakana Unicode character block, 372
KeepSocketOpen Xerces sample class, 433
key element, 101, 102, 342, 343, 408, 862
  attributes of, 347–348
  content options for, 348
  example of, 346–347
  function of, 346
Key sequence, in XML validation, 339
keyref element, 101, 102, 343, 408, 862
  attributes of, 350–352

content options for, 352
example of, 349–350
function of, 349
**Khmer Unicode character block, 371**

# L

**L Unicode character category, 364**
**L& Unicode character category, 364**
**Language, specifying, 113**
**language datatype**
  derivation of, 318
  and relational database, 604–608
  treatment of whitespace in, 319
**Lao Unicode character block, 371**
**Latin character set, 359–360**
**Latin-1Supplement Unicode character block, 370**
**LatinExtendedA Unicode character block, 370**
**LatinExtendedAdditional Unicode character block, 371**
**LatinExtendedB Unicode character block, 370**
**Lax validation, 415**
**length constraining facet, 90, 220**
  and relational database, 599, 682–686
**LENGTHC (SQL) function, 600**
**LetterLikeSymbols Unicode character block, 371**
**Lexical analyzer, 29**
**Lexical constraint, 84**
**Lexical space, 294**
  of simple type, 202, 206
**List**
  constrained, 221

delimited nature of, 216
sample program for, 219, 221
**list element, 91, 215–216, 862**
  attributes of, 216–218
  constraining facets of, 220–221, 682–689
  content options for, 218–219
  example of, 216
  and relational databases, 674, 678–689
  single-column implementation of, 678, 679–680
  table implementation of, 678, 680–682
**Ll Unicode character category, 364**
**Lm Unicode character category, 364**
**Lo Unicode character category, 364**
**Local component, 82**
**Local element type, 138, 139**
**Local name, 13**
**Local name property, 15**
  of attribute information item, 64, 66
  of element information item, 63
**Local part, of name, 39**
**Location path, 47**
**Location set, 51**
**Locator interface (SAX), 444**
**LocatorImpl class (SAX), 445**
**long datatype, 297, 302**
  constraining facets of, 303–304
  derivation relationships of, 304
  and relational database, 630
  use of, 302, 303, 304
**LowSurrogates Unicode character block, 372**
**Lt Unicode character category, 364**

**Lu Unicode character category, 364**

# M

**M Unicode character category, 365**
**Magic string-derived datatypes**
  constraining facets of, 322
  derivation of, 321
  function of, 321
**Malayalam Unicode character block, 371**
  Markup, 927
**Markup punctuation, 61, 927**
**MathematicalAlphanumericSymbols Unicode character block, 373**
**MathematicalOperators Unicode character block, 371**
**maxExclusive constraining facet, 90**
  Oracle8*i* compatibility issues, 905–906, 908, 910, 912–913, 915, 917, 919, 921
  and relational database, 627, 639, 643–644, 648, 652, 656–657, 661, 665, 669
**maxInclusive constraining facet, 90**
  Oracle8*i* compatibility issues, 905, 907–908, 910, 912, 915, 916–917, 919–919, 920–921
  and relational database, 626–627, 638, 642–643, 647, 651–652, 655–656, 660, 664, 668
**maxLength constraining facet, 90, 220**
  and relational database, 599, 687–689

# Index

**maxOccurs attribute**
   of all element, 272–273, 722
   of element element, 149, 160–161
   of choice element, 275, 276
   of group element, 289, 290
   of sequence element, 278, 280

**Mc Unicode character category, 365**

**Me Unicode character category, 365**

**Member type definition, 395**

**memberTypes attribute, of union element, 224**

**message element, in WDSL document, 570**

**Metacharacters, 361–362**

**Metadata string, 61, 927**

**Method, of object, 924**

**Microsoft Common Dialog Control, 493**

**Microsoft .NET XML Web Services, 762**
   *See also* .NET Framework.

**Microsoft Windows Common Controls, 493**

**Microsoft XML Core Services.** *See* MSXML.

**minExclusive constraining facet, 90**
   Oracle8*i* compatibility issues, 906, 908, 910–911, 913, 915, 917, 919, 921
   and relational database, 628–629, 640–641, 645, 649–650, 653–654, 658, 662–663, 666, 670–671

**minInclusive constraining facet, 90**
   Oracle8*i* compatibility issues, 906, 908, 910, 913, 915, 917, 919, 921
   and relational database, 627–628, 640, 644–645,
648–649, 653, 657, 661–662, 665–666, 669–670

**minLength constraining facet, 90, 220**
   and relational database, 687

**minOccurs attribute**
   of all element, 272, 273, 722
   of choice element, 275, 277
   of element element, 149, 162
   of group element, 289, 290–291
   of sequence element, 279, 280

**Misc, of XML document, 58**

**MiscellaneousSymbols Unicode character block, 372**

**MiscellaneousTechnical Unicode character block, 371**

**mixed attribute**
   of complexContent element, 258, 259
   of complexType element, 247, 253, 709

**Mixed content, 86–87, 230**
   mapping to database schema, 713–718
   specification of, 237–238

**Mn Unicode character category, 365**

**Model group, 96–98**
   characteristics of, 407
   named, 410–411
   properties of, 407
   redefined, 133

**Model group definitions, of schema, 391**

**Mongolian Unicode character block, 371**

**msxm14.dll, 472, 473**

**MSXML (Microsoft XML Core Services), 576, 580**
   downloading, 472, 493
   example of use of, 493–503
   for parsing, 472
   proprietary features of, 474
   structure of, 473
   using DOM with, 476–478
   using SAX with, 478–483
   validation in, 488–493
   Visual Basic and, 475
   XSLT processor in, 472

**Multiple character escape (regular expression), 367–368**
   examples of, 368

**MusicalSymbols Unicode character block, 373**

**Myanmar Unicode character block, 371**

# N

**N Unicode character category, 365**

**n-tier architecture, 775**
   XML and, 776–777

**Name**
   defined, 39
   of element, 14
   locally scoped, 79
   namespace, 390, 929
   qualified *vs.* unqualified, 38, 79
   of schema-defined element type, 17

**name attribute**
   of attribute element, 182, 187–188
   of attributeGroup element, 194–195
   of complexType element, 247, 253, 720
   of element element, 149, 163
   of group element, 289, 291
   of key element, 347, 348
   of keyref element, 351
   of notation element, 130
   of simpleType element, 209, 210–211

of unique element, 344, 345
**Name datatype, 317, 937**
   derivation of, 318, 320
   and relational database, 608–609
   treatment of whitespace in, 319
**Named attribute use-group, 88, 174, 193, 391, 409–410**
   example of, 176–177
   function of, 410
   representation of, 410
**Named model group, 96, 98, 391, 410–411**
**NamedNodeMap interface (DOM), 443**
**Namespace, 36**
   and attribute type, 181–182
   components of, 38
   declaration of, 38–39, 780, 929
   default, 39, 40, 41, 43, 79–80
   defined, 929
   element type and, 147–148
   qualifier of, 79
   importance of specifying, 107–108
   scoping rules for, 42
   specifying, 78
   target, 17, 80
   and XML instance, 80–81
   XPointer and, 51–52
**namespace attribute**
   of any element, 168, 169–170
   of anyAttribute element, 197–198
   of import element, 126, 127
**Namespace attributes property, of element information item, 63, 64**
**namespace (XPath axis), 54**
**Namespace declaration, 38–39, 780**
   defined, 929
   scope of, 929

**Namespace identifier (NID), 36**
   registering, 37
**Namespace information item, 62**
**Namespace name, 390, 929**
**Namespace name property**
   of attribute information item, 64, 66
   of element information item, 63
**Namespace Recommendation, of W3C, 8, 36**
**Namespace schema information, added by PSVI, 424, 425**
**Namespace URI, 39**
**Namespace-specific string (NSS), 36**
**NamespaceSupport class (SAX), 445**
**NaN (not a number), 295, 298, 631**
**Natural numbers, 295**
**NCHAR datatype, 598**
**NCLOB datatype, 599, 902**
**NCName datatype, 317, 937**
   defined, 13
   derivation of, 320
   derivative datatypes of, 321
   use of, 317–318, 320
   and relational database, 609–612
   treatment of whitespace in, 319
**Nd Unicode character category, 365**
**Negative character ranges, 379**
**Negative infinity (Inf-), 295, 298, 631**
**negativeInteger datatype, 300, 302**
   and relational database, 629

   use of, 302
**Nested elements, 85**
   complex type and, 234–237
**.NET Framework, 536, 557, 759**
   programming languages for, 801
   as replacement for COM, 770
   schema and DTD support of, 849
   transport protocols for, 563
   validation in, 781, 849
**Netscape (AOL), XML compatibility of, 800**
**NID (Namespace identifier), 36**
   registering, 37
**nil attribute, 147**
**Nil PSVI property, 68, 69**
**nillable attribute, 146, 398**
   of element element, 149, 163
**Nl Unicode character category, 365**
**NMTOKEN datatype, 317**
   derivation of, 318
   and relational database, 618–619
   treatment of whitespace in, 319
**NMTOKENS datatype, 317**
   derivation of, 318, 320
   and relational database, 590, 620–624
   single-column implementation of, 620–621
   table implementation of, 620, 622–624
   treatment of whitespace in, 319
   VARRAY implementation of, 620
**No Unicode character category, 365**
**NO VALUE value, 67**
**Node, in XML, 339**

# Index

Node ID, 48–49
Node interface (DOM), 443
Node set, 47
   use of predicates on, 47–48
NodeFilter interface (DOM), 444
NodeIterator interface (DOM), 444
NodeList interface (DOM), 443
Non-instantiable class, 12, 926
Non-instantiable types, 207–208, 400, 935
   explicitly, 238–240
   implicitly, 240–244
   mapping to object-oriented language, 512–513
nonNegativeInteger datatype, 297, 300, 302
   and relational database, 630
   use of, 302
Nonnegative integers, 295
nonPositiveInteger datatype, 297, 300, 302
   and relational database, 629
   use of, 302
Normal characters, 363
Normalized value property, of attribute information item, 64, 66
normalizedString datatype, 317
   derivation of, 318, 320
   Oracle8*i* compatibility issues, 903–904
   and relational database, 602
   treatment of whitespace in, 319
Not a number (NaN), 295, 298, 631
Notation
   described, 411–412, 417, 936
   properties of, 412
   XML, 102

notation content option for schema element, 116
notation datatype, 322
   constraining facets of, 339
   function of, 389
   non-instantiability of, 329
   and relational database, 633
   use of, 329–330
Notation declaration, 936
   of schema, 391
notation element, 128–129, 862
   attributes of, 130–132
   content options for, 132
Notation information item, 62, 932
Notation interface (DOM), 443
NSS (Namespace-specific string), 36
NumberForms Unicode character block, 371
Numbers
   characteristics of, 295
   as datatype, 89
   treatment in relational database, 589
Numeric range, 376
NVARCHAR2 datatype, 598

## O

Object, 14
   characteristics of, 924–925
Object-oriented (OO) programming, 508–509
   described, 509
   design patterns and, 527–528
   encapsulation in, 509
   examples of, 529–539
   extensional *vs.* intensional, 924
   inheritance in, 509
   polymorphism in, 510

   and XML, 510–527
Ogham Unicode character block, 371
OldItalic Unicode character block, 373
Operators, precedence of, 380–381
OpticalCharacterRecognition Unicode character block, 371
Optional property, 67
Optional quantifiers, 375
Optional repeating quantifiers, 375
OPTIONS, HTTP verb, 565
or (regular expression) operator, 361, 362
Oracle8*i*
   features not supported by, 902–903
   workarounds in, 903–921
Oracle9*i*
   column datatype support, 598
   PL/SQL functions in, 678
   XML compatibility, 588–671, 815
org.apache.xerces package, 446
org.apache.xerces.parsers package, 446–447
org.apache.xml.serialize package, 438, 445–446
org.w3c.dom package, 443
org.w3c.dom.Document interface, 447–449
org.w3c.dom.Element interface, 453
org.w3c.dom.events package, 459
org.w3c.dom.htmls package, 459
org.w3c.dom.Node interface, 454–456
org.w3c.dom.ranges package, 459

Index 957

org.w3c.dom.traversal package, 444, 459
org.w3c.sax package, 444–445
org.w3c.sax.helpers package, 445
org.xml example file, 525–526
Oriya Unicode character block, 370
Output, 557
Output token, 29
OutputFormat class (DOM and SAX), 446
Owner element property, of attribute information item, 64

## P

P Unicode character category, 365
parent (XPath axis), 54
Parent property
    of character information item, 66
    of element information item, 63, 64
parse function, in DocumentBuilder, 440–441
Parser, 28–29
    nonvalidating, 31
    for SGML, 30
    syntax-driven, 31
    for XML, 30
ParserAdaptor class (SAX), 445
ParserConfigurationException, 442
Parsing, 13
Parsing event, 31
Parsing-event token, 31
Particle
    described, 406
    properties of, 406
Party, defined, 521
party.xsd example file, 521–525
Pattern, enforcement of, 588
pattern constraining facet, 90, 220, 381
    use of multiple, 382–383
    and relational database, 590–592, 689, 706
    use of, 382
pattern element, within restriction element, 358
Pattern facet, 294, 302
Pattern-constrained simple type, 203
Pc Unicode character category, 365
PCDATA strings, 406
Pd Unicode character category, 365
Pe Unicode character category, 365
Perl, regular expressions in, 360
Pf Unicode character category, 365
Pi Unicode character category, 365
Picklist tables, 594–597
Po Unicode character category, 365
Point in Polygon sample application, 572–583
Polymorphism, 510
    mapping to object-oriented language, 515–517
Positive character groups, 377–379
Positive infinity (Inf+), 295, 298, 631
positiveInteger datatype, 300, 302
    and relational database, 630
    use of, 302

POST, HTTP verb, 565
Post-schema-validation infoset (PSVI). *See* PSVI.
Potential substitution group, 398
Precedence of operators, 380–381
preceding (XPath axis), 54
preceding-sibling (XPath axis), 54
Predicate, 47–48
    validity of, 48
Prefix, 13, 38, 39
    absence of in schema, 390
Prefix property
    of attribute information item, 64
    of element information item, 63
pricing.xsd explanation, 176–177, 207, 230–233, 238–240, 257–258, 274, 282–289
    complete listing, 895–899
Primitive, defined, 394–395
Primitive type definition, 394, 395
Printer class (DOM and SAX), 446
PrivateUse Unicode character block, 372, 373
processContents attribute, of any element, 168, 170
    and relational database, 708, 723
    values of, 170
processContents attribute, of anyAttribute element, 198
Processing instruction information item, 62, 932
ProcessingInstruction interface (DOM), 443
Production software
    formatting-markup based, 552–553
    stylesheet-based, 551–552
PROGID, 476, 477

# Index

Prolog, of XML document, 58
Properties, 15
   of objects, 924
   values of, 67
propertyMethods, 59, 924–925
Provide, defined, 925
Ps Unicode character category, 365
PSVI (Post-schema-validation infoset), 34, 520
   characteristics of, 67
   construction of, 415
   described, 928
   distinguished from basic infoset, 416
   information items added by, 423–426
   properties of, 68–69
   properties added by, 418–423
ptinpoly.xsd sample application, 574–575, 580–583
pttest.htm example file, 577–578
public attribute, of notation element, 130, 131
PUT, HTTP verb, 565
putFeature method, 482
putProperty method, 482

## Q

QName datatype, 13, 40, 937
   alternatives to, 324
   constraining facets of, 324
   defined, 13
   and relational database, 633
   structure of, 323
   unique features of, 322
   use of, 317–318, 320, 323
Qualified attribute, 181
Qualified element, 147
Qualified name, 13, 38, 39
   defined, 79, 937

   as value, 40–41
Qualifier, of namespace, 79
Quantifier, 868, 869
Query types, SQL support of, 768–769

## R

range-to function (XPointer), 53
Rational numbers, 295
Real numbers, 295
redefine content option for schema element, 116
redefine element, 71, 862
   attributes of, 134–135
   content options for, 135–136
   function of, 132–134
ref attribute, 81
   of attribute element, 182, 188, 191
   of attributeGroup element, 195
   of element element, 149, 164
   of group element, 289, 291
refer attribute, of keyref element, 351, 352
Reference, entity, 29
References property, of attribute information item, 64, 65
Referential integrity, 343
regexpDemo.xml online example file, 359
regexpDemo.xsd online example file, 359
Regular expressions
   constraint of simple content using, 381–384
   grammar for, 868–876
   guidelines for, 359
   Perl, 360
   syntax of, 361–381
Relational database

   check constraints *vs.* triggers in, 598
   facet restrictions and, 590–597
   mapping complex types to, 708–754
   mapping schemas to, 815–823
   mapping simple types to, 674–706
   Oracle PL/SQL functions and, 678
   XML datatypes and, 598–671
   XML schema design considerations regarding, 588–590, 674–675, 708–709
Repeating dates and times, 314–315
   constraining facets of, 315
REPLACE process, 318
Request-response application, 561, 562
Required repeating quantifiers, 376
Resource Directory Description Language (RDDL), 38
Restriction
   of complex type, 94–96
   of simple type, 89
   in XML, 10
restriction element, 212, 243, 260, 358, 514, 863–864
   attributes of, 212–213, 267–268
   constraining facets of, 215
   content options for, 213–215, 268–271
   examples of use of, 739–745
   function of, 266–267, 738
   and object-oriented languages, 515
   and relational database, 738–745
Restrictor, 925
Result-oriented schemas, 505
   application-oriented, 556–584

document-oriented, 542–553
object-oriented, 508–539
**Reusable datatypes**
creating, 786–789
identifying, 783–786
XML schema support for, 782–783
**Rich Text Format (RTF), 552–553**
**Routing application, 561, 562, 563**
**Runic Unicode character block, 371**

## S

**S Unicode character category, 365**
**SAX (Simple API for XML), 428**
advantages and disadvantages of, 460
ContentHandler interface of, 459–469
**SAX-compliant token, 28**
**SAX2, 478–483**
validation using, 492–493
**SAXContent VB class, 479**
**SAXException, 445**
**SAXNotRecognizedException, 445**
**SAXNotSupportedException, 445**
**SAXParseException, 445**
**SAXParser class (SAX), 442, 447, 465**
**SaxParserFactory class (SAX), 442**
**SAXTest.cls example file, 500–501**
**SAXXMLReader40 (Microsoft)**
configuration of, 482
handler interfaces of, 479
handler properties of, 481–482

parsing errors in, 482–483
reading XML with, 479–482
**Sc Unicode character category, 365**
**Scalability, 760**
**Schema(s)**
abstract vs. concrete, 58
benefits of, 6
characteristics of, 10, 388
combining, 840
compared with DTDs, 14
creating, 779
database design using, 810–823
data-oriented, 585–754
default namespace of, 114
for describing applications, 560, 569–572
for describing arguments, 558–559
document-oriented, 542–553
drawbacks of, 6–7
locating components of, 125
mapping to object-oriented language, 518–520
object-oriented, 508–536
properties of, 69–70
purpose of, 5
reasons for using, 761, 776
regular expressions in, 360
result-oriented, 505–580
role in applications, 558
set-valued properties of, 391
testing using, 764
validation of, 771, 780–782
for validation of data, 558
WDSL and, 570–572
**Schema component, 34, 388**
as declaration, 389
defined, 933
as definition, 389
types of, 390
**Schema document. See XML schema document.**

**Schema document information, added by PSVI, 424, 426**
**schema element, 78, 571, 864**
attributes of, 108–114
content options for, 115–116
sample, 106–107
**Schema normalized value, PSVI property, 68**
**Schema Object Model. See SOM.**
**Schema processing, 33–34, 414**
steps of, 415
**Schema Recommendation, of W3C, 9–10**
online resources regarding, 26
**Schema schema component, 69, 388, 391**
**Schema value, 12–13**
**Schema-defined element types, 18**
abstract, 17
concrete, 18
name of, 17
**schemaLocation attribute, 51**
of import element, 127
of include element, 123
of redefine element, 134, 135
**SchemaTreeForm.frm example file, 495–499**
**Schema-valid document, 936**
**Schmuller, Joseph, 760**
**Scientific notation, 295**
**Scope, of component, 81**
anonymous, 82
global, 81–82
local, 82
of namespace declaration, 929
**Scoping, 42**
**Scripting languages, 557**
**Selector, in XML schema, 339**
XPaths for, 340–341
**selector element, 865**
attributes of, 353–354
content options for, 354

# Index

**self (XPath axis), 54**
**sequence element, 255, 865**
    attributes of, 278–280, 731
    content options for, 280–281
    examples of use of, 731–738
    function of, 278, 731
    and relational database, 731–738
**Sequence model group, 96, 98**
**sequence.xsd explanation, 153–156, 241–243**
    complete listing, 899–900
**Serializer classes, 439**
**Serializer interface (DOM), 445**
**SGML, 8, 29**
    characteristics of, 405
    ISO 8879 standard for, 14, 30
    parsing, 30
**short datatype, 297**
    constraining facets of, 303–304
    derivation relationships of, 304
    and relational database, 630
    use of, 302, 303, 304
**Sign, of number, 295**
**Simple attribute values, 87**
**Simple content, 84, 405, 408**
    and attribute types, 85
    constraint with regular expressions, 381–384
    lexically constrained values, 84
**Simple Object Access Protocol (SOAP), 557**
    references on, 762
    sample of, 762–763
**Simple type, 11, 79, 358, 936**
    adding attributes to, 231–233
    annotations in, 396
    anonymous, 208
    base type definition of, 394–395
    blocking of, 208

    constraining facets of, 88–89, 205
    custom, 89
    defined, 935
    derivation data of, 394
    derivation from token datatype, 202–203
    derivation from user-derived simple type, 204
    derivation by restriction, 89
    examples of, 202–204, 207
    functions of, 407
    global *vs.* local, 208
    instantiability of, 101, 240
    lexical space of, 202, 206
    list in, 91
    mapping to database schema, 675–677
    mapping to object-oriented language, 520
    name of, 394
    non-instantiable, 207–208
    pattern-constrained, 203
    redefined, 133
    and relational databases, 674–677
    structure of, 204
    union in, 91, 690–697
    value space of, 202, 205–206
**Simple-API-for-XML (SAX)-compliant token, 28**
**simpleContent element, 244, 245, 255, 865**
    attributes of, 256
    content options for, 256–258
    and relational database, 738
**simpleSchema.xsd example file, 106**
**simpleType content option for schema element, 116**
**simpleType element, 84, 208, 865**
    attributes of, 208–211
    constraining facets of, 212
    content options for, 211

**Single character escape (regular expression), 366–367**
    examples of, 367
**Sinhala Unicode character block, 371**
**Sk Unicode character category, 365**
**Skip validation, 415**
**Sm Unicode character category, 365**
**SmallFormVariants Unicode character block, 373**
**So Unicode character category, 365**
**SOAP (Simple Object Access Protocol), 557**
    references on, 762
    sample of, 762–763
    XML subproject, 428
**SoftModeler (Softera), 24**
**SOM (Schema Object Model), 474**
    advantages and disadvantages of, 488
    creating schemas using, 488
    interfaces of, 483–488
    structure of, 485
**source attribute**
    of appinfo element, 119–120
    of documentation element, 121
**Sovereign application, 561**
**SpacingModifierLetters Unicode character block, 370**
**Specials Unicode character block, 373**
**Specified property, of attribute information item, 64**
**SQL 2000, 767**
    template-based queries in, 769
    XML support in, 768, 815
**SQL XML View Mapper, 816–819**

# Index

**SQLXML3 (Microsoft), 815, 818, 819**
   Configure IIS Support tool in, 824–829
**Standard Time, 310**
**Start-tag, 14, 29, 930**
   of concrete element, 59
**STL (Standard Template Library), 534**
**strict keyword, importance of, 632**
**Strict validation, 415**
**String**
   as datatype, 89
   length of, 589
   treatment in relational database, 589
**string datatype, 89**
   alternatives to, 317
   constraining facets of, 317
   datatypes derived from, 317–322
   derivation relationships of, 317
   use of, 316–317
**String datatypes, 316**
   constraining facets of, 317, 320
   derivation relationships of, 317, 320
   treatment in relational database, 589
   use of, 316–317
**string-derived datatypes, 318–319**
   alternatives, 320
   constraining facets of, 320
   derivation relationships of, 320
   magic, 321–322
**Structure type, 11, 66, 935**
   element type and, 138
**Stylesheet, 551**
**Subelement, 930**
   immediate, 60, 930

**Subelement sequence, 52**
**substGroup.xsd example file, 142–143, 144–146**
**Substitution group, 99–100, 139, 389, 398**
   in derived type, 142–143
   of element type, 398
   examples of, 139–141, 153–156
   features of, 141
   potential, 398
**substitution value, in blockDefault attribute, 109**
**substitutionGroup attribute of element element, 149, 166**
**Subtraction, character class, 380**
**Superclass, 12**
**SuperscriptsandSubscripts Unicode character block, 371**
**Supporting Database Sequence Schema explanation, 153–156, 241–243**
   complete listing, 899–900
**Supporting Pricing Schema Document explanation, 176–177, 207, 230–233, 238–240, 257–258, 274, 282–289**
   complete listing, 895–899
**Syriac Unicode character block, 370**
**SYS.AnyData Oracle type, 903**
**SYS.AnyData type database mapping, 702–705**
   column inserts in, 704
   column retrieval in, 705
**SYS.UriType Oracle type, 903**
**system attribute, of notation element, 130, 132**

# T

**Tags Unicode character block, 373**
**Tamil Unicode character block, 370**
**Target namespace, 17, 80**
**Target node set, in XML validation, 339**
**targetNamespace attribute, 42, 80**
   of schema element, 108, 112
**Teach Yourself UML in 24 Hours, 760**
**T$_E$X-based systems, 552–553.**
**Telugu Unicode character block, 370**
**Template files, 824**
   use of, 845, 846
**Template-based queries, 769, 824**
   implementation of, 851–952
**Terminology, questions of, 11–12**
**Testing, using schemas, 764**
**TestShapeTrue.xml example file, 578–579**
**Text editors, 24**
**Text interface (DOM), 443**
**TextSerializer class (DOM and SAX), 446**
**Thaana Unicode character block, 370**
**Thai Unicode character block, 371**
**Thematic Address Schema Document.** See **address.xsd.**
**Thematic Catalog Schema Document.** See **catalog.xsd.**
**Tibetan Unicode character block, 371**
**time datatype, 913–915**
   constraining facets of, 655–658
   and relational database, 6654–658

## Index

Time line, 304–305
Time zones, 308–310, 902
    treatment in relational database, 590, 641, 646
Time-line-based datatypes
    constraining facets of, 310
    derivation relationships of, 311
    integralization of, 307–308
    ordering of, 310, 311
    syntax of, 306
    time zones and, 308–310
    using, 306–307
TIMESTAMP datatype, 637, 902
Token, 28
    output, 29
    parsing-event, 31
token datatype, 84, 317
    derivation of, 318, 320
    and relational database, 603–604
    simple type derived from, 202–203
    treatment of whitespace in, 319
    use of, 320, 329
tokenAttribute attribute, 85, 88
tokenElement element, 85, 88
totalDigits constraining facet, 90, 625
TRACE, HTTP verb, 565
Transport protocols, 563–569
    for input and output, 557
TreeView Xerces sample class, 433
TreeWalker interface (DOM), 444
Triggers
    *vs.* check constraints, 598
    for picklist table, 595–597
Type
    avoiding use of term, 66

defined, 389
types of, 11, 926, 935
*See also* Complex type; Simple type.
type attribute, 81, 84
    of attribute element, 182, 188
    of element element, 149
Type generator, 926
Type name, 396
    of attribute, 931
    of element, 14, 15, 16, 81, 389, 930
types element, 571

## U

UIBroker, 842
    function of, 842, 845–846
    implementation of, 842, 843–844
UML (Unified Modeling Language), 760
    component model of, 837
UML-style editing tools, 24
Unexpanded entity preference information item, 62
Unicode Regular Expression Guidelines, 359
Unicode Standard, 359, 873–876
    character blocks in, 370–373
    character references in, 374
Unified Modeling Language (UML), 760
    component model of, 837
UnifiedCanadianAboriginalSyllabics Unicode character block, 371
Uniform Record Locator. *See* URL.
Uniform Resource Name, 36, 37
union element, 91, 221, 865
    attributes of, 223–226

    constraining facets of, 227, 706
    content options for, 226
    of enumerations, 690–694
    examples of, 221–223, 225–226, 227
    multiple column database mapping of, 697–702
    and relational databases, 675, 690–706
    single column database mapping of, 696–697
    of single-valued simple types, 694–696
    SYS.AnyData type mapping of, 702–705
unionExamples.xsd example file, 225–226, 227
unique element, 101, 342, 343, 408, 865
    attributes of, 344–345
    content options for, 345–346
    example of, 344
    function of, 343–344
Uniqueness
    aspects of, 343
    enforcing with identity constraints, 342
UNISTR function, 903
Unparsed entity declaration, 321
Unparsed entity information item, 62
Unqualified
    attribute, 39, 181
    element, 147
    name, 38, 79
unsignedByte datatype, 302
    constraining facets of, 303–304
    derivation relationships of, 304
    and relational database, 631
    use of, 302, 303, 304
unsignedInt datatype, 297, 302

## V

constraining facets of, 303–304
derivation relationships of, 304
and relational database, 630
use of, 302, 303, 304
**unsignedLong datatype, 297, 302**
constraining facets of, 303–304
derivation relationships of, 304
and relational database, 630
use of, 302, 303, 304
**unsignedShort datatype, 297, 302**
constraining facets of, 303–304
derivation relationships of, 304
and relational database, 631
use of, 302, 303, 304
**Updategrams, 832–833**
**URI, 36**
creating, 37
namespace, 39
**URI class (Xerces), 446**
**URL (Uniform Record Locator), 36**
to locate schema and components, 103
RFCs about, 37
using RDDL with, 37–38
**URL Schema Validation Service, 771**
**URN (Uniform Resource Name), 36**
RFCs about, 37
**use attribute, of attribute element, 182, 189**
values for, 189–190
**UTF-8, 598, 902**
**UTF-16, 598, 902**
**UTL_ENCODE PL/SQL package, 902**

**Valid document, 936**
**validateOnParse property, in DOMDocument40, 478**
**Validation, 414, 849–850**
catching errors in, 851
defined, 389
of list element, 683, 685, 686
in MSXML, 488–493
results of, 416
schemas for, 558
types of, 414–415
**Validation root, 414, 415**
**Validator, 30, 32, 332**
**Value, defined, 931**
**Value constraint, 389**
on attribute type, 393
on element type, 397
**Value model, 389**
**Value space, 294**
of simple type, 202, 205–206
**VARCHAR datatype, 902**
**VARCHAR2 datatype, 598, 599**
use of, 600
**Variety, of simple type, 395**
**VBScript, 581**
**version attribute, of schema element, 108, 112–113**
**Visual Basic**
use with MSXML, 475
XML implementation using, 530–533
**Visual Studio .NET, 770, 788**
table creation using, 811–812
Web page views of, 840
**Vlissides, John, 527**

## W

**Web Services Definition Language (WDSL), 569**
described, 570

files, 824
using, 571–572
**Web tier, 775**
construction of, 838–842
views of, 840
**Well-formed XML document, defined, 929**
**Whitespace character**
in strings, 318–319
treatment of, 67
treatment in relational database, 589
**whiteSpace constraining facet, 90, 220**
characteristics of, 317
and relational database, 597
**Wildcard**
attribute, 88, 174
element, 87, 407
properties of, 404
uses of, 407
**Wildcard escape (regular expressions), 369, 377**
**Wilson, Flip, 550**
**World Wide Web Consortium (W3C)**
Infoset Recommendation of, 8–9, 58, 59, 61
Namespace Recommendation of, 8, 36
Schema Recommendation of, 9–10, 26
**World Wide Web Consortium (continued)**
XML Recommendation of, 7–8
XPath Recommendation of, 9, 46
**Writer Xerces sample class (SAX), 433**

## X

# Index

Xalan, Apache XML subproject, 428
Xang, Apache XML subproject, 428
XDR (XML Data Reduced), Microsoft, 474, 811
   schemas, 818
Xerces, 781
Xerces Java XML parser, 428
   content handler interface of, 459–469
   document interface of, 447–449
   downloading, 430–431
   element interface of, 452–454
   exceptions in, 441
   package contents, 431–432
   running, 432–435
   sample classes in package, 433
   versions of, 429
Xerces Native Interface (XNI), 429
XHTMLSerializer class (DOM and SAX), 446
XLink Recommendation, 38
xlink:arcrole attribute, 38
xlink:href attribute, 38
XML
   characteristics of, 4–5
   context-based markup, 542
   conversion to, 763–764
   Data Reduced (XDR), Microsoft, 474, 811, 818
   declarations in, 8
   document analysis for, 544–548
   document processing in, 548–553
   documents in, 542–544
   DTDs, 932–936
   mapping to relational databases, 815–823
   Microsoft compatibility of, 472–504
   and object-oriented programming, 508–539
   parsing, 30
   reduced versions of, 474
   and SQL 2000, 767–770
   subprojects of, 428
   XSLT and, 766, 767
XML application
   architecture of, 556
   business logic of, 557
   described using schemas, 560, 569–572
   client code in, 575–580
   defined, 937
   example of, 572–583
   input and output for, 557
   role of schemas in, 558
   scripting languages and, 557
   server code in, 580–583
   structure of, 561–563
   transport protocols and, 563–569
XML document
   defined, 927
   DTD-valid, 936
   insertion of bit strings into, 325–327
   schema-valid, 936
   structure of, 32–33
   valid, 936
   well-formed, 929
XML document information item, 31
XML information set (infoset), 33
   characteristics of, 61, 66–67
   defined, 928
   importance of, 61
   structure of, 61
XML instance, 12
   defined, 927–928
   example of, 77–78
   namespace and, 80–81
   quantity of elements in, 276, 279
   validating, 24–25
XML Parser 4.0 (Microsoft), 576, 580. *See also* MSXML (Microsoft XML Core Services).
XML Recommendation, of W3C, 7–8
XML representation, defined, 19
XML schema. *See* Schema; XML schema document.
XML schema document, 5
   characteristics of, 70–71
   creating, 24–25
   defined, 34
   documenting, 82–83
   editing, 24
   element IDs for, 103
   elements of, 70
   examples of, 76–77, 106
   imports and includes in, 102–103
   locating, 103
   notations in, 102
   processing, 34
   validating, 18, 24–25
XML Spy (Altova), 24, 771
   sample creation facility of, 794–795
   table creation using, 812–814
   validation using, 780, 788
   XDR mapping schemas using, 818
XML validator, 12, 936
xml:lang attribute
   of documentation element, 121, 122
   of schema element, 108, 113
XMLFilter interface (SAX), 444
XMLFilterImpl class (SAX), 445
XMLHTTP object, 576–577
xmlns attribute, 79

# Index

of schema element, 108, 113–114
**XMLReader interface (SAX), 444**
**XMLReaderAdaptor class (SAX), 445**
**XMLReaderFactory class (SAX), 445**
**XMLSerializer class (DOM), 438, 446**
**XNI (Xerces Native Interface), 429**
**XPath**
 defined, 937
 evaluation of, 46, 48
 and identity constraints, 49–50, 340
 to locate schemas, 53
 location paths of, 47
 XPointer extensions to, 53
**xpath attribute, of field element, 355–356**
**XPath queries, executing, 824**
**XPath Recommendation, of W3C, 9, 46**
**XPointer, 46, 51**
 examples of, 55
 function of, 47
 to locate schemas, 53
 and namespaces, 51–52
**XPointer Recommendation, 46**
**xsd.exe, 536**
**xsi:type attribute, 240, 244**
**XSL (Extensible Stylesheet Language), 552, 553**
**XSL Transformations (XSLT), 552**
 advantages of, 765
 business uses for, 766, 767
 characteristics of, 764–766, 800
 conversion of XML to relational data, 766, 767
 debugging templates in, 771
 HTML creation in, 795–800
 using System.XML classes, 846

## Y

**YiRadicals Unicode character block, 372**
**YiSyllables Unicode character block, 372**

## Z

**Z Unicode character category, 365**
**zip format, 431**
**Zl Unicode character category, 365**
**Zp Unicode character category, 365**
**Zs Unicode character category, 365**

# informIT

www.informit.com

## YOUR GUIDE TO IT REFERENCE

### Articles

Keep your edge with thousands of free articles, in-depth features, interviews, and IT reference recommendations – all written by experts you know and trust.

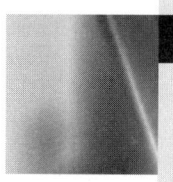

### Online Books

Answers in an instant from **InformIT Online Book's** 600+ fully searchable on line books. For a limited time, you can get your first 14 days **free**.

**Safari**
POWERED BY
TECH BOOKS ONLINE

### Catalog

Review online sample chapters, author biographies and customer rankings and choose exactly the right book from a selection of over 5,000 titles.

# Wouldn't it be great

if the world's leading technical publishers joined forces to deliver their best tech books in a common digital reference platform?

They have. Introducing
**InformIT Online Books
powered by Safari.**

**Safari** TECH BOOKS ONLINE

**InformIT Online Books**

**informit.com/onlinebooks**

- **Specific answers to specific questions.**
InformIT Online Books' powerful search engine gives you relevance-ranked results in a matter of seconds.

- **Immediate results.**
With InformIT Online Books, you can select the book you want and view the chapter or section you need immediately.

- **Cut, paste and annotate.**
Paste code to save time and eliminate typographical errors. Make notes on the material you find useful and choose whether or not to share them with your work group.

- **Customized for your enterprise.**
Customize a library for you, your department or your entire organization. You only pay for what you need.

## Get your first 14 days **FREE!**

For a limited time, InformIT Online Books is offering its members a 10 book subscription risk-free for 14 days. Visit http://www.informit.com/onlinebooks for details.

# Register Your Book

## at www.awprofessional.com/register

You may be eligible to receive:

- Advance notice of forthcoming editions of the book
- Related book recommendations
- Chapter excerpts and supplements of forthcoming titles
- Information about special contests and promotions throughout the year
- Notices and reminders about author appearances, tradeshows, and online chats with special guests

## Contact us

If you are interested in writing a book or reviewing manuscripts prior to publication, please write to us at:

Editorial Department
Addison-Wesley Professional
75 Arlington Street, Suite 300
Boston, MA 02116 USA
Email: AWPro@aw.com

Visit us on the Web: http://www.awprofessional.com